Key to map pages

Shetland Islands
160
Lerwick

Fair Isle

Orkney Islands
Kirkwall **159**

Thurso
Lewis
Stornoway
154 155
Scourie
156 157
Wick
158
Harris
Ullapool
Dornoch
North Uist
Skye
A87
A835
Elgin
Fraserburgh
Inverness
150 151
152 153
South Uist
148 149
Kyle of Lochalsh
A87 A82
A95
Aberdeen
A86
Mallaig
136 137
138 139
140 141
A830
Coll
Tiree
146 147
Fort William
A9
A90
Mull
130 131
132 133
134 135
A828
Dundee
Oban
A85
Perth
St Andrews
124 125
126 127
A83
A82
Colonsay
M9
128 129
Stirling
A90 A92
144 145
Glasgow
M90
Jura
118 119
Edinburgh
122 123
Islay
M74
M8
A702
Berwick-upon-Tweed
142 143
Arran
Ayr
A76
Hawick
Alnwick
Campbeltown
112 113
114 115
A77
A74(M)
A7
116 117

◆ Town plan and urban approach map

● Town plan

XVIII

Derry/
Londonderry
Coleraine
Ballymena
Sligo
Enniskillen
Belfast
Portadown
Newry
Newcastle upon Tyne
110 111
Stranraer
Dumfries
104 105
106 107
Carlisle
Sunderland
A75
A69
Durham
A19
Whitehaven
A66
Middlesbrough
M6
98 99
100 101
102 103
Kendal
A595
A1
A19
Scarborough
A171
Isle of
Man
84
Douglas
Barrow in Furness
Lancaster
Harrogate
York
A64
A165
Drogheda
92 93
94 95
96 97
Galway
Athlone
Blackpool
Bradford
Leeds
M62
A63
Hull
Dublin
Preston
86 87
88
M180
Grimsby
Dun Laoghaire
85
Manchester
89 90 91
Liverpool
M62
Doncaster
Lincoln
Holyhead
82 83
Sheffield
A16
Limerick
A55
Anglesey
Macclesfield
M1
Skegness
Kilkenny
Llandudno
Chester
A49
74 75 76 77 78 79
XIX
Bangor
72 73
Hanley
A6
Mansfield
80 81
Waterford
A487
Wrexham
Stoke
Derby
Nottingham
Boston
Cromer
Wexford
70 71
A5
A50
A17
Great
Yarmouth
Killarney
Dolgellau
Stafford
Leicester
A16
King's Lynn
Norwich
Rosslare
A458
60 61 62 63 64 65 66 67 68 69
Shrewsbury
M54
A47
Cork
Newtown
Telford
Birmingham
A43
Peterborough
A11 A12
58 59
Wolverhampton
Coventry
A1(M)
M1
Aberystwyth
A44
Stratford-upon-Avon
Kettering
Newmarket
Bury St Edmunds
45 46 47 48 49
Worcester
Northampton
Cambridge
56 57
Builth Wells
Hereford
50 51 52 53 54 55
Ipswich
Felixstowe
A487
A470
Banbury
Milton Keynes
M11
A12
Fishguard
A483
M50
M5
A14
Luton
A1(M)
Colchester
44
Merthyr Tydfil
Gloucester
Cheltenham
M40
40 41
Chelmsford
42 43
Pembroke
32 33 34 35 36 37 38 39
M1
London
Southend-on-Sea
Llanelli
A470
Newport
Swindon
Oxford
M25
30 31
Swansea
A4
Heathrow
28 29
Canterbury
A49
A34 A40
Croydon
Maidstone
Cardiff
Bristol
Bath
M4
Reading
Windsor
M2
Lundy
20 21 22 23 24 25 26 27
Gatwick
Ashford
Dover
Ilfracombe
A36
Newbury
M3
Winchester
Lewes
A259
M5
A37
Salisbury
A3
Southampton
14 15 16 17 18 19
Bideford
Taunton
A303
M27
Chichester
Brighton
8 9 10 11 12 13
Dorchester
Poole
Portsmouth
A39
A386
Weymouth
Bournemouth
Exeter
A35
Isle of Wight
A30
Newquay
Plymouth
Torquay
4 5 6 7
Truro
A38
Penzance
2 3
A30
Isles of
Scilly

Alderney

Channel
Islands
Guernsey

Jersey

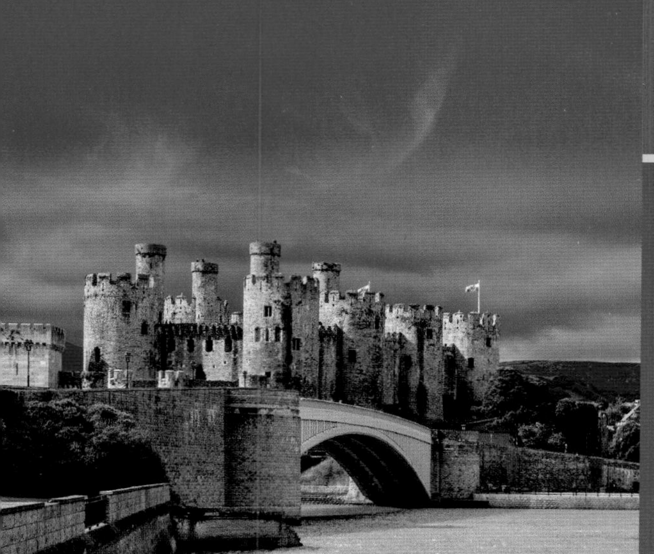
Ian Dagnall / Alamy

PHILIP'S | ROAD ATLAS

2016 COMPLETE BRITAIN & IRELAND

www.philips-maps.co.uk

First published in 2009 by Philip's
a division of Octopus Publishing Group Ltd
www.octopusbooks.co.uk
Carmelite House, 50 Victoria Embankment
London EC4Y 0DZ
An Hachette UK Company
www.hachette.co.uk

Seventh edition 2015
First impression 2015

ISBN 978-1-84907-372-1 (spiral)
ISBN 978-1-84907-373-8 (hardback)

Cartography by Philip's
Copyright © 2015 Philip's

Ordnance Survey® This product includes mapping data licensed from Ordnance Survey®, with the permission of the Controller of Her Majesty's Stationery Office. © Crown copyright 2015. All rights reserved. Licence number 100011710

The map of Ireland on pages XVIII-XIX is based upon the Crown Copyright and is reproduced with the permission of Land & Property Services under delegated authority from the Controller of Her Majesty's Stationery Office, © Crown Copyright and database right 2015, PMLPA No 100503, and on Ordnance Survey Ireland by permission of the Government © Ordnance Survey Ireland / Government of Ireland Permit number 8982.

Data for the speed cameras provided by PocketGPSWorld.com Ltd.

Information for National Parks, Areas of Outstanding Natural Beauty, National Trails and Country Parks in Wales supplied by the Countryside Council for Wales.

Information for National Parks, Areas of Outstanding Natural Beauty, National Trails and Country Parks in England supplied by Natural England. Data for Regional Parks, Long Distance Footpaths and Country Parks in Scotland provided by Scottish Natural Heritage.

Gaelic name forms used in the Western Isles provided by Comhairle nan Eilean.

Data for the National Nature Reserves in England provided by Natural England. Data for the National Nature Reserves in Wales provided by Countryside Council for Wales. Darparwyd data'n ymwneud â Gwarchodfeydd Natur Cenedlaethol Cymru gan Gyngor Cefn Gwlad Cymru.

Information on the location of National Nature Reserves in Scotland was provided by Scottish Natural Heritage.

Data for National Scenic Areas in Scotland provided by the Scottish Executive Office. Crown copyright material is reproduced with the permission of the Controller of HMSO and the Queen's Printer for Scotland. Licence number C02W0003960.

Printed in China

*Independent research survey, from research carried out by Outlook Research Limited, 2005/06.

**Nielsen BookScan Travel Publishing Year Book 2014 data

Inside back cover: **County and unitary authority boundaries**

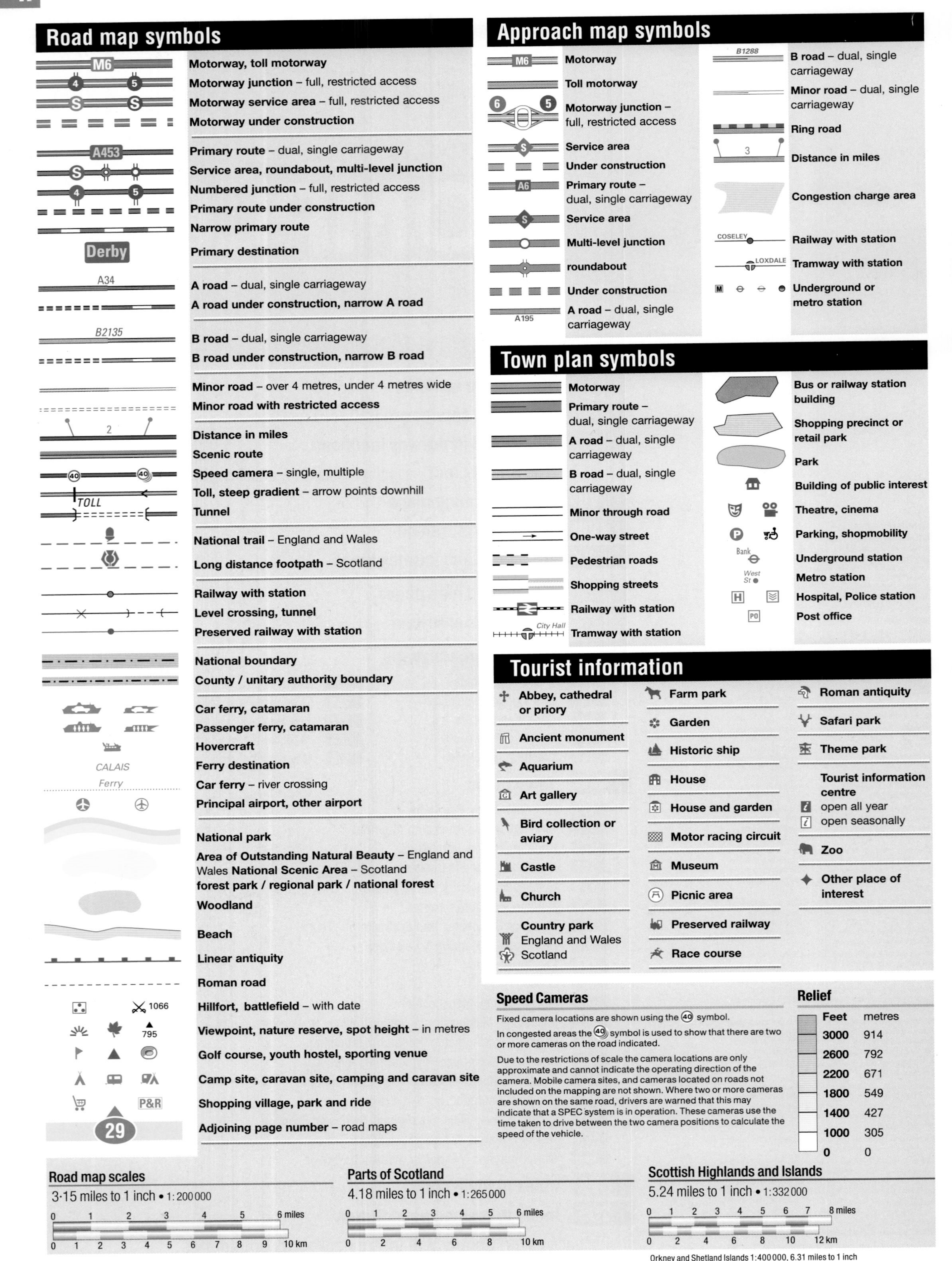

Road map symbols

- Motorway, toll motorway
- Motorway junction – full, restricted access
- Motorway service area – full, restricted access
- Motorway under construction

- Primary route – dual, single carriageway
- Service area, roundabout, multi-level junction
- Numbered junction – full, restricted access
- Primary route under construction
- Narrow primary route
- Primary destination — **Derby**

- A road – dual, single carriageway — A34
- A road under construction, narrow A road
- B road – dual, single carriageway — B2135
- B road under construction, narrow B road

- Minor road – over 4 metres, under 4 metres wide
- Minor road with restricted access

- Distance in miles
- Scenic route
- Speed camera – single, multiple
- Toll, steep gradient – arrow points downhill
- Tunnel

- National trail – England and Wales
- Long distance footpath – Scotland

- Railway with station
- Level crossing, tunnel
- Preserved railway with station

- National boundary
- County / unitary authority boundary

- Car ferry, catamaran
- Passenger ferry, catamaran
- Hovercraft
- Ferry destination — CALAIS / Ferry
- Car ferry – river crossing
- Principal airport, other airport

- National park
- Area of Outstanding Natural Beauty – England and Wales National Scenic Area – Scotland
- forest park / regional park / national forest
- Woodland

- Beach
- Linear antiquity
- Roman road

- Hillfort, battlefield – with date
- Viewpoint, nature reserve, spot height – in metres
- Golf course, youth hostel, sporting venue
- Camp site, caravan site, camping and caravan site
- Shopping village, park and ride
- Adjoining page number – road maps — 29

Approach map symbols

- Motorway — M6
- Toll motorway
- Motorway junction – full, restricted access
- Service area
- Under construction
- Primary route – dual, single carriageway — A6
- Service area
- Multi-level junction
- roundabout
- Under construction
- A road – dual, single carriageway — A195

- B road – dual, single carriageway — B1288
- Minor road – dual, single carriageway
- Ring road
- Distance in miles — 3
- Congestion charge area
- Railway with station — COSELEY
- Tramway with station — LOXDALE
- Underground or metro station

Town plan symbols

- Motorway
- Primary route – dual, single carriageway
- A road – dual, single carriageway
- B road – dual, single carriageway
- Minor through road
- One-way street
- Pedestrian roads
- Shopping streets
- Railway with station
- Tramway with station — City Hall

- Bus or railway station building
- Shopping precinct or retail park
- Park
- Building of public interest
- Theatre, cinema
- Parking, shopmobility — Bank
- Underground station — West St
- Metro station
- Hospital, Police station — H
- Post office — PO

Tourist information

- Abbey, cathedral or priory
- Ancient monument
- Aquarium
- Art gallery
- Bird collection or aviary
- Castle
- Church
- Country park — England and Wales / Scotland

- Farm park
- Garden
- Historic ship
- House
- House and garden
- Motor racing circuit
- Museum
- Picnic area
- Preserved railway
- Race course

- Roman antiquity
- Safari park
- Theme park
- Tourist information centre — i open all year / i open seasonally
- Zoo
- Other place of interest

Speed Cameras

Fixed camera locations are shown using the 40 symbol.

In congested areas the 40 symbol is used to show that there are two or more cameras on the road indicated.

Due to the restrictions of scale the camera locations are only approximate and cannot indicate the operating direction of the camera. Mobile camera sites, and cameras located on roads not included on the mapping are not shown. Where two or more cameras are shown on the same road, drivers are warned that this may indicate that a SPEC system is in operation. These cameras use the time taken to drive between the two camera positions to calculate the speed of the vehicle.

Relief

Feet	metres
3000	914
2600	792
2200	671
1800	549
1400	427
1000	305
0	0

Road map scales
3·15 miles to 1 inch • 1:200 000

0 1 2 3 4 5 6 miles
0 1 2 3 4 5 6 7 8 9 10 km

Parts of Scotland
4.18 miles to 1 inch • 1:265 000

0 1 2 3 4 5 6 miles
0 2 4 6 8 10 km

Scottish Highlands and Islands
5.24 miles to 1 inch • 1:332 000

0 1 2 3 4 5 6 7 8 miles
0 2 4 6 8 10 12 km

Orkney and Shetland Islands 1:400 000, 6.31 miles to 1 inch

Motorway service areas

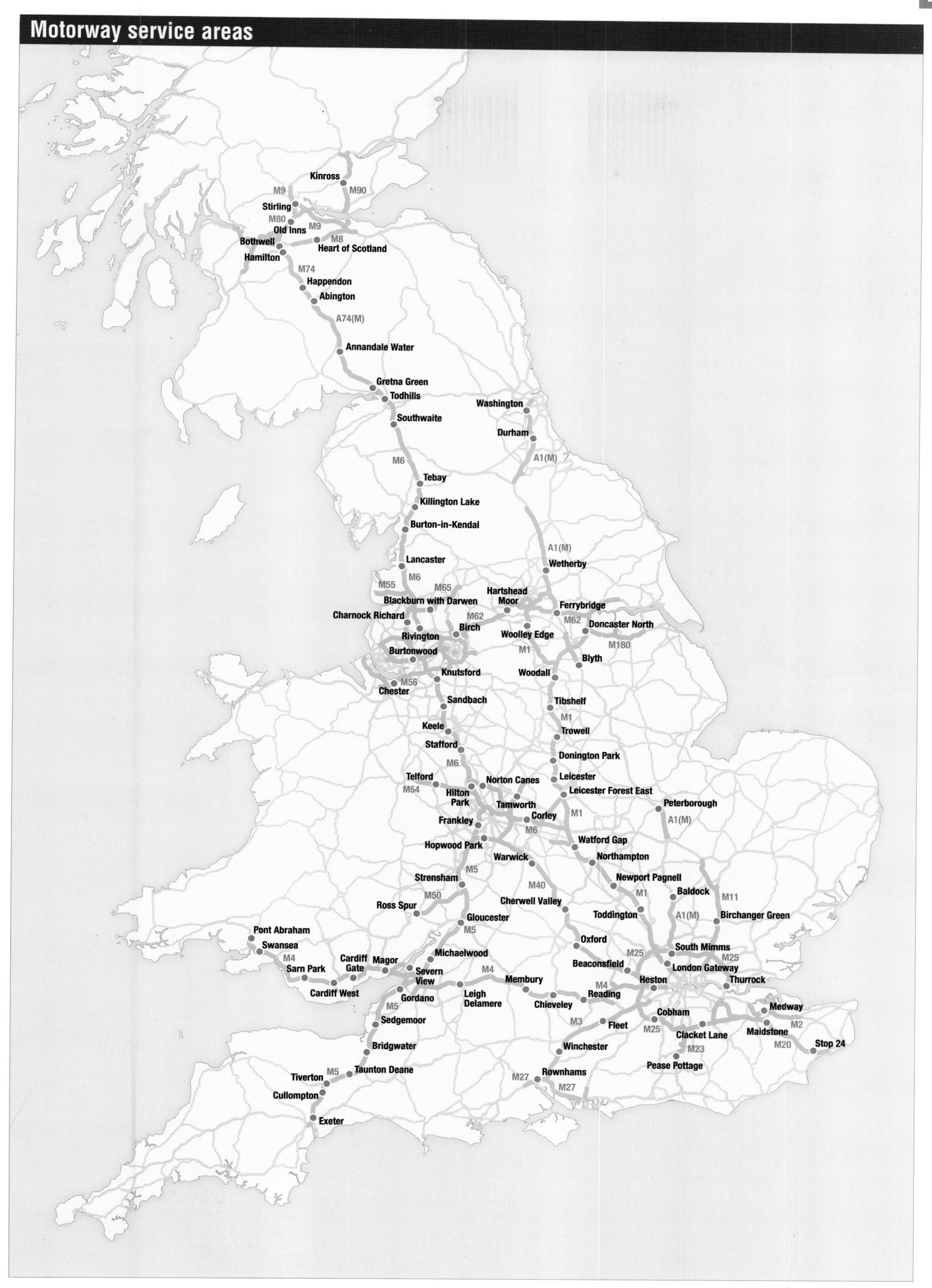

Restricted motorway junctions

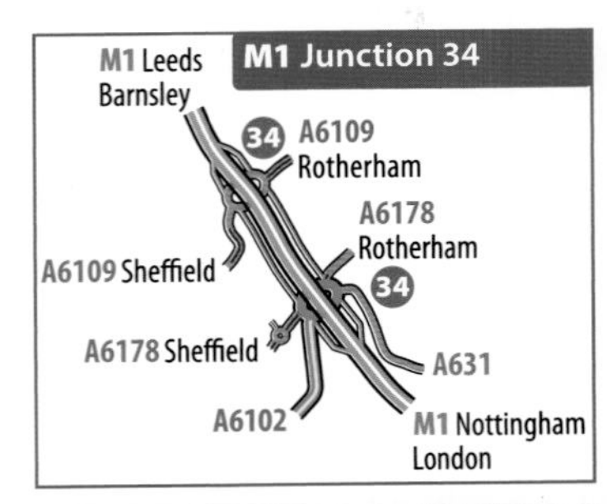

M1 Junction 34

M1 Leeds Barnsley • 34 • A6109 Rotherham • A6178 Rotherham • A6109 Sheffield • A6178 Sheffield • 34 • A631 • A6102 • M1 Nottingham London

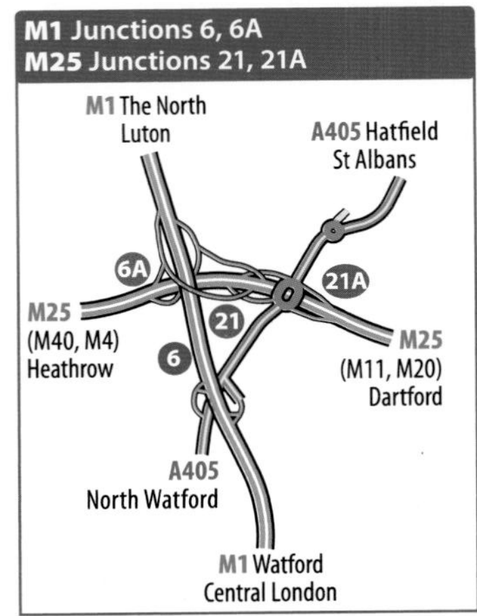

M1 Junctions 6, 6A
M25 Junctions 21, 21A

M1 The North Luton • A405 Hatfield St Albans • 6A • 21A • M25 (M40, M4) Heathrow • 21 • 6 • M25 (M11, M20) Dartford • A405 North Watford • M1 Watford Central London

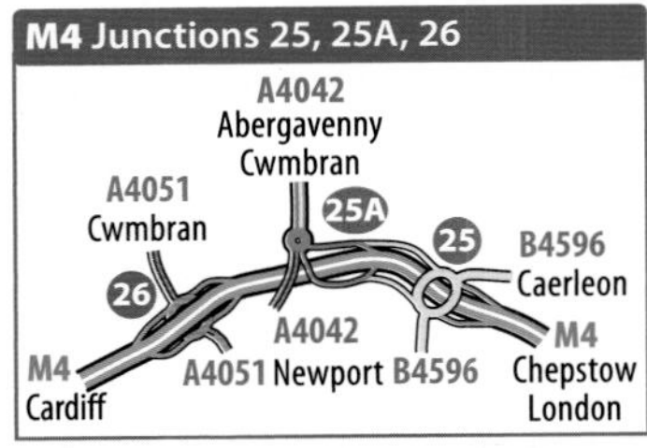

M4 Junctions 25, 25A, 26

A4042 Abergavenny Cwmbran • A4051 Cwmbran • 25A • 25 • B4596 Caerleon • 26 • A4042 • A4051 Newport • B4596 • M4 Cardiff • Chepstow London

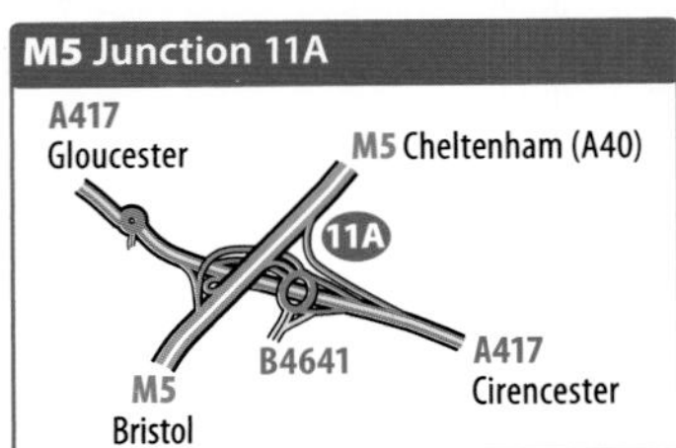

M5 Junction 11A

A417 Gloucester • M5 Cheltenham (A40) • 11A • B4641 • M5 Bristol • A417 Cirencester

M8 Junctions 8, 9 · M73 Junctions 1, 2
M74 Junctions 2A, 3, 3A, 4

M8 Glasgow • 9 • M73 Stirling • 8 • 2 • A89 Coatbridge • A8 Edinburgh • B7058 • A74 • B765 • A74 • M73 • M74 Glasgow • 2A • 3 • M74 • 3A • 1/4 • B7001 • A763 • B758 • A721 • M74 Carlisle • B7071

M1	Northbound	Southbound
2	No exit	No access
4	No exit	No access
6A	No exit. Access from M25 only	No access. Exit to M25 only
7	No exit. Access from A414 only	No access. Exit to A414 only
17	No access. Exit to M45 only	No exit. Access from M45 only
19	No exit to A14	No access from A14
21A	No access	No exit
23A		Exit to A42 only
24A	No exit	No access
35A	No access	No exit
43	No access. Exit to M621 only	No exit. Access from M621 only
48	No exit to A1(M) southbound	

M3	Eastbound	Westbound
8	No exit	No access
10	No access	No exit
13	No access to M27 eastbound	
14	No exit	No access

M4	Eastbound	Westbound
1	Exit to A4 eastbound only	Access from A4 westbound only
2	Access from A4 eastbound only	Access to A4 westbound only
21	No exit	No access
23	No access	No exit
25	No exit	No access
25A	No exit	No access
29	No exit	No access
38		No access
39	No exit or access	No exit
41	No access	No exit
41A	No exit	No access
42	Access from A483 only	Exit to A483 only

M5	Northbound	Southbound
10	No exit	No access
11A	No access from A417 eastbound	No exit to A417 westbound

M6	Northbound	Southbound
3A	No access. Exit to M42 northbound only	No exit. Access from M6 eastbound only
4A	No exit. Access from M42 southbound only	No access. Exit to M42 only
5	No access	No exit
10A	No access. Exit to M54 only	No exit. Access from M54 only
11A	No exit. Access from M6 Toll only	No access. Exit to M6 Toll only
20	No exit to M56 eastbound	No access from M56 westbound
24	No exit	No access
25	No access	No exit
30	No exit. Access from M61 northbound only	No access. Exit to M61 southbound only
31A	No access	No exit
45	No access	No exit

M6 Toll	Northbound	Southbound
T1		No exit
T2	No exit, no access	No access
T5	No exit	No access
T7	No access	No exit
T8	No access	No exit

M8	Eastbound	Westbound
8	No exit to M73 northbound	No access from M73 southbound
9	No access	No exit
13	No exit southbound	Access from M73 southbound only
14	No access	No exit
16	No exit	No access
17	No exit	No access
18		No exit
19	No exit to A814 eastbound	No access from A814 westbound
20	No exit	No access
21	No access from M74	No exit
22	No exit. Access from M77 only	No access. Exit to M77 only
23	No exit	No access
25	Exit to A739 northbound only. Access from A739 southbound only	Access from A739 southbound only
25A	No exit	No access
28	No exit	No access
28A	No exit	No access

M9	Eastbound	Westbound
1A	No exit	No access
2	No access	No exit
3	No exit	No access
6	No access	No exit
8	No exit	No access

M11	Northbound	Southbound
4	No exit. Access from A406 only	No access. Exit to A406 only
5	No access	No exit
9	No access	No exit
13	No access	No exit
14	No exit to A428 westbound	No exit. Access from A14 westbound only

M20	Eastbound	Westbound
2	No access	No exit
3	No exit Access from M26 eastbound only	No access Exit to M26 westbound only
11A	No access	No exit

M23	Northbound	Southbound
7	No exit to A23 southbound	No access from A23 northbound
10A	No exit	No access

M25	Clockwise	Anticlockwise
5	No exit to M26 eastbound	No access from M26 westbound
19	No access	No exit
21	No exit to M1 southbound. Access from M1 southbound only	No exit to M1 southbound. Access from M1 southbound only
31	No exit	No access

M27	Eastbound	Westbound
10	No exit	No access
12	No access	No exit

M40	Eastbound	Westbound
3	No exit	No access
7	No exit	No access
8	No exit	No access
13	No exit	No access
14	No access	No exit
16	No access	No exit

M42	Northbound	Southbound
1	No exit	No access
7	No access Exit to M6 northbound only	No exit Access from M6 northbound only
7A	No access. Exit to M6 southbound only	No exit
8	No exit. Access from M6 southbound only	Exit to M6 northbound only. Access from M6 southbound only

M45		Eastbound	Westbound
M1 J17		Access to M1 southbound only	No access from M1 southbound
With A45		No access	No exit

M48	Eastbound	Westbound
M4 J21	No exit to M4 westbound	No access from M4 eastbound
M4 J23	No access from M4 westbound	No exit to M4 eastbound

M49	Southbound	Northbound
18A	No exit to M5 northbound	No access from M5 southbound

M53	Northbound	Southbound
11	Exit to M56 eastbound only. Access from M56 westbound only	Exit to M56 eastbnd only. Access from M56 westbound only

M56	Eastbound	Westbound
2	No exit	No access
3	No access	No exit
4	No exit	No access
7		No access
8	No exit or access	No access
9	No access from M6 northbound	No access to M6 southbound
15	No exit to M53	No access from M53 northbound

M57	Northbound	Southbound
3	No exit	No access
5	No exit	No access

M58	Eastbound	Westbound
1	No exit	No access

M60	Clockwise	Anticlockwise
2	No exit	No access
3	No exit to A34 northbound	No exit to A34 northbound
4	No access from M56	No exit to M56
5	No exit to A5103 southbound	No exit to A5103 northbound
14	No exit	No access
16	No exit	No access
20	No access	No exit
22		No access
25	No access	
26		No exit or access
27	No exit	No access

M61	Northbound	Southbound
2	No access from A580 eastbound	No exit to A580 westbound
3	No access from A580 eastbound. No access from A666 southbound	No exit to A580 westbound
M6 J30	No exit to M6 southbound	No access from M6 northbound

M62	Eastbound	Westbound
23	No access	No exit

M65	Eastbound	Westbound
9	No access	No exit
11	No exit	No access

M66	Northbound	Southbound
1	No access	No exit

M67	Eastbound	Westbound
1A	No access	No exit
2	No exit	No access

M69	Northbound	Southbound
2	No access	No access

M73	Northbound	Southbound
2	No access from M8 or A89 eastbound. No exit to A89	No exit to M8 or A89 westbound. No access from A89

M74	Northbound	Southbound
3	No access	No exit
3A	No exit	No access
7	No exit	No access
9	No exit or access	No access
10		No exit
11	No exit	No access
12	No access	No exit

M77	Northbound	Southbound
4	No exit	No access
6	No exit	No access
7	No exit or access	
8	No access	No access

M80	Northbound	Southbound
4A	No access	No exit
6A	No exit	
8	Exit to M876 northbound only. No access	Access from M876 southbound only. No exit

M90	Northbound	Southbound
2A	No access	No exit
7	No exit	No access
8	No access	No exit
10	No access from A912	No exit to A912

M180	Eastbound	Westbound
1	No access	No exit

M621	Eastbound	Westbound
2A	No exit	No access
4	No exit	
5	No exit	No access
6	No access	No exit

M876	Northbound	Southbound
2	No access	No exit

A1(M)	Northbound	Southbound
2	No access	No exit
3		No access
5	No exit	No access
14	No exit	No access
40	No access	No exit
43	No exit. Access from M1 only	No access. Exit to M1 only
57	No access	No exit
65	No access	No exit

A3(M)	Northbound	Southbound
1	No exit	No access
4	No access	No exit

A38(M)	Northbound	Southbound
With Victoria Rd, (Park Circus) Birmingham	No exit	No access

A48(M)	Northbound	Southbound
M4 Junc 29	Exit to M4 eastbound only	Access from M4 westbound only
29A	Access from A48 eastbound only	Exit to A48 westbound only

A57(M)	Eastbound	Westbound
With A5103	No access	No exit
With A34	No access	No exit

A58(M)		Southbound
With Park Lane and Westgate, Leeds		No access

A64(M)	Eastbound	Westbound
With A58 Clay Pit Lane, Leeds	No access	No exit
With Regent Street, Leeds	No access	No access

A74(M)	Northbound	Southbound
18	No access	No exit
22		No exit

A194(M)	Northbound	Southbound
A1(M) J65 Gateshead Western Bypass	Access from A1(M) northbound only	Exit to A1(M) southbound only

M3 Junctions 13, 14
M27 Junction 4

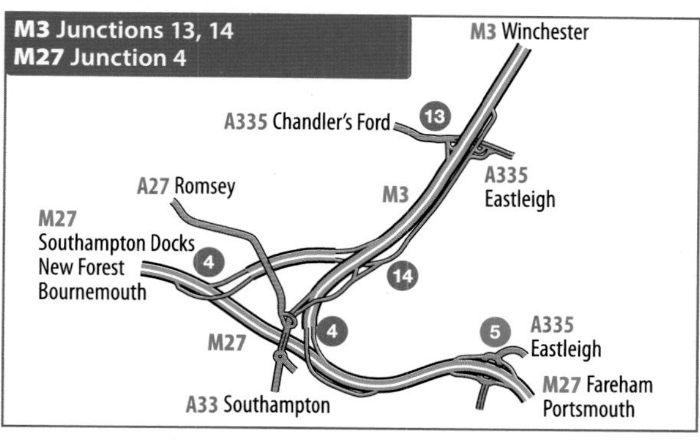

M6 Junctions 3A, 4A · M42 Junctions 7, 7A, 8, 9
M6 Toll Junctions T1, T2

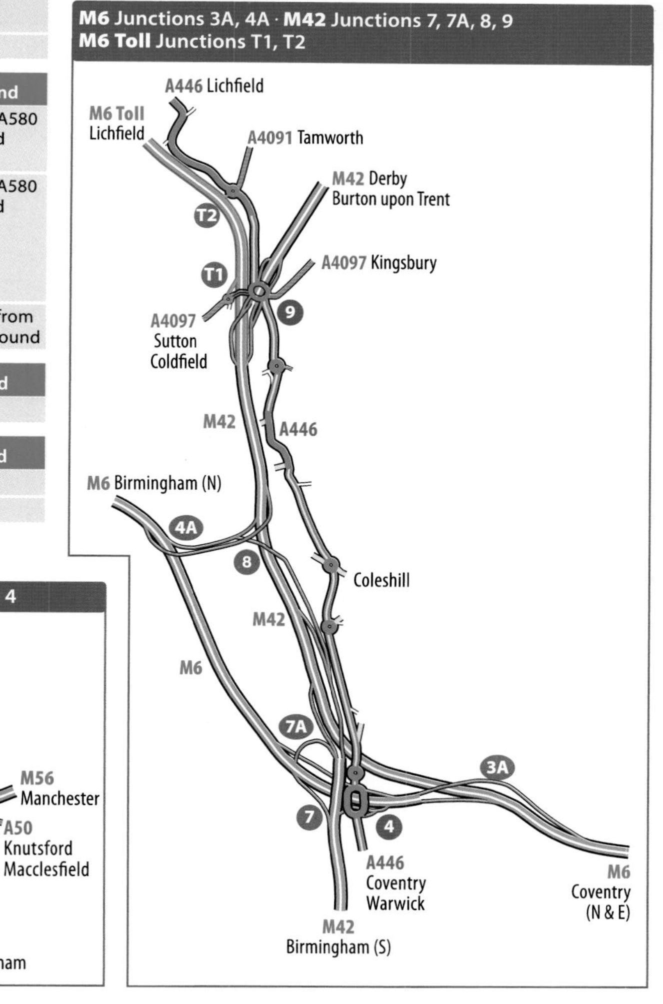

M6 Junction 20 · M56 Junction 4

M62 Junctions 32A, 33 · A1(M) Junctions 40, 41

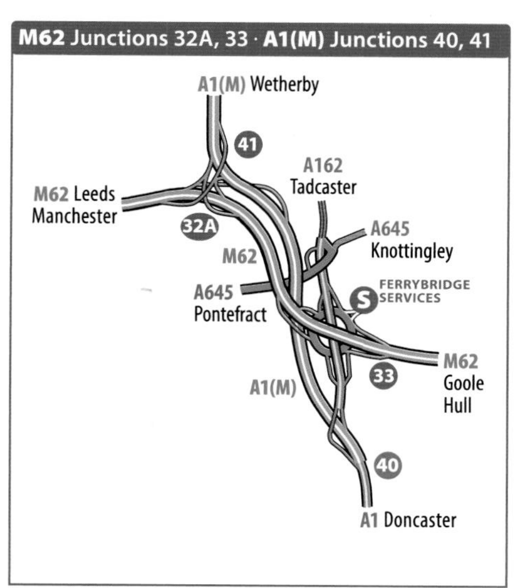

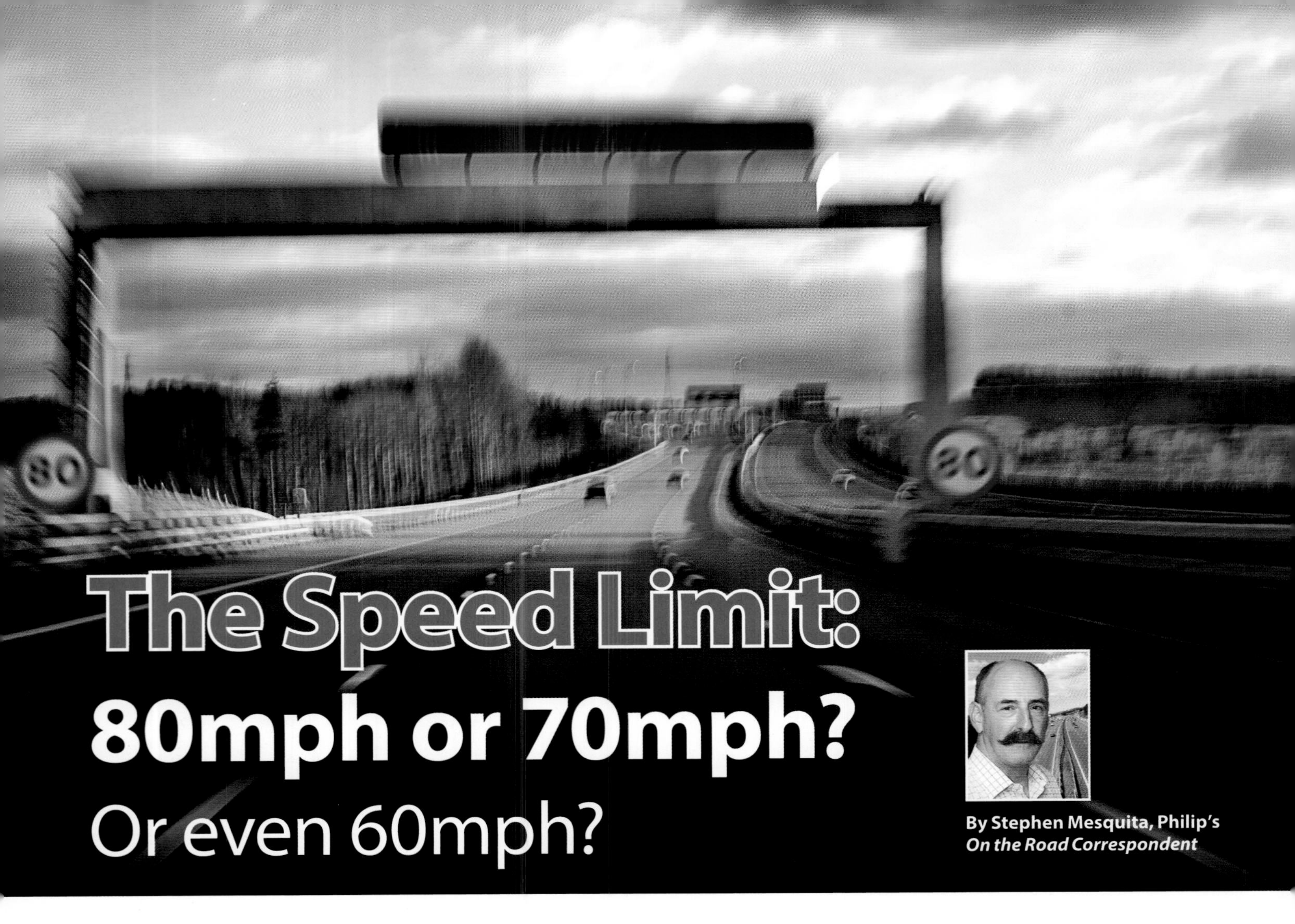

The Speed Limit:

80mph or 70mph?

Or even 60mph?

By Stephen Mesquita, Philip's
On the Road Correspondent

I t was one of those moments, described in phrasebooks as 'At the Car Hire Desk'. A moment to make the heart sink and the spirit to travel wither. It was at Frankfurt airport. 'I'm very sorry, sir, we don't have the Compact you ordered.' Visions of scooters and mopeds appeared before my eyes.
'But we do have a Mercedes blah blah blah, which we can offer you in its place at no extra charge' (sorry Mercedes fans, the specification escapes me).

So there I was, on the autobahn, with over 100 miles to drive to my appointment. An autobahn with no speed limit and a Mercedes blah blah blah which also seemed to have no speed limit. It was a pleasant autumn's afternoon. The traffic was relatively light.

We have reached the stage in this tale where I need to break the flow to state my credentials. I am not a boy racer. I never have been a boy racer (except for an incident in my long lost youth which I may decide to relate later). Speed comes a very poor second to safety when I am driving. I'm normally very happy to pootle along the motorway at 70mph, if not a bit slower.

But here I was with an opportunity to conduct an experiment – purely for the sake of research, you understand. How fast could I go in this speed machine at whose wheel I now found myself? Looking in my mirror at the outside lane I could see another Merc way back on the autobahn. Within a few seconds it passed me in a blur. Now was my chance. I put the pedal to the metal, manoeuvred into the outside lane and held on tight.

 … even at 240kph, there were still cars appearing with alarming speed in my rear view mirror

From a quick calculation, 240kph is 150mph. That was the stage at which I decided that my driving skills probably weren't up to going any faster. The worrying thing was that, even at 240kph, there were still cars appearing with alarming speed in my rear view mirror, impatient to overtake.

Where is all this leading?

This year, the government has again floated the idea of raising the speed limit on motorways to 80mph. When I heard this, my mind went back to my experience outside Frankfurt. But it also went back even further. To my first driving experience, in the mid 1970s, on the freeways of the Mid West. It was just after the oil crisis and the speed limit, even on the freeway, was 55mph. My job entailed a lot of driving in a car with automatic everything – a car that more or less drove itself.

The freeways were, for the most part, empty and the journeys were long. 55mph seemed

mind-numbingly slow. The radio played the same hits over and over. Combating boredom was nearly impossible.

So which was it to be? The German experience, the status quo or the US experience of the mid-70s?

To try to answer this question, I left my house at 4.40am on a damp February morning. The first challenge was to find a stretch of road where I could conduct my experiment. Out here, in deepest East Anglia, there are no three-lane motorways. There are also, in some areas, forests of speed cameras. I needed to drive on an east-west axis to neutralise the effect of a north wind. And I needed to be out at a time of day when lorries were least likely to be overtaking each other in the outside lane and when all good law enforcement officers were tucked up in bed.

This was the plan – to drive 30 miles at 80mph and 30 miles at 60mph and a bit in between at regulation 70mph. I chose the A14, A11 and M11 from Bury St Edmunds and back. It's dual carriageway all the way. It's comparatively speed camera free on the outward leg (at least I hope so) and, although it's busy, it's not too busy at 5.30am when I started the 80mph stretch.

The advantage of driving faster is that you get there faster. So you save time. The advantage of driving slower is that you use less petrol, so you save money. I am not qualified to talk about road safety, although the Road Safety Pressure Groups all argue that faster is more dangerous. I am also not qualified to comment on the environmental issues, although it follows that less petrol means less pollution.

I would not normally bore you with spreadsheets – but, on this occasion, it seems to be the simplest way to express the argument.

The important thing is to understand – as all motorists surely do – that the faster you drive, the more petrol you consume. In my trusty 10-year-old VW Passat Estate 1.9 TDi (I do remember the specification of my own car), I would normally expect to do about 45 miles per gallon on a long journey.

At 80mph, over 30 miles, the petrol consumption was 36.6mpg; at 70mph over 20 miles (10 miles into the wind and 10 miles with the wind behind) the average was 42.9mpg; and, at 60mph, the consumption was 47.3mpg.

> ### It may not sound much – but multiply it up over a year and it turns into a sum of money that you notice

Now for the maths. At the time of going to press, diesel costs £1.12 per litre (and long may it last). So my 30 miles at 80mph cost me £4.17 and my 30 miles at 60mph cost me £3.23. It may not sound much – but multiply it up over a year and it turns into a sum of money that you notice. In fact, if you're a professional driver clocking up 25,000 miles a year, it totals out at nearly £1,000 more.

So here is my Ready Reckoner (table 1)

Based on my experience, if I drove at 60mph on long journeys, it could save me 23% on my fuel costs compared with driving at 80mph and 9% compared with driving at 70mph. You'll notice that the differential is greater between 70 and 80 than between 60 and 70mph.

But time is also money. Is it possible that the savings in petrol would be wiped out by the cost of the additional journey time? Back to the spreadsheet (table 2).

So you'll see that, although it's 23% cheaper to drive at 60mph compared with 80, it takes 32% longer. The 104 hours lost by the professional driver would cost considerably more than the £983 gained in the petrol saving.

'Hours lost' is a concept that is not always easy to quantify. How many of those hours would otherwise be downtime, so not really lost? If this is what the bean counters call a Cost Benefit Analysis, it doesn't really give us a conclusive answer.

1	(80)	(70)	(60)	(70)	(60)	(70)	(60)
	36.6mpg	42.9mpg	47.3mpg	Amount saved*			% Saved*
5,000 miles	£696	£593	£538	£102.15	£157.35	17%	23%
10,000 miles	£1,391	£1,187	£1,076	£204.30	£314.70	17%	23%
15,000 miles	£2,087	£1,780	£1,615	£306.44	£472.05	17%	23%
20,000 miles	£2,782	£2,374	£2,153	£408.59	£629.40	17%	23%
25,000 miles	£3,478	£2,967	£2,691	£510.74	£786.75	17%	23%

Price per litre – diesel: £1.12
Price per gallon – diesel: £5.09
*compared to 80mph

2	Time taken (hours)			Additional time taken (hours)			% Additional time taken at 60mph compared to:	
	(80)	(70)	(60)	(80)	(70)	(60)	(80)	(70)
5,000 miles	62.50	71.43	83.33	0	8.93	20.83	32%	13%
10,000 miles	125.00	142.86	166.67	0	17.86	41.67	32%	13%
15,000 miles	187.50	214.29	250.00	0	26.79	62.50	32%	13%
20,000 miles	250.00	285.71	333.33	0	35.71	83.33	32%	13%
25,000 miles	312.50	357.14	416.67	0	44.64	104.17	32%	13%

> ### …my speedometer was set to register 3–4mph faster than I was actually driving

Back to the A14. Here are some considerations which you can't deduce from the spreadsheets. First, I didn't actually drive at 80mph. The needle of my speedometer was at, or over, 80mph for most of the journey. But when I came to check my average speed, I had actually driven the 30 miles at 77mph. Thanks to those nice people at VW, my speedometer was set to register 3–4mph faster than I was actually driving. Anyone who uses sat nav can see this as they drive. Their speedometer registers a higher speed than the sat nav tells them they are actually driving.

But I was happy not to be averaging 80. If it had been a fine day on an empty motorway, I would probably have been very comfortable doing 80. But on a dual carriageway, with overtaking lorries which threw up spray, and in the dark, 77mph was fast enough. Actually, it was probably too fast.

And then I had a surprise when I was driving at 60mph on the return leg. Quite a few other drivers – and not just lorries – were also keeping to 60. In these tough times, many drivers have already worked out for themselves the economies of driving more slowly – without a law being needed to stop those who want or need to drive faster. The law does not force you to drive at 70.

It may make for a dull conclusion to this otherwise sparkling article (spreadsheets and all) – but my vote is to keep the speed limit at 70mph. If we were really trying to be green in this country, we would reduce it – but that's currently left to you as an individual. My dawn sortie has convinced me that raising the speed limit to 80mph on our crowded motorways does not have my vote. Sorry all you budding Jensons and Lewis's out there.

So, after breaking the law to bring you this research, I'll be going back to driving at 70mph – or, now I've done the sums, maybe a little bit slower.

Oh yes – that incident from my long lost past. I nearly forgot. Well, I didn't always keep to the 55mph speed limit during my stint on the road in the USA. In fact, on an empty freeway between Chicago and Minneapolis, I got stopped. Despite my poor impression of Bertie Wooster pleading ignorance as a foreigner, a request for $115 arrived from a court in Wisconsin. I remember thinking as I wrote the cheque, that in 1975 $115 was quite a lot of money.

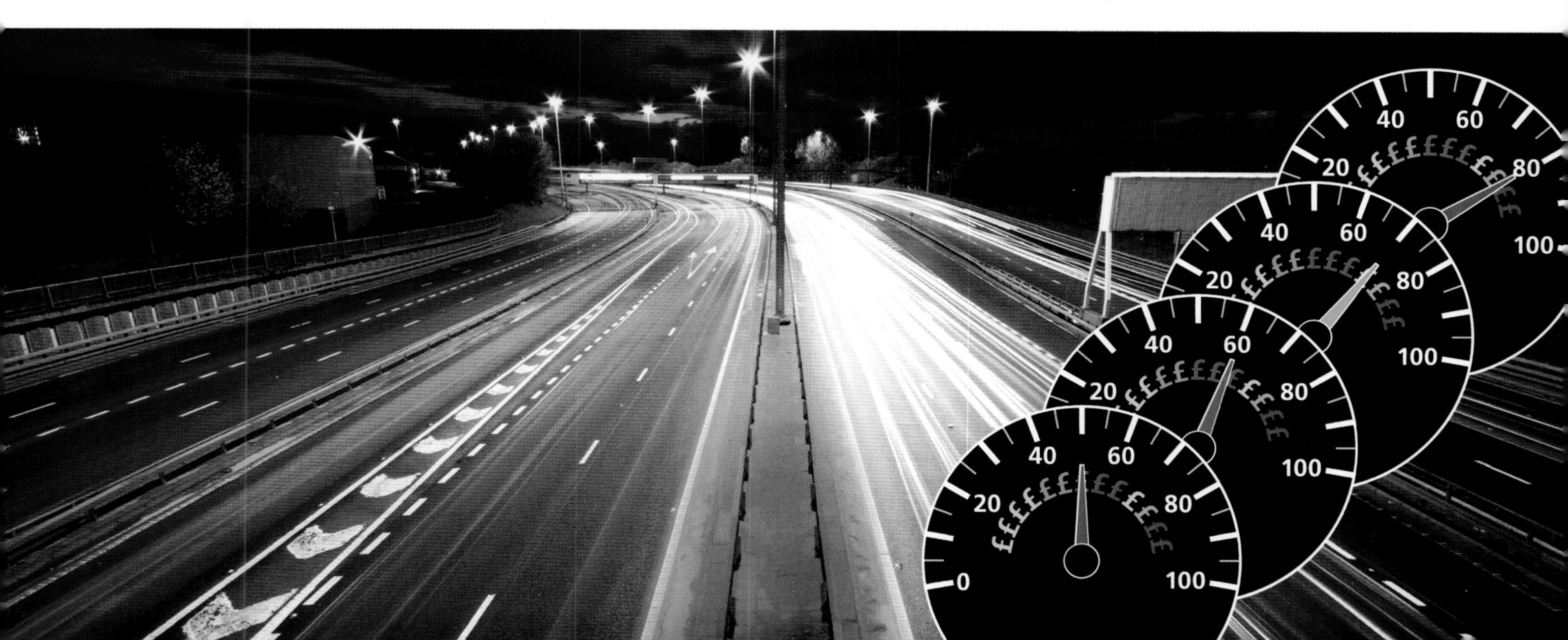

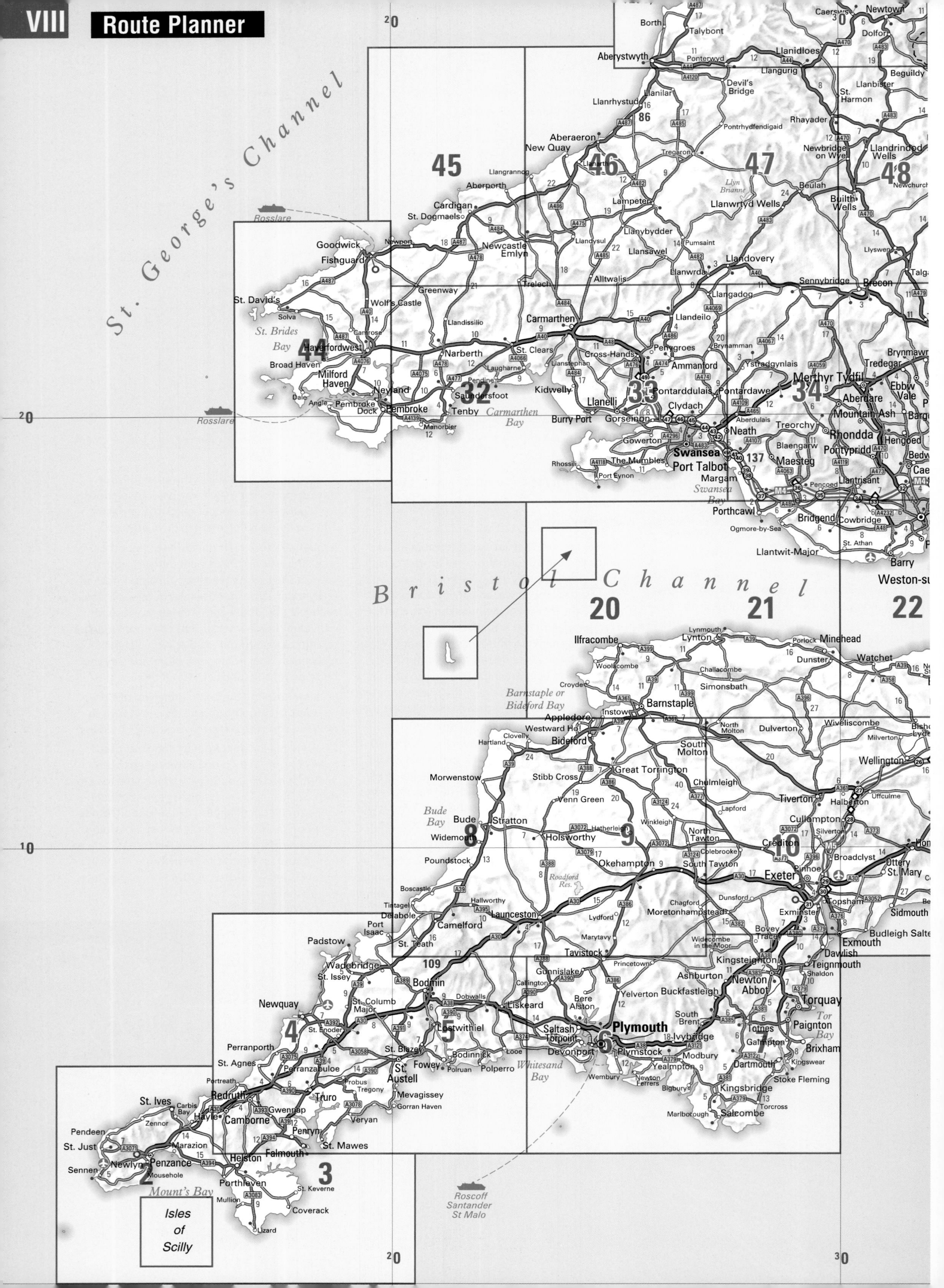
St. George's Channel
Bristol Channel
45
46
47
48
44
32
33
34
20
21
22
8
9
10
4
5
6
7
2
3
Borth
Talybont
Aberystwyth
Ponterwyd
Llanidloes
Llangurig
Newtown
Caersws
Dolfor
Devil's Bridge
Llanilar
Llanrhystud
Pontrhydfendigaid
Rhayader
St. Harmon
Llanbister
Beguildy
Aberaeron
New Quay
Tregaron
Newbridge on Wye
Llandrindod Wells
Llangrannog
Aberporth
Llyn Brianne
Beulah
Builth Wells
Newchurch
Lampeter
Llanwrtyd Wells
Cardigan
St. Dogmaels
Llanybydder
Llanfair
Llansawel
Pumsaint
Llyswen
Rosslare
Goodwick
Fishguard
Newport
Newcastle Emlyn
Llandysul
Llandovery
Llanwrda
Alltwalis
Trelech
Sennybridge
Brecon
Talgarth
St. David's
Solva
Greenway
Wolf's Castle
Llangadog
Carmarthen
Llandeilo
Llandissilio
St. Brides Bay
Camrose
Haverfordwest
Narberth
St. Clears
Cross Hands
Penygroes
Brynamman
Ammanford
Ystradgynlais
Merthyr Tydfil
Brynmawr
Tredegar
Ebbw Vale
Broad Haven
Milford Haven
Neyland
Laugharne
Llanstephan
Pendine
Kidwelly
Saundersfoot
Pontarddulais
Pontardawe
Aberdare
Mountain Ash
Dale
Angle
Pembroke Dock
Pembroke
Tenby
Manorbier
Carmarthen Bay
Burry Port
Llanelli
Gorseinon
Clydach
Neath
Aberdulais
Treorchy
Rhondda
Hengoed
Gowerton
Swansea
Blaengarw
Pontypridd
Rhossili
The Mumbles
Port Eynon
Port Talbot
Maesteg
Margam
Swansea Bay
Pencoed
Llantrisant
Porthcawl
Bridgend
Cowbridge
Ogmore-by-Sea
St. Athan
Llantwit-Major
Barry
Weston-su
Lynmouth
Lynton
Porlock
Minehead
Ilfracombe
Watchet
Dunster
Woolacombe
Challacombe
Simonsbath
Croyde
Barnstaple or Bideford Bay
Barnstaple
Instow
Appledore
Westward Ho!
Bideford
Clovelly
Hartland
North Molton
Dulverton
Wiveliscombe
South Molton
Milverton
Wellington
Morwenstow
Stibb Cross
Great Torrington
Chulmleigh
Tiverton
Halberton
Uffculme
Venn Green
Lapford
Bude Bay
Bude
Stratton
Hatherleigh
Winkleigh
Cullompton
Widemouth
Holsworthy
North Tawton
Crediton
Silverton
Poundstock
Okehampton
Colebrooke
South Tawton
Broadclyst
Ottery St. Mary
Roadford Res.
Pinhoe
Exeter
Boscastle
Tintagel
Delabole
Hallworthy
Launceston
Chagford
Moretonhampstead
Dunsford
Exminster
Topsham
Sidmouth
Camelford
Port Isaac
Lydford
Marytavy
Bovey Tracey
Exmouth
Budleigh Salterton
Padstow
St. Teath
Tavistock
Widecombe in the Moor
Dawlish
Teignmouth
Wadebridge
St. Issey
Gunnislake
Princetown
Ashburton
Kingsteignton
Shaldon
Bodmin
Callington
Newton Abbot
Torquay
Newquay
St. Columb Major
Dobwalls
Liskeard
Bere Alston
Yelverton
Buckfastleigh
Tor Bay
Paignton
St. Enoder
Lostwithiel
Saltash
Torpoint
Plymouth
South Brent
Ivybridge
Totnes
Galmpton
Perranporth
St. Blazey
Bodinnick
Looe
Devonport
Plymstock
Modbury
Brixham
St. Agnes
Perranzabuloe
Fowey
Polruan
Polperro
Whitesand Bay
Yealmpton
Dartmouth
Kingswear
Portreath
Probus
Tregony
St. Austell
Wembury
Newton Ferrers
Bigbury
Stoke Fleming
Redruth
Truro
Mevagissey
Kingsbridge
Torcross
St. Ives
Carbis Bay
Hayle
Gwennap
Gorran Haven
Marlborough
Salcombe
Zennor
Camborne
Veryan
Pendeen
Penryn
St. Just
Marazion
St. Mawes
Falmouth
Sennen
Newlyn
Penzance
Helston
Mousehole
Porthleven
St. Keverne
Mount's Bay
Mullion
Coverack
Lizard
Isles of Scilly
Roscoff
Santander
St Malo

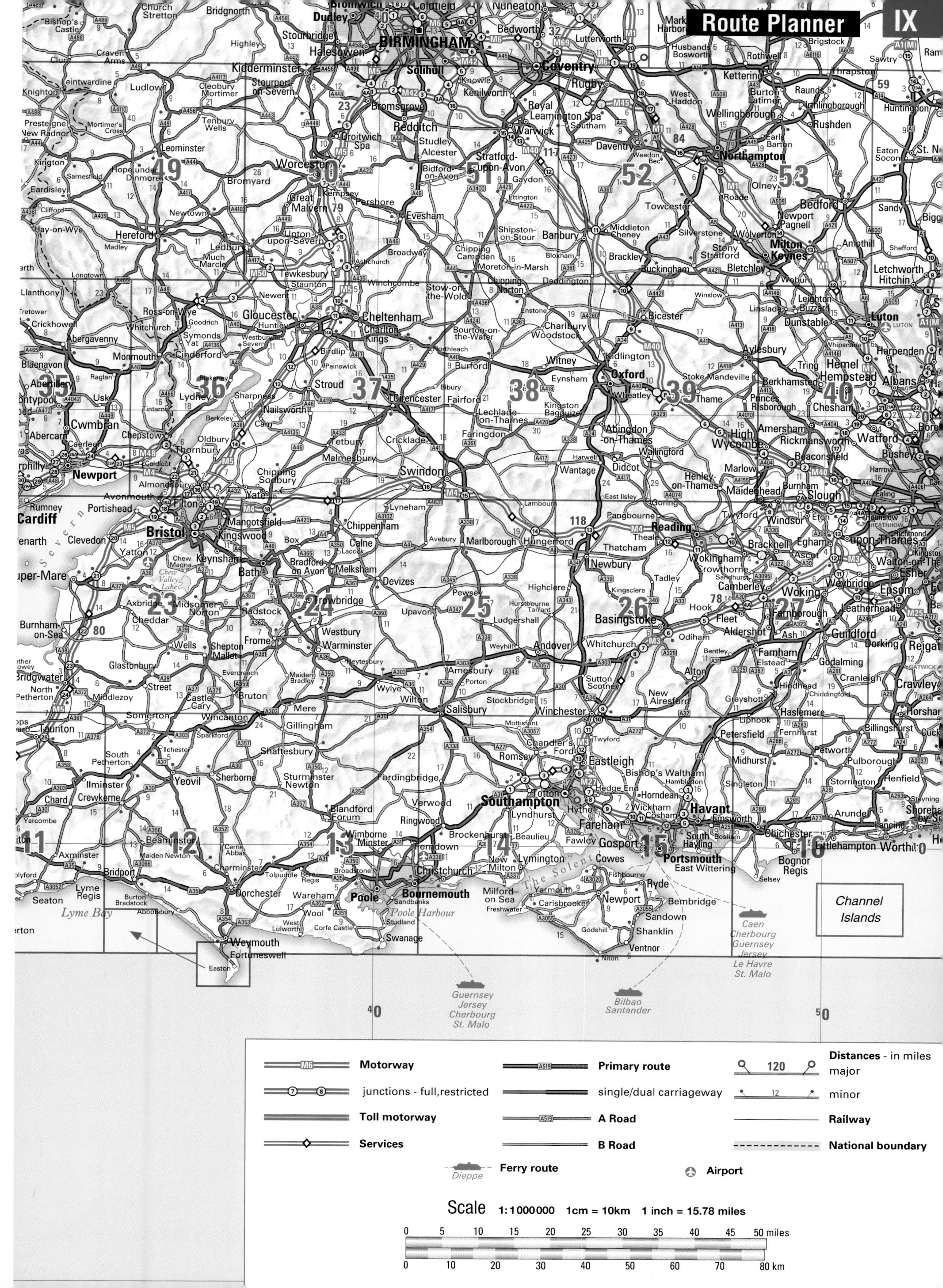

Scale

1:1000000   1cm = 10km   1 inch = 15.78 miles

	Motorway		Primary route		Distances - in miles major
	junctions - full, restricted		single/dual carriageway		minor
	Toll motorway		A Road		Railway
	Services		B Road		National boundary
	Ferry route		Airport		

Channel Islands

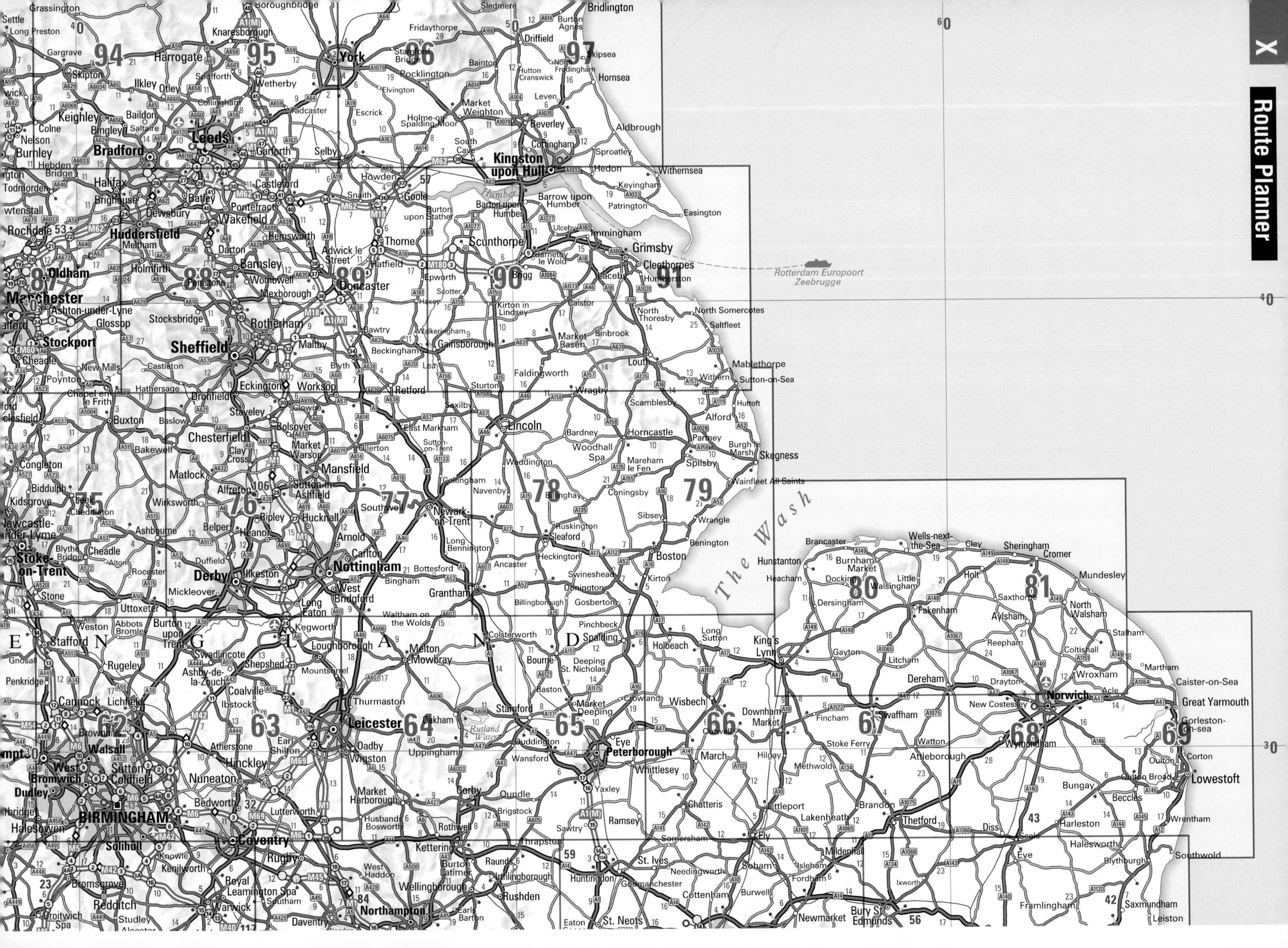

Rotterdam Europoort
Zeebrugge
The Wash
York
Leeds
Bradford
Huddersfield
Sheffield
Doncaster
Kingston upon Hull
Grimsby
Scunthorpe
Lincoln
Nottingham
Derby
Leicester
Peterborough
Norwich
Great Yarmouth
Lowestoft
King's Lynn
Boston
Skegness
Cromer
Coventry
BIRMINGHAM
Northampton
Stoke-on-Trent
Stockport
Oldham
Manchester

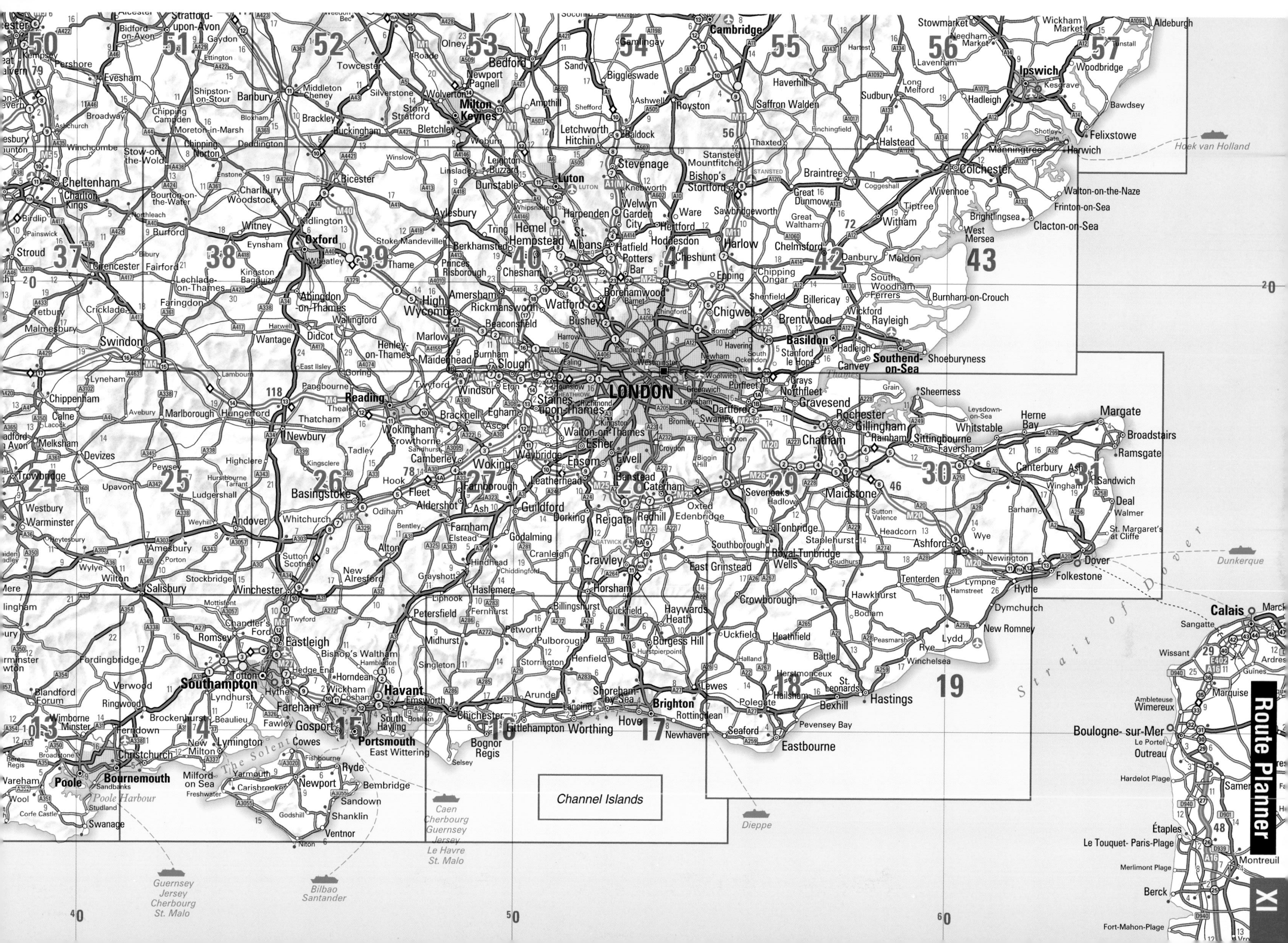

LONDON
Cambridge
Ipswich
Felixstowe
Harwich
Hoek van Holland
Colchester
Chelmsford
Basildon
Southend-on-Sea
Margate
Ramsgate
Canterbury
Dover
Dunkerque
Folkestone
Calais
Boulogne-sur-Mer
Ashford
Maidstone
Hastings
Eastbourne
Brighton
Worthing
Chichester
Portsmouth
Southampton
Bournemouth
Poole
Salisbury
Winchester
Basingstoke
Reading
Oxford
Swindon
Cheltenham
Bedford
Milton Keynes
Luton
Guildford
Channel Islands
Dieppe
Bilbao
Santander
Guernsey
Jersey
Cherbourg
St. Malo
Caen
Le Havre
The Solent
Poole Harbour
Strait of Dover

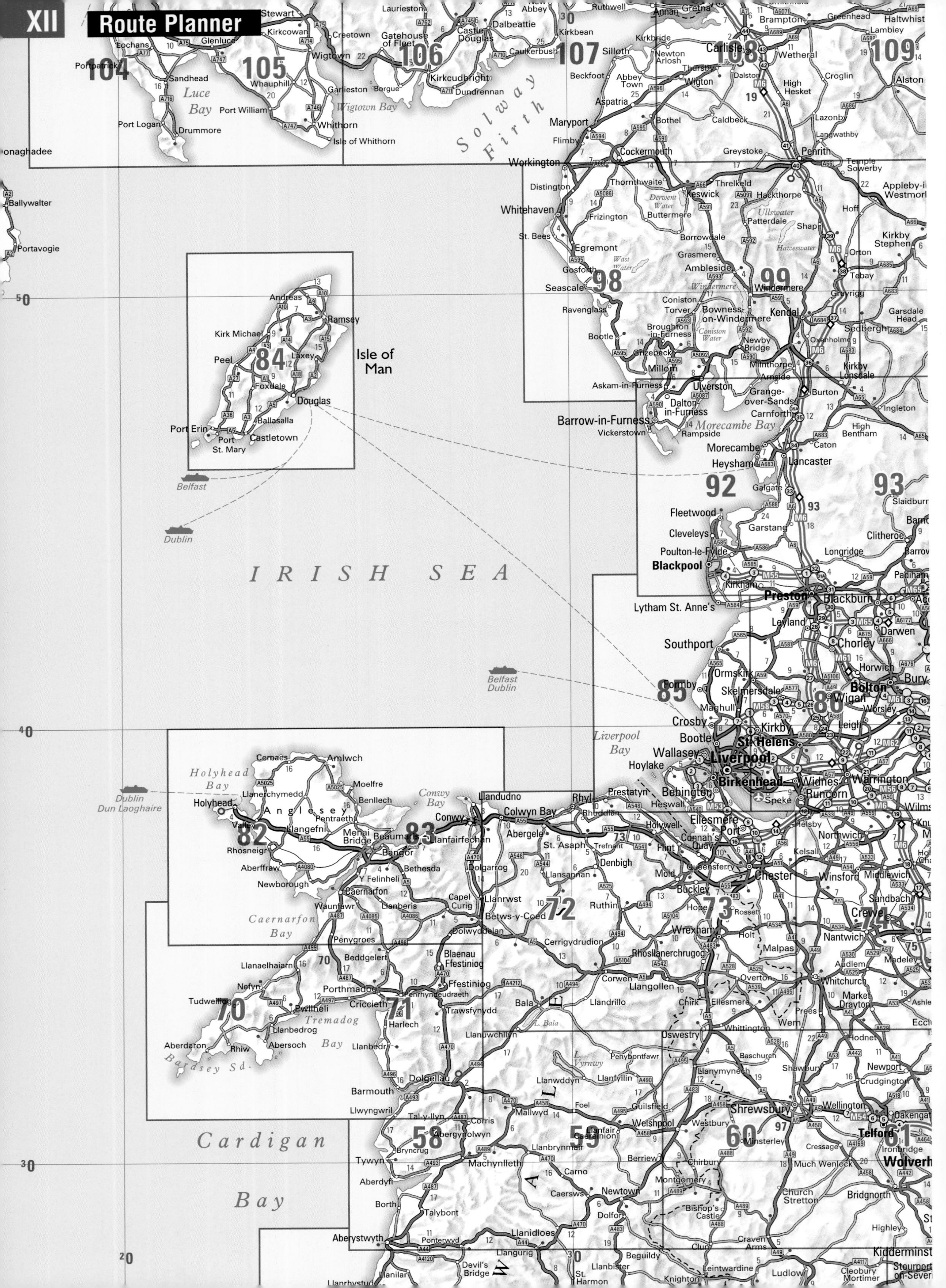

Stewart
Kirkcowan
Glenluce
Lochans
Portpatrick
104
105
106
107
108
109
Sandhead
Luce Bay
Port William
Port Logan
Drummore
Whauphill
Wigtown
Garlieston
Whithorn
Isle of Whithorn
Wigtown Bay
Creetown
Gatehouse of Fleet
Lauriesto
Castle Douglas
Dalbeattie
Kirkcudbright
Borgue
Dundrennan
Caulkerbush
Kirkbean
Solway Firth
Ruthwell
Annan
Gretna
Silloth
Kirkbride
Newton Arlosh
Abbey Town
Beckfoot
Aspatria
Maryport
Flimby
Workington
Carlisle
Thursby
Wigton
Dalston
Wetheral
Brampton
Greenhead
Haltwhistle
Lambley
Croglin
Alston
High Hesket
Caldbeck
Bothel
Cockermouth
Lazonby
Langwathby
Greystoke
Penrith
Temple Sowerby
Appleby-in-Westmorland
Distington
Whitehaven
Thornthwaite
Derwent Water
Keswick
Threlkeld
Hackthorpe
Frizington
Buttermere
Ullswater
Patterdale
Shap
Hoff
St. Bees
Egremont
Borrowdale
Grasmere
Haweswater
Orton
Kirkby Stephen
Tebay
Wast Water
Gosforth
Ambleside
Seascale
98
99
Windermere
Grayrigg
Ravenglass
Coniston
Torver
Bowness-on-Windermere
Kendal
Garsdale Head
Sedbergh
Broughton-in-Furness
Coniston Water
Bootle
Newby Bridge
Oxenholme
Grizebeck
Millom
Milnthorpe
Arnside
Kirkby Lonsdale
Askam-in-Furness
Ulverston
Grange-over-Sands
Burton
Dalton-in-Furness
Carnforth
Ingleton
Barrow-in-Furness
Vickerstown
Rampside
Morecambe Bay
High Bentham
Caton
Morecambe
Heysham
Lancaster
Galgate
92
93
Slaidburn
Fleetwood
Garstang
Cleveleys
Clitheroe
Poulton-le-Fylde
Longridge
Blackpool
Kirkham
Preston
Blackburn
Padiham
Lytham St. Anne's
Leyland
Darwen
Southport
Chorley
Horwich
Ormskirk
Skelmersdale
Bolton
Bury
Formby
85
86
Wigan
Maghull
Worsley
Crosby
Kirkby
Leigh
Bootle
St. Helens
Liverpool Bay
Wallasey
Liverpool
Hoylake
Birkenhead
Widnes
Warrington
Prestatyn
Bebington
Heswall
Speke
Runcorn
Isle of Man
Andreas
Ramsey
Kirk Michael
Peel
84
Laxey
Foxdale
Douglas
Ballasalla
Port Erin
Port St. Mary
Castletown
Belfast
Dublin
IRISH SEA
Belfast Dublin
Cemaes
Amlwch
Holyhead Bay
Moelfre
Llanerchymedd
Benllech
Dublin Dun Laoghaire
Holyhead
Anglesey
Pentraeth
Conwy Bay
Valley
Llangefni
Menai Bridge
Beaumaris
82
83
Rhosneigr
Bangor
Aberffraw
Bethesda
Y Felinheli
Newborough
Caernarfon
Llanberis
Waunfawr
Caernarfon Bay
Penygroes
Llandudno
Conwy
Llanfairfechan
Colwyn Bay
Abergele
Rhyl
Rhuddlan
St. Asaph
Trefnant
Holywell
Flint
Ellesmere Port
Connah's Quay
Denbigh
Dolgarrog
Llansannan
Mold
Queensferry
Chester
Buckley
Ruthin
Llanrwst
Capel Curig
Betws-y-Coed
72
73
Hope
Rossett
Wrexham
Holt
Dolwyddelan
Cerrigydrudion
Rhosllanerchrugog
Malpas
Blaenau Ffestiniog
Beddgelert
Llanaelhaearn
Nefyn
Porthmadog
Penrhyndeudraeth
Ffestiniog
Corwen
Llangollen
Overton
Whitchurch
Tudweiliog
70
Pwllheli
Criccieth
71
Harlech
Trawsfynydd
Bala
L. Bala
Llandrillo
Chirk
Ellesmere
Prees
Market Drayton
Tremadog Bay
Llanbedrog
Abersoch
Aberdaron
Rhiw
Bardsey Sd.
Llanbedr
Llanuwchllyn
Oswestry
Whittington
Wem
Hodnet
Penybontfawr
L. Vyrnwy
Llanymynech
Baschurch
Shawbury
Newport
Crudgington
Llanwddyn
Llanfyllin
Dolgellau
Barmouth
Llwyngwril
Tal-y-llyn
Corris
Mallwyd
Foel
Guilsfield
Welshpool
Shrewsbury
Wellington
Telford
Oakengates
Westbury
Minsterley
Cressage
Ironbridge
58
59
60
61
Abergynolwyn
Bryncrug
Tywyn
Llanfair Caereinion
Llanbrynmair
Machynlleth
Berriew
Chirbury
Much Wenlock
Wolverhampton
Aberdyfi
Carno
Caersws
Montgomery
Newtown
Church Stretton
Bridgnorth
Borth
Talybont
Dolfor
Bishop's Castle
Highley
Aberystwyth
Llanidloes
Ponterwyd
Llangurig
Clun
Craven Arms
Kidderminster
Devil's Bridge
Llanilar
Llanbister
Beguildy
Leintwardine
Ludlow
Cleobury Mortimer
Stourport-on-Severn
St. Harmon
Knighton
Cardigan Bay
WALES
Ballywalter
Portavogie
Donaghadee
Nantwich
Crewe
Sandbach
Middlewich
Winsford
Northwich
Kelsall
Helsby
Madeley
Audlem

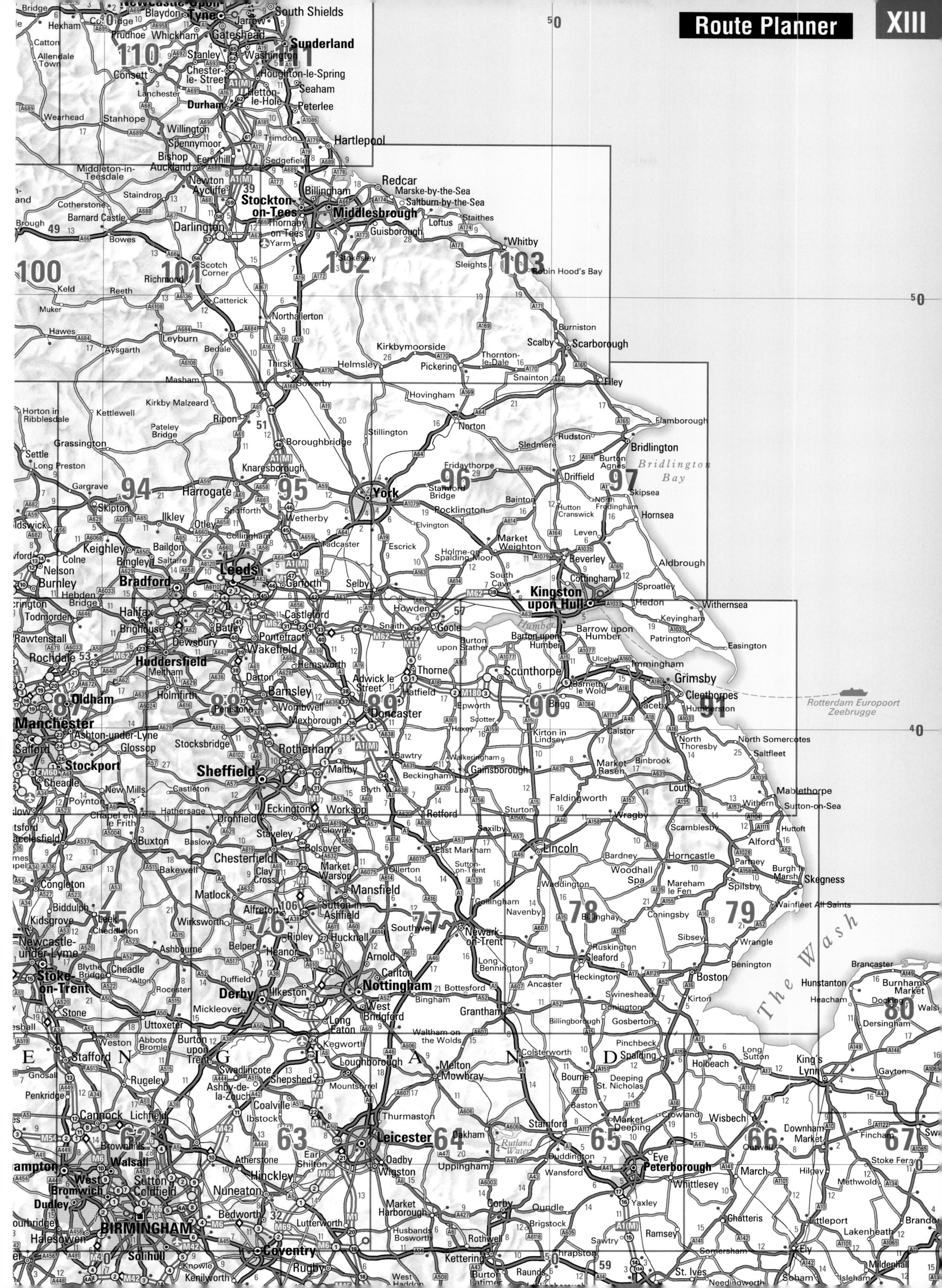

Newcastle-upon-Tyne
South Shields
Jarrow
Blaydon
Hexham
Prudhoe
Whickham
Gateshead
Sunderland
Catton
Allendale Town
110
Stanley
Washington
111
Consett
Chester-le-Street
Houghton-le-Spring
Seaham
Lanchester
Hetton-le-Hole
Durham
Peterlee
Wearhead
Stanhope
Willington
Spennymoor
Trimdon
Hartlepool
Bishop Auckland
Ferryhill
Sedgefield
Middleton-in-Teesdale
Newton Aycliffe
Billingham
Redcar
Marske-by-the-Sea
Saltburn-by-the-Sea
Staindrop
Cotherstone
Stockton-on-Tees
Middlesbrough
Barnard Castle
Thornaby on Tees
Loftus
Staithes
Brough
Darlington
Guisborough
Bowes
Yarm
Whitby
Stokesley
102
103
Robin Hood's Bay
Sleights
100
101
Scotch Corner
Richmond
Keld
Reeth
Catterick
Muker
Northallerton
Burniston
Hawes
Leyburn
Scalby
Scarborough
Aysgarth
Bedale
Kirkbymoorside
Thornton-le-Dale
Thirsk
Helmsley
Pickering
Masham
Snainton
Sowerby
Filey
Hovingham
Horton in Ribblesdale
Kettlewell
Kirkby Malzeard
Ripon
Pateley Bridge
Norton
Flamborough
Stillington
Rudston
Grassington
Boroughbridge
Sledmere
Bridlington
Settle
Long Preston
Knaresborough
Fridaythorpe
Burton Agnes
Bridlington Bay
Driffield
Gargrave
94
Harrogate
95
York
96
97
Skipton
Stamford Bridge
Skipsea
Ilkley
Spofforth
Wetherby
Pocklington
Bainton
Hutton Cranswick
North Frodingham
Hornsea
Otley
Elvington
Collingham
Market Weighton
Leven
Keighley
Baildon
Escrick
Colne
Bingley
Saltaire
Tadcaster
Holme-on-Spalding-Moor
Beverley
Nelson
Aldbrough
Leeds
Garforth
Cottingham
Burnley
Bradford
Selby
South Cave
Sproatley
Hebden Bridge
Kingston upon Hull
Hedon
Withernsea
Todmorden
Halifax
Castleford
Howden
Keyingham
Brighouse
Batley
Pontefract
Snaith
Goole
Barrow upon Humber
Patrington
Rawtenstall
Dewsbury
Wakefield
Burton upon Stather
Barton-upon-Humber
Easington
Rochdale
Huddersfield
Hemsworth
Thorne
Scunthorpe
Immingham
Meltham
Darton
Adwick le Street
Grimsby
Barnetby le Wold
Holmfirth
Barnsley
Hatfield
Cleethorpes
Oldham
87
88
Penistone
Wombwell
89
Doncaster
Epworth
90
Brigg
Laceby
Humberston
91
Rotterdam Europoort
Zeebrugge
Manchester
Mexborough
Scotter
Haxey
Kirton in Lindsey
Caistor
Ashton-under-Lyne
Stocksbridge
North Somercotes
Salford
Glossop
Rotherham
Bawtry
North Thoresby
Saltfleet
Stockport
Sheffield
Maltby
Walkeringham
Binbrook
Market Rasen
Cheadle
Beckingham
Gainsborough
Louth
Castleton
New Mills
Blyth
Lea
Mablethorpe
Poynton
Faldingworth
Withern
Sutton-on-Sea
Chapel en le Frith
Hathersage
Eckington
Worksop
Retford
Sturton
Wragby
Huttoft
Dronfield
Scamblesby
Macclesfield
Buxton
Staveley
Saxilby
Clowne
Alford
Baslow
Bolsover
East Markham
Lincoln
Horncastle
Partney
Chesterfield
Bardney
Burgh le Marsh
Bakewell
Market Warsop
Ollerton
Sutton-on-Trent
Woodhall Spa
Skegness
Clay Cross
Mareham le Fen
Spilsby
Congleton
Waddington
Matlock
Mansfield
Biddulph
Collingham
Wainfleet All Saints
75
Alfreton
106
Sutton-in-Ashfield
Navenby
78
Coningsby
79
Billinghay
Leek
Kidsgrove
Cheddleton
Wirksworth
76
77
Southwell
The Wash
Ripley
Hucknall
Newark-on-Trent
Sibsey
Newcastle-under-Lyme
Ruskington
Wrangle
Ashbourne
Belper
Heanor
Arnold
Sleaford
Stoke-on-Trent
Cheadle
Blythe Bridge
Long Bennington
Benington
Alton
Carlton
Heckington
Brancaster
Boston
Duffield
Nottingham
Ancaster
Hunstanton
Burnham Market
Rocester
Derby
Ilkeston
Bottesford
Swineshead
Kirton
Heacham
Docking
Stone
West Bridgford
Bingham
80
Mickleover
Grantham
Donington
Walsingham
Uttoxeter
Long Eaton
Billingborough
Gosberton
Dersingham
Weston
Abbots Bromley
Waltham on the Wolds
Kegworth
Colsterworth
Pinchbeck
Long Sutton
Stafford
ENGLAND
Burton upon Trent
Spalding
King's Lynn
Loughborough
Melton Mowbray
Holbeach
Gnosall
Rugeley
Swadlincote
Shepshed
Bourne
Deeping St. Nicholas
Gayton
Penkridge
Ashby-de-la-Zouch
Mountsorrel
Coalville
Baston
Cannock
Lichfield
Ibstock
Thurmaston
Market Deeping
Crowland
Wisbech
Brownhills
62
63
Leicester
64
Oakham
Rutland Water
Stamford
65
66
Downham Market
Fincham
67
Walsall
Atherstone
Earl Shilton
Oadby
Duddington
Eye
Outwell
Wolverhampton
West Bromwich
Sutton Coldfield
Hinckley
Wigston
Uppingham
Wansford
Peterborough
March
Hilgay
Stoke Ferry
Methwold
Dudley
Nuneaton
Whittlesey
Yaxley
Corby
Oundle
Stourbridge
Bedworth
Market Harborough
Chatteris
Littleport
Brandon
Halesowen
Birmingham
Lutterworth
Husbands Bosworth
Brigstock
Ramsey
Lakenheath
Coventry
Rothwell
Sawtry
Solihull
Rugby
Kettering
Thrapston
Somersham
Ely
Mildenhall
Knowle
Kenilworth
West Haddon
Burton Latimer
Raunds
St. Ives
Soham
Isleham
Needingworth

Route Planner

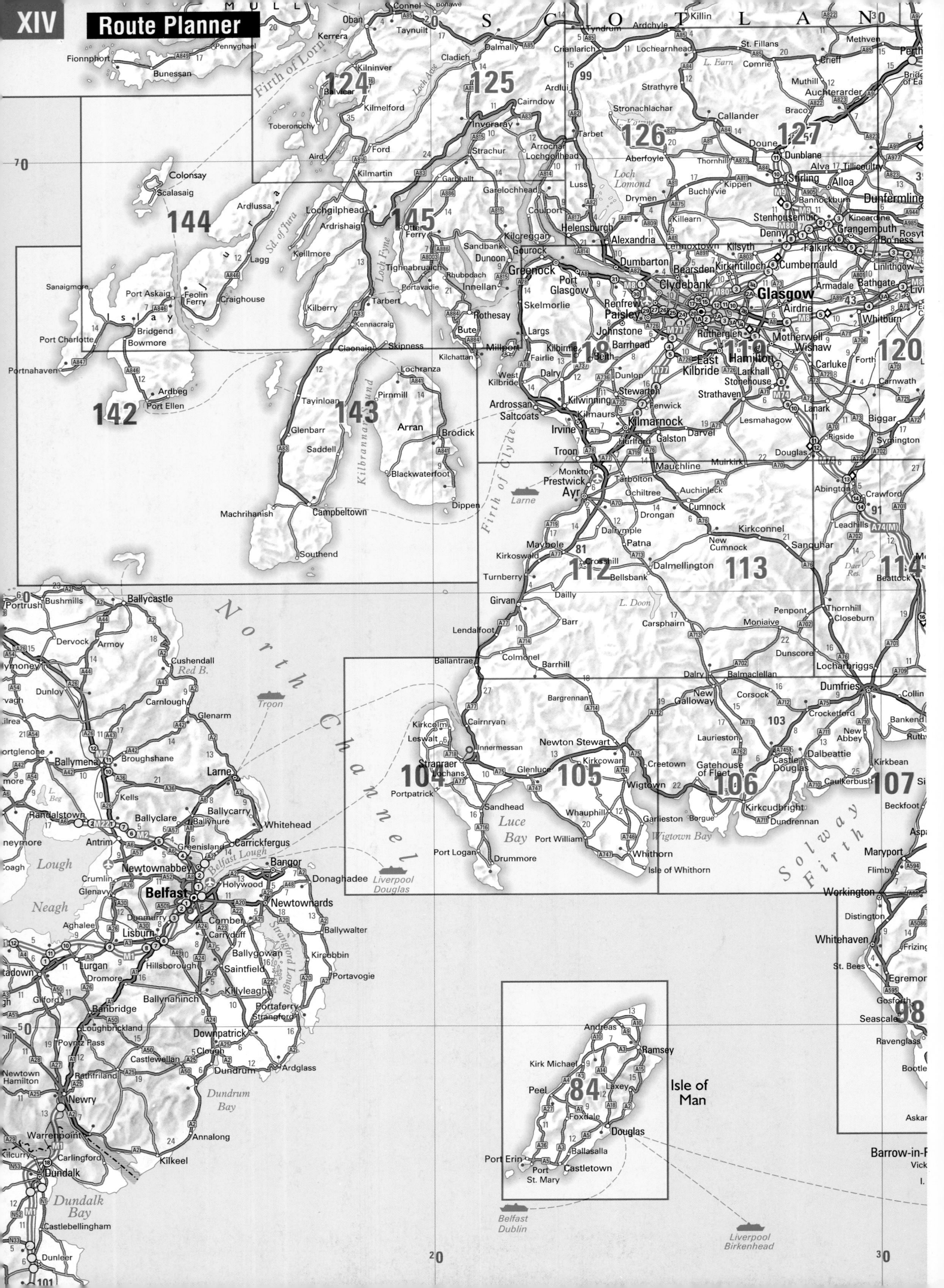

SCOTLAND
MULL
Oban
Connel
Bonawe
Taynuilt
Kerrera
Pennyghael
Fionnphort
Bunessan
Firth of Lorn
Kilninver
Balvicar
Kilmelford
Toberonochy
Aird
Ford
Kilmartin
Cladich
Dalmally
Loch Awe
Cairndow
Inveraray
Strachur
Arrochar
Lochgoilhead
Tyndrum
Ardchyle
Killin
Crianlarich
Lochearnhead
St. Fillans
Comrie
L. Earn
Methven
Perth
Crieff
Muthill
Auchterarder
Braco
Strathyre
Stronachlachar
Callander
Tarbet
Aberfoyle
Doune
Dunblane
Ardlui
Thornhill
Stirling
Alloa
Alva
Tillicoultry
Dunfermline
Bannockburn
Kippen
Buchlyvie
Drymen
Killearn
Luss
Loch Lomond
Stenhousemuir
Kincardine
Grangemouth
Bo'ness
Rosyth
Denny
Falkirk
Linlithgow
Cumbernauld
Kilsyth
Lennoxtown
Kirkintilloch
Bearsden
Clydebank
Glasgow
Dumbarton
Alexandria
Helensburgh
Garelochhead
Coulport
Kilcreggan
Gourock
Greenock
Port Glasgow
Dunoon
Sandbank
Innellan
Rhubodach
Rothesay
Bute
Millport
Kilchattan
Tighnabruaich
Portavadie
Otter Ferry
Garbhallt
Lochgilphead
Ardrishaig
Kellmore
Loch Fyne
Tarbert
Kilberry
Kennacraig
Claonaig
Skipness
Colonsay
Scalasaig
Ardlussa
Jura
Sd. of Jura
Lagg
Craighouse
Port Askaig
Feolin Ferry
Islay
Bridgend
Bowmore
Port Charlotte
Portnahaven
Sanaigmore
Ardbeg
Port Ellen
Lochranza
Pirnmill
Arran
Brodick
Blackwaterfoot
Kilbrannan Sound
Tayinloan
Glenbarr
Saddell
Machrihanish
Campbeltown
Southend
Dippen
Skelmorlie
Largs
Fairlie
West Kilbride
Ardrossan
Saltcoats
Irvine
Kilwinning
Kilbirnie
Beith
Dalry
Renfrew
Paisley
Johnstone
Barrhead
Dunlop
Stewarton
Fenwick
Kilmaurs
Kilmarnock
Hurlford
Galston
Darvel
East Kilbride
Rutherglen
Airdrie
Motherwell
Wishaw
Hamilton
Larkhall
Stonehouse
Strathaven
Carluke
Lanark
Lesmahagow
Forth
Carnwath
Biggar
Whitburn
Bathgate
Armadale
Troon
Monkton
Prestwick
Ayr
Tarbolton
Mauchline
Muirkirk
Douglas
Rigside
Symington
Abington
Crawford
Leadhills
Ochiltree
Auchinleck
Cumnock
Drongan
Dalrymple
Patna
Maybole
Kirkoswald
Crosshill
Turnberry
Girvan
Dailly
Bellsbank
Dalmellington
New Cumnock
Kirkconnel
Sanquhar
Firth of Clyde
Larne
L. Doon
Barr
Carsphairn
Penpont
Moniaive
Thornhill
Closeburn
Dunscore
Lochanbriggs
Lendalfoot
Colmonel
Barrhill
Ballantrae
Dalry
Balmaclellan
New Galloway
Corsock
Crocketford
Dumfries
Collin
Bargrennan
Cairnryan
Innermessan
Kirkcolm
Leswalt
Stranraer
Lochans
Portpatrick
Newton Stewart
Glenluce
Kirkcowan
Creetown
Wigtown
Gatehouse of Fleet
Laurieston
Castle Douglas
Dalbeattie
New Abbey
Kirkbean
Caulkerbush
Kirkcudbright
Dundrennan
Borgue
Garlieston
Whauphill
Sandhead
Luce Bay
Port William
Wigtown Bay
Whithorn
Isle of Whithorn
Port Logan
Drummore
Solway Firth
Beckfoot
Maryport
Flimby
Workington
Distington
Whitehaven
St. Bees
Egremont
Gosforth
Seascale
Ravenglass
Bootle
Barrow-in-F
North Channel
Troon
Liverpool Douglas
Ballycastle
Portrush
Bushmills
Dervock
Armoy
Cushendall
Red B.
Dunloy
Carnlough
Glenarm
Ballymena
Broughshane
Portglenone
Kells
Larne
Ballyclare
Ballycarry
Ballynure
Whitehead
Randalstown
Antrim
Greenisland
Carrickfergus
Belfast Lough
Bangor
Newtownabbey
Crumlin
Glenavy
Lough Neagh
Belfast
Holywood
Donaghadee
Newtownards
Dunmurry
Comber
Carryduff
Ballywalter
Lisburn
Aghalee
Ballygowan
Kircubbin
Strangford Lough
Saintfield
Hillsborough
Portavogie
Lurgan
Dromore
Killyleagh
Ballynahinch
Portaferry
Strangford
Gilford
Banbridge
Loughbrickland
Downpatrick
Poyntz Pass
Castlewellan
Clough
Dundrum
Ardglass
Rathfriland
Dundrum Bay
Newry
Warrenpoint
Annalong
Carlingford
Kilkeel
Dundalk
Dundalk Bay
Castlebellingham
Dunleer
Isle of Man
Andreas
Ramsey
Kirk Michael
Peel
Laxey
Foxdale
Douglas
Ballasalla
Port Erin
Port St. Mary
Castletown
Belfast Dublin
Liverpool Birkenhead
124
125
126
127
144
145
142
143
118
119
120
112
113
114
104
105
106
107
103
84
98
81
91
99

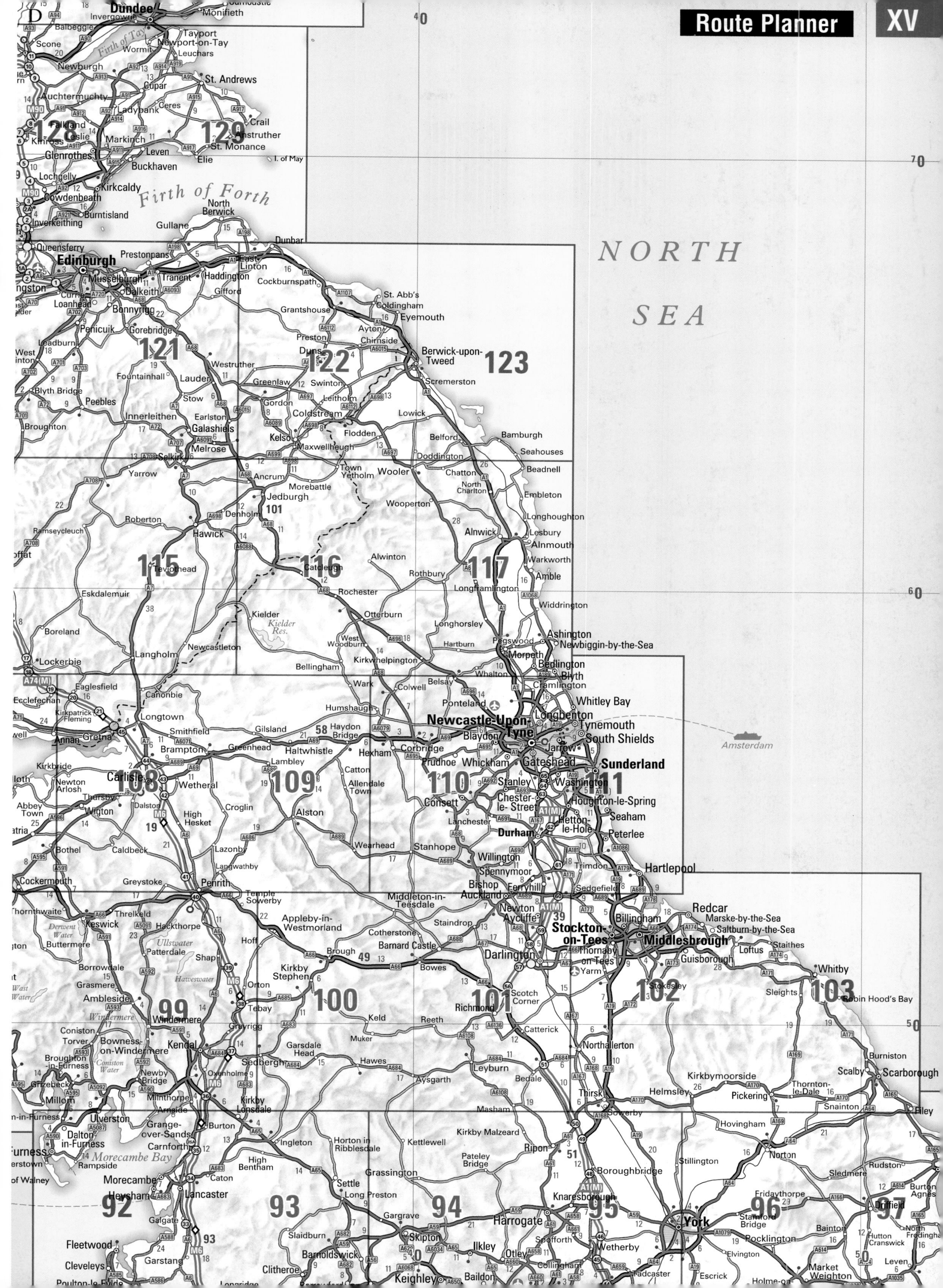
NORTH SEA
Firth of Forth
Firth of Tay
Dundee
Perth
St. Andrews
Cupar
Kirkcaldy
Glenrothes
Dunfermline
Edinburgh
Musselburgh
Dalkeith
Haddington
North Berwick
Dunbar
Penicuik
Peebles
Galashiels
Melrose
Selkirk
Kelso
Coldstream
Duns
Eyemouth
Berwick-upon-Tweed
Jedburgh
Hawick
Langholm
Lockerbie
Annan
Gretna
Carlisle
Brampton
Haltwhistle
Hexham
Bellingham
Kielder
Otterburn
Rothbury
Alnwick
Amble
Bamburgh
Wooler
Morpeth
Ashington
Newcastle-Upon-Tyne
Gateshead
Tynemouth
South Shields
Sunderland
Washington
Durham
Consett
Hartlepool
Stockton-on-Tees
Middlesbrough
Redcar
Darlington
Whitby
Scarborough
Penrith
Keswick
Cockermouth
Ambleside
Windermere
Kendal
Ulverston
Barrow-in-Furness
Morecambe
Lancaster
Fleetwood
Settle
Skipton
Keighley
Ilkley
Otley
Harrogate
Ripon
Knaresborough
Wetherby
York
Thirsk
Northallerton
Richmond
Pickering
Malton
Driffield
Filey
Amsterdam
Kielder Res.
Ullswater
Morecambe Bay
92
93
94
95
96
97
99
100
101
102
103
108
109
110
111
115
116
117
121
122
123
128
129

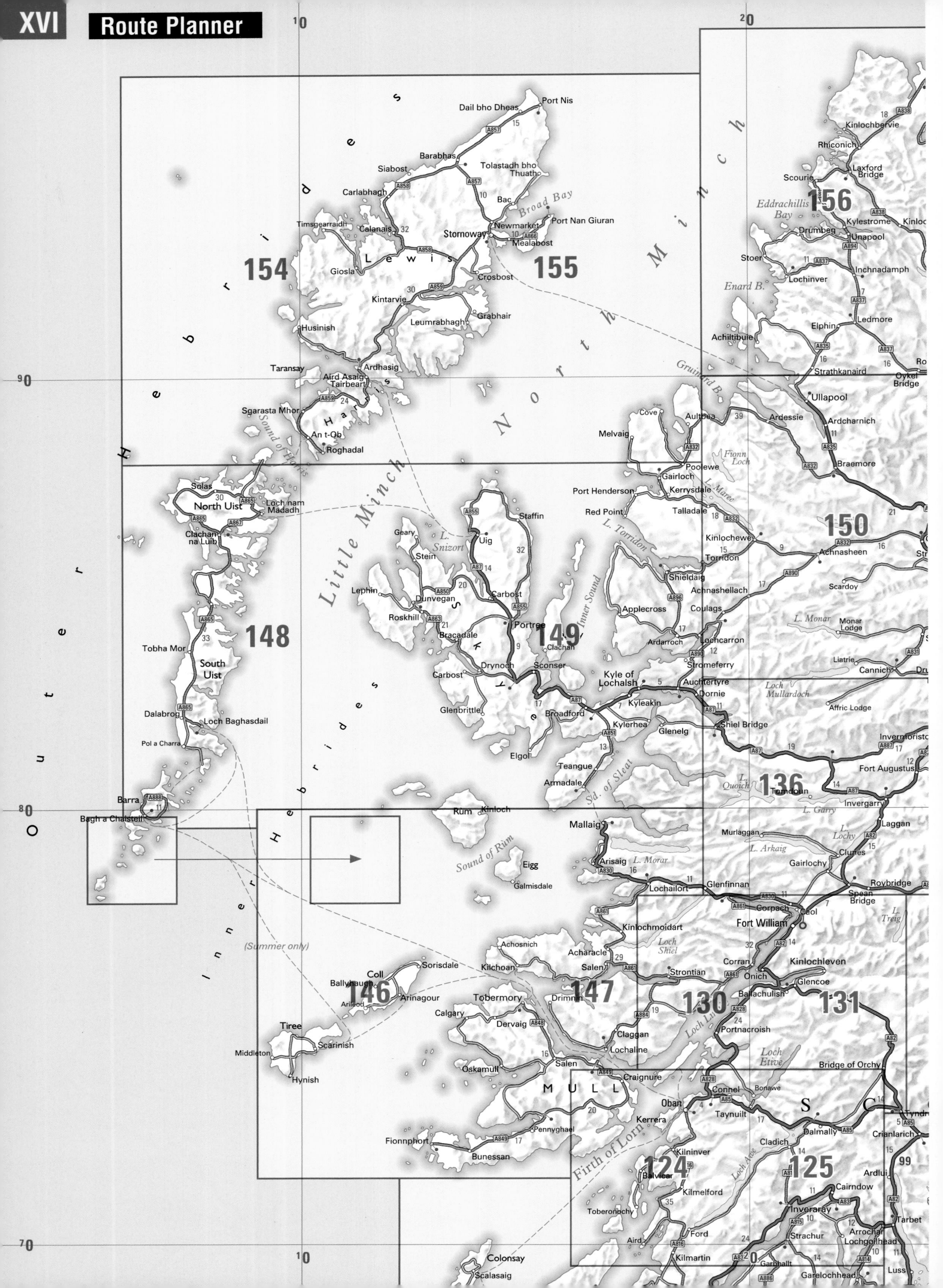

Outer Hebrides
Inner Hebrides
North Minch
Little Minch
Lewis
Harris
North Uist
South Uist
Skye
Mull
154
155
156
148
149
150
136
146
147
130
131
124
125
Port Nis
Dail bho Dheas
Barabhas
Siabost
Tolastadh bho Thuath
Carlabhagh
Bac
Broad Bay
Timsgearraidh
Calanais
Stornoway
Newmarket
Port Nan Giuran
Mealabost
Giosla
Crosbost
Kintarvie
Grabhair
Leumrabhagh
Husinish
Taransay
Ardhasig
Aird Asaig
Tairbeart
Sgarasta Mhor
An t-Ob
Roghadal
Sound of Harris
Solas
Loch nam Madadh
Clachan na Luib
Tobha Mor
Dalabrog
Loch Baghasdail
Pol a Charra
Barra
Bagh a Chaisteil
Kinlochbervie
Rhiconich
Laxford Bridge
Scourie
Eddrachillis Bay
Kylestrome
Drumbeg
Unapool
Stoer
Lochinver
Inchnadamph
Enard B.
Elphin
Ledmore
Achiltibuie
Strathkanaird
Oykel Bridge
Ullapool
Ardcharnich
Ardessie
Gruinard B.
Cove
Aultbea
Melvaig
Fionn Loch
Poolewe
Braemore
Gairloch
Port Henderson
Kerrysdale
L. Maree
Red Point
Talladale
Staffin
Geary
L. Snizort
Uig
Stein
L. Torridon
Kinlochewe
Torridon
Achnasheen
Shieldaig
Achnashellach
Scardoy
Lephin
Dunvegan
Applecross
Coulags
Carbost
Roskhill
Portree
Inner Sound
L. Monar
Monar Lodge
Bracadale
Clachan
Ardarroch
Lochcarron
Drynoch
Sconser
Stromeferry
Liatrie
Cannich
Carbost
Kyle of Lochalsh
Auchtertyre
Loch Mullardoch
Dornie
Kyleakin
Glenbrittle
Broadford
Affric Lodge
Kylerhea
Glenelg
Shiel Bridge
Invermoriston
Elgol
Teangue
Sd. of Sleat
Fort Augustus
Armadale
L. Quoich
Tomdoun
Invergarry
L. Garry
Rum
Kinloch
Mallaig
Laggan
Murlaggan
L. Arkaig
L. Lochy
Sound of Rum
Clunes
Eigg
Arisaig
L. Morar
Gairlochy
Galmisdale
Lochailort
Glenfinnan
Roybridge
Spean Bridge
Corpach
Caol
L. Treig
Kinlochmoidart
Fort William
(Summer only)
Achosnich
Loch Shiel
Acharacle
Corran
Kinlochleven
Salen
Kilchoan
Strontian
Coll
Sorisdale
Onich
Glencoe
Ballyhaugh
Arinagour
Tobermory
Drimnin
Ballachulish
Arileod
Calgary
Dervaig
Loch Linnhe
Portnacroish
Tiree
Claggan
Scarinish
Middleton
Lochaline
Loch Etive
Hynish
Oskamull
Salen
Bridge of Orchy
Craignure
Connel
Bonawe
Oban
Taynuilt
Kerrera
Pennyghael
Dalmally
Crianlarich
Tyndrum
Fionnphort
Cladich
Bunessan
Kilninver
Firth of Lorn
Loch Awe
Ardlui
Balvicar
Kilmelford
Cairndow
Toberonochy
Inveraray
Tarbet
Arrochar
Lochgoilhead
Strachur
Aird
Ford
Colonsay
Scalasaig
Kilmartin
Garbhallt
Garelochhead
Luss
A857
A858
A859
A866
A838
A837
A894
A835
A832
A890
A87
A855
A850
A863
A851
A887
A82
A830
A861
A884
A848
A849
A828
A85
A816
A815
A83
A814
A886
A865
A867
A888
A896
A831

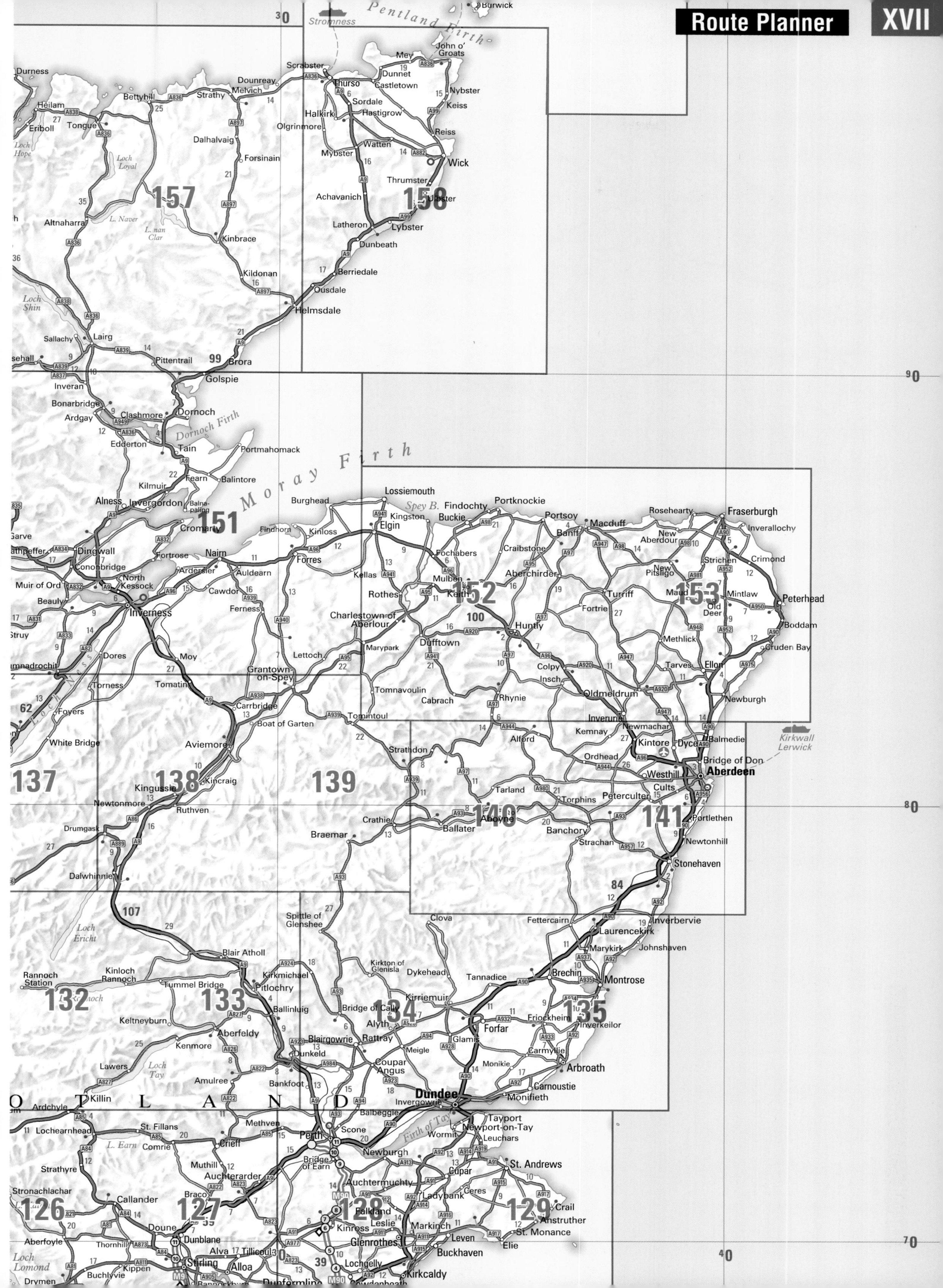

Pentland Firth
Stromness
Burwick
Mey
John o' Groats
Dunnet
Scrabster
Thurso
Castletown
Nybster
Keiss
Dounreay
Melvich
Strathy
Bettyhill
Durness
Heilam
Eriboll
Tongue
Sordale
Hastigrow
Halkirk
Olgrinmore
Reiss
Watten
Mybster
Wick
Thrumster
Ulbster
Achavanich
Dalhalvaig
Forsinain
Loch Loyal
Loch Hope
157
158
Altnaharra
L. Naver
Kinbrace
Latheron
Lybster
Dunbeath
Berriedale
Kildonan
Ousdale
Helmsdale
Loch Shin
Lairg
Sallachy
Pittentrail
Brora
Golspie
Inveran
Bonarbridge
Ardgay
Clashmore
Dornoch
Dornoch Firth
Edderton
Tain
Portmahomack
Moray Firth
Balintore
Fearn
Kilmuir
Alness
Invergordon
Cromarty
151
Garve
Dingwall
Conon Bridge
Fortrose
Nairn
North Kessock
Muir of Ord
Ardersier
Auldearn
Beauly
Cawdor
Inverness
Ferness
Dores
Moy
Struy
Findhorn
Kinloss
Burghead
Lossiemouth
Elgin
Kingston
Forres
Kellas
Rothes
Charlestown-of-Aberlour
Lettoch
Grantown-on-Spey
Tomatin
Torness
Foyers
White Bridge
62
Carrbridge
Boat of Garten
Aviemore
Kincraig
Kingussie
Newtonmore
Ruthven
137
138
139
Drumgask
Dalwhinnie
Spey B.
Findochty
Portknockie
Buckie
Fochabers
Mulben
Keith
152
Craibstone
Portsoy
Banff
Macduff
Aberchirder
Rosehearty
Fraserburgh
Inverallochy
New Aberdour
New Pitsligo
Strichen
Crimond
153
Maud
Mintlaw
Old Deer
Peterhead
Boddam
Cruden Bay
Turriff
Fortrie
Methlick
Tarves
Ellon
Huntly
Dufftown
Marypark
Tomnavoulin
Cabrach
Rhynie
Colpy
Insch
Oldmeldrum
Newburgh
Inverurie
Newmachar
Kintore
Dyce
Balmedie
Kemnay
Alford
Tomintoul
Strathdon
Kirkwall Lerwick
Bridge of Don
Aberdeen
Westhill
Ordhead
Cults
Peterculter
Tarland
Torphins
Aboyne
140
141
Crathie
Ballater
Banchory
Portlethen
Braemar
Strachan
Newtonhill
Stonehaven
Loch Ericht
Spittle of Glenshee
Clova
Fettercairn
Inverbervie
Laurencekirk
Johnshaven
Marykirk
Brechin
Montrose
Blair Atholl
Kirkmichael
Kirkton of Glenisla
Dykehead
Tannadice
Kirriemuir
Rannoch Station
Kinloch Rannoch
Tummel Bridge
Pitlochry
132
133
134
135
Ballinluig
Bridge of Cally
Alyth
Forfar
Friockheim
Inverkeilor
Keltneyburn
Aberfeldy
Blairgowrie
Rattray
Glamis
Kenmore
Dunkeld
Meigle
Carmyllie
Arbroath
Loch Tay
Lawers
Amulree
Coupar Angus
Monikie
Carnoustie
Bankfoot
Dundee
Monifieth
Killin
Invergowrie
SCOTLAND
Ardchyle
Balbeggie
Tayport
Methven
Newport-on-Tay
Lochearnhead
St. Fillans
Perth
Scone
Firth of Tay
Wormit
Leuchars
L. Earn
Comrie
Crieff
Newburgh
St. Andrews
Strathyre
Muthill
Bridge of Earn
Cupar
Auchterarder
Auchtermuchty
Ceres
Stronachlachar
Callander
Braco
Ladybank
126
127
128
129
Falkland
Crail
Anstruther
Kinross
Leslie
Markinch
St. Monance
Doune
Dunblane
Glenrothes
Leven
Elie
Aberfoyle
Thornhill
Tillicoultry
Alva
Buckhaven
Loch Lomond
Stirling
Alloa
Lochgelly
Kippen
Buchlyvie
Kirkcaldy
Drymen

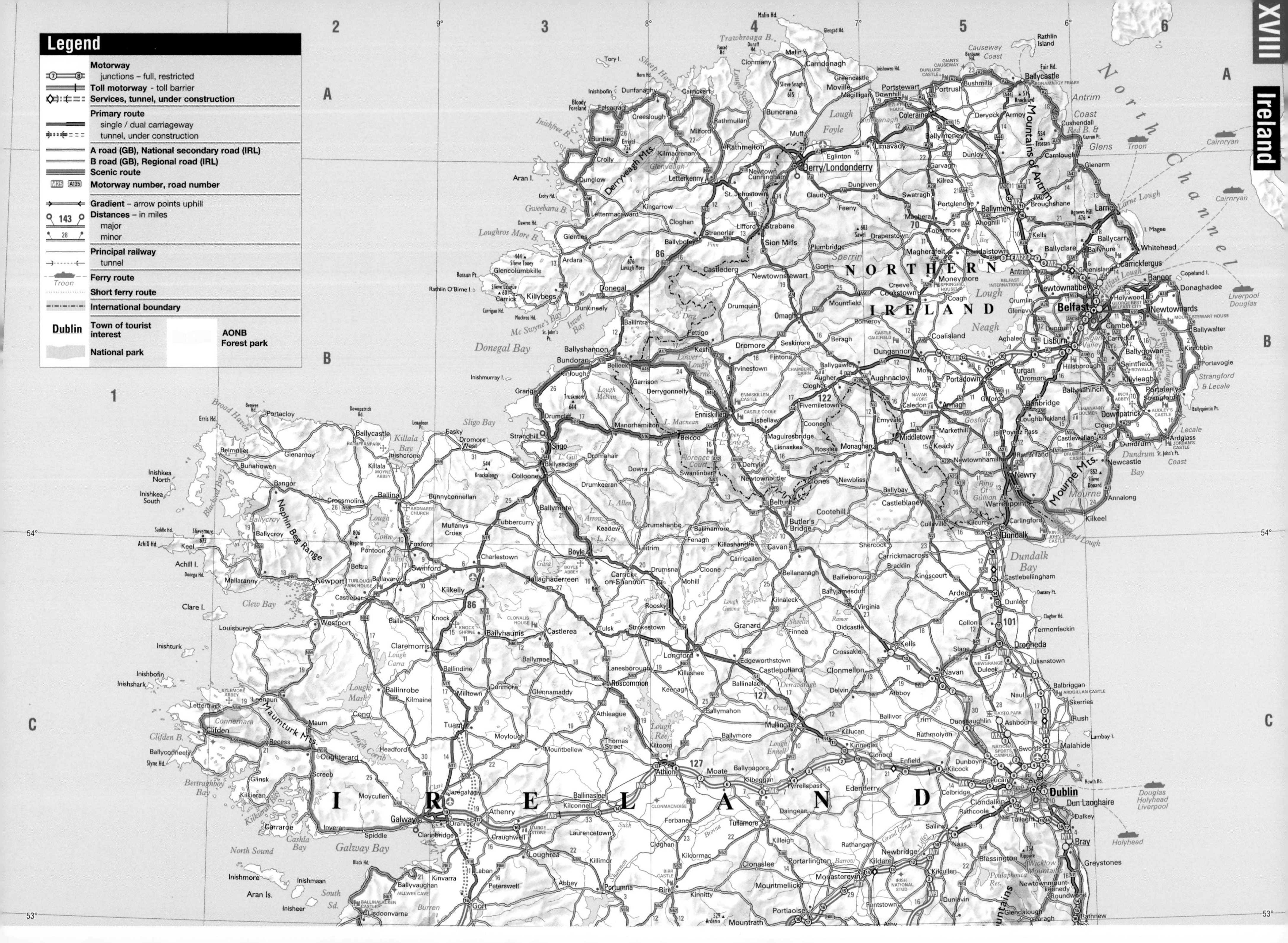

Legend

Motorway
junctions – full, restricted

Toll motorway – toll barrier

Services, tunnel, under construction

Primary route
single / dual carriageway

tunnel, under construction

A road (GB), National secondary road (IRL)

B road (GB), Regional road (IRL)

Scenic route

Motorway number, road number

Gradient – arrow points uphill

Distances – in miles

major

minor

Principal railway

tunnel

Ferry route

Short ferry route

International boundary

Dublin Town of tourist interest

National park

AONB

Forest park

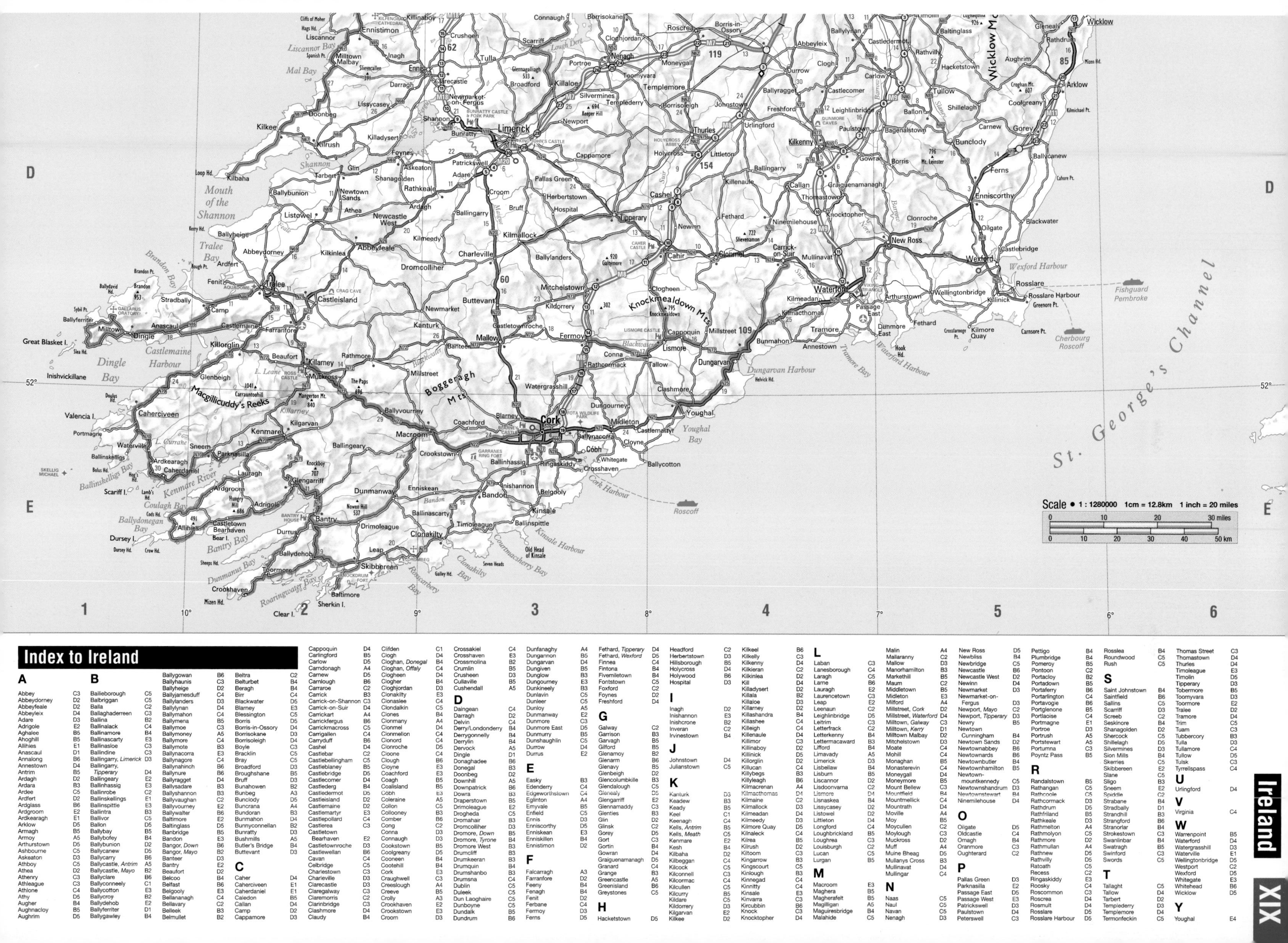

Distance table

How to use this table

Distances are shown in miles and kilometres with estimated journey times in hours and minutes.

For example: the distance between Dover and Fishguard is 331 miles or 533 kilometres with an estimated journey time of 6 hours, 20 minutes.

Estimated driving times are based on an average speed of 60mph on Motorways and 40mph on other roads. Drivers should allow extra time when driving at peak periods or through areas likely to be congested.

Map labels: John o' Groats, Kyle of Lochalsh, Inverness, Aberdeen, Braemar, Fort William, Dundee, Oban, Edinburgh, Glasgow, Berwick-upon-Tweed, Ayr, Stranraer, Carlisle, Newcastle upon Tyne, York, Kingston upon Hull, Leeds, Blackpool, Manchester, Doncaster, Liverpool, Sheffield, Lincoln, Holyhead, Shrewsbury, Nottingham, Leicester, Norwich, Great Yarmouth, Aberystwyth, Birmingham, Cambridge, Fishguard, Gloucester, Oxford, Harwich, Swansea, Cardiff, Bristol, London, Exeter, Southampton, Brighton, Dover, Bournemouth, Portsmouth, Plymouth, Land's End

Distance matrix (each cell: miles / kilometres / hours:minutes). Column headers run diagonally, left-to-right: London, Aberdeen, Aberystwyth, Ayr, Berwick-upon-Tweed, Birmingham, Blackpool, Bournemouth, Braemar, Brighton, Bristol, Cambridge, Cardiff, Carlisle, Doncaster, Dover, Dundee, Edinburgh, Exeter, Fishguard, Fort William, Glasgow, Gloucester, Great Yarmouth, Harwich, Holyhead, Inverness, John o' Groats, Kingston upon Hull, Kyle of Lochalsh, Land's End, Leeds, Leicester, Lincoln, Liverpool, Manchester, Newcastle upon Tyne, Norwich, Nottingham, Oban, Oxford, Plymouth, Portsmouth, Sheffield, Shrewsbury, Southampton, Stranraer, Swansea, York.

Row city	Distances (miles / km / time)
London	—
Aberdeen	517 / 832 / 11:20
Aberystwyth	445 211 / 716 340 / 8:40 4:40
Ayr	317 183 394 / 510 295 634 / 6:10 4:40 7:20
Berwick-upon-Tweed	134 311 182 352 / 216 501 293 567 / 3:00 6:20 4:40 7:30
Birmingham	274 289 114 420 117 / 441 465 183 676 188 / 5:30 5:30 2:50 8:30 2:50
Blackpool	123 181 180 153 308 52 / 198 291 290 246 496 84 / 2:40 3:50 2:50 3:20 6:50 2:20
Bournemouth	270 447 412 436 207 564 107 / 435 237 663 702 333 908 172 / 5:00 5:10 7:50 8:10 4:00 10:50 2:10
Braemar	524 281 385 148 143 405 59 482 / 843 452 620 238 230 652 95 776 / 9:30 5:20 7:10 3:20 3:00 7:50 1:50 10:30
Brighton	534 92 286 163 446 573 52 / 859 148 460 262 658 718 407 922 84 / 9:40 2:10 5:20 3:20 5:20 7:40 5:10 10:30 1:50
Bristol	147 477 82 204 81 362 370 125 493 122 / 237 768 132 328 130 583 595 201 793 196 / 4:10 8:40 2:30 3:50 2:00 6:50 6:40 3:00 9:10 3:20
Cambridge	169 116 438 157 208 100 306 357 214 471 54 / 272 187 705 248 335 161 493 575 344 758 87 / 3:50 2:20 7:50 3:00 5:20 2:40 6:50 6:20 4:20 10:50 1:30
Cardiff	190 45 182 483 117 209 103 368 382 105 169 253 / 306 72 293 778 336 592 201 655 813 / 3:30 1:20 3:40 8:40 3:00 4:40 2:20 7:00 7:00 2:40 3:20
Carlisle	289 264 277 370 360 87 196 87 93 224 221 / 465 425 446 596 316 552 140 315 140 150 360 / 5:20 4:40 5:00 8:00 6:20 2:20 5:00 2:10 3:50 2:10 4:30 5:40
Doncaster	142 209 116 175 236 310 163 94 94 235 176 344 171 / 229 336 187 282 380 499 378 151 151 296 378 283 554 275 / 3:00 4:00 3:10 4:00 5:20 7:00 4:40 2:10 2:20 5:40 4:00 8:00 4:20
Dover	242 389 238 125 202 82 553 174 312 194 424 478 297 588 71 / 390 626 383 201 325 132 890 280 502 312 683 769 478 947 114 / 4:30 7:00 4:30 3:50 3:20 2:20 9:50 4:30 5:40 3:50 7:50 8:30 5:50 10:40 2:10
Dundee	523 56 462 219 96 385 345 373 456 91 439 183 292 57 320 125 390 / 842 443 245 710 654 692 832 84 797 385 562 182 188 605 108 721 / 9:10 1:30 8:10 4:00 2:00 7:00 5:50 6:50 8:20 2:10 8:40 3:40 1:40 1:50 8:40
Edinburgh	56 462 219 96 385 345 373 456 91 439 183 292 57 320 125 462 / 90 744 555 600 734 146 707 295 470 92 117 515 201 / 1:30 8:10 4:00 2:00 7:00 5:50 6:50 8:20 2:10 8:40 3:40 1:40 1:50 8:40
Exeter	450 518 251 353 121 249 76 121 249 76 82 185 239 349 113 121 82 84 / 724 834 399 404 568 195 401 122 96 885 132 454 253 689 718 323 916 / 8:00 9:10 4:30 4:30 6:20 2:30 5:40 5:00 9:40 2:20 3:10 1:50 7:50 7:40 6:40 10:20 3:40
Fishguard	230 399 460 331 247 297 112 270 154 281 493 222 157 90 371 373 56 504 260 / 370 642 740 533 398 478 180 435 248 468 794 357 336 144 597 600 90 811 418 / 4:30 7:30 8:30 6:20 4:50 5:40 2:40 5:40 3:10 3:40 7:40 4:40 3:10 3:40 6:40 10:10 3:10
Fort William	486 560 144 204 596 / 782 901 232 204 959 / 9:30 10:20 3:10 3:10 11:00
Glasgow	101 376 449 44 83 488 249 96 385 372 373 468 310 439 183 292 101 33 320 145 397 / 163 605 723 71 134 786 401 154 620 599 600 753 177 707 295 470 163 53 515 233 639 / 2:50 7:10 8:00 1:20 2:00 8:40 4:40 1:50 7:00 6:50 6:50 8:40 3:10 8:40 3:40 2:40 1:10 3:30 7:30
Gloucester	346 454 153 111 410 191 150 247 56 123 159 443 419 170 343 87 196 87 93 224 221 701 / 557 731 246 179 660 307 241 398 90 198 256 713 280 90 512 531 164 753 175 / 6:10 8:30 3:10 2:10 7:10 3:30 3:20 5:40 1:40 3:20 3:10 7:00 7:00 2:40 5:50 2:10 3:50 2:10 4:30 5:30 2:30
Great Yarmouth	225 419 527 366 335 386 484 185 167 320 284 82 275 180 240 290 180 345 402 294 517 128 / 362 674 848 589 539 621 779 298 269 515 457 132 443 290 386 406 290 555 647 473 832 206 / 4:40 8:00 10:20 7:20 6:30 6:30 9:00 4:00 3:40 6:20 4:40 3:10 5:40 2:50 3:40 5:50 3:40 7:40 6:50 10:50 3:40
Harwich	82 196 432 543 337 279 413 469 125 194 336 217 167 372 425 281 535 76 / 132 316 695 874 542 449 665 755 201 312 541 396 108 349 269 599 684 452 861 122 / 2:10 4:00 8:10 10:30 6:40 5:20 7:40 8:40 2:50 4:00 5:40 3:40 2:50 6:10 7:20 5:50 11:20 2:40
Holyhead	349 334 191 330 438 167 282 333 394 360 181 231 216 270 206 334 328 141 148 310 305 111 439 269 / 562 538 307 531 705 269 454 536 634 580 297 372 348 435 332 538 686 463 227 238 501 491 179 707 433 / 7:10 7:00 4:00 6:40 8:50 4:00 5:40 6:40 7:00 7:30 3:50 5:40 4:20 5:00 5:40 7:40 8:20 4:20 4:20 6:20 8:40 2:40 8:50 5:30
Inverness	474 569 553 504 166 66 542 618 158 132 622 383 262 549 505 539 75 597 348 458 215 199 486 105 550 / 763 916 890 811 267 106 872 995 254 212 1001 617 422 884 813 867 993 121 961 560 737 346 320 782 169 885 / 10:50 11:30 11:30 11:00 3:50 1:00 11:00 12:40 3:50 3:10 12:50 8:10 10:20 10:00 10:20 2:00 11:20 2:00 2:00 9:40 2:50
John o' Groats	129 603 693 677 628 295 195 671 744 285 259 746 507 391 680 697 680 1094 769 924 550 528 967 373 1067 / 208 970 1116 1090 1011 475 314 1080 1197 459 417 1201 816 629 1094 1014 1075 1193 1165 769 924 550 528 967 373 1067 / 3:20 12:40 14:00 14:00 14:00 7:10 5:00 14:40 16:00 7:10 6:10 16:10 11:50 10:00 14:30 13:30 15:50
Kingston upon Hull	518 394 231 196 207 169 254 369 280 309 284 295 47 158 244 139 245 327 264 127 134 185 251 223 364 184 / 834 634 372 316 333 409 594 497 497 457 475 412 76 254 393 224 375 394 526 204 216 298 404 359 586 296 / 10:50 7:50 4:50 4:10 5:20 3:10 4:50 5:40 5:40 5:40 4:50 4:50 1:20 2:50 4:20 2:30 4:20 4:40 4:20 2:30 2:20 3:50 5:10 4:50 6:00 3:50
Kyle of Lochalsh	445 189 84 611 602 528 179 79 567 628 319 216 186 671 432 158 995 372 479 189 586 / 716 304 135 827 983 969 850 288 127 913 1011 348 609 1080 695 443 904 553 888 1048 159 995 758 423 341 803 943 / 9:00 4:20 2:10 10:40 12:10 12:10 10:40 2:10 5:20 13:30 4:50 4:20 11:10 10:10 5:10 2:40 6:10 15:10 10:20
Land's End	763 421 868 741 405 390 446 235 573 686 353 123 574 642 381 374 681 245 308 665 297 552 507 313 692 297 / 1228 678 1397 1193 652 628 718 922 1164 548 198 924 1033 613 602 768 394 602 322 496 330 1070 452 888 917 504 1114 478 / 15:10 8:20 17:20 14:20 8:30 8:00 9:00 5:00 13:20 3:20 12:00 4:30 9:40 6:30 6:10 7:00 5:40 11:40 7:20 7:20 8:20
Leeds	394 148 487 360 176 174 215 329 314 422 288 141 148 311 305 111 439 269 / 634 652 634 89 784 579 283 359 315 280 346 530 381 435 418 29 192 373 145 312 419 472 410 716 113 341 272 526 304 / 8:20 1:30 8:20 4:00 2:20 3:20 4:40 6:40 6:40 8:40 5:00 2:30 2:30 5:00 4:40 1:50 3:20 6:10 5:50 3:50
Leicester	95 320 500 102 588 461 190 147 140 85 314 422 209 196 296 349 185 74 206 124 68 166 389 158 39 252 299 153 414 98 / 153 515 805 164 947 742 306 237 225 137 505 679 336 315 476 562 298 119 332 267 109 193 267 626 254 63 406 481 246 666 156 / 2:00 6:30 9:50 2:10 11:50 8:50 4:00 3:10 3:20 1:40 6:30 8:00 4:00 3:30 4:40 7:00 3:00 1:50 3:10 2:50 1:20 2:30 6:20 4:20 0:40
Lincoln	51 68 371 476 44 554 427 216 155 128 159 299 389 106 37 179 240 80 258 297 137 51 183 197 208 145 360 441 320 616 211 / 82 109 597 766 71 892 687 348 249 206 256 468 642 438 398 81 505 202 39 307 478 137 82 295 317 330 233 568 213 311 568 / 1:20 1:50 7:30 9:40 1:20 12:00 9:40 4:40 3:10 3:10 3:20 5:40 8:00 4:40 2:30 2:50 0:50 1:40 4:40 7:00 9:40 3:40
Liverpool	129 130 75 361 407 130 511 382 102 265 124 140 329 160 237 216 286 88 120 169 194 161 272 104 341 202 / 208 209 121 581 655 209 822 615 164 427 386 226 425 348 257 381 348 460 481 142 195 272 312 259 438 167 550 325 / 2:50 2:40 1:50 7:20 8:20 2:40 10:40 7:40 2:40 5:40 2:50 2:40 6:40 2:30 5:20 3:00 3:20 1:50 1:50 3:50 4:30 3:20 5:20 2:20
Manchester	35 84 92 40 340 430 95 500 373 124 269 148 128 329 197 206 65 61 119 183 166 157 318 207 335 208 / 56 135 148 64 581 654 153 805 600 200 367 341 203 355 329 191 203 329 196 215 98 192 295 266 254 514 365 77 129 315 208 547 298 / 1:10 2:00 2:00 1:10 7:20 8:40 2:20 10:50 7:40 2:40 5:40 2:50 2:40 6:40 3:30 3:20 3:40 3:00 1:40 1:40 2:30 5:20 3:00 5:50 3:20
Newcastle upon Tyne	132 168 159 187 92 498 318 132 395 268 274 308 220 130 110 166 358 114 57 325 388 567 123 400 107 240 414 378 460 / 212 270 256 301 148 802 512 212 636 431 438 496 452 407 529 586 177 576 580 92 523 627 558 394 333 103 240 414 378 460 / 2:50 3:20 3:40 3:40 1:40 9:40 7:40 2:50 8:40 5:40 5:40 5:30 5:40 2:20 2:40 3:40 7:20 2:10 1:00 6:20 7:40 11:00 2:50 9:20
Norwich	264 185 220 105 119 176 421 582 149 654 529 311 73 168 185 135 111 80 233 103 240 414 276 496 114 / 425 298 354 169 192 283 678 937 240 1053 852 501 117 270 298 217 179 129 375 166 386 666 444 798 183 / 5:20 4:30 4:40 2:10 2:10 3:30 10:30 14:40 3:00 16:30 13:40 7:40 1:40 3:40 4:30 3:20 2:40 2:10 5:20 2:30 6:10 9:40
Nottingham	130 157 73 98 35 25 70 345 419 90 692 528 241 246 177 472 646 354 422 528 300 312 172 80 233 103 240 264 633 196 / 209 253 118 158 56 40 113 555 692 241 1056 852 388 396 285 760 1040 570 679 850 483 502 277 129 375 166 386 425 1019 315 / 3:10 3:40 1:40 2:10 1:10 0:50 1:40 8:40 10:30 2:30 16:00 13:00 6:30 6:00 4:40 9:50 14:00 7:30 9:10 11:30 6:20 6:50 3:20 1:30 5:30 2:30 6:10
Oban	390 492 253 308 387 419 307 665 128 346 244 117 427 524 515 49 481 556 117 346 465 141 530 234 94 178 499 / 628 792 375 494 496 623 674 1070 206 557 393 188 687 843 829 710 79 774 889 188 557 748 227 853 376 151 286 803 / 7:30 9:40 4:50 6:00 6:00 7:50 6:20 16:00 8:00 5:40 4:40 3:10 9:40 11:50 11:40 2:00 3:20 6:20 3:50 6:50 9:10
Oxford	462 109 145 260 144 172 137 73 168 274 160 52 346 221 156 156 301 599 167 233 314 108 134 119 108 749 145 301 103 521 568 248 777 92 / 744 175 233 418 232 277 221 117 270 441 885 309 1056 356 383 233 50 200 583 760 30 213 201 1067 145 301 103 521 568 248 777 148 / 8:30 2:10 3:40 5:40 4:00 4:30 3:40 2:50 5:00 6:30 3:10 1:30 8:40 6:50 5:20 5:20 3:20 5:30 3:10 4:10 4:50 2:20 2:00 1:50
Plymouth	199 587 267 343 410 283 283 293 242 316 89 674 355 790 664 328 309 166 167 495 495 216 167 293 167 602 474 474 217 615 218 / 320 945 430 552 660 455 455 472 389 509 143 1085 571 1271 1069 528 497 588 253 797 798 408 477 196 301 763 792 382 990 351 / 4:00 11:00 4:50 6:20 7:50 5:20 5:20 5:20 4:30 6:20 2:00 12:00 6:50 16:00 14:00 6:20 6:10 3:10 3:10 10:10 10:00 5:20 6:20 5:20
Portsmouth	176 77 545 191 309 180 162 259 269 162 448 591 414 417 1019 433 1186 983 501 267 356 192 721 893 404 217 759 307 881 84 425 401 430 357 901 113 / 283 124 877 307 497 290 261 417 433 261 721 951 667 671 1639 697 1908 1582 806 430 573 309 1160 1437 650 349 1221 494 1417 135 684 645 692 575 1450 182 / 4:50 1:40 12:40 4:30 7:10 3:40 3:20 5:00 4:40 3:20 7:50 10:40 7:30 7:20 17:00 11:00 20:00 17:00 9:00 5:20 6:20 3:30 13:10 16:10 7:20 3:40 13:40 5:40 16:20 2:10
Sheffield	230 283 135 339 37 146 62 33 361 427 259 269 189 64 171 259 181 237 193 18 176 190 159 360 159 / 370 455 217 546 60 235 100 53 581 687 417 433 304 103 275 417 291 402 312 193 28 306 256 579 256 / 4:20 5:30 3:30 6:40 1:00 3:00 1:30 0:50 8:00 9:40 6:00 5:30 4:00 1:30 4:20 6:10 4:20 5:40 4:30
Shrewsbury	82 207 106 363 155 200 111 69 214 135 488 272 108 158 352 43 426 433 124 642 258 / 132 333 362 590 361 250 322 111 93 214 135 786 417 172 442 531 404 70 178 364 597 166 681 697 200 1033 415 / 2:40 5:20 4:20 7:20 3:10 4:30 2:40 2:40 5:10 3:20 10:10 6:00 2:40 3:40 7:20 1:10 9:00 6:50
Southampton	185 199 21 151 64 309 77 181 46 256 73 160 421 159 200 204 189 57 426 433 388 417 181 547 77 / 298 320 34 243 103 353 124 329 74 412 1164 257 677 256 322 328 304 92 686 705 624 671 291 880 124 / 4:10 4:30 0:40 3:50 2:30 7:20 1:50 4:40 1:10 6:40 4:10 4:00 10:40 4:10 5:00 5:20 4:40 1:20
Stranraer	445 277 263 461 500 379 269 269 309 158 43 416 610 402 267 101 269 414 444 303 478 478 553 367 / 716 446 423 742 805 610 433 433 497 254 69 669 982 647 430 162 433 667 716 488 769 769 890 591 / 8:20 5:10 4:40 8:30 9:20 6:50 4:40 4:40 5:20 2:40 0:50 7:50 11:00 7:20 4:50 2:20 4:40 7:10 7:10
Swansea	417 161 118 217 182 206 141 505 192 301 347 187 195 51 248 594 204 696 572 269 56 161 412 473 309 379 73 507 194 / 671 259 189 349 293 332 227 815 309 485 559 301 314 82 399 956 328 1121 921 433 90 259 663 761 497 610 117 816 312 / 7:50 3:30 2:50 4:10 3:30 4:00 3:10 9:40 5:00 7:10 8:20 4:30 4:50 1:20 5:00 14:10 7:20 16:10 13:10 6:20 1:40 3:00 4:40
York	272 222 258 128 77 181 46 108 24 411 407 665 60 180 189 221 189 357 443 459 154 209 238 344 314 513 333 / 438 357 415 214 84 448 53 291 497 124 291 661 655 60 771 566 328 302 189 237 349 531 462 392 402 454 195 393 165 357 / 5:10 4:40 5:10 2:40 1:40 3:20 2:10 2:30 5:40 2:10 0:50 8:00 10:10 10:10 2:30 3:20 4:00 3:30 5:10 7:10 7:20 2:50 3:30 3:10 4:10 4:40

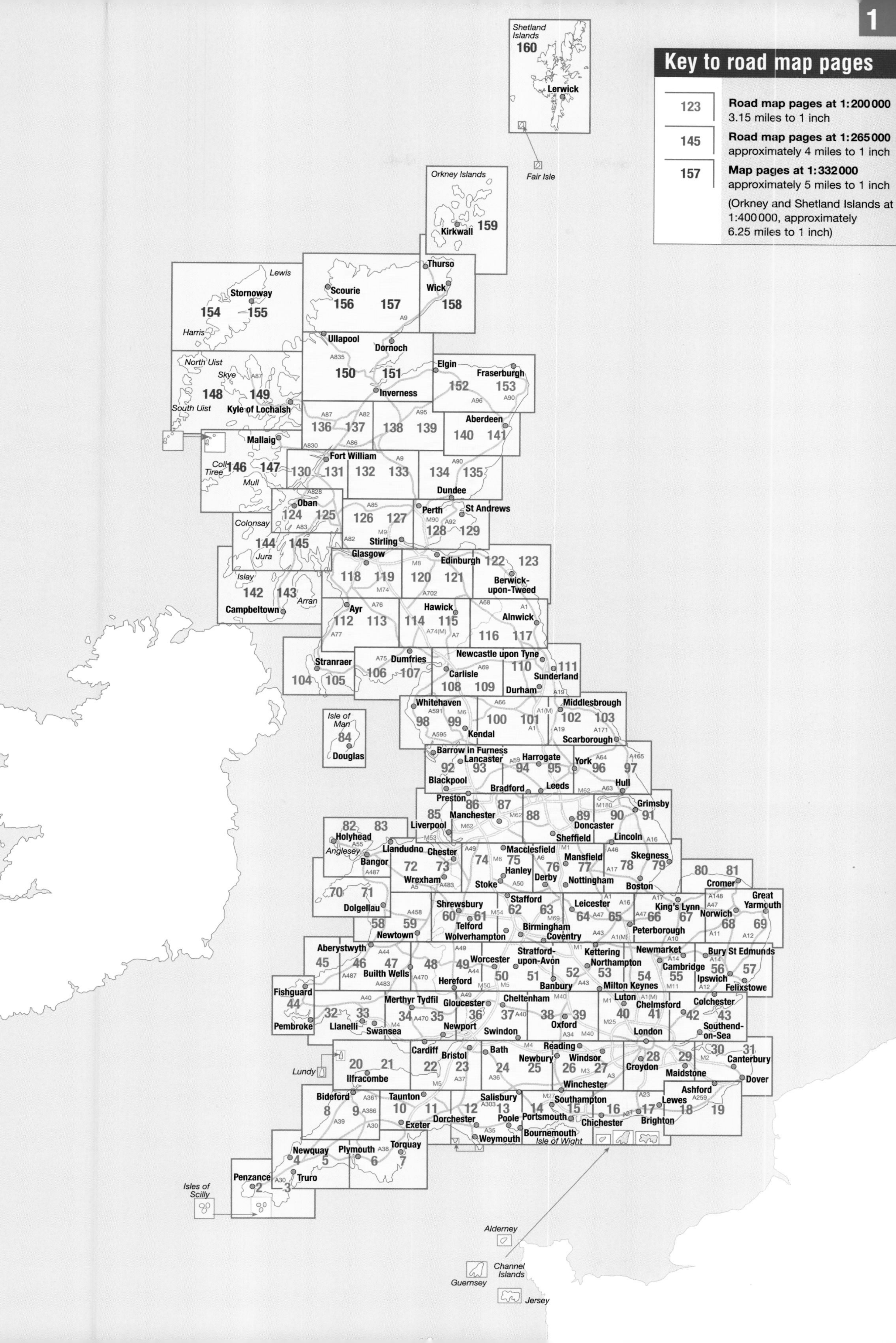

Key to road map pages

123	**Road map pages at 1:200 000** 3.15 miles to 1 inch
145	**Road map pages at 1:265 000** approximately 4 miles to 1 inch
157	**Map pages at 1:332 000** approximately 5 miles to 1 inch (Orkney and Shetland Islands at 1:400 000, approximately 6.25 miles to 1 inch)

Shetland Islands
160
Lerwick

Fair Isle

Orkney Islands
Kirkwall **159**

Lewis
Stornoway
154 – **155**
Harris

Scourie **156** **157** Thurso Wick **158**

North Uist
Skye
148 **149**
South Uist
Kyle of Lochalsh

Ullapool **150** **151** Dornoch Inverness Elgin **152** Fraserburgh **153**

Mallaig
Coll Tiree **146** **147** **130** **131** Fort William **132** **133** **134** **135** Aberdeen **140** **141**

136 **137** **138** **139**

Mull
Oban **124** **125** **126** **127** Perth **128** Dundee St Andrews **129**

Colonsay
144 **145** Stirling

Islay
142 **143** Arran Glasgow **118** **119** **120** **121** Edinburgh **122** **123** Berwick-upon-Tweed

Campbeltown

Ayr **112** **113** **114** **115** Hawick Alnwick **116** **117**

Stranraer **104** **105** **106** **107** Dumfries Carlisle **108** **109** Durham Newcastle upon Tyne **110** **111** Sunderland

Isle of Man
84
Douglas

Whitehaven **98** **99** **100** **101** **102** **103** Middlesbrough Kendal Scarborough

Barrow in Furness
92 **93** Lancaster Harrogate **94** **95** York **96** **97**
Blackpool Bradford Leeds Hull

Preston **85** **86** Manchester **87** **88** **89** Doncaster **90** Grimsby **91**
Liverpool Sheffield Lincoln

82 **83**
Holyhead
Anglesey Llandudno Chester **74** Macclesfield **75** Mansfield **77** **78** Skegness **79** **80** **81** Cromer
Bangor **72** **73** Hanley Derby **76** Nottingham Boston Great Yarmouth
70 **71** Wrexham Stoke
Dolgellau Shrewsbury **60** **61** Stafford **62** **63** Leicester **64** **65** **66** King's Lynn **67** Norwich **68** **69**
58 **59** Telford Birmingham Peterborough
Newtown Wolverhampton Coventry

Aberystwyth Stratford-upon-Avon Kettering Northampton Newmarket Bury St Edmunds
45 **46** **47** **48** **49** Worcester **51** **52** **53** **54** **55** Cambridge **56** **57** Ipswich
Builth Wells Hereford Banbury Milton Keynes Felixstowe

Fishguard
44 **32** **33** **34** **35** Merthyr Tydfil Gloucester **36** **37** Cheltenham **38** **39** Oxford Luton Chelmsford **41** Colchester **42** **43** Southend-on-Sea
Pembroke Llanelli Swansea Newport Swindon London
Cardiff Bristol Bath Newbury Reading Windsor **27** **28** Croydon **29** **30** Canterbury **31**
Lundy **20** **21** **22** **23** **24** **25** **26** Maidstone Dover
Ilfracombe Winchester Ashford **18** **19**
Bideford **8** **9** Taunton **10** **11** **12** Salisbury **13** **14** Southampton **15** **16** **17** Lewes Brighton
Exeter Dorchester Poole Portsmouth Chichester
Newquay **4** **5** Plymouth **6** **7** Weymouth Bournemouth Isle of Wight
Penzance **2** Truro **3**
Isles of Scilly

Alderney

Channel Islands
Guernsey Jersey

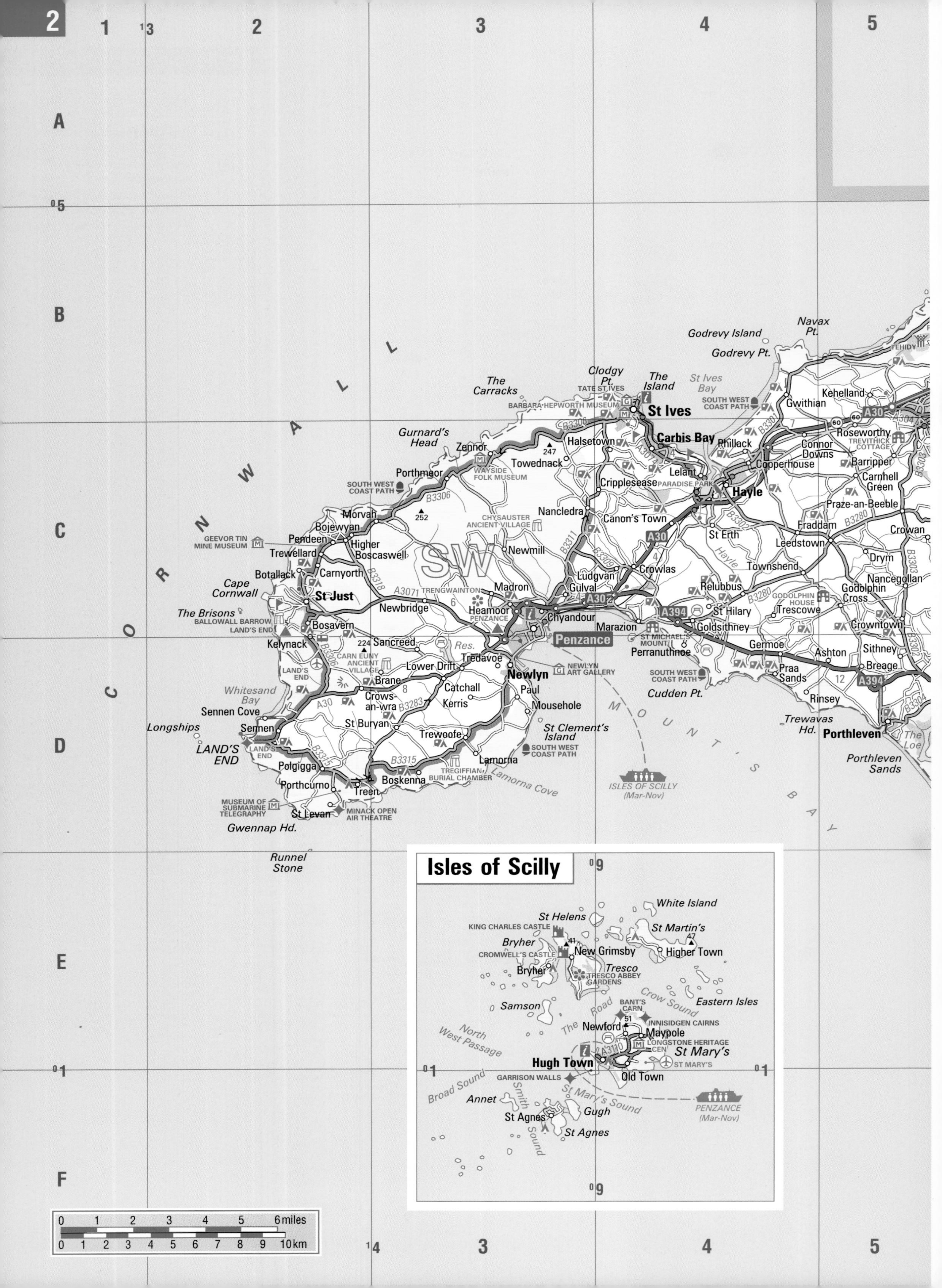

CORNWALL
SW
St Ives
Carbis Bay
Hayle
Penzance
Newlyn
St Just
Marazion
Porthleven
LAND'S END
Sennen Cove
Sennen
Mousehole
Lamorna
Zennor
Gurnard's Head
The Carracks
Clodgy Pt.
The Island
St Ives Bay
Godrevy Island
Godrevy Pt.
Navax Pt.
Cape Cornwall
The Brisons
Whitesand Bay
Longships
Gwennap Hd.
Runnel Stone
Cudden Pt.
Trewavas Hd.
Porthleven Sands
The Loe
MOUNT'S BAY
Lamorna Cove
St Clement's Island
Isles of Scilly
St Helens
White Island
St Martin's
Higher Town
Bryher
New Grimsby
Tresco
Samson
Eastern Isles
Crow Sound
The Road
North West Passage
Newford
Maypole
Hugh Town
St Mary's
Old Town
Broad Sound
Annet
Smith Sound
St Mary's Sound
St Agnes
Gugh
PENZANCE (Mar-Nov)
ISLES OF SCILLY (Mar-Nov)
0 1 2 3 4 5 6 miles
0 1 2 3 4 5 6 7 8 9 10 km

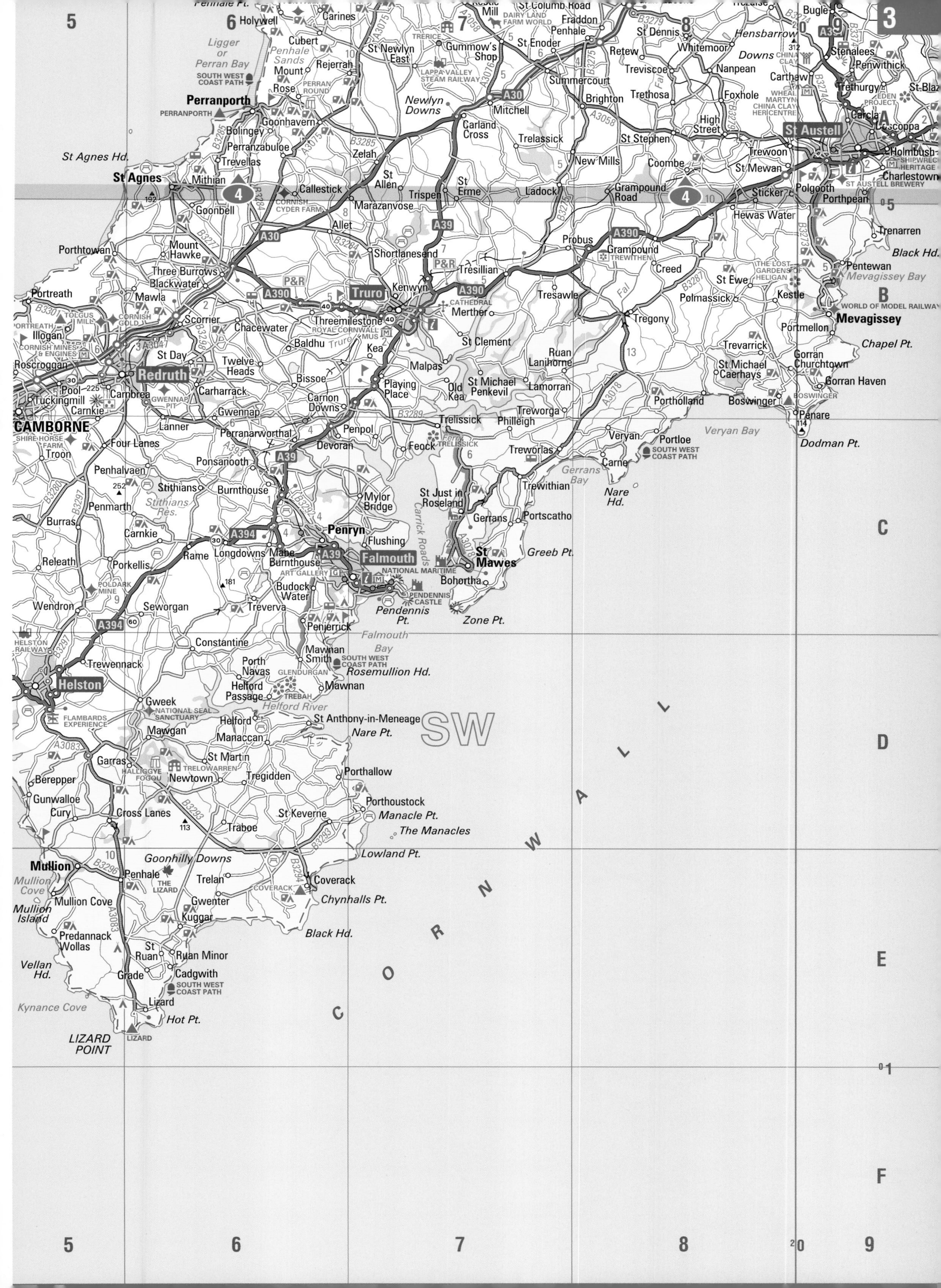
5
6
7
8
9
0
A
B
C
D
E
F
Holywell
Carines
Cubert
Ligger or Perran Bay
Penhale Sands
Mount
Rose
Rejerrah
Perran Round
SOUTH WEST COAST PATH
Perranporth
PERRANPORTH
St Newlyn East
Trerice
Gummow's Shop
Lappa Valley Steam Railway
St Columb Road
Dairy Land Farm World
Fraddon
Penhale
St Enoder
Summercourt
St Dennis
Whitemoor
Retew
Treviscoe
Nanpean
Hensbarrow Downs
China Clay
Bugle
Stenalees
Penwithick
Carthew
Trethurgy
St Blazey
Wheal Martyn China Clay Heritage Centre
Eden Project
Carclaze
Boscoppa
St Austell
Holmbush
Shipwreck Heritage
Charlestown
St Austell Brewery
Foxhole
Brighton
Trethosa
High Street
Newlyn Downs
Mitchell
Carland Cross
Trelassick
St Stephen
Coombe
Trewoon
St Mewan
New Mills
Goonhavern
Bolingey
Perranzabuloe
Trevellas
Zelah
St Agnes Hd.
St Agnes
Mithian
Callestick
Cornish Cyder Farm
St Allen
Trispen
St Erme
Ladock
Grampound Road
Sticker
Polgooth
Porthpean
Hewas Water
Trenarren
Black Hd.
Goonbell
Marazanvose
Allet
Shortlanesend
Porthtowan
Mount Hawke
Three Burrows
Blackwater
Tresillian
Probus
Grampound
Trewithen
Creed
St Ewe
The Lost Gardens of Heligan
Pentewan
Mevagissey Bay
Portreath
Mawla
Tolgus Mill
Cornish Gold
Truro
Kenwyn
Threemilestone
Royal Cornwall Mus
Cathedral
Merther
Tresawle
Fal
Polmassick
Kestle
World of Model Railway
Mevagissey
Illogan
Cornish Mines & Engines
Scorrier
Chacewater
Baldhu
Kea
St Clement
Tregony
Portmellon
Chapel Pt.
Roscroggan
Redruth
St Day
Twelve Heads
Bissoe
Malpas
Ruan Lanihorne
Trevarrick
St Michael Caerhays
Gorran Churchtown
Gorran Haven
Pool
Tuckingmill
Carnkie
Camborne
Cambrea
Gwennap Pit
Carharrack
Gwennap
Carnon Downs
Playing Place
Old Kea
St Michael Penkevil
Lamorran
Portholland
Boswinger
Penare
Dodman Pt.
Lanner
Perranarworthal
Penpol
Devoran
Trelissick
Philleigh
Treworga
Veryan
Portloe
Veryan Bay
Shire Horse Farm
Troon
Four Lanes
Ponsanooth
Feock
Trelissick
Treworlas
Carne
Gerrans Bay
Penhalvaen
Stithians
Burnthouse
Mylor Bridge
St Just in Roseland
Trewithian
Nare Hd.
Stithians Res.
Penmarth
Burras
Carnkie
Penryn
Flushing
Carrick Roads
Gerrans
Portscatho
Releath
Porkellis
Rame
Longdowns
Mabe Burnthouse
Falmouth
National Maritime
St Mawes
Greeb Pt.
Art Gallery
Bohortha
Poldark Mine
Wendron
Seworgan
Treverva
Budock Water
Pendennis Castle
Pendennis Pt.
Zone Pt.
Helston Railway
Constantine
Penjerrick
Falmouth Bay
Mawnan Smith
Trewennack
Porth Navas
Glendurgan
Rosemullion Hd.
Helston
Helford Passage
Trebah
Mawnan
Gweek
National Seal Sanctuary
Helford River
Flambards Experience
St Anthony-in-Meneage
Nare Pt.
SW
Mawgan
Helford
Manaccan
Garras
St Martin
Trelowarren
Halliggye Fogou
Newtown
Tregidden
Porthallow
Berepper
Gunwalloe
Porthoustock
Manacle Pt.
Cury
Cross Lanes
Traboe
St Keverne
The Manacles
Lowland Pt.
Mullion
Goonhilly Downs
Penhale
The Lizard
Trelan
Coverack
Mullion Cove
Mullion Island
Gwenter
Chynhalls Pt.
Kuggar
Predannack Wollas
Black Hd.
St Ruan
Ruan Minor
Vellan Hd.
Grade
Cadgwith
SOUTH WEST COAST PATH
Kynance Cove
Lizard
Hot Pt.
LIZARD POINT
LIZARD
C O R N W A L L
A30
A39
A390
A394
A3047
A3075
A3076
A3078
A3083
A3058
B3279
B3274
B3285
B3284
B3277
B3300
B3298
B3280
B3297
B3292
B3289
B3287
B3275
B3273
B3293
B3294
B3296
P&R
4

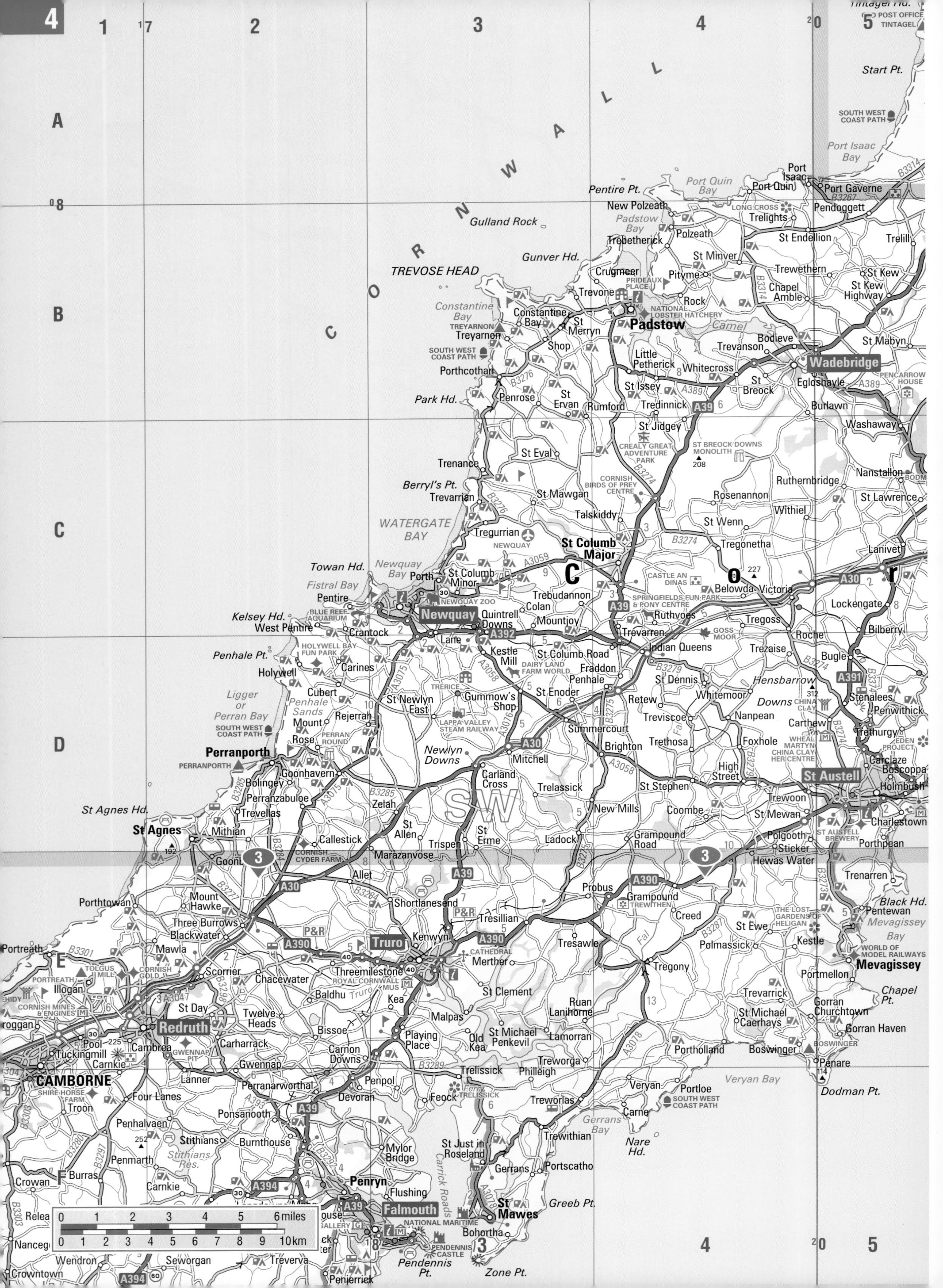
CORNWALL
Tintagel Hd.
OLD POST OFFICE TINTAGEL
Start Pt.
SOUTH WEST COAST PATH
Port Isaac Bay
Port Isaac
Port Quin
Port Quin Bay
Port Gaverne
Pentire Pt.
New Polzeath
Padstow Bay
Gulland Rock
LONG CROSS
Trelights
Pendoggett
Trebetherick
Polzeath
St Endellion
Trelill
Gunver Hd.
St Minver
TREVOSE HEAD
Crugmeer
Pityme
Trewethern
St Kew
St Kew Highway
Chapel Amble
Trevone
PRIDEAUX PLACE
Rock
NATIONAL LOBSTER HATCHERY
Constantine Bay
Constantine Bay
St Merryn
Padstow
Camel
TREYARNON
Treyarnon
Shop
Bodieve
Trevanson
St Mabyn
SOUTH WEST COAST PATH
Little Petherick
Whitecross
Wadebridge
Porthcothan
St Breock
Egloshayle
PENCARROW HOUSE
Park Hd.
Penrose
St Ervan
Rumford
St Issey
Tredinnick
Burlawn
St Jidgey
Washaway
CREALY GREAT ADVENTURE PARK
ST BREOCK DOWNS MONOLITH
208
St Eval
Trenance
CORNISH BIRDS OF PREY CENTRE
Nanstallon
Ruthernbridge
Berryl's Pt.
Trevarrian
St Mawgan
Rosenannon
St Lawrence
Withiel
Talskiddy
St Wenn
WATERGATE BAY
Tregurrian
NEWQUAY
St Columb Major
Tregonetha
Lanivet
Towan Hd.
Newquay Bay
Porth
St Columb Minor
CASTLE AN DINAS
227
Fistral Bay
Pentire
NEWQUAY ZOO
Trebudannon
SPRINGFIELDS FUN PARK & PONY CENTRE
Belowda
Victoria
Lockengate
Kelsey Hd.
BLUE REEF AQUARIUM
Newquay
Quintrell Downs
Colan
Mountjoy
Ruthvoes
West Pentire
Crantock
Lane
Trevarren
Tregoss
Roche
Bilberry
HOLYWELL BAY FUN PARK
Kestle Mill
St Columb Road
Indian Queens
GOSS MOOR
Trezaise
Penhale Pt.
Bugle
Holywell
Carines
DAIRY LAND FARM WORLD
Fraddon
St Dennis
Hensbarrow Downs
Penhale
Cubert
TRERICE
Gummow's Shop
St Enoder
Whitemoor
312
Stenalees
Ligger or Perran Bay
Penhale Sands
St Newlyn East
Retew
CHINA CLAY
Penwithick
Rejerrah
Treviscoe
Nanpean
SOUTH WEST COAST PATH
Mount
LAPPA VALLEY STEAM RAILWAY
Summercourt
Carthew
Trethurgy
Rose
PERRAN ROUND
Brighton
Trethosa
Foxhole
WHEAL MARTYN CHINA CLAY HERITAGE CENTRE
EDEN PROJECT
Perranporth
Newlyn Downs
Mitchell
Carclaze
Boscoppa
PERRANPORTH
Goonhavern
Carland Cross
High Street
St Austell
Bolingey
Holmbush
Perranzabuloe
Trelassick
St Stephen
St Agnes Hd.
Trevellas
Zelah
New Mills
Coombe
Trewoon
St Mewan
Charlestown
St Agnes
Mithian
St Allen
St Erme
Ladock
Grampound Road
ST AUSTELL BREWERY
Polgooth
Porthpean
192
Callestick
Trispen
Sticker
CORNISH CYDER FARM
Marazanvose
Hewas Water
Goonbell
Allet
Trenarren
Mount Hawke
Shortlanesend
Probus
Grampound
TREWITHEN
Black Hd.
Porthtowan
THE LOST GARDENS OF HELIGAN
Pentewan
Three Burrows
P&R
Tresillian
Creed
St Ewe
Mevagissey Bay
Blackwater
Kenwyn
Truro
Tresawle
Kestle
Portreath
Mawla
CATHEDRAL
Polmassick
WORLD OF MODEL RAILWAYS
TOLGUS MILL
CORNISH GOLD
Scorrier
Threemilestone
Merther
Tregony
Mevagissey
PORTREATH
Chacewater
ROYAL CORNWALL MUS
Portmellon
Illogan
St Clement
Trevarrick
Chapel Pt.
CORNISH MINES & ENGINES
St Day
Baldhu
Truro
Kea
Ruan Lanihorne
Gorran Churchtown
Twelve Heads
Malpas
St Michael Caerhays
Redruth
Bissoe
Playing Place
Old Kea
St Michael Penkevil
Lamorran
Gorran Haven
Pool
225
Carharrack
Carnon Downs
Portholland
Boswinger
BOSWINGER
Tuckingmill
Cambrea
GWENNAP PIT
Penare
Carnkie
Gwennap
Trelissick
Treworga
CAMBORNE
Lanner
Perranarwothal
Penpol
Philleigh
Veryan Bay
114
SHIRE HORSE FARM
Four Lanes
Devoran
Feock
Ferry TRELISSICK
Veryan
Portloe
Dodman Pt.
Troon
Treworlas
SOUTH WEST COAST PATH
Ponsanooth
Carne
Penhalvaen
Gerrans Bay
252
Stithians
Burnthouse
Trewithian
Nare Hd.
Stithians Res.
Mylor Bridge
St Just in Roseland
Penmarth
Carrick Roads
Gerrans
Portscatho
Crowan
Burras
Penryn
Carnkie
Flushing
St Mawes
Greeb Pt.
Falmouth
NATIONAL MARITIME
Bohortha
PENDENNIS CASTLE
Pendennis Pt.
Wendron
Seworgan
Treverva
Crowntown
Penjerrick
Zone Pt.
0 1 2 3 4 5 6 miles
0 1 2 3 4 5 6 7 8 9 10 km
A30
A39
A389
A392
A3059
A3075
A3058
A3076
A390
A393
A394
A3047
A3078
B3314
B3267
B3276
B3274
B3279
B3275
B3285
B3284
B3277
B3298
B3301
B3300
B3303
B3280
B3297
B3291
B3289
B3287
B3273
B3374
SW
1
2
3
4
5
A
B
C
D
E
F

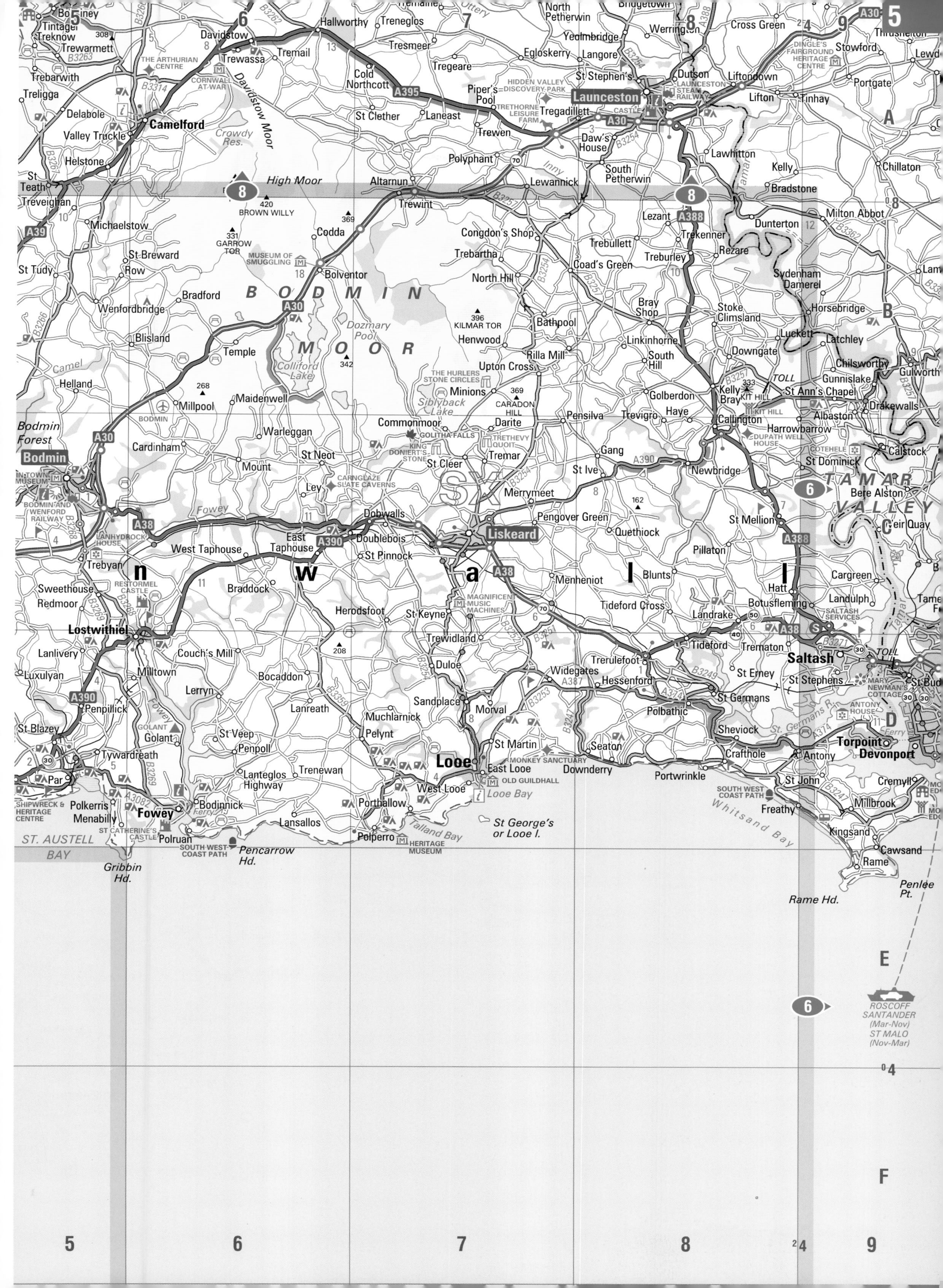

5
Tintagel
Treknow
Trewarmett
Trebarwith
Treligga
Delabole
Camelford
Valley Truckle
Helstone
St Teath
Davidstow
Trewassa
THE ARTHURIAN CENTRE
CORNWALL AT WAR
Crowdy Res.
Davidstow Moor
Hallworthy
Treneglos
Tremail
Tresmeer
Tregeare
Cold Northcott
A395
St Clether
Laneast
Trewen
Polyphant
North Petherwin
Yeolmbridge
Werrington
Egloskerry
Langore
St Stephen's
Dutson
Launceston
LAUNCESTON STEAM RAILWAY
HIDDEN VALLEY DISCOVERY PARK
Piper's Pool
TRETHORNE LEISURE FARM
Tregadillett
CASTLE
A30
Daw's House
Cross Green
DINGLE'S FAIRGROUND HERITAGE CENTRE
Stowford
Liftondown
Lifton
Portgate
Tinhay
Lawhitton
South Petherwin
Kelly
Chillaton
Bradstone
High Moor
BROWN WILLY
420
GARROW TOR
331
369
Altarnun
Trewint
Lewannick
Inny
Lezant
A388
Trekenner
Dunterton
Milton Abbot
Treveighan
Michaelstow
A39
St Breward
Row
St Tudy
MUSEUM OF SMUGGLING
Codda
Bolventor
Congdon's Shop
Trebartha
North Hill
Trebullett
Treburley
Coad's Green
Rezare
Sydenham Damerel
B O D M I N
M O O R
Bradford
Wenfordbridge
A30
Dozmary Pool
KILMAR TOR
396
Henwood
Bathpool
Bray Shop
Stoke Climsland
Horsebridge
Blisland
Temple
Colliford Lake
342
Rilla Mill
Linkinhorne
South Hill
Downgate
Luckett
Latchley
Camel
Helland
268
Millpool
Maidenwell
THE HURLERS STONE CIRCLES
Upton Cross
Minions
Siblyback Lake
369
CARADON HILL
Golberdon
Haye
Kelly Bray
KIT HILL
333
TOLL
Chilsworthy
Gunnislake
St Ann's Chapel
Gulworthy
Albaston
Drakewalls
Bodmin Forest
BODMIN
Warleggan
Cardinham
Commonmoor
GOLITHA FALLS
TRETHEVY QUOIT
Darite
Pensilva
Trevigro
Callington
Harrowbarrow
DUPATH WELL HOUSE
COTEHELE
Calstock
Bodmin
IN TOWN MUSEUM
Mount
St Neot
KING DONIERT'S STONE
St Cleer
Tremar
Gang
A390
St Ive
Newbridge
St Dominick
TAMAR VALLEY
Bere Alston
Ley
CARNGLAZE SLATE CAVERNS
SX
Merrymeet
162
BODMIN AND WENFORD RAILWAY
Fowey
A38
Dobwalls
Liskeard
Pengover Green
St Mellion
Weir Quay
LANHYDROCK HOUSE
West Taphouse
East Taphouse
A390
Doublebois
St Pinnock
Quethiock
A388
Trebyan
n
w
a
l
l
Pillaton
Sweethouse
RESTORMEL CASTLE
Braddock
Menheniot
Blunts
Hatt
Cargreen
Redmoor
MAGNIFICENT MUSIC MACHINES
Tideford Cross
Botusfleming
Landulph
Lostwithiel
Herodsfoot
St Keyne
Landrake
SALTASH SERVICES
Trewidland
A38
Tideford
Trematon
Saltash
TOLL
Lanlivery
Couch's Mill
208
Duloe
Trerulefoot
Luxulyan
Milltown
Widegates
A387
Hessenford
St Erney
St Stephens
MARY NEWMAN'S COTTAGE
St Budeaux
A390
Lerryn
Bocaddon
Penpillick
Sandplace
Morval
St Germans
Lanreath
Muchlarnick
Polbathic
ANTONY HOUSE
St Blazey
GOLANT
Golant
St Veep
Pelynt
Sheviock
St Germans R.
Penpoll
St Martin
Seaton
Torpoint
Devonport
Tywardreath
Looe
East Looe
MONKEY SANCTUARY
Downderry
Crafthole
Antony
Par
Lanteglos Highway
Trenewan
OLD GUILDHALL
Portwrinkle
St John
Cremyll
SHIPWRECK & HERITAGE CENTRE
Polkerris
Menabilly
Fowey
Bodinnick
West Looe
Looe Bay
SOUTH WEST COAST PATH
Freathy
Millbrook
ST CATHERINE'S CASTLE
Polruan
Lansallos
Porthallow
St George's or Looe I.
Whitsand Bay
Kingsand
ST. AUSTELL BAY
SOUTH WEST COAST PATH
Pencarrow Hd.
Polperro
HERITAGE MUSEUM
Talland Bay
Cawsand
Rame
Gribbin Hd.
Penlee Pt.
Rame Hd.
E
ROSCOFF
SANTANDER
(Mar-Nov)
ST MALO
(Nov-Mar)
F
5
6
7
8
9

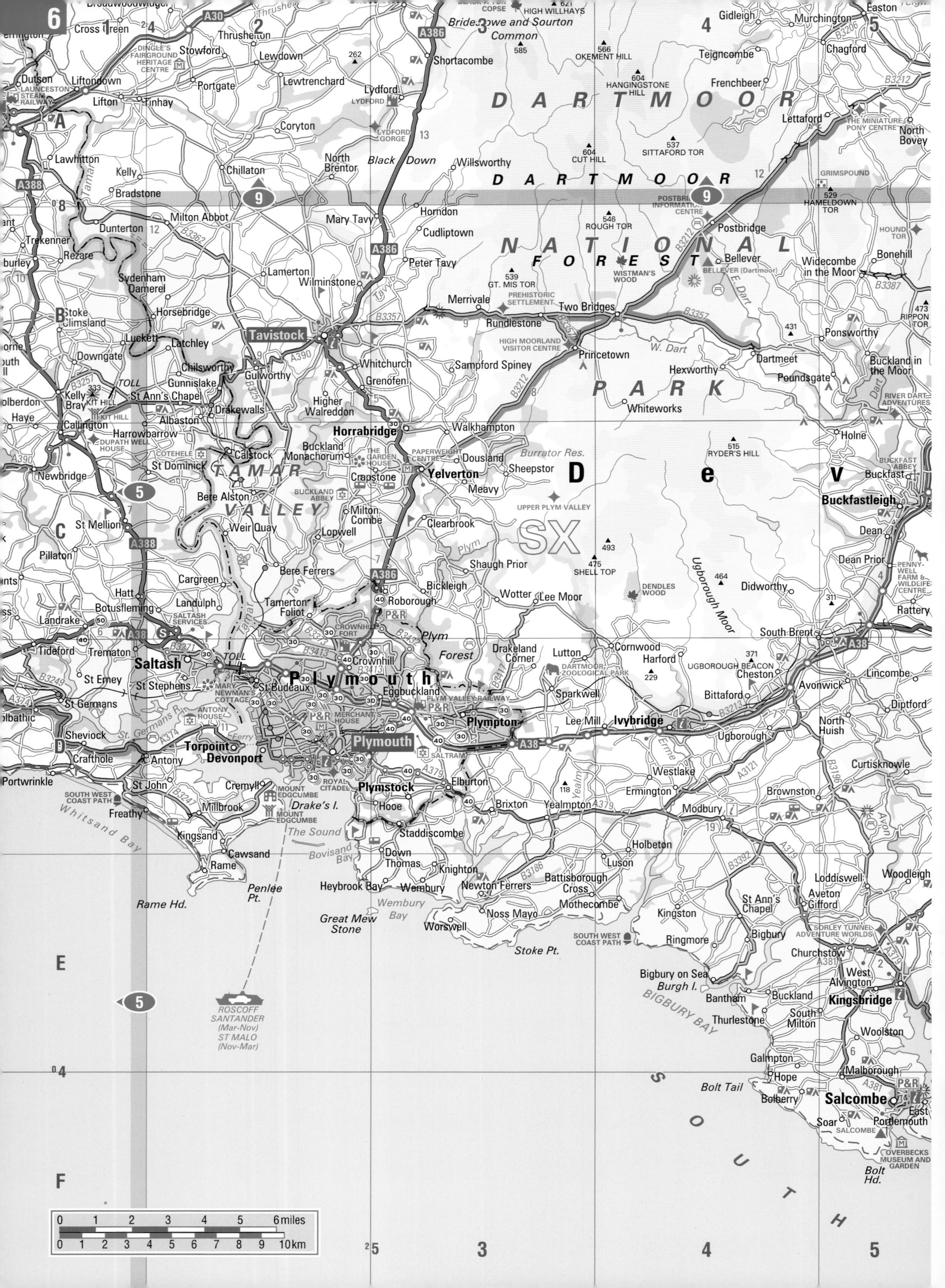
6
DARTMOOR
DARTMOOR NATIONAL PARK
FOREST
TAMAR VALLEY
Devon
SX
SOUTH
Bridestowe and Sourton Common
HIGH WILLHAYS
OKEMENT HILL
HANGINGSTONE HILL
CUT HILL
SITTAFORD TOR
ROUGH TOR
GT. MIS TOR
WISTMAN'S WOOD
RYDER'S HILL
SHELL TOP
UPPER PLYM VALLEY
DENDLES WOOD
Ugborough Moor
UGBOROUGH BEACON
HAMELDOWN TOR
RIPPON TOR
GRIMSPOUND
HOUND TOR
POSTBRIDGE INFORMATION CENTRE
HIGH MOORLAND VISITOR CENTRE
PREHISTORIC SETTLEMENT
BELLEVER (Dartmoor)
THE MINIATURE PONY CENTRE
RIVER DART ADVENTURES
BUCKFAST ABBEY
PENNYWELL FARM & WILDLIFE CENTRE
DARTMOOR ZOOLOGICAL PARK
PLYM VALLEY RAILWAY
SALTRAM
MERCHANT'S HOUSE
MARY NEWMAN'S COTTAGE
ANTONY HOUSE
COTEHELE
BUCKLAND ABBEY
THE GARDEN HOUSE
PAPERWEIGHT CENTRE
CROWNHILL FORT
DINGLE'S FAIRGROUND HERITAGE CENTRE
LAUNCESTON STEAM RAILWAY
LYDFORD GORGE
DUPATH WELL HOUSE
KIT HILL
SALTASH SERVICES
MOUNT EDGCUMBE
ROYAL CITADEL
SOUTH WEST COAST PATH
SORLEY TUNNEL ADVENTURE WORLDS
OVERBECKS MUSEUM AND GARDEN
SALCOMBE
ROSCOFF SANTANDER (Mar-Nov) ST MALO (Nov-Mar)
Plymouth
Tavistock
Saltash
Torpoint
Devonport
Plymstock
Plympton
Ivybridge
Horrabridge
Yelverton
Buckfastleigh
Kingsbridge
Salcombe
Launceston
Dutson
Liftondown
Lifton
Tinhay
Cross Green
Stowford
Thrushelton
Lewdown
Portgate
Lewtrenchard
Lydford
Shortacombe
Coryton
Lawhitton
Kelly
Bradstone
Chillaton
North Brentor
Black Down
Willsworthy
Mary Tavy
Horndon
Cudliptown
Peter Tavy
Milton Abbot
Dunterton
Trekenner
Rezare
Sydenham Damerel
Horsebridge
Lamerton
Wilminstone
Merrivale
Rundlestone
Two Bridges
Princetown
Stoke Climsland
Luckett
Latchley
Downgate
Chilsworthy
Gunnislake
Gulworthy
Whitchurch
Grenofen
Sampford Spiney
Kelly Bray
St Ann's Chapel
Drakewalls
Albaston
Higher Walreddon
Callington
Harrowbarrow
Calstock
St Dominick
Buckland Monachorum
Crapstone
Dousland
Walkhampton
Sheepstor
Meavy
Burrator Res.
Newbridge
Bere Alston
Milton Combe
Clearbrook
St Mellion
Weir Quay
Lopwell
Pillaton
Bere Ferrers
Shaugh Prior
Cargreen
Hatt
Landulph
Botusfleming
Tamerton Foliot
Roborough
Bickleigh
Wotter
Lee Moor
Landrake
Tideford
Trematon
St Erney
St Stephens
St Budeaux
Crownhill
Eggbuckland
Plym Forest
Drakeland Corner
Lutton
Cornwood
Harford
Sparkwell
Lee Mill
St Germans
Sheviock
Crafthole
Antony
Portwrinkle
St John
Cremyll
Millbrook
Freathy
Kingsand
Cawsand
Rame
Rame Hd.
Penlee Pt.
Whitsand Bay
Drake's I.
The Sound
Bovisand Bay
Hooe
Staddiscombe
Elburton
Brixton
Yealmpton
Down Thomas
Knighton
Heybrook Bay
Wembury
Wembury Bay
Great Mew Stone
Newton Ferrers
Noss Mayo
Worswell
Stoke Pt.
Battisborough Cross
Mothecombe
Holbeton
Luson
Ermington
Westlake
Ugborough
Bittaford
Cheston
Avonwick
Modbury
Kingston
Ringmore
Bigbury
Bigbury on Sea
Burgh I.
BIGBURY BAY
Bantham
Thurlestone
Buckland
South Milton
St Ann's Chapel
Aveton Gifford
Loddiswell
Woodleigh
Churchstow
West Alvington
Woolston
Galmpton
Hope
Bolt Tail
Bolberry
Malborough
Soar
East Portlemouth
Bolt Hd.
Gidleigh
Murchington
Easton
Chagford
Teigncombe
Frenchbeer
Lettaford
North Bovey
Postbridge
Bellever
Widecombe in the Moor
Bonehill
Ponsworthy
Dartmeet
Hexworthy
Poundsgate
Buckland in the Moor
Whiteworks
Holne
Buckfast
Dean
Dean Prior
Didworthy
Rattery
South Brent
Lincombe
Diptford
North Huish
Curtisknowle
Brownston
Haye
Holne
W. Dart
E. Dart
Dart
Tamar
Tavy
Plym
Yealm
Erme
Avon
St Germans R.
Ferry
Tamar
TOLL
A30
A386
A388
A390
A38
A374
A379
A3121
A381
B3212
B3357
B3362
B3257
B3271
B3249
B3247
B3413
B3432
B3417
B3213
B3186
B3392
B3196
B3387
B3206
B3212
P&R
0 1 2 3 4 5 6 miles
0 1 2 3 4 5 6 7 8 9 10 km

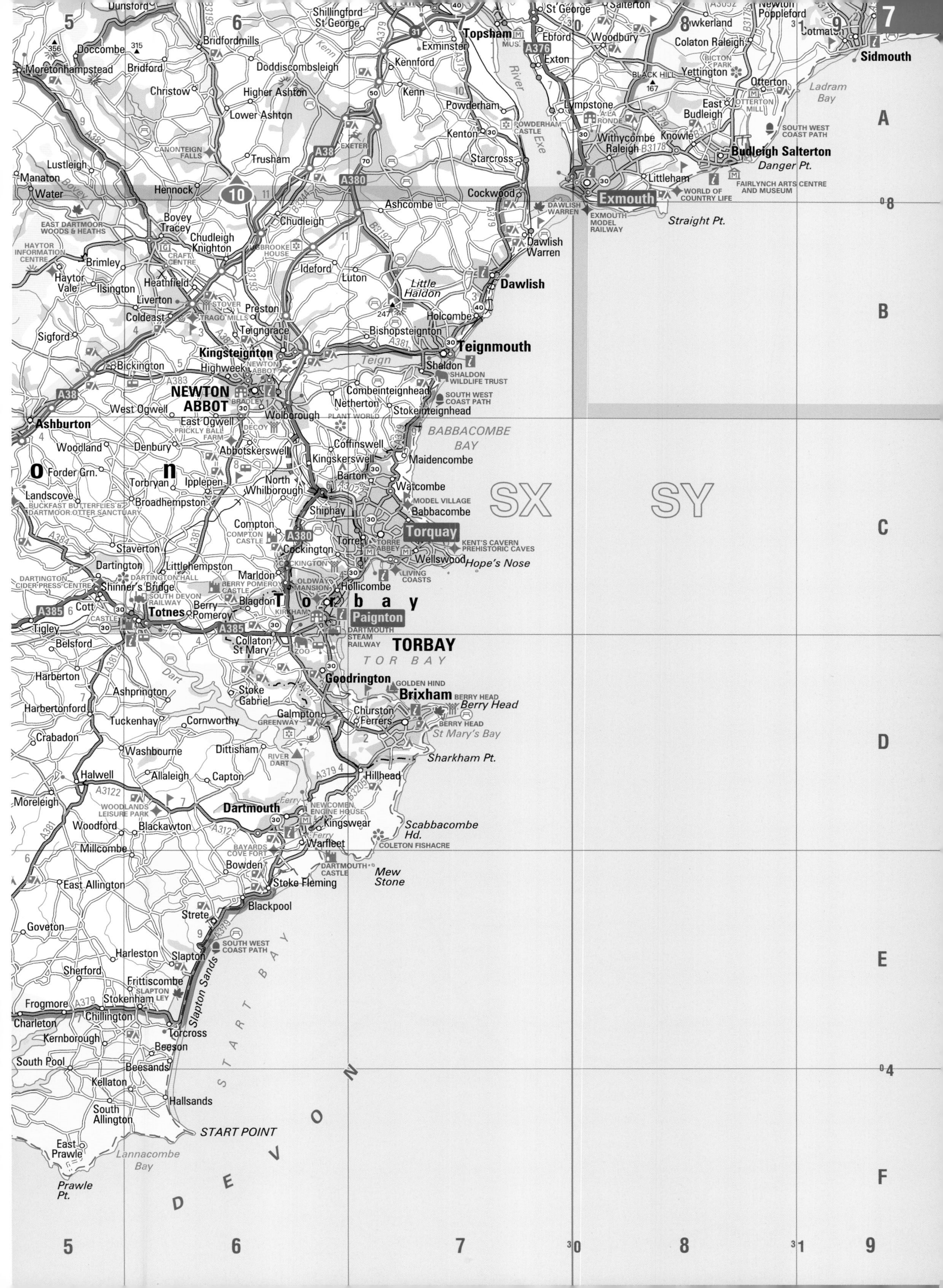
7
Dunsford
Shillingford St George
Topsham
St George
Salterton
Newton Poppleford
Woodbury
Colaton Raleigh
Cotmaton
Sidmouth
Doccombe
Moretonhampstead
Bridford
Bridfordmills
Doddiscombsleigh
Exminster
Kennford
Kenn
Ebford
Exton
Christow
Higher Ashton
Lower Ashton
Powderham
Powderham Castle
Lympstone
Bicton Park
Black Hill
Yettington
Otterton
Otterton Mill
Ladram Bay
East Budleigh
South West Coast Path
Withycombe Raleigh
Knowle
A La Ronde
Kenton
Starcross
River Exe
Canonteign Falls
Trusham
Exeter
Budleigh Salterton
Danger Pt.
Lustleigh
Manaton
Water
Bovey
Hennock
Cockwood
Littleham
Fairlynch Arts Centre and Museum
World of Country Life
Exmouth
Dawlish Warren
Exmouth Model Railway
Straight Pt.
Ashcombe
Chudleigh
East Dartmoor Woods & Heaths
Bovey Tracey
Chudleigh Knighton
Haytor Information Centre
Craft Centre
Ugbrooke House
Brimley
Haytor Vale
Ilsington
Heathfield
Ideford
Luton
Little Haldon
Dawlish
Liverton
Stover
Trago Mills
Coldeast
Preston
Holcombe
Sigford
Teigngrace
Bishopsteignton
Teignmouth
Teign
Bickington
Kingsteignton
Highweek
Newton Abbot
Shaldon
Shaldon Wildlife Trust
Newton Abbot
Bradley
Combeinteignhead
South West Coast Path
West Ogwell
Netherton
Wolborough
Stokeinteignhead
Plant World
Ashburton
East Ogwell
Decoy
Prickly Ball Farm
Babbacombe Bay
Woodland
Denbury
Abbotskerswell
Coffinswell
Maidencombe
Forder Grn.
Kingskerswell
Barton
Torbryan
Ipplepen
North Whilborough
Watcombe
Landscove
Buckfast Butterflies & Dartmoor Otter Sanctuary
Broadhempston
Model Village
Babbacombe
SX
SY
Shiphay
Compton
Compton Castle
Torre
Torre Abbey
Torquay
Kent's Cavern Prehistoric Caves
Staverton
Cockington
Wellswood
Hope's Nose
Dartington
Littlehempston
Dartington Cider Press Centre
Dartington Hall
Berry Pomeroy Castle
Marldon
Living Coasts
Shinner's Bridge
Oldway Mansion
Hollicombe
South Devon Railway
Cott
Berry Pomeroy
Blagdon
Torbay
Castle
Totnes
Kirkham
Paignton
Tigley
Dartmouth Steam Railway
Belsford
Collaton St Mary
Zoo
TORBAY
Tor Bay
Harberton
Dart
Goodrington
Golden Hind
Brixham
Berry Head
Ashprington
Stoke Gabriel
Harbertonford
Galmpton
Churston Ferrers
Tuckenhay
Cornworthy
Greenway
St Mary's Bay
Crabadon
Washbourne
Dittisham
River Dart
Sharkham Pt.
Halwell
Allaleigh
Capton
Hillhead
Moreleigh
Woodlands Leisure Park
Dartmouth
Ferry
Newcomen Engine House
Woodford
Blackawton
Kingswear
Scabbacombe Hd.
Bayards Cove Fort
Warfleet
Coleton Fishacre
Millcombe
Bowden
Dartmouth Castle
Mew Stone
East Allington
Stoke Fleming
Blackpool
Strete
Goveton
South West Coast Path
Harleston
Slapton
Sherford
Slapton Sands
Start Bay
Frittiscombe
Slapton Ley
Frogmore
Stokenham
Chillington
Charleton
Torcross
Kernborough
Beeson
South Pool
Beesands
Kellaton
Hallsands
South Allington
Start Point
East Prawle
Lannacombe Bay
Prawle Pt.
DEVON
A B C D E F
5 6 7 8 9

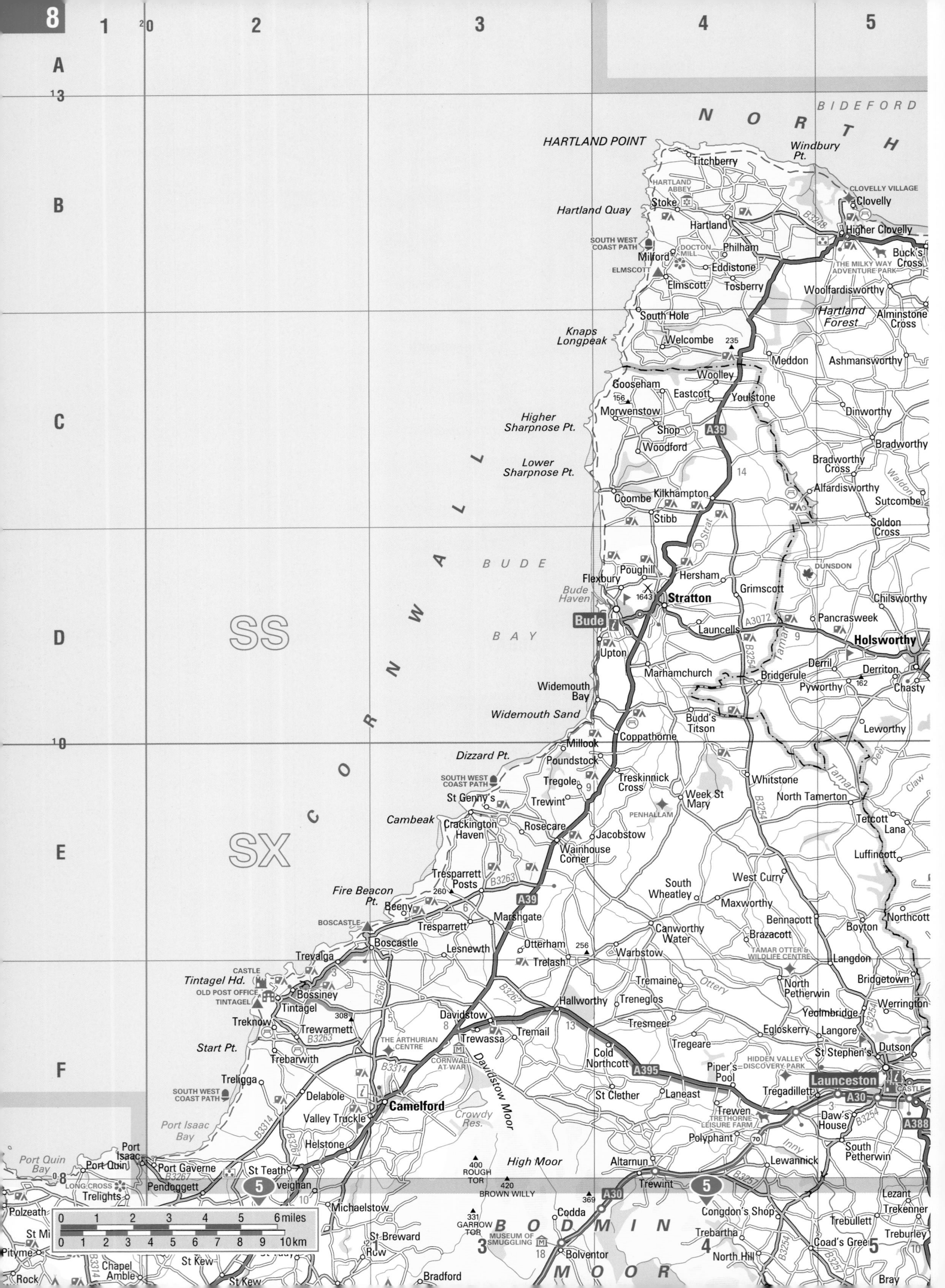

1
2
3
4
5
A
B
C
D
E
F
BIDEFORD
NORTH
HARTLAND POINT
Windbury Pt.
Titchberry
HARTLAND ABBEY
CLOVELLY VILLAGE
Clovelly
Stoke
Hartland Quay
Hartland
B3248
Higher Clovelly
SOUTH WEST COAST PATH
DOCTON MILL
Philham
Milford
Eddistone
THE MILKY WAY ADVENTURE PARK
Buck's Cross
ELMSCOTT
Elmscott
Tosberry
Woolfardisworthy
South Hole
Hartland Forest
Alminstone Cross
Knaps Longpeak
Welcombe
235
Meddon
Ashmansworthy
Gooseham
Woolley
156
Eastcott
Youlstone
Morwenstow
Dinworthy
Higher Sharpnose Pt.
Shop
A39
Woodford
Bradworthy
Lower Sharpnose Pt.
14
Bradworthy Cross
Waldon
Alfardisworthy
Coombe
Kilkhampton
Sutcombe
Stibb
Soldon Cross
Strat
DUNSDON
BUDE
Poughill
Flexbury
Hersham
Grimscott
Bude Haven
1643
Stratton
Chilsworthy
Bude
A3072
Pancrasweek
SS
BAY
Launcells
Tamar
9
Holsworthy
B3254
Upton
Derril
Marhamchurch
Derriton
Bridgerule
Pyworthy
162
Chasty
Widemouth Bay
Widemouth Sand
Budd's Titson
Leworthy
Coppathorne
Millook
Dizzard Pt.
Poundstock
Deer
SOUTH WEST COAST PATH
Tregole
9
Treskinnick Cross
Whitstone
Week St Mary
North Tamerton
Claw
St Genny's
Trewint
PENHALLAM
Tetcott
Lana
Cambeak
Crackington Haven
Rosecare
Jacobstow
SX
Wainhouse Corner
Luffincott
Tresparrett Posts
West Curry
South Wheatley
Fire Beacon Pt.
260
B3263
Maxworthy
Beeny
6
A39
BOSCASTLE
Tresparrett
Marshgate
Bennacott
Northcott
Boyton
Brazacott
Canworthy Water
Boscastle
Otterham
256
Lesnewth
Warbstow
TAMAR OTTER & WILDLIFE CENTRE
Trevalga
Trelash
Langdon
CASTLE
Tintagel Hd.
Bridgetown
OLD POST OFFICE
Bossiney
B3266
B3262
Tremaine
North Petherwin
Ottery
TINTAGEL
Tintagel
Hallworthy
Treneglos
Werrington
308
Yeolmbridge
Treknow
Davidstow
13
Tresmeer
B3254
Trewarmett
Trewassa
Tremail
Egloskerry
Langore
B3263
8
Start Pt.
THE ARTHURIAN CENTRE
Tregeare
St Stephen's
Dutson
Trebarwith
CORNWALL AT WAR
Davidstow Moor
Cold Northcott
HIDDEN VALLEY DISCOVERY PARK
B3314
A395
Piper's Pool
Launceston
Treligga
CASTLE
SOUTH WEST COAST PATH
Delabole
St Clether
Laneast
Tregadillett
A30
Camelford
Trewen
Port Isaac Bay
Valley Truckle
Crowdy Res.
TRETHORNE LEISURE FARM
Daw's House
B3254
A388
B3314
B3267
Helstone
Polyphant
70
Inny
South Petherwin
Port Quin Bay
Port Isaac
Port Quin
400 ROUGH TOR
High Moor
Altarnun
Lewannick
Port Gaverne
St Teath
B3267
LONG CROSS
Pendoggett
5
veighan
420 BROWN WILLY
Trewint
5
B3257
Trelights
369
A30
Lezant
Polzeath
10
Michaelstow
Codda
Congdon's Shop
Trekenner
0 1 2 3 4 5 6 miles
0 1 2 3 4 5 6 7 8 9 10 km
331 GARROW TOR
BODMIN
Trebullett
St Mi
St Breward
MUSEUM OF SMUGGLING
Trebartha
Treburley
Pityme
3
18
4
B3254
Coad's Green
5
Row
Bolventor
North Hill
B3314
Chapel Amble
St Kew
Rock
St Kew
Bradford
MOOR
B3257
Bray

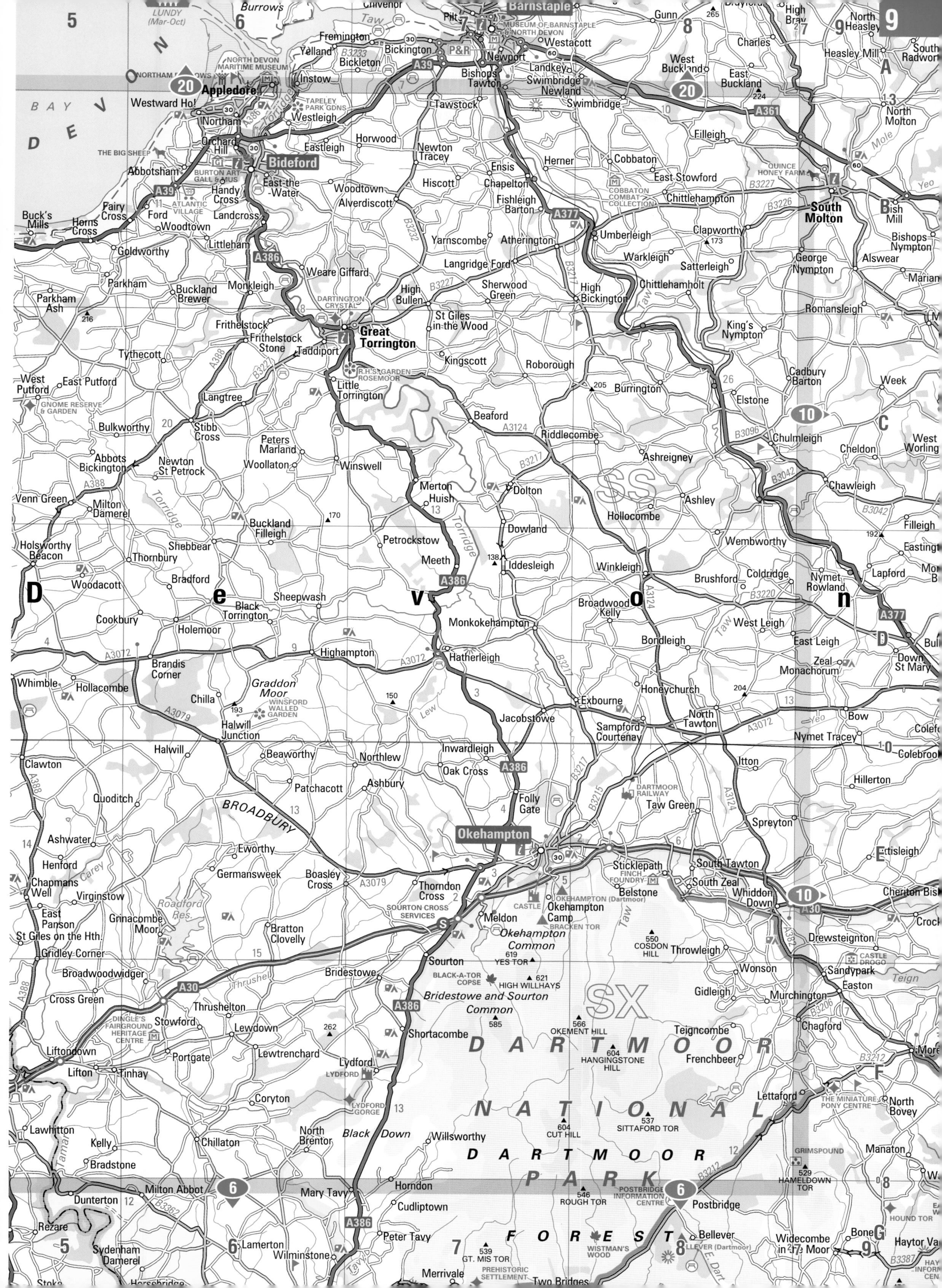

Barnstaple
Bideford
Great Torrington
Okehampton
South Molton
Appledore
Westward Ho!
Northam
Fremington
Bickington
Instow
Newport
Bishops Tawton
Landkey
Swimbridge
Westacott
West Buckland
East Buckland
Filleigh
Chittlehampton
Umberleigh
Atherington
Chittlehamholt
High Bickington
Burrington
Chulmleigh
Beaford
Dolton
Merton
Winkleigh
Hatherleigh
Holsworthy Beacon
Shebbear
Sheepwash
Black Torrington
Highampton
Halwill Junction
Jacobstowe
Exbourne
North Tawton
Sampford Courtenay
Northlew
Ashbury
Sticklepath
South Zeal
Belstone
Okehampton Camp
Sourton
Bridestowe
Lydford
Lewdown
Lifton
Milton Abbot
Mary Tavy
Peter Tavy
Postbridge
Chagford
Moretonhampstead
North Bovey
Widecombe in the Moor
Two Bridges
DARTMOOR
DARTMOOR NATIONAL PARK
DARTMOOR FOREST
Okehampton Common
Bridestowe and Sourton Common
BROADBURY
Graddon Moor
Black Down
D e v o n
BAY
SS
SX
YES TOR
HIGH WILLHAYS
CUT HILL
SITTAFORD TOR
HANGINGSTONE HILL
OKEMENT HILL
ROUGH TOR
GT. MIS TOR
COSDON HILL
HAMELDOWN TOR
A39
A386
A377
A3124
A3072
A3079
A388
A30
A361
A382
B3227
B3217
B3215
B3212

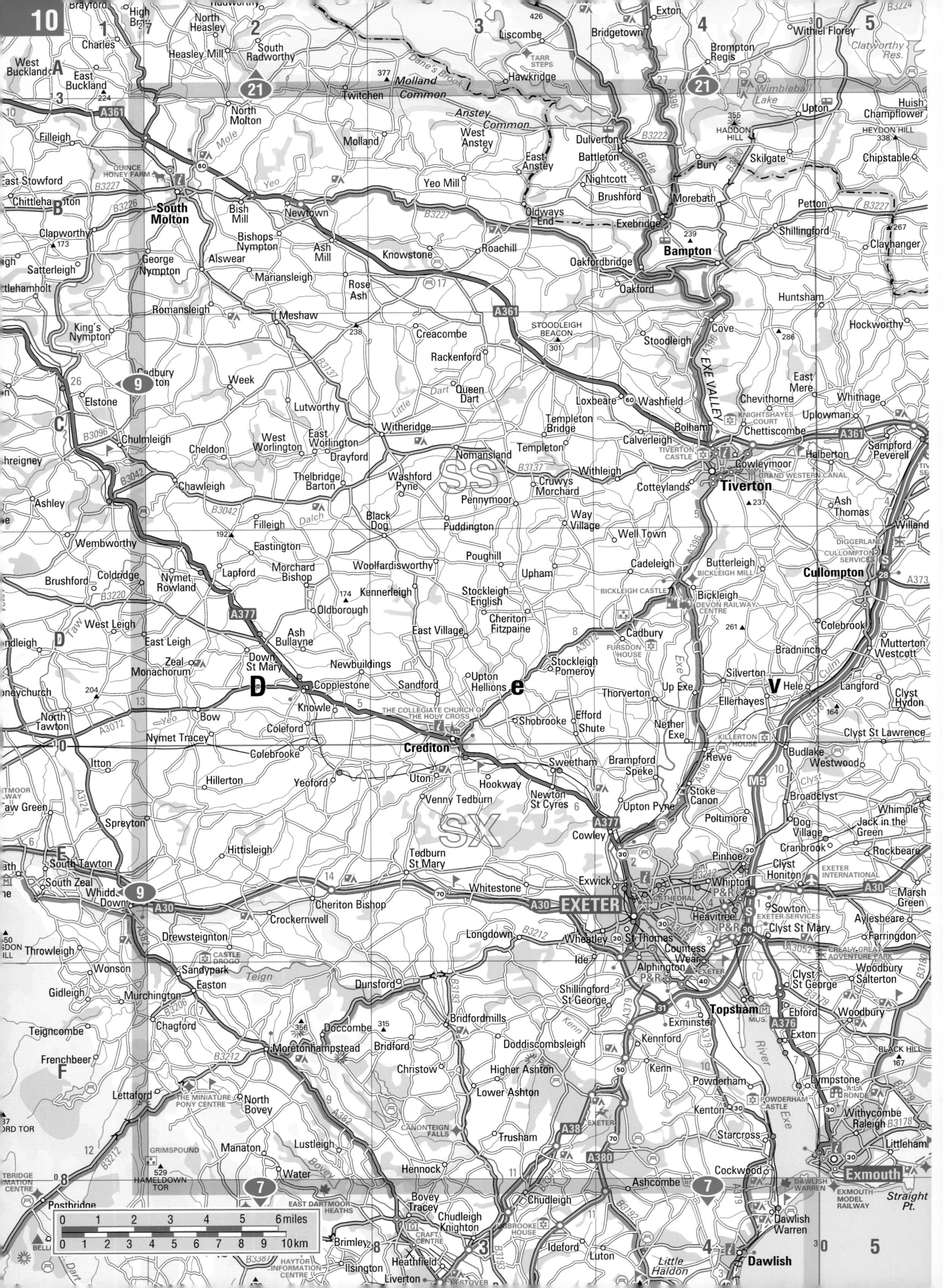
Brayford
High Bray
North Heasley
Heasley Mill
South Radworthy
Charles
West Buckland
East Buckland
Molland Common
Twitchen
Liscombe
Tarr Steps
Hawkridge
Exton
Bridgetown
Brompton Regis
Withiel Florey
Clatworthy Res.
Wimbleball Lake
Upton
Huish Champflower
Haddon Hill
Heydon Hill
North Molton
Anstey Common
West Anstey
East Anstey
Molland
Dulverton
Battleton
Barle
Skilgate
Chipstable
Bury
Quince Honey Farm
East Stowford
Chittlehampton
South Molton
Bish Mill
Newtown
Yeo Mill
Nightcott
Brushford
Oldways End
Exebridge
Morebath
Petton
Shillingford
Clayhanger
Bampton
Clapworthy
Satterleigh
George Nympton
Alswear
Bishops Nympton
Ash Mill
Knowstone
Roachill
Oakfordbridge
Oakford
Mariansleigh
Rose Ash
Huntsham
Romansleigh
Meshaw
King's Nympton
Creacombe
Stoodleigh Beacon
Stoodleigh
Cove
Hockworthy
Rackenford
Exe Valley
East Mere
Cadbury Barton
Elstone
Week
Lutworthy
Queen Dart
Little Dart
Loxbeare
Washfield
Chevithorne
Whitnage
Knightshayes Court
Uplowman
Templeton Bridge
Bolham
Chettiscombe
Chulmleigh
Cheldon
West Worlington
East Worlington
Drayford
Witheridge
Nomansland
Templeton
Calverleigh
Tiverton Castle
Cowleymoor
Halberton
Sampford Peverell
Grand Western Canal
Chawleigh
Thelbridge Barton
Washford Pyne
Cruwys Morchard
Withleigh
Cotteylands
Tiverton
Pennymoor
Ash Thomas
Ashley
Filleigh
Dalch
Black Dog
Puddington
Way Village
Well Town
Willand
Wembworthy
Eastington
Poughill
Cadeleigh
Butterleigh
Diggerland
Cullompton Services
Cullompton
Brushford
Coldridge
Nymet Rowland
Lapford
Morchard Bishop
Woolfardisworthy
Upham
Bickleigh Mill
Bickleigh Castle
Bickleigh
Devon Railway Centre
Kennerleigh
Stockleigh English
Oldborough
Cheriton Fitzpaine
East Village
Cadbury
Fursdon House
Colebrook
West Leigh
East Leigh
Ash Bullayne
Bradninch
Mutterton
Westcott
Zeal Monachorum
Down St Mary
Newbuildings
Stockleigh Pomeroy
Exe
Silverton
Hele
Langford
Copplestone
Sandford
Upton Hellions
Thorverton
Up Exe
Ellerhayes
Clyst Hydon
North Tawton
Bow
Knowle
The Collegiate Church of the Holy Cross
Shobrooke
Efford Shute
Nether Exe
Clyst St Lawrence
Nymet Tracey
Coleford
Crediton
Killerton House
Colebrooke
Itton
Budlake
Westwood
Sweetham
Rewe
Hillerton
Yeoford
Uton
Hookway
Brampford Speke
Broadclyst
Taw Green
Venny Tedburn
Newton St Cyres
Stoke Canon
Spreyton
Upton Pyne
Whimple
Poltimore
Jack in the Green
Dog Village
Cowley
Cranbrook
Rockbeare
Hittisleigh
Tedburn St Mary
Pinhoe
Clyst Honiton
Exeter International
South Tawton
South Zeal
Whiddon Down
Whitestone
Exwick
Whipton
Marsh Green
Cheriton Bishop
Exeter
Cathedral
Sowton
Exeter Services
Heavitree
Crockernwell
Aylesbeare
Drewsteignton
Longdown
Wheatley
St Thomas
Clyst St Mary
Farringdon
Throwleigh
Castle Drogo
Ide
Countess Wear
Crealy Great Adventure Park
Wonson
Sandypark
Alphington
Easton
Teign
Dunsford
Shillingford St George
Clyst St George
Woodbury Salterton
Gidleigh
Murchington
Topsham
Exminster
Bridfordmills
Chagford
Ebford
Woodbury
Teigncombe
Doccombe
Kenn
Kennford
Exton
Moretonhampstead
Bridford
Doddiscombsleigh
Black Hill
Frenchbeer
Christow
Higher Ashton
Powderham
Lympstone
A La Ronde
Lettaford
The Miniature Pony Centre
North Bovey
Lower Ashton
Powderham Castle
Kenton
Withycombe Raleigh
Canonteign Falls
Trusham
Starcross
Grimspound
Manaton
Lustleigh
Littleham
Hameldown Tor
Water
Hennock
Chudleigh
Ashcombe
Cockwood
Dawlish Warren
Exmouth
Exmouth Model Railway
Straight Pt.
Postbridge
East Dartmoor Heaths
Bovey Tracey
Chudleigh Knighton
Ugbrooke House
Brimley
Craft Centre
Ideford
Luton
Little Haldon
Dawlish
Heathfield
Haytor Information Centre
Ilsington
Liverton
Bovey
Dart
SS
SX
0 1 2 3 4 5 6 miles
0 1 2 3 4 5 6 7 8 9 10 km

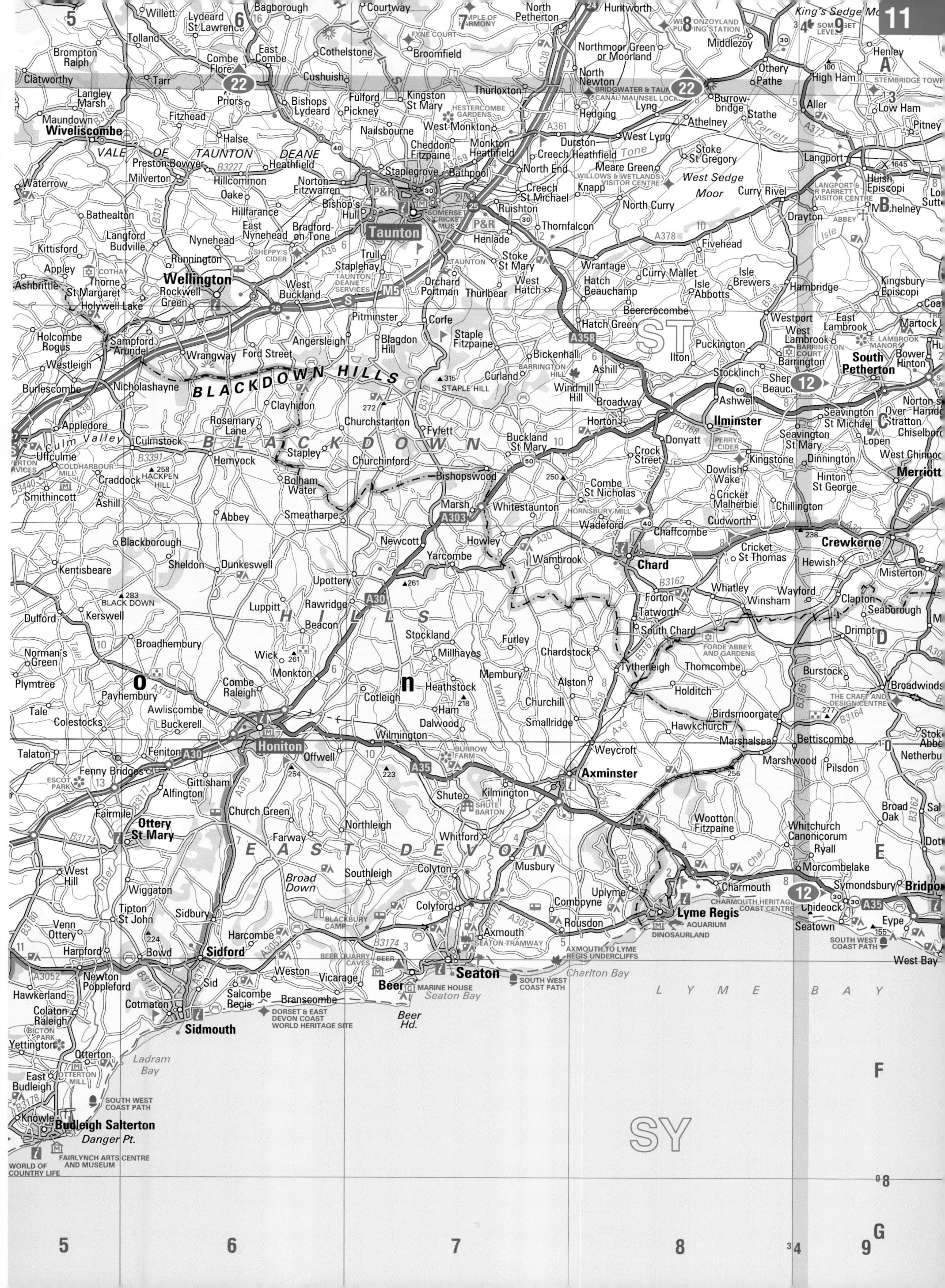

Willett
Lydeard St Lawrence
Bagborough
Courtway
TEMPLE OF HARMONY
North Petherton
Huntworth
WESTONZOYLAND PUMPING STATION
King's Sedge Moor
SOMERSET LEVELS
Tolland
Combe Florey
East Combe
Cothelstone
FYNE COURT
Broomfield
Northmoor Green or Moorland
Middlezoy
Othery
Henley
Brompton Ralph
Clatworthy
Tarr
Cushuish
Thurloxton
North Newton
BRIDGWATER & TAUNTON CANAL
MAUNSEL LOCK
Burrow-bridge
Pathe
High Ham
STEMBRIDGE TOWER
Langley Marsh
Priors
Bishops Lydeard
Fulford
Pickney
Kingston St Mary
HESTERCOMBE GARDENS
Hedging
Lyng
Stathe
Aller
Low Ham
Maundown
Wiveliscombe
Fitzhead
Nailsbourne
West Monkton
Athelney
Pitney
Halse
Cheddon Fitzpaine
Monkton Heathfield
Durston
West Lyng
Stoke St Gregory
VALE OF TAUNTON DEANE
Creech Heathfield
Tone
Parrett
Langport
Preston Bowyer
Heathfield
Staplegrove
Bathpool
North End
Meare Green
WILLOWS & WETLANDS VISITOR CENTRE
West Sedge Moor
Huish Episcopi
Waterrow
Milverton
Hillcommon
Norton Fitzwarren
Creech St Michael
Knapp
Curry Rivel
LANGPORT & R PARRETT VISITOR CENTRE
Oake
Bishop's Hull
Taunton
SOMERSET CRICKET MUS
Ruishton
North Curry
Drayton
ABBEY
Muchelney
Bathealton
Hillfarance
East Nynehead
Bradford-on-Tone
Henlade
Thornfalcon
Isle
Langford Budville
Nynehead
SHEPPY'S CIDER
Trull
Stoke St Mary
A378
Fivehead
Kittisford
Runnington
Staplehay
TAUNTON
Wrantage
Curry Mallet
Isle Brewers
Appley
COTHAY
Thorne St Margaret
Wellington
West Buckland
TAUNTON DEANE SERVICES
Orchard Portman
Thurlbear
West Hatch
Hatch Beauchamp
Isle Abbotts
Hambridge
Kingsbury Episcopi
Ashbrittle
Rockwell Green
Holywell Lake
Pitminster
Corfe
Beercrocombe
Westport
East Lambrook
Martock
Holcombe Rogus
Sampford Arundel
Angersleigh
Blagdon Hill
Staple Fitzpaine
Hatch Green
ST
West Lambrook
E. LAMBROOK MANOR
BARRINGTON COURT
Westleigh
Wrangway
Ford Street
Bickenhall
BARRINGTON HILL
Puckington
Ilton
Barrington
South Petherton
Bower Hinton
Burlescombe
Nicholashayne
BLACKDOWN HILLS
STAPLE HILL
Curland
Ashill
Stocklinch
Shepton Beauchamp
Windmill Hill
Ashwell
Broadway
Norton sub Hamdon
Clayhidon
Seavington St Michael
Over Stratton
Appledore
Rosemary Lane
Churchstanton
Fyfett
Horton
Ilminster
Culm Valley
Culmstock
BLACKDOWN
Buckland St Mary
Donyatt
Seavington St Mary
Lopen
Chiselborough
Uffculme
Hemyock
Stapley
Churchinford
Crock Street
PERRY'S CIDER
Kingstone
Dinnington
West Chinnock
COLDHARBOUR MILL
HACKPEN HILL
Bishopswood
Combe St Nicholas
Dowlish Wake
Hinton St George
Merriott
Craddock
Bolham Water
Cricket Malherbie
Smithincott
Ashill
Marsh
A303
Whitestaunton
HORNSBURY MILL
Chillington
Abbey
Smeatharpe
Wadeford
Cudworth
Chaffcombe
Crewkerne
Blackborough
Newcott
Howley
Wambrook
Cricket St Thomas
Sheldon
Dunkeswell
Yarcombe
Chard
Hewish
Misterton
Kentisbeare
Upottery
B3162
Whatley
Wayford
BLACK DOWN
A30
Forton
Winsham
Clapton
Dulford
Kerswell
Luppitt
Rawridge
HILLS
Tatworth
Seaborough
Beacon
Stockland
Furley
South Chard
Drimpton
Broadhembury
FORDE ABBEY AND GARDENS
Norman's Green
Wick
Millhayes
Chardstock
Burstock
Tale
Monkton
Membury
Tytherleigh
Thorncombe
Plymtree
Combe Raleigh
Heathstock
Yarty
Alston
Broadwindsor
Payhembury
Cotleigh
Holditch
THE CRAFT AND DESIGN CENTRE
Tale
Awliscombe
Ham
Churchill
Birdsmoorgate
Colestocks
Buckerell
Dalwood
Smallridge
Hawkchurch
Wilmington
Bettiscombe
Talaton
Feniton
Honiton
Offwell
Weycroft
Marshalsea
BURROW FARM
Marshwood
Pilsdon
Fenny Bridges
ESCOT PARK
Gittisham
A35
Axminster
Alfington
Shute
Kilmington
SHUTE BARTON
Fairmile
Ottery St Mary
Church Green
Northleigh
Wootton Fitzpaine
Whitchurch Canonicorum
Broad Oak
Farway
Whitford
Ryall
EAST DEVON
West Hill
Broad Down
Southleigh
Colyton
Musbury
Morcombelake
Char
Wiggaton
Uplyme
Charmouth
Symondsbury
Bridport
Tipton St John
Colyford
Combpyne
CHARMOUTH HERITAGE COAST CENTRE
Chideock
Sidbury
BLACKBURY CAMP
Axmouth
Rousdon
Lyme Regis
AQUARIUM
Eype
Venn Ottery
Harcombe
SEATON TRAMWAY
DINOSAURLAND
Seatown
Harpford
Bowd
Sidford
BEER QUARRY CAVES
AXMOUTH TO LYME REGIS UNDERCLIFFS
SOUTH WEST COAST PATH
West Bay
Newton Poppleford
Weston
Vicarage
Beer
Seaton
Charlton Bay
Sid
MARINE HOUSE
Seaton Bay
LYME BAY
Hawkerland
Salcombe Regis
Branscombe
Colaton Raleigh
Cotmaton
DORSET & EAST DEVON COAST WORLD HERITAGE SITE
Beer Hd.
Sidmouth
BICTON PARK
Yettington
Otterton
Ladram Bay
OTTERTON MILL
East Budleigh
SOUTH WEST COAST PATH
Knowle
Budleigh Salterton
Danger Pt.
SY
WORLD OF COUNTRY LIFE
FAIRLYNCH ARTS CENTRE AND MUSEUM
A
B
C
D
E
F
G
5
6
7
8
9

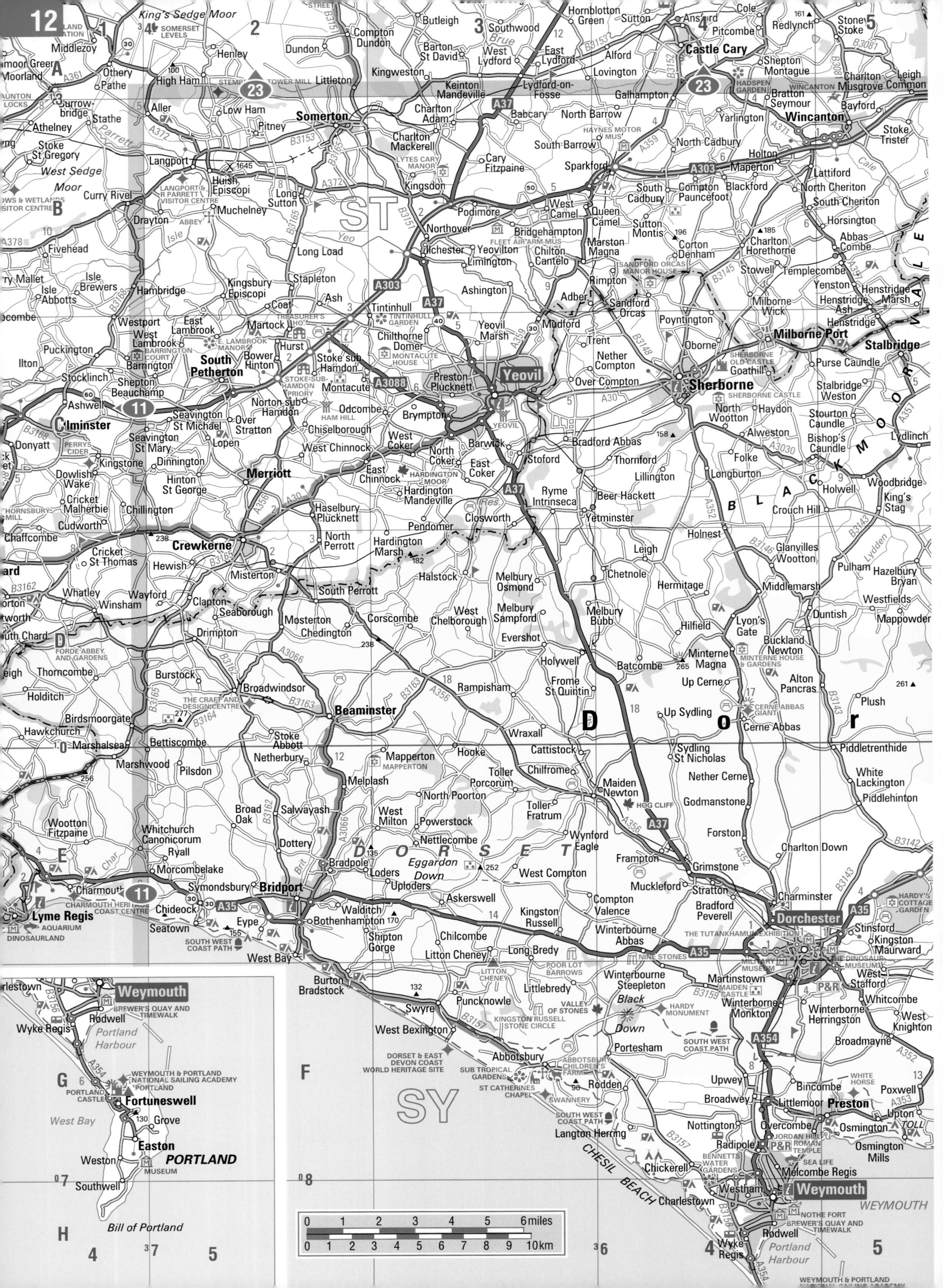
King's Sedge Moor
SOMERSET LEVELS
Middlezoy
Othery
Pathe
Moorland
Burrowbridge
Stathe
Athelney
Stoke St Gregory
West Sedge Moor
Curry Rivel
Henley
High Ham
STEMBRIDGE TOWER MILL
Low Ham
Aller
Pitney
Langport
Huish Episcopi
LANGPORT & R PARRETT VISITOR CENTRE
Muchelney
Drayton
ABBEY
Fivehead
Isle Brewers
Isle Abbotts
Hambridge
Kingsbury Episcopi
Westport
West Lambrook
East Lambrook
E. LAMBROOK MANOR
BARRINGTON COURT
Barrington
Puckington
Ilton
Stocklinch
Shepton Beauchamp
South Petherton
Ashwell
Ilminster
Donyatt
PERRYS CIDER
Kingstone
Dowlish Wake
Cricket Malherbie
Chillington
Cudworth
HORNSBURY MILL
Chaffcombe
Seavington St Michael
Seavington St Mary
Lopen
Over Stratton
Dinnington
Hinton St George
Merriott
Crewkerne
Cricket St Thomas
Hewish
Misterton
Whatley
Winsham
Wayford
Clapton
Seaborough
Drimpton
South Chard
FORDE ABBEY AND GARDENS
Thorncombe
Holditch
Burstock
Broadwindsor
THE CRAFT AND DESIGN CENTRE
Birdsmoorgate
Hawkchurch
Marshalsea
Bettiscombe
Marshwood
Pilsdon
Wootton Fitzpaine
Whitchurch Canonicorum
Ryall
Morcombelake
Charmouth
CHARMOUTH HERITAGE COAST CENTRE
Lyme Regis
AQUARIUM
DINOSAURLAND
Chideock
Symondsbury
Seatown
Eype
SOUTH WEST COAST PATH
Bridport
Bothenhampton
West Bay
Burton Bradstock
Dundon
Compton Dundon
Butleigh
Barton St David
Littleton
Kingweston
Somerton
Charlton Adam
Charlton Mackerell
LYTES CARY MANOR
Kingsdon
Long Sutton
Long Load
Stapleton
Ash
Coat
Martock
TREASURER'S HOUSE
Hurst
Bower Hinton
Stoke sub Hamdon
STOKE-SUB-HAMDON PRIORY
HAM HILL
Montacute
MONTACUTE HOUSE
Norton sub Hamdon
Odcombe
Chiselborough
West Chinnock
East Chinnock
Haselbury Plucknett
North Perrott
South Perrott
Mosterton
Chedington
Corscombe
Southwood
Brue
West Lydford
East Lydford
Keinton Mandeville
Lydford-on-Fosse
Cary Fitzpaine
Podimore
Northover
Ilchester
Yeovilton
FLEET AIR ARM MUS
Limington
Bridgehampton
Tintinhull
TINTINHULL GARDEN
Chilthorne Domer
Ashington
Yeovil Marsh
Preston Plucknett
Yeovil
Brympton
West Coker
North Coker
East Coker
HARDINGTON MOOR
Hardington Mandeville
Pendomer
Closworth
Hardington Marsh
Halstock
Hornblotton Green
Sutton
Alford
Lovington
Galhampton
Babcary
North Barrow
HAYNES MOTOR MUS
South Barrow
Sparkford
West Camel
Queen Camel
Marston Magna
Chilton Cantelo
Rimpton
Adber
Mudford
Trent
Nether Compton
Over Compton
Bradford Abbas
Stoford
Barwick
Thornford
Ryme Intrinseca
Beer Hackett
Yetminster
Ansford
Castle Cary
Pitcombe
Cole
Redlynch
Stoney Stoke
Shepton Montague
HADSPEN GARDEN
Bratton Seymour
Yarlington
Wincanton
Charlton Musgrove
Leigh Common
Bayford
Stoke Trister
North Cadbury
Holton
Maperton
South Cadbury
Compton Pauncefoot
Blackford
Lattiford
North Cheriton
South Cheriton
Sutton Montis
Corton Denham
Charlton Horethorne
Horsington
Abbas Combe
Templecombe
SANDFORD ORCAS MANOR HOUSE
Sandford Orcas
Stowell
Yenston
Henstridge Marsh
Henstridge Ash
Henstridge
Milborne Wick
Poyntington
Oborne
Milborne Port
Stalbridge
SHERBORNE OLD CASTLE
Goathill
Sherborne
SHERBORNE CASTLE
Purse Caundle
Stalbridge Weston
North Wootton
Haydon
Stourton Caundle
Alweston
Bishop's Caundle
Lydlinch
Folke
Longburton
Lillington
Holwell
Woodbridge
King's Stag
Crouch Hill
BLACKMOOR VALE
Holnest
Glanvilles Wootton
Pulham
Hazelbury Bryan
Leigh
Chetnole
Hermitage
Middlemarsh
Westfields
Dunstish
Mappowder
Melbury Osmond
West Chelborough
Melbury Sampford
Melbury Bubb
Evershot
Hilfield
Lyon's Gate
Buckland Newton
Minterne Magna
MINTERNE HOUSE & GARDENS
Batcombe
Holywell
Up Cerne
Alton Pancras
Plush
Frome St Quintin
Rampisham
Up Sydling
CERNE ABBAS GIANT
Cerne Abbas
Beaminster
Stoke Abbott
Netherbury
Mapperton
MAPPERTON
Hooke
Wraxall
Cattistock
Chilfrome
Toller Porcorum
Maiden Newton
Sydling St Nicholas
Nether Cerne
Piddletrenthide
White Lackington
Piddlehinton
Melplash
North Poorton
Broad Oak
Salwayash
West Milton
Powerstock
Toller Fratrum
HOG CLIFF
Godmanstone
Nettlecombe
Dottery
Wynford Eagle
Forston
Charlton Down
DORSET
Eggardon Down
Bradpole
Loders
Uploders
West Compton
Frampton
Grimstone
Muckleford
Stratton
Charminster
Walditch
Askerswell
Kingston Russell
Compton Valence
Bradford Peverell
Dorchester
HARDY'S COTTAGE GARDEN
Stinsford
Kingston Maurward
Shipton Gorge
Chilcombe
Litton Cheney
Long Bredy
Winterbourne Abbas
THE TUTANKHAMUN EXHIBITION
NINE STONES
MILITARY MUSEUM
DINOSAUR MUSEUM
West Stafford
POOR LOT BARROWS
Littlebredy
Winterbourne Steepleton
Martinstown
MAIDEN CASTLE
Winterborne Monkton
Winterborne Herringston
Whitcombe
West Knighton
Puncknowle
Swyre
VALLEY OF STONES
KINGSTON RUSSELL STONE CIRCLE
Black Down
HARDY MONUMENT
West Bexington
Portesham
SOUTH WEST COAST PATH
Broadmayne
Abbotsbury
ABBOTSBURY CHILDREN'S FARM
DORSET & EAST DEVON COAST WORLD HERITAGE SITE
SUB TROPICAL GARDENS
ST CATHERINES CHAPEL
SWANNERY
Rodden
Upwey
Bincombe
WHITE HORSE
Poxwell
Broadwey
Littlemoor
Preston
Upton
SOUTH WEST COAST PATH
Langton Herring
Nottington
Overcombe
Osmington
Osmington Mills
Radipole
JORDAN HILL ROMAN TEMPLE
BENNETTS WATER GARDENS
SEA LIFE
Chickerell
Melcombe Regis
CHESIL BEACH
Westham
Weymouth
Charlestown
NOTHE FORT
BREWER'S QUAY AND TIMEWALK
Rodwell
WEYMOUTH
Wyke Regis
Portland Harbour
WEYMOUTH & PORTLAND
ST
SY
Charlestown
Weymouth
BREWER'S QUAY AND TIMEWALK
Rodwell
Wyke Regis
Portland Harbour
WEYMOUTH & PORTLAND NATIONAL SAILING ACADEMY
PORTLAND CASTLE
Fortuneswell
West Bay
Grove
Easton
PORTLAND
Weston
MUSEUM
Southwell
Bill of Portland
0 1 2 3 4 5 6 miles
0 1 2 3 4 5 6 7 8 9 10 km

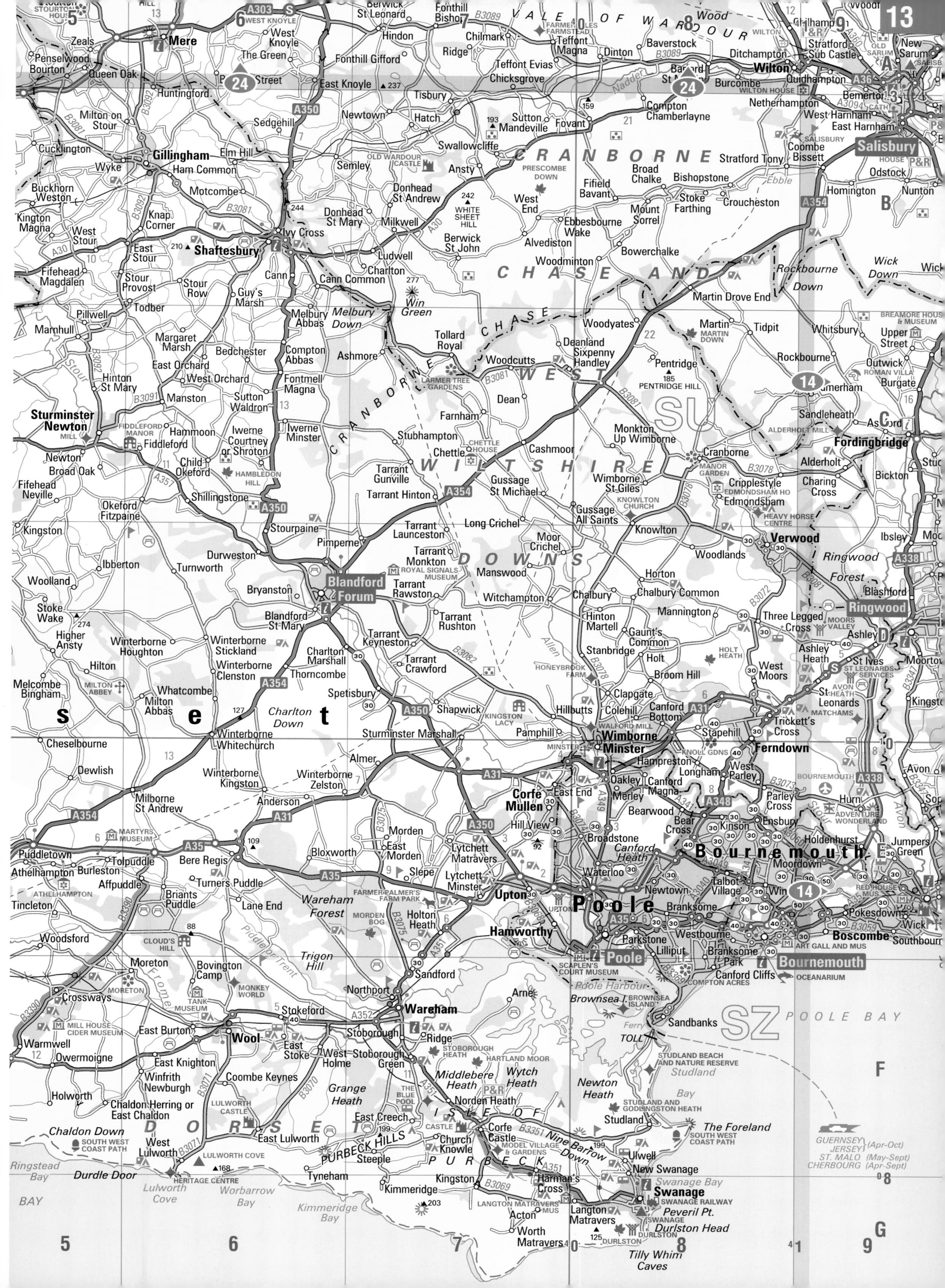

Stourton House
Mere
Zeals
Penselwood
Bourton
Queen Oak
West Knoyle
The Green
Street
Huntingford
Milton on Stour
Sedgehill
Cucklington
Gillingham
Elm Hill
Wyke
Ham Common
Buckhorn Weston
Motcombe
Kington Magna
Knap Corner
West Stour
East Stour
Shaftesbury
Ivy Cross
Fifehead Magdalen
Stour Provost
Stour Row
Guy's Marsh
Todber
Pillwell
Marnhull
Margaret Marsh
East Orchard
West Orchard
Hinton St Mary
Manston
Bedchester
Sturminster Newton
Fiddleford Manor
Fiddleford
Hammoon
Iwerne Courtney or Shroton
Child Okeford
Newton
Broad Oak
Fifehead Neville
Okeford Fitzpaine
Shillingstone
Hambledon Hill
Kingston
Ibberton
Turnworth
Durweston
Woolland
Stoke Wake
Higher Ansty
Winterborne Houghton
Winterborne Stickland
Hilton
Melcombe Bingham
Milton Abbey
Whatcombe
Milton Abbas
Winterborne Clenston
Cheselbourne
Dewlish
Winterborne Whitechurch
Winterborne Kingston
Milborne St Andrew
Martyrs Museum
Puddletown
Tolpuddle
Athelhampton
Burleston
Affpuddle
Briants Puddle
Tincleton
Turners Puddle
Bere Regis
Lane End
Woodsford
Cloud's Hill
Moreton
Crossways
Bovington Camp
Tank Museum
Monkey World
Warmwell
Mill House Cider Museum
Owermoigne
East Burton
Wool
East Knighton
Winfrith Newburgh
Holworth
Chaldon Herring or East Chaldon
Chaldon Down
South West Coast Path
West Lulworth
Lulworth Castle
Lulworth Cove
Heritage Centre
Durdle Door
Ringstead Bay
Worbarrow Bay
Kimmeridge Bay
East Lulworth
Coombe Keynes
Tyneham
Steeple
Kimmeridge
Purbeck Hills
Stokeford
East Stoke
West Holme
Grange Heath
East Creech
Stoborough
Stoborough Green
Stoborough Heath
Wareham
Northport
Sandford
Ridge
Arne
Hartland Moor
Middlebere Heath
Wytch Heath
Norden Heath
The Blue Pool
Isle of Purbeck
Corfe Castle
Model Village & Gardens
Church Knowle
Kingston
Nine Barrow Down
Harman's Cross
Langton Matravers
Acton
Worth Matravers
Durlston
Durlston Head
Peveril Pt.
Tilly Whim Caves
Swanage
Swanage Railway
Swanage Bay
New Swanage
Ulwell
Studland
Studland Bay
Studland and Godlingston Heath
Studland Beach and Nature Reserve
The Foreland
Newton Heath
Sandbanks
Toll
Ferry
Brownsea I.
Brownsea Island
Poole Harbour
Poole Bay
SZ
Guernsey (Apr-Oct)
Jersey (May-Sept)
St. Malo (Apr-Sept)
Cherbourg
Hindon
Berwick St Leonard
Fonthill Bishop
Fonthill Gifford
Vale of Wardour
Chilmark
Ridge
Teffont Magna
Teffont Evias
Chicksgrove
Dinton
Baverstock
Barford St Martin
Burcombe
Wilton
Wilton House
Ditchampton
Quidhampton
Bemerton
Netherhampton
West Harnham
East Harnham
Salisbury
Old Sarum
Stratford sub Castle
New Sarum
Coombe Bissett
Odstock
Homington
Nunton
Stratford Tony
Bishopstone
Croucheston
Stoke Farthing
Broad Chalke
Fifield Bavant
Ebbesbourne Wake
Mount Sorrel
Alvediston
Bowerchalke
Woodminton
Compton Chamberlayne
Fovant
Sutton Mandeville
Tisbury
East Knoyle
Newtown
Hatch
Swallowcliffe
Old Wardour Castle
Semley
Ansty
Donhead St Andrew
Donhead St Mary
Milkwell
White Sheet Hill
Berwick St John
Ludwell
Charlton
Cann
Cann Common
Win Green
Melbury Abbas
Melbury Down
Compton Abbas
Ashmore
Tollard Royal
Fontmell Magna
Sutton Waldron
Iwerne Minster
Larmer Tree Gardens
Woodcutts
Dean
Farnham
Stubhampton
Chettle
Chettle House
Tarrant Gunville
Tarrant Hinton
Stourpaine
Pimperne
Tarrant Launceston
Tarrant Monkton
Royal Signals Museum
Blandford Forum
Bryanston
Blandford St Mary
Tarrant Rawston
Tarrant Rushton
Tarrant Keyneston
Charlton Marshall
Tarrant Crawford
Thorncombe
Spetisbury
Charlton Down
Shapwick
Kingston Lacy
Sturminster Marshall
Almer
Winterborne Zelston
Anderson
Morden
East Morden
Bloxworth
Slepe
Lytchett Matravers
Lytchett Minster
Farmer Palmer's Farm Park
Morden Bog
Holton Heath
Wareham Forest
Trigon Hill
Cranborne Chase
West Wiltshire Downs
Martin Drove End
Martin
Martin Down
Tidpit
Woodyates
Deanland
Sixpenny Handley
Pentridge
Pentridge Hill
Cashmoor
Gussage St Michael
Long Crichel
Moor Crichel
Manswood
Witchampton
Gussage All Saints
Wimborne St Giles
Monkton Up Wimborne
Cranborne
Manor Garden
Knowlton
Knowlton Church
Chalbury
Chalbury Common
Hinton Martell
Gaunt's Common
Holt
Holt Heath
Stanbridge
Honeybrook Farm
Broom Hill
Clapgate
Colehill
Canford Bottom
Hillbutts
Pamphill
Walford Mill
Wimborne Minster
Minster
Hampreston
Knoll Gdns
Stapehill
Ferndown
Trickett's Cross
Longham
West Parley
Oakley
Canford Magna
Merley
Corfe Mullen
East End
Hill View
Broadstone
Canford Heath
Bearwood
Bear Cross
Kinson
Ensbury
Parley Cross
Hurn
Adventure Wonderland
Holdenhurst
Bournemouth
Moordown
Jumpers Green
Waterloo
Newtown
Talbot Village
Upton
Poole
Hamworthy
Branksome
Parkstone
Lilliput
Westbourne
Branksome Park
Canford Cliffs
Compton Acres
Scaplen's Court Museum
Oceanarium
Art Gall and Mus
Boscombe
Southbourne
Pokesdown
Wick
Red House Mus
Rockbourne
Rockbourne Down
Whitsbury
Breamore House & Museum
Upper Street
Outwick
Roman Villa
Burgate
Damerham
Sandleheath
Alderholt Mill
Ashford
Fordingbridge
Alderholt
Cripplestyle
Edmondsham Ho
Edmondsham
Heavy Horse Centre
Charing Cross
Bickton
Verwood
Woodlands
Ibsley
Ringwood Forest
Ringwood
Blashford
Three Legged Cross
Moors Valley
Mannington
Ashley
Ashley Heath
St Ives
St Leonards Services
Moortown
Avon Heath
St Leonards
West Moors
Matchams
Kingston
Avon
Sopley
Wick Down
Wick
Dorset

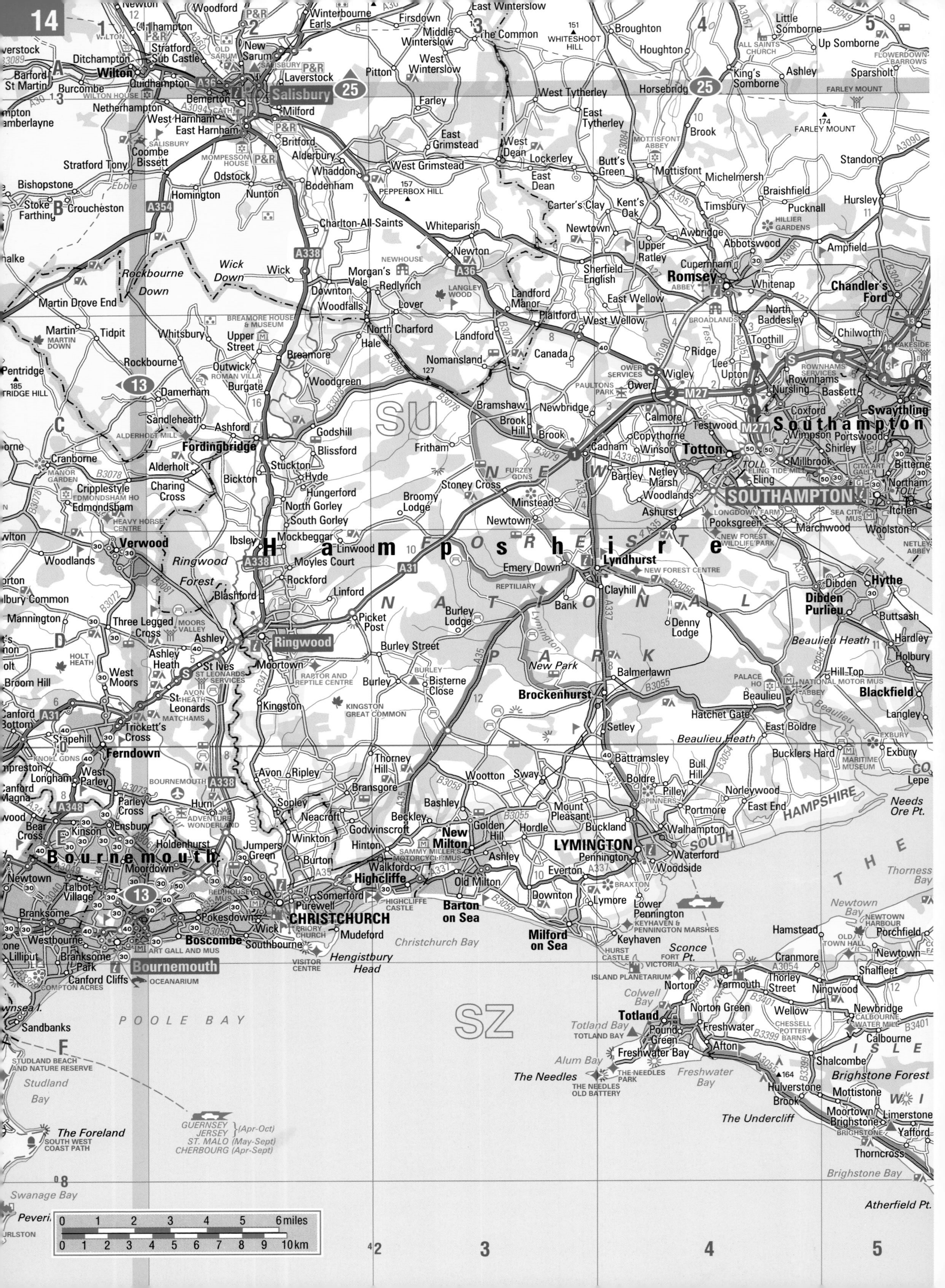

Salisbury
Wilton
Romsey
Southampton
SOUTHAMPTON
Totton
Lyndhurst
Ringwood
Fordingbridge
Verwood
Ferndown
Bournemouth
CHRISTCHURCH
New Milton
LYMINGTON
Brockenhurst
Highcliffe
Barton on Sea
Milford on Sea
Hythe
Dibden Purlieu
Blackfield
Beaulieu
Chandler's Ford
Totland
Yarmouth
Hampshire
NEW FOREST NATIONAL PARK
SU
SZ
POOLE BAY
Christchurch Bay
Hengistbury Head
The Needles
Alum Bay
Freshwater Bay
The Undercliff
Brightstone Bay
Atherfield Pt.
Studland Bay
Swanage Bay
The Foreland
GUERNSEY JERSEY (Apr-Oct)
ST. MALO (May-Sept)
CHERBOURG (Apr-Sept)
0 1 2 3 4 5 6 miles
0 1 2 3 4 5 6 7 8 9 10 km

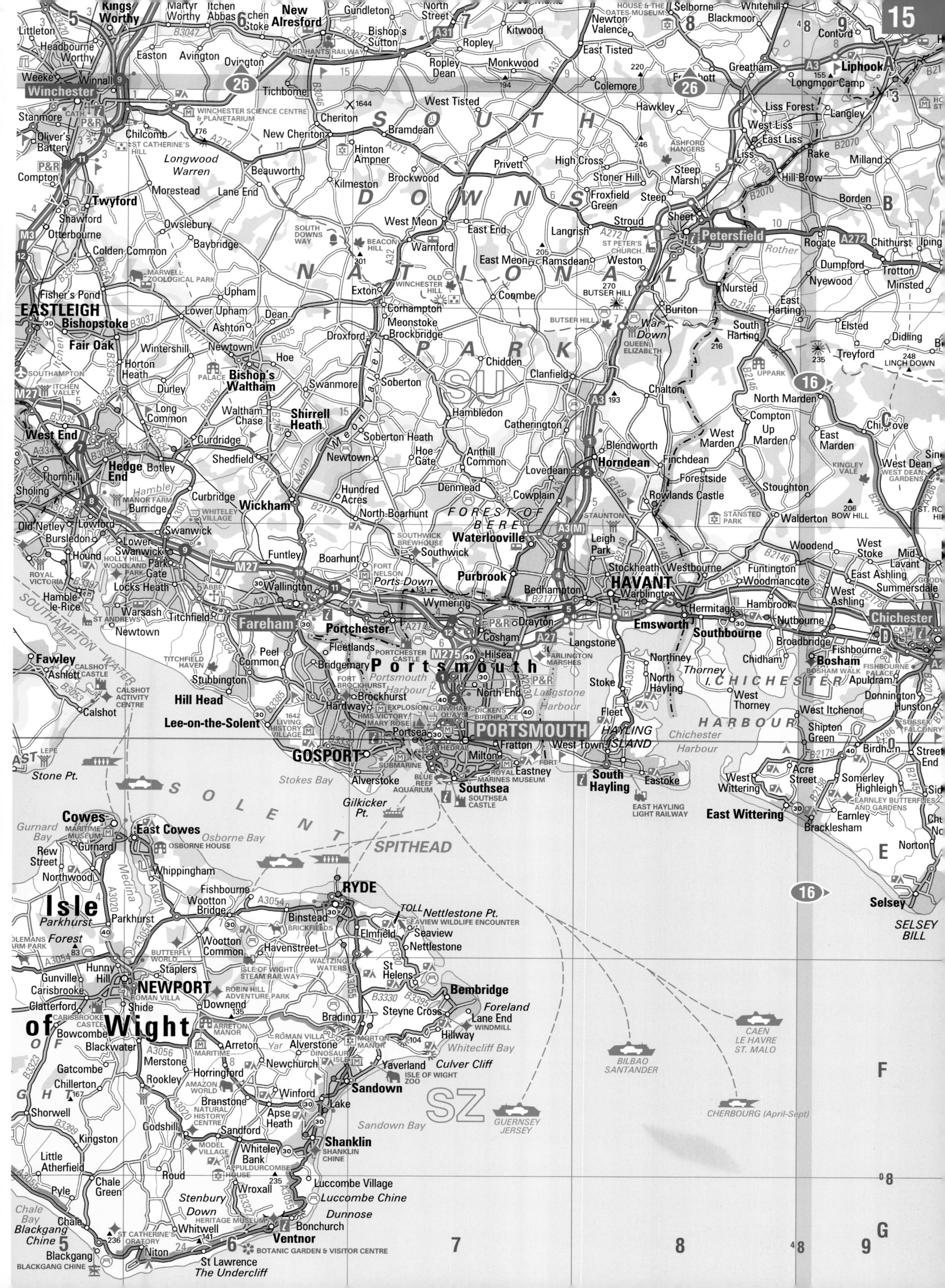
Kings Worthy
Martyr Worthy
Itchen Abbas
Itchen Stoke
New Alresford
Gundleton
North Street
Newton Valence
Selborne
Blackmoor
Whitehill
Conford
Littleton
Headbourne Worthy
Bishop's Sutton
Ropley
Kitwood
East Tisted
Greatham
Liphook
Weeke
Winnall
Easton
Avington
Ovington
MID-HANTS RAILWAY
Ropley Dean
Monkwood
Longmoor Camp
Winchester
Tichborne
Colemore
WINCHESTER SCIENCE CENTRE & PLANETARIUM
West Tisted
Hawkley
Liss Forest
Langley
Stanmore
Cheriton
Bramdean
West Liss
East Liss
Oliver's Battery
Chilcomb
ST CATHERINE'S HILL
New Cheriton
Hinton Ampner
ASHFORD HANGERS
Rake
Milland
Compton
Longwood Warren
Beauworth
Privett
High Cross
Steep Marsh
Liss
Stoner Hill
Hill Brow
Morestead
Lane End
Kilmeston
Brockwood
Froxfield Green
Steep
Borden
Twyford
Shawford
Owslebury
West Meon
Stroud
Sheet
Otterbourne
SOUTH DOWNS WAY
BEACON HILL
East End
Langrish
Petersfield
Rogate
Chithurst
Iping
Baybridge
Warnford
ST PETER'S CHURCH
Rother
Colden Common
East Meon
Ramsdean
Weston
Dumpford
Trotton
MARWELL ZOOLOGICAL PARK
OLD WINCHESTER HILL
Nyewood
Minsted
Upham
Exton
Coombe
BUTSER HILL
Nursted
Fisher's Pond
Corhampton
Buriton
East Harting
EASTLEIGH
Lower Upham
Dean
Meonstoke
War Down
South Harting
Elsted
Bishopstoke
Ashton
Brockbridge
QUEEN ELIZABETH
Didling
Fair Oak
Wintershill
Newtown
Droxford
Treyford
Hoe
Chidden
LINCH DOWN
SOUTHAMPTON
Horton Heath
Bishop's Waltham
Swanmore
Clanfield
UPPARK
ITCHEN VALLEY
Durley
Soberton
Chalton
North Marden
Long Common
Waltham Chase
Shirrell Heath
Hambledon
Catherington
Compton
Up Marden
West Marden
Chilgrove
West End
Curdridge
Soberton Heath
Blendworth
East Marden
Shedfield
Hoe Gate
Anthill Common
Newtown
Horndean
Finchdean
KINGLEY VALE
West Dean
WEST DEAN GARDENS
Hedge End
Botley
Lovedean
Forestside
Thornhill
Hamble
Hundred Acres
Denmead
Stoughton
Sholing
MANOR FARM
Burridge
Curbridge
Wickham
Cowplain
Rowlands Castle
BOW HILL
WHITELEY VILLAGE
FOREST OF BERE
STAUNTON
STANSTED PARK
Walderton
Old Netley
Lowford
North Boarhunt
Bursledon
Swanwick
Waterlooville
Leigh Park
Woodend
West Stoke
Mid Lavant
SOUTHWICK BREWHOUSE
Southwick
Hound
Lower Swanwick
HOLLY HILL WOODLAND PARK
Funtley
Boarhunt
Stockheath
Westbourne
Funtington
East Ashling
ROYAL VICTORIA
Park Gate
FORT NELSON
Purbrook
Woodmancote
Summersdale
Locks Heath
ABBEY
Wallington
Ports Down
Bedhampton
HAVANT
West Ashling
Hamble-le-Rice
Warblington
Hambrook
Warsash
Wymering
Hermitage
SOUTHAMPTON WATER
ST ANDREWS
Titchfield
Fareham
Portchester
Drayton
Emsworth
Southbourne
Nutbourne
Chichester
Newtown
Cosham
Langstone
Broadbridge
Fishbourne
Fleetlands
PORTCHESTER CASTLE
Hilsea
FARLINGTON MARSHES
Northney
Chidham
Bosham
Fawley
CALSHOT CASTLE
TITCHFIELD HAVEN
Peel Common
Bridgemary
Portsmouth
Thorney I.
BOSHAM WALK
FISHBOURNE ROMAN PALACE
Ashlett
Stubbington
Portsmouth Harbour
FORT BROCKHURST
North End
Langstone Harbour
Stoke
North Hayling
CHICHESTER
Apuldram
CALSHOT ACTIVITY CENTRE
Hill Head
Brockhurst
Hardway
West Thorney
Donnington
Calshot
HMS VICTORY
MARY ROSE
EXPLOSION
GUNWHARF QUAYS
DICKENS BIRTHPLACE
Hunston
Lee-on-the-Solent
LIVING HISTORY VILLAGE
Fleet
HARBOUR
West Itchenor
Portsea
PORTSMOUTH
HAYLING ISLAND
Chichester Harbour
Shipton Green
SUSSEX FALCONRY
LEPE
GOSPORT
CATHEDRAL
Fratton
West Town
Birdham
Street End
Stone Pt.
SUBMARINE
Milton
FORT
Acre Street
Eastney
South Hayling
Eastoke
West Wittering
Somerley
Highleigh
Sidlesham
Stokes Bay
Alverstoke
BLUE REEF AQUARIUM
ROYAL MARINES MUSEUM
Southsea
SOUTHSEA CASTLE
EARNLEY BUTTERFLIES AND GARDENS
SOLENT
Gilkicker Pt.
EAST HAYLING LIGHT RAILWAY
East Wittering
Earnley
Cowes
Gurnard Bay
MARITIME MUSEUM
East Cowes
Bracklesham
Gurnard
Osborne Bay
OSBORNE HOUSE
SPITHEAD
Norton
Rew Street
Northwood
Whippingham
Medina
Fishbourne
RYDE
Selsey
Isle
Wootton Bridge
TOLL
Nettlestone Pt.
Parkhurst Forest
Parkhurst
Binstead
SEAVIEW WILDLIFE ENCOUNTER
SELSEY BILL
BRICKFIELDS
Elmfield
Seaview
Wootton Common
Havenstreet
Nettlestone
BUTTERFLY WORLD
Gunville
Hunny Hill
Staplers
ISLE OF WIGHT STEAM RAILWAY
WALTZING WATERS
St Helens
Carisbrooke
NEWPORT
ROBIN HILL ADVENTURE PARK
Bembridge
ROMAN VILLA
Foreland
Clatterford
Shide
Downend
CARISBROOKE CASTLE
Steyne Cross
Lane End
WINDMILL
of Wight
Bowcombe
ARRETON MANOR
Brading
ROMAN VILLA
MORTON MANOR
CAEN
LE HAVRE
ST. MALO
Hillway
Blackwater
Arreton
Yar
Alverstone
DINOSAUR ISLE
Whitecliff Bay
MARITIME
Merstone
BILBAO
SANTANDER
Gatcombe
Horringford
Newchurch
Yaverland
Culver Cliff
ISLE OF WIGHT ZOO
Chillerton
Rookley
AMAZON WORLD
Sandown
Winford
Branstone
NATURAL HISTORY CENTRE
Lake
SZ
Shorwell
Apse Heath
GUERNSEY
JERSEY
CHERBOURG (April-Sept)
Godshill
Sandown Bay
Kingston
Sandford
Shanklin
SHANKLIN CHINE
MODEL VILLAGE
Whiteley Bank
Little Atherfield
APPULDURCOMBE HOUSE
Roud
Chale Green
Luccombe Village
Wroxall
Luccombe Chine
Pyle
Stenbury Down
Dunnose
Chale Bay
Chale
HERITAGE MUSEUM
Bonchurch
Blackgang Chine
ST CATHERINE'S ORATORY
Whitwell
Ventnor
Blackgang
Niton
BOTANIC GARDEN & VISITOR CENTRE
St Lawrence
The Undercliff
BLACKGANG CHINE
SOUTH DOWNS NATIONAL PARK

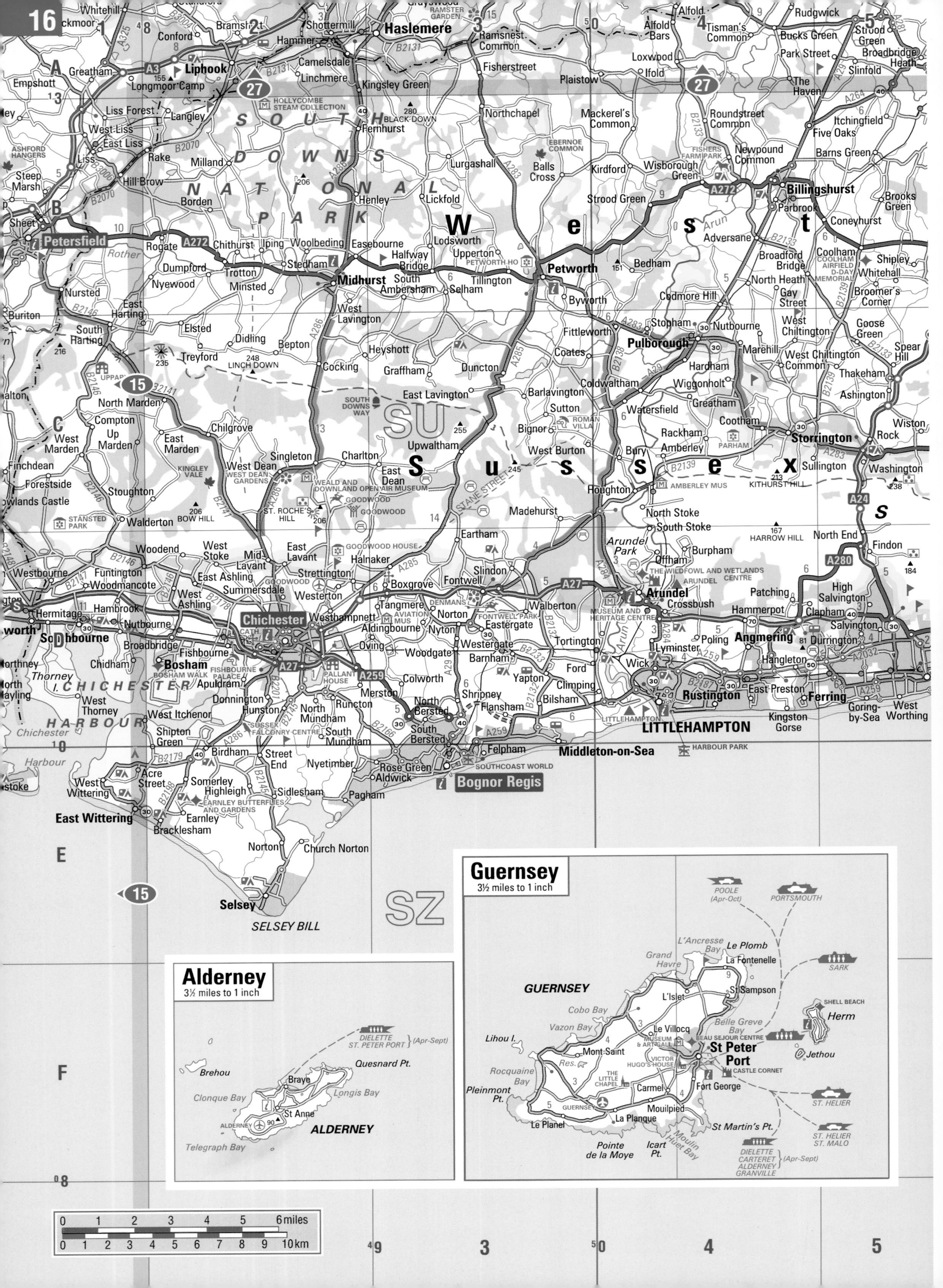

Haslemere
Liphook
Longmoor Camp
Greatham
Empshott
Conford
Bramshott
Shottermill
Hammer
Camelsdale
Linchmere
Kingsley Green
Ramsnest Common
Fisherstreet
Plaistow
Loxwood
Ifold
Alfold
Alfold Bars
Tisman's Common
Rudgwick
Bucks Green
Park Street
Strood Green
Broadbridge Heath
Slinfold
The Haven
HOLLYCOMBE STEAM COLLECTION
Liss Forest
Langley
West Liss
East Liss
Liss
Rake
ASHFORD HANGERS
Steep Marsh
Hill Brow
Milland
Borden
SOUTH DOWNS NATIONAL PARK
BLACK DOWN
Fernhurst
Northchapel
Lurgashall
Henley
Lickfold
Balls Cross
EBERNOE COMMON
Mackerel's Common
Kirdford
Wisborough Green
FISHERS FARM PARK
Roundstreet Common
Newpound Common
Itchingfield
Five Oaks
Barns Green
Billingshurst
Strood Green
Parbrook
Brooks Green
Coneyhurst
Sheet
Petersfield
Rogate
Chithurst
Iping
Woolbeding
Easebourne
Halfway Bridge
Lodsworth
Upperton
PETWORTH HO
Petworth
Bedham
Adversane
Broadford Bridge
Coolham
COOLHAM AIRFIELD D-DAY MEMORIAL
Shipley
Whitehall
Rother
Dumpford
Trotton
Nyewood
Minsted
Stedham
Midhurst
South Ambersham
Selham
Tillington
Byworth
Codmore Hill
North Heath
Gay Street
Broomer's Corner
Nursted
Buriton
East Harting
South Harting
Elsted
Didling
Bepton
West Lavington
Heyshott
Graffham
Cocking
Duncton
Fittleworth
Coates
Stopham
Pulborough
Nutbourne
Marehill
West Chiltington
West Chiltington Common
Goose Green
Spear Hill
Thakeham
Ashington
Treyford
LINCH DOWN
Hardham
Wiggonholt
Greatham
Coldwaltham
Barlavington
East Lavington
SOUTH DOWNS WAY
North Marden
Compton
Up Marden
West Marden
Chilgrove
East Marden
Sutton
ROMAN VILLA
Bignor
Waterfield
Rackham
Amberley
PARHAM
Cootham
Storrington
Wiston
Rock
SU
Upwaltham
West Burton
Bury
Washington
Sullington
KITHURST HILL
AMBERLEY MUS
Finchdean
Forestside
Rowlands Castle
STANSTED PARK
KINGLEY VALE
West Dean
WEST DEAN GARDENS
Singleton
Charlton
East Dean
WEALD AND DOWNLAND OPEN AIR MUSEUM
GOODWOOD
ST. ROCHE'S HILL
STANE STREET
Houghton
Stoughton
Walderton
BOW HILL
Madehurst
North Stoke
South Stoke
HARROW HILL
North End
Findon
Eartham
Arundel Park
Offham
Burpham
Woodend
West Stoke
Mid Lavant
East Lavant
GOODWOOD HOUSE
Halnaker
Westbourne
Funtington
Woodmancote
East Ashling
West Ashling
Summersdale
Strettington
Slindon
Fontwell
Boxgrove
Westerton
Tangmere
DENMANS
THE WILDFOWL AND WETLANDS CENTRE
ARUNDEL
Arundel
Crossbush
Patching
High Salvington
Hermitage
Hambrook
Nutbourne
Chichester
Westhampnett
AVIATION MUS
Aldingbourne
Norton
Nyton
FONTWELL PARK
Eastergate
Walberton
MUSEUM AND HERITAGE CENTRE
Tortington
Hammerpot
Clapham
Salvington
Southbourne
Broadbridge
Fishbourne
Bosham
FISHBOURNE PALACE
BOSHAM WALK
Oving
Woodgate
Westergate
Barnham
Lyminster
Poling
Angmering
Durrington
Thorney
Chidham
CHICHESTER HARBOUR
West Thorney
Apuldram
PALLANT HOUSE
Colworth
Yapton
Ford
Wick
Climping
Bilsham
Hangleton
Rustington
East Preston
Ferring
Goring-by-Sea
West Worthing
Kingston Gorse
Donnington
Hunston
North Mundham
Runcton
Merston
North Bersted
Shripney
Flansham
West Itchenor
Shipton Green
SUSSEX FALCONRY CENTRE
South Mundham
South Bersted
LITTLEHAMPTON
Felpham
Middleton-on-Sea
HARBOUR PARK
Birdham
Street End
Nyetimber
Rose Green
Aldwick
SOUTHCOAST WORLD
Bognor Regis
Acre Street
West Wittering
Somerley
Highleigh
Sidlesham
Pagham
East Wittering
EARNLEY BUTTERFLIES AND GARDENS
Earnley
Bracklesham
Norton
Church Norton
Selsey
SELSEY BILL
SZ
Guernsey
3½ miles to 1 inch
POOLE (Apr-Oct)
PORTSMOUTH
L'Ancresse Bay
Le Plomb
Grand Havre
La Fontenelle
SARK
GUERNSEY
St Sampson
L'Islet
SHELL BEACH
Herm
Cobo Bay
Belle Greve Bay
Vazon Bay
Le Villocq
BEAU SEJOUR CENTRE
Lihou I.
Mont Saint
St Peter Port
Jethou
CASTLE CORNET
Rocquaine Bay
THE LITTLE CHAPEL
Carmel
Fort George
Pleinmont Pt.
ST. HELIER
La Planque
Le Planel
Mouilpied
St Martin's Pt.
ST. HELIER ST. MALO
Pointe de la Moye
Icart Pt.
Moulin Huet Bay
DIELETTE CARTERET ALDERNEY GRANVILLE
(Apr-Sept)
Alderney
3½ miles to 1 inch
DIELETTE ST. PETER PORT
(Apr-Sept)
Quesnard Pt.
Brehou
Braye
Clonque Bay
Longis Bay
St Anne
ALDERNEY
Telegraph Bay
0 1 2 3 4 5 6 miles
0 1 2 3 4 5 6 7 8 9 10 km

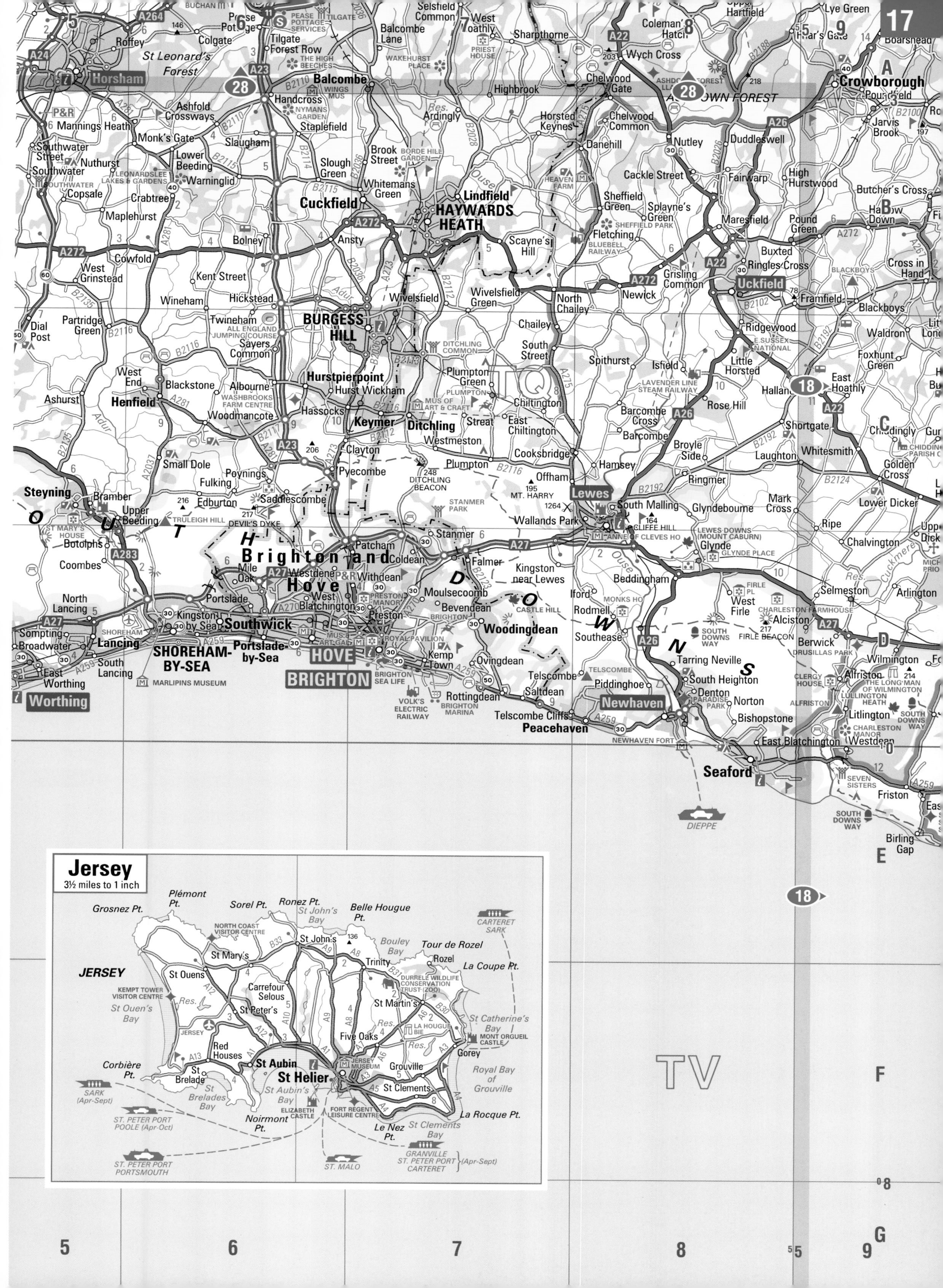

Horsham
Roffey
Colgate
St Leonard's Forest
Pease Pottage Services
Tilgate
Tilgate Forest Row
Balcombe Lane
Selsfield Common
West Hoathly
Sharpthorne
Priest House
Wakehurst Place
The High Beeches
Balcombe
Wings Mus
Coleman's Hatch
Wych Cross
Chelwood Gate
Ashdown Forest
Crowborough
Poundfield
Jarvis Brook
Highbrook
Ardingly
Handcross
Nymans Garden
Ashfold Crossways
Mannings Heath
Monk's Gate
Slaugham
Staplefield
Horsted Keynes
Chelwood Common
Danehill
Nutley
Duddleswell
Southwater Street
Southwater
Nuthurst
Lower Beeding
Leonardslee Lakes & Gardens
Warninglid
Copsale
Crabtree
Brook Street
Borde Hill Garden
Slough Green
Whitemans Green
Cuckfield
Heaven Farm
Lindfield
Haywards Heath
Cackle Street
Fairwarp
High Hurstwood
Butcher's Cross
Sheffield Green
Splayne's Green
Sheffield Park
Fletching
Bluebell Railway
Maresfield
Pound Green
Maplehurst
Bolney
Ansty
Scayne's Hill
Cowfold
West Grinstead
Kent Street
Buxted
Ringles Cross
Blackboys
Cross in Hand
Grisling Common
Newick
Uckfield
Framfield
Blackboys
Wineham
Hickstead
Twineham
All England Jumping Course
Burgess Hill
Wivelsfield
Wivelsfield Green
North Chailey
Dial Post
Partridge Green
Sayers Common
Ditchling Common
Chailey
South Street
Spithurst
Isfield
Ridgewood
E. Sussex National
Little Horsted
Waldron
Foxhunt Green
West End
Henfield
Blackstone
Albourne
Washbrooks Farm Centre
Hurstpierpoint
Hurst Wickham
Plumpton Green
Plumpton
Mus of Art & Craft
Chiltington
Lavender Line Steam Railway
Rose Hill
Halland
East Hoathly
Ashurst
Woodmancote
Hassocks
Keymer
Ditchling
Streat
East Chiltington
Barcombe Cross
Barcombe
Shortgate
Chiddingly
Westmeston
Broyle Side
Laughton
Whitesmith
Golden Cross
Small Dole
Clayton
Pyecombe
Cooksbridge
Hamsey
Fulking
Poynings
Ditchling Beacon
Offham
Mt. Harry
Ringmer
Mark Cross
Lower Dicker
Steyning
Bramber
Upper Beeding
Edburton
Truleigh Hill
Devil's Dyke
Saddlescombe
Stanmer Park
Lewes
South Malling
Glyndebourne
Wallands Park
Cliffe Hill
Anne of Cleves Ho
Ripe
St Mary's House
Botolphs
Stanmer
Lewes Downs (Mount Caburn)
Glynde
Glynde Place
Chalvington
Coombes
Brighton and Hove
Patcham
Coldean
Falmer
Kingston near Lewes
Mile Oak
Westdene
Withdean
Beddingham
Selmeston
Arlington
Firle Pl
West Firle
North Lancing
Portslade
West Blatchington
Preston Manor
Moulsecoomb
Bevendean
Iford
Rodmell
Monks Ho
Charleston Farmhouse
Alciston
Sompting
Broadwater
Shoreham
Kingston by Sea
Southwick
Preston
Castle Hill
Woodingdean
Southease
South Downs Way
Firle Beacon
Berwick
Drusillas Park
Wilmington
Lancing
Shoreham-by-Sea
Portslade-by-Sea
Hove
Royal Pavilion
Kemp Town
Ovingdean
Tarring Neville
East Worthing
South Lancing
Marlipins Museum
Brighton
Brighton Sea Life
Telscombe
Piddinghoe
South Heighton
Clergy House
Alfriston
The Long Man of Wilmington
Lullington Heath
Worthing
Volk's Electric Railway
Rottingdean
Brighton Marina
Saltdean
Newhaven
Denton
Paradise Park
Norton
Telscombe Cliffs
Peacehaven
Bishopstone
Litlington
Charleston Manor
Newhaven Fort
East Blatchington
Westdean
Seaford
Seven Sisters
Friston
Dieppe
South Downs Way
Birling Gap
South Downs
TQ
TV
Jersey
3½ miles to 1 inch
Plémont Pt.
Grosnez Pt.
Sorel Pt.
Ronez Pt.
St John's Bay
Belle Hougue Pt.
North Coast Visitor Centre
St John's
Carteret Sark
Bouley Bay
Tour de Rozel
Rozel
St Mary's
Trinity
La Coupe Pt.
Jersey
St Ouens
Kempt Tower Visitor Centre
Carrefour Selous
Durrell Wildlife Conservation Trust (Zoo)
St Martin's
St Ouen's Bay
St Peter's
St Catherine's Bay
La Hougue Bie
Five Oaks
Mont Orgueil Castle
Red Houses
Gorey
Corbière Pt.
St Aubin
Jersey Museum
Grouville
Royal Bay of Grouville
St Brelade
St Helier
St Clements
Sark (Apr-Sept)
St Brelades Bay
St Aubin's Bay
Elizabeth Castle
Fort Regent Leisure Centre
La Rocque Pt.
St. Peter Port Poole (Apr-Oct)
Noirmont Pt.
Le Nez Pt.
St Clements Bay
Granville St. Peter Port Carteret (Apr-Sept)
St. Peter Port Portsmouth
St. Malo

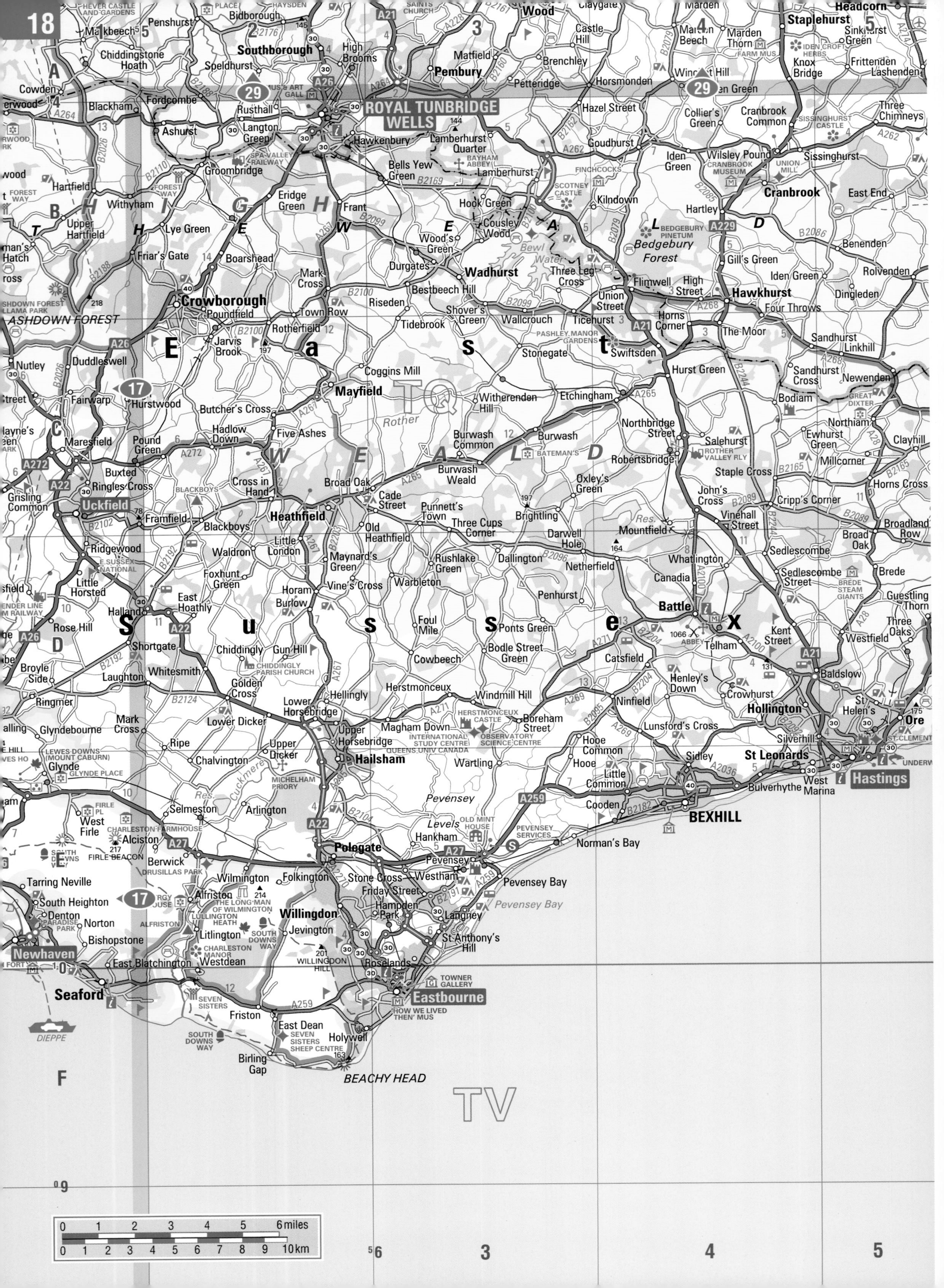

ROYAL TUNBRIDGE WELLS
Southborough
Crowborough
Uckfield
Heathfield
Mayfield
Wadhurst
Hawkhurst
Cranbrook
Battle
Hailsham
Polegate
Willingdon
Eastbourne
BEXHILL
St Leonards
Hastings
Hollington
Seaford
Newhaven
East Sussex
Bedgebury Forest
ASHDOWN FOREST
Pevensey Levels
Pevensey Bay
BEACHY HEAD
TQ
TV
DIEPPE
0 1 2 3 4 5 6 miles
0 1 2 3 4 5 6 7 8 9 10 km

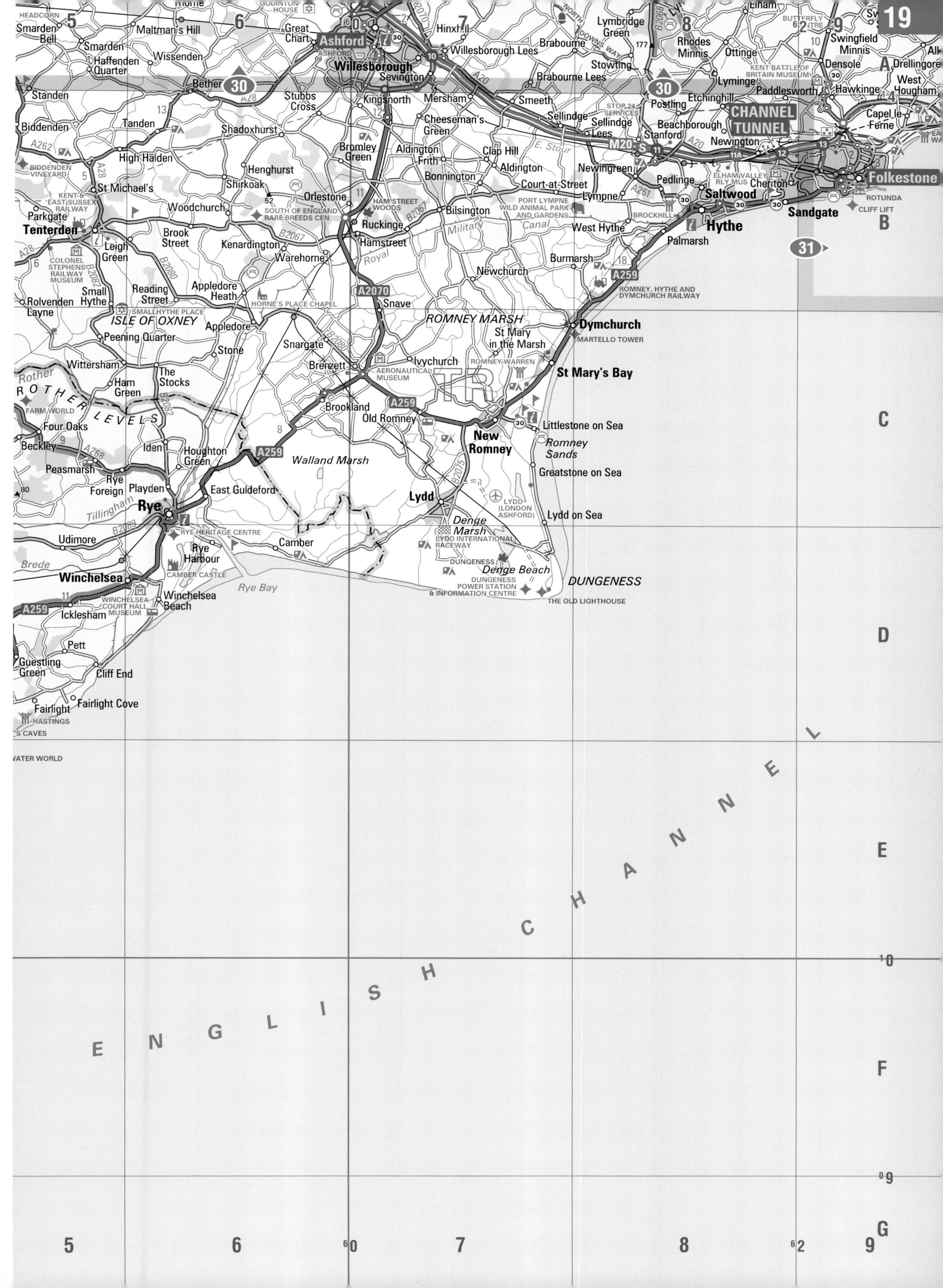
Ashford
Willesborough
Sevington
Kingsnorth
Mersham
Hinxhill
Willesborough Lees
Brabourne
Brabourne Lees
Smeeth
Sellindge
Stowting
Lymbridge Green
Rhodes Minnis
Ottinge
Swingfield Minnis
Densole
Drellingore
West Hougham
Hawkinge
Paddlesworth
Lyminge
Etchinghill
Postling
CHANNEL TUNNEL
Beachborough
Stanford
Newington
Capel le Ferne
Folkestone
Cheriton
Saltwood
Hythe
Sandgate
Pedlinge
Newingreen
Lympne
Court-at-Street
Aldington
Clap Hill
Bonnington
Aldington Frith
Cheeseman's Green
Bromley Green
Orlestone
Ruckinge
Hamstreet
Bilsington
PORT LYMPNE WILD ANIMAL PARK AND GARDENS
West Hythe
Palmarsh
Burmarsh
Newchurch
Dymchurch
MARTELLO TOWER
ROMNEY, HYTHE AND DYMCHURCH RAILWAY
St Mary in the Marsh
St Mary's Bay
ROMNEY MARSH
ROMNEY WARREN
Snave
Ivychurch
Brenzett
AERONAUTICAL MUSEUM
Snargate
Brookland
Old Romney
New Romney
Littlestone on Sea
Romney Sands
Greatstone on Sea
Lydd
LYDD (LONDON ASHFORD)
Lydd on Sea
Denge Marsh
LYDD INTERNATIONAL RACEWAY
Denge Beach
DUNGENESS
DUNGENESS POWER STATION & INFORMATION CENTRE
THE OLD LIGHTHOUSE
Walland Marsh
Camber
East Guldeford
Rye
RYE HERITAGE CENTRE
Rye Harbour
CAMBER CASTLE
Rye Bay
Winchelsea
Winchelsea Beach
WINCHELSEA COURT HALL MUSEUM
Icklesham
Pett
Guestling Green
Cliff End
Fairlight
Fairlight Cove
HASTINGS
Udimore
Playden
Rye Foreign
Peasmarsh
Iden
Houghton Green
Beckley
Four Oaks
ROTHER LEVELS
FARM WORLD
Ham Green
The Stocks
Wittersham
Peening Quarter
Stone
Appledore
ISLE OF OXNEY
SMALLHYTHE PLACE
Small Hythe
Rolvenden Layne
Reading Street
Appledore Heath
HORNE'S PLACE CHAPEL
Warehorne
Kenardington
Brook Street
Leigh Green
Tenterden
COLONEL STEPHENS RAILWAY MUSEUM
Parkgate
KENT & EAST SUSSEX RAILWAY
St Michael's
Woodchurch
SOUTH OF ENGLAND RARE BREEDS CEN
HAM STREET WOODS
Shirkoak
Henghurst
High Halden
Shadoxhurst
Tanden
Biddenden
BIDDENDEN VINEYARD
Standen
Bethersden
Stubbs Cross
Haffenden Quarter
Smarden
Smarden Bell
Wissenden
Maltman's Hill
Great Chart
HEADCORN
ENGLISH CHANNEL
Royal Military Canal
E. Stour
Tillingham
Brede
Rother
M20
A20
A28
A259
A2070
A261
A262
A268
B2067
B2080
B2082
B2089
B2075
B2068
TR
5
6
60
7
8
62
9
A
B
C
D
E
F
G
10
09
30
31

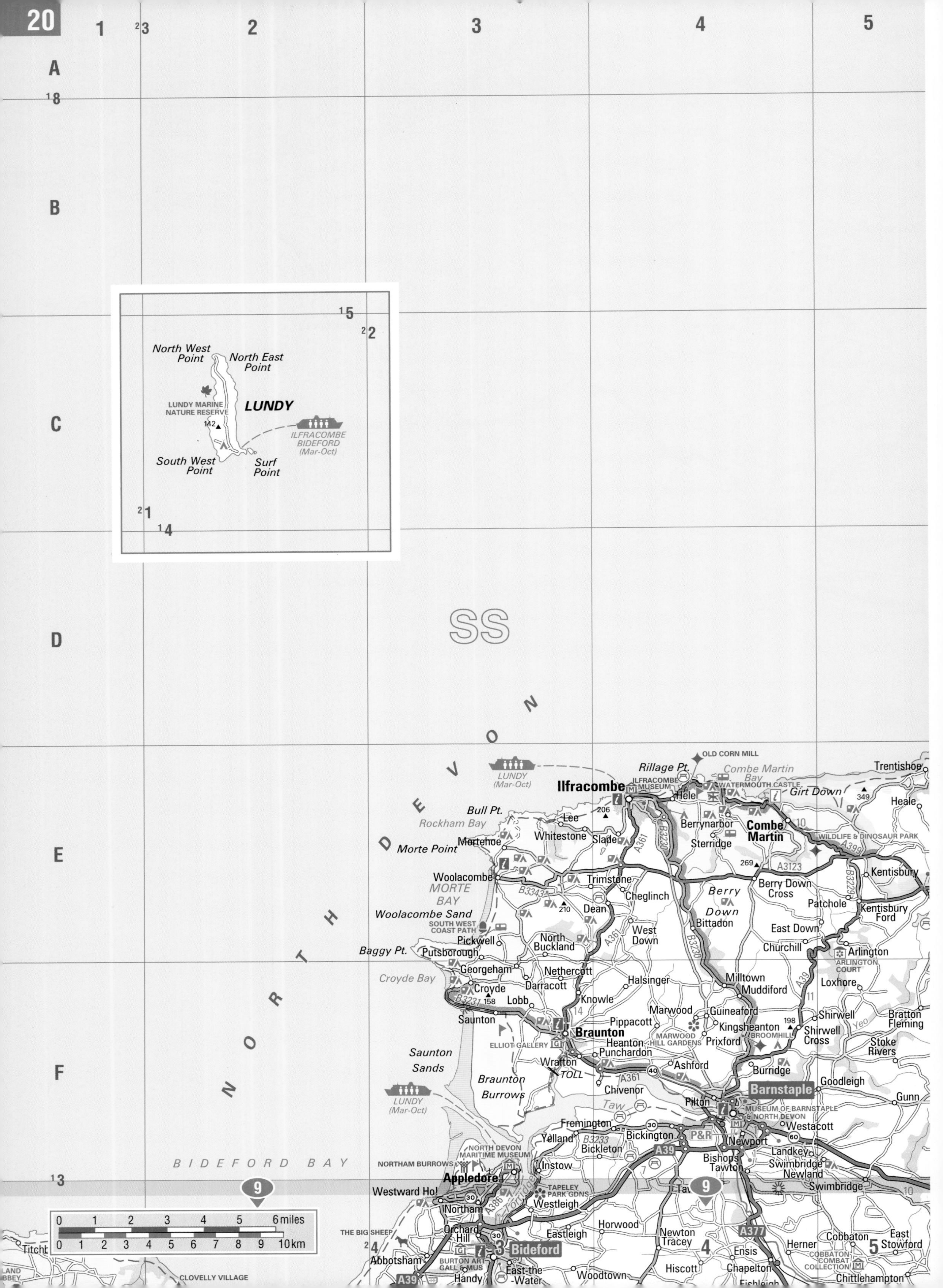

1 ²3   2   3   4   5

A

¹8

B

C

North West
Point   North East
              Point

LUNDY MARINE
NATURE RESERVE   **LUNDY**

                142 ▲   ILFRACOMBE
                             BIDEFORD
                             (Mar-Oct)

South West   Surf
Point   Point

¹5
²2

²1
¹4

D

SS

DEVON

LUNDY
(Mar-Oct)   Rillage Pt.   OLD CORN MILL   Combe Martin
                                                 Bay   Trentishoe
                 Ilfracombe   ILFRACOMBE   WATERMOUTH CASTLE
                                  MUSEUM   Hele   Girt Down   349 ▲   Heale
            Bull Pt.   Berrynarbor   **Combe**   WILDLIFE & DINOSAUR PARK
Rockham Bay   Lee   Sterridge   **Martin** A399
            Whitestone   Slade   206 ▲   A3123   Kentisbury
Morte Point Mortehoe   269 ▲   Berry Down
E   Trimstone   Berry   Cross   Patchole   Kentisbury
Woolacombe   Cheglinch   Down   Ford
MORTE   210 ▲   Dean   Bittadon   East Down
BAY   West   Churchill   Arlington
Woolacombe Sand   North   Down   Milltown   ARLINGTON
SOUTH WEST   Buckland   Muddiford   COURT
COAST PATH   Pickwell   Halsinger   11   Loxhore
Baggy Pt.   Putsborough   Marwood Guineaford   198 ▲ Shirwell   Bratton
Croyde Bay   Georgeham   Nethercott   Kingsheanton   Shirwell   Fleming
             Croyde 158   Darracott   Pippacott MARWOOD Prixford Cross   Stoke
                    Lobb   Knowle   HILL GARDENS   Rivers
             Saunton   14   Heanton   Ashford   Burridge   Goodleigh   Gunn
F   ELLIOT GALLERY   **Braunton**   Punchardon
Saunton   Wrafton   Chivenor   Pilton   **Barnstaple** Westacott
Sands   TOLL   A361 40   MUSEUM OF
       Braunton   BARNSTAPLE
       Burrows   LUNDY   Taw   30   Bickington P&R Newport   Landkey
                  (Mar-Oct)   Fremington B3233   Bishops   Swimbridge
¹3   NORTHAM BURROWS   Yelland Bickleton A39 7 Tawton Newland Swimbridge
B I D E F O R D   B A Y   NORTH DEVON Instow
                          MARITIME MUSEUM
9   **Appledore** TAPELEY   **9**
                          Westward Ho! PARK GDNS   Ta
                          Northam   A386 Westleigh   Newton   Ensis Herner Cobbaton
     0 1 2 3 4 5 6 miles THE BIG SHEEP Orchard 30   Tracey   East
     0 1 2 3 4 5 6 7 8 9 10km   Hill   BURTON ART **Bideford** Horwood Hiscott A377 Cobbaton Stowford
Titch   GALL & MUS East-the-   Woodtown   COMBAT
              CLOVELLY VILLAGE Abbotsham Handy Water   Chapelton COLLECTION Chittlehampton
                                                                     Fishleigh

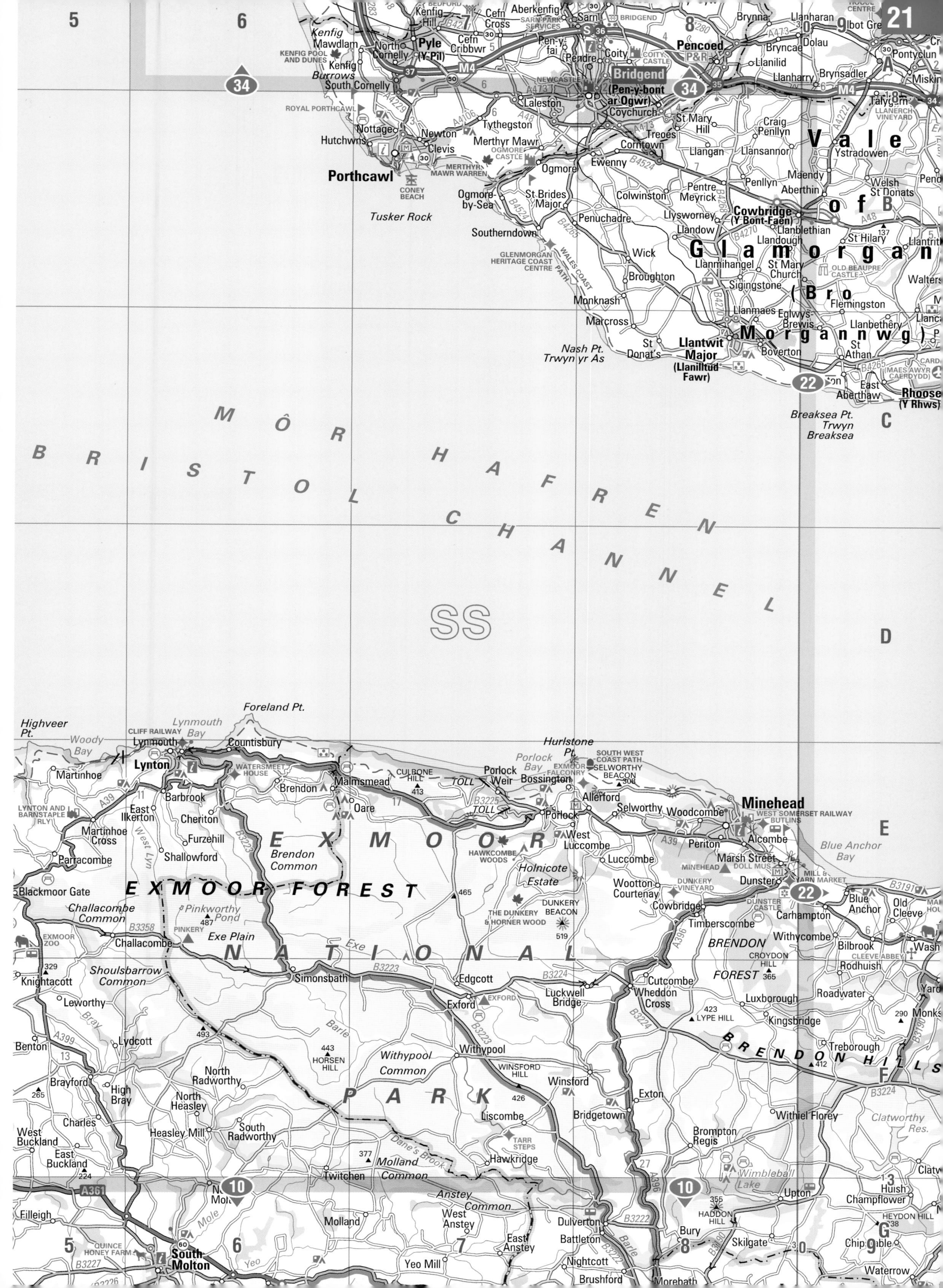
5
6
7
8
9
Kenfig Hill
Cefn Cross
Aberkenfig
Sarn
Bridgend
Brynna
Llanharan
Kenfig
Mawdlam
Pyle
(Y Pil)
North Cornelly
Cefn Cribbwr
Pen-y-fai
Pendre
Coity
Pencoed
Bryncae
Dolau
Pontyclun
Kenfig Pool and Dunes
Kenfig Burrows
South Cornelly
Llanilid
Llanharry
Brynsadler
Miskin
Sarn Park Services
Coity Castle
Newcastle
Bridgend
(Pen-y-bont ar Ogwr)
Coychurch
Talygarn
Llanerch Vineyard
34
M4
Royal Porthcawl
Laleston
Tythegston
Nottage
Hutchwns
Newton
Clevis
Merthyr Mawr
Ogmore Castle
Merthyr Mawr Warren
St Mary Hill
Treoes
Corntown
Craig Penllyn
Llangan
Llansannor
Vale
Ystradowen
Porthcawl
Coney Beach
Ogmore
Ewenny
Maendy
Aberthin
Penllyn
Pentre Meyrick
Welsh St Donats
Ogmore-by-Sea
St Brides Major
Colwinston
Cowbridge
(Y Bont-Faen)
of
Tusker Rock
Penuchadre
Llysworney
Llanblethian
Llandow
Llandough
St Hilary
Southerndown
Glenmorgan Heritage Coast Centre
Wales Coast Path
Wick
Glamorgan
Llanmihangel
St Mary Church
Old Beaupre Castle
Broughton
Sigingstone
(Bro
Flemingston
Monknash
Llanmaes
Eglwys-Brewis
Llanbethery
Marcross
Morgannwg)
Nash Pt.
Trwyn yr As
St Donat's
Llantwit Major
(Llanilltud Fawr)
Boverton
St Athan
East Aberthaw
Rhoose
(Y Rhws)
22
Breaksea Pt.
Trwyn Breaksea
C
MÔR HAFREN
BRISTOL CHANNEL
SS
D
Foreland Pt.
Highveer Pt.
Lynmouth Bay
Woody Bay
Cliff Railway
Lynmouth
Countisbury
Hurlstone Pt.
Porlock Bay
South West Coast Path
Exmoor Falconry
Selworthy Beacon
Martinhoe
Lynton
Watersmeet House
Culbone Hill
Malmsmead
Toll
Porlock Weir
Bossington
Allerford
Brendon
Oare
Porlock
Selworthy
Woodcombe
Minehead
West Somerset Railway
Butlins
Lynton and Barnstaple Rly
Barbrook
East Ilkerton
Cheriton
Martinhoe Cross
West Lyn
Furzehill
Shallowford
EXMOOR
Brendon Common
Hawkcombe Woods
West Luccombe
Luccombe
Periton
Alcombe
Marsh Street
Blue Anchor Bay
E
Parracombe
Holnicote Estate
Minehead
Doll Mus
Dunster
Mill & Yarn Market
Blackmoor Gate
EXMOOR FOREST
465
Wootton Courtenay
Dunkery Vineyard
Dunster Castle
Blue Anchor
Old Cleeve
Challacombe Common
Pinkworthy Pond
487
Pinkery
Exe Plain
The Dunkery & Horner Wood
Dunkery Beacon
519
Cowbridge
Timberscombe
Carhampton
Exmoor Zoo
Challacombe
Exe
NATIONAL
BRENDON
Withycombe
Bilbrook
Cleeve Abbey
Washford
329
Knightacott
Shoulsbarrow Common
Simonsbath
Edgcott
Cutcombe
Croydon Hill
365
FOREST
Rodhuish
Leworthy
Exford
Luckwell Bridge
Wheddon Cross
Luxborough
Roadwater
Bray
423
Lype Hill
Kingsbridge
290
Benton
Lydcott
493
Barle
443
Horsen Hill
BRENDON HILLS
Treborough
412
13
North Radworthy
Withypool Common
Withypool
Winsford Hill
Winsford
F
Brayford
High Bray
265
North Heasley
PARK
426
Exton
Charles
Liscombe
Bridgetown
Withiel Florey
Clatworthy Res.
West Buckland
Heasley Mill
South Radworthy
Tarr Steps
Brompton Regis
East Buckland
224
377
Molland Common
Dane's Brook
Hawkridge
Twitchen
Wimbleball Lake
10
A361
Upton
Huish Champflower
Anstey Common
West Anstey
355
Haddon Hill
Filleigh
Mole
Molland
Dulverton
Heydon Hill
Quince Honey Farm
South Molton
East Anstey
Battleton
Bury
Skilgate
Chipstable
Yeo Mill
Nightcott
Brushford
Morebath
Waterrow
Yeo
Barle

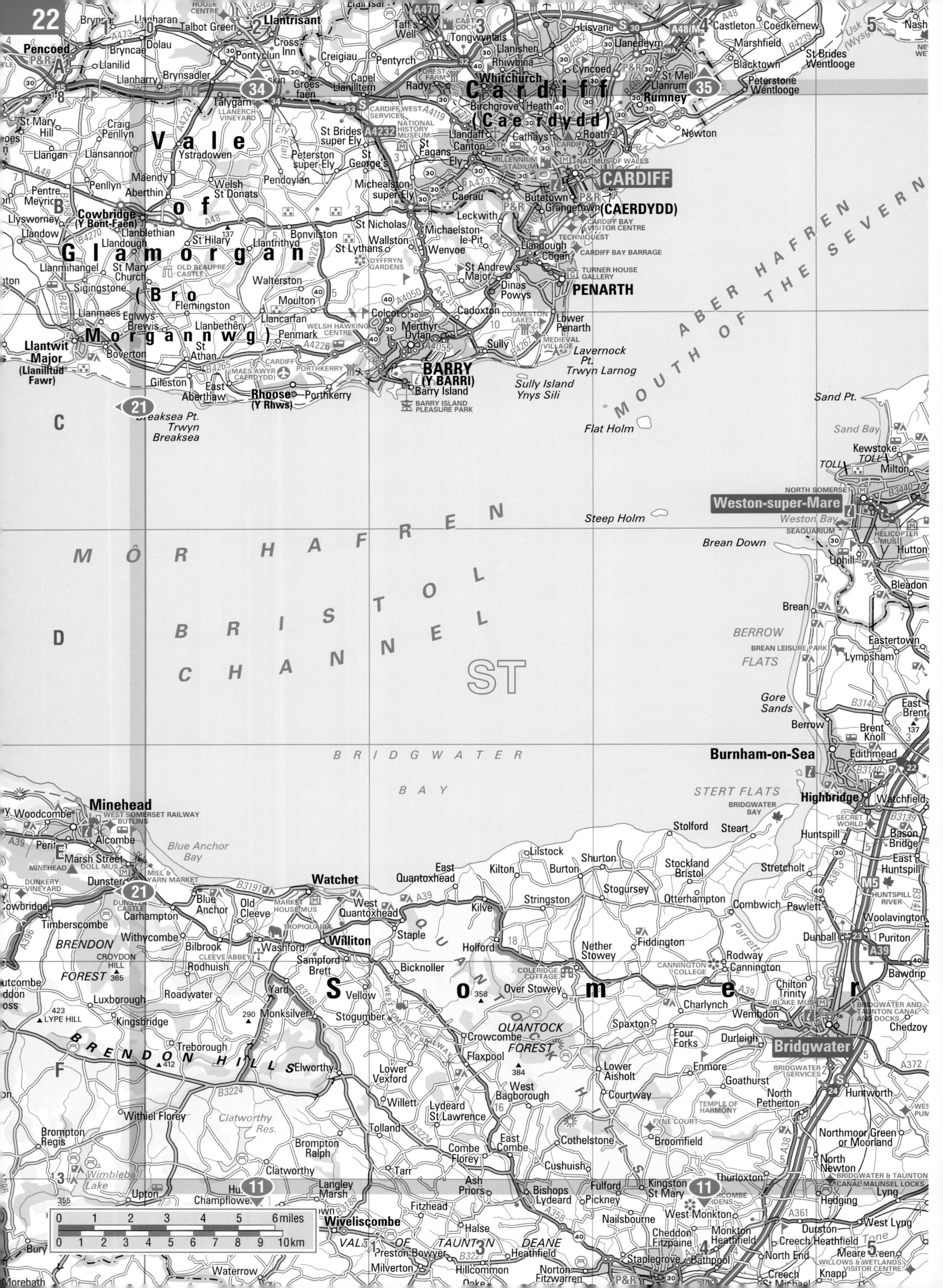

Pencoed
Llantrisant
Talbot Green
Pontyclun
Creigiau
Pentyrch
Taff's Well
Tongwynlais
Lisvane
Castleton
Coedkernew
Nash
Marshfield
Llanishen
Rhiwbina
Llanedeyrn
St Brides Wentlooge
Blacktown
Whitchurch
Cyncoed
Radyr
Capel Llanilltern
Peterstone Wentlooge
Cardiff
(Caerdydd)
Rumney
Llanrumney
St Mellons
Newton
Llanharry
Brynsadler
Talygarn
Groes-faen
St Mary Hill
Craig Penllyn
Vale
of
Glamorgan
(Bro
Morgannwg)
Ystradowen
St Brides super Ely
Peterston super-Ely
St George's
St Fagans
Llandaff
Cathays
Roath
Canton
Ely
Llangan
Llansannor
Maendy
Aberthin
Welsh St Donats
Pendoylan
Michaelston-super-Ely
Caerau
CARDIFF
Pentre Meyrick
Penllyn
Cowbridge
(Y Bont-Faen)
Butetown
Grangetown
(CAERDYDD)
Llysworney
Llandow
Llanblethian
St Hilary
Bonvilston
St Nicholas
Leckwith
Michaelston-le-Pit
Llandough
Llantrithyd
Wallston
St Lythans
Wenvoe
Cogan
CARDIFF BAY BARRAGE
Llanmihangel
St Mary Church
OLD BEAUPRE CASTLE
DYFFRYN GARDENS
St Andrews Major
Dinas Powys
PENARTH
Sigingstone
Walterston
Moulton
Flemingston
Llancarfan
Colcot
Cadoxton
Llanmaes
Eglwys-Brewis
Llanbethery
Penmark
Merthyr-Dyfan
Lower Penarth
Llantwit Major
(Llanilltud Fawr)
St Athan
Boverton
Sully
Lavernock Pt.
Trwyn Larnog
BARRY
(Y BARRI)
Barry Island
Gileston
East Aberthaw
Rhoose
(Y Rhws)
Porthkerry
Sully Island
Ynys Sili
Breaksea Pt.
Trwyn Breaksea
Flat Holm
ABER HAFREN
MOUTH OF THE SEVERN
Sand Pt.
Sand Bay
Kewstoke
Milton
Weston-super-Mare
Weston Bay
Steep Holm
Brean Down
Uphill
Hutton
MÔR HAFREN
BRISTOL CHANNEL
Bleadon
Brean
BERROW FLATS
Eastertown
Lympsham
ST
Gore Sands
Berrow
East Brent
Brent Knoll
Burnham-on-Sea
Edithmead
BRIDGWATER BAY
STERT FLATS
Highbridge
Watchfield
Minehead
Woodcombe
WEST SOMERSET RAILWAY
Alcombe
Blue Anchor Bay
Stolford
Steart
Huntspill
Bason Bridge
Marsh Street
Dunster
Watchet
East Quantoxhead
Kilton
Lilstock
Burton
Shurton
Stockland Bristol
Stretcholt
East Huntspill
Blue Anchor
Old Cleeve
West Quantoxhead
Kilve
Stringston
Stogursey
Otterhampton
Combwich
Pawlett
Timberscombe
Carhampton
Woolavington
BRENDON
Withycombe
Williton
Staple
Holford
Nether Stowey
Fiddington
Dunball
Puriton
Bilbrook
Washford
Sampford Brett
Rodway
Cannington
FOREST
Rodhuish
Bicknoller
Bawdrip
Roadwater
Yard
Vellow
Over Stowey
Chilton Trinity
Somerset
Luxborough
Monksilver
Stogumber
Charlynch
Wembdon
LYPE HILL
Kingsbridge
QUANTOCK FOREST
Spaxton
Four Forks
Durleigh
Bridgwater
Chedzoy
BRENDON HILLS
Treborough
Crowcombe
Flaxpool
Elworthy
Lower Vexford
Lower Aisholt
Enmore
Goathurst
Huntworth
West Bagborough
Courtway
North Petherton
Withiel Florey
Clatworthy Res.
Willett
Lydeard St Lawrence
Brompton Regis
Tolland
Cothelstone
Broomfield
Northmoor Green or Moorland
Brompton Ralph
Combe Florey
East Combe
Cushuish
North Newton
Wimbleball Lake
Clatworthy
Tarr
Thurloxton
Upton
Champflower
Langley Marsh
Ash Priors
Bishops Lydeard
Fulford
Pickney
Kingston St Mary
Lyng
Hedging
Fitzhead
Wiveliscombe
Halse
Nailsbourne
West Monkton
Durston
West Lyng
Cheddon Fitzpaine
Monkton Heathfield
Creech Heathfield
VALE OF TAUNTON DEANE
Preston Bowyer
Heathfield
Staplegrove
Bathpool
North End
Meare Green
Milverton
Hillcommon
Norton Fitzwarren
Creech St Michael
Knapp
Waterrow
Bury
Morebath
0 1 2 3 4 5 6 miles
0 1 2 3 4 5 6 7 8 9 10 km

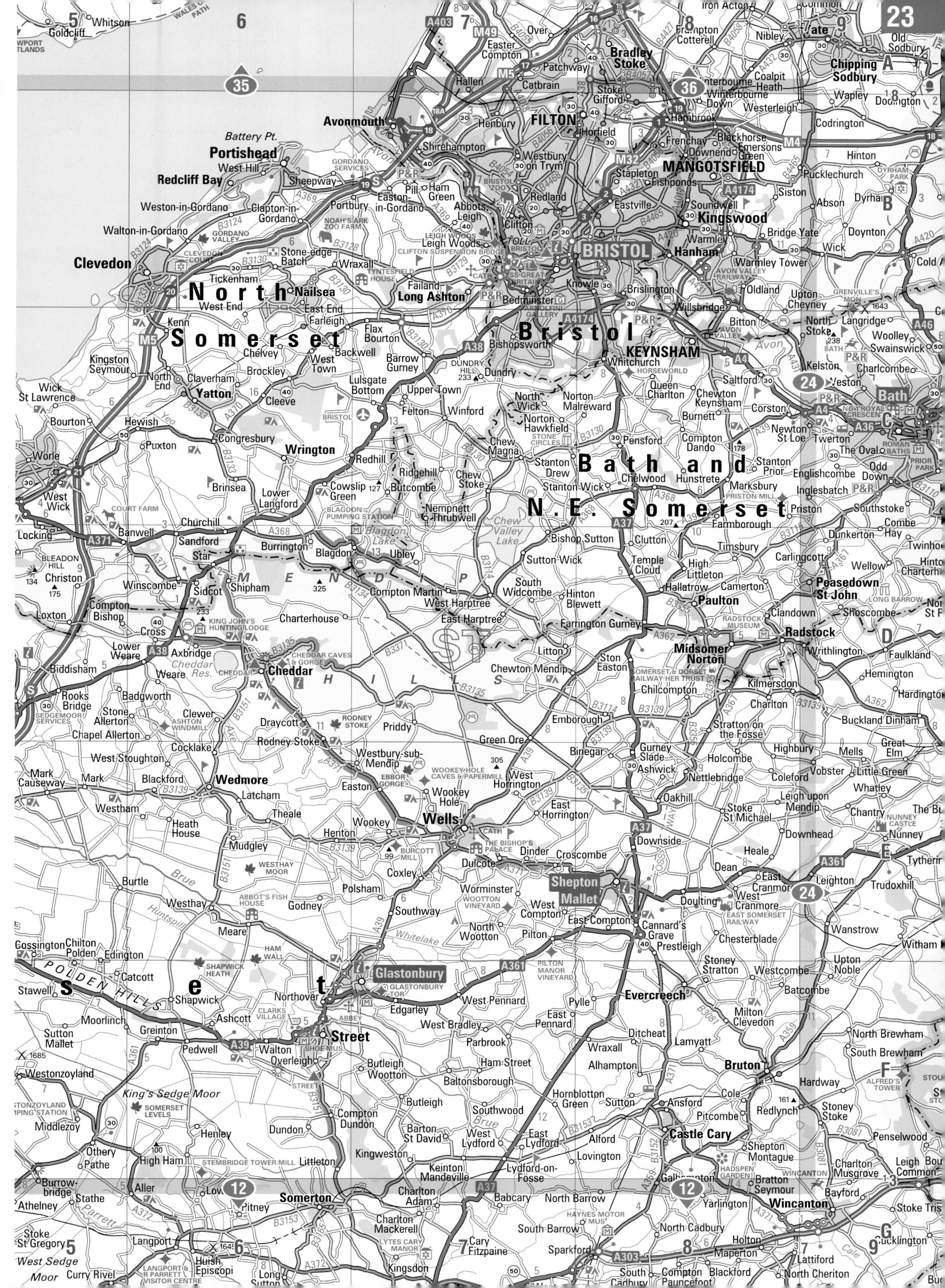

Goldcliff
Whitson
6
Over
Frampton Cotterell
Iron Acton
Nibley
Yate
Old Sodbury
Easter Compton
Bradley Stoke
Patchway
35
36
Chipping Sodbury
Hallen
Catbrain
Stoke Gifford
Winterbourne
Coalpit Heath
Winterbourne Down
Westerleigh
Wapley
Dodington
Avonmouth
Henbury
FILTON
Horfield
Hambrook
Codrington
Battery Pt.
Portishead
Shirehampton
Frenchay
Blackhorse
Emersons Green
Downend
West Hill
Westbury on Trym
MANGOTSFIELD
Hinton
Redcliff Bay
Sheepway
Pill
Ham Green
Stapleton
Fishponds
Pucklechurch
Weston-in-Gordano
Clapton-in-Gordano
Portbury
Easton-in-Gordano
Abbots Leigh
Redland
Eastville
Siston
Abson
Dyrham
Soundwell
Kingswood
Walton-in-Gordano
Clifton
Leigh Woods
Bridge Yate
Doynton
Clevedon
Stone-edge Batch
Wraxall
BRISTOL
Hanham
Warmley
Wick
Cold
Warmley Tower
Tickenham
Failand
Knowle
Oldland
North
Nailsea
Long Ashton
Bedminster
Brislington
Upton Cheyney
West End
East End
Farleigh
Willsbridge
Bitton
Kenn
Flax Bourton
Bristol
North Stoke
Langridge
Somerset
Backwell
Bishopsworth
KEYNSHAM
Woolley
Swainswick
Chelvey
West Town
Barrow Gurney
Whitchurch
Kelston
Charlcombe
Kingston Seymour
North End
Claverham
Brockley
Dundry
Saltford
Weston
Yatton
Lulsgate Bottom
Queen Charlton
Chewton Keynsham
Bath
Wick St Lawrence
Cleeve
Upper Town
North Wick
Norton Malreward
Corston
Bourton
Hewish
Felton
Winford
Norton Hawkfield
Burnett
Newton St Loe
Twerton
Puxton
Congresbury
Chew Magna
Pensford
Compton Dando
The Oval
Worle
Wrington
Redhill
Stanton Drew
Bath and
Stanton Prior
Odd Down
Ridgehill
Chew Stoke
Chelwood
Hunstrete
Englishcombe
West Wick
Brinsea
Lower Langford
Cowslip Green
Butcombe
Stanton Wick
Marksbury
Inglesbatch
Nempnett Thrubwell
N.E. Somerset
Priston
Southstoke
Combe Hay
Locking
Churchill
Banwell
Sandford
Burrington
Blagdon Lake
Bishop Sutton
Clutton
Farmborough
Dunkerton
Star
Blagdon
Ubley
Chew Valley Lake
Timsbury
Twinhoe
Christon
Winscombe
Sidcot
Shipham
Sutton Wick
Temple Cloud
High Littleton
Carlingcott
Wellow
Hinton Charterhouse
MENDIP
Compton Martin
South Widcombe
Hinton Blewett
Hallatrow
Camerton
Peasedown St John
Compton Bishop
Loxton
West Harptree
Paulton
Cross
Charterhouse
East Harptree
Farrington Gurney
Clandown
Shoscombe
Lower Weare
Axbridge
Radstock
Biddisham
Cheddar
Litton
Midsomer Norton
Writhlington
Faulkland
Weare
Cheddar Res.
Chewton Mendip
Ston Easton
Hemington
Rooks Bridge
Badgworth
HILLS
Chilcompton
Kilmersdon
Hardington
Stone Allerton
Clewer
Charlton
Chapel Allerton
Draycott
Priddy
Emborough
Stratton on the Fosse
Buckland Dinham
Cocklake
Rodney Stoke
Green Ore
Binegar
Gurney Slade
Highbury
Mells
Great Elm
West Stoughton
Westbury-sub-Mendip
Ashwick
Holcombe
Vobster
Little Green
Mark Causeway
Mark
Blackford
Wedmore
West Horrington
Nettlebridge
Coleford
Whatley
Latcham
Easton
Wookey Hole
Oakhill
Leigh upon Mendip
Westham
Theale
East Horrington
Stoke St Michael
Chantry
Heath House
Wookey
Wells
Downside
Downhead
Mudgley
Henton
Dinder
Croscombe
Heale
Nunney
Burtle
Coxley
Dulcote
Dean
East Cranmore
Leighton
Tytherington
Polsham
Worminster
Shepton Mallet
Trudoxhill
Westhay
Godney
Southway
West Compton
Doulting
West Cranmore
Meare
North Wootton
East Compton
Cannard's Grave
Wanstrow
Cossington
Chilton Polden
Edington
Pilton
Prestleigh
Chesterblade
Witham
Catcott
Glastonbury
Stoney Stratton
Westcombe
Upton Noble
Stawell
Shapwick
POLDEN HILLS
Northover
West Pennard
Pylle
Evercreech
Batcombe
Moorlinch
Ashcott
Edgarley
East Pennard
Milton Clevedon
Sutton Mallet
Greinton
Street
West Bradley
Ditcheat
Lamyatt
North Brewham
Pedwell
Walton
Overleigh
Parbrook
Wraxall
South Brewham
Westonzoyland
Butleigh Wootton
Ham Street
Alhampton
Bruton
Baltonsborough
Hardway
King's Sedge Moor
Hornblotton Green
Sutton
Ansford
Cole
Butleigh
Southwood
Redlynch
Pitcombe
Stoney Stoke
Middlezoy
Compton Dundon
Dundon
Barton St David
West Lydford
East Lydford
Alford
Castle Cary
Othery
Henley
Penselwood
Pathe
High Ham
Littleton
Kingweston
Lovington
Shepton Montague
Keinton Mandeville
Lydford-on-Fosse
Charlton Musgrove
Leigh Common
Burrowbridge
Aller
12
Charlton Adam
Galhampton
Bratton Seymour
Stathe
Low Ham
Somerton
Babcary
North Barrow
Yarlington
Wincanton
Bayford
Athelney
Pitney
Charlton Mackerell
Stoke Trister
South Barrow
North Cadbury
Stoke St Gregory
Langport
Cary Fitzpaine
Sparkford
Holton
Cucklington
West Sedge Moor
Huish Episcopi
Maperton
Lattiford
Curry Rivel
Long Sutton
Kingsdon
South Cadbury
Compton Pauncefoot
Blackford
North Cheriton

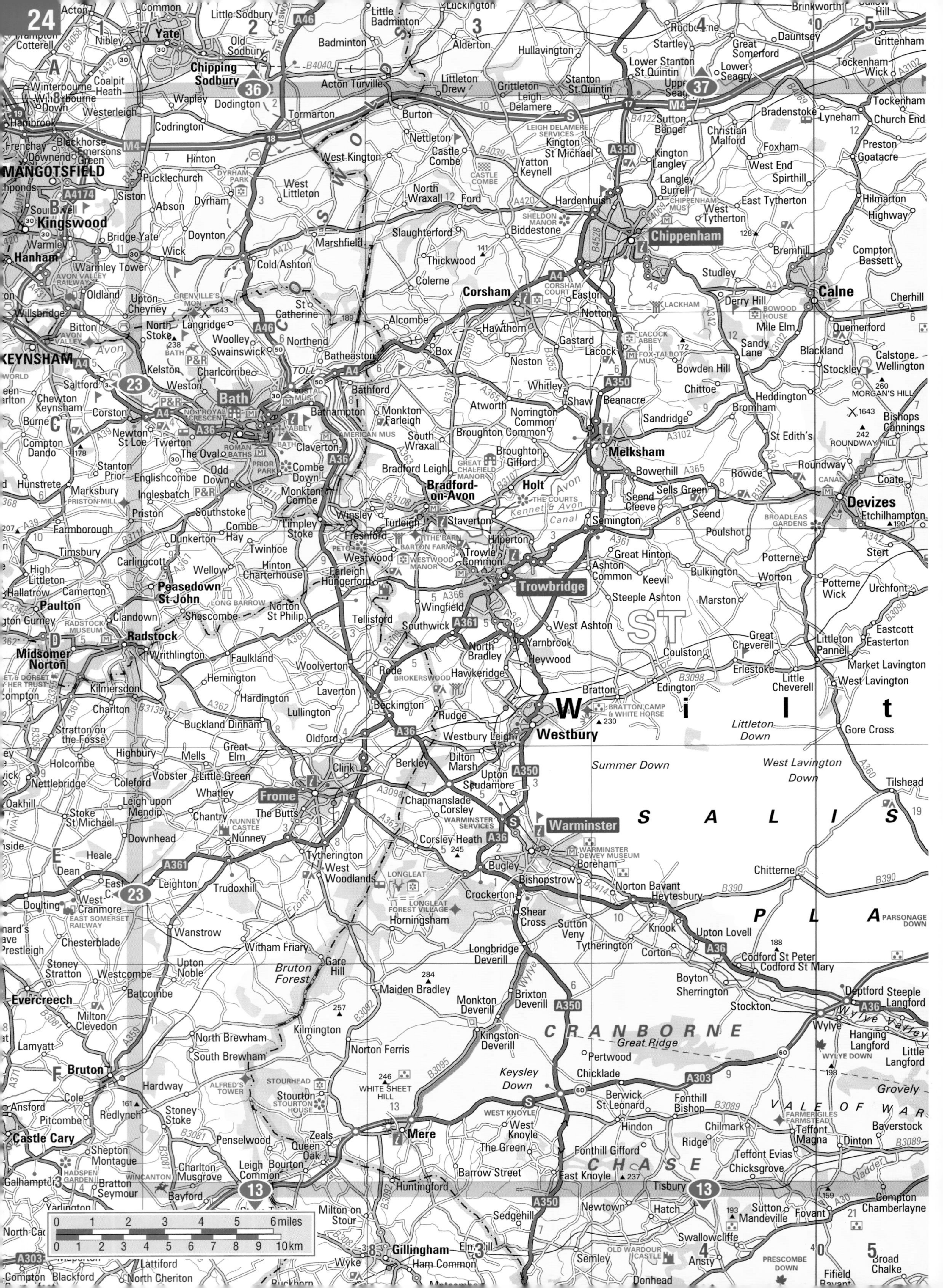
Yate
Chipping Sodbury
Little Sodbury
Old Sodbury
Badminton
Little Badminton
Luckington
Alderton
Hullavington
Acton Turville
Littleton Drew
Grittleton
Leigh Delamere
Stanton St Quintin
Lower Stanton St Quintin
Startley
Great Somerford
Dauntsey
Brinkworth
Grittenham
Tockenham Wick
Tockenham
Lyneham
Bradenstoke
Christian Malford
Sutton Benger
Kington St Michael
Kington Langley
Yatton Keynell
Castle Combe
Nettleton
Burton
West Kington
Tormarton
Dodington
Wapley
Westerleigh
Codrington
Hinton
Pucklechurch
Dyrham
Abson
Siston
Kingswood
MANGOTSFIELD
Winterbourne
Frenchay
Downend
Emersons Green
Hambrook
Coalpit Heath
Hanham
Warmley
Bridge Yate
Doynton
Wick
Cold Ashton
Marshfield
West Littleton
North Wraxall
Ford
Slaughterford
Biddestone
Hardenhuish
Chippenham
West Tytherton
East Tytherton
Langley Burrell
Foxham
West End
Spirthill
Preston
Goatacre
Church End
Hilmarton
Highway
Compton Bassett
Bremhill
Studley
Calne
Cherhill
Derry Hill
Mile Elm
Quemerford
Blackland
Sandy Lane
Calstone Wellington
Stockley
Heddington
Bromham
Chittoe
Bowden Hill
Lacock
Gastard
Neston
Notton
Easton
Corsham
Thickwood
Colerne
Box
Hawthorn
Alcombe
Northend
Batheaston
Bathford
Bathampton
Bath
St Catherine
Langridge
North Stoke
Swainswick
Woolley
Charlcombe
Kelston
Weston
Saltford
KEYNSHAM
Bitton
Oldland
Upton Cheyney
Willsbridge
Chewton Keynsham
Corston
Newton St Loe
Twerton
The Oval
Claverton
Combe Down
Monkton Combe
Odd Down
Englishcombe
Stanton Prior
Compton Dando
Burnett
Hunstrete
Marksbury
Inglesbatch
Priston
Southstoke
Combe Hay
Dunkerton
Farmborough
Timsbury
Carlingcott
Wellow
Twinhoe
Hinton Charterhouse
High Littleton
Hallatrow
Camerton
Peasedown St John
Paulton
Shoscombe
Clandown
Radstock
Writhlington
Midsomer Norton
Kilmersdon
Faulkland
Hemington
Hardington
Charlton
Buckland Dinham
Stratton on the Fosse
Holcombe
Nettlebridge
Highbury
Coleford
Vobster
Mells
Great Elm
Little Green
Whatley
Leigh upon Mendip
Stoke St Michael
Oakhill
Chantry
Nunney
Downhead
Frome
The Butts
Clink
Berkley
Oldford
Lullington
Laverton
Beckington
Rudge
Woolverton
Rode
Norton St Philip
Tellisford
Southwick
Farleigh Hungerford
Westwood
Freshford
Limpley Stoke
Winsley
Turleigh
Bradford-on-Avon
Staverton
Holt
Monkton Farleigh
South Wraxall
Bradford Leigh
Atworth
Broughton Common
Broughton Gifford
Norrington Common
Whitley
Shaw
Beanacre
Melksham
Sandridge
Bowerhill
Sells Green
Seend
Seend Cleeve
Semington
Hilperton
Trowle Common
Trowbridge
Wingfield
North Bradley
Yarnbrook
Heywood
West Ashton
Steeple Ashton
Ashton Common
Keevil
Great Hinton
Bulkington
Poulshot
Rowde
Roundway
Devizes
Coate
Etchilhampton
Stert
Potterne
Potterne Wick
Worton
Marston
Urchfont
Eastcott
Easterton
Littleton Pannell
Market Lavington
West Lavington
Great Cheverell
Little Cheverell
Erlestoke
Coulston
Edington
Bratton
Westbury
Westbury Leigh
Hawkeridge
Dilton Marsh
Upton Scudamore
Chapmanslade
Corsley
Corsley Heath
Warminster
Boreham
Bugley
Bishopstrow
Crockerton
Norton Bavant
Heytesbury
Knook
Upton Lovell
Codford St Peter
Codford St Mary
Sutton Veny
Tytherington
Corton
Boyton
Sherrington
Stockton
Shear Cross
Longbridge Deverill
Horningsham
Tytherington
West Woodlands
Trudoxhill
Leighton
Heale
Dean
East Cranmore
West Cranmore
Doulting
Chesterblade
Prestleigh
Stoney Stratton
Westcombe
Batcombe
Evercreech
Milton Clevedon
Lamyatt
Bruton
Wanstrow
Upton Noble
Witham Friary
Gare Hill
Bruton Forest
Maiden Bradley
Monkton Deverill
Brixton Deverill
Kingston Deverill
Kilmington
North Brewham
South Brewham
Hardway
Redlynch
Cole
Pitcombe
Castle Cary
Ansford
Stoney Stoke
Stourton
Zeals
Penselwood
Queen Oak
Mere
Charlton Musgrove
Bratton Seymour
Shepton Montague
Leigh Common
Bourton
Bayford
Huntingford
Barrow Street
West Knoyle
The Green
East Knoyle
Sedgehill
Milton on Stour
Gillingham
Ham Common
Wyke
Semley
Donhead
Ansty
Swallowcliffe
Hatch
Newtown
Tisbury
Fonthill Gifford
Fonthill Bishop
Berwick St Leonard
Hindon
Chicklade
Pertwood
Chilmark
Ridge
Teffont Evias
Teffont Magna
Chicksgrove
Dinton
Baverstock
Sutton Mandeville
Fovant
Compton Chamberlayne
Broad Chalke
Fifield Bavant
Wylye
Hanging Langford
Little Langford
Deptford
Steeple Langford
Tilshead
Chitterne
Gore Cross
Summer Down
West Lavington Down
Littleton Down
Keysley Down
Great Ridge
Grovely
CRANBORNE CHASE
VALE OF WARDOUR
Wylye Valley
SALISBURY PLAIN
WILTS
COTSWOLDS
Kennet & Avon Canal
Avon
Frome
Wylye
Nadder
0 1 2 3 4 5 6 miles
0 1 2 3 4 5 6 7 8 9 10 km

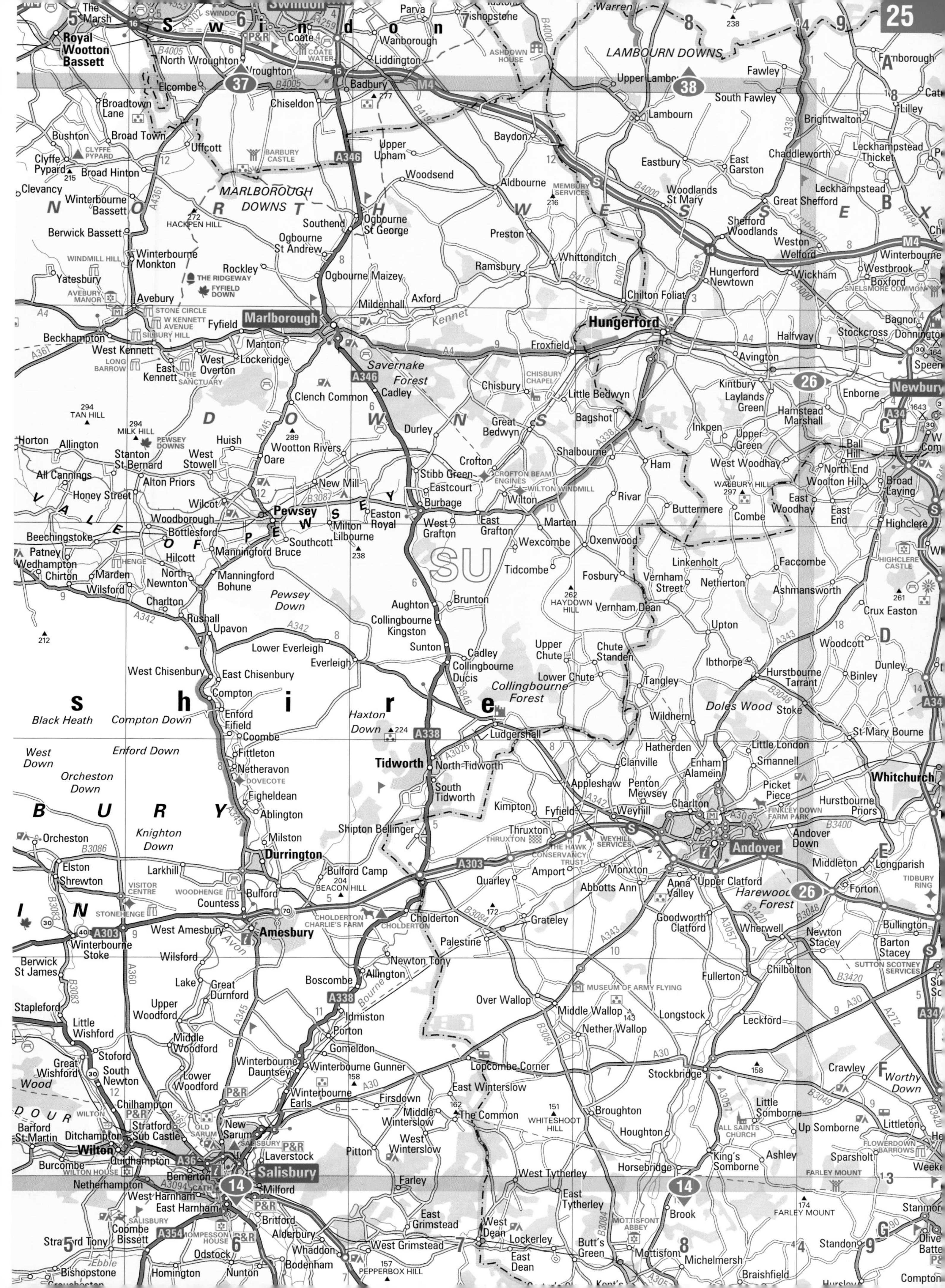
Swindon
Parva
Bishopstone
Royal Wootton Bassett
The Marsh
P&R
Coate
COATE WATER
Wanborough
Liddington
ASHDOWN HOUSE
LAMBOURN DOWNS
Farnborough
North Wroughton
Wroughton
Elcombe
Badbury
Upper Lambourn
Fawley
South Fawley
Lilley
Broadtown Lane
Chiseldon
Lambourn
Brightwalton
Bushton
Broad Town
Baydon
Clyffe Pypard
CLYFFE PYPARD
Uffcott
BARBURY CASTLE
Upper Upham
Eastbury
East Garston
Chaddleworth
Leckhampstead Thicket
Broad Hinton
Woodsend
Clevancy
MARLBOROUGH DOWNS
Aldbourne
MEMBURY SERVICES
Woodlands St Mary
Leckhampstead
Great Shefford
Winterbourne Bassett
HACKPEN HILL
Southend
Ogbourne St George
Shefford Woodlands
Berwick Bassett
Ogbourne St Andrew
Preston
Weston
Welford
Winterbourne
WINDMILL HILL
Winterbourne Monkton
Whittonditch
Hungerford Newtown
Westbrook
Wickham
Boxford
Yatesbury
Rockley
THE RIDGEWAY
FYFIELD DOWN
Ogbourne Maizey
Ramsbury
SNELSMORE COMMON
AVEBURY MANOR
Avebury
Mildenhall
Axford
Chilton Foliat
STONE CIRCLE
W KENNETT AVENUE
Fyfield
Marlborough
Kennet
Hungerford
Bagnor
Donnington
SILBURY HILL
Beckhampton
West Kennett
Manton
Froxfield
Halfway
Stockcross
LONG BARROW
East Kennett
THE SANCTUARY
West Overton
Lockeridge
Savernake Forest
Avington
Speen
CHISBURY CHAPEL
Chisbury
Kintbury
Laylands Green
Enborne
Newbury
Clench Common
Cadley
Little Bedwyn
Hamstead Marshall
TAN HILL
MILK HILL
PEWSEY DOWNS
Wootton Rivers
Durley
Great Bedwyn
Bagshot
Inkpen
Upper Green
Horton
Allington
Huish
Stanton St Bernard
West Stowell
Oare
Shalbourne
Ball Hill
All Cannings
Stibb Green
Crofton
CROFTON BEAM ENGINES
Ham
West Woodhay
North End
Broad Laying
Alton Priors
New Mill
Eastcourt
WILTON WINDMILL
WALBURY HILL
Woolton Hill
Honey Street
Wilton
Rivar
East Woodhay
Wilcot
Burbage
Buttermere
Pewsey
Easton Royal
West Grafton
East Grafton
Marten
Combe
East End
Highclere
Woodborough
Milton Lilbourne
Beechingstoke
Bottlesford
Southcott
Wexcombe
Oxenwood
Patney
Wedhampton
HENGE
Hilcott
Manningford Bruce
Tidcombe
Linkenholt
Faccombe
HIGHCLERE CASTLE
Chirton
Marden
North Newnton
Manningford Bohune
Fosbury
Vernham Street
Netherton
Wilsford
Pewsey Down
Ashmansworth
HAYDOWN HILL
Vernham Dean
Charlton
Brunton
Aughton
Rushall
Upavon
Collingbourne Kingston
Upton
Crux Easton
Lower Everleigh
Sunton
Everleigh
Cadley
Upper Chute
Chute Standen
Woodcott
West Chisenbury
East Chisenbury
Collingbourne Ducis
Lower Chute
Ibthorpe
Dunley
Hurstbourne Tarrant
Binley
Tangley
Compton
Collingbourne Forest
Black Heath
Compton Down
Enford
Fifield
Haxton Down
Ludgershall
Wildhern
Doles Wood
Stoke
Coombe
St Mary Bourne
West Down
Enford Down
Fittleton
Tidworth
North Tidworth
Hatherden
Little London
Clanville
Enham Alamein
Smannell
Orcheston Down
Netheravon
DOVECOTE
Appleshaw
Penton Mewsey
Picket Piece
Whitchurch
South Tidworth
Figheldean
Kimpton
Fyfield
Weyhill
Charlton
Hurstbourne Priors
Knighton Down
Ablington
FINKLEY DOWN FARM PARK
Orcheston
Milston
Shipton Bellinger
Thruxton
THRUXTON
THE HAWK CONSERVANCY TRUST
WEYHILL SERVICES
Andover
Andover Down
Elston
Shrewton
Durrington
Larkhill
Bulford Camp
Amport
Monxton
Middleton
Longparish
BEACON HILL
Quarley
Abbotts Ann
Anna Valley
Upper Clatford
VISITOR CENTRE
WOODHENGE
Bulford
Countess
TIDBURY RING
Forton
Harewood Forest
STONEHENGE
CHOLDERTON CHARLIE'S FARM
CHOLDERTON
Cholderton
Grateley
Goodworth Clatford
Bullington
Winterbourne Stoke
West Amesbury
Amesbury
Avon
Wherwell
Newton Stacey
Palestine
Barton Stacey
Berwick St James
Wilsford
Newton Tony
Allington
Chilbolton
SUTTON SCOTNEY SERVICES
Boscombe
Fullerton
Lake
Great Durnford
Bourne
MUSEUM OF ARMY FLYING
Stapleford
Upper Woodford
Over Wallop
Middle Wallop
Longstock
Leckford
Little Wishford
Idmiston
Porton
Nether Wallop
Middle Woodford
Gomeldon
Stoford
Great Wishford
Wood
South Newton
Winterbourne Dauntsey
Winterbourne Gunner
Lopcombe Corner
Stockbridge
Crawley
Worthy Down
Lower Woodford
East Winterslow
Winterbourne Earls
Chilhampton
WILTON
Firsdown
Middle Winterslow
The Common
WHITESHOOT HILL
Broughton
Little Somborne
Littleton
Barford St Martin
Ditchampton
Wilton
Stratford sub Castle
OLD SARUM
New Sarum
Houghton
ALL SAINTS CHURCH
Up Somborne
Laverstock
West Winterslow
Pitton
King's Somborne
Ashley
FLOWERDOWN BARROWS
Sparsholt
Burcombe
Quidhampton
Salisbury
WILTON HOUSE
Bemerton
Horsebridge
Netherhampton
FARLEY MOUNT
West Harnham
Milford
Farley
West Tytherley
East Tytherley
East Harnham
Britford
Brook
Stanmore
SALISBURY
MOTTISFONT ABBEY
Stratford Tony
Coombe Bissett
LONGFORD CASTLE
MOMPESSON HOUSE
Alderbury
East Grimstead
West Dean
Lockerley
Butt's Green
Mottisfont
Standon
Olivers Battery
Odstock
Whaddon
West Grimstead
Michelmersh
Bishopstone
Ebble
Homington
Nunton
Bodenham
PEPPERBOX HILL
East Dean
Braishfield
Compton
NORTH WESSEX DOWNS
VALE OF PEWSEY
Wiltshire
SALISBURY PLAIN
SU
M4
A346
A338
A303
A36
A343
A30
A4
A34
B4000
37
38
26
14

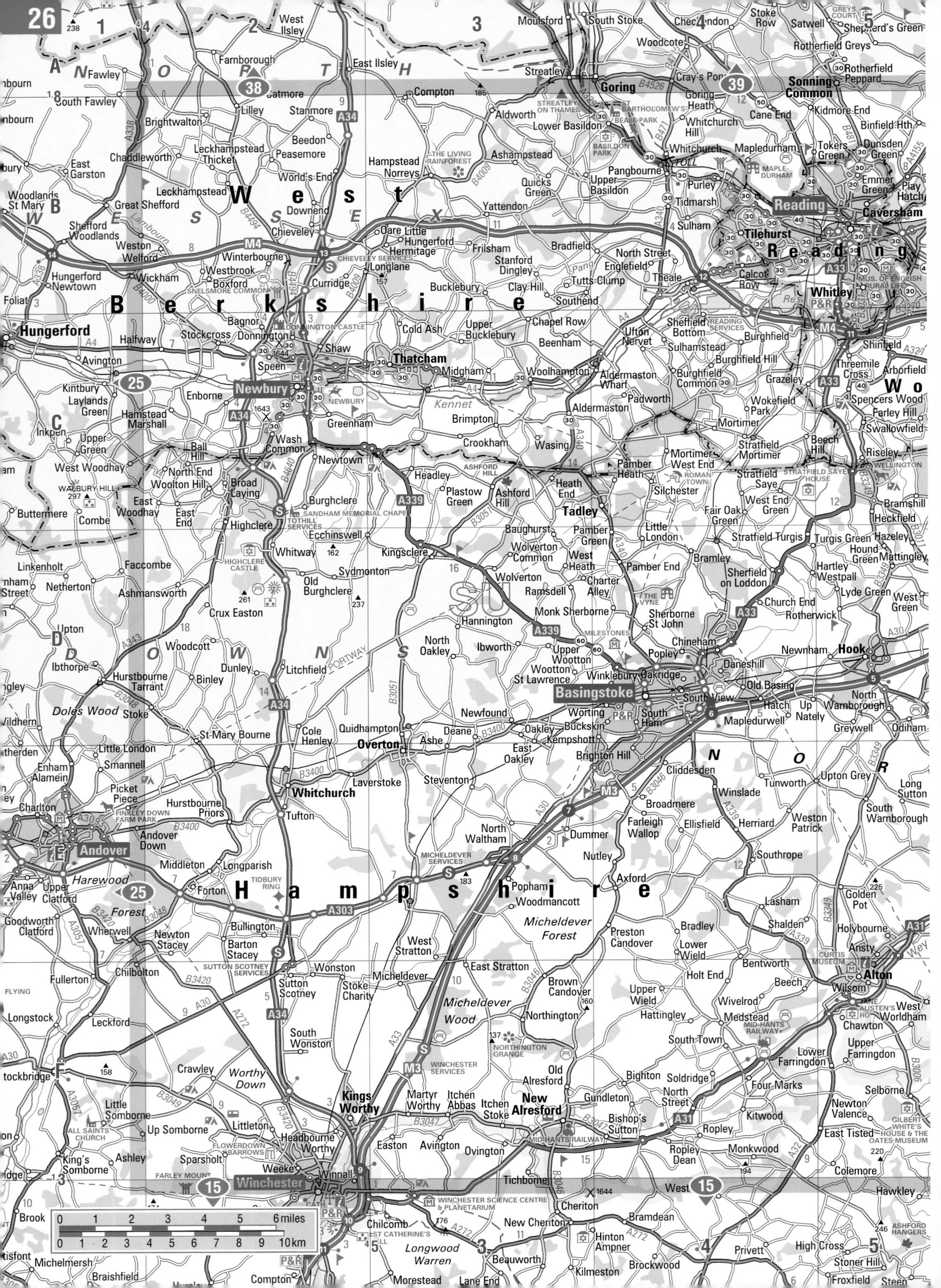
West Ilsley
Moulsford
South Stoke
Checkendon
Stoke Row
Satwell
Shepherd's Green
Farnborough
East Ilsley
Woodcote
Rotherfield Greys
Fawley
Streatley
Goring
Cray's Pond
Rotherfield Peppard
Sonning Common
South Fawley
Catmore
Compton
Goring Heath
Kidmore End
Lilley
Stanmore
Aldworth
Lower Basildon
Cane End
Brightwalton
Whitchurch Hill
Binfield Hth.
Beedon
Chaddleworth
Leckhampstead Thicket
Peasemore
Hampstead Norreys
Ashampstead
Whitchurch
Mapledurham
Tokers Green
Dunsden Green
East Garston
World's End
THE LIVING RAINFOREST
BASILDON PARK
Pangbourne
Woodlands St Mary
Leckhampstead
Quicks Green
Upper Basildon
Purley
Emmer Green
Play Hatch
Great Shefford
Downend
Yattendon
Tidmarsh
Reading
Caversham
Shefford Woodlands
Chieveley
Oare
Little Hungerford
Sulham
Tilehurst
Weston
Welford
Winterbourne
Hermitage
Frilsham
Bradfield
North Street
Westbrook
Longlane
Stanford Dingley
Englefield
Hungerford Newtown
Wickham
Boxford
Curridge
Bucklebury
Clay Hill
Tutts Clump
Theale
Calcot Row
Whitley
SNELSMORE COMMON
Southend
Berkshire
West
Bagnor
Chapel Row
Sheffield Bottom
Hungerford
Halfway
Stockcross
Donnington
DONNINGTON CASTLE
Cold Ash
Upper Bucklebury
Beenham
Ufton Nervet
Sulhamstead
Burghfield
Shinfield
Avington
Speen
Shaw
Thatcham
Midgham
Woolhampton
Aldermaston Wharf
Burghfield Hill
Threemile Cross
Arborfield
Kintbury
Newbury
Enborne
Burghfield Common
Grazeley
Laylands Green
Padworth
Wokefield Park
Spencers Wood
Hamstead Marshall
Kennet
Aldermaston
Farley Hill
Inkpen
Greenham
Brimpton
Mortimer
Swallowfield
Upper Green
Wash Common
Crookham
Wasing
Stratfield Mortimer
Beech Hill
Ball Hill
Newtown
Pamber Heath
Mortimer West End
Riseley
West Woodhay
North End
Headley
ASHFORD HILL
ROMAN TOWN
Stratfield Saye
STRATFIELD SAYE HOUSE
Woolton Hill
Broad Laying
Plastow Green
Ashford Hill
Heath End
Silchester
WALBURY HILL
East Woodhay
Burghclere
Tadley
Fair Oak Green
West End Green
Bramshill
Buttermere
Combe
East End
Highclere
SANDHAM MEMORIAL CHAPEL
TOTHILL SERVICES
Baughurst
Pamber Green
Little London
Heckfield
Ecchinswell
Stratfield Turgis
Turgis Green
Hazeley
Whitway
Kingsclere
Wolverton Common
West Heath
Bramley
Hound Green
Mattingley
Linkenholt
Faccombe
HIGHCLERE CASTLE
Sydmonton
Pamber End
Hartley Westpall
Netherton
Wolverton
Charter Alley
Sherfield on Loddon
Ashmansworth
Old Burghclere
Ramsdell
THE VYNE
Lyde Green
West Green
Church End
Crux Easton
Hannington
Monk Sherborne
Sherborne St John
Rotherwick
Upton
MILESTONES
Woodcott
North Oakley
Ibworth
Upper Wootton
Chineham
Newnham
Hook
Ibthorpe
Dunley
Litchfield
PORTWAY
Popley
Daneshill
Hurstbourne Tarrant
Binley
Wootton St Lawrence
Winklebury
Oakridge
Old Basing
North Warnborough
Basingstoke
South View
Up Nately
Doles Wood
Stoke
Newfound
Worting
South Ham
Hatch
Mapledurwell
Greywell
Odiham
St Mary Bourne
Cole Henley
Quidhampton
Deane
Oakley
Buckskin
Kempshott
Little London
Overton
Ashe
East Oakley
Brighton Hill
Smannell
Enham Alamein
Laverstoke
Steventon
Cliddesden
Tunworth
Upton Grey
Long Sutton
Picket Piece
Whitchurch
Winslade
Charlton
Hurstbourne Priors
Broadmere
South Warnborough
FINKLEY DOWN FARM PARK
Tufton
Farleigh Wallop
Ellisfield
Herriard
Weston Patrick
Andover Down
North Waltham
Dummer
Andover
Middleton
Longparish
Nutley
Southrope
MICHELDEVER SERVICES
Harewood
TIDBURY RING
Axford
Golden Pot
Anna Valley
Upper Clatford
Forton
Popham
Woodmancott
Lasham
Hampshire
Forest
Goodworth Clatford
Wherwell
Bullington
Micheldever Forest
Preston Candover
Bradley
Shalden
Holybourne
Newton Stacey
Barton Stacey
West Stratton
Lower Wield
Ansty
CURTIS MUSEUM
Chilbolton
SUTTON SCOTNEY SERVICES
Wonston
East Stratton
Holt End
Bentworth
Alton
Fullerton
Sutton Scotney
Stoke Charity
Micheldever
Brown Candover
Beech
Wilsom
FLYING
Upper Wield
Micheldever Wood
Northington
Wivelrod
JANE AUSTEN'S HO
West Worldham
Longstock
Leckford
Hattingley
Medstead
MID-HANTS RAILWAY
Chawton
South Wonston
NORTHINGTON GRANGE
South Town
Lower Farringdon
Upper Farringdon
Stockbridge
Crawley
Worthy Down
WINCHESTER SERVICES
Old Alresford
Bighton
Soldridge
Four Marks
Selborne
Little Somborne
Kings Worthy
Martyr Worthy
Itchen Abbas
Itchen Stoke
New Alresford
Gundleton
North Street
Newton Valence
Up Somborne
Littleton
Bishop's Sutton
Kitwood
ALL SAINTS CHURCH
Headbourne Worthy
Easton
Avington
Ovington
Ropley
East Tisted
GILBERT WHITE'S & THE OATES MUSEUM
FLOWERDOWN BARROWS
MID-HANTS RAILWAY
Ropley Dean
Monkwood
King's Somborne
Ashley
Sparsholt
Weeke
Winnall
Colemore
FARLEY MOUNT
Winchester
Tichborne
West
Hawkley
Brook
CATH.
WINCHESTER SCIENCE CENTRE & PLANETARIUM
Cheriton
Chilcomb
New Cheriton
Bramdean
ASHFORD HANGERS
ST CATHERINE'S
Hinton Ampner
Longwood Warren
Beauworth
Privett
High Cross
Michelmersh
Stoner Hill
Braishfield
Compton
Morestead
Lane End
Kilmeston
Brockwood
Froxfield
Steep
0 1 2 3 4 5 6 miles
0 1 2 3 4 5 6 7 8 9 10 km

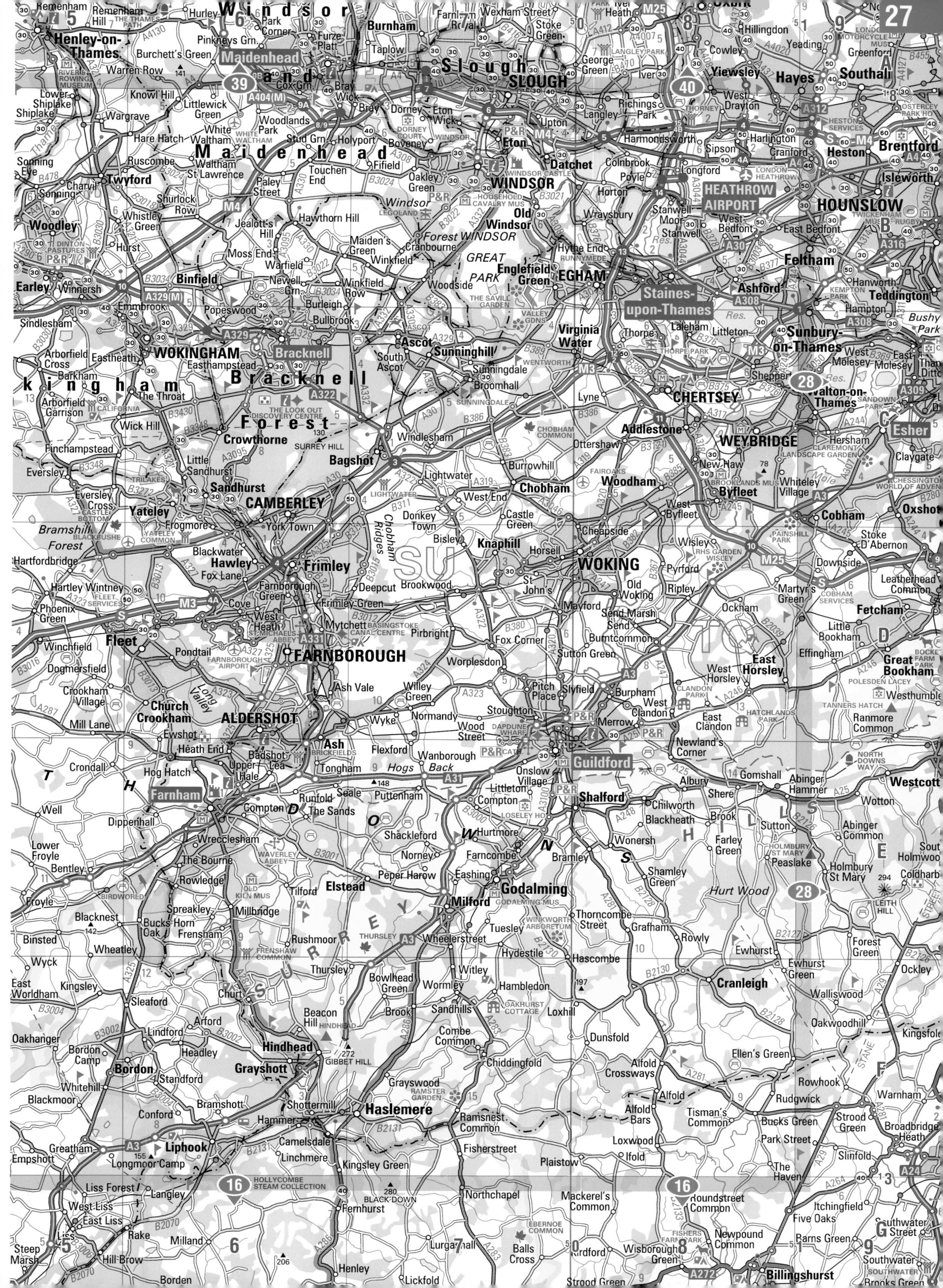

Remenham
Remenham Hill
Hurley
Windsor
Burnham
Farnham Royal
Wexham Street
Iver Heath
Hillingdon
Yeading
Henley-on-Thames
Pinkneys Grn.
Park Corner
Furze Platt
Taplow
Stoke Green
George Green
Iver
Cowley
Greenford
Burchett's Green
Maidenhead
Warren Row
Slough
SLOUGH
Yiewsley
Hayes
Southall
Lower Shiplake
Shiplake
Knowl Hill
Littlewick Green
Cox Grn.
Bray Wick
Bray
Dorney
Eton Wick
Richings Park
Langley
West Drayton
Wargrave
White Waltham
Woodlands Park
Holyport
Stud Grn.
Boveney
Upton
Eton
Harmondsworth
Harlington
Cranford
Heston
Brentford
Hare Hatch
Sonning Eye
Ruscombe
Waltham St Lawrence
Maidenhead
Fifield
Touchen End
Oakley Green
Datchet
Colnbrook
Poyle
Sipson
Longford
Isleworth
Twyford
Charvil
Sonning
Paley Street
WINDSOR
Horton
HEATHROW AIRPORT
HOUNSLOW
Woodley
Shurlock Row
Whistley Green
Hurst
Jealott's Hill
Hawthorn Hill
Windsor
Old Windsor
Wraysbury
Stanwell Moor
Stanwell
West Bedfont
East Bedfont
Maiden's Green
Cranbourne
Forest
WINDSOR GREAT PARK
Moss End
Warfield
Winkfield
Hythe End
Englefield Green
EGHAM
Feltham
Hanworth
Earley
Winnersh
Binfield
Newell Grn.
Winkfield Row
Woodside
Ashford
Teddington
Staines-upon-Thames
Sindlesham
Emmbrook
Popeswood
Burleigh
Bullbrook
Hampton
Bushy Park
Virginia Water
Thorpe
Laleham
Littleton
Sunbury-on-Thames
WOKINGHAM
Bracknell
Ascot
Sunninghill
Arborfield Cross
Eastheath
Easthampstead
South Ascot
Sunningdale
West Molesey
East Molesey
Barkham
Bracknell
Broomhall
Shepperton
Arborfield Garrison
The Throat
Lyne
CHERTSEY
Walton-on-Thames
Forest
Wick Hill
Addlestone
Esher
Finchampstead
Crowthorne
Windlesham
Ottershaw
WEYBRIDGE
Hersham
Eversley
Little Sandhurst
Bagshot
Lightwater
Burrowhill
New Haw
Claygate
Sandhurst
Chobham
Woodham
Byfleet
Whiteley Village
Eversley Cross
Yateley
CAMBERLEY
West End
West Byfleet
Cobham
Oxshott
Frogmore
York Town
Donkey Town
Castle Green
Bramshill Forest
Bisley
Knaphill
Horsell
Cheapside
Wisley
Stoke D'Abernon
Hartfordbridge
Blackwater
Hawley
Frimley
WOKING
Pyrford
Downside
Fox Lane
Farnborough Green
Deepcut
Brookwood
St John's
Old Woking
Ripley
Leatherhead Common
Hartley Wintney
Phoenix Green
Cove
Frimley Green
Mayford
Martyr's Green
Fetcham
West Heath
Mytchett
Send Marsh
Send
Ockham
Winchfield
Fleet
Pondtail
Pirbright
Burntcommon
Little Bookham
FARNBOROUGH
Fox Corner
Effingham
Dogmersfield
Worplesdon
Sutton Green
East Horsley
West Horsley
Great Bookham
Crookham Village
Church Crookham
Long Valley
Ash Vale
Willey Green
Pitch Place
Slyfield
Burpham
West Clandon
Westhumble
ALDERSHOT
Normandy
Stoughton
Merrow
East Clandon
Ranmore Common
Mill Lane
Ewshot
Wyke
Wood Street
Heath End
Ash
Flexford
Wanborough
Hogs Back
Guildford
Newland's Corner
Crondall
Badshot Lea
Upper Hale
Tongham
Onslow Village
Gomshall
Abinger Hammer
Westcott
Hog Hatch
Farnham
Seale
Puttenham
Littleton
Albury
Shere
Runfold
The Sands
Compton
Shalford
Chilworth
Wotton
Well
Dippenhall
Shackleford
Hurtmore
Blackheath
Brook
Sutton
Abinger Common
Lower Froyle
Wrecclesham
Norney
Farncombe
Wonersh
Farley Green
Holmbury St Mary
Peaslake
Bentley
The Bourne
Bramley
Rowledge
Peper Harow
Eashing
Shamley Green
South Holmwood
Froyle
Tilford
Elstead
Godalming
Milford
Hurt Wood
Coldharbour
Blacknest
Spreakley
Millbridge
Bucks Horn Oak
Frensham
Tuesley
Thorncombe Street
Grafham
Binsted
Rushmoor
Wheelerstreet
Hydestile
Rowly
Forest Green
Wyck
Wheatley
Thursley
Witley
Hascombe
Ewhurst
Ewhurst Green
Ockley
East Worldham
Kingsley
Bowlhead Green
Wormley
Hambledon
Cranleigh
Sleaford
Churt
Sandhills
Loxhill
Walliswood
Arford
Beacon Hill
Brook
Oakwoodhill
Oakhanger
Lindford
Headley
Combe Common
Dunsfold
Kingsfold
Bordon Camp
Hindhead
Ellen's Green
Bordon
Grayshott
Chiddingfold
Alfold Crossways
Whitehill
Standford
Grayswood
Rowhook
Blackmoor
Bramshott
Shottermill
Haslemere
Alfold
Rudgwick
Warnham
Conford
Hammer
Ramsnest Common
Alfold Bars
Tisman's Common
Bucks Green
Strood Green
Broadbridge Heath
Greatham
Liphook
Camelsdale
Fisherstreet
Loxwood
Park Street
Empshott
Longmoor Camp
Linchmere
Kingsley Green
Plaistow
Ifold
Slinfold
The Haven
Liss Forest
Langley
Northchapel
Mackerel's Common
Roundstreet Common
Itchingfield
West Liss
Fernhurst
Five Oaks
East Liss
Liss
Rake
Milland
Lurgashall
Balls Cross
Wisborough Green
Newpound Common
Barns Green
Southwater Street
Steep Marsh
Hill Brow
Kirdford
Southwater
Borden
Henley
Lickfold
Strood Green
Billingshurst
Brooks Green
SURREY
SU
TQ

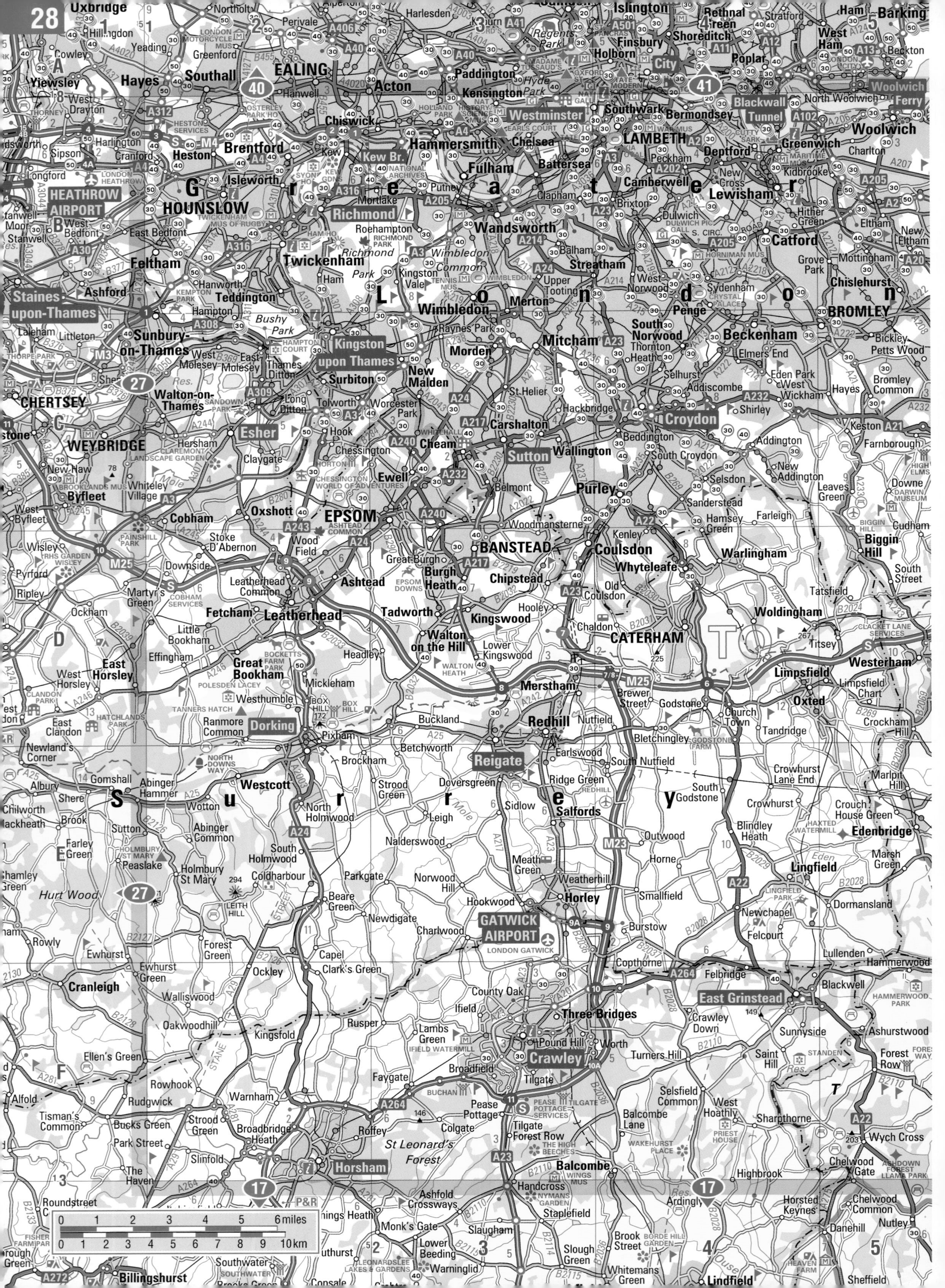
Uxbridge
Hillingdon
Northolt
Perivale
Alperton
Harlesden
Islington
Bethnal Green
Stratford
Ham
Barking
Cowley
Yeading
Greenford
Regent's Park
Finsbury
Shoreditch
West Ham
Beckton
Yiewsley
Hayes
Southall
EALING
Hanwell
Acton
Paddington
Holborn
City
Poplar
West Drayton
Kensington
Hyde Park
Westminster
Southwark
Bermondsey
Blackwall Tunnel
North Woolwich
Woolwich Ferry
Woolwich
Chiswick
Hammersmith
Chelsea
LAMBETH
Greenwich
Charlton
Harlington
Sipson
Cranford
Heston
Brentford
Kew
Kew Br.
Fulham
Battersea
Peckham
Deptford
Longford
HEATHROW AIRPORT
Isleworth
HOUNSLOW
Putney
Mortlake
Richmond
Clapham
Camberwell
New Cross
Lewisham
Kidbrooke
Stanwell
West Bedfont
East Bedfont
Roehampton
Richmond Park
Wandsworth
Brixton
Dulwich
Hither Green
Eltham
New Eltham
Feltham
Twickenham
Wimbledon Common
Balham
Streatham
Catford
Grove Park
Mottingham
Hanworth
Ham
Kingston Vale
Upper Tooting
West Norwood
Sydenham
Chislehurst
Staines upon-Thames
Ashford
Teddington
Hampton
Bushy Park
Wimbledon
Merton
Penge
BROMLEY
Laleham
Littleton
Sunbury-on-Thames
Raynes Park
Morden
Mitcham
South Norwood
Thornton Heath
Beckenham
Bickley
Petts Wood
Kingston upon Thames
West Molesey
East Molesey
Thames Ditton
Elmers End
Surbiton
New Malden
Selhurst
Eden Park
West Wickham
Hayes
Bromley Common
Shepperton
CHERTSEY
Walton-on-Thames
Long Ditton
Tolworth
Worcester Park
St Helier
Addiscombe
Shirley
Hook
Carshalton
Hackbridge
Croydon
Keston
Esher
Hersham
WEYBRIDGE
Cheam
Sutton
Wallington
Beddington
Addington
Farnborough
Claygate
Chessington
South Croydon
New Addington
New Haw
Ewell
Selsdon
Byfleet
Whiteley Village
Belmont
Purley
Downe
Leaves Green
West Byfleet
Oxshott
EPSOM
Sanderstead
Farleigh
Cobham
Woodmansterne
Hamsey Green
Cudham
Stoke D'Abernon
Wood Field
BANSTEAD
Kenley
Coulsdon
Biggin Hill
Wisley
Great Burgh
Warlingham
Pyrford
Downside
Ashtead
Burgh Heath
Chipstead
Whyteleafe
South Street
Ripley
Martyr's Green
Leatherhead Common
Old Coulsdon
Tatsfield
Ockham
Fetcham
Leatherhead
Tadworth
Kingswood
Hooley
Woldingham
Little Bookham
Chaldon
CATERHAM
Walton on the Hill
Lower Kingswood
Headley
Titsey
Effingham
Great Bookham
East Horsley
West Horsley
Mickleham
Merstham
Limpsfield
Westerham
Limpsfield Chart
Brewer Street
Godstone
Oxted
Westhumble
Box Hill
Buckland
Redhill
Nutfield
Church Town
Crockham Hill
East Clandon
Ranmore Common
Dorking
Pixham
Betchworth
Bletchingley
Tandridge
Newland's Corner
Brockham
Reigate
Earlswood
South Nutfield
Crowhurst Lane End
Marlpit Hill
Albury
Gomshall
Abinger Hammer
Westcott
Strood Green
Doversgreen
Ridge Green
South Godstone
Shere
Wotton
North Holmwood
Sidlow
Salfords
Crowhurst
Crouch House Green
Chilworth
Brook
Leigh
Sutton
Abinger Common
Blindley Heath
Outwood
Edenbridge
Farley Green
South Holmwood
Nalderswood
Peaslake
Holmbury St Mary
Horne
Marsh Green
Meath Green
Coldharbour
Parkgate
Norwood Hill
Weatherhill
Lingfield
Hurt Wood
Leith Hill
Beare Green
Hookwood
Horley
Smallfield
Dormansland
Newdigate
GATWICK AIRPORT
Burstow
Newchapel
Charlwood
Felcourt
Rowly
Ewhurst
Forest Green
Capel
Lullenden
Ewhurst Green
Ockley
Clark's Green
Copthorne
Hammerwood
Felbridge
Cranleigh
County Oak
Blackwell
Walliswood
Ifield
East Grinstead
Three Bridges
Oakwoodhill
Kingsfold
Rusper
Lambs Green
Crawley Down
Pound Hill
Sunnyside
Ashurstwood
Worth
Ellen's Green
Crawley
Turners Hill
Saint Hill
Forest Row
Broadfield
Faygate
Tilgate
Rowhook
Selsfield Common
Alfold
Rudgwick
Warnham
Pease Pottage
West Hoathly
Sharpthorne
Tisman's Common
Bucks Green
Strood Green
Broadbridge Heath
Roffey
Colgate
Balcombe Lane
Wych Cross
Park Street
Slinfold
St Leonard's Forest
Tilgate Forest Row
The Haven
Horsham
Balcombe
Chelwood Gate
Highbrook
Roundstreet Common
Handcross
Ashfold Crossways
Ardingly
Horsted Keynes
Chelwood Common
Monk's Gate
Staplefield
Slaugham
Danehill
Nutley
Lower Beeding
Brook Street
Slough Green
Southwater
Warninglid
Whitemans Green
Lindfield
Sheffield
Billingshurst
Woolwich
Thamesmead
M25
M23
M3
M4
A3
A22
A23
A24
A25
A264
miles
km
0 1 2 3 4 5 6 miles
0 1 2 3 4 5 6 7 8 9 10 km
G r e a t e r
L o n d o n
S u r r e y

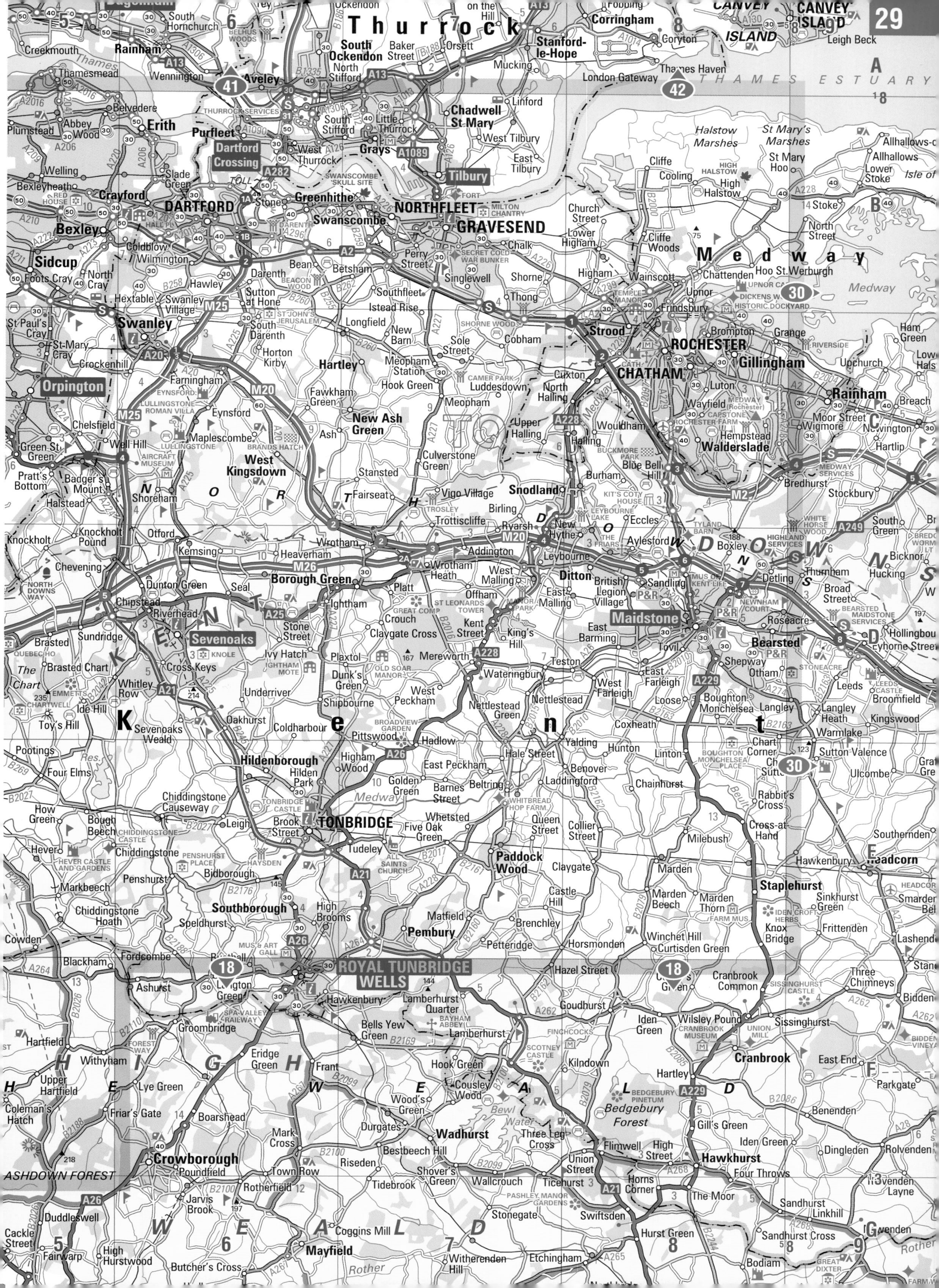
Thurrock
South Hornchurch
Rainham
Creekmouth
Thames
Thamesmead
Wennington
Aveley
South Ockendon
North Stifford
Baker Street
Orsett
Stanford-le-Hope
Corringham
Fobbing
Coryton
CANVEY ISLAND
Leigh Beck
Mucking
London Gateway
Thames Haven
THAMES ESTUARY
Linford
Chadwell St Mary
West Tilbury
East Tilbury
Tilbury
Belvedere
Erith
Abbey Wood
Plumstead
Purfleet
Dartford Crossing
THURROCK SERVICES
South Stifford
Little Thurrock
West Thurrock
Grays
Welling
Bexleyheath
Crayford
Slade Green
DARTFORD
Stone
Greenhithe
Swanscombe
NORTHFLEET
GRAVESEND
MILTON CHANTRY
SWANSCOMBE SKULL SITE
Bexley
Coldblow
Wilmington
Sidcup
Foots Cray
North Cray
Hawley
Darenth
Bean
Betsham
Perry Street
SECRET COLD WAR BUNKER
Chalk
Singlewell
Shorne
Thong
Hextable
Swanley Village
Sutton at Hone
South Darenth
Swanley
Horton Kirby
Southfleet
Istead Rise
Longfield
New Barn
Hartley
Sole Street
Cobham
SHORNE WOODS
Meopham Station
Hook Green
Meopham
St Paul's Cray
St Mary Cray
Crockenhill
Farningham
Orpington
EYNSFORD
LULLINGSTONE ROMAN VILLA
Eynsford
Maplescombe
LULLINGSTONE
BRANDS HATCH
Fawkham Green
New Ash Green
Ash
West Kingsdown
Chelsfield
Well Hill
Green St Green
Pratt's Bottom
Badger's Mount
AIRCRAFT MUSEUM
Halstead
Shoreham
NORTH DOWNS
Stansted
Culverstone Green
Fairseat
Vigo Village
TROSLEY
Trottiscliffe
Knockholt
Knockholt Pound
Otford
Kemsing
Heaverham
Wrotham
Chevening
Dunton Green
Seal
Borough Green
Wrotham Heath
Platt
Addington
Chipstead
Riverhead
Sevenoaks
Stone Street
Ightham
Sundridge
Brasted
Brasted Chart
The Chart
EMMETTS
CHARTWELL
Ide Hill
Toy's Hill
KNOLE
Cross Keys
Whitley Row
Sevenoaks Weald
Underriver
Ivy Hatch
IGHTHAM MOTE
Plaxtol
Dunk's Green
Shipbourne
Oakhurst
Coldharbour
Kent
Hildenborough
Hilden Park
Pootings
Four Elms
How Green
Bough Beech
Chiddingstone Causeway
Leigh
TONBRIDGE CASTLE
TONBRIDGE
Brook Street
Hever
HEVER CASTLE AND GARDENS
Chiddingstone
CHIDDINGSTONE CASTLE
PENSHURST PLACE
Penshurst
Bidborough
HAYSDEN
Markbeech
Chiddingstone Hoath
Speldhurst
Southborough
High Brooms
Cowden
Blackham
Fordcombe
Ashurst
Langton Green
ROYAL TUNBRIDGE WELLS
Hawkenbury
Groombridge
SPA VALLEY RAILWAY
Hartfield
Withyham
Upper Hartfield
Lye Green
Coleman's Hatch
Friar's Gate
Eridge Green
Frant
Boarshead
Crowborough
ASHDOWN FOREST
Poundfield
Jarvis Brook
Rotherfield
Town Row
Duddleswell
Cackle Street
Fairwarp
High Hurstwood
Butcher's Cross
Mayfield
Coggins Mill
Rother
WEALD
Mark Cross
Durgates
Wadhurst
Wood's Green
Cousley Wood
Bewl Water
Best Beech Hill
Riseden
Tidebrook
Shover's Green
Wallcrouch
Ticehurst
Stonegate
PASHLEY MANOR GARDENS
Witherenden Hill
Etchingham
Swiftsden
Union Street
Flimwell
High Street
Three Leg Cross
Hurst Green
Horns Corner
The Moor
Hawkhurst
Four Throws
Bodiam
Sandhurst
Sandhurst Cross
Linkhill
Newenden
Rolvenden Layne
Dingleden
Rolvenden
GREAT DIXTER
Iden Green
Gill's Green
Bedgebury Forest
BEDGEBURY PINETUM
Kilndown
SCOTNEY CASTLE
Lamberhurst
Lamberhurst Quarter
BAYHAM ABBEY
Bells Yew Green
Hook Green
FINCHCOCKS
Goudhurst
Iden Green
CRANBROOK MUSEUM
Wilsley Pound
Cranbrook
Hartley
Sissinghurst
SISSINGHURST CASTLE
UNION MILL
Cranbrook Common
Three Chimneys
Benenden
East End
Parkgate
Frittenden
Biddenden
Hazel Street
Curtisden Green
Winchet Hill
Horsmonden
Pembury
Petteridge
Matfield
Brenchley
Castle Hill
Paddock Wood
Claygate
Marden
Marden Beech
Marden Thorn
FARM MUS
Staplehurst
IDEN CROFT HERBS
Knox Bridge
Sinkhurst Green
Headcorn
Smarden
Lashenden
Hawkenbury
Cross-at-Hand
Milebush
Chainhurst
Collier Street
Queen Street
Beltring
WHITBREAD HOP FARM
Laddingford
Benover
Five Oak Green
Whetsted
Tudeley
ALL SAINTS CHURCH
Golden Green
Barnes Street
East Peckham
Hale Street
Hadlow
Pittswood
BROADVIEW GARDEN
Higham Wood
Medway
Yalding
Hunton
Linton
BOUGHTON MONCHELSEA PLACE
Chart Corner
Chart Sutton
Sutton Valence
Ulcombe
Rabbit's Cross
Southernden
West Peckham
Nettlestead
Nettlestead Green
Wateringbury
Mereworth
OLD SOAR MANOR
GREAT COMP
Crouch
Claygate Cross
Offham
ST LEONARDS TOWER
Kent Street
King's Hill
Teston
West Farleigh
East Farleigh
Coxheath
Loose
Boughton Monchelsea
Langley
Langley Heath
Warmlake
Kingswood
Leeds
LEEDS CASTLE
Broomfield
Otham
Shepway
Tovil
Maidstone
East Barming
Bearsted
STONEACRE
MAIDSTONE SERVICES
Hollingbourne
Eyhorne Street
Roseacre
NEWNHAM COURT
Thurnham
Detling
Broad Street
Bicknor
Hucking
Sandling
MUS OF KENT LIFE
Boxley
Aylesford
Ditton
British Legion Village
East Malling
West Malling
MANOR PARK
Leybourne
New Hythe
Ryarsh
Birling
Snodland
Eccles
KIT'S COTY HOUSE
LEYBOURNE LAKE
THE FRIARS
TYLAND BARN
Burham
Blue Bell Hill
BUCKMORE PARK
Wouldham
Halling
Upper Halling
North Halling
Cuxton
Luddesdown
CAMER PARK
Strood
ROCHESTER
CHATHAM
Gillingham
Luton
Wayfield
CAPSTONE
Walderslade
Hempstead
Wigmore
Moor Street
Rainham
Hartlip
Bredhurst
Stockbury
MEDWAY SERVICES
South Green
Upchurch
Grange
RIVERSIDE
Brompton
Frindsbury
Upnor
Chattenden
Hoo St Werburgh
UPNOR CASTLE
DICKENS WORLD
HISTORIC DOCKYARD
Wainscott
TEMPLE MANOR
Higham
Lower Higham
Church Street
Cliffe
Cliffe Woods
Cooling
High Halstow
Halstow Marshes
St Mary's Marshes
St Mary Hoo
Allhallows
Lower Stoke
Stoke
North Street
Isle of Grain
Medway
Ham Green
Breach
Newington
HEADCORN

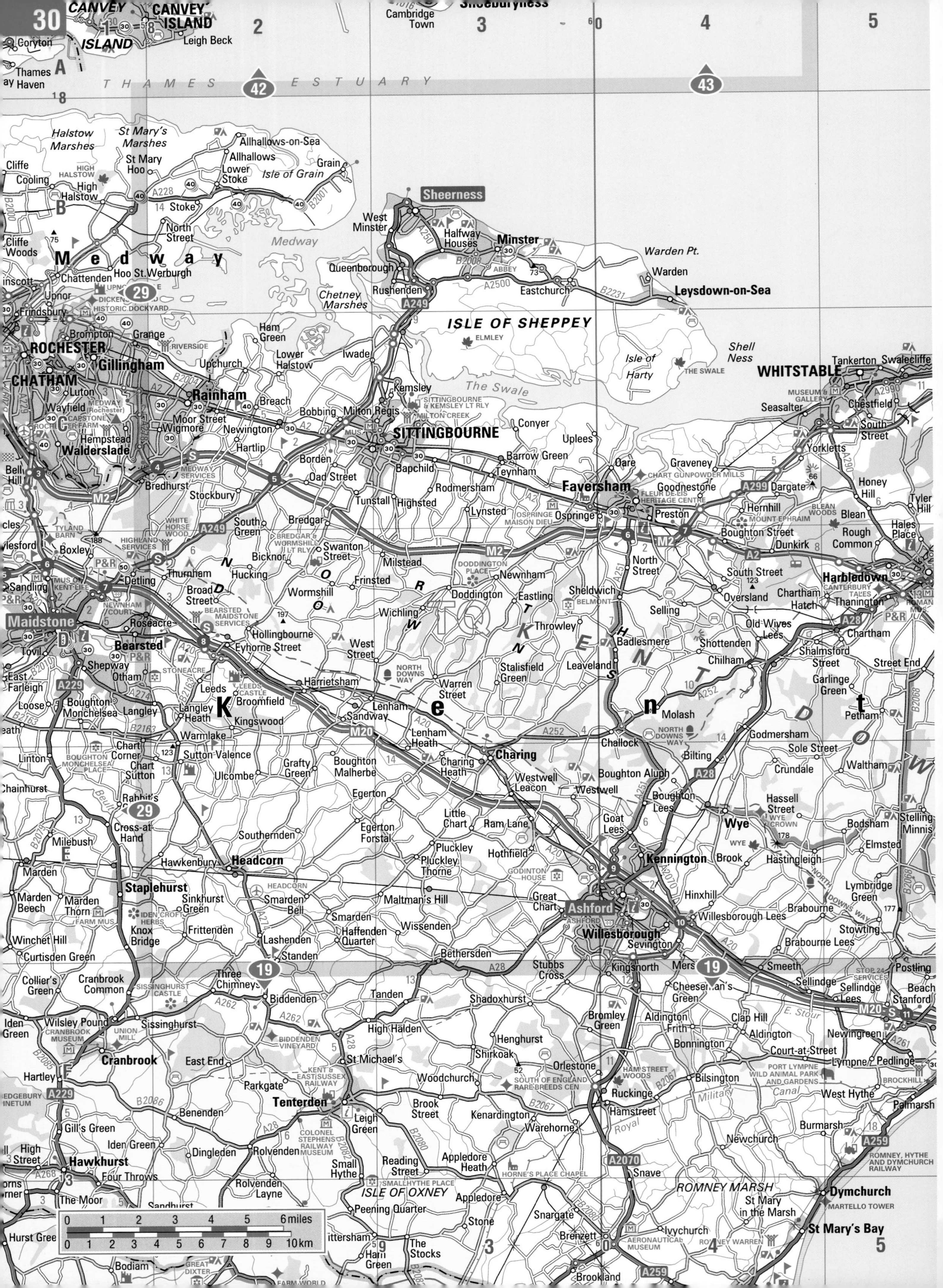

CANVEY ISLAND
Coryton
Thames Haven
Leigh Beck
Cambridge Town
Shoeburyness
THAMES ESTUARY
42
43
Halstow Marshes
St Mary's Marshes
Allhallows-on-Sea
Allhallows
Grain
St Mary Hoo
Lower Stoke
Isle of Grain
Cliffe
Cooling
High Halstow
Stoke
North Street
Medway
Cliffe Woods
Sheerness
West Minster
Halfway Houses
Minster
Warden Pt.
Warden
Queenborough
Rushenden
Eastchurch
Leysdown-on-Sea
ABBEY
Chattenden
Hoo St.Werburgh
Upnor
Frindsbury
HISTORIC DOCKYARD
Chetney Marshes
ISLE OF SHEPPEY
ELMLEY
Brompton
Grange
ROCHESTER
Gillingham
CHATHAM
Ham Green
Lower Halstow
Iwade
Upchurch
RIVERSIDE
Shell Ness
Isle of Harty
THE SWALE
WHITSTABLE
Tankerton
Swalecliffe
Luton
Rainham
Breach
Kemsley
SITTINGBOURNE & KEMSLEY LT RLY
MILTON CREEK
The Swale
Wayfield
Moor Street
Bobbing
Milton Regis
SITTINGBOURNE
Conyer
Seasalter
Chestfield
Hempstead
Wigmore
Newington
Walderslade
Hartlip
Uplees
South Street
Yorkletts
Borden
Barrow Green
Oare
Graveney
CHART GUNPOWDER MILLS
Bell Hill
MEDWAY SERVICES
Bredhurst
Oad Street
Bapchild
Teynham
Stockbury
Rodmersham
Faversham
Goodnestone
FLEUR DE LIS HERITAGE CENTRE
Dargate
Honey Hill
Tyler Hill
Tunstall
Highsted
Lynsted
OSPRINGE MAISON DIEU
Ospringe
Preston
Hernhill
MOUNT EPHRAIM
BLEAN WOODS
Blean
WHITE HORSE WOOD
South Green
Bredgar
BREDGAR & WORMSHILL LT RLY
TYLAND BARN
HIGHLAND SERVICES
Boxley
Swanton Street
Boughton Street
Rough Common
Hales Place
Dunkirk
Bicknor
Milstead
DODDINGTON PLACE
North Street
South Street
Harbledown
Thurnham
Hucking
Detling
Fristed
Newnham
Sheldwich
BELMONT
Sandling
MUS OF KENT LIFE
Broad Street
Wormshill
Doddington
Eastling
Oversland
Chartham Hatch
Thanington
CANTERBURY TALES
NEWNHAM COURT
Maidstone
Roseacre
BEARSTED MAIDSTONE SERVICES
Hollingbourne
Wichling
Throwley
Selling
Old Wives Lees
Chartham
Tovil
Bearsted
Eyhorne Street
West Street
Badlesmere
Shottenden
Shalmsford Street
Shepway
Otham
STONEACRE
NORTH DOWNS WAY
Stalisfield Green
Leaveland
Chilham
Street End
East Farleigh
Leeds
LEEDS CASTLE
Harrietsham
Warren Street
Garlinge Green
Loose
Boughton Monchelsea
Langley
Langley Heath
Broomfield
Lenham
Sandway
Molash
Petham
Kingswood
Lenham Heath
Warmlake
Challock
NORTH DOWNS WAY
Godmersham
Chart Corner
Chart Sutton
Sutton Valence
BOUGHTON MONCHELSEA PLACE
Linton
Charing
Charing Heath
Grafty Green
Boughton Malherbe
Sole Street
Waltham
Bilting
Ulcombe
Westwell Leacon
Westwell
Boughton Aluph
Crundale
Chainhurst
Rabbit's Cross
Cross-at-Hand
Egerton
Boughton Lees
Hassell Street
Little Chart
Ram Lane
Goat Lees
Wye
WYE CROWN
Bodsham
Stelling Minnis
Milebush
Southernden
Egerton Forstal
Pluckley
Hothfield
WYE
Elmsted
Marden
Hawkenbury
Headcorn
Pluckley Thorne
Kennington
Brook
Hastingleigh
GODINTON HOUSE
Staplehurst
HEADCORN
Lymbridge Green
Marden Beech
Marden Thorn
FARM MUS
IDEN CROFT HERBS
Sinkhurst Green
Smarden Bell
Maltman's Hill
Great Chart
Ashford
Hinxhill
Brabourne
Smarden
Haffenden Quarter
Wissenden
Willesborough
Willesborough Lees
Stowting
Winchet Hill
Knox Bridge
Frittenden
Lashenden
Sevington
Brabourne Lees
Curtisden Green
Standen
Bethersden
Stubbs Cross
Kingsnorth
Mersham
Smeeth
Postling
Collier's Green
Cranbrook Common
SISSINGHURST CASTLE
Three Chimneys
Biddenden
Tanden
Shadoxhurst
Cheeseman's Green
Sellindge
STOP 24 SERVICES
Beach
Stanford
Iden Green
Wilsley Pound
CRANBROOK MUSEUM
UNION MILL
Sissinghurst
BIDDENDEN VINEYARD
High Halden
Bromley Green
Aldington Frith
Clap Hill
E. Stour
Aldington
Newingreen
Henghurst
Bonnington
Court-at-Street
Cranbrook
East End
Shirkoak
Orlestone
HAM STREET WOODS
PORT LYMPNE WILD ANIMAL PARK AND GARDENS
Lympne
Pedlinge
Hartley
KENT & EAST SUSSEX RAILWAY
St Michael's
Parkgate
Woodchurch
SOUTH OF ENGLAND RARE BREEDS CEN
Ruckinge
Bilsington
BROCKHILL
BEDGEBURY PINETUM
Tenterden
Leigh Green
Brook Street
Kenardington
Hamstreet
Military Canal
West Hythe
Palmarsh
Benenden
Warehorne
Royal
Gill's Green
COLONEL STEPHENS RAILWAY MUSEUM
Burmarsh
Iden Green
Newchurch
High Street
Dingleden
Rolvenden
Small Hythe
Reading Street
Appledore Heath
HORNE'S PLACE CHAPEL
ROMNEY, HYTHE AND DYMCHURCH RAILWAY
Hawkhurst
Four Throws
Snave
Rolvenden Layne
SMALLHYTHE PLACE
ISLE OF OXNEY
Appledore
ROMNEY MARSH
Dymchurch
MARTELLO TOWER
The Moor
Sandhurst
Peening Quarter
St Mary in the Marsh
Stone
Snargate
Ivychurch
Hurst Green
Wittersham
Hare Green
The Stocks
Brenzett
AERONAUTICAL MUSEUM
ROMNEY WARREN
St Mary's Bay
Bodiam
GREAT DIXTER
FARM WORLD
Brookland
Medway
Kent
NORTH DOWNS
TQ
0 1 2 3 4 5 6 miles
0 1 2 3 4 5 6 7 8 9 10km

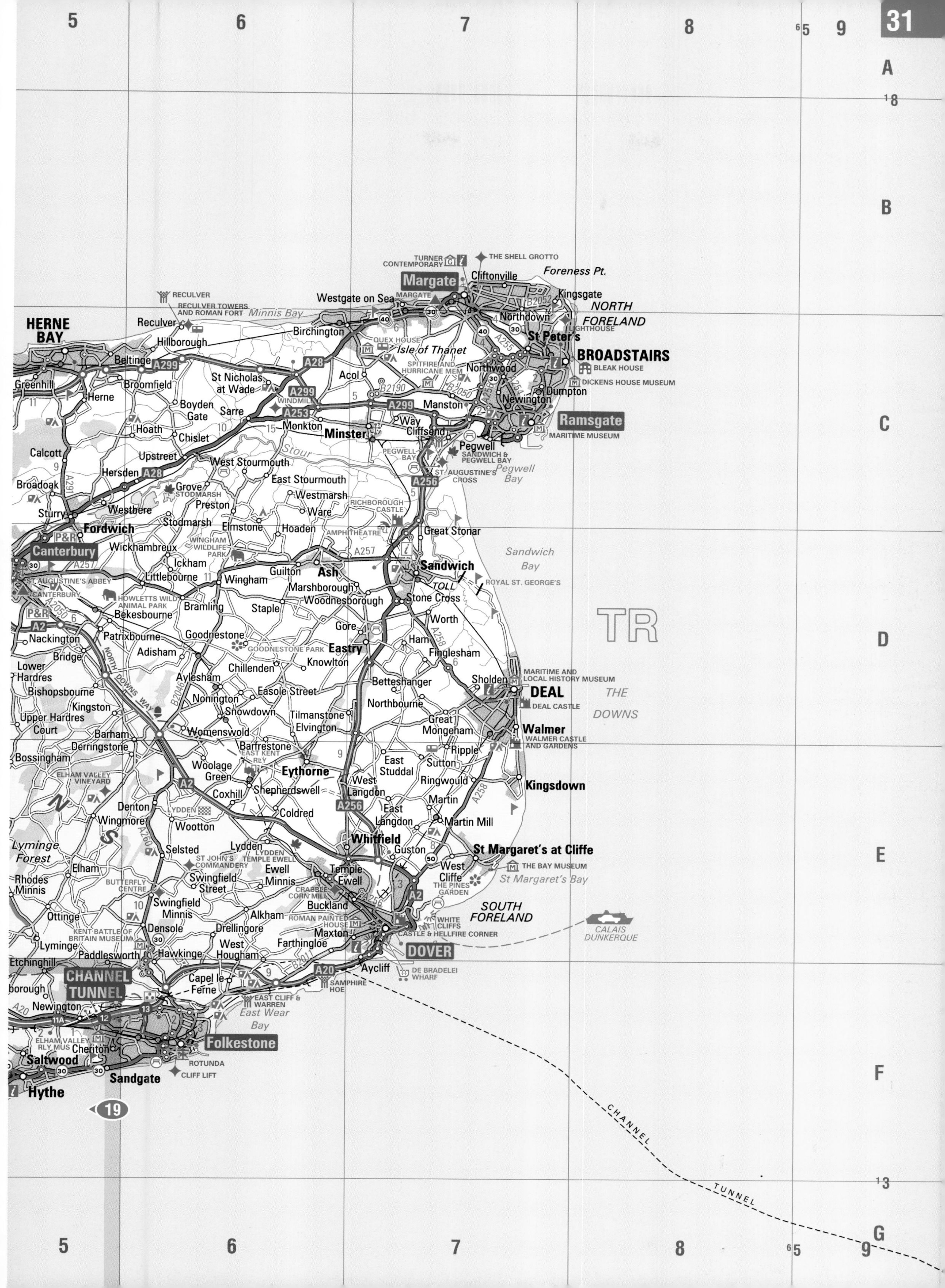

5
6
7
8
9
A
B
C
D
E
F
G
TR
Margate
Cliftonville
Foreness Pt.
TURNER CONTEMPORARY
THE SHELL GROTTO
Westgate on Sea
Kingsgate
NORTH FORELAND
Northdown
St Peter's
BROADSTAIRS
BLEAK HOUSE
DICKENS HOUSE MUSEUM
Dumpton
Newington
Ramsgate
MARITIME MUSEUM
Northwood
Isle of Thanet
QUEX HOUSE
SPITFIRE AND HURRICANE MEM
Acol
Manston
Birchington
RECULVER
RECULVER TOWERS AND ROMAN FORT
Minnis Bay
Reculver
HERNE BAY
Hillborough
Beltinge
Greenhill
Broomfield
Herne
St Nicholas at Wade
Sarre
Boyden Gate
Hoath
Chislet
Monkton
Minster
Way
Cliffsend
Pegwell
SANDWICH & PEGWELL BAY
Pegwell Bay
ST. AUGUSTINE'S CROSS
Calcott
Upstreet
Hersden
West Stourmouth
East Stourmouth
Stour
Broadoak
Grove
STODMARSH
Preston
Westmarsh
Ware
RICHBOROUGH CASTLE
Sturry
Westbere
Fordwich
Stodmarsh
Elmstone
Hoaden
AMPHITHEATRE
Great Stonar
Canterbury
Wickhambreux
WINGHAM WILDLIFE PARK
Ickham
Littlebourne
Wingham
Guilton
Ash
Sandwich
Sandwich Bay
ROYAL ST. GEORGE'S
TOLL
ST. AUGUSTINE'S ABBEY
CANTERBURY
HOWLETTS WILD ANIMAL PARK
Bekesbourne
Bramling
Staple
Marshborough
Woodnesborough
Stone Cross
Worth
Nackington
Patrixbourne
Goodnestone
GOODNESTONE PARK
Gore
Eastry
Ham
Finglesham
Bridge
Adisham
Knowlton
Lower Hardres
Chillenden
Bishopsbourne
Aylesham
Easole Street
Betteshanger
Sholden
MARITIME AND LOCAL HISTORY MUSEUM
DEAL
DEAL CASTLE
THE DOWNS
Kingston
Nonington
Northbourne
Upper Hardres Court
Snowdown
Tilmanstone
Elvington
Great Mongeham
Walmer
WALMER CASTLE AND GARDENS
Barham
Womenswold
Derringstone
Barfrestone
EAST KENT RLY
Ripple
Bossingham
Woolage Green
Eythorne
East Studdal
Sutton
ELHAM VALLEY VINEYARD
Shepherdswell
West Langdon
Ringwould
Kingsdown
Coxhill
Martin
Denton
LYDDEN PARK
Coldred
East Langdon
Martin Mill
Wingmore
Wootton
Whitfield
Lyminge Forest
Selsted
Lydden
LYDDEN TEMPLE EWELL
Guston
St Margaret's at Cliffe
THE BAY MUSEUM
ST JOHN'S COMMANDERY
Elham
Swingfield Street
Ewell Minnis
Temple Ewell
West Cliffe
THE PINES GARDEN
St Margaret's Bay
Rhodes Minnis
BUTTERFLY CENTRE
CRABBLE CORN MILL
Buckland
SOUTH FORELAND
Swingfield Minnis
Ottinge
Alkham
ROMAN PAINTED HOUSE
WHITE CLIFFS
CASTLE & HELLFIRE CORNER
CALAIS DUNKERQUE
KENT BATTLE OF BRITAIN MUSEUM
Densole
Drellingore
Maxton
Lyminge
Farthingloe
West Hougham
Hawkinge
Paddlesworth
DOVER
Etchinghill
CHANNEL TUNNEL
Capel le Ferne
Aycliff
DE BRADELEI WHARF
SAMPHIRE HOE
EAST CLIFF & WARREN
East Wear Bay
Newington
ELHAM VALLEY RLY MUS
Cheriton
Folkestone
ROTUNDA
CLIFF LIFT
Saltwood
Sandgate
Hythe
19
CHANNEL TUNNEL
A299
A28
A253
A257
A2
A20
A256
A258
A255
A254
B2052
B2190
B2050
A291
A2050
B2046
A260
B2011
P&R
NORTH DOWNS WAY

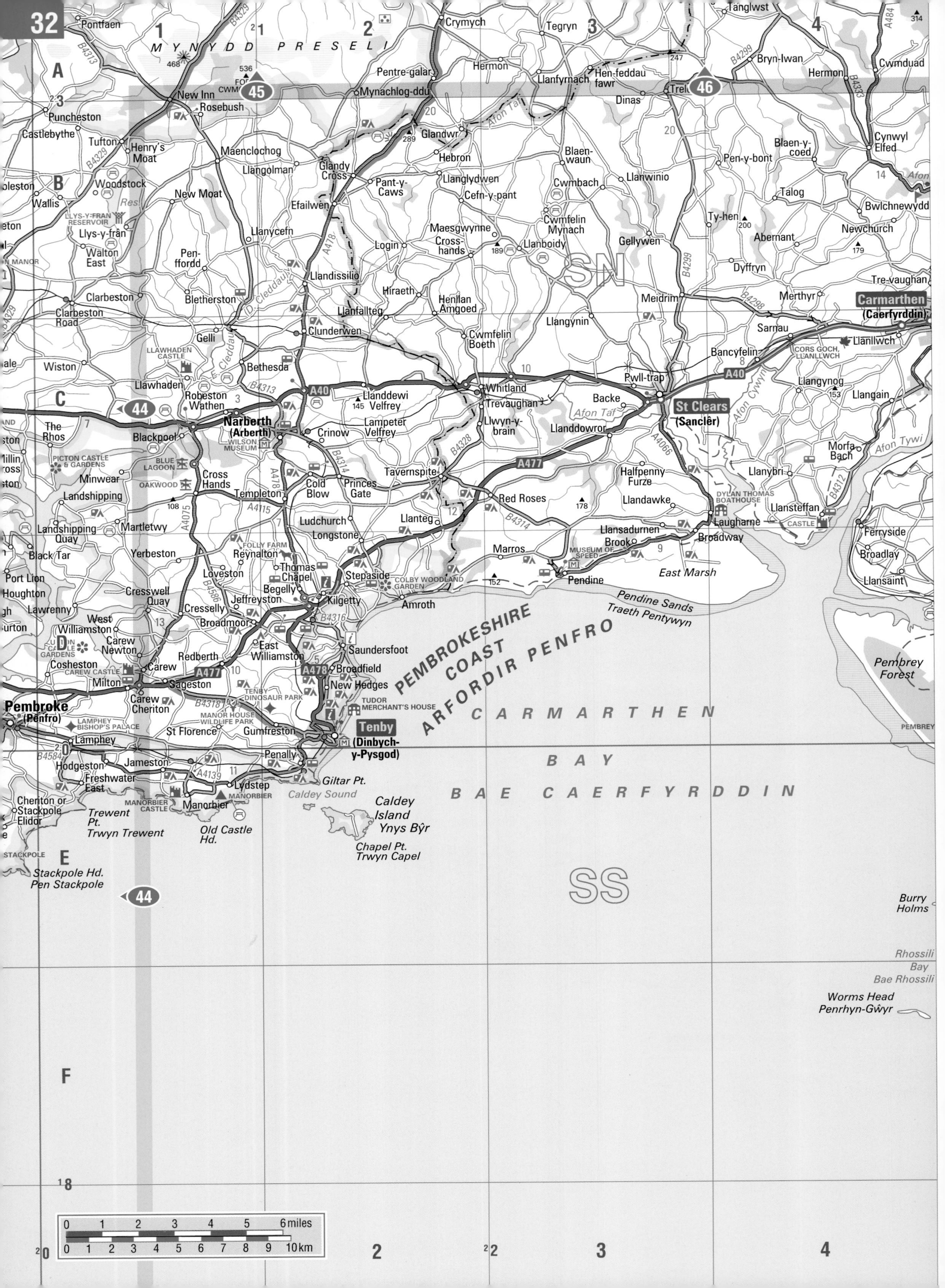

MYNYDD PRESELI
Pontfaen
Crymych
Tegryn
Tanglwst
Pentre-galar
Hermon
Llanfyrnach
Hen-feddau fawr
Bryn-Iwan
Cwmduad
New Inn
Rosebush
Mynachlog-ddu
Dinas
Trelech
Puncheston
Castlebythe
Tufton
Henry's Moat
Maenclochog
Glandwr
Hebron
Blaen-waun
Pen-y-bont
Blaen-y-coed
Cynwyl Elfed
Llangolman
Glandy Cross
Pant-y-Caws
Llanglydwen
Cefn-y-pant
Cwmbach
Llanwinio
Talog
Woodstock
Wallis
New Moat
Efailwen
Bwlchnewydd
LLYS-Y-FRAN RESERVOIR
Llys-y-frân
Walton East
Llanycefn
Maesgwynne
Cross-hands
Cwmfelin Mynach
Llanboidy
Gellywen
Ty-hen
Abernant
Newchurch
Login
Pen-ffordd
Dyffryn
Llandissilio
Hiraeth
Henllan Amgoed
Meidrim
Merthyr
Tre-vaughan
Carmarthen (Caerfyrddin)
Clarbeston
Bletherston
Clarbeston Road
Llanfallteg
Clunderwen
Cwmfelin Boeth
Llangynin
Sarnau
Bancyfelin
Llanllwch
CORS GOCH, LLANLLWCH
Gelli
LLAWHADEN CASTLE
Wiston
Bethesda
Llawhaden
Robeston Wathen
Llanddewi Velfrey
Whitland
Trevaughan
Pwll-trap
Backe
St Clears (Sanclêr)
Llangynog
Llangain
The Rhos
Narberth (Arberth)
WILSON MUSEUM
Crinow
Lampeter Velfrey
Llwyn-y-brain
Llanddowror
Afon Taf
Afon Cywyn
Afon Tywi
Blackpool
PICTON CASTLE & GARDENS
BLUE LAGOON
Minwear
OAKWOOD
Cross Hands
Templeton
Cold Blow
Princes Gate
Tavernspite
Halfpenny Furze
Llanybri
Morfa Bach
Landshipping
Red Roses
Landshipping Quay
Martletwy
Ludchurch
Llanteg
Llandawke
DYLAN THOMAS BOATHOUSE
Llansteffan
Laugharne
CASTLE
Ferryside
Black Tar
Yerbeston
FOLLY FARM
Reynalton
Longstone
Llansadurnen
Brook
Broadway
Broadlay
Port Lion
Houghton
Loveston
Thomas Chapel
Stepaside
COLBY WOODLAND GARDEN
Marros
MUSEUM OF SPEED
Pendine
East Marsh
Llansaint
Cresswell Quay
Begelly
Jeffreyston
Kilgetty
Amroth
Pendine Sands
Traeth Pentywyn
Lawrenny
Cresselly
West Williamston
Broadmoor
Carew Newton
East Williamston
Saundersfoot
PEMBROKESHIRE COAST
ARFORDIR PENFRO
Cosheston
CAREW CASTLE
Carew
Redberth
Milton
Sageston
Broadfield
New Hedges
TENBY DINOSAUR PARK
TUDOR MERCHANT'S HOUSE
Pembroke (Penfro)
LAMPHEY BISHOP'S PALACE
Carew Cheriton
MANOR HOUSE WILDLIFE PARK
St Florence
Gumfreston
Tenby (Dinbych-y-Pysgod)
CARMARTHEN BAY
BAE CAERFYRDDIN
Pembrey Forest
PEMBREY
Lamphey
Hodgeston
Jameston
Penally
Freshwater East
Lydstep
Giltar Pt.
Caldey Sound
MANORBIER CASTLE
Manorbier
Cheriton or Stackpole Elidor
Trewent Pt.
Trwyn Trewent
Old Castle Hd.
Caldey Island
Ynys Bŷr
Chapel Pt.
Trwyn Capel
STACKPOLE
Stackpole Hd.
Pen Stackpole
SN
SS
Burry Holms
Rhossili Bay
Bae Rhossili
Worms Head
Penrhyn-Gŵyr
A40
A477
A478
A4075
A4115
A4066
A4139
B4313
B4329
B4314
B4328
B4316
B4318
B4586
B4584
B4299
B4298
B4312
B4333
A484
44
45
46
0 1 2 3 4 5 6 miles
0 1 2 3 4 5 6 7 8 9 10 km

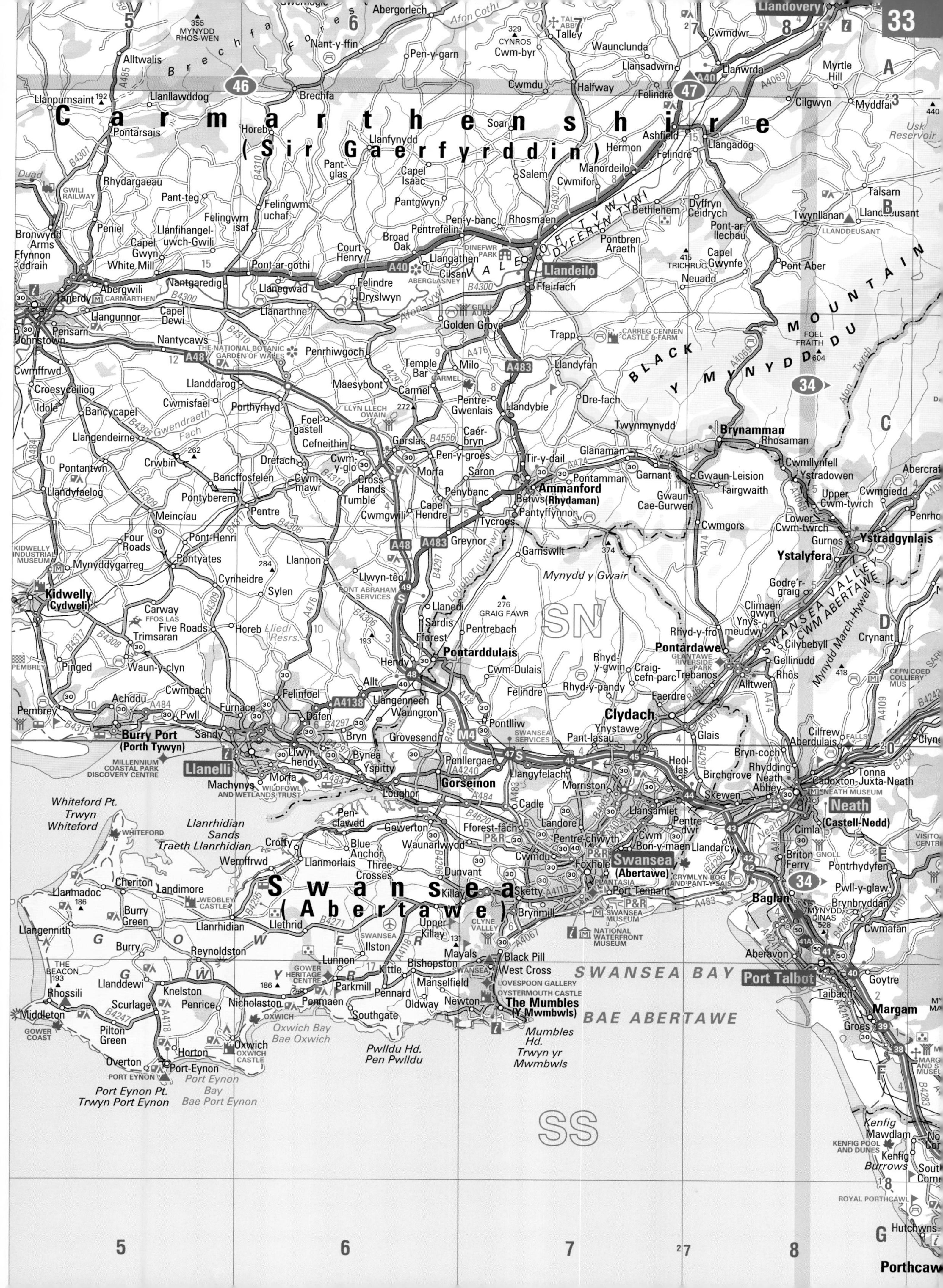

33
Carmarthenshire
(Sir Gaerfyrddin)
Swansea
(Abertawe)
Brechfa Forest
VALE OF TYWI
DYFFRYN TYWI
BLACK MOUNTAIN
Y MYNYDD DU
SWANSEA VALLEY
CWM ABERTAWE
Mynydd March-Hywel
Mynydd y Gwair
SWANSEA BAY
BAE ABERTAWE
GOWER
SN
SS
Llandovery
Abergorlech
Nant-y-ffin
Alltwalis
Brechfa
Llanllawddog
Llanpumsaint
Pontarsais
Horeb
Llanfynydd
Talley
Cwm-byr
Pen-y-garn
Cwmdu
Halfway
Waunclunda
Llansadwrn
Llanwrda
Cwmdwr
Myrtle Hill
Cilgwyn
Myddfai
Felindre
Ashfield
Llangadog
Usk Reservoir
Soar
Hermon
Manordeilo
Salem
Cwmifor
Capel Isaac
Pant-glas
Pantgwyn
Rhydargaeau
Pant-teg
Felingwm uchaf
Felingwm isaf
Peniel
Capel Gwyn
Llanfihangel-uwch-Gwili
Bronwydd Arms
Ffynnon ddrain
White Mill
Pont-ar-gothi
Court Henry
Broad Oak
Pentrefelin
Pen-y-banc
Rhosmaen
Bethlehem
Dyffryn Ceidrych
Pont-ar-llechau
Talsarn
Twynllanan
Llanddeusant
Llangathen
Cilsan
Llandeilo
Ffairfach
Capel Gwynfe
Pont Aber
Neuadd
Abergwili
Nantgaredig
Llanegwad
Felindre
Dryslwyn
Llanarthne
Golden Grove
Trapp
Carreg Cennen Castle & Farm
Foel Fraith
Llangunnor
Capel Dewi
Pensarn
Johnstown
Nantycaws
The National Botanic Garden of Wales
Penrhiwgoch
Temple Bar
Milo
Llandyfan
Cwmffrwd
Croesyceiliog
Llanddarog
Maesybont
Carmel
Pentre-Gwenlais
Llandybie
Dre-fach
Idole
Bancycapel
Cwmisfael
Porthyrhyd
Foel-gastell
Llyn Llech Owain
Twynmynydd
Brynamman
Rhosaman
Llangendeirne
Cefneithin
Gorslas
Caer-bryn
Glanaman
Cwmllynfell
Ystradowen
Pontantwn
Crwbin
Drefach
Cwm-y-glo
Morfa
Pen-y-groes
Tir-y-dail
Pontamman
Garnant
Gwaun-Leision
Tairgwaith
Llandyfaelog
Bancffosfelen
Cwm-mawr
Cross Hands
Saron
Ammanford
Betws (Rhydaman)
Gwaun-Cae-Gurwen
Upper Cwm-twrch
Cwmgiedd
Pontyberem
Tumble
Penybanc
Pantyffynnon
Lower Cwm-twrch
Meinciau
Pentre
Cwmgwili
Capel Hendre
Tycroes
Cwmgors
Gurnos
Ystradgynlais
Four Roads
Pont-Henri
Greynor
Garnswllt
Ystalyfera
Kidwelly Industrial Museum
Mynyddygarreg
Pontyates
Llannon
Llwyn-teg
Kidwelly (Cydweli)
Cynheidre
Sylen
Pont Abraham Services
Godre'r-graig
Carway
Ffos Las
Llanedi
Graig Fawr
Climaen gwyn
Five Roads
Trimsaran
Horeb
Lliedi Resrs.
Sardis
Fforest
Pentrebach
Ynys-meudwy
Crynant
Pembrey
Pinged
Waun-y-clyn
Hendy
Pontarddulais
Rhyd-y-fro
Pontardawe
Cilybebyll
Gellinudd
Rhos
Rhyd-y-gwin
Craig-cefn-parc
Glantawe Riverside Park
Trebanos
Alltwen
Cwm-Dulais
Rhyd-y-pandy
Felindre
Cefn Coed Colliery Mus
Cwmbach
Achddu
Pwll
Furnace
Felinfoel
Allt
Llangennech
Faerdre
Clydach
Waungron
Pontlliw
Ynystawe
Glais
Burry Port (Porth Tywyn)
Sandy
Dafen
Bryn
Grovesend
Swansea Services
Pant-lasau
Cilfrew
Aberdulais
Millennium Coastal Park Discovery Centre
Llanelli
Llwyn-hendy
Bynea
Yspitty
Penllergaer
Llangyfelach
Heol-las
Bryn-coch
Rhydding
Neath Abbey
Cadoxton-Juxta-Neath
Neath Museum
Neath (Castell-Nedd)
Machynys
Wildfowl and Wetlands Trust
Morfa
Loughor
Gorseinon
Morriston
Birchgrove
Skewen
Whiteford Pt.
Trwyn Whiteford
Llanrhidian Sands
Traeth Llanrhidian
Pen-clawdd
Gowerton
Cadle
Llansamlet
Pentre-dwr
Cimla
Whiteford
Crofty
Fforest-fach
Landore
Pentre-chwyth
Cwm
Bon-y-maen
Llandarcy
Blue Anchor
Waunarlwydd
Cwmdu
Foxhole
Briton Ferry
Pontrhydyfen
Wernffrwd
Llanmorlais
Three Crosses
Dunvant
Swansea (Abertawe)
Crymlyn Bog and Pant-y-Sais
Llanmadoc
Cheriton
Landimore
Killay
Sketty
Plantasia
Port Tennant
Pwll-y-glaw
Baglan
Weobley Castle
Brynbryddan
Burry Green
Llethrid
Upper Killay
Clyne Valley
Brynmill
Swansea Museum
Mynydd Dinas
Llangennith
Llanrhidian
National Waterfront Museum
Cwmafan
Burry
Reynoldston
Ilston
Mayals
Black Pill
Aberavon
The Beacon
Llanddewi
Lunnon
Gower Heritage Centre
Kittle
Bishopston
West Cross
Port Talbot
Goytre
Rhossili
Knelston
Parkmill
Pennard
Manselfield
Lovespoon Gallery
Oystermouth Castle
Taibach
Middleton
Scurlage
Penrice
Nicholaston
Penmaen
Oldway
Newton
The Mumbles (Y Mwmbwls)
Margam
Gower Coast
Pilton Green
Oxwich
Southgate
Oxwich Bay
Bae Oxwich
Mumbles Hd.
Trwyn yr Mwmbwls
Groes
Horton
Oxwich Castle
Pwlldu Hd.
Pen Pwlldu
Overton
Port-Eynon
Port Eynon
Port Eynon Bay
Bae Port Eynon
Port Eynon Pt.
Trwyn Port Eynon
Kenfig
Mawdlam
Kenfig Pool and Dunes
Kenfig Burrows
Royal Porthcawl
Hutchwns
Porthcawl
Tonna
Clyne
Penrhos
Abercraf
Afon Cothi
Afon Tywi
Afon Aman
Gwendraeth Fach
Loughor
Neath
A40
A48
A483
A476
A484
A4138
M4
B4300
B4310
B4306
B4297
46
47
34
5
6
7
8
A
B
C
D
E
F
G

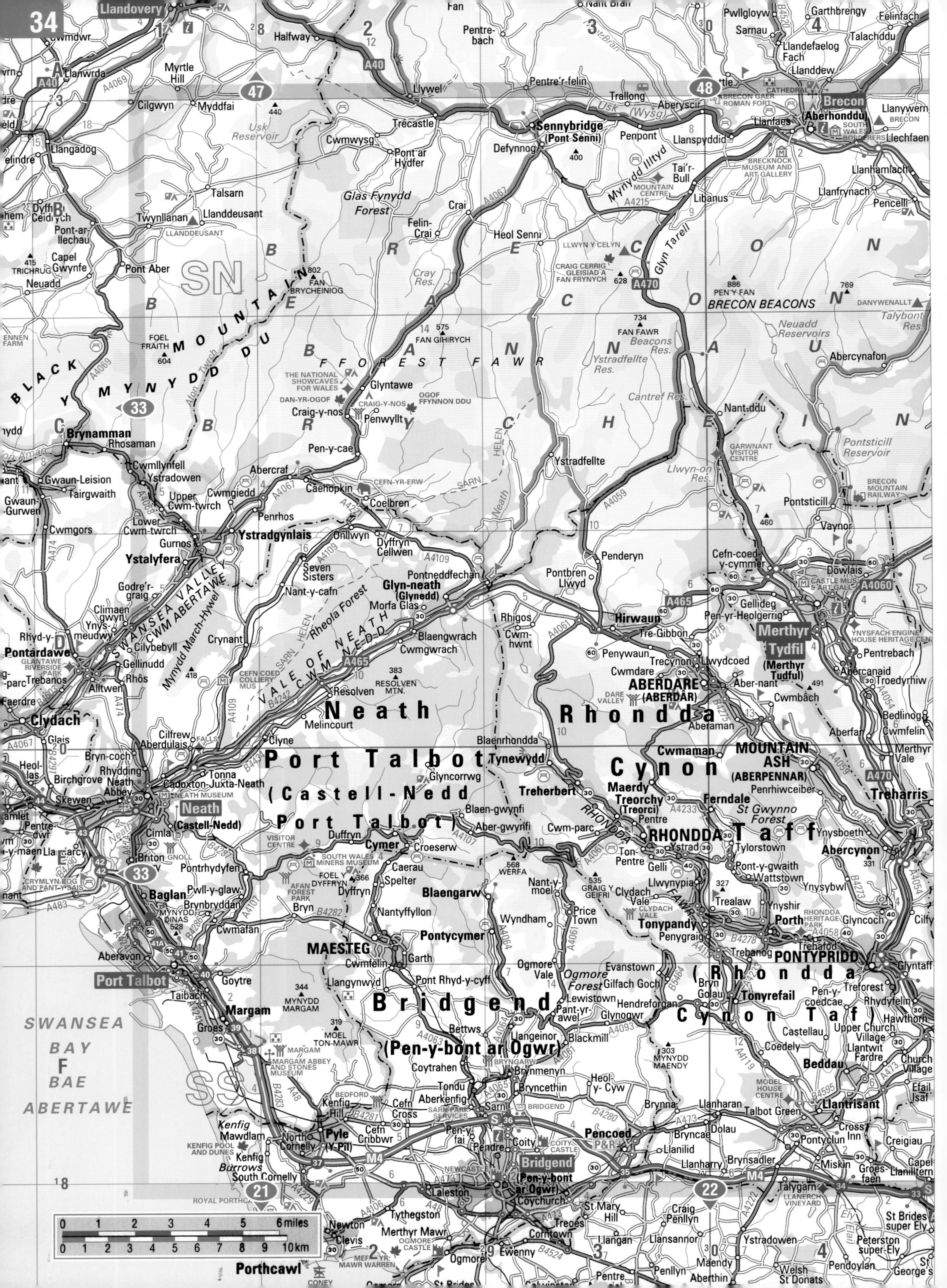
Llandovery
Cwmdwr
Halfway
Pentre-bach
Pwllgloyw
Garthbrengy
Felinfach
Sarnau
Llandefaelog Fach
Talachddu
Llanwrda
Myrtle Hill
Llywel
Pentre'r-felin
Trallong
Aberyscir
Llanddew
Brecon (Aberhonddu)
BRECON GAER ROMAN FORT
CATHEDRAL
Llanywern
Cilgwyn
Myddfai
Usk Reservoir
Trecastle
Sennybridge (Pont Senni)
Penpont
Llanspyddid
Llanfaes
SOUTH WALES BORDERERS
Llechfaen
Llangadog
Cwmwysg
Pont ar Hydfer
Defynnog
BRECKNOCK MUSEUM AND ART GALLERY
Llanhamlach
Tai'r-Bull
Mynydd Illtyd
MOUNTAIN CENTRE
Libanus
Llanfrynach
Pencelli
Talsarn
Glas Fynydd Forest
Crai
Twynllanan
Llanddeusant
Dyffryn Ceidrych
Pont-ar-llechau
Capel Gwynfe
TRICHRUG
Pont Aber
Neuadd
Felin-Crai
Heol Senni
LLWYN Y CELYN
CRAIG CERRIG GLEISIAD A FAN FRYNYCH
Glyn Tarell
SN
FAN BRYCHEINIOG
Cray Res.
PEN Y FAN
BRECON BEACONS
DANYWENALLT
Talybont Res.
BLACK MOUNTAIN
FOEL FRAITH
Y MYNYDD DU
FAN GIHIRYCH
FAN FAWR
Beacons Res.
Ystradfellte Res.
Neuadd Reservoirs
Abercynafon
FFOREST FAWR
THE NATIONAL SHOWCAVES FOR WALES
DAN-YR-OGOF
Glyntawe
CRAIG-Y-NOS
OGOF FFYNNON DDU
Craig-y-nos
Penwyllt
Cantref Res.
Nant-ddu
BRECON BEACONS
Brynamman
Rhosaman
Pen-y-cae
Ystradfellte
GARWNANT VISITOR CENTRE
Llwyn-on Res.
Pontsticill Reservoir
BRECON MOUNTAIN RAILWAY
Gwaun-Leision
Cwmllynfell
Ystradowen
Tairgwaith
Abercraf
Cwmgiedd
Upper Cwm-twrch
Caehopkin
CEFN-YR-ERW
Coelbren
Pontsticill
Gwaun-Cae-Gurwen
Cwmgors
Lower Cwm-twrch
Penrhos
Gurnos
Ystradgynlais
Onllwyn
Dyffryn Cellwen
Vaynor
Ystalyfera
Seven Sisters
Penderyn
Cefn-coed-y-cymmer
Dowlais
CASTLE MUSEUM & ART GALLERY
Pontneddfechan
Pontbren Llwyd
Godre'r-graig
Nant-y-cafn
Glyn-neath (Glynedd)
Gellideg
Pen-yr-Heolgerrig
Climaen gwyn
Ynysmeudwy
SWANSEA VALLEY CWM ABERTAWE
Morfa Glas
Rhigos
Hirwaun
Tre-Gibbon
Merthyr Tydfil (Merthyr Tudful)
YNYSFACH ENGINE HOUSE HERITAGE CENTRE
Rhyd-y-fro
Pontardawe
GLANTAWE RIVERSIDE PARK
Cilybebyll
Gellinudd
Mynydd March-Hywel
Crynant
Rheola Forest
VALE OF NEATH CWM NEDD
Blaengwrach
Cwmgwrach
Cwm-hwnt
Penywaun
Trecynon
Llwydcoed
Pentrebach
Abercanaid
Troedyrhiw
Trebanos
Alltwen
Rhôs
CEFN COED COLLIERY MUS
Resolven
RESOLVEN MTN.
Cwmdare
ABERDARE (ABERDÂR)
DARE VALLEY
Aber-nant
Cwmbâch
Clydach
Glais
Melincourt
Neath Port Talbot (Castell-Nedd Port Talbot)
Rhondda Cynon Taf (Rhondda Cynon Taf)
Aberaman
Bedlinog
Aberfan
Cwmfelin
Cilfrew
Aberdulais
FALLS
Clyne
Blaenrhondda
Heol-las
Bryn-coch
Rhydding
Birchgrove
Neath Abbey
Tonna
Cadoxton-Juxta-Neath
Tynewydd
Glyncorrwg
Cwmaman
MOUNTAIN ASH (ABERPENNAR)
Penrhiwceiber
Merthyr Vale
Treharris
Skewen
NEATH MUSEUM
Neath (Castell-Nedd)
Treherbert
Maerdy
Treorchy (Treorci)
Pentre
Ferndale
St Gwynno Forest
Blaen-gwynfi
Aber-gwynfi
Cwm-parc
RHONDDA
Ystrad
Tylorstown
Ynysboeth
Abercynon
Pentre-dwr
Llansamlet
Cimla
Duffryn
Cymer
Croeserw
VISITOR CENTRE
SOUTH WALES MINERS MUSEUM
Ton-Pentre
Gelli
Pont-y-gwaith
Wattstown
Ynysybwl
Briton Ferry
GNOLL
Pontrhydyfen
Caerau
Spelter
WERFA
Nant-y-moel
GRAIG Y GEIFR
Llwynypia
Clydach Vale
Trealaw
Ynyshir
CRYMLYN BOG AND PANT-Y-SAIS
Baglan
Pwll-y-glaw
FOEL Y DYFFRYN
AFAN FOREST PARK
Dyffryn
Blaengarw
Price Town
CLYDACH VALE
Tonypandy
Porth
RHONDDA HERITAGE PARK
Glyncoch
Brynbryddan
MYNYDD DINAS
Bryn
Nantyffyllon
Wyndham
Penygraig
Cwmafan
Pontycymer
Trehafod
Trebanog
PONTYPRIDD
Aberavon
MAESTEG
Cwmfelin
Garth
Ogmore Vale
Ogmore Forest
Evanstown
Gilfach Goch
Glyntaff
Port Talbot
Goytre
Pont Rhyd-y-cyff
Llangynwyd
MYNYDD MARGAM
Bryn Golau
Tonyrefail
Pen-y-coedcae
Treforest
Rhydyfelin
Taibach
Margam
Bridgend (Pen-y-bont ar Ogwr)
Lewistown
Pant-yr-awel
Hendreforgan
Glynogwr
Castellau
Upper Church Village
Hawthorn
SWANSEA BAY
BAE ABERTAWE
Groes
MOEL TON-MAWR
Bettws
Llangeinor
Blackmill
MYNYDD MAENDY
Coedely
Llantwit Fardre
Church Village
MARGAM
MARGAM ABBEY AND STONES MUSEUM
Coytrahen
BRYNGARW
Brynmenyn
Heol-y-Cyw
Beddau
Tondu
Aberkenfig
Bryncethin
MODEL HOUSE CENTRE
Efail Isaf
BEDFORD
Kenfig Hill
Cefn Cross
SARN PARK SERVICES
Sarn
BRIDGEND
Brynna
Llanharan
Talbot Green
Llantrisant
Kenfig
Mawdlam
Pyle (Y Pîl)
North Cornelly
Cefn Cribbwr
Pen-y-fai
Coity
COITY CASTLE
Pencoed
Bryncae
Dolau
Cross Inn
Pontyclun
Creigiau
KENFIG POOL AND DUNES
Kenfig Burrows
South Cornelly
Pendre
Llanilid
Llanharry
Brynsadler
Miskin
Groes-faen
Capel Llanilltern
NEWCASTLE
Bridgend (Pen-y-bont ar Ogwr)
ROYAL PORTHCAWL
Laleston
Coychurch
Talygarn
LLANERCH VINEYARD
St Brides super Ely
Tythegston
St Mary Hill
Craig-Penllyn
Treoes
Corntown
Newton
Merthyr Mawr
OGMORE CASTLE
Llangan
Llansannor
Ystradowen
Peterston super-Ely
Clevis
MERTHYR MAWR WARREN
Ogmore
Ewenny
Penllyn
Maendy
Welsh St Donats
Pendoylan
St George's
Porthcawl
CONEY
Aberthin
Pentre
0 1 2 3 4 5 6 miles
0 1 2 3 4 5 6 7 8 9 10 km

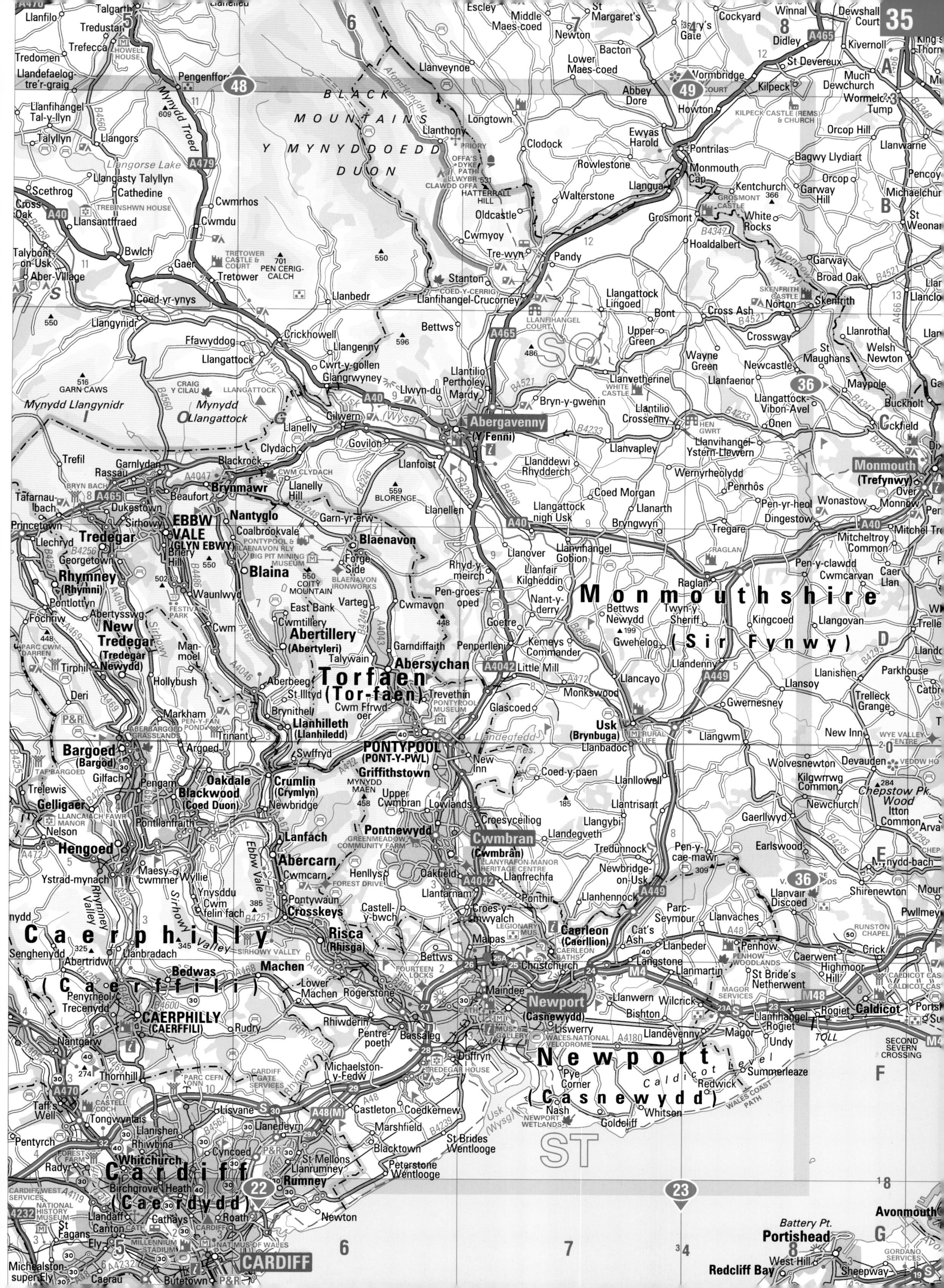
BLACK MOUNTAINS
Y MYNYDDOEDD DUON
Monmouthshire
(Sir Fynwy)
Torfaen
(Tor-faen)
Caerphilly
(Caerffili)
Newport
(Casnewydd)
Cardiff
(Caerdydd)
CARDIFF
Abergavenny
(Y Fenni)
Monmouth
(Trefynwy)
Newport
(Casnewydd)
Talgarth
Llanfilo
Tredustan
Trefecca
Tredomen
Llandefaelog-tre'r-graig
Pengenffordd
Llanfihangel Tal-y-llyn
Talyllyn
Llangors
Llangorse Lake
Llangasty Talyllyn
Cathedine
Scethrog
Cross Oak
Llansantffraed
Cwmrhos
Cwmdu
Bwlch
Talybont-on-Usk
Aber-Village
Gaer
Tretower
TRETOWER CASTLE & COURT
PEN CERIG-CALCH
Coed-yr-ynys
Llangynidr
Llanbedr
Crickhowell
Ffawyddog
Llangattock
Llangenny
Cwrt-y-gollen
Glangrwyney
GARN CAWS
Mynydd Llangynidr
Mynydd Llangattock
Llanelly
Gilwern
Govilon
Clydach
Llanfoist
Blackrock
Trefil
Rassau
Garnlydan
Brynmawr
Beaufort
Tafarnau-bach
Dukestown
Sirhowy
EBBW VALE
(GLYN EBWY)
Nantyglo
Coalbrookvale
Princetown
Llechryd
Tredegar
Georgetown
Briery Hill
Blaina
Blaenavon
Forge Side
COITY MOUNTAIN
BLAENAVON IRONWORKS
BIG PIT MINING MUSEUM
Garn-yr-erw
BLORENGE
Llanelly Hill
Rhymney
(Rhymni)
Pontlottyn
Waunlwyd
Varteg
Cwmavon
East Bank
Fochriw
Abertysswg
New Tredegar
(Tredegar Newydd)
Cwm
Cwmtillery
Abertillery
(Abertyleri)
Tirphil
Man-moel
Hollybush
Garndiffaith
Talywain
Abersychan
Aberbeeg
St Illtyd
Brynithel
Cwm Ffrwd-oer
Trevethin
Llanhilleth
(Llanhiledd)
Deri
Markham
Trinant
Argoed
Bargoed
(Bargod)
Gilfach
Swffryd
PONTYPOOL
(PONT-Y-PŴL)
Griffithstown
Crumlin
(Crymlyn)
Oakdale
Pengam
Blackwood
(Coed Duon)
Trelewis
Gelligaer
Nelson
Pontllanfraith
Newbridge
MYNYDD MAEN
Upper Cwmbran
Lowlands
Hengoed
Lanfach
Pontnewydd
Cwmbran
(Cwmbrân)
Abercarn
Cwmcarn
Henllys
Oakfield
Llantarnam
Ystrad-mynach
Maesy-cwmmer
Wyllie
Ynysddu
Cwm felin fach
Pontywaun
Crosskeys
Risca
(Rhisga)
Castell-y-bwch
Croes-y-mwyalch
Malpas
Rhymney Valley
Sirhowy Valley
Ebbw Vale
Senghenydd
Llanbradach
Abertridwr
Bedwas
Machen
Lower Machen
Rogerstone
Bettws
Penyrheol
Trecenydd
CAERPHILLY
(CAERFFILI)
Rudry
Rhiwderin
Pentre-poeth
Bassaleg
Nantgarw
Thornhill
Michaelston-y-Fedw
Castleton
Coedkernew
Marshfield
St Brides Wentlooge
Blacktown
Peterstone Wentlooge
Duffryn
TREDEGAR HOUSE
Taff's Well
Tongwynlais
Lisvane
Llanishen
Llanedeyrn
Rhiwbina
Cyncoed
Pentyrch
Radyr
Whitchurch
St Mellons
Llanrumney
Rumney
Birchgrove
Heath
Llandaff
Canton
Cathays
Roath
St Fagans
Ely
Caerau
Butetown
Michaelston-super-Ely
MILLENNIUM STADIUM
NAT MUS OF WALES
Newton
Escley
Middle Maes-coed
Newton
St Margaret's
Bacton
Lower Maes-coed
Llanveynoe
Abbey Dore
Longtown
Llanthony
PRIORY
OFFA'S DYKE PATH
HATTERRALL HILL
Clodock
Ewyas Harold
Pontrilas
Rowlestone
Walterstone
Llangua
Monmouth Cap
Oldcastle
Cwmyoy
Tre-wyn
Pandy
Stanton
Llanfihangel-Crucorney
Bettws
Llantilio Pertholey
Mardy
Llwyn-du
Bryn-y-gwenin
Llanvetherine
WHITE CASTLE
Llanfaenor
Llantilio Crossenny
Llanvapley
Llanddewi Rhydderch
Coed Morgan
Llanarth
Llanellen
Llangattock nigh Usk
Bryngwyn
Llanover
Llanvihangel Gobion
Llanfair Kilgheddin
Rhyd-y-meirch
Pen-groes-oped
Goetre
Nant-y-derry
Penperlleni
Kemeys Commander
Bettws Newydd
Gwehelog
Little Mill
Llandenny
Llancayo
Monkswood
Glascoed
Usk
(Brynbuga)
Llanbadoc
New Inn
Coed-y-paen
Llanllowell
Llantrisant
Croesyceiliog
Llangybi
Llandegveth
Tredunnock
Llanfrechfa
Newbridge-on-Usk
Ponthir
Llanhennock
Caerleon
(Caerllion)
Christchurch
Maindee
Liswerry
Llanwern
Bishton
Wilcrick
Langstone
Llanbeder
Llanmartin
Llandevenny
Magor
Undy
Llanfihangel Rogiet
Rogiet
Caldicot
Pye Corner
Nash
Goldcliff
Whitson
Redwick
Summerleaze
NEWPORT WETLANDS
WALES NATIONAL VELODROME
Caldicot Level
Cat's Ash
Parc-Seymour
Llanvaches
Penhow
St Bride's Netherwent
Caerwent
Crick
Highmoor Hill
Llanvair Discoed
Shirenewton
Pen-y-cae-mawr
Earlswood
Gaerllwyd
Newchurch
Itton Common
Kilgwrrwg Common
Chepstow Pk. Wood
Devauden
Wolvesnewton
New Inn
Llangwm
Gwernesney
Llansoy
Llanishen
Trelleck Grange
Parkhouse
Kingcoed
Llangovan
Twyn-y-Sheriff
Raglan
Tregare
Dingestow
Pen-yr-heol
Wonastow
Mitcheltroy Common
Pen-y-clawdd
Cwmcarvan
Caer Llan
Penrhôs
Wernyrheolydd
Llanvihangel-Ystern-Llewern
Llangattock-Vibon-Avel
Onen
Maypole
Buckholt
Llanrothal
Welsh Newton
St Maughans
Newcastle
Wayne Green
Upper Green
Crossway
Bont
Llangattock Lingoed
Cross Ash
Norton
Skenfrith
Broad Oak
Garway
White Rocks
Hoaldalbert
Grosmont
Kentchurch
Garway Hill
Orcop
Orcop Hill
Bagwy Llydiart
Llanwarne
Kilpeck
Howton
Wormbridge
St Devereux
Didley
Cockyard
Winnal
Dewshall Court
Kivernoll
Much Dewchurch
Wormelow Tump
Michaelchurch
Second Severn Crossing
Avonmouth
Battery Pt.
Portishead
West Hill
Redcliff Bay
Sheepway
SO
ST

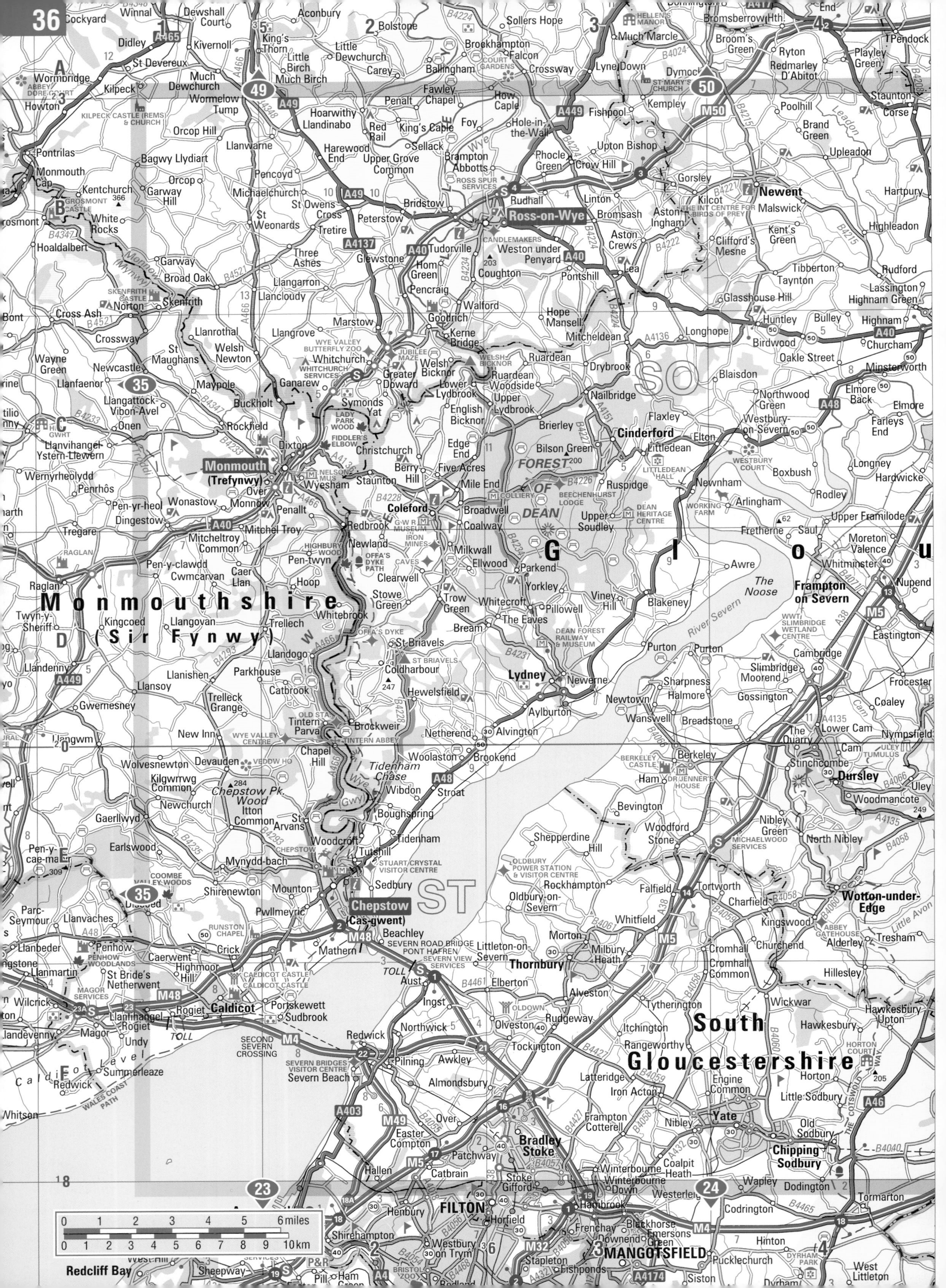

Cockyard
Winnal
Dewshall Court
Aconbury
Bolstone
Sollers Hope
Much Marcle
Bromsberrow Hth.
Pendock
Didley
Kivernoll
King's Thorn
Little Dewchurch
Brockhampton
Falcon
Lyne Down
Broom's Green
Ryton
Playley Green
St Devereux
Little Birch
Much Birch
Carey
Ballingham
Crossway
Dymock
Redmarley D'Abitot
Wormbridge
Kilpeck
Much Dewchurch
Wormelow Tump
Fawley Chapel
How Caple
Kempley
Staunton
Corse
Howton
Kilpeck Castle (Rems) & Church
Hoarwithy
Llandinabo
Penalt
Foy
Fishpool
Poolhill
Brand Green
Orcop Hill
Llanwarne
Red Rail
King's Caple
Hole-in-the-Wall
Upton Bishop
Upleadon
Pontrilas
Bagwy Llydiart
Harewood End
Upper Grove Common
Sellack
Brampton Abbotts
Phocle Green
Crow Hill
Gorsley
Monmouth Cap
Orcop
Pencoyd
Ross Spur Services
Kentchurch
Garway Hill
Michaelchurch
St Owens Cross
Bridstow
Rudhall
Linton
Kilcot
Newent
Hartpury
Grosmont Castle
Grosmont
White Rocks
St Weonards
Tretire
Peterstow
Ross-on-Wye
Bromsash
Aston Ingham
The Int Centre for Birds of Prey
Malswick
Highleadon
Hoaldalbert
Candlemakers
Weston under Penyard
Aston Crews
Kent's Green
Clifford's Mesne
Garway
Three Ashes
Tudorville
Glewstone
Hom Green
Coughton
Lea
Tibberton
Taynton
Rudford
Broad Oak
Llangarron
Llancloudy
Pencraig
Pontshill
Lassington
Highnam Green
Glasshouse Hill
Skenfrith Castle
Norton
Skenfrith
Walford
Hope Mansell
Bont
Cross Ash
Marstow
Goodrich
Kerne Bridge
Mitcheldean
Longhope
Huntley
Bulley
Highnam
Crossway
Llanrothal
Llangrove
Wye Valley Butterfly Zoo
Jubilee Maze
Welsh Bicknor
Ruardean
Drybrook
Birdwood
Churcham
Wayne Green
St Maughans
Welsh Newton
Whitchurch
Whitchurch Services
Greater Doward
Welsh Bicknor
Ruardean Woodside
Blaisdon
Oakle Street
Minsterworth
Newcastle
Llanfaenor
Ganarew
Lower Lydbrook
Upper Lydbrook
Nailbridge
Northwood Green
Elmore Back
Elmore
Llangattock-Vibon-Avel
Maypole
Buckholt
Symonds Yat
Lady Park Wood
English Bicknor
Flaxley
Westbury-on-Severn
Onen
Rockfield
Brierley
Cinderford
Farleys End
Llanvihangel Ystern-Llewern
Fiddler's Elbow
Dixton
Christchurch
Edge End
Bilson Green
Littledean
Elton
Westbury Court
Monmouth (Trefynwy)
Berry Hill
Five Acres
Forest
Littledean Hall
Longney
Boxbush
Hardwicke
Wernyrheolydd
Nelson Mus
Wyesham
Staunton
Mile End
Colliery
Of
Beechenhurst Lodge
Ruspidge
Newnham
Penrhôs
Over Monnow
Penallt
Coleford
Broadwell
Dean
Dean Heritage Centre
Arlingham
Rodley
Pen-yr-heol
Wonastow
Dingestow
Redbrook
G W R Museum
Coalway
Upper Soudley
Working Farm
Upper Framilode
Tregare
Mitchel Troy
Fretherne
Saul
Newland
Iron Mines
Moreton Valence
Mitcheltroy Common
Highbury Wood
Raglan
Pen-y-clawdd
Cwmcarvan
Offa's Dyke Path
Pen-twyn
Milkwall
Caves
Ellwood
Parkend
Awre
Whitminster
Frampton on Severn
Nupend
Caer Llan
Raglan
Hoop
Clearwell
Yorkley
The Noose
Monmouthshire
(Sir Fynwy)
Stowe Green
Trow Green
Whitecroft
Pillowell
Viney Hill
Blakeney
Twyn-y-Sheriff
Kingcoed
Llangovan
Trellech
Whitebrook
The Eaves
River Severn
WWT Slimbridge Wetland Centre
Eastington
Offa's Dyke
St Briavels
Bream
Dean Forest Railway & Museum
Purton
Cambridge
Llandenny
Llanishen
Parkhouse
Llandogo
St Briavels
Coldharbour
Lydney
Slimbridge
Moorend
Frocester
Llansoy
Catbrook
Hewelsfield
Newerne
Sharpness
Halmore
Gossington
Trelleck Grange
Aylburton
Newtown
Coaley
Gwernesney
Old Sta
Tintern Parva
Brockweir
Wanswell
Breadstone
New Inn
Llangwm
Wye Valley Centre
Tintern Abbey
Netherend
Alvington
The Quarry
Lower Cam
Nympsfield
Cam
Uley Tumulus
Wolvesnewton
Devauden
Veddw Ho
Chapel Hill
Tidenham Chase
Woolaston
Brookend
Berkeley Castle
Berkeley
Stinchcombe
Dursley
Kilgwrrwg Common
Chepstow Pk. Wood
Wibdon
Stroat
Ham
Dr Jenner's House
Uley
Woodmancote
Newchurch
Itton Common
Boughspring
Bevington
Gaerllwyd
St Arvans
Nibley Green
Woodford
Stone
Earlswood
Tidenham
Shepperdine
Hill
Michaelwood Services
North Nibley
Pen-y-cae-mawr
Woodcroft
Tutshill
Stuart Crystal Visitor Centre
Mynydd-bach
Chepstow
Oldbury Power Station & Visitor Centre
Coombe Valley Woods
Shirenewton
Mounton
Sedbury
Rockhampton
Falfield
Tortworth
Wotton-under-Edge
Parc-Seymour
Llanvaches
Pwllmeyric
Chepstow (Cas-gwent)
Oldbury-on-Severn
Charfield
Kingswood
Abbey Gatehouse
Whitfield
Tresham
Runston Chapel
Beachley
Morton
Alderley
Little Avon
Llanbeder
Penhow
Penhow Woodlands
Crick
Severn Road Bridge
Pont Hafren
Severn View Services
Littleton-on-Severn
Milbury Heath
Cromhall
Churchend
Caerwent
Mathern
Thornbury
Cromhall Common
Hillesley
Highmoor Hill
Caldicot Castle
Toll
Aust
Elberton
Llanmartin
St Bride's Netherwent
Magor Services
Ingst
Alveston
Wickwar
Hawkesbury Upton
Wilcrick
Llanfihangel Rogiet
Rogiet
Caldicot
Portskewett
Sudbrook
Tytherington
Magor
Undy
Oldown
Olveston
Rudgeway
South
Hawkesbury
Llandevenny
Second Severn Crossing
Redwick
Northwick
Itchington
Rangeworthy
Horton Court
Gloucestershire
Caldicot Level
Summerleaze
Severn Bridges Visitor Centre
Pilning
Awkley
Tockington
Latteridge
Horton
Redwick
Severn Beach
Almondsbury
Iron Acton
Engine Common
Wales Coast Path
Little Sodbury
Whitson
Over
Frampton Cotterell
Nibley
Yate
The Cotswold Way
Easter Compton
Bradley Stoke
Old Sodbury
Patchway
Chipping Sodbury
Hallen
Catbrain
Stoke Gifford
Winterbourne
Coalpit Heath
Winterbourne Down
Westerleigh
Wapley
Dodington
Tormarton
Henbury
Filton
Horfield
Hambrook
Codrington
Shirehampton
Westbury on Trym
Frenchay
Blackhorse
Emersons Green
Downend
Hinton
Dyrham Park
Redcliff Bay
West Hill
Sheepway
Pill
Ham Green
Bristol Zoo
Stapleton
Fishponds
Mangotsfield
Pucklechurch
Siston
Dyrham
West Littleton
SO
ST
0 1 2 3 4 5 6 miles
0 1 2 3 4 5 6 7 8 9 10 km

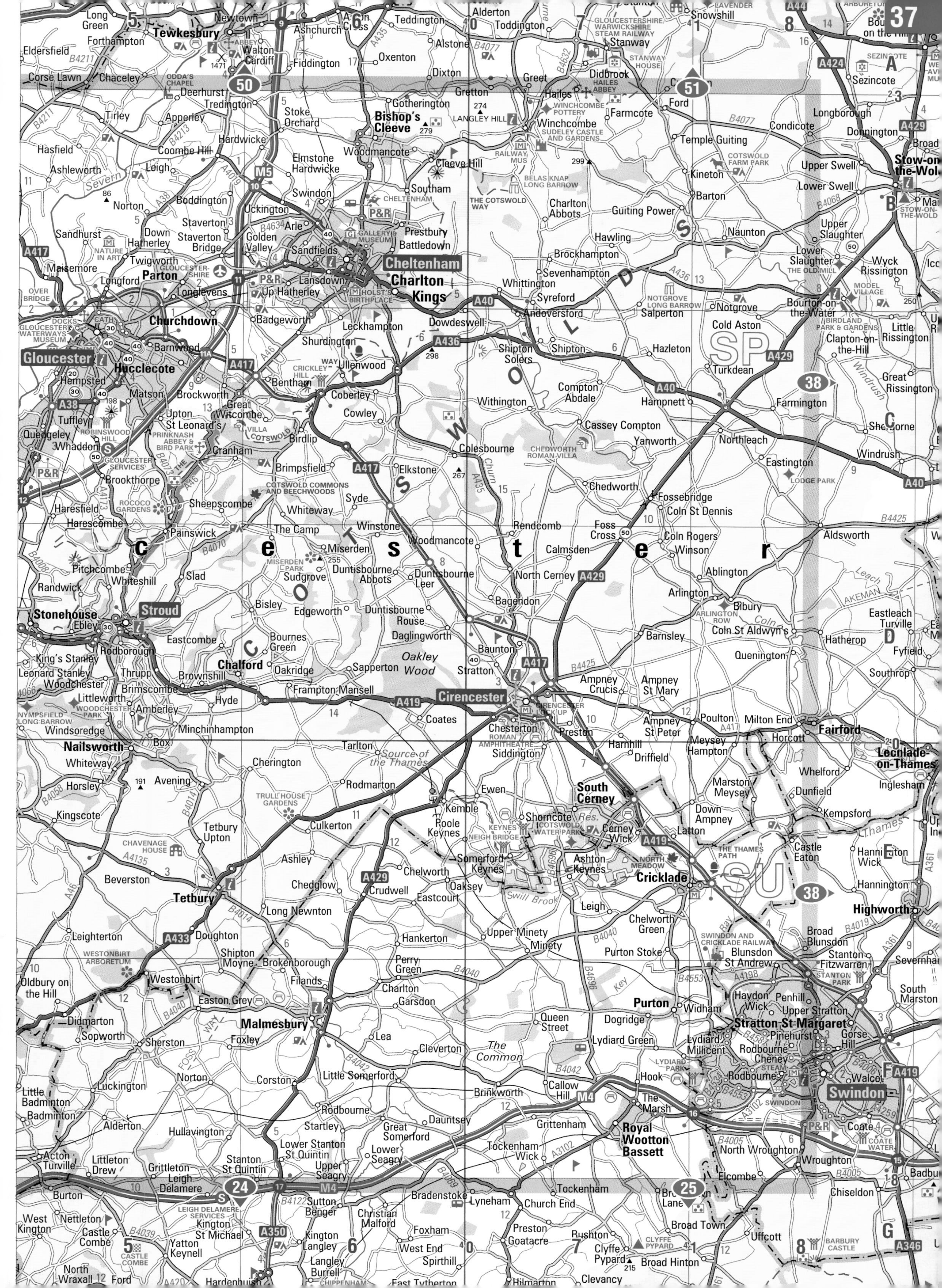

Long Green
Tewkesbury
Newtown
Ashchurch
Aston Cross
Teddington
Alderton
Toddington
Snowshill
Gloucestershire Warwickshire Steam Railway
Stanway
Eldersfield
Forthampton
Walton Cardiff
Fiddington
Oxenton
Alstone
Dixton
Corse Lawn
Chaceley
Odda's Chapel
Deerhurst
Tredington
Gretton
Greet
Hailes
Hailes Abbey
Didbrook
Stanway House
Ford
Sezincote
Sezincote
Longborough
Condicote
Donnington
Broad
Stow-on-the-Wold
Tirley
Apperley
Stoke Orchard
Gotherington
Bishop's Cleeve
Langley Hill
Winchcombe
Winchcombe Pottery
Sudeley Castle and Gardens
Farmcote
Temple Guiting
Cotswold Farm Park
Hasfield
Coombe Hill
Hardwicke
Elmstone Hardwicke
Woodmancote
Cleeve Hill
Railway Mus
Belas Knap Long Barrow
Kineton
Upper Swell
Lower Swell
Ashleworth
Leigh
Severn
Norton
Boddington
Swindon
Southam
Uckington
Cheltenham
The Cotswold Way
Charlton Abbots
Barton
Guiting Power
Stow-on-the-Wold
Sandhurst
Staverton
Down Hatherley
Staverton Bridge
Arle
Golden Valley
Gallery & Museum
Prestbury
Battledown
Hawling
Naunton
Upper Slaughter
Lower Slaughter
The Old Mill
Wyck Rissington
Nature in Art
Twigworth
Gloucestershire
Maisemore
Longford
Parton
Sandfields
Cheltenham
Lansdown
Charlton Kings
Up Hatherley
Holst's Birthplace
Brockhampton
Sevenhampton
Whittington
Syreford
Model Village
Over Bridge
Longlevens
Andoversford
Notgrove Long Barrow
Notgrove
Salperton
Bourton-on-the-Water
Churchdown
Badgeworth
Leckhampton
Dowdeswell
Birdland Park & Gardens
Little Rissington
Docks
Cath
Gloucester Waterways Museum
Gloucester
Barnwood
Hucclecote
Shurdington
Crickley Hill
Ullenwood
Shipton Solers
Shipton
Hazleton
Cold Aston
Clapton-on-the-Hill
Hempsted
Bentham
Turkdean
Great Rissington
Matson
Brockworth
Great Witcombe
Coberley
Compton Abdale
Hampnett
Farmington
Tuffley
Upton St Leonard's
Cowley
Withington
Cassey Compton
Sherborne
Quedgeley
Robinswood Hill
Whaddon
Prinknash Abbey & Bird Park
Villa
Birdlip
Colesbourne
Yanworth
Northleach
Windrush
Cranham
Chedworth Roman Villa
Eastington
Gloucester Services
Brookthorpe
Brimpsfield
Elkstone
Lodge Park
Cotswold Commons and Beechwoods
Chedworth
Fossebridge
Coln St Dennis
Haresfield
Harescombe
Rococo Gardens
Sheepscombe
Whiteway
Syde
Rendcomb
Foss Cross
Coln Rogers
Winson
Aldsworth
Painswick
The Camp
Winstone
Woodmancote
Calmsden
Pitchcombe
Whiteshill
Miserden
Miserden Park
Duntisbourne Abbots
Duntisbourne Leer
North Cerney
Ablington
Randwick
Slad
Sudgrove
Bisley
Bagendon
Arlington
Bibury
Arlington Row
Akeman
Leach
Stonehouse
Ebley
Stroud
Edgeworth
Duntisbourne Rouse
Coln
Coln St Aldwyn's
Eastleach Turville
Eastcombe
Bournes Green
Daglingworth
Barnsley
Hatherop
King's Stanley
Rodborough
Chalford
Oakley Wood
Baunton
Quenington
Fyfield
Leonard Stanley
Thrupp
Brownshill
Oakridge
Sapperton
Stratton
Southrop
Woodchester
Brimscombe
Frampton Mansell
Ampney Crucis
Ampney St Mary
Littleworth
Woodchester Park
Nympsfield Long Barrow
Amberley
Hyde
Cirencester
Cirencester Lock Up
Windsoredge
Minchinhampton
Coates
Chesterton
Roman Amphitheatre
Preston
Ampney St Peter
Poulton
Milton End
Fairford
Nailsworth
Box
Tarlton
Source of the Thames
Siddington
Harnhill
Driffield
Meysey Hampton
Horcott
Lechlade-on-Thames
Whiteway
Cherington
Whelford
Horsley
Avening
Rodmarton
Ewen
South Cerney
Marston Meysey
Dunfield
Inglesham
Trull House Gardens
Kemble
Kingscote
Tetbury Upton
Culkerton
Poole Keynes
Shorncote
Keynes
Cotswold Water Park
Cerney Wick
Down Ampney
Kempsford
Latton
Chavenage House
Neigh Bridge
Ashley
Somerford Keynes
Ashton Keynes
North Meadow
The Thames Path
Castle Eaton
Hannington Wick
Thames
Beverston
Tetbury
Chedglow
Chelworth
Crudwell
Oaksey
Cricklade
Hannington
Long Newnton
Eastcourt
Swill Brook
Leigh
Chelworth Green
Highworth
Leighterton
Doughton
Hankerton
Upper Minety
Minety
Purton Stoke
Swindon and Cricklade Railway
Blunsdon St Andrew
Broad Blunsdon
Stanton Fitzwarren
Stanton Park
Sevenhampton
Westonbirt Arboretum
Shipton Moyne
Brokenborough
Perry Green
Filands
Charlton
Garsdon
Haydon Wick
Penhill
Upper Stratton
South Marston
Oldbury on the Hill
Westonbirt
Easton Grey
Purton
Widham
Stratton St Margaret
Pinehurst
Gorse Hill
Didmarton
Malmesbury
Queen Street
Dogridge
Sopworth
Sherston
Foxley
Lea
Cleverton
The Common
Lydiard Green
Lydiard Millicent
Rodbourne Cheney
Lydiard Park
Norton
Corston
Little Somerford
Hook
Rodbourne
Walcot
Swindon
Little Badminton
Luckington
Brinkworth
Callow Hill
The Marsh
Badminton
Rodbourne
Alderton
Hullavington
Startley
Dauntsey
Great Somerford
Grittenham
Royal Wootton Bassett
Coate
Coate Water
Acton Turville
Littleton Drew
Grittleton
Stanton St Quintin
Lower Stanton St Quintin
Lower Seagry
Upper Seagry
Tockenham Wick
North Wroughton
Wroughton
Badbury
Leigh Delamere
Burton
Leigh Delamere Services
Bradenstoke
Lyneham
Tockenham
Church End
Broad Town Lane
Elcombe
Chiseldon
Sutton Benger
West Kington
Nettleton
Castle Combe
Castle Combe
Kington St Michael
Christian Malford
Foxham
Preston
Goatacre
Broad Town
Uffcott
Barbury Castle
Yatton Keynell
Kington Langley
West End
Spirthill
Bushton
Clyffe Pypard
Clyffe Pypard
Broad Hinton
North Wraxall
Ford
Hardenhuish
Langley Burrell
Chippenham
East Tytherton
Hilmarton
Clevancy
Cotswolds

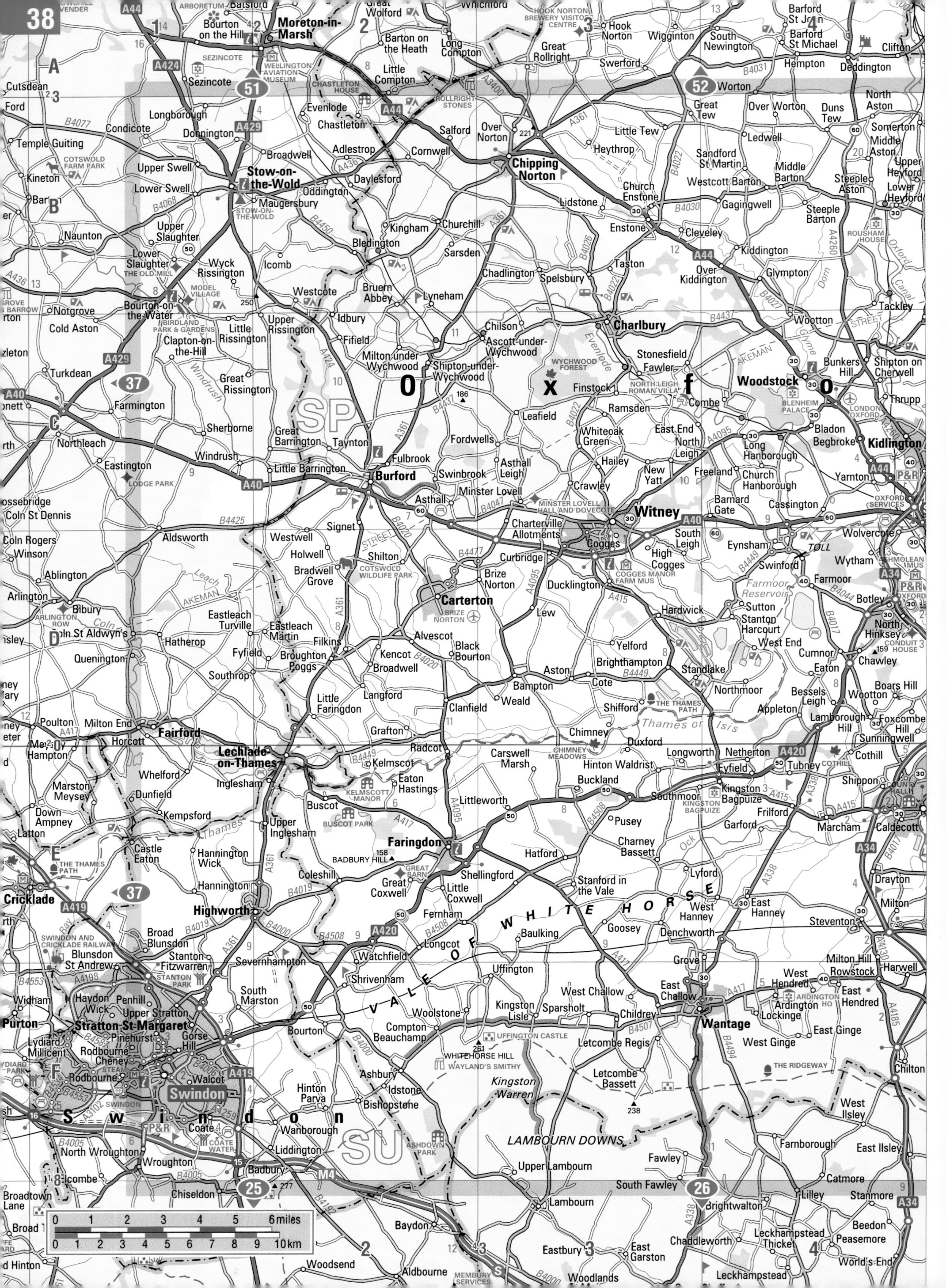
Bourton on the Hill
Moreton-in-Marsh
Great Wolford
Barton on the Heath
Long Compton
Little Compton
Hook Norton Brewery Visitor Centre
Hook Norton
Great Rollright
Wigginton
South Newington
Swerford
Barford St John
Barford St Michael
Hempton
Deddington
Clifton
Sezincote
Wellington Aviation Museum
Chastleton House
Rollright Stones
Worton
Cutsdean
Ford
Longborough
Condicote
Donnington
Evenlode
Chastleton
Salford
Over Norton
Great Tew
Over Worton
Duns Tew
North Aston
Little Tew
Heythrop
Ledwell
Somerton
Middle Aston
Temple Guiting
Cotswold Farm Park
Kineton
Upper Swell
Lower Swell
Broadwell
Adlestrop
Cornwell
Chipping Norton
Sandford St Martin
Middle Barton
Steeple Aston
Upper Heyford
Lower Heyford
Stow-on-the-Wold
Oddington
Daylesford
Maugersbury
Westcott Barton
Church Enstone
Lidstone
Gagingwell
Steeple Barton
Barton
Naunton
Upper Slaughter
Kingham
Churchill
Enstone
Cleveley
Rousham House
Lower Slaughter
The Old Mill
Wyck Rissington
Icomb
Bledington
Sarsden
Kiddington
Taston
Over Kiddington
Glympton
Chadlington
Spelsbury
Model Village
Bourton-on-the-Water
Birdland Park & Gardens
Westcote
Bruern Abbey
Lyneham
Notgrove
Cold Aston
Upper Rissington
Idbury
Little Rissington
Clapton-on-the-Hill
Fifield
Chilson
Ascott-under-Wychwood
Charlbury
Wootton
Tackley
Stonesfield
Fawler
Bunkers Hill
Shipton on Cherwell
Milton under Wychwood
Shipton-under-Wychwood
Wychwood Forest
Evenlode
Turkdean
Great Rissington
Windrush
Finstock
North Leigh Roman Villa
Woodstock
Combe
Thrupp
Blenheim Palace
London Oxford
Farmington
Oxfordshire
Leafield
Ramsden
Whiteoak Green
East End
North Leigh
Bladon
Begbroke
Kidlington
Northleach
Sherborne
Great Barrington
Taynton
Fordwells
Long Hanborough
Eastington
Lodge Park
Windrush
Little Barrington
Fulbrook
Burford
Swinbrook
Asthall Leigh
Hailey
New Yatt
Freeland
Church Hanborough
Yarnton
Asthall
Minster Lovell
Minster Lovell Hall and Dovecote
Crawley
Witney
Barnard Gate
Cassington
Oxford Services
Fossebridge
Coln St Dennis
Signet
Charterville Allotments
Cogges
South Leigh
Eynsham
Wolvercote
Aldsworth
Westwell
Holwell
Shilton
Cotswold Wildlife Park
Curbridge
Brize Norton
High Cogges
Cogges Manor Farm Mus
Swinford
Toll
Wytham
Ashmolean Mus
Coln Rogers
Winson
Ablington
Bradwell Grove
Ducklington
Farmoor
Farmoor Reservoir
Arlington
Bibury
Arlington Row
Coln St Aldwyn's
Akeman
Eastleach Turville
Eastleach Martin
Carterton
Brize Norton
Lew
Hardwick
Sutton
Stanton Harcourt
Botley
North Hinksey
Conduit House
Hatherop
Quenington
Fyfield
Filkins
Broughton Poggs
Alvescot
Kencot
Broadwell
Black Bourton
Yelford
Brighthampton
West End
Cumnor
Chawley
Southrop
Aston
Cote
Standlake
Eaton
Bampton
Weald
Northmoor
Bessels Leigh
Wootton
Boars Hill
Little Faringdon
Langford
Clanfield
Shifford
The Thames Path
Appleton
Lamborough Hill
Foxcombe Hill
Sunningwell
Poulton
Milton End
Fairford
Horcott
Grafton
Chimney
Thames or Isis
Duxford
Meysey Hampton
Lechlade-on-Thames
Radcot
Kelmscott
Carswell Marsh
Chimney Meadows
Hinton Waldrist
Longworth
Netherton
Fyfield
Tubney
Cothill
Shippon
Whelford
Inglesham
Eaton Hastings
Kelmscott Manor
Buckland
Kingston Bagpuize
Southmoor
Marston Meysey
Dunfield
Buscot
Buscot Park
Littleworth
Frilford
Garford
Marcham
Caldecott
Down Ampney
Kempsford
Upper Inglesham
Pusey
Latton
Castle Eaton
Hannington Wick
Faringdon
Badbury Hill
Hatford
Charney Bassett
Ock
The Thames Path
Hannington
Coleshill
Great Barn
Great Coxwell
Shellingford
Little Coxwell
Stanford in the Vale
Lyford
Drayton
Cricklade
Highworth
Fernham
Vale of White Horse
West Hanney
East Hanney
Milton
Broad Blunsdon
Goosey
Steventon
Swindon and Cricklade Railway
Blunsdon St Andrew
Stanton Fitzwarren
Stanton Park
Sevenhampton
Watchfield
Longcot
Baulking
Denchworth
Grove
Milton Hill
Rowstock
Harwell
Shrivenham
Uffington
West Hendred
East Hendred
Ardington
Ardington House
Widham
Haydon Wick
Penhill
South Marston
West Challow
East Challow
Purton
Stratton St Margaret
Upper Stratton
Woolstone
Kingston Lisle
Sparsholt
Childrey
Wantage
Locking
Lydiard Millicent
Pinehurst
Gorse Hill
Rodbourne Cheney
Bourton
Compton Beauchamp
Uffington Castle
Letcombe Regis
West Ginge
East Ginge
Steam
Rodbourne
Walcot
Swindon
Ashbury
Whitehorse Hill
Wayland's Smithy
Letcombe Bassett
The Ridgeway
Chilton
Hinton Parva
Idstone
Bishopstone
Kingston Warren
West Ilsley
Coate
Coate Water
Wanborough
P&R
North Wroughton
Liddington
Ashdown Park
Lambourn Downs
Farnborough
East Ilsley
Wroughton
Badbury
Upper Lambourn
Fawley
Elcombe
Chiseldon
South Fawley
Catmore
Broadtown Lane
Lambourn
Lilley
Stanmore
Brightwalton
Broad Town
Baydon
Leckhampstead Thicket
Beedon
Chaddleworth
Peasemore
Eastbury
East Garston
World's End
Woodsend
Aldbourne
Membury Services
Woodlands
Leckhampstead
SP
SU
A44
A424
A429
A436
A40
A361
A3400
A417
A419
A420
A4095
A415
A338
A34
A4260
A417
A4185
A3102
A4259
A4130
B4077
B4068
B4450
B4437
B4026
B4022
B4030
B4031
B4027
B4425
B4047
B4020
B4477
B4449
B4044
B4017
B4019
B4000
B4508
B4553
B4587
B4006
B4005
B4192
B4507
B4494
M4
Akeman Street
Oxford Canal
Cherwell
Glyme
Dorn
Windrush
Leach
Coln
Thames
Ray
51
52
37
25
26
0 1 2 3 4 5 6 miles
0 1 2 3 4 5 6 7 8 9 10 km

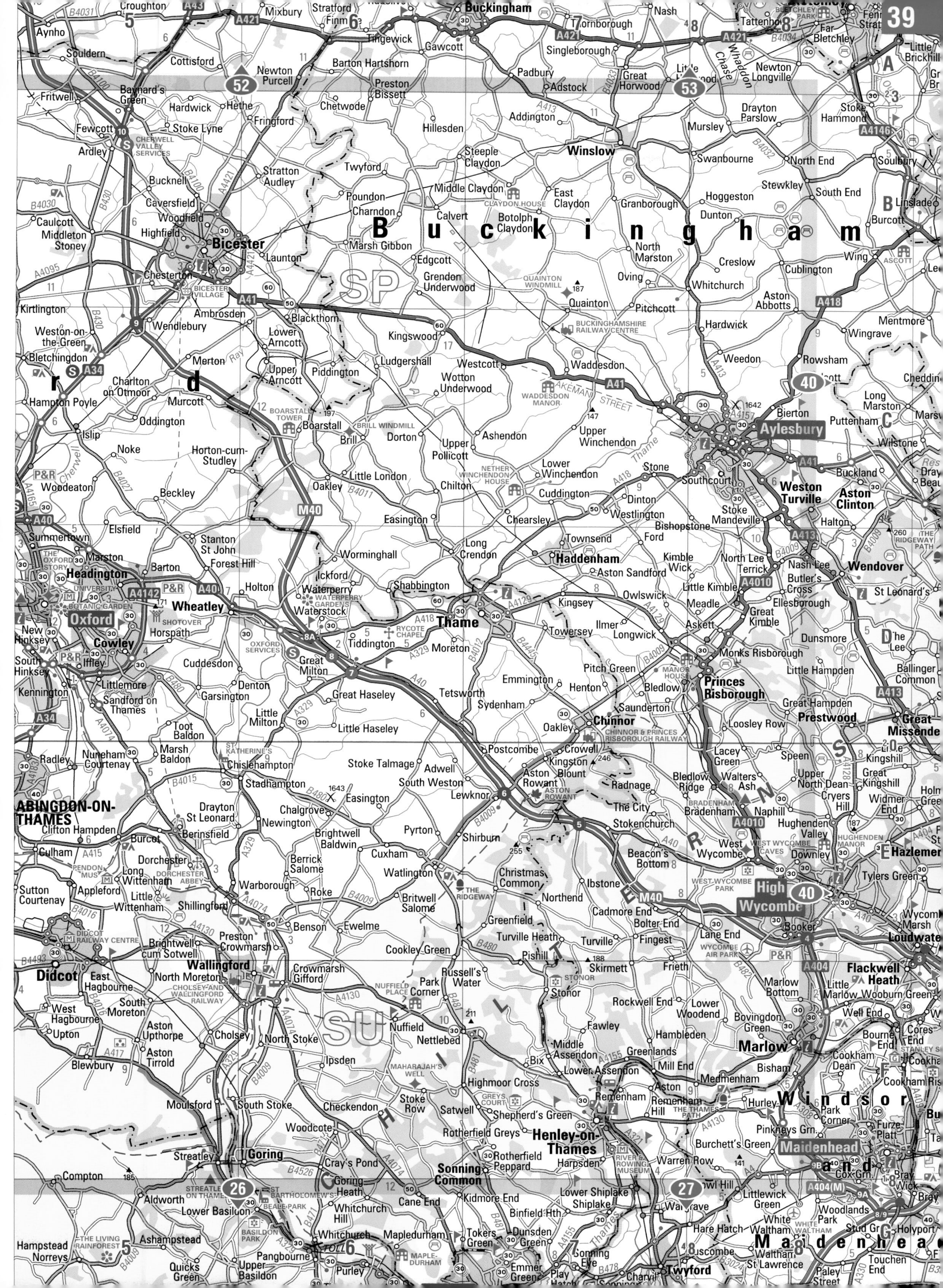
Buckingham
Aynho
Souldern
Croughton
Mixbury
Stratford
Tingewick
Gawcott
Thornborough
Nash
Tattenhoe
Bletchley
Far Bletchley
Little Brickhill
Cottisford
Newton Purcell
Barton Hartshorn
Preston Bissett
Padbury
Adstock
Singleborough
Great Horwood
Whaddon Chase
Newton Longville
Fritwell
Baynard's Green
Hardwick
Hethe
Chetwode
Addington
Drayton Parslow
Stoke Hammond
Fewcott
Stoke Lyne
Fringford
Hillesden
Mursley
Ardley
CHERWELL VALLEY SERVICES
Steeple Claydon
Winslow
Swanbourne
North End
Soulbury
Bucknell
Stratton Audley
Twyford
Middle Claydon
East Claydon
Hoggeston
Stewkley
South End
Caversfield
Poundon
CLAYDON HOUSE
Granborough
Dunton
Linslade
Caulcott
Woodfield
Charndon
Calvert
Botolph Claydon
Burcott
Middleton Stoney
Highfield
Bicester
Marsh Gibbon
Buckingham
North Marston
Launton
Edgcott
Creslow
Cublington
Wing
ASCOTT
Chesterton
SP
Grendon Underwood
QUAINTON WINDMILL
Oving
Whitchurch
BICESTER VILLAGE
Quainton
Aston Abbotts
Kirtlington
Ambrosden
Blackthorn
Pitchcott
Mentmore
Wendlebury
Kingswood
BUCKINGHAMSHIRE RAILWAY CENTRE
Hardwick
Wingrave
Weston-on-the-Green
Lower Arncott
Bletchingdon
Merton
Upper Arncott
Ludgershall
Westcott
Waddesdon
Weedon
Rowsham
Piddington
Charlton on Otmoor
Wotton Underwood
WADDESDON MANOR
AKEMAN STREET
Long Marston
Hampton Poyle
Murcott
BOARSTALL TOWER
Bierton
Oddington
Boarstall
BRILL WINDMILL
Ashendon
Upper Winchendon
Aylesbury
Puttenham
Islip
Brill
Dorton
Upper Pollicott
Wilstone
Noke
Horton-cum-Studley
Thame
Buckland
Little London
NETHER WINCHENDON HOUSE
Lower Winchendon
Stone
Southcourt
Weston Turville
Aston Clinton
Woodeaton
Oakley
Chilton
Cuddington
Beckley
Dinton
Stoke Mandeville
Halton
Westlington
Easington
Chearsley
Bishopstone
Elsfield
Townsend
Ford
Summertown
Stanton St John
Long Crendon
Worminghall
Haddenham
Kimble Wick
North Lee
Terrick
Marston
Forest Hill
Aston Sandford
Nash Lee
Wendover
Headington
Barton
Ickford
THE OXFORD STORY
UNIVERSITY
Holton
Waterperry
Shabbington
Owlswick
Little Kimble
Butler's Cross
St Leonard's
BOTANIC GARDEN
Wheatley
WATERPERRY GARDENS
Kingsey
Meadle
Ellesborough
Oxford
SHOTOVER
Waterstock
Great Kimble
New Hinksey
Horspath
RYCOTE CHAPEL
Towersey
Ilmer
Longwick
Askett
Dunsmore
Cowley
OXFORD SERVICES
Tiddington
Moreton
The Lee
South Hinksey
Iffley
Cuddesdon
Great Milton
Monks Risborough
Little Hampden
Littlemore
Pitch Green
MANOR HOUSE
Ballinger Common
Kennington
Denton
Emmington
Henton
Bledlow
Princes Risborough
Sandford on Thames
Garsington
Great Haseley
Tetsworth
Sydenham
Great Hampden
Saunderton
Prestwood
Great Missenden
Little Milton
Chinnor
Oakley
CHINNOR & PRINCES RISBOROUGH RAILWAY
Loosley Row
Toot Baldon
Little Haseley
Marsh Baldon
Radley
Nuneham Courtenay
ST KATHERINE'S
Chiselhampton
Postcombe
Crowell
Lacey Green
Speen
Kingshill
Stoke Talmage
Adwell
Kingston Blount
Stadhampton
South Weston
Aston Rowant
Radnage
Bledlow Ridge
Walters Ash
Upper North Dean
Great Kingshill
Easington
Lewknor
ASTON ROWANT
Cryers Hill
Widmer End
ABINGDON-ON-THAMES
Drayton St Leonard
Chalgrove
The City
Bradenham
Naphill
Clifton Hampden
Newington
Hughenden Valley
Berinsfield
Brightwell Baldwin
Pyrton
Shirburn
Stokenchurch
West Wycombe
HUGHENDEN MANOR
Burcot
Culham
Dorchester
Berrick Salome
Cuxham
Beacon's Bottom
WEST WYCOMBE CAVES
Downley
Hazlemere
PENDON MUS
Long Wittenham
DORCHESTER ABBEY
Watlington
Christmas Common
Ibstone
Tylers Green
Sutton Courtenay
Appleford
Warborough
Roke
THE RIDGEWAY
WEST WYCOMBE PARK
High Wycombe
Little Wittenham
Shillingford
Britwell Salome
Northend
Cadmore End
Bolter End
Booker
Wycombe Marsh
Benson
Ewelme
Greenfield
Turville Heath
Turville
Fingest
Lane End
Loudwater
DIDCOT RAILWAY CENTRE
Brightwell cum Sotwell
Preston Crowmarsh
Cookley Green
Pishill
Skirmett
WYCOMBE AIR PARK
Didcot
East Hagbourne
Wallingford
Crowmarsh Gifford
Russell's Water
STONOR
Frieth
Flackwell Heath
North Moreton
CHOLSEY AND WALLINGFORD RAILWAY
NUFFIELD PLACE
Park Corner
Marlow Bottom
Little Marlow
Wooburn Green
West Hagbourne
South Moreton
Stonor
Rockwell End
Lower Woodend
Upton
Aston Upthorpe
Nuffield
Well End
SU
Fawley
Bovingdon Green
Bourne End
Cores End
Cholsey
North Stoke
Nettlebed
Hambleden
Marlow
Aston Tirrold
Middle Assendon
Greenlands
Cookham Dean
Cookham
Blewbury
Ipsden
MAHARAJAH'S WELL
Bix
Lower Assendon
Mill End
Bisham
Highmoor Cross
Medmenham
Cookham Rise
Moulsford
South Stoke
Checkendon
Stoke Row
Satwell
GREYS COURT
Shepherd's Green
Remenham
Aston
Remenham Hill
THE THAMES PATH
Hurley
Windsor
Park Corner
Woodcote
Rotherfield Greys
Henley-on-Thames
Burchett's Green
Pinkneys Grn.
Furze Platt
Streatley
Goring
Cray's Pond
Sonning Common
Rotherfield Peppard
Harpsden
RIVER & ROWING MUSEUM
Warren Row
Maidenhead
Compton
STREATLEY ON THAMES
Goring Heath
ST BARTHOLOMEW'S
Cane End
Kidmore End
Lower Shiplake
Shiplake
Wargrave
Littlewick Green
Cox Grn.
Bray Wick
Aldworth
Lower Basildon
BEALE PARK
Whitchurch Hill
Binfield Hth.
Hare Hatch
White Waltham
WHITE WALTHAM
Woodlands Park
Holyport
Hampstead Norreys
THE LIVING RAINFOREST
Ashampstead
BASILDON PARK
Whitchurch
Mapledurham
Tokers Green
Dunsden Green
Maidenhead
Pangbourne
MAPLE-DURHAM
Sonning Eye
Waltham St Lawrence
Touchen End
Quicks Green
Upper Basildon
Purley
Emmer Green
Play Hatch
Twyford
Paley Street
Bray
Cherwell
Thame
Thames
Ray
Oxford
Buckingham
RIDGEWAY PATH
Hampden
CHILTERN HILLS
M40
A40
A41
A413
A418
A421
A4010
A404
A404(M)
A34
A4142
A4146
A4157
A329
A4074
A4130
A4155
A415
A417
A4129
A4009
A4095
A4421
A43
B4030
B4031
B4100
B4011
B4015
B4016
B4027
B4032
B4033
B4034
B4009
B4012
B4443
B4445
B480
B481
B482
B4493
B4526
B471
B478
B3024
52
53
26
27
40
1643
1642
187
197
147
171
246
255
211
188
141
185
260
187

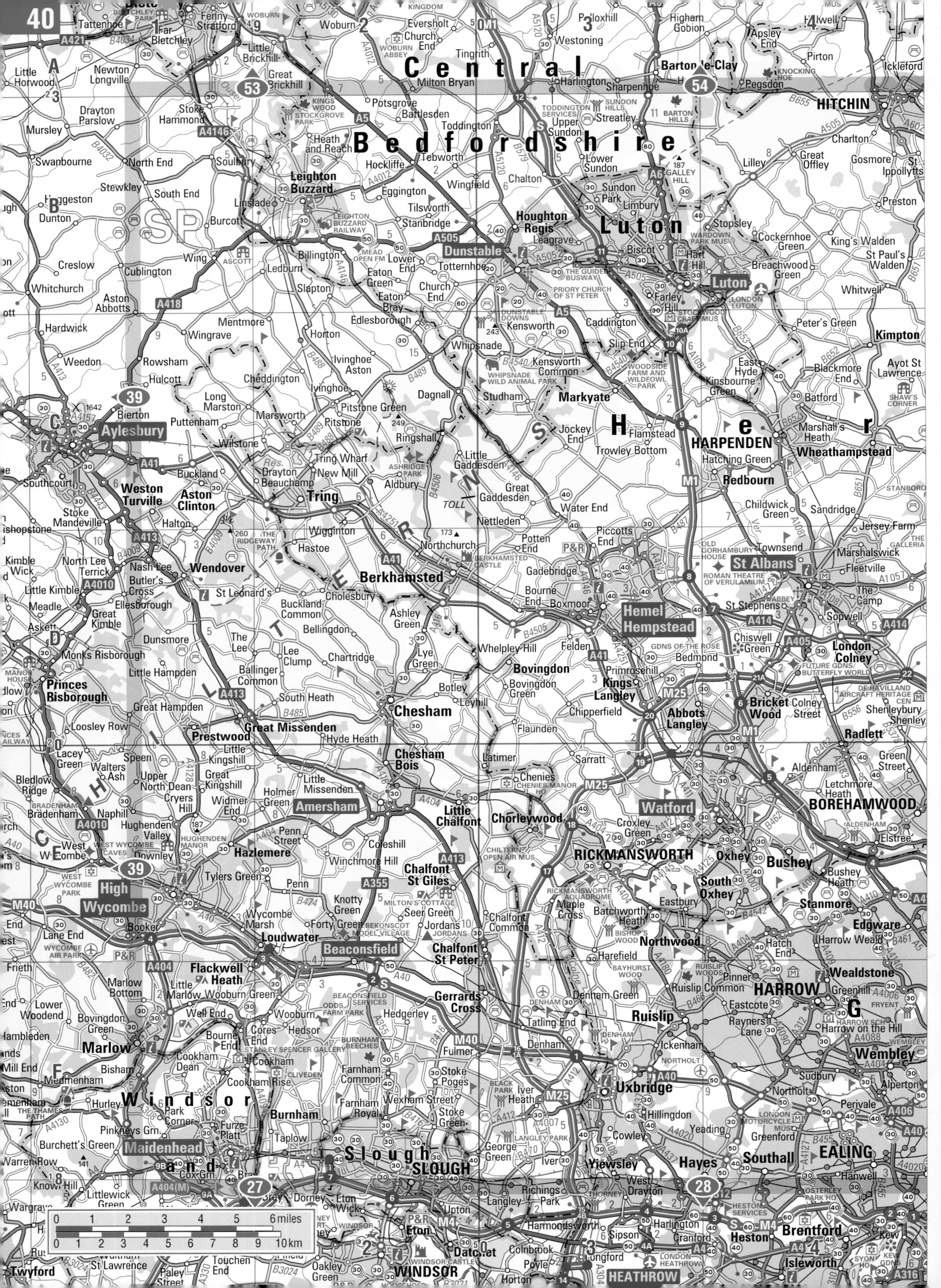

40
Central Bedfordshire
Hertfordshire
Chilterns
Windsor and Maidenhead
Slough
Tattenhoe
Fenny Stratford
Bletchley
Woburn
Eversholt
Church End
Tingrith
Milton Bryan
Westoning
Pulloxhill
Harlington
Higham Gobion
Barton-le-Clay
Sharpenhoe
Apsley End
Pirton
Ickleford
Pegsdon
HITCHIN
Little Horwood
Newton Longville
Little Brickhill
Great Brickhill
Drayton Parslow
Stoke Hammond
Potsgrove
Battlesden
Toddington
Upper Sundon
Streatley
Mursley
Swanbourne
North End
Soulbury
Heath and Reach
Leighton Buzzard
Hockliffe
Tebworth
Chalton
Lower Sundon
Sundon Park
Limbury
Lilley
Great Offley
Charlton
Gosmore
St Ippolyts
Stewkley
South End
Dunton
Linslade
Eggington
Tilsworth
Stanbridge
Wingfield
Houghton Regis
Leagrave
Luton
Stopsley
Cockernhoe Green
King's Walden
St Paul's Walden
Preston
Burcott
Wing
Creslow
Cublington
Whitchurch
Aston Abbotts
Billington
Ledburn
Slapton
Eaton Bray
Eaton Green
Lower End
Totternhoe
Dunstable
Church End
Biscot
Hart Hill
Farley Hill
Breachwood Green
Whitwell
Hardwick
Mentmore
Wingrave
Edlesborough
Horton
Whipsnade
Kensworth
Caddington
Slip End
Peter's Green
Kimpton
Weedon
Rowsham
Hulcott
Cheddington
Ivinghoe Aston
Ivinghoe
Kensworth Common
East Hyde
Kinsbourne Green
Blackmore End
Ayot St Lawrence
Bierton
Aylesbury
Long Marston
Puttenham
Marsworth
Pitstone Green
Pitstone
Dagnall
Studham
Markyate
Batford
Ringshall
Jockey End
Flamstead
Trowley Bottom
HARPENDEN
Marshall's Heath
Wheathampstead
Wilstone
Buckland
Drayton Beauchamp
Tring Wharf
New Mill
Tring
Aldbury
Little Gaddesden
Great Gaddesden
Hatching Green
Redbourn
Southcourt
Weston Turville
Aston Clinton
Stoke Mandeville
Halton
Water End
Nettleden
Childwick Green
Sandridge
Jersey Farm
Wigginton
Hastoe
Northchurch
Potten End
Piccotts End
Townsend
Marshalswick
Kimble Wick
North Lee
Terrick
Nash Lee
Wendover
Butler's Cross
Little Kimble
Ellesborough
St Leonard's
Berkhamsted
Gadebridge
St Albans
Fleetville
Meadle
Great Kimble
Buckland Common
Cholesbury
Ashley Green
Bourne End
Boxmoor
Hemel Hempstead
St.Stephens
The Camp
Sopwell
Askett
Monks Risborough
Dunsmore
The Lee
Lee Clump
Bellingdon
Chartridge
Lye Green
Whelpley Hill
Felden
Bovingdon
Chiswell Green
Bedmond
London Colney
Princes Risborough
Little Hampden
Ballinger Common
Bovingdon Green
Primrosehill
Kings Langley
Great Hampden
South Heath
Chesham
Botley
Leyhill
Chipperfield
Abbots Langley
Bricket Wood
Colney Street
Shenleybury
Shenley
Loosley Row
Prestwood
Great Missenden
Hyde Heath
Flaunden
Radlett
Lacey Green
Speen
Walters Ash
Little Kingshill
Great Kingshill
Chesham Bois
Latimer
Sarratt
Aldenham
Green Street
Bledlow Ridge
Upper North Dean
Little Missenden
Holmer Green
Cryers Hill
Widmer End
Amersham
Chenies
Little Chalfont
Chorleywood
Watford
Letchmore Heath
BOREHAMWOOD
Bradenham
Naphill
Hughenden Valley
Penn Street
Coleshill
Croxley Green
Elstree
West Wycombe
Downley
Hazlemere
Winchmore Hill
Chalfont St Giles
RICKMANSWORTH
Oxhey
Bushey
High Wycombe
Tylers Green
Penn
Knotty Green
Seer Green
Jordans
Maple Cross
South Oxhey
Bushey Heath
Eastbury
Stanmore
Lane End
Booker
Wycombe Marsh
Loudwater
Forty Green
Chalfont Common
Batchworth Heath
Edgware
Beaconsfield
Chalfont St Peter
Northwood
Harefield
Hatch End
Harrow Weald
Frieth
Marlow Bottom
Flackwell Heath
Little Marlow
Wooburn Green
Gerrards Cross
Denham Green
Ruislip Common
Pinner
HARROW
Wealdstone
Greenhill
Lower Woodend
Bovingdon Green
Well End
Wooburn
Hedsor
Hedgerley
Tatling End
Ruislip
Eastcote
Rayners Lane
Harrow on the Hill
Marlow
Bourne End
Cores End
Denham
Ickenham
Wembley
Bisham
Medmenham
Cookham Dean
Cookham
Cookham Rise
Farnham Common
Stoke Poges
Fulmer
Uxbridge
Sudbury
Alperton
Hurley
Park Corner
Furze Platt
Burnham
Farnham Royal
Wexham Street
Stoke Green
Iver Heath
Hillingdon
Northolt
Perivale
Pinkneys Grn.
Maidenhead
Taplow
George Green
Iver
Cowley
Yeading
Greenford
Burchett's Green
Cox Grn.
Bray
SLOUGH
Yiewsley
West Drayton
Hayes
Southall
EALING
Knowl Hill
Littlewick Green
Dorney
Eton Wick
Upton
Langley
Richings Park
Hanwell
Wargrave
Eton
Datchet
Harmondsworth
Sipson
Harlington
Cranford
Heston
Brentford
Kew
Twyford
St Lawrence Waltham
Paley Street
Touchen End
Oakley Green
WINDSOR
Colnbrook
Poyle
Horton
Longford
HEATHROW
Isleworth
0 1 2 3 4 5 6 miles
0 1 2 3 4 5 6 7 8 9 10 km

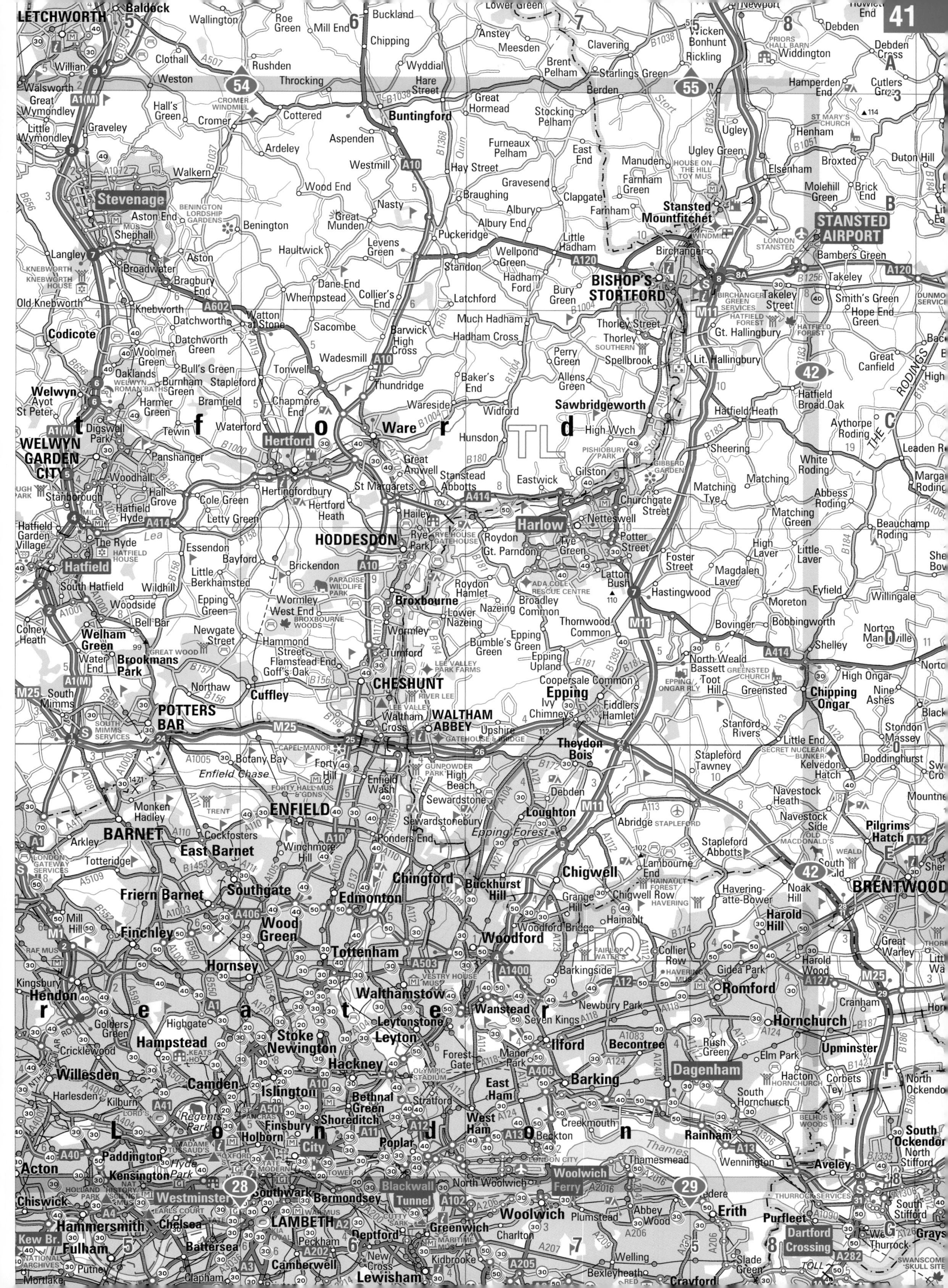

41
LETCHWORTH
Baldock
Wallington
Roe Green
Mill End
Buckland
Chipping
Anstey
Meesden
Clavering
Wicken Bonhunt
Rickling
Debden
Widdington
Debden Cross
Willian
Clothall
Rushden
Weston
Throcking
Wyddial
Hare Street
Brent Pelham
Starlings Green
Berden
Cutlers Green
Hamperden End
Walsworth
Great Wymondley
Little Wymondley
Hall's Green
Cromer
Cottered
Buntingford
Great Hormead
Stocking Pelham
Henham
Ugley
Ugley Green
Graveley
Aspenden
Ardeley
Westmill
Furneaux Pelham
Hay Street
East End
Manuden
Elsenham
Broxted
Duton Hill
Walkern
Stevenage
Wood End
Gravesend
Farnham Green
Clapgate
Molehill Green
Brick End
Aston End
Shephall
Benington
Nasty
Great Munden
Braughing
Albury
Albury End
Farnham
Stansted Mountfitchet
STANSTED AIRPORT
Langley
Aston
Haultwick
Levens Green
Puckeridge
Wellpond Green
Little Hadham
Birchanger
Bambers Green
Broadwater
Knebworth
Bragbury End
Dane End
Standon
Hadham Ford
Bury Green
BISHOP'S STORTFORD
Takeley
Takeley Street
Smith's Green
Old Knebworth
Whempstead
Collier's End
Latchford
Hope End Green
Codicote
Datchworth
Datchworth Green
Watton at Stone
Sacombe
Barwick
High Cross
Much Hadham
Hadham Cross
Thorley Street
Thorley
Gt. Hallingbury
Woolmer Green
Bull's Green
Wadesmill
Tonwell
Perry Green
Spellbrook
Lit. Hallingbury
Great Canfield
Oaklands
Burnham Green
Stapleford
Thundridge
Baker's End
Allens Green
Welwyn
Ayot St Peter
Harmer Green
Bramfield
Chapmore End
Wareside
Widford
Sawbridgeworth
Hatfield Heath
Hatfield Broad Oak
High Roding
Digswell Park
Tewin
Waterford
Ware
Hunsdon
High Wych
Aythorpe Roding
WELWYN GARDEN CITY
Hertford
Panshanger
Great Amwell
Stanstead Abbotts
Eastwick
Gilston
Sheering
White Roding
Leaden Roding
Woodhall
Stanborough
Hall Grove
Hertingfordbury
St Margarets
Matching
Matching Tye
Abbess Roding
Margaret Roding
Hatfield Hyde
Cole Green
Hertford Heath
Hailey
Churchgate Street
Letty Green
Harlow
Netteswell
Matching Green
Beauchamp Roding
Hatfield Garden Village
The Ryde
HODDESDON
Rye Park
Roydon
Gt. Parndon
Tye Green
Potter Street
Essendon
Bayford
Hatfield
Brickendon
Foster Street
High Laver
Little Laver
Magdalen Laver
Latton Bush
South Hatfield
Little Berkhamsted
Wildhill
Roydon Hamlet
Hastingwood
Fyfield
Willingale
Woodside
Epping Green
Wormley West End
Broxbourne
Broadley Common
Nazeing
Lower Nazeing
Moreton
Colney Heath
Bell Bar
Welham Green
Newgate Street
Hammond Street
Wormley
Bumble's Green
Epping Green
Thornwood Common
Bovinger
Bobbingworth
Norton Mandeville
Water End
Brookmans Park
Flamstead End
Goff's Oak
Turnford
Epping Upland
North Weald Bassett
Toot Hill
Greensted
Shelley
High Ongar
Chipping Ongar
Nine Ashes
South Mimms
Northaw
Cuffley
CHESHUNT
Coopersale Common
Epping
Ivy Chimneys
Fiddlers Hamlet
POTTERS BAR
Waltham Cross
WALTHAM ABBEY
Upshire
Theydon Bois
Stanford Rivers
Little End
Stondon Massey
Doddinghurst
Botany Bay
Enfield Chase
Forty Hill
Enfield Wash
High Beach
Stapleford Tawney
Kelvedon Hatch
Sewardstone
Debden
Loughton
Navestock Heath
Navestock Side
Monken Hadley
ENFIELD
Sewardstonebury
Epping Forest
Abridge
Stapleford Abbotts
Pilgrims Hatch
BARNET
Arkley
Cockfosters
East Barnet
Winchmore Hill
Ponders End
Lambourne End
Totteridge
Chigwell
Chigwell Row
Havering-atte-Bower
Noak Hill
South Weald
BRENTWOOD
Friern Barnet
Southgate
Edmonton
Chingford
Buckhurst Hill
Grange Hill
Hainault
Harold Hill
Mill Hill
Finchley
Wood Green
Woodford
Woodford Bridge
Collier Row
Great Warley
Hornsey
Tottenham
Barkingside
Gidea Park
Harold Wood
Kingsbury
Hendon
Walthamstow
Romford
Wanstead
Newbury Park
Seven Kings
Cranham
Golders Green
Highgate
Hampstead
Stoke Newington
Leytonstone
Leyton
Ilford
Becontree
Hornchurch
Cricklewood
Hackney
Forest Gate
Manor Park
Rush Green
Elm Park
Upminster
Willesden
Harlesden
Camden
Islington
Bethnal Green
Stratford
East Ham
Barking
Dagenham
Hacton
South Hornchurch
Corbets Tey
North Ockendon
Kilburn
Regents Park
Finsbury
Shoreditch
West Ham
Creekmouth
Beckton
Rainham
South Ockendon
Paddington
Holborn
City
Poplar
Thames
Thamesmead
Wennington
Aveley
North Stifford
Acton
Kensington
Hyde Park
Westminster
Southwark
Bermondsey
Blackwall Tunnel
North Woolwich
Woolwich Ferry
Erith
Chiswick
Hammersmith
Chelsea
LAMBETH
Deptford
Greenwich
Woolwich
Plumstead
Abbey Wood
Purfleet
Dartford Crossing
South Stifford
Grays
West Thurrock
Kew Br.
Fulham
Battersea
Peckham
Charlton
Welling
Putney
Camberwell
New Cross
Kidbrooke
Bexleyheath
Slade Green
Mortlake
Clapham
Lewisham
Crayford

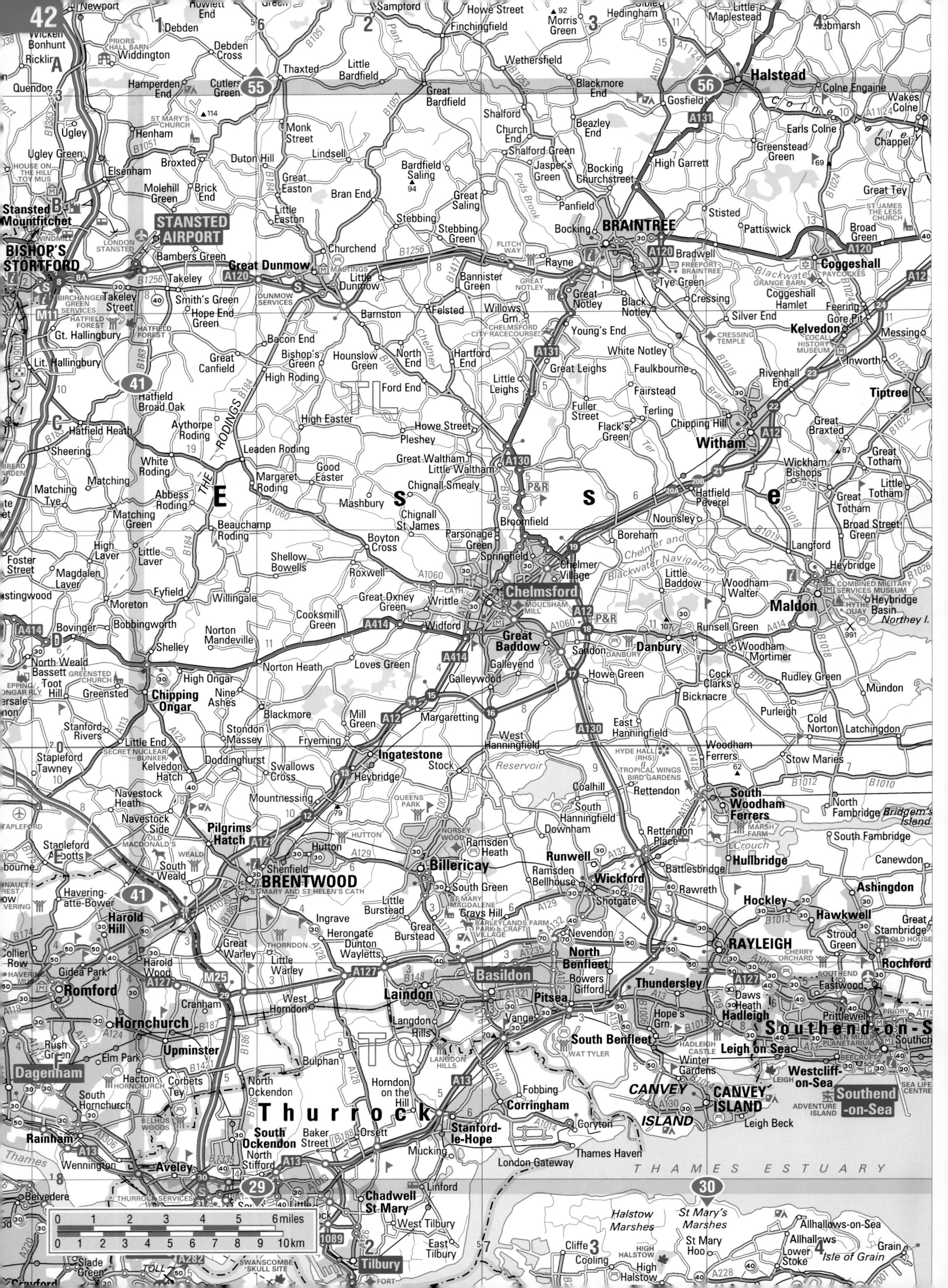
Newport
Debden
Samptord
Howe Street
Finchingfield
Morris Green
Hedingham
Little Maplestead
Wicken Bonhunt
Ricklin
Widdington
Debden Cross
Thaxted
Little Bardfield
Wethersfield
Halstead
Quendon
Hampenden End
Cutlers Green
55
56
Great Bardfield
Blackmore End
Gosfield
Colne Engaine
Wakes Colne
Shalford
Ugley
Henham
Monk Street
Church End
Beazley End
Earls Colne
Chappel
Ugley Green
Broxted
Duton Hill
Lindsell
Shalford Green
Jasper's Green
Bocking Churchstreet
High Garrett
Greenstead Green
Elsenham
Bardfield Saling
Molehill Green
Brick End
Great Easton
Bran End
Great Saling
Panfield
Great Tey
Stansted Mountfitchet
STANSTED AIRPORT
Little Easton
Stebbing
Stebbing Green
Stisted
Pattiswick
Bocking
BRAINTREE
Broad Green
BISHOP'S STORTFORD
Bambers Green
Churchend
Great Dunmow
Rayne
Bradwell
Coggeshall
Takeley
Little Dunmow
Bannister Green
Tye Green
Coggeshall Hamlet
Takeley Street
Smith's Green
Hope End Green
Barnston
Felsted
Willows Grn.
Great Notley
Black Notley
Cressing
Feering
Gore Pit
Gt. Hallingbury
Silver End
Kelvedon
Messing
Young's End
Bacon End
Bishop's Green
Hounslow Green
North End
Hartford End
White Notley
Lit. Hallingbury
Great Canfield
High Roding
Great Leighs
Faulkbourne
Inworth
Rivenhall End
Ford End
Little Leighs
Fairstead
Tiptree
Hatfield Broad Oak
Fuller Street
Terling
Aythorpe Roding
High Easter
Howe Street
Chipping Hill
Great Braxted
Hatfield Heath
Pleshey
Flack's Green
Witham
Sheering
Leaden Roding
Great Waltham
Little Waltham
Great Totham
White Roding
Good Easter
Wickham Bishops
Little Totham
Matching
Margaret Roding
Chignall Smealy
Hatfield Peverel
Matching Tye
Abbess Roding
Mashbury
Great Totham
Matching Green
E
s
s
e
Chignall St James
Broomfield
Nounsley
Broad Street Green
Beauchamp Roding
Boreham
Langford
High Laver
Parsonage Green
Foster Street
Little Laver
Boyton Cross
Springfield
Heybridge
Magdalen Laver
Shellow Bowells
Chelmer Village
Roxwell
Little Baddow
Woodham Walter
Fyfield
Chelmsford
Heybridge Basin
Moreton
Willingale
Great Oxney Green
Writtle
Maldon
Northey I.
Bovinger
Bobbingworth
Cooksmill Green
Widford
Norton Mandeville
Great Baddow
Sandon
Danbury
Runsell Green
Woodham Mortimer
North Weald Bassett
Shelley
Norton Heath
Loves Green
Galleyend
Howe Green
Cock Clarks
Rudley Green
Toot Hill
Greensted
High Ongar
Galleywood
Mundon
Chipping Ongar
Nine Ashes
Bicknacre
Blackmore
Mill Green
Margaretting
Purleigh
Cold Norton
Stanford Rivers
Latchingdon
Stondon Massey
Fryerning
East Hanningfield
West Hanningfield
Little End
Woodham Ferrers
Stapleford Tawney
Doddinghurst
Ingatestone
Stow Maries
Kelvedon Hatch
Swallows Cross
Stock
Reservoir
Heybridge
Coalhill
Rettendon
South Woodham Ferrers
North Fambridge
Navestock Heath
Mountnessing
South Hanningfield
Downham
Navestock Side
Ramsden Heath
Rettendon Place
South Fambridge
Pilgrims Hatch
Hutton
Runwell
Stapleford Abbotts
Shenfield
Billericay
Ramsden Bellhouse
Battlesbridge
Hullbridge
Canewdon
South Weald
BRENTWOOD
South Green
Wickford
Rawreth
Ashingdon
Havering-atte-Bower
Little Burstead
Shotgate
Hockley
Hawkwell
Harold Hill
Ingrave
Great Burstead
Crays Hill
Nevendon
Great Stambridge
Great Warley
Herongate
Dunton Wayletts
RAYLEIGH
Stroud Green
North Benfleet
Harold Wood
Little Warley
Rochford
Gidea Park
Basildon
Bowers Gifford
Thundersley
Romford
Eastwood
Laindon
Daws Heath
Cranham
West Horndon
Pitsea
Hope's Grn.
Prittlewell
Hadleigh
Hornchurch
Langdon Hills
Vange
Southend-on-S
Rush Green
Elm Park
Upminster
South Benfleet
Leigh on Sea
Southch
Bulphan
Dagenham
Westcliff-on-Sea
Hacton
Corbets Tey
North Ockendon
Horndon on the Hill
Fobbing
CANVEY ISLAND
Southend-on-Sea
South Hornchurch
Corringham
CANVEY ISLAND
Thurrock
Leigh Beck
Rainham
South Ockendon
Baker Street
Orsett
Stanford-le-Hope
Coryton
Wennington
North Stifford
Mucking
Thames Haven
Aveley
London Gateway
THAMES ESTUARY
Thames
29
30
Linford
Belvedere
Chadwell St Mary
Halstow Marshes
St Mary's Marshes
Allhallows-on-Sea
West Tilbury
Allhallows
St Mary Hoo
Lower Stoke
Grain
East Tilbury
Cliffe
Cooling
High Halstow
Isle of Grain
Slade Green
Tilbury
High Halstow
Crayford
0 1 2 3 4 5 6 miles
0 1 2 3 4 5 6 7 8 9 10 km

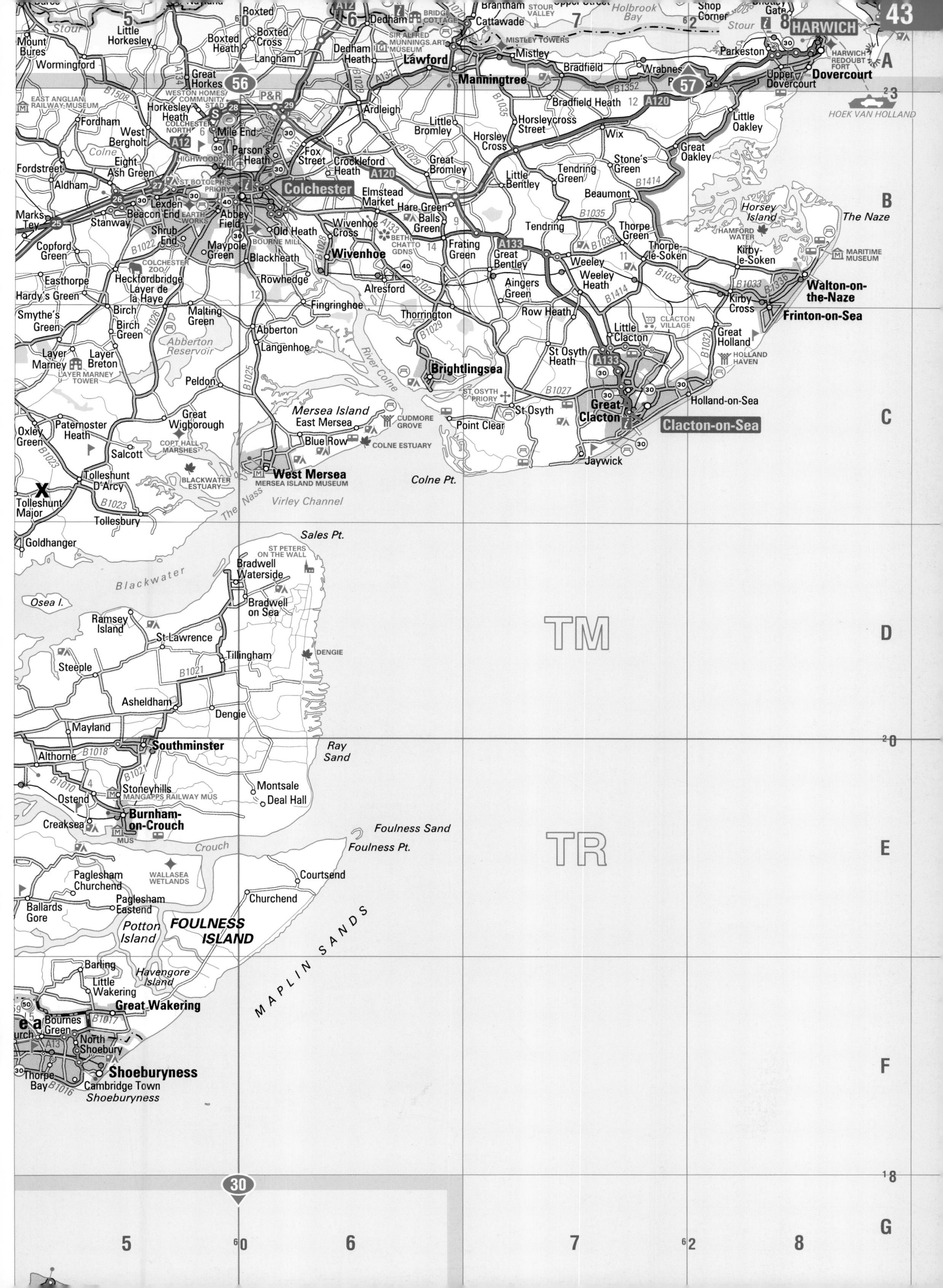
HARWICH
Dovercourt
Upper Dovercourt
Parkeston
HARWICH REDOUBT FORT
HOEK VAN HOLLAND
Brantham
STOUR VALLEY
Holbrook Bay
Shop Corner
Stour
Cattawade
Dedham
BRIDGE COTTAGE
SIR ALFRED MUNNINGS ART MUSEUM
Dedham Heath
Lawford
MISTLEY TOWERS
Mistley
Manningtree
Bradfield
Wrabness
Bradfield Heath
Boxted
Boxted Cross
Boxted Heath
Langham
Little Horkesley
Mount Bures
Wormingford
Great Horkes
WESTON HOMES COMMUNITY STAD
EAST ANGLIAN RAILWAY MUSEUM
Horkesley Heath
COLCHESTER NORTH
Fordham
West Bergholt
Mile End
Ardleigh
Little Bromley
Horsleycross Street
Horsley Cross
Wix
Little Oakley
Great Oakley
Stone's Green
Tendring Green
Little Bentley
Great Bromley
Crockleford Heath
Fox Street
Parson's Heath
HIGHWOODS
Colne
Eight Ash Green
Fordstreet
Aldham
ST BOTOLPH'S PRIORY
Colchester
Elmstead Market
Hare Green
Balls Green
Beaumont
Horsey Island
The Naze
HAMFORD WATER
MARITIME MUSEUM
Kirby-le-Soken
Thorpe Green
Thorpe-le-Soken
Tendring
Marks Tey
Stanway
Lexden
Beacon End
EARTH WORKS
Abbey Field
Shrub End
Maypole Green
Old Heath
BOURNE MILL
Wivenhoe Cross
Wivenhoe
BETH CHATTO GDNS
Frating Green
Great Bentley
Weeley
Weeley Heath
Walton-on-the-Naze
Kirby Cross
Frinton-on-Sea
Copford Green
COLCHESTER ZOO
Blackheath
Rowhedge
Alresford
Aingers Green
Row Heath
Easthorpe
Heckfordbridge
Layer de la Haye
Hardy's Green
Smythe's Green
Birch
Birch Green
Malting Green
Fingringhoe
Thorrington
CLACTON VILLAGE
Little Clacton
Great Holland
HOLLAND HAVEN
Abberton
Langenhoe
Abberton Reservoir
Layer Marney
Layer Breton
LAYER MARNEY TOWER
River Colne
St Osyth Heath
Brightlingsea
Peldon
ST OSYTH PRIORY
St Osyth
Great Clacton
Holland-on-Sea
Clacton-on-Sea
Mersea Island
East Mersea
CUDMORE GROVE
Point Clear
Oxley Green
Paternoster Heath
Great Wigborough
COPT HALL MARSHES
Salcott
Blue Row
COLNE ESTUARY
Jaywick
Tolleshunt D'Arcy
BLACKWATER ESTUARY
West Mersea
MERSEA ISLAND MUSEUM
Colne Pt.
Tolleshunt Major
The Nass
Virley Channel
Tollesbury
Goldhanger
Sales Pt.
ST PETERS ON THE WALL
Bradwell Waterside
Blackwater
Osea I.
Bradwell on Sea
Ramsey Island
St Lawrence
Tillingham
DENGIE
Steeple
TM
Asheldham
Dengie
Mayland
Southminster
Althorne
Ray Sand
Stoneyhills
MANGAPPS RAILWAY MUS
Montsale
Deal Hall
Ostend
Burnham-on-Crouch
Creaksea
Foulness Sand
Foulness Pt.
Crouch
TR
Paglesham Churchend
WALLASEA WETLANDS
Courtsend
Ballards Gore
Paglesham Eastend
Churchend
Potton Island
FOULNESS ISLAND
MAPLIN SANDS
Barling
Havengore Island
Little Wakering
Great Wakering
Bournes Green
North Shoebury
Shoeburyness
Thorpe Bay
Cambridge Town
Shoeburyness
A12
A120
A133
A134
A137
A13
B1508
B1029
B1035
B1352
B1414
B1035
B1033
B1028
B1027
B1022
B1026
B1025
B1029
B1027
B1032
B1033
B1336
B1023
B1021
B1018
B1010
B1017
B1016
56
57
30
A
B
C
D
E
F
G
5
6
7
8

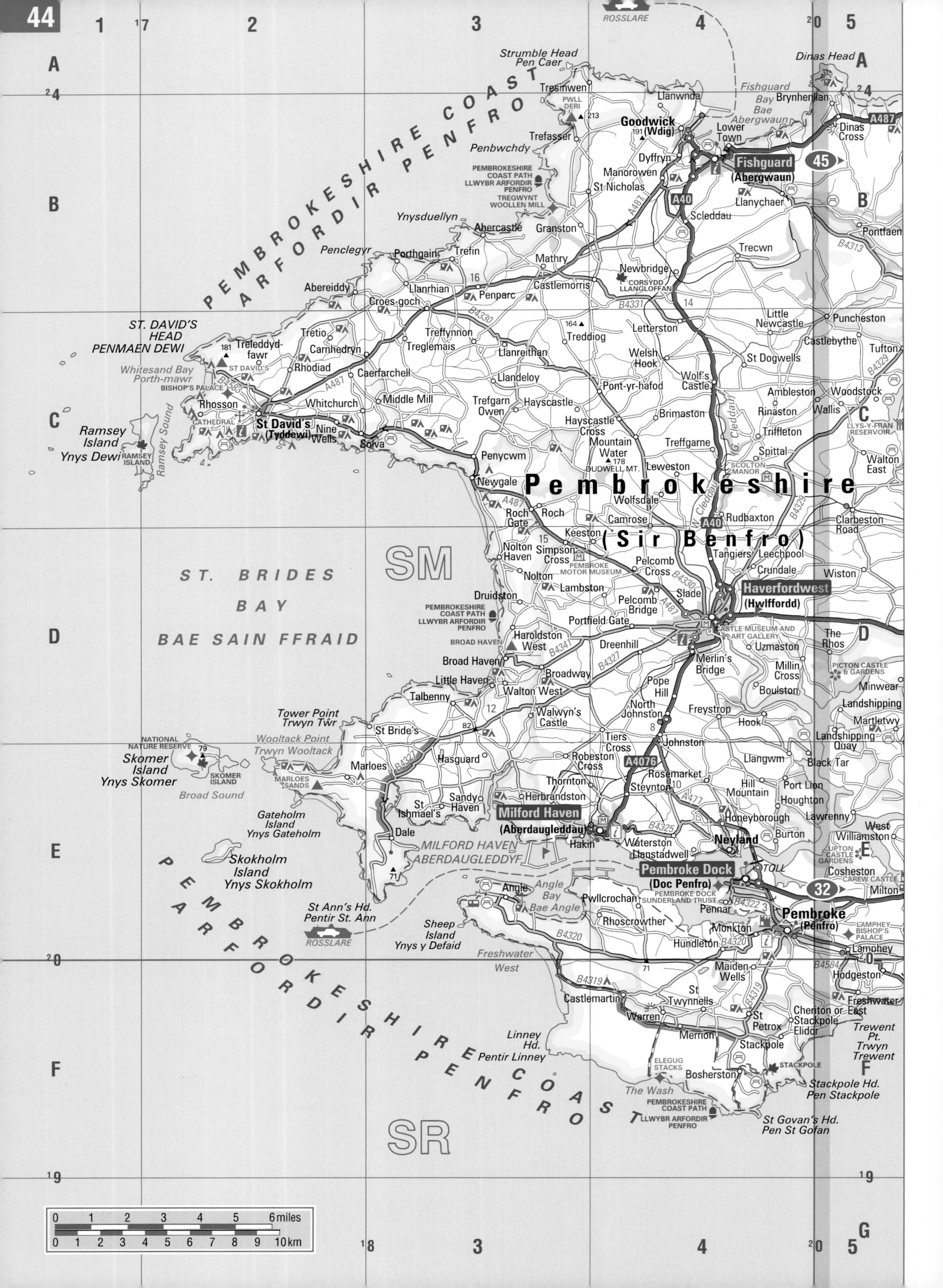
ROSSLARE
Strumble Head
Pen Caer
Dinas Head
PEMBROKESHIRE COAST
ARFORDIR PENFRO
Tresinwen
Llanwnda
Fishguard Bay
Bae Abergwaun
Brynhenllan
Dinas Cross
A487
PWLL DERI
Goodwick
(Wdig)
Lower Town
Trefasser
Penbwchdy
Dyffryn
Fishguard
(Abergwaun)
45
PEMBROKESHIRE COAST PATH
LLWYBR ARFORDIR PENFRO
Manorowen
St Nicholas
A40
TREGWYNT WOOLLEN MILL
Llanychaer
Ynysduellyn
Scleddau
Abercastle
Granston
Pontfaen
B4313
Penclegyr
Porthgain
Trefin
Trecwn
Mathry
Newbridge
Abereiddy
Llanrhian
Castlemorris
CORSYDD LLANGLOFFAN
Penparc
Croes-goch
B4331
Little Newcastle
Puncheston
B4330
ST. DAVID'S HEAD
PENMAEN DEWI
Tretio
Treffynnon
Letterston
Treddiog
Castlebythe
Tufton
Treleddyd-fawr
Carnhedryn
Treglemais
Llanreithan
Welsh Hook
St Dogwells
B4329
Whitesand Bay
Porth-mawr
ST DAVID'S
Rhodiad
Caerfarchell
Llandeloy
Wolf's Castle
Pont-yr-hafod
Ambleston
Woodstock
BISHOP'S PALACE
A487
Rhosson
Middle Mill
Whitchurch
Trefgarn Owen
Hayscastle
Rinaston
Wallis
Ramsey Island
Ynys Dewi
RAMSEY ISLAND
Ramsey Sound
CATHEDRAL
St David's
(Tyddewi)
Nine Wells
Solva
Hayscastle Cross
Brimaston
Triffleton
LLYS-Y-FRAN RESERVOIR
Mountain Water
Treffgarne
Spittal
Penycwm
DUDWELL MT.
Leweston
SCOLTON MANOR
Walton East
Newgale
Pembrokeshire
Wolfsdale
Roch Gate
Roch
Camrose
Rudbaxton
Clarbeston Road
Keeston
(Sir Benfro)
Nolton Haven
Simpson Cross
Tangiers
Leechpool
SM
ST. BRIDES BAY
BAE SAIN FFRAID
PEMBROKE MOTOR MUSEUM
Pelcomb Cross
Crundale
Wiston
Nolton
Lambston
Haverfordwest
(Hwlffordd)
Druidston
Pelcomb Bridge
Slade
Portfield Gate
CASTLE MUSEUM AND ART GALLERY
The Rhos
Haroldston West
BROAD HAVEN
B4341
Dreenhill
Uzmaston
Merlin's Bridge
PICTON CASTLE & GARDENS
Millin Cross
Broad Haven
B4327
Broadway
Pope Hill
Minwear
Little Haven
Walton West
Boulston
Talbenny
Landshipping
North Johnston
Freystrop
Martletwy
Tower Point
Trwyn Twr
Walwyn's Castle
Hook
St Bride's
Landshipping Quay
NATIONAL NATURE RESERVE
Wooltack Point
Trwyn Wooltack
Tiers Cross
Johnston
Skomer Island
Ynys Skomer
SKOMER ISLAND
Marloes
Hasguard
Robeston Cross
A4076
Llangwm
Black Tar
MARLOES SANDS
Rosemarket
Thornton
Hill Mountain
Port Lion
Broad Sound
Sandy Haven
Herbrandston
Steynton
Houghton
Gateholm Island
Ynys Gateholm
St Ishmael's
Milford Haven
(Aberdaugleddau)
A477
Honeyborough
Lawrenny
Dale
Hakin
B4325
Neyland
Burton
West Williamston
MILFORD HAVEN
ABERDAUGLEDDYF
Waterston
Llanstadwell
UPTON CASTLE GARDENS
Skokholm Island
Ynys Skokholm
Pembroke Dock
(Doc Penfro)
TOLL
Cosheston
CAREW CASTLE
Angle
Angle Bay
Bae Angle
Pwllcrochan
PEMBROKE DOCK SUNDERLAND TRUST
32
Milton
St Ann's Hd.
Pentir St. Ann
Pennar
B4322
Pembroke
(Penfro)
Rhoscrowther
Sheep Island
Ynys y Defaid
ROSSLARE
B4320
Monkton
LAMPHEY BISHOP'S PALACE
Hundleton
Lamphey
Freshwater West
B4584
Hodgeston
Maiden Wells
B4319
Castlemartin
St Twynnells
Freshwater East
Warren
St Petrox
Cheriton or Stackpole Elidor
Linney Hd.
Pentir Linney
Merrion
Trewent Pt.
Trwyn Trewent
Stackpole
ELEGUG STACKS
STACKPOLE
Bosherston
Stackpole Hd.
Pen Stackpole
The Wash
PEMBROKESHIRE COAST PATH
LLWYBR ARFORDIR PENFRO
St Govan's Hd.
Pen St Gofan
SR
0 1 2 3 4 5 6 miles
0 1 2 3 4 5 6 7 8 9 10 km

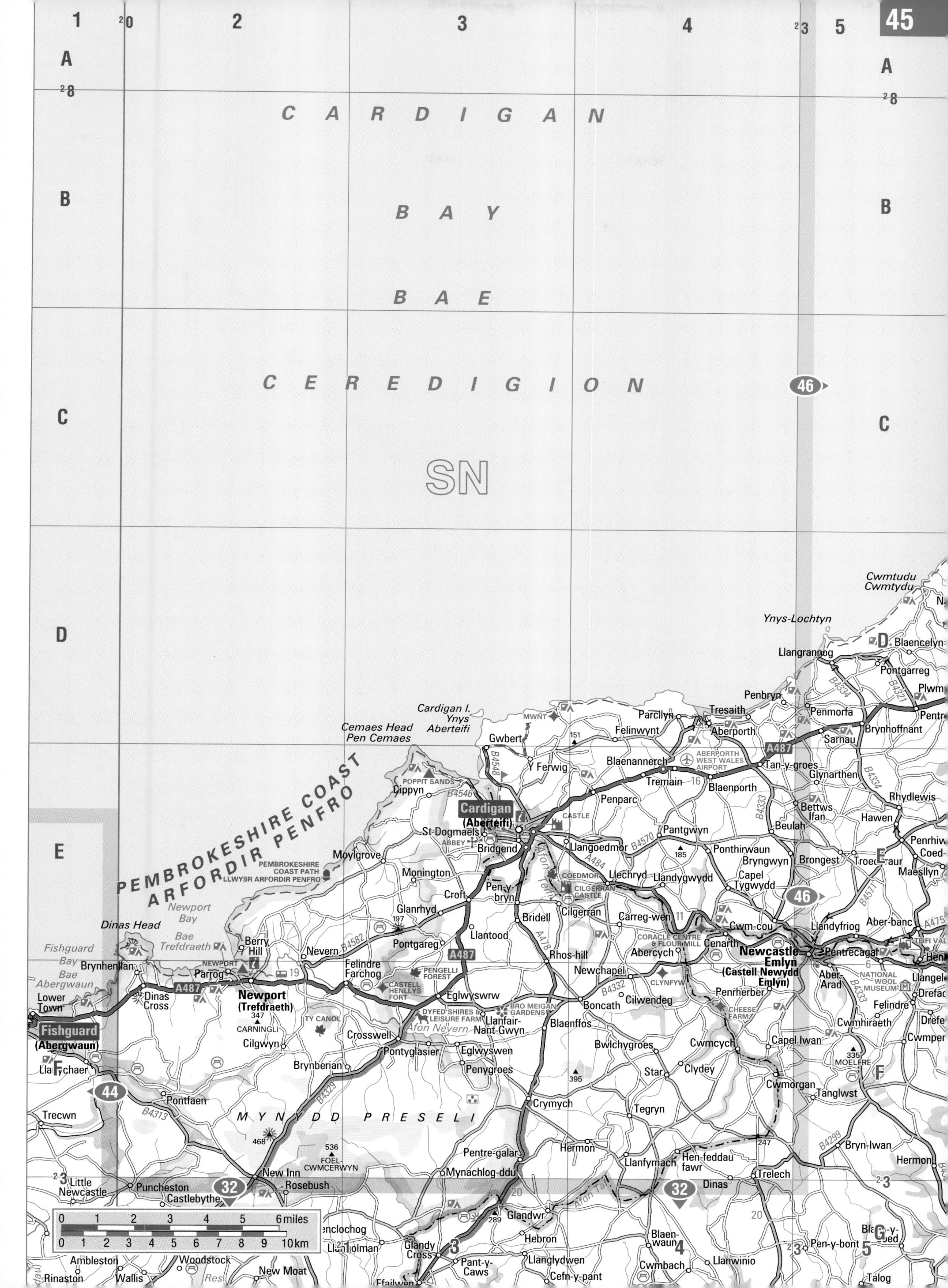

CARDIGAN

BAY

BAE

CEREDIGION

SN

Cwmtudu
Cwmtydu

Ynys-Lochtyn

Llangrannog   Blaencelyn

Pontgarreg   Plwm

Penbryn   Penmorfa   Pentr

Cardigan I.   MWNT   Parcllyn   Tresaith
Ynys   151   Brynhoffnant
Aberteifi   Felinwynt   Aberporth   Sarnau
Cemaes Head   Gwbert   ABERPORTH WEST WALES AIRPORT   Tan-y-groes
Pen Cemaes   Blaenannerch   A487   Glynarthen   Rhydlewis
Y Ferwig   Tremain   16   Blaenporth   Bettws   Hawen
POPPIT SANDS   B4548   Penparc   Ifan   Beulah
Cippyn   B4546   Pantgwyn   Penrhiw-
Cardigan   CASTLE   185   Ponthirwaun   Coed
(Aberteifi)   Llangoedmor   B4570   Bryngwyn   Brongest   Troed-
St-Dogmaels   Bridgend   A484   Llechryd   Llandygwydd   Capel   r-aur
ABBEY   COEDMOR   Tygwydd   Maesllyn
Moylgrove   CILGERRAN   46
                    CASTLE   Carreg-wen   11   Cwm-cou   Aber-banc
Monington   Pen-y-   Bridell   Cilgerran   Llandyfriog   A475
Croft   bryn   Newcastle
Glanrhyd   Llantood   CORACLE CENTRE   Emlyn   Pentrecagal
197   & FLOURMILL   (Castell Newydd   TEIFI VAL
Berry   Rhos-hill   Genarth   Emlyn)
Dinas Head   Hill   Pontgareg   Newchapel   Abercych   Aber-   NATIONAL
Nevern   B4582   CLYNFYW   Arad   WOOL   Llangele
Fishguard   NEWPORT   19   Felindre   PENGELLI   Penrherber   MUSEUM   M   Drefac
Bay   Brynhenllan   Parrog   Farchog   FOREST   Newchapel   CHEESE   Felindre
Bae Abergwaun   A487   CASTELL   Boncath   Cilwendeg   FARM   Drefe
Lower   Dinas   Newport   HENLLYS FORT   Bwlchygroes   Cwmhiraeth   Cwmper
Town   Cross   (Trefdraeth)   DYFED SHIRES &   BRO MEIGAN   Cwmcych   Capel Iwan
Fishguard   347   LEISURE FARM   GARDENS   Star   335
(Abergwaun)   CARNINGLI   TY CANOL   Llanfair-   Clydey   MOELFRE
Cilgwyn   Crosswell   Nant-Gwyn   Blaenffos   Cwmorgan
Lla F chaer   Brynberian   Afon Nevern   Cwmbach   Tanglwst
44   Pontyglasier   Eglwyswen   Penygroes   Cwmcych
Pontfaen   B4329   Crymych   Tegryn   B4299   Bryn-Iwan
Trecwn   B4313   468   MYNYDD   PRESELI   395   Hermon
536   Pentre-galar   Llanfyrnach   Hen-feddau   247   Hermon
FOEL-   fawr
CWMCERWYN   Mynachlog-ddu   32   Dinas   Trelech
Little   New Inn   Hermon   Blaen-
Newcastle   Puncheston   32   Rosebush   Glandwr   waun   Pen-y-bont
Castlebythe   289   Glandy   Hebron   Llanglydwen   Talog
Ambleston   Woodstock   Glandwr   Cross   Pant-y-   Cefn-y-pant
Rinaston   Wallis   New Moat   Res   Caws   Cwmbach   Llanwinio

0   1   2   3   4   5   6 miles
0 1 2 3 4 5 6 7 8 9 10km

PEMBROKESHIRE COAST
ARFORDIR PENFRO

PEMBROKESHIRE
COAST PATH
LLWYBR ARFORDIR PENFRO

Newport Bay
Bae Trefdraeth

46

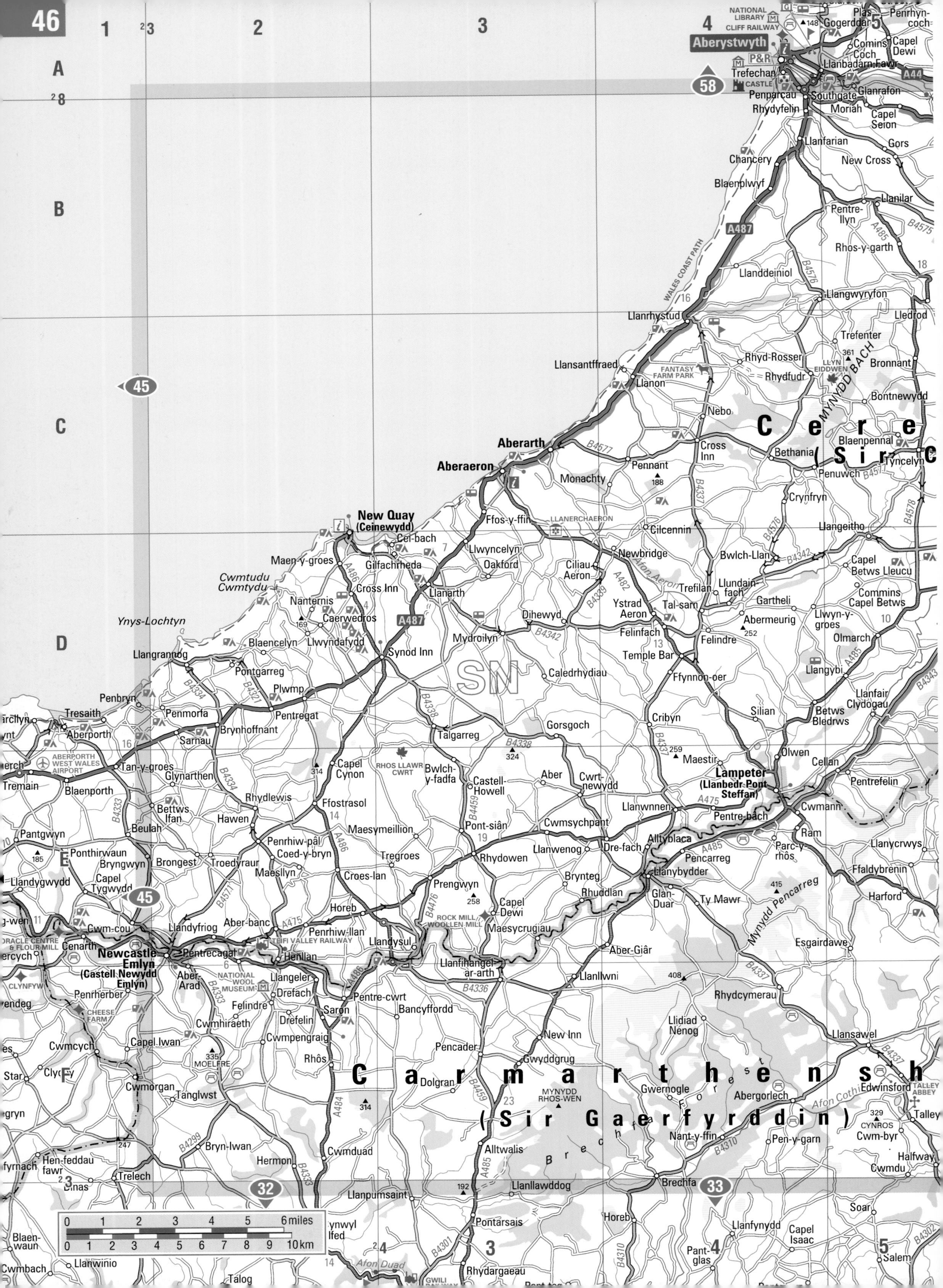
1
2
3
4
5
A
B
C
D
E
F
58
45
32
33
NATIONAL LIBRARY
CLIFF RAILWAY
Aberystwyth
P&R
Trefechan
CASTLE
Penparcau
Southgate
Glanrafon
Rhydyfelin
Moriah
Gogerddan
Plas
Penrhyn-coch
Comins Coch
Capel Dewi
Llanbadarn Fawr
A44
Capel Seion
Llanfarian
Gors
Chancery
New Cross
Blaenplwyf
Llanilar
Pentre-llyn
A487
B4575
A485
Rhos-y-garth
WALES COAST PATH
Llanddeiniol
B4576
Llangwyryfon
Llanrhystud
Lledrod
Trefenter
Llansantffraed
FANTASY FARM PARK
Rhyd-Rosser
LLYN EIDDWEN
MYNYDD BACH
Bronnant
Llanon
Rhydfudr
Bontnewydd
Nebo
Cere
Aberarth
Cross Inn
Blaenpennal
B4577
Bethania
(Sir C
Tyncelyn
Aberaeron
Pennant
Penuwch
Monachty
188
B4337
Crynfryn
B4578
New Quay
(Ceinewydd)
Ffos-y-ffin
LLANERCHAERON
Cilcennin
Cei-bach
Llangeitho
Llwyncelyn
Newbridge
Maen-y-groes
Gilfachrheda
B4342
Bwlch-Llan
Capel Betws Lleucu
Oakford
Ciliau Aeron
Afon Aeron
Cwmtudu
Cwmtydu
A486
Cross Inn
Llanarth
A482
Trefilan
Llundain-fach
Commins Capel Betws
Nanternis
B4339
Ystrad Aeron
Tal-sarn
Gartheli
Caerwedros
Dihewyd
Llwyn-y-groes
Ynys-Lochtyn
169
Abermeurig
Mydroilyn
Felinfach
Olmarch
Llwyndafydd
252
Llangrannog
Blaencelyn
Synod Inn
Temple Bar
Felindre
Pontgarreg
Ffynnon-oer
Llangybi
SN
Caledrhydiau
Plwmp
B4334
B4321
Penbryn
Llanfair Clydogau
B4343
Tresaith
Penmorfa
Pentregat
B4338
Cribyn
Silian
Betws Bledrws
Aberporth
Brynhoffnant
Gorsgoch
Sarnau
Talgarreg
B4338
Olwen
16
ABERPORTH WEST WALES AIRPORT
324
259
Maestir
Cellan
Tan-y-groes
Capel Cynon
RHOS LLAWR CWRT
Aber
Cwrt-newydd
Lampeter
(Llanbedr Pont Steffan)
Pentrefelin
Tremain
Glynarthen
314
Bwlch-y-fadfa
Castell-Howell
Blaenporth
B4333
Rhydlewis
Ffostrasol
B4459
Llanwnnen
A475
Cwmann
Bettws Ifan
Hawen
Pentre-bach
Maesymeillion
Pont-siân
Cwmsychpant
Ram
Beulah
Pantgwyn
Penrhiw-pâl
Coed-y-bryn
A486
Alltyblaca
Llanycrwys
Ponthirwaun
Tregroes
Rhydowen
Llanwenog
Dre-fach
A485
Parc-y-rhôs
185
Bryngwyn
Brongest
Troedyraur
Pencarreg
Llandygwydd
Maesllyn
Capel Tygwydd
Croes-lan
Prengwyn
Brynteg
Llanybydder
Ffaldybrenin
415
Mynydd Pencarreg
Rhuddlan
Glan-Duar
Ty Mawr
Harford
258
Capel Dewi
Horeb
B4476
B4571
ROCK MILL WOOLLEN MILL
Cwm-cou
Llandyfriog
Aber-banc
A475
Penrhiw-llan
Maesycrugiau
Esgairdawe
TEIFI VALLEY RAILWAY
Llandysul
Cenarth
Newcastle Emlyn
(Castell Newydd Emlyn)
Pentrecagal
Henllan
Llanfihangel-ar-arth
Aber-Giâr
Aber-Arad
NATIONAL WOOL MUSEUM
Llangeler
B4336
Llanllwni
408
B4337
CLYNFYW
Penrherber
Drefach
Pentre-cwrt
Rhydcymerau
B4333
CHEESE FARM
Felindre
Saron
Bancyffordd
Cwmhiraeth
Drefelin
Llidiad Nenog
New Inn
Cwmpengraig
Llansawel
Cwmcych
Capel Iwan
Pencader
335
MOELFRE
Rhôs
Gwyddgrug
B4337
Star
Clydey
Carmarthensh
Cwmorgan
Dolgran
Forest
Gwernogle
Edwinsford
TALLEY ABBEY
MYNYDD RHOS-WEN
Tanglwst
B4459
Abergorlech
A484
314
23
Afon Cothi
329
CYNROS
Talley
(Sir Gaerfyrddin)
Brechfa
Nant-y-ffin
Pen-y-garn
B4299
Bryn-Iwan
B4310
Cwm-byr
247
Alltwalis
Cwmduad
Halfway
Hermon
A485
Hen-feddau fawr
Cwmdu
Trelech
B4333
Llanllawddog
Brechfa
Llanpumsaint
192
Soar
0 1 2 3 4 5 6 miles
0 1 2 3 4 5 6 7 8 9 10 km
Pontarsais
Horeb
Llanfynydd
Capel Isaac
Blaen-waun
B4301
B4310
Pant-glas
B4302
Salem
Cwmbach
Llanwinio
Afon Duad
Rhydargaeau
Talog
GWILI RAILWAY

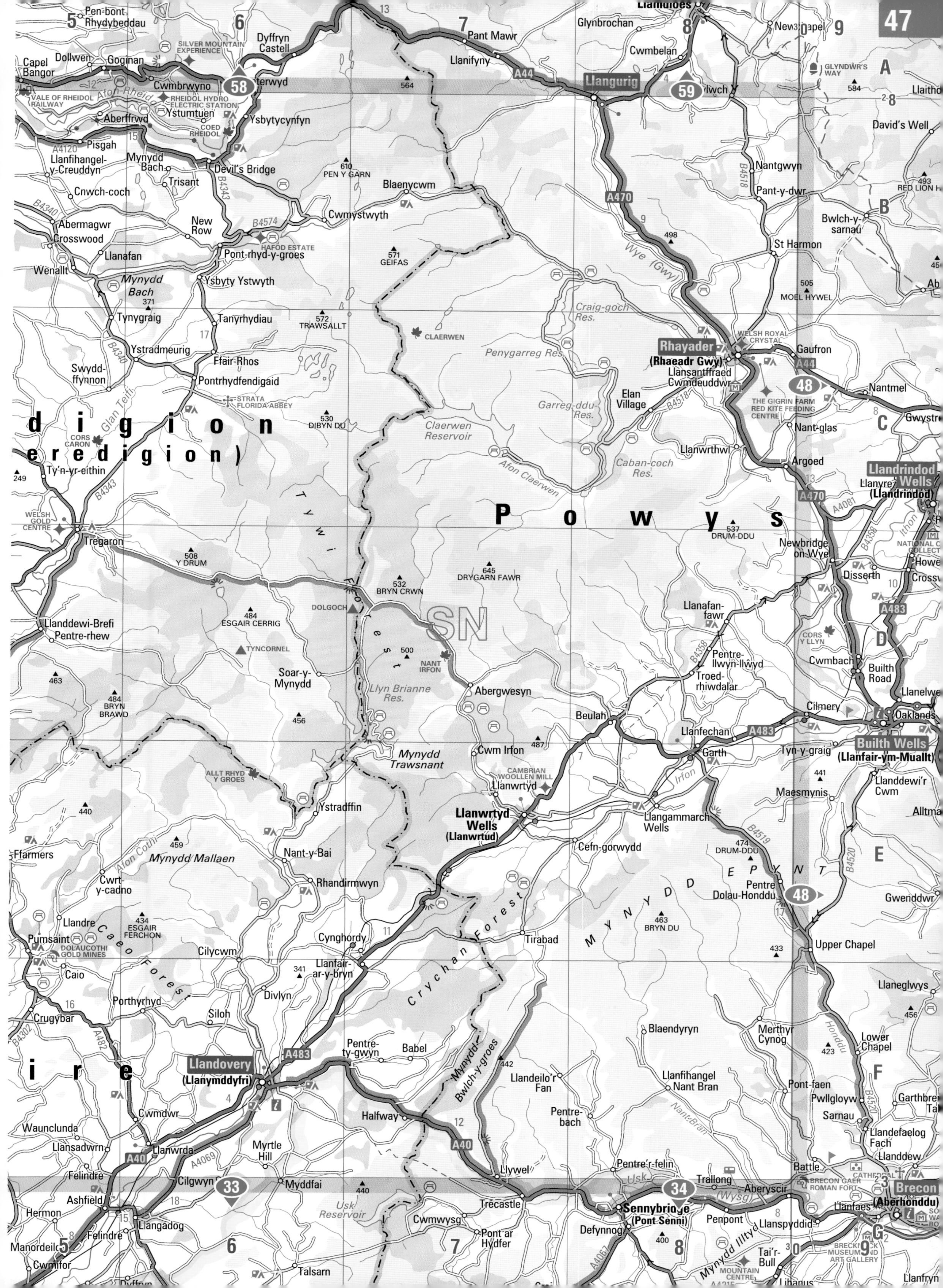

47
Pen-bont Rhydybeddau
Dyffryn Castell
Pant Mawr
Glynbrochan
Newchapel
Capel Bangor
Dollwen
Goginan
SILVER MOUNTAIN EXPERIENCE
Llanifyny
Cwmbelan
GLYNDWR'S WAY
Cwmbrwyno
VALE OF RHEIDOL RAILWAY
RHEIDOL HYDRO ELECTRIC STATION
Ystumtuen
Aberffrwd
COED RHEIDOL
Ysbytycynfyn
Llangurig
A44
564
584
Llaithddu
David's Well
Pisgah
Llanfihangel-y-Creuddyn
Mynydd Bach
Devil's Bridge
Trisant
610 PEN Y GARN
Blaenycwm
Nantgwyn
Pant-y-dwr
493 RED LION HILL
Cnwch-coch
A470
B4518
B4343
B4340
B4574
Abermagwr
Crosswood
New Row
HAFOD ESTATE
Cwmystwyth
Bwlch-y-sarnau
St Harmon
498
Llanafan
Pont-rhyd-y-groes
Wenallt
571 GEIFAS
Wye (Gwy)
Mynydd Bach
371
Ysbyty Ystwyth
505 MOEL HYWEL
Tynygraig
Tanyrhydiau
572 TRAWSALLT
Craig-goch Res.
CLAERWEN
WELSH ROYAL CRYSTAL
Rhayader
(Rhaeadr Gwy)
Gaufron
Ystradmeurig
Ffair-Rhos
Penygarreg Res.
Llansantffraed Cwmdeuddwr
Swydd-ffynnon
Pontrhydfendigaid
Elan Village
Nantmel
STRATA FLORIDA ABBEY
Glan Teifi
530 DIBYN DU
Garreg-ddu Res.
THE GIGRIN FARM RED KITE FEEDING CENTRE
B4518
Claerwen Reservoir
Nant-glas
digion
eredigion)
CORS CARON
Llanwrthwl
Argoed
249
Ty'n-yr-eithin
Afon Claerwen
Caban-coch Res.
Llandrindod Wells
Llanyre
(Llandrindod)
Tywi Forest
Powys
A4081
WELSH GOLD CENTRE
Tregaron
537 DRUM-DDU
Newbridge on Wye
508 Y DRUM
645 DRYGARN FAWR
532 BRYN CRWN
Disserth
Howey
Crossway
DOLGOCH
SN
Llanafan-fawr
A483
Llanddewi-Brefi
Pentre-rhew
484 ESGAIR CERRIG
TYNCORNEL
500
NANT IRFON
CORS Y LLYN
Pentre-llwyn-llwyd
463
484 BRYN BRAWD
Soar-y-Mynydd
Llyn Brianne Res.
Abergwesyn
Troed-rhiwdalar
Cwmbach
Builth Road
456
Beulah
Cilmery
Llanelwedd
Oaklands
487
Llanfechan
Garth
Builth Wells
(Llanfair-ym-Muallt)
Tyn-y-graig
ALLT RHYD Y GROES
Mynydd Trawsnant
Cwm Irfon
CAMBRIAN WOOLLEN MILL
Llanwrtyd
441
Llanddewi'r Cwm
Maesmynis
440
Ystradffin
Llanwrtyd Wells
(Llanwrtud)
Llangammarch Wells
Alltmawr
Ffarmers
459
Afon Cothi
Mynydd Mallaen
Nant-y-Bai
Cefn-gorwydd
474 DRUM-DDU
B4519
Cwrt-y-cadno
Rhandirmwyn
MYNYDD EPYNT
Pentre Dolau-Honddu
48
B4520
Gwenddwr
Llandre
434 ESGAIR FERCHON
Caeo Forest
Cynghordy
Crychan Forest
Tirabad
463 BRYN DU
Pumsaint
DOLAUCOTHI GOLD MINES
Cilycwm
433
Upper Chapel
Caio
341
Llanfair-ar-y-bryn
Llaneglwys
Porthyrhyd
Divlyn
Crugybar
Siloh
456
Blaendyryn
Merthyr Cynog
Honddu
Lower Chapel
B4302
A482
Pentre-ty-gwyn
Babel
Mynydd Bwlch-y-groes
442
423
Llandovery
(Llanymddyfri)
Llandeilo'r Fan
Llanfihangel Nant Bran
Pont-faen
Garthbrengy
Pwllgloyw
Cwmdwr
Pentre-bach
Sarnau
Halfway
Nant Bran
Wauncluda
Llandefaelog Fach
Llansadwrn
Llanwrda
A40
A4069
Myrtle Hill
Llywel
Llanddew
Felindre
Cilgwyn
Myddfai
440
Pentre'r-felin
Trallong
Battle
BRECON GAER ROMAN FORT
CATHEDRAL
Brecon
(Aberhonddu)
Ashfield
33
34
Usk (Wysg)
Aberyscir
Hermon
Llangadog
Usk Reservoir
Trecastle
Sennybridge
(Pont Senni)
Penpont
Llanspyddid
Llanfaes
Manordeilo
Felindre
Cwmwysg
Pont ar Hydfer
Defynnog
400
Mynydd Illtyd
BRECKNOCK MUSEUM AND ART GALLERY
Cwmifor
Talsarn
A4067
MOUNTAIN CENTRE
Tai'r-Bull
Libanus
Llanfrynach
58
59
48
A
B
C
D
E
F
G
5
6
7
8
9

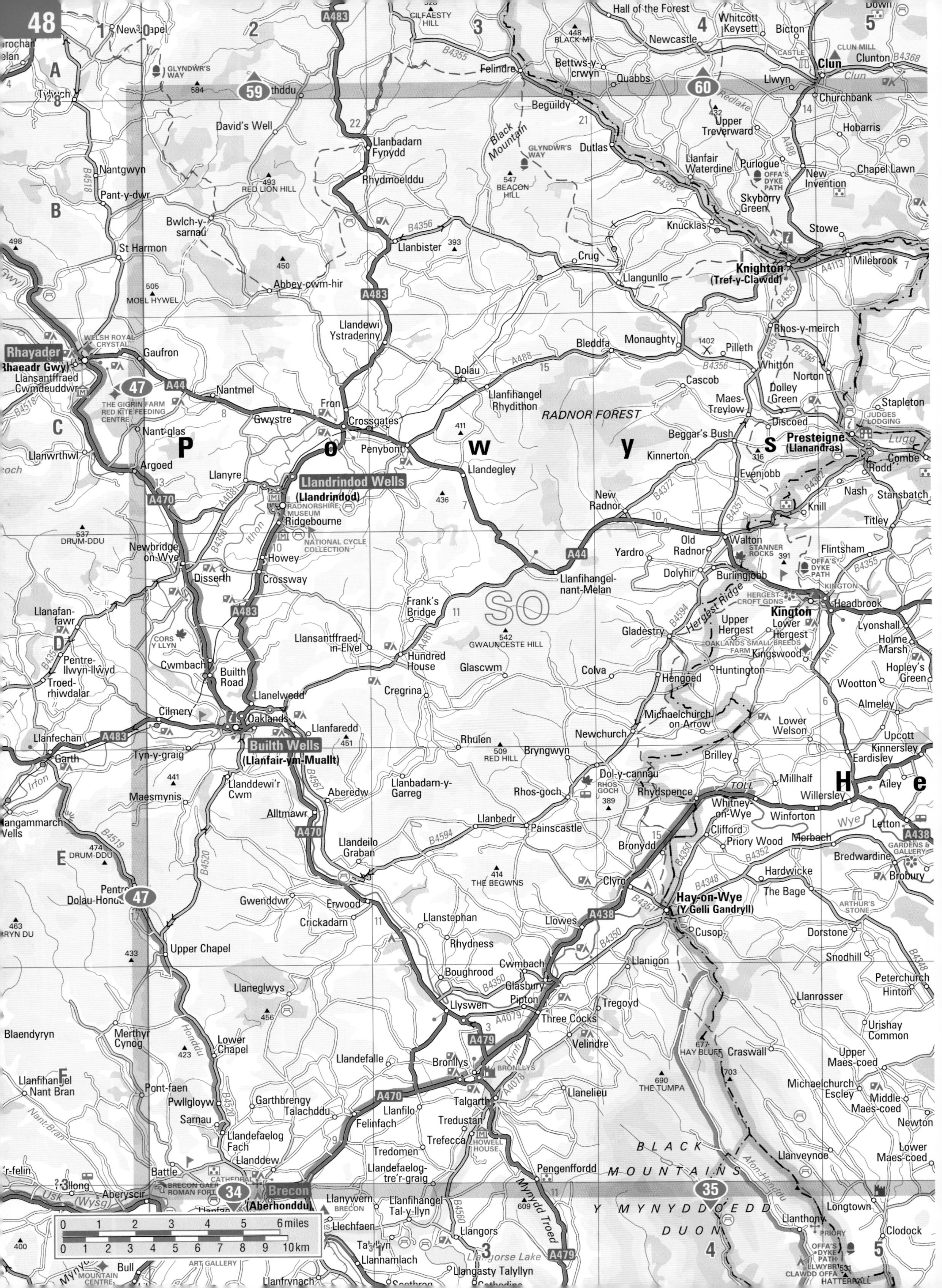

Hall of the Forest
Whitcott Keysett
Bicton
CILFAESTY HILL
448 BLACK MT
Newcastle
CLUN MILL
CASTLE
Clun
Clunton
B4368
GLYNDŴR'S WAY
584
59
Felindre
Bettws-y-crwyn
Quabbs
60
Llwyn
Churchbank
Tylwch
Redlake
Beguildy
432
Upper Treverward
Hobarris
David's Well
Llanbadarn Fynydd
Black Mountain
GLYNDŴR'S WAY
Dutlas
Llanfair Waterdine
Purlogue
OFFA'S DYKE PATH
New Invention
Chapel Lawn
Nantgwyn
493 RED LION HILL
Rhydmoelddu
547 BEACON HILL
B4355
Skyborry Green
Pant-y-dwr
B4518
Bwlch-y-sarnau
B4356
Knucklas
Stowe
498
St Harmon
Llanbister
393
Crug
Knighton
(Tref-y-Clawdd)
A4113
Milebrook
450
Abbey-cwm-hir
Llangunllo
505 MOEL HYWEL
A483
Llandewi Ystradenny
Rhos-y-meirch
WELSH ROYAL CRYSTAL
Rhayader
Rhaeadr Gwy)
Gaufron
Bleddfa
Monaughty
1402
Pilleth
Llansantffraed Cwmdeuddwr
A488
Dolau
15
B4356
Whitton
Norton
47
A44
Nantmel
Cascob
Dolley Green
THE GIGRIN FARM RED KITE FEEDING CENTRE
Fron
Llanfihangel Rhydithon
Maes-Treylow
Stapleton
B4518
RADNOR FOREST
Discoed
JUDGES LODGING
Nant-glas
Gwystre
Crossgates
411
Beggar's Bush
Presteigne
(Llanandras)
Lugg
Penybont
P
o
w
y
s
Llanwrthwl
Kinnerton
316
Combe
Argoed
Llanyre
Llandrindod Wells
(Llandrindod)
Llandegley
Rodd
Evenjobb
Nash
Stansbatch
A470
A4081
RADNORSHIRE MUSEUM
436
New Radnor
B4372
B4362
Knill
Ridgebourne
7
10
B4357
Titley
537 DRUM-DDU
Ithon
NATIONAL CYCLE COLLECTION
Old Radnor
Walton
STANNER ROCKS
391
Flintsham
Newbridge on Wye
B4358
Howey
A44
Yardro
OFFA'S DYKE PATH
B4355
Disserth
Llanfihangel-nant-Melan
Dolyhir
Burlingjobb
KINGTON
Crossway
SO
Hergest Ridge
HERGEST CROFT GDNS
Headbrook
Llanafan-fawr
A483
Frank's Bridge
11
Kington
B4594
Upper Hergest
Lower Hergest
Lyonshall
CORS Y LLYN
Llansantffraed-in-Elvel
A481
542 GWAUNCESTE HILL
Gladestry
OAKLANDS SMALL BREEDS FARM
Holme Marsh
D
Pentre-llwyn-llŵyd
Hundred House
Kingswood
Cwmbach
Builth Road
Glascwm
Colva
Huntington
Hopley's Green
Troed-rhiwdalar
Cregrina
Hengoed
Wootton
A4111
Llanelwedd
6
Almeley
Cilmery
Oaklands
Michaelchurch-on-Arrow
Lower Welson
Llanfaredd
Llanfechan
A483
Builth Wells
(Llanfair-ym-Muallt)
451
Rhulen
Newchurch
Upcott
Kinnersley
Garth
Tyn-y-graig
509 RED HILL
Bryngwyn
Brilley
Eardisley
441
Dol-y-cannau
Irfon
B4567
Millhalf
H
e
Aberedw
Llanbadarn-y-Garreg
RHOS GOCH
Rhos-goch
Rhydspence
TOLL
Willersley
Ailey
Maesmynis
Llanddewi'r Cwm
389
Whitney-on-Wye
Winforton
Alltmawr
Llanbedr
Painscastle
Clifford
Wye
Letton
A470
A438
B4519
B4594
15
Priory Wood
Merbach
474 DRUM-DDU
Llandeilo Graban
Bronydd
B4350
B4352
GARDENS & GALLERY
E
Bredwardine
B4520
414 THE BEGWNS
Hardwicke
Clyro
B4348
Brobury
Pentre
Dolau-Honddu
47
Gwenddwr
Erwood
The Bage
Hay-on-Wye
(Y Gelli Gandryll)
ARTHUR'S STONE
Crickadarn
11
Llanstephan
Llowes
A438
B4351
463
Cusop
Dorstone
Rhydness
B4350
Upper Chapel
433
Snodhill
Boughrood
Cwmbach
Llanigon
B4348
Glasbury
Peterchurch
Hinton
B4350
Llaneglwys
Pipton
Tregoyd
Llanrosser
Llyswen
A4079
456
Three Cocks
Urishay Common
Blaendyryn
Merthyr Cynog
Honddu
Lower Chapel
3
A479
Velindre
677 HAY BLUFF
Craswall
Upper Maes-coed
423
Llandefalle
Bronllys
Lynfi
BRONLLYS
703
F
690 THE TUMPA
Michaelchurch Escley
Llanfihangel Nant Bran
Pont-faen
A4078
Llanelieu
Middle Maes-coed
A470
Talgarth
Pwllgloyw
B4520
Garthbrengy
Talachddu
Llanfilo
Nant-Bran
Sarnau
Felinfach
Tredustan
Newton
Llandefaelog Fach
Trefecca
HOWELL HOUSE
BLACK
Lower Maes-coed
Llanddew
Tredomen
Llanveynoe
Llandefaelog-tre'r-graig
Afon Honddu
Battle
CATHEDRAL
Pengenfforddd
MOUNTAINS
BRECON GAER ROMAN FORT
34
Brecon
(Aberhonddu)
35
Aberyscir
Usk
Wysg
Llanywern
Llanfihangel Tal-y-llyn
B4560
11
609
Mynydd Troed
Y MYNYDDOEDD DUON
Longtown
BRECON
Llechfaen
Llanthony
Llangors
PRIORY
Clodock
400
Tal-y-llyn
3
Llangorse Lake
A479
4
OFFA'S DYKE PATH
5
Llannamlach
ART GALLERY
Bull
MOUNTAIN CENTRE
Llangasty Talyllyn
Llanfrynach
Cathedine
LLWYBR CLAWDD OFFA
HATTERRALL
0 1 2 3 4 5 6 miles
0 1 2 3 4 5 6 7 8 9 10 km

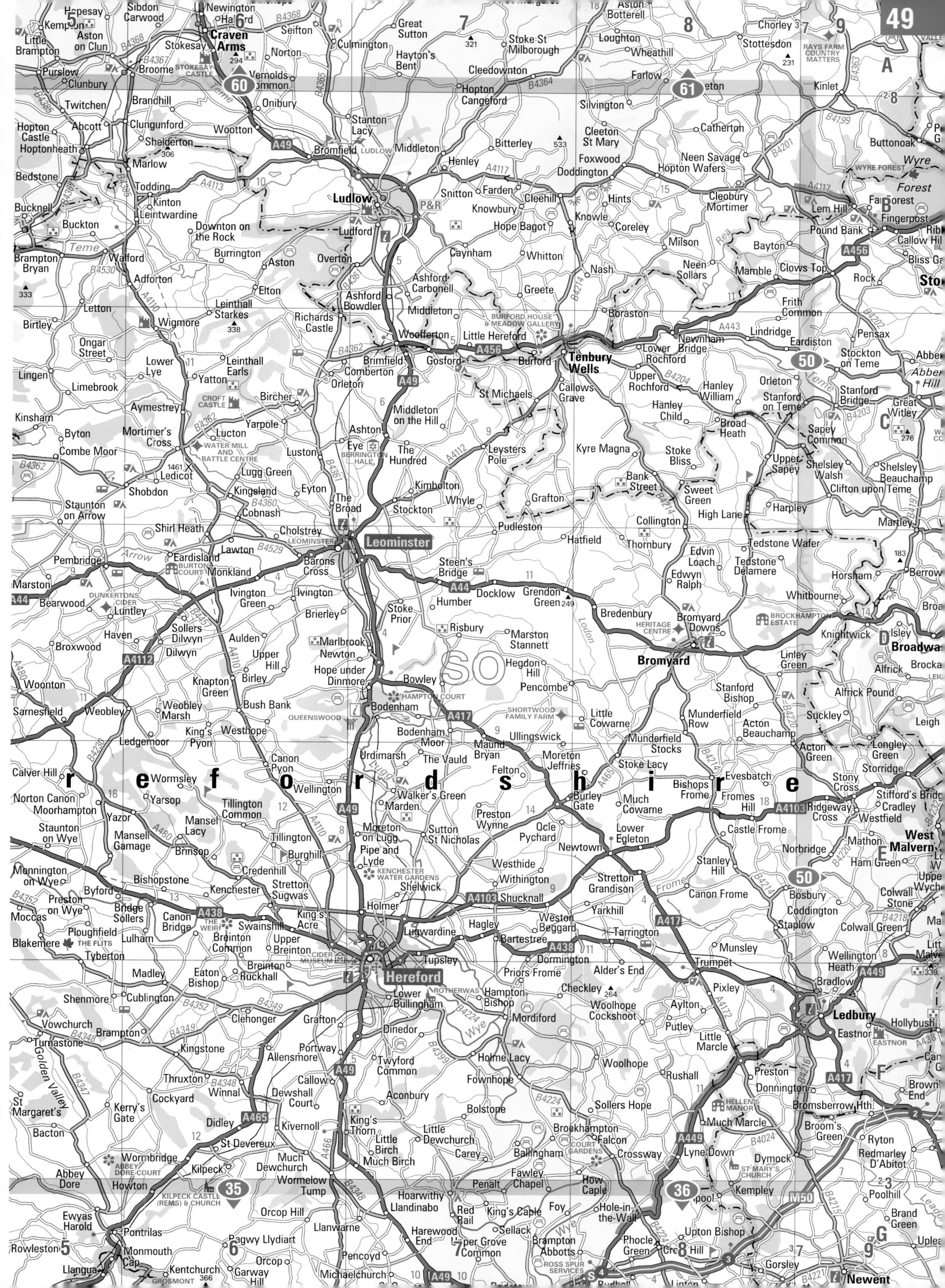

Hopesay
Sibdon Carwood
Newington
Kempton
Aston on Clun
Little Brampton
Craven Arms
Seifton
Great Sutton
Culmington
Hayton's Bent
Stokesay
Stokesay Castle
Broome
Norton
Vernolds Common
Stoke St Milborough
Asterton
Loughton
Wheathill
Chorley
Stottesdon
Rays Farm Country Matters
Purslow
Clunbury
Cleedownton
Farlow
Hopton Cangeford
Kinlet
Silvington
Twitchen
Brandhill
Onibury
Stanton Lacy
Clungunford
Abcott
Hopton Castle
Hoptonheath
Sheldeton
Wootton
Bromfield
Ludlow
Middleton
Bitterley
Cleeton St Mary
Catherton
Buttonoak
Wyre Forest
Bedstone
Marlow
Henley
Foxwood
Doddington
Neen Savage
Hopton Wafers
Todding
Kinton
Leintwardine
Bucknell
Snitton
Farden
Knowbury
Cleehill
Hints
Cleobury Mortimer
Lem Hill
Far Forest
Fingerpost
Pound Bank
Callow Hill
Buckton
Downton on the Rock
Ludford
Hope Bagot
Knowle
Coreley
Milson
Bayton
Brampton Bryan
Burrington
Aston
Overton
Caynham
Whitton
Nash
Neen Sollars
Mamble
Clows Top
Bliss Gate
Walford
Adforton
Ashford Carbonell
Rock
Elton
Ashford Bowdler
Greete
Frith Common
Letton
Leinthall Starkes
Wigmore
Richards Castle
Middleton
Boraston
Burford House & Meadow Gallery
Birtley
Ongar Street
Woofferton
Little Hereford
Newnham Bridge
Lindridge
Eardiston
Pensax
Lower Lye
Leinthall Earls
Brimfield
Gosford
Burford
Tenbury Wells
Lower Rochford
Stockton on Teme
Lingen
Yatton
Comberton
Orleton
Upper Rochford
Hanley William
Orleton
Stanford Bridge
Limebrook
Croft Castle
Bircher
St Michaels
Callows Grave
Stanford on Teme
Great Witley
Kinsham
Aymestrey
Yarpole
Middleton on the Hill
Hanley Child
Broad Heath
Sapey Common
Byton
Mortimer's Cross
Lucton
Water Mill and Battle Centre
Ashton
Eye
Berrington Hall
The Hundred
Leysters Pole
Kyre Magna
Stoke Bliss
Upper Sapey
Shelsley Walsh
Shelsley Beauchamp
Combe Moor
Luston
Ledicot
Lugg Green
Kimbolton
Bank Street
Sweet Green
Clifton upon Teme
Shobdon
Kingsland
Eyton
Whyle
Grafton
High Lane
Harpley
Staunton on Arrow
Cobnash
The Broad
Stockton
Collington
Martley
Shirl Heath
Cholstrey
Leominster
Pudleston
Hatfield
Thornbury
Tedstone Wafer
Pembridge
Eardisland
Lawton
Barons Cross
Edvin Loach
Tedstone Delamere
Horsham
Marston
Burton Court
Monkland
Steen's Bridge
Edwyn Ralph
Dunkertons Cider
Ivington Green
Ivington
Docklow
Grendon Green
Whitbourne
Bearwood
Luntley
Stoke Prior
Humber
Bredenbury
Bromyard Downs
Brockhampton Estate
Heritage Centre
Sollers Dilwyn
Brierley
Risbury
Marston Stannett
Knightwick
Isley
Broadwas
Broxwood
Haven
Dilwyn
Aulden
Marlbrook
Newton
Bromyard
Linley Green
Upper Hill
Hope under Dinmore
Hegdon Hill
Alfrick
Woonton
Birley
Bowley
Pencombe
Stanford Bishop
Alfrick Pound
Knapton Green
Hampton Court
Sarnesfield
Weobley
Weobley Marsh
Bush Bank
Queenswood
Bodenham
Shortwood Family Farm
Little Cowarne
Munderfield Row
Suckley
Acton Beauchamp
Leigh
Ledgemoor
King's Pyon
Westhope
Bodenham Moor
Ullingswick
Munderfield Stocks
Canon Pyon
Urdimarsh
The Vauld
Maund Bryan
Moreton Jeffries
Acton Green
Longley Green
Calver Hill
Felton
Stoke Lacy
Storridge
Wormsley
Wellington
Evesbatch
Stony Cross
Herefordshire
Norton Canon
Yarsop
Burley Gate
Bishops Frome
Fromes Hill
Stifford's Bridge
Cradley
Moorhampton
Tillington Common
Walker's Green
Much Cowarne
Ridgeway Cross
Westfield
Yazor
Marden
Preston Wynne
Staunton on Wye
Mansel Lacy
Moreton on Lugg
Sutton St Nicholas
Ocle Pychard
Lower Egleton
Castle Frome
Mathon
West Malvern
Mansell Gamage
Tillington
Newtown
Norbridge
Brinsop
Burghill
Pipe and Lyde
Westhide
Stanley Hill
Ham Green
Monnington on Wye
Credenhill
Kenchester Water Gardens
Withington
Bishopstone
Stretton Sugwas
Shelwick
Stretton Grandison
Canon Frome
Bosbury
Colwall Stone
Kenchester
Byford
Preston on Wye
Holmer
Shucknall
Coddington
Moccas
Bridge Sollers
Canon Bridge
The Weir
Swainshill
King's Acre
Yarkhill
Staplow
Colwall Green
Ploughfield
Breinton Common
Lugwardine
Hagley
Weston Beggard
Tarrington
Blakemere
The Flits
Lulham
Upper Breinton
Bartestree
Tyberton
Cider Museum
Tupsley
Dormington
Munsley
Wellington Heath
Madley
Eaton Bishop
Breinton
Ruckhall
Hereford
Priors Frome
Alder's End
Trumpet
Bradlow
Rotherwas
Hampton Bishop
Checkley
Pixley
Shenmore
Cublington
Lower Bullingham
Woolhope Cockshoot
Aylton
Ledbury
Hollybush
Vowchurch
Brampton
Clehonger
Grafton
Mordiford
Putley
Eastnor
Turnastone
Dinedor
Little Marcle
Golden Valley
Kingstone
Portway
Allensmore
Holme Lacy
Twyford Common
Woolhope
Preston
Donnington
Brown End
Thruxton
Winnal
Callow
Fownhope
Rushall
St Margaret's
Cockyard
Dewshall Court
Aconbury
Kerry's Gate
Bolstone
Sollers Hope
Hellens Manor
Bromsberrow Hth.
Bacton
Didley
Kivernoll
King's Thorn
Much Marcle
Broom's Green
Ryton
Wormbridge
St Devereux
Little Dewchurch
Brockhampton
Falcon
Redmarley D'Abitot
Abbey Dore Court
Much Dewchurch
Little Birch
Carey
Ballingham
Court Gardens
Crossway
Lyne Down
Dymock
St Mary's Church
Abbey Dore
Kilpeck
Much Birch
Howton
Wormelow Tump
Penalt
Fawley Chapel
How Caple
Kempley
Poolhill
Kilpeck Castle (rems) & Church
Hoarwithy
Llandinabo
Red Rail
King's Caple
Foy
Hole-in-the-Wall
Orcop Hill
Sellack
Upton Bishop
Brand Green
Ewyas Harold
Llanwarne
Harewood End
Upper Grove Common
Brampton Abbotts
Phocle Green
Pontrilas
Rowlestone
Pagwy Llydiart
Upleadon
Monmouth Cap
Orcop
Ross Spur Services
Gorsley
Llangua
Kentchurch
Garway Hill
Pencoyd
Grosmont
Michaelchurch
Newent
Teme
Arrow
Lugg
Wye
Frome
Rea
Lodon
Leadon
SO

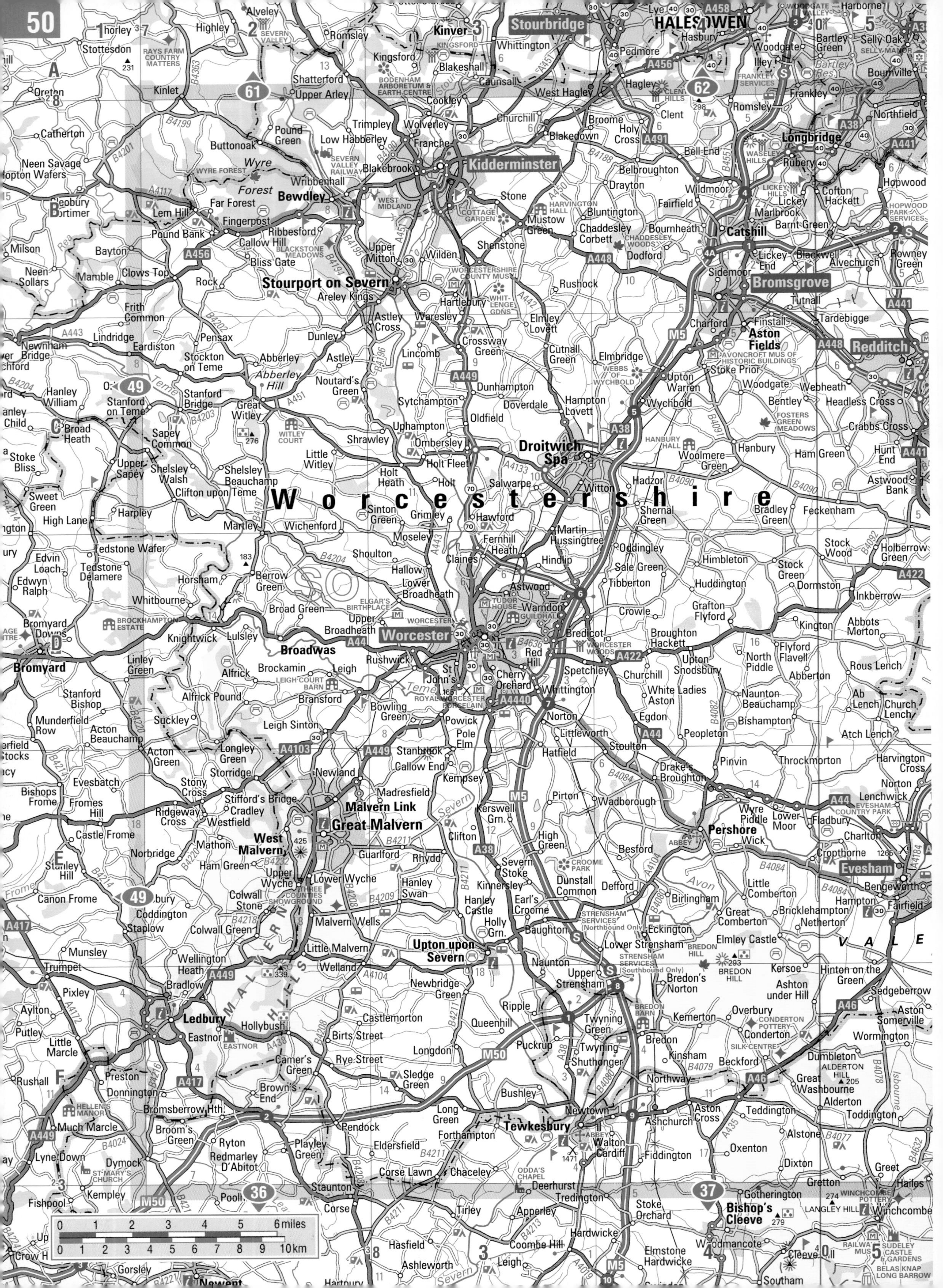
Worcestershire
Alveley
Highley
Chorley
Stottesdon
RAYS FARM COUNTRY MATTERS
SEVERN VALLEY
Romsley
Kinver
KINGSFORD
Stourbridge
Whittington
Lye
HALESOWEN
Harborne
Hasbury
Bartley Green
Selly Oak
SELLY MANOR
Kingsford
Pedmore
Woodgate
Illey
Bartley Res.
Bournville
Oreton
Kinlet
Shatterford
Upper Arley
BODENHAM ARBORETUM & EARTH CENTRE
Blakeshall
Caunsall
West Hagley
Hagley
CLENT HILLS
FRANKLEY SERVICES
Frankley
Clent
Romsley
Northfield
Catherton
Pound Green
Low Habberley
Trimpley
Wolverley
Cookley
Churchill
Blakedown
Broome
Holy Cross
Longbridge
Buttonoak
Franche
Bell End
WASELEY HILLS
Rubery
Neen Savage
Wyre
WYRE FOREST
SEVERN VALLEY RAILWAY
Blakebrook
Kidderminster
Belbroughton
Hopwood
Hopton Wafers
Wribbenhall
Forest
Drayton
Wildmoor
Cofton Hackett
Cleobury Mortimer
Far Forest
Bewdley
WEST MIDLAND
Stone
HARVINGTON HALL
Fairfield
LICKEY HILLS
Lickey
HOPWOOD PARK SERVICES
Lem Hill
Fingerpost
COTTAGE GARDEN
Mustow Green
Bluntington
Marlbrook
Barnt Green
Pound Bank
Ribbesford
Chaddesley Corbett
Bournheath
Catshill
Milson
Callow Hill
BLACKSTONE MEADOWS
Upper Mitton
Wilden
Shenstone
CHADDESLEY WOODS
Dodford
Lickey End
Blackwell
Alvechurch
Rowney Green
Bayton
Bliss Gate
Neen Sollars
Mamble
Clows Top
Rock
Stourport on Severn
WORCESTERSHIRE COUNTY MUSEUM
Rushock
Sidemoor
Bromsgrove
Areley Kings
Hartlebury
WHITLENGE GDNS
Tutnall
Frith Common
Astley Cross
Waresley
Elmley Lovett
Finstall
Tardebigge
Lindridge
Pensax
Dunley
Charford
Aston Fields
Newnham Bridge
Eardiston
Astley
Crossway Green
Cutnall Green
Elmbridge
AVONCROFT MUS OF HISTORIC BUILDINGS
Redditch
Stockton on Teme
Abberley
Lincomb
WEBBS OF WYCHBOLD
Stoke Prior
Abberley Hill
Noutard's Green
Dunhampton
Upton Warren
Woodgate
Webheath
Hanley William
Stanford on Teme
Stanford Bridge
Sytchampton
Doverdale
Hampton Lovett
Wychbold
Bentley
Headless Cross
Great Witley
Oldfield
FOSTERS GREEN MEADOWS
Hanley Child
Broad Heath
Sapey Common
WITLEY COURT
Uphampton
Shrawley
Ombersley
Droitwich Spa
HANBURY HALL
Crabbs Cross
Stoke Bliss
Upper Sapey
Little Witley
Holt Fleet
Hanbury
Woolmere Green
Ham Green
Hunt End
Shelsley Walsh
Shelsley Beauchamp
Holt Heath
Holt
Salwarpe
Hadzor
Astwood Bank
Sweet Green
Clifton upon Teme
Witton
High Lane
Harpley
Sinton Green
Grimley
Hawford
Shernal Green
Bradley Green
Feckenham
Martley
Wichenford
Martin Hussingtree
Moseley
Fernhill Heath
Stock Wood
Holberrow Green
Edvin Loach
Tedstone Wafer
Tedstone Delamere
Shoulton
Claines
Oddingley
Hindlip
Himbleton
Stock Green
Edwyn Ralph
Horsham
Berrow Green
Hallow
Sale Green
Tibberton
Dormston
Huddington
Whitbourne
Lower Broadheath
Astwood
Inkberrow
Broad Green
ELGAR'S BIRTHPLACE
TUDOR HOUSE
Warndon
GUILDHALL
Grafton Flyford
Crowle
Bromyard Downs
BROCKHAMPTON ESTATE
Upper Broadheath
WORCESTER
Kington
Abbots Morton
Knightwick
Lulsley
Worcester
Bredicot
Broughton Hackett
Broadwas
Red Hill
WORCESTER WOODS
Flyford Flavell
Bromyard
Linley Green
Alfrick
Brockamin
Leigh
Rushwick
Spetchley
Upton Snodsbury
North Piddle
Rous Lench
LEIGH COURT BARN
St John's
Cherry Orchard
Churchill
Abberton
Stanford Bishop
Alfrick Pound
Bransford
ROYAL WORCESTER PORCELAIN
Whittington
White Ladies Aston
Naunton Beauchamp
Ab Lench
Church Lench
Munderfield Row
Suckley
Bowling Green
Norton
Egdon
Bishampton
Acton Beauchamp
Leigh Sinton
Powick
Littleworth
Peopleton
Atch Lench
Pole Elm
Stoulton
Longley Green
Acton Green
Stanbrook
Hatfield
Pinvin
Throckmorton
Harvington Cross
Callow End
Drake's Broughton
Storridge
Newland
Kempsey
Evesbatch
Stony Cross
Madresfield
Norton
Bishops Frome
Stifford's Bridge
Pirton
Wadborough
Lenchwick
Fromes Hill
Cradley
Malvern Link
Kerswell Grn.
EVESHAM COUNTRY PARK
Ridgeway Cross
Westfield
Great Malvern
Wyre Piddle
Lower Moor
Fladbury
Castle Frome
Mathon
West Malvern
Clifton
High Green
Pershore
Wick
Charlton
Norbridge
Guarlford
Rhydd
Besford
ABBEY
Cropthorne
Ham Green
Severn Stoke
CROOME PARK
Evesham
Stanley Hill
Upper Wyche
Lower Wyche
Hanley Swan
Dunstall Common
Defford
Little Comberton
Bengeworth
Canon Frome
Colwall Stone
THREE COUNTIES SHOWGROUND
Kinnersley
Birlingham
Hampton
Hanley Castle
Earl's Croome
Great Comberton
Bricklehampton
Fairfield
Coddington
Malvern Wells
Holly Grn.
STRENSHAM SERVICES (Northbound Only)
Eckington
Netherton
Staplow
Colwall Green
Baughton
Elmley Castle
VALE
Munsley
Little Malvern
Upton upon Severn
Lower Strensham
BREDON HILL
Trumpet
Wellington Heath
Welland
Naunton
STRENSHAM SERVICES (Southbound Only)
Kersoe
Hinton on the Green
Upper Strensham
Bredon's Norton
Ashton under Hill
Pixley
Bradlow
Newbridge Green
Sedgeberrow
Aylton
Ledbury
Castlemorton
Ripple
Overbury
Aston Somerville
Putley
Hollybush
Queenhill
Twyning Green
Kemerton
CONDERTON POTTERY
Wormington
Little Marcle
Eastnor
EASTNOR
Birts Street
Longdon
Puckrup
Twyning
Bredon
Conderton
SILK CENTRE
Dumbleton
Camer's Green
Rye Street
Shuthonger
Kinsham
Beckford
ALDERTON HILL
Rushall
Preston
Sledge Green
Northway
Great Washbourne
Donnington
Brown's End
Bushley
Alderton
HELLEN'S MANOR
Bromsberrow Hth.
Long Green
Newtown
Aston Cross
Teddington
Toddington
Much Marcle
Broom's Green
Pendock
Tewkesbury
Ashchurch
Ryton
Playley Green
Eldersfield
Forthampton
ABBEY
Walton Cardiff
Alstone
Oxenton
Lyne Down
Dymock
ST MARY'S CHURCH
Redmarley D'Abitot
Fiddington
Dixton
Greet
Corse Lawn
Chaceley
ODDA'S CHAPEL
Gretton
Hailes
Kempley
Staunton
Deerhurst
Tredington
Gotherington
WINCHCOMBE POTTERY
Fishpool
Poolhill
Corse
Tirley
Apperley
Stoke Orchard
Bishop's Cleeve
LANGLEY HILL
Winchcombe
Hasfield
Coombe Hill
Hardwicke
Woodmancote
RAILWAY MUS
SUDELEY CASTLE & GARDENS
Crow Hill
Ashleworth
Leigh
Elmstone Hardwicke
Cleeve Hill
BELAS KNAP LONG BARROW
Gorsley
Newent
Hartpury
Southam
Severn
Teme
Avon
Rea
Frome
Isbourne
SO
MALVERN HILLS
0 1 2 3 4 5 6 miles
0 1 2 3 4 5 6 7 8 9 10 km

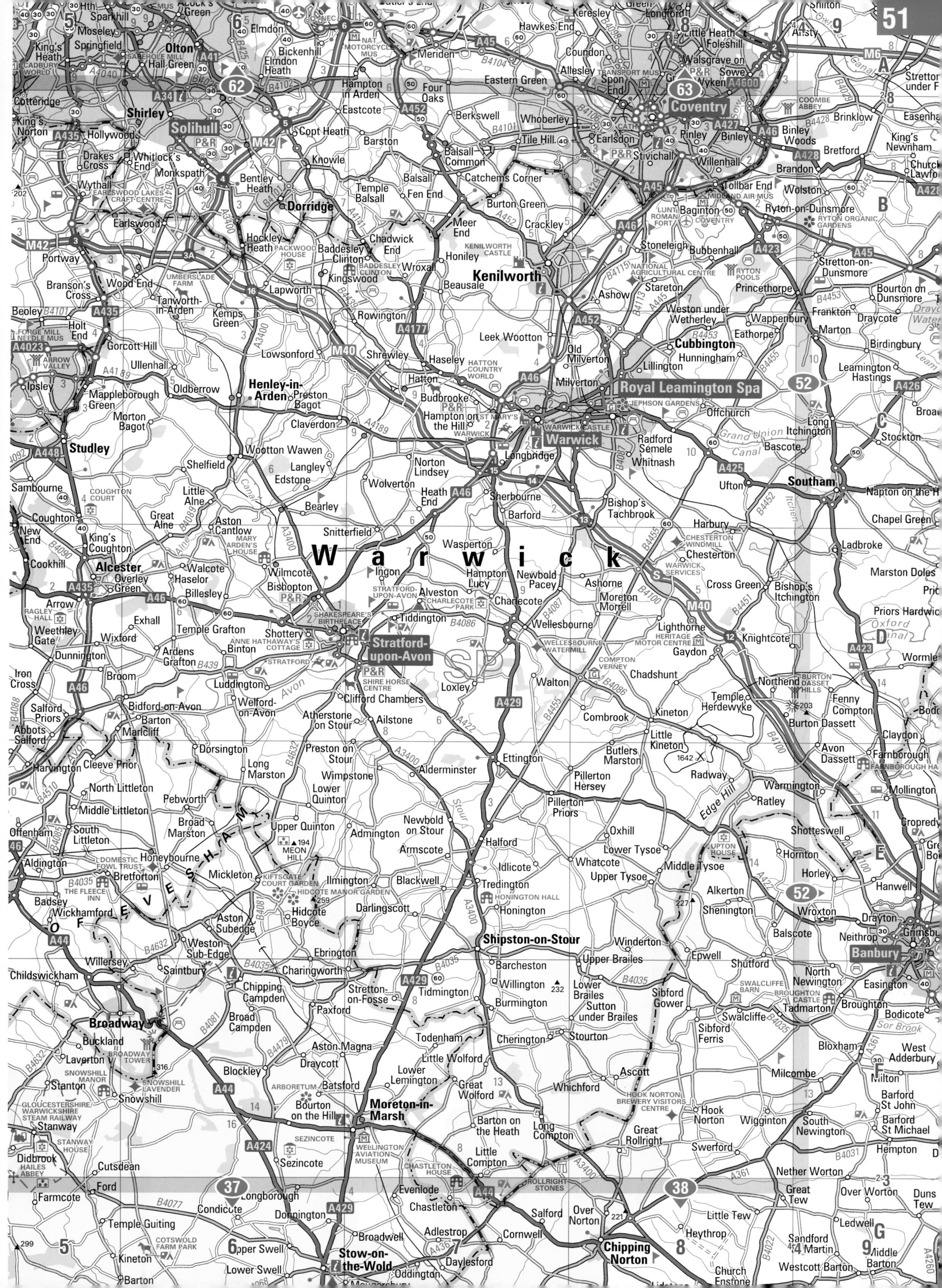
Warwick
Coventry
Solihull
Shirley
Olton
Kenilworth
Royal Leamington Spa
Warwick
Stratford-upon-Avon
Southam
Banbury
Shipston-on-Stour
Moreton-in-Marsh
Chipping Norton
Stow-on-the-Wold
Broadway
Alcester
Studley
Henley-in-Arden
Dorridge
Cubbington
Sparkhill
Moseley
Springfield
King's Heath
Hall Green
Elmdon
Bickenhill
Elmdon Heath
Hampton in Arden
Eastcote
Meriden
Four Oaks
Berkswell
Eastern Green
Hawkes End
Keresley
Longford
Coundon
Allesley
Little Heath
Foleshill
Walsgrave on Sowe
Wyken
Ansty
Stretton under Fosse
Cotteridge
King's Norton
Hollywood
Drakes Cross
Whitlock's End
Monkspath
Wythall
Earlswood
Bentley Heath
Copt Heath
Knowle
Barston
Balsall Common
Temple Balsall
Balsall
Fen End
Catchems Corner
Burton Green
Whoberley
Tile Hill
Earlsdon
Stivichall
Pinley
Binley
Binley Woods
Willenhall
Brinklow
Easenhall
King's Newnham
Bretford
Brandon
Church Lawford
Tollbar End
Wolston
Ryton-on-Dunsmore
Baginton
Crackley
Meer End
Chadwick End
Baddesley Clinton
Hockley Heath
Portway
Branson's Cross
Wood End
Tanworth-in-Arden
Lapworth
Kingswood
Wroxall
Honiley
Beausale
Stoneleigh
Bubbenhall
Stareton
Ashow
Princethorpe
Stretton-on-Dunsmore
Bourton on Dunsmore
Frankton
Draycote
Weston under Wetherley
Wappenbury
Eathorpe
Marton
Birdingbury
Hunningham
Lillington
Leamington Hastings
Beoley
Holt End
Gorcott Hill
Kemps Green
Rowington
Shrewley
Haseley
Lowsonford
Ullenhall
Ipsley
Mappleborough Green
Oldberrow
Preston Bagot
Hatton
Budbrooke
Hampton on the Hill
Leek Wootton
Old Milverton
Milverton
Offchurch
Long Itchington
Stockton
Morton Bagot
Claverdon
Wootton Wawen
Norton Lindsey
Longbridge
Radford Semele
Whitnash
Bascote
Ufton
Napton on the Hill
Sambourne
Shelfield
Langley
Edstone
Wolverton
Heath End
Sherbourne
Barford
Bishop's Tachbrook
Harbury
Chapel Green
Coughton
Little Alne
Great Alne
Aston Cantlow
Bearley
Snitterfield
Wasperton
Chesterton
Ladbroke
New End
King's Coughton
Cookhill
Walcote
Haselor
Wilmcote
Ingon
Hampton Lucy
Newbold Pacey
Ashorne
Cross Green
Bishop's Itchington
Marston Doles
Overley Green
Billesley
Bishopton
Alveston
Charlecote
Moreton Morrell
Arrow
Weethley Gate
Exhall
Wixford
Temple Grafton
Shottery
Tiddington
Wellesbourne
Lighthorne
Knightcote
Priors Hardwick
Dunnington
Ardens Grafton
Binton
Gaydon
Iron Cross
Broom
Luddington
Welford-on-Avon
Clifford Chambers
Loxley
Walton
Chadshunt
Northend
Fenny Compton
Salford Priors
Abbots Salford
Bidford-on-Avon
Barton
Marlcliff
Atherstone on Stour
Ailstone
Combrook
Kineton
Temple Herdewyke
Burton Dassett
Little Kineton
Dorsington
Preston on Stour
Ettington
Butlers Marston
Avon Dassett
Claydon
Farnborough
Harvington
Cleeve Prior
Long Marston
Wimpstone
Alderminster
Pillerton Hersey
Radway
Warmington
Mollington
North Littleton
Middle Littleton
Lower Quinton
Pebworth
Pillerton Priors
Ratley
Offenham
South Littleton
Broad Marston
Upper Quinton
Admington
Newbold on Stour
Halford
Oxhill
Shotteswell
Cropredy
Aldington
Honeybourne
Meon Hill
Armscote
Lower Tysoe
Whatcote
Middle Tysoe
Upper Tysoe
Hornton
Horley
Hanwell
Badsey
Bretforton
Mickleton
Ilmington
Blackwell
Idlicote
Tredington
Honington
Alkerton
Shenington
Wroxton
Drayton
Wickhamford
Aston Subedge
Hidcote Boyce
Darlingscott
Balscote
Neithrop
Grimsbury
Weston-Sub-Edge
Willersey
Saintbury
Ebrington
Charingworth
Winderton
Epwell
Shutford
North Newington
Childswickham
Chipping Campden
Stretton-on-Fosse
Barcheston
Willington
Upper Brailes
Lower Brailes
Sutton under Brailes
Sibford Gower
Tidmington
Burmington
Easington
Broughton
Tadmarton
Bodicote
Swalcliffe
Sibford Ferris
Broad Campden
Paxford
Buckland
Laverton
Aston Magna
Todenham
Cherington
Stourton
Bloxham
West Adderbury
Draycott
Little Wolford
Great Wolford
Lower Lemington
Ascott
Milcombe
Milton
Stanton
Snowshill
Blockley
Batsford
Whichford
Hook Norton
Wigginton
South Newington
Barford St John
Barford St Michael
Stanway
Bourton on the Hill
Barton on the Heath
Long Compton
Great Rollright
Swerford
Hempton
Didbrook
Cutsdean
Sezincote
Little Compton
Nether Worton
Over Worton
Duns Tew
Farmcote
Ford
Condicote
Longborough
Evenlode
Chastleton
Great Tew
Donnington
Salford
Over Norton
Little Tew
Ledwell
Temple Guiting
Broadwell
Adlestrop
Cornwell
Heythrop
Sandford St Martin
Middle Barton
Kineton
Upper Swell
Lower Swell
Oddington
Daylesford
Church Enstone
Westcott Barton
Evesham
Vale of Evesham

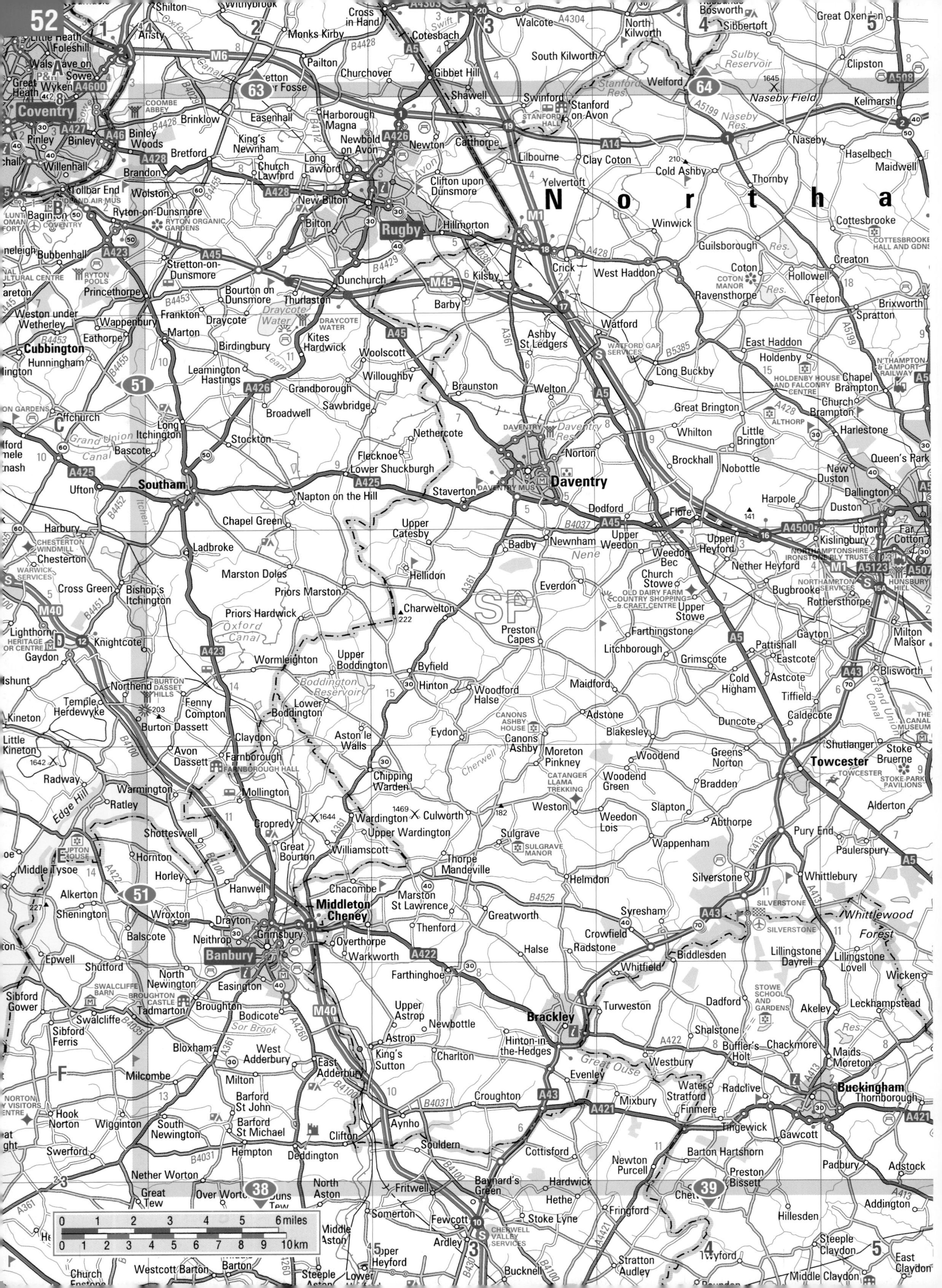
Shilton
Withybrook
Cross in Hand
Walcote
North Kilworth
Husbands Bosworth
Sibbertoft
Great Oxendon
Ansty
Monks Kirby
Cotesbach
Little Heath
Foleshill
Walsgrave on Sowe
Wyken
Great Heath
Coventry
Pailton
Churchover
Gibbet Hill
Shawell
South Kilworth
Welford
Sulby Reservoir
Clipston
Stanford Res.
Naseby Field
Kelmarsh
Coombe Abbey
Brinklow
Easenhall
Harborough Magna
Newbold on Avon
Newton
Catthorpe
Swinford
Stanford Hall
Stanford on Avon
Naseby Res.
Naseby
Haselbech
Maidwell
Pinley
Binley
Binley Woods
King's Newnham
Bretford
Church Lawford
Long Lawford
Lilbourne
Clay Coton
Cold Ashby
Thornby
Willenhall
Brandon
Wolston
Tollbar End
Clifton upon Dunsmore
Yelvertoft
Northa
Baginton
Ryton-on-Dunsmore
Ryton Organic Gardens
New Bilton
Bilton
Rugby
Hillmorton
Winwick
Cottesbrooke
Cottesbrooke Hall and Gdns
Bubbenhall
Stretton-on-Dunsmore
Crick
West Haddon
Guilsborough
Coton
Coton Manor
Creaton
Hollowell
Ryton Pools
Princethorpe
Bourton on Dunsmore
Dunchurch
Thurlaston
Kilsby
Barby
Ravensthorpe
Teeton
Brixworth
Spratton
Weston under Wetherley
Wappenbury
Frankton
Draycote
Draycote Water
Marton
Eathorpe
Cubbington
Hunningham
Birdingbury
Kites Hardwick
Woolscott
Ashby St Ledgers
Watford
Watford Gap Services
East Haddon
Holdenby
Long Buckby
Holdenby House and Falconry Centre
N'hampton & Lamport Railway
Chapel Brampton
Church Brampton
Leamington Hastings
Grandborough
Willoughby
Braunston
Welton
Great Brington
Broadwell
Sawbridge
Offchurch
Long Itchington
Grand Union Canal
Stockton
Bascote
Nethercote
Daventry
Daventry Res.
Whilton
Little Brington
Althorp
Harlestone
Norton
Brockhall
Nobottle
New Duston
Queen's Park
Ufton
Southam
Napton on the Hill
Flecknoe
Lower Shuckburgh
Staverton
Daventry Mus
Dodford
Harpole
Dallington
Duston
Flore
Upton
Far Cotton
Kislingbury
Harbury
Chapel Green
Upper Catesby
Badby
Newnham
Upper Weedon
Weedon Bec
Upper Heyford
Nether Heyford
Northamptonshire Ironstone Rly Trust
Chesterton Windmill
Chesterton
Ladbroke
Nene
Warwick Services
Marston Doles
Hellidon
Church Stowe
Upper Stowe
Everdon
Old Dairy Farm Country Shopping & Craft Centre
Bugbrooke
Northampton Services
Rothersthorpe
Hunsbury Hill
Cross Green
Bishop's Itchington
Priors Marston
Charwelton
SP
Priors Hardwick
Oxford Canal
Preston Capes
Farthingstone
Gayton
Milton Malsor
Lighthorne
Heritage Motor Centre
Knightcote
Gaydon
Wormleighton
Upper Boddington
Byfield
Litchborough
Grimscote
Pattishall
Eastcote
Blisworth
Astcote
Cold Higham
Tiffield
Northend
Burton Dassett Hills
Boddington Reservoir
Hinton
Woodford Halse
Maidford
Temple Herdewycke
Fenny Compton
Lower Boddington
Canons Ashby House
Adstone
Kineton
Burton Dassett
Eydon
Blakesley
Duncote
Caldecote
Canal Museum
Little Kineton
Avon Dassett
Claydon
Aston le Walls
Canons Ashby
Moreton Pinkney
Woodend
Greens Norton
Shutlanger
Stoke Bruerne
Farnborough
Farnborough Hall
Chipping Warden
Cherwell
Catanger Llama Trekking
Woodend Green
Bradden
Towcester
Radway
Warmington
Mollington
Stoke Park Pavilions
Edge Hill
Ratley
Cropredy
Wardington
Culworth
Weston
Slapton
Alderton
Shotteswell
Upper Wardington
Sulgrave
Sulgrave Manor
Weedon Lois
Abthorpe
Pury End
Upton House
Great Bourton
Williamscott
Wappenham
Paulerspury
Hornton
Thorpe Mandeville
Middle Tysoe
Horley
Helmdon
Silverstone
Whittlebury
Hanwell
Chacombe
Marston St Lawrence
Alkerton
Middleton Cheney
Greatworth
Syresham
Silverstone
Whittlewood Forest
Shenington
Wroxton
Drayton
Grimsbury
Thenford
Crowfield
Balscote
Neithrop
Overthorpe
Radstone
Lillingstone Dayrell
Lillingstone Lovell
Epwell
Banbury
Warkworth
Halse
Biddlesden
Shutford
North Newington
Farthinghoe
Whitfield
Wicken
Swalcliffe Barn
Easington
Stowe School and Gardens
Sibford Gower
Broughton Castle
Tadmarton
Broughton
Upper Astrop
Brackley
Turweston
Dadford
Akeley
Leckhampstead
Swalcliffe
Bodicote
Newbottle
Sor Brook
Shalstone
Sibford Ferris
Astrop
Hinton-in-the-Hedges
Chackmore
Res.
Bloxham
West Adderbury
King's Sutton
Charlton
Great Ouse
Westbury
Buffler's Holt
Maids Moreton
Milcombe
East Adderbury
Evenley
Water Stratford
Radclive
Buckingham
Milton
Croughton
Mixbury
Thornborough
Barford St John
Finmere
Norton Visitors Centre
Hook Norton
Wigginton
South Newington
Barford St Michael
Aynho
Tingewick
Gawcott
Clifton
Souldern
Cottisford
Swerford
Hempton
Deddington
Barton Hartshorn
Padbury
Adstock
Newton Purcell
Nether Worton
North Aston
Hardwick
Preston Bissett
Great Tew
Over Worton
Fritwell
Baynard's Green
Hethe
Addington
Somerton
Fewcott
Stoke Lyne
Fringford
Hillesden
Middle Aston
Ardley
Cherwell Valley Services
Upper Heyford
Steeple Claydon
Twyford
Stratton Audley
Bucknell
East Claydon
Middle Claydon
Church Enstone
Westcott Barton
Steeple Aston
Lower Heyford
Canal
Oxford
Avon
Swift
Leam
Itchen
Res.
0 1 2 3 4 5 6 miles
0 1 2 3 4 5 6 7 8 9 10 km

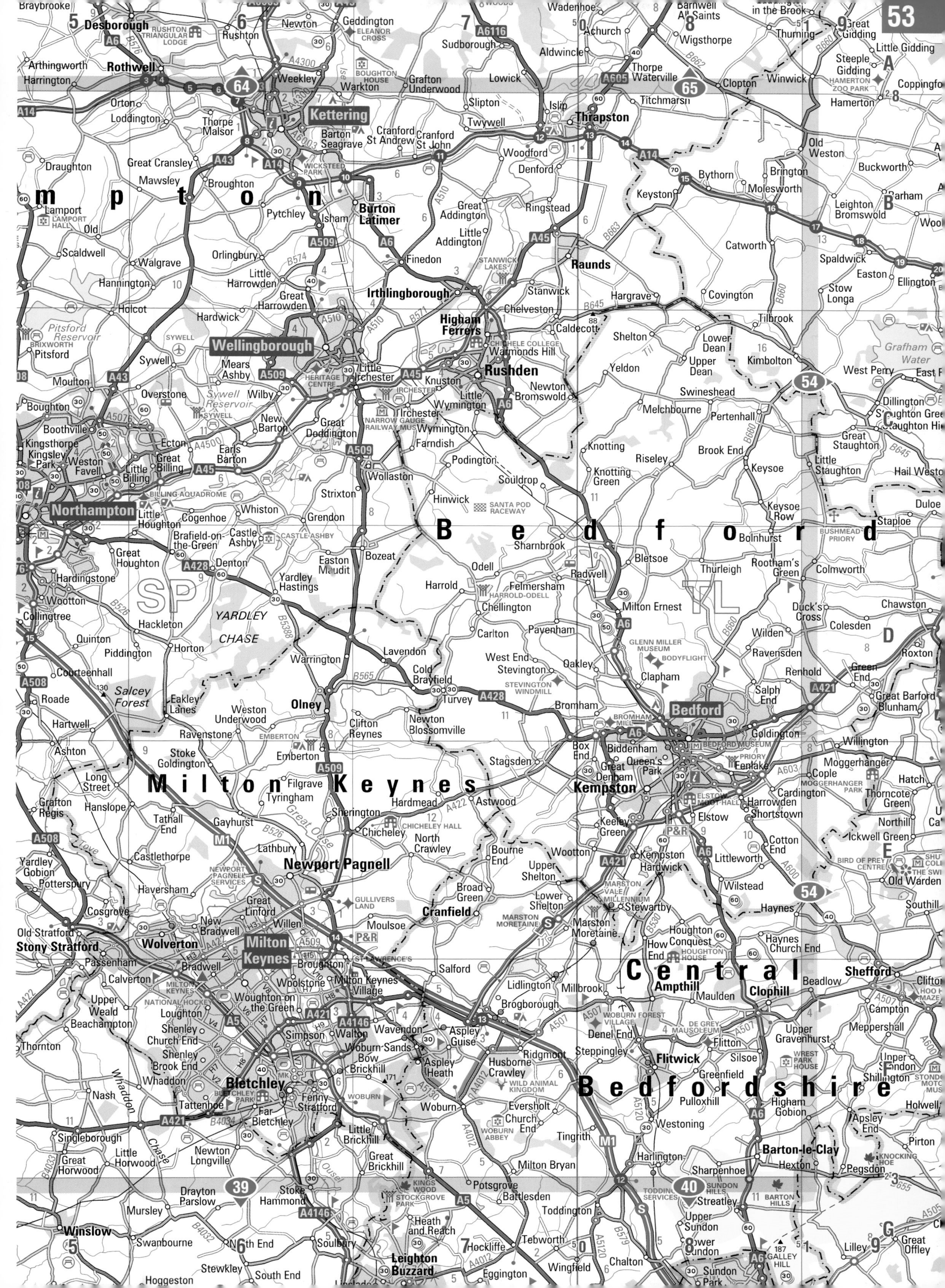
Braybrooke
Desborough
Rushton Triangular Lodge
Rushton
Newton
Geddington
Eleanor Cross
Sudborough
Wadenhoe
Achurch
Barnwell All Saints
Wigsthorpe
in the Brook
Thurning
Great Gidding
Little Gidding
Steeple Gidding
Hamerton Zoo Park
Coppingford
Hamerton
Rothwell
Arthingworth
Harrington
Weekley
Boughton House
Warkton
Grafton Underwood
Lowick
Aldwincle
Thorpe Waterville
Clopton
Winwick
Titchmarsh
Thrapston
Islip
Slipton
Twywell
Orton
Loddington
Thorpe Malsor
Kettering
Barton Seagrave
Cranford St Andrew
Cranford St John
Woodford
Denford
Old Weston
Draughton
Great Cransley
Mawsley
Broughton
Wicksteed Park
Bythorn
Brington
Molesworth
Buckworth
Keyston
Barham
Lamport
Lamport Hall
Old
Scaldwell
Pytchley
Isham
Burton Latimer
Great Addington
Little Addington
Ringstead
Leighton Bromswold
Catworth
Orlingbury
Walgrave
Finedon
Stanwick Lakes
Raunds
Spaldwick
Easton
Ellington
Hannington
Little Harrowden
Great Harrowden
Irthlingborough
Stanwick
Hargrave
Covington
Stow Longa
Holcot
Hardwick
Higham Ferrers
Chelveston
Caldecott
Tilbrook
Pitsford Reservoir
Brixworth
Pitsford
Sywell
Wellingborough
Chichele College
Shelton
Lower Dean
Upper Dean
Kimbolton
Grafham Water
Mears Ashby
Little Irchester
Rushden
Yeldon
West Perry
Moulton
Overstone
Sywell Reservoir
Wilby
Heritage Centre
Knuston
Newton Bromswold
Swineshead
Dillington
Boughton
Irchester
Little Wymington
Melchbourne
Pertenhall
Staughton
New Barton
Great Doddington
Narrow Gauge Railway Mus
Wymington
Great Staughton
Boothville
Kingsthorpe
Kingsley Park
Weston Favell
Ecton
Earls Barton
Farndish
Knotting
Riseley
Brook End
Little Staughton
Little Billing
Great Billing
Podington
Souldrop
Knotting Green
Keysoe
Hail Weston
Billing Aquadrome
Wollaston
Strixton
Hinwick
Santa Pod Raceway
Northampton
Whiston
Little Houghton
Cogenhoe
Grendon
Keysoe Row
Duloe
Brafield-on-the-Green
Castle Ashby
Bedford
Bolnhurst
Bushmead Priory
Staploe
Great Houghton
Denton
Easton Maudit
Bozeat
Sharnbrook
Bletsoe
Thurleigh
Rootham's Green
Colmworth
Hardingstone
SP
Yardley Hastings
Harrold
Odell
Radwell
Felmersham
Harrold-Odell
Wootton
Chellington
Milton Ernest
TL
Duck's Cross
Chawston
Collingtree
Yardley Chase
Hackleton
Carlton
Pavenham
Wilden
Colesden
Quinton
Piddington
Horton
Warrington
Lavendon
Glenn Miller Museum
Bodyflight
Ravensden
Roxton
Courteenhall
West End
Stevington
Oakley
Clapham
Renhold
Cold Brayfield
Turvey
Stevington Windmill
Great Barford
Salcey Forest
Roade
Eakley Lanes
Olney
Salph End
Green End
Blunham
Hartwell
Weston Underwood
Clifton Reynes
Newton Blossomville
Bromham
Bromham Mill
Ravenstone
Emberton
Goldington
Willington
Ashton
Stoke Goldington
Box End
Biddenham
Bedford Museum
Priory
Stagsden
Queen's Park
Fenlake
Moggerhanger
Hatch
Long Street
Milton Keynes
Filgrave
Tyringham
Great Denham
Kempston
Cople
Moggerhanger Park
Cardington
Thorncote Green
Grafton Regis
Hanslope
Hardmead
Astwood
Elstow
Moot Hall
Harrowden
Shortstown
Sherington
Tathall End
Gayhurst
Great Ouse
Chicheley Hall
Chicheley
Keeley Green
Northill
Ickwell Green
North Crawley
Lathbury
Cotton End
Castlethorpe
Yardley Gobion
Bourne End
Wootton
Kempston Hardwick
Littleworth
Bird of Prey Centre
Old Warden
Newport Pagnell
Newport Pagnell Services
Upper Shelton
Potterspury
Haversham
Broad Green
Wilstead
Lower Shelton
Marston Vale Millennium
Gullivers Land
Haynes
Southill
Cosgrove
Great Linford
Cranfield
Stewartby
Old Stratford
New Bradwell
Willen
Moulsoe
Marston Moretaine
Houghton Conquest
Stony Stratford
Wolverton
Haynes Church End
How End
Houghton House
Central
Passenham
St Lawrence's
Bradwell
Broughton
Salford
Shefford
Calverton
Milton Keynes Village
Woolstone
Ampthill
Clophill
Beadlow
Clifton
Lidlington
Millbrook
Maulden
Upper Weald
National Hockey
Woughton on the Green
Brogborough
Campton
Beachampton
Loughton
Woburn Forest Village
De Grey Mausoleum
Denel End
Flitton
Upper Gravenhurst
Meppershall
Shenley Church End
Simpson
Walton
Wavendon
Aspley Guise
Ridgmont
Steppingley
Silsoe
Wrest Park House
Thornton
Shenley Brook End
Woburn Sands
Bow Brickhill
Aspley Heath
Husborne Crawley
Flitwick
Greenfield
Upper Stondon
Shillington
Whaddon
Wild Animal Kingdom
Bedfordshire
Bletchley
Bletchley Park
Fenny Stratford
Woburn
Pulloxhill
Higham Gobion
Nash
Tattenhoe
Far Bletchley
Woburn
Eversholt
Church End
Holwell
Westoning
Apsley End
Singleborough
Little Horwood
Newton Longville
Little Brickhill
Woburn Abbey
Tingrith
Pirton
Great Horwood
Great Brickhill
Milton Bryan
Harlington
Barton-le-Clay
Knocking Hoe
Hexton
Pegsdon
Sharpenhoe
Drayton Parslow
Stoke Hammond
Kings Wood
Stockgrove Park
Potsgrove
Battlesden
Toddington Services
Sundon Hills
Barton Hills
Mursley
Heath and Reach
Toddington
Streatley
Upper Sundon
Winslow
Swanbourne
North End
Soulbury
Hockliffe
Tebworth
Lower Sundon
Galley Hill
Lilley
Great Offley
Leighton Buzzard
Chalton
Stewkley
South End
Wingfield
Sundon Park
Hoggeston
Eggington
Whaddon Chase
Ouzel
A6116
A605
A14
A43
A509
A6
A45
A510
A4500
A5076
A428
A508
A5
A421
A4146
A422
A603
A600
A507
A4012
A5120
A505
M1
B576
B662
B660
B663
B645
B574
B571
B5388
B526
B565
B4034
B4033
B4032
B530
B579
B655
64
65
54
39
40
5
6
7
8
9
A
B
C
D
E
F
G

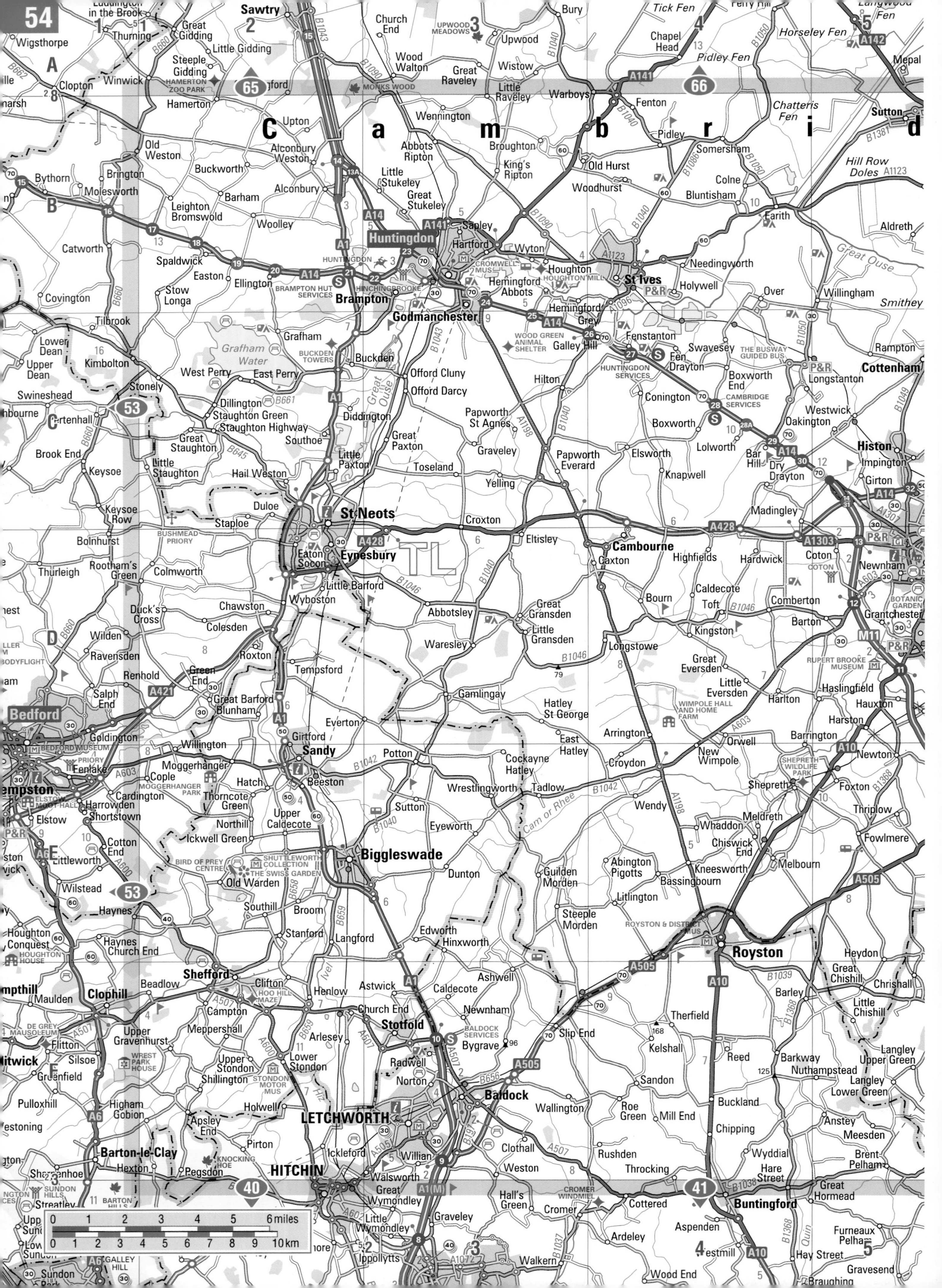
Cambridge
Luddington in the Brook
Sawtry
Church End
UPWOOD MEADOWS
Upwood
Bury
Tick Fen
Langwood Fen
Thurning
Great Gidding
Little Gidding
Wigsthorpe
Steeple Gidding
HAMERTON ZOO PARK
Wood Walton
Great Raveley
Wistow
Chapel Head
Pidley Fen
Horseley Fen
Mepal
Clopton
Winwick
MONKS WOOD
Little Raveley
Warboys
Fenton
Chatteris Fen
Sutton
Hamerton
Upton
Wennington
Pidley
Somersham
Alconbury Weston
Abbots Ripton
Broughton
Old Weston
King's Ripton
Old Hurst
Hill Row Doles
Bythorn
Brington
Molesworth
Buckworth
Little Stukeley
Woodhurst
Colne
Bluntisham
Alconbury
Great Stukeley
Barham
Leighton Bromswold
Woolley
Huntingdon
Sapley
Hartford
Wyton
Earith
Aldreth
Catworth
HUNTINGDON
CROMWELL MUS
Houghton
HOUGHTON MILL
St Ives
Needingworth
Great Ouse
Spaldwick
Easton
Ellington
BRAMPTON HUT SERVICES
HINCHINGBROOKE
Brampton
Hemingford Abbots
Holywell
Over
Willingham
Smithey
Covington
Stow Longa
Godmanchester
Hemingford Grey
Tilbrook
Grafham
WOOD GREEN ANIMAL SHELTER
Galley Hill
Fenstanton
Swavesey
THE BUSWAY GUIDED BUS
Rampton
Lower Dean
Upper Dean
Grafham Water
BUCKDEN TOWERS
Buckden
Offord Cluny
HUNTINGDON SERVICES
Fen Drayton
Boxworth End
Longstanton
Cottenham
Kimbolton
West Perry
East Perry
Offord Darcy
Hilton
Conington
CAMBRIDGE SERVICES
Swineshead
Stonely
Dillington
Staughton Green
Staughton Highway
Papworth St Agnes
Westwick
Oakington
Pertenhall
Diddington
Southoe
Great Paxton
Boxworth
Lolworth
Histon
Brook End
Great Staughton
Graveley
Papworth Everard
Elsworth
Bar Hill
Dry Drayton
Impington
Keysoe
Little Staughton
Hail Weston
Little Paxton
Toseland
Knapwell
Girton
Yelling
Duloe
St Neots
Croxton
Madingley
Keysoe Row
Staploe
BUSHMEAD PRIORY
Eltisley
Cambourne
Highfields
Hardwick
Coton
Bolnhurst
Eaton Socon
Eynesbury
TL
Caxton
COTON
Newnham
Thurleigh
Rootham's Green
Colmworth
Little Barford
Caldecote
Wyboston
Bourn
Toft
Comberton
BOTANIC GARDEN
Chawston
Abbotsley
Great Gransden
Grantchester
Duck's Cross
Colesden
Little Gransden
Kingston
Barton
Wilden
Waresley
Longstowe
Ravensden
Roxton
Great Eversden
RUPERT BROOKE MUSEUM
Tempsford
Renhold
Green End
Little Eversden
Harlton
Haslingfield
Hauxton
Salph End
Great Barford
Gamlingay
Hatley St George
WIMPOLE HALL AND HOME FARM
Blunham
Harston
Bedford
Goldington
Everton
Arrington
Barrington
BEDFORD MUSEUM
Girtford
Orwell
PRIORY
Willington
Sandy
Potton
East Hatley
New Wimpole
Newton
Fenlake
Moggerhanger
Cockayne Hatley
Croydon
SHEPRETH WILDLIFE PARK
Kempston
Cople
MOGGERHANGER PARK
Hatch
Beeston
Tadlow
Shepreth
Foxton
ELSTOW MOOT HALL
Cardington
Thorncote Green
Wrestlingworth
Wendy
Harrowden
Shortstown
Upper Caldecote
Sutton
Thriplow
Elstow
Northill
Meldreth
Whaddon
Fowlmere
Cotton End
Ickwell Green
Eyeworth
Cam or Rhee
Chiswick End
Littleworth
BIRD OF PREY CENTRE
SHUTTLEWORTH COLLECTION
THE SWISS GARDEN
Biggleswade
Abington Pigotts
Kneesworth
Melbourn
Old Warden
Dunton
Guilden Morden
Bassingbourn
Wilstead
Southill
Litlington
Haynes
Broom
Steeple Morden
ROYSTON & DISTRICT MUS
Houghton Conquest
Stanford
Langford
Edworth
Hinxworth
Haynes Church End
Royston
Heydon
HOUGHTON HOUSE
Great Chishill
Chrishall
Ampthill
Beadlow
Shefford
Clifton
Ashwell
Barley
Maulden
Clophill
HOO HILL MAZE
Henlow
Astwick
Caldecote
Little Chishill
DE GREY MAUSOLEUM
Campton
Church End
Newnham
Therfield
Upper Gravenhurst
Meppershall
Stotfold
BALDOCK SERVICES
Flitton
Arlesey
Bygrave
Slip End
Kelshall
Langley Upper Green
Silsoe
WREST PARK HOUSE
Upper Stondon
Lower Stondon
Radwell
Reed
Barkway
Nuthampstead
Flitwick
Greenfield
Shillington
STONDON MOTOR MUS
Norton
Sandon
Langley Lower Green
Pulloxhill
Higham Gobion
Holwell
Baldock
Wallington
Buckland
Westoning
Apsley End
LETCHWORTH
Roe Green
Mill End
Chipping
Anstey
Meesden
Barton-le-Clay
Pirton
KNOCKING HOE
Ickleford
Willian
Clothall
Wyddial
Brent Pelham
Hexton
Pegsdon
HITCHIN
Weston
Rushden
Throcking
Hare Street
Sharpenhoe
SUNDON HILLS
Walsworth
Great Wymondley
CROMER WINDMILL
Buntingford
Great Hormead
BARTON HILLS
Streatley
Hall's Green
Cromer
Cottered
Graveley
Little Wymondley
Aspenden
Furneaux Pelham
Ardeley
Ippollytts
Walkern
Westmill
Hay Street
Sundon
GALLEY HILL
Wood End
Braughing
Gravesend
Quin
Ivel
Hiz
A1
A1(M)
A14
A141
A142
A1123
A1096
A1198
A1303
A421
A428
A505
A507
A600
A602
A603
A6
A10
M11
B1043
B1090
B1040
B1050
B1086
B1381
B1049
B660
B662
B661
B645
B1046
B1042
B658
B659
B656
B1037
B1039
B1368
B1038
B197
P&R
65
66
53
40
41
0 1 2 3 4 5 6 miles
0 1 2 3 4 5 6 7 8 9 10 km

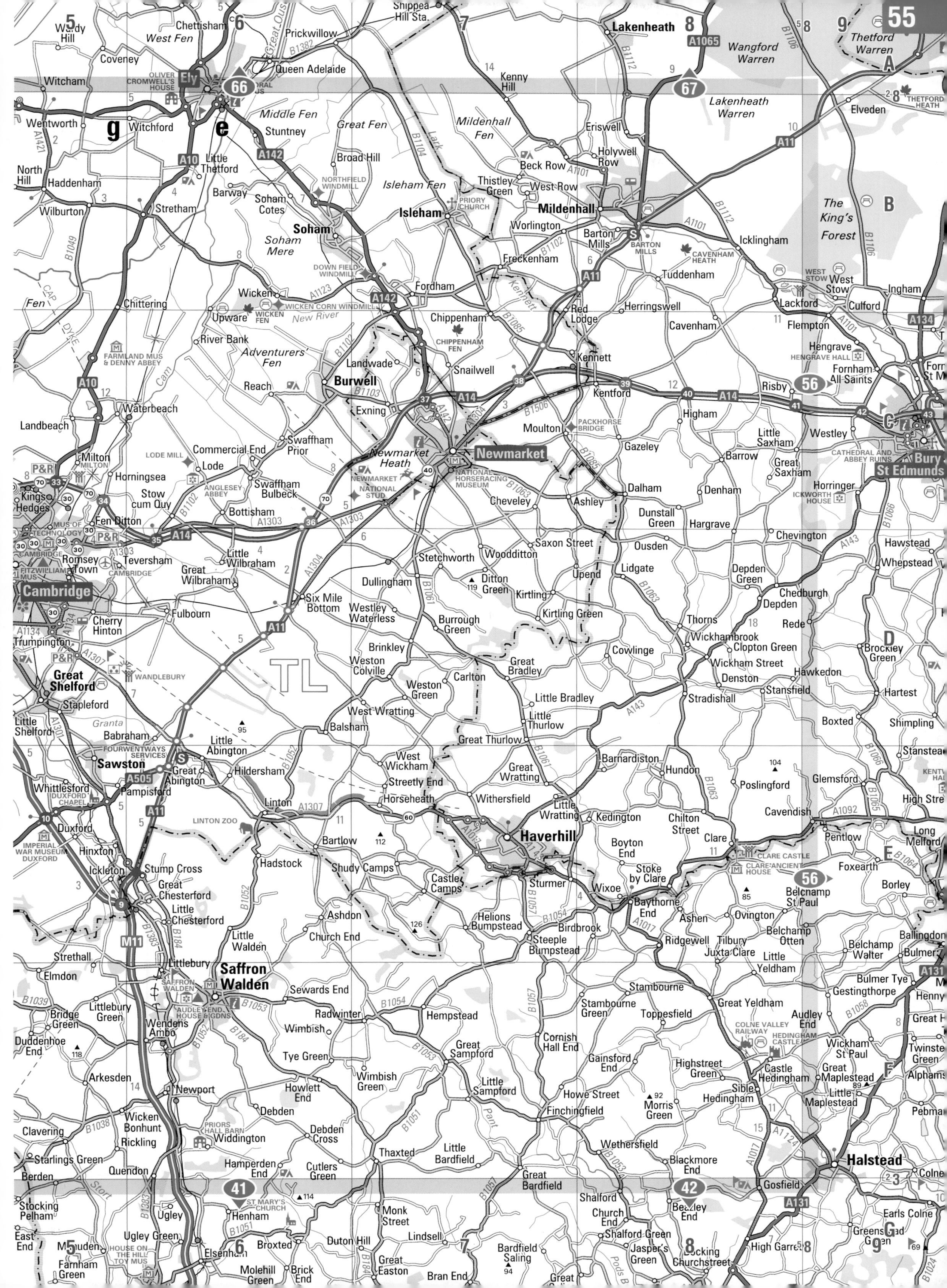
Shippea Hill Sta.
Lakenheath
Thetford Warren
Wangford Warren
Chettisham
West Fen
Prickwillow
Queen Adelaide
Coveney
Witcham
Oliver Cromwell's House
Ely
Kenny Hill
Lakenheath Warren
Elveden
Thetford Heath
Wentworth
Witchford
Middle Fen
Stuntney
Great Fen
Mildenhall Fen
Eriswell
Holywell Row
Beck Row
West Row
Thistley Green
North Hill
Haddenham
Little Thetford
Barway
Soham Cotes
Northfield Windmill
Isleham Fen
Priory Church
Isleham
Mildenhall
The King's Forest
Wilburton
Stretham
Soham
Soham Mere
Worlington
Barton Mills
Icklingham
Freckenham
Cavenham Heath
Tuddenham
Down Field Windmill
Wicken
Wicken Corn Windmill
Wicken Fen
New River
Fordham
Red Lodge
Herringswell
West Stow
Ingham
Lackford
Culford
Fen
Chittering
Upware
Chippenham
Chippenham Fen
Cavenham
Flempton
River Bank
Adventurers' Fen
Landwade
Snailwell
Kennett
Hengrave
Hengrave Hall
Farmland Mus & Denny Abbey
Burwell
Fornham All Saints
Reach
Kentford
Risby
Waterbeach
Exning
Higham
Landbeach
Moulton
Packhorse Bridge
Little Saxham
Westley
Commercial End
Swaffham Prior
Lode Mill
Lode
Newmarket Heath
Newmarket
National Horseracing Museum
Gazeley
Barrow
Great Saxham
Cathedral and Abbey Ruins
Bury St Edmunds
Milton
Horningsea
Swaffham Bulbeck
National Stud
Dalham
Denham
Horringer
Ickworth House
Kings Hedges
Stow cum Quy
Anglesey Abbey
Cheveley
Ashley
Dunstall Green
Hargrave
Bottisham
Fen Ditton
Mus of Technology
Chevington
Hawstead
Whepstead
Teversham
Romsey Town
Cambridge
Fitzwilliam Mus
Little Wilbraham
Great Wilbraham
Stetchworth
Woodditton
Saxon Street
Ousden
Ditton Green
Upend
Lidgate
Depden Green
Dullingham
Six Mile Bottom
Kirtling
Chedburgh
Depden
Cherry Hinton
Fulbourn
Westley Waterless
Kirtling Green
Trumpington
Burrough Green
Thorns
Rede
Wickhambrook
Clopton Green
Brockley Green
Brinkley
Cowlinge
Great Bradley
Wickham Street
Hawkedon
Great Shelford
Wandlebury
Weston Colville
Carlton
Denston
Stansfield
Stapleford
Weston Green
Stradishall
Hartest
Little Bradley
Little Shelford
Granta
West Wratting
Little Thurlow
Babraham
Balsham
Boxted
Shimpling
Great Thurlow
Fourwentways Services
Little Abington
Sawston
Great Abington
West Wickham
Hildersham
Great Wratting
Barnardiston
Hundon
Poslingford
Glemsford
Streetly End
Whittlesford
Duxford Chapel
Pampisford
Horseheath
Withersfield
Little Wratting
Kedington
Chilton Street
Cavendish
Linton
Linton Zoo
Haverhill
Clare
Long Melford
Duxford
Bartlow
Boyton End
Pentlow
Imperial War Museum Duxford
Hinxton
Clare Castle
Clare Ancient House
Foxearth
Ickleton
Stump Cross
Hadstock
Shudy Camps
Stoke by Clare
Great Chesterford
Castle Camps
Sturmer
Wixoe
Borley
Belchamp St Paul
Little Chesterford
Ashdon
Baythorne End
Helions Bumpstead
Ashen
Ovington
Birdbrook
Little Walden
Church End
Steeple Bumpstead
Ridgewell
Tilbury Juxta Clare
Belchamp Otten
Belchamp Walter
Ballingdon
Bulmer
Strethall
Little Yeldham
Elmdon
Littlebury
Saffron Walden
Bulmer Tye
Stambourne
Gestingthorpe
Sewards End
Audley End House & Gdns
Bridge Green
Littlebury Green
Wendens Ambo
Radwinter
Hempstead
Stambourne Green
Toppesfield
Great Yeldham
Audley End
Henny
Great Henny
Wimbish
Colne Valley Railway
Hedingham Castle
Duddenhoe End
Great Sampford
Cornish Hall End
Wickham St Paul
Tye Green
Gainsford End
Highstreet Green
Castle Hedingham
Great Maplestead
Twinstead Green
Arkesden
Wimbish Green
Little Sampford
Sible Hedingham
Little Maplestead
Alphamstone
Newport
Howlett End
Howe Street
Morris Green
Pebmarsh
Wicken Bonhunt
Debden
Finchingfield
Clavering
Priors Hall Barn
Widdington
Debden Cross
Rickling
Thaxted
Little Bardfield
Wethersfield
Blackmore End
Halstead
Starlings Green
Quendon
Hamperden End
Cutlers Green
Great Bardfield
Gosfield
Berden
St. Mary's Church
Shalford
Beazley End
Stocking Pelham
Henham
Ugley
Monk Street
Church End
Earls Colne
East End
Ugley Green
Lindsell
Shalford Green
Greenstead Green
Maunden
House on the Hill Toy Mus
Broxted
Duton Hill
Bardfield Saling
Jasper's Green
Bocking Churchstreet
High Garrett
Farnham Green
Elsenham
Molehill Green
Brick End
Great Easton
Bran End

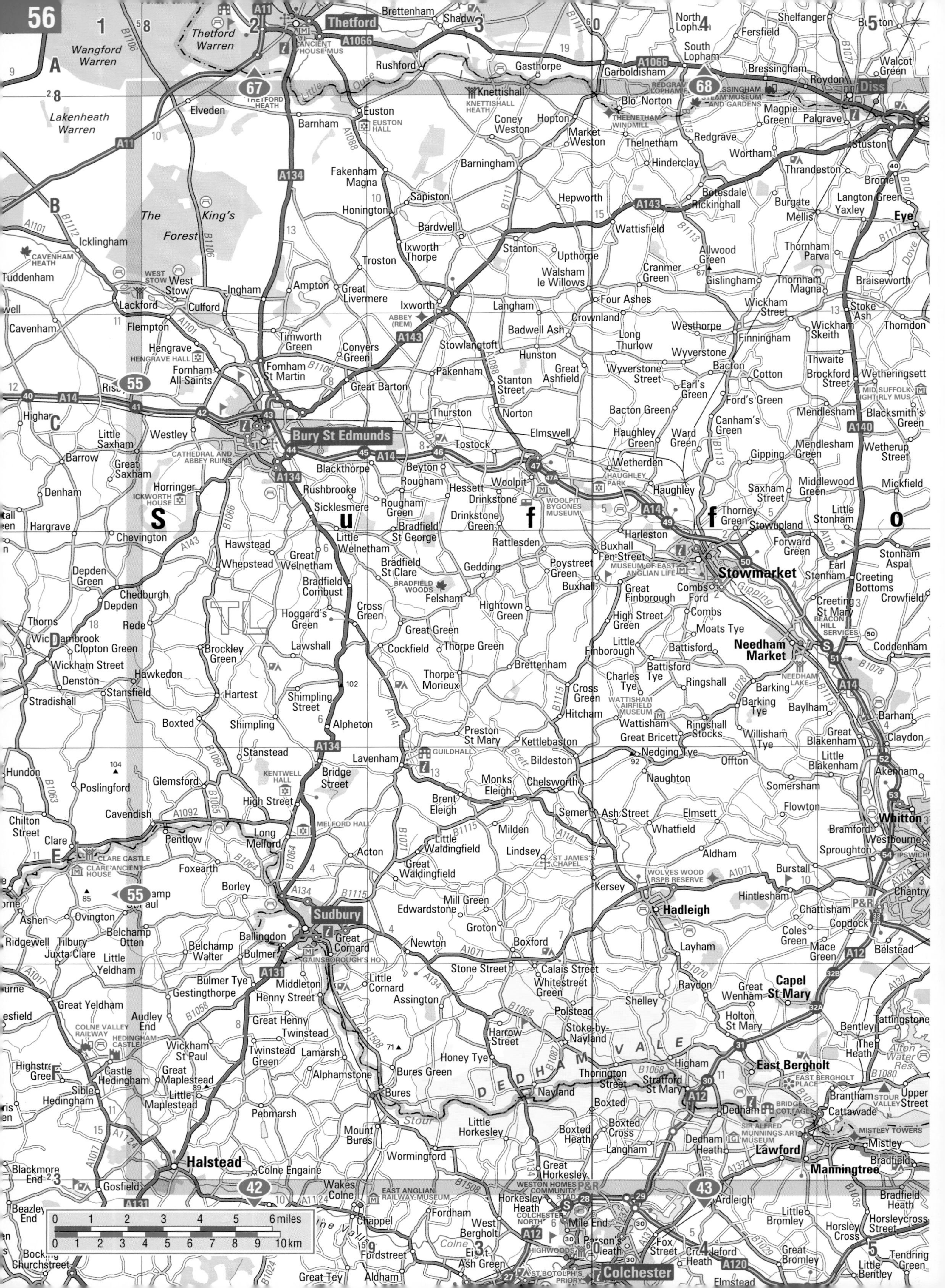

Wangford Warren
Thetford Warren
Thetford
Brettenham
Shadwell
North Lopham
Shelfanger
Fersfield
Bressingham
Roydon
Diss
Walcot Green
South Lopham
Rushford
Gasthorpe
Garboldisham
ANCIENT HOUSE MUS
Lakenheath Warren
Elveden
THETFORD HEATH
Knettishall
KNETTISHALL HEATH
Blo' Norton
THELNETHAM WINDMILL
BRESSINGHAM STEAM MUSEUM AND GARDENS
Magpie Green
Palgrave
Euston
EUSTON HALL
Barnham
Coney Weston
Hopton
Market Weston
Thelnetham
Redgrave
Wortham
Stuston
Hinderclay
Thrandeston
Brome
Fakenham Magna
Barningham
Botesdale
Rickinghall
Burgate
Langton Green
Yaxley
Mellis
Eye
Sapiston
Honington
Hepworth
Wattisfield
The King's Forest
Icklingham
CAVENHAM HEATH
Tuddenham
Bardwell
Ixworth Thorpe
Troston
Stanton
Upthorpe
Allwood Green
Thornham Parva
Cranmer Green
Walsham le Willows
Gislingham
Thornham Magna
Braiseworth
WEST STOW
West Stow
Lackford
Culford
Ingham
Ampton
Great Livermere
Ixworth
ABBEY (REM)
Langham
Four Ashes
Wickham Street
Stoke Ash
Cavenham
Flempton
Timworth Green
Conyers Green
Crownland
Long Thurlow
Westhorpe
Finningham
Wickham Skeith
Thorndon
Hengrave
HENGRAVE HALL
Fornham All Saints
Fornham St Martin
Stowlangtoft
Badwell Ash
Hunston
Wyverstone
Wyverstone Street
Thwaite
Pakenham
Great Ashfield
Bacton
Cotton
Brockford Street
Wetheringsett
MID SUFFOLK LIGHT RLY MUS
Great Barton
Stanton Street
Earl's Green
Ford's Green
Risby
Higham
Westley
Little Saxham
Bury St Edmunds
Thurston
Norton
Bacton Green
Mendlesham
Blacksmith's Green
Canham's Green
Barrow
CATHEDRAL AND ABBEY RUINS
Great Saxham
Tostock
Elmswell
Haughley Green
Ward Green
Mendlesham Green
Wetherup Street
Gipping
Beyton
Blackthorpe
Wetherden
HAUGHLEY PARK
Denham
Horringer
ICKWORTH HOUSE
Rushbrooke
Rougham
Hessett
Woolpit
Drinkstone
WOOLPIT BYGONES MUSEUM
Haughley
Saxham Street
Middlewood Green
Mickfield
Sicklesmere
Rougham Green
Drinkstone Green
Thorney Green
Stowupland
Little Stonham
Hargrave
Chevington
Bradfield St George
Harleston
Forward Green
Suffolk
Little Welnetham
Rattlesden
Buxhall Fen Street
Earl Stonham
Stonham Aspal
Hawstead
Great Welnetham
Whepstead
Bradfield St Clare
Gedding
Poystreet Green
Stowmarket
Creeting Bottoms
Depden Green
Chedburgh
Depden
Bradfield Combust
BRADFIELD WOODS
Felsham
MUSEUM OF EAST ANGLIAN LIFE
Buxhall
Great Finborough
Combs Ford
Gipping
Crowfield
Creeting St Mary
BEACON HILL SERVICES
Thorns
Rede
Cross Green
Hoggard's Green
Hightown Green
Combs
High Street Green
Wickhambrook
Clopton Green
Great Green
Lawshall
Moats Tye
Little Finborough
Battisford
Needham Market
Coddenham
Cockfield
Thorpe Green
Brockley Green
Wickham Street
Brettenham
Battisford Tye
NEEDHAM LAKE
Denston
Hawkedon
Thorpe Morieux
Charles Tye
Ringshall
Barking
Stradishall
Stansfield
Hartest
Shimpling Street
Cross Green
WATTISHAM AIRFIELD MUSEUM
Barking Tye
Baylham
Hitcham
Wattisham
Ringshall Stocks
Barham
Boxted
Shimpling
Alpheton
Preston St Mary
Kettlebaston
Great Bricett
Willisham Tye
Great Blakenham
Claydon
Stanstead
GUILDHALL
Nedging Tye
Offton
Little Blakenham
Hundon
Lavenham
Bildeston
Akenham
Poslingford
Glemsford
KENTWELL HALL
Bridge Street
Monks Eleigh
Chelsworth
Naughton
Somersham
High Street
Brent Eleigh
Flowton
Whitton
Chilton Street
Cavendish
Semer
Ash Street
Elmsett
Bramford
Clare
Pentlow
Long Melford
MELFORD HALL
Milden
Whatfield
Westbourne
Little Waldingfield
Sproughton
IPSWICH
CLARE CASTLE
CLARE ANCIENT HOUSE
Acton
Lindsey
ST JAMES'S CHAPEL
Aldham
Foxearth
Great Waldingfield
WOLVES WOOD RSPB RESERVE
Burstall
Chantry
Borley
Kersey
Hintlesham
Mill Green
Hadleigh
Ashen
Ovington
Sudbury
Edwardstone
Chattisham
Copdock
Belchamp Otten
Groton
Coles Green
Ridgewell
Tilbury Juxta Clare
Belchamp Walter
Ballingdon
Great Cornard
Newton
Boxford
Layham
Mace Green
Belstead
Bulmer
GAINSBOROUGH'S HO
Little Yeldham
Stone Street
Calais Street
Bulmer Tye
Little Cornard
Whitestreet Green
Raydon
Capel St Mary
Gestingthorpe
Middleton
Assington
Great Wenham
Great Yeldham
Henny Street
Polstead
Shelley
Audley End
Great Henny
Holton St Mary
Tattingstone
Bentley
COLNE VALLEY RAILWAY
HEDINGHAM CASTLE
Twinstead
Stoke-by-Nayland
Harrow Street
Wickham St Paul
Twinstead Green
Lamarsh
Dedham Vale
The Heath
Alton Water Res
Honey Tye
Higham
Castle Hedingham
Great Maplestead
Alphamstone
Thorington Street
East Bergholt
Stratford St Mary
EAST BERGHOLT PLACE
Sible Hedingham
Little Maplestead
Bures Green
Bures
Nayland
Brantham
Upper Street
STOUR VALLEY
Boxted
Dedham
BRIDGE COTTAGE
Cattawade
Pebmarsh
Stour
Little Horkesley
Boxted Cross
SIR ALFRED MUNNINGS ART MUSEUM
MISTLEY TOWERS
Mount Bures
Boxted Heath
Dedham Heath
Lawford
Mistley
Langham
Wormingford
Manningtree
Bradfield
Blackmore End
Halstead
Colne Engaine
Great Horkesley
Gosfield
Wakes Colne
EAST ANGLIAN RAILWAY MUSEUM
WESTON HOMES COMMUNITY STAD
Horkesley Heath
COLCHESTER NORTH
Ardleigh
Bradfield Heath
Beazley End
Chappel
Fordham
West Bergholt
Mile End
Little Bromley
Horsleycross Street
Horsley Cross
Colne
Parson's Heath
Fox Street
Crockleford Heath
Great Bromley
Tendring Green
Little Bentley
Bocking Churchstreet
Fordstreet
Eight Ash Green
HIGHWOODS
ST BOTOLPH'S PRIORY
Colchester
Great Tey
Aldham
Elmstead
A11
A1066
A134
A143
A14
A1088
A1101
A1092
A140
A1120
A12
A131
A1124
A1017
A1141
A1071
A1214
A137
A1232
A120
B1106
B1112
B1111
B1113
B1066
B1063
B1065
B1064
B1115
B1071
B1058
B1508
B1068
B1087
B1070
B1078
B1077
B1117
B1080
B1035
B1029
B1024
67
68
55
42
43
TL
0 1 2 3 4 5 6 miles
0 1 2 3 4 5 6 7 8 9 10 km

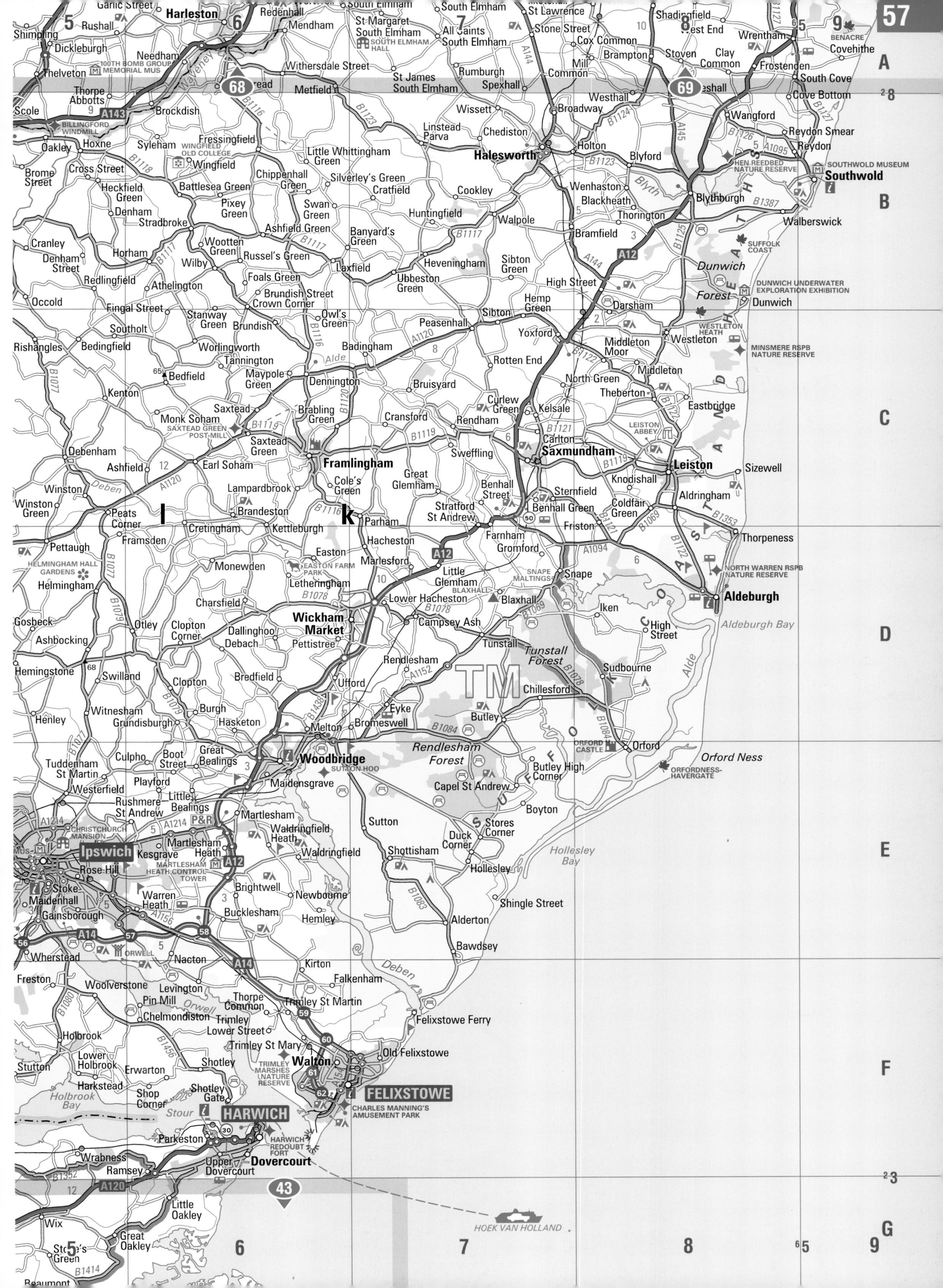
Harleston
Rushall
Redenhall
Mendham
South Elmham
St Margaret South Elmham
South Elmham Hall
All Saints South Elmham
St Lawrence
Stone Street
Cox Common
Brampton
Mill Common
Shadingfield
West End
Wrentham
Benacre
Covehithe
Stoven
Clay Common
Frostenden
South Cove
Cove Bottom
Shimpling
Dickleburgh
Needham
100th Bomb Group Memorial Mus
Thelveton
Withersdale Street
St James South Elmham
Rumburgh
Spexhall
Westhall
Metfield
Thorpe Abbotts
Scole
Brockdish
Billingford Windmill
Wissett
Broadway
Wangford
Reydon Smear
Reydon
Linstead Parva
Chediston
Holton
Halesworth
Blyford
Oakley
Hoxne
Syleham
Wingfield Old College
Fressingfield
Wingfield
Little Whittingham Green
Brome Street
Cross Street
Hen Reedbed Nature Reserve
Southwold Museum
Southwold
Heckfield Green
Chippenhall Green
Silverley's Green
Cratfield
Battlesea Green
Cookley
Wenhaston
Blackheath
Blythburgh
Walberswick
Thorington
Denham
Stradbroke
Pixey Green
Swan Green
Huntingfield
Walpole
Bramfield
Ashfield Green
Banyard's Green
Cranley
Horham
Wootten Green
Russel's Green
Wilby
Laxfield
Heveningham
Sibton Green
Suffolk Coast
Dunwich
Dunwich Forest
Dunwich Underwater Exploration Exhibition
Denham Street
Redlingfield
Athelington
Foals Green
Ubbeston Green
High Street
Hemp Green
Darsham
Occold
Brundish Street
Crown Corner
Fingal Street
Stanway Green
Brundish
Owl's Green
Sibton
Peasenhall
Yoxford
Westleton Heath
Westleton
Southolt
Bedingfield
Rishangles
Worlingworth
Tannington
Badingham
Middleton Moor
Minsmere RSPB Nature Reserve
Rotten End
Bedfield
Maypole Green
Dennington
Middleton
North Green
Theberton
Kenton
Bruisyard
Eastbridge
Curlew Green
Kelsale
Saxtead
Brabling Green
Cransford
Monk Soham
Saxtead Green Post Mill
Rendham
Leiston Abbey
Carlton
Saxmundham
Debenham
Saxtead Green
Sweffling
Leiston
Framlingham
Sizewell
Ashfield
Earl Soham
Knodishall
Great Glemham
Benhall Street
Sternfield
Cole's Green
Winston
Deben
Lampardbrook
Aldringham
Winston Green
Peats Corner
Brandeston
Stratford St Andrew
Benhall Green
Coldfair Green
Parham
Friston
Thorpeness
Framsden
Cretingham
Kettleburgh
Hacheston
Farnham
Gromford
Pettaugh
Easton
Marlesford
Helmingham Hall Gardens
Monewden
Easton Farm Park
Little Glemham
Snape Maltings
Snape
North Warren RSPB Nature Reserve
Helmingham
Letheringham
Blaxhall
Aldeburgh
Charsfield
Lower Hacheston
Iken
Gosbeck
Wickham Market
Campsey Ash
High Street
Aldeburgh Bay
Ashbocking
Otley
Clopton Corner
Dallinghoo
Debach
Pettistree
Tunstall
Tunstall Forest
Rendlesham
Sudbourne
Hemingstone
Swilland
Clopton
Bredfield
Ufford
Chillesford
Alde
Witnesham
Grundisburgh
Burgh
Hasketon
Eyke
Butley
Henley
Melton
Bromeswell
Orford Castle
Orford
Tuddenham St Martin
Culpho
Boot Street
Great Bealings
Woodbridge
Rendlesham Forest
Orford Ness
Sutton Hoo
Butley High Corner
Playford
Maidensgrave
Capel St Andrew
Orfordness-Havergate
Westerfield
Rushmere St Andrew
Little Bealings
Boyton
Martlesham
Christchurch Mansion
Waldringfield Heath
Sutton
Stores Corner
Duck Corner
Ipswich
Kesgrave
Martlesham Heath
Waldringfield
Shottisham
Hollesley
Hollesley Bay
Rose Hill
Martlesham Heath Control Tower
Stoke
Maidenhall
Brightwell
Newbourne
Warren Heath
Shingle Street
Gainsborough
Bucklesham
Hemley
Alderton
Bawdsey
Wherstead
Orwell
Nacton
Kirton
Freston
Woolverstone
Levington
Falkenham
Pin Mill
Thorpe Common
Trimley St Martin
Chelmondiston
Trimley Lower Street
Felixstowe Ferry
Holbrook
Trimley St Mary
Lower Holbrook
Walton
Old Felixstowe
Stutton
Erwarton
Shotley
Trimley Marshes Nature Reserve
Harkstead
Shotley Gate
Shop Corner
Holbrook Bay
Felixstowe
Stour
Harwich
Charles Manning's Amusement Park
Parkeston
Harwich Redoubt Fort
Wrabness
Ramsey
Upper Dovercourt
Dovercourt
Little Oakley
Hoek van Holland
Wix
Great Oakley
Stone's Green
Beaumont
TM
A B C D E F G
5 6 7 8 9

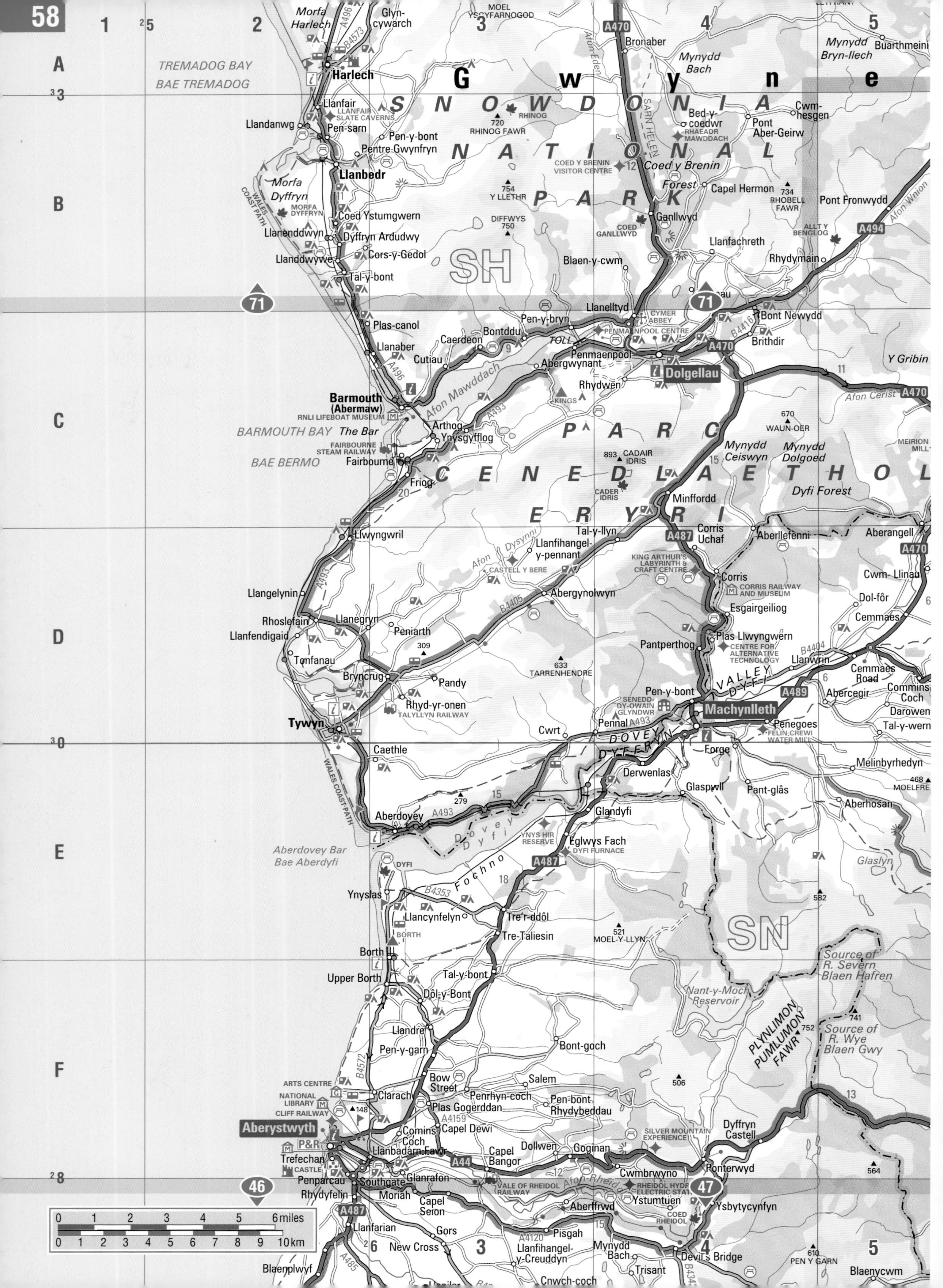

TREMADOG BAY
BAE TREMADOG
Morfa Harlech
Harlech
Glyn-cywarch
MOEL YSGYFARNOGOD
Bronaber
Afon Eden
Mynydd Bach
Mynydd Bryn-llech
Buarthmeini
Gwynedd
SNOWDONIA NATIONAL PARK
Llanfair
LLANFAIR SLATE CAVERNS
Llandanwg
Pen-sarn
Pen-y-bont
Pentre Gwynfryn
720 RHINOG FAWR
RHINOG
SARN HELEN
Bed-y-coedwr
RHAEADR MAWDDACH
Cwm-hesgen
Pont Aber-Geirw
COED Y BRENIN VISITOR CENTRE
Coed y Brenin Forest
Capel Hermon
734 RHOBELL FAWR
Pont Fronwydd
Llanbedr
Morfa Dyffryn
MORFA DYFFRYN
WALES COAST PATH
754 Y LLETHR
Coed Ystumgwern
DIFFWYS 750
COED GANLLWYD
Ganllwyd
ALLT Y BENGLOG
Afon Wnion
A494
Llanenddwyn
Dyffryn Ardudwy
Cors-y-Gedol
Llanddwywe
Llanfachreth
Rhydymain
Blaen-y-cwm
SH
Tal-y-bont
71
Plas-canol
Llanelltyd
CYMER ABBEY
Bont Newydd
Pen-y-bryn
Bontddu
Caerdeon
TOLL
PENMAENPOOL CENTRE
Brithdir
B4416
A470
Llanaber
Cutiau
Penmaenpool
Abergwynant
Dolgellau
Y Gribin
A496
Afon Mawddach
Rhydwen
KINGS
Afon Cerist
Barmouth (Abermaw)
RNLI LIFEBOAT MUSEUM
BARMOUTH BAY
The Bar
Arthog
Ynysgyfflog
A493
PARC CENEDLAETHOL ERYRI
670 WAUN-OER
MEIRION MILL
FAIRBOURNE STEAM RAILWAY
Fairbourne
BAE BERMO
893 CADAIR IDRIS
Mynydd Ceiswyn
Mynydd Dolgoed
Friog
CADER IDRIS
Dyfi Forest
Minffordd
Llwyngwril
Tal-y-llyn
A487
Corris Uchaf
Aberllefenni
Aberangell
Afon Dysynni
Llanfihangel-y-pennant
CASTELL Y BERE
KING ARTHUR'S LABYRINTH & CRAFT CENTRE
Corris
CORRIS RAILWAY AND MUSEUM
Cwm-Llinau
Llangelynin
Abergynolwyn
B4405
Esgairgeiliog
Dol-fôr
Cemmaes
Rhoslefain
Llanegryn
Peniarth
Llanfendigaid
Plas Llwyngwern
CENTRE FOR ALTERNATIVE TECHNOLOGY
Pantperthog
B4404
Llanwrin
Tonfanau
309
633 TARRENHENDRE
Cemmaes Road
Bryncrug
Pandy
VALLEY DYFI
Rhyd-yr-onen
TALYLLYN RAILWAY
SENEDD-DY-OWAIN GLYNDWR
Pen-y-bont
Machynlleth
A489
Abercegir
Commins Coch
Darowen
Tywyn
Pennal
Cwrt
Penegoes
FELIN CREWI WATER MILL
Tal-y-wern
Caethle
DOVEY DYFFRYN
Forge
Melinbyrhedyn
Derwenlas
Glaspwll
Pant-glâs
468 MOELFRE
279
Aberdovey
Glandyfi
Aberhosan
Dovey Dyfi
YNYS HIR RESERVE
Eglwys Fach
DYFI FURNACE
Aberdovey Bar
Bae Aberdyfi
DYFI
Fochno
18
Glaslyn
Ynyslas
B4353
582
Llancynfelyn
Tre'r-ddôl
BORTH
Tre-Taliesin
521 MOEL-Y-LLYN
SN
Borth
Source of R. Severn Blaen Hafren
Upper Borth
Tal-y-bont
Nant-y-Moch Reservoir
Dôl-y-Bont
PLYNLIMON PUMLUMON FAWR
752
741
Source of R. Wye Blaen Gwy
Llandre
Pen-y-garn
Bont-goch
B4572
ARTS CENTRE
Bow Street
Salem
506
NATIONAL LIBRARY
Clarach
Penrhyn-coch
Pen-bont Rhydybeddau
CLIFF RAILWAY
148
Plas Gogerddan
A4159
Aberystwyth
Comins Coch
Capel Dewi
SILVER MOUNTAIN EXPERIENCE
Dyffryn Castell
P&R
Llanbadarn Fawr
Dollwen
Goginan
Trefechan
CASTLE
A44
Capel Bangor
Ponterwyd
564
Penparcau
Southgate
Glanrafon
Cwmbrwyno
Rhydyfelin
Moriah
VALE OF RHEIDOL RAILWAY
Afon Rheidol
RHEIDOL HYDRO ELECTRIC STATION
46
47
Capel Seion
Aberffrwd
Ystumtuen
Ysbyty Cynfyn
A487
Llanfarian
Gors
COED RHEIDOL
Pisgah
A4120
New Cross
Llanfihangel-y-Creuddyn
Mynydd Bach
Devil's Bridge
610 PEN Y GARN
Blaenplwyf
A485
Trisant
Cnwch-coch
Blaenycwm
0 1 2 3 4 5 6 miles
0 1 2 3 4 5 6 7 8 9 10 km

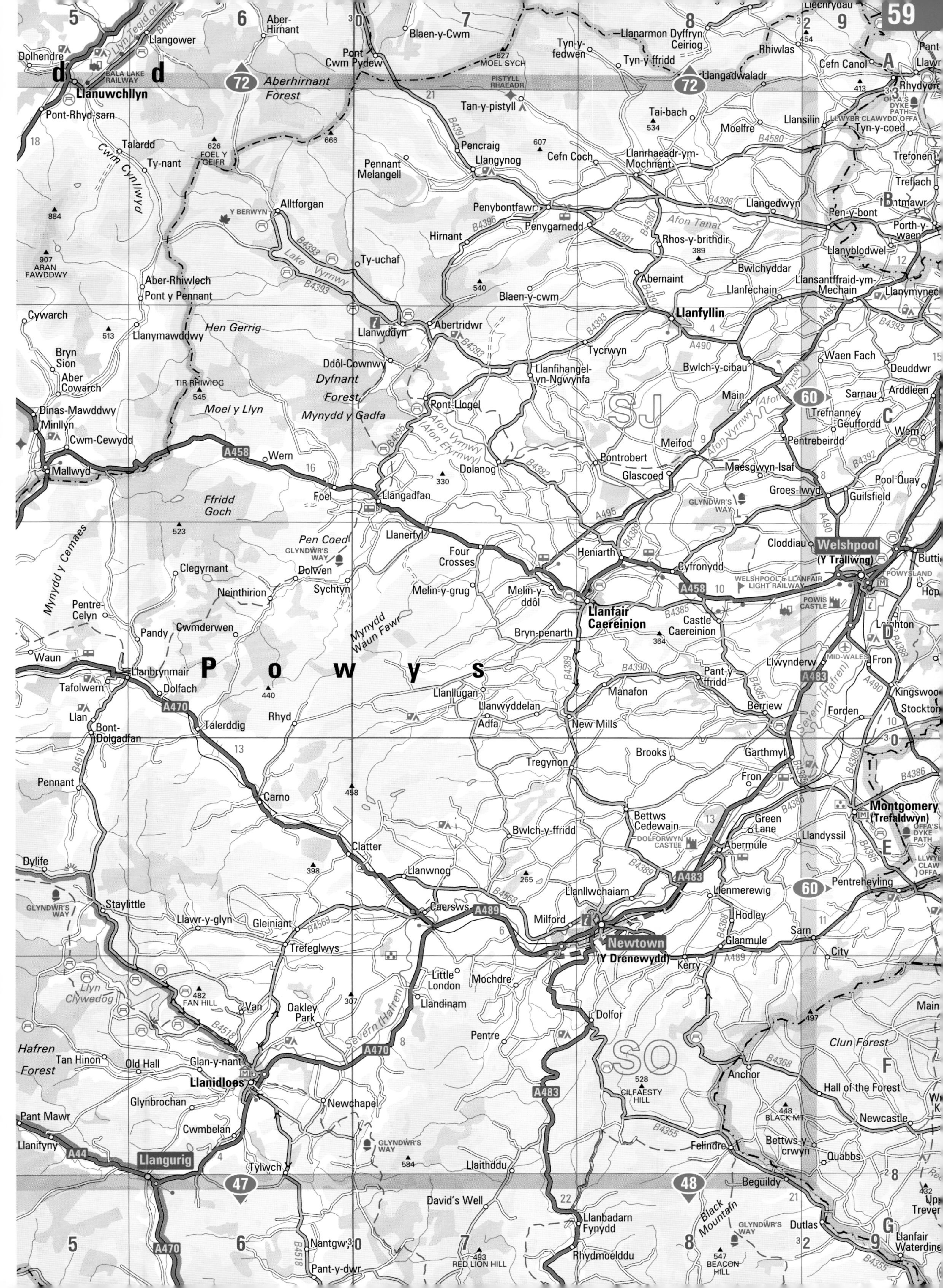
Llanuwchllyn
Llangower
Dolhendre
Pont-Rhyd-sarn
Talardd
Ty-nant
Cwm Cynllwyd
Aber-Hirnant
Aberhirnant Forest
Pont Cwm Pydew
Blaen-y-Cwm
MOEL SYCH
PISTYLL RHAEADR
Tan-y-pistyll
Tyn-y-fedwen
Llanarmon Dyffryn Ceiriog
Tyn-y-ffridd
Llangadwaladr
Rhiwlas
Cefn Canol
Rhydycroesau
Tai-bach
Moelfre
Llansilin
Tyn-y-coed
Trefonen
Treflach
LLWYBR CLAWDD OFFA
OFFA'S DYKE PATH
FOEL Y GEIFR
Pencraig
Llangynog
Pennant Melangell
Cefn Coch
Llanrhaeadr-ym-Mochnant
Llangedwyn
Pen-y-bont
Porth-y-waen
Penybontfawr
Penygarnedd
Afon Tanat
Rhos-y-brithdir
Llanyblodwel
Y BERWYN
Alltforgan
Hirnant
Lake Vyrnwy
Ty-uchaf
ARAN FAWDDWY
Aber-Rhiwlech
Pont y Pennant
Abernaint
Bwlchyddar
Llanfechain
Llansantffraid-ym-Mechain
Llanymynech
Blaen-y-cwm
Cywarch
Llanymawddwy
Hen Gerrig
Llanwddyn
Abertridwr
Llanfyllin
Bryn Sion
Aber Cowarch
Ddôl-Cownwy
Dyfnant Forest
Tycrwyn
Bwlch-y-cibau
Waen Fach
Deuddwr
TIR RHIWIOG
Llanfihangel-yn-Ngwynfa
Sarnau
Arddleen
Dinas-Mawddwy
Minllyn
Moel y Llyn
Mynydd y Gadfa
Pont Llogel
SJ
Main
Trefnanney
Geufforddd
Cwm-Cewydd
Afon Vyrnwy (Afon Efyrnwy)
Meifod
Pentrebeirdd
Wern
Mallwyd
Wern
Dolanog
Pontrobert
Glascoed
Maesgwyn-Isaf
Pool Quay
Ffridd Goch
Foel
Llangadfan
Groes-lwyd
Guilsfield
GLYNDWR'S WAY
Mynydd y Cemaes
Pen Coed
Llanerfyl
Heniarth
Cloddiau
Welshpool (Y Trallwng)
Buttington
Four Crosses
Clegyrnant
Dolwen
Sychtyn
Melin-y-grug
Melin-y-ddôl
Cyfronydd
WELSHPOOL & LLANFAIR LIGHT RAILWAY
POWYSLAND
Neinthirion
Llanfair Caereinion
POWIS CASTLE
Pentre-Celyn
Cwmderwen
Mynydd Waun Fawr
Castle Caereinion
Leighton
Pandy
Bryn-penarth
Waun
Llanbrynmair
P o w y s
MID-WALES
Llwynderw
Fron
Tafolwern
Dolfach
Llanllugan
Pant-y-ffridd
Manafon
Kingswood
Llan
Bont-Dolgadfan
Talerddig
Rhyd
Llanwyddelan
Adfa
New Mills
Berriew
Forden
Stockton
Severn (Hafren)
Pennant
Tregynon
Brooks
Garthmyl
Fron
Carno
Montgomery (Trefaldwyn)
Bettws Cedewain
Green Lane
Bwlch-y-ffridd
DOLFORWYN CASTLE
Abermule
Llandyssil
Dylife
Clatter
Llanwnog
Llanllwchaiarn
Llanmerewig
Pentreheyling
GLYNDWR'S WAY
Staylittle
Caersws
Milford
Hodley
Llawr-y-glyn
Gleiniant
Newtown (Y Drenewydd)
Sarn
Trefeglwys
Glanmule
Kerry
City
Llyn Clywedog
Little London
Mochdre
FAN HILL
Van
Llandinam
Dolfor
Main
Oakley Park
Hafren Forest
Tan Hinon
Old Hall
Glan-y-nant
Pentre
Clun Forest
SO
Llanidloes
Anchor
CILFAESTY HILL
Hall of the Forest
Glynbrochan
Newchapel
BLACK MT
Newcastle
Pant Mawr
Cwmbelan
Felindre
Bettws-y-crwyn
Quabbs
Llanifyny
Llangurig
Tylwch
Llaithddu
Beguildy
David's Well
Black Mountain
Llanbadarn Fynydd
Dutlas
Llanfair Waterdine
Nantgwyn
RED LION HILL
Rhydmoelddu
BEACON HILL
Pant-y-dwr
A458
A470
A489
A483
A495
A490
A44
B4391
B4393
B4396
B4580
B4382
B4395
B4389
B4390
B4385
B4388
B4386
B4392
B4518
B4569
B4568
B4368
B4355
B4403
72
60
47
48

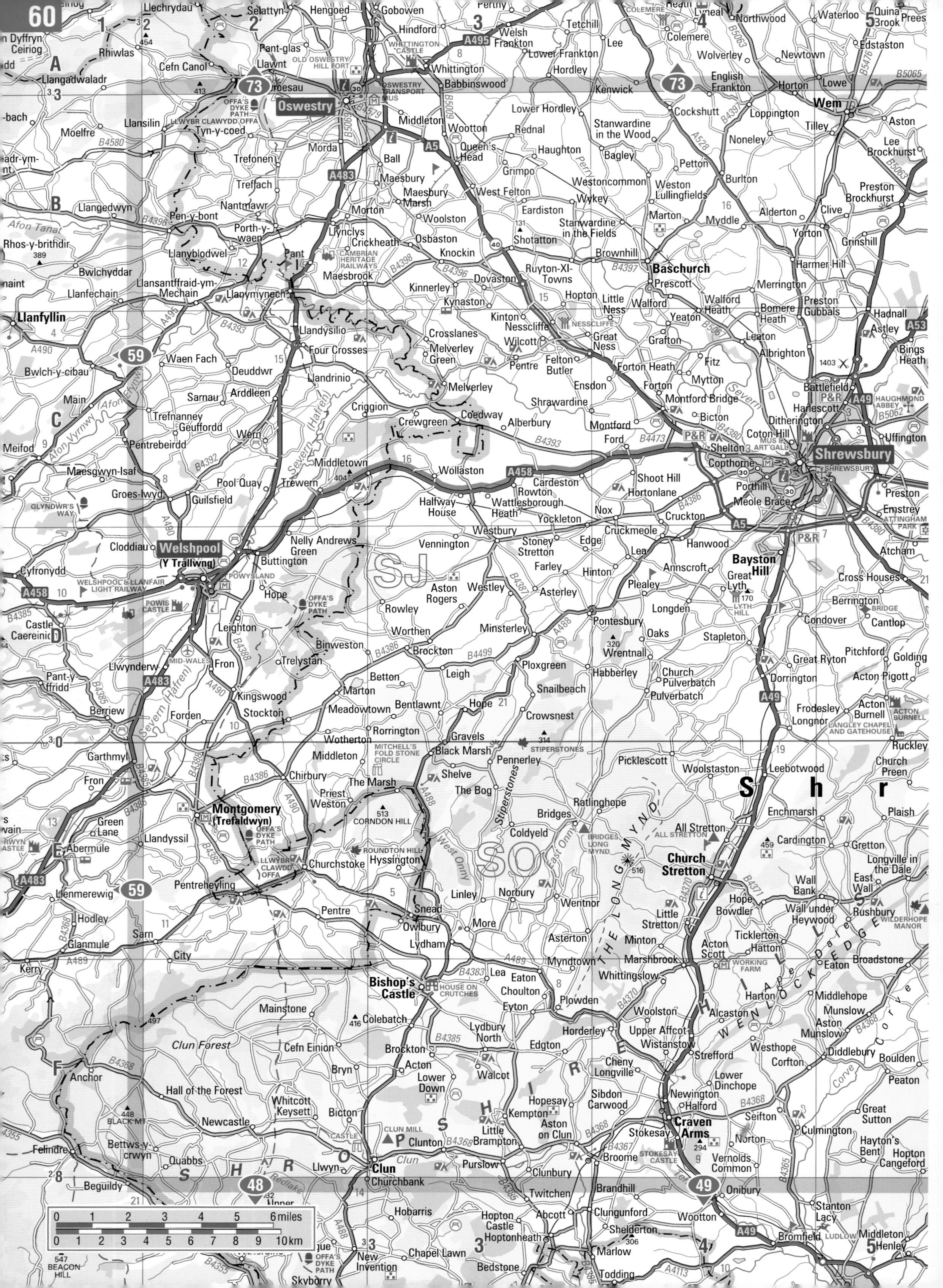

Llechrydau
Selattyn
Hengoed
Gobowen
Tetchill
Lyneal
Northwood
Waterloo
Quina Brook
Welsh Frankton
Lee
Colemere
Hindford
WHITTINGTON CASTLE
A495
Lower Frankton
Wolverley
Newtown
Edstaston
Dyffryn Ceiriog
Rhiwlas
Pant-glas
Llawnt
OLD OSWESTRY HILL FORT
Whittington
Hordley
English Frankton
Horton
Lowe
Llangadwaladr
Cefn Canol
Babbinswood
Kenwick
73
Wem
Oswestry
OSWESTRY TRANSPORT MUS
OFFA'S DYKE PATH
Lower Hordley
Cockshutt
Loppington
Aston
Llansilin
LLWYBR CLAWDD OFFA
Middleton
Wootton
Stanwardine in the Wood
Tilley
Moelfre
Tyn-y-coed
Rednal
Noneley
Lee Brockhurst
B4580
Morda
A5
Queen's Head
Haughton
Bagley
Trefonen
Ball
Petton
A483
Maesbury
Grimpo
Burlton
Treflach
Maesbury Marsh
West Felton
Westoncommon
Weston Lullingfields
Preston Brockhurst
Llangedwyn
Nantmawr
Wykey
Morton
Eardiston
Marton
Myddle
Alderton
Clive
Pen-y-bont
Woolston
Afon Tanat
Porth-y-waen
Llynclys
Osbaston
Shotatton
Stanwardine in the Fields
Yorton
Rhos-y-brithdir
389
Crickheath
Grinshill
Llanyblodwel
Pant
CAMBRIAN HERITAGE RAILWAYS
Knockin
Brownhill
Bwlchyddar
B4398
Maesbrook
Ruyton-XI-Towns
B4397
Baschurch
Harmer Hill
Llansantffraid-ym-Mechain
Kinnerley
Dovaston
Prescott
Merrington
Llanfechain
Llanymynech
Kynaston
Hopton
Little Ness
Walford
Walford Heath
Preston Gubbals
Llanfyllin
Kinton
Nesscliffe
NESSCLIFFE
Yeaton
Bomere Heath
Hadnall
Crosslanes
Great Ness
Leaton
Astley
Llandysilio
Melverley Green
Wilcott
Grafton
Bings Heath
A490
Four Crosses
Pentre
Felton Butler
Fitz
Albrighton
59
Waen Fach
Forton Heath
Bwlch-y-cibau
Deuddwr
Llandrinio
Mytton
Battlefield
Melverley
Ensdon
Forton
Main
Sarnau
Arddleen
Shrawardine
Montford Bridge
HAUGHMOND ABBEY
Criggion
Coedway
Harlescott
Trefnanney
Geuffordd
Crewgreen
Alberbury
Montford
Bicton
Ditherington
Wern
Ford
Coton Hill
Uffington
Meifod
Pentrebeirdd
B4393
Shelton
MUS & ART GALL
Shrewsbury
Maesgwyn-Isaf
Middletown
Copthorne
SHREWSBURY
A458
Shoot Hill
Pool Quay
Trewern
Wollaston
Cardeston
Porthill
Preston
Groes-lwyd
Guilsfield
Rowton
Hortonlane
GLYNDWR'S WAY
Halfway House
Wattlesborough Heath
Meole Brace
Emstrey
Nox
Cruckton
ATTINGHAM PARK
Yockleton
Nelly Andrews Green
Vennington
Westbury
Cruckmeole
Hanwood
Cloddiau
Welshpool
(Y Trallwng)
Buttington
Stoney Stretton
Edge
Bayston Hill
Atcham
Lea
Farley
Hinton
Annscroft
Great Lyth
Cross Houses
Cyfronydd
POWYSLAND
SJ
Aston Rogers
Westley
Asterley
Plealey
WELSHPOOL & LLANFAIR LIGHT RAILWAY
LYTH HILL
Berrington
Hope
OFFA'S DYKE PATH
BRIDGE
POWIS CASTLE
Rowley
Longden
Condover
Cantlop
Castle Caereinion
Pontesbury
Leighton
Worthen
Minsterley
Oaks
Stapleton
Wrentnall
Binweston
Brockton
Pitchford
Golding
Llwynderw
MID-WALES
Fron
Trelystan
Ploxgreen
Habberley
Church Pulverbatch
Great Ryton
Leigh
Pant-y-ffridd
Betton
Dorrington
Acton Pigott
Snailbeach
Pulverbatch
Kingswood
Marton
Bentlawnt
Acton Burnell
ACTON BURNELL
Berriew
Forden
Stockton
Meadowtown
Hope
Frodesley
Crowsnest
Longnor
LANGLEY CHAPEL AND GATEHOUSE
Rorrington
Gravels
Wotherton
314
STIPERSTONES
Ruckley
Garthmyl
Middleton
MITCHELL'S FOLD STONE CIRCLE
Black Marsh
Pennerley
Picklescott
Woolstaston
Leebotwood
Church Preen
Fron
Chirbury
Shelve
The Marsh
The Bog
Stiperstones
Priest Weston
Ratlinghope
Enchmarsh
Plaish
Montgomery
(Trefaldwyn)
CORNDON HILL
Bridges
All Stretton
ALL STRETTON
Cardington
Green Lane
OFFA'S DYKE PATH
Coldyeld
BRIDGES LONG MYND
Gretton
Llandyssil
ROUNDTON HILL
West Onny
SO
East Onny
THE LONG MYND
Church Stretton
Longville in the Dale
Abermule
LLWYBR CLAWDD OFFA
Churchstoke
Hyssington
East Wall
Wall Bank
Llanmerewig
Pentreheyling
Linley
Norbury
Hope Bowdler
Rushbury
Wentnor
Little Stretton
Wall under Heywood
WILDERHOPE MANOR
Hodley
Pentre
Snead
Owlbury
More
Ticklerton
Sarn
Asterton
Minton
Acton Scott
Hatton
Glanmule
Lydham
Marshbrook
WENLOCK EDGE
City
Myndtown
WORKING FARM
Eaton
Broadstone
Kerry
A489
Bishop's Castle
HOUSE ON CRUTCHES
Lea
Eaton
Choulton
Whittingslow
Eyton
Plowden
Harton
Middlehope
Munslow
Mainstone
Colebatch
Woolston
Alcaston
Aston Munslow
497
Lydbury North
Upper Affcot
Clun Forest
Cefn Einion
Edgton
Horderley
Wistanstow
Westhope
Diddlebury
Boulden
Brockton
Strefford
Corfton
Anchor
Acton
Lower Down
Walcot
Cheny Longville
Lower Dinchope
Peaton
Bryn
Hall of the Forest
Whitcott Keysett
Hopesay
Sibdon Carwood
Newington
Halford
Great Sutton
BLACK MT
Newcastle
Bicton
Kempton
Aston on Clun
Little Brampton
Stokesay
Craven Arms
Seifton
Culmington
CLUN MILL
CASTLE
Clunton
Norton
Hayton's Bent
Felindre
Bettws-y-crwyn
Quabbs
Clun
Purslow
Broome
STOKESAY CASTLE
Vernolds Common
Cangeford
Llwyn
Churchbank
Clunbury
48
49
Beguildy
Redlake
Twitchen
Brandhill
Onibury
Hobarris
Hopton Castle
Abcott
Clungunford
Stanton Lacy
Hoptonheath
Shelderton
Wootton
Bromfield
LUDLOW
Middleton
Henley
547 BEACON HILL
OFFA'S DYKE PATH
New Invention
Chapel Lawn
Marlow
Bedstone
Skyborry
Todding
A4113
0 1 2 3 4 5 6 miles
0 1 2 3 4 5 6 7 8 9 10 km

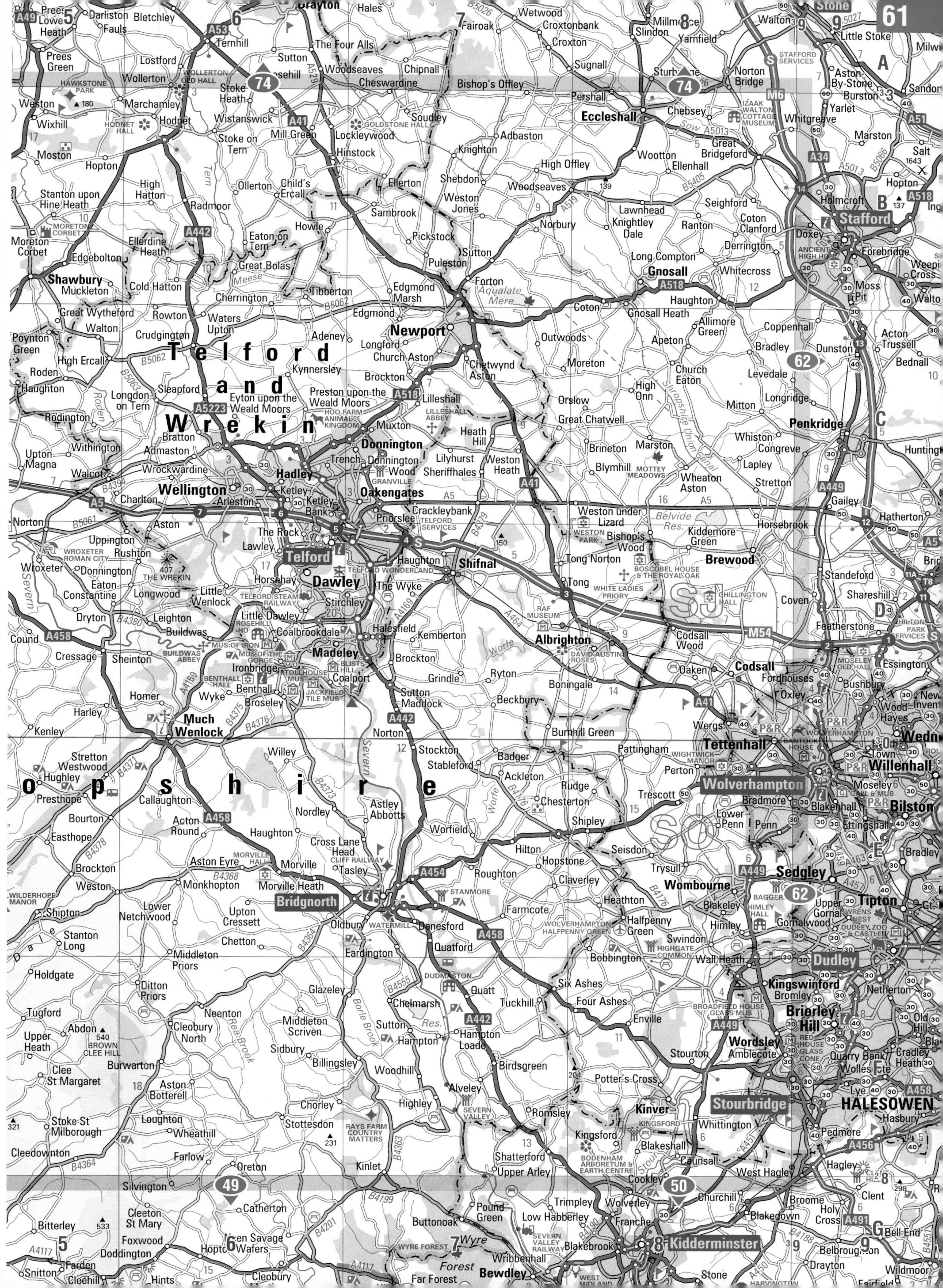
Telford and Wrekin
Shropshire
Prees Lower Heath
Darliston
Fauls
Bletchley
Ternhill
Drayton
Hales
Fairoak
Wetwood
Croxtonbank
Croxton
Millmeece
Slindon
Yarnfield
Walton
Stone
Little Stoke
Prees Green
Lostford
Sutton
The Four Alls
Woodseaves
Chipnall
Cheswardine
Bishop's Offley
Sugnall
Norton Bridge
Stafford Services
Hawkstone Park
Wollerton
Wollerton Old Hall
Stoke Heath
Pershall
Eccleshall
Chebsey
Izaak Walton Cottage Museum
Aston-By-Stone
Burston
Yarlet
Whitgreave
Sandon
Weston
Wixhill
Marchamley
Hodnet Hall
Hodnet
Wistanswick
Goldstone Hall
Soudley
Mill Green
Lockleywood
Adbaston
Great Bridgeford
Marston
Salt
Moston
Hopton
Stoke on Tern
Hinstock
Knighton
High Offley
Wootton
Ellenhall
High Hatton
Stanton upon Hine Heath
Ollerton
Child's Ercall
Ellerton
Shebdon
Woodseaves
Seighford
Holmcroft
Radmoor
Sambrook
Weston Jones
Lawnhead
Knightley Dale
Ranton
Coton Clanford
Stafford
Moreton Corbet
Ellerdine Heath
Eaton on Tern
Howle
Pickstock
Norbury
Derrington
Doxey
Ancient High House
Forebridge
Edgebolton
Great Bolas
Sutton
Puleston
Long Compton
Gnosall
Whitecross
Weeping Cross
Moss Pit
Shawbury
Muckleton
Cold Hatton
Meese
Tibberton
Edgmond Marsh
Forton
Aqualate Mere
Cherrington
Haughton
Great Wytheford
Rowton
Waters Upton
Edgmond
Newport
Coton
Gnosall Heath
Allimore Green
Coppenhall
Acton Trussell
Walton
Crudgington
Adeney
Longford
Outwoods
Apeton
Bradley
Dunston
Bednall
Poynton Green
High Ercall
Church Aston
Chetwynd Aston
Moreton
Church Eaton
Roden
Kynnersley
Brockton
Levedale
Haughton
Longdon on Tern
Sleapford
Eyton upon the Weald Moors
Preston upon the Weald Moors
Lilleshall
Orslow
High Onn
Longridge
Mitton
Rodington
Hoo Farm Animal Kingdom
Lilleshall Abbey
Great Chatwall
Penkridge
Withington
Bratton
Admaston
Muxton
Heath Hill
Whiston
Congreve
Upton Magna
Wrockwardine
Donnington
Trench
Donnington Wood
Granville
Lilyhurst
Sheriffhales
Weston Heath
Brineton
Marston
Blymhill
Mottey Meadows
Wheaton Aston
Lapley
Stretton
Huntington
Walcot
Hadley
Wellington
Ketley
Oakengates
Shropshire Union Canal
Charlton
Arleston
Ketley Bank
Crackleybank
Gailey
Norton
Priorslee
Telford Services
Weston under Lizard
Weston Park
Belvide Res.
Kiddemore Green
Horsebrook
Hatherton
Uppington
Aston
The Rock
Lawley
Bishop's Wood
Brewood
Wroxeter Roman City
Rushton
Telford
Haughton
Shifnal
Tong Norton
Boscobel House & The Royal Oak
Wroxeter
Donnington
Dawley
Telford Wonderland
The Wrekin
Eaton Constantine
Longwood
Little Wenlock
Horsehay
Telford Steam Railway
The Wyke
Tong
White Ladies Priory
Chillington Hall
Standeford
Coven
Shareshill
Dryton
Leighton
Little Dawley
Stirchley
RAF Museum
Buildwas
Rosehill
Coalbrookdale
Halesfield
Kemberton
Albrighton
Codsall Wood
Featherstone
Hilton Park Services
Cound
Cressage
Sheinton
Buildwas Abbey
Mus of Iron
Mus of the Gorge
Madeley
Blists Hill
David Austin Roses
Oaken
Codsall
Moseley Old Hall
Essington
Ironbridge
Benthall Hall
Tollhouse
Brockton
Ryton
Fordhouses
Bushbury
Coalport
Jackfield Tile Mus
Grindle
Boningale
Oxley
Wood Hayes
Homer
Wyke
Benthall
Broseley
Sutton Maddock
Beckbury
Harley
Much Wenlock
Norton
Burnhill Green
Wergs
Tettenhall
Wolverhampton
Bantock House
Wednesfield
Kenley
Willey
Stockton
Stableford
Badger
Pattingham
Wightwick Manor
Perton
Willenhall
Stretton Westwood
Hughley
Ackleton
Rudge
Chesterton
Trescott
Moseley
Bilston
Presthope
Callaughton
Nordley
Astley Abbotts
Bradmore
Blakenhall
Lower Penn
Penn
Ettingshall
Bourton
Acton Round
Worfield
Shipley
Easthope
Haughton
Cross Lane Head
Cliff Railway
Hilton
Hopstone
Seisdon
Aston Eyre
Morville Hall
Morville
Tasley
Roughton
Claverley
Trysull
Sedgley
Bradley
Brockton
Monkhopton
Morville Heath
Stanmore
Wombourne
Tipton
Weston
Bridgnorth
Farmcote
Heathton
Bagger
Upper Gornal
Wilderhope Manor
Shipton
Lower Netchwood
Upton Cressett
Oldbury
Watermill
Danesford
Wolverhampton Halfpenny Green
Halfpenny Green
Blakeley
Himley
Himley Hall
Gornalwood
Wrens Nest
Dudley Zoo & Castle
Stanton Long
Chetton
Eardington
Quatford
Swindon
Highgate Common
Bobbington
Wall Heath
Dudley
Middleton Priors
Holdgate
Dudmaston
Quatt
Six Ashes
Kingswinford
Bromley
Netherton
Ditton Priors
Glazeley
Chelmarsh
Tuckhill
Four Ashes
Broadfield House Glass Mus
Brierley Hill
Old Hill
Tugford
Neenton
Middleton Scriven
Sutton
Enville
Wordsley
Amblecote
Red House Glass Cone
Abdon
Brown Clee Hill
Upper Heath
Cleobury North
Rea Brook
Hampton
Hampton Loade
Sidbury
Borle Brook
Stourton
Quarry Bank
Cradley Heath
Clee St Margaret
Burwarton
Billingsley
Woodhill
Birdsgreen
Potter's Cross
Wollescote
Lye
Aston Botterell
Alveley
Severn Valley
Highley
Stourbridge
Halesowen
Stoke St Milborough
Loughton
Chorley
Romsley
Kinver
Whittington
Hasbury
Wheathill
Stottesdon
Rays Farm Country Matters
Kingsford
Pedmore
Cleedownton
Farlow
Shatterford
Blakeshall
Hagley
Oreton
Kinlet
Upper Arley
Bodenham Arboretum & Earth Centre
Caunsall
Cookley
West Hagley
Clent
Silvington
Pound Green
Trimpley
Wolverley
Churchill
Broome
Cleeton St Mary
Catherton
Bitterley
Buttonoak
Low Habberley
Franche
Blakedown
Holy Cross
Bell End
Foxwood
Doddington
Hopton Wafers
Neen Savage
Wyre Forest
Severn Valley Railway
Blakebrook
Kidderminster
Belbroughton
Farden
Snitton
Cleehill
Hints
Cleobury
Far Forest
Wribbenhall
Bewdley
Stone
Drayton
Wildmoor
Fairfield
Severn
Tern
Roden
Worfe
Stour
Sow
74
62
49
50
M6
M54
A5
A41
A442
A458
A518
A449
SJ
SO

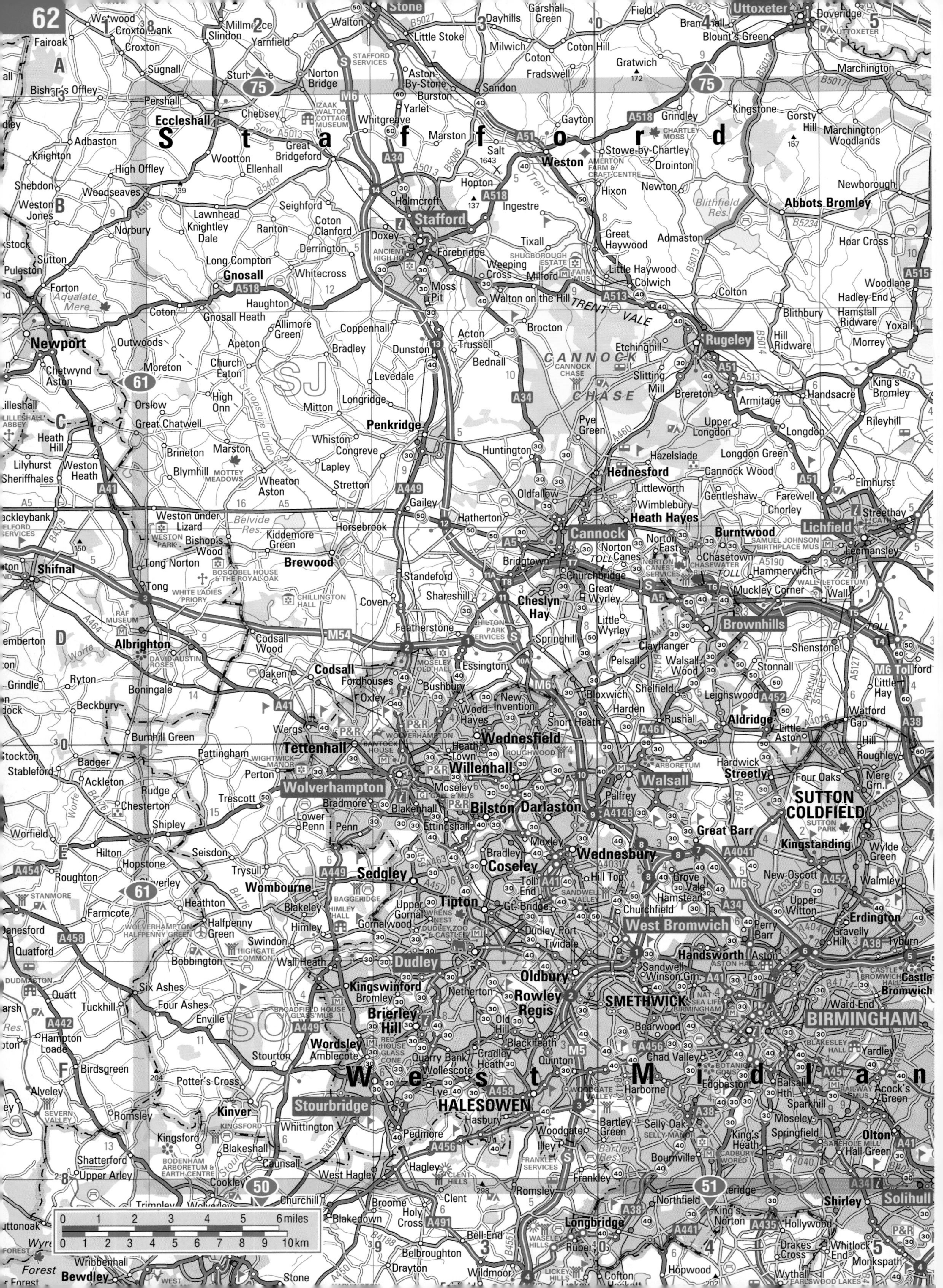
Stone
Uttoxeter
Stafford
Staffordshire
Stafford
Eccleshall
Newport
Gnosall
Penkridge
Cannock
Cannock Chase
Rugeley
Abbots Bromley
Lichfield
Brownhills
Hednesford
Heath Hayes
Burntwood
Cheslyn Hay
Shifnal
Albrighton
Brewood
Codsall
Tettenhall
Wolverhampton
Wednesfield
Willenhall
Walsall
Bilston
Darlaston
Wednesbury
Sedgley
Coseley
Tipton
Wombourne
Dudley
Kingswinford
Brierley Hill
Oldbury
Rowley Regis
Smethwick
West Bromwich
Handsworth
Sutton Coldfield
Aldridge
Streetly
Kingstanding
Erdington
Birmingham
Stourbridge
Halesowen
Kinver
Harborne
Edgbaston
Selly Oak
Northfield
Longbridge
Solihull
Shirley
Olton
Castle Bromwich
Bewdley
West Midlands
Dayhills
Garshall Green
Field
Bramshall
Doveridge
Blount's Green
Marchington
Marchington Woodlands
Little Stoke
Walton
Milwich
Coton
Coton Hill
Fradswell
Gratwich
Aston-By-Stone
Burston
Yarlet
Sandon
Norton Bridge
Izaak Walton Cottage Museum
Whitgreave
Marston
Salt
Weston
Gayton
Grindley
Kingstone
Gorsty Hill
Chartley Moss
Stowe-by-Chartley
Drointon
Amerton Farm & Craft Centre
Hixon
Newton
Blithfield Res.
Newborough
Admaston
Hoar Cross
Great Haywood
Little Haywood
Colwich
Tixall
Shugborough Estate
Ingestre
Hopton
Holmcroft
Doxey
Forebridge
Coton Clanford
Seighford
Derrington
Weeping Cross
Milford
Moss Pit
Walton on the Hill
Trent Vale
Colton
Woodlane
Hadley End
Hamstall Ridware
Yoxall
Blithbury
Hill Ridware
Morrey
Etchinghill
Slitting Mill
Brereton
Armitage
Handsacre
King's Bromley
Rileyhill
Longdon
Upper Longdon
Longdon Green
Cannock Wood
Hazelslade
Farewell
Chorley
Gentleshaw
Elmhurst
Streethay
Leomansley
Hammerwich
Chasetown
Muckley Corner
Wall
Shenstone
Stonnall
Little Hay
Watford Gap
Hill
Roughley
Four Oaks
Mere Grn.
Wylde Green
Walmley
New Oscott
Upper Witton
Gravelly Hill
Tyburn
Perry Barr
Great Barr
Hamstead
Grove Vale
Churchfield
Aston
Ward End
Yardley
Acock's Green
Sparkhill
Moseley
Springfield
Hall Green
Balsall Hth
King's Heath
Bournville
Cofton Hackett
Hollywood
Drakes Cross
Whitlock's End
Monkspath
Wythall
Hopwood
Rubery
Frankley
Bartley Green
Woodgate
Illey
Hasbury
Romsley
Clent
Hagley
West Hagley
Broome
Holy Cross
Blakedown
Belbroughton
Drayton
Bell End
Wildmoor
Pedmore
Lye
Wollescote
Cradley Heath
Quarry Bank
Amblecote
Wordsley
Stourton
Whittington
Kingsford
Blakeshall
Caunsall
Cookley
Churchill
Wolverley
Trimpley
Upper Arley
Shatterford
Romsley
Alveley
Birdsgreen
Hampton Loade
Quatt
Quatford
Danesford
Tuckhill
Six Ashes
Four Ashes
Enville
Potter's Cross
Bobbington
Halfpenny Green
Farmcote
Heathton
Swindon
Wall Heath
Himley
Gornalwood
Upper Gornal
Blakeley
Bromley
Netherton
Old Hill
Blackheath
Quinton
Tividale
Dudley Port
Gt. Bridge
Toll End
Hill Top
Moxley
Bradley
Ettingshall
Blakenhall
Penn
Lower Penn
Bradmore
Trescott
Perton
Pattingham
Rudge
Chesterton
Shipley
Worfield
Hilton
Hopstone
Seisdon
Trysull
Roughton
Claverley
Badger
Ackleton
Stableford
Stockton
Burnhill Green
Beckbury
Ryton
Grindle
Boningale
Oaken
Codsall Wood
Bushbury
Fordhouses
Oxley
Wergs
Essington
Featherstone
Shareshill
Coven
Standeford
Bridgtown
Churchbridge
Great Wyrley
Little Wyrley
Norton Canes
Norton East
Springhill
Pelsall
Clayhanger
Walsall Wood
Shelfield
Leighswood
Rushall
Little Aston
Hardwick
Palfrey
Bloxwich
Harden
Short Heath
New Invention
Wood Hayes
Heath Town
Horsebrook
Hatherton
Gailey
Kiddemore Green
Bishop's Wood
Boscobel House & The Royal Oak
White Ladies Priory
Chillington Hall
Tong
Tong Norton
Weston Park
Weston under Lizard
Belvide Res.
Wheaton Aston
Stretton
Lapley
Congreve
Whiston
Mitton
Longridge
Levedale
Dunston
Bradley
Coppenhall
Acton Trussell
Bednall
Brocton
Huntington
Pye Green
Oldfallow
Littleworth
Wimblebury
Church Eaton
High Onn
Apeton
Allimore Green
Haughton
Gnosall Heath
Coton
Outwoods
Moreton
Orslow
Great Chatwell
Brineton
Blymhill
Marston
Mottey Meadows
Lilleshall
Heath Hill
Lilyhurst
Weston Heath
Sheriffhales
Chetwynd Aston
Forton
Aqualate Mere
Puleston
Sutton
Norbury
Weston Jones
Shebdon
Woodseaves
High Offley
Knighton
Adbaston
Wootton
Ellenhall
Great Bridgeford
Chebsey
Pershall
Bishop's Offley
Sugnall
Croxton
Croxtonbank
Fairoak
Wetwood
Slindon
Millmeece
Yarnfield
Lawnhead
Knightley Dale
Ranton
Long Compton
Whitecross
Moseley Old Hall
Wightwick Manor
Bantock House
Roughwood
Arboretum
Himley Hall
Baggeridge
Wrens Nest
Dudley Zoo & Castle
Sandwell Valley
Winson Grn.
Nat. Sea Life Birmingham
Bearwood
Chad Valley
Botanical Gdns
Sutton Park
Aston Hall
Castle Bromwich Hall
Blakesley Hall
Sarehole Mill
Cadbury World
Selly Manor
Waseley Hills
Lickey Hills
Clent Hills
Kingsford
Bodenham Arboretum & Earth Centre
Severn Valley
Dudmaston
Stanmore
Wolverhampton Halfpenny Green
Highgate Common
Broadfield House Glass Mus
Red House Glass Cone
RAF Museum
David Austin Roses
Samuel Johnson Birthplace Mus
Chasewater
Norton Canes Services
Hilton Park Services
Stafford Services
Frankley Services
M6 Toll
M54
M6
M5
M42
A449
A34
A518
A5
A41
A51
A513
A515
A38
A452
A453
A4041
A454
A458
A442
A456
A491
A4148
A461
A460
A5013
A5190
A5127
A4026
A4040
A435
A441
A45
B5027
B5026
B5066
B5405
B5013
B5234
B5014
B4379
B4176
B4154
B4124
B4188
B4551
0 1 2 3 4 5 6 miles
0 1 2 3 4 5 6 7 8 9 10 km

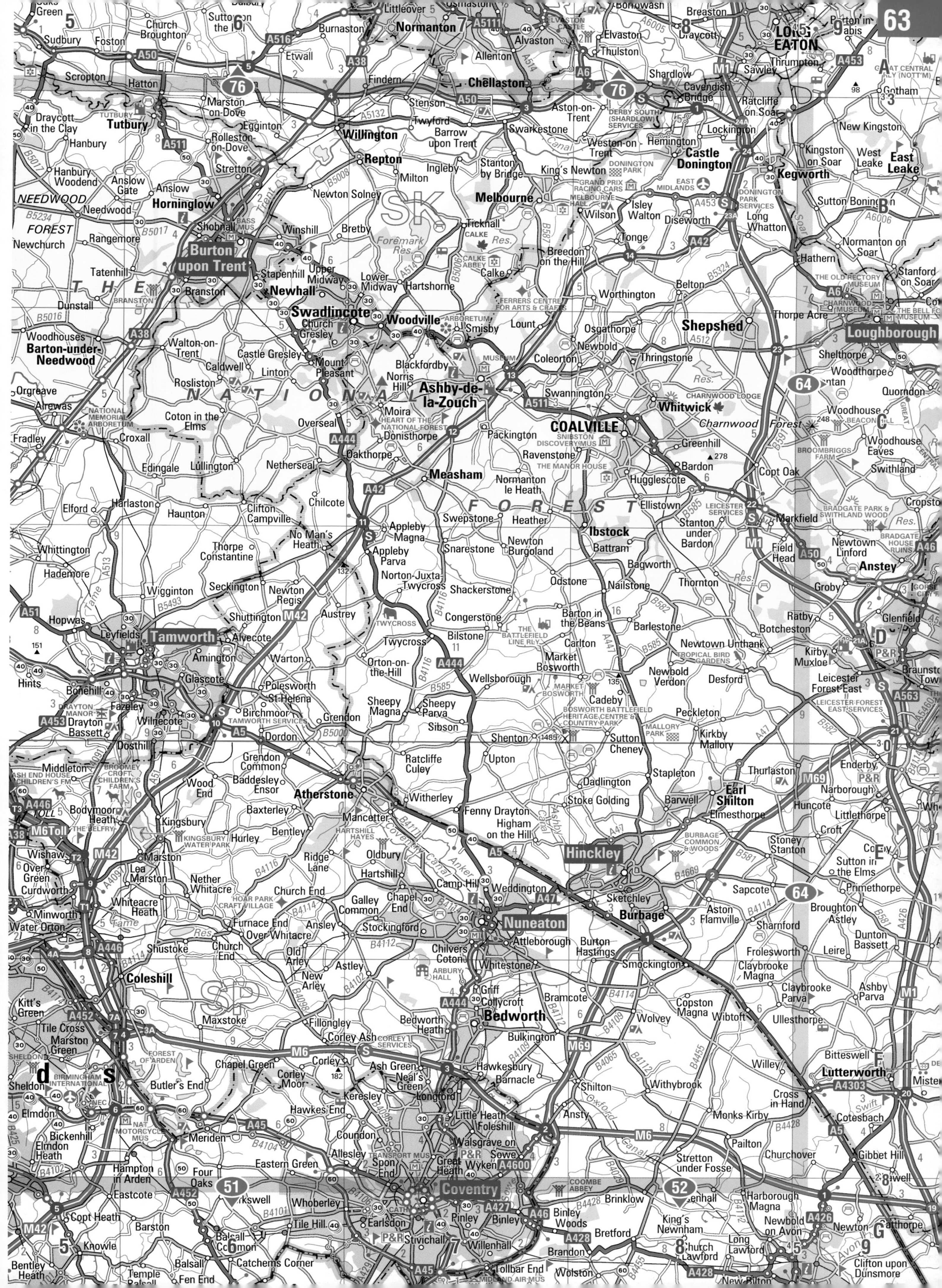
Sudbury
Foston
Church Broughton
Sutton on the Hill
Burnaston
Littleover
Normanton
Alvaston
Elvaston
Elvaston Castle
Borrowash
Breaston
Draycott
Long Eaton
Thrumpton
Sawley
Etwall
Allenton
Thulston
Scropton
Hatton
Findern
Chellaston
Shardlow
Cavendish Bridge
Gotham
Marston on Dove
Stenson
Aston-on-Trent
Derby South (Shardlow) Services
Ratcliffe on Soar
Draycott in the Clay
Tutbury
Egginton
Twyford
Barrow upon Trent
Swarkestone
Lockington
New Kingston
Hanbury
Rolleston-on-Dove
Willington
Weston-on-Trent
Hemington
Castle Donington
Kingston on Soar
West Leake
East Leake
Hanbury Woodend
Stretton
Repton
Milton
Ingleby
Stanton by Bridge
King's Newton
Donington Park
Grand Prix Racing Cars
East Midlands
Kegworth
Anslow Gate
Anslow
Needwood
Horninglow
Newton Solney
Melbourne
Melbourne Hall
Isley Walton
Diseworth
Donington Park Services
Long Whatton
Sutton Bonington
Forest
Rangemore
Shobnall
Bass Mus
Winshill
Bretby
Ticknall
Calke
Wilson
Tonge
Normanton on Soar
Newchurch
Burton upon Trent
Foremark Res.
Staunton Harold Res.
Calke Abbey
Breedon on the Hill
Hathern
Tatenhill
Stapenhill
Upper Midway
Lower Midway
Hartshorne
The Old Rectory Museum
Stanford on Soar
Dunstall
Branston
Newhall
Swadlincote
Woodville
Arboretum
Smisby
Lount
Worthington
Belton
Charnwood Museum
The Bell Foundry Museum
Ferrers Centre for Arts & Crafts
Church Gresley
Thorpe Acre
Shepshed
Loughborough
Woodhouses
Barton-under-Needwood
Walton-on-Trent
Castle Gresley
Caldwell
Mount Pleasant
Blackfordby
Osgathorpe
Newbold
Coleorton
Thringstone
Shelthorpe
Woodthorpe
Rosliston
Linton
Norris Hill
Ashby-de-la-Zouch
Museum
Swannington
Quorndon
Orgreave
Alrewas
National Memorial Arboretum
Coton in the Elms
Moira
Heart of the National Forest
Whitwick
Charnwood Lodge
Charnwood Forest
Woodhouse
Beacon Hill
Overseal
Donisthorpe
Packington
Coalville
Snibston Discovery Mus
Greenhill
Woodhouse Eaves
Fradley
Croxall
Edingale
Lullington
Netherseal
Oakthorpe
Ravenstone
The Manor House
Bardon
Broombriggs Farm
Copt Oak
Swithland
Measham
Normanton le Heath
Hugglescote
Elford
Harlaston
Haunton
Clifton Campville
Chilcote
Ellistown
Leicester Services
Markfield
Bradgate Park & Swithland Wood
Cropston
Appleby Magna
Swepstone
Heather
Ibstock
Stanton under Bardon
Whittington
Thorpe Constantine
No Man's Heath
Appleby Parva
Snarestone
Newton Burgoland
Battram
Field Head
Newtown Linford
Bradgate House Ruins
Hademore
Norton-Juxta-Twycross
Bagworth
Anstey
Wigginton
Seckington
Newton Regis
Shackerstone
Odstone
Nailstone
Thornton
Groby
Hopwas
Shuttington
Austrey
Twycross
Congerstone
Barton in the Beans
Barlestone
Ratby
Glenfield
Leyfields
Tamworth
Alvecote
Bilstone
The Battlefield Line Rly
Botcheston
Amington
Warton
Carlton
Newtown Unthank
Tropical Bird Gardens
Kirby Muxloe
Hints
Glascote
Polesworth
St Helena
Orton-on-the-Hill
Market Bosworth
Wellsborough
Newbold Verdon
Desford
Leicester Forest East
Braunstone Town
Bonehill
Fazeley
Drayton Manor
Drayton Bassett
Wilnecote
Birchmoor
Tamworth Services
Sheepy Magna
Sheepy Parva
Cadeby
Leicester Forest East Services
Dosthill
Dordon
Grendon
Sibson
Bosworth Battlefield Heritage Centre & Country Park
Peckleton
Mallory Park
Kirkby Mallory
Middleton
Ash End House Children's Fm
Broomey Croft Children's Farm
Grendon Common
Baddesley Ensor
Ratcliffe Culey
Shenton
Upton
Sutton Cheney
Stapleton
Thurlaston
Enderby
Wood End
Atherstone
Witherley
Dadlington
Earl Shilton
Narborough
Bodymoor Heath
The Belfry
Baxterley
Mancetter
Fenny Drayton
Stoke Golding
Barwell
Elmesthorpe
Huncote
Littlethorpe
Kingsbury
Kingsbury Water Park
Hurley
Bentley
Hartshill Hayes
Higham on the Hill
Ashby Canal
Burbage Common & Woods
Croft
Wishaw
Marston
Ridge Lane
Oldbury
Coventry Canal
Hinckley
Stoney Stanton
Cosby
Over Green
Lea Marston
Curdworth
Nether Whitacre
Hartshill
Camp Hill
Weddington
Sutton in the Elms
Whiteacre Heath
Hoar Park Craft Village
Church End
Galley Common
Chapel End
Sketchley
Burbage
Sapcote
Primethorpe
Minworth
Water Orton
Furnace End
Over Whitacre
Ansley
Stockingford
Nuneaton
Attleborough
Burton Hastings
Aston Flamville
Sharnford
Broughton Astley
Shustoke
Old Arley
Chilvers Coton
Smockington
Frolesworth
Leire
Dunton Bassett
Coleshill
New Arley
Astley
Arbury Hall
Whitestone
Claybrooke Magna
Griff
Collycroft
Bramcote
Claybrooke Parva
Ashby Parva
Kitt's Green
Maxstoke
Fillongley
Bedworth Heath
Bedworth
Copston Magna
Wolvey
Wibtoft
Ullesthorpe
Tile Cross
Marston Green
Corley Ash
Corley Services
Bulkington
Forest of Arden
Chapel Green
Corley
Ash Green
Hawkesbury
Barnacle
Willey
Bitteswell
Sheldon
Birmingham International
Corley Moor
Neal's Green
Withybrook
Lutterworth
Misterton
Butler's End
Keresley
Longford
Shilton
Cross in Hand
Elmdon
NEC
Hawkes End
Little Heath
Foleshill
Ansty
Monks Kirby
Cotesbach
Bickenhill
Nat Motorcycle Mus
Meriden
Coundon
Walsgrave on Sowe
Pailton
Elmdon Heath
Allesley
Transport Mus
Wyken
Stretton under Fosse
Churchover
Gibbet Hill
Eastern Green
Spon End
Great Heath
Hampton in Arden
Four Oaks
Combe Abbey
Brinklow
Harborough Magna
Shawell
Eastcote
Berkswell
Whoberley
Coventry
Binley Woods
Newbold on Avon
Copt Heath
Barston
Tile Hill
Earlsdon
Cath
Binley
Pinley
King's Newnham
Newton
Catthorpe
Knowle
Balsall Common
Stivichall
Willenhall
Bretford
Church Lawford
Long Lawford
Brandon
Bentley Heath
Temple Balsall
Catchems Corner
Tollbar End
Midland Air Mus
Wolston
New Bilton
Clifton upon Dunsmore
Fen End
Avon
Anker
Tame
Soar
Trent
Swift
Oxford Canal
Canal
Res.
Calke Res.
The National Forest
SK
SP
76
64
51
52
M1
M6
M6 Toll
M42
M69
A50
A38
A42
A444
A5
A47
A46
A453
A511
A512
A6
A426
A4303
A45
A46
A428
A427
A4600
A452
A446
A447
A563
A51
A513
A516
A5111
A514
A5132
A453
A6006
A6005
A4091
A4097
B5008
B5017
B5016
B5234
B5006
B587
B5324
B585
B582
B591
B4116
B4111
B4114
B4112
B4102
B4098
B4104
B4101
B4106
B4109
B4065
B4029
B4428
B4455
B4669
B581
B5000
B5493
B4114
B4112
B4027
A5460
A5199
A5460
A5199

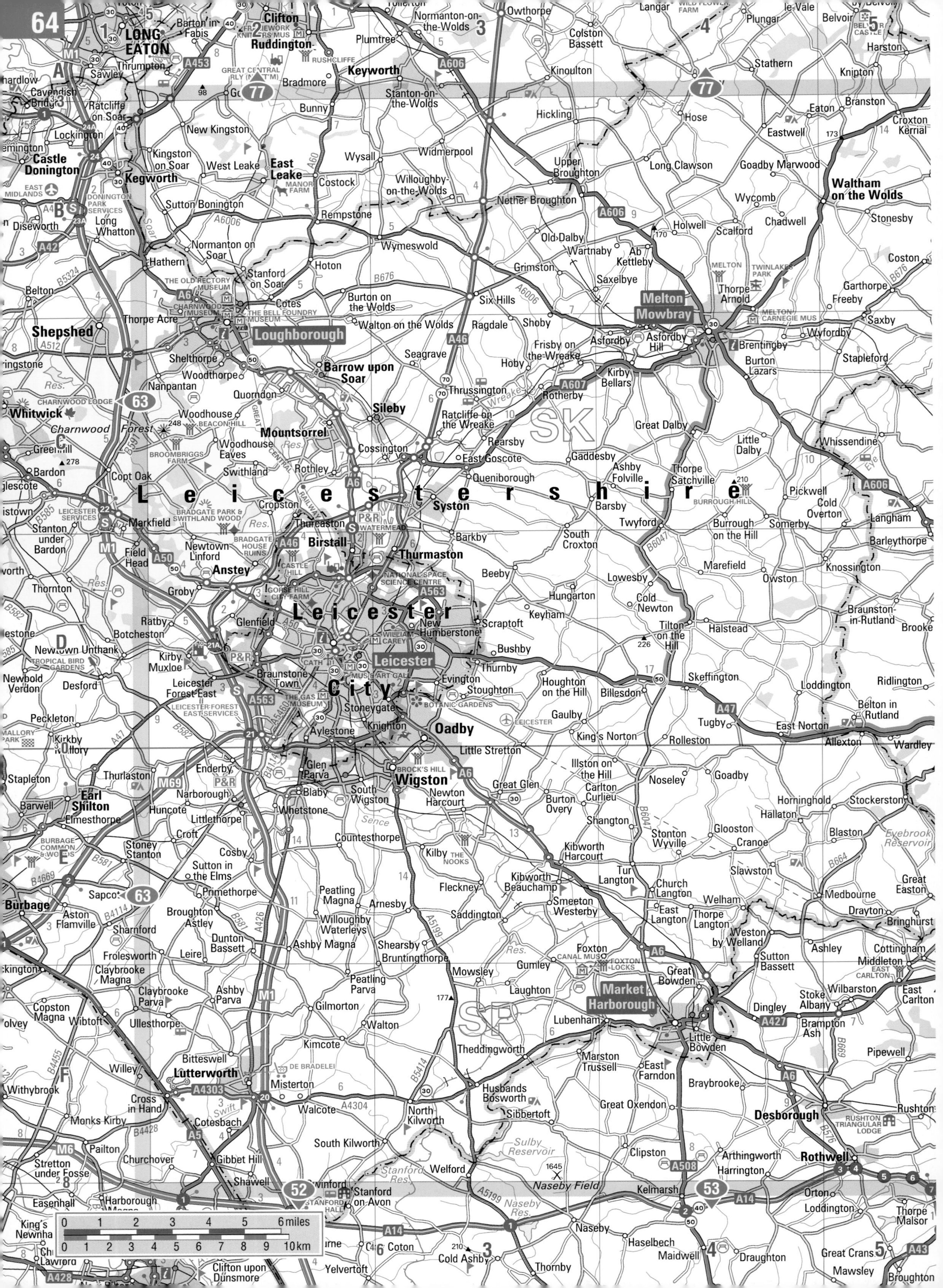

LONG EATON
Barton in Fabis
Clifton
Ruddington
Normanton-on-the-Wolds
Owthorpe
Langar
Plungar
Belvoir
Colston Bassett
Harston
Thrumpton
Sawley
Plumtree
RUSHCLIFFE
Keyworth
Bradmore
Kinoulton
Stathern
Knipton
Cavendish Bridge
Ratcliffe on Soar
Bunny
Stanton-on-the-Wolds
Hickling
Hose
Eaton
Branston
Croxton Kerrial
Lockington
New Kingston
Eastwell
Castle Donington
Kingston on Soar
West Leake
East Leake
Costock
Wysall
Widmerpool
Upper Broughton
Long Clawson
Goadby Marwood
Kegworth
EAST MIDLANDS
MANOR FARM
Willoughby-on-the-Wolds
Nether Broughton
Wycomb
Waltham on the Wolds
Sutton Bonington
DONINGTON PARK SERVICES
Long Whatton
Diseworth
Rempstone
Chadwell
Stonesby
Holwell
Scalford
Wymeswold
Old Dalby
Wartnaby
Ab Kettleby
Normanton on Soar
Hathern
Hoton
Grimston
Coston
Stanford on Soar
Saxelbye
Thorpe Arnold
Garthorpe
Freeby
Belton
THE OLD RECTORY MUSEUM
Cotes
Burton on the Wolds
Six Hills
Melton Mowbray
CHARNWOOD MUSEUM
THE BELL FOUNDRY
Thorpe Acre
Shepshed
Walton on the Wolds
Ragdale
Shoby
Asfordby
Asfordby Hill
Saxby
Wyfordby
Loughborough
Brentingby
Shelthorpe
Seagrave
Frisby on the Wreake
Burton Lazars
Stapleford
Barrow upon Soar
Hoby
Woodthorpe
Nanpantan
Quorndon
Thrussington
Rotherby
Kirby Bellars
CHARNWOOD LODGE
Whitwick
Woodhouse
Sileby
Ratcliffe on the Wreake
Charnwood Forest
BEACON HILL
Mountsorrel
Rearsby
Great Dalby
Greenhill
Woodhouse Eaves
Cossington
SK
Little Dalby
Whissendine
Bardon
BROOMBRIGGS FARM
Swithland
East Goscote
Gaddesby
Copt Oak
Rothley
Queniborough
Ashby Folville
Thorpe Satchville
Leicestershire
Pickwell
Cold Overton
LEICESTER SERVICES
Markfield
BRADGATE PARK & SWITHLAND WOOD
Cropston
Syston
Barsby
BURROUGH HILL
Langham
Stanton under Bardon
Thurcaston
WATERMEAD
Twyford
Burrough on the Hill
Somerby
Barkby
South Croxton
Barleythorpe
Field Head
Newtown Linford
BRADGATE HOUSE RUINS
Birstall
Thurmaston
Marefield
Knossington
Thornton
Anstey
CASTLE HILL
NATIONAL SPACE SCIENCE CENTRE
Beeby
Lowesby
Owston
Groby
GORSE HILL CITY FARM
Hungarton
Cold Newton
Braunston-in-Rutland
Ratby
Glenfield
Leicester
Keyham
Scraptoft
Tilton on the Hill
Halstead
Brooke
Botcheston
WILLIAM CAREY
New Humberstone
Newtown Unthank
TROPICAL BIRD GARDENS
Kirby Muxloe
CATH
Leicester City
Bushby
Thurnby
Newbold Verdon
Desford
Braunstone Town
MUS & ART GALL
Evington
Houghton on the Hill
Skeffington
Loddington
Ridlington
Leicester Forest East
LEICESTER FOREST EAST SERVICES
THE GAS MUSEUM
Stoughton
Billesdon
Belton in Rutland
Stoneygate
BOTANIC GARDENS
Gaulby
Peckleton
LEICESTER
Tugby
Knighton
Oadby
King's Norton
East Norton
Kirkby Mallory
Aylestone
Rolleston
Allexton
Wardley
Little Stretton
Illston on the Hill
Stapleton
Thurlaston
Enderby
Glen Parva
BROCK'S HILL
Wigston
Noseley
Goadby
Narborough
Great Glen
Carlton Curlieu
Earl Shilton
Blaby
South Wigston
Newton Harcourt
Burton Overy
Horninghold
Stockerston
Barwell
Huncote
Elmesthorpe
Whetstone
Hallaton
Littlethorpe
Sence
Shangton
Glooston
BURBAGE COMMON & WOODS
Croft
Countesthorpe
Stonton Wyville
Cranoe
Blaston
Eyebrook Reservoir
Stoney Stanton
Cosby
Kilby
THE NOOKS
Kibworth Harcourt
Sutton in the Elms
Tur Langton
Slawston
Great Easton
Sapcote
Primethorpe
Peatling Magna
Fleckney
Kibworth Beauchamp
Church Langton
Medbourne
Burbage
Aston Flamville
Broughton Astley
Arnesby
Smeeton Westerby
Welham
East Langton
Drayton
Sharnford
Willoughby Waterleys
Saddington
Thorpe Langton
Bringhurst
Dunton Bassett
Weston by Welland
Frolesworth
Leire
Ashby Magna
Shearsby
Bruntingthorpe
Foxton
CANAL MUS
FOXTON LOCKS
Sutton Bassett
Ashley
Cottingham
Claybrooke Magna
Peatling Parva
Mowsley
Gumley
Great Bowden
Middleton
EAST CARLTON
Claybrooke Parva
Ashby Parva
Laughton
Market Harborough
Stoke Albany
Wilbarston
East Carlton
Copston Magna
Wibtoft
Gilmorton
SP
Lubenham
Dingley
Brampton Ash
Ullesthorpe
Walton
Little Bowden
Kimcote
Theddingworth
Pipewell
Bitteswell
Marston Trussell
East Farndon
Willey
Lutterworth
DE BRADELEI
Misterton
Husbands Bosworth
Braybrooke
Withybrook
Cross in Hand
Walcote
North Kilworth
Sibbertoft
Great Oxendon
Desborough
Rushton
RUSHTON TRIANGULAR LODGE
Monks Kirby
Cotesbach
Swift
South Kilworth
Sulby Reservoir
Pailton
Churchover
Gibbet Hill
Stanford Res.
Welford
Clipston
Arthingworth
Rothwell
Stretton under Fosse
Shawell
Swinford
Stanford on Avon
STANFORD HALL
Naseby Field
Kelmarsh
Harrington
Easenhall
Harborough Magna
Naseby Res.
Orton
Loddington
Thorpe Malsor
King's Newnham
Naseby
Haselbech
Coton
Cold Ashby
Maidwell
Draughton
Great Cransley
Mawsley
Clifton upon Dunsmore
Yelvertoft
Thornby
Broughton
M1
M6
M69
A6
A46
A47
A50
A60
A426
A427
A428
A453
A508
A512
A563
A606
A607
A4303
A4304
A5199
A14
A42
A43
A5
B5324
B676
B6047
B664
B669
B581
B582
B585
B4114
B4669
B4428
B4455
B5414
B6047
0 1 2 3 4 5 6 miles
0 1 2 3 4 5 6 7 8 9 10 km

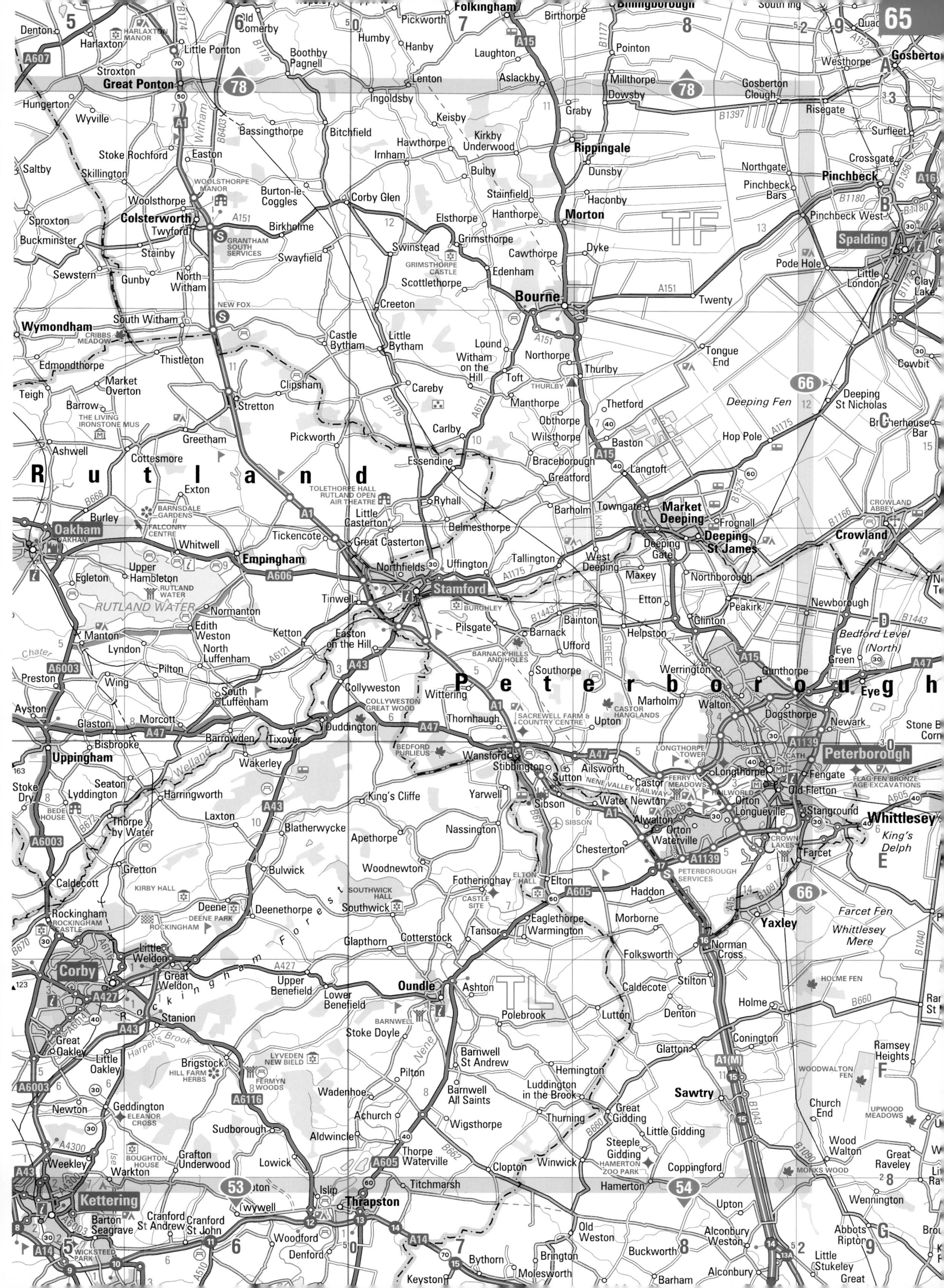

Denton
Harlaxton
HARLAXTON MANOR
Old Somerby
Pickworth
Folkingham
Birthorpe
Billingborough
Quadring
Gosberton
Little Ponton
Humby
Hanby
Boothby Pagnell
Laughton
Pointon
Westhorpe
Stroxton
Great Ponton
Lenton
Aslackby
Millthorpe
Dowsby
Gosberton Clough
Risegate
Hungerton
Ingoldsby
Graby
Surfleet
Wyville
Bassingthorpe
Bitchfield
Keisby
Hawthorpe
Kirkby Underwood
Rippingale
Crossgate
Stoke Rochford
Easton
Irnham
Dunsby
Northgate
Pinchbeck
Saltby
Skillington
Bulby
Pinchbeck Bars
WOOLSTHORPE MANOR
Burton-le-Coggles
Corby Glen
Stainfield
Haconby
Woolsthorpe
Hanthorpe
Morton
Pinchbeck West
Sproxton
Colsterworth
Elsthorpe
TF
Twyford
Birkholme
Grimsthorpe
Spalding
Buckminster
GRANTHAM SOUTH SERVICES
Swinstead
Cawthorpe
Dyke
Stainby
Swayfield
GRIMSTHORPE CASTLE
Pode Hole
Little London
Sewstern
Gunby
North Witham
Edenham
Scottlethorpe
Clay Lake
Bourne
Twenty
NEW FOX
Creeton
Wymondham
South Witham
CRIBBS MEADOW
Castle Bytham
Little Bytham
Lound
Tongue End
Edmondthorpe
Thistleton
Northorpe
Cowbit
Witham on the Hill
Thurlby
Teigh
Market Overton
Clipsham
Careby
Toft
THURLBY
Deeping St Nicholas
Deeping Fen
Barrow
Stretton
Manthorpe
Thetford
THE LIVING IRONSTONE MUS
Obthorpe
Brotherhouse Bar
Carlby
Wilsthorpe
Hop Pole
Ashwell
Greetham
Pickworth
Baston
Cottesmore
Essendine
Braceborough
Langtoft
Rutland
Greatford
Exton
TOLETHORPE HALL RUTLAND OPEN AIR THEATRE
Ryhall
Barholm
Towngate
Market Deeping
CROWLAND ABBEY
BARNSDALE GARDENS
Little Casterton
Burley
Frognall
FALCONRY CENTRE
Oakham
Belmesthorpe
Crowland
Tickencote
Deeping St James
Deeping Gate
Whitwell
Great Casterton
Empingham
Tallington
West Deeping
Egleton
Upper Hambleton
Northfields
Uffington
RUTLAND WATER
Maxey
Northborough
Stamford
Tinwell
Etton
Newborough
Normanton
BURGHLEY
Peakirk
Edith Weston
Bainton
Glinton
Manton
Ketton
Easton on the Hill
Pilsgate
Barnack
Helpston
Bedford Level (North)
Lyndon
Ufford
Eye Green
BARNACK HILLS AND HOLES
Chater
North Luffenham
Southorpe
Werrington
Gunthorpe
Preston
Pilton
Eye
Wing
Peterborough
Collyweston
Wittering
Marholm
South Luffenham
Walton
Ayston
CASTOR HANGLANDS
COLLYWESTON GREAT WOOD
Dogsthorpe
Glaston
Morcott
SACREWELL FARM & COUNTRY CENTRE
Newark
Thornhaugh
Upton
Stone Bridge Corner
Duddington
Barrowden
Tixover
Bisbrooke
BEDFORD PURLIEUS
Wansford
LONGTHORPE TOWER
Uppingham
Stibbington
Ailsworth
Longthorpe
Fengate
Wakerley
Sutton
Castor
FERRY MEADOWS
Seaton
Welland
NENE VALLEY RAILWAY
RAILWORLD
Old Fletton
FLAG FEN BRONZE AGE EXCAVATIONS
Stoke Dry
Harringworth
King's Cliffe
Yarwell
Lyddington
Water Newton
Orton Longueville
Stanground
Whittlesey
BEDE HOUSE
Sibson
Alwalton
King's Delph
Thorpe by Water
Laxton
SIBSON
Orton Waterville
Blatherwycke
Nassington
CROWN LAKES
Apethorpe
Chesterton
Farcet
Gretton
Bulwick
Woodnewton
PETERBOROUGH SERVICES
Caldecott
KIRBY HALL
Fotheringhay
ELTON HALL
Elton
Haddon
SOUTHWICK HALL
Southwick
CASTLE SITE
Farcet Fen
Rockingham
ROCKINGHAM CASTLE
Deene
Deenethorpe
DEENE PARK
Morborne
Yaxley
ROCKINGHAM
Eaglethorpe
Warmington
Whittlesey Mere
Tansor
Glapthorn
Cotterstock
Norman Cross
Little Weldon
Folksworth
Corby
Great Weldon
Upper Benefield
Lower Benefield
Oundle
Ashton
TL
Caldecote
Stilton
HOLME FEN
Holme
Stanion
BARNWELL
Polebrook
Lutton
Denton
Great Oakley
Stoke Doyle
Conington
Little Oakley
Harper's Brook
Barnwell St Andrew
Glatton
Ramsey Heights
Brigstock
LYVEDEN NEW BIELD
HILL FARM HERBS
FERMYN WOODS
Pilton
Hemington
WOODWALTON FEN
Geddington
Wadenhoe
Barnwell All Saints
Luddington in the Brook
Sawtry
Church End
ELEANOR CROSS
Newton
Achurch
Thurning
Great Gidding
UPWOOD MEADOWS
Sudborough
Wigsthorpe
Aldwincle
Little Gidding
Steeple Gidding
Wood Walton
BOUGHTON HOUSE
Grafton Underwood
Lowick
Thorpe Waterville
Winwick
Clopton
HAMERTON ZOO PARK
Coppingford
Great Raveley
Weekley
Warkton
MONKS WOOD
Titchmarsh
Hamerton
Kettering
Islip
Twywell
Thrapston
Upton
Wennington
Barton Seagrave
Cranford St Andrew
Cranford St John
Woodford
Old Weston
Alconbury Weston
Abbots Ripton
WICKSTEED PARK
Denford
Bythorn
Brington
Buckworth
Little Stukeley
Keyston
Molesworth
Barham
Alconbury
Great

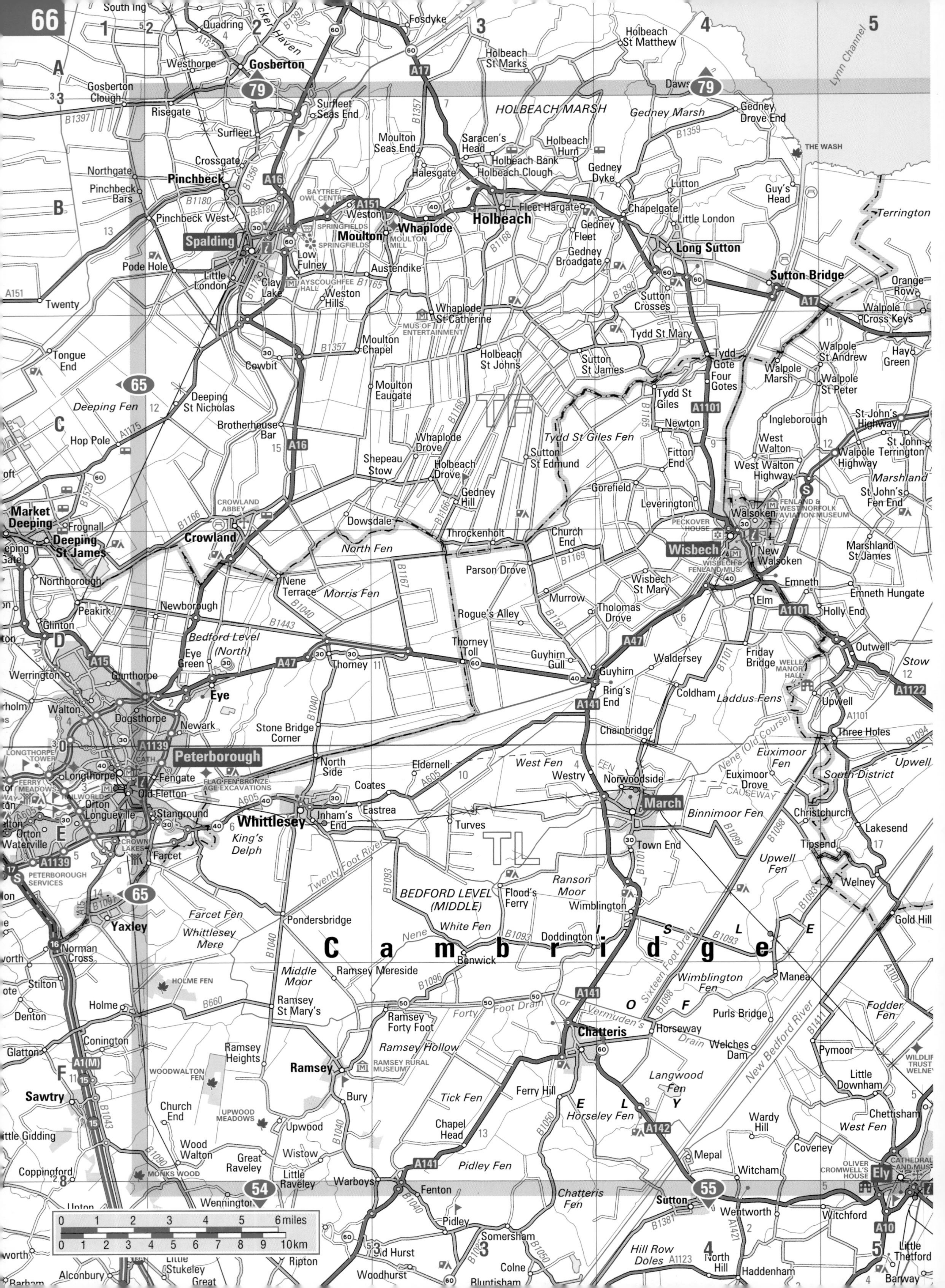
South Ing
Quadring
Westhorpe
Gosberton
Gosberton Clough
Risegate
Surfleet Seas End
Surfleet
Crossgate
Fosdyke
Holbeach St Marks
Holbeach St Matthew
HOLBEACH MARSH
Gedney Marsh
Gedney Drove End
THE WASH
Lynn Channel
Moulton Seas End
Saracen's Head
Holbeach Bank
Holbeach Hurn
Holbeach Clough
Halesgate
Gedney Dyke
Lutton
Guy's Head
Northgate
Pinchbeck
Pinchbeck Bars
Pinchbeck West
BAYTREE OWL CENTRE
Weston
SPRINGFIELDS
Moulton
Whaplode
MOULTON MILL
Holbeach
Fleet Hargate
Gedney
Fleet
Chapelgate
Little London
Terrington
Spalding
Pode Hole
Little London
Low Fulney
Austendike
Gedney Broadgate
Long Sutton
Sutton Bridge
Orange Row
Twenty
Clay Lake
AYSCOUGHFEE HALL
Weston Hills
Whaplode St Catherine
MUS OF ENTERTAINMENT
Sutton Crosses
Walpole Cross Keys
Tydd St Mary
Tongue End
Cowbit
Moulton Chapel
Holbeach St Johns
Sutton St James
Tydd Gote
Four Gotes
Walpole Marsh
Walpole St Andrew
Walpole St Peter
Hay Green
Deeping Fen
Deeping St Nicholas
Moulton Eaugate
Tydd St Giles
Hop Pole
Brotherhouse Bar
Whaplode Drove
Tydd St Giles Fen
Newton
Ingleborough
St John's Highway
West Walton
St John
Terrington
Walpole Highway
West Walton Highway
Marshland
Shepeau Stow
Holbeach Drove
Sutton St Edmund
Fitton End
Gedney Hill
Gorefield
St John's Fen End
Market Deeping
Frognall
CROWLAND ABBEY
Dowsdale
Leverington
Walsoken
FENLAND & WEST NORFOLK AVIATION MUSEUM
PECKOVER HOUSE
Deeping St James
Crowland
Throckenholt
Church End
North Fen
Wisbech
WISBECH & FENLAND MUS.
New Walsoken
Marshland St James
Northborough
Nene Terrace
Morris Fen
Parson Drove
Wisbech St Mary
Emneth
Emneth Hungate
Peakirk
Newborough
Murrow
Tholomas Drove
Elm
Holly End
Glinton
Rogue's Alley
Bedford Level (North)
Eye Green
Thorney
Thorney Toll
Guyhirn Gull
Guyhirn
Waldersey
Friday Bridge
WELLE MANOR HALL
Outwell
Stow
Werrington
Gunthorpe
Eye
Ring's End
Coldham
Laddus Fens
Upwell
Walton
Dogsthorpe
Newark
Stone Bridge Corner
Chainbridge
Three Holes
LONGTHORPE TOWER
Peterborough
CATH.
Fengate
FLAG FEN BRONZE AGE EXCAVATIONS
North Side
Eldernell
West Fen
Westry
Norwoodside
Euximoor Fen
Upwell
FERRY MEADOWS
Longthorpe
RAILWORLD
Old Fletton
Orton Longueville
Coates
Nene (Old Course)
Euximoor Drove
CAUSEWAY
South District
Stanground
Whittlesey
Inham's End
Eastrea
March
Binnimoor Fen
Christchurch
Orton Waterville
King's Delph
Turves
Town End
Lakesend
CROWN LAKES
Farcet
Tipsend
PETERBOROUGH SERVICES
Twenty Foot River
Upwell Fen
Welney
BEDFORD LEVEL (MIDDLE)
Flood's Ferry
Ranson Moor
Wimblington
Yaxley
Farcet Fen
Pondersbridge
Whittlesey Mere
White Fen
Doddington
ISLE
Gold Hill
Norman Cross
Cambridge
Benwick
Manea
Stilton
HOLME FEN
Middle Moor
Ramsey Mereside
Sixteen Foot Drain
Wimblington Fen
OF
Holme
Ramsey St Mary's
Forty Foot Drain
Vermuden's Drain
Purls Bridge
Fodder Fen
Denton
Ramsey Forty Foot
Chatteris
Horseway
Welches Dam
Conington
Ramsey Heights
Ramsey Hollow
Pymoor
Glatton
WOODWALTON FEN
Ramsey
RAMSEY RURAL MUSEUM
New Bedford River
Langwood Fen
Little Downham
WILDLIFE TRUST WELNEY
Sawtry
Bury
Tick Fen
Ferry Hill
ELY
Church End
UPWOOD MEADOWS
Upwood
Chapel Head
Horseley Fen
Wardy Hill
Chettisham
West Fen
Little Gidding
Wood Walton
Wistow
Mepal
Coveney
Coppingford
MONKS WOOD
Great Raveley
Little Raveley
Pidley Fen
Witcham
OLIVER CROMWELL'S HOUSE
CATHEDRAL AND MUS
Ely
Warboys
Fenton
Chatteris Fen
Sutton
Wentworth
Witchford
Upton
Wennington
Pidley
Somersham
Hill Row Doles
North Hill
Haddenham
Little Thetford
Little Stukeley
Old Hurst
Ripton
Colne
Bluntisham
Woodhurst
Alconbury
Great
Barway
0 1 2 3 4 5 6 miles
0 1 2 3 4 5 6 7 8 9 10 km

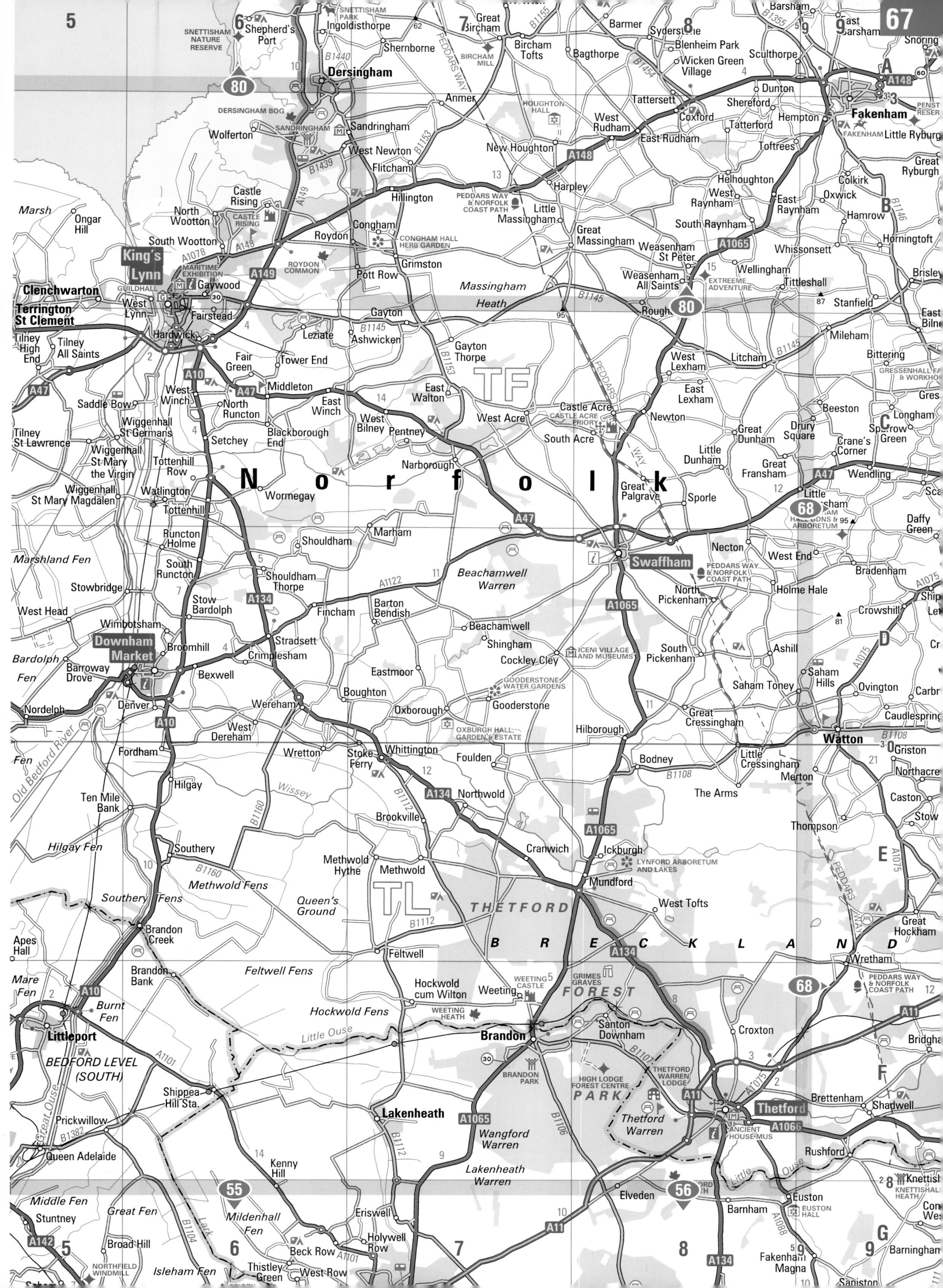
5
6
7
8
9
SNETTISHAM NATURE RESERVE
Shepherd's Port
SNETTISHAM PARK
Ingoldisthorpe
Great Bircham
Barmer
Syderstone
Barsham
East Barsham
Shernborne
BIRCHAM MILL
Bircham Tofts
Bagthorpe
Blenheim Park
Wicken Green Village
Sculthorpe
Snoring
Dersingham
PEDDARS WAY
80
B1440
B1155
B1355
B1454
DERSINGHAM BOG
SANDRINGHAM
Sandringham
Anmer
HOUGHTON HALL
West Rudham
Tattersett
Coxford
Dunton
Shereford
Hempton
Fakenham
FAKENHAM
Little Ryburgh
Great Ryburgh
PENSTHORPE NATURE RESERVE
A148
A
Wolferton
West Newton
New Houghton
East Rudham
Tatterford
Toftrees
B1439
B1153
Flitcham
Hillington
Harpley
Helhoughton
Colkirk
Castle Rising
CASTLE RISING
North Wootton
Marsh
Ongar Hill
PEDDARS WAY & NORFOLK COAST PATH
Little Massingham
West Raynham
East Raynham
Oxwick
Hamrow
B1146
B
Congham
CONGHAM HALL HERB GARDEN
Roydon
South Wootton
A149
A1078
MARITIME EXHIBITION
King's Lynn
Great Massingham
South Raynham
Horningtoft
Weasenham St Peter
Whissonsett
A1065
Grimston
ROYDON COMMON
Pott Row
Wellingham
Weasenham All Saints
EXTREEME ADVENTURE
Tittleshall
Brisley
Clenchwarton
GUILDHALL
Gaywood
West Lynn
Massingham Heath
B1145
Rough
Stanfield
Terrington St Clement
Fairstead
Gayton
East Bilney
Hardwick
Leziate
Ashwicken
Mileham
Tilney High End
Tilney All Saints
Fair Green
Tower End
Gayton Thorpe
West Lexham
Litcham
Bittering
GRESSENHALL FARM & WORKHOUSE
A47
A10
Middleton
TF
East Walton
East Lexham
Gressenhall
Saddle Bow
West Winch
North Runcton
East Winch
West Acre
Castle Acre
CASTLE ACRE PRIORY
Newton
Beeston
Longham
C
Tilney St Lawrence
Wiggenhall St Germans
Setchey
Blackborough End
West Bilney
Pentney
South Acre
Great Dunham
Drury Square
Sparrow Green
Wiggenhall St Mary the Virgin
Tottenhill Row
Narborough
Little Dunham
Crane's Corner
Wendling
Wiggenhall St Mary Magdalen
Watlington
Norfolk
Great Palgrave
Sporle
Great Fransham
Little Fransham
Tottenhill
Wormegay
HALL GDNS & ARBORETUM
Daffy Green
Runcton Holme
Shouldham
Marham
Swaffham
Necton
West End
Marshland Fen
South Runcton
Shouldham Thorpe
Beachamwell Warren
PEDDARS WAY & NORFOLK COAST PATH
Bradenham
Stowbridge
A1122
North Pickenham
Holme Hale
A1075
West Head
Stow Bardolph
A134
Fincham
Barton Bendish
Crowshill
Wimbotsham
Beachamwell
Downham Market
Broomhill
Stradsett
Shingham
ICENI VILLAGE AND MUSEUMS
South Pickenham
Ashill
D
Bardolph Fen
Barroway Drove
Crimplesham
Cockley Cley
Saham Hills
Bexwell
Eastmoor
GOODERSTONE WATER GARDENS
Saham Toney
Ovington
Carbrooke
Nordelph
Denver
Boughton
Wereham
Oxborough
Gooderstone
Great Cressingham
Caudlesprings
West Dereham
OXBURGH HALL, GARDEN & ESTATE
Hilborough
Watton
B1108
Griston
Old Bedford River
Fordham
Wretton
Stoke Ferry
Whittington
Foulden
Bodney
Little Cressingham
Merton
Northacre
Hilgay
Wissey
B1112
Northwold
The Arms
Caston
Ten Mile Bank
B1160
Brookville
Thompson
Stow
Hilgay Fen
Southery
Methwold Hythe
Methwold
Cranwich
Ickburgh
LYNFORD ARBORETUM AND LAKES
E
Methwold Fens
Mundford
Southery Fens
Queen's Ground
TL
THETFORD
West Tofts
Great Hockham
Brandon Creek
B R E C K L A N D
Feltwell
Apes Hall
Wretham
Brandon Bank
Feltwell Fens
GRIMES GRAVES
WEETING CASTLE
Weeting
FOREST
Mare Fen
Hockwold cum Wilton
Burnt Fen
Hockwold Fens
WEETING HEATH
Santon Downham
Croxton
Bridgham
Littleport
Little Ouse
Brandon
A11
BEDFORD LEVEL (SOUTH)
A1101
BRANDON PARK
B1107
THETFORD WARREN LODGE
HIGH LODGE FOREST CENTRE
PARK
A1075
Brettenham
Shadwell
F
Shippea Hill Sta.
Lakenheath
A1065
Thetford Warren
Thetford
ANCIENT HOUSE MUS
A1066
Prickwillow
Great Ouse
B1382
Wangford Warren
B1106
Rushford
Queen Adelaide
Kenny Hill
Lakenheath Warren
Knettishall
KNETTISHALL HEATH
55
56
Elveden
Euston
EUSTON HALL
Middle Fen
Great Fen
Mildenhall Fen
Eriswell
Barnham
A1088
Stuntney
B1104
Lark
Holywell Row
A142
Broad Hill
Beck Row
G
Barningham
NORTHFIELD WINDMILL
Isleham Fen
Thistley Green
West Row
Fakenham Magna
Sapiston
68

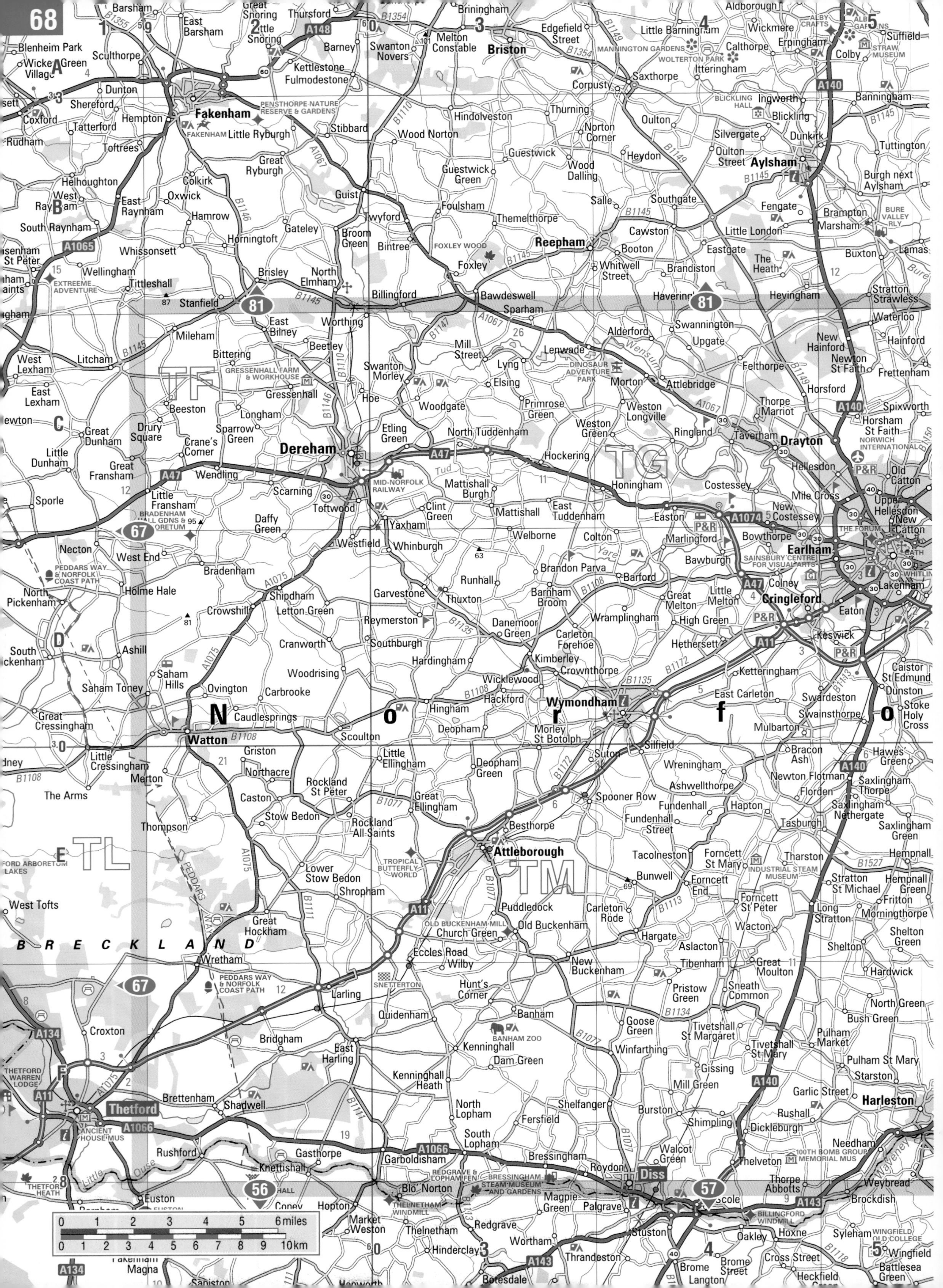
Barsham
East Barsham
Great Snoring
Little Snoring
Thursford
Briningham
Aldborough
Blenheim Park
Wicken Green Village
Sculthorpe
Kettlestone
Fulmodestone
Barney
Swanton Novers
Melton Constable
Briston
Edgefield Street
Little Barningham
Wickmere
Calthorpe
Erpingham
Suffield
Colby
MANNINGTON GARDENS
WOLTERTON PARK
Itteringham
Saxthorpe
Corpusty
Dunton
Shereford
Coxford
Tatterford
Hempton
Fakenham
PENSTHORPE NATURE RESERVE & GARDENS
Little Ryburgh
Stibbard
Hindolveston
Thurning
Norton Corner
Wood Norton
Oulton
BLICKLING HALL
Ingworth
Blickling
Banningham
Rudham
Toftrees
Great Ryburgh
Guestwick
Heydon
Silvergate
Oulton Street
Aylsham
Dunkirk
Tuttington
Burgh next Aylsham
Helhoughton
Colkirk
Guestwick Green
Wood Dalling
West Raynham
East Raynham
Oxwick
Guist
Foulsham
Salle
Southgate
Fengate
Brampton
BURE VALLEY RLY
South Raynham
Hamrow
Twyford
Themelthorpe
Cawston
Little London
Marsham
Horningtoft
Gateley
Broom Green
Bintree
FOXLEY WOOD
Reepham
Booton
Eastgate
The Heath
Buxton
Lamas
Whissonsett
Foxley
Whitwell Street
Brandiston
Wellingham
EXTREEME ADVENTURE
Tittleshall
Brisley
North Elmham
Billingford
Bawdeswell
Haveringland
Hevingham
Stratton Strawless
Stanfield
Sparham
East Bilney
Worthing
Alderford
Swanington
Waterloo
Mileham
Beetley
Mill Street
Upgate
New Hainford
Hainford
West Lexham
Litcham
Bittering
Lyng
Lenwade
DINOSAUR ADVENTURE PARK
Wensum
Felthorpe
Newton St Faith
Frettenham
GRESSENHALL FARM & WORKHOUSE
Swanton Morley
Elsing
Morton
Attlebridge
East Lexham
Gressenhall
Hoe
Horsford
Beeston
Woodgate
Primrose Green
Weston Longville
Thorpe Marriot
Spixworth
Longham
Ringland
Horsham St Faith
NORWICH INTERNATIONAL
Newton
Great Dunham
Drury Square
Sparrow Green
Etling Green
North Tuddenham
Weston Green
Taverham
Drayton
Little Dunham
Crane's Corner
Dereham
Hockering
Hellesdon
Old Catton
Great Fransham
Wendling
Tud
Mattishall Burgh
Honingham
Costessey
Mile Cross
Sporle
Little Fransham
Scarning
MID-NORFOLK RAILWAY
Toftwood
Clint Green
Mattishall
East Tuddenham
Easton
New Costessey
Upper Hellesdon
BRADENHAM HALL GDNS & ARBORETUM
Daffy Green
Yaxham
Welborne
Colton
Marlingford
Bowthorpe
Earlham
THE FORUM
New Catton
Necton
West End
Westfield
Whinburgh
Yare
Bawburgh
SAINSBURY CENTRE FOR VISUAL ARTS
PEDDARS WAY & NORFOLK COAST PATH
Bradenham
Brandon Parva
Barford
Holme Hale
Runhall
Garvestone
Little Melton
Colney
Lakenham
North Pickenham
Shipdham
Thuxton
Barnham Broom
Great Melton
Cringleford
Eaton
Crowshill
Letton Green
Reymerston
Danemoor Green
Wramplingham
High Green
Keswick
South Pickenham
Ashill
Cranworth
Southburgh
Carleton Forehoe
Hethersett
Hardingham
Kimberley
Caistor St Edmund
Saham Hills
Woodrising
Crownthorpe
Ketteringham
Dunston
Saham Toney
Ovington
Carbrooke
Wicklewood
Hackford
East Carleton
Swardeston
Great Cressingham
Caudlesprings
Hingham
Wymondham
Swainsthorpe
Stoke Holy Cross
Watton
Deopham
Morley St Botolph
Mulbarton
Scoulton
Sifield
Bracon Ash
Little Cressingham
Griston
Little Ellingham
Suton
Hawes' Green
The Arms
Merton
Northacre
Rockland St Peter
Deopham Green
Wreningham
Newton Flotman
Saxlingham Thorpe
Caston
Great Ellingham
Spooner Row
Ashwellthorpe
Florden
Stow Bedon
Fundenhall
Hapton
Saxlingham Nethergate
Thompson
Rockland All Saints
Besthorpe
Fundenhall Street
Tasburgh
Saxlingham Green
FORD ARBORETUM LAKES
Attleborough
Tacolneston
Forncett St Mary
Tharston
INDUSTRIAL STEAM MUSEUM
Hempnall
Lower Stow Bedon
TROPICAL BUTTERFLY WORLD
Bunwell
Forncett End
Stratton St Michael
Hempnall Green
Shropham
Forncett St Peter
Fritton
West Tofts
Puddledock
Carleton Rode
Long Stratton
Morningthorpe
Great Hockham
OLD BUCKENHAM MILL
Old Buckenham
Wacton
Shelton Green
BRECKLAND
Church Green
Hargate
Aslacton
Shelton
Wretham
Eccles Road
Wilby
New Buckenham
Tibenham
Great Moulton
Hardwick
SNETTERTON
Hunt's Corner
Pristow Green
Sneath Common
North Green
Larling
Quidenham
Banham
Goose Green
Tivetshall St Margaret
Bush Green
Croxton
Bridgham
BANHAM ZOO
Kenninghall
Winfarthing
Tivetshall St Mary
Pulham Market
East Harling
Dam Green
Gissing
Pulham St Mary
THETFORD WARREN LODGE
Kenninghall Heath
Mill Green
Starston
Brettenham
Shadwell
Garlic Street
Harleston
Thetford
North Lopham
Shelfanger
Burston
Rushall
ANCIENT HOUSE MUS
Fersfield
Shimpling
Dickleburgh
South Lopham
Rushford
Gasthorpe
Garboldisham
Bressingham
Walcot Green
Needham
Knettishall
REDGRAVE & LOPHAM FEN
BRESSINGHAM STEAM MUSEUM AND GARDENS
Roydon
Thelveton
100TH BOMB GROUP MEMORIAL MUS
Thorpe Abbotts
Weybread
Euston
Blo' Norton
Diss
Magpie Green
Palgrave
Scole
Brockdish
THETFORD HEATH
Little Ouse
Coney Weston
Hopton
THELNETHAM WINDMILL
BILLINGFORD WINDMILL
Market Weston
Thelnetham
Redgrave
Stuston
Oakley
Hoxne
Syleham
WINGFIELD OLD COLLEGE
Hinderclay
Wortham
Thrandeston
Brome Street
Cross Street
Wingfield
Fakenham Magna
Botesdale
Brome
Langton
Heckfield Green
Battlesea Green
Waveney
TF
TG
TL
TM
N o r f o
A148
A1067
A1065
A47
A1075
A11
A140
A1074
A134
A1066
A143
A1062
B1355
B1354
B1110
B1149
B1145
B1146
B1147
B1108
B1135
B1172
B1077
B1113
B1111
B1134
B1527
B1118
B1150
B1113
B1108
81
67
56
57
0 1 2 3 4 5 6 miles
0 1 2 3 4 5 6 7 8 9 10 km

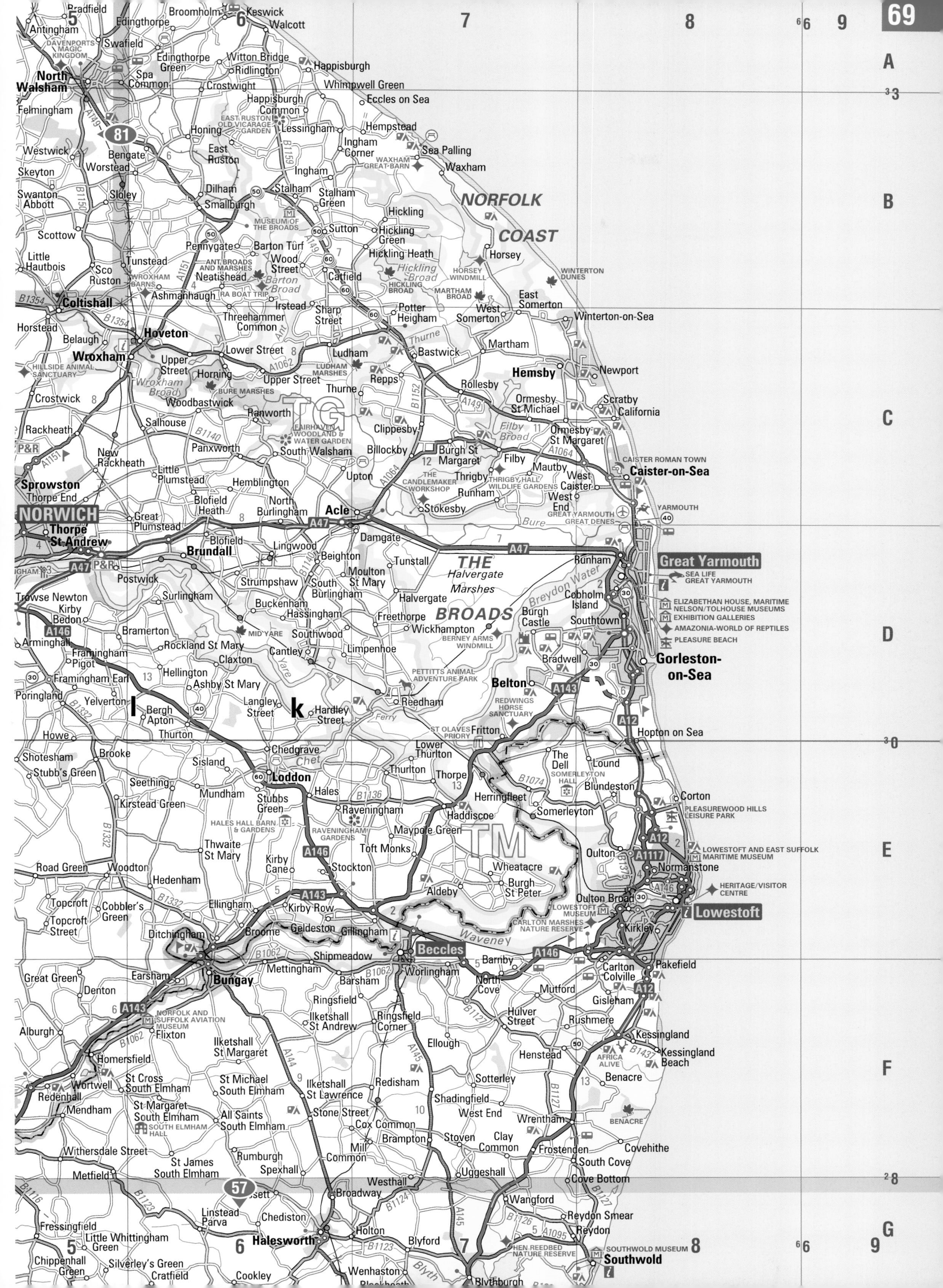
Bradfield
Antingham
Edingthorpe
Broomholm
Keswick
Walcott
Davenports Magic Kingdom
Swafield
Edingthorpe Green
Witton Bridge
Ridlington
Happisburgh
North Walsham
Spa Common
Crostwight
Whimpwell Green
Felmingham
Happisburgh Common
Eccles on Sea
East Ruston Old Vicarage Garden
Lessingham
Hempstead
Honing
Ingham Corner
Sea Palling
Westwick
Bengate
East Ruston
Waxham Great Barn
Waxham
Worstead
Skeyton
Ingham
Swanton Abbott
Dilham
Stalham
Stalham Green
Sloley
Smallburgh
NORFOLK
Museum of the Broads
Hickling
Scottow
Sutton
Hickling Green
COAST
Pennygate
Barton Turf
Hickling Heath
Horsey
Little Hautbois
Tunstead
Wood Street
Hickling Broad
Horsey Windmill
Winterton Dunes
Sco Ruston
Ant Broads and Marshes
Neatishead
Barton Broad
Catfield
Wroxham Barns
Hickling Broad
Martham Broad
Ashmanhaugh
RA Boat Trip
East Somerton
Coltishall
Irstead
Sharp Street
Potter Heigham
West Somerton
Winterton-on-Sea
Threehammer Common
Horstead
Hoveton
Belaugh
Thurne
Bastwick
Martham
Lower Street
Ludham
Wroxham
Upper Street
Hillside Animal Sanctuary
Horning
Ludham Marshes
Repps
Hemsby
Newport
Wroxham Broad
Upper Street
Rollesby
Thurne
Bure Marshes
Crostwick
Woodbastwick
Ormesby St Michael
Scratby
California
TG
Ranworth
Rackheath
Salhouse
Fairhaven Woodland & Water Garden
Clippesby
Filby Broad
Ormesby St Margaret
P&R
Panxworth
South Walsham
Billockby
Burgh St Margaret
New Rackheath
Filby
Caister Roman Town
Caister-on-Sea
Little Plumstead
Upton
Mautby
West Caister
Sprowston
Hemblington
The Candlemaker Workshop
Thrigby
Thrigby Hall Wildlife Gardens
Runham
Thorpe End
Blofield Heath
North Burlingham
Acle
Stokesby
West End
Yarmouth
NORWICH
Great Plumstead
Great Yarmouth Great Denes
Bure
Thorpe St Andrew
Blofield
Damgate
Brundall
Lingwood
Beighton
Runham
THE
Great Yarmouth
Tunstall
Halvergate Marshes
Sea Life Great Yarmouth
Postwick
Moulton St Mary
Strumpshaw
South Burlingham
Breydon Water
Trowse Newton
Surlingham
Halvergate
Cobholm Island
Elizabethan House, Maritime
Kirby Bedon
Buckenham
Hassingham
Freethorpe
BROADS
Burgh Castle
Nelson/Tolhouse Museums
Exhibition Galleries
Bramerton
Wickhampton
Southtown
Amazonia-World of Reptiles
Mid Yare
Southwood
Berney Arms Windmill
Pleasure Beach
Arminghall
Framingham Pigot
Rockland St Mary
Cantley
Limpenhoe
Bradwell
Gorleston-on-Sea
Claxton
Pettitts Animal Adventure Park
Framingham Earl
Hellington
Poringland
Ashby St Mary
Belton
Yelverton
Langley Street
Bergh Apton
Hardley Street
Reedham
Redwings Horse Sanctuary
Ferry
Howe
Thurton
St Olaves Priory
Fritton
Hopton on Sea
Shotesham
Brooke
Chedgrave
Lower Thurlton
Stubb's Green
Sisland
Chet
The Dell
Lound
Thurlton
Thorpe
Somerleyton Hall
Seething
Loddon
Blundeston
Mundham
Stubbs Green
Hales
Herringfleet
Corton
Kirstead Green
Raveningham
Haddiscoe
Somerleyton
Pleasurewood Hills Leisure Park
Hales Hall Barn & Gardens
Raveningham Gardens
Maypole Green
TM
Thwaite St Mary
Toft Monks
Oulton
Lowestoft and East Suffolk Maritime Museum
Kirby Cane
Road Green
Woodton
Stockton
Wheatacre
Normanstone
Hedenham
Burgh St Peter
Heritage/Visitor Centre
Aldeby
Oulton Broad
Topcroft
Cobbler's Green
Ellingham
Kirby Row
Lowestoft Museum
Lowestoft
Topcroft Street
Carlton Marshes Nature Reserve
Kirkley
Ditchingham
Broome
Geldeston
Gillingham
Waveney
Beccles
Shipmeadow
Barnby
Great Green
Earsham
Mettingham
Worlingham
Carlton Colville
Pakefield
Denton
Bungay
Barsham
North Cove
Mutford
Gisleham
Ringsfield
Norfolk and Suffolk Aviation Museum
Flixton
Alburgh
Ilketshall St Andrew
Ringsfield Corner
Hulver Street
Rushmere
Ilketshall St Margaret
Ellough
Kessingland
Homersfield
Henstead
Africa Alive
Kessingland Beach
Wortwell
St Cross South Elmham
St Michael South Elmham
Ilketshall St Lawrence
Redisham
Sotterley
Benacre
Redenhall
Mendham
St Margaret South Elmham
All Saints South Elmham
Stone Street
Shadingfield
West End
Wrentham
South Elmham Hall
Cox Common
Brampton
Stoven
Clay Common
Benacre
Withersdale Street
Mill Common
Frostenden
Covehithe
St James South Elmham
Rumburgh
Spexhall
South Cove
Metfield
Westhall
Uggeshall
Cove Bottom
Broadway
Wangford
Linstead Parva
Chediston
Reydon Smear
Fressingfield
Holton
Reydon
Little Whittingham Green
Halesworth
Blyford
Hen Reedbed Nature Reserve
Southwold Museum
Chippenhall Green
Silverley's Green
Southwold
Cratfield
Cookley
Wenhaston
Blyth
Blythburgh

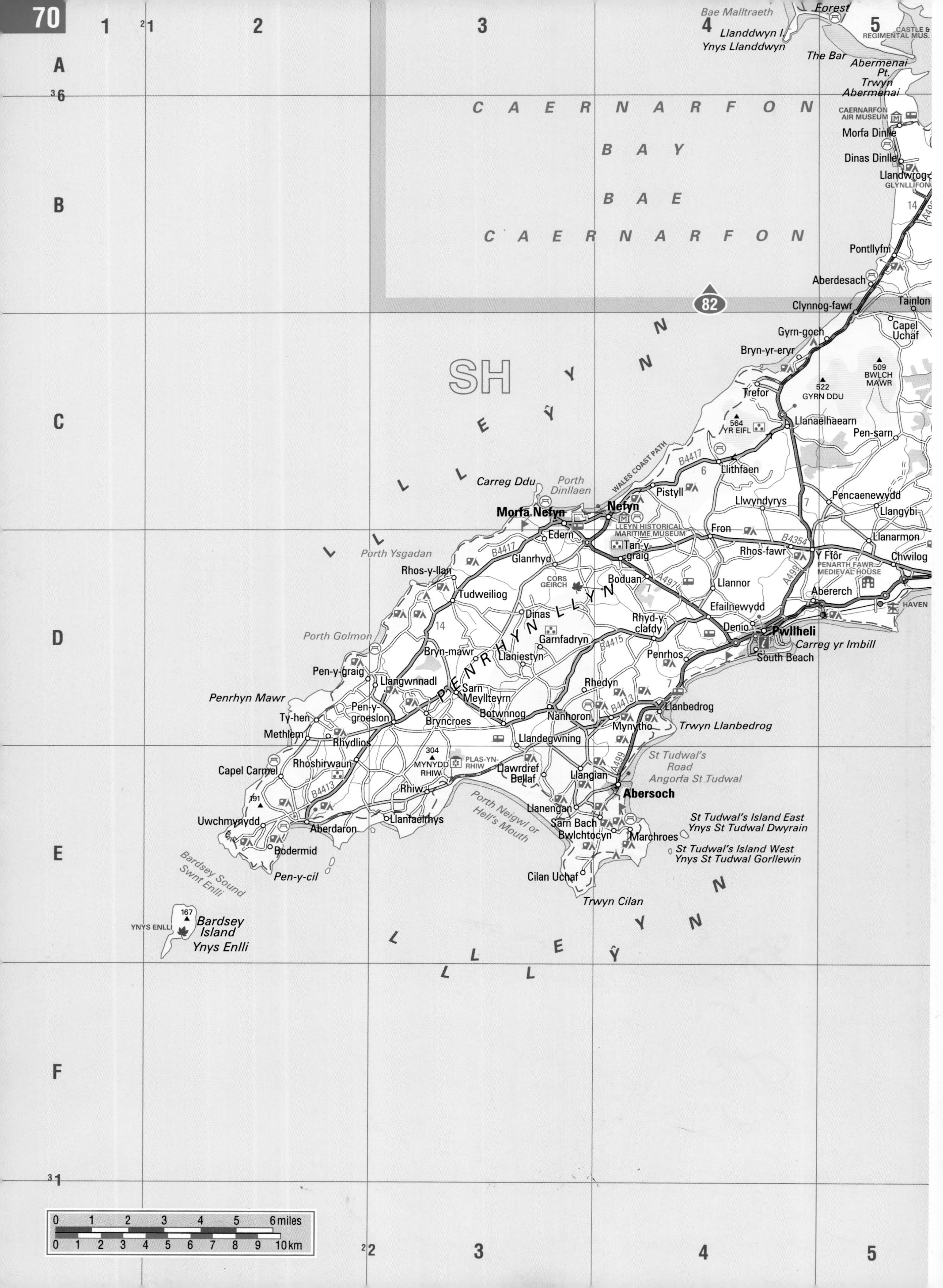
CAERNARFON BAY
BAE CAERNARFON
LLEYN
SH
82
Bae Malltraeth
Forest
Llanddwyn I.
Ynys Llanddwyn
The Bar
Abermenai Pt.
Trwyn Abermenai
CASTLE & REGIMENTAL MUS.
CAERNARFON AIR MUSEUM
Morfa Dinlle
Dinas Dinlle
Llandwrog
GLYNLLIFON
Pontllyfni
Aberdesach
Clynnog-fawr
Tainlon
Capel Uchaf
Gyrn-goch
Bryn-yr-eryr
509 BWLCH MAWR
522 GYRN DDU
Trefor
564 YR EIFL
Llanaelhaearn
Pen-sarn
WALES COAST PATH
B4417
Llithfaen
Carreg Ddu
Porth Dinllaen
Pistyll
Llwyndyrys
Pencaenewydd
Llangybi
Morfa Nefyn
Nefyn
LLEYN HISTORICAL MARITIME MUSEUM
Edern
Fron
B4354
Llanarmon
Porth Ysgadan
Tan-y-graig
Rhos-fawr
Y Ffôr
Chwilog
PENARTH FAWR MEDIEVAL HOUSE
Glanrhyd
Rhos-y-llan
CORS GEIRCH
Boduan
A497
Llannor
A499
Abererch
HAVEN
Tudweiliog
Efailnewydd
PENRHYN LLYN
Dinas
Rhyd-y-clafdy
Denio
Pwllheli
Porth Golmon
Garnfadryn
B4415
Carreg yr Imbill
Bryn-mawr
Llaniestyn
Penrhos
South Beach
Pen-y-graig
Llangwnnadl
Rhedyn
Penrhyn Mawr
Sarn Meyllteyrn
B4413
Llanbedrog
Ty-hen
Pen-y-groeslon
Bryncroes
Botwnnog
Nanhoron
Mynytho
Trwyn Llanbedrog
Methlem
Rhydlios
Llandegwning
St Tudwal's Road
Angorfa St Tudwal
304 MYNYDD RHIW
PLAS-YN-RHIW
Capel Carmel
Rhoshirwaun
Llawrdref Bellaf
Llangian
Abersoch
Rhiw
Porth Neigwl or Hell's Mouth
191
Llanengan
St Tudwal's Island East
Ynys St Tudwal Dwyrain
Uwchmynydd
Aberdaron
Llanfaelrhys
Sarn Bach
Bwlchtocyn
Marchroes
St Tudwal's Island West
Ynys St Tudwal Gorllewin
Bodermid
Bardsey Sound
Swnt Enlli
Pen-y-cil
Cilan Uchaf
Trwyn Cilan
167
YNYS ENLLI
Bardsey Island
Ynys Enlli
A B C D E F
1 2 3 4 5
0 1 2 3 4 5 6 miles
0 1 2 3 4 5 6 7 8 9 10 km

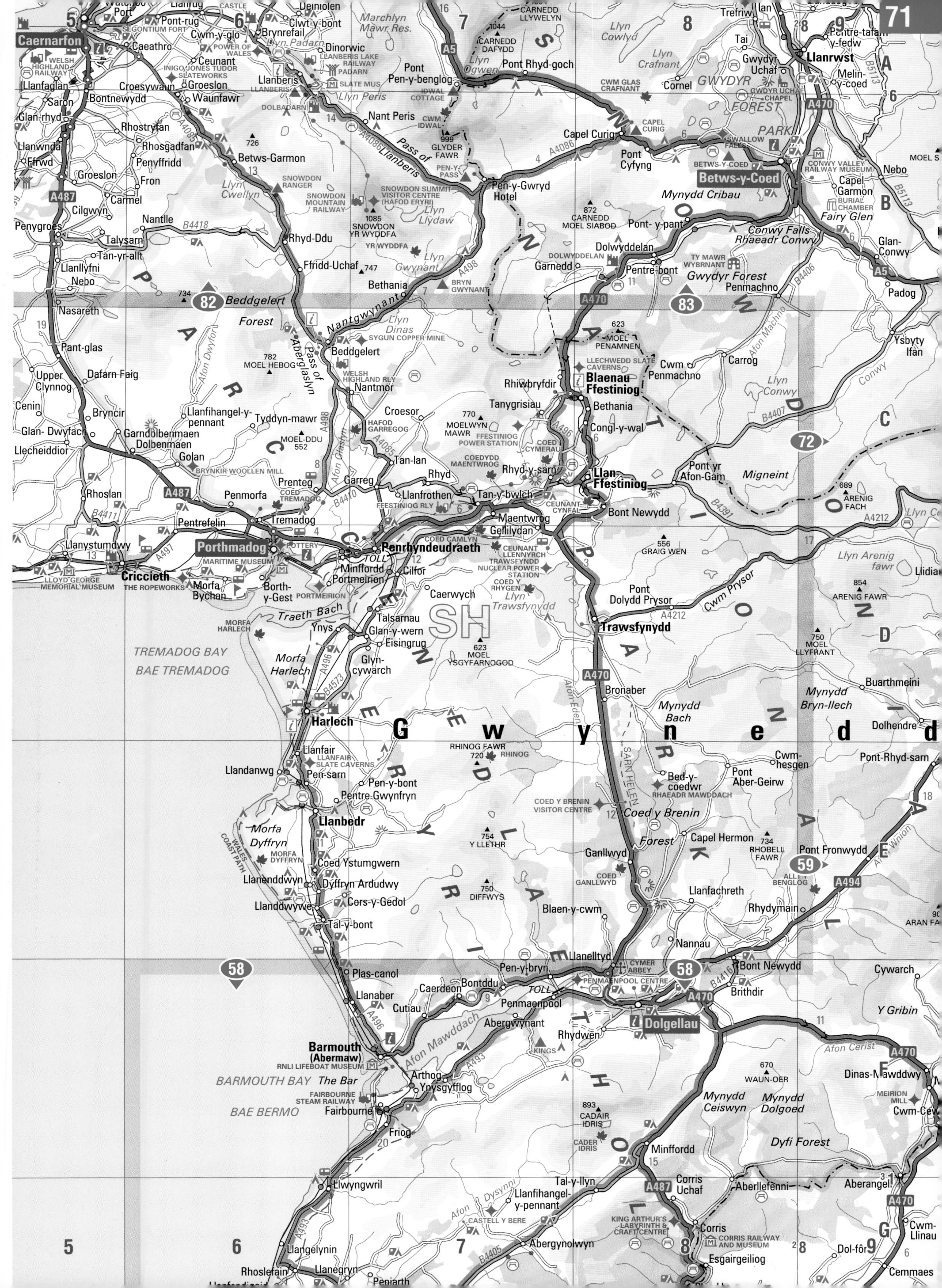
Caernarfon
Pont-rug
Cwm-y-glo
Brynrefail
Clwt-y-bont
Deiniolen
Caeathro
Dinorwic
Ceunant
Llanberis
Pont Pen-y-benglog
Pont Rhyd-goch
Llyn Padarn
Llyn Peris
Llyn Ogwen
Llyn Cowlyd
Llyn Crafnant
Marchlyn Mawr Res.
CARNEDD LLYWELYN
CARNEDD DAFYDD
Trefriw
Tai
Gwydyr Uchaf
Llanrwst
Melin-y-coed
Pentre-tafarn-y-fedw
Cornel
GWYDYR FOREST
PARK
WELSH HIGHLAND RAILWAY
SEGONTIUM FORT
POWER OF WALES
LLANBERIS LAKE RAILWAY
PADARN
SLATE MUS
INIGO JONES TUDOR SLATEWORKS
IDWAL COTTAGE
CWM IDWAL
GLYDER FAWR
CWM GLAS CRAFNANT
Llanfaglan
Croesywaun
Groeslon
Waunfawr
Bontnewydd
Saron
Glan-rhyd
Rhostryfan
Rhosgadfan
Llanwnda
Ffrwd
Groeslon
Penyffridd
Fron
Betws-Garmon
Nant Peris
Pass of Llanberis
PEN-Y-PASS
Pen-y-Gwryd Hotel
Capel Curig
Pont Cyfyng
SWALLOW FALLS
Betws-y-Coed
CONWY VALLEY RAILWAY MUSEUM
Nebo
Capel Garmon
BURIAL CHAMBER
Fairy Glen
Mynydd Cribau
Llyn Cwellyn
SNOWDON RANGER
SNOWDON MOUNTAIN RAILWAY
SNOWDON SUMMIT VISITOR CENTRE (HAFOD ERYRI)
SNOWDON YR WYDDFA
YR WYDDFA
Llyn Llydaw
CARNEDD MOEL SIABOD
Pont-y-pant
Conwy Falls
Rhaeadr Conwy
Glan-Conwy
Carmel
Cilgwyn
Penygroes
Nantlle
Talysarn
Tan-yr-allt
Llanllyfni
Nebo
Rhyd-Ddu
Ffridd-Uchaf
Llyn Gwynant
Bethania
BRYN GWYNANT
Dolwyddelan
DOLWYDDELAN
Garnedd
Pentre-bont
TY MAWR WYBRNANT
Gwydyr Forest
Penmachno
Padog
Beddgelert Forest
Nasareth
Nantgwynant
Llyn Dinas
SYGUN COPPER MINE
Beddgelert
Pass of Aberglaslyn
MOEL HEBOG
Afon Dwyfor
MOEL PENAMNEN
LLECHWEDD SLATE CAVERNS
Cwm Penmachno
Carrog
Ysbyty Ifan
Llyn Conwy
Conwy
Pant-glas
Upper Clynnog
Dafarn Faig
WELSH HIGHLAND RLY
Nantmor
Rhiwbryfdir
Blaenau Ffestiniog
Bethania
Congl-y-wal
Cenin
Bryncir
Glan-Dwyfach
Llecheiddior
Garndolbenmaen
Dolbenmaen
Llanfihangel-y-pennant
Tyddyn-mawr
MOEL-DDU
HAFOD GARREGOG
Croesor
MOELWYN MAWR
FFESTINIOG POWER STATION
Tanygrisiau
COED CYMERAU
Golan
BRYNKIR WOOLLEN MILL
Tan-lan
Rhyd
COEDYDD MAENTWROG
Rhyd-y-sarn
Llan-Ffestiniog
Pont yr Afon-Gam
Migneint
ARENIG FACH
Llyn Celyn
Rhoslan
Penmorfa
Prenteg
COED TREMADOG
Garreg
Llanfrothen
FFESTINIOG RLY
Tan-y-bwlch
CEUNANT CYNFAL
Bont Newydd
Pentrefelin
Tremadog
Maentwrog
Gellilydan
COED CAMLYN
Llanystumdwy
Porthmadog
POTTERY
Penrhyndeudraeth
TOLL
GRAIG WEN
Llyn Arenig fawr
Llidiardau
LLOYD GEORGE MEMORIAL MUSEUM
Criccieth
THE ROPEWORKS
MARITIME MUSEUM
Morfa Bychan
Borth-y-Gest
Minffordd
Portmeirion
PORTMEIRION
Cilfor
Caerwych
CEUNANT LLENNYRCH
TRAWSFYNYDD NUCLEAR POWER STATION
COED Y RHYGEN
Llyn Trawsfynydd
Pont Dolydd Prysor
Cwm Prysor
ARENIG FAWR
Trawsfynydd
MOEL LLYFRANT
MORFA HARLECH
Traeth Bach
Talsarnau
Ynys
Glan-y-wern
Eisingrug
SH
TREMADOG BAY
BAE TREMADOG
Morfa Harlech
Glyn-cywarch
MOEL YSGYFARNOGOD
Afon Eden
Bronaber
Mynydd Bach
Mynydd Bryn-llech
Buarthmeini
Harlech
Gwynedd
Dolhendre
Llanfair
LLANFAIR SLATE CAVERNS
RHINOG FAWR
RHINOG
SARN HELEN
Cwm-hesgen
Pont-Rhyd-sarn
Llandanwg
Pen-sarn
Pen-y-bont
Pentre Gwynfryn
Bed-y-coedwr
RHAEADR MAWDDACH
Pont Aber-Geirw
COED Y BRENIN VISITOR CENTRE
Coed y Brenin Forest
Llanbedr
Morfa Dyffryn
WALES COAST PATH
MORFA DYFFRYN
Y LLETHR
Capel Hermon
RHOBELL FAWR
Pont Fronwydd
Afon Wnion
Coed Ystumgwern
Ganllwyd
COED GANLLWYD
ALLT Y BENGLOG
Llanenddwyn
Dyffryn Ardudwy
DIFFWYS
Llanfachreth
Rhydymain
Llanddwywe
Cors-y-Gedol
Blaen-y-cwm
ARAN FAWDDWY
Tal-y-bont
Nannau
Plas-canol
Pen-y-bryn
Llanelltyd
CYMER ABBEY
Bont Newydd
Cywarch
PENMAENPOOL CENTRE
Brithdir
Caerdeon
Bontddu
TOLL
Llanaber
Cutiau
Penmaenpool
Dolgellau
Y Gribin
Abergwynant
Rhydwen
Afon Mawddach
KINGS
Barmouth (Abermaw)
RNLI LIFEBOAT MUSEUM
Afon Cerist
BARMOUTH BAY
The Bar
Arthog
Ynysgyffflog
WAUN-OER
Dinas-Mawddwy
FAIRBOURNE STEAM RAILWAY
BAE BERMO
Fairbourne
CADAIR IDRIS
Mynydd Ceiswyn
Mynydd Dolgoed
MEIRION MILL
Cwm-Cewydd
Friog
CADER IDRIS
Dyfi Forest
Minfordd
Llwyngwril
Tal-y-llyn
Corris Uchaf
Aberllefenni
Aberangell
Afon Dysynni
Llanfihangel-y-pennant
CASTELL Y BERE
KING ARTHUR'S LABYRINTH & CRAFT CENTRE
Corris
CORRIS RAILWAY AND MUSEUM
Cwm-Llinau
Abergynolwyn
Dol-fôr
Llangelynin
Esgairgeiliog
Rhoslefain
Llanegryn
Peniarth
Cemmaes
82
83
72
59
58
A5
A470
A487
A4085
A4086
A498
A496
A497
A4212
A494
A493
B4418
B4410
B4411
B4391
B4407
B4406
B4573
B4416
B4405
B5113
SNOWDONIA
ERYRI
MEIRIONNYDD

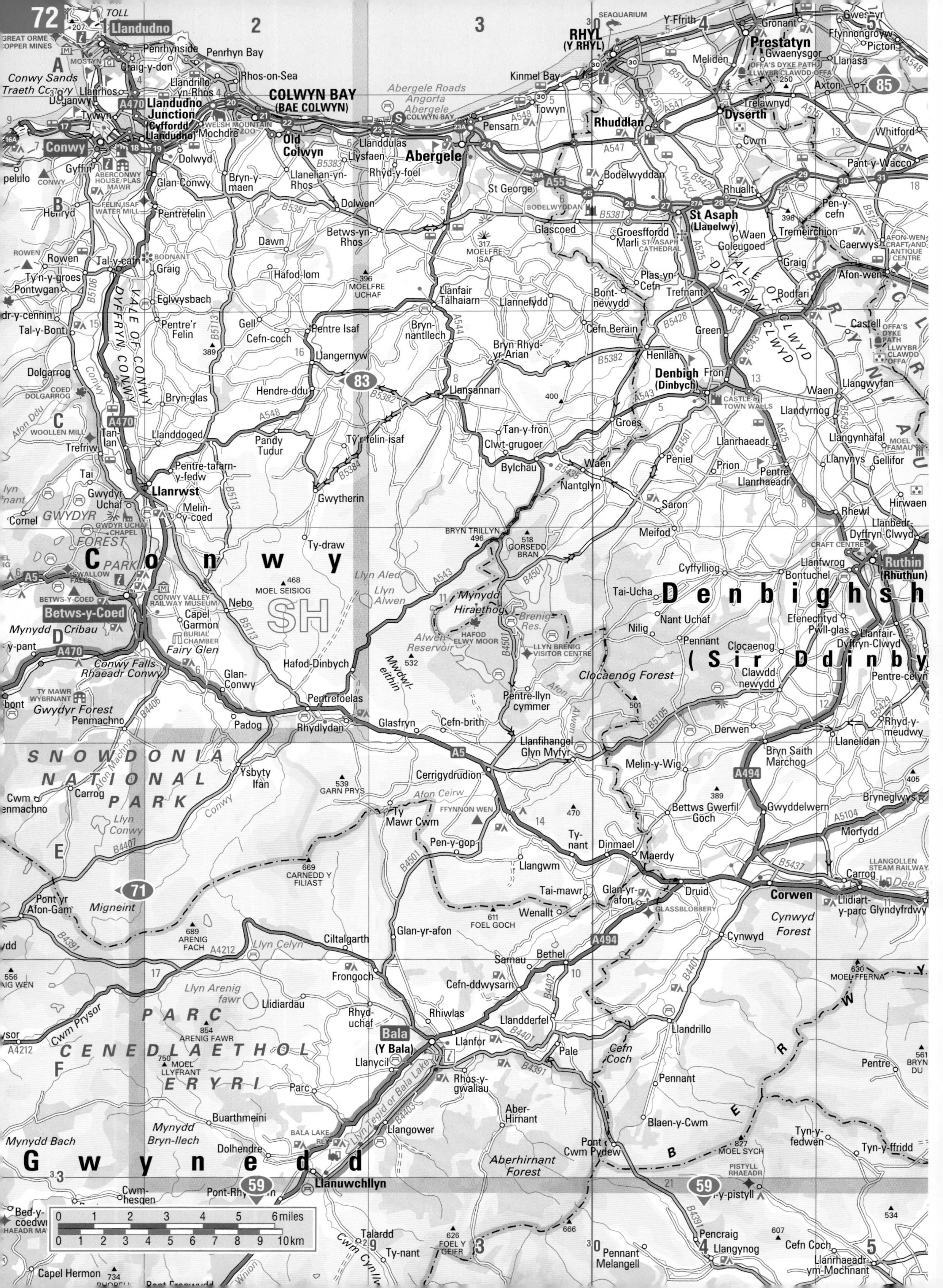

72
2
3
4
5
Llandudno
GREAT ORME COPPER MINES
TOLL
Penrhynside
Penrhyn Bay
Craig-y-don
Rhos-on-Sea
Llandrillo-yn-Rhos
Conwy Sands
Traeth Conwy
Llanrhos
Deganwy
Tywyn
Llandudno Junction (Cyffordd Llandudno)
COLWYN BAY (BAE COLWYN)
WELSH MOUNTAIN ZOO
Mochdre
Old Colwyn
Llanddulas
Llysfaen
Abergele
Abergele Roads
Angorfa Abergele
Pensarn
Conwy
ABERCONWY HOUSE/PLAS MAWR
Gyffin
Dolwyd
Glan-Conwy
Bryn-y-maen
Llanelian-yn-Rhos
Rhyd-y-foel
Dolwen
Henryd
FELIN ISAF WATER MILL
Pentrefelin
Dawn
Betws-yn-Rhos
ROWEN
Rowen
Tal-y-cafn
BODNANT
Graig
Ty'n-y-groes
Pontwgan
Eglwysbach
Hafod-lom
396 MOELFRE UCHAF
317 MOELFRE ISAF
Llanfair Talhaiarn
VALE OF CONWY
DYFFRYN CONWY
Tal-y-Bont
Pentre'r Felin
Gell
Cefn-coch
Pentre Isaf
Bryn-nantllech
Llangernyw
Dolgarrog
COED DOLGARROG
Bryn-glas
Hendre-ddu
83
Llansannan
Afon Ddu
WOOLLEN MILL
Trefriw
Tan-lan
Llanddoged
Pandy Tudur
Tŷ'n-felin-isaf
Pentre-tafarn-y-fedw
Llanrwst
Tai
Gwydyr Uchaf
Melin-y-coed
Gwytherin
Cornel
GWYDYR
GWYDYR UCHAF CHAPEL
FOREST PARK
Conwy
Ty-draw
SWALLOW FALLS
BETWS-Y-COED
Betws-y-Coed
CONWY VALLEY RAILWAY MUSEUM
Nebo
468 MOEL SEISIOG
SH
Llyn Aled
Llyn Alwen
Capel Garmon
BURIAL CHAMBER
Fairy Glen
Mynydd Cribau
Conwy Falls
Rhaeadr Conwy
TY MAWR WYBRNANT
Gwydyr Forest
Penmachno
Glan-Conwy
Hafod-Dinbych
Pentrefoelas
Padog
Rhydlydan
Glasfryn
SNOWDONIA NATIONAL PARK
Ysbyty Ifan
Carrog
Afon Machno
Cwm Penmachno
Llyn Conwy
539 GARN PRYS
Ty Mawr Cwm
Afon Ceirw
FFYNNON WEN
Pen-y-gop
669 CARNEDD Y FILIAST
71
Pont yr Afon-Gam
Migneint
689 ARENIG FACH
Llyn Celyn
Ciltalgarth
556 MIG WEN
Llyn Arenig fawr
Llidiardau
Frongoch
PARC CENEDLAETHOL ERYRI
854 ARENIG FAWR
750 MOEL LLYFRANT
Cwm Prysor
Rhyd-uchaf
Bala (Y Bala)
Llanycil
Parc
Buarthmeini
Mynydd Bryn-llech
Mynydd Bach
BALA LAKE RLY
Llyn Tegid or Bala Lake
Dolhendre
Gwynedd
Llanuwchllyn
Pont-Rhyd-y-fen
59
Cwm-hesgen
Bed-y-coedwr
Talardd
Ty-nant
Cwm Cynllwyd
626 FOEL Y GEIFR
Capel Hermon
734
Wnion
RHYL (Y RHYL)
SEAQUARIUM
Kinmel Bay
Towyn
Y-Ffrith
Gronant
Prestatyn
Gwaenysgor
Meliden
OFFA'S DYKE PATH
LLWYBR CLAWDD OFFA
Llanasa
Gwespyr
Ffynnongroyw
Picton
Axton
85
Trelawnyd
Dyserth
Rhuddlan
Cwm
Whitford
Bodelwyddan
BODELWYDDAN
St George
Rhuallt
Pant-y-Wacco
St Asaph (Llanelwy)
ST ASAPH CATHEDRAL
Glascoed
Groesffordd Marli
Waen
Goleugoed
Tremeirchion
398
Pen-y-cefn
Caerwys
AFON-WEN CRAFT AND ANTIQUE CENTRE
Afon-wen
Plas-yn-Cefn
Trefnant
VALE OF CLWYD
DYFFRYN CLWYD
Graig
Bodfari
Llannefydd
Bont-newydd
Cefn Berain
Green
Castell
Bryn Rhyd-yr-Arian
Henllan
Denbigh (Dinbych)
Fron
CASTLE & TOWN WALLS
Llangwyfan
Waen
Llandyrnog
400
Groes
Tan-y-fron
Clwt-grugoer
Bylchau
Waen
Nantglyn
Peniel
Llanrhaeadr
Prion
Pentre Llanrhaeadr
Llangynhafal
MOEL FAMAU
Llanynys
Gellifor
Saron
Rhewl
Hirwaen
Llanbedr-Dyffryn-Clwyd
BRYN TRILLYN 496
518 GORSEDD BRAN
Meifod
CRAFT CENTRE
Ruthin (Rhuthun)
Llanfwrog
Cyffylliog
Bontuchel
Tai-Ucha
Denbighshire (Sir Ddinbych)
Mynydd Hiraethog
Brenig Res.
HAFOD ELWY MOOR
LLYN BRENIG VISITOR CENTRE
Alwen Reservoir
Nant Uchaf
Nilig
Pennant
Efenechtyd
Pwll-glas
Llanfair-Dyffryn-Clwyd
Clocaenog
Mwdwl-eithin
532
Clocaenog Forest
Clawdd-newydd
Pentre-celyn
Pentre-llyn cymmer
Cefn-brith
501
Derwen
Rhyd-y-meudwy
Llanelidan
Llanfihangel Glyn Myfyr
Bryn Saith Marchog
Melin-y-Wig
Cerrigydrudion
389
405
Bryneglwys
Bettws Gwerfil Goch
Gwyddelwern
470
Ty-nant
Dinmael
Maerdy
Morfydd
Llangwm
LLANGOLLEN STEAM RAILWAY
Carrog
Dee
Tai-mawr
Glan-yr-afon
Druid
Corwen
Llidiart-y-parc
Glyndyfrdwy
GLASSBLOBBERY
Wenallt
611 FOEL GOCH
Cynwyd Forest
Glan-yr-afon
Cynwyd
Bethel
Sarnau
Cefn-ddwysarn
630 MOEL FFERNA
Rhiwlas
Llandderfel
Llanfor
Pale
Cefn Coch
Llandrillo
Rhos-y-gwaliau
561 BRYN DU
Pentre
Pennant
Aber-Hirnant
Llangower
Blaen-y-Cwm
BERWYN
Tyn-y-fedwen
Tyn-y-ffridd
Pont Cwm Pydew
827 MOEL SYCH
Aberhirnant Forest
PISTYLL RHAEADR
Tan-y-pistyll
666
534
Pencraig
Llangynog
607
Cefn Coch
Pennant Melangell
Llanrhaeadr-ym-Mochnant
0 1 2 3 4 5 6 miles
0 1 2 3 4 5 6 7 8 9 10 km
A55
A470
A5
A543
A548
A547
A525
A541
A494
A5104
A4212
B5381
B5382
B5383
B5113
B5384
B5106
B5429
B5428
B5435
B4501
B4391
B4401
B4402
B4403
B4406
B4407
B5105
B5437
B5119
B5429
B5122

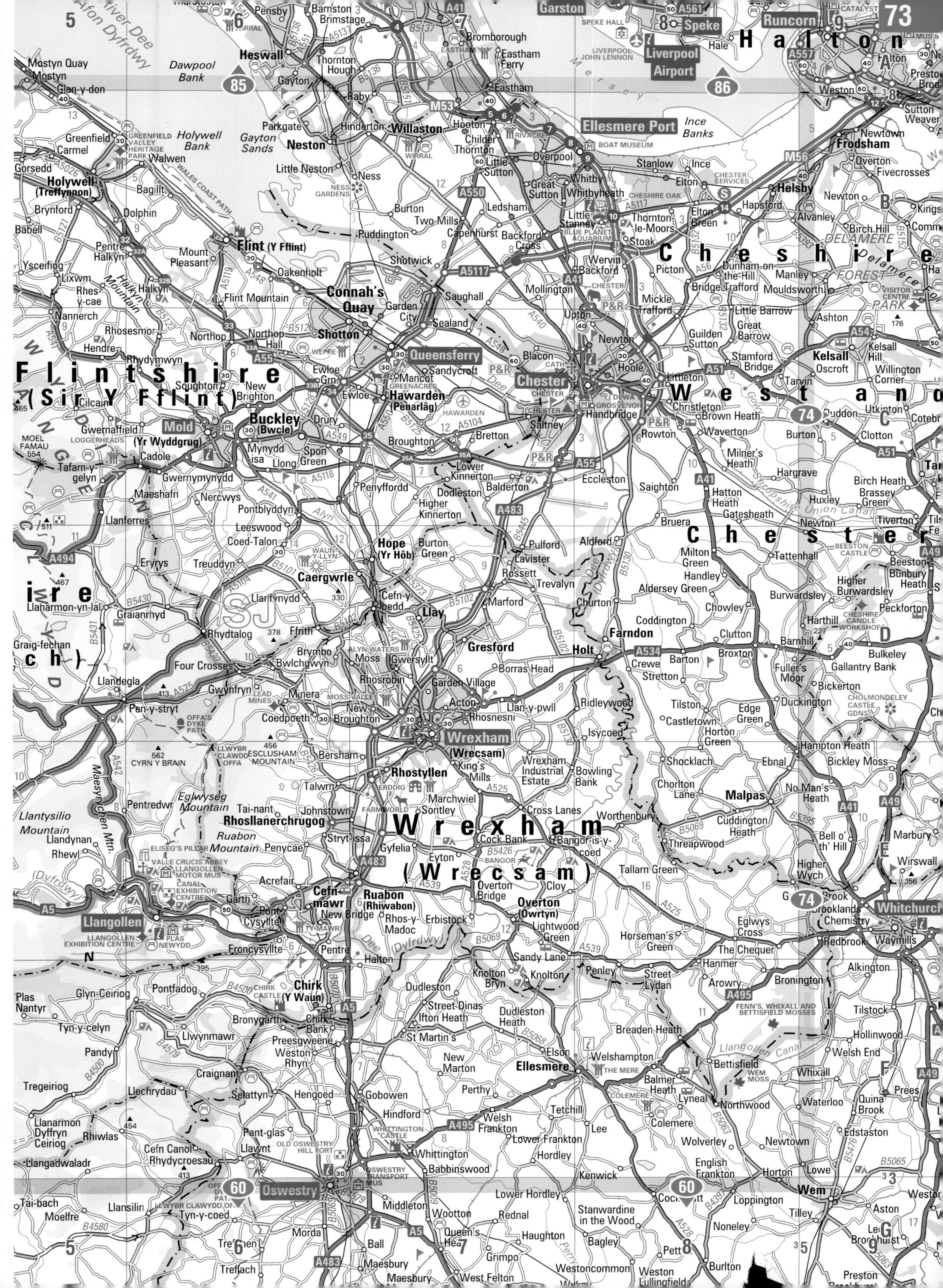

73
5
6
7
8
9
Garston
Speke
Speke Hall
Liverpool John Lennon
Liverpool Airport
Runcorn
Halton
Hale
Pensby
Barnston
Brimstage
Bromborough
Eastham
Eastham Ferry
Heswall
Thornton Hough
Dawpool Bank
Mostyn Quay
Mostyn
Glan-y-don
Gayton
Raby
M53
Weston
Sutton Weaver
Frodsham
Newtown
Ellesmere Port
Boat Museum
Ince Banks
Parkgate
Hinderton
Willaston
Hooton
Childer Thornton
Greenfield
Carmel
Greenfield Valley Heritage Park
Holywell Bank
Gayton Sands
Neston
Walwen
Gorsedd
Holywell (Treffynnon)
Little Neston
Ness
Ness Gardens
Little Sutton
Overpool
Stanlow
Ince
Elton
Chester Services
Helsby
Overton
Fivecrosses
Wales Coast Path
Bagillt
Great Sutton
Whitby
Whitbyheath
Cheshire Oak
Brynford
Dolphin
Burton
Two Mills
Ledsham
Capenhurst
Backford Cross
Little Stanney
Blue Planet Aquarium
Thornton-le-Moors
Elton Green
Hapsford
Alvanley
Newton
Birch Hill
Delamere
Babell
Pentre Halkyn
Mount Pleasant
Flint (Y Fflint)
Puddington
Stoak
Cheshire
Ysceifiog
Lixwm
Rhes-y-cae
Halkyn Mountain
Halkyn
Flint Mountain
Oakenholt
Shotwick
Connah's Quay
Garden City
Saughall
Mollington
Wervin
Backford
Picton
Dunham-on-the-Hill
Manley
Mouldsworth
Bridge Trafford
Forest
Visitor Centre
Park
Nannerch
Rhosesmor
Northop
Northop Hall
Shotton
Sealand
Upton
Mickle Trafford
Little Barrow
Great Barrow
Ashton
Guilden Sutton
Kelsall
Kelsall Hill
Oscroft
Willington Corner
Hendre
Rhydymwyn
Flintshire (Sir Y Fflint)
Soughton
New Brighton
Ewloe Grn
Ewloe
Queensferry
Mancot
Sandycroft
Hawarden (Penarlâg)
Blacon
Chester
Hoole
Littleton
Stamford Bridge
Tarvin
West and Chester
Cilcain
Buckley (Bwcle)
Mold (Yr Wyddgrug)
Gwernaffield
Loggerheads
Moel Famau
Drury
Mynydd-isa
Spon Green
Broughton
Bretton
Saltney
Handbridge
Christleton
Brown Heath
Waverton
Rowton
Duddon
Utkinton
Burton
Clotton
Cadole
Tafarn-y-gelyn
Llong
Gwernymynydd
Maeshafn
Nercwys
Pontblyddyn
Leeswood
Coed-Talon
Llanferres
Penyffordd
Lower Kinnerton
Dodleston
Higher Kinnerton
Balderton
Eccleston
Saighton
Milner's Heath
Hargrave
Birch Heath
Brassey Green
Huxley
Hatton Heath
Gatesheath
Bruera
Newton
Tiverton
Shropshire Union Canal
Hope (Yr Hôb)
Burton Green
Caergwrle
Pulford
Lavister
Rossett
Trevalyn
Aldford
Milton Green
Handley
Tattenhall
Beeston Castle
Beeston
Bunbury Heath
Higher Burwardsley
Burwardsley
Peckforton
Eryrys
Treuddyn
Llanarmon-yn-Ial
Llanfynydd
Cefn-y-bedd
Llay
Marford
Churton
Aldersey Green
Chowley
Coddington
Farndon
Harthill
Cheshire Candle Workshops
Graianrhyd
Rhydtalog
Ffrith
Brymbo
Alyn Waters
Moss
Gwersyllt
Gresford
Holt
Crewe
Barton
Stretton
Clutton
Broxton
Barnhill
Bulkeley
Fuller's Moor
Gallantry Bank
Bickerton
Graig-fechan
Four Crosses
Bwlchgwyn
Borras Head
Llandegla
Gwynfryn
Lead Mines
Minera
Moss Valley
Rhosrobin
Garden Village
Acton
Llan-y-pwll
Ridleywood
Tilston
Castletown
Edge Green
Duckington
Cholmondeley Castle Gdns
Pen-y-stryt
Offa's Dyke Path
Coedpoeth
New Broughton
Rhosnesni
Wrexham (Wrecsam)
Isycoed
Horton Green
Hampton Heath
Bickley Moss
Cyrn y Brain
Llwybr Clawdd Offa
Esclusham Mountain
Bersham
King's Mills
Wrexham Industrial Estate
Bowling Bank
Shocklach
Ebnal
Chorlton Lane
Malpas
No Man's Heath
Rhostyllen
Talwrn
Erddig
Marchwiel
Sontley
Farmworld
Cross Lanes
Worthenbury
Llantysilio Mountain
Pentredwr
Eglwyseg Mountain
Tai-nant
Johnstown
Rhosllanerchrugog
Ruabon Mountain
Penycae
Stryt-issa
Gyfelia
Wrexham (Wrecsam)
Cock Bank
Bangor-is-y-coed
Cuddington Heath
Threapwood
Bell o' th' Hill
Marbury
Llandynan
Rhewl
Eliseg's Pillar
Valle Crucis Abbey
Llangollen Motor Mus
Canal Exhibition Centre
Eyton
Bangor
Tallarn Green
Higher Wych
Wirswall
Acrefair
Cefn-mawr
Ruabon (Rhiwabon)
Overton Bridge
Overton (Owrtyn)
Cloy
Garth
Pont Cysyllte
New Bridge
Rhos-y-Madoc
Erbistock
Lightwood Green
Horseman's Green
Eglwys Cross
Brookland
Chemistry
Whitchurch
Redbrook
Waymills
Llangollen
Llangollen Exhibition Centre
Plas Newydd
Ty Mawr
Froncysyllte
Pentre
Halton
Sandy Lane
Penley
The Chequer
Hanmer
Arowry
Alkington
Bronington
Street Lydan
Knolton
Knolton Bryn
Plas Nantyr
Glyn-Ceiriog
Pontfadog
Chirk Castle
Chirk (Y Waun)
Dudleston
Street Dinas
Ifton Heath
Dudleston Heath
Fenn's, Whixall and Bettisfield Mosses
Tilstock
Tyn-y-celyn
Bronygarth
Chirk Bank
Llwynmawr
Preesgweene
Weston Rhyn
St Martin's
Breaden Heath
Hollinwood
Pandy
Welshampton
The Mere
Ellesmere
Elson
New Marton
Llangollen Canal
Bettisfield
Wem Moss
Welsh End
Whixall
Tregeiriog
Craignant
Selattyn
Hengoed
Gobowen
Perthy
Balmer Heath
Lyneal
Northwood
Waterloo
Quina Brook
Prees
Llechrydau
Llanarmon Dyffryn Ceiriog
Rhiwlas
Pant-glas
Hindford
Whittington Castle
Welsh Frankton
Tetchill
Lee
Colemere
Lower Frankton
Wolverley
Edstaston
Newtown
Cefn Canol
Rhydycroesau
Llangadwaladr
Llawnt
Old Oswestry Hill Fort
Whittington
Babbinswood
Hordley
English Frankton
Horton
Lowe
Kenwick
Oswestry
Oswestry Transport Mus
Lower Hordley
Cockshutt
Loppington
Wem
Weston
Tai-bach
Llansilin
Moelfre
Llwybr Clawdd Offa
Tyn-y-coed
Middleton
Wootton
Rednal
Stanwardine in the Wood
Tilley
Aston
Noneley
Lee Brockhurst
Morda
Queen's Head
Haughton
Bagley
Trefonen
Ball
Grimpo
Pett
Burlton
Maesbury
Westoncommon
Weston Lullingfields
Preston
Maesbury Marsh
West Felton
Treflach
85
86
60
74

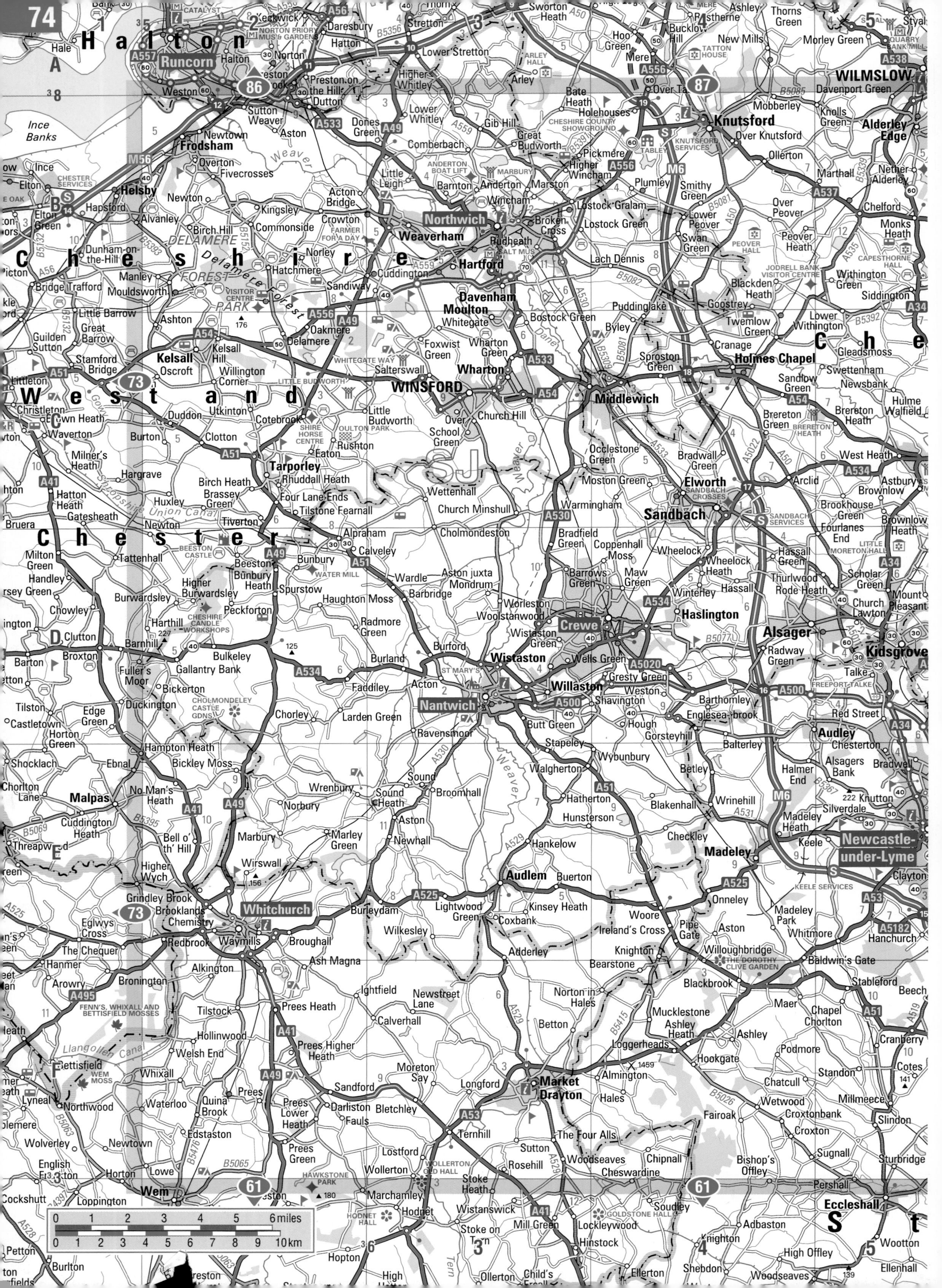

Halton
Runcorn
Halton
Norton
Weston
Keckwick
Daresbury
Hatton
Stretton
Lower Stretton
Preston on the Hill
Dutton
Sutton Weaver
Aston
Higher Whitley
Lower Whitley
Sworton Heath
Arley
Arley Hall
Hoo Green
Mere
Bucklow Hill
Rostherne
Ashley
Thorns Green
Styal
Morley Green
New Mills
Tatton House
Wilmslow
Davenport Green
Mobberley
Knolls Green
Alderley Edge
Knutsford
Over Knutsford
Ollerton
Over Tabley
Bate Heath
Holehouses
Cheshire County Showground
Great Budworth
Pickmere
Higher Wincham
Gib Hill
Comberbach
Dones Green
Frodsham
Newtown
Overton
Fivecrosses
Ince Banks
Ince
Elton
Chester Services
Helsby
Hapsford
Alvanley
Newton
Kingsley
Acton Bridge
Crowton
Little Leigh
Anderton Boat Lift
Marbury
Barnton
Anderton
Marston
Wincham
Northwich
Weaverham
Lostock Gralam
Lostock Green
Plumley
Smithy Green
Lower Peover
Swan Green
Peover Hall
Over Peover
Peover Heath
Marthall
Nether Alderley
Chelford
Monks Heath
Capesthorne Hall
Withington Green
Jodrell Bank Visitor Centre
Siddington
Lower Withington
Goostrey
Blackden Heath
Twemlow Green
Cranage
Holmes Chapel
Gleadsmoss
Swettenham
Sandlow Green
Newsbank
Hulme Walfield
Brereton Green
Brereton Heath
Cheshire
Delamere Forest
Delamere Forest Park Visitor Centre
Birch Hill
Commonside
Norley
Dunham-on-the-Hill
Picton
Bridge Trafford
Manley
Mouldsworth
Hatchmere
Sandiway
Cuddington
Hartford
Rudheath
Salt Mus
Broken Cross
Lach Dennis
Davenham
Moulton
Whitegate
Bostock Green
Byley
Puddinglake
Sproston Green
Middlewich
Foxwist Green
Wharton Green
Wharton
Winsford
Whitegate Way
Salterswall
Little Budworth
Oakmere
Delamere
Ashton
Little Barrow
Great Barrow
Guilden Sutton
Kelsall
Kelsall Hill
Oscroft
Willington Corner
Stamford Bridge
Littleton
Christleton
Cotton Heath
Waverton
West and Chester
Duddon
Utkinton
Cotebrook
Shire Horse Centre
Oulton Park
Rushton
Eaton
Over
School Green
Church Hill
Occlestone Green
Bradwall Green
Moston Green
Elworth
Sandbach
Sandbach Crosses
Sandbach Services
Arclid
West Heath
Astbury
Brownlow
Brookhouse Green
Fourlanes End
Brownlow Heath
Little Moreton Hall
Burton
Clotton
Milner's Heath
Hargrave
Tarporley
Rhuddall Heath
Birch Heath
Brassey Green
Huxley
Four Lane Ends
Tilstone Fearnall
Tiverton
Wettenhall
Church Minshull
Warmingham
Hatton Heath
Gatesheath
Newton
Shropshire Union Canal
Bruera
Milton Green
Handley
Tattenhall
Beeston Castle
Beeston
Bunbury
Bunbury Heath
Water Mill
Alpraham
Calveley
Cholmondeston
Bradfield Green
Coppenhall Moss
Wheelock
Wheelock Heath
Hassall Green
Thurlwood
Rode Heath
Scholar Green
Mount Pleasant
Church Lawton
Chowley
Burwardsley
Higher Burwardsley
Spurstow
Haughton Moss
Wardle
Aston juxta Mondrum
Barbridge
Barrows Green
Maw Green
Winterley
Hassall
Haslington
Crewe
Worleston
Woolstanwood
Wistaston Green
Alsager
Kidsgrove
Harthill
Cheshire Candle Workshops
Peckforton
Radmore Green
Clutton
Barnhill
Broxton
Barton
Fuller's Moor
Gallantry Bank
Bulkeley
Burland
Burford
Wistaston
Wells Green
Radway Green
Talke
Freeport Talke
Gresty Green
Willaston
Weston
Shavington
Bickerton
Cholmondeley Castle Gdns
Duckington
Faddiley
Acton
St Mary's
Nantwich
Barthomley
Englesea-brook
Hough
Red Street
Tilston
Castletown
Horton Green
Edge Green
Chorley
Larden Green
Ravensmoor
Butt Green
Gorstyhill
Audley
Balterley
Chesterton
Stapeley
Wybunbury
Shocklach
Ebnal
Hampton Heath
Bickley Moss
Chorlton Lane
Malpas
No Man's Heath
Wrenbury
Sound
Sound Heath
Broomhall
Walgherton
Betley
Halmer End
Alsagers Bank
Bradwell
Knutton
Silverdale
Cuddington Heath
Threapwood
Norbury
Aston
Newhall
Hatherton
Hunsterson
Blakenhall
Wrinehill
Madeley Heath
Keele
Newcastle-under-Lyme
Bell o' th' Hill
Marbury
Marley Green
Hankelow
Checkley
Madeley
Higher Wych
Wirswall
Audlem
Buerton
Clayton
Keele Services
Grindley Brook
Brooklands
Chemistry
Whitchurch
Burleydam
Lightwood Green
Coxbank
Kinsey Heath
Onneley
Madeley Park
Woore
Pipe Gate
Aston
Whitmore
Hanchurch
Eglwys Cross
The Chequer
Redbrook
Waymills
Broughall
Wilkesley
Adderley
Ireland's Cross
Knighton
Bearstone
Willoughbridge
The Dorothy Clive Garden
Baldwin's Gate
Hanmer
Arowry
Bronington
Alkington
Ash Magna
Ightfield
Newstreet Lane
Norton in Hales
Blackbrook
Stableford
Maer
Beech
Chapel Chorlton
Fenn's, Whixall and Bettisfield Mosses
Tilstock
Prees Heath
Calverhall
Betton
Mucklestone
Ashley Heath
Ashley
Hollinwood
Welsh End
Llangollen Canal
Prees Higher Heath
Loggerheads
Hookgate
Podmore
Cranberry
Bettisfield
Wem Moss
Whixall
Moreton Say
Longford
Market Drayton
Almington
Hales
Chatcull
Standon
Cotes
Lyneal
Northwood
Waterloo
Quina Brook
Prees
Sandford
Prees Lower Heath
Darliston
Bletchley
Fauls
Wetwood
Croxtonbank
Millmeece
Fairoak
Croxton
Slindon
Welshampton
Wolverley
Newtown
Edstaston
Prees Green
Ternhill
Sutton
The Four Alls
Woodseaves
Chipnall
Cheswardine
Rosehill
Lostford
Wollerton
Wollerton Old Hall
Bishop's Offley
Sugnall
Sturbridge
English Frankton
Horton
Lowe
Wem
Hawkstone Park
Marchamley
Stoke Heath
Pershall
Eccleshall
Cockshutt
Loppington
Hodnet
Hodnet Hall
Wistanswick
Goldstone Hall
Soudley
Adbaston
Mill Green
Stoke on Tern
Lockleywood
Hinstock
Knighton
High Offley
Wootton
Petton
Burlton
Hopton
Ollerton
Child's Ercall
Ellerton
Shebdon
Woodseaves
Ellenhall
Tern
Weaver
Dane
Gowy
Staffordshire
SJ
86
87
73
61
0 1 2 3 4 5 6 miles
0 1 2 3 4 5 6 7 8 9 10 km

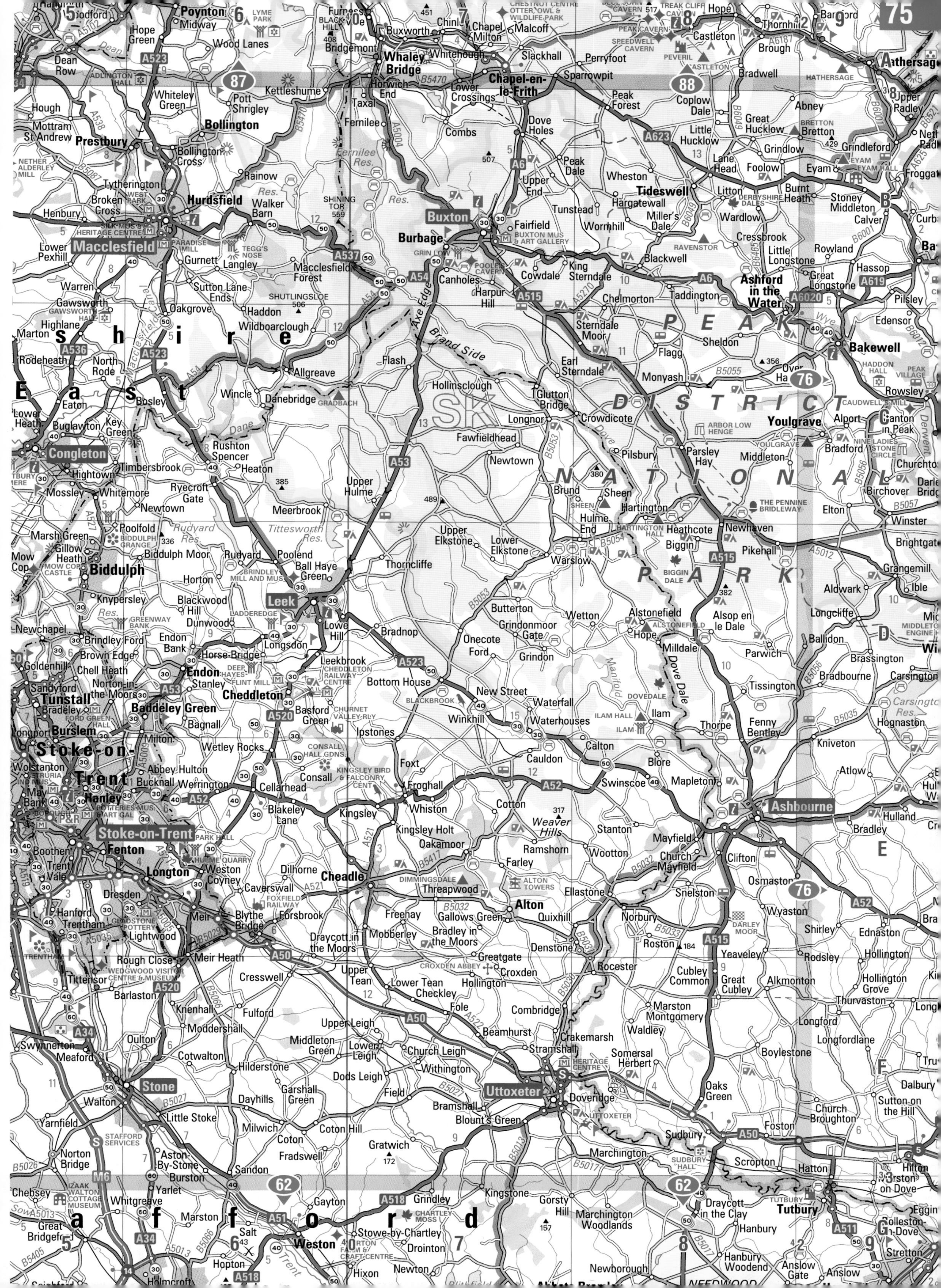
Poynton
Midway
Hope Green
Wood Lanes
Dean Row
Adlington Hall
Whiteley Green
Pott Shrigley
Kettleshume
Bollington
Hough
Mottram St Andrew
Prestbury
Bollington Cross
Rainow
Tytherington
Hurdsfield
Broken Cross
Walker Barn
Henbury
Silk Mus & Heritage Centre
Macclesfield
Lower Pexhill
Gurnett
Langley
Macclesfield Forest
Warren
Sutton Lane Ends
Gawsworth
Oakgrove
Haddon
Shutlingsloe
Wildboarclough
Highlane
Marton
Rodeheath
North Rode
Allgreave
Wincle
Danebridge
Bosley
Gradbach
Eaton
Lower Heath
Buglawton
Key Green
Congleton
Rushton Spencer
Heaton
Timbersbrook
Hightown
Mossley
Whitemore
Ryecroft Gate
Newtown
Meerbrook
Poolfold
Biddulph Grange
Marsh Green
Gillow Heath
Mow Cop
Biddulph
Biddulph Moor
Rudyard
Rudyard Res.
Tittesworth Res.
Poolend
Ball Haye Green
Horton
Knypersley
Blackwood Hill
Dunwood
Leek
Newchapel
Brindley Ford
Brown Edge
Endon Bank
Horse Bridge
Longsdon
Goldenhill
Chell Heath
Norton-in-the-Moors
Endon
Stanley
Cheddleton
Sandyford
Tunstall
Bradeley
Baddeley Green
Burslem
Bagnall
Basford Green
Stoke-on-Trent
Milton
Wetley Rocks
Abbey Hulton
Bucknall
Werrington
Cellarhead
Wolstanton
Hanley
Blakeley Lane
Fenton
Longton
Weston Coyney
Boothen
Trent Vale
Caverswall
Dresden
Hanford
Trentham
Meir
Blythe Bridge
Lightwood
Rough Close
Meir Heath
Tittensor
Barlaston
Cresswell
Forsbrook
Knenhall
Fulford
Moddershall
Oulton
Swynnerton
Meaford
Cotwalton
Hilderstone
Stone
Walton
Yarnfield
Little Stoke
Dayhills
Garshall Green
Milwich
Coton
Stafford Services
Norton Bridge
Aston-By-Stone
Burston
Sandon
Fradswell
Chebsey
Yarlet
Whitgreave
Marston
Great Bridgeford
Salt
Weston
Hopton
Hixon
Stowe-by-Chartley
Drointon
Newton
Gayton
Grindley
Chartley Moss
Kingstone
Gratwich
Coton Hill
Uttoxeter
Bramshall
Blount's Green
Field
Dods Leigh
Lower Leigh
Middleton Green
Upper Leigh
Church Leigh
Withington
Upper Tean
Lower Tean
Checkley
Fole
Beamhurst
Hollington
Croxden
Croxden Abbey
Greatgate
Draycott in the Moors
Mobberley
Bradley in the Moors
Freehay
Cheadle
Dilhorne
Threapwood
Alton
Alton Towers
Gallows Green
Quixhill
Denstone
Rocester
Stramshall
Crakemarsh
Combridge
Doveridge
Somersal Herbert
Marchington
Marchington Woodlands
Gorsty Hill
Draycott in the Clay
Hanbury
Hanbury Woodend
Newborough
Anslow
Anslow Gate
Tutbury
Rolleston-on-Dove
Stretton
Hatton
Hilton
Marston on Dove
Scropton
Sudbury
Sudbury Hall
Foston
Church Broughton
Sutton on the Hill
Dalbury
Boylestone
Longford
Longfordlane
Thurvaston
Hollington Grove
Alkmonton
Great Cubley
Cubley Common
Marston Montgomery
Waldley
Roston
Norbury
Ellastone
Snelston
Wyaston
Osmaston
Clifton
Church Mayfield
Mayfield
Ashbourne
Shirley
Ednaston
Yeaveley
Rodsley
Hollington
Bradley
Hulland
Atlow
Kniveton
Hognaston
Carsington
Carsington Res.
Bradbourne
Tissington
Fenny Bentley
Thorpe
Mapleton
Blore
Ilam
Ilam Hall
Dove Dale
Dovedale
Milldale
Hope
Alstonefield
Wetton
Grindon
Grindonmoor Gate
Butterton
Onecote
Ford
Bradnop
Lowe Hill
Leekbrook
Bottom House
New Street
Winkhill
Waterfall
Waterhouses
Calton
Cauldon
Ipstones
Foxt
Consall
Froghall
Kingsley
Whiston
Kingsley Holt
Oakamoor
Cotton
Weaver Hills
Ramshorn
Farley
Wootton
Stanton
Swinscoe
Parwich
Alsop en le Dale
Ballidon
Brassington
Longcliffe
Aldwark
Grangemill
Ible
Brightgate
Pikehall
Newhaven
Biggin
Heathcote
Hartington
Hulme End
Sheen
Brund
Warslow
Upper Elkstone
Lower Elkstone
Thorncliffe
Upper Hulme
Newtown
Fawfieldhead
Longnor
Crowdicote
Glutton Bridge
Hollinsclough
Flash
Earl Sterndale
Pilsbury
Parsley Hay
Arbor Low Henge
Middleton
Youlgrave
Alport
Bradford
Birchover
Elton
Winster
Stanton in Peak
Rowsley
Bakewell
Over Haddon
Monyash
Flagg
Sheldon
Sterndale Moor
Chelmorton
Taddington
Ashford in the Water
Great Longstone
Little Longstone
Hassop
Rowland
Pilsley
Edensor
Cressbrook
Wardlow
Litton
Tideswell
Miller's Dale
Wormhill
Blackwell
King Sterndale
Cowdale
Harpur Hill
Canholes
Burbage
Buxton
Fairfield
Tunstead
Hargatewall
Wheston
Peak Dale
Upper End
Dove Holes
Combs
Chapel-en-le-Frith
Sparrowpit
Perryfoot
Slackhall
Chapel Milton
Malcoff
Chinley
Buxworth
Bridgemont
Whaley Bridge
Whitehough
Horwich End
Taxal
Fernilee
Lower Crossings
Peak Forest
Castleton
Hope
Bradwell
Brough
Thornhill
Bamford
Hathersage
Abney
Upper Padley
Great Hucklow
Little Hucklow
Bretton
Grindleford
Grindlow
Foolow
Eyam
Lane Head
Stoney Middleton
Calver
Froggatt
Burnt Heath
Curbar
Coplow Dale
Axe Edge
Brand Side
Shining Tor
Cheshire
East
Stafford
PEAK DISTRICT NATIONAL PARK
SK

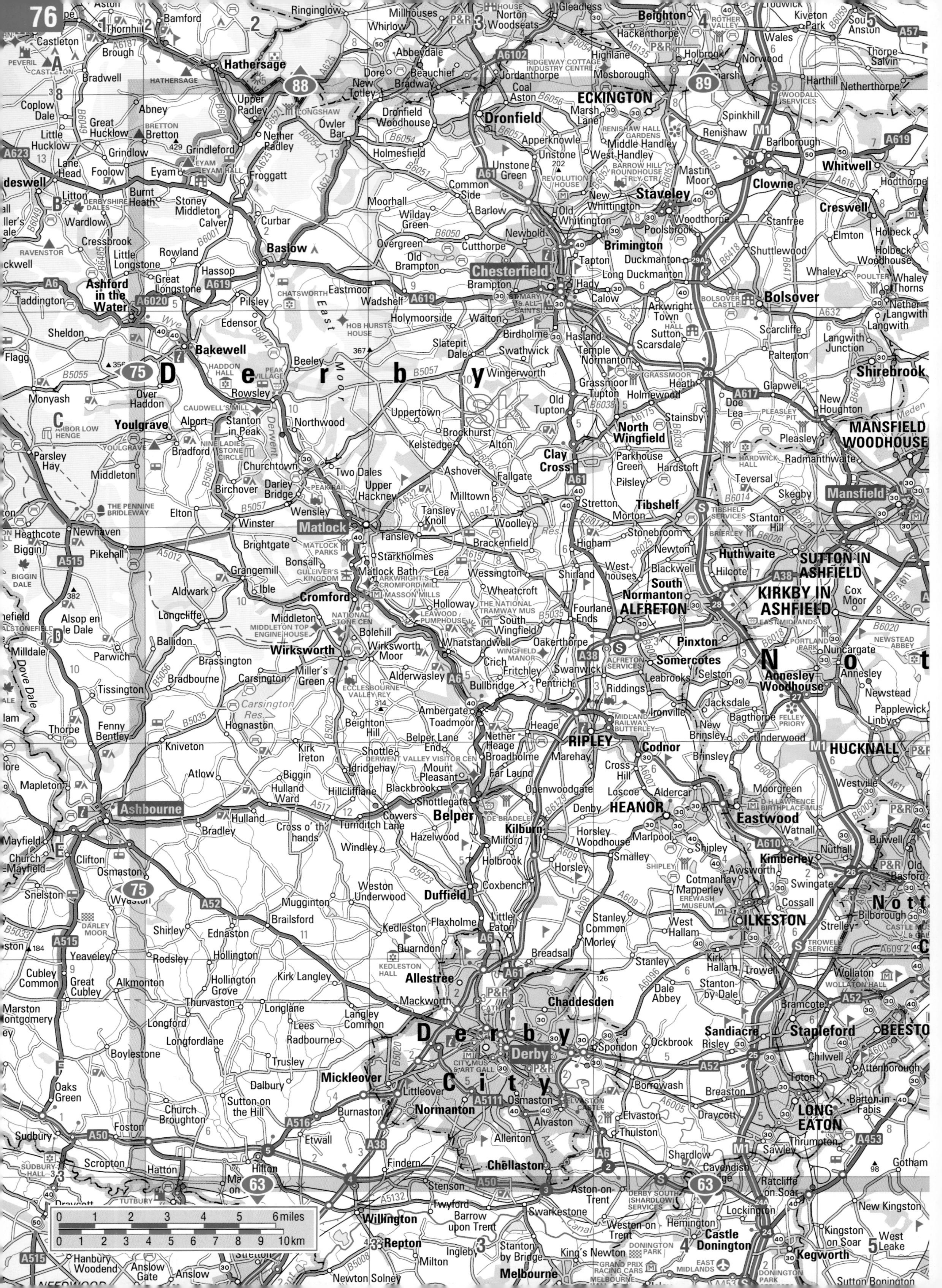

Derby
Derby City
Nott
SK
Castleton
Brough
Hathersage
Bamford
Thornhill
Ringinglow
Millhouses
Whirlow
Norton
Woodseats
Gleadless
Beighton
Hackenthorpe
Kiveton Park
South Anston
Wales
Thorpe Salvin
Highlane
Mosborough
Holbrook
Norwood
Harthill
Netherthorpe
Abbeydale
Dore
Beauchief
Bradway
Jordanthorpe
Coal Aston
ECKINGTON
Marsh Lane
Spinkhill
Renishaw
Barlborough
Whitwell
Clowne
Creswell
Hodthorpe
Bradwell
Abney
Upper Padley
Longshaw
Owler Bar
Nether Padley
Totley
Dronfield Woodhouse
Dronfield
Apperknowle
Unstone
West Handley
Middle Handley
Mastin Moor
Staveley
Coplow Dale
Great Hucklow
Little Hucklow
Bretton
Grindleford
Grindlow
Foolow
Eyam
Froggatt
Holmesfield
Unstone Green
Common Side
New Whittington
Old Whittington
Woodthorpe
Poolsbrook
Stanfree
Elmton
Holbeck
Holbeck Woodhouse
Lane Head
Litton
Wardlow
Stoney Middleton
Calver
Curbar
Burnt Heath
Moorhall
Barlow
Wilday Green
Overgreen
Cutthorpe
Old Brampton
Newbold
Brimington
Tapton
Duckmanton
Long Duckmanton
Shuttlewood
Whaley
Whaley Thorns
Nether Langwith
Langwith
Cressbrook
Little Longstone
Rowland
Hassop
Great Longstone
Baslow
Chesterfield
Brampton
Hady
Calow
Bolsover
Ashford in the Water
Taddington
Pilsley
Eastmoor
Wadshelf
Chatsworth
Edensor
Holymoorside
Walton
Birdholme
Arkwright Town
Sutton Scarsdale
Scarcliffe
Langwith Junction
Sheldon
Bakewell
Hob Hursts House
Slatepit Dale
Swathwick
Hasland
Temple Normanton
Palterton
Shirebrook
Flagg
Haddon Hall
Beeley
Wingerworth
Grassmoor
Heath
Glapwell
Monyash
Over Haddon
Rowsley
Tupton
Old Tupton
Holmewood
Doe Lea
New Houghton
Arbor Low Henge
Youlgrave
Alport
Stanton in Peak
Northwood
Uppertown
Brockhurst
Alton
North Wingfield
Stainsby
Pleasley
MANSFIELD WOODHOUSE
Parsley Hay
Bradford
Middleton
Churchtown
Two Dales
Kelstedge
Ashover
Fallgate
Clay Cross
Parkhouse Green
Hardstoft
Radmanthwaite
Pilsley
Teversal
Skegby
Mansfield
Birchover
Darley Bridge
Upper Hackney
Milltown
Elton
Wensley
Tansley Knoll
Stretton
Tibshelf
Morton
Stanton Hill
Winster
Matlock
Tansley
Woolley
Stonebroom
Newton
Huthwaite
SUTTON IN ASHFIELD
Heathcote
Newhaven
Biggin
Pikehall
Brightgate
Starkholmes
Brackenfield
Higham
Bonsall
Grangemill
Matlock Bath
Lea
Wessington
Shirland
West houses
Blackwell
Hilcote
South Normanton
KIRKBY IN ASHFIELD
Cox Moor
Aldwark
Ible
Cromford
Wheatcroft
Holloway
Fourlane Ends
ALFRETON
Alsop en le Dale
Longcliffe
Middleton
Bolehill
South Wingfield
Oakerthorpe
Pinxton
Nuncargate
Ballidon
Wirksworth
Wirksworth Moor
Whatstandwell
Crich
Fritchley
Swanwick
Somercotes
Annesley
Annesley Woodhouse
Milldale
Parwich
Brassington
Carsington
Miller's Green
Alderwasley
Bullbridge
Pentrich
Riddings
Leabrooks
Selston
Newstead
Tissington
Bradbourne
Carsington Res.
Ambergate
Toadmoor
Ironville
Jacksdale
Bagthorpe
Papplewick
Linby
Thorpe
Fenny Bentley
Hognaston
Beighton Hill
Heage
Nether Heage
RIPLEY
Codnor
New Brinsley
Underwood
HUCKNALL
Kniveton
Kirk Ireton
Shottle
Belper Lane End
Broadholme
Marehay
Cross Hill
Brinsley
Mapleton
Atlow
Biggin
Hulland Ward
Idridgehay
Mount Pleasant
Far Laund
Loscoe
Aldercar
Moorgreen
Westville
Ashbourne
Hillcliffane
Blackbrook
Shottlegate
Openwoodgate
Denby
HEANOR
Eastwood
Watnall
Hulland
Bradley
Cross o' th' hands
Turnditch
Cowers Lane
Belper
Kilburn
Horsley Woodhouse
Marlpool
Bulwell
Mayfield
Church Mayfield
Clifton
Osmaston
Windley
Hazelwood
Milford
Holbrook
Horsley
Smalley
Shipley
Kimberley
Nuthall
Awsworth
Swingate
Old Basford
Snelston
Wyaston
Weston Underwood
Duffield
Coxbench
Cotmanhay
Mapperley
Cossall
Mugginton
Brailsford
Flaxholme
Little Eaton
Stanley Common
Morley
West Hallam
ILKESTON
Strelley
Bilborough
Shirley
Ednaston
Kedleston
Quarndon
Breadsall
Stanley
Kirk Hallam
Trowell
Yeaveley
Rodsley
Hollington
Kedleston Hall
Allestree
Wollaton
Cubley Common
Great Cubley
Alkmonton
Hollington Grove
Kirk Langley
Dale Abbey
Stanton-by-Dale
Thurvaston
Longlane
Mackworth
Chaddesden
Marston Montgomery
Longford
Lees
Langley Common
Bramcote
Stapleford
BEESTON
Longfordlane
Radbourne
Spondon
Ockbrook
Sandiacre
Risley
Boylestone
Trusley
Chilwell
Attenborough
Mickleover
Littleover
Dalbury
Borrowash
Toton
Oaks Green
Sutton on the Hill
Normanton
Osmaston
Elvaston
Breaston
Barton in Fabis
Church Broughton
Burnaston
Alvaston
Thulston
Draycott
LONG EATON
Foston
Sudbury
Etwall
Allenton
Thrumpton
Sawley
Scropton
Hatton
Hilton
Findern
Chellaston
Shardlow
Cavendish Bridge
Gotham
Stenson
Aston-on-Trent
Ratcliffe on Soar
Twyford
Barrow upon Trent
Swarkestone
Lockington
New Kingston
Willington
Weston-on-Trent
Hemington
Castle Donington
Kingston on Soar
West Leake
Repton
Ingleby
Stanton by Bridge
King's Newton
Kegworth
Milton
Melbourne
Hanbury Woodend
Anslow Gate
Anslow
Newton Solney
Sutton Bonington
Peak District National Park
Matlock Parks
Gulliver's Kingdom
Masson Mills
Arkwright's Cromford Mill
National Stone Cen
Middleton Top Engine House
Leawood Pumphouse
The National Tramway Mus
Wingfield Manor
Ecclesbourne Valley Rly
Derwent Valley Visitor Cen
Midland Railway Butterley
Felley Priory
D.H. Lawrence Birthplace Mus
Erewash Museum
Wollaton Hall
Elvaston Castle
Donington Park
East Midlands
Derby South (Shardlow) Services
Tibshelf Services
Alfreton Services
Trowell Services
Woodall Services
Hardwick Hall
Bolsover Castle
Sutton Hall
Renishaw Hall Gardens
Barrow Hill Roundhouse Rly Ctr
Revolution House
Ridgeway Cottage Industry Centre
Caudwell's Mill
Nine Ladies Stone Circle
The Pennine Bridleway
Peveril Castle
Peak Village
Peak Rail
City Mus & Art Gall
Kedleston Hall
Darley Moor
Sudbury Hall
Tutbury
Carsington Res.
Dove Dale
East Moor
Derwent
Wye
0 1 2 3 4 5 6 miles
0 1 2 3 4 5 6 7 8 9 10 km

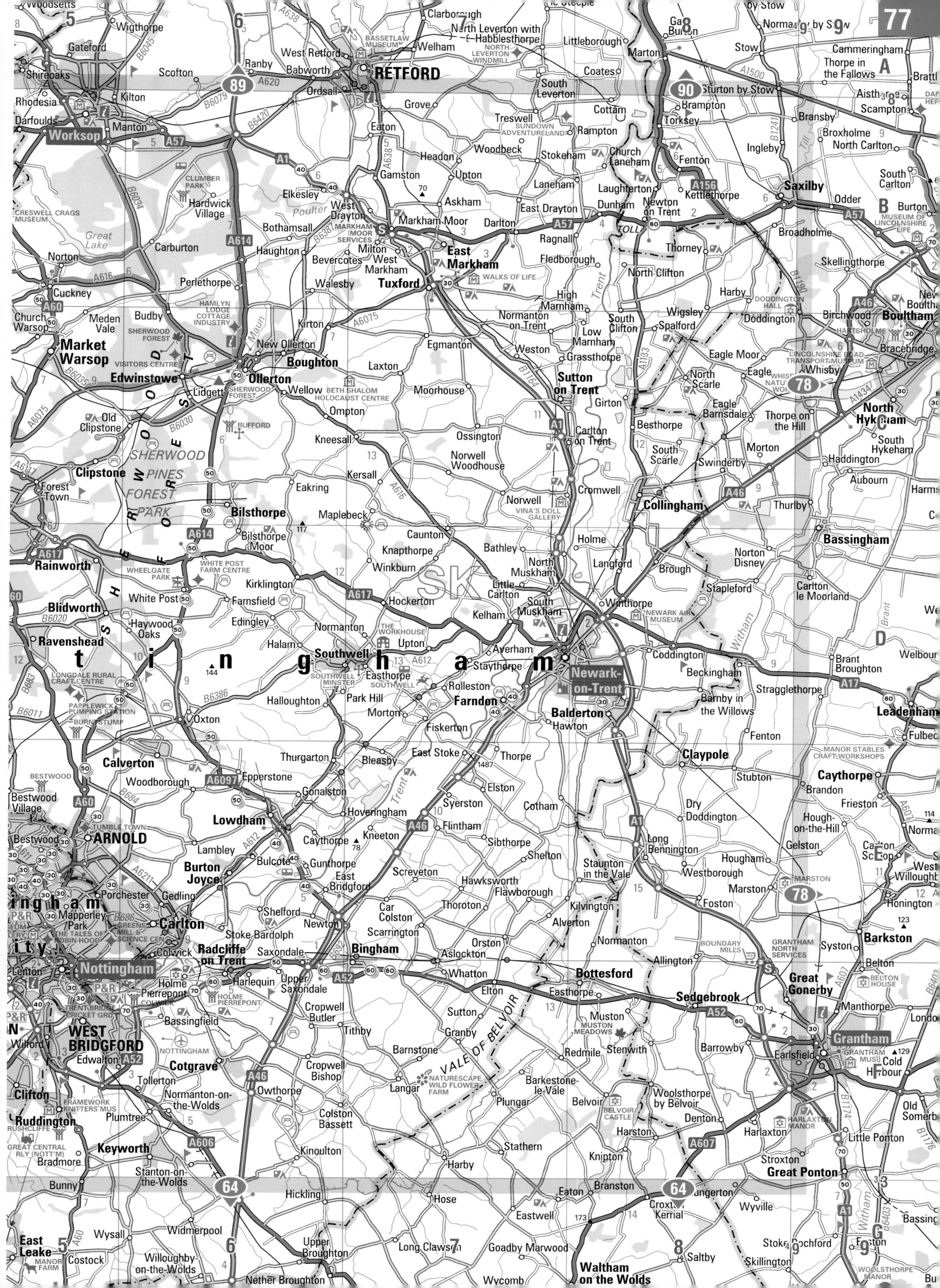

RETFORD
Worksop
Clarborough
North Leverton with Habblesthorpe
Littleborough
Marton
Stow
Normanby by Stow
Cammeringham
Thorpe in the Fallows
Wigthorpe
Gateford
Shireoaks
Rhodesia
Darfoulds
Kilton
Manton
Scofton
Ranby
West Retford
Babworth
Ordsall
Welham
BASSETLAW MUSEUM
NORTH LEVERTON WINDMILL
South Leverton
Coates
Sturton by Stow
Aisthorpe
Scampton
Brampton
Torksey
Bransby
Broxholme
North Carlton
Grove
Treswell
SUNDOWN ADVENTURELAND
Rampton
Cottam
Eaton
Headon
Woodbeck
Stokeham
Church Laneham
Fenton
Ingleby
South Carlton
Gamston
Elkesley
Upton
Laneham
Laughterton
Kettlethorpe
Saxilby
Odder
Burton
CLUMBER PARK
Hardwick Village
CRESWELL CRAGS MUSEUM
Great Lake
Carburton
West Drayton
Poulter
Askham
Markham Moor
Darlton
East Drayton
Dunham
Newton on Trent
MUSEUM OF LINCOLNSHIRE LIFE
Bothamsall
MARKHAM MOOR SERVICES
Ragnall
Broadholme
Norton
Haughton
Milton
East Markham
Thorney
Skellingthorpe
Bevercotes
West Markham
Fledborough
North Clifton
Tuxford
WALKS OF LIFE
Cuckney
Perlethorpe
Walesby
Harby
DODDINGTON HALL
Church Warsop
Meden Vale
Budby
HAMLYN LODGE COTTAGE INDUSTRY
Kirton
High Marnham
Wigsley
Doddington
Birchwood
Boultham
SHERWOOD FOREST
Normanton on Trent
South Clifton
Spalford
HARTSHOLME
Market Warsop
New Ollerton
Egmanton
Low Marnham
Weston
Eagle Moor
LINCOLNSHIRE ROAD TRANSPORT MUSEUM
Bracebridge
VISITORS CENTRE
Boughton
Grassthorpe
Edwinstowe
Ollerton
Laxton
North Scarle
Eagle
Whisby
Lidgett
SHERWOOD FOREST
Wellow
BETH SHALOM HOLOCAUST CENTRE
Moorhouse
Sutton on Trent
Girton
Eagle Barnsdale
Thorpe on the Hill
North Hykeham
Old Clipstone
Ompton
Besthorpe
RUFFORD
Kneesall
Ossington
Carlton on Trent
South Scarle
Morton
South Hykeham
SHERWOOD PINES FOREST PARK
Norwell Woodhouse
Swinderby
Haddington
Clipstone
Forest Town
Kersall
Aubourn
Eakring
Cromwell
Norwell
Collingham
Thurlby
VINA'S DOLL GALLERY
Bilsthorpe
Maplebeck
Bilsthorpe Moor
Caunton
Holme
Bassingham
Rainworth
Knapthorpe
Bathley
Norton Disney
WHITE POST FARM CENTRE
WHEELGATE PARK
Winkburn
North Muskham
Langford
Brough
Kirklington
Little Carlton
Stapleford
Carlton le Moorland
Bildworth
White Post
Farnsfield
Hockerton
South Muskham
Winthorpe
Kelham
NEWARK AIR MUSEUM
Haywood Oaks
Edingley
Ravenshead
Normanton
THE WORKHOUSE
Halam
Upton
Averham
Coddington
Brant Broughton
Southwell
Staythorpe
Newark-on-Trent
Beckingham
LONGDALE RURAL CRAFT CENTRE
SOUTHWELL MINSTER
Easthorpe
Rolleston
Stragglethorpe
PAPPLEWICK PUMPING STATION
Halloughton
Park Hill
Farndon
Barnby in the Willows
Leadenham
BURNTSTUMP
Oxton
Morton
Balderton
Hawton
Fiskerton
Fenton
Fulbeck
MANOR STABLES CRAFT WORKSHOPS
Thurgarton
East Stoke
Thorpe
Claypole
Calverton
Bleasby
BESTWOOD
Woodborough
Epperstone
Stubton
Caythorpe
Elston
Brandon
Gonalston
Bestwood Village
Syerston
Cotham
Dry Doddington
Frieston
Hoveringham
Lowdham
Flintham
Hough-on-the-Hill
ARNOLD
TUMBLE TOWN
Caythorpe
Kneeton
Sibthorpe
Long Bennington
Gelston
Carlton Scroop
Lambley
Shelton
Hougham
Burton Joyce
Bulcote
Gunthorpe
Screveton
Staunton in the Vale
Westborough
West Willoughby
Porchester
East Bridgford
Hawksworth
Marston
MARSTON
Gedling
Flawborough
Foston
Honington
Mapperley Park
Carlton
Car Colston
Thoroton
Kilvington
Shelford
Newton
Alverton
Barkston
THE TALES OF ROBIN HOOD
GREEN'S MILL & SCIENCE CENTRE
Stoke Bardolph
Scarrington
Orston
Normanton
BOUNDARY MILLS
GRANTHAM NORTH SERVICES
Syston
Colwick
Radcliffe on Trent
Saxondale
Bingham
Aslockton
Allington
Nottingham
Belton
Lenton
Holme Pierrepont
Harlequin
Upper Saxondale
Whatton
Bottesford
Great Gonerby
BELTON HOUSE
TRENT BRIDGE CRICKET GRD
HOLME PIERREPONT
Elton
Easthorpe
Sedgebrook
Manthorpe
Bassingfield
Cropwell Butler
Sutton
Muston
MUSTON MEADOWS
WEST BRIDGFORD
Tithby
Granby
Stenwith
Grantham
Wilford
NOTTINGHAM
Barnstone
Redmile
Barrowby
Earlsfield
GRANTHAM MUSEUM
Cold Harbour
Edwalton
Cotgrave
VALE OF BELVOIR
Cropwell Bishop
NATURESCAPE WILD FLOWER FARM
Barkestone-le-Vale
Tollerton
Clifton
Owthorpe
Langar
Plungar
Belvoir
Woolsthorpe by Belvoir
Normanton-on-the-Wolds
FRAMEWORK KNITTERS' MUS
BELVOIR CASTLE
Old Somerby
Ruddington
Plumtree
Colston Bassett
Denton
HARLAXTON MANOR
Harlaxton
RUSHCLIFFE GREAT CENTRAL RLY (NOTT'M)
Keyworth
Kinoulton
Harston
Little Ponton
Bradmore
Stathern
Knipton
Stroxton
Stanton-on-the-Wolds
Harby
Great Ponton
Bunny
Hickling
Eaton
Branston
Croxton Kerrial
Hungerton
Wyville
Hose
Eastwell
Widmerpool
Wysall
East Leake
Costock
MANOR FARM
Upper Broughton
Long Clawson
Goadby Marwood
Saltby
Stoke Rochford
Easton
Bassingham
Willoughby-on-the-Wolds
Nether Broughton
Wycomb
Waltham on the Wolds
Skillington
WOOLSTHORPE MANOR
SK
Nottingham
Trent
Witham
Brant
Maun
Till

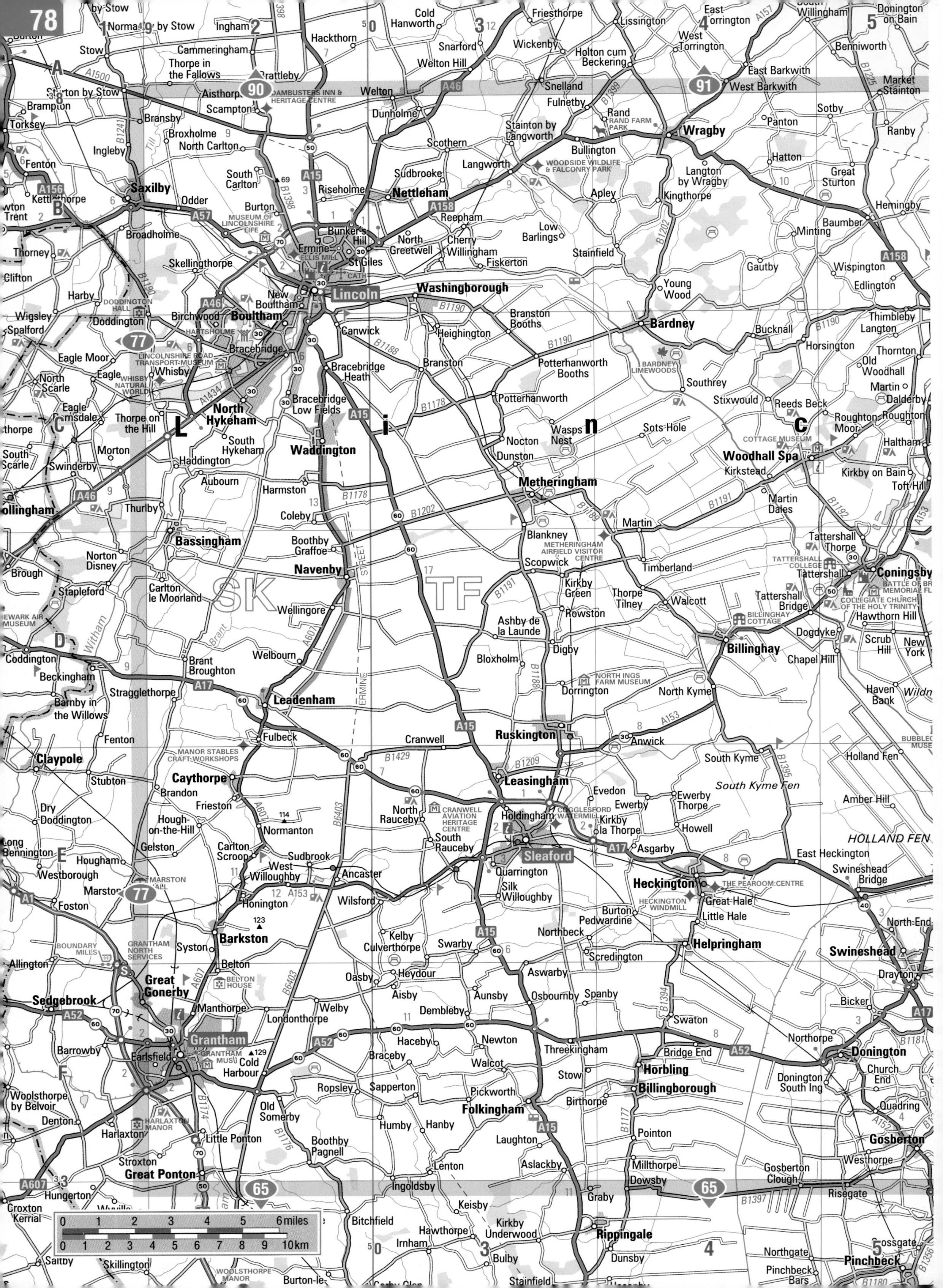
Stow
Ingham
Cold Hanworth
Friesthorpe
Lissington
East Torrington
South Willingham
Donington on Bain
Cammeringham
Hackthorn
Snarford
Wickenby
Holton cum Beckering
West Torrington
Benniworth
Thorpe in the Fallows
Brattleby
Welton Hill
East Barkwith
West Barkwith
Market Stainton
Sturton by Stow
Aisthorpe
90
DAMBUSTERS INN & HERITAGE CENTRE
Welton
A46
Snelland
91
Brampton
Scampton
Dunholme
Fulnetby
Rand
RAND FARM PARK
Sotby
Torksey
Bransby
Stainton by Langworth
Wragby
Panton
Ranby
Broxholme
North Carlton
Scothern
Bullington
Ingleby
Langworth
WOODSIDE WILDLIFE & FALCONRY PARK
Hatton
Fenton
South Carlton
Sudbrooke
Langton by Wragby
Great Sturton
Saxilby
Riseholme
Nettleham
Apley
Kingthorpe
Kettlethorpe
Odder
Burton
A158
Hemingby
Newton on Trent
A57
MUSEUM OF LINCOLNSHIRE LIFE
Reepham
Low Barlings
Baumber
Broadholme
Bunker's Hill
North Greetwell
Cherry Willingham
Minting
Thorney
Ermine
ELLIS MILL
St Giles
Fiskerton
Stainfield
Skellingthorpe
CATH
Gautby
Wispington
Clifton
A158
Harby
Lincoln
Washingborough
Young Wood
Edlington
DODDINGTON HALL
New Boultham
B1190
Branston Booths
Thimbleby
Wigsley
A46
Birchwood
Boultham
Canwick
Heighington
Bardney
Bucknall
Langton
Spalford
Doddington
HARTSHOLME
77
Bracebridge
B1188
B1190
Horsington
Thornton
LINCOLNSHIRE ROAD TRANSPORT MUSEUM
Eagle Moor
Whisby
Bracebridge Heath
Branston
Potterhanworth Booths
BARDNEY LIMEWOODS
Old Woodhall
North Scarle
Eagle
WHISBY NATURAL WORLD
Southrey
Martin
Eagle Barnsdale
A1434
Bracebridge Low Fields
B1178
Potterhanworth
Stixwould
Reeds Beck
Dalderby
Thorpe on the Hill
North Hykeham
A15
Roughton Moor
Roughton
L
i
n
Wasps Nest
Sots Hole
C
South Hykeham
Waddington
Nocton
COTTAGE MUSEUM
Haltham
Morton
Woodhall Spa
South Scarle
Swinderby
Haddington
Dunston
Kirkstead
Kirkby on Bain
Aubourn
Metheringham
Toft Hill
A46
Harmston
B1178
Martin Dales
Collingham
Thurlby
Coleby
B1202
B1189
B1191
Martin
B1192
A153
Bassingham
Boothby Graffoe
Blankney
METHERINGHAM AIRFIELD VISITOR CENTRE
Tattershall Thorpe
Norton Disney
TATTERSHALL COLLEGE
Tattershall
Coningsby
Brough
Navenby
STREET
Scopwick
Timberland
BATTLE OF BRITAIN MEMORIAL FLIGHT
Stapleford
Carlton le Moorland
SK
TF
B1191
Kirkby Green
Thorpe Tilney
Walcott
Tattershall Bridge
COLLEGIATE CHURCH OF THE HOLY TRINITY
NEWARK AIR MUSEUM
Wellingore
Rowston
BILLINGHAY COTTAGE
Hawthorn Hill
Witham
Brant
A607
Ashby de la Launde
Dogdyke
Scrub Hill
New York
D
Billinghay
Coddington
Welbourn
Brant Broughton
Bloxholm
Digby
Chapel Hill
Beckingham
A17
B1188
NORTH INGS FARM MUSEUM
Dorrington
North Kyme
Haven Bank
Wildmore
Stragglethorpe
Barnby in the Willows
Leadenham
ERMINE
A15
Ruskington
A153
Fenton
Cranwell
Anwick
BUBBLECAR MUSEUM
MANOR STABLES CRAFT WORKSHOPS
Fulbeck
South Kyme
B1395
Holland Fen
Claypole
B1429
B1209
Stubton
Caythorpe
Leasingham
South Kyme Fen
Brandon
Evedon
Ewerby Thorpe
Amber Hill
Frieston
Ewerby
Dry Doddington
Hough-on-the-Hill
A607
Normanton
B6403
North Rauceby
CRANWELL AVIATION HERITAGE CENTRE
Holdingham
COGGLESFORD WATERMILL
Kirkby la Thorpe
Howell
Long Bennington
Gelston
Carlton Scroop
South Rauceby
Asgarby
HOLLAND FEN
E
Hougham
Sudbrook
Sleaford
A17
East Heckington
Westborough
West Willoughby
Ancaster
Quarrington
Swineshead Bridge
MARSTON HALL
Heckington
THE PEAROOM CENTRE
Marston
77
A153
Silk Willoughby
HECKINGTON WINDMILL
Great Hale
A1
Foston
Honington
Wilsford
Burton Pedwardine
Little Hale
North End
Barkston
Kelby
Culverthorpe
Swarby
Northbeck
Helpringham
BOUNDARY MILLS
GRANTHAM NORTH SERVICES
Syston
A15
Scredington
Swineshead
Allington
Belton
Heydour
Aswarby
Drayton
Great Gonerby
A607
BELTON HOUSE
Oasby
Aisby
Aunsby
Osbournby
Spanby
B1394
Bicker
Sedgebrook
Manthorpe
Welby
Dembleby
A17
A52
Londonthorpe
Swaton
Grantham
A52
Haceby
Newton
Northorpe
Barrowby
GRANTHAM MUSEUM
Cold Harbour
Braceby
Threekingham
Bridge End
A52
Donington
Earlsfield
Walcot
Horbling
Church End
F
Stow
Donington South Ing
Woolsthorpe by Belvoir
B1174
Ropsley
Sapperton
Pickworth
Billingborough
Old Somerby
Birthorpe
Quadring
HARLAXTON MANOR
Folkingham
B1176
Denton
Harlaxton
Humby
Hanby
B1177
Little Ponton
Pointon
Boothby Pagnell
Laughton
Gosberton
Stroxton
Lenton
Aslackby
Millthorpe
Westhorpe
Great Ponton
A607
Hungerton
Dowsby
Gosberton Clough
65
Ingoldsby
Graby
65
B1397
Risegate
Croxton Kerrial
Wyville
Keisby
0 1 2 3 4 5 6 miles
0 1 2 3 4 5 6 7 8 9 10 km
Bitchfield
Kirkby Underwood
Rippingale
Hawthorpe
Irnham
Cossgate
Saltby
Skillington
Bulby
Dunsby
Northgate
Pinchbeck
Pinchbeck Bars
WOOLSTHORPE MANOR
Burton-le-Coggles
Stainfield
B1356
B1180

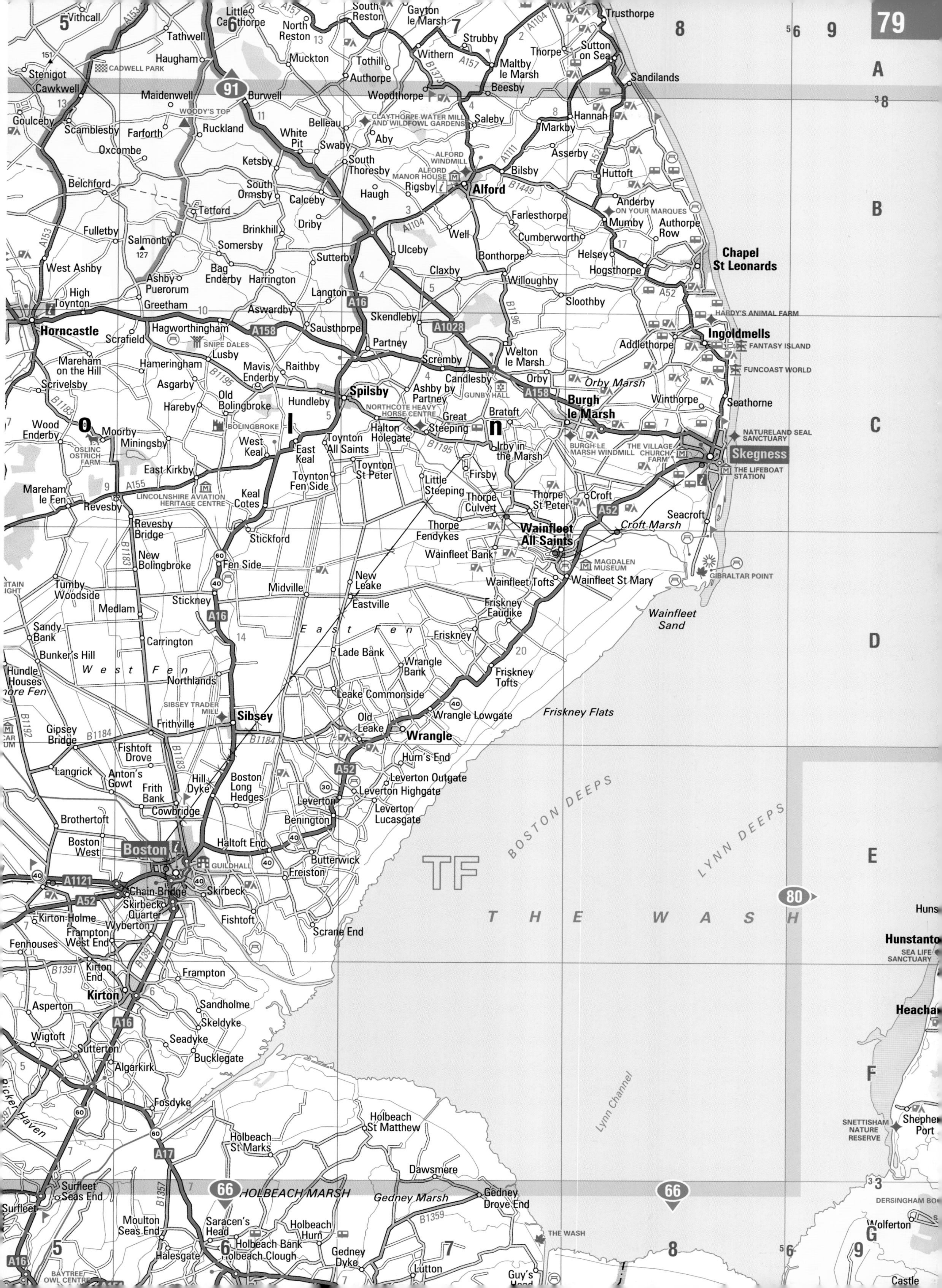
Vithcall
Little Cawthorpe
South Reston
Gayton le Marsh
Trusthorpe
Tathwell
North Reston
Strubby
Thorpe
Sutton on Sea
Haugham
Muckton
Tothill
Withern
Maltby le Marsh
Stenigot
CADWELL PARK
Authorpe
Sandilands
Cawkwell
Maidenwell
Burwell
Woodthorpe
Beesby
WOODY'S TOP
Hannah
Goulceby
CLAYTHORPE WATER MILL AND WILDFOWL GARDENS
Saleby
Scamblesby
Farforth
Ruckland
White Pit
Belleau
Markby
Aby
Oxcombe
Swaby
ALFORD WINDMILL
Asserby
Ketsby
South Thoresby
ALFORD MANOR HOUSE
Bilsby
Huttoft
Belchford
South Ormsby
Rigsby
Alford
Calceby
Haugh
Anderby
ON YOUR MARQUES
Tetford
Farlesthorpe
Mumby
Authorpe Row
Fulletby
Brinkhill
Driby
Well
Salmonby
Somersby
Cumberworth
Ulceby
Helsey
Chapel St Leonards
Sutterby
Bonthorpe
West Ashby
Bag Enderby
Claxby
Hogsthorpe
Ashby Puerorum
Harrington
Willoughby
High Toynton
Langton
Sloothby
Greetham
Aswardby
Skendleby
HARDY'S ANIMAL FARM
Horncastle
Hagworthingham
Sausthorpe
Ingoldmells
Scrafield
SNIPE DALES
Partney
Welton le Marsh
Addlethorpe
FANTASY ISLAND
Mareham on the Hill
Hameringham
Lusby
Scremby
FUNCOAST WORLD
Mavis Enderby
Raithby
Candlesby
Orby
Orby Marsh
Scrivelsby
Asgarby
Ashby by Partney
GUNBY HALL
Spilsby
Old Bolingbroke
Hundleby
Burgh le Marsh
Winthorpe
Seathorne
Hareby
NORTHCOTE HEAVY HORSE CENTRE
Great Steeping
Bratoft
Wood Enderby
Moorby
BOLINGBROKE
Halton Holegate
NATURELAND SEAL SANCTUARY
Miningsby
West Keal
East Keal
Toynton All Saints
Irby in the Marsh
BURGH LE MARSH WINDMILL
THE VILLAGE CHURCH FARM
Skegness
OSLINC OSTRICH FARM
East Kirkby
Toynton St Peter
Firsby
THE LIFEBOAT STATION
Toynton Fen Side
Little Steeping
Mareham le Fen
LINCOLNSHIRE AVIATION HERITAGE CENTRE
Keal Cotes
Thorpe Culvert
Thorpe St Peter
Croft
Revesby
Seacroft
Revesby Bridge
Thorpe Fendykes
Wainfleet All Saints
Croft Marsh
Stickford
New Bolingbroke
Wainfleet Bank
MAGDALEN MUSEUM
Fen Side
GIBRALTAR POINT
Tumby Woodside
New Leake
Wainfleet Tofts
Wainfleet St Mary
Midville
Stickney
Eastville
Friskney Eaudike
Wainfleet Sand
Medlam
Sandy Bank
East Fen
Friskney
Carrington
Bunker's Hill
Lade Bank
Wrangle Bank
West Fen
Hundle Houses
Northlands
Friskney Tofts
Leake Commonside
SIBSEY TRADER MILL
Sibsey
Wrangle Lowgate
Friskney Flats
Gipsey Bridge
Frithville
Old Leake
Wrangle
Fishtoft Drove
Hurn's End
Langrick
Anton's Gowt
Leverton Outgate
Hill Dyke
Boston Long Hedges
Leverton Highgate
Frith Bank
Leverton
BOSTON DEEPS
Cowbridge
Leverton Lucasgate
Brothertoft
Benington
LYNN DEEPS
Boston West
Boston
Haltoft End
Butterwick
TF
GUILDHALL
Freiston
Chain Bridge
Skirbeck
Skirbeck Quarter
THE WASH
Kirton Holme
Wyberton
Fishtoft
Hunstanton
Frampton West End
Scrane End
Fenhouses
SEA LIFE SANCTUARY
Kirton End
Frampton
Kirton
Sandholme
Heacham
Asperton
Skeldyke
Wigtoft
Seadyke
Sutterton
Bucklegate
Algarkirk
Fosdyke
Lynn Channel
Holbeach St Matthew
SNETTISHAM NATURE RESERVE
Shepherds Port
Holbeach St Marks
Dawsmere
Surfleet Seas End
HOLBEACH MARSH
Gedney Marsh
Gedney Drove End
DERSINGHAM BOG
Surfleet
Moulton Seas End
Saracen's Head
Holbeach Hurn
Holbeach Bank
THE WASH
Wolferton
Halesgate
Holbeach Clough
Gedney Dyke
Lutton
Guy's Head
Castle
BAYTREE OWL CENTRE

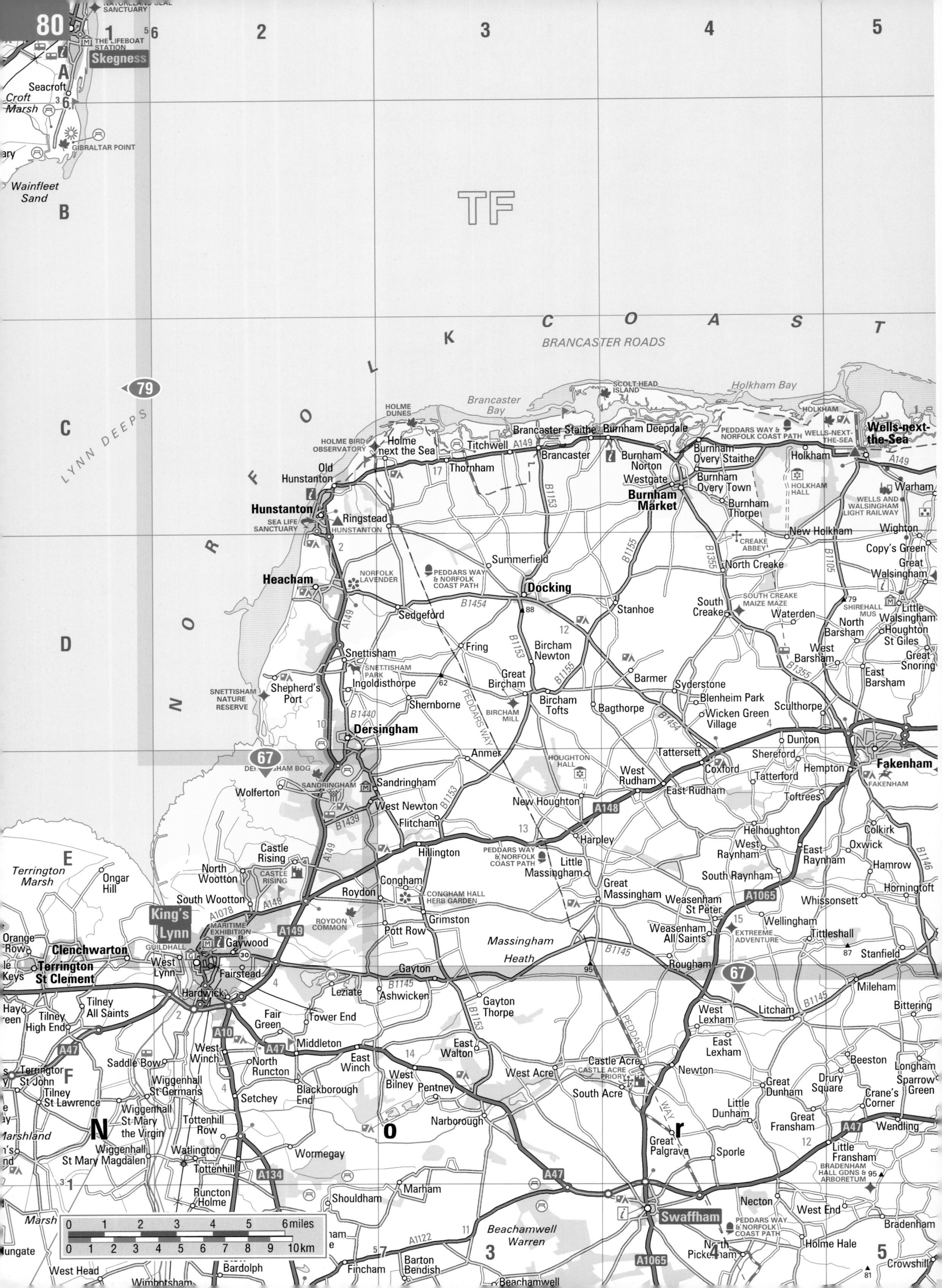

NATURELAND SEAL SANCTUARY
THE LIFEBOAT STATION
Skegness
Seacroft
Croft Marsh
GIBRALTAR POINT
Wainfleet Sand
TF
LYNN DEEPS
79
N O R F O L K C O A S T
BRANCASTER ROADS
SCOLT HEAD ISLAND
Holkham Bay
Brancaster Bay
HOLME DUNES
HOLME BIRD OBSERVATORY
Holme next the Sea
Titchwell
Brancaster Staithe
Burnham Deepdale
PEDDARS WAY & NORFOLK COAST PATH
HOLKHAM
WELLS-NEXT-THE-SEA
Wells-next-the-Sea
Old Hunstanton
Thornham
Brancaster
Burnham Norton
Burnham Overy Staithe
Holkham
Warham
Burnham Westgate
Burnham Overy Town
HOLKHAM HALL
WELLS AND WALSINGHAM LIGHT RAILWAY
Burnham Market
Burnham Thorpe
Hunstanton
SEA LIFE SANCTUARY
Ringstead
HUNSTANTON
New Holkham
Wighton
CREAKE ABBEY
Copy's Green
Summerfield
North Creake
Great Walsingham
NORFOLK LAVENDER
PEDDARS WAY & NORFOLK COAST PATH
Heacham
Docking
South Creake
SOUTH CREAKE MAIZE MAZE
Stanhoe
Waterden
SHIREHALL MUS
Little Walsingham
North Barsham
Houghton St Giles
Sedgeford
Fring
Bircham Newton
West Barsham
Great Snoring
Snettisham
SNETTISHAM PARK
Great Bircham
Barmer
East Barsham
Ingoldisthorpe
Syderstone
SNETTISHAM NATURE RESERVE
Shepherd's Port
Blenheim Park
Bircham Tofts
Shernborne
BIRCHAM MILL
Bagthorpe
Wicken Green Village
Sculthorpe
PEDDARS WAY
Dersingham
Dunton
67
DERSINGHAM BOG
Anmer
HOUGHTON HALL
Tattersett
Shereford
Coxford
Fakenham
West Rudham
Hempton
Sandringham
SANDRINGHAM
Tatterford
Wolferton
East Rudham
FAKENHAM
West Newton
New Houghton
Toftrees
Flitcham
Harpley
Helhoughton
Colkirk
Castle Rising
Hillington
West Raynham
East Raynham
Oxwick
PEDDARS WAY & NORFOLK COAST PATH
Little Massingham
Hamrow
Terrington Marsh
Ongar Hill
North Wootton
CASTLE RISING
South Raynham
Congham
Great Massingham
Horningtoft
Roydon
CONGHAM HALL HERB GARDEN
Weasenham St Peter
South Wootton
Whissonsett
King's Lynn
MARITIME EXHIBITION
ROYDON COMMON
Grimston
Wellingham
Pott Row
Weasenham All Saints
EXTREEME ADVENTURE
Tittleshall
GUILDHALL
Gaywood
Massingham Heath
Stanfield
Orange Row
Clenchwarton
Terrington St Clement
West Lynn
Fairstead
Gayton
Rougham
Hardwick
Leziate
Ashwicken
Mileham
Gayton Thorpe
Tilney All Saints
West Lexham
Litcham
Bittering
Tilney High End
Fair Green
Tower End
East Lexham
PEDDARS
West Winch
Middleton
East Walton
Castle Acre
Beeston
Saddle Bow
East Winch
CASTLE ACRE PRIORY
Newton
Longham
North Runcton
West Acre
Great Dunham
Drury Square
Sparrow Green
Terrington St John
Wiggenhall St Germans
West Bilney
Pentney
Tilney St Lawrence
Blackborough End
South Acre
Crane's Corner
Setchey
Little Dunham
WAY
Wiggenhall St Mary the Virgin
Tottenhill Row
Great Fransham
Wendling
Marshland
Narborough
Great Palgrave
Little Fransham
Wiggenhall St Mary Magdalen
Watlington
Wormegay
Sporle
BRADENHAM HALL GDNS & ARBORETUM
Tottenhill
Runcton Holme
Shouldham
Marham
Necton
West End
Swaffham
Bradenham
Marsh
Beachamwell Warren
PEDDARS WAY & NORFOLK COAST PATH
North Pickenham
Holme Hale
Barton Bendish
Fincham
Crowshill
West Head
Bardolph
Wimbotsham
Beachamwell
0 1 2 3 4 5 6 miles
0 1 2 3 4 5 6 7 8 9 10 km

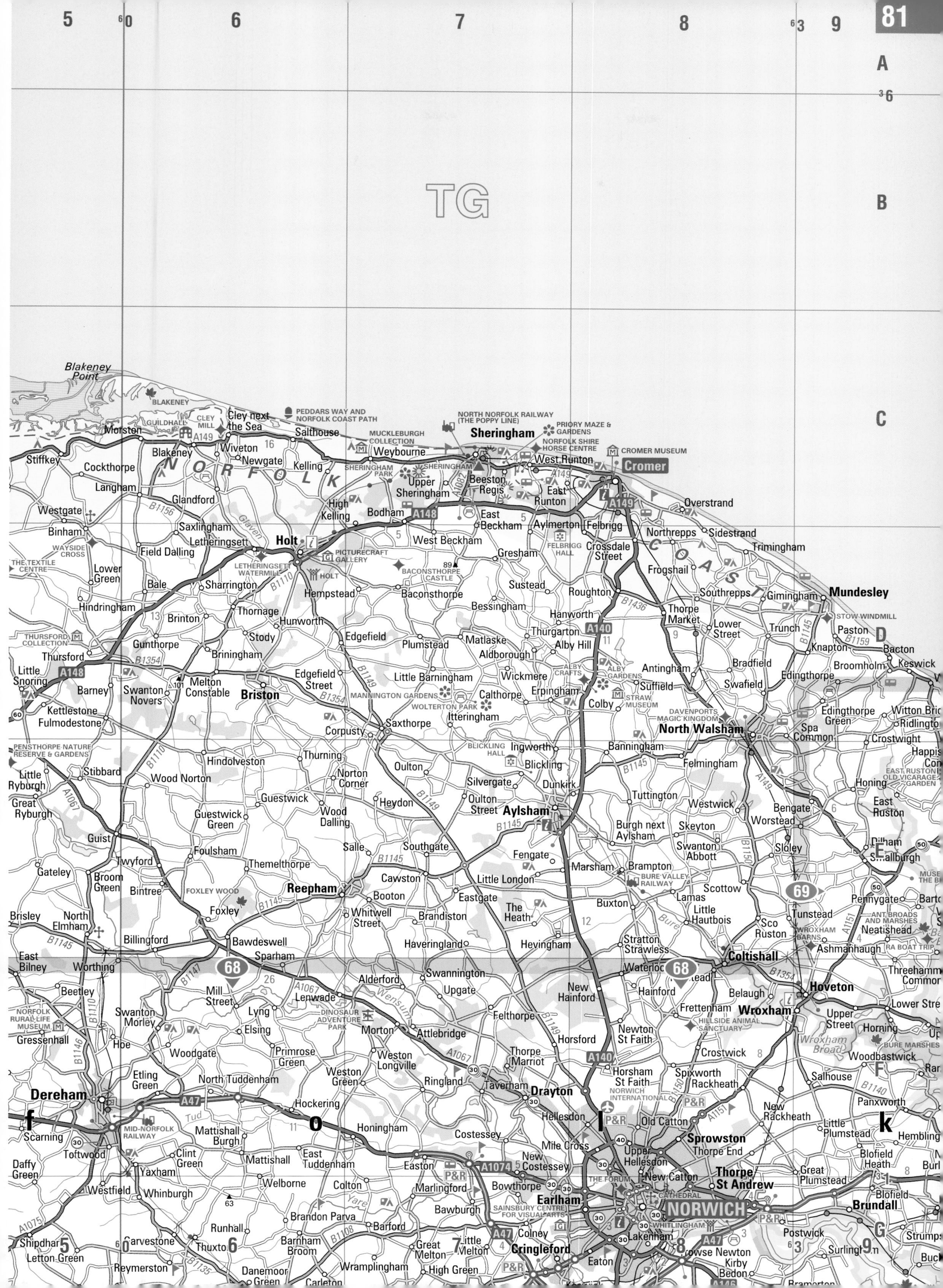
5
6
7
8
9
A
B
C
D
E
F
G
TG
Blakeney Point
BLAKENEY
PEDDARS WAY AND NORFOLK COAST PATH
NORTH NORFOLK RAILWAY (THE POPPY LINE)
GUILDHALL
CLEY MILL
Cley next the Sea
Morston
Salthouse
MUCKLEBURGH COLLECTION
Sheringham
PRIORY MAZE & GARDENS
NORFOLK SHIRE HORSE CENTRE
CROMER MUSEUM
Cromer
Stiffkey
Blakeney
Wiveton
Newgate
Weybourne
West Runton
Cockthorpe
NORFOLK
Kelling
SHERINGHAM PARK
SHERINGHAM
Upper Sheringham
Beeston Regis
East Runton
Langham
Glandford
High Kelling
Bodham
A148
A149
Overstrand
Westgate
Binham
Saxlingham
Letheringsett
Holt
East Beckham
Aylmerton
Felbrigg
Northrepps
Sidestrand
Trimingham
WAYSIDE CROSS
Field Dalling
PICTURECRAFT GALLERY
West Beckham
Gresham
FELBRIGG HALL
Crossdale Street
COAST
THE TEXTILE CENTRE
Lower Green
LETHERINGSETT WATERMILL
HOLT
BACONSTHORPE CASTLE
Frogshail
Bale
Sharrington
Hempstead
Baconsthorpe
Sustead
Roughton
Southrepps
Gimingham
Mundesley
Hindringham
Thornage
Bessingham
B1436
Thorpe Market
STOW WINDMILL
Brinton
Hunworth
Hanworth
Lower Street
Trunch
Paston
THURSFORD COLLECTION
Stody
Edgefield
Plumstead
Matlaske
Thurgarton
A140
Alby Hill
Knapton
Bacton
Gunthorpe
Aldborough
Thursford
Briningham
Antingham
Bradfield
Broomholm
Keswick
Little Snoring
B1354
Melton Constable
Edgefield Street
Little Barningham
Wickmere
ALBY CRAFTS
ALBY GARDENS
Suffield
Swafield
Edingthorpe
Barney
Swanton Novers
Briston
MANNINGTON GARDENS
Calthorpe
Erpingham
STRAW MUSEUM
Colby
DAVENPORTS MAGIC KINGDOM
Edingthorpe Green
Kettlestone
Fulmodestone
WOLTERTON PARK
Itteringham
Corpusty
Saxthorpe
North Walsham
Spa Common
Crostwight
PENSTHORPE NATURE RESERVE & GARDENS
BLICKLING HALL
Ingworth
Banningham
Hindolveston
Thurning
Blickling
Felmingham
Stibbard
Little Ryburgh
Wood Norton
Norton Corner
Oulton
Silvergate
Dunkirk
Honing
EAST RUSTON OLD VICARAGE GARDEN
Great Ryburgh
Guestwick
Heydon
Oulton Street
Aylsham
Tuttington
Westwick
Bengate
East Ruston
Guestwick Green
Wood Dalling
Worstead
Burgh next Aylsham
Skeyton
Guist
Salle
Southgate
Fengate
Swanton Abbott
Sloley
Dilham
Smallburgh
Foulsham
Twyford
Themelthorpe
Marsham
Brampton
Gateley
BURE VALLEY RAILWAY
Broom Green
Bintree
Cawston
Little London
Reepham
Booton
Scottow
69
Pennygate
FOXLEY WOOD
Eastgate
Lamas
Whitwell Street
The Heath
Buxton
Little Hautbois
Brisley
North Elmham
Foxley
Brandiston
Tunstead
ANT BROADS AND MARSHES
Neatishead
Sco Ruston
Billingford
Bawdeswell
Haveringland
Hevingham
Stratton Strawless
WROXHAM BARNS
Ashmanhaugh
East Bilney
Worthing
Sparham
Coltishall
68
Waterloo
Threehammer Common
Beetley
Mill Street
Alderford
Swannington
Upgate
New Hainford
Hainford
Belaugh
Hoveton
NORFOLK RURAL LIFE MUSEUM
Swanton Morley
Lyng
Lenwade
DINOSAUR ADVENTURE PARK
Frettenham
Wroxham
Lower Street
Upper Street
Elsing
Morton
Felthorpe
HILLSIDE ANIMAL SANCTUARY
Newton St Faith
Horning
BURE MARSHES
Gressenhall
Hoe
Woodgate
Primrose Green
Weston Longville
Attlebridge
Horsford
Crostwick
Wroxham Broad
Woodbastwick
Etling Green
Thorpe Marriot
Horsham St Faith
Spixworth
Rackheath
Salhouse
Dereham
North Tuddenham
Weston Green
Ringland
Taverham
Drayton
NORWICH INTERNATIONAL
New Rackheath
Panxworth
A47
Hockering
Hellesdon
P&R
Old Catton
Little Plumstead
MID-NORFOLK RAILWAY
Mattishall Burgh
Honingham
Costessey
Sprowston
Thorpe End
Scarning
Toftwood
Clint Green
Mile Cross
Upper Hellesdon
Blofield Heath
Daffy Green
Yaxham
Mattishall
East Tuddenham
Easton
A1074
New Costessey
New Catton
Thorpe St Andrew
Great Plumstead
Westfield
Whinburgh
Welborne
Colton
Marlingford
Bowthorpe
THE FORUM
Earlham
CATHEDRAL
NORWICH
Blofield
Brundall
Bawburgh
SAINSBURY CENTRE FOR VISUAL ARTS
Brandon Parva
Barford
Runhall
WHITLINGHAM
Colney
Postwick
Shipdham
Carvestone
Thuxton
Barnham Broom
Great Melton
Little Melton
Cringleford
Lakenham
Trowse Newton
Surlingham
Letton Green
Reymerston
Danemoor Green
Wramplingham
High Green
Eaton
Kirby Bedon

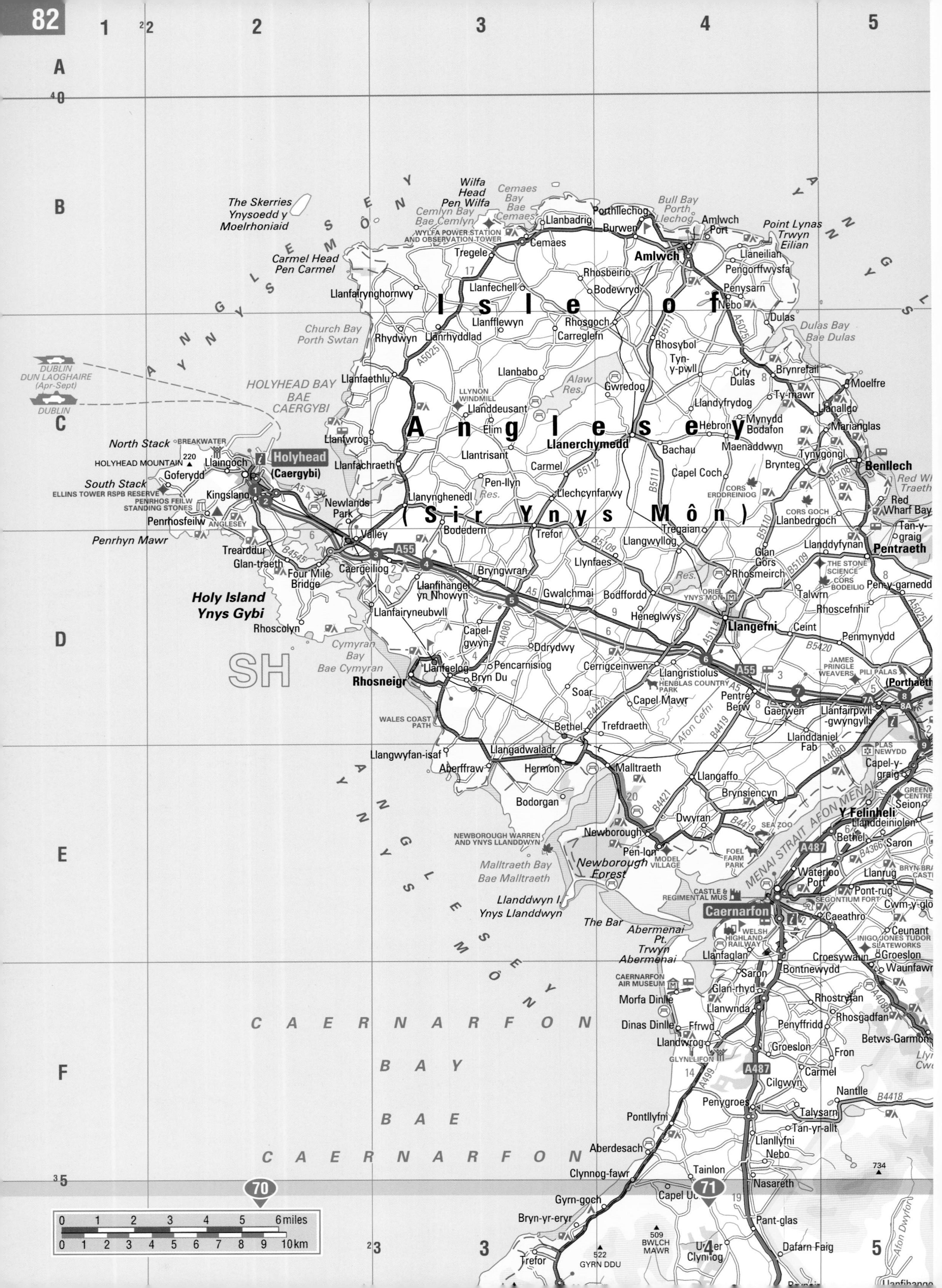

Isle of Anglesey
(Sir Ynys Môn)
ANGLESEY YNYS MÔN
CAERNARFON BAY
BAE CAERNARFON
The Skerries
Ynysoedd y Moelrhoniaid
Carmel Head
Pen Carmel
Wilfa Head
Pen Wilfa
Cemlyn Bay
Bae Cemlyn
Cemaes Bay
Bae Cemaes
WYLFA POWER STATION AND OBSERVATION TOWER
Llanbadrig
Porthllechog
Bull Bay
Porth Llechog
Burwen
Amlwch
Amlwch Port
Point Lynas
Trwyn Eilian
Cemaes
Tregele
Llaneilian
Pengorffwysfa
Rhosbeirio
Bodewryd
Llanfechell
Penysarn
Nebo
Llanfairynghornwy
Llanfflewyn
Rhosgoch
Carreglefn
Dulas
Dulas Bay
Bae Dulas
Church Bay
Porth Swtan
Rhydwyn
Llanrhyddlad
Rhosybol
Tyn-y-pwll
City Dulas
Brynrefail
Moelfre
Llanbabo
Alaw Res.
Gwredog
Ty-mawr
DUBLIN DUN LAOGHAIRE (Apr-Sept)
DUBLIN
HOLYHEAD BAY
BAE CAERGYBI
Llanfaethlu
LLYNON WINDMILL
Llanddeusant
Llandyfrydog
Mynydd Bodafon
Llanallgo
Marianglas
Elim
Hebron
Llanfwrog
Llanerchymedd
Bachau
Maenaddwyn
Tynygongl
Benllech
North Stack
BREAKWATER
HOLYHEAD MOUNTAIN
220
Llaingoch
Holyhead
(Caergybi)
Llantrisant
Carmel
Capel Coch
Brynteg
Red Wharf Bay
South Stack
ELLINS TOWER RSPB RESERVE
Goferydd
Llanfachraeth
Pen-llyn
CORS ERDDREINIOG
Kingsland
PENRHOS FEILW STANDING STONES
Newlands Park
Llanynghenedl
Llechcynfarwy
CORS GOCH
Llanbedrgoch
Penrhosfeilw
ANGLESEY
Bodedern
Tregaian
Tan-y-graig
Penrhyn Mawr
Valley
Trefor
Llangwyllog
Llanddyfnan
Pentraeth
Trearddur
Glan-traeth
Four Mile Bridge
Caergeiliog
A55
Bryngwran
Llynfaes
Glan Gors
THE STONE SCIENCE
Rhosmeirch
CORS BODEILIO
Pen-y-garnedd
Llanfihangel yn Nhowyn
Gwalchmai
Bodffordd
ORIEL YNYS MÔN
Talwrn
Holy Island
Ynys Gybi
Llanfairyneubwll
Heneglwys
Llangefni
Rhoscefnhir
Rhoscolyn
Capel-gwyn
Ceint
Penmynydd
Ddrydwy
SH
Cymyran Bay
Bae Cymyran
Llanfaelog
Pencarnisiog
Cerrigceinwen
Llangristiolus
JAMES PRINGLE WEAVERS
PILI PALAS
(Porthaethwy)
Rhosneigr
Bryn Du
HENBLAS COUNTRY PARK
Soar
Capel Mawr
Pentre Berw
Gaerwen
Llanfairpwll-gwyngyll
WALES COAST PATH
Bethel
Trefdraeth
Afon Cefni
Llanddaniel Fab
Llangwyfan-isaf
Llangadwaladr
PLAS NEWYDD
Aberffraw
Hermon
Malltraeth
Capel-y-graig
Llangaffo
Brynsiencyn
Bodorgan
Y Felinheli
Seion
Llanddeiniolen
Dwyran
SEA ZOO
NEWBOROUGH WARREN AND YNYS LLANDDWYN
Newborough
Bethel
Saron
MENAI STRAIT AFON MENAI
A487
Pen-lon
MODEL VILLAGE
FOEL FARM PARK
Malltraeth Bay
Bae Malltraeth
Newborough Forest
Waterloo Port
Llanrug
Pont-rug
CASTLE & REGIMENTAL MUS
SEGONTIUM FORT
Cwm-y-glo
Llanddwyn I.
Ynys Llanddwyn
Caernarfon
Caeathro
The Bar
Abermenai Pt.
Trwyn Abermenai
WELSH HIGHLAND RAILWAY
Ceunant
INIGO JONES TUDOR SLATEWORKS
Llanfaglan
Croesywaun
Groeslon
Saron
Bontnewydd
Waunfawr
CAERNARFON AIR MUSEUM
Glan-rhyd
Morfa Dinlle
Llanwnda
Rhostryfan
Rhosgadfan
Dinas Dinlle
Ffrwd
Penyffridd
Betws-Garmon
Llandwrog
Groeslon
Fron
GLYNLLIFON
A487
Carmel
Cilgwyn
Nantlle
B4418
Penygroes
Pontllyfni
Talysarn
Tan-yr-allt
Llanllyfni
Aberdesach
Nebo
734
Tainlon
Clynnog-fawr
Nasareth
70
71
Capel Uchaf
Gyrn-goch
Bryn-yr-eryr
Pant-glas
509
BWLCH MAWR
522
GYRN DDU
Uwchaf Clynnog
Dafarn Faig
Afon Dwyfor
Trefor
0 1 2 3 4 5 6 miles
0 1 2 3 4 5 6 7 8 9 10 km

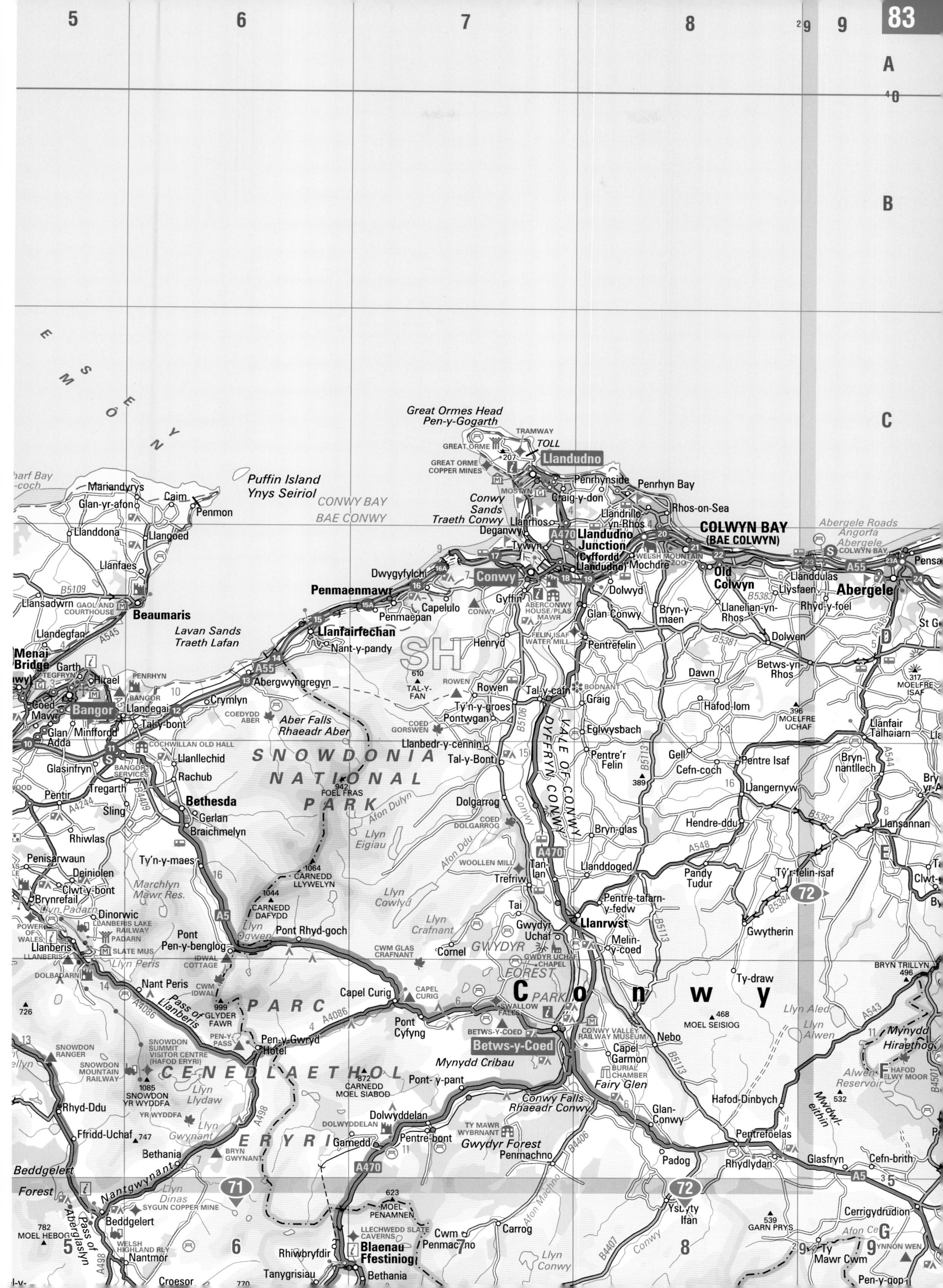

5
6
7
8
9
A
B
C
D
E
F
G
MENAI STRAIT
ANGLESEY
Puffin Island
Ynys Seiriol
CONWY BAY
BAE CONWY
Great Ormes Head
Pen-y-Gogarth
TRAMWAY
GREAT ORME
TOLL
GREAT ORME COPPER MINES
Llandudno
MOSTYN
Conwy Sands
Traeth Conwy
Penrhynside
Penrhyn Bay
Craig-y-don
Llandrillo-yn-Rhos
Rhos-on-Sea
COLWYN BAY
(BAE COLWYN)
Abergele Roads
Angorfa Abergele
Llanrhos
Deganwy
Tywyn
Llandudno Junction
(Cyffordd Llandudno)
WELSH MOUNTAIN ZOO
Mochdre
Old Colwyn
Llanddulas
Abergele
Pensarn
Mariandyrys
Caim
Penmon
Glan-yr-afon
Llanddona
Llangoed
Llanfaes
Llansadwrn
GAOL AND COURTHOUSE
Beaumaris
Llandegfan
Lavan Sands
Traeth Lafan
Menai Bridge
Garth
Hirael
PENRHYN
Bangor
Llandegai
Glan Adda
Minffordd
Tal-y-bont
Coed Mawr
BANGOR SERVICES
COCHWILLAN OLD HALL
Llanllechid
Rachub
Glasinfryn
Pentir
Tregarth
Sling
Bethesda
Gerlan
Braichmelyn
Rhiwlas
Penisarwaun
Deiniolen
Clwt-y-bont
Brynrefail
Llyn Padarn
Dinorwic
LLANBERIS LAKE RAILWAY
PADARN
POWER OF WALES
Llanberis
SLATE MUS
DOLBADARN
Llyn Peris
Nant Peris
Pass of Llanberis
Dwygyfylchi
Penmaenmawr
Capelulo
Penmaenan
Llanfairfechan
Nant-y-pandy
Abergwyngregyn
Crymlyn
COEDYDD ABER
Aber Falls
Rhaeadr Aber
SH
610
TAL-Y-FAN
ROWEN
Rowen
Ty'n-y-groes
Pontwgan
COED GORSWEN
Llanbedr-y-cennin
Tal-y-Bont
Henryd
Conwy
Gyffin
ABERCONWY HOUSE/PLAS MAWR
FELIN ISAF WATER MILL
Glan-Conwy
Dolwyd
Pentrefelin
Tal-y-cafn
BODNANT
Graig
Eglwysbach
VALE OF CONWY
DYFFRYN CONWY
SNOWDONIA NATIONAL PARK
942
FOEL FRAS
Afon Dulyn
Llyn Eigiau
Dolgarrog
COED DOLGARROG
Afon Ddu
WOOLLEN MILL
Trefriw
Tan-lan
1064
CARNEDD LLYWELYN
1044
CARNEDD DAFYDD
Llyn Cowlyd
Llyn Crafnant
Marchlyn Mawr Res.
Ty'n-y-maes
Llyn Ogwen
Pont Rhyd-goch
Pont Pen-y-benglog
IDWAL COTTAGE
CWM IDWAL
999
GLYDER FAWR
CWM GLAS CRAFNANT
Cornel
GWYDYR FOREST
GWYDYR UCHAF CHAPEL
Tai
Gwydyr Uchaf
Llanrwst
Melin-y-coed
PARC
Capel Curig
CAPEL CURIG
SWALLOW FALLS
Pont Cyfyng
BETWS-Y-COED
Betws-y-Coed
CONWY VALLEY RAILWAY MUSEUM
PEN-Y-PASS
Pen-y-Gwryd Hotel
SNOWDON SUMMIT VISITOR CENTRE (HAFOD ERYRI)
SNOWDON RANGER
SNOWDON MOUNTAIN RAILWAY
1085
SNOWDON YR WYDDFA
CENEDLAETHOL
ERYRI
Llyn Llydaw
Llyn Gwynant
Mynydd Cribau
872
CARNEDD MOEL SIABOD
Pont-y-pant
Dolwyddelan
DOLWYDDELAN
Garnedd
Pentre-bont
TY MAWR WYBRNANT
Gwydyr Forest
Penmachno
Conwy Falls
Rhaeadr Conwy
Fairy Glen
Capel Garmon
BURIAL CHAMBER
Nebo
Glan-Conwy
726
Rhyd-Ddu
Ffridd-Uchaf
747
Bethania
BRYN GWYNANT
Beddgelert Forest
Nantgwynant
Llyn Dinas
SYGUN COPPER MINE
Beddgelert
782
MOEL HEBOG
Pass of Aberglaslyn
WELSH HIGHLAND RLY
Nantmor
Croesor
623
MOEL PENAMNEN
LLECHWEDD SLATE CAVERNS
Blaenau Ffestiniog
Rhiwbryfdir
Tanygrisiau
Bethania
Cwm Penmachno
Carrog
Afon Machno
Llyn Conwy
Ysbyty Ifan
Padog
Rhydlydan
Pentrefoelas
Hafod-Dinbych
Glasfryn
Cefn-brith
Cerrigydrudion
539
GARN PRYS
Ty Mawr Cwm
Pen-y-gop
Conwy
468
MOEL SEISIOG
Ty-draw
Gwytherin
Llyn Aled
Llyn Alwen
Alwen Reservoir
Mynydd Hiraethog
HAFOD ELWY MOOR
532
Mwdwl-eithin
BRYN TRILLYN
496
Llansannan
Tŷ'r-felin-isaf
Pandy Tudur
Pentre-tafarn-y-fedw
Llanddoged
Bryn-glas
Hendre-ddu
Llangernyw
Pentre Isaf
Cefn-coch
Gell
389
Pentre'r Felin
Bryn-nantllech
Llanfair Talhaiarn
396
MOELFRE UCHAF
Hafod-lom
Dawn
Betws-yn-Rhos
317
MOELFRE ISAF
Dolwen
Rhyd-y-foel
Llysfaen
Llanelian-yn-Rhos
Bryn-y-maen
St George
Clwt-y-bont
Mynydd

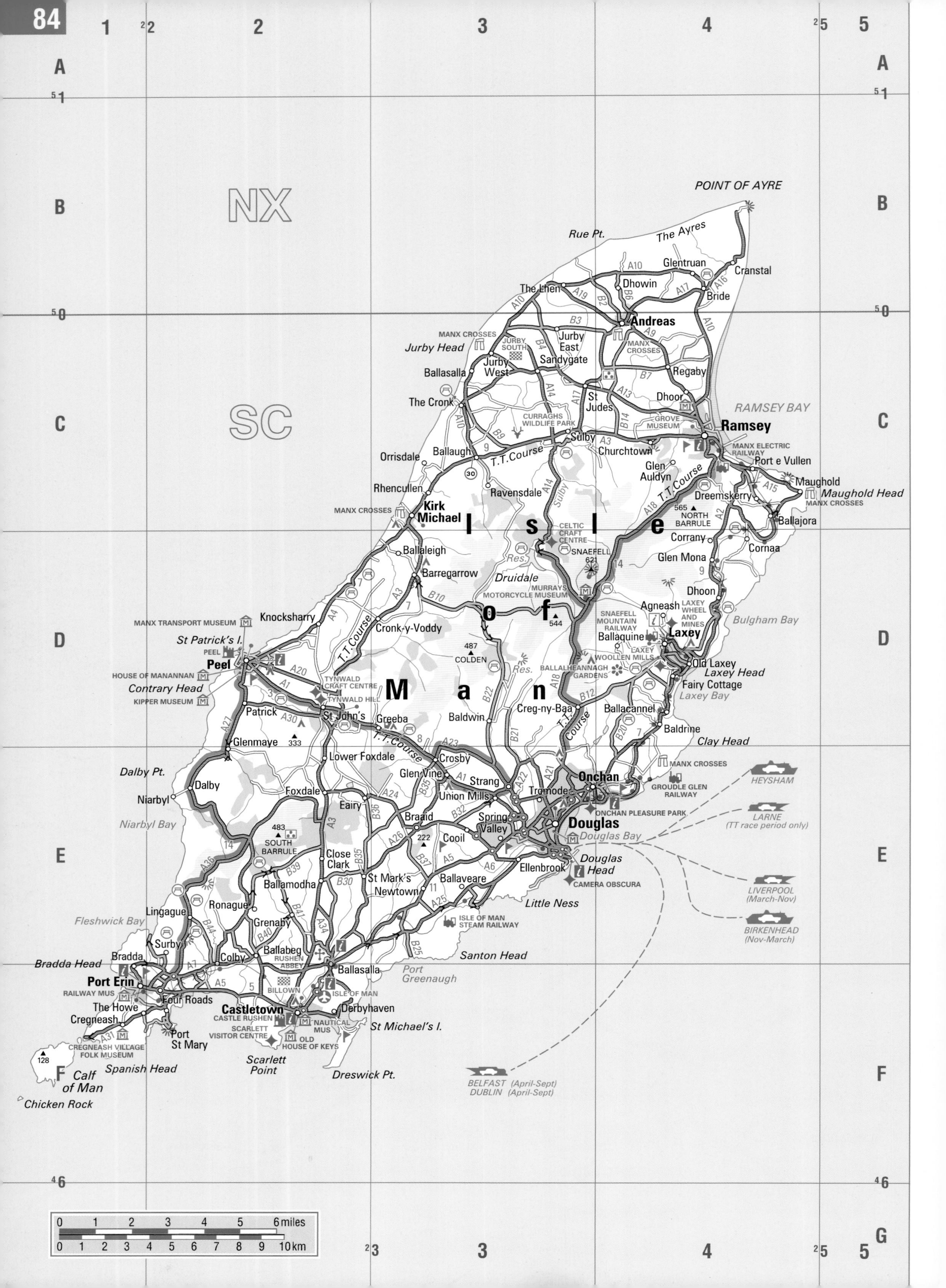
NX
SC
POINT OF AYRE
Rue Pt.
The Ayres
Glentruan
Cranstal
Dhowin
The Lhen
Bride
Andreas
MANX CROSSES
Jurby Head
JURBY SOUTH
Jurby East
Sandygate
MANX CROSSES
Jurby West
Ballasalla
Regaby
The Cronk
St Judes
Dhoor
RAMSEY BAY
CURRAGHS WILDLIFE PARK
GROVE MUSEUM
Ramsey
Sulby
Churchtown
MANX ELECTRIC RAILWAY
Orrisdale
Ballaugh
T.T.Course
Glen Auldyn
Port e Vullen
Maughold
Rhencullen
Ravensdale
Maughold Head
MANX CROSSES
MANX CROSSES
Kirk Michael
Dreemskerry
565 NORTH BARRULE
Ballajora
Isle of Man
CELTIC CRAFT CENTRE
Corrany
SNAEFELL 621
Ballaleigh
Res.
Glen Mona
Cornaa
Barregarrow
Druidale
Dhoon
MURRAYS MOTORCYCLE MUSEUM
Agneash
LAXEY WHEEL AND MINES
MANX TRANSPORT MUSEUM
Knockshary
SNAEFELL MOUNTAIN RAILWAY
Bulgham Bay
544
Cronk-y-Voddy
St Patrick's I.
Ballaquine
Laxey
PEEL
487 COLDEN
LAXEY WOOLLEN MILLS
Peel
Res.
BALLALHEANNAGH GARDENS
Old Laxey
HOUSE OF MANANNAN
Laxey Head
TYNWALD CRAFT CENTRE
Contrary Head
Fairy Cottage
KIPPER MUSEUM
TYNWALD HILL
Laxey Bay
Patrick
St John's
Greeba
Baldwin
Creg-ny-Baa
Ballacannel
Baldrine
Glenmaye
333
Clay Head
Lower Foxdale
Crosby
MANX CROSSES
Dalby Pt.
Glen Vine
Strang
Onchan
HEYSHAM
Dalby
GROUDLE GLEN RAILWAY
Niarbyl
Foxdale
Union Mills
Tromode
ONCHAN PLEASURE PARK
Eairy
Spring Valley
LARNE
(TT race period only)
Braaid
Douglas
Niarbyl Bay
483 SOUTH BARRULE
222
Cooil
Douglas Bay
Close Clark
Douglas Head
Ellenbrook
Ballamodha
St Mark's
Newtown
Ballaveare
CAMERA OBSCURA
LIVERPOOL (March-Nov)
Ronague
Little Ness
Lingague
Fleshwick Bay
Grenaby
ISLE OF MAN STEAM RAILWAY
BIRKENHEAD (Nov-March)
Surby
Bradda
Colby
Ballabeg
RUSHEN ABBEY
Santon Head
Bradda Head
Ballasalla
Port Greenaugh
Port Erin
BILLOWN
RAILWAY MUS
ISLE OF MAN
Four Roads
The Howe
Castletown
Derbyhaven
Cregneash
CASTLE RUSHEN
NAUTICAL MUS
St Michael's I.
SCARLETT VISITOR CENTRE
OLD HOUSE OF KEYS
Port St Mary
CREGNEASH VILLAGE FOLK MUSEUM
128
Scarlett Point
Spanish Head
Dreswick Pt.
Calf of Man
BELFAST (April-Sept)
DUBLIN (April-Sept)
Chicken Rock
0 1 2 3 4 5 6 miles
0 1 2 3 4 5 6 7 8 9 10 km

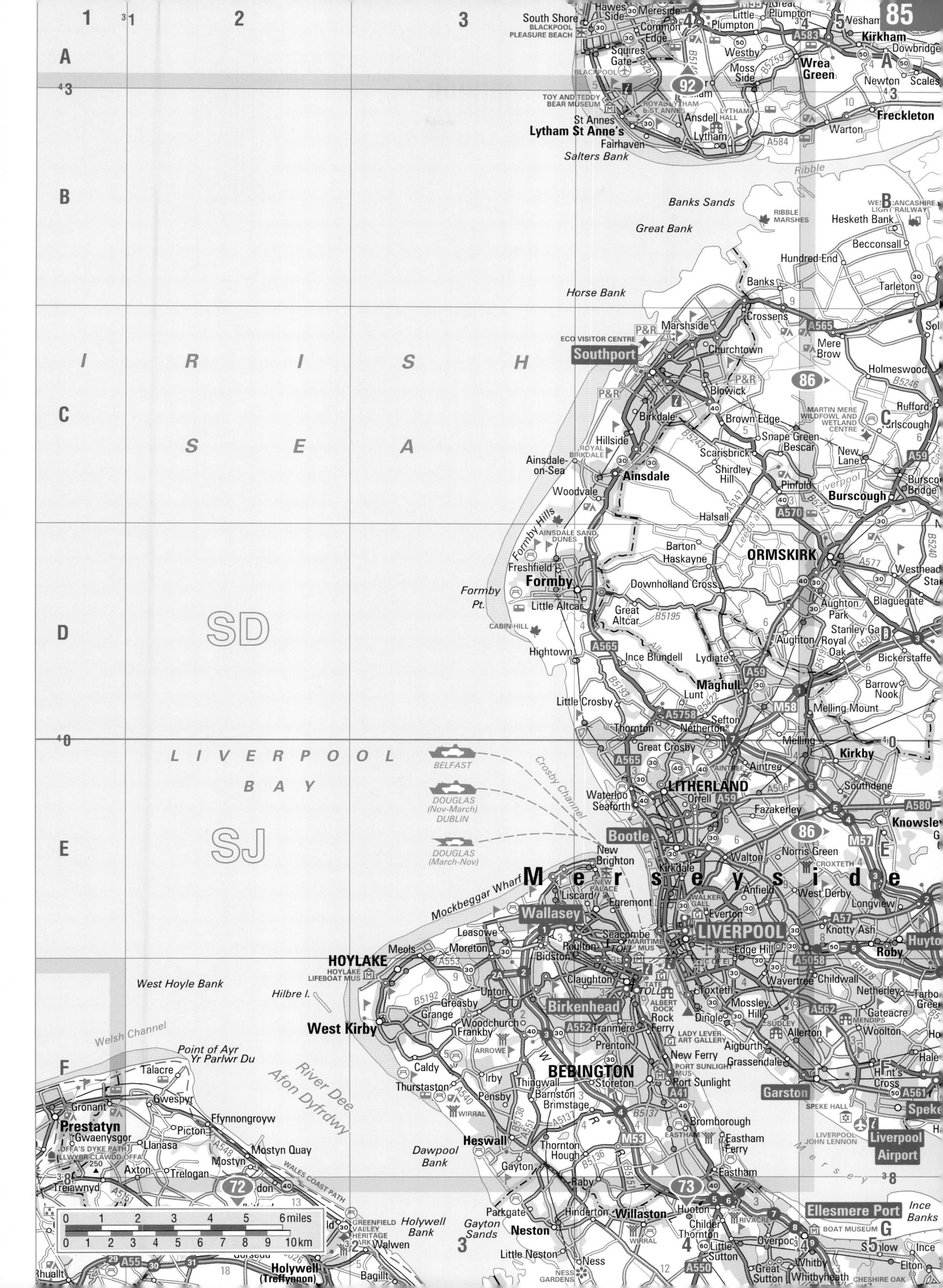
IRISH SEA
LIVERPOOL BAY
SD
SJ
Merseyside
South Shore
BLACKPOOL PLEASURE BEACH
Squires Gate
Common Edge
Mereside
Little Plumpton
Plumpton
Westby
Wrea Green
Moss Side
Kirkham
Dowbridge
Newton
Scales
Freckleton
Warton
TOY AND TEDDY BEAR MUSEUM
St Annes
Lytham St Anne's
Ansdell
Lytham
LYTHAM HALL
Fairhaven
Salters Bank
Ribble
Banks Sands
RIBBLE MARSHES
WEST LANCASHIRE LIGHT RAILWAY
Hesketh Bank
Great Bank
Becconsall
Hundred End
Banks
Tarleton
Horse Bank
Crossens
Marshside
ECO VISITOR CENTRE
Southport
Churchtown
Mere Brow
Holmeswood
Blowick
Rufford
Birkdale
Brown Edge
MARTIN MERE WILDFOWL AND WETLAND CENTRE
Snape Green
Bescar
Hillside
ROYAL BIRKDALE
Scarisbrick
New Lane
Ainsdale-on-Sea
Ainsdale
Shirdley Hill
Pinfold
Burscough
Burscough Bridge
Woodvale
Halsall
Formby Hills
AINSDALE SAND DUNES
Barton
Haskayne
ORMSKIRK
Westhead
Freshfield
Formby
Downholland Cross
Formby Pt.
Little Altcar
Great Altcar
Aughton Park
Blaguegate
CABIN HILL
Stanley Gate
Hightown
Ince Blundell
Lydiate
Aughton
Royal Oak
Bickerstaffe
Maghull
Barrow Nook
Little Crosby
Lunt
Melling Mount
Sefton
Thornton
Netherton
Melling
Great Crosby
Aintree
Kirkby
BELFAST
DOUGLAS (Nov-March) DUBLIN
DOUGLAS (March-Nov)
Crosby Channel
Waterloo
Seaforth
LITHERLAND
Orrell
Southdene
Fazakerley
Knowsley
Bootle
New Brighton
Kirkdale
Walton
Norris Green
CROXTETH
Mockbeggar Wharf
Liscard
Egremont
Anfield
West Derby
Longview
Wallasey
Everton
Knotty Ash
Huyton
Leasowe
Seacombe
LIVERPOOL
Roby
Meols
Moreton
Poulton
Edge Hill
HOYLAKE
HOYLAKE LIFEBOAT MUS
Bidston
Childwall
West Hoyle Bank
Claughton
Wavertree
Netherley
Tarbock Green
Hilbre I.
Upton
TATE
ALBERT DOCK
Toxteth
Greasby
Birkenhead
Mossley Hill
Gateacre
Grange
Dingle
SUDLEY
MENDIPS
Woolton
West Kirby
Woodchurch
Tranmere
Rock Ferry
Allerton
Welsh Channel
Frankby
ARROWE
LADY LEVER ART GALLERY
Prenton
Aigburth
Point of Ayr
Yr Parlwr Du
New Ferry
PORT SUNLIGHT MUS
Grassendale
Hale
Talacre
River Dee
Afon Dyfrdwy
Caldy
Irby
BEBINGTON
Hunt's Cross
Thurstaston
Thingwall
Storeton
Port Sunlight
Garston
Gwespyr
Pensby
Barnston
Brimstage
Gronant
WIRRAL
Bromborough
SPEKE HALL
Speke
Ffynnongroyw
Prestatyn
Gwaenysgor
Picton
OFFA'S DYKE PATH
LLWYBR CLAWDD OFFA
Llanasa
Heswall
Thornton Hough
Eastham Ferry
EASTHAM
LIVERPOOL JOHN LENNON
Liverpool Airport
Mostyn Quay
Mostyn
Dawpool Bank
Gayton
Axton
Trelogan
Trelawnyd
WALES COAST PATH
Eastham
Mersey
Raby
Parkgate
Hinderton
Willaston
Hooton
Ellesmere Port
Ince Banks
GREENFIELD VALLEY HERITAGE PARK
Holywell Bank
Gayton Sands
Neston
Childer Thornton
RIVACRE
Overpool
BOAT MUSEUM
Walwen
WIRRAL
Little Sutton
Ince
Elton
Little Neston
Ness
NESS GARDENS
Rhuallt
Holywell (Treffynnon)
Bagillt
Great Sutton
Whitby
Whitbyheath
CHESHIRE OAK
92
86
72
73
0 1 2 3 4 5 6 miles
0 1 2 3 4 5 6 7 8 9 10 km

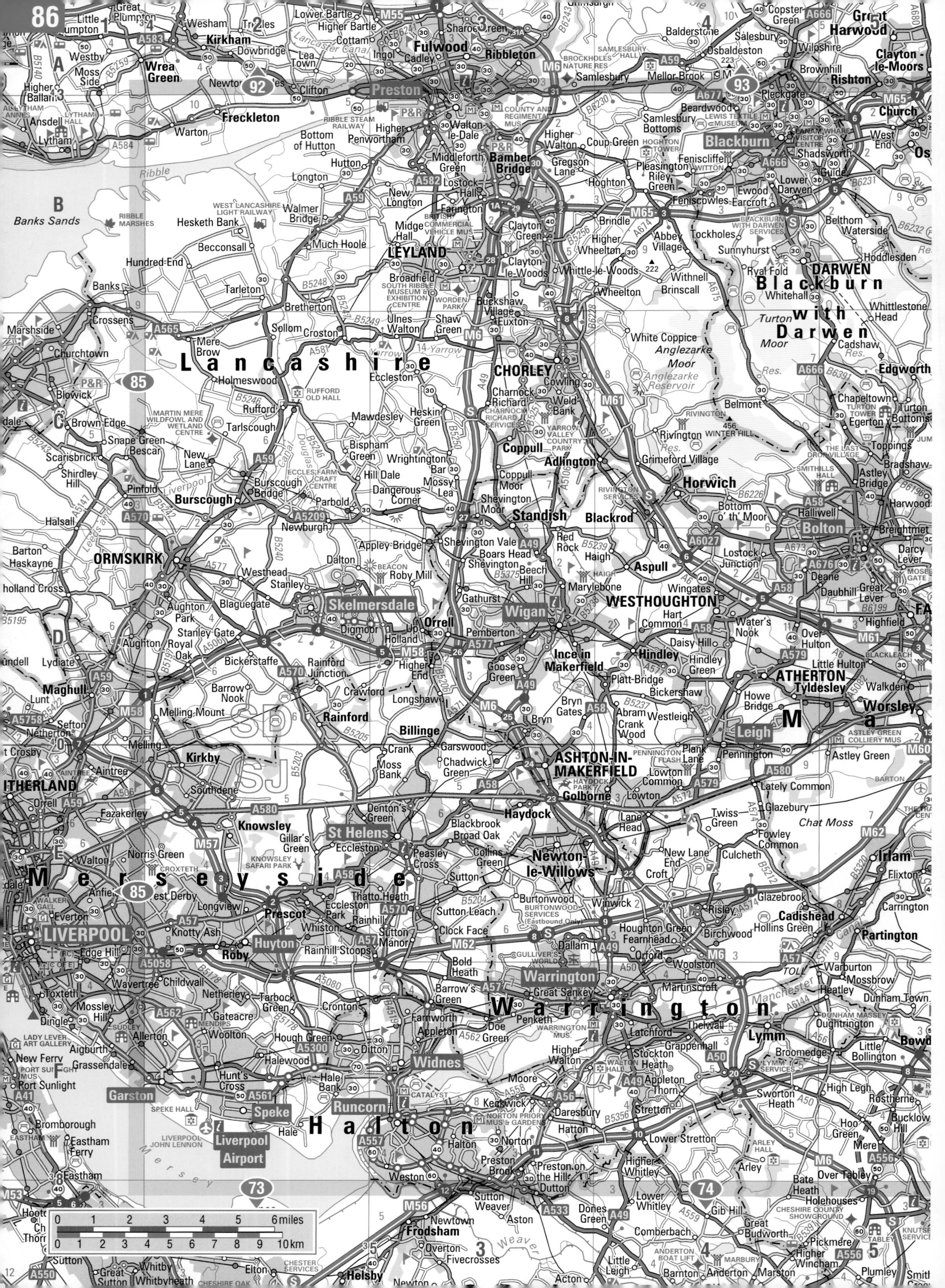

Kirkham
Wrea Green
Freckleton
Lytham
Ansdell
Warton
Preston
Fulwood
Ribbleton
Samlesbury
Balderstone
Salesbury
Great Harwood
Clayton-le-Moors
Rishton
Blackburn
Church
Darwen
Blackburn with Darwen
Banks Sands
Ribble
Hesketh Bank
Becconsall
Hundred End
Banks
Tarleton
Longton
Walmer Bridge
Much Hoole
Leyland
Bamber Bridge
Lostock Hall
Farington
Clayton Green
Clayton-le-Woods
Whittle-le-Woods
Wheelton
Brinscall
Withnell
Croston
Bretherton
Eccleston
Euxton
Chorley
Lancashire
Churchtown
Crossens
Marshside
Holmeswood
Rufford
Mawdesley
Heskin Green
Coppull
Adlington
Horwich
Belmont
Edgworth
Turton Moor
Anglezarke Moor
Anglezarke Reservoir
Rivington
Scarisbrick
Burscough
Parbold
Standish
Blackrod
Bolton
Ormskirk
Halsall
Skelmersdale
Orrell
Wigan
Aspull
Westhoughton
Hindley
Atherton
Tyldesley
Walkden
Worsley
Leigh
Maghull
Aughton
Kirkby
Rainford
Billinge
Ashton-in-Makerfield
Golborne
Haydock
Newton-le-Willows
St Helens
Knowsley
Prescot
Huyton
Merseyside
Liverpool
Bootle
Croxteth
Irlam
Cadishead
Partington
Chat Moss
Warrington
Great Sankey
Penketh
Lymm
Widnes
Runcorn
Halton
Speke
Garston
Liverpool John Lennon Airport
Frodsham
Helsby
Sutton Weaver
Lower Stretton
Great Budworth
Bate Heath
Over Tabley
Mere
Rostherne
M6
M61
M65
M58
M62
M56
M57
M55
0 1 2 3 4 5 6 miles
0 1 2 3 4 5 6 7 8 9 10 km

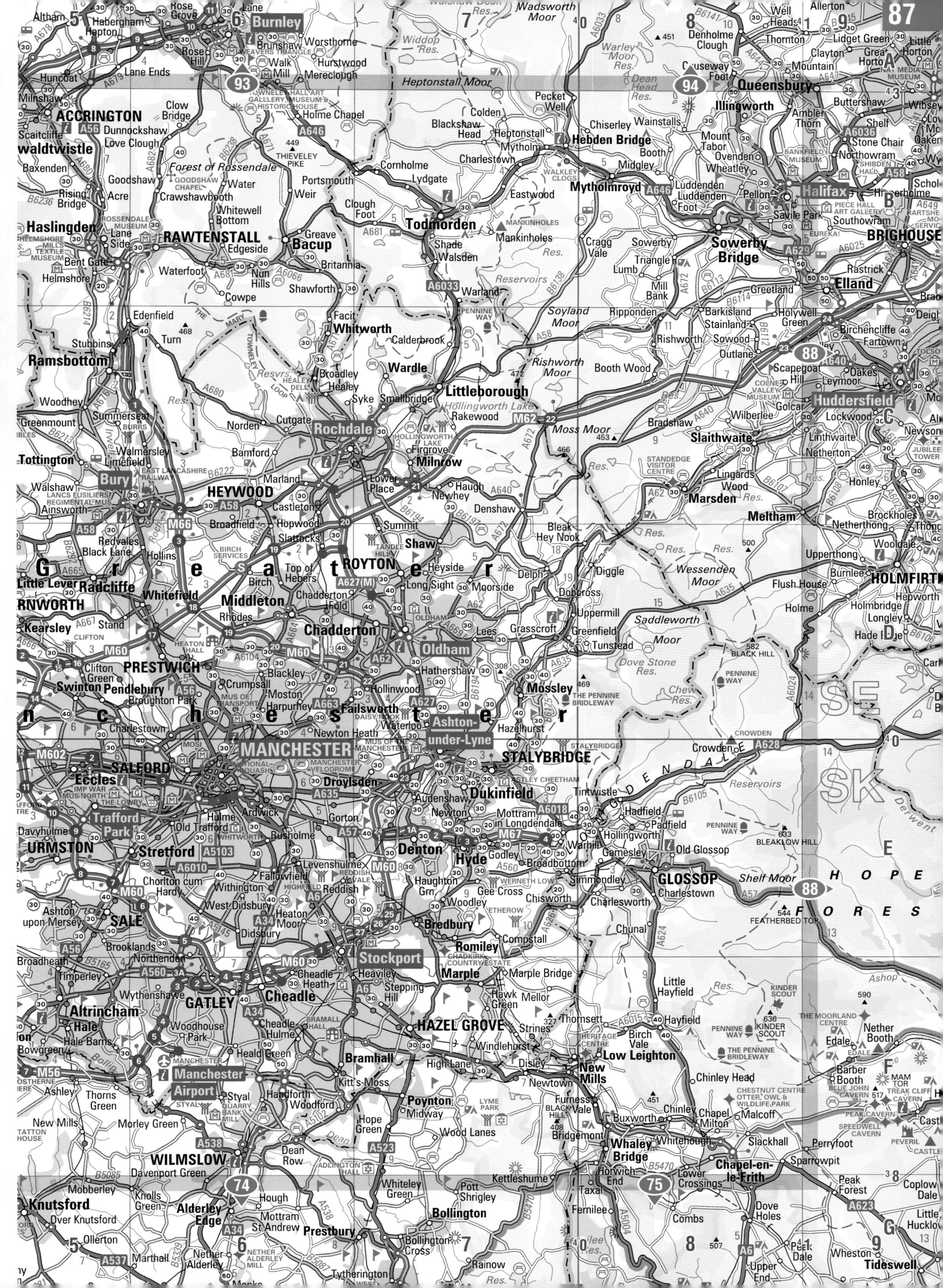
Burnley
Heptonstall Moor
ACCRINGTON
Forest of Rossendale
Hebden Bridge
Queensbury
Illingworth
Mytholmroyd
Halifax
Haslingden
RAWTENSTALL
Bacup
Todmorden
Sowerby Bridge
BRIGHOUSE
Elland
Whitworth
Soyland Moor
Rishworth Moor
Ramsbottom
Wardle
Littleborough
Huddersfield
Rochdale
Hollingworth Lake
Moss Moor
Slaithwaite
Milnrow
Bury
HEYWOOD
Marsden
Meltham
ROYTON
Shaw
Wessenden Moor
HOLMFIRTH
Radcliffe
Whitefield
Middleton
Chadderton
Saddleworth Moor
Oldham
PRESTWICH
Swinton
Pendlebury
Mossley
Ashton-under-Lyne
MANCHESTER
SALFORD
STALYBRIDGE
Eccles
Droylsden
Dukinfield
Trafford Park
URMSTON
Stretford
Denton
Hyde
GLOSSOP
Shelf Moor
HOPE FOREST
SALE
Bredbury
Romiley
Stockport
Marple
Altrincham
GATLEY
Cheadle
HAZEL GROVE
Low Leighton
New Mills
Bramhall
Manchester Airport
Poynton
Whaley Bridge
Chapel-en-le-Frith
WILMSLOW
Knutsford
Alderley Edge
Bollington
Prestbury
Tideswell

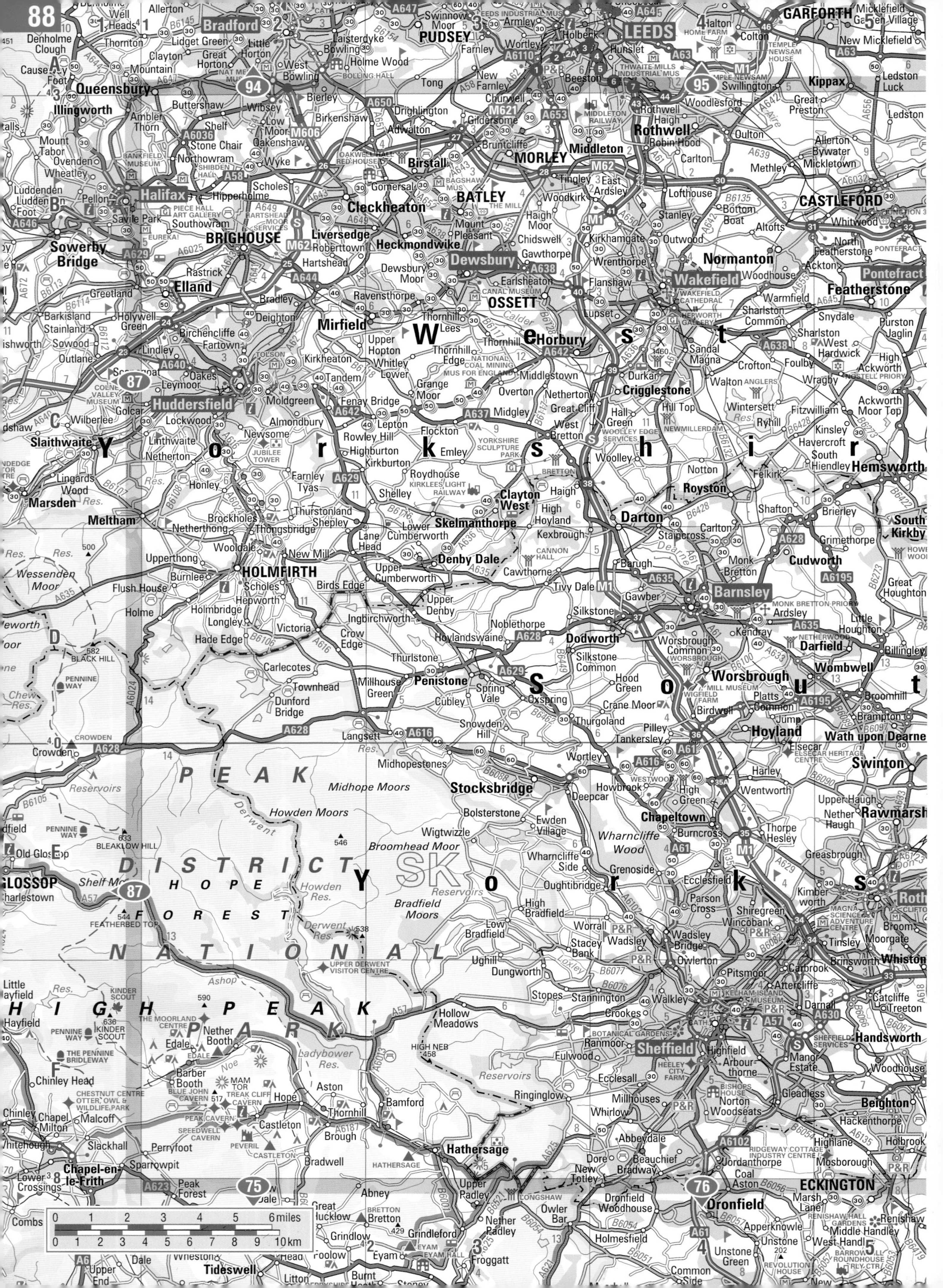

Bradford
PUDSEY
LEEDS
GARFORTH
Queensbury
Illingworth
Halifax
Sowerby Bridge
BRIGHOUSE
Elland
Cleckheaton
Heckmondwike
BATLEY
MORLEY
Rothwell
Middleton
Dewsbury
OSSETT
Wakefield
Normanton
CASTLEFORD
Pontefract
Featherstone
Kippax
Mirfield
Horbury
Huddersfield
Slaithwaite
Marsden
Meltham
HOLMFIRTH
Skelmanthorpe
Denby Dale
Darton
Royston
Hemsworth
South Kirkby
Cudworth
Barnsley
Penistone
Dodworth
Worsbrough
Wombwell
Hoyland
Wath upon Dearne
Swinton
Stocksbridge
Chapeltown
Rawmarsh
GLOSSOP
Sheffield
ECKINGTON
Dronfield
Hathersage
Castleton
Chapel-en-le-Frith
Tideswell
West Yorkshire
South Yorkshire
PEAK DISTRICT NATIONAL PARK
HIGH PEAK
HOPE FOREST
Howden Moors
Midhope Moors
Broomhead Moor
Bradfield Moors
Ladybower Res.
Derwent Res.
Howden Res.
Wessenden Moor
BLACK HILL
BLEAKLOW HILL
FEATHERBED TOP
KINDER SCOUT
Reservoirs
0 1 2 3 4 5 6 miles
0 1 2 3 4 5 6 7 8 9 10 km

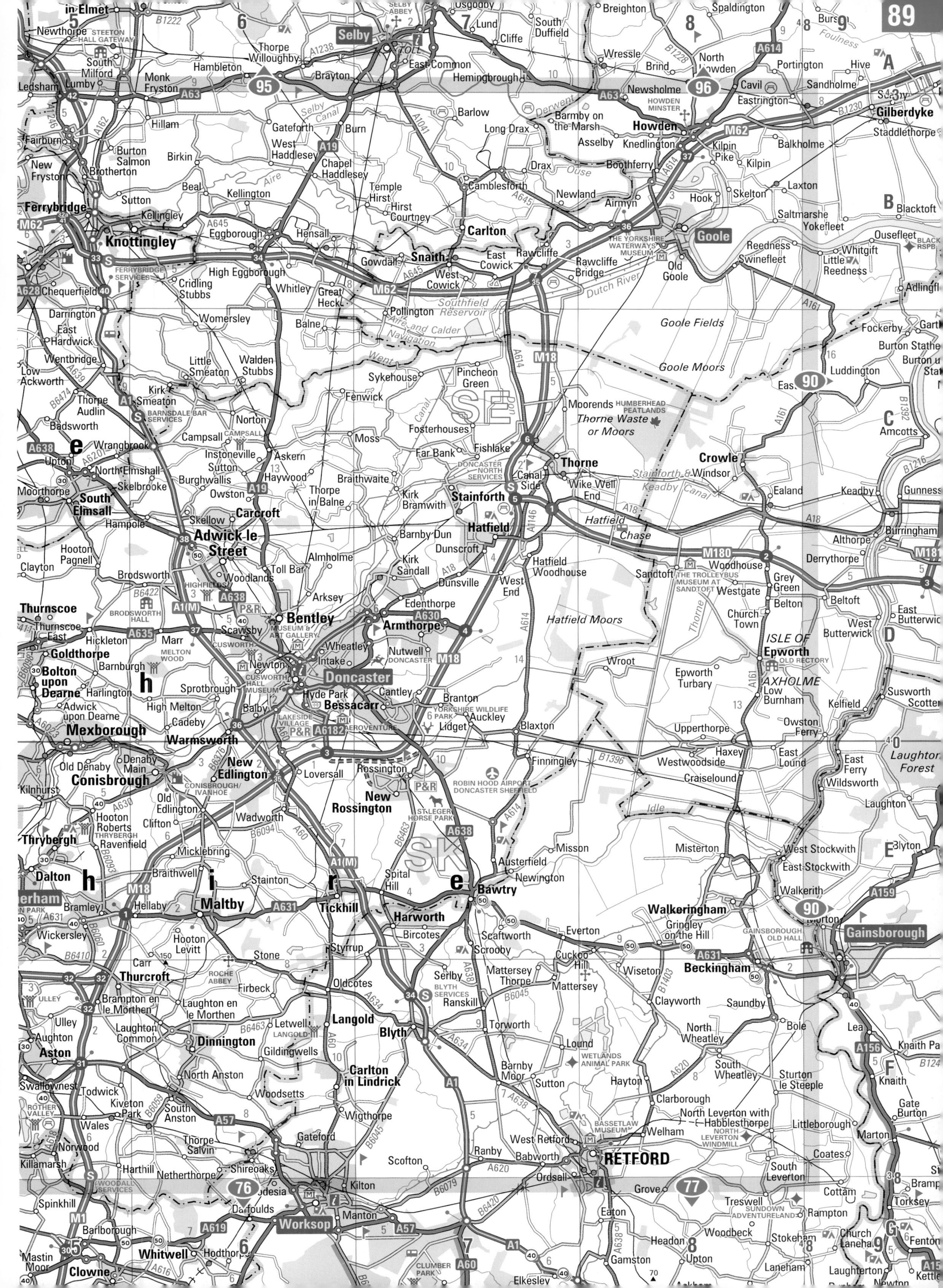

Selby
Selby Abbey
Osgodby
Lund
South Duffield
Cliffe
Breighton
Spaldington
Bursea
Foulness
in Elmet
Newthorpe
Steeton Hall Gateway
South Milford
Thorpe Willoughby
Hambleton
Brayton
East Common
Hemingbrough
Wressle
Brind
North Howden
Portington
Hive
Monk Fryston
Lumby
Ledsham
Newsholme
Howden Minster
Cavil
Sandholme
Eastrington
Gilberdyke
Hillam
Gateforth
Burn
Barlow
Barmby on the Marsh
Long Drax
Howden
Knedlington
Asselby
Kilpin Pike
Kilpin
Balkholme
Staddlethorpe
Fairburn
Burton Salmon
Birkin
West Haddlesey
Chapel Haddlesey
Temple Hirst
Hirst Courtney
Drax
Boothferry
New Fryston
Brotherton
Camblesforth
Newland
Airmyn
Hook
Skelton
Laxton
Blacktoft
Sutton
Beal
Kellington
Ferrybridge
Kellingley
Knottingley
Eggborough
Hensall
Carlton
Goole
Saltmarshe
Yokefleet
Ousefleet
Blacktoft RSPB
Whitgift
Reedness
Little Reedness
Swinefleet
Snaith
East Cowick
Rawcliffe
West Cowick
Rawcliffe Bridge
The Yorkshire Waterways Museum
Old Goole
Gowdall
Ferrybridge Services
High Eggborough
Cridling Stubbs
Whitley
Great Heck
Chequerfield
Dutch River
Adlingfleet
Southfield Reservoir
Pollington
Aire and Calder Navigation
Balne
Darrington
East Hardwick
Womersley
Goole Fields
Fockerby
Garthorpe
Burton Stather
Wentbridge
Little Smeaton
Walden Stubbs
Goole Moors
Luddington
Low Ackworth
Kirk Smeaton
Sykehouse
Pincheon Green
Thorpe Audlin
Barnsdale Bar Services
Fenwick
Moorends
Humberhead Peatlands
Thorne Waste or Moors
Amcotts
Badsworth
Norton
Campsall
Fosterhouses
Moss
Wrangbrook
Upton
Instoneville
Askern
Fishlake
Far Bank
Doncaster North Services
Thorne
Crowle
North Elmsall
Skelbrooke
Sutton
Haywood
Braithwaite
Canal Side
Stainforth & Keadby Canal
Windsor
Moorthorpe
South Elmsall
Burghwallis
Owston
Thorpe in Balne
Kirk Bramwith
Stainforth
Wike Well End
Ealand
Keadby
Gunness
Hampole
Skellow
Carcroft
Hatfield
Hatfield Chase
Burringham
Adwick le Street
Barnby Dun
Dunscroft
Althorpe
Hooton Pagnell
Almholme
Clayton
Brodsworth
Toll Bar
Kirk Sandall
Hatfield Woodhouse
Sandtoft
Woodhouse
Derrythorpe
Woodlands
Dunsville
West End
The Trolleybus Museum at Sandtoft
Grey Green
Westgate
Thurnscoe
Brodsworth Hall
Arksey
Edenthorpe
Belton
Beltoft
East Butterwick
Thurnscoe East
Hickleton
Marr
Scawsby
Bentley
Museum & Art Gallery
Armthorpe
Hatfield Moors
Church Town
West Butterwick
Goldthorpe
Melton Wood
Cusworth
Wheatley
Nutwell
Isle of Axholme
Epworth
Old Rectory
Bolton upon Dearne
Barnburgh
Newton
Intake
Doncaster
Wroot
Epworth Turbary
Harlington
Sprotbrough
Cusworth Hall Museum
Hyde Park
Cantley
Branton
Low Burnham
Kelfield
Susworth
Scotter
Adwick upon Dearne
High Melton
Balby
Bessacarr
Yorkshire Wildlife Park
Auckley
Mexborough
Cadeby
Lakeside Village
Aeroventure
Lidget
Blaxton
Upperthorpe
Owston Ferry
Warmsworth
Haxey
East Lound
East Ferry
Laughton Forest
Old Denaby
Denaby Main
New Edlington
Loversall
Rossington
Finningley
Westwoodside
Craiselound
Wildsworth
Conisbrough
Conisbrough/Ivanhoe
Robin Hood Airport Doncaster Sheffield
Kilnhurst
New Rossington
Old Edlington
Idle
Laughton
Hooton Roberts
Clifton
Wadworth
St. Leger Horse Park
Thrybergh
Ravenfield
Misson
Misterton
West Stockwith
Blyton
Micklebring
Austerfield
East Stockwith
Dalton
Braithwell
Stainton
Spital Hill
Newington
Bawtry
Walkerith
Bramley
Hellaby
Maltby
Tickhill
Harworth
Walkeringham
Gringley on the Hill
Morton
Gainsborough
Gainsborough Old Hall
Wickersley
Hooton Levitt
Bircotes
Scaftworth
Everton
Carr
Styrrup
Scrooby
Stone
Cuckoo Hill
Wiseton
Beckingham
Thurcroft
Roche Abbey
Firbeck
Oldcotes
Serlby
Mattersey Thorpe
Mattersey
Ulley
Brampton en le Morthen
Laughton en le Morthen
Blyth Services
Ranskill
Clayworth
Saundby
Aughton
Letwell
Langold
Blyth
Torworth
North Wheatley
Bole
Lea
Laughton Common
Dinnington
Gildingwells
Lound
Wetlands Animal Park
Aston
Carlton in Lindrick
Barnby Moor
Sutton
Hayton
South Wheatley
Sturton le Steeple
Knaith Park
Knaith
Swallownest
North Anston
Todwick
Woodsetts
Clarborough
Gate Burton
Kiveton Park
Rother Valley
South Anston
Wales
Wigthorpe
North Leverton with Habblesthorpe
Littleborough
Bassetlaw Museum
Welham
North Leverton Windmill
Marton
Norwood
Thorpe Salvin
Gateford
West Retford
Ranby
Coates
Killamarsh
Harthill
Shireoaks
Scofton
Babworth
Retford
South Leverton
Netherthorpe
Woodall Services
Rhodesia
Kilton
Ordsall
Grove
Cottam
Torksey
Spinkhill
Darfoulds
Worksop
Manton
Treswell
Sundown Adventureland
Rampton
Barlborough
Eaton
Woodbeck
Headon
Stokeham
Church Laneham
Fenton
Mastin Moor
Whitwell
Hodthorpe
Upton
Gamston
Laneham
Laughterton
Clowne
Clumber Park
Elkesley
Kettle
SE
SK
Derwent
Ouse
Aire
Went
Canal
Thorne

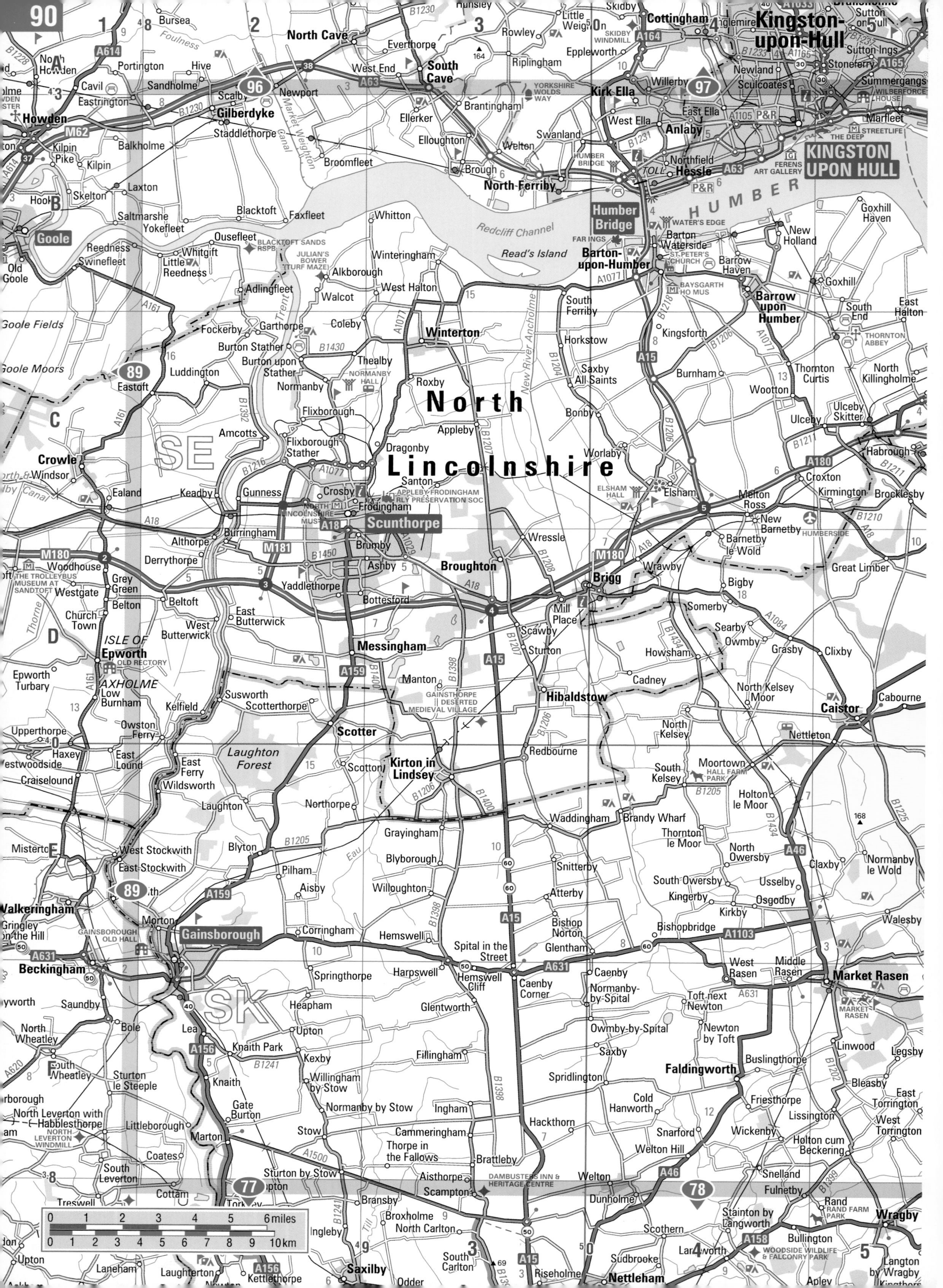
Kingston-upon-Hull
KINGSTON UPON HULL
North Cave
Cottingham
Bursea
Everthorpe
South Cave
Rowley
Little Weighton
Skidby
Skidby Windmill
Eppleworth
Riplingham
Brantingham
Ellerker
Elloughton
Welton
Brough
North Ferriby
Swanland
Kirk Ella
West Ella
Willerby
Anlaby
East Ella
Hessle
Northfield
Newland
Sculcoates
Stoneferry
Sutton Ings
Summergangs
Wilberforce House
Marfleet
The Deep
Streetlife
Ferens Art Gallery
Humber Bridge
Humber
North Howden
Portington
Hive
Sandholme
Cavil
Eastrington
Scalby
Newport
Gilberdyke
Staddlethorpe
West End
Howden
Kilpin Pike
Kilpin
Balkholme
Broomfleet
Laxton
Skelton
Hook
Goole
Saltmarshe
Yokefleet
Blacktoft
Faxfleet
Whitton
Redcliff Channel
Read's Island
Ousefleet
Blacktoft Sands RSPB
Whitgift
Reedness
Swinefleet
Little Reedness
Old Goole
Julian's Bower (Turf Maze)
Alkborough
Winteringham
Far Ings
Barton-upon-Humber
Barton Waterside
Water's Edge
St Peter's Church
Barrow Haven
New Holland
Goxhill Haven
Goxhill
West Halton
Walcot
Adlingfleet
Goole Fields
Fockerby
Garthorpe
Coleby
Winterton
South Ferriby
Baysgarth Ho Mus
Barrow upon Humber
South End
East Halton
Thornton Abbey
Kingsforth
Horkstow
Burton Stather
Burton upon Stather
Thealby
Normanby
Normanby Hall
Roxby
Saxby All Saints
Burnham
Thornton Curtis
North Killingholme
Goole Moors
Eastoft
Luddington
North Lincolnshire
Wootton
Bonby
Flixborough
Ulceby
Ulceby Skitter
Appleby
Amcotts
Flixborough Stather
Dragonby
Worlaby
Habrough
Crowle
SE
Croxton
Santon
Elsham Hall
Elsham
Kirmington
Brocklesby
Ealand
Keadby
Gunness
Crosby
Appleby-Frodingham Rly Preservation Soc
North Lincolnshire Mus
Frodingham
Scunthorpe
Melton Ross
New Barnetby
Humberside
Althorpe
Burringham
Wressle
Barnetby le Wold
Woodhouse
The Trolleybus Museum at Sandtoft
Grey Green
Derrythorpe
Brumby
Ashby
Broughton
Wrawby
Great Limber
Brigg
Bigby
Westgate
Belton
Beltoft
Yaddlethorpe
Bottesford
Somerby
Church Town
West Butterwick
East Butterwick
Mill Place
Scawby
Searby
Owmby
Grasby
Clixby
Isle of Axholme
Epworth
Old Rectory
Messingham
Sturton
Howsham
Epworth Turbary
Manton
Cadney
North Kelsey Moor
Cabourne
Low Burnham
Susworth
Scotterthorpe
Gainsthorpe Deserted Medieval Village
Hibaldstow
Caistor
Kelfield
Owston Ferry
Scotter
North Kelsey
Nettleton
Upperthorpe
Haxey
East Lound
Laughton Forest
Scotton
Kirton in Lindsey
Redbourne
South Kelsey
Moortown
Hall Farm Park
Westwoodside
Craiselound
East Ferry
Wildsworth
Holton le Moor
Laughton
Northorpe
Waddingham
Brandy Wharf
Thornton le Moor
Misterton
West Stockwith
East Stockwith
Blyton
Grayingham
North Owersby
Claxby
Normanby le Wold
Blyborough
Snitterby
South Owersby
Usselby
Pilham
Aisby
Willoughton
Atterby
Kingerby
Osgodby
Walkeringham
Morton
Gainsborough
Gainsborough Old Hall
Gringley on the Hill
Corringham
Hemswell
Bishop Norton
Bishopbridge
Kirkby
Walesby
Glentham
Beckingham
Springthorpe
Harpswell
Spital in the Street
Hemswell Cliff
Caenby Corner
Caenby
Normanby-by-Spital
West Rasen
Middle Rasen
Market Rasen
Saundby
SK
Heapham
Glentworth
Toft next Newton
Bole
North Wheatley
Lea
Upton
Owmby-by-Spital
Newton by Toft
Knaith Park
Fillingham
Saxby
Linwood
Legsby
South Wheatley
Sturton le Steeple
Knaith
Kexby
Willingham by Stow
Spridlington
Buslingthorpe
Faldingworth
Bleasby
Gate Burton
Normanby by Stow
Ingham
Cold Hanworth
Friesthorpe
East Torrington
West Torrington
North Leverton with Habblesthorpe
North Leverton Windmill
Littleborough
Stow
Cammeringham
Hackthorn
Snarford
Wickenby
Lissington
Marton
Thorpe in the Fallows
Welton Hill
Holton cum Beckering
Coates
Brattleby
South Leverton
Sturton by Stow
Aisthorpe
Dambusters Inn & Heritage Centre
Welton
Snelland
Treswell
Cottam
Scampton
Dunholme
Fulnetby
Rand
Rand Farm Park
Wragby
Bransby
Broxholme
North Carlton
Ingleby
Stainton by Langworth
Scothern
Bullington
Upton
South Carlton
Woodside Wildlife & Falconry Park
Lanworth
Laneham
Laughterton
Kettlethorpe
Saxilby
Riseholme
Sudbrooke
Nettleham
Langton by Wragby
Odder
Apley
0 1 2 3 4 5 6 miles
0 1 2 3 4 5 6 7 8 9 10 km

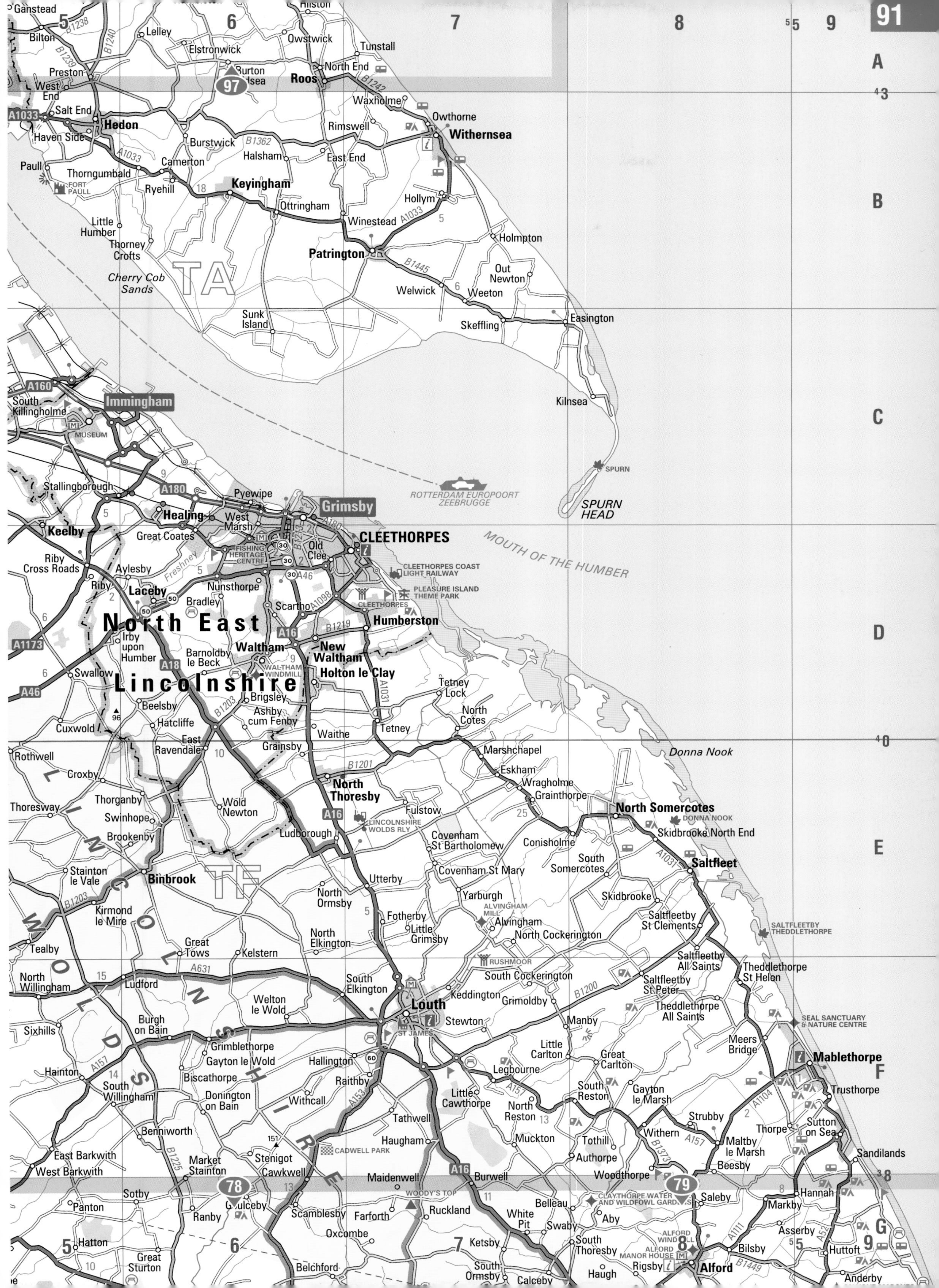

Ganstead
Bilton
Lelley
Elstronwick
Owstwick
Hilston
Tunstall
North End
Roos
Burton
Preston
West End
Salt End
A1033
Hedon
Haven Side
Waxholme
Owthorne
Withernsea
Rimswell
Burstwick
B1362
Halsham
East End
Camerton
Paull
Thorngumbald
FORT PAULL
Ryehill
Keyingham
Ottringham
Hollym
Winestead
Little Humber
Thorney Crofts
Patrington
Holmpton
B1445
Out Newton
Cherry Cob Sands
TA
Welwick
Weeton
Sunk Island
Skeffling
Easington
A160
South Killingholme
Immingham
MUSEUM
Kilnsea
SPURN
Stallingborough
A180
Pyewipe
Grimsby
ROTTERDAM EUROPOORT ZEEBRUGGE
SPURN HEAD
Healing
West Marsh
Keelby
Great Coates
CLEETHORPES
MOUTH OF THE HUMBER
FISHING HERITAGE CENTRE
Old Clee
Riby Cross Roads
Aylesby
Freshney
A46
CLEETHORPES COAST LIGHT RAILWAY
Riby
Laceby
Nunsthorpe
PLEASURE ISLAND THEME PARK
Bradley
Scartho
A1098
CLEETHORPES
North East
Humberston
B1219
A1173
Irby upon Humber
Waltham
New Waltham
Barnoldby le Beck
A18
WALTHAM WINDMILL
Holton le Clay
Swallow
Lincolnshire
Tetney Lock
A1031
Brigsley
Beelsby
Ashby cum Fenby
North Cotes
Cuxwold
Hatcliffe
Waithe
Tetney
B1203
East Ravendale
Grainsby
Rothwell
Marshchapel
Donna Nook
Croxby
B1201
Eskham
North Thoresby
Wragholme
Grainthorpe
Thoresway
Thorganby
Wold Newton
Swinhope
Fulstow
North Somercotes
A16
LINCOLNSHIRE WOLDS RLY
DONNA NOOK
Brookenby
Ludborough
Covenham St Bartholomew
Conisholme
Skidbrooke North End
South Somercotes
Saltfleet
Stainton le Vale
Binbrook
TF
Covenham St Mary
Utterby
North Ormsby
Yarburgh
Skidbrooke
Kirmond le Mire
ALVINGHAM MILL
Fotherby
Saltfleetby St Clements
Alvingham
SALTFLEETBY THEDDLETHORPE
Little Grimsby
North Cockerington
Tealby
Great Tows
North Elkington
Kelstern
Saltfleetby All Saints
RUSHMOOR
Theddlethorpe St Helen
North Willingham
Ludford
A631
South Elkington
South Cockerington
Saltfleetby St Peter
Keddington
Grimoldby
B1200
Welton le Wold
Louth
Theddlethorpe All Saints
Sixhills
Burgh on Bain
Stewton
SEAL SANCTUARY & NATURE CENTRE
ST JAMES
Manby
Grimblethorpe
Little Carlton
Meers Bridge
Gayton le Wold
Great Carlton
Hallington
Mablethorpe
Hainton
A157
Legbourne
Biscathorpe
Raithby
South Willingham
Donington on Bain
South Reston
Trusthorpe
Withcall
Little Cawthorpe
Gayton le Marsh
A153
North Reston
A1104
Tathwell
Strubby
Thorpe
Sutton on Sea
Benniworth
Withern
Haugham
Muckton
Tothill
Maltby le Marsh
Sandilands
East Barkwith
B1225
Market Stainton
Stenigot
CADWELL PARK
B1373
Authorpe
West Barkwith
Cawkwell
Beesby
Maidenwell
Burwell
Woodthorpe
WOODY'S TOP
CLAYTHORPE WATER AND WILDFOWL GARDENS
Saleby
Hannah
Sotby
Panton
Goulceby
Scamblesby
Farforth
Ruckland
White Pit
Belleau
Markby
Ranby
Swaby
Aby
Oxcombe
A1111
Asserby
Hatton
Ketsby
ALFORD WINDMILL
South Thoresby
Bilsby
Huttoft
Great Sturton
ALFORD MANOR HOUSE
B1449
Belchford
South Ormsby
Haugh
Rigsby
Alford
Anderby
Calceby
A52

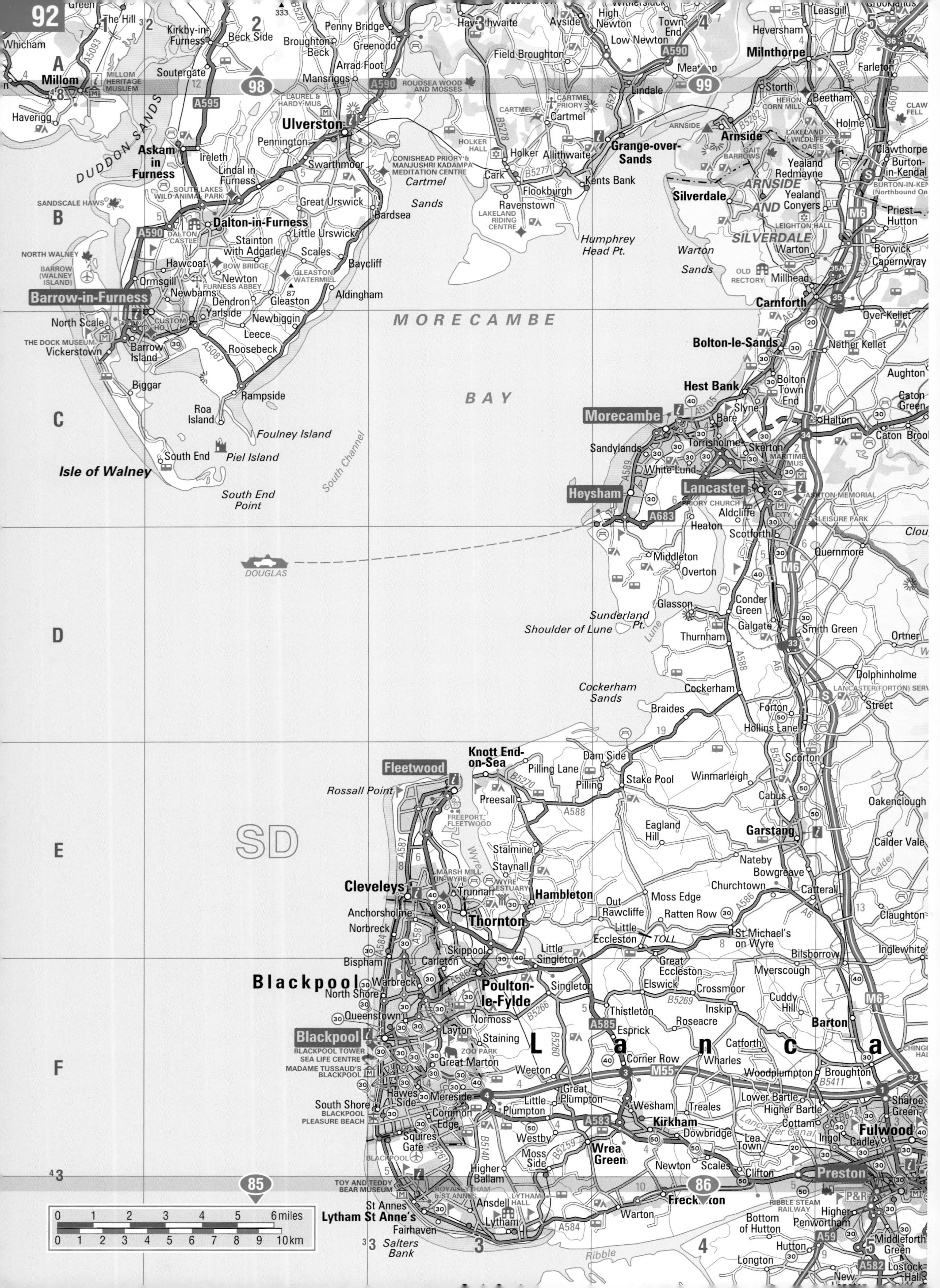
Whicham
Millom
MILLOM HERITAGE MUSEUM
Haverigg
The Hill
Kirkby-in-Furness
Beck Side
Soutergate
Broughton Beck
Penny Bridge
Greenodd
Arrad Foot
Mansriggs
Haverthwaite
Ayside
High Newton
Low Newton
Town End
Field Broughton
Meathop
Lindale
Heversham
Milnthorpe
Leasgill
Farleton
Storth
Beetham
HERON CORN MILL
CLAW FELL
Holme
LAURELL & HARDY MUS
ROUDSEA WOOD AND MOSSES
Ulverston
CARTMEL
CARTMEL PRIORY
Cartmel
Grange-over-Sands
ARNSIDE
Arnside
GAIT BARROWS
LAKELAND WILDLIFE OASIS
Yealand Redmayne
Clawthorpe
Burton-in-Kendal
BURTON-IN-KENDAL (Northbound Only)
DUDDON SANDS
Askam in Furness
Ireleth
Pennington
HOLKER HALL
Holker
Allithwaite
Lindal in Furness
Swarthmoor
CONISHEAD PRIORY & MANJUSHRI KADAMPA MEDITATION CENTRE
Cartmel Sands
Cark
Flookburgh
Kents Bank
Silverdale
ARNSIDE AND SILVERDALE
Yealand Conyers
Priest Hutton
SOUTH LAKES WILD ANIMAL PARK
SANDSCALE HAWS
Great Urswick
Bardsea
Ravenstown
LAKELAND RIDING CENTRE
Dalton-in-Furness
DALTON CASTLE
Little Urswick
LEIGHTON HALL
Warton
Borwick
Capernwray
NORTH WALNEY
BARROW (WALNEY ISLAND)
Stainton with Adgarley
Scales
Humphrey Head Pt.
Warton Sands
Hawcoat
BOW BRIDGE
Baycliff
GLEASTON WATERMILL
OLD RECTORY
Millhead
Ormsgill
FURNESS ABBEY
Newton
Newbarns
Dendron
Gleaston
Aldingham
Barrow-in-Furness
Yarlside
Newbiggin
Carnforth
Over Kellet
North Scale
CUSTOM HO
MORECAMBE
THE DOCK MUSEUM
Vickerstown
Barrow Island
Leece
Roosebeck
Bolton-le-Sands
Nether Kellet
Biggar
Rampside
Bolton Town End
Aughton
BAY
Hest Bank
Slyne
Bare
Halton
Caton Green
Caton
Brookhouse
Roa Island
Foulney Island
Morecambe
Torrisholme
Skerton
South End
Piel Island
South Channel
Sandylands
MARITIME MUS
Isle of Walney
White Lund
Lancaster
South End Point
Heysham
PRIORY CHURCH
ASHTON MEMORIAL
Aldcliffe
CITY
LEISURE PARK
Heaton
Scotforth
Quernmore
DOUGLAS
Middleton
Overton
Conder Green
Glasson
Sunderland Pt.
Shoulder of Lune
Lune
Galgate
Smith Green
Thurnham
Ortner
Dolphinholme
Cockerham Sands
Cockerham
LANCASTER (FORTON) SERV
Braides
Forton
Street
Hollins Lane
Knott End-on-Sea
Dam Side
Fleetwood
Pilling Lane
Pilling
Stake Pool
Winmarleigh
Scorton
Rossall Point
Preesall
Cabus
Oakenclough
FREEPORT FLEETWOOD
Eagland Hill
Garstang
SD
Stalmine
Nateby
Calder Vale
Staynall
Bowgreave
MARSH MILL-IN-WYRE
WYRE ESTUARY
Cleveleys
Trunnah
Hambleton
Churchtown
Catterall
Anchorsholme
Moss Edge
Out Rawcliffe
Ratten Row
Claughton
Thornton
Norbreck
Little Eccleston
TOLL
St Michael's on Wyre
Skippool
Little Singleton
Bispham
Carleton
Great Eccleston
Bilsborrow
Inglewhite
Blackpool
Warbreck
Poulton-le-Fylde
Singleton
Elswick
Crossmoor
Myerscough
North Shore
Thistleton
Cuddy Hill
Queenstown
Normoss
Inskip
Roseacre
Barton
Layton
Staining
Esprick
Blackpool
BLACKPOOL TOWER
SEA LIFE CENTRE
ZOO PARK
Lancashire
Catforth
MADAME TUSSAUD'S BLACKPOOL
Great Marton
Corner Row
Wharles
Weeton
Woodplumpton
Broughton
Hawes Side
Mereside
Little Plumpton
Great Plumpton
Lower Bartle
Sharoe Green
South Shore
BLACKPOOL PLEASURE BEACH
Common Edge
Wesham
Treales
Higher Bartle
Kirkham
Cottam
Fulwood
Westby
Dowbridge
Lancaster Canal
Ingol
Cadley
Squires Gate
Wrea Green
Lea Town
BLACKPOOL
Moss Side
Scales
Higher Ballam
Newton
Clifton
Preston
TOY AND TEDDY BEAR MUSEUM
ROYAL LYTHAM & ST. ANNES
LYTHAM HALL
Freckleton
RIBBLE STEAM RAILWAY
P&R
St Annes
Ansdell
Higher Penwortham
Lytham St Anne's
Lytham
Warton
Bottom of Hutton
Fairhaven
Middleforth Green
Salters Bank
Ribble
Hutton
Longton
Lostock Hall
New
0 1 2 3 4 5 6 miles
0 1 2 3 4 5 6 7 8 9 10 km
98
99
85
86
M6
M55
A590
A595
A5087
A588
A683
A6
A585
A583
A584
A587
A586
A589
A59
A582
B5269
B5270
B5266
B5260
B5259
B5261
B5140
B5411
B5278
B5277
B5271

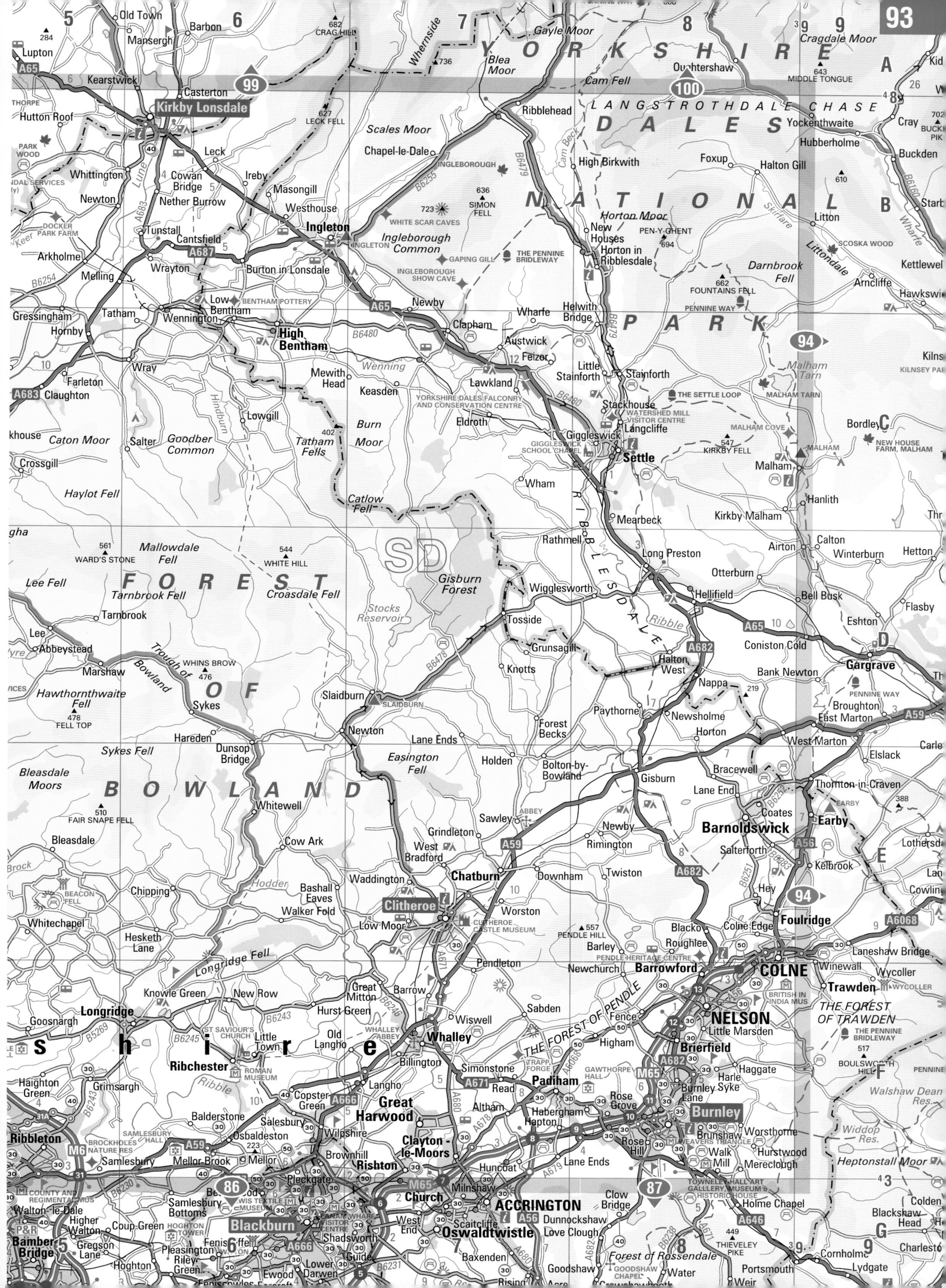
YORKSHIRE DALES NATIONAL PARK
FOREST OF BOWLAND
LANGSTROTHDALE CHASE
SD
Kirkby Lonsdale
Old Town
Mansergh
Barbon
Lupton
Kearstwick
Casterton
Hutton Roof
Leck
Cowan Bridge
Ireby
Whittington
Newton
Nether Burrow
Masongill
Westhouse
Ingleton
Tunstall
Cantsfield
Arkholme
Melling
Wrayton
Burton in Lonsdale
Low Bentham
Gressingham
Hornby
Tatham
Wennington
High Bentham
Wray
Farleton
Claughton
Caton Moor
Salter
Goodber Common
Lowgill
Tatham Fells
Burn Moor
Crossgill
Haylot Fell
Catlow Fell
Mewith Head
Keasden
Wenning
Newby
Clapham
Austwick
Feizor
Lawkland
Eldroth
YORKSHIRE DALES FALCONRY AND CONSERVATION CENTRE
Scales Moor
Chapel-le-Dale
INGLEBOROUGH
SIMON FELL
WHITE SCAR CAVES
Ingleborough Common
GAPING GILL
INGLEBOROUGH SHOW CAVE
THE PENNINE BRIDLEWAY
Whernside
CRAG HILL
LECK FELL
Blea Moor
Gayle Moor
Cam Fell
Ribblehead
High Birkwith
Horton Moor
New Houses
Horton in Ribblesdale
PEN-Y-GHENT
Helwith Bridge
Wharfe
Little Stainforth
Stainforth
Stackhouse
WATERSHED MILL VISITOR CENTRE
Langcliffe
Giggleswick
GIGGLESWICK SCHOOL CHAPEL
Settle
Wham
Mearbeck
Rathmell
Long Preston
Wigglesworth
Tosside
Gisburn Forest
Stocks Reservoir
Grunsagill
Knotts
Halton West
Hellifield
Otterburn
Oughtershaw
Cragdale Moor
MIDDLE TONGUE
Yockenthwaite
Hubberholme
Buckden
Cray
Foxup
Halton Gill
Litton
Littondale
SCOSKA WOOD
Kettlewell
Arncliffe
Darnbrook Fell
FOUNTAINS FELL
PENNINE WAY
Malham Tarn
MALHAM TARN
THE SETTLE LOOP
MALHAM COVE
KIRKBY FELL
Malham
NEW HOUSE FARM, MALHAM
Bordley
Hanlith
Kirkby Malham
Airton
Calton
Winterburn
Hetton
Bell Busk
Flasby
Eshton
Coniston Cold
Gargrave
Bank Newton
Broughton
East Marton
West Marton
Elslack
Thornton-in-Craven
Earby
Barnoldswick
Salterforth
Kelbrook
Coates
Bracewell
Lane End
Gisburn
Newsholme
Horton
Nappa
Paythorne
Forest Becks
Bolton-by-Bowland
Holden
Sawley
Rimington
Newby
Twiston
Downham
Chatburn
Grindleton
West Bradford
Waddington
Clitheroe
CLITHEROE CASTLE MUSEUM
Low Moor
Worston
PENDLE HILL
Barley
Blacko
Roughlee
Colne Edge
Foulridge
Laneshaw Bridge
Winewall
Wycoller
Trawden
THE FOREST OF TRAWDEN
COLNE
NELSON
BRITISH IN INDIA MUS
Little Marsden
Brierfield
Barrowford
PENDLE HERITAGE CENTRE
Newchurch
Pendleton
Sabden
Fence
Higham
THE FOREST OF PENDLE
Simonstone
Read
Padiham
GAWTHORPE HALL
Burnley
Harle Syke
Haggate
Rose Grove
Habergham
Hapton
Rose Hill
Brunshaw
Worsthorne
Hurstwood
Mereclough
WEAVERS TRIANGLE
Walk Mill
Lane Ends
Huncoat
TOWNELEY HALL ART GALLERY, MUSEUM & HISTORIC HOUSE
Holme Chapel
Walshaw Dean Res.
Widdop Res.
Heptonstall Moor
BOULSWORTH HILL
Colden
Blackshaw Head
Charlestown
Cornholme
Lydgate
Portsmouth
THIEVELEY PIKE
Forest of Rossendale
Goodshaw
Water
Weir
Clow Bridge
Dunnockshaw
Love Clough
ACCRINGTON
Oswaldtwistle
Baxenden
Scaitcliffe
West End
Church
Milnshaw
Clayton-le-Moors
Rishton
Altham
Great Harwood
Whalley
WHALLEY ABBEY
Billington
Langho
Wiswell
Barrow
Great Mitton
Hurst Green
Old Langho
Copster Green
Salesbury
Wilpshire
Osbaldeston
Mellor
Mellor Brook
Samlesbury
SAMLESBURY HALL
Balderstone
Ribchester
ROMAN MUSEUM
Little Town
ST SAVIOUR'S CHURCH
Longridge
Longridge Fell
Knowle Green
New Row
Goosnargh
Grimsargh
Haighton Green
Ribbleton
BROCKHOLES NATURE RES
Blackburn
Pleckgate
Brownhill
Shadsworth
Guide
Lower Darwen
Feniscowles
Pleasington
Riley Green
Hoghton
Samlesbury Bottoms
Walton-le-Dale
Higher Walton
Coup Green
Gregson Lane
Bamber Bridge
Chipping
BEACON FELL
Whitechapel
Hesketh Lane
Cow Ark
Bashall Eaves
Walker Fold
Whitewell
Bleasdale
Bleasdale Moors
FAIR SNAPE FELL
Dunsop Bridge
Hareden
Sykes Fell
Sykes
Trough of Bowland
WHINS BROW
Hawthornthwaite Fell
FELL TOP
Marshaw
Abbeystead
Lee
Tarnbrook
Tarnbrook Fell
Lee Fell
Mallowdale Fell
WARD'S STONE
WHITE HILL
Croasdale Fell
Slaidburn
Newton
Lane Ends
Easington Fell
Ribble
Hodder
Lune
Hindburn
RIBBLESDALE
Skirfare
Wharfe
A65
A683
A687
A682
A59
A56
A6068
A646
A671
A666
A680
A678
A679
M65
M6
B6480
B6479
B6255
B6478
B6254
B6243
B6245
B6246
B6251
B6383
B6160
B5269
86
87
94
99
100

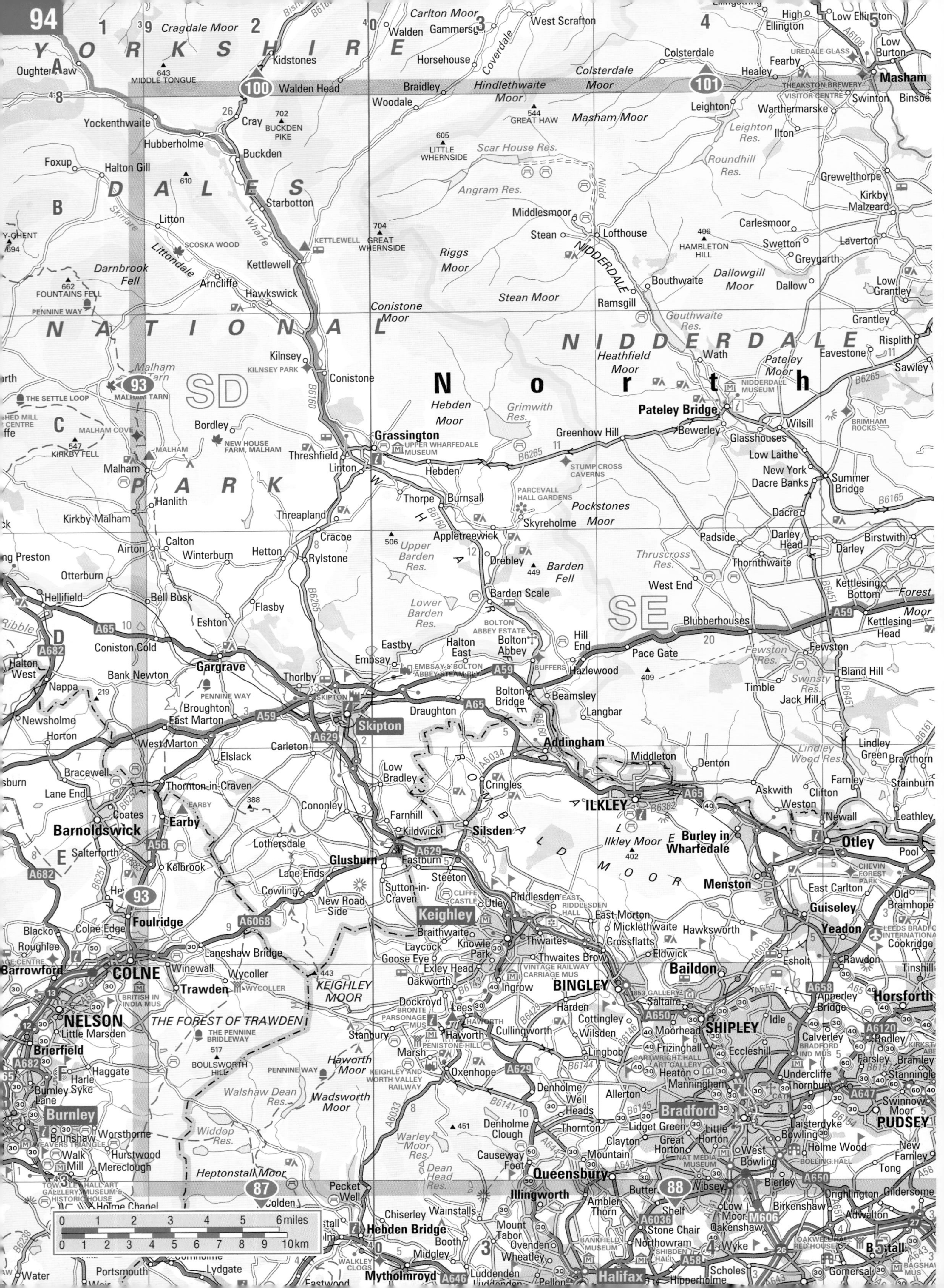
YORKSHIRE
DALES
NATIONAL
PARK
NIDDERDALE
North
SD
SE
Cragdale Moor
Carlton Moor
Walden
Gammersgill
West Scrafton
High Ellington
Low Ellington
Low Burton
Oughtershaw
643 MIDDLE TONGUE
Kidstones
Horsehouse
Coverdale
Colsterdale
Colsterdale Moor
Healey
Fearby
UREDALE GLASS
THEAKSTON BREWERY VISITOR CENTRE
Masham
100
Walden Head
Braidley
Hindlethwaite Moor
101
Woodale
Leighton
Warthermarske
Swinton
Binsoe
Yockenthwaite
Cray
702 BUCKDEN PIKE
544 GREAT HAW
Masham Moor
Leighton Res.
Ilton
Hubberholme
Buckden
605 LITTLE WHERNSIDE
Scar House Res.
Roundhill Res.
Foxup
Halton Gill
610
Angram Res.
Grewelthorpe
Kirkby Malzeard
Starbotton
Nidd
Litton
Middlesmoor
Carlesmoor
Y-GHENT 694
SCOSKA WOOD
Wharfe
KETTLEWELL
704 GREAT WHERNSIDE
Stean
Lofthouse
406 HAMBLETON HILL
Swetton
Laverton
Littondale
Riggs Moor
NIDDERDALE
Greygarth
Darnbrook Fell
Kettlewell
Dallowgill Moor
Arncliffe
Hawkswick
Bouthwaite
Dallow
Low Grantley
662 FOUNTAINS FELL
Stean Moor
Ramsgill
PENNINE WAY
Conistone Moor
GoDalewaite Res.
Grantley
Risplith
Eavestone
Sawley
Heathfield Moor
Wath
Pateley Moor
Kilnsey
KILNSEY PARK
Malham Tarn
93
MALHAM TARN
Conistone
B6160
NIDDERDALE MUSEUM
B6265
THE SETTLE LOOP
Hebden Moor
Grimwith Res.
Pateley Bridge
Bordley
Greenhow Hill
Bewerley
Wilsill
Glasshouses
BRIMHAM ROCKS
MALHAM COVE
547 KIRKBY FELL
NEW HOUSE FARM, MALHAM
Grassington
UPPER WHARFEDALE MUSEUM
Threshfield
MALHAM
Malham
Linton
Hebden
STUMP CROSS CAVERNS
Low Laithe
New York
Dacre Banks
Summer Bridge
B6165
Hanlith
Thorpe
Burnsall
PARCEVALL HALL GARDENS
Pockstones Moor
Kirkby Malham
Threapland
Dacre
Skyreholme
Cracoe
506
Appletreewick
Padside
Darley Head
Birstwith
Darley
Airton
Calton
Winterburn
Hetton
Rylstone
Upper Barden Res.
Drebley
449
Barden Fell
Thruscross Res.
Thornthwaite
Long Preston
Otterburn
West End
Kettlesing Bottom
Forest Moor
Hellifield
Bell Busk
Flasby
Lower Barden Res.
Barden Scale
B6451
Eshton
A65
Ribble
BOLTON ABBEY ESTATE
Bolton Abbey
Blubberhouses
A59
Kettlesing Head
A682
Coniston Cold
Eastby
Halton East
Hill End
Pace Gate
Fewston Res.
Fewston
Halton West
Gargrave
Embsay
EMBSAY & BOLTON ABBEY STEAM RLY
BUFFERS
Hazlewood
409
Bland Hill
Swinsty Res.
Bank Newton
Thorlby
Timble
Nappa
219
PENNINE WAY
Broughton
SKIPTON
Bolton Bridge
Beamsley
Jack Hill
Newsholme
East Marton
Draughton
Langbar
Skipton
Horton
A629
West Marton
Carleton
Addingham
Elslack
Middleton
Denton
Lindley Wood Res.
Lindley Green
Braythorn
Bracewell
Low Bradley
A6034
Thornton-in-Craven
Cringles
Askwith
Farnley
Stainburn
Clifton
Lane End
EARBY
388
A65
ILKLEY
B6382
Weston
Newall
Leathley
Coates
Cononley
Farnhill
Barnoldswick
Earby
Kildwick
Silsden
RUMBALDS MOOR
Ilkley Moor
Burley in Wharfedale
Otley
Pool
A56
Lothersdale
Salterforth
Glusburn
Eastburn
402
B6383
Kelbrook
Lane Ends
Steeton
Menston
CHEVIN FOREST PARK
East Carlton
Old Bramhope
Cowling
Sutton-in-Craven
CLIFFE CASTLE
Riddlesden
EAST RIDDLESDEN HALL
Guiseley
New Road Side
Utley
93
Foulridge
A6068
Keighley
East Morton
Micklethwaite
Yeadon
LEEDS BRADFORD INTERNATIONAL
Cookridge
Blacko
Colne Edge
Braithwaite
Crossflatts
Hawksworth
Roughlee
Laycock
Knowle Park
Thwaites
Goose Eye
Thwaites Brow
Eldwick
A6038
Esholt
Rawdon
Barrowford
COLNE
Laneshaw Bridge
Exley Head
Baildon
Tinshill
Winewall
Wycoller
443
VINTAGE RAILWAY CARRIAGE MUS
Oakworth
BINGLEY
Ingrow
1853 GALLERY
A658
Horsforth
Trawden
WYCOLLER
KEIGHLEY MOOR
BRITISH IN INDIA MUS
Dockroyd
Lees
Harden
Saltaire
Apperley Bridge
NELSON
THE FOREST OF TRAWDEN
BRONTE PARSONAGE MUS
HAWORTH
B6429
Cottingley
A650
SHIPLEY
Idle
Little Marsden
THE PENNINE BRIDLEWAY
Stanbury
Haworth
Cullingworth
Wilsden
Moorhead
Calverley
Rodley
A6120
Brierfield
517 BOULSWORTH HILL
PENNINE WAY
Haworth Moor
PENISTONE HILL
Marsh
Lingbob
Frizinghall
Eccleshill
Farsley
Bramley
A682
Haggate
KEIGHLEY AND WORTH VALLEY RAILWAY
Oxenhope
A629
B6144
CARTWRIGHT HALL ART GALLERY
Heaton
Manningham
Undercliffe
Thornbury
Stanningley
Harle Syke
Burnley Lane
Walshaw Dean Res.
Wadsworth Moor
Denholme
Allerton
A647
Swinnow Moor
Burnley
A6033
B6141
Well Heads
B6145
Bradford
PUDSEY
Brunshaw
Worsthorne
Widdop Res.
451
Denholme Clough
Thornton
Lidget Green
Little Horton
Laisterdyke
Bowling
WEAVERS TRIANGLE
Hurstwood
Warley Moor Res.
Clayton
Great Horton
Holme Wood
Walk Mill
Mereclough
Causeway Foot
A644
Mountain
NAT MEDIA MUSEUM
West Bowling
BOLLING HALL
New Farnley
Tong
TOWNELEY HALL ART GALLERY & HISTORIC HOUSE
Heptonstall Moor
Dean Head Res.
Queensbury
A647
Bierley
87
Colden
Pecket Well
Illingworth
Butter
88
Wibsey
A650
Drighlington
Gildersome
Holme Chapel
Ambler Thorn
Shelf
Low Moor
Birkenshaw
Chiserley
Wainstalls
Adwalton
Hebden Bridge
Mount Tabor
A6036
Stone Chair
Oakenshaw
M606
Booth
Ovenden
BANKFIELD MUSEUM
Northowram
Wyke
OAKWELL HALL
RED HOUSE
Birstall
Midgley
Wheatley
SHIBDEN HALL
A58
Portsmouth
Lydgate
WALKLEY CLOGS
Mytholmroyd
A646
Luddenden
Pellon
Halifax
Hipperholme
Scholes
Gomersal
BAGSHAW MUS
Water
0 1 2 3 4 5 6 miles
0 1 2 3 4 5 6 7 8 9 10 km

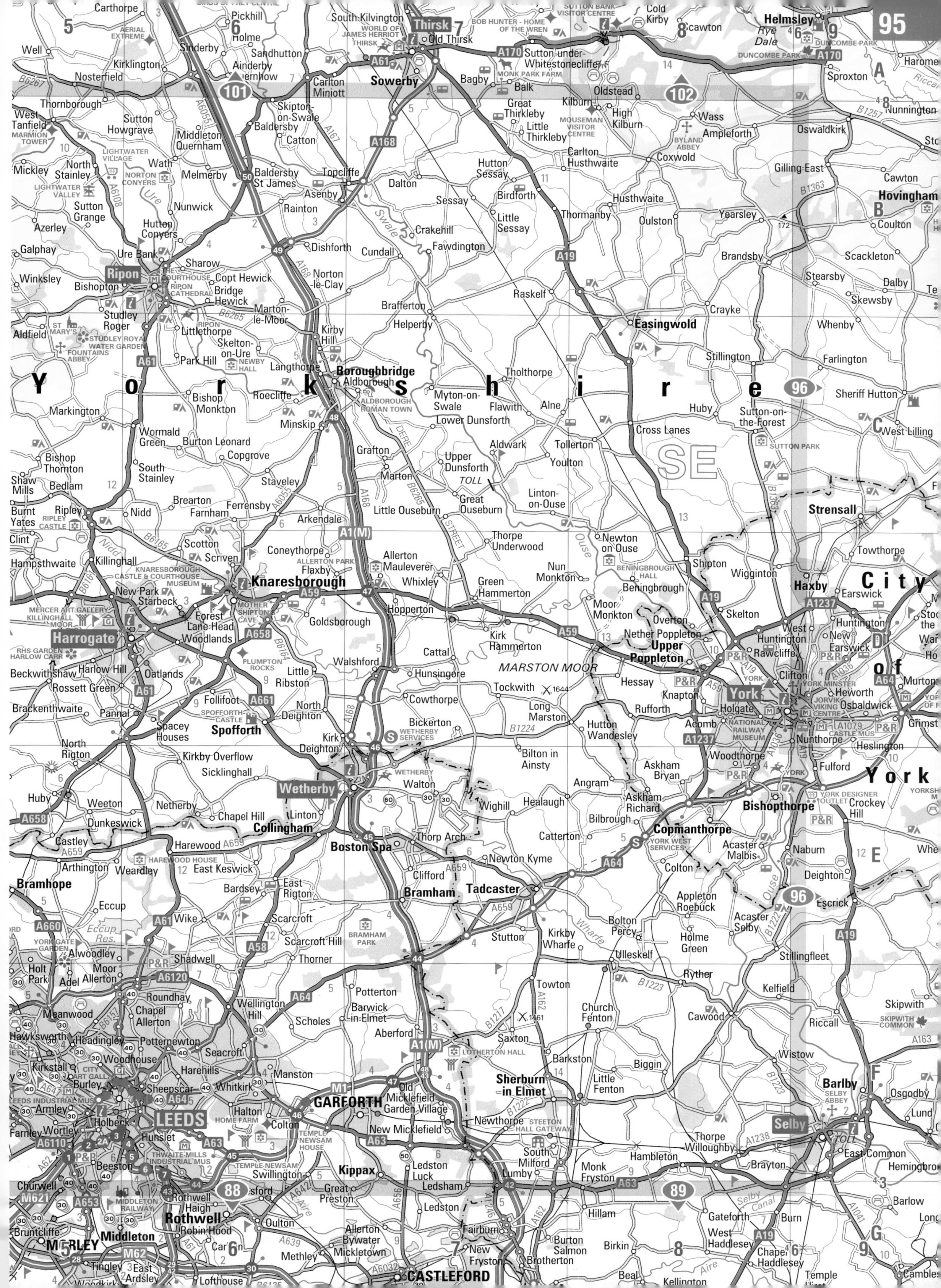
Carthorpe
Pickhill
South Kilvington
WORLD OF JAMES HERRIOT
Thirsk
BOB HUNTER - HOME OF THE WREN
SUTTON BANK VISITOR CENTRE
Cold Kirby
Scawton
Helmsley
Rye Dale
DUNCOMBE PARK
Harome
Well
AERIAL EXTREME
Sinderby
Holme
Old Thirsk
Sutton-under-Whitestonecliffe
Kirklington
Ainderby Quernhow
Sandhutton
Carlton Miniott
Sowerby
Bagby
MONK PARK FARM
Balk
Oldstead
Sproxton
Nosterfield
Thornborough
West Tanfield
MARMION TOWER
Sutton Howgrave
Middleton Quernham
Skipton-on-Swale
Baldersby
Catton
Great Thirkleby
Little Thirkleby
Kilburn
High Kilburn
MOUSEMAN VISITOR CENTRE
Wass
Ampleforth
BYLAND ABBEY
Nunnington
Oswaldkirk
LIGHTWATER VILLAGE
Mickley
North Stainley
NORTON CONYERS
Wath
Melmerby
Baldersby St James
Topcliffe
Carlton Husthwaite
Coxwold
Gilling East
Cawton
LIGHTWATER VALLEY
Sutton Grange
Nunwick
Asenby
Rainton
Dalton
Hutton Sessay
Sessay
Birdforth
Husthwaite
Thormanby
Oulston
Yearsley
Hovingham
Coulton
Azerley
Hutton Conyers
Crakehill
Little Sessay
Fawdington
Galphay
Ure Bank
Sharow
Dishforth
Cundall
Brandsby
Scackleton
Ripon
RIPON CATHEDRAL
Winksley
Bishopton
Copt Hewick
Bridge Hewick
Norton-le-Clay
Raskelf
Stearsby
Dalby
Skewsby
Studley Roger
Marton-le-Moor
Brafferton
Helperby
Crayke
Easingwold
Whenby
Aldfield
ST MARY'S
STUDLEY ROYAL WATER GARDEN
FOUNTAINS ABBEY
Littlethorpe
Skelton-on-Ure
NEWBY HALL
Kirby Hill
Park Hill
Langthorpe
Boroughbridge
Aldborough
ALDBOROUGH ROMAN TOWN
Tholthorpe
Stillington
Farlington
Y o r k s h i r e
Bishop Monkton
Roecliffe
Myton-on-Swale
Flawith
Alne
Huby
Sutton-on-the-Forest
Sheriff Hutton
Markington
Minskip
Lower Dunsforth
Cross Lanes
SUTTON PARK
West Lilling
Wormald Green
Burton Leonard
Aldwark
Tollerton
Bishop Thornton
Copgrove
Grafton
Upper Dunsforth
Youlton
SE
South Stainley
Marton
TOLL
Shaw Mills
Bedlam
Staveley
Linton-on-Ouse
Great Ouseburn
Burnt Yates
Ripley
RIPLEY CASTLE
Nidd
Brearton
Farnham
Ferrensby
Little Ouseburn
Arkendale
Strensall
Clint
Scotton
Scriven
Coneythorpe
Allerton Mauleverer
ALLERTON PARK
Thorpe Underwood
Newton on Ouse
Towthorpe
Hampsthwaite
Killinghall
KNARESBOROUGH CASTLE & COURTHOUSE MUSEUM
Knaresborough
Flaxby
Whixley
Nun Monkton
BENINGBROUGH HALL
Beningbrough
Shipton
Wigginton
Haxby
Earswick
City of York
New Park
Starbeck
MOTHER SHIPTON'S CAVE
Green Hammerton
Moor Monkton
Skelton
Huntington
MERCER ART GALLERY
KILLINGHALL MOOR
Forest Lane Head
Goldsborough
Hopperton
Overton
West Huntington
Harrogate
Woodlands
Kirk Hammerton
Nether Poppleton
Upper Poppleton
Rawcliffe
New Earswick
RHS GARDEN HARLOW CARR
PLUMPTON ROCKS
Cattal
MARSTON MOOR
Clifton
YORK MINSTER
Murton
Harlow Hill
Oatlands
Little Ribston
Walshford
Hunsingore
Hessay
York
Heworth
Beckwithshaw
Rossett Green
Tockwith
Knapton
Osbaldwick
Brackenthwaite
Follifoot
Cowthorpe
Long Marston
Rufforth
Holgate
JORVIK VIKING CENTRE
Grimston
Pannal
SPOFFORTH CASTLE
Spofforth
North Deighton
Bickerton
Hutton Wandesley
Acomb
NATIONAL RAILWAY MUSEUM
CASTLE MUS
Spacey Houses
Kirk Deighton
WETHERBY SERVICES
Nunthorpe
Heslington
North Rigton
Kirkby Overflow
Bilton in Ainsty
Woodthorpe
Askham Bryan
Fulford
Sicklinghall
WETHERBY
Walton
Angram
Askham Richard
York
Huby
Weeton
Wetherby
Wighill
Healaugh
Bishopthorpe
YORK DESIGNER OUTLET
Crockey Hill
Netherby
Chapel Hill
Linton
Bilbrough
Dunkeswick
Collingham
Copmanthorpe
YORK WEST SERVICES
Castley
Harewood
Thorp Arch
Catterton
Acaster Malbis
Naburn
Boston Spa
HAREWOOD HOUSE
Newton Kyme
Arthington
Weardley
East Keswick
Clifford
Colton
Deighton
Bramhope
Bardsey
East Rigton
Bramham
Tadcaster
Appleton Roebuck
Escrick
Eccup
Scarcroft
Bolton Percy
Acaster Selby
Wike
Stutton
Kirkby Wharfe
Holme Green
Eccup Res.
BRAMHAM PARK
YORK GATE GARDEN
Scarcroft Hill
Alwoodley
Shadwell
Thorner
Ulleskelf
Stillingfleet
Holt Park
Adel
Moor Allerton
Rythe
Towton
Kelfield
Potterton
Roundhay
Meanwood
Chapel Allerton
Wellington Hill
Barwick in-Elmet
Church Fenton
Cawood
Skipwith
SKIPWITH COMMON
Scholes
Hawksworth
Headingley
Potternewton
Aberford
Saxton
Riccall
Seacroft
LOTHERTON HALL
Wistow
Woodhouse
Harehills
Barkston
Biggin
Kirkstall
CITY ART GALLERY
Manston
Burley
Sheepscar
Whitkirk
Sherburn in Elmet
Little Fenton
Barlby
Old Micklefield
LEEDS INDUSTRIAL MUS
GARFORTH
Garden Village
SELBY ABBEY
Osgodby
Armley
Halton
Colton
HOME FARM
LEEDS
TEMPLE NEWSAM HOUSE
Newthorpe
STEETON HALL GATEWAY
Thorpe Willoughby
Selby
Lund
Farnley
Wortley
Holbeck
Hunslet
New Micklefield
South Milford
Hambleton
THWAITE MILLS INDUSTRIAL MUS
Beeston
TEMPLE NEWSAM
Swillington
Kippax
Ledston Luck
Monk Fryston
Brayton
East Common
Hemingbrough
Lumby
Churwell
MIDDLETON RAILWAY
Rothwell
Great Preston
Ledsham
Hillam
Barlow
Rothwell Haigh
Ledston
Gateforth
Burn
Bruntcliffe
Middleton
Robin Hood
Oulton
Allerton Bywater
Fairburn
Burton Salmon
West Haddlesey
MORLEY
Carlton
Methley
Mickletown
New Fryston
Birkin
Chapel Haddlesey
Tingley
East Ardsley
Lofthouse
CASTLEFORD
Brotherton
Beal
Kellington
Temple Hirst
Camblesforth
Woodkirk
Selby Canal

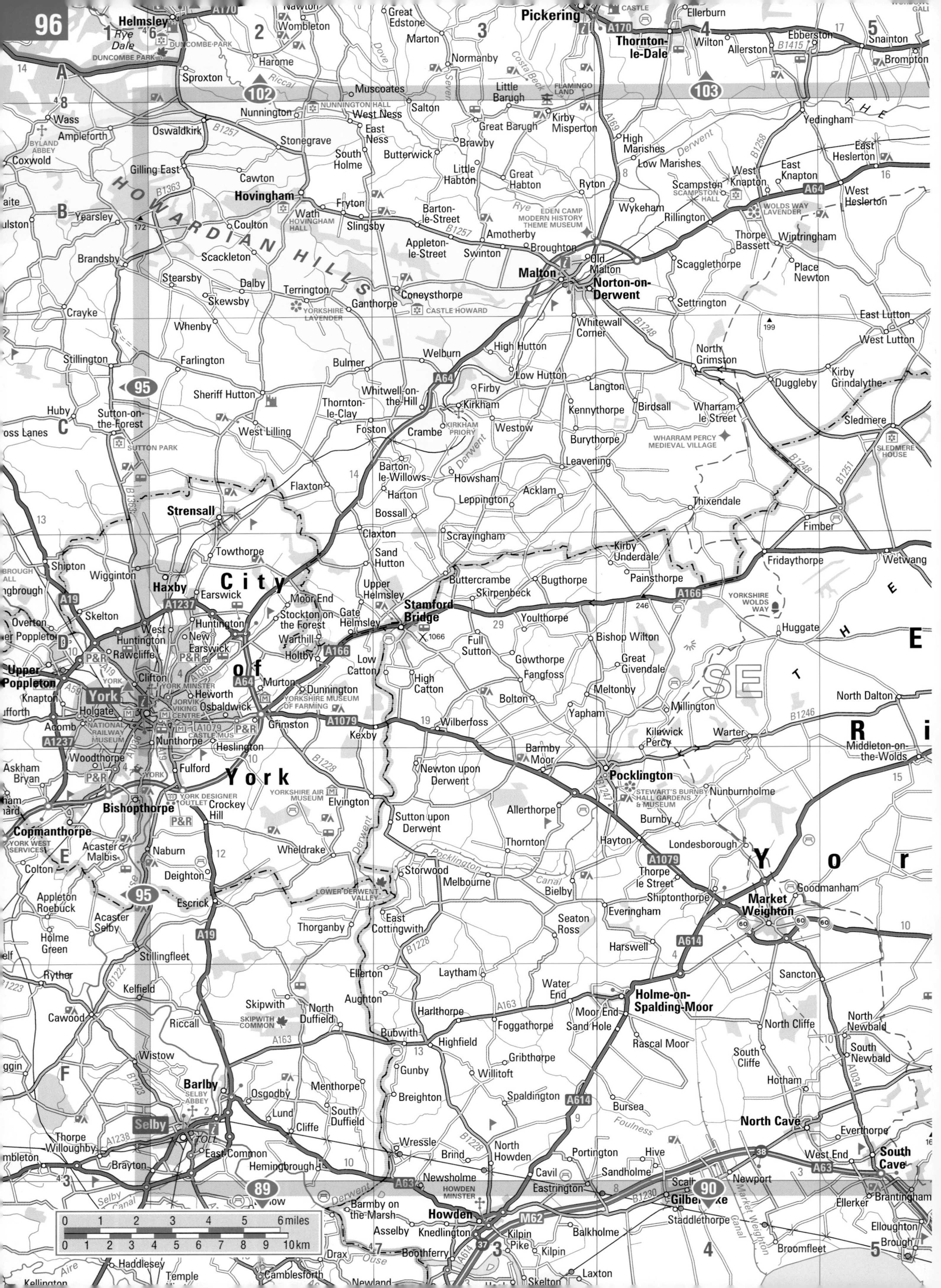

Helmsley
Rye Dale
Duncombe Park
Nawton
Wombleton
Great Edstone
Marton
Pickering
Castle
Ellerburn
Thornton-le-Dale
Wilton
Allerston
Ebberston
Snainton
Brompton
Harome
Normanby
Sproxton
Riccal
Muscoates
Little Barugh
Flamingo Land
Nunnington
Nunnington Hall
Salton
West Ness
East Ness
Great Barugh
Kirby Misperton
Wass
Ampleforth
Byland Abbey
Oswaldkirk
Stonegrave
South Holme
Butterwick
Brawby
High Marishes
Low Marishes
Yedingham
East Heslerton
Coxwold
Gilling East
Cawton
Little Habton
Great Habton
Ryton
Scampston
Scampston Hall
West Knapton
East Knapton
West Heslerton
Howardian Hills
Hovingham
Hovingham Hall
Wath
Fryton
Slingsby
Barton-le-Street
Eden Camp Modern History Theme Museum
Wykeham
Rillington
Wolds Way Lavender
Yearsley
Coulton
Amotherby
Thorpe Bassett
Wintringham
Brandsby
Scackleton
Appleton-le-Street
Swinton
Broughton
Old Malton
Malton
Norton-on-Derwent
Scagglethorpe
Place Newton
Stearsby
Dalby
Terrington
Skewsby
Yorkshire Lavender
Ganthorpe
Coneysthorpe
Castle Howard
Settrington
Crayke
Whenby
Whitewall Corner
East Lutton
West Lutton
Stillington
Farlington
Bulmer
Welburn
High Hutton
Low Hutton
North Grimston
Duggleby
Kirby Grindalythe
Huby
Sutton-on-the-Forest
Sutton Park
Sheriff Hutton
Thornton-le-Clay
Whitwell-on-the-Hill
Firby
Kirkham
Kirkham Priory
Langton
Kennythorpe
Birdsall
Wharram le Street
Sledmere
Sledmere House
West Lilling
Foston
Crambe
Westow
Burythorpe
Wharram Percy Medieval Village
Barton-le-Willows
Howsham
Leavening
Flaxton
Harton
Acklam
Leppington
Thixendale
Strensall
Bossall
Fimber
Claxton
Scrayingham
Towthorpe
Sand Hutton
Kirby Underdale
Fridaythorpe
Wetwang
Shipton
Wigginton
Haxby
City of York
Earswick
Upper Helmsley
Buttercrambe
Skirpenbeck
Bugthorpe
Painsthorpe
Yorkshire Wolds Way
Skelton
Moor End
Stockton on the Forest
Gate Helmsley
Stamford Bridge
Youlthorpe
Huggate
Overton
Nether Poppleton
Huntington
West Huntington
New Earswick
Warthill
Full Sutton
Bishop Wilton
Rawcliffe
Holtby
Low Catton
Gowthorpe
Great Givendale
Upper Poppleton
Clifton
York
York Minster
Jorvik Viking Centre
Murton
High Catton
Fangfoss
Meltonby
Knapton
Heworth
Dunnington
Yorkshire Museum of Farming
Bolton
North Dalton
Holgate
Osbaldwick
Grimston
Wilberfoss
Yapham
Millington
Acomb
National Railway Museum
Castle Mus
Kexby
Kilnwick Percy
Warter
Nunthorpe
Heslington
Barmby Moor
Middleton-on-the-Wolds
Woodthorpe
Fulford
Newton upon Derwent
Pocklington
Askham Bryan
Bishopthorpe
York Designer Outlet
Crockey Hill
Yorkshire Air Museum
Elvington
Stewart's Burnby Hall Gardens & Museum
Nunburnholme
Copmanthorpe
York West Services
Sutton upon Derwent
Allerthorpe
Burnby
Acaster Malbis
Naburn
Wheldrake
Thornton
Hayton
Londesborough
Colton
Deighton
Storwood
Melbourne
Pocklington Canal
Bielby
Thorpe le Street
Goodmanham
Appleton Roebuck
Lower Derwent Valley
Shiptonthorpe
Market Weighton
Escrick
Everingham
Acaster Selby
East Cottingwith
Seaton Ross
Thorganby
Holme Green
Harswell
Stillingfleet
Rythor
Kelfield
Ellerton
Laytham
Sancton
Water End
Holme-on-Spalding-Moor
Cawood
Skipwith
Skipwith Common
North Duffield
Aughton
Harlthorpe
Foggathorpe
Moor End
Sand Hole
North Cliffe
North Newbald
Riccall
Bubwith
Highfield
Rascal Moor
South Cliffe
South Newbald
Wistow
Gunby
Gribthorpe
Willitoft
Hotham
Barlby
Selby Abbey
Osgodby
Menthorpe
Breighton
Spaldington
Bursea
Lund
South Duffield
Selby
Cliffe
Foulness
North Cave
Everthorpe
Thorpe Willoughby
Wressle
Brind
North Howden
Portington
Hive
West End
South Cave
East Common
Brayton
Hemingbrough
Cavil
Sandholme
Newport
Newsholme
Eastrington
Scalby
Gilberdyke
Howden Minster
Brantingham
Ellerker
Barmby on the Marsh
Howden
Staddlethorpe
Market Weighton Canal
Asselby
Knedlington
Kilpin
Balkholme
Elloughton
Kilpin Pike
Brough
Broomfleet
Drax
Boothferry
Haddlesey
Temple
Camblesforth
Laxton
Skelton
Newland
Kellington
Ouse
Aire
Derwent
Selby Canal
Dove
Seven
Costa Beck
Rye
Foulness

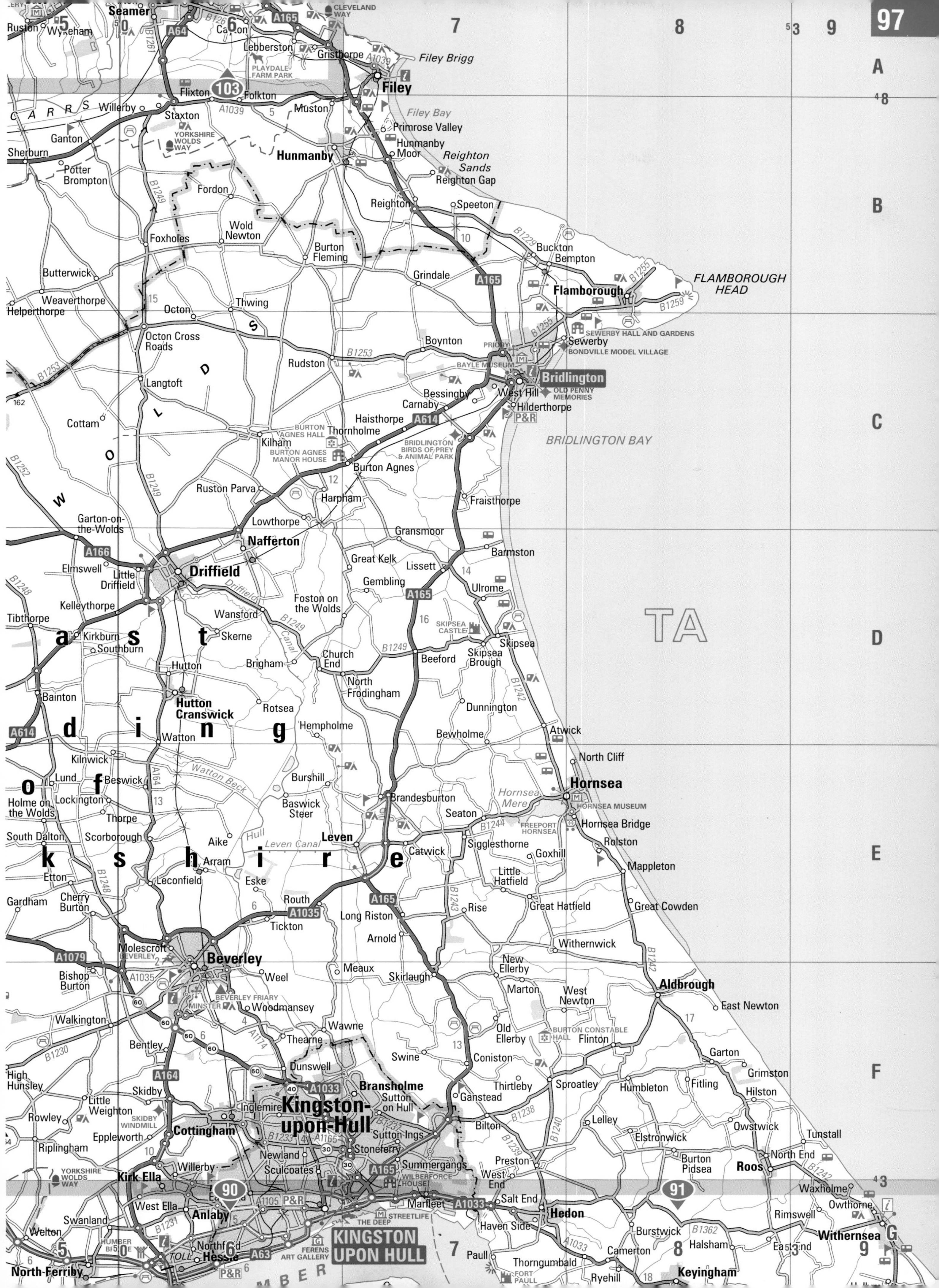
Seamer
Ruston
Wykeham
Cayton
A64
A165
B1261
CLEVELAND WAY
Lebberston
Gristhorpe
A1039
Filey Brigg
PLAYDALE FARM PARK
Filey
Flixton
103
Folkton
CARRS
Willerby
Staxton
A1039
Muston
Filey Bay
Primrose Valley
YORKSHIRE WOLDS WAY
Ganton
Hunmanby
Hunmanby Moor
Reighton Sands
Sherburn
Potter Brompton
Reighton Gap
Fordon
B1249
Reighton
Speeton
Wold Newton
Foxholes
Burton Fleming
B1229
Buckton
Bempton
Butterwick
Grindale
A165
B1255
FLAMBOROUGH HEAD
Flamborough
B1259
Weaverthorpe
Helperthorpe
Thwing
Octon
SEWERBY HALL AND GARDENS
Octon Cross Roads
Boynton
Sewerby
BONDVILLE MODEL VILLAGE
B1253
PRIORY
Rudston
BAYLE MUSEUM
Bridlington
Langtoft
West Hill
OLD PENNY MEMORIES
Bessingby
Carnaby
Hilderthorpe
P&R
Haisthorpe
A614
Cottam
BURTON AGNES HALL
Thornholme
BRIDLINGTON BAY
Kilham
BRIDLINGTON BIRDS OF PREY & ANIMAL PARK
BURTON AGNES MANOR HOUSE
Burton Agnes
B1252
Ruston Parva
Harpham
Fraisthorpe
Garton-on-the-Wolds
Lowthorpe
Gransmoor
Nafferton
A166
Barmston
Great Kelk
Elmswell
Little Driffield
Driffield
Lissett
Gembling
B1248
Foston on the Wolds
A165
Ulrome
Kelleythorpe
Wansford
Tibthorpe
B1249
SKIPSEA CASTLE
TA
Kirkburn
Skerne
Skipsea
Southburn
Church End
Skipsea Brough
Hutton
Brigham
B1249
Beeford
North Frodingham
B1242
Bainton
Hutton Cranswick
Rotsea
Dunnington
A614
Hempholme
Atwick
Watton
Bewholme
Kilnwick
North Cliff
Watton Beck
Burshill
Lund
Beswick
Hornsea
A164
Hornsea Mere
Brandesburton
HORNSEA MUSEUM
Holme on the Wolds
Lockington
Baswick Steer
Seaton
Thorpe
B1244
FREEPORT HORNSEA
Hornsea Bridge
South Dalton
Scorborough
Aike
Hull
Leven Canal
Leven
Rolston
Catwick
Sigglesthorpe
Goxhill
Arram
Mappleton
Etton
Leconfield
Eske
Little Hatfield
B1243
Gardham
Cherry Burton
Routh
A165
Rise
Great Hatfield
Great Cowden
A1035
Long Riston
Tickton
Arnold
Withernwick
Molescroft
A1079
BEVERLEY
Beverley
Bishop Burton
Weel
Meaux
Skirlaugh
New Ellerby
B1242
A1035
Marton
Aldbrough
BEVERLEY FRIARY
West Newton
East Newton
MINSTER
Woodmansey
Walkington
Wawne
Old Ellerby
BURTON CONSTABLE HALL
Flinton
A1174
Bentley
B1230
Thearne
Swine
Coniston
Garton
Dunswell
A164
Thirtleby
Sproatley
Grimston
High Hunsley
A1033
Bransholme
Humbleton
Fitling
Skidby
Sutton on Hull
Ganstead
Hilston
Little Weighton
Inglemire
Kingston-upon-Hull
Rowley
SKIDBY WINDMILL
Bilton
B1238
Lelley
Cottingham
Owstwick
Eppleworth
B1233
A1165
Sutton Ings
B1240
Elstronwick
Tunstall
Riplingham
Newland
Stoneferry
B1239
Preston
Burton Pidsea
North End
YORKSHIRE WOLDS WAY
Willerby
Summergangs
Roos
B1242
Kirk Ella
Sculcoates
A165
WILBERFORCE HOUSE
West End
90
91
Waxholme
West Ella
A1105
P&R
Salt End
Owthorne
Marfleet
A1033
Anlaby
Hedon
Swanland
B1231
STREETLIFE
THE DEEP
Haven Side
Rimswell
Welton
HUMBER BRIDGE
KINGSTON UPON HULL
A1033
Burstwick
B1362
Withernsea
FERENS ART GALLERY
Halsham
TOLL
Hessle
A63
Camerton
Easington
North Ferriby
P&R
Paull
Thorngumbald
FORT PAULL
Ryehill
Keyingham
HUMBER

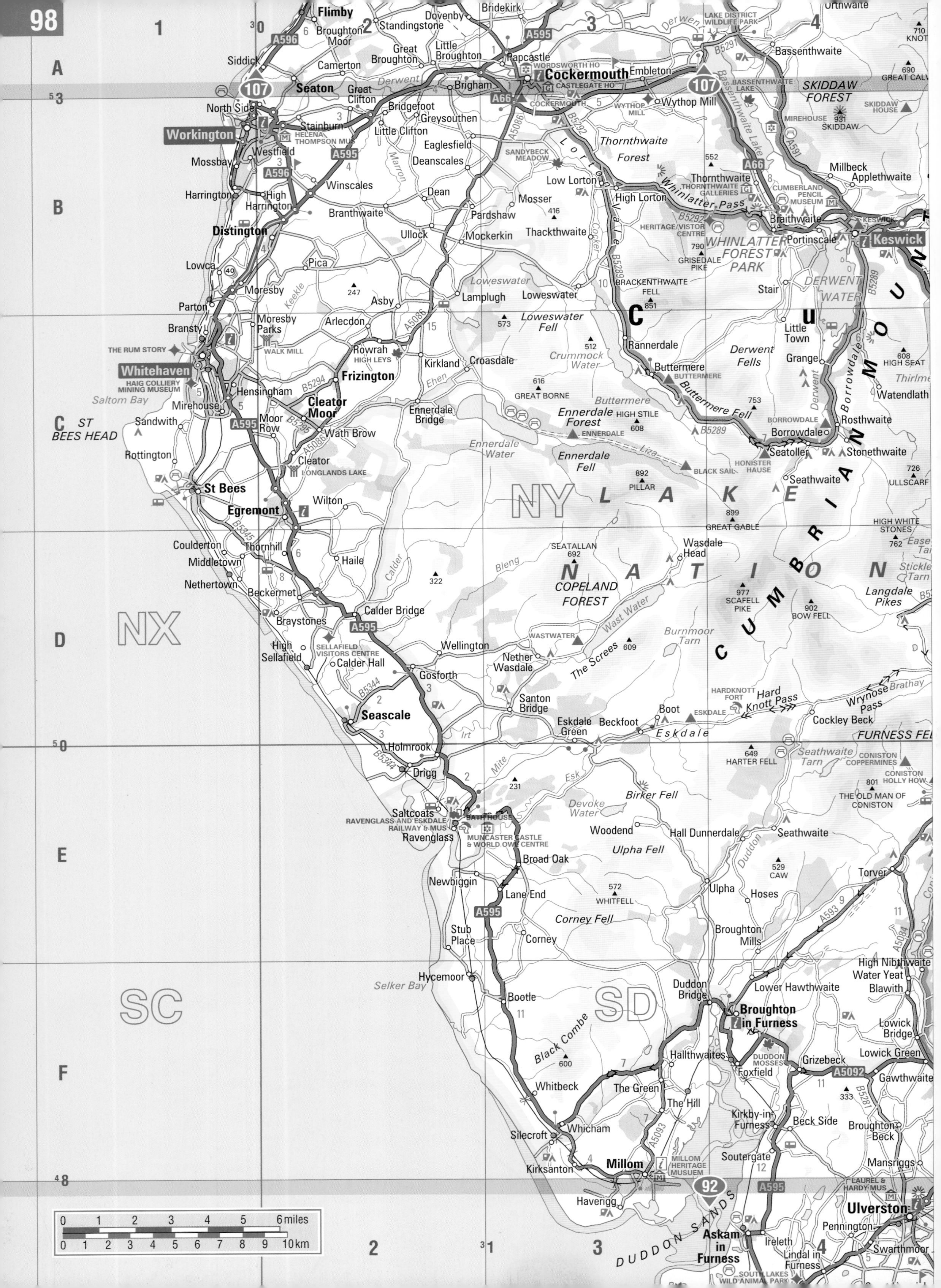

98
Flimby
Broughton Moor
Standingstone
Dovenby
Bridekirk
Siddick
Camerton
Great Broughton
Little Broughton
Papcastle
Cockermouth
Embleton
Wythop Mill
Bassenthwaite
SKIDDAW FOREST
SKIDDAW
Seaton
Great Clifton
Brigham
North Side
Bridgefoot
Greysouthen
Workington
Stainburn
Little Clifton
Eaglesfield
Westfield
Deanscales
Mossbay
Thornthwaite Forest
Winscales
Harrington
High Harrington
Dean
Low Lorton
Mosser
High Lorton
Thornthwaite
Millbeck
Applethwaite
Whinlatter Pass
Braithwaite
Branthwaite
Pardshaw
Distington
Ullock
Mockerkin
Thackthwaite
WHINLATTER FOREST PARK
Portinscale
Keswick
Lowca
Pica
Moresby
Asby
Lamplugh
Loweswater
BRACKENTHWAITE FELL
Stair
DERWENT WATER
Parton
Moresby Parks
Arlecdon
Loweswater Fell
Little Town
Bransty
THE RUM STORY
Rowrah
Kirkland
Croasdale
Crummock Water
Rannerdale
Derwent Fells
Grange
HIGH SEAT
Whitehaven
HAIG COLLIERY MINING MUSEUM
Frizington
GREAT BORNE
Buttermere
Buttermere Fell
Watendlath
Saltom Bay
Hensingham
Cleator Moor
Ennerdale Bridge
Ennerdale Forest
HIGH STILE
Mirehouse
Moor Row
Rosthwaite
ST BEES HEAD
Sandwith
Wath Brow
Ennerdale Water
Borrowdale
Rottington
Cleator
Ennerdale Fell
Seatoller
Stonethwaite
HONISTER HAUSE
BLACK SAIL
PILLAR
Seathwaite
ULLSCARF
St Bees
NY
LAKE
Egremont
Wilton
GREAT GABLE
HIGH WHITE STONES
Coulderton
Thornhill
SEATALLAN
Wasdale Head
Middletown
Haile
NATIONAL
CUMBRIAN MOUNTAINS
Nethertown
COPELAND FOREST
SCAFELL PIKE
BOW FELL
Langdale Pikes
Beckermet
Calder Bridge
Braystones
NX
WASTWATER
Burnmoor Tarn
High Sellafield
SELLAFIELD VISITORS CENTRE
Wellington
Calder Hall
Nether Wasdale
The Screes
Gosforth
HARDKNOTT FORT
Hard Knott Pass
Wrynose Pass
Santon Bridge
Seascale
Eskdale Green
Beckfoot
Boot
Eskdale
Cockley Beck
FURNESS FELLS
Holmrook
HARTER FELL
Seathwaite Tarn
CONISTON COPPERMINES
Drigg
CONISTON HOLLY HOW
THE OLD MAN OF CONISTON
Birker Fell
Saltcoats
RAVENGLASS AND ESKDALE RAILWAY & MUS
Ravenglass
MUNCASTER CASTLE & WORLD OWL CENTRE
Devoke Water
Woodend
Hall Dunnerdale
Seathwaite
Broad Oak
Ulpha Fell
CAW
Torver
Newbiggin
Lane End
WHITFELL
Ulpha
Hoses
Corney Fell
Stub Place
Corney
Broughton Mills
High Nibthwaite
Water Yeat
Blawith
Hycemoor
Selker Bay
Lower Hawthwaite
SC
Bootle
SD
Duddon Bridge
Broughton in Furness
Lowick Bridge
Black Combe
Hallthwaites
DUDDON MOSSES
Foxfield
Grizebeck
Lowick Green
Gawthwaite
Whitbeck
The Green
The Hill
Kirkby-in-Furness
Beck Side
Broughton Beck
Whicham
Silecroft
Soutergate
Millom
MILLOM HERITAGE MUSEUM
Mansriggs
Kirksanton
LAUREL & HARDY MUS
Haverigg
Ulverston
DUDDON SANDS
Askam in Furness
Ireleth
Pennington
Lindal in Furness
Swarthmoor
SOUTH LAKES WILD ANIMAL PARK
0 1 2 3 4 5 6 miles
0 1 2 3 4 5 6 7 8 9 10 km

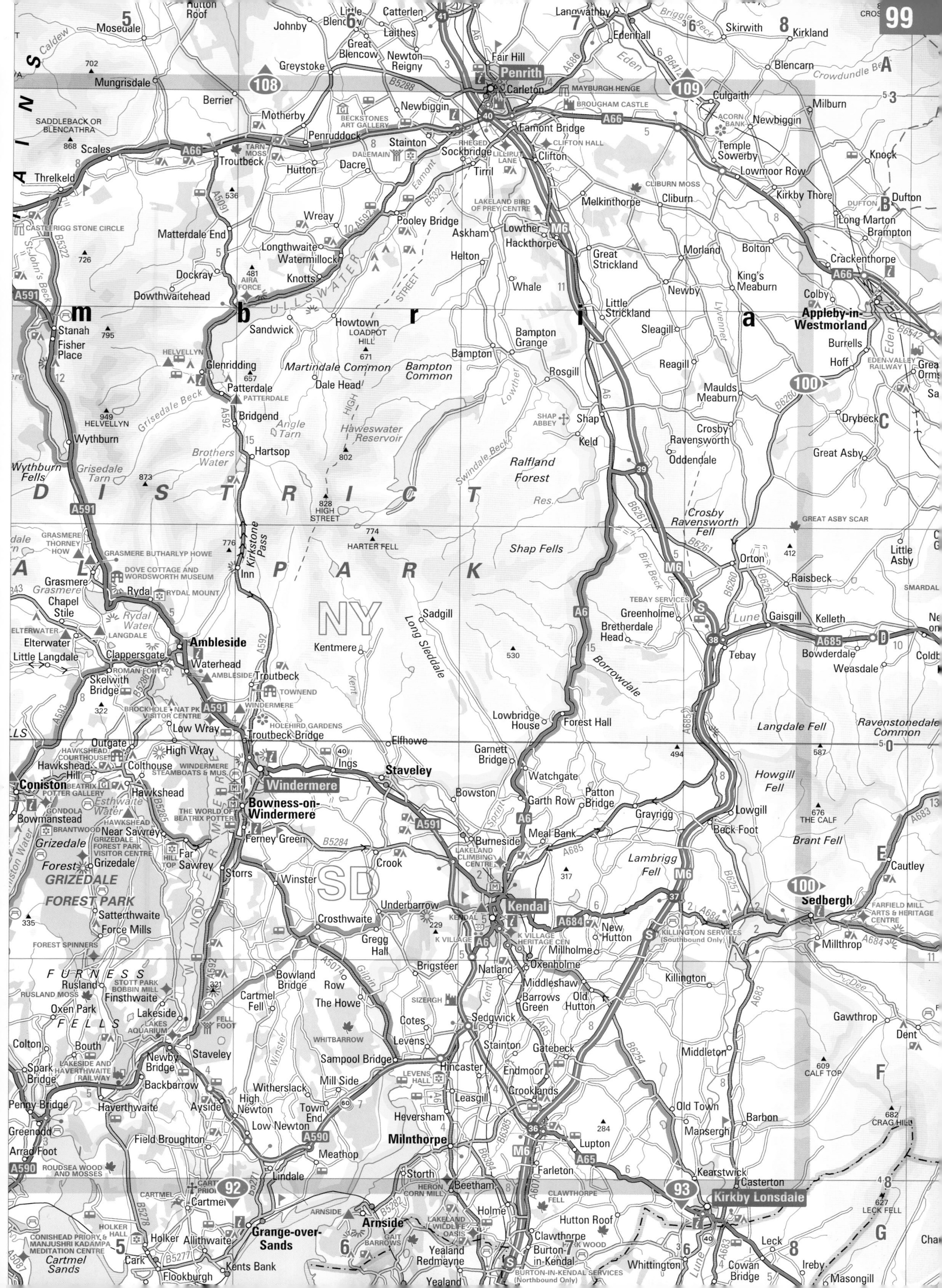
Hutton Roof
Mosedale
Johnby
Little Blencow
Catterlen
Langwathby
Skirwith
Kirkland
Laithes
Great Blencow
Newton Reigny
Edenhall
Fair Hill
Penrith
Carleton
MAYBURGH HENGE
BROUGHAM CASTLE
Culgaith
Blencarn
Crowdundle Beck
Mungrisdale
Greystoke
Berrier
Motherby
Newbiggin
BECKSTONES ART GALLERY
Eamont Bridge
Milburn
ACORN BANK
Newbiggin
SADDLEBACK OR BLENCATHRA
868
Scales
Penruddock
Stainton
RHEGED
CLIFTON HALL
Temple Sowerby
Knock
Threlkeld
Troutbeck
TARN MOSS
DALEMAIN
Sockbridge
LILLIPUT LANE
Clifton
Hutton
Dacre
Tirril
Lowmoor Row
CLIBURN MOSS
Kirkby Thore
Dufton
Melkinthorpe
Cliburn
DUFTON
CASTLERIGG STONE CIRCLE
Matterdale End
Wreay
Pooley Bridge
LAKELAND BIRD OF PREY CENTRE
Askham
Lowther
Hackthorpe
Long Marton
Brampton
Longthwaite
Watermillock
Helton
Great Strickland
Morland
Bolton
Crackenthorpe
St John's Beck
Dockray
AIRA FORCE
Knotts
Whale
King's Meaburn
Newby
Colby
Dowthwaitehead
ULLSWATER
STREET
Little Strickland
Appleby-in-Westmorland
Stanah
Fisher Place
Sandwick
Howtown
LOADPOT HILL
Bampton Grange
Sleagill
Burrells
Hoff
HELVELLYN
Glenridding
Martindale Common
Bampton
Bampton Common
Rosgill
Reagill
EDEN VALLEY RAILWAY
Patterdale
PATTERDALE
Dale Head
Maulds Meaburn
Grisedale Beck
Bridgend
Angle Tarn
Haweswater Reservoir
SHAP ABBEY
Shap
Keld
Crosby Ravensworth
Drybeck
HELVELLYN
Wythburn
Hartsop
Oddendale
Great Asby
Brothers Water
Ralfland Forest
Swindale Beck
Wythburn Fells
Grisedale Tarn
DISTRICT
HIGH STREET
Res.
Crosby Ravensworth Fell
GREAT ASBY SCAR
GRASMERE THORNEY HOW
GRASMERE BUTHARLYP HOWE
Kirkstone Pass
Inn
HARTER FELL
Shap Fells
Orton
Little Asby
DOVE COTTAGE AND WORDSWORTH MUSEUM
PARK
Birk Beck
Raisbeck
Grasmere
Rydal
RYDAL MOUNT
SMARDAL
Chapel Stile
NY
Sadgill
TEBAY SERVICES
Greenholme
Gaisgill
Kelleth
Rydal Water
Long Sleddale
Bretherdale Head
Lune
Elterwater
ELTERWATER
LANGDALE
Ambleside
Kentmere
Tebay
Bowderdale
Little Langdale
Clappersgate
Waterhead
AMBLESIDE
Borrowdale
Weasdale
Skelwith Bridge
ROMAN FORT
Troutbeck
TOWNEND
Kent
BROCKHOLE NAT PK VISITOR CENTRE
WINDERMERE
Lowbridge House
Forest Hall
Low Wray
HOLEHIRD GARDENS
Langdale Fell
Ravenstonedale Common
Outgate
High Wray
Troutbeck Bridge
Elfhowe
Garnett Bridge
HAWKSHEAD COURTHOUSE
Hawkshead Hill
Colthouse
WINDERMERE STEAMBOATS & MUS.
Ings
Staveley
Watchgate
Howgill Fell
Coniston
BEATRIX POTTER GALLERY
Hawkshead
Windermere
Bowston
Patton Bridge
Esthwaite Water
Bowness-on-Windermere
Garth Row
Grayrigg
Lowgill
GONDOLA
THE WORLD OF BEATRIX POTTER
THE CALF
Bowmanstead
BRANTWOOD
HAWKSHEAD GRIZEDALE FOREST PARK VISITOR CENTRE
Near Sawrey
Ferney Green
Burneside
Meal Bank
Beck Foot
Brant Fell
Grizedale
Far Sawrey
HILL TOP
Crook
LAKELAND CLIMBING CENTRE
Lambrigg Fell
Cautley
Forest
Grizedale
GRIZEDALE FOREST PARK
Storrs
Winster
SD
Kendal
Underbarrow
Sedbergh
FARFIELD MILL ARTS & HERITAGE CENTRE
Satterthwaite
Force Mills
Crosthwaite
KENDAL
New Hutton
KILLINGTON SERVICES (Southbound Only)
Millthrop
FOREST SPINNERS
Gregg Hall
K VILLAGE
K VILLAGE HERITAGE CEN
Millholme
Oxenholme
FURNESS
STOTT PARK BOBBIN MILL
Rusland
Bowland Bridge
Brigsteer
Natland
Killington
RUSLAND MOSS
Finsthwaite
Row
Middleshaw
Cartmel Fell
Gilpin
SIZERGH
Barrows Green
Old Hutton
Dee
Oxen Park
The Howe
Lakeside
LAKES AQUARIUM
FELL FOOT
FELLS
Cotes
Sedgwick
Gawthrop
Dent
Colton
Booth
Staveley
WHITBARROW
Levens
Stainton
Gatebeck
Middleton
Newby Bridge
LAKESIDE AND HAVERTHWAITE RAILWAY
Spark Bridge
Winster
Sampool Bridge
Hincaster
Endmoor
CALF TOP
Backbarrow
Witherslack
Mill Side
LEVENS HALL
Leasgill
Crooklands
Penny Bridge
Haverthwaite
Ayside
High Newton
Town End
Old Town
Barbon
Heversham
Greenodd
Low Newton
Mansergh
CRAG HILL
Field Broughton
Milnthorpe
Lupton
Arrad Foot
Meathop
Farleton
ROUDSEA WOOD AND MOSSES
Storth
Kearstwick
Casterton
Lindale
CARTMEL PRIORY
CARTMEL
Cartmel
HERON CORN MILL
Beetham
CLAWTHORPE FELL
Kirkby Lonsdale
LECK FELL
ARNSIDE
Arnside
Holme
Hutton Roof
HOLKER HALL
LAKELAND WILDLIFE OASIS
CONISHEAD PRIORY & MANJUSHRI KADAMPA MEDITATION CENTRE
Holker
Allithwaite
Grange-over-Sands
GAIT BARROWS
Yealand Redmayne
Clawthorpe
HK WOOD
Leck
Cartmel Sands
Cark
Flookburgh
Kents Bank
Burton-in-Kendal
BURTON-IN-KENDAL SERVICES (Northbound Only)
Whittington
Cowan Bridge
Ireby
Masongill
Yealand
A66
A591
A592
A5091
A592
B5288
B6412
A686
B5320
B5322
A6
M6
A685
A684
A683
A65
A590
A5074
A593
B5285
B5284
B6261
B6260
B6254
B6385
B6384
B5277
B5278
B5282
A6070
A5087
B6257
B6542
108
109
100
92
93

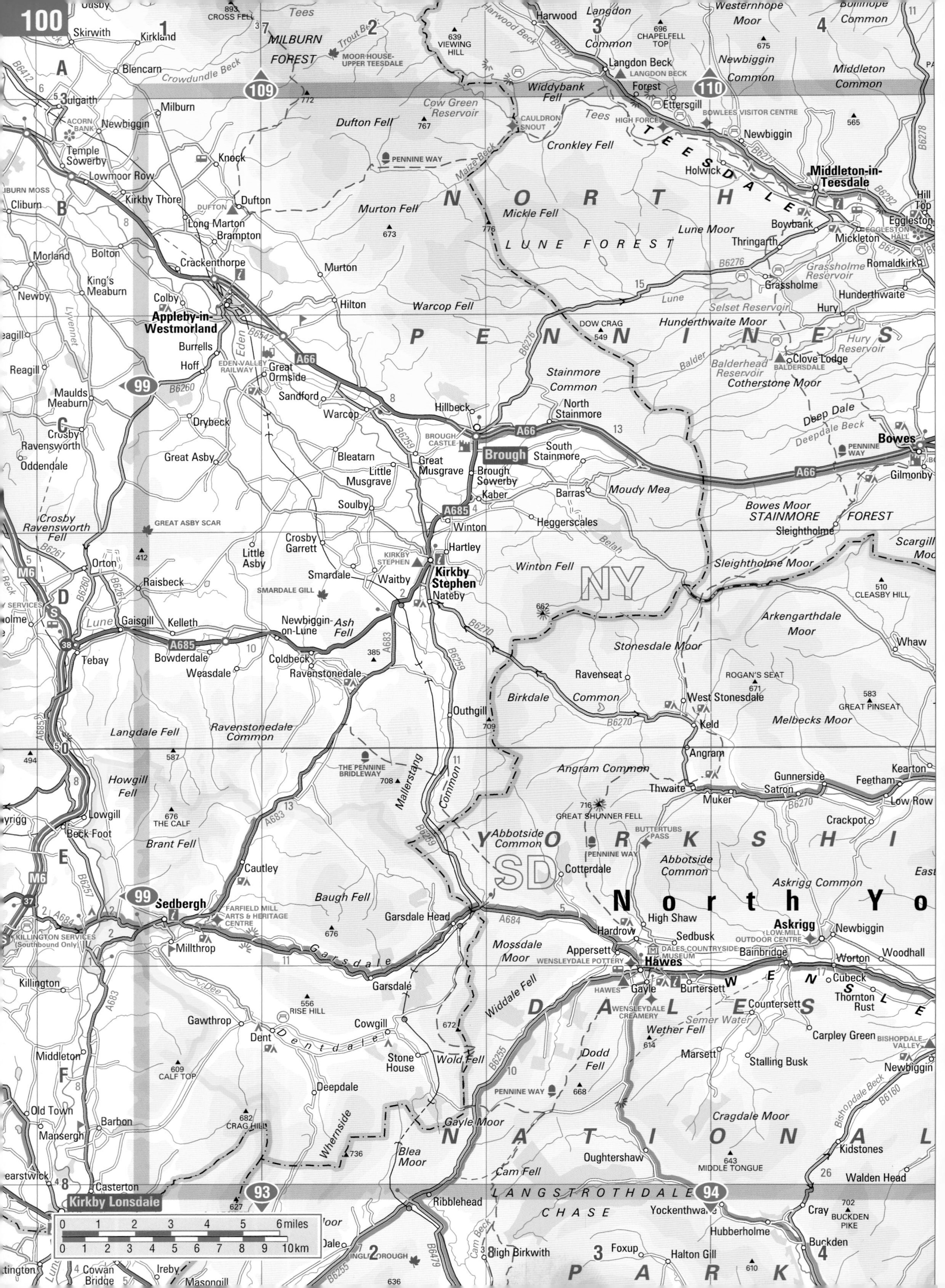
Skirwith
Kirkland
893 CROSS FELL
Tees
MILBURN FOREST
Trout Beck
MOOR HOUSE-UPPER TEESDALE
639 VIEWING HILL
Harwood Beck
Harwood
Langdon Common
696 CHAPELFELL TOP
Westernhope Moor
675
Newbiggin Common
Bollihope Common
Middleton Common
Blencarn
Crowdundle Beck
109
772
Langdon Beck
LANGDON BECK
Forest
110
Widdybank Fell
Ettersgill
Culgaith
Milburn
Cow Green Reservoir
CAULDRON SNOUT
Tees
HIGH FORCE
BOWLEES VISITOR CENTRE
565
ACORN BANK
Newbiggin
Dufton Fell
767
Newbiggin
Temple Sowerby
Knock
PENNINE WAY
Cronkley Fell
TEESDALE
B6277
B6278
Lowmoor Row
Maize Beck
Holwick
Middleton-in-Teesdale
B6282
Hill Top
KIRKBY THORE
Cliburn
Kirkby Thore
DUFTON
Dufton
NORTH
Murton Fell
Mickle Fell
Eggleston
Long Marton
Brampton
Lune Moor
Bowbank
EGGLESTON HALL
Mickleton
673
776
LUNE FOREST
Thringarth
Morland
Bolton
Romaldkirk
Crackenthorpe
B6276
Grassholme Reservoir
Murton
King's Meaburn
15
Grassholme
Newby
Colby
Hilton
Warcop Fell
Lune
Hunderthwaite
Lyvennet
Appleby-in-Westmorland
Selset Reservoir
Hury
DOW CRAG 549
Hunderthwaite Moor
Reagill
Eden
B6542
PENNINES
Hury Reservoir
Burrells
A66
B6276
Balder
Balderhead Reservoir
Clove Lodge
BALDERSDALE
Reagill
Hoff
EDEN VALLEY RAILWAY
Great Ormside
Stainmore Common
99
B6260
Cotherstone Moor
Maulds Meaburn
Sandford
8
North Stainmore
Deep Dale
Warcop
Hillbeck
13
Deepdale Beck
Drybeck
A66
Bowes
PENNINE WAY
Crosby Ravensworth
BROUGH CASTLE
B6259
Brough
South Stainmore
Oddendale
Great Asby
Bleatarn
Great Musgrave
Brough Sowerby
A66
Gilmonby
Little Musgrave
Barras
Moudy Mea
Kaber
Soulby
A685
Bowes Moor
STAINMORE
FOREST
Crosby Ravensworth Fell
GREAT ASBY SCAR
Winton
Heggerscales
Sleightholme
Crosby Garrett
Belah
Scargill Moor
Hartley
B6261
412
KIRKBY STEPHEN
Little Asby
Winton Fell
NY
Sleightholme Moor
Orton
M6
Smardale
Kirkby Stephen
Waitby
510 CLEASBY HILL
B6260
B6261
Raisbeck
SMARDALE GILL
Nateby
662
SERVICES
D
Newbiggin-on-Lune
Ash Fell
Arkengarthdale Moor
Lune
Gaisgill
Kelleth
B6270
38
Tebay
A685
10
385
A683
B6259
Stonesdale Moor
Whaw
Bowderdale
Coldbeck
Weasdale
Ravenstonedale
Ravenseat
ROGAN'S SEAT 671
Birkdale
Common
West Stonesdale
583 GREAT PINSEAT
Outhgill
B6270
Keld
Melbecks Moor
Langdale Fell
Ravenstonedale Common
709
A685
494
587
THE PENNINE BRIDLEWAY
708
Mallerstang
11
Common
Angram
Angram Common
Kearton
Howgill Fell
Gunnerside
Feetham
Thwaite
Satron
Muker
B6270
Low Row
676 THE CALF
A683
13
716
GREAT SHUNNER FELL
Crackpot
Lowgill
B6259
BUTTERTUBS PASS
Beck Foot
Brant Fell
Abbotside Common
YORKSHIRE
PENNINE WAY
Abbotside Common
M6
B6257
Cautley
SD
Cotterdale
Askrigg Common
East
99
Sedbergh
Baugh Fell
North Yo
37
FARFIELD MILL ARTS & HERITAGE CENTRE
A684
5
High Shaw
Askrigg
A684
Garsdale Head
Hardrow
LOW MILL OUTDOOR CENTRE
Newbiggin
KILLINGTON SERVICES (Southbound Only)
676
Sedbusk
Millthrop
Mossdale Moor
Appersett
DALES COUNTRYSIDE MUSEUM
Bainbridge
Woodhall
WENSLEYDALE POTTERY
Hawes
Worton
Garsdale
11
Killington
Dee
Garsdale
17
Cubeck
HAWES
Gayle
Burtersett
WENSLEYDALE
A683
556 RISE HILL
Widdale Fell
Thornton Rust
Countersett
WENSLEYDALE CREAMERY
Semer Water
Gawthrop
Cowgill
672
Wether Fell
Carpley Green
BISHOPDALE VALLEY
Dent
Dentdale
614
Middleton
Stone House
Wold Fell
Dodd Fell
Marsett
Stalling Busk
B6255
Newbiggin
609 CALF TOP
10
Deepdale
PENNINE WAY
668
Bishopdale Beck
B6160
Old Town
Whernside
Cragdale Moor
Barbon
682 CRAG HILL
Gayle Moor
NATIONAL
Mansergh
736
Blea Moor
Oughtershaw
Kidstones
643 MIDDLE TONGUE
Cam Fell
Casterton
26
Walden Head
Kirkby Lonsdale
93
627
Ribblehead
LANGSTROTHDALE
94
CHASE
Yockenthwaite
Cray
702 BUCKDEN PIKE
Hubberholme
0 1 2 3 4 5 6 miles
0 1 2 3 4 5 6 7 8 9 10 km
Cam Beck
Buckden
B6479
B6255
High Birkwith
Foxup
Halton Gill
INGLEBOROUGH
610
Cowan Bridge
Ireby
Masongill
636
PARK

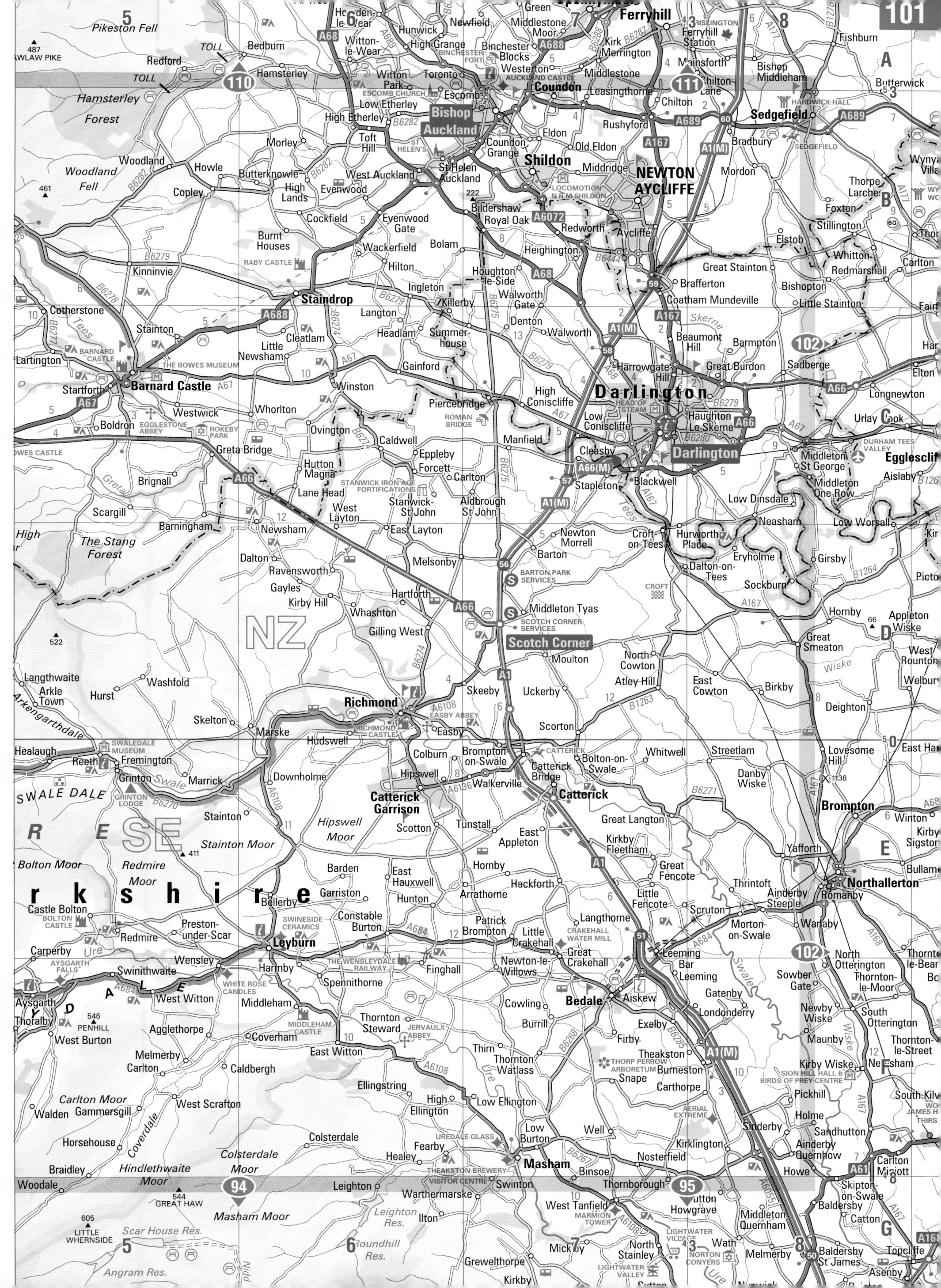
Pikeston Fell
Bedburn
Redford
Hamsterley
Hamsterley Forest
Woodland
Woodland Fell
Howle
Copley
Butterknowle
High Lands
Morley
Toft Hill
High Etherley
Low Etherley
Witton Park
Witton-le-Wear
Hunwick
High Grange
Newfield
Binchester
Blocks
Westerton
Middlestone Moor
Ferryhill
Ferryhill Station
Kirk Merrington
Middlestone
Coundon
Leasingthorne
Chilton
Chilton Lane
Mainsforth
Bishop Middleham
Fishburn
Butterwick
Sedgefield
Bradbury
Mordon
Rushyford
Eldon
Old Eldon
Shildon
Middridge
NEWTON AYCLIFFE
Aycliffe
Redworth
Heighington
Bishop Auckland
Escomb
Toronto
Coundon Grange
St Helen Auckland
West Auckland
Evenwood
Evenwood Gate
Cockfield
Burnt Houses
Wackerfield
Hilton
Bolam
Bildershaw
Royal Oak
Kinninvie
Staindrop
Ingleton
Killerby
Langton
Headlam
Summerhouse
Houghton-le-Side
Walworth Gate
Denton
Walworth
Cotherstone
Stainton
Cleatlam
Little Newsham
Lartington
Barnard Castle
Startforth
Gainford
Winston
Piercebridge
High Coniscliffe
Low Coniscliffe
Darlington
Harrowgate Hill
Beaumont Hill
Barmpton
Great Burdon
Sadberge
Haughton-le-Skerne
Great Stainton
Brafferton
Coatham Mundeville
Bishopton
Little Stainton
Elstob
Stillington
Whitton
Redmarshall
Carlton
Foxton
Thorpe Larches
Elton
Longnewton
Urlay Nook
Middleton St George
Middleton One Row
Egglescliffe
Aislaby
Westwick
Whorlton
Boldron
Greta Bridge
Ovington
Caldwell
Eppleby
Forcett
Carlton
Manfield
Cleasby
Stapleton
Blackwell
Brignall
Hutton Magna
Lane Head
West Layton
Stanwick-St-John
Aldbrough St John
Scargill
Barningham
Newsham
East Layton
Newton Morrell
Barton
Croft-on-Tees
Hurworth Place
Neasham
Low Dinsdale
Low Worsall
Eryholme
Dalton-on-Tees
Girsby
Sockburn
The Stang Forest
Dalton
Ravensworth
Gayles
Kirby Hill
Melsonby
Hartforth
Whashton
Gilling West
Middleton Tyas
Scotch Corner
Moulton
North Cowton
Atley Hill
East Cowton
Birkby
Great Smeaton
Hornby
Appleton Wiske
West Rounton
Welbury
Deighton
Langthwaite
Arkle Town
Hurst
Washfold
Arkengarthdale
Skelton
Marske
Richmond
Easby
Skeeby
Uckerby
Scorton
Hudswell
Colburn
Brompton-on-Swale
Catterick Bridge
Bolton-on-Swale
Whitwell
Streetlam
Danby Wiske
Lovesome Hill
East Harlsey
Healaugh
Reeth
Fremington
Grinton
Marrick
Downholme
Hipswell
Walkerville
Catterick
Catterick Garrison
Scotton
Tunstall
Great Langton
Brompton
Winton
Kirby Sigston
SWALE DALE
Stainton
Stainton Moor
Hipswell Moor
East Appleton
Kirkby Fleetham
Great Fencote
Little Fencote
Yafforth
Northallerton
Romanby
Bullamoor
Bolton Moor
Redmire Moor
Barden
East Hauxwell
Hornby
Hackforth
Arrathorne
Hunton
Garriston
Bellerby
Thrintoft
Ainderby Steeple
Scruton
Morton-on-Swale
Warlaby
Castle Bolton
Preston-under-Scar
Redmire
Constable Burton
Patrick Brompton
Little Crakehall
Langthorne
Great Crakehall
Leyburn
Carperby
Wensley
Harmby
Finghall
Newton-le-Willows
Leeming
Leeming Bar
North Otterington
Thornton-le-Beans
Thornton-le-Moor
Sowber Gate
Swinithwaite
West Witton
Spennithorne
Middleham
Cowling
Bedale
Aiskew
Gatenby
Londonderry
Newby Wiske
South Otterington
Aysgarth
Thoralby
Agglethorpe
West Burton
Coverham
Thornton Steward
Burrill
Exelby
Firby
Maunby
Thornton-le-Street
East Witton
Thirn
Thornton Watlass
Theakston
Burneston
Snape
Carthorpe
Kirby Wiske
Newsham
Melmerby
Carlton
Caldbergh
Pickhill
Carlton Moor
Walden
Gammersgill
West Scrafton
Ellingstring
High Ellington
Low Ellington
Holme
Sandhutton
South Kilvington
Sinderby
Horsehouse
Colsterdale
Fearby
Low Burton
Well
Kirklington
Ainderby Quernhow
Howe
Carlton Miniott
Braidley
Hindlethwaite Moor
Colsterdale Moor
Healey
Masham
Nosterfield
Binsoe
Thornborough
Woodale
Leighton
Warthermarske
Swinton
Sutton Howgrave
Skipton-on-Swale
Baldersby
Catton
Great Haw
Masham Moor
West Tanfield
Middleton Quernham
Little Whernside
Scar House Res.
Leighton Res.
Ilton
Roundhill Res.
Mickley
North Stainley
Wath
Melmerby
Baldersby St James
Topcliffe
Asenby
Angram Res.
Grewelthorpe
Kirkby
NZ
SE
Yorkshire
A68
A688
A689
A167
A1(M)
A6072
A67
A66
A66(M)
A1
A6108
A6136
A684
A61
A168
A177
B6282
B6279
B6278
B6277
B6274
B6275
B6287
B6288
B6444
B6280
B6271
B6270
B6285
B6268
B6267
B1263
B1264
102
110
111
94
95

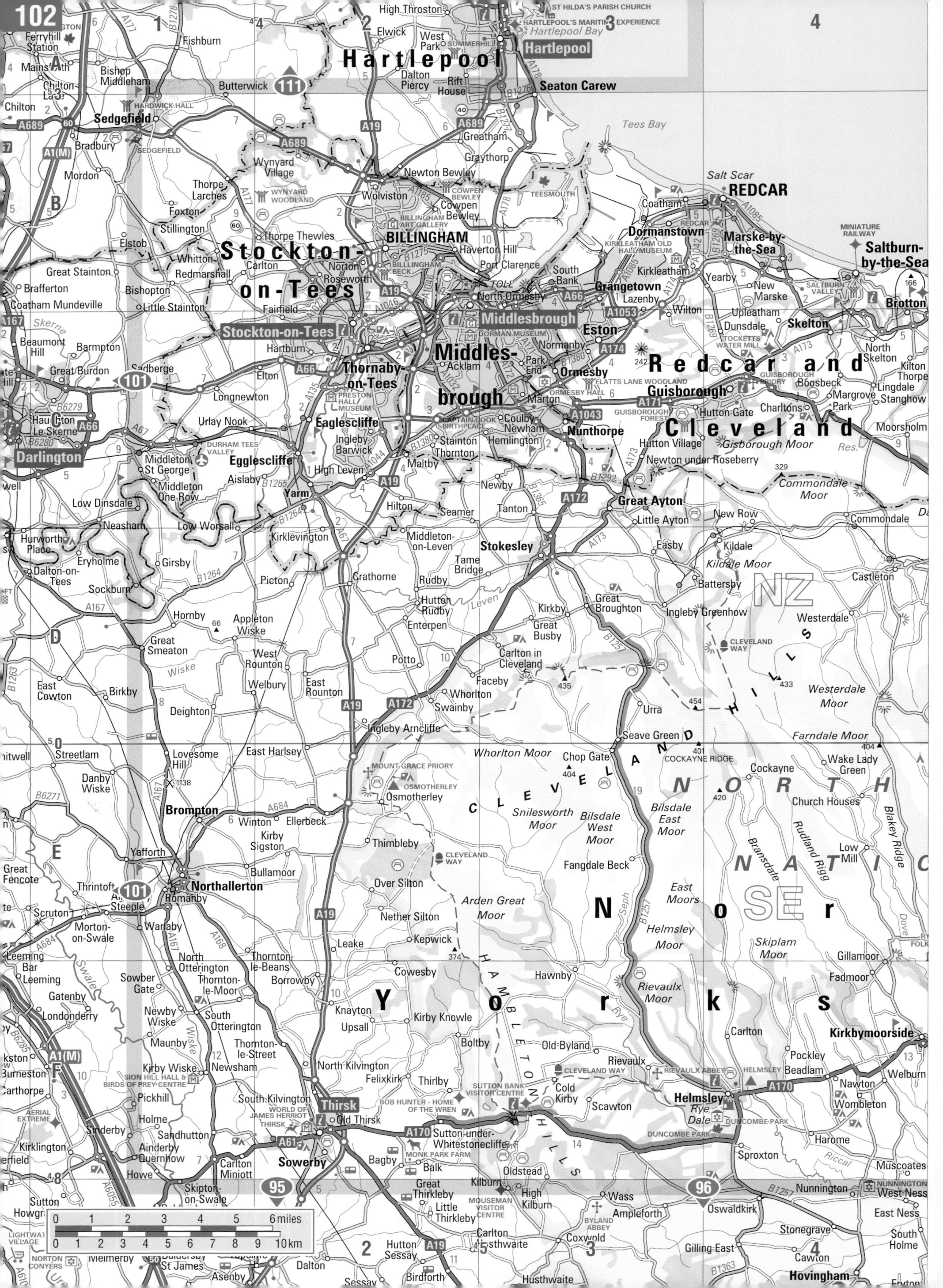
Hartlepool
Stockton-on-Tees
Middlesbrough
Redcar and Cleveland
North York Moors National Park
Cleveland Hills
Hambleton Hills
Cleveland Way
NZ
SE
High Throston
St Hilda's Parish Church
Hartlepool's Maritime Experience
Hartlepool Bay
Elwick
West Park
Summerhill
Dalton Piercy
Rift House
Seaton Carew
Tees Bay
Greatham
Graythorp
Newton Bewley
Wolviston
Cowpen Bewley
Teesmouth
Billingham
Billingham Art Gallery
Haverton Hill
Port Clarence
Norton
Roseworth
Fairfield
Hartburn
Thornaby-on-Tees
Preston Hall Museum
Acklam
Eaglescliffe
Egglescliffe
Ingleby Barwick
Yarm
High Leven
Maltby
Stainton
Thornton
Captain Cook Birthplace
Coulby Newham
Hemlington
Marton
Nunthorpe
Ormesby
Ormesby Hall
Park End
Normanby
Eston
South Bank
North Ormesby
Dorman Museum
Grangetown
Lazenby
Wilton
Kirkleatham
Kirkleatham Old Hall Museum
Dormanstown
Coatham
Salt Scar
Redcar
Marske-by-the-Sea
Saltburn-by-the-Sea
Miniature Railway
Saltburn Valley
Brotton
New Marske
Yearby
Upleatham
Dunsdale
Tocketts Water Mill
Skelton
North Skelton
Kilton Thorpe
Lingdale
Boosbeck
Margrove Park
Stanghow
Charltons
Guisborough
Guisborough Priory
Guisborough Forest
Flatts Lane Woodland
Hutton Gate
Hutton Village
Gisborough Moor
Moorsholm
Newton under Roseberry
Commondale Moor
Commondale
Great Ayton
Little Ayton
New Row
Easby
Kildale
Kildale Moor
Battersby
Castleton
Ingleby Greenhow
Westerdale
Westerdale Moor
Farndale Moor
Wake Lady Green
Cockayne
Cockayne Ridge
Church Houses
Blakey Ridge
Rudland Rigg
Bransdale
Low Mill
East Moors
Skiplam Moor
Gillamoor
Fadmoor
Kirkbymoorside
Carlton
Pockley
Beadlam
Nawton
Wombleton
Welburn
Harome
Helmsley
Duncombe Park
Rye Dale
Rievaulx
Rievaulx Abbey
Rievaulx Moor
Sproxton
Muscoates
Nunnington
West Ness
East Ness
Oswaldkirk
Stonegrave
South Holme
Gilling East
Cawton
Hovingham
Ampleforth
Wass
Byland Abbey
Coxwold
Husthwaite
Carlton Husthwaite
High Kilburn
Kilburn
Mouseman Visitor Centre
Oldstead
Sutton Bank Visitor Centre
Cold Kirby
Scawton
Old Byland
Hawnby
Boltby
Kirby Knowle
Cowesby
Kepwick
Nether Silton
Over Silton
Arden Great Moor
Bilsdale West Moor
Bilsdale East Moor
Snilesworth Moor
Fangdale Beck
Helmsley Moor
Chop Gate
Whorlton Moor
Seave Green
Urra
Faceby
Whorlton
Swainby
Carlton in Cleveland
Great Busby
Kirkby
Great Broughton
Stokesley
Tame Bridge
Rudby
Hutton Rudby
Enterpen
Potto
Middleton-on-Leven
Seamer
Tanton
Newby
Hilton
Crathorne
Kirklevington
Picton
Low Worsall
Ingleby Arncliffe
Mount Grace Priory
Osmotherley
East Harlsey
Thimbleby
Winton
Ellerbeck
Kirby Sigston
Bullamoor
Northallerton
Romanby
Brompton
Lovesome Hill
Deighton
Welbury
West Rounton
East Rounton
Appleton Wiske
Hornby
Great Smeaton
Birkby
East Cowton
Danby Wiske
Streetlam
Yafforth
Thrintoft
Ainderby Steeple
Warlaby
Morton-on-Swale
Scruton
Great Fencote
Leeming Bar
Leeming
Gatenby
Londonderry
Newby Wiske
Sowber Gate
North Otterington
Thornton-le-Moor
Thornton-le-Beans
South Otterington
Maunby
Thornton-le-Street
Kirby Wiske
Newsham
Sion Hill Hall & Birds of Prey Centre
Pickhill
Holme
Sandhutton
Sinderby
Ainderby Quernhow
Kirklington
Howe
Carlton Miniott
Skipton-on-Swale
Thirsk
Old Thirsk
World of James Herriot
Sowerby
Bagby
Monk Park Farm
Balk
Great Thirkleby
Little Thirkleby
Sutton-under-Whitestonecliffe
Bob Hunter - Home of the Wren
North Kilvington
South Kilvington
Felixkirk
Thirlby
Knayton
Upsall
Borrowby
Leake
Hutton Sessay
Sessay
Birdforth
Dalton
Asenby
Baldersby St James
Norton Conyers
Lightwater Valley
Aerial Extreme
Sutton Howgrave
Burneston
Carthorpe
Wath
Darlington
Durham Tees Valley
Middleton St George
Middleton One Row
Aislaby
Low Dinsdale
Neasham
Hurworth Place
Eryholme
Dalton-on-Tees
Sockburn
Girsby
Hurworth
Urlay Nook
Longnewton
Elton
Sadberge
Great Burdon
Barmpton
Beaumont Hill
Haughton Le Skerne
Coatham Mundeville
Brafferton
Great Stainton
Little Stainton
Bishopton
Redmarshall
Carlton
Whitton
Stillington
Elstob
Foxton
Thorpe Larches
Thorpe Thewles
Wynyard Village
Wynyard Woodland
Mordon
Bradbury
Sedgefield
Hardwick Hall
Chilton
Mainsforth
Bishop Middleham
Ferryhill Station
Fishburn
Butterwick
0 1 2 3 4 5 6 miles
0 1 2 3 4 5 6 7 8 9 10 km

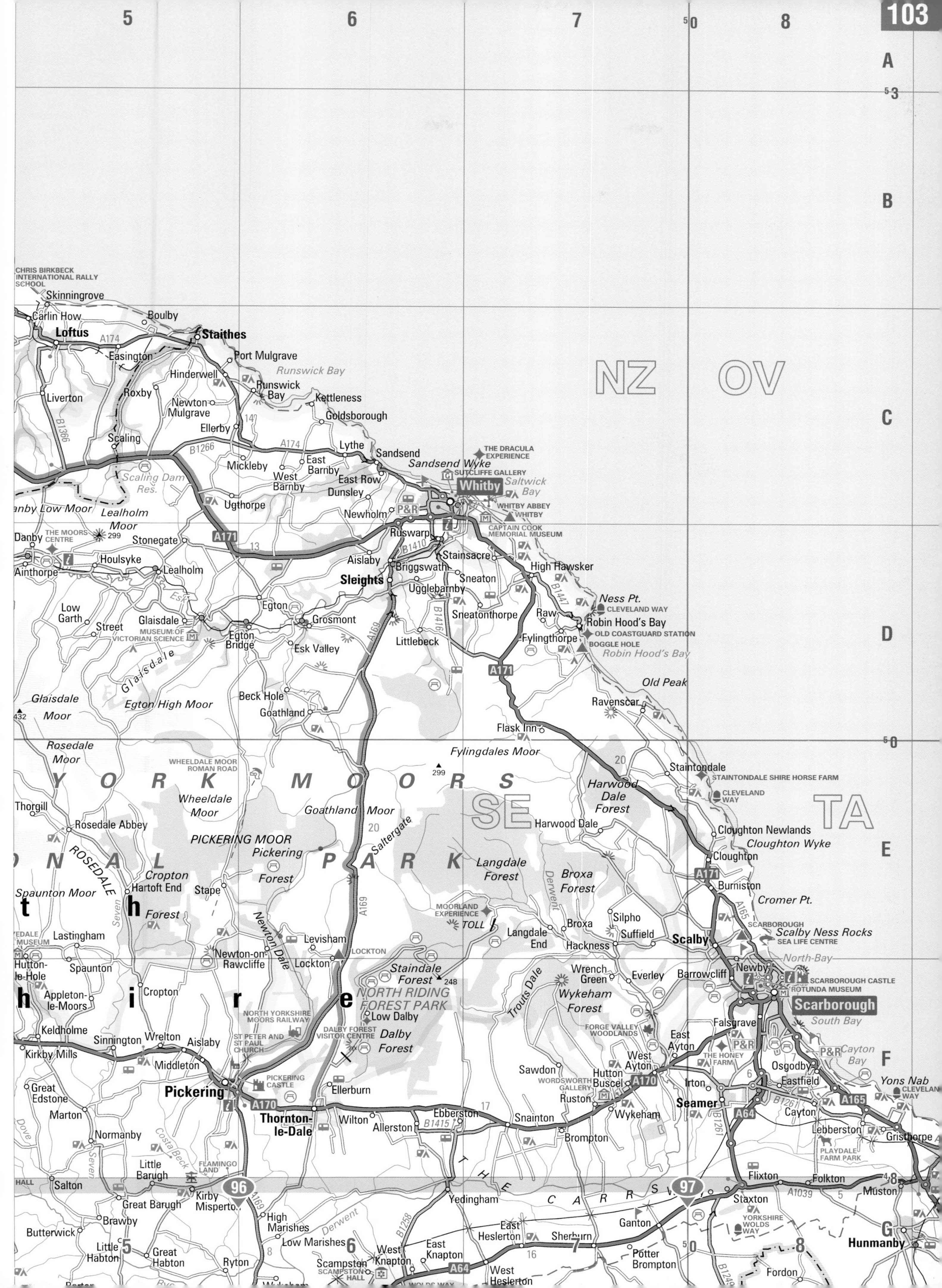
5
6
7
8
A
B
C
D
E
F
G
NZ
OV
SE
TA
CHRIS BIRKBECK INTERNATIONAL RALLY SCHOOL
Skinningrove
Carlin How
Boulby
Loftus
Staithes
Easington
Port Mulgrave
Runswick Bay
Hinderwell
Runswick Bay
Kettleness
Liverton
Roxby
Newton Mulgrave
Goldsborough
Ellerby
Scaling
Lythe
Sandsend
Mickleby
East Barnby
West Barnby
Sandsend Wyke
THE DRACULA EXPERIENCE
SUTCLIFFE GALLERY
Whitby
Saltwick Bay
Scaling Dam Res.
East Row
Dunsley
WHITBY ABBEY
WHITBY
Ugthorpe
Newholm
Danby Low Moor
Lealholm Moor
CAPTAIN COOK MEMORIAL MUSEUM
Danby
THE MOORS CENTRE
Stonegate
Ruswarp
Ainthorpe
Houlsyke
Lealholm
Aislaby
Stainsacre
High Hawsker
Briggswath
Sleights
Sneaton
Ugglebarnby
Ness Pt.
CLEVELAND WAY
Low Garth
Egton
Sneatonthorpe
Raw
Robin Hood's Bay
Street
Glaisdale
Grosmont
OLD COASTGUARD STATION
MUSEUM OF VICTORIAN SCIENCE
Egton Bridge
Littlebeck
Fylingthorpe
BOGGLE HOLE
Robin Hood's Bay
Esk Valley
Glaisdale
Old Peak
Glaisdale Moor
Egton High Moor
Beck Hole
Goathland
Ravenscar
Flask Inn
Rosedale Moor
Fylingdales Moor
WHEELDALE MOOR ROMAN ROAD
Staintondale
STAINTONDALE SHIRE HORSE FARM
YORK MOORS
Harwood Dale Forest
CLEVELAND WAY
Thorgill
Wheeldale Moor
Goathland Moor
Harwood Dale
Rosedale Abbey
Saltergate
Cloughton Newlands
Cloughton Wyke
PICKERING MOOR
Pickering Forest
ROSEDALE
Cloughton
NAL PARK
Langdale Forest
Broxa Forest
Cropton Forest
Hartoft End
Burniston
Spaunton Moor
Stape
Cromer Pt.
Forest
MOORLAND EXPERIENCE
TOLL
Silpho
Broxa
Langdale End
Suffield
Scalby
Lastingham
Levisham
SCARBOROUGH SEA LIFE CENTRE
Scalby Ness Rocks
Hackness
Newton-on-Rawcliffe
LOCKTON
Newton Dale
North Bay
Hutton-le-Hole
Spaunton
Lockton
Staindale Forest
Wrench Green
Everley
Barrowcliff
Newby
SCARBOROUGH CASTLE
ROTUNDA MUSEUM
Trouts Dale
Wykeham Forest
Cropton
NORTH RIDING FOREST PARK
Scarborough
Appleton-le-Moors
NORTH YORKSHIRE MOORS RAILWAY
Low Dalby
South Bay
Keldholme
DALBY FOREST VISITOR CENTRE
Dalby Forest
FORGE VALLEY WOODLANDS
Falsgrave
Kirkby Mills
Sinnington
Wrelton
Aislaby
ST PETER AND ST PAUL CHURCH
East Ayton
Cayton Bay
West Ayton
THE HONEY FARM
Osgodby
Middleton
Sawdon
Hutton Buscel
Eastfield
Yons Nab
Great Edstone
Pickering
PICKERING CASTLE
Ellerburn
WORDSWORTH GALLERY
Irton
CLEVELAND WAY
Ruston
Seamer
Marton
Thornton-le-Dale
Wilton
Allerston
Ebberston
Snainton
Wykeham
Cayton
Normanby
Brompton
Lebberston
Gristhorpe
PLAYDALE FARM PARK
Little Barugh
FLAMINGO LAND
Flixton
Folkton
HALL
Salton
Kirby Misperton
Yedingham
THE CARRS
Staxton
Muston
Great Barugh
YORKSHIRE WOLDS WAY
Brawby
High Marishes
Ganton
Butterwick
Low Marishes
East Heslerton
Sherburn
Little Habton
Great Habton
Scampston
SCAMPSTON HALL
West Knapton
East Knapton
Potter Brompton
Ryton
West Heslerton
Fordon
Hunmanby
Derwent
Esk
Seven
Dove
Costa Beck
A171
A174
A169
A170
A165
A64
A1039
B1266
B1366
B1410
B1416
B1447
B1415
B1261
B1258
B1249
96
97
299
432
248

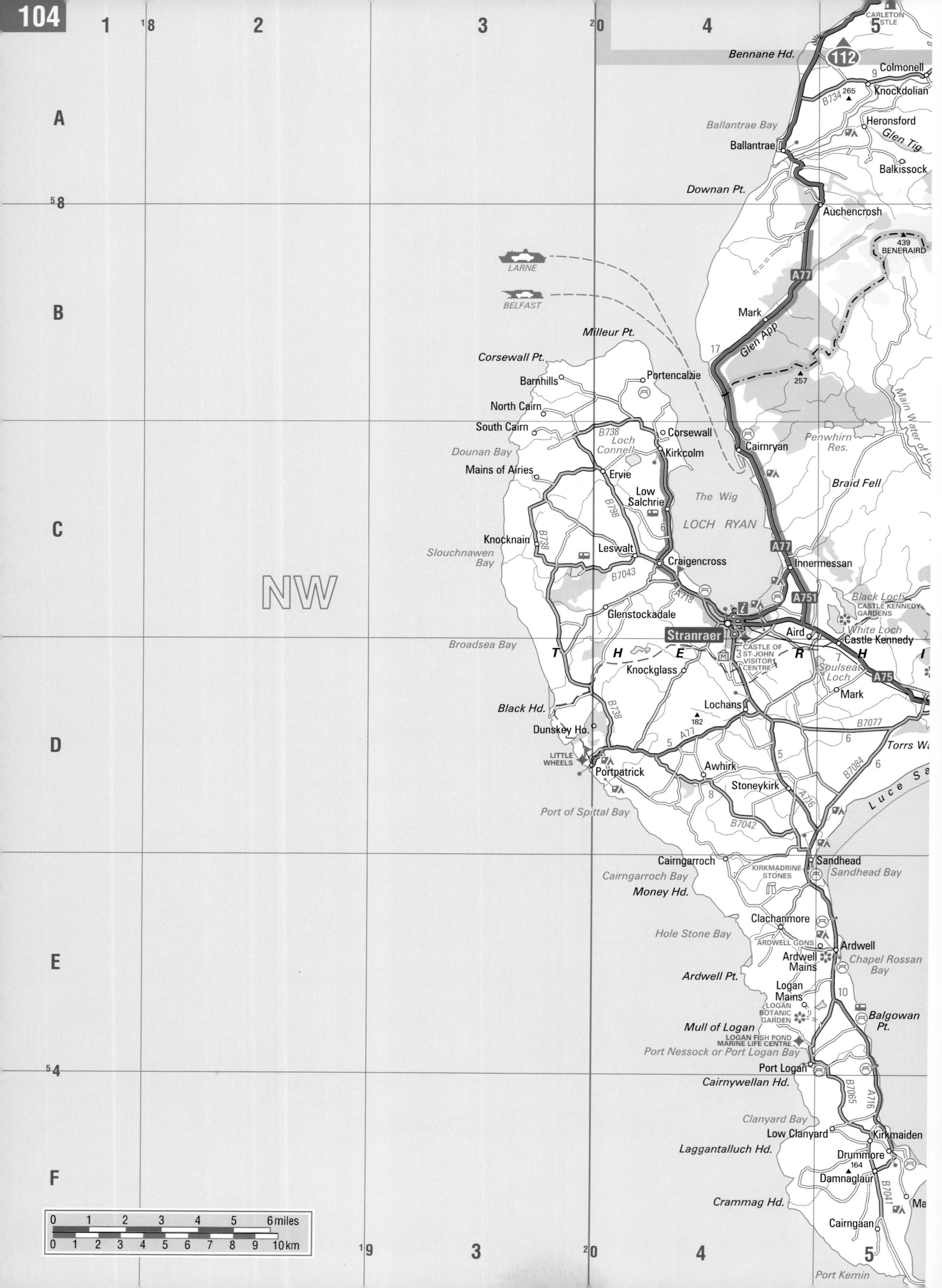

1 8 2 3 0 4 5

A

Bennane Hd.

CARLETON STLE

112

Colmonell

B734 265

Knockdolian

Heronsford

Glen Tig

Balkissock

Ballantrae Bay

58

Ballantrae

Downan Pt.

Auchencrosh

439 BENERAIRD

LARNE

BELFAST

A77

Mark

Glen App

Benet

B

17

257

Milleur Pt.

Corsewall Pt.

Barnhills

Portencalzie

North Cairn

South Cairn

Corsewall

Cairnryan

Penwhirn Res.

B738

Loch Connell

Kirkcolm

The Wig

Braid Fell

Dounan Bay

Mains of Airies

Ervie

Low Salchrie

LOCH RYAN

Main Water of Lu

B798

6

Knocknain

B738

Leswalt

Craigencross

Innermessan

C

Slouchnawen Bay

B7043

A718

A77

A751

Black Loch

CASTLE KENNEDY GARDENS

White Loch

Glenstockadale

Stranraer

Aird

Castle Kennedy

Broadsea Bay

T H E   R H I

CASTLE OF ST·JOHN VISITOR CENTRE

Black Hd.

Knockglass

Soulseat Loch

A75

Dunskey Ho.

B738

Lochans

Mark

LITTLE WHEELS

182

A77

B7077

Torrs Wa

Portpatrick

5

Awhirk

5

B7084

6

D

Stoneykirk

A716

Luce Sa

8

Port of Spittal Bay

B7042

Cairngarroch

Sandhead

KIRKMADRINE STONES

Sandhead Bay

Cairngarroch Bay

Money Hd.

Clachanmore

Hole Stone Bay

ARDWELL GDNS

Ardwell

Ardwell Mains

Chapel Rossan Bay

E

Ardwell Pt.

Logan Mains

10

LOGAN BOTANIC GARDEN

Balgowan Pt.

Mull of Logan

LOGAN FISH POND MARINE LIFE CENTRE

Port Nessock or Port Logan Bay

54

Port Logan

A716

Cairnywellan Hd.

B7065

Clanyard Bay

Low Clanyard

Kirkmaiden

Laggantalluch Hd.

Drummore

F

164

Damnaglaur

B7041

Ma

Crammag Hd.

Cairngaan

NW

Port Kemin

0 1 2 3 4 5 6 miles
0 1 2 3 4 5 6 7 8 9 10 km

19 3 0 4 5

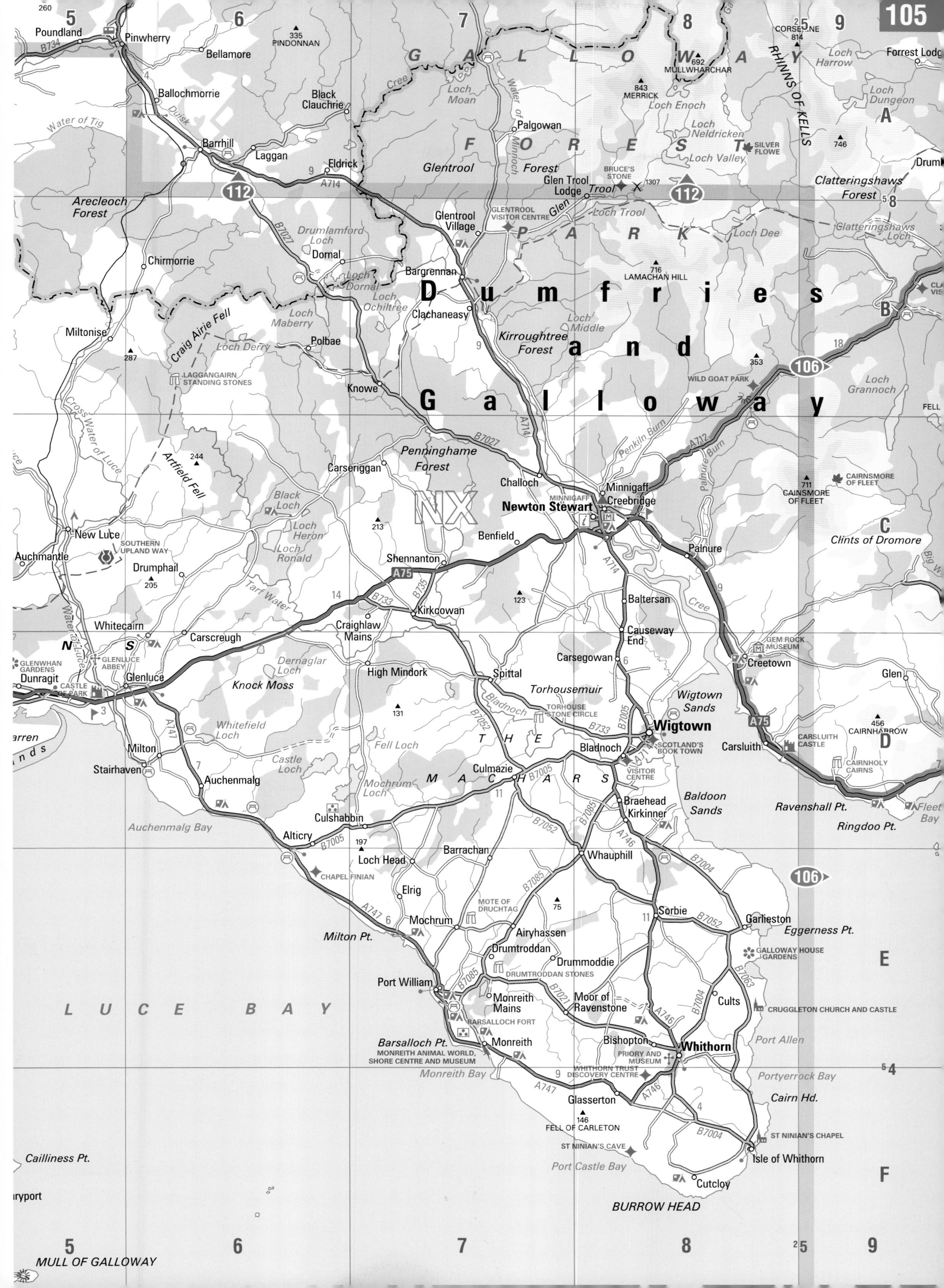
Dumfries and Galloway
GALLOWAY FOREST PARK
NX
Poundland
Pinwherry
Bellamore
Ballochmorrie
Black Clauchrie
Barrhill
Laggan
Eldrick
Arecleoch Forest
Chirmorrie
Dornal
Glentrool
Glentrool Village
Glen Trool Lodge
Palgowan
Loch Moan
Loch Enoch
Loch Neldricken
Loch Valley
Loch Trool
Loch Dee
Loch Harrow
Loch Dungeon
Forrest Lodge
MULLWHARCHAR
MERRICK
CORSERINE
RHINNS OF KELLS
SILVER FLOWE
BRUCE'S STONE
GLENTROOL VISITOR CENTRE
Clatteringshaws Forest
Clatteringshaws Loch
LAMACHAN HILL
PINDONNAN
Bargrennan
Clachaneasy
Kirroughtree Forest
Loch Middle
Loch Dornal
Loch Ochiltree
Loch Maberry
Loch Derry
Drumlamford Loch
Polbae
Miltonise
Craig Airie Fell
LAGGANGAIRN STANDING STONES
Knowe
WILD GOAT PARK
Loch Grannoch
Cross Water of Luce
Artfield Fell
Penninghame Forest
Carseriggan
Challoch
Minnigaff
Creebridge
Newton Stewart
CAIRNSMORE OF FLEET
Clints of Dromore
Black Loch
Loch Heron
Loch Ronald
New Luce
SOUTHERN UPLAND WAY
Auchmantle
Drumphail
Benfield
Shennanton
Palnure
Tarf Water
Kirkcowan
Baltersan
Craighlaw Mains
Causeway End
Whitecairn
Carscreugh
GLENWHAN GARDENS
GLENLUCE ABBEY
Dunragit
CASTLE OF PARK
Glenluce
Knock Moss
Dernaglar Loch
High Mindork
Spittal
Carsegowan
Torhousemuir
GEM ROCK MUSEUM
Creetown
Glen
Whitefield Loch
TORHOUSE STONE CIRCLE
Wigtown Sands
Wigtown
SCOTLAND'S BOOK TOWN
Bladnoch
Carsluith
CARSLUITH CASTLE
CAIRNHARROW
CAIRNHOLY CAIRNS
Milton
Stairhaven
Fell Loch
Castle Loch
Auchenmalg
Culmazie
THE MACHARS
VISITOR CENTRE
Mochrum Loch
Baldoon Sands
Braehead
Kirkinner
Ravenshall Pt.
Ringdoo Pt.
Fleet Bay
Culshabbin
Auchenmalg Bay
Alticry
Loch Head
Barrachan
Whauphill
CHAPEL FINIAN
Elrig
MOTE OF DRUCHTAG
Sorbie
Garlieston
Eggerness Pt.
Mochrum
Airyhassen
Milton Pt.
Drumtroddan
Drummoddie
GALLOWAY HOUSE GARDENS
DRUMTRODDAN STONES
Port William
Monreith Mains
Moor of Ravenstone
Cults
CRUGGLETON CHURCH AND CASTLE
LUCE BAY
BARSALLOCH FORT
Barsalloch Pt.
Monreith
MONREITH ANIMAL WORLD, SHORE CENTRE AND MUSEUM
Bishopton
PRIORY AND MUSEUM
Whithorn
Port Allen
WHITHORN TRUST DISCOVERY CENTRE
Monreith Bay
Portyerrock Bay
Glasserton
Cairn Hd.
FELL OF CARLETON
ST NINIAN'S CHAPEL
ST NINIAN'S CAVE
Isle of Whithorn
Port Castle Bay
Cutcloy
BURROW HEAD
Cailliness Pt.
MULL OF GALLOWAY
A75
A714
A712
A747
A746
B7027
B7005
B7052
B7085
B7004
B7063
B7021
B733
B735
B734
112
106

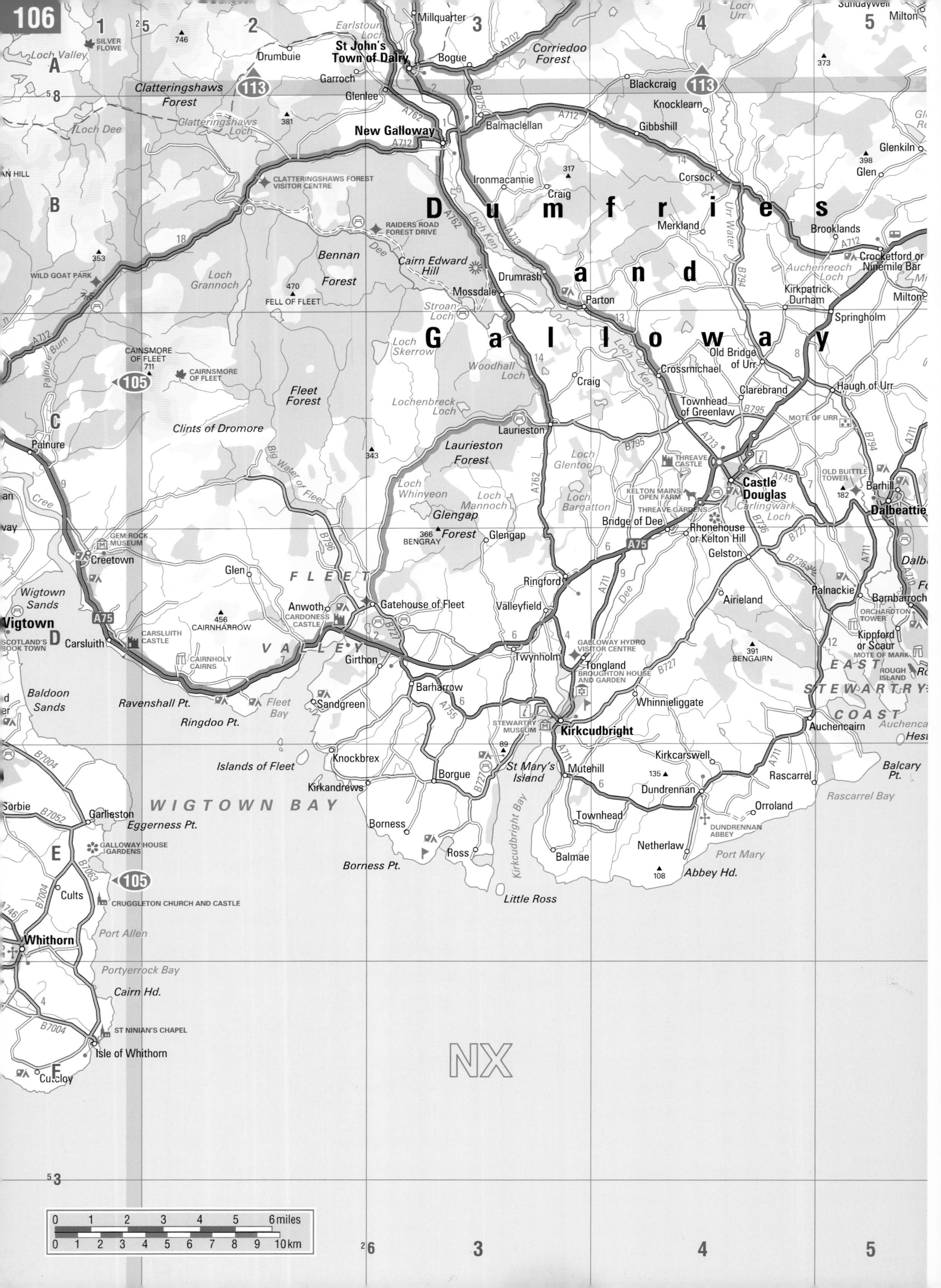

Dumfries and Galloway
St John's Town of Dalry
New Galloway
Balmaclellan
Corriedoo Forest
Millquarter
Bogue
Earlstoun Loch
Drumbuie
Garroch
Glenlee
Clatteringshaws Forest
Clatteringshaws Loch
Loch Dee
Loch Valley
SILVER FLOWE
Blackcraig
Knocklearn
Gibbshill
Corsock
Glenkiln
Glen
Ironmacannie
Craig
Merkland
Urr Water
Brooklands
Crocketford or Ninemile Bar
Auchenreoch Loch
Kirkpatrick Durham
Milton
Springholm
CLATTERINGSHAWS FOREST VISITOR CENTRE
RAIDERS ROAD FOREST DRIVE
Bennan Forest
Cairn Edward Hill
Loch Ken
Drumrash
Mossdale
Parton
Stroan Loch
Loch Grannoch
FELL OF FLEET
WILD GOAT PARK
Palnure Burn
CAINSMORE OF FLEET
CAIRNSMORE OF FLEET
Loch Skerrow
Woodhall Loch
Craig
Crossmichael
Old Bridge of Urr
Clarebrand
Haugh of Urr
Fleet Forest
Lochenbreck Loch
Townhead of Greenlaw
MOTE OF URR
Palnure
Clints of Dromore
Laurieston
Laurieston Forest
Loch Glentoo
THREAVE CASTLE
Castle Douglas
OLD BUITTLE TOWER
Barhill
Dalbeattie
Big Water of Fleet
Loch Whinyeon
Loch Mannoch
KELTON MAINS OPEN FARM
THREAVE GARDENS
Loch Bargatton
Carlingwark Loch
Cree
Glengap Forest
BENGRAY
Glengap
Bridge of Dee
Rhonehouse or Kelton Hill
Gelston
GEM ROCK MUSEUM
Creetown
Glen
FLEET VALLEY
Ringford
Airieland
Palnackie
Barnbarroch
Wigtown Sands
Wigtown
Anwoth
CARDONESS CASTLE
Gatehouse of Fleet
Valleyfield
ORCHARDTON TOWER
Kippford or Scaur
MOTE OF MARK
SCOTLAND'S BOOK TOWN
Carsluith
CARSLUITH CASTLE
CAIRNHARROW
CAIRNHOLY CAIRNS
Girthon
Twynholm
GALLOWAY HYDRO VISITOR CENTRE
Tongland
BROUGHTON HOUSE AND GARDEN
BENGAIRN
ROUGH ISLAND
EAST STEWARTRY COAST
Baldoon Sands
Ravenshall Pt.
Ringdoo Pt.
Fleet Bay
Sandgreen
Barharrow
Whinnieligate
STEWARTRY MUSEUM
Kirkcudbright
Auchencairn
Islands of Fleet
Knockbrex
Borgue
St Mary's Isle
Mutehill
Kirkcarswell
Rascarrel
Balcary Pt.
Rascarrel Bay
Kirkandrews
Dundrennan
Orroland
Sorbie
Garlieston
WIGTOWN BAY
Eggerness Pt.
GALLOWAY HOUSE GARDENS
Borness
Ross
Townhead
Kirkcudbright Bay
DUNDRENNAN ABBEY
Netherlaw
Port Mary
Balmae
Abbey Hd.
Borness Pt.
Little Ross
Cults
CRUGGLETON CHURCH AND CASTLE
Port Allen
Whithorn
Portyerrock Bay
Cairn Hd.
ST NINIAN'S CHAPEL
Isle of Whithorn
Cutcloy
NX
0 1 2 3 4 5 6 miles
0 1 2 3 4 5 6 7 8 9 10 km

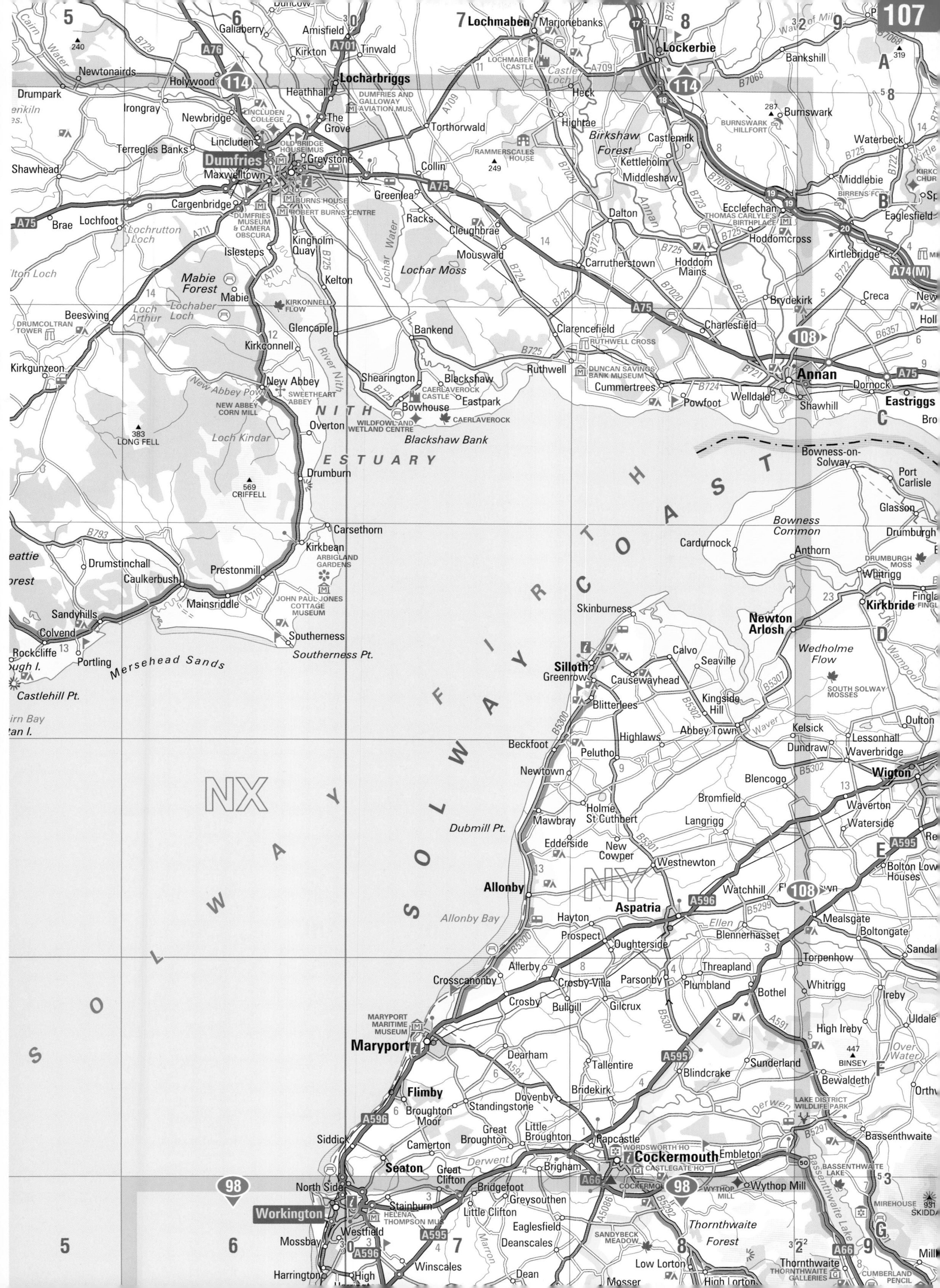
Lochmaben
Marjoriebanks
Lockerbie
Amisfield
Tinwald
Kirkton
Galiaberry
Newtonairds
Holywood
Locharbriggs
Drumpark
Heathhall
Irongray
Newbridge
Lincluden
The Grove
Terregles Banks
Dumfries
Maxwelltown
Greystone
Shawhead
Cargenbridge
Brae
Lochfoot
Lochrutton Loch
Islesteps
Kingholm Quay
Kelton
Mabie Forest
Mabie
Loch Arthur
Lochaber Loch
Beeswing
Drumcoltran Tower
Kirkconnell
Glencaple
Kirkgunzeon
New Abbey
Sweetheart Abbey
New Abbey Corn Mill
Long Fell
Loch Kindar
Criffell
Overton
Drumburn
Carsethorn
Kirkbean
Arbigland Gardens
Drumstinchall
Caulkerbush
Prestonmill
Mainsriddle
John Paul Jones Cottage Museum
Sandyhills
Colvend
Rockcliffe
Portling
Southerness
Southerness Pt.
Mersehead Sands
Castlehill Pt.
Lochmaben Castle
Castle Loch
Heck
Hightae
Torthorwald
Collin
Rammerscales House
Greenlea
Racks
Cleughbrae
Mouswald
Lochar Moss
Lochar Water
Bankend
Shearington
Blackshaw
Caerlaverock Castle
Eastpark
Bowhouse
Wildfowl and Wetland Centre
Caerlaverock
Blackshaw Bank
Nith Estuary
Birkshaw Forest
Castlemilk
Kettleholm
Middleshaw
Dalton
Carrutherstown
Hoddom Mains
Clarencefield
Ruthwell Cross
Ruthwell
Duncan Savings Bank Museum
Cummertrees
Powfoot
Bankshill
Burnswark
Burnswark Hillfort
Waterbeck
Middlebie
Ecclefechan
Thomas Carlyle's Birthplace
Hoddomcross
Eaglesfield
Kirtlebridge
Brydekirk
Creca
Charlesfield
Annan
Welldale
Shawhill
Dornock
Eastriggs
Bowness-on-Solway
Port Carlisle
Glasson
Bowness Common
Drumburgh
Cardurnock
Anthorn
Drumburgh Moss
Whitrigg
Kirkbride
Skinburness
Newton Arlosh
Silloth
Greenrow
Calvo
Seaville
Causewayhead
Blitterlees
Kingside Hill
Wedholme Flow
South Solway Mosses
Abbey Town
Beckfoot
Highlaws
Pelutho
Kelsick
Dundraw
Lessonhall
Waverbridge
Newtown
Blencogo
Wigton
Bromfield
Holme St Cuthbert
Mawbray
Langrigg
Waverton
Waterside
Dubmill Pt.
Edderside
New Cowper
Westnewton
Allonby
Aspatria
Watchhill
Allonby Bay
Hayton
Prospect
Oughterside
Blennerhasset
Mealsgate
Boltongate
Allerby
Crosby Villa
Parsonby
Threapland
Plumbland
Torpenhow
Crosscanonby
Crosby
Bullgill
Gilcrux
Bothel
Whitrigg
Ireby
Uldale
High Ireby
Binsey
Maryport Maritime Museum
Maryport
Dearham
Tallentire
Blindcrake
Sunderland
Bewaldeth
Flimby
Bridekirk
Dovenby
Broughton Moor
Standingstone
Lake District Wildlife Park
Siddick
Camerton
Great Broughton
Little Broughton
Papcastle
Wordsworth Ho
Cockermouth
Embleton
Bassenthwaite
Seaton
Great Clifton
Brigham
Castlegate Ho
North Side
Bridgefoot
Stainburn
Greysouthen
Wythop Mill
Bassenthwaite Lake
Mirehouse
Workington
Helena Thompson Mus
Little Clifton
Eaglesfield
Thornthwaite Forest
Westfield
Mossbay
Deanscales
Sandybeck Meadow
Harrington
Winscales
Dean
Low Lorton
Thornthwaite
Thornthwaite Galleries
Cumberland Pencil
Solway Firth
Solway Coast
NX
NY
A75
A76
A701
A709
A710
A711
A74(M)
A595
A596
A66
A591
A594
A5086
B725
B724
B7020
B5300
B5301
B5302
B5307
B5299
108
114
98

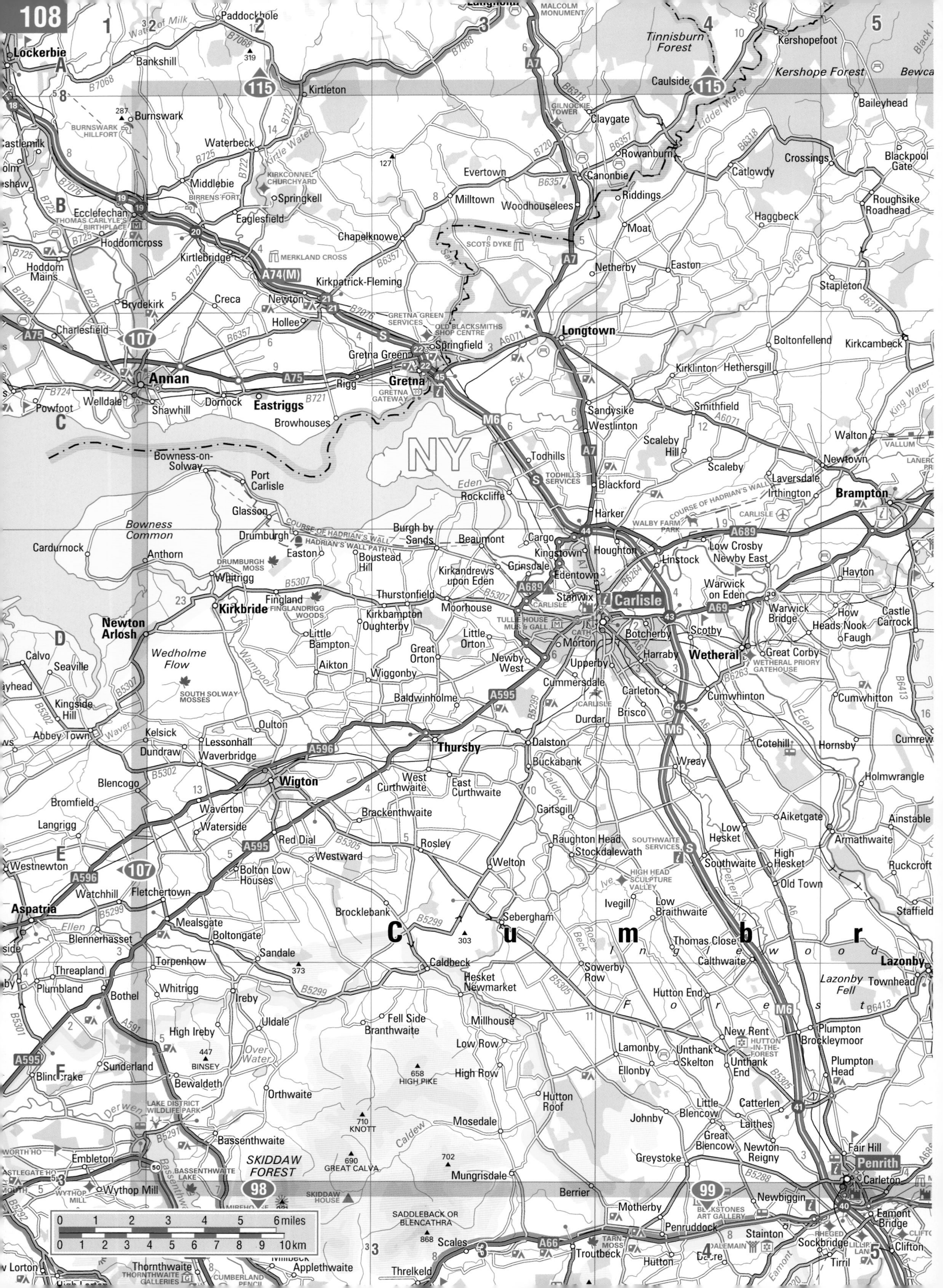
Lockerbie
Paddockhole
Kirtleton
Bankshill
Burnswark
Burnswark Hillfort
Castlemilk
Waterbeck
Middlebie
Kirkconnel Churchyard
Springkell
Birrens Fort
Ecclefechan
Thomas Carlyle's Birthplace
Eaglesfield
Hoddomcross
Kirtlebridge
Merkland Cross
Hoddom Mains
Brydekirk
Creca
Newton
Kirkpatrick-Fleming
Chapelknowe
Milltown
Evertown
Woodhouselees
Canonbie
Rowanburn
Riddings
Claygate
Gilnockie Tower
Malcolm Monument
Tinnisburn Forest
Caulside
Kershopefoot
Kershope Forest
Baileyhead
Crossings
Blackpool Gate
Catlowdy
Roughsike
Roadhead
Haggbeck
Moat
Scots Dyke
Netherby
Easton
Stapleton
Hollee
Charlesfield
Gretna Green Services
Old Blacksmiths Shop Centre
Springfield
Gretna Green
Gretna
Gretna Gateway
Rigg
Annan
Welldale
Powfoot
Shawhill
Dornock
Eastriggs
Browhouses
Longtown
Boltonfellend
Kirkcambeck
Kirklinton
Hethersgill
Sandysike
Westlinton
Smithfield
Scaleby Hill
Scaleby
Walton
Vallum
Newtown
Laversdale
Irthington
Brampton
Carlisle
Walby Farm Park
Todhills
Todhills Services
Blackford
Harker
Rockcliffe
Bowness-on-Solway
Port Carlisle
Glasson
Bowness Common
Drumburgh
Course of Hadrian's Wall
Hadrian's Wall Path
Cardurnock
Anthorn
Easton
Drumburgh Moss
Whitrigg
Burgh by Sands
Boustead Hill
Beaumont
Cargo
Kingstown
Houghton
Grinsdale
Kirkandrews upon Eden
Edentown
Stanwix
Linstock
Low Crosby
Newby East
Hayton
Warwick on Eden
Warwick Bridge
How
Heads Nook
Faugh
Castle Carrock
Fingland
Finglandrigg Woods
Kirkbride
Thurstonfield
Moorhouse
Kirkbampton
Oughterby
Tullie House Mus & Gall.
Newton Arlosh
Little Bampton
Little Orton
Great Orton
Botcherby
Scotby
Morton
Harraby
Wetheral
Great Corby
Wetheral Priory Gatehouse
Calvo
Seaville
Wedholme Flow
Aikton
Newby West
Upperby
Wiggonby
Cummersdale
Kingside Hill
South Solway Mosses
Baldwinholme
Carleton
Cumwhinton
Cumwhitton
Brisco
Durdar
Abbey Town
Kelsick
Lessonhall
Oulton
Thursby
Dalston
Cotehill
Hornsby
Cumrew
Dundraw
Waverbridge
Buckabank
Wreay
Blencogo
Wigton
West Curthwaite
East Curthwaite
Holmwrangle
Bromfield
Waverton
Brackenthwaite
Gaitsgill
Aiketgate
Ainstable
Langrigg
Waterside
Red Dial
Rosley
Raughton Head
Stockdalewath
Southwaite Services
Low Hesket
Armathwaite
Westnewton
Westward
Bolton Low Houses
Welton
High Head Sculpture Valley
Southwaite
High Hesket
Ruckcroft
Old Town
Watchhill
Fletchertown
Aspatria
Mealsgate
Brocklebank
Sebergham
Ivegill
Low Braithwaite
Staffield
Blennerhasset
Boltongate
Sandale
Cumbria
Inglewood Forest
Thomas Close
Calthwaite
Lazonby
Torpenhow
Caldbeck
Hesket Newmarket
Sowerby Row
Lazonby Fell
Townhead
Threapland
Plumbland
Whitrigg
Bothel
Ireby
Hutton End
Uldale
Fell Side
Branthwaite
Millhouse
Plumpton
Brockleymoor
High Ireby
Low Row
Lamonby
Unthank
Skelton
New Rent
Hutton-in-the-Forest
Unthank End
Plumpton Head
Sunderland
Binsey
Over Water
High Row
High Pike
Ellonby
Blindcrake
Bewaldeth
Orthwaite
Hutton Roof
Lake District Wildlife Park
Little Blencow
Catterlen
Johnby
Laithes
Knott
Mosedale
Great Blencow
Newton Reigny
Fair Hill
Penrith
Bassenthwaite
Embleton
Great Calva
Skiddaw Forest
Greystoke
Mungrisdale
Carleton
Wythop Mill
Bassenthwaite Lake
Skiddaw House
Berrier
Motherby
Newbiggin
Eamont Bridge
Blencathra or Saddleback
Blackstones Art Gallery
Penruddock
Stainton
Dalemain
Sockbridge
Scales
Tarn Moss
Troutbeck
Hutton
Dacre
Tirril
Clifton
Lorton
Thornthwaite
Thornthwaite Galleries
Applethwaite
Cumberland Pencil
Threlkeld
NY
miles
km

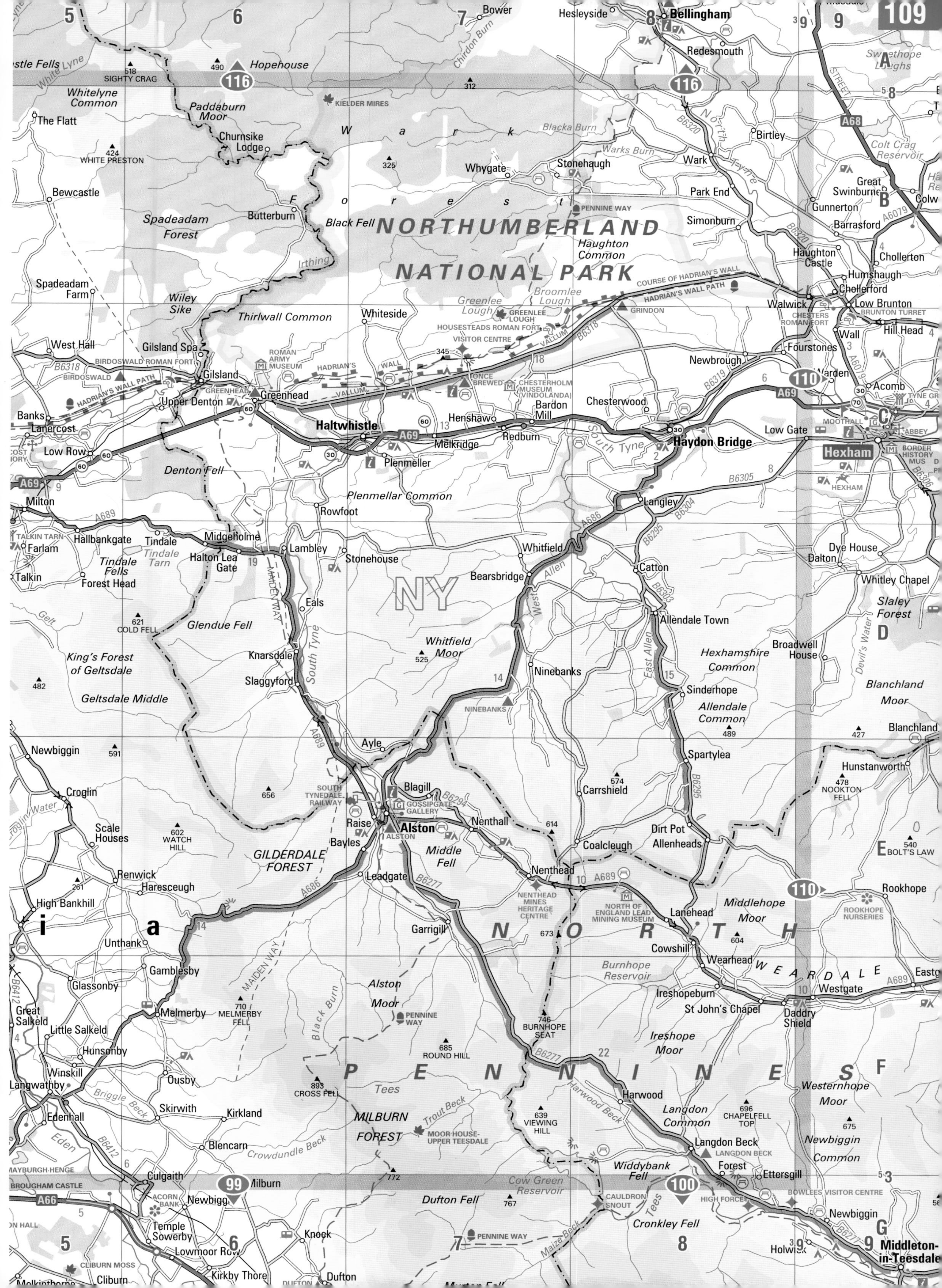
Bower
Hesleyside
Bellingham
Redesmouth
Hopehouse
116
Whitelyne Common
SIGHTY CRAG
KIELDER MIRES
Paddaburn Moor
The Flatt
Churnsike Lodge
WHITE PRESTON
W a r k
F o r e s t
Blacka Burn
Warks Burn
North Tyne
Birtley
Wark
Whygate
Stonehaugh
Colt Crag Reservoir
Great Swinburne
Gunnerton
Barrasford
Park End
Simonburn
Bewcastle
Spadeadam Forest
Butterburn
Black Fell
NORTHUMBERLAND NATIONAL PARK
PENNINE WAY
Haughton Common
Haughton Castle
Humshaugh
Chollerton
Chollerford
Irthing
Spadeadam Farm
Wiley Sike
Thirlwall Common
Whiteside
Greenlee Lough
Broomlee Lough
GREENLEE LOUGH
COURSE OF HADRIAN'S WALL
HADRIAN'S WALL PATH
GRINDON
Walwick
CHESTERS ROMAN FORT
Low Brunton
BRUNTON TURRET
HOUSESTEADS ROMAN FORT
VISITOR CENTRE
VALLUM
Wall
Hill Head
West Hall
Gilsland Spa
ROMAN ARMY MUSEUM
HADRIAN'S WALL
Fourstones
Newbrough
Warden
B6318
BIRDOSWALD ROMAN FORT
BIRDOSWALD
Gilsland
GREENHEAD
Greenhead
ONCE BREWED
CHESTERHOLM MUSEUM (VINDOLANDA)
Acomb
HADRIAN'S WALL PATH
Upper Denton
Banks
Lanercost
Haltwhistle
Henshaw
Bardon Mill
Chesterwood
A69
Melkridge
Redburn
South Tyne
Haydon Bridge
Low Gate
MOOTHALL
ABBEY
Hexham
BORDER HISTORY MUS
HEXHAM
Low Row
Plenmeller
Denton Fell
Plenmellar Common
B6305
Milton
Rowfoot
Langley
A689
A686
B6304
TALKIN TARN
Hallbankgate
Tindale
Midgeholme
Lambley
Stonehouse
Whitfield
Farlam
Tindale Fells
Tindale Tarn
Halton Lea Gate
Catton
Dye House
Dalton
Talkin
Forest Head
MAIDEN WAY
Bearsbridge
West Allen
B6295
Whitley Chapel
NY
Eals
Slaley Forest
COLD FELL
Glendue Fell
Allendale Town
Gelt
Whitfield Moor
Broadwell House
Devil's Water
King's Forest of Geltsdale
Knarsdale
Hexhamshire Common
Slaggyford
Ninebanks
East Allen
Sinderhope
Blanchland Moor
Geltsdale Middle
Allendale Common
NINEBANKS
Blanchland
Ayle
A689
Newbiggin
Spartylea
Hunstanworth
Croglin
Carrshield
NOOKTON FELL
Blagill
SOUTH TYNEDALE RAILWAY
GOSSIPGATE GALLERY
B6294
Croglin Water
Scale Houses
WATCH HILL
Raise
Alston
ALSTON
Nenthall
Dirt Pot
Allenheads
Bayles
Middle Fell
Coalcleugh
BOLT'S LAW
GILDERDALE FOREST
Renwick
Haresceugh
Leadgate
Nenthead
B6277
A689
Rookhope
NENTHEAD MINES HERITAGE CENTRE
NORTH OF ENGLAND LEAD MINING MUSEUM
ROOKHOPE NURSERIES
High Bankhill
Middlehope Moor
Lanehead
Garrigill
N O R T H
Unthank
Cowshill
Wearhead
Gamblesby
WEARDALE
Burnhope Reservoir
Glassonby
Alston Moor
Ireshopeburn
Westgate
Great Salkeld
Melmerby
MELMERBY FELL
St John's Chapel
Daddry Shield
Little Salkeld
PENNINE WAY
BURNHOPE SEAT
Black Burn
Ireshope Moor
Hunsonby
ROUND HILL
B6277
Winskill
Langwathby
Ousby
CROSS FELL
P E N N I N E S
Tees
Harwood
Westernhope Moor
Briggle Beck
Skirwith
Kirkland
Trout Beck
Langdon Common
CHAPELFELL TOP
Edenhall
MILBURN FOREST
VIEWING HILL
Harwood Beck
Eden
B6412
Blencarn
MOOR HOUSE-UPPER TEESDALE
Langdon Beck
LANGDON BECK
Newbiggin Common
Crowdundle Beck
Widdybank Fell
Forest
Ettersgill
MAYBURGH HENGE
Culgaith
Milburn
99
Cow Green Reservoir
100
BROUGHAM CASTLE
HIGH FORCE
BOWLEES VISITOR CENTRE
A66
ACORN BANK
Newbiggin
Dufton Fell
CAULDRON SNOUT
Tees
Newbiggin
Temple Sowerby
Knock
Cronkley Fell
PENNINE WAY
Maize Beck
Lowmoor Row
Holwick
B6277
Middleton-in-Teesdale
CLIBURN MOSS
Cliburn
Kirkby Thore
Dufton

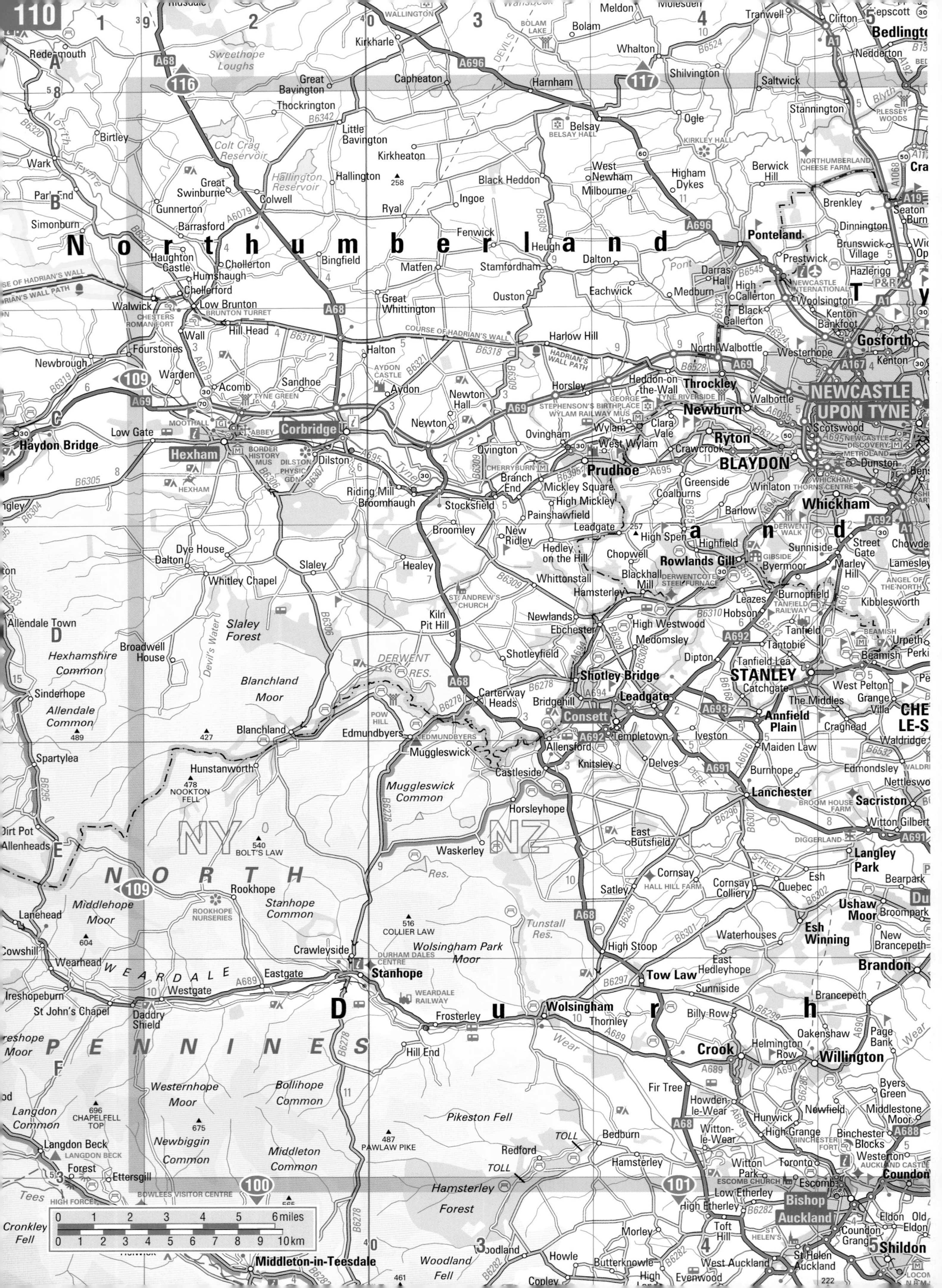

Northumberland
Tyne and Wear
Durham
NORTH PENNINES
WEARDALE
NY
NZ
Redesmouth
Sweethope Loughs
Kirkharle
Great Bavington
Capheaton
Harnham
Bolam
Meldon
Whalton
Shilvington
Tranwell
Clifton
Bedlington
Saltwick
Stannington
Thockrington
Little Bavington
Belsay
Ogle
Birtley
Colt Crag Reservoir
Kirkheaton
Hallington Reservoir
Hallington
Black Heddon
West Newham
Milbourne
Higham Dykes
Berwick Hill
Wark
Park End
Great Swinburne
Gunnerton
Colwell
Ryal
Ingoe
Brenkley
Simonburn
Barrasford
Fenwick
Ponteland
Dinnington
Haughton Castle
Chollerton
Humshaugh
Chollerford
Bingfield
Matfen
Stamfordham
Heugh
Dalton
Prestwick
Hazlerigg
Walwick
Low Brunton
Great Whittington
Ouston
Eachwick
Medburn
Darras Hall
High Callerton
Black Callerton
Woolsington
Kenton Bankfoot
Wall
Hill Head
Fourstones
Halton
Harlow Hill
North Walbottle
Westerhope
Gosforth
Kenton
Newbrough
Warden
Acomb
Sandhoe
Aydon
Newton Hall
Horsley
Heddon-on-the-Wall
Throckley
Walbottle
NEWCASTLE UPON TYNE
Haydon Bridge
Low Gate
Hexham
Corbridge
Dilston
Newton
Ovingham
Wylam
West Wylam
Clara Vale
Newburn
Ryton
Crawcrook
BLAYDON
Scotswood
Dunston
Ovington
Branch End
Prudhoe
Mickley Square
High Mickley
Greenside
Coalburns
Winlaton
Riding Mill
Broomhaugh
Stocksfield
Painshawfield
Barlow
Whickham
Broomley
New Ridley
Leadgate
High Spen
Highfield
Sunniside
Street Gate
Dye House
Dalton
Slaley
Healey
Hedley on the Hill
Chopwell
Rowlands Gill
Byermoor
Marley Hill
Lamesley
Whitley Chapel
Whittonstall
Blackhall Mill
Hamsterley
Burnopfield
Kibblesworth
Allendale Town
Slaley Forest
Kiln Pit Hill
Newlands
Ebchester
Leazes
Hobson
High Westwood
Medomsley
Tanfield
Tantobie
Beamish
Urpeth
Hexhamshire Common
Broadwell House
Shotleyfield
Dipton
Tanfield Lea
STANLEY
West Pelton
Blanchland Moor
Derwent Res.
Carterway Heads
Shotley Bridge
Leadgate
Catchgate
The Middles
Grange Villa
Sinderhope
Allendale Common
Bridgehill
Consett
Annfield Plain
Craghead
Blanchland
Edmundbyers
Allensford
Templetown
Iveston
Maiden Law
Waldridge
Spartylea
Hunstanworth
Muggleswick
Castleside
Knitsley
Delves
Burnhope
Edmondsley
Nettlesworth
Muggleswick Common
Lanchester
Sacriston
Nookton Fell
Horsleyhope
Dirt Pot
Allenheads
Bolt's Law
Waskerley
East Butsfield
Witton Gilbert
Langley Park
Cornsay
Cornsay Colliery
Esh
Rookhope
Satley
Quebec
Bearpark
Middlehope Moor
Stanhope Common
Ushaw Moor
Broompark
Lanehead
Collier Law
Tunstall Res.
Waterhouses
Esh Winning
New Brancepeth
Cowshill
Crawleyside
Wolsingham Park Moor
High Stoop
Wearhead
Eastgate
Stanhope
Tow Law
East Hedleyhope
Brandon
Westgate
Sunniside
Ireshopeburn
St John's Chapel
Daddry Shield
Frosterley
Wolsingham
Thornley
Billy Row
Brancepeth
Oakenshaw
Page Bank
Westernhope Moor
Hill End
Crook
Helmington Row
Willington
Langdon Common
Chapelfell Top
Bollihope Common
Fir Tree
Howden-le-Wear
Byers Green
Newfield
Middlestone Moor
Pikeston Fell
Hunwick
High Grange
Binchester Blocks
Langdon Beck
Newbiggin Common
Pawlaw Pike
Witton-le-Wear
Westerton
Middleton Common
Redford
Bedburn
Hamsterley
Witton Park
Toronto
Coundon
Forest
Ettersgill
Escomb
Hamsterley Forest
Low Etherley
High Etherley
Bishop Auckland
Cronkley Fell
Toft Hill
Eldon
Coundon Grange
Middleton-in-Teesdale
Woodland Fell
Howle
Morley
Butterknowle
West Auckland
St Helen Auckland
Shildon
Evenwood
Copley
Woodland
0 1 2 3 4 5 6 miles
0 1 2 3 4 5 6 7 8 9 10 km

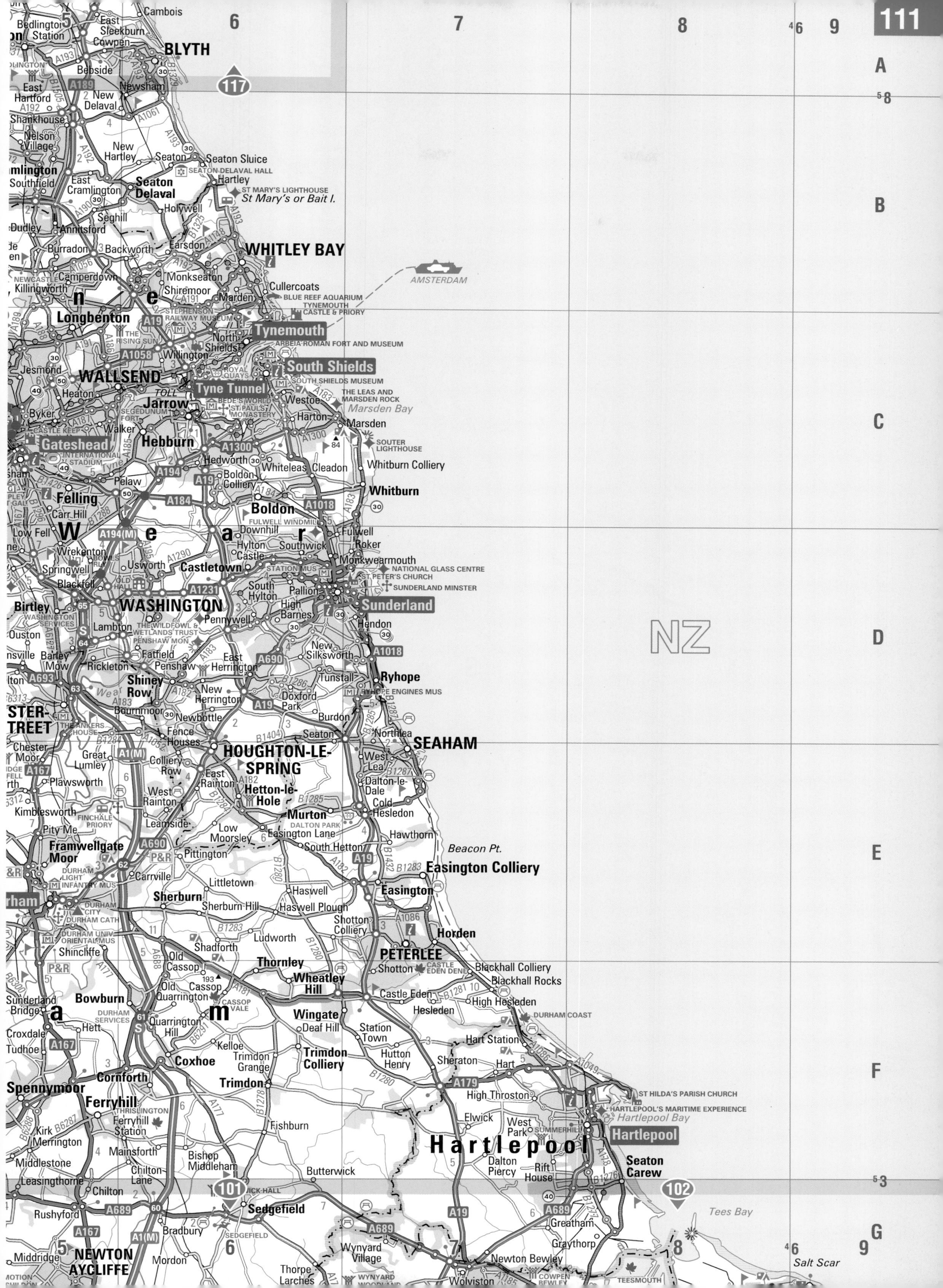
6
7
8
9
A
B
C
D
E
F
G
117
101
102
NZ
Cambois
East Sleekburn
Bedlington Station
Cowpen
BLYTH
Bebside
East Hartford
New Delaval
Newsham
Shankhouse
Nelson Village
New Hartley
Seaton
Seaton Sluice
SEATON DELAVAL HALL
Cramlington
East Cramlington
Seaton Delaval
Hartley
ST MARY'S LIGHTHOUSE
St Mary's or Bait I.
Southfield
Holywell
Seghill
Dudley
Annitsford
Burradon
Backworth
Earsdon
WHITLEY BAY
Camperdown
Monkseaton
Killingworth
Shiremoor
Cullercoats
Marden
BLUE REEF AQUARIUM
TYNEMOUTH CASTLE & PRIORY
AMSTERDAM
Longbenton
STEPHENSON RAILWAY MUSEUM
Tynemouth
North Shields
ARBEIA ROMAN FORT AND MUSEUM
THE RISING SUN
Willington
South Shields
SOUTH SHIELDS MUSEUM
Jesmond
WALLSEND
ROYAL QUAYS
Heaton
Tyne Tunnel
TOLL
THE LEAS AND MARSDEN ROCK
Marsden Bay
Jarrow
Westoe
Byker
SEGEDUNUM FORT
BEDE'S WORLD
ST PAUL'S MONASTERY
Harton
Marsden
CASTLE KEEP
Walker
Gateshead
Hebburn
SOUTER LIGHTHOUSE
INTERNATIONAL STADIUM
Hedworth
Whitburn Colliery
Whiteleas
Cleadon
Boldon Colliery
Pelaw
Whitburn
Felling
Boldon
Carr Hill
FULWELL WINDMILL
Low Fell
Wear
Downhill
Fulwell
Roker
Hylton Castle
Southwick
Wrekenton
Monkwearmouth
NATIONAL GLASS CENTRE
Springwell
Usworth
Castletown
ST PETER'S CHURCH
SUNDERLAND MINSTER
Blackfell
South Hylton
Pallion
Sunderland
Birtley
WASHINGTON
High Barnes
WASHINGTON SERVICES
Pennywell
Hendon
Lambton
THE WILDFOWL & WETLANDS TRUST
Ouston
PENSHAW MON
New Silksworth
Barley Mow
Fatfield
East Herrington
Rickleton
Penshaw
Ryhope
Shiney Row
Tunstall
RYHOPE ENGINES MUS
New Herrington
Doxford Park
Bournmoor
Newbottle
Burdon
THE ANKERS HOUSE
Fence Houses
Seaton
Northlea
SEAHAM
Chester Moor
Great Lumley
HOUGHTON-LE-SPRING
Colliery Row
West Lea
East Rainton
Dalton-le-Dale
Plawsworth
West Rainton
Hetton-le-Hole
Cold Hesledon
Kimblesworth
Murton
FINCHALE PRIORY
Leamside
DALTON PARK
Pity Me
Low Moorsley
Easington Lane
Hawthorn
Framwellgate Moor
South Hetton
Beacon Pt.
Pittington
Easington Colliery
DURHAM LIGHT INFANTRY MUS
Carrville
Littletown
Easington
Durham
Sherburn
Haswell
Sherburn Hill
Haswell Plough
DURHAM CITY
DURHAM CATH
Shotton Colliery
Horden
DURHAM UNIV ORIENTAL MUS
Ludworth
Shadforth
Shincliffe
PETERLEE
Old Cassop
Thornley
Shotton
CASTLE EDEN DENE
Blackhall Colliery
Blackhall Rocks
Cassop
Wheatley Hill
Old Quarrington
CASSOP VALE
Castle Eden
High Hesleden
Sunderland Bridge
Bowburn
DURHAM SERVICES
Hesleden
DURHAM COAST
Wingate
Quarrington Hill
Hett
Deaf Hill
Station Town
Croxdale
Tudhoe
Kelloe
Hart Station
Trimdon Grange
Trimdon Colliery
Hutton Henry
Coxhoe
Sheraton
Hart
Cornforth
Trimdon
Spennymoor
High Throston
ST HILDA'S PARISH CHURCH
Ferryhill
HARTLEPOOL'S MARITIME EXPERIENCE
THRISLINGTON
Hartlepool Bay
Ferryhill Station
Elwick
West Park
SUMMERHILL
Hartlepool
Kirk Merrington
Fishburn
Mainsforth
Middlestone
Bishop Middleham
Chilton Lane
Dalton Piercy
Rift House
Seaton Carew
Leasingthorne
Butterwick
Chilton
HICK HALL
Rushyford
Sedgefield
Tees Bay
Greatham
SEDGEFIELD
Bradbury
Graythorp
Middridge
NEWTON AYCLIFFE
Mordon
Wynyard Village
Newton Bewley
Salt Scar
Thorpe Larches
WYNYARD WOODLAND
Wolviston
COWPEN BEWLEY
TEESMOUTH

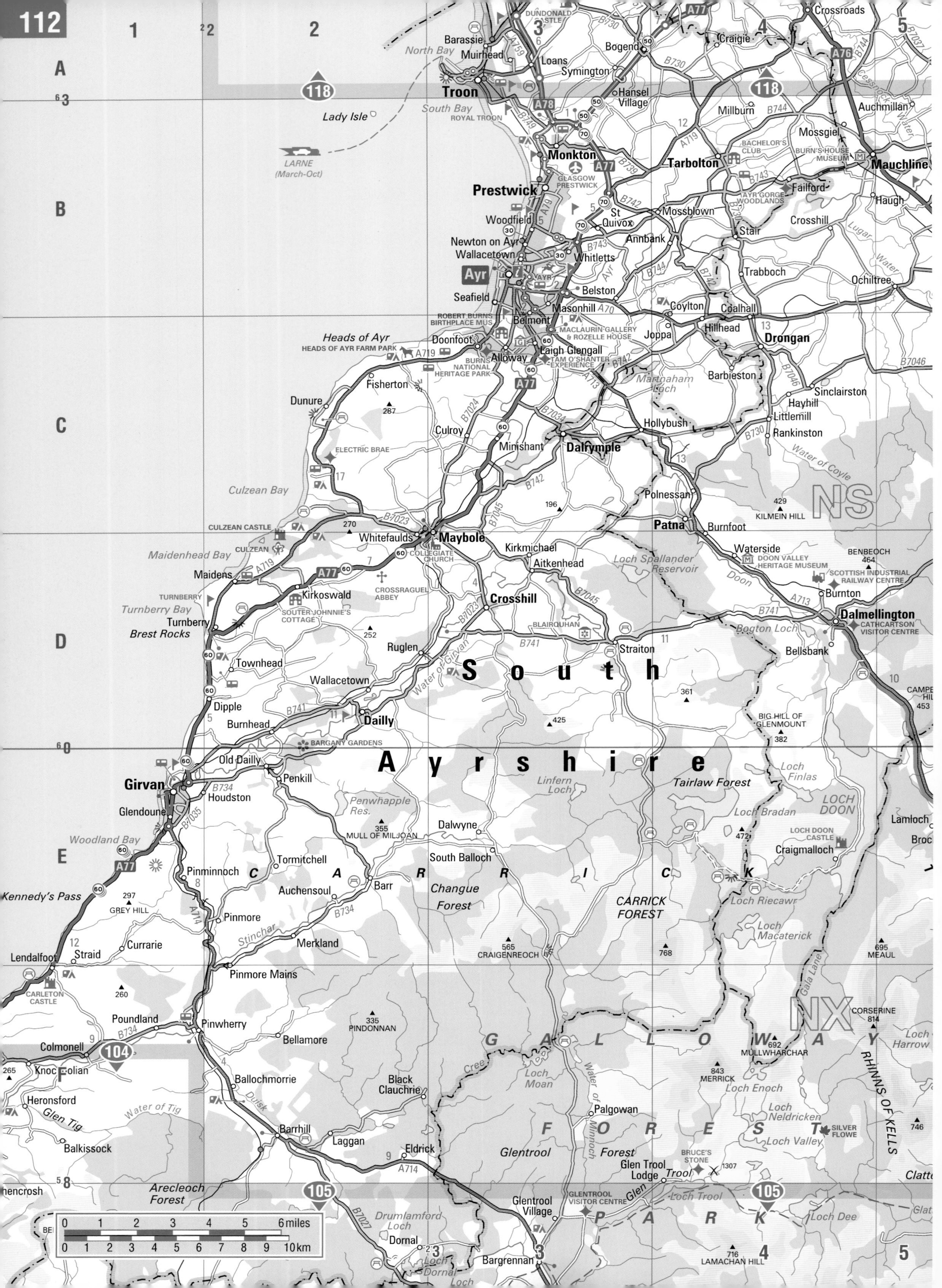

Barassie
Muirhead
North Bay
Troon
Lady Isle
South Bay
ROYAL TROON
LARNE
(March-Oct)
Dundonald Castle
Loans
Symington
Bogend
Craigie
Crossroads
Hansel Village
Millburn
Auchmillan
Mossgiel
Mauchline
Bachelor's Club
Burn's House Museum
Monkton
Glasgow Prestwick
Tarbolton
Prestwick
Failford
Ayr Gorge Woodlands
Haugh
Mossblown
St Quivox
Woodfield
Newton on Ayr
Wallacetown
Annbank
Stair
Crosshill
Whitletts
Trabboch
Ayr
Ochiltree
Seafield
Belston
Coylton
Coalhall
Robert Burns Birthplace Mus
Belmont
Masonhill
Maclaurin Gallery & Rozelle House
Hillhead
Joppa
Drongan
Heads of Ayr
Heads of Ayr Farm Park
Doonfoot
Alloway
Laigh Glengall
Burns National Heritage Park
Tam O'Shanter Experience
Martnaham Loch
Barbieston
Fisherton
Sinclairston
Dunure
Hayhill
Littlemill
Culroy
Hollybush
Rankinston
Minishant
Dalrymple
Electric Brae
Water of Coyle
Culzean Bay
Polnessan
NS
Kilmein Hill
Patna
Burnfoot
Culzean Castle
Whitefaulds
Maybole
Collegiate Church
Culzean
Maidenhead Bay
Kirkmichael
Aitkenhead
Loch Spallander Reservoir
Waterside
Doon Valley Heritage Museum
Benbeoch
Scottish Industrial Railway Centre
Maidens
Kirkoswald
Crossraguel Abbey
Crosshill
Burnton
Turnberry
Turnberry Bay
Souter Johnnie's Cottage
Dalmellington
Cathcartson Visitor Centre
Brest Rocks
Blairquhan
Bogton Loch
Bellsbank
Townhead
Ruglen
Straiton
Water of Girvan
South
Wallacetown
Dipple
Burnhead
Dailly
Big Hill of Glenmount
Bargany Gardens
Old Dailly
Ayrshire
Girvan
Penkill
Houdston
Linfern Loch
Tairlaw Forest
Loch Finlas
Glendoune
Penwhapple Res.
Loch Bradan
Loch Doon
Lamloch
Mull of Miljoan
Dalwyne
Loch Doon Castle
Woodland Bay
South Balloch
Craigmalloch
Tormitchell
Pinminnoch
Carrick
Barr
Auchensoul
Changue Forest
Carrick Forest
Loch Riecawr
Kennedy's Pass
Grey Hill
Pinmore
Loch Macaterick
Stinchar
Merkland
Craigenreoch
Meaul
Lendalfoot
Straid
Currarie
Pinmore Mains
Carleton Castle
Gala Lane
NX
Corserine
Poundland
Pinwherry
Pindonnan
Bellamore
Galloway
Loch Harrow
Colmonell
Mullwharchar
Knockdolian
Rhinns of Kells
Cree
Loch Moan
Merrick
Loch Enoch
Ballochmorrie
Black Clauchrie
Heronsford
Glen Tig
Water of Tig
Duisk
Palgowan
Water of Minnoch
Loch Neldricken
Forest
Silver Flowe
Barrhill
Laggan
Loch Valley
Balkissock
Eldrick
Glentrool
Bruce's Stone
Glen Trool Lodge
Trool
Arecleoch Forest
Loch Trool
Glentrool Village
Glentrool Visitor Centre
Park
Drumlamford Loch
Loch Dee
Dornal
Bargrennan
Lamachan Hill
0 1 2 3 4 5 6 miles
0 1 2 3 4 5 6 7 8 9 10 km

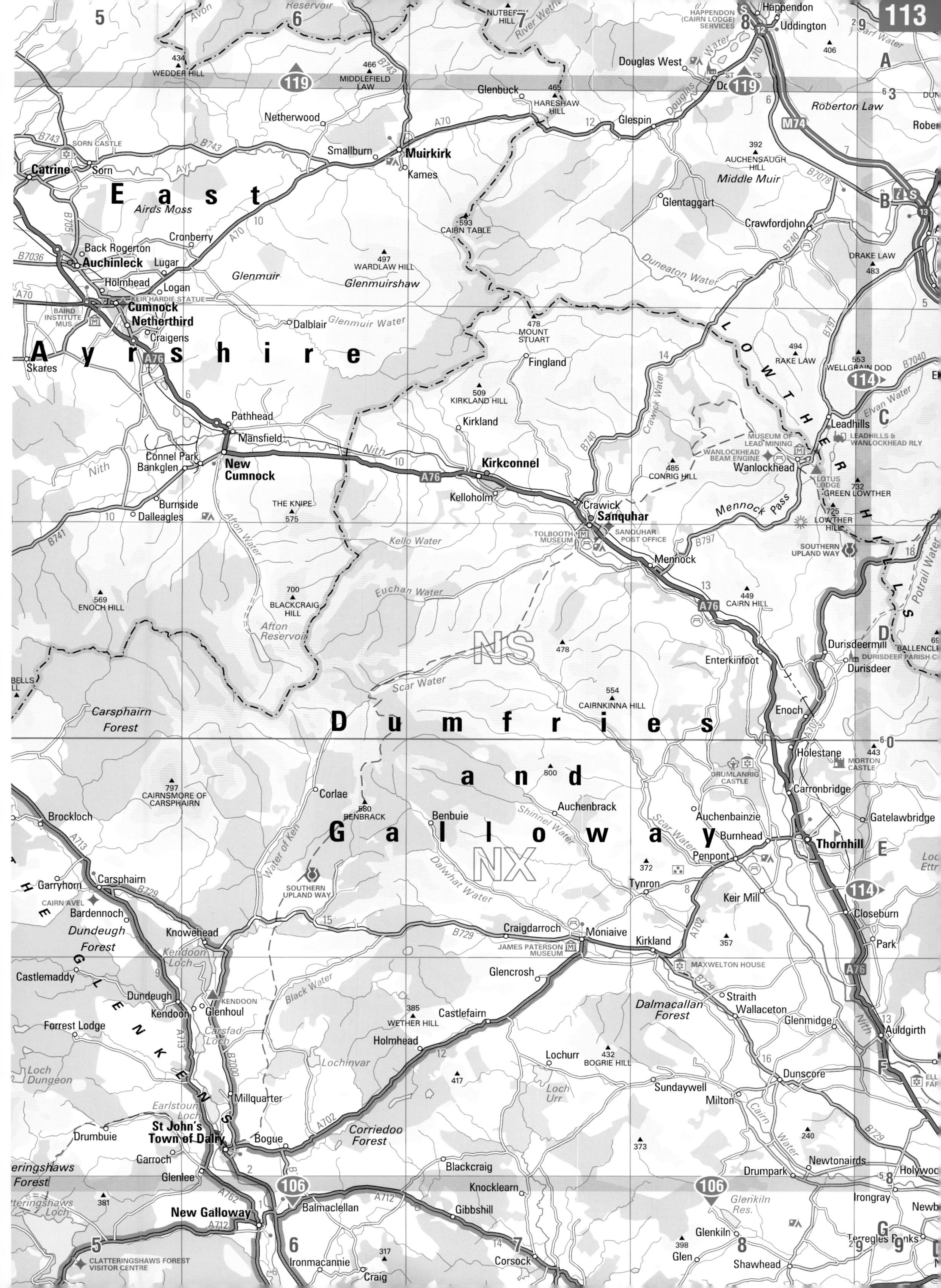
East Ayrshire
Dumfries and Galloway
Catrine
Sorn
Sorn Castle
Airds Moss
Muirkirk
Smallburn
Kames
Netherwood
Glenbuck
Hareshaw Hill
Glespin
Douglas West
Happendon
Uddington
Happendon (Cairn Lodge) Services
Robertson Law
Middle Muir
Auchensaugh Hill
Glentaggart
Crawfordjohn
Duneaton Water
Drake Law
Cronberry
Back Rogerton
Auchinleck
Lugar
Holmhead
Logan
Glenmuir
Glenmuirshaw
Wardlaw Hill
Cairn Table
Keir Hardie Statue
Baird Institute Mus.
Cumnock
Netherthird
Craigens
Dalblair
Glenmuir Water
Mount Stuart
Fingland
Skares
Lowther Hills
Rake Law
Wellgrain Dod
Kirkland Hill
Kirkland
Pathhead
Mansfield
Connel Park
Bankglen
New Cumnock
Kirkconnel
Kelloholm
Crawick
Sanquhar
Tolbooth Museum
Sanquhar Post Office
Conrig Hill
Museum of Lead Mining
Wanlockhead Beam Engine
Wanlockhead
Leadhills
Leadhills & Wanlockhead Rly
Lotus Lodge
Green Lowther
Lowther Hill
Mennock Pass
Southern Upland Way
Mennock
Burnside
Dalleagles
The Knipe
Afton Water
Kello Water
Euchan Water
Cairn Hill
Enoch Hill
Blackcraig Hill
Afton Reservoir
Enterkinfoot
Durisdeermill
Durisdeer
Durisdeer Parish Ch
Cairnkinna Hill
Scar Water
Enoch
Carsphairn Forest
Holestane
Morton Castle
Drumlanrig Castle
Cairnsmore of Carsphairn
Corlae
Benbrack
Benbuie
Auchenbrack
Shinnel Water
Auchenbainzie
Carronbridge
Gatelawbridge
Burnhead
Thornhill
Penpont
Brockloch
Garryhorn
Carsphairn
Cairn Avel
Bardennoch
Dundeugh Forest
Knowehead
Kendoon Loch
Southern Upland Way
Dalwhat Water
Tynron
Keir Mill
Closeburn
Craigdarroch
Moniaive
James Paterson Museum
Kirkland
Park
Maxwelton House
Glencrosh
Castlemaddy
Dundeugh
Kendoon
Glenhoul
Black Water
Straith
Wallaceton
Dalmacallan Forest
Glenmidge
Auldgirth
Forrest Lodge
Carsfad Loch
Wether Hill
Castlefairn
Holmhead
Lochinvar
Lochurr
Bogrie Hill
Loch Urr
Dunscore
Loch Dungeon
Glenkens
Millquarter
Earlstoun Loch
Sundaywell
Milton
Cairn Water
St John's Town of Dalry
Drumbuie
Bogue
Corriedoo Forest
Garroch
Blackcraig
Newtonairds
Drumpark
Glenlee
Knocklearn
Irongray
Balmaclellan
Gibbshill
Glenkiln Res.
New Galloway
Glenkiln
Terregles Banks
Ironmacannie
Corsock
Glen
Shawhead
Craig
Clatteringshaws Forest Visitor Centre
Wedder Hill
Middlefield Law
Nutberry Hill
River Nith
NS
NX

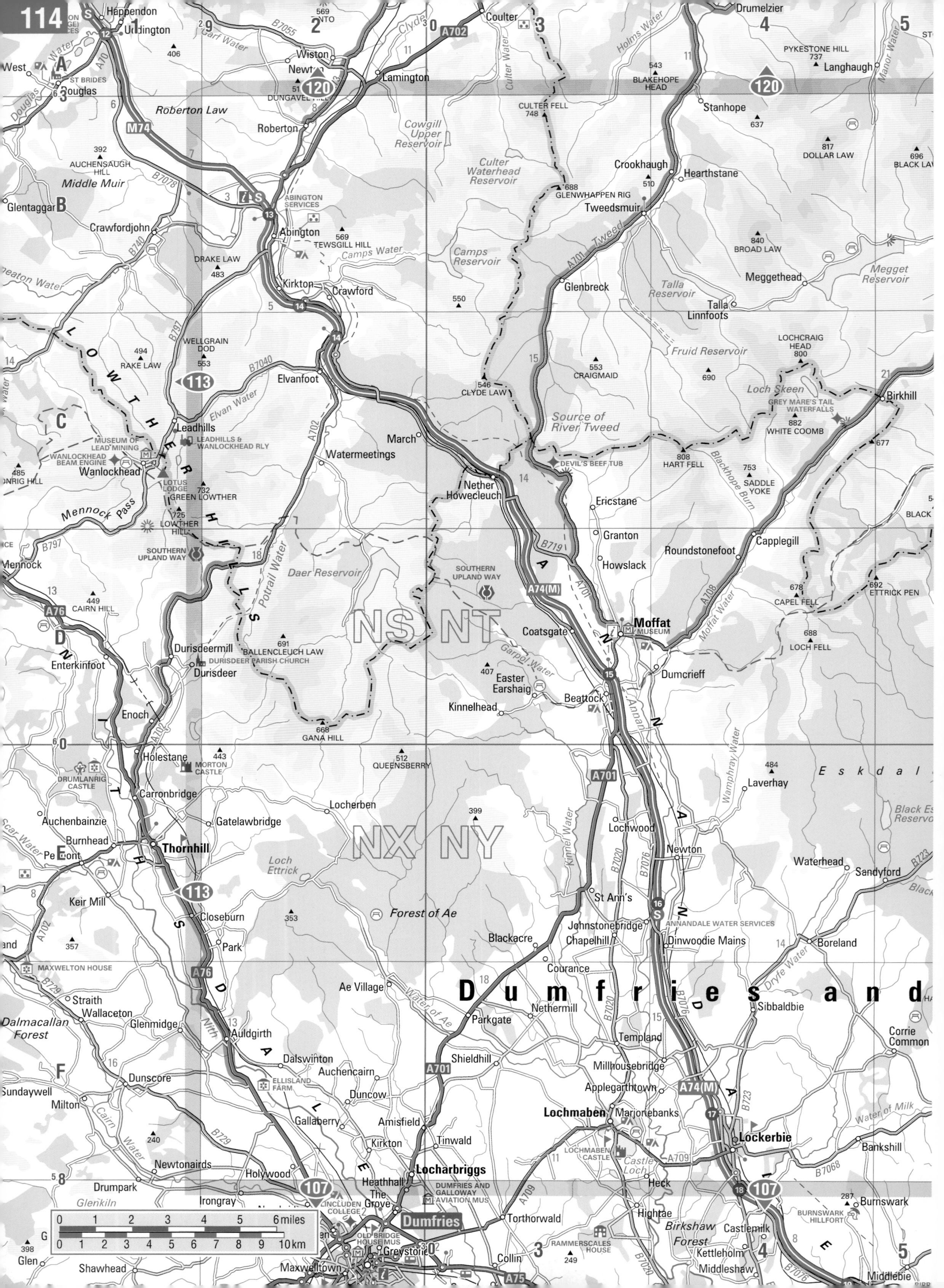
114
Happendon
Uddington
Douglas
St Brides
West
Roberton Law
M74
406
Wiston
Newton
Dungavel Hill
120
Lamington
Coulter
A702
Clyde
Culter Water
Holms Water
Drumelzier
Pykestone Hill
737
Langhaugh
Manor Water
543
Blakehope Head
Stanhope
637
Culter Fell
748
Cowgill Upper Reservoir
Roberton
B7055
Garf Water
392
Auchensaugh Hill
Middle Muir
B7078
Glentaggar
Culter Waterhead Reservoir
Crookhaugh
510
Hearthstane
817
Dollar Law
696
Black Law
688
Glenwhappen Rig
Tweedsmuir
Abington Services
Abington
569
Tewsgill Hill
Camps Water
Crawfordjohn
Camps Reservoir
Tweed
A701
840
Broad Law
Megget Reservoir
Meggethead
Drake Law
483
Kirkton
Crawford
550
Glenbreck
Talla Reservoir
Talla
Linnfoots
Lowther Hills
Wellgrain Dod
553
494
Rake Law
B797
B7040
113
Elvanfoot
Fruid Reservoir
553
Craigmaid
690
Lochcraig Head
800
Loch Skeen
Birkhill
Clyde Law
546
Source of River Tweed
Grey Mare's Tail Waterfalls
882
White Coomb
677
Elvan Water
Leadhills
Museum of Lead Mining
Leadhills & Wanlockhead Rly
Wanlockhead Beam Engine
Wanlockhead
485
Lotus Lodge
732
Green Lowther
725
Lowther Hill
Mennock Pass
A702
March
Watermeetings
Nether Howecleuch
Devil's Beef Tub
808
Hart Fell
753
Saddle Yoke
Blackhope Burn
Ericstane
Granton
Howslack
B719
Roundstonefoot
Capplegill
Black
Southern Upland Way
Mennock
Potrail Water
Daer Reservoir
Southern Upland Way
A74(M)
A708
678
Capel Fell
692
Ettrick Pen
Moffat Water
449
Cairn Hill
A76
NS NT
Coatsgate
Moffat
Museum
688
Loch Fell
Durisdeermill
Durisdeer Parish Church
Durisdeer
691
Ballencleuch Law
Enterkinfoot
407
Easter Earshaig
Garpol Water
Beattock
Dumcrieff
Kinnelhead
Annan
Enoch
668
Gana Hill
Holestane
443
Morton Castle
512
Queensberry
A701
484
Laverhay
Wamphray Water
Eskdale
Drumlanrig Castle
Carronbridge
Locherben
399
Auchenbainzie
Gatelawbridge
Lochwood
Black Esk Reservoir
Scar Water
Burnhead
Penpont
Thornhill
NX NY
Kinnel Water
Newton
Loch Ettrick
B7020
B7076
Waterhead
Sandyford
B723
Keir Mill
113
Closeburn
353
Forest of Ae
St Ann's
Annandale Water Services
Johnstonebridge
Chapelhill
Dinwoodie Mains
Boreland
Dryfe Water
357
Park
Blackacre
Courance
Maxwelton House
A76
B729
Ae Village
Water of Ae
Dumfries and
Straith
Wallaceton
Parkgate
Nethermill
Sibbaldbie
Dalmacallan Forest
Glenmidge
Auldgirth
Nith
Templand
Corrie Common
Shieldhill
Dalswinton
Auchencairn
Millhousebridge
Dunscore
Ellisland Farm
Applegarthtown
Sundaywell
Milton
Duncow
Lochmaben
Marjoriebanks
Cairn Water
Gallaberry
Amisfield
Lockerbie
Water of Milk
240
Kirkton
Tinwald
Lochmaben Castle
Castle Loch
A709
Bankshill
Newtonairds
Holywood
Locharbriggs
B7068
Drumpark
107
Heathhall
Heck
Glenkiln
Irongray
The Grove
Dumfries and Galloway Aviation Mus
Torthorwald
Hightae
287
Burnswark
Burnswark Hillfort
Lincluden College
Dumfries
Birkshaw Forest
Castlemilk
Old Bridge House Mus
Greystone
Rammerscales House
Kettleholm
398
Glen
249
Shawhead
Maxwelltown
Collin
A75
Middleshaw
Middlebie
0 1 2 3 4 5 6 miles
0 1 2 3 4 5 6 7 8 9 10 km

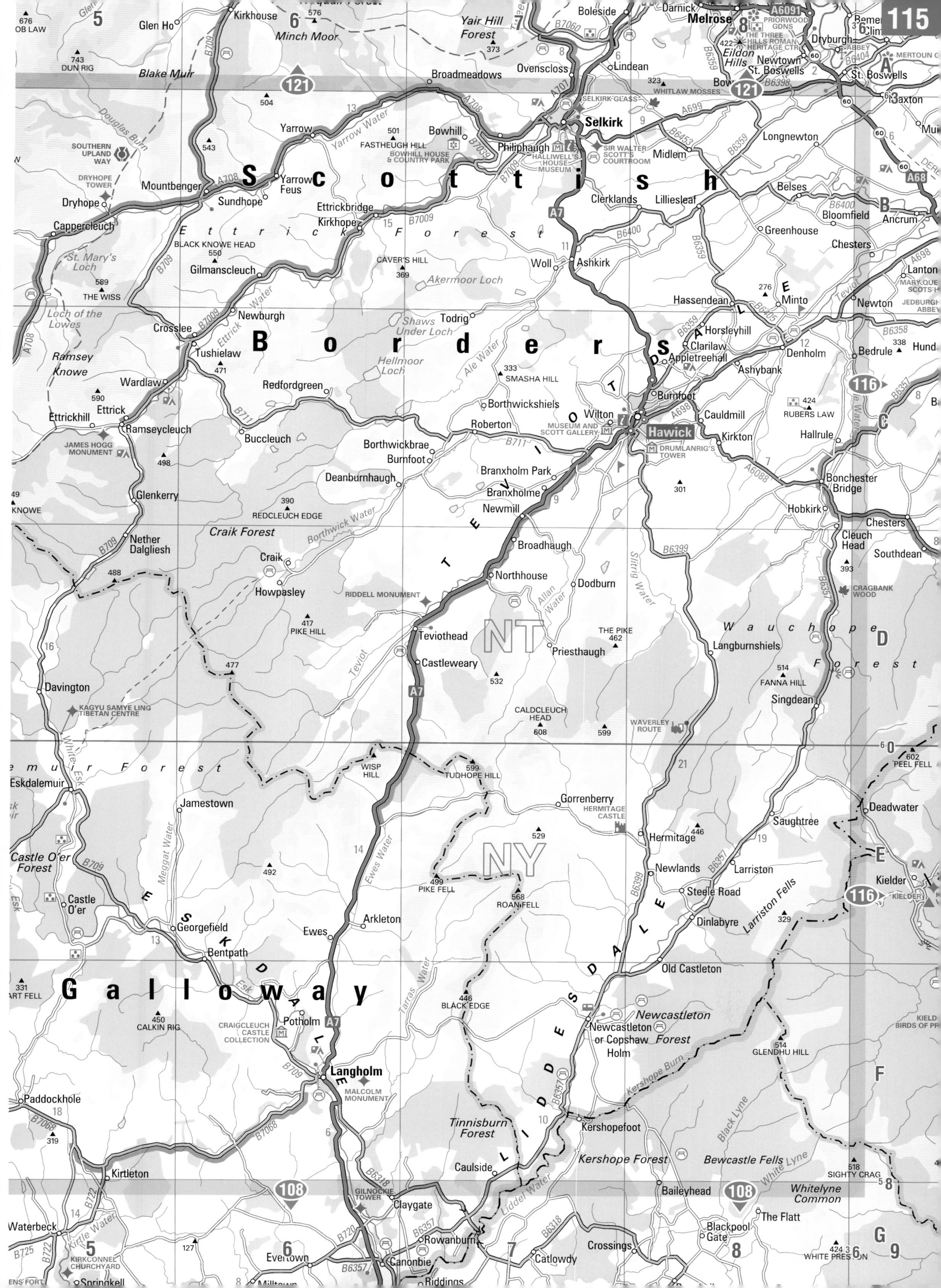
Scottish Borders
Dumfries and Galloway
Ettrick Forest
Wauchope Forest
Eskdalemuir Forest
TEVIOTDALE
ESKDALE
LIDDESDALE
NT
NY
Kirkhouse
Glen Ho
Minch Moor
Yair Hill Forest
Boleside
Darnick
Melrose
A6091
PRIORWOOD GDNS
THE THREE HILLS ROMAN HERITAGE CTR
Eildon Hills
Dryburgh
Newtown St. Boswells
St. Boswells
Maxton
743 DUN RIG
Blake Muir
121
Broadmeadows
Ovenscloss
Lindean
323 WHITLAW MOSSES
SELKIRK GLASS
Selkirk
Yarrow
Yarrow Water
501 FASTHEUGH HILL
Bowhill
BOWHILL HOUSE & COUNTRY PARK
Philiphaugh
HALLIWELL'S HOUSE MUSEUM
SIR WALTER SCOTT'S COURTROOM
Midlem
Longnewton
SOUTHERN UPLAND WAY
Douglas Burn
DRYHOPE TOWER
Dryhope
Mountbenger
Yarrow Feus
Sundhope
Ettrickbridge
Kirkhope
Clerklands
Lilliesleaf
Belses
Bloomfield
Ancrum
Cappercleuch
St. Mary's Loch
BLACK KNOWE HEAD 550
Gilmanscleuch
CAVER'S HILL 369
Akermoor Loch
Woll
Ashkirk
Greenhouse
Chesters
589 THE WISS
Loch of the Lowes
Newburgh
Ettrick Water
Shaws Under Loch
Todrig
Hassendean
Minto
Newton
Lanton
Crosslee
Tushielaw
Horsleyhill
Clarilaw
Appletreehall
Denholm
Bedrule
Hundalee
Ramsey Knowe
Hellmoor Loch
Ale Water
333 SMASHA HILL
Ashybank
Wardlaw
Redfordgreen
Burnfoot
116
424 RUBERS LAW
Ettrick
Ettrickhill
Ramseycleuch
Borthwickshiels
Wilton
MUSEUM AND SCOTT GALLERY
Hawick
Cauldmill
Hallrule
JAMES HOGG MONUMENT
Buccleuch
Roberton
Borthwickbrae
Burnfoot
DRUMLANRIG'S TOWER
Kirkton
Branxholm Park
Branxholme
Deanburnhaugh
Newmill
Bonchester Bridge
Hobkirk
Glenkerry
390 REDCLEUCH EDGE
Borthwick Water
Craik Forest
Chesters
Cleuch Head
Southdean
Nether Dalgliesh
Craik
Broadhaugh
Northhouse
Howpasley
RIDDELL MONUMENT
Dodburn
Allan Water
Slitrig Water
CRAGBANK WOOD
417 PIKE HILL
Teviothead
Teviot
THE PIKE 462
Priesthaugh
Langburnshiels
Castleweary
514 FANNA HILL
Singdean
Davington
KAGYU SAMYE LING TIBETAN CENTRE
White Esk
CALDCLEUCH HEAD 608
599
WAVERLEY ROUTE
WISP HILL
599 TUDHOPE HILL
602 PEEL FELL
Eskdalemuir
Jamestown
Gorrenberry
HERMITAGE CASTLE
Deadwater
Saughtree
Hermitage
Meggat Water
Castle O'er Forest
Castle O'er
492
Ewes Water
499 PIKE FELL
529
Newlands
Larriston
Kielder
568 ROAN FELL
Steele Road
Dinlabyre
Larriston Fells
Georgefield
Arkleton
Ewes
Bentpath
Old Castleton
331
450 CALKIN RIG
CRAIGCLEUCH CASTLE COLLECTION
Potholm
Tarras Water
446 BLACK EDGE
Newcastleton
Newcastleton or Copshaw Holm
Newcastleton Forest
KIELDER BIRDS OF PREY
514 GLENDHU HILL
Langholm
MALCOLM MONUMENT
Paddockhole
Kershope Burn
Black Lyne
Tinnisburn Forest
Kershopefoot
Kershope Forest
Bewcastle Fells
White Lyne
518 SIGHTY CRAG
Kirtleton
Caulside
108
GILNOCKIE TOWER
Claygate
Liddel Water
Baileyhead
Whitelyne Common
The Flatt
Waterbeck
Kirtle Water
Rowanburn
Blackpool Gate
KIRKCONNEL CHURCHYARD
Evertown
Canonbie
Catlowdy
Crossings
424 WHITE PRESTON
Springkell
Riddings
A7
A68
A698
A699
A708
A707
A6088
B709
B7009
B711
B6399
B6357
B6318
B7068
B722
B720
B725
B6359
B6400
B6453
B6405
B6358
B7039
B7060
B6398
B6404

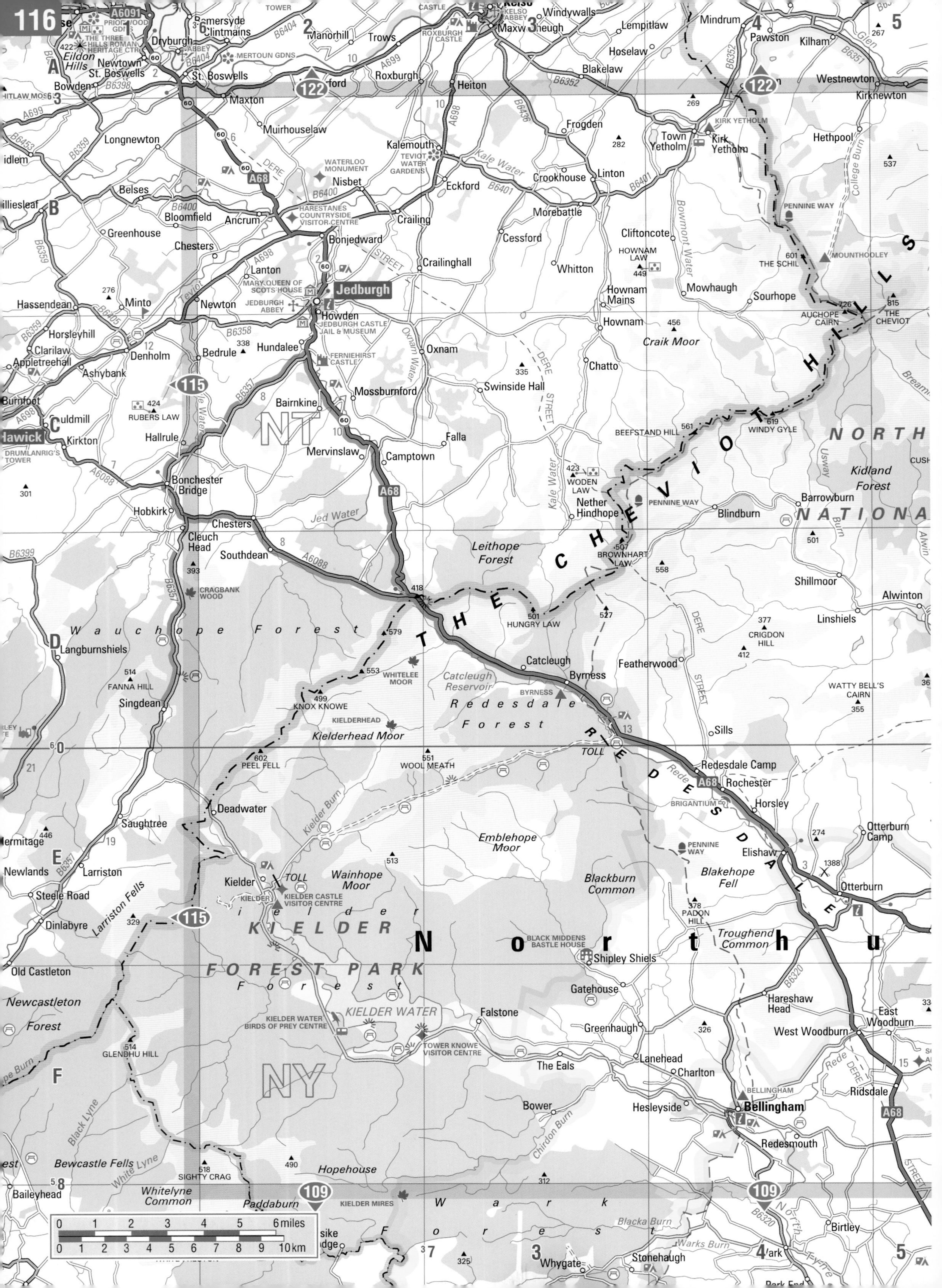
A6091
PRIORWOOD GDNS
THE THREE HILLS ROMAN HERITAGE CTR
Eildon Hills
Newtown St. Boswells
Dryburgh
DRYBURGH ABBEY
Clintmains
MERTOUN GDNS
St. Boswells
Bowden
B6398
Manorhill
Trows
ROXBURGH CASTLE
KELSO ABBEY
Windywalls
Maxwheugh
Lempitlaw
Hoselaw
Roxburgh
Blakelaw
B6352
Heiton
122
Mindrum
Pawston
Kilham
Westnewton
Kirknewton
Glen
B6351
Maxton
A699
Muirhouselaw
Longnewton
Frogden
KIRK YETHOLM
Town Yetholm
Kirk Yetholm
Hethpool
College Burn
Kalemouth
TEVIOT WATER GARDENS
WATERLOO MONUMENT
Kale Water
Crookhouse
Linton
DERE
A68
Nisbet
Eckford
B6401
B6400
Belses
Bloomfield
Ancrum
HARESTANES COUNTRYSIDE VISITOR CENTRE
Crailing
Morebattle
Cessford
Cliftoncote
Bowmont Water
PENNINE WAY
Greenhouse
Chesters
Bonjedward
Crailinghall
STREET
HOWNAM LAW
Whitton
Lanton
MARY QUEEN OF SCOTS' HOUSE
Jedburgh
JEDBURGH ABBEY
Minto
Hassendean
Newton
Howden
JEDBURGH CASTLE JAIL & MUSEUM
FERNIEHIRST CASTLE
Hownam Mains
Hownam
Mowhaugh
Sourhope
THE SCHIL
MOUNTHOOLEY
AUCHOPE CAIRN
THE CHEVIOT
Horsleyhill
Clarilaw
Appletreehall
Denholm
Ashybank
Bedrule
Hundalee
B6358
Oxnam
Oxnam Water
Craik Moor
Chatto
Swinside Hall
Mossburnford
115
RUBERS LAW
Bairnkine
Burnfoot
Culdmill
Hawick
Kirkton
Hallrule
NT
Mervinslaw
Camptown
Falla
BEEFSTAND HILL
WINDY GYLE
NORTH
DRUMLANRIG'S TOWER
A6088
Bonchester Bridge
Hobkirk
Chesters
Jed Water
WODEN LAW
Kale Water
Nether Hindhope
PENNINE WAY
Blindburn
Barrowburn
Kidland Forest
NATIONA
Usway
Cleuch Head
Southdean
Leithope Forest
BROWNHART LAW
THE CHEVIOT HILLS
Shillmoor
Alwinton
Linshiels
B6399
B6357
CRAGBANK WOOD
HUNGRY LAW
CRIGDON HILL
Wauchope Forest
Langburnshiels
FANNA HILL
Singdean
WHITELEE MOOR
Catcleugh
Catcleugh Reservoir
Byrness
Featherwood
KNOX KNOWE
BYRNESS
WATTY BELL'S CAIRN
KIELDERHEAD
Kielderhead Moor
Redesdale Forest
TOLL
Sills
PEEL FELL
WOOL MEATH
REDESDALE
Redesdale Camp
Rochester
BRIGANTIUM
Horsley
Deadwater
Saughtree
Kielder Burn
Emblehope Moor
Otterburn Camp
Hermitage
Newlands
Larriston
PENNINE WAY
Elishaw
Wainhope Moor
Blackburn Common
Blakehope Fell
Kielder
KIELDER CASTLE VISITOR CENTRE
Otterburn
Steele Road
Larriston Fells
PADON HILL
Dinlabyre
KIELDER
BLACK MIDDENS BASTLE HOUSE
Troughend Common
Northumberland
Shipley Shiels
Old Castleton
FOREST PARK
Gatehouse
Newcastleton Forest
KIELDER WATER
Falstone
Hareshaw Head
East Woodburn
West Woodburn
Greenhaugh
KIELDER WATER BIRDS OF PREY CENTRE
TOWER KNOWE VISITOR CENTRE
GLENDHU HILL
The Eals
Lanehead
Charlton
BELLINGHAM
Ridsdale
Rede
NY
Bower
Hesleyside
Bellingham
Chirdon Burn
Black Lyne
Redesmouth
Bewcastle Fells
White Lyne
SIGHTY CRAG
Hopehouse
Baileyhead
Whitelyne Common
Paddaburn
109
KIELDER MIRES
Wark Forest
Blacka Burn
Warks Burn
Birtley
North Tyne
Whygate
Stonehaugh
Wark
B6320
0 1 2 3 4 5 6 miles
0 1 2 3 4 5 6 7 8 9 10 km

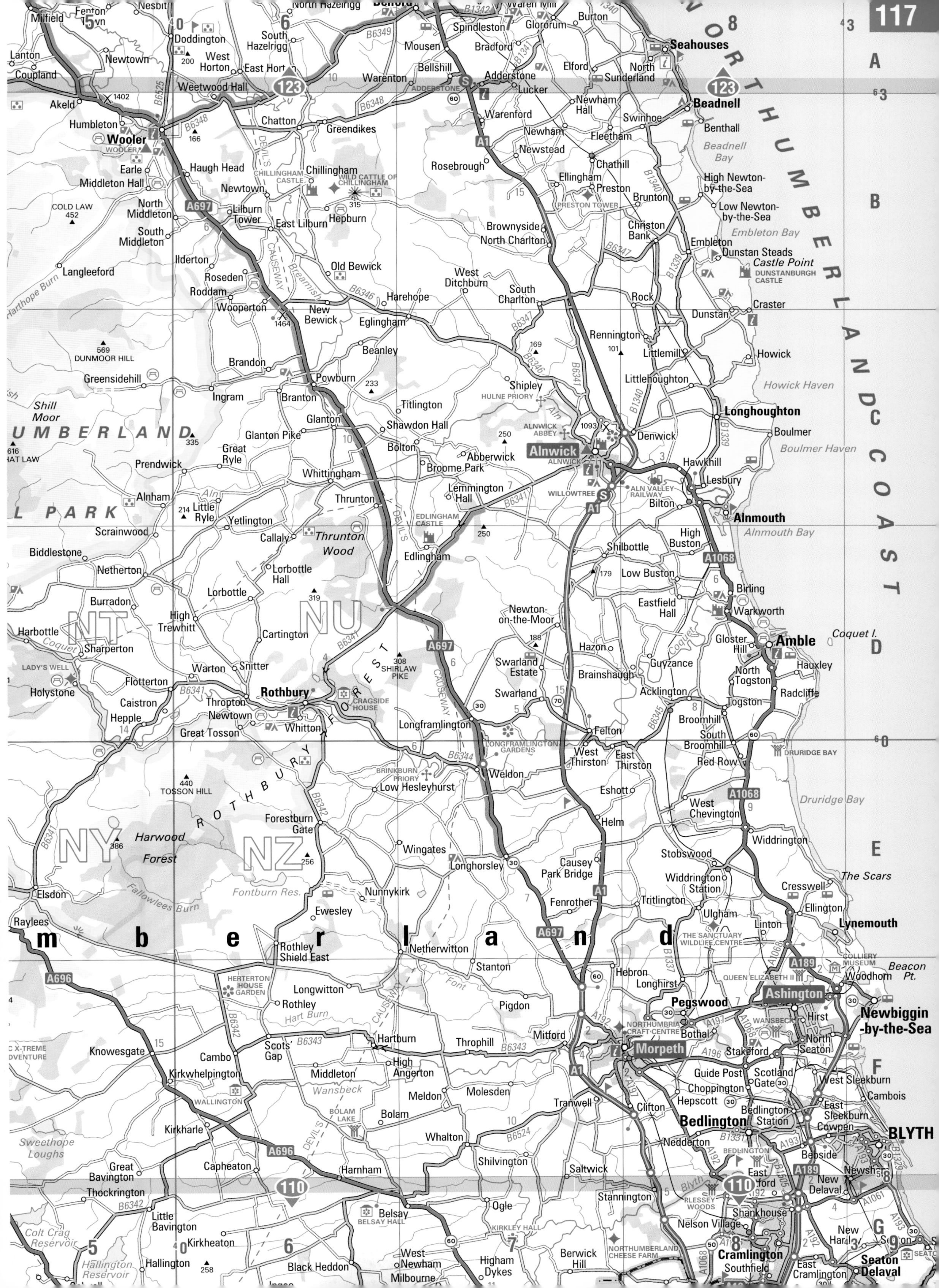

A
B
C
D
E
F
G
NORTHUMBERLAND COAST
NT
NU
NY
NZ
Northumberland
NATIONAL PARK
ROTHBURY FOREST
Milfield
Fenton Town
Nesbit
North Hazelrigg
Belford
Warenmill
Burton
Spindleston
Glororum
Seahouses
Doddington
South Hazelrigg
Mousen
Bradford
Lanton
Newtown
West Horton
East Horton
Bellshill
Adderstone
North Sunderland
Elford
Coupland
Warenton
Lucker
Weetwood Hall
Newham Hall
Beadnell
Akeld
Chatton
Warenford
Swinhoe
Benthall
Humbleton
Greendikes
Newham
Fleetham
Beadnell Bay
Wooler
Newstead
Chathill
Earle
Haugh Head
Chillingham
Rosebrough
Ellingham
High Newton-by-the-Sea
Middleton Hall
CHILLINGHAM CASTLE
WILD CATTLE OF CHILLINGHAM
Preston
Newtown
PRESTON TOWER
Brunton
COLD LAW
North Middleton
Lilburn Tower
Hepburn
Low Newton-by-the-Sea
South Middleton
East Lilburn
Brownyside
Christon Bank
Embleton Bay
North Charlton
Embleton
Dunstan Steads
Castle Point
Ilderton
Old Bewick
DUNSTANBURGH CASTLE
Langleeford
West Ditchburn
Roseden
Roddam
South Charlton
Harehope
Rock
Wooperton
New Bewick
Craster
Eglingham
Dunstan
Rennington
DUNMOOR HILL
Beanley
Littlemill
Howick
Brandon
Powburn
Greensidehill
Shipley
Littlehoughton
Howick Haven
Ingram
Branton
HULNE PRIORY
Shill Moor
Titlington
Longhoughton
Glanton
Shawdon Hall
Boulmer
ALNWICK ABBEY
Denwick
Glanton Pike
Bolton
Alnwick
Boulmer Haven
HAT LAW
Great Ryle
Abberwick
Hawkhill
Prendwick
Broome Park
Whittingham
Lesbury
Lemmington Hall
ALN VALLEY RAILWAY
WILLOWTREE
Alnham
Thrunton
Bilton
Little Ryle
Alnmouth
Yetlington
EDLINGHAM CASTLE
Scrainwood
Thrunton Wood
Alnmouth Bay
Callaly
High Buston
Edlingham
Biddlestone
Shilbottle
Netherton
Lorbottle Hall
Low Buston
Birling
Lorbottle
Burradon
Eastfield Hall
Newton-on-the-Moor
Warkworth
High Trewhitt
Harbottle
Cartington
Coquet I.
Sharperton
Gloster Hill
Amble
Hazon
SHIRLAW PIKE
Swarland Estate
Guyzance
LADY'S WELL
Hauxley
Warton
Snitter
North Togston
Brainshaugh
Flotterton
Holystone
Radcliffe
Rothbury
Acklington
Caistron
Thropton
CRAGSIDE HOUSE
Swarland
Togston
Newtown
Broomhill
Hepple
Whitton
Longframlington
Felton
South Broomhill
Great Tosson
LONGFRAMLINGTON GARDENS
West Thirston
East Thirston
DRURIDGE BAY
Red Row
BRINKBURN PRIORY
Weldon
TOSSON HILL
Low Hesleyhurst
Eshott
West Chevington
Druridge Bay
Forestburn Gate
Helm
Harwood Forest
Wingates
Widdrington
Stobswood
Longhorsley
Causey Park Bridge
Widdrington Station
The Scars
Fontburn Res.
Nunnykirk
Elsdon
Cresswell
Fallowlees Burn
Fenrother
Tritlington
Ellington
Ewesley
Raylees
Ulgham
Lynemouth
Linton
Netherwitton
THE SANCTUARY WILDLIFE CENTRE
Rothley Shield East
COLLIERY MUSEUM
Stanton
Beacon Pt.
Woodhorn
HERTERTON HOUSE GARDEN
Hebron
QUEEN ELIZABETH II
Longwitton
Longhirst
Ashington
Pegswood
Pigdon
Rothley
Newbiggin-by-the-Sea
Hart Burn
NORTHUMBRIA CRAFT CENTRE
Hirst
WANSBECK
Bothal
Mitford
Hartburn
Throphill
North Seaton
Morpeth
Knowesgate
Scots' Gap
Stakeford
Cambo
High Angerton
Guide Post
Scotland Gate
West Sleekburn
Middleton
Kirkwhelpington
Choppington
Cambois
Wansbeck
Meldon
Molesden
Hepscott
WALLINGTON
Tranwell
East Sleekburn
Clifton
Bedlington Station
Bedlington
BOLAM LAKE
Bolam
Cowpen
Kirkharle
BLYTH
Whalton
Nedderton
Sweethope Loughs
Bebside
Shilvington
Great Bavington
Capheaton
Saltwick
Newsham
Harnham
East Hartford
Thockrington
New Delaval
Ogle
Stannington
Belsay
BELSAY HALL
PLESSEY WOODS
Little Bavington
Shankhouse
Nelson Village
Colt Crag Reservoir
Kirkheaton
KIRKLEY HALL
New Hartley
NORTHUMBERLAND CHEESE FARM
Seaton
West Newham
Berwick Hill
Cramlington
Seaton Delaval
Hallington Reservoir
Hallington
Black Heddon
Higham Dykes
Southfield
East Cramlington
Milbourne

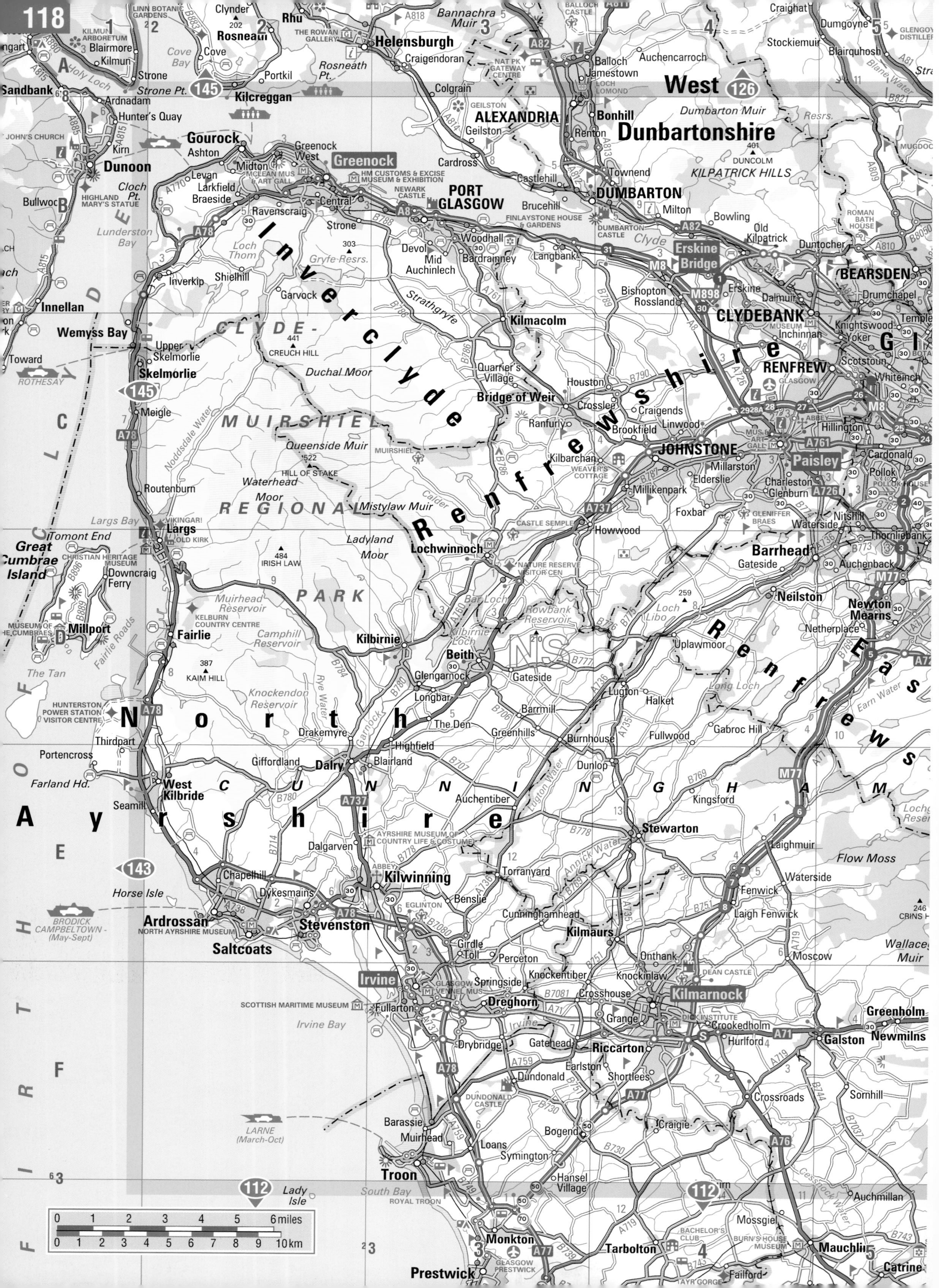
Helensburgh
Rhu
Rosneath
Clynder
Kilcreggan
Cove
Dunoon
Sandbank
Hunter's Quay
Kirn
Innellan
Gourock
Greenock
PORT GLASGOW
ALEXANDRIA
Balloch
Jamestown
Bonhill
Renton
DUMBARTON
West
Dunbartonshire
KILPATRICK HILLS
Dumbarton Muir
Old Kilpatrick
Bowling
Duntocher
BEARSDEN
CLYDEBANK
Erskine Bridge
Erskine
RENFREW
Paisley
JOHNSTONE
Linwood
Houston
Bridge of Weir
Kilmacolm
Kilbarchan
Elderslie
Barrhead
Neilston
Newton Mearns
Inverclyde
Renfrewshire
East Renfrewshire
CLYDE-MUIRSHIEL REGIONAL PARK
Wemyss Bay
Skelmorlie
Largs
Great Cumbrae Island
Millport
Fairlie
Lochwinnoch
Kilbirnie
Beith
Glengarnock
Dalry
Lugton
Dunlop
Stewarton
Kilmaurs
West Kilbride
Seamill
North Ayrshire
CUNNINGHAM
Ardrossan
Saltcoats
Stevenston
Kilwinning
Irvine
Dreghorn
Kilmarnock
Riccarton
Hurlford
Galston
Newmilns
Fenwick
Dundonald
Troon
Monkton
Prestwick
Tarbolton
Mauchline
Catrine
Symington
FIRTH OF CLYDE
Horse Isle
Lady Isle
Irvine Bay
BRODICK CAMPBELTOWN (May-Sept)
LARNE (March-Oct)
ROTHESAY
0 1 2 3 4 5 6 miles
0 1 2 3 4 5 6 7 8 9 10 km

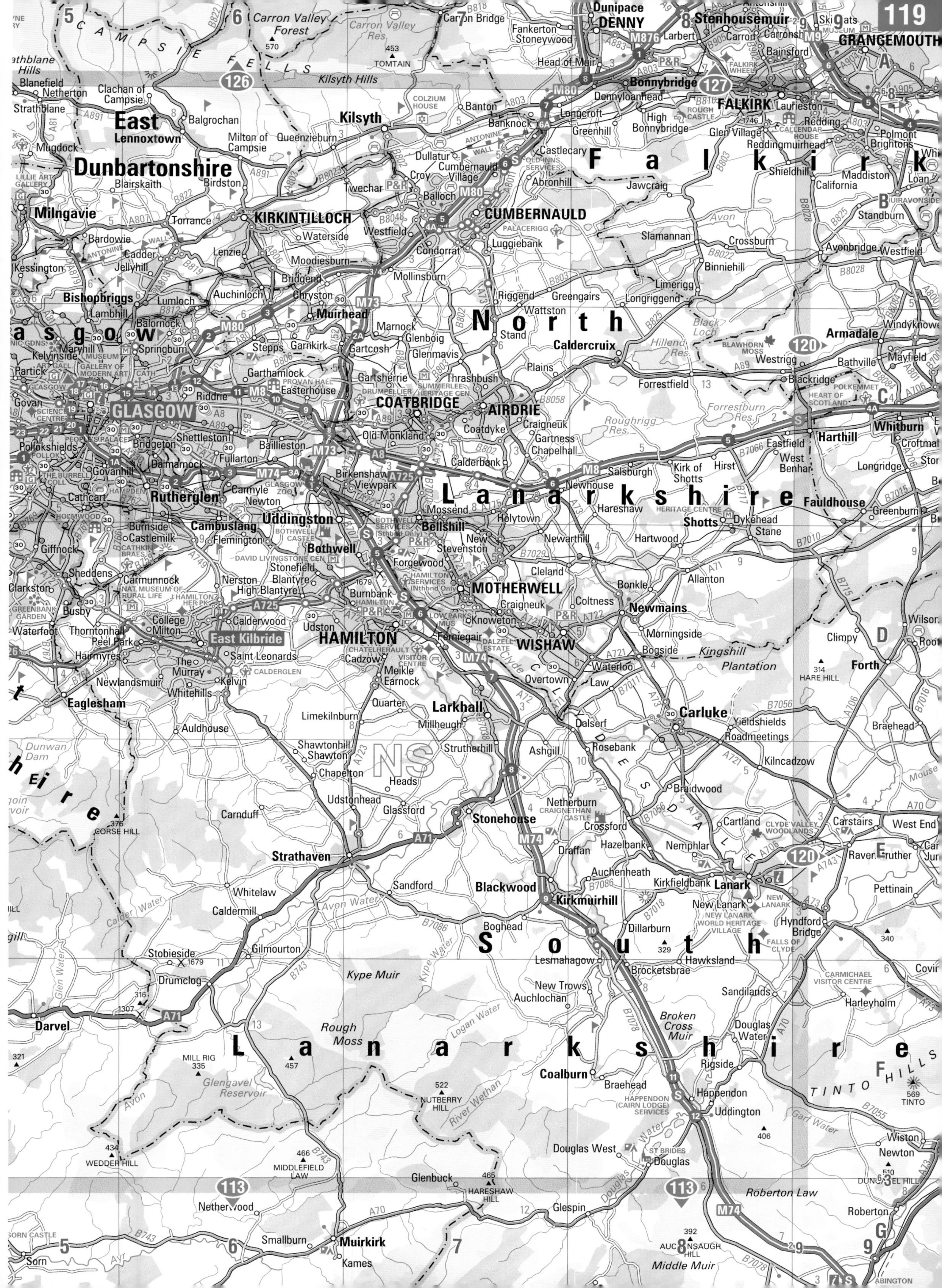

119
Campsie Fells
Carron Valley Forest
Carron Valley Res.
Carron Bridge
Dunipace
DENNY
Stenhousemuir
Larbert
Carron
Carronshore
GRANGEMOUTH
Fankerton
Stoneywood
Head of Muir
Bainsford
Falkirk Wheel
Bonnybridge
Dennyloanhead
FALKIRK
Laurieston
Polmont
Redding
Brightons
Blanefield
Netherton
Strathblane
Clachan of Campsie
Kilsyth Hills
Tomtain
Colzium House
Banton
Kilsyth
Queenzieburn
Milton of Campsie
Balgrochan
East Dunbartonshire
Lennoxtown
Mugdock
Blairskaith
Birdston
Milngavie
Torrance
KIRKINTILLOCH
Waterside
Bardowie
Cadder
Lenzie
Jellyhill
Kessington
Bishopbriggs
Lumloch
Auchinloch
Moodiesburn
Bridgend
Chryston
Muirhead
Lambhill
Balornock
Glasgow
Maryhill
Springburn
Kelvinside
Partick
Govan
GLASGOW
Riddrie
Easterhouse
Stepps
Garnkirk
Gartcosh
Glenboig
Marnock
Glenmavis
Gartsherrie
Thrashbush
Garthamlock
Provan Hall
Dullatur
Croy
Cumbernauld Village
Twechar
Balloch
Westfield
Condorrat
CUMBERNAULD
Palacerigg
Luggiebank
Mollinsburn
Castlecary
Banknock
Longcroft
Greenhill
High Bonnybridge
Glen Village
Reddingmuirhead
Shieldhill
Maddiston
California
Falkirk
Abronhill
Jawcraig
Slamannan
Avon
Crossburn
Avonbridge
Binniehill
Limerigg
Longriggend
Riggend
Greengairs
Wattston
North
Stand
Caldercruix
Plains
Black Loch
Hillend Res.
Blawhorn Moss
Westrigg
Armadale
Bathville
Mayfield
Blackridge
Forrestfield
Forrestburn Res.
Heart of Scotland
Polkemmet
Whitburn
Harthill
COATBRIDGE
AIRDRIE
Coatdyke
Craigneuk
Gartness
Chapelhall
Roughrigg Res.
Old Monkland
Calderbank
Baillieston
Shettleston
Bridgeton
Fullarton
Dalmarnock
Govanhill
Pollokshields
Cathcart
Rutherglen
Carmyle
Newton
Birkenshaw
Viewpark
Uddingston
Cambuslang
Flemington
Burnside
Castlemilk
Bothwell
Bellshill
Mossend
Holytown
New Stevenston
Newarthill
Salsburgh
Kirk of Shotts
Hirst
Eastfield
West Benhar
Longridge
Fauldhouse
Greenburn
Newhouse
Lanarkshire
Hareshaw
Shotts
Dykehead
Stane
Hartwood
Giffnock
Sheddens
Clarkston
Carmunnock
Busby
Waterfoot
Thorntonhall
Peel Park
Hairmyres
Newlandsmuir
Eaglesham
East Kilbride
College Milton
Calderwood
Nerston
High Blantyre
Blantyre
Stonefield
Burnbank
Forgewood
MOTHERWELL
Cleland
Bonkle
Allanton
Craigneuk
Coltness
Newmains
Morningside
Udston
HAMILTON
Knowetop
Ferniegair
WISHAW
Chatelherault
Cadzow
Meikle Earnock
Saint Leonards
The Murray
Kelvin
Whitehills
Auldhouse
Bogside
Waterloo
Overtown
Law
Kingshill Plantation
Hare Hill
Forth
Clydesdale
Quarter
Limekilnburn
Larkhall
Millheugh
Strutherhill
Dalserf
Ashgill
Rosebank
Carluke
Yieldshields
Roadmeetings
Braehead
Kilncadzow
Shawtonhill
Shawton
Chapelton
Heads
Udstonhead
Glassford
Carnduff
Corse Hill
Dunwan Dam
Stonehouse
Netherburn
Craignethan Castle
Crossford
Braidwood
Cartland
Clyde Valley Woodlands
Carstairs
West End
Strathaven
Hazelbank
Draffan
Nemphlar
Ravenstruther
Sandford
Blackwood
Auchenheath
Kirkmuirhill
Kirkfieldbank
Lanark
New Lanark
New Lanark World Heritage Village
Hyndford Bridge
Falls of Clyde
Pettinain
Whitelaw
Caldermill
Calder Water
Avon Water
Boghead
Dillarburn
South
Stobieside
Gilmourton
Lesmahagow
Brocketsbrae
Hawksland
Carmichael Visitor Centre
Covington
Drumclog
Kype Muir
New Trows
Auchlochan
Sandilands
Harleyholm
Darvel
Rough Moss
Broken Cross Muir
Douglas Water
Lanarkshire
Mill Rig
Glengavel Reservoir
Nutberry Hill
River Wethan
Coalburn
Braehead
Rigside
Tinto Hills
Tinto
Happendon (Cairn Lodge) Services
Happendon
Uddington
Wedder Hill
Middlefield Law
Douglas West
St Brides
Douglas
Wiston
Newton
Glenbuck
Hareshaw Hill
Roberton Law
Roberton
Netherwood
Glespin
Sorn Castle
Sorn
Smallburn
Muirkirk
Kames
Middle Muir
Abington

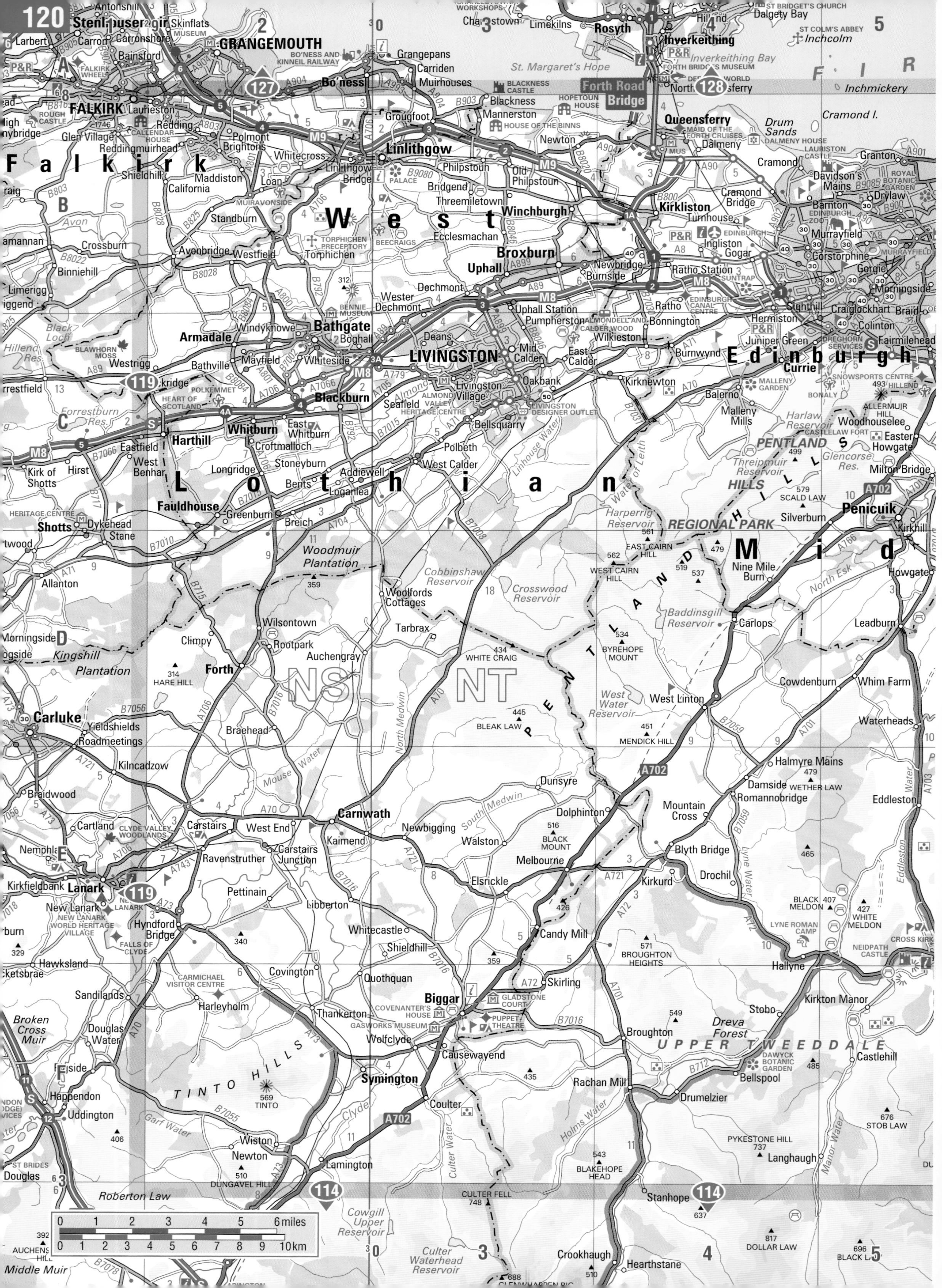

GRANGEMOUTH
Larbert
Carron
Carronshore
Bainsford
FALKIRK
Laurieston
Redding
Polmont
Brightons
Reddingmuirhead
Glen Village
Grangepans
Carriden
Muirhouses
Bo'ness
BO'NESS AND KINNEIL RAILWAY
Charlestown
Limekilns
Rosyth
Inverkeithing
Dalgety Bay
ST BRIDGET'S CHURCH
ST COLM'S ABBEY
Inchcolm
Inverkeithing Bay
St. Margaret's Hope
FORTH BRIDGES MUSEUM
Forth Road Bridge
Inchmickery
BLACKNESS CASTLE
Blackness
HOPETOUN HOUSE
Mannerston
HOUSE OF THE BINNS
Queensferry
MAID OF THE FORTH CRUISES
Drum Sands
Cramond I.
DALMENY HOUSE
Dalmeny
Newton
Grougfoot
Whitecross
Linlithgow
Linlithgow Bridge
PALACE
Philpstoun
Old Philpstoun
Bridgend
Threemiletown
Winchburgh
Kirkliston
Turnhouse
Cramond
Cramond Bridge
Granton
Davidson's Mains
ROYAL BOTANIC GARDEN
Barnton
Drylaw
EDINBURGH ZOO
Murrayfield
Ingliston
Gogar
Corstorphine
MURRAYFIELD
Gorgie
Falkirk
Shieldhill
Maddiston
California
Loan
MUIRAVONSIDE
Standburn
Avon
West
Lothian
Ecclesmachan
TORPHICHEN PRECEPTORY
BEECRAIGS
Crossburn
Avonbridge
Westfield
Torphichen
Broxburn
Uphall
Newbridge
Burnside
Ratho Station
SUNTRAP
Binniehill
Dechmont
Wester Dechmont
Uphall Station
Pumpherston
ALMONDELL AND CALDER WOOD
Ratho
EDINBURGH CANAL CENTRE
Bonnington
Hermiston
Sighthill
Craiglockhart
Braid
Morningside
Colinton
Fairmilehead
Juniper Green
DREGHORN SERVICES
Currie
Edinburgh
Limerigg
Black Loch
BENNIE MUSEUM
Armadale
Windyknowe
Bathgate
Boghall
Deans
LIVINGSTON
Mid Calder
East Calder
Wilkieston
Burnwynd
BLAWHORN MOSS
Westrigg
Bathville
Mayfield
Whiteside
Kirknewton
MALLENY GARDEN
SNOWSPORTS CENTRE
HILLEND
Balerno
Malleny Mills
BONALY
ALLERMUIR HILL
Woodhouselee
Easter Howgate
HEART OF SCOTLAND
POLKEMMET
Forrestburn Res.
Blackburn
Seafield
ALMOND VALLEY HERITAGE CENTRE
Livingston Village
Oakbank
LIVINGSTON DESIGNER OUTLET
Bellsquarry
Harlaw Reservoir
CASTLELAW FORT
PENTLAND HILLS
Threipmuir Reservoir
Glencorse Res.
Milton Bridge
Harthill
Whitburn
East Whitburn
Croftmalloch
Eastfield
West Benhar
Polbeth
West Calder
Kirk of Shotts
Hirst
Longridge
Stoneyburn
Addiewell
Loganlea
Bents
Linhouse Water
Water of Leith
SCALD LAW
Penicuik
HERITAGE CENTRE
Shotts
Dykehead
Stane
Fauldhouse
Greenburn
Breich
Harperrig Reservoir
REGIONAL PARK
Silverburn
Kirkhill
EAST CAIRN HILL
WEST CAIRN HILL
Mid
Allanton
Woodmuir Plantation
Cobbinshaw Reservoir
Crosswood Reservoir
Nine Mile Burn
Howgate
North Esk
Woolfords Cottages
Baddinsgill Reservoir
Carlops
Leadburn
Wilsontown
Tarbrax
BYREHOPE MOUNT
Morningside
Climpy
Rootpark
Auchengray
WHITE CRAIG
Kingshill Plantation
HARE HILL
Forth
NS
NT
Cowdenburn
Whim Farm
West Linton
West Water Reservoir
Carluke
Yieldshields
Roadmeetings
Braehead
BLEAK LAW
MENDICK HILL
Waterheads
Kilncadzow
Mouse Water
North Medwin
Dunsyre
Halmyre Mains
WETHER LAW
Damside
Romannobridge
Eddleston
Braidwood
Dolphinton
Mountain Cross
Cartland
CLYDE VALLEY WOODLANDS
Carstairs
West End
Carnwath
Newbigging
South Medwin
Kaimend
Walston
BLACK MOUNT
Nemphlar
Ravenstruther
Carstairs Junction
Melbourne
Blyth Bridge
Drochil
Lyne Water
Kirkfieldbank
Lanark
New Lanark
NEW LANARK WORLD HERITAGE VILLAGE
Pettinain
Elsrickle
Kirkurd
BLACK MELDON
WHITE MELDON
LYNE ROMAN CAMP
CROSS KIRK
Hyndford Bridge
FALLS OF CLYDE
Libberton
Whitecastle
Candy Mill
BROUGHTON HEIGHTS
NEIDPATH CASTLE
Hawksland
Shieldhill
Hallyne
Covington
Skirling
CARMICHAEL VISITOR CENTRE
Sandilands
Quothquan
Biggar
GLADSTONE COURT
Kirkton Manor
Harleyholm
Thankerton
COVENANTER'S HOUSE
GASWORKS MUSEUM
PUPPET THEATRE
Stobo
Broken Cross Muir
Douglas Water
Wolfclyde
Broughton
Dreva Forest
UPPER TWEEDDALE
Causewayend
DAWYCK BOTANIC GARDEN
Castlehill
TINTO HILLS
Symington
Rachan Mill
Bellspool
Happendon
TINTO
Coulter
Drumelzier
Uddington
Garf Water
Holms Water
STOB LAW
Wiston
Newton
Lamington
Culter Water
PYKESTONE HILL
Langhaugh
Manor Water
BLAKEHOPE HEAD
ST BRIDES
Douglas
DUNGAVEL HILL
Robertson Law
CULTER FELL
Stanhope
Cowgill Upper Reservoir
DOLLAR LAW
AUCHENS HILL
Culter Waterhead Reservoir
Crookhaugh
Hearthstane
BLACK LAW
Middle Muir
0 1 2 3 4 5 6 miles
0 1 2 3 4 5 6 7 8 9 10 km

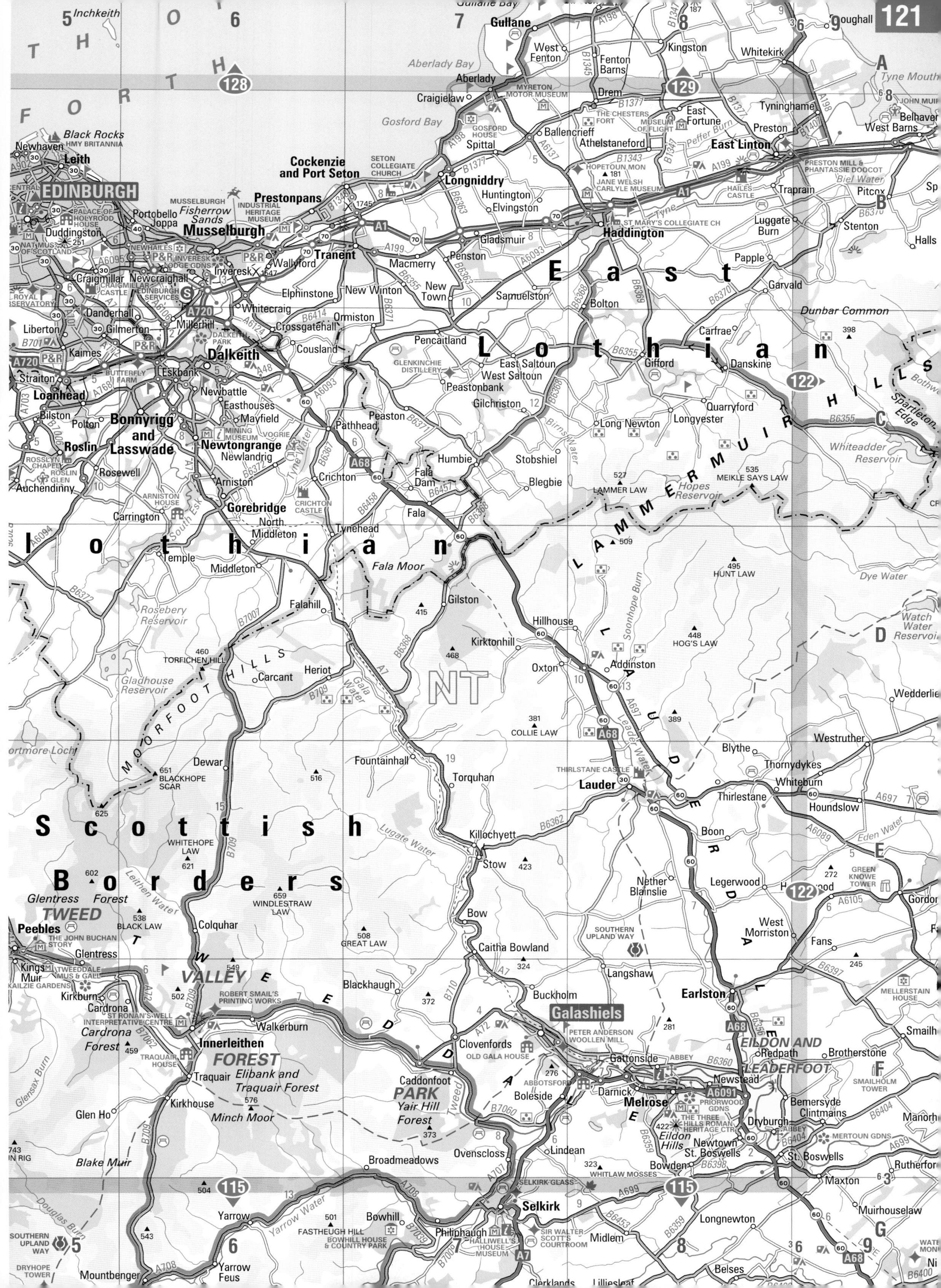
FIRTH OF FORTH
Inchkeith
Gullane Bay
Gullane
West Fenton
Fenton Barns
Kingston
Whitekirk
Aberlady Bay
Aberlady
Tyne Mouth
128
129
Craigielaw
MYRETON MOTOR MUSEUM
Drem
THE CHESTERS FORT
MUSEUM OF FLIGHT
East Fortune
Tyninghame
JOHN MUIR
Belhaven
West Barns
Gosford Bay
GOSFORD HOUSE
Spittal
Ballencrieff
Athelstaneford
Peffer Burn
Preston
East Linton
Black Rocks
HMY BRITANNIA
Newhaven
Leith
Cockenzie and Port Seton
SETON COLLEGIATE CHURCH
Longniddry
HOPETOUN MON
JANE WELSH CARLYLE MUSEUM
PRESTON MILL & PHANTASSIE DOOCOT
Biel Water
HAILES CASTLE
Traprain
Pitcox
EDINBURGH
MUSSELBURGH
Fisherrow Sands
Prestonpans
INDUSTRIAL HERITAGE MUSEUM
Huntington
Elvingston
PALACE OF HOLYROOD HOUSE
Portobello
Joppa
Duddingston
Musselburgh
Gladsmuir
Haddington
ST MARY'S COLLEGIATE CH
Luggate Burn
Stenton
Halls
NAT MUSEUM OF SCOTLAND
NEWHAILES
INVERESK LODGE GDNS
Wallyford
Tranent
Macmerry
Penston
Papple
Craigmillar
Newcraighall
CRAIGMILLAR CASTLE
EDINBURGH SERVICES
Inveresk
ROYAL OBSERVATORY
Elphinstone
New Winton
New Town
Samuelston
East
Garvald
Danderhall
Whitecraig
Ormiston
Bolton
Dunbar Common
Liberton
Gilmerton
Millerhill
Crossgatehall
DALKEITH PARK
Cousland
Pencaitland
Carfrae
Kaimes
Dalkeith
Lothian
Gifford
Danskine
GLENKINCHIE DISTILLERY
East Saltoun
West Saltoun
Straiton
BUTTERFLY FARM
Eskbank
Loanhead
Newbattle
Peastonbank
Bothwell
Quarryford
LAMMERMUIR HILLS
Bilston
Polton
Bonnyrigg and Lasswade
Easthouses
Mayfield
Peaston
Pathhead
Gilchriston
Long Newton
Longyester
Spartleton Edge
MINING MUSEUM
VOGRIE
Newtongrange
Newlandrig
Birns Water
Roslin
ROSSLYN CHAPEL
ROSLIN GLEN
Rosewell
Tyne Water
Humbie
Stobshiel
Whiteadder Reservoir
Crichton
Fala Dam
Blegbie
527 LAMMER LAW
Hopes Reservoir
535 MEIKLE SAYS LAW
Auchendinny
Arniston
ARNISTON HOUSE
Gorebridge
CRICHTON CASTLE
Fala
Carrington
South Esk
North Middleton
Tynehead
Lothian
Temple
Middleton
Fala Moor
509
495 HUNT LAW
Dye Water
Rosebery Reservoir
Falahill
Gilston
415
Hillhouse
Watch Water Reservoir
460 TORFICHEN HILL
MOORFOOT HILLS
Carcant
Heriot
468
Kirktonhill
Oxton
Addinston
448 HOG'S LAW
Soonhope Burn
Gladhouse Reservoir
Gala Water
NT
Wedderlie
381 COLLIE LAW
389
Leader Water
Portmore Loch
Dewar
651 BLACKHOPE SCAR
516
Fountainhall
Torquhan
THIRLSTANE CASTLE
Lauder
Blythe
Westruther
Thornydykes
Whiteburn
Thirlestane
Houndslow
Eden Water
625
Scottish Borders
WHITEHOPE LAW 621
Lugate Water
Killochyett
Stow
423
Boon
Nether Blainslie
Legerwood
272
GREEN KNOWE TOWER
Gordon
602
Glentress Forest
TWEED
Leithen Water
659 WINDLESTRAW LAW
538 BLACK LAW
Colquhar
Bow
508 GREAT LAW
SOUTHERN UPLAND WAY
West Morriston
Fans
245
Peebles
THE JOHN BUCHAN STORY
Glentress
TWEEDDALE
Kings Muir
TWEEDDALE MUS & GALL
KAILZIE GARDENS
549
VALLEY
Caitha Bowland
324
Langshaw
Kirkburn
Cardrona
502
ROBERT SMAIL'S PRINTING WORKS
Blackhaugh
372
Buckholm
Earlston
MELLERSTAINE HOUSE
ST RONAN'S WELL INTERPRETATIVE CENTRE
Cardrona Forest
459
Innerleithen
Walkerburn
Galashiels
PETER ANDERSON WOOLLEN MILL
281
Smailholm
TRAQUAIR HOUSE
FOREST
Clovenfords
OLD GALA HOUSE
Gattonside
ABBEY
EILDON AND LEADERFOOT
Redpath
Brotherstone
Traquair
Elibank and Traquair Forest
276
ABBOTSFORD
Newstead
SMAILHOLM TOWER
Kirkhouse
Caddonfoot
PARK
Yair Hill Forest
Boleside
Darnick
Melrose
PRIORWOOD GDNS
Bemersyde
Clintmains
Glensax Burn
Glen Ho
576 Minch Moor
373
THE THREE HILLS ROMAN HERITAGE CTR
Eildon Hills
422
Dryburgh
Manorhill
743
Lindean
Newtown St. Boswells
MERTOUN GDNS
St. Boswells
Blake Muir
Broadmeadows
Ovenscloss
323 WHITLAW MOSSES
Bowden
Rutherford
504
115
SELKIRK GLASS
Maxton
Douglas Burn
Yarrow
Yarrow Water
501 FASTHEUGH HILL
Bowhill
BOWHILL HOUSE & COUNTRY PARK
Selkirk
Philiphaugh
HALLIWELL'S HOUSE MUSEUM
SIR WALTER SCOTT'S COURTROOM
Midlem
Longnewton
Muirhouselaw
543
SOUTHERN UPLAND WAY
DRYHOPE TOWER
Mountbenger
Yarrow Feus
Clerklands
Lilliesleaf
Belses
LAUDERDALE
TWEEDDALE
122
A1
A68
A7
A72
A697
A6091
A699
A708
A720

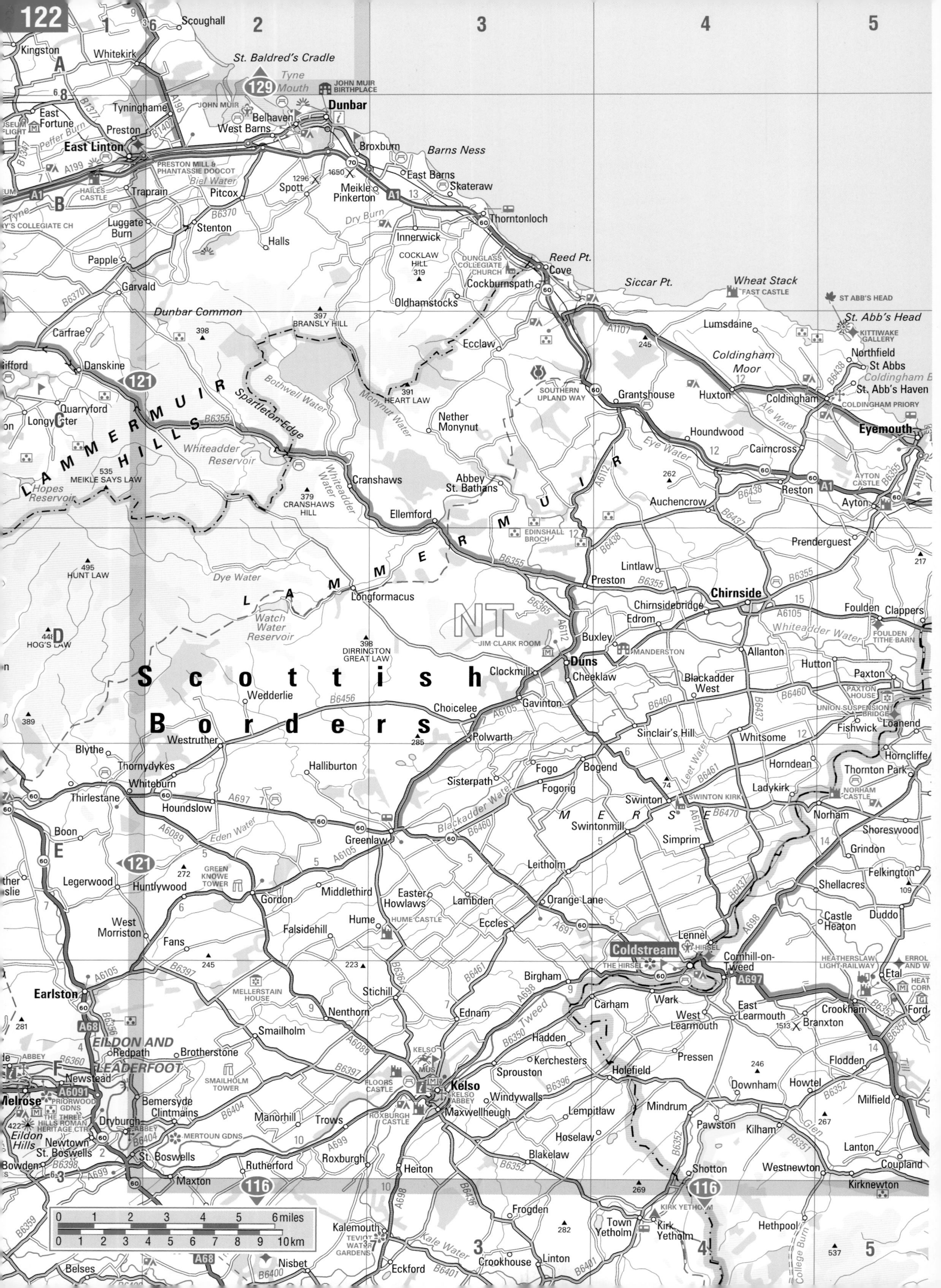
1
2
3
4
5
A
B
C
D
E
F
Scoughall
Kingston
Whitekirk
St. Baldred's Cradle
Tyne Mouth
129
JOHN MUIR BIRTHPLACE
Dunbar
Tyninghame
JOHN MUIR
Belhaven
West Barns
East Fortune
Preston
East Linton
Broxburn
Barns Ness
PRESTON MILL & PHANTASSIE DOOCOT
Biel Water
East Barns
Skateraw
HAILES CASTLE
Traprain
Pitcox
Spott
Meikle Pinkerton
A1
Thorntonloch
Luggate Burn
Stenton
Dry Burn
Innerwick
Halls
Papple
COCKLAW HILL 319
DUNGLASS COLLEGIATE CHURCH
Reed Pt.
Cove
Garvald
Cockburnspath
Siccar Pt.
Wheat Stack
FAST CASTLE
ST ABB'S HEAD
St. Abb's Head
KITTIWAKE GALLERY
Oldhamstocks
Dunbar Common
397 BRANSLY HILL
Carfrae
398
Ecclaw
A1107
245
Lumsdaine
Northfield
St Abbs
Coldingham Moor
Coldingham
St. Abb's Haven
COLDINGHAM PRIORY
Danskine
121
LAMMERMUIR HILLS
Quarryford
Longyester
Spartleton Edge
Bothwell Water
Monynut Water
391 HEART LAW
Nether Monynut
SOUTHERN UPLAND WAY
Grantshouse
Huxton
Houndwood
Cairncross
Eyemouth
Eye Water
Ale Water
Whiteadder Reservoir
B6355
535 MEIKLE SAYS LAW
Hopes Reservoir
379 CRANSHAWS HILL
Whiteadder Water
Cranshaws
Abbey St. Bathans
262
Reston
AYTON CASTLE
Ayton
Auchencrow
Ellemford
EDINSHALL BROCH
Prenderguest
217
495 HUNT LAW
Dye Water
LAMMERMUIR
Longformacus
Lintlaw
Preston
Chirnside
Chirnsidebridge
Edrom
Foulden
Clappers
Whiteadder Water
FOULDEN TITHE BARN
Watch Water Reservoir
448 HOG'S LAW
NT
398 DIRRINGTON GREAT LAW
JIM CLARK ROOM
Buxley
MANDERSTON
Allanton
Duns
Hutton
Paxton
PAXTON HOUSE
UNION SUSPENSION BRIDGE
Scottish Borders
Clockmill
Cheeklaw
Blackadder West
Wedderlie
B6456
Choicelee
Gavinton
Fishwick
Loanend
389
Westruther
Polwarth
285
Sinclair's Hill
Whitsome
Blythe
Thornydykes
Halliburton
Fogo
Bogend
Horndean
Horncliffe
Thornton Park
Sisterpath
Fogorig
Ladykirk
NORHAM CASTLE
Whiteburn
Thirlestane
Houndslow
A697
Swinton
SWINTON KIRK
Norham
MERSE
Swintonmill
Blackadder Water
Simprim
Shoreswood
Boon
Greenlaw
Eden Water
Grindon
Legerwood
272
GREEN KNOWE TOWER
Huntlywood
Leitholm
Felkington
Gordon
Middlethird
Easter Howlaws
Lambden
Orange Lane
Shellacres
109
West Morriston
Hume
HUME CASTLE
Eccles
Castle Heaton
Duddo
Falsidehill
Lennel
Fans
245
223
Coldstream
HIRSEL
Cornhill-on-Tweed
THE HIRSEL
HEATHERSLAW LIGHT RAILWAY
ERROL AND W
Etal
Earlston
MELLERSTAIN HOUSE
Stichill
Birgham
Carham
Wark
Nenthorn
Ednam
West Learmouth
East Learmouth
Crookham
Ford
281
Smailholm
Tweed
Hadden
1513
Branxton
EILDON AND LEADERFOOT
Redpath
Brotherstone
Kerchesters
Pressen
ABBEY
KELSO MUS
SMAILHOLM TOWER
FLOORS CASTLE
Sprouston
Holefield
246
Flodden
Newstead
Kelso
KELSO ABBEY
Windywalls
Downham
Howtel
Melrose
PRIORWOOD GDNS
THE THREE HILLS ROMAN HERITAGE CTR
Bemersyde
Clintmains
Milfield
Maxwellheugh
Mindrum
Eildon Hills
422
Dryburgh
ABBEY
Manorhill
Trows
ROXBURGH CASTLE
Lempitlaw
Pawston
Kilham
267
Glen
Newtown St. Boswells
MERTOUN GDNS
Hoselaw
Bowden
St. Boswells
Rutherford
Roxburgh
Blakelaw
Lanton
Coupland
Heiton
Shotton
Westnewton
Maxton
116
269
116
Kirknewton
KIRK YETHOLM
Frogden
282
Town Yetholm
Kirk Yetholm
Hethpool
Kalemouth
TEVIOT WATER GARDENS
Kale Water
College Burn
537
Belses
Nisbet
Eckford
Crookhouse
Linton
0 1 2 3 4 5 6 miles
0 1 2 3 4 5 6 7 8 9 10 km

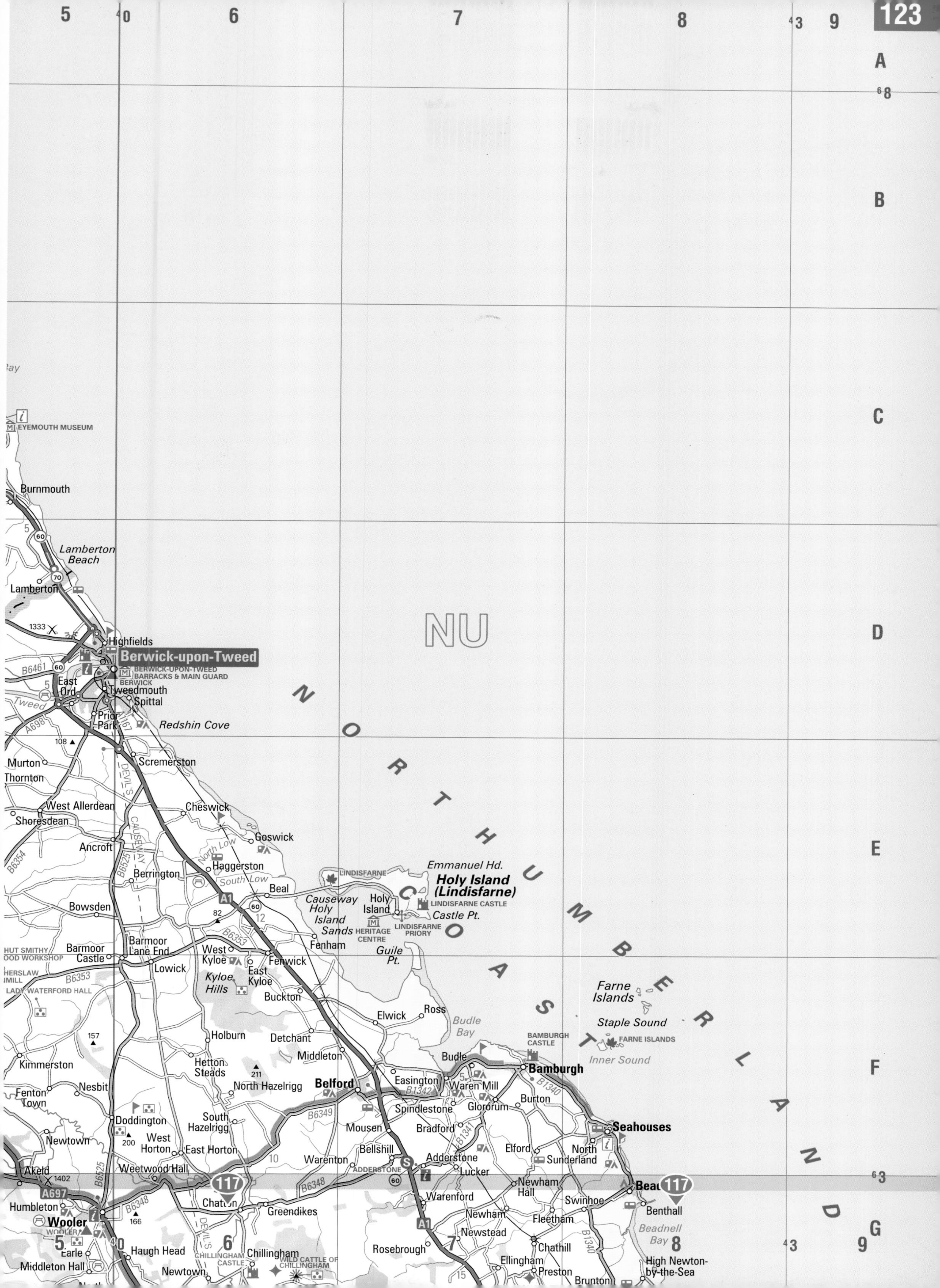
123
5
6
7
8
9
A
B
C
D
E
F
G
NU
NORTHUMBERLAND COAST
EYEMOUTH MUSEUM
Burnmouth
Lamberton Beach
Lamberton
Highfields
Berwick-upon-Tweed
BERWICK-UPON-TWEED BARRACKS & MAIN GUARD
BERWICK
East Ord
Tweedmouth
Spittal
Tweed
Prior Park
Redshin Cove
A698
B6461
A1167
Murton
Thornton
Scremerston
West Allerdean
Shoresdean
Cheswick
Goswick
Ancroft
DEVIL'S CAUSEWAY
B6354
B6525
North Low
Haggerston
Berrington
South Low
Beal
A1
Bowsden
LINDISFARNE
Emmanuel Hd.
Holy Island (Lindisfarne)
LINDISFARNE CASTLE
Causeway
Holy Island Sands
Holy Island
Castle Pt.
HERITAGE CENTRE
LINDISFARNE PRIORY
Fenham
Guile Pt.
Barmoor Lane End
Barmoor Castle
HUT SMITHY WOOD WORKSHOP
B6353
West Kyloe
Fenwick
Lowick
East Kyloe
Kyloe Hills
LADY WATERFORD HALL
Buckton
Elwick
Ross
Budle Bay
Farne Islands
Staple Sound
FARNE ISLANDS
BAMBURGH CASTLE
Inner Sound
Holburn
Detchant
Middleton
Kimmerston
Hetton Steads
Budle
Bamburgh
B1340
Belford
Easington
B1342
Waren Mill
Nesbit
North Hazelrigg
Fenton Town
Spindlestone
Glororum
Burton
Doddington
South Hazelrigg
B6349
Mousen
Bradford
B1341
Seahouses
Newtown
West Horton
East Horton
Bellshill
Elford
North Sunderland
Akeld
Weetwood Hall
Warenton
ADDERSTONE
Adderstone
Lucker
A697
117
Chatton
B6348
Warenford
Newham Hall
Beadnell
Humbleton
Greendikes
Swinhoe
Benthall
Wooler
WOOLER
Newham
Fleetham
Beadnell Bay
Newstead
Chathill
Earle
Haugh Head
CHILLINGHAM CASTLE
Chillingham
WILD CATTLE OF CHILLINGHAM
Rosebrough
Ellingham
Preston
High Newton-by-the-Sea
Middleton Hall
Newtown
Brunton

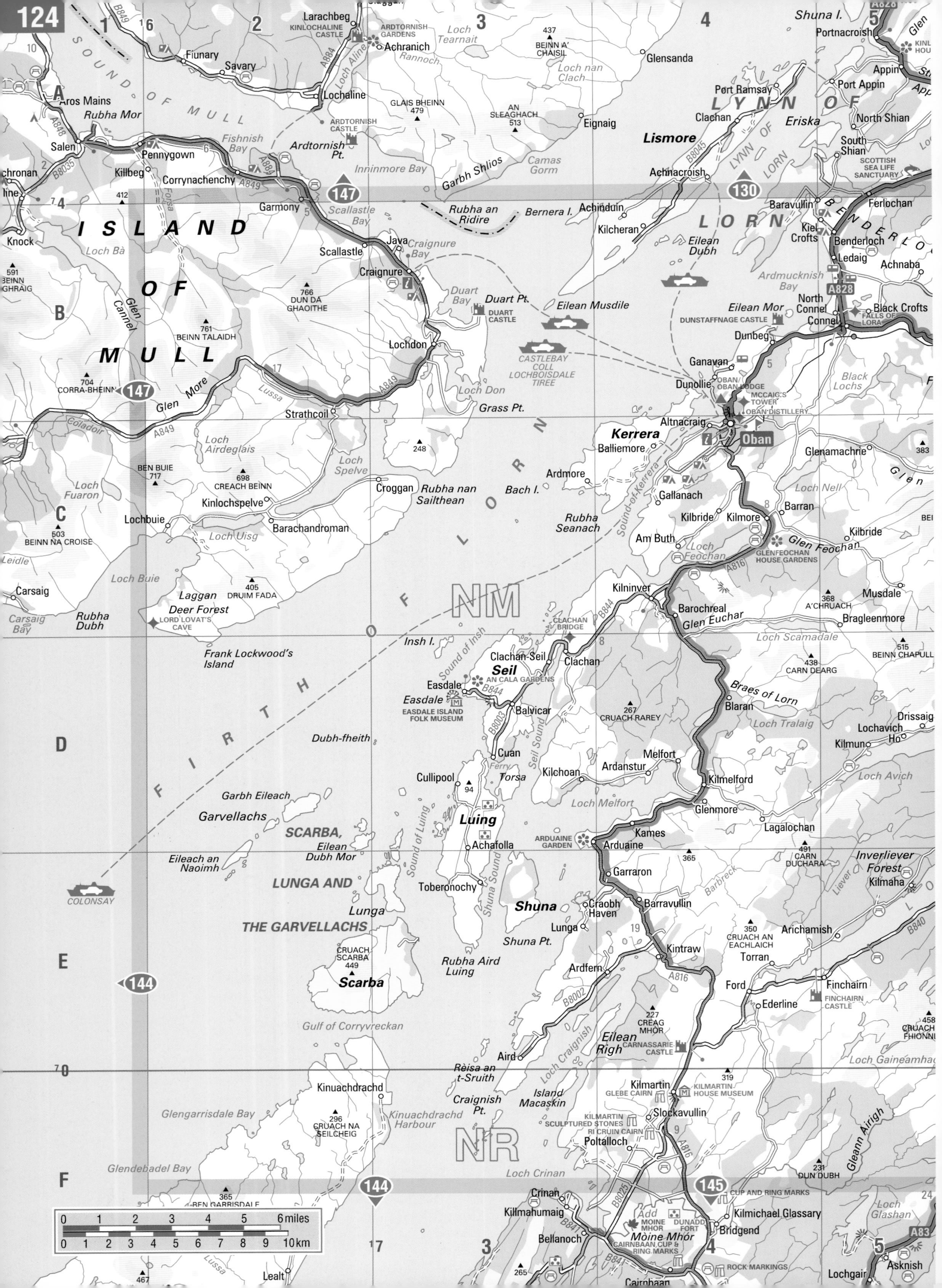

SOUND OF MULL
Larachbeg
KINLOCHALINE CASTLE
ARDTORNISH GARDENS
Achranich
Loch Tearnait
Rannoch
437 BEINN A' CHAISIL
Glensanda
Shuna I.
Portnacroish
Fiunary
Savary
Loch Aline
Lochaline
Loch nan Clach
Appin
Port Appin
Port Ramsay
Aros Mains
Rubha Mor
GLAIS BHEINN 479
AN SLEAGHACH 513
Eignaig
LYNN OF
Clachan
Eriska
North Shian
South Shian
Salen
Fishnish Bay
Pennygown
ARDTORNISH CASTLE
Ardtornish Pt.
Lismore
LYNN OF LORN
SCOTTISH SEA LIFE SANCTUARY
Killbeg
Corrynachenchy
Inninmore Bay
Garbh Shlios
Camas Gorm
Achnacroish
Forsa
412
147
130
Garmony
Scallastle Bay
Rubha an Ridire
Bernera I.
Achinduin
Baravullin
Ferlochan
ISLAND OF MULL
Knock
Loch Bà
LORN
Kilcheran
Kiel Crofts
Benderloch
BENDERLOCH
Scallastle
Java
Craignure Bay
Eilean Dubh
Ledaig
Achnaba
591 BEINN GHRAIG
Craignure
Ardmucknish Bay
766 DUN DA GHAOITHE
Duart Bay
Duart Pt.
DUART CASTLE
Eilean Musdile
Eilean Mor
North Connel
A828
Black Crofts
Glen Cannel
DUNSTAFFNAGE CASTLE
Connel
FALLS OF LORA
761 BEINN TALAIDH
Lochdon
Dunbeg
CASTLEBAY COLL LOCHBOISDALE TIREE
Ganavan
Dunollie
OBAN LODGE
MCCAIG'S TOWER
OBAN DISTILLERY
Black Lochs
704 CORRA-BHEINN
Glen More
Lussa
A849
Loch Don
Grass Pt.
Strathcoil
Coladoir
Loch Airdeglais
248
Altnacraig
Kerrera
Oban
Balliemore
Glenamachrie
383
Loch Spelve
BEN BUIE 717
698 CREACH BEINN
Ardmore
Gallanach
Loch Nell
Glen
Loch Fuaron
Croggan
Rubha nan Sailthean
Bach I.
Kinlochspelve
Barran
Lochbuie
Barachandroman
Rubha Seanach
Sound of Kerrera
Kilbride
Kilmore
503 BEINN NA CROISE
Loch Uisg
Am Buth
Loch Feochan
Glen Feochan
GLENFEOCHAN HOUSE GARDENS
Kilbride
Carsaig
Loch Buie
405 DRUIM FADA
Laggan Deer Forest
NM
Kilninver
A816
Musdale
368 A'CHRUACH
Barochreal
Glen Euchar
Bragleenmore
Carsaig Bay
Rubha Dubh
LORD LOVAT'S CAVE
CLACHAN BRIDGE
B844
Loch Scamadale
515 BEINN CHAPULL
Frank Lockwood's Island
Insh I.
Sound of Insh
Clachan-Seil
Seil
Clachan
438 CARN DEARG
FIRTH OF LORN
Easdale
AN CALA GARDENS
Easdale
EASDALE ISLAND FOLK MUSEUM
Balvicar
B8003
Braes of Lorn
267 CRUACH RAREY
Blaran
Loch Tralaig
Drissaig
Lochavich
Dubh-fheith
Kilmun
Cuan
Seil Sound
Melfort
Ardanstur
Kilchoan
Kilmelford
Ferry
Torsa
Cullipool
94
Loch Avich
Garbh Eileach
Garvellachs
Loch Melfort
Glenmore
SCARBA, LUNGA AND THE GARVELLACHS
Luing
Kames
Lagalochan
Eilean Dubh Mor
ARDUAINE GARDEN
Arduaine
Achafolla
Sound of Luing
365
491 CARN DUCHARA
Inverliever Forest
Eileach an Naoimh
Garraron
Kilmaha
COLONSAY
Toberonochy
Shuna Sound
Barbreck
Liever
Shuna
Craobh Haven
Barravullin
Lunga
Lunga
350 CRUACH AN EACHLAICH
Arichamish
B840
Shuna Pt.
19
Kintraw
Torran
CRUACH SCARBA 449
Scarba
Rubha Aird Luing
144
Ardfern
Ford
Finchairn
B8002
Ederline
FINCHAIRN CASTLE
227 CREAG MHOR
458 CRUACH FHIONN
Gulf of Corryvreckan
Eilean Righ
Loch Craignish
CARNASSARIE CASTLE
Aird
Loch Gaineamhach
Rèisa an t-Sruith
319
Kinuachdrachd
Kilmartin
GLEBE CAIRN
KILMARTIN HOUSE MUSEUM
Craignish Pt.
Island Macaskin
Glengarrisdale Bay
296 CRUACH NA SEILCHEIG
Kinuachdrachd Harbour
Slockavullin
KILMARTIN SCULPTURED STONES
RI CRUIN CAIRN
Gleann Airigh
NR
Poltalloch
Glendebadel Bay
Loch Crinan
231 DUN DUBH
365 BEN GARRISDALE
144
Crinan
145
CUP AND RING MARKS
Killmahumaig
B8025
Add
MOINE MHOR
DUNADD FORT
Kilmichael Glassary
Loch Glashan
Bridgend
Moine Mhor
Bellanoch
B841
CAIRNBAAN CUP & RING MARKS
A83
Lussa
467
Lealt
265
ROCK MARKINGS
Lochgair
Asknish
Cairnbaan
0 1 2 3 4 5 6 miles
0 1 2 3 4 5 6 7 8 9 10 km

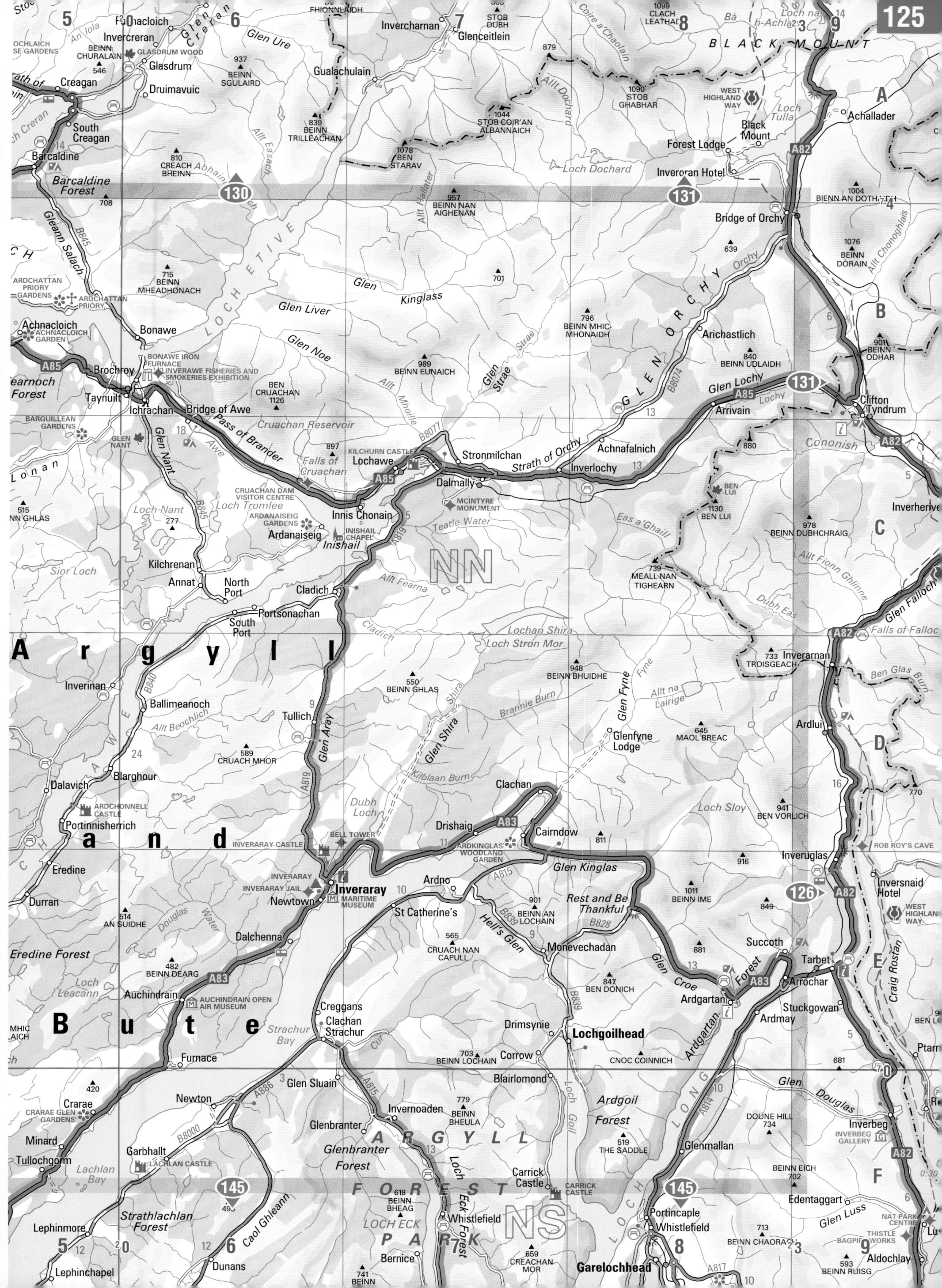
Invercharnan
Glenceitlein
STOB DUBH
1099 CLACH LEATHAD
Coire a'Chaolain
Loch na h-Achlaise
BLACK MOUNT
Invercreran
Glen Creran
Glen Ure
BEINN CHURALAIN
GLASDRUM WOOD
Glasdrum
937 BEINN SGULAIRD
Gualachulain
879
Creagan
Druimavuic
1090 STOB GHABHAR
WEST HIGHLAND WAY
Loch Tulla
Achallader
South Creagan
839 BEINN TRILLEACHAN
1044 STOB COIR'AN ALBANNAICH
Allt Dochard
Black Mount
Forest Lodge
Barcaldine
810 CREACH BHEINN
Allt Easach
1078 BEN STARAV
Loch Dochard
Inveroran Hotel
A82
Barcaldine Forest
708
130
957 BEINN NAN AIGHENAN
Allt Hallater
131
1004 BIENN AN DOTHAIDH
Bridge of Orchy
Gleann Salach
B845
LOCH ETIVE
639
1076 BEINN DORAIN
Allt Chonoghlais
ARDCHATTAN PRIORY GARDENS
ARDCHATTAN PRIORY
715 BEINN MHEADHONACH
Glen Kinglass
701
Glen Orchy
Orchy
Achnacloich
ACHNACLOICH GARDEN
Glen Liver
796 BEINN MHIC MHONAIDH
Arichastlich
Bonawe
Glen Noe
989 BEINN EUNAICH
Glen Strae
840 BEINN UDLAIDH
901 BEINN ODHAR
A85
Brochroy
BONAWE IRON FURNACE
INVERAWE FISHERIES AND SMOKERIES EXHIBITION
BEN CRUACHAN 1126
Allt Mhoille
B8074
Glen Lochy
Clifton
Tyndrum
Taynuilt
Ichrachan
Bridge of Awe
Pass of Brander
Arrivain
Lochy
BARGUILLEAN GARDENS
GLEN NANT
Glen Nant
Awe
Cruachan Reservoir
897
Falls of Cruachan
KILCHURN CASTLE
Lochawe
B8077
Stronmilchan
Strath of Orchy
Achnafalnich
Inverlochy
880
Cononish
Loch Nant
Loch Tromlee
CRUACHAN DAM VISITOR CENTRE
Dalmally
MCINTYRE MONUMENT
BEN LUI
1130 BEN LUI
Inverherive
515 BEINN GHLAS
277
ARDANAISEIG GARDENS
Innis Chonain
Teatle Water
Eas a'Ghaill
978 BEINN DUBHCHRAIG
Ardanaiseig
INISHAIL CHAPEL
Inishail
A819
NN
Allt Fionn Ghlinne
Kilchrenan
Sior Loch
739 MEALL NAN TIGHEARN
Annat
North Port
Cladich
Allt Fearna
Glen Falloch
Dubh Eas
South Port
Portsonachan
Cladich
Lochan Shira
Falls of Falloch
Argyll
Loch Stron Mor
733 TROISGEACH
Inverarnan
948 BEINN BHUIDHE
Inverinan
B840
550 BEINN GHLAS
Glen Fyne
Fyne
Allt na Lairige
Ben Glas Burn
Ballimeanoch
Tullich
Shira
Brannie Burn
Allt Beochlich
Glen Aray
Glen Shira
Glenfyne Lodge
645 MAOL BREAC
Ardlui
589 CRUACH MHOR
Dalavich
Blarghour
Kilblaan Burn
Clachan
770
ARDCHONNELL CASTLE
Portinnisherrich
Dubh Loch
Drishaig
A83
Loch Sloy
941 BEN VORLICH
and
INVERARAY CASTLE
BELL TOWER
ARDKINGLAS WOODLAND GARDEN
Cairndow
811
ROB ROY'S CAVE
Eredine
INVERARAY
INVERARAY JAIL
Inveraray
MARITIME MUSEUM
Ardno
A815
Glen Kinglas
916
Inveruglas
Inversnaid Hotel
Durran
Newtown
St Catherine's
901 BEINN AN LOCHAIN
Rest and Be Thankful
B828
1011 BEINN IME
126
849
WEST HIGHLAND WAY
514 AN SUIDHE
Douglas Water
Dalchenna
B839
Hell's Glen
565 CRUACH NAN CAPULL
Monevechadan
Glen Croe
881
Succoth
Tarbet
Eredine Forest
482 BEINN DEARG
847 BEN DONICH
Forest
Arrochar
Craig Rostan
Loch Leacann
Auchindrain
AUCHINDRAIN OPEN AIR MUSEUM
Creggans
Ardgartan
Stuckgowan
Bute
Clachan Strachur
Strachur Bay
Drimsynie
Lochgoilhead
Ardgartan
Ardmay
703 BEINN LOCHAIN
Corrow
CNOC COINNICH
Furnace
Cur
681
Glen Douglas
420
Glen Sluain
Blairlomond
Loch Goil
Newton
A886
779 BEINN BHEULA
Invernoaden
Ardgoil Forest
Loch Long
A814
DOUNE HILL 734
Crarae
CRARAE GLEN GARDENS
Glenbranter
ARGYLL
Inverbeg
INVERBEG GALLERY
Minard
B8000
Glenbranter Forest
519 THE SADDLE
Glenmallan
Tullochgorm
Garbhallt
LACHLAN CASTLE
Lachlan Bay
Loch Eck
Carrick Castle
CARRICK CASTLE
BEINN EICH 702
145
FOREST
618 BEINN BHEAG
Edentaggart
495
Strathlachlan Forest
Caol Ghleann
LOCH ECK
Whistlefield
Eck Forest
NS
Portincaple
Whistlefield
Glen Luss
NAT PARK CENTRE
Lephinmore
PARK
713 BEINN CHAORACH
THISTLE BAGPIPE WORKS
Bernice
659 CREACHAN MOR
Garelochhead
593 BEINN RUISG
Aldochlay
Lephinchapel
Dunans
741 BEINN
A817

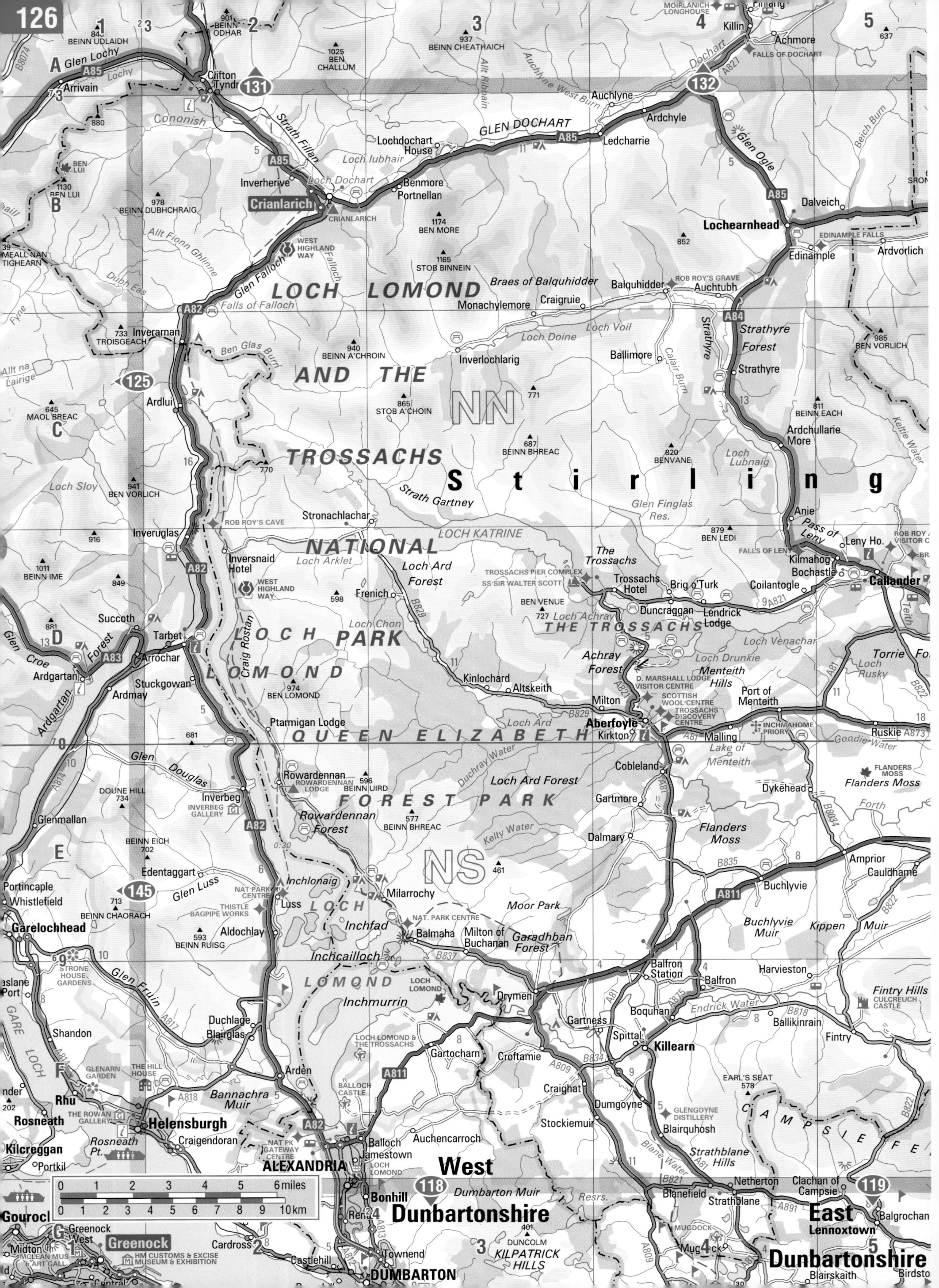

BEINN UDLAIDH
BEINN ODHAR
1025 BEN CHALLUM
937 BEINN CHEATHAICH
MOIRLANICH LONGHOUSE
Killin
Achmore
FALLS OF DOCHART
Glen Lochy
A85
Arrivain
Clifton
Tyndrum
131
132
Dochart
Auchlyne
Auchlyne West Burn
Allt Ribhain
Ardchyle
Cononish
Strath Fillan
GLEN DOCHART
Ledcharrie
Glen Ogle
Lochdochart House
Loch Iubhair
880
BEN LUI
1130 BEN LUI
Inverherive
Loch Dochart
Benmore
Portnellan
Crianlarich
CRIANLARICH
978 BEINN DUBHCHRAIG
1174 BEN MORE
Dalveich
Lochearnhead
852
EDINAMPLE FALLS
Edinample
Ardvorlich
MEALL NAN TIGHEARN
Allt Fionn Ghlinne
WEST HIGHLAND WAY
Glen Falloch
1165 STOB BINNEIN
Dubh Eas
LOCH LOMOND
Braes of Balquhidder
Balquhidder
ROB ROY'S GRAVE
Auchtubh
Monachylemore
Craigruie
Falls of Falloch
A82
A84
Strathyre Forest
733 TROISGEACH
Inverarnan
Loch Voil
Loch Doine
985 BEN VORLICH
940 BEINN A'CHROIN
Ben Glas Burn
Inverlochlarig
Ballimore
Calair Burn
Strathyre
AND THE
125
Ardlui
865 STOB A'CHOIN
NN
771
811 BEINN EACH
645 MAOL BREAC
Ardchullarie More
687 BEINN BHREAC
820 BENVANE
Loch Lubnaig
TROSSACHS
770
Stirling
Loch Sloy
941 BEN VORLICH
Strath Gartney
Glen Finglas Res.
Anie
Pass of Leny
Stronachlachar
ROB ROY'S CAVE
879 BEN LEDI
Leny Ho.
Inveruglas
916
LOCH KATRINE
NATIONAL
FALLS OF LENY
ROB ROY VISITOR CENTRE
Inversnaid Hotel
Loch Arklet
Loch Ard Forest
The Trossachs
Kilmahog
Bochastle
1011 BEINN IME
849
WEST HIGHLAND WAY
TROSSACHS PIER COMPLEX
SS SIR WALTER SCOTT
Trossachs Hotel
Brig o'Turk
Coilantogle
Callander
598
Frenich
BEN VENUE
727
Duncraggan
Lendrick Lodge
A821
881
Succoth
Tarbet
Loch Achray
THE TROSSACHS
Loch Chon
LOCH PARK
Craig Rostan
B829
Loch Venachar
Glen Croe
Forest
A83
Arrochar
Achray Forest
Loch Drunkie
Torrie
Loch Rusky
Ardgartan
Ardmay
Stuckgowan
LOMOND
974 BEN LOMOND
Kinlochard
Altskeith
Menteith Hills
D. MARSHALL LODGE VISITOR CENTRE
SCOTTISH WOOL CENTRE
TROSSACHS DISCOVERY CENTRE
Milton
Port of Menteith
Ardgartan
Ptarmigan Lodge
Loch Ard
Aberfoyle
Kirkton
681
QUEEN ELIZABETH
A81
Malling
INCHMAHOME PRIORY
Ruskie
A873
Goodie Water
Lake of Menteith
Glen Douglas
A814
Rowardennan
ROWARDENNAN LODGE
596 BEINN UIRD
Duchray Water
Loch Ard Forest
Cobleland
FLANDERS MOSS
Flanders Moss
DOUNE HILL 734
Inverbeg
INVERBEG GALLERY
FOREST PARK
Gartmore
Dykehead
Forth
Glenmallan
Rowardennan Forest
577 BEINN BHREAC
Kelty Water
Flanders Moss
B8034
A82
Dalmary
BEINN EICH 702
NS
461
B835
Arnprior
Cauldhame
Edentaggart
Glen Luss
Inchlonaig
Milarrochy
Buchlyvie
Portincaple
Whistlefield
145
NAT PARK CENTRE
Luss
LOCH
Moor Park
A811
THISTLE BAGPIPE WORKS
713 BEINN CHAORACH
NAT. PARK CENTRE
Buchlyvie Muir
Kippen
Muir
Garelochhead
593 BEINN RUISG
Aldochlay
Inchfad
Balmaha
Milton of Buchanan
Garadhban Forest
STRONE HOUSE GARDENS
Inchcailloch
B837
Balfron Station
Balfron
Harvieston
Glen Fruin
LOMOND
LOCH LOMOND
Drymen
Fintry Hills
CULCREUCH CASTLE
Inchmurrin
Endrick Water
Boquhan
B818
Ballikinrain
GARE LOCH
A817
Duchlage
Blairglas
Gartness
Spittal
Killearn
Fintry
Shandon
LOCH LOMOND & THE TROSSACHS
Gartocharn
Croftamie
A809
B834
GLENARN GARDEN
THE HILL HOUSE
Arden
A811
EARL'S SEAT 578
Rhu
BALLOCH CASTLE
Craighat
CAMPSIE FELLS
A818
Bannachra Muir
Dumgoyne
GLENGOYNE DISTILLERY
Rosneath
THE ROWAN GALLERY
Helensburgh
A82
Stockiemuir
Blairquhosh
Blane Water
Craigendoran
Auchencarroch
Kilcreggan
Rosneath Pt.
NAT PK GATEWAY CENTRE
Balloch
Jamestown
Strathblane Hills
Portkil
ALEXANDRIA
LOCH LOMOND
West
Netherton
Clachan of Campsie
119
118
B821
Blanefield
Strathblane
A891
Gourock
Bonhill
Dumbarton Muir
Resrs.
East Lennoxtown
Balgrochan
Greenock
West
Renton
Dunbartonshire
Greenock
HM CUSTOMS & EXCISE MUSEUM & EXHIBITION
MUGDOCK
Mugdock
Dunbartonshire
Midton
MCLEAN MUS & ART GALL
Cardross
DUNCOLM
KILPATRICK HILLS
Castlehill
Townend
A813
DUMBARTON
Blairskaith
0 1 2 3 4 5 6 miles
0 1 2 3 4 5 6 7 8 9 10 km

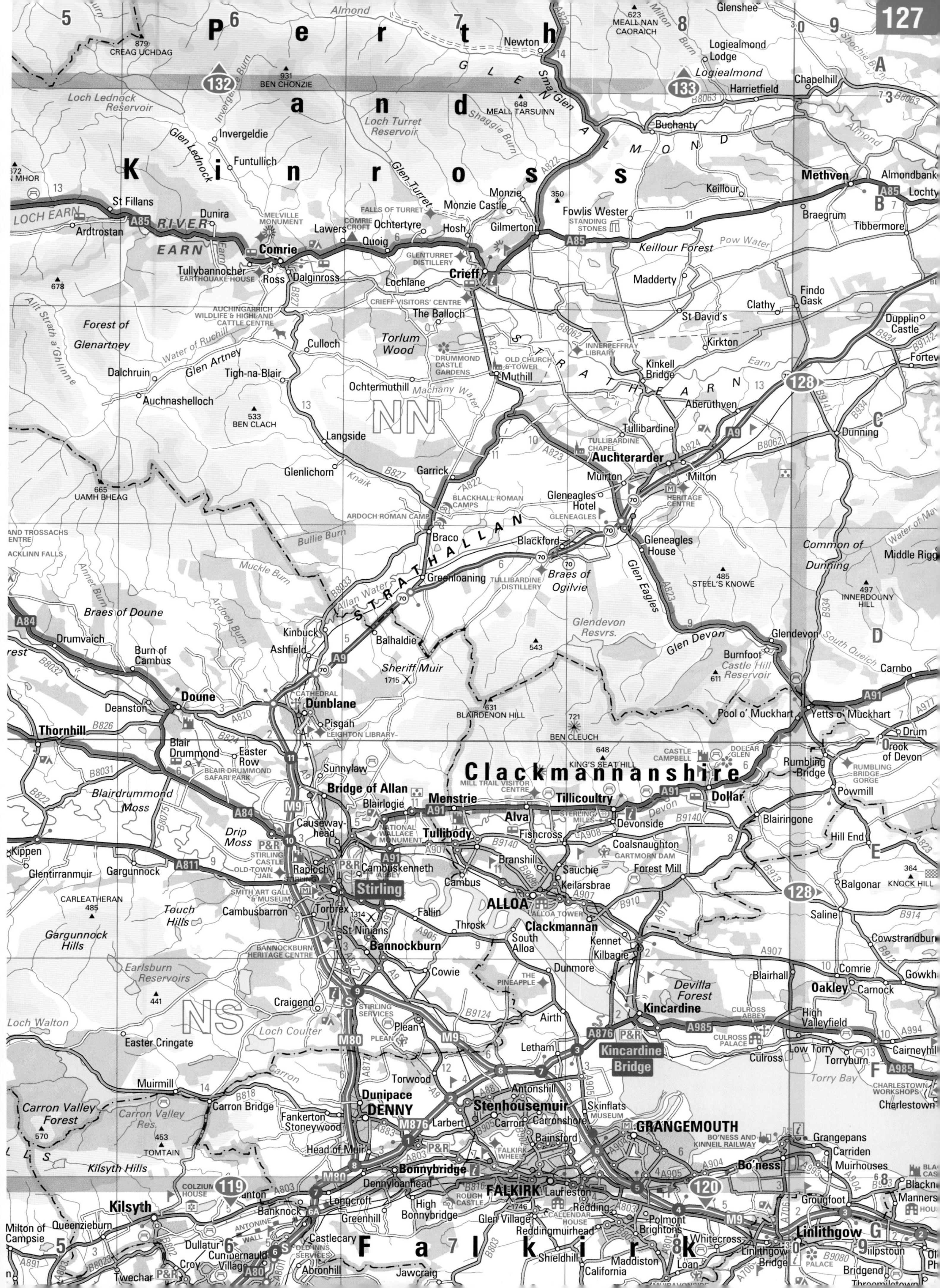
Perth and Kinross
Clackmannanshire
Falkirk
NN
NS
Almond
Glenshee
623 MEALL NAN CAORAICH
879 CREAG UCHDAG
Newton
Logiealmond Lodge
Logiealmond
931 BEN CHONZIE
132
133
Chapelhill
Harrietfield
Loch Lednock Reservoir
GLEN ALMOND
648 MEALL TARSUINN
Shaggie Burn
Loch Turret Reservoir
Invergeldie
Glen Lednock
Funtullich
Glen Turret
Buchanty
Methven
Almondbank
Lochty
Keillour
Monzie
Monzie Castle
350
Fowlis Wester
STANDING STONES
Gilmerton
St Fillans
LOCH EARN
Dunira
Ardtrostan
RIVER EARN
MELVILLE MONUMENT
FALLS OF TURRET
COMRIE CROFT
Ochtertyre
Lawers
Quoig
Hosh
Comrie
Tullybannocher
EARTHQUAKE HOUSE
Ross
Dalginross
GLENTURRET DISTILLERY
Lochlane
Crieff
CRIEFF VISITORS' CENTRE
Keillour Forest
Pow Water
Braegrum
Tibbermore
Madderty
Findo Gask
Clathy
St David's
Dupplin Castle
678
Alt Strath a'Ghlinne
AUCHINGARRICH WILDLIFE & HIGHLAND CATTLE CENTRE
Forest of Glenartney
Water of Ruchill
Glen Artney
Culloch
The Balloch
Torlum Wood
DRUMMOND CASTLE GARDENS
OLD CHURCH & TOWER
Muthill
STRATHEARN
INNERPEFFRAY LIBRARY
Kirkton
Kinkell Bridge
Forteviot
128
Dalchruin
Tigh-na-Blair
Auchnashelloch
Ochtermuthill
Machany Water
533 BEN CLACH
Aberuthven
Tullibardine
TULLIBARDINE CHAPEL
Auchterarder
Dunning
Langside
Knaik
Glenlichorn
Garrick
Muirton
Milton
HERITAGE CENTRE
665 UAMH BHEAG
BLACKHALL ROMAN CAMPS
Gleneagles Hotel
GLENEAGLES
ARDOCH ROMAN CAMP
STRATHALLAN
Braco
Blackford
Gleneagles House
Common of Dunning
Middle Rigg
Bullie Burn
Muckle Burn
Greenloaning
TULLIBARDINE DISTILLERY
Braes of Ogilvie
Glen Eagles
485 STEEL'S KNOWE
497 INNERDOUNY HILL
Allan Water
Annet Burn
Braes of Doune
Ardoch Burn
Kinbuck
Balhaldie
Glendevon Resvrs.
Glen Devon
Glendevon
South Queich
Drumvaich
Burn of Cambus
Ashfield
543
Burnfoot
Castle Hill Reservoir
611
Carnbo
Sheriff Muir
1715
Doune
Deanston
CATHEDRAL
Dunblane
631 BLAIRDENON HILL
721 BEN CLEUCH
Pool o' Muckhart
Yetts o' Muckhart
Drum
Crook of Devon
Thornhill
Pisgah
LEIGHTON LIBRARY
648 KING'S SEAT HILL
CASTLE CAMPBELL
DOLLAR GLEN
Rumbling Bridge
RUMBLING BRIDGE GORGE
Blair Drummond
Easter Row
BLAIR DRUMMOND SAFARI PARK
Sunnylaw
Bridge of Allan
MILL TRAIL VISITOR CENTRE
Menstrie
Tillicoultry
Dollar
Powmill
Blairdrummond Moss
Drip Moss
Blairlogie
NATIONAL WALLACE MONUMENT
Tullibody
Alva
STERLING MILLS
Devonside
Causewayhead
Fishcross
Coalsnaughton
GARTMORN DAM
Blairingone
Hill End
Kippen
Glentirranmuir
Gargunnock
STIRLING CASTLE
OLD TOWN JAIL
Raploch
Cambuskenneth ABBEY
Branshill
Sauchie
Forest Mill
364 KNOCK HILL
Balgonar
SMITH ART GALL & MUSEUM
Stirling
Cambus
Keilarsbrae
CARLEATHERAN 485
Touch Hills
Cambusbarron
Torbrex
1314
Fallin
ALLOA
ALLOA TOWER
Saline
Gargunnock Hills
St Ninians
Throsk
Clackmannan
South Alloa
Kennet
Kilbagie
Cowstrandburn
BANNOCKBURN HERITAGE CENTRE
Bannockburn
Earlsburn Reservoirs
Cowie
Dunmore
THE PINEAPPLE
Blairhall
Comrie
Gowkhall
Oakley
Carnock
Devilla Forest
441
Craigend
STIRLING SERVICES
Airth
Kincardine
CULROSS ABBEY
High Valleyfield
Loch Walton
Loch Coulter
Plean
PLEAN
Easter Cringate
Letham
Kincardine Bridge
CULROSS PALACE
Low Torry
Torryburn
Culross
Cairneyhill
Carron
Torwood
Torry Bay
CHARLESTOWN WORKSHOPS
Charlestown
Muirmill
Carron Bridge
Dunipace
DENNY
Antonshill
Stenhousemuir
Skinflats MUSEUM
Carron Valley Forest
Carron Valley Res.
570
Fankerton
Stoneywood
Larbert
Carron
Carronshore
GRANGEMOUTH
BO'NESS AND KINNEIL RAILWAY
453 TOMTAIN
Head of Muir
Bainsford
FALKIRK WHEEL
Grangepans
Carriden
Kilsyth Hills
Bonnybridge
Bo'ness
Muirhouses
COLZIUM HOUSE
Banton
Dennyloanhead
FALKIRK
Laurieston
119
120
Kilsyth
Longcroft
Banknock
High Bonnybridge
ROUGH CASTLE
1746
Redding
Polmont
Grougfoot
Manners
Queenzieburn
ANTONINE WALL
Greenhill
Glen Village
CALLENDAR HOUSE
Reddingmuirhead
Brightons
Linlithgow
Milton of Campsie
Dullatur
Cumbernauld Village
Croy
Castlecary
OLD INNS SERVICES
Shieldhill
Whitecross
Linlithgow Bridge
PALACE
Philpstoun
Twechar
Abronhill
Jawcraig
California
Maddiston
Loan
Bridgend
M9
M80
M876
A9
A84
A85
A91
A811
A822
A823
A824
A876
A977
A985
A907
B8033
B827
B8062
B934
B9140
B824
B826
B8031
B822
B8032
B913
B914
B9124
B816
A803
A883
A872
A905
A904
A993
A706
A801
A80
A994

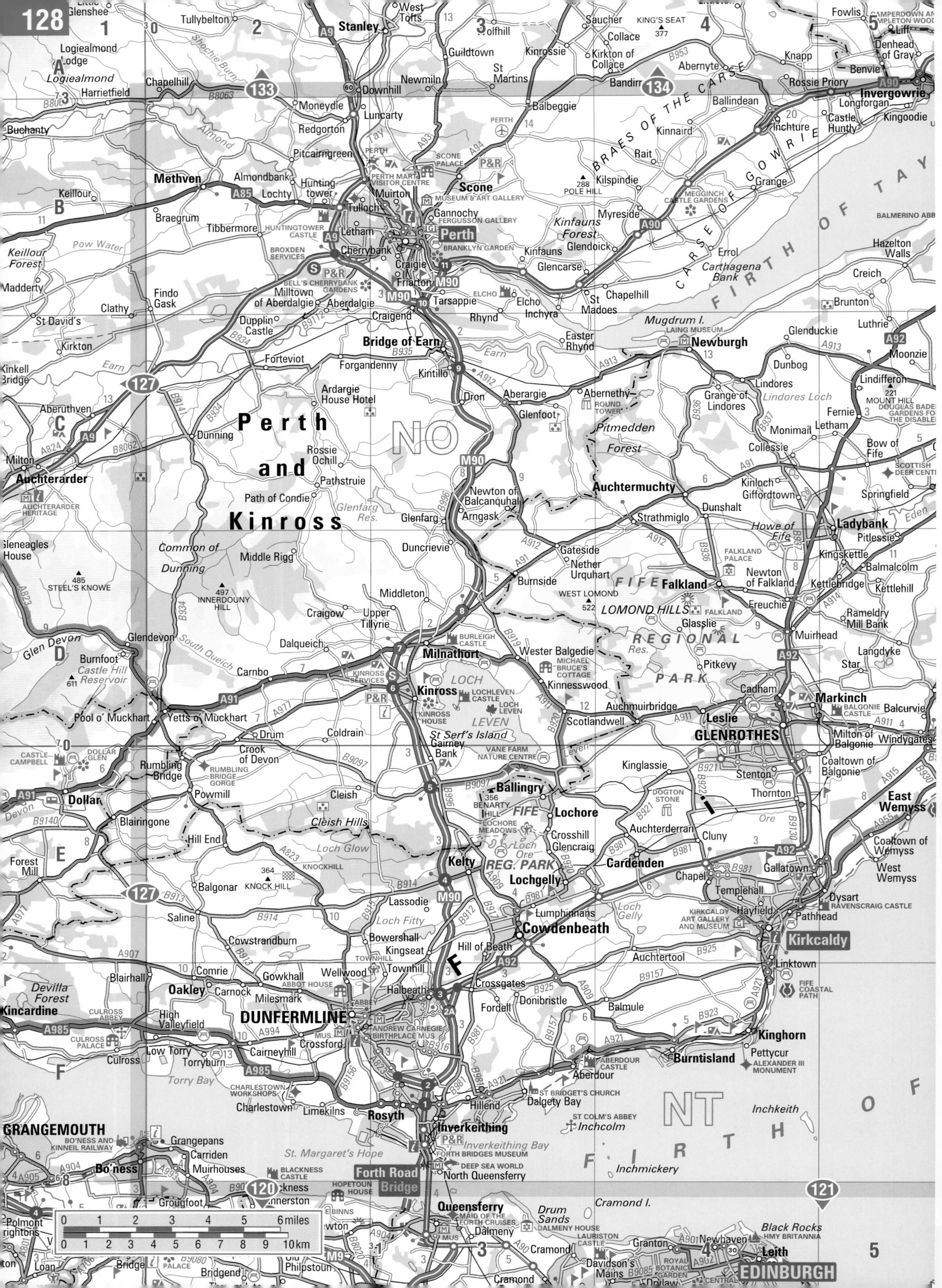

Perth and Kinross
NO
NT
Glenshee
Tullybelton
Stanley
West Tofts
Wolfhill
Saucher
KING'S SEAT 377
Collace
Kinrossie
Kirkton of Collace
Abernyte
Knapp
Fowlis
Liff
Denhead of Gray
Benvie
Rossie Priory
Invergowrie
Longforgan
Castle Huntly
Kingoodie
Logiealmond Lodge
Logiealmond
Harrietfield
Chapelhill
Downhill
Newmiln
Guildtown
St Martins
Bandirran
Balbeggie
Ballindean
Inchture
Kinnaird
BRAES OF THE CARSE
CARSE OF GOWRIE
FIRTH OF TAY
Buchanty
Moneydie
Luncarty
Redgorton
Pitcairngreen
Almond
Tay
PERTH
SCONE PALACE
Rait
Kilspindie
288 POLE HILL
Grange
MEGGINCH CASTLE GARDENS
Methven
Almondbank
Huntingtower
Lochty
Tulloch
Muirton
PERTH MART VISITOR CENTRE
MUSEUM & ART GALLERY
Scone
Gannochy
FERGUSSON GALLERY
Perth
Keillour
Braegrum
Tibbermore
HUNTINGTOWER CASTLE
Letham
Kinfauns Forest
Myreside
BALMERINO ABBEY
Keillour Forest
Pow Water
BROXDEN SERVICES
Cherrybank
Craigie
BRANKLYN GARDEN
Kinfauns
Glendoick
Errol
Hazelton Walls
Madderty
BELL'S CHERRYBANK GARDENS
Friarton
Glencarse
Carthagena Bank
Creich
Findo Gask
Milltown of Aberdalgie
Aberdalgie
Tarsappie
ELCHO
Elcho
Chapelhill
Brunton
Clathy
St David's
Dupplin Castle
Craigend
Rhynd
Inchyra
St Madoes
Mugdrum I.
Luthrie
LAING MUSEUM
Glenduckie
Kirkton
Bridge of Earn
Easter Rhynd
Newburgh
Kinkell Bridge
Forteviot
Forgandenny
Earn
Kintillo
Dunbog
Moonzie
Lindores
Lindores Loch
Lindifferon
MOUNT HILL 221
DOUGLAS BADER GARDENS FOR THE DISABLED
Aberuthven
Ardargie House Hotel
Dron
Aberargie
Abernethy
ROUND TOWER
Glenfoot
Grange of Lindores
Fernie
Monimail
Letham
Pitmedden Forest
Collessie
Bow of Fife
Milton
Auchterarder
Dunning
Rossie Ochill
SCOTTISH DEER CENTRE
AUCHTERARDER HERITAGE
Pathstruie
Path of Condie
Newton of Balcanquhal
Auchtermuchty
Kinloch
Giffordtown
Springfield
Glenfarg Res.
Glenfarg
Arngask
Dunshalt
Strathmiglo
Ladybank
Howe of Fife
Pitlessie
Eden
Gleneagles House
Kinross
Common of Dunning
Middle Rigg
Duncrievie
Gateside
Nether Urquhart
FALKLAND PALACE
Kingskettle
Balmalcolm
485 STEEL'S KNOWE
Burnside
FIFE
Falkland
Newton of Falkland
Kettlebridge
Kettlehill
497 INNERDOUNY HILL
Middleton
WEST LOMOND 522
LOMOND HILLS
FALKLAND
Freuchie
Rameldry Mill Bank
Craigow
Upper Tillyrie
Glasslie
REGIONAL PARK
Muirhead
Glendevon
Glen Devon
South Queich
Dalqueich
BURLEIGH CASTLE
Milnathort
Wester Balgedie
MICHAEL BRUCE'S COTTAGE
Res.
Langdyke
Burnfoot
Castle Hill Reservoir
611
Carnbo
KINROSS SERVICES
LOCH
Kinnesswood
Pitkevy
Star
Cadham
Markinch
BALGONIE CASTLE
Balcurvie
Kinross
LOCHLEVEN CASTLE
LOCH LEVEN
KINROSS HOUSE
Auchmuirbridge
Leslie
GLENROTHES
Milton of Balgonie
Windygates
Pool o' Muckhart
Yetts o' Muckhart
Drum
Coldrain
St Serf's Island
Scotlandwell
CASTLE CAMPBELL
DOLLAR GLEN
Crook of Devon
Gairney Bank
VANE FARM NATURE CENTRE
Kinglassie
Coaltown of Balgonie
Rumbling Bridge
RUMBLING BRIDGE GORGE
Stenton
Dollar
Powmill
Cleish
Ballingry
DOGTON STONE
Thornton
East Wemyss
356 BENARTY HILL
FIFE
Lochore
Blairingone
Cleish Hills
LOCHORE MEADOWS
Auchterderran
Devon
Hill End
Loch Ore
Crosshill
Glencraig
Cluny
Coaltown of Wemyss
Forest Mill
Loch Glow
KNOCKHILL
Kelty
REG. PARK
Cardenden
Gallatown
West Wemyss
364 KNOCK HILL
Lochgelly
Chapel
Templehall
Dysart
RAVENSCRAIG CASTLE
Balgonar
Lassodie
Lumphinnans
Loch Gelly
KIRKCALDY ART GALLERY AND MUSEUM
Hayfield
Pathhead
Saline
Loch Fitty
Cowdenbeath
Kirkcaldy
Cowstrandburn
Bowershall
Kingseat
Hill of Beath
TOWNHILL
Townhill
Auchtertool
Comrie
Blairhall
Linktown
Devilla Forest
Oakley
Carnock
Gowkhall
Wellwood
ABBOT HOUSE
Halbeath
Crossgates
FIFE COASTAL PATH
Kincardine
CULROSS ABBEY
High Valleyfield
Milesmark
DUNFERMLINE
ABBEY
Fordell
Donibristle
Balmule
ANDREW CARNEGIE BIRTHPLACE MUS
CULROSS PALACE
Crossford
Kinghorn
Low Torry
Torryburn
Cairneyhill
Pettycur
ALEXANDER III MONUMENT
Culross
Torry Bay
Burntisland
ABERDOUR CASTLE
Aberdour
CHARLESTOWN WORKSHOPS
ST BRIDGET'S CHURCH
Charlestown
Limekilns
Rosyth
Hillend
Dalgety Bay
Inchkeith
GRANGEMOUTH
ST COLM'S ABBEY
Inchcolm
Inverkeithing
BO'NESS AND KINNEIL RAILWAY
Grangepans
Carriden
St. Margaret's Hope
Inverkeithing Bay
FORTH BRIDGES MUSEUM
FIRTH OF FORTH
Bo'ness
Muirhouses
BLACKNESS CASTLE
Forth Road Bridge
DEEP SEA WORLD
North Queensferry
Inchmickery
Blackness
HOPETOUN HOUSE
Grougfoot
Abercorn
Queensferry
Cramond I.
Drum Sands
Polmont
Brightons
MAID OF THE FORTH CRUISES
DALMENY HOUSE
Black Rocks
HMY BRITANNIA
Dalmeny
LAURISTON CASTLE
Granton
Newhaven
Leith
Cramond
Davidson's Mains
ROYAL BOTANIC GARDEN
EDINBURGH
Loan
Bridge
Bridgend
Philpstoun
0 1 2 3 4 5 6 miles
0 1 2 3 4 5 6 7 8 9 10 km

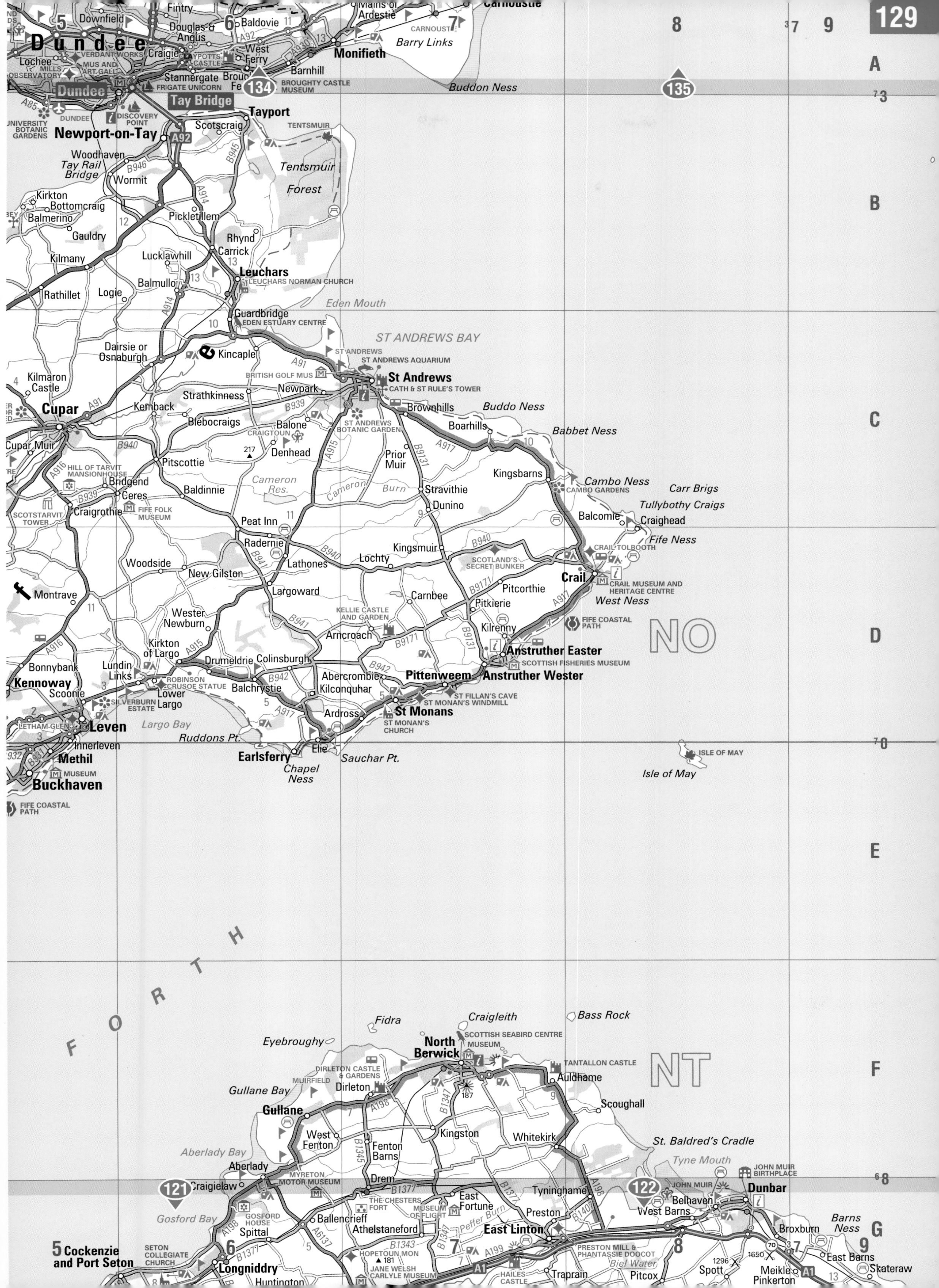
Fintry
Downfield
Douglas & Angus
Baldovie
Mains of Ardestie
Carnoustie
Dundee
Lochee
Verdant Works
Craigie
Mus and Art Gall
Mills Observatory
Claypotts Castle
West Ferry
Monifieth
Carnoustie
Barry Links
Barnhill
Stannergate
Broughty Ferry
Frigate Unicorn
Broughty Castle Museum
Buddon Ness
134
135
Dundee
Tay Bridge
Discovery Point
Tayport
University Botanic Gardens
Newport-on-Tay
Scotscraig
Tentsmuir
Woodhaven
Tay Rail Bridge
Wormit
Tentsmuir Forest
Kirkton
Bottomcraig
Balmerino
Gauldry
Pickletillem
Rhynd
Carrick
Kilmany
Lucklawhill
Leuchars
Leuchars Norman Church
Balmullo
Rathillet
Logie
Eden Mouth
Guardbridge
Eden Estuary Centre
St Andrews Bay
Dairsie or Osnaburgh
Kincaple
St Andrews
St Andrews Aquarium
British Golf Mus
St Andrews
Cath & St Rule's Tower
Kilmaron Castle
Cupar
Kemback
Strathkinness
Newpark
Brownhills
Buddo Ness
Blebocraigs
Balone
St Andrews Botanic Garden
Boarhills
Babbet Ness
Cupar Muir
Craigtoun
Denhead
Prior Muir
Hill of Tarvit Mansionhouse
Pitscottie
Cameron Res.
Cameron Burn
Kingsbarns
Cambo Ness
Cambo Gardens
Carr Brigs
Bridgend
Baldinnie
Stravithie
Tullybothy Craigs
Ceres
Dunino
Scotstarvit Tower
Craigrothie
Fife Folk Museum
Peat Inn
Balcomie
Craighead
Fife Ness
Radernie
Kingsmuir
Crail Tolbooth
Woodside
Lathones
Lochty
Scotland's Secret Bunker
New Gilston
Crail
Crail Museum and Heritage Centre
Montrave
Largoward
Carnbee
Pitcorthie
West Ness
Pitkierie
Kellie Castle and Garden
Wester Newburn
Kilrenny
Fife Coastal Path
NO
Arncroach
Kirkton of Largo
Anstruther Easter
Scottish Fisheries Museum
Bonnybank
Lundin Links
Drumeldrie
Colinsburgh
Kennoway
Robinson Crusoe Statue
Abercrombie
Pittenweem
Anstruther Wester
Balchrystie
Kilconquhar
St Fillan's Cave
Scoonie
Lower Largo
St Monan's Windmill
Silverburn Estate
Ardross
St Monans
St Monan's Church
Letham Glen
Leven
Largo Bay
Ruddons Pt.
Innerleven
Methil
Earlsferry
Elie
Sauchar Pt.
Isle of May
Isle of May
Chapel Ness
Museum
Buckhaven
Fife Coastal Path
F O R T H
Fidra
Craigleith
Bass Rock
Eyebroughy
Scottish Seabird Centre
Museum
North Berwick
Tantallon Castle
NT
Dirleton Castle & Gardens
Muirfield
Dirleton
Auldhame
Gullane Bay
Gullane
Scoughall
West Fenton
Kingston
Whitekirk
St. Baldred's Cradle
Fenton Barns
Aberlady Bay
Tyne Mouth
Aberlady
John Muir Birthplace
Myreton Motor Museum
Drem
121
Craigielaw
Tyninghame
122
John Muir
Dunbar
The Chesters Fort
Museum of Flight
East Fortune
Belhaven
Gosford House
West Barns
Barns Ness
Gosford Bay
Ballencrieff
Preston
Broxburn
Spittal
Athelstaneford
East Linton
5 Cockenzie and Port Seton
Seton Collegiate Church
Hopetoun Mon
Preston Mill & Phantassie Doocot
East Barns
Biel Water
Spott
Meikle Pinkerton
Skateraw
Longniddry
Jane Welsh Carlyle Museum
Hailes Castle
Traprain
Pitcox
Huntington
A
B
C
D
E
F
G
5
6
7
8
9

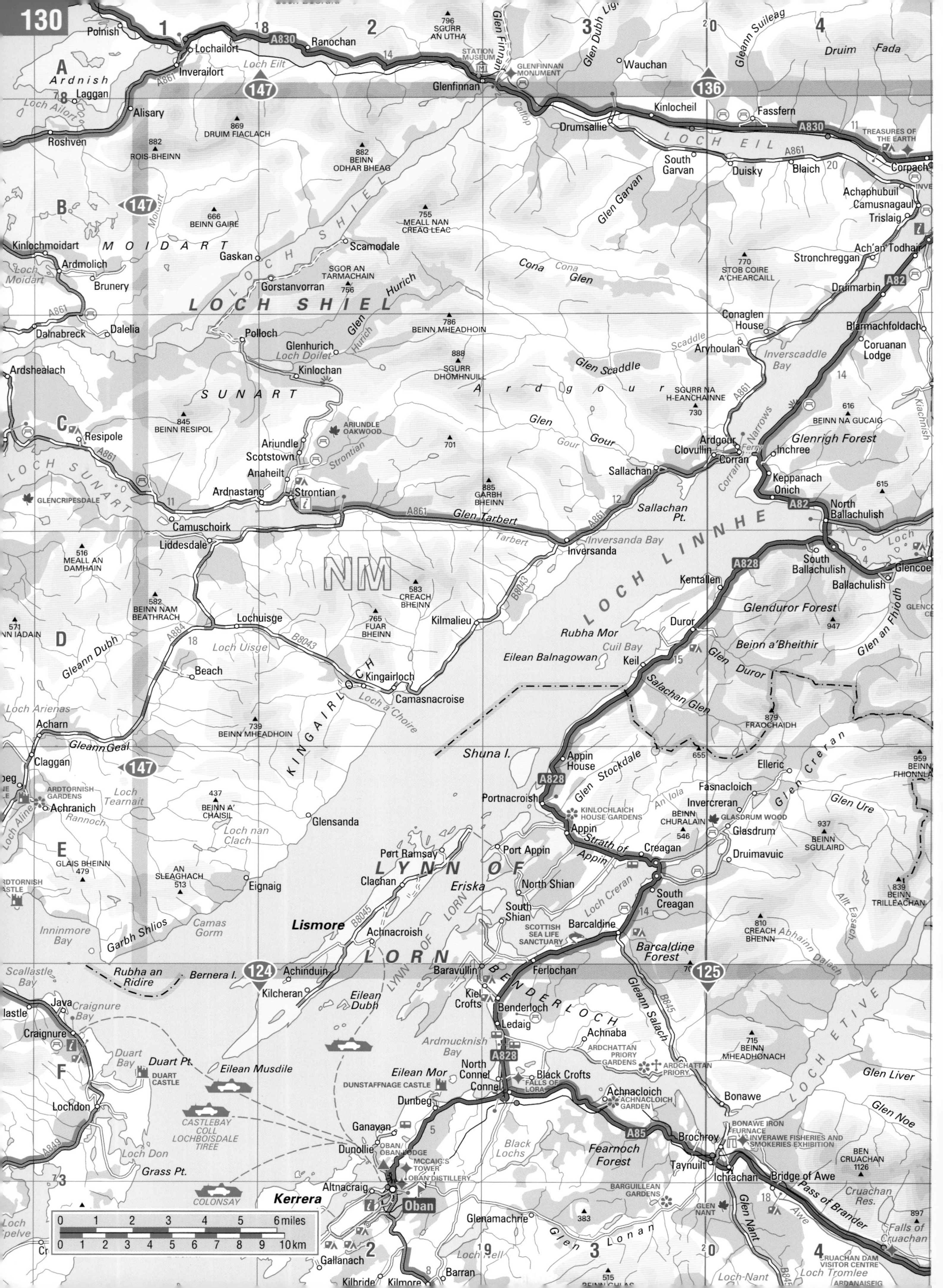
Polnish
Lochailort
Inverailort
Ranochan
A830
Loch Eilt
147
Ardnish
Laggan
Loch Ailort
Alisary
Roshven
796 SGURR AN UTHA
STATION MUSEUM
Glen Finnan
GLENFINNAN MONUMENT
Glenfinnan
Callop
Glen Dubh Lighe
Wauchan
Gleann Suileag
Druim Fada
136
Kinlocheil
Fassfern
Drumsallie
LOCH EIL
A861
TREASURES OF THE EARTH
Corpach
South Garvan
Duisky
Blaich
869 DRUIM FIACLACH
882 ROIS-BHEINN
882 BEINN ODHAR BHEAG
666 BEINN GAIRE
755 MEALL NAN CREAG LEAC
Moidart
MOIDART
Kinlochmoidart
Ardmolich
Loch Moidart
Brunery
Gaskan
Scamodale
LOCH SHIEL
SGOR AN TARMACHAIN 756
Gorstanvorran
Glen Hurich
Cona Glen
Glen Garvan
770 STOB COIRE A'CHEARCAILL
Achaphubuil
Camusnagaul
Trislaig
Stronchreggan
Ach'an Todhair
Druimarbin
A82
Dalnabreck
Dalelia
Polloch
Glenhurich
Loch Doilet
786 BEINN MHEADHOIN
888 SGURR DHOMHNUILL
Conaglen House
Aryhoulan
Scaddle
Glen Scaddle
Inverscaddle Bay
Blarmachfoldach
Coruanan Lodge
Ardshealach
Kinlochan
SUNART
Ardgour
SGURR NA H-EANCHAINNE 730
616 BEINN NA GUCAIG
Kiachnish
845 BEINN RESIPOL
Resipole
ARIUNDLE OAKWOOD
Ariundle
Scotstown
Strontian
Anaheilt
701
Glen Gour
Ardgour
Clovullin
Corran
Corran Narrows
Inchree
Glenrigh Forest
LOCH SUNART
GLENCRIPESDALE
Ardnastang
885 GARBH BHEINN
Sallachan
Keppanach
Onich
615
North Ballachulish
Camuschoirk
Glen Tarbert
Sallachan Pt.
LOCH LINNHE
Liddesdale
Tarbert
Inversanda Bay
Inversanda
South Ballachulish
Glencoe
Ballachulish
516 MEALL AN DAMHAIN
NM
583 CREACH BHEINN
A828
Kentallen
582 BEINN NAM BEATHRACH
B8043
Glen an Fhiodh
Glendurор Forest
571
Lochuisge
765 FUAR BHEINN
Kilmalieu
Duror
947
Gleann Dubh
Loch Uisge
Rubha Mor
Cuil Bay
Beinn a'Bheithir
Eilean Balnagowan
Keil
Glen Duror
Beach
Kingairloch
Salachan Glen
Loch Arienas
Camasnacroise
Loch a' Choire
879 FRAOCHAIDH
Acharn
739 BEINN MHEADHOIN
KINGAIRLOCH
Gleann Geal
Shuna I.
655
Glen Creran
959 BEINN FHIONNLAIDH
Claggan
Appin House
Glen Stockdale
Elleric
ARDTORNISH GARDENS
Achranich
Loch Tearnait
Rannoch
Loch Aline
437 BEINN A' CHAISIL
Portnacroish
Fasnacloich
An Iola
Invercreran
Glen Ure
KINLOCHLAICH HOUSE GARDENS
BEINN CHURALAIN 546
GLASDRUM WOOD
Glasdrum
937 BEINN SGULAIRD
Glensanda
Loch nan Clach
Appin
Strath of Appin
Creagan
Druimavuic
Port Ramsay
Port Appin
GLAIS BHEINN 479
LYNN OF LORN
AN SLEAGHACH 513
Eignaig
Clachan
Eriska
North Shian
South Creagan
839 BEINN TRILLEACHAN
Allt Easach
Loch Creran
South Shian
Barcaldine
Lismore
B8045
SCOTTISH SEA LIFE SANCTUARY
810 CREACH BHEINN
Abhainn Dalach
Inninmore Bay
Garbh Shlios
Camas Gorm
Achnacroish
Barcaldine Forest
LORN
Scallastle Bay
Rubha an Ridire
Bernera I.
124
Achinduin
Baravullin
BENDERLOCH
Ferlochan
125
Gleann Salach
B845
LOCH ETIVE
Java
Craignure Bay
Kilcheran
Eilean Dubh
Kiel Crofts
Benderloch
Craignure
Ledaig
Achnaba
715 BEINN MHEADHONACH
Ardmucknish Bay
Duart Bay
Duart Pt.
Eilean Musdile
ARDCHATTAN PRIORY GARDENS
ARDCHATTAN PRIORY
Glen Liver
DUART CASTLE
Eilean Mor
North Connel
Black Crofts
FALLS OF LORA
DUNSTAFFNAGE CASTLE
Connel
Achnacloich
ACHNACLOICH GARDEN
Bonawe
Glen Noe
Lochdon
Dunbeg
CASTLEBAY COLL LOCHBOISDALE TIREE
Ganavan
A85
BONAWE IRON FURNACE
INVERAWE FISHERIES AND SMOKERIES EXHIBITION
Brochroy
A849
Loch Don
Dunollie
OBAN LODGE
Black Lochs
Fearnoch Forest
BEN CRUACHAN 1126
Grass Pt.
MCCAIG'S TOWER
OBAN DISTILLERY
Taynuilt
Ichrachan
Bridge of Awe
Pass of Brander
Altnacraig
COLONSAY
Kerrera
Oban
BARGUILLEAN GARDENS
GLEN NANT
Glen Nant
Cruachan Res.
Awe
383
Glenamachrie
Glen Lonan
Falls of Cruachan
897
Loch Spelve
0 1 2 3 4 5 6 miles
0 1 2 3 4 5 6 7 8 9 10 km
Gallanach
Loch Nell
CRUACHAN DAM VISITOR CENTRE
Loch Tromlee
Loch Nant
Barran
Kilbride
Kilmore
515
ARDANAISEIG
B845

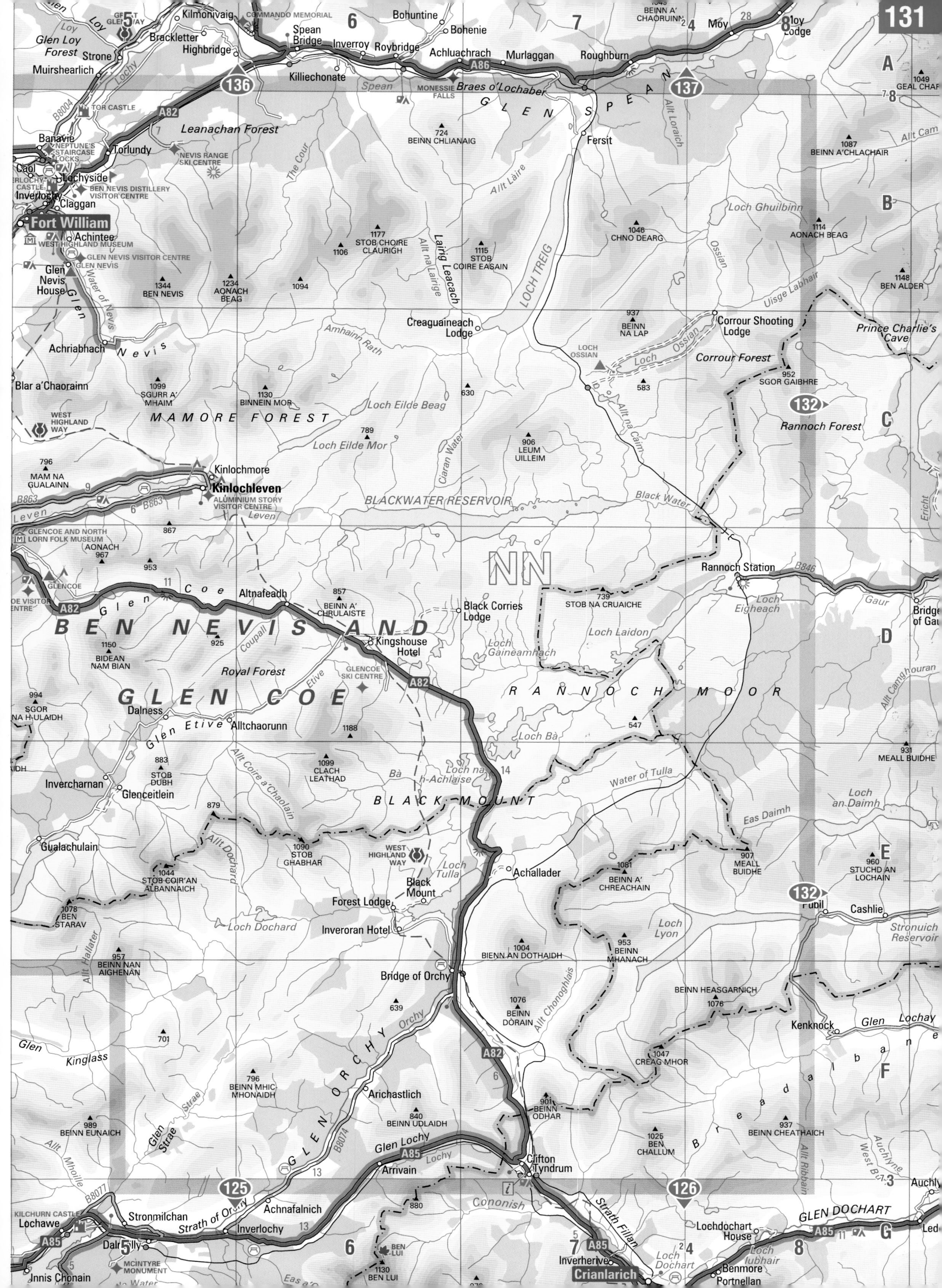

Kilmonivaig
COMMANDO MEMORIAL
Bohuntine
Bohenie
BEINN A' CHAORUINN
Moy
Loy Lodge
Glen Loy Forest
Strone
Brackletter
Highbridge
Spean Bridge
Inverroy
Roybridge
Achluachrach
Murlaggan
Roughburn
Muirshearlich
Killiechonate
A86
136
137
Spean
MONESSIE FALLS
Braes o'Lochaber
GLEN SPEAN
Allt Loraich
GEAL CHAR
TOR CASTLE
B8004
A82
Leanachan Forest
724
BEINN CHLIANAIG
Fersit
1087
BEINN A'CHLACHAIR
Allt Cam
Banavie
NEPTUNE'S STAIRCASE LOCKS
Torlundy
NEVIS RANGE SKI CENTRE
Caol
Lochyside
The Cour
Allt Laire
Inverlochy
BEN NEVIS DISTILLERY VISITOR CENTRE
Claggan
Fort William
Achintee
WEST HIGHLAND MUSEUM
GLEN NEVIS VISITOR CENTRE
GLEN NEVIS
Glen Nevis House
1177
STOB CHOIRE CLAURIGH
1106
Allt na Lairige
Lairig Leacach
1115
STOB COIRE EASAIN
LOCH TREIG
Loch Ghuilbinn
1046
CHNO DEARG
Ossian
1114
AONACH BEAG
1148
BEN ALDER
Water of Nevis
1344
BEN NEVIS
1234
AONACH BEAG
1094
Uisge Labhair
Creaguaineach Lodge
937
BEINN NA LAP
Corrour Shooting Lodge
Prince Charlie's Cave
Achriabhach
Nevis
Amhainn Rath
LOCH OSSIAN
Loch Ossian
Corrour Forest
952
SGOR GAIBHRE
132
Rannoch Forest
Blar a'Chaorainn
1099
SGURR A' MHAIM
1130
BINNEIN MOR
630
583
WEST HIGHLAND WAY
MAMORE FOREST
Loch Eilde Beag
Allt na Cainn
789
Loch Eilde Mor
Ciaran Water
906
LEUM UILLEIM
796
MAM NA GUALAINN
Kinlochmore
Kinlochleven
ALUMINIUM STORY VISITOR CENTRE
B863
Leven
BLACKWATER RESERVOIR
Black Water
Ericht
GLENCOE AND NORTH LORN FOLK MUSEUM
867
AONACH
967
953
NN
Rannoch Station
B846
GLENCOE
Glen Coe
Altnafeadh
857
BEINN A' CHRULAISTE
Black Corries Lodge
739
STOB NA CRUAICHE
Loch Eigheach
Gaur
Bridge of Gaur
A82
BEN NEVIS AND
Coupall
925
Kingshouse Hotel
Loch Laidon
1150
BIDEAN NAM BIAN
Royal Forest
Loch Gaineamhach
GLENCOE SKI CENTRE
Etive
994
SGOR NA H-ULAIDH
GLEN COE
RANNOCH MOOR
Allt Camghouran
Dalness
Glen Etive
Alltchaorunn
1188
547
Loch Bà
931
MEALL BUIDHE
883
STOB DUBH
1099
CLACH LEATHAD
Allt Coire a'Chaolain
Loch na h-Achlaise
Water of Tulla
Invercharnan
Glenceitlein
Bà
BLACK MOUNT
Loch an Daimh
879
Eas Daimh
Gualachulain
Allt Dochard
1090
STOB GHABHAR
WEST HIGHLAND WAY
907
MEALL BUIDHE
960
STUCHD AN LOCHAIN
1044
STOB COIR'AN ALBANNAICH
Loch Tulla
Achallader
1081
BEINN A' CHREACHAIN
Black Mount
Forest Lodge
Pubil
Cashlie
1078
BEN STARAV
Loch Dochard
Inveroran Hotel
Loch Lyon
Stronuich Reservoir
Allt Hallater
957
BEINN NAN AIGHENAN
1004
BIENN AN DOTHAIDH
953
BEINN MHANACH
Bridge of Orchy
Allt Chonoghlais
BEINN HEASGARNICH
1076
639
1076
BEINN DORAIN
Kenknock
Glen Lochay
701
Glen
Kinglass
Orchy
1047
CREAG MHOR
Breadalbane
796
BEINN MHIC MHONAIDH
GLEN ORCHY
Arichastlich
901
BEINN ODHAR
989
BEINN EUNAICH
840
BEINN UDLAIDH
937
BEINN CHEATHAICH
Glen Strae
1025
BEN CHALLUM
Auchlyne
West Burn
Allt Mhoille
B8074
Glen Lochy
A85
Lochy
Clifton
Tyndrum
Arrivain
Allt Ribbain
125
126
KILCHURN CASTLE
B8077
Stronmilchan
Achnafalnich
880
Cononish
Strath Fillan
GLEN DOCHART
Lochawe
Strath of Orchy
Inverlochy
Lochdochart House
A85
Dalmally
MCINTYRE MONUMENT
BEN LUI
Inverherive
Loch Dochart
Loch Iubhair
Innis Chonain
1130
BEN LUI
Crianlarich
Benmore
Portnellan
A
B
C
D
E
F
G
6
7
8

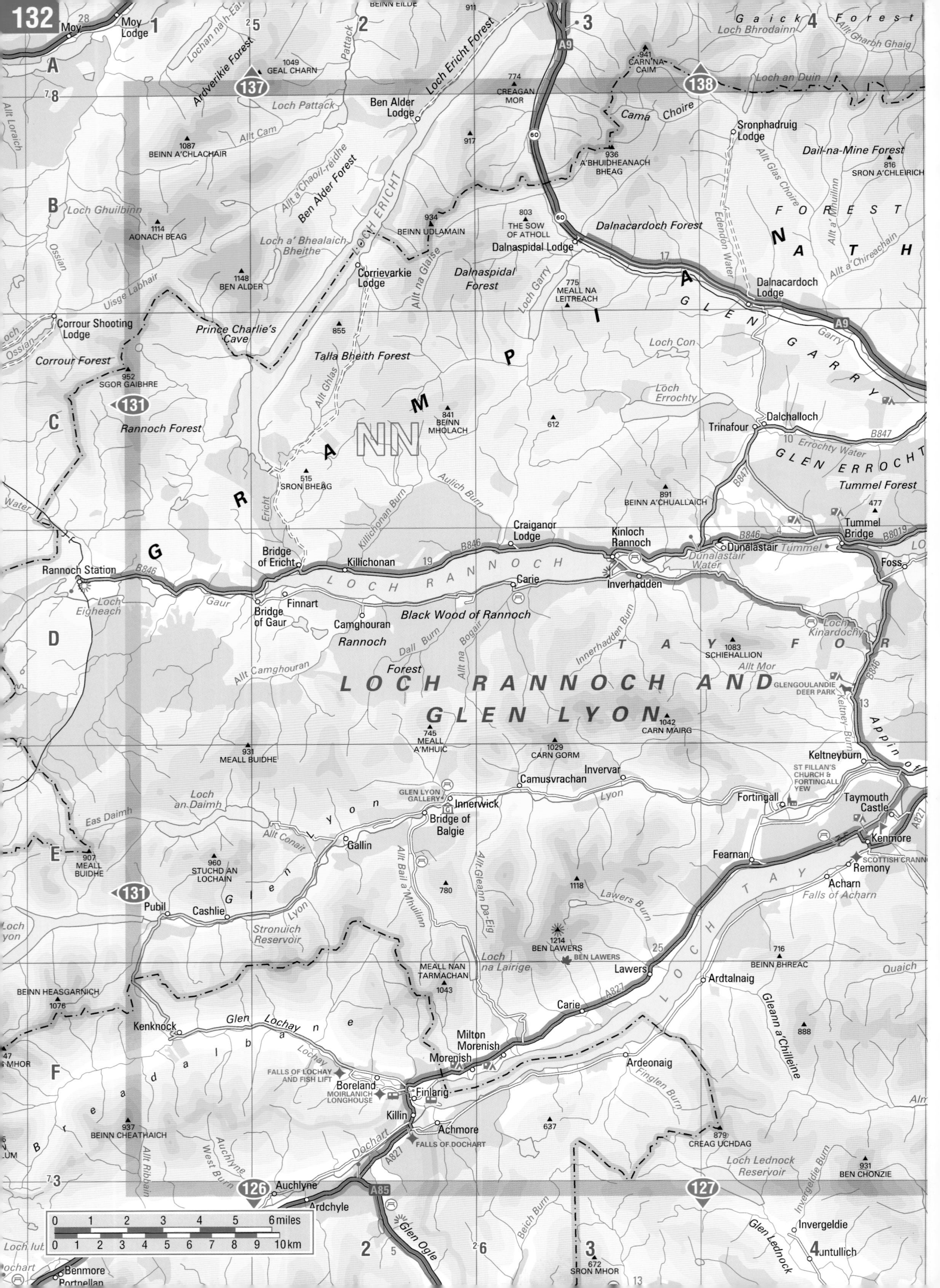
Moy
Moy Lodge
Lochan na h-Earba
Ardverikie Forest
1049
GEAL CHARN
Pattack
Loch Pattack
Loch Ericht Forest
Ben Alder Lodge
911
774
CREAGAN MOR
A9
941
CARN NA CAIM
Gaick Forest
Loch Bhrodainn
Allt Gharbh Ghaig
Loch an Duin
Cama Choire
Sronphadruig Lodge
Dail-na-Mine Forest
816
SRON A'CHLEIRICH
Allt Loraich
1087
BEINN A'CHLACHAIR
Allt Cam
917
936
A'BHUIDHEANACH BHEAG
Allt Glas Choire
Loch Ghuilbinn
1114
AONACH BEAG
Allt a'Chaoil-reidhe
Ben Alder Forest
LOCH ERICHT
934
BEINN UDLAMAIN
803
THE SOW OF ATHOLL
Dalnacardoch Forest
FOREST
Allt a'Mhuillinn
Edendon Water
Allt a'Chireachain
Ossian
Loch a' Bhealaich Bheithe
1148
BEN ALDER
Uisge Labhair
Corrievarkie Lodge
Allt na Glaise
Dalnaspidal Lodge
Dalnaspidal Forest
Loch Garry
775
MEALL NA LEITREACH
17
Dalnacardoch Lodge
GLEN GARRY
Corrour Shooting Lodge
Loch Ossian
Prince Charlie's Cave
855
Talla Bheith Forest
Loch Con
Corrour Forest
952
SGOR GAIBHRE
GRAMPIAN MOUNTAINS
Loch Errochty
Allt Ghlas
841
BEINN MHOLACH
612
Rannoch Forest
Dalchalloch
Trinafour
B847
Errochty Water
GLEN ERROCHTY
515
SRON BHEAG
Aulich Burn
Killichonan Burn
891
BEINN A'CHUALLAICH
Tummel Forest
477
Water
Ericht
Craiganor Lodge
Kinloch Rannoch
Tummel Bridge
B8019
Bridge of Ericht
B846
Killichonan
19
LOCH RANNOCH
Dunalastair
Dunalastair Water
Tummel
Foss
Rannoch Station
Carie
Inverhadden
Loch Eigheach
Gaur
Bridge of Gaur
Finnart
Camghouran
Black Wood of Rannoch
Loch Kinardochy
Rannoch
Dall Burn
Allt na Bogair
Innerhadden Burn
TAY FOREST
1083
SCHIEHALLION
Allt Mor
Allt Camghouran
Forest
LOCH RANNOCH AND GLEN LYON
GLENGOULANDIE DEER PARK
B846
13
Keltney Burn
1042
CARN MAIRG
745
MEALL A'MHUIC
931
MEALL BUIDHE
1029
CARN GORM
Appin of
Keltneyburn
Invervar
Camusvrachan
ST FILLAN'S CHURCH & FORTINGALL YEW
Loch an Daimh
GLEN LYON GALLERY
Innerwick
Lyon
Fortingall
Taymouth Castle
Eas Daimh
Bridge of Balgie
Allt Conait
Gallin
Kenmore
A827
907
MEALL BUIDHE
960
STUCHD AN LOCHAIN
Glen Lyon
Allt Bail a'Mhuilinn
Allt Gleann Da-Eig
Fearnan
SCOTTISH CRANNOG
Remony
LOCH TAY
780
1118
Acharn
Falls of Acharn
Pubil
Cashlie
Lawers Burn
Loch Lyon
Stronuich Reservoir
1214
BEN LAWERS
Loch na Lairige
25
MEALL NAN TARMACHAN
716
BEINN BHREAC
Quaich
Lawers
Ardtalnaig
BEINN HEASGARNICH
1076
1043
Gleann a'Chilleine
Carie
Kenknock
Glen Lochay
Breadalbane
888
Milton Morenish
Morenish
Ardeonaig
FALLS OF LOCHAY AND FISH LIFT
Boreland
MOIRLANICH LONGHOUSE
Finlarig
Finglen Burn
Killin
Achmore
937
BEINN CHEATHAICH
Allt Ribhain
Auchlyne West Burn
Dochart
FALLS OF DOCHART
637
879
CREAG UCHDAG
Loch Lednock Reservoir
Invergeldie Burn
931
BEN CHONZIE
A827
Auchlyne
Ardchyle
A85
Glen Ogle
Beich Burn
Glen Lednock
Invergeldie
Comrie
Loch Iubhair
Dochart
Benmore
Portnellan
672
SRON MHOR
0 1 2 3 4 5 6 miles
0 1 2 3 4 5 6 7 8 9 10 km
137
138
131
126
127
A B C D E F
1 2 3 4

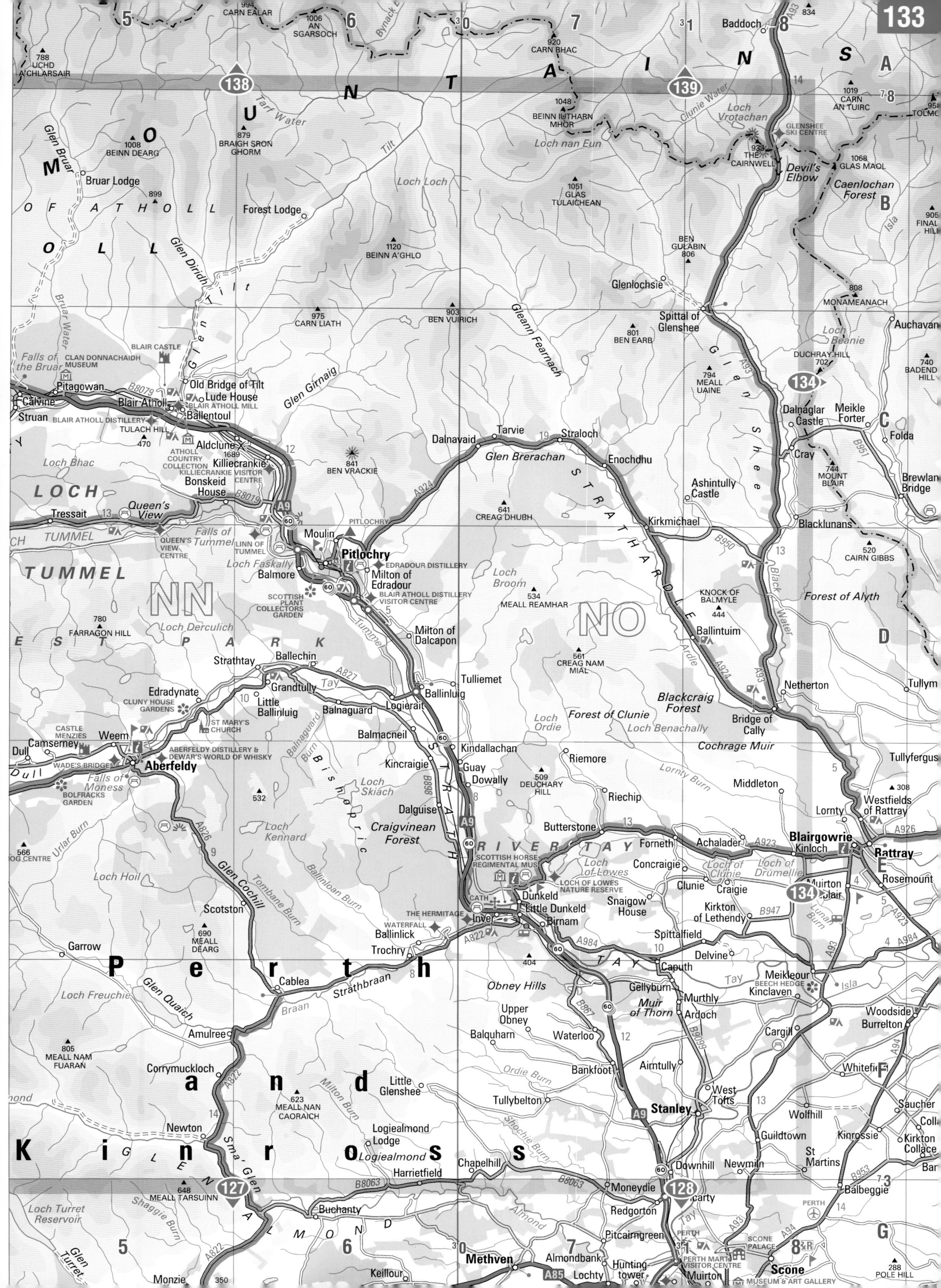
CARN EALAR
AN SGARSOCH
CARN BHAC
Baddoch
UCHD A'CHLARSAIR
138
139
M O U N T A I N S
CARN AN TUIRC
Tarf Water
BEINN IUTHARN MHOR
Clunie Water
Loch Vrotachan
GLENSHEE SKI CENTRE
Glen Bruar
BEINN DEARG
BRAIGH SRON GHORM
Loch nan Eun
THE CAIRNWELL
GLAS MAOL
Bruar Lodge
Tilt
Devil's Elbow
Caenlochan Forest
Loch Loch
GLAS TULAICHEAN
FOREST OF ATHOLL
Forest Lodge
Isla
FINAL HILL
BEINN A'GHLO
BEN GULABIN
Glen Diridh
Glen Tilt
Glenlochsie
MONAMEANACH
CARN LIATH
BEN VUIRICH
Gleann Fearnach
Spittal of Glenshee
Auchavan
BEN EARB
Loch Beanie
Bruar Water
BLAIR CASTLE
Falls of the Bruar
CLAN DONNACHAIDH MUSEUM
DUCHRAY HILL
BADEND HILL
Glen Girnaig
MEALL UAINE
134
Glen Shee
Pitagowan
Old Bridge of Tilt
Lude House
Calvine
Blair Atholl
BLAIR ATHOLL MILL
Struan
Ballentoul
BLAIR ATHOLL DISTILLERY
TULACH HILL
Dalnaglar Castle
Meikle Forter
Tarvie
Straloch
Dalnavaid
Folda
Aldclune
ATHOLL COUNTRY COLLECTION
Killiecrankie
KILLIECRANKIE VISITOR CENTRE
BEN VRACKIE
Glen Brerachan
Enochdhu
Cray
MOUNT BLAIR
Brewlands Bridge
Loch Bhac
LOCH TUMMEL
Bonskeid House
A924
STRATHARDLE
Ashintully Castle
Queen's View
Tressait
CREAG DHUBH
Kirkmichael
Blacklunans
QUEEN'S VIEW CENTRE
Falls of Tummel
LINN OF TUMMEL
PITLOCHRY
Moulin
Pitlochry
EDRADOUR DISTILLERY
B950
CAIRN GIBBS
Loch Faskally
Balmore
Milton of Edradour
Loch Broom
Black Water
SCOTTISH PLANT COLLECTORS GARDEN
BLAIR ATHOLL DISTILLERY VISITOR CENTRE
MEALL REAMHAR
KNOCK OF BALMYLE
Forest of Alyth
NN
NO
FARRAGON HILL
Loch Derculich
Tummel
TAY FOREST PARK
Milton of Dalcapon
Ballintuim
CREAG NAM MIAL
Ardle
Strathtay
Ballechin
A827
Tulliemet
Netherton
Tullymurdoch
Edradynate
Grandtully
Tay
CLUNY HOUSE GARDENS
Little Ballinluig
Balnaguard
Logierait
Ballinluig
Blackcraig Forest
Loch Ordie
Forest of Clunie
Loch Benachally
Bridge of Cally
CASTLE MENZIES
ST MARY'S CHURCH
Weem
Balmacneil
Dull
Camserney
ABERFELDY DISTILLERY & DEWAR'S WORLD OF WHISKY
Kindallachan
Riemore
Cochrage Muir
Tullyfergus
WADE'S BRIDGE
Aberfeldy
Balnaguard Burn
Bishopric
Kincraigie
Guay
Lornty Burn
Falls of Moness
Dowally
DEUCHARY HILL
Middleton
BOLFRACKS GARDEN
Loch Skiach
B898
STRATH TAY
Riechip
Westfields of Rattray
Dalguise
Lornty
Craigvinean Forest
Loch Kennard
Urlar Burn
A826
Butterstone
A926
RIVER TAY
Forneth
Achalader
A923
Blairgowrie
Kinloch
Rattray
SCOTTISH HORSE REGIMENTAL MUS
Loch of Lowes
Concraigie
Loch of Clunie
Loch of Drumellie
Loch Hoil
Glen Cochill
LOCH OF LOWES NATURE RESERVE
Clunie
Craigie
Rosemount
Tombane Burn
Ballinloan Burn
Dunkeld
Little Dunkeld
Snaigow House
Kirkton of Lethendy
B947
Scotston
THE HERMITAGE
Inver
Birnam
WATERFALL
Ballinlick
A822
A984
Spittalfield
MEALL DEARG
Garrow
Trochry
Delvine
Caputh
Perth and Kinross
Glen Quaich
Cablea
Strathbraan
Obney Hills
Gellyburn
Meikleour
Loch Freuchie
Braan
Murthly
BEECH HEDGE
Kinclaven
Isla
Upper Obney
Muir of Thorn
Ardoch
Amulree
B867
Woodside
Burrelton
Balquharn
Waterloo
Cargill
B9099
A94
MEALL NAM FUARAN
Ordie Burn
Corrymuckloch
Airntully
Whitefield
Bankfoot
Little Glenshee
West Tofts
Milton Burn
MEALL NAN CAORAICH
Tullybelton
Stanley
Saucher
Wolfhill
Shochie Burn
Newton
Logiealmond Lodge
Collace
Kinrossie
Guildtown
Kirkton of Collace
GLEN ALMOND
Sma' Glen
Logiealmond
St Martins
Chapelhill
Downhill
Newmiln
Harrietfield
B8063
B953
MEALL TARSUINN
127
Moneydie
128
Balbeggie
Loch Turret Reservoir
Shaggie Burn
Buchanty
Redgorton
Almond
PERTH
Glen Turret
Pitcairngreen
SCONE PALACE
Methven
Almondbank
PERTH MART VISITOR CENTRE
Scone
Huntingtower
POLE HILL
Monzie
Keillour
A85
Lochty
Muirton
MUSEUM & ART GALLERY

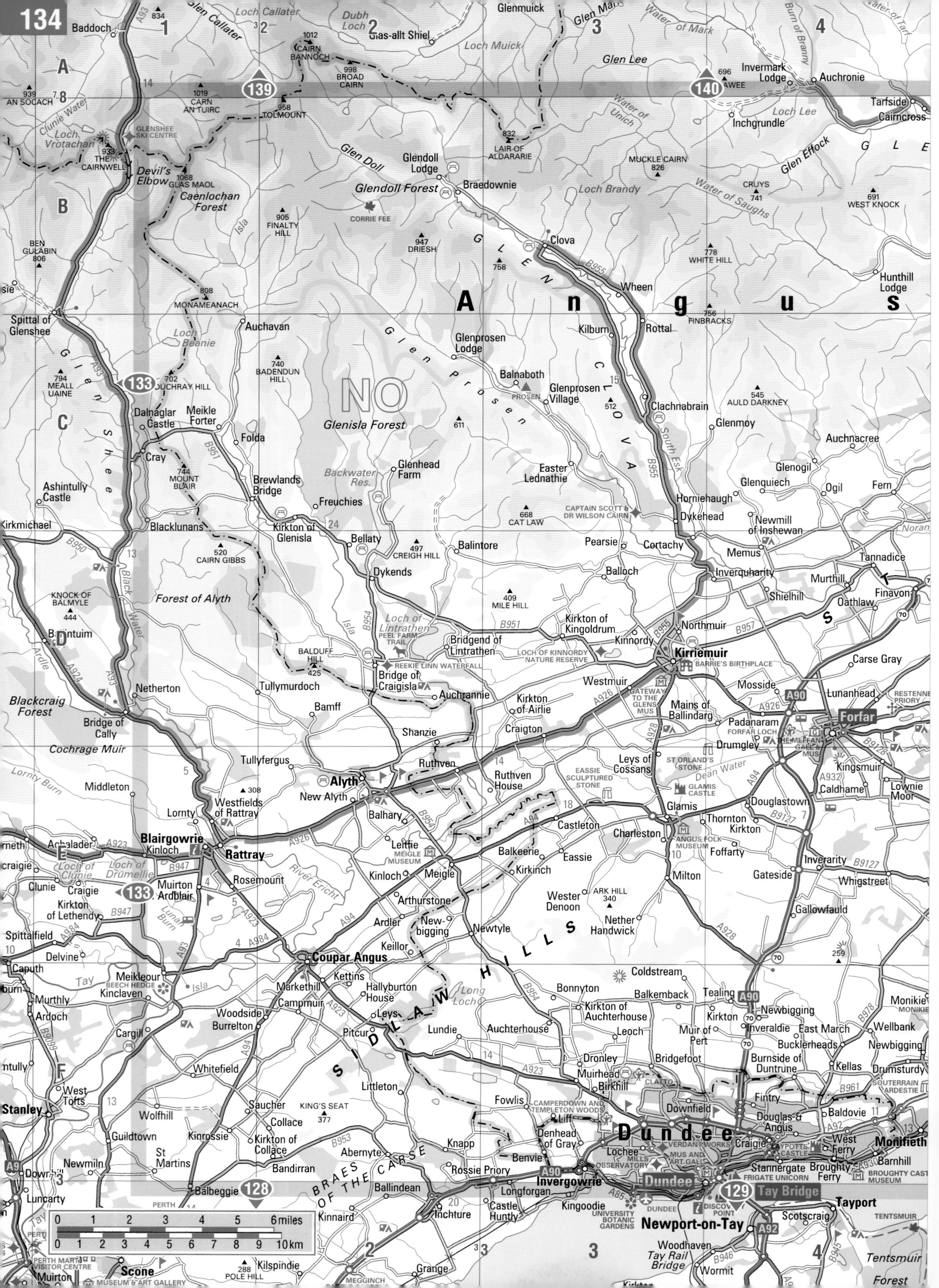
Baddoch
Glen Callater
Loch Callater
Dubh Loch
Glas-allt Shiel
Glenmuick
Loch Muick
Glen Lee
Water of Mark
Burn of Branny
Invermark Lodge
Auchronie
1012 CAIRN BANNOCH
998 BROAD CAIRN
139
140
939 AN SOCACH
1019 CARN AN TUIRC
958 TOLMOUNT
Clunie Water
Loch Vrotachan
GLENSHEE SKI CENTRE
933 THE CAIRNWELL
Devil's Elbow
1068 GLAS MAOL
Caenlochan Forest
832 LAIR OF ALDARARIE
Glen Doll
Glendoll Lodge
Glendoll Forest
Braedownie
CORRIE FEE
Water of Unich
Inchgrundle
Loch Lee
Tarfside
Cairncross
Glen Effock
MUCKLE CAIRN 826
Loch Brandy
Water of Saughs
CRUYS 741
691 WEST KNOCK
905 FINALTY HILL
947 DRIESH
758
Clova
778 WHITE HILL
Hunthill Lodge
BEN GULABIN 806
808 MONAMEANACH
Spittal of Glenshee
Glen Shee
Loch Beanie
Auchavan
740 BADENDUN HILL
Angus
Wheen
Kilburn
Rottal
756 FINBRACKS
Glenprosen Lodge
Glen Prosen
Balnaboth
Glenprosen Village
794 MEALL UAINE
133
702 DUCHRAY HILL
NO
Glenisla Forest
611
512
Clachnabrain
545 AULD DARKNEY
Glenmoy
Auchnacree
Dalnaglar Castle
Meikle Forter
Folda
Cray
744 MOUNT BLAIR
B951
Backwater Res.
Glenhead Farm
Easter Lednathie
Glen Clova
South Esk
B955
Glenogil
Glenquiech
Ogil
Fern
Ashintully Castle
Brewlands Bridge
Freuchies
668 CAT LAW
CAPTAIN SCOTT & DR WILSON CAIRN
Horniehaugh
Dykehead
Newmill of Inshewan
Kirkmichael
Blacklunans
Kirkton of Glenisla
Bellaty
497 CREIGH HILL
Balintore
Pearsie
Cortachy
Memus
Tannadice
B950
520 CAIRN GIBBS
Dykends
Balloch
Inverquharity
Murthill
Finavon
Black Water
Forest of Alyth
409 MILE HILL
Shielhill
Oathlaw
KNOCK OF BALMYLE 444
Isla
B954
Loch of Lintrathen
PEEL FARM TRAIL
Bridgend of Lintrathen
Kirkton of Kingoldrum
Kinnordy
Northmuir
B957
Ardle
A924
A93
BALDUFF HILL 425
REEKIE LINN WATERFALL
LOCH OF KINNORDY NATURE RESERVE
Kirriemuir
BARRIE'S BIRTHPLACE
Carse Gray
Netherton
Tullymurdoch
Bridge of Craigisla
Auchrannie
Westmuir
GATEWAY TO THE GLENS MUS
Mosside
Lunanhead
RESTENNETH PRIORY
Blackcraig Forest
Bridge of Cally
Bamff
Kirkton of Airlie
A926
Mains of Ballindarg
Padanaram
A90
Forfar
FORFAR LOCH
Cochrage Muir
Shanzie
Craigton
A928
Drumgley
THE MEFFAN GALLERY & MUS
Kingsmuir
B9128
Lornty Burn
Tullyfergus
Ruthven
Ruthven House
Leys of Cossans
ST ORLAND'S STONE
EASSIE SCULPTURED STONE
Dean Water
A94
A932
Middleton
308
Alyth
New Alyth
GLAMIS CASTLE
Caldhame
Lownie Moor
Lornty
Westfields of Rattray
Balhary
Castleton
Glamis
Douglastown
Thornton
Kirkton
Charleston
B9127
Blairgowrie
Rattray
Kinloch
Achalader
A923
B947
Loch of Clunie
Loch of Drumellie
Leitfie
MEIGLE MUSEUM
Balkeerie
Eassie
ANGUS FOLK MUSEUM
Foffarty
Inverarity
Clunie
Craigie
Muirton of Ardblair
Rosemount
River Ericht
Kinloch
Meigle
Kirkinch
Milton
Gateside
Whigstreet
Kirkton of Lethendy
Lunan Burn
Arthurstone
Wester Denoon
ARK HILL 340
Nether Handwick
Gallowfauld
Spittalfield
A984
Ardler
New-bigging
Newtyle
SIDLAW HILLS
Delvine
Keillor
Coupar Angus
259
Caputh
Meikleour
BEECH HEDGE
Tay
Kinclaven
Murthly
Ardoch
Markethill
Kettins
Hallyburton House
Campmuir
Long Loch
B954
Coldstream
Bonnyton
Balkemback
Tealing
Kirkton of Auchterhouse
Newbigging
Monikie
Woodside
Burrelton
Leys
Lundie
Auchterhouse
Leoch
Kirkton
Muir of Pert
Inveraldie
East March
Wellbank
Bucklerheads
Newbigging
Cargill
B9099
Pitcur
Dronley
Bridgefoot
Burnside of Duntrune
Kellas
Drumsturdy
Whitefield
Muirhead
Birkhill
CLATTO
SOUTERRAIN ARDESTIE
Fintry
B961
Littleton
West Tofts
Stanley
Wolfhill
Saucher
KING'S SEAT 377
Collace
Fowlis
CAMPERDOWN AND TEMPLETON WOODS
Downfield
Baldovie
Liff
Douglas & Angus
Guildtown
Kinrossie
Kirkton of Collace
Dundee
Denhead of Gray
Lochee
VERDANT WORKS
MILLS OBSERVATORY
MUS AND ART GALL
Craigie
BROUGHTY CASTLE
West Ferry
Monifieth
Barnhill
Broughty Ferry
Stannergate
FRIGATE UNICORN
Newmiln
Dowrie
St Martins
B953
Abernyte
Knapp
Benvie
Rossie Priory
Bandirran
BRAES OF THE CARSE
A90
Invergowrie
Longforgan
A85
Kingoodie
UNIVERSITY BOTANIC GARDENS
DUNDEE
DISCOVERY POINT
129 Tay Bridge
Tayport
BROUGHTY CASTLE MUSEUM
Balbeggie
128
Ballindean
Luncarty
PERTH
Kinnaird
Inchture
Castle Huntly
Newport-on-Tay
Scotscraig
TENTSMUIR
A92
Tentsmuir Forest
Woodhaven
Tay Rail Bridge
B946
Wormit
B945
PERTH MART VISITOR CENTRE
Scone
MUSEUM & ART GALLERY
Muirton
288 POLE HILL
Kilspindie
Grange
MEGGINCH
0 1 2 3 4 5 6 miles
0 1 2 3 4 5 6 7 8 9 10 km

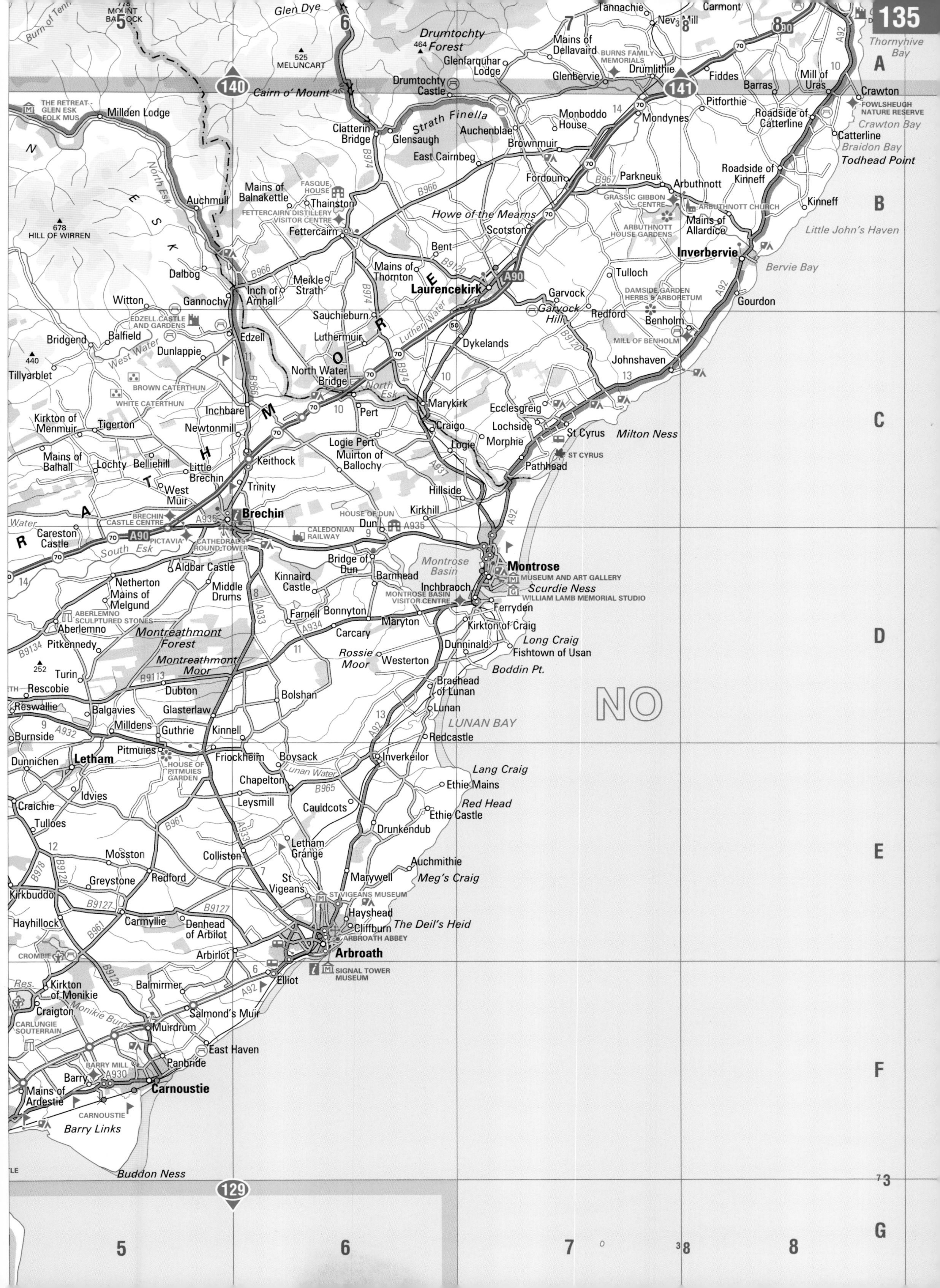

Glen Dye
Drumtochty Forest
Tannachie
Carmont
Thornyhive Bay
Mains of Dellavaird
Burns Family Memorials
Drumlithie
Glenfarquhar Lodge
Glenbervie
Fiddes
Mill of Uras
Barras
Crawton
Fowlsheugh Nature Reserve
Crawton Bay
525 Meluncart
Cairn o' Mount
Drumtochty Castle
Pitforthie
Mondynes
Roadside of Catterline
Catterline
Braidon Bay
Todhead Point
The Retreat Glen Esk Folk Mus
Millden Lodge
Strath Finella
Monboddo House
Clatterin Bridge
Glensaugh
Auchenblae
Brownmuir
East Cairnbeg
Fordoun
Parkneuk
Arbuthnott
Roadside of Kinneff
Kinneff
Grassic Gibbon Centre
Arbuthnott Church
Mains of Allardice
Arbuthnott House Gardens
Little John's Haven
Fasque House
Mains of Balnakettle
Thainston
Fettercairn Distillery Visitor Centre
Fettercairn
Auchmull
678 Hill of Wirren
Howe of the Mearns
Scotston
Inverbervie
Bervie Bay
Bent
Mains of Thornton
Tulloch
Dalbog
Meikle Strath
Inch of Arnhall
Laurencekirk
Damside Garden Herbs & Arboretum
Gourdon
Witton
Gannochy
Garvock
Garvock Hill
Redford
Benholm
Edzell Castle and Gardens
Sauchieburn
Bridgend
Balfield
Edzell
Luthermuir
Luther Water
Dykelands
Mill of Benholm
Johnshaven
West Water
Dunlappie
440
Tillyarblet
North Water Bridge
North Esk
Brown Caterthun
White Caterthun
Inchbare
Pert
Marykirk
Ecclesgreig
Kirkton of Menmuir
Tigerton
Newtonmill
Craigo
Lochside
St Cyrus
Milton Ness
Logie Pert
Logie
Morphie
Mains of Balhall
Lochty
Bellichill
Keithock
Little Brechin
Muirton of Ballochy
Pathhead
West Muir
Trinity
Hillside
Brechin Castle Centre
Brechin
Kirkhill
House of Dun
Dun
Careston Castle
Caledonian Railway
Pictavia
Cathedral & Round Tower
South Esk
Montrose Basin
Montrose
Bridge of Dun
Aldbar Castle
Museum and Art Gallery
Scurdie Ness
Kinnaird Castle
Barnhead
Inchbraoch
William Lamb Memorial Studio
Netherton
Mains of Melgund
Middle Drums
Montrose Basin Visitor Centre
Ferryden
Aberlemno Sculptured Stones
Farnell
Bonnyton
Maryton
Kirkton of Craig
Aberlemno
Montreathmont Forest
Carcary
Pitkennedy
Dunninald
Long Craig
Fishtown of Usan
252
Montreathmont Moor
Rossie Moor
Westerton
Boddin Pt.
Turin
Braehead of Lunan
Rescobie
Dubton
Bolshan
NO
Reswallie
Balgavies
Glasterlaw
Lunan
Milldens
Guthrie
Kinnell
LUNAN BAY
Burnside
Redcastle
Pitmuies
Dunnichen
Letham
House of Pitmuies Garden
Friockheim
Boysack
Inverkeilor
Lang Craig
Lunan Water
Chapelton
Ethie Mains
Idvies
Craichie
Leysmill
Cauldcots
Red Head
Ethie Castle
Tulloes
Drunkendub
Letham Grange
Mosston
Colliston
Auchmithie
Greystone
Redford
St Vigeans
Marywell
Meg's Craig
Kirkbuddo
St Vigeans Museum
Hayshead
Carnyllie
Denhead of Arbilot
The Deil's Heid
Hayhillock
Cliffburn
Arbroath Abbey
Crombie
Arbirlot
Arbroath
Signal Tower Museum
Elliot
Kirkton of Monikie
Balmirmer
Salmond's Muir
Craigton
Monikie Burn
Carlungie Souterrain
Muirdrum
East Haven
Barry Mill
Panbride
Barry
Carnoustie
Mains of Ardestie
Barry Links
Buddon Ness

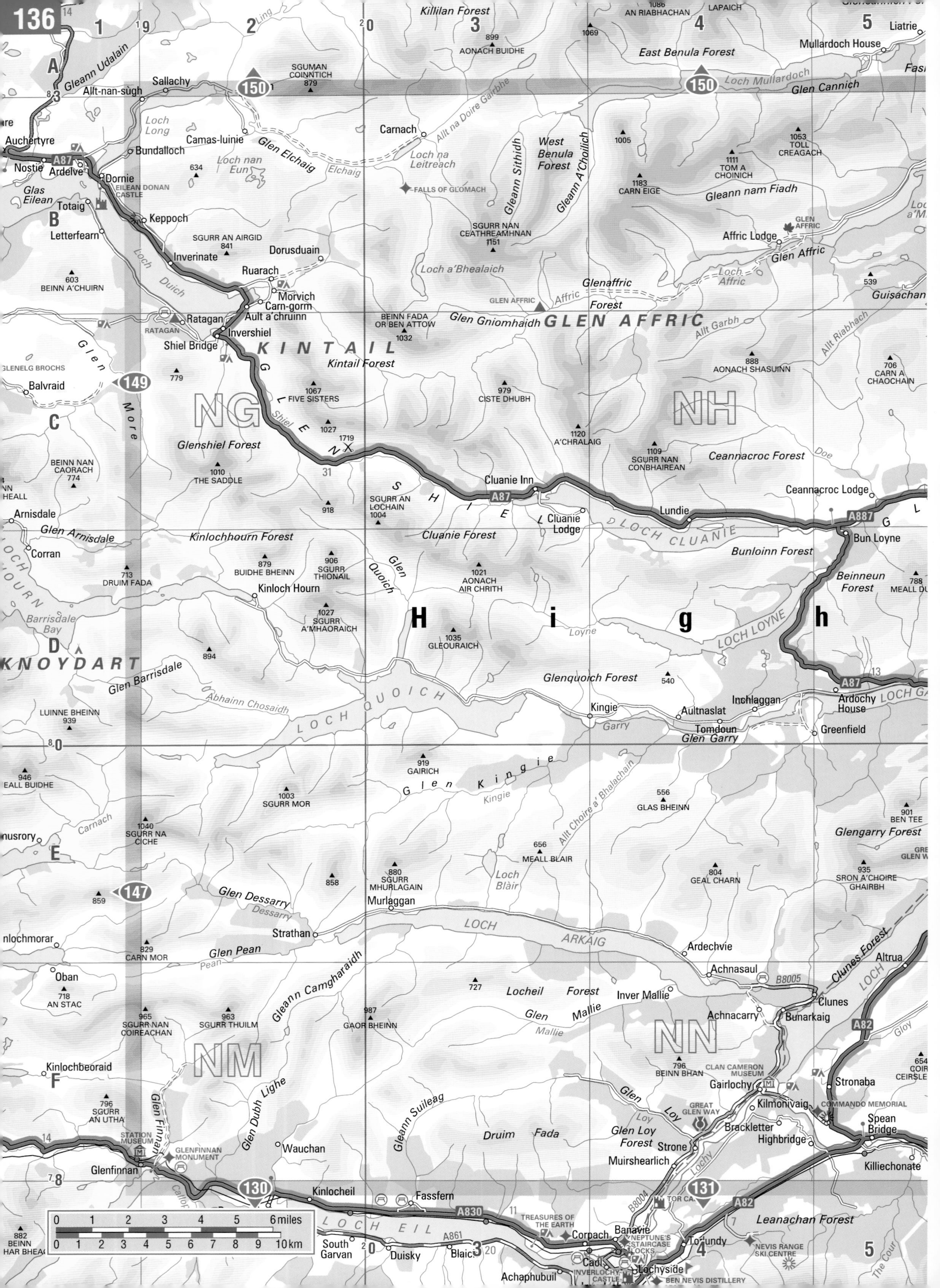

Killilan Forest
AN RIABHACHAN
LAPAICH
Liatrie
AONACH BUIDHE
Mullardoch House
East Benula Forest
Gleann Udalain
Sallachy
SGUMAN COINNTICH
150
Loch Mullardoch
Glen Cannich
Allt-nan-sugh
Allt na Doire Gairbhe
Loch Long
Carnach
West Benula Forest
Gleann Sithidh
Gleann A'Choilich
Auchertyre
Camas-luinie
Glen Elchaig
TOLL CREAGACH
Bundalloch
Loch nan Eun
Loch na Leitreach
A87
Nostie
Ardelve
Dornie
EILEAN DONAN CASTLE
Elchaig
TOM A CHOINICH
CARN EIGE
FALLS OF GLOMACH
Glas Eilean
Totaig
Gleann nam Fiadh
Keppoch
GLEN AFFRIC
Letterfearn
SGURR AN AIRGID
Affric Lodge
SGURR NAN CEATHREAMHNAN
Loch Duich
Inverinate
Dorusduain
Glen Affric
Loch a'Bhealaich
Loch Affric
BEINN A'CHUIRN
Ruarach
Glenaffric Forest
Morvich
Guisachan
Carn-gorm
Ault a'chruinn
Ratagan
RATAGAN
Invershiel
BEINN FADA OR BEN ATTOW
Glen Gniomhaidh
GLEN AFFRIC
Allt Garbh
Allt Riabhach
KINTAIL
Shiel Bridge
Kintail Forest
Glen More
GLENELG BROCHS
149
AONACH SHASUINN
CARN A CHAOCHAIN
Balvraid
FIVE SISTERS
CISTE DHUBH
NG
NH
Glen Shiel
A'CHRALAIG
Glenshiel Forest
SGURR NAN CONBHAIREAN
Ceannacroc Forest
Doe
BEINN NAN CAORACH
THE SADDLE
Cluanie Inn
Ceannacroc Lodge
SGURR AN LOCHAIN
Lundie
A887
Arnisdale
Cluanie Lodge
LOCH CLUANIE
Glen Arnisdale
Kinlochhourn Forest
Cluanie Forest
Bun Loyne
Corran
Bunloinn Forest
BUIDHE BHEINN
SGURR THIONAIL
Glen Quoich
AONACH AIR CHRITH
Beinneun Forest
DRUIM FADA
Kinloch Hourn
Loch Hourn
SGURR A'MHAORAICH
High
Barrisdale Bay
Loyne
LOCH LOYNE
GLEOURAICH
KNOYDART
Glen Barrisdale
Glenquoich Forest
Abhainn Chosaidh
LOCH QUOICH
Kingie
Inchlaggan
Ardochy House
LOCH GARRY
LUINNE BHEINN
Aultnaslat
Garry
Tomdoun
Glen Garry
Greenfield
GAIRICH
Glen Kingie
Kingie
SGURR MOR
GLAS BHEINN
Allt Choire a' Bhalachain
BEN TEE
Carnach
SGURR NA CICHE
Glengarry Forest
MEALL BLAIR
Loch Blàir
SGURR MHURLAGAIN
GEAL CHARN
SRON A'CHOIRE GHAIRBH
147
Glen Dessarry
Dessarry
Murlaggan
Strathan
LOCH ARKAIG
CARN MOR
Glen Pean
Pean
Ardechvie
Clunes Forest
Altrua
Oban
Achnasaul
B8005
AN STAC
Gleann Camgharaidh
Locheil Forest
Inver Mallie
Clunes
Glen Mallie
Mallie
Achnacarry
Bunarkaig
A82
Gloy
SGURR NAN COIREACHAN
SGURR THUILM
GAOR BHEINN
NM
NN
Kinlochbeoraid
BEINN BHAN
CLAN CAMERON MUSEUM
Gairlochy
Stronaba
Glen Dubh Lighe
Glen Finnan
Gleann Suileag
Glen Loy
Kilmonivaig
COMMANDO MEMORIAL
SGURR AN UTHA
GREAT GLEN WAY
Spean Bridge
STATION MUSEUM
Wauchan
Druim Fada
Glen Loy Forest
Brackletter
Highbridge
GLENFINNAN MONUMENT
Strone
Muirshearlich
Killiechonate
Glenfinnan
Loch Lochy
130
Kinlocheil
131
Fassfern
B8004
TOR CASTLE
A830
Leanachan Forest
LOCH EIL
TREASURES OF THE EARTH
Corpach
Banavie
NEPTUNE'S STAIRCASE LOCKS
A861
Tomlundy
NEVIS RANGE SKI CENTRE
South Garvan
Duisky
Blaich
Lochyside
The Cour
BEINN HAR BHEAG
Achaphubuil
Caol
INVERLOCHY CASTLE
BEN NEVIS DISTILLERY
0 1 2 3 4 5 6 miles
0 1 2 3 4 5 6 7 8 9 10 km

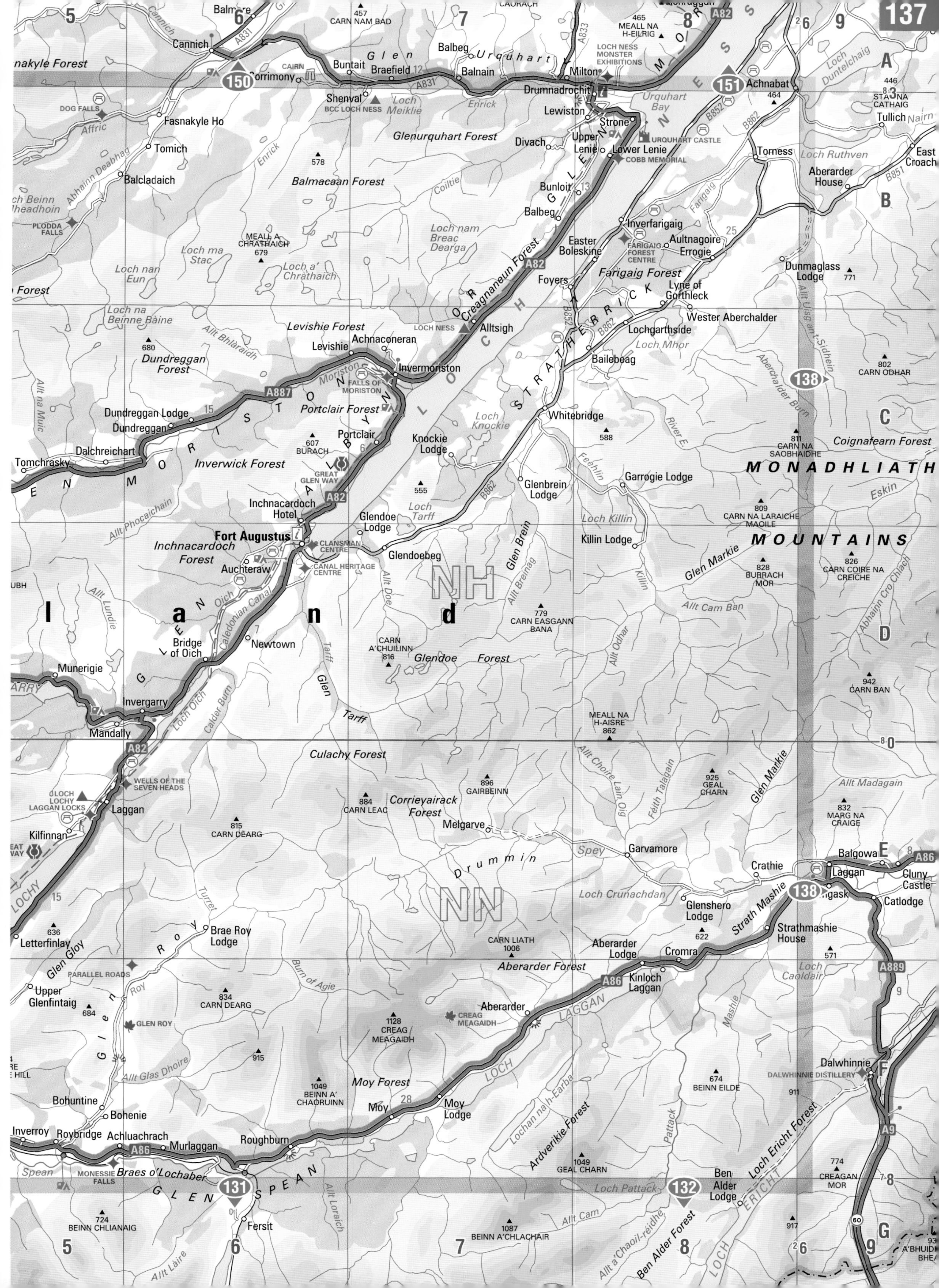

Cannich
Balmore
457 CARN NAM BAD
CAURACH
465 MEALL NA H-EILRIG
A82
A831
A833
Glen Urquhart
Balbeg
Buntait
Braefield
Balnain
Milton
LOCH NESS MONSTER EXHIBITIONS
Drumnadrochit
Achnabat
150
151
CAIRN
Corrimony
Shenval
BCC LOCH NESS
Loch Meiklie
Enrick
Urquhart Bay
Lewiston
Strone
URQUHART CASTLE
Loch Duntelchaig
446
464
STAC NA CATHAIG
Tullich
Nairn
DOG FALLS
Affric
Fasnakyle Ho
Tomich
Glenurquhart Forest
Divach
Upper Lenie
Lower Lenie
COBB MEMORIAL
Torness
Loch Ruthven
East Croachy
Aberarder House
B851
B852
B862
Abhainn Deabhag
Balcladaich
578
Balmacaan Forest
Coiltie
Bunloit
Balbeg
GLEN
Inverfarigaig
Farigaig
Aultnagoire
Errogie
FARIGAIG FOREST CENTRE
Easter Boleskine
PLODDA FALLS
Loch nam Breac Dearga
MEALL A' CHRATHAICH 679
Loch ma Stac
Loch a' Chrathaich
Loch nan Eun
Creagnaneun Forest
Foyers
Farigaig Forest
Lyne of Gorthleck
Dunmaglass Lodge
771
Forest
Loch na Beinne Bàine
Allt Bhlàraidh
680
Dundreggan Forest
Levishie Forest
Levishie
Achnaconeran
LOCH NESS
Alltsigh
Wester Aberchalder
Lochgarthside
Loch Mhor
Bailebeag
Allt Uisg an t-Sidhein
802 CARN ODHAR
138
Aberchalder Burn
Moriston
Invermoriston
FALLS OF MORISTON
A887
Allt na Muic
Dundreggan Lodge
Dundreggan
Portclair Forest
Portclair
LOCH
STRATHERRICK
Loch Knockie
Whitebridge
588
River E.
C
811 CARN NA SAOBHAIDHE
Coignafearn Forest
Tomchrasky
Dalchreichart
Inverwick Forest
607 BURACH
GREAT GLEN WAY
Knockie Lodge
Feehlin
Garrogie Lodge
MONADHLIATH
MORISTON
555
Glenbrein Lodge
Eskin
Allt Phocaichain
Inchnacardoch Hotel
Loch Tarff
Loch Killin
809 CARN NA LARAICHE MAOILE
Fort Augustus
CLANSMAN CENTRE
Glendoe Lodge
Killin Lodge
MOUNTAINS
Inchnacardoch Forest
Glendoebeg
Glen Brein
Glen Markie
826 CARN COIRE NA CREICHE
828 BURRACH MOR
Auchteraw
CANAL HERITAGE CENTRE
NH
Allt Breinag
Killin
Abhainn Cro Chlach
Allt Lundie
Caledonian Canal
Oich
Allt Doe
Highland
779 CARN EASGANN BANA
Allt Cam Ban
D
Bridge of Oich
Newtown
CARN A'CHUILINN 816
Glendoe Forest
Allt Odhar
942 CARN BAN
Munerigie
Invergarry
Mandally
Loch Oich
Calder Burn
Glen Tarff
MEALL NA H-AISRE 862
Culachy Forest
Allt Choire Lain Oig
Féith Talagain
Glen Markie
925 GEAL CHARN
896 GAIRBEINN
884 CARN LEAC
Corrieyairack Forest
Allt Madagain
832 MARG NA CRAIGE
WELLS OF THE SEVEN HEADS
LOCH LOCHY
LAGGAN LOCKS
Laggan
Kilfinnan
815 CARN DEARG
Melgarve
Spey
Garvamore
Crathie
Balgowan
E
A86
Drummin
Laggan
Cluny Castle
Catlodge
NN
Loch Crunachdan
Glenshero Lodge
Strath Mashie
Strathmashie House
636
Letterfinlay
Turret
Brae Roy Lodge
Glen Roy
622
CARN LIATH 1006
Aberarder Lodge
Cromra
571
Aberarder Forest
Loch Caoldair
A889
PARALLEL ROADS
Glen Gloy
Upper Glenfintaig
684
Burn of Agie
834 CARN DEARG
Kinloch Laggan
Roy
GLEN ROY
1128 CREAG MEAGAIDH
CREAG MEAGAIDH
Aberarder
LAGGAN
Mashie
915
Allt Glas Dhoire
LOCH
Dalwhinnie
DALWHINNIE DISTILLERY
F
674 BEINN EILDE
911
1049 BEINN A' CHAORUINN
Moy Forest
Lochan na h-Earba
Bohuntine
Bohenie
Moy
Moy Lodge
Pattack
Loch Ericht Forest
Ardverikie Forest
Inverroy
Roybridge
Achluachrach
Murlaggan
Roughburn
A9
Spean
MONESSIE FALLS
Braes o'Lochaber
1049 GEAL CHARN
774 CREAGAN MOR
GLEN SPEAN
131
132
Loch Pattack
Ben Alder Lodge
ERICHT
Allt Loraich
724 BEINN CHLIANAIG
Fersit
1087 BEINN A'CHLACHAIR
Allt Cam
Allt a' Chaoil-reidhe
Ben Alder Forest
LOCH
917
G
Allt Làire

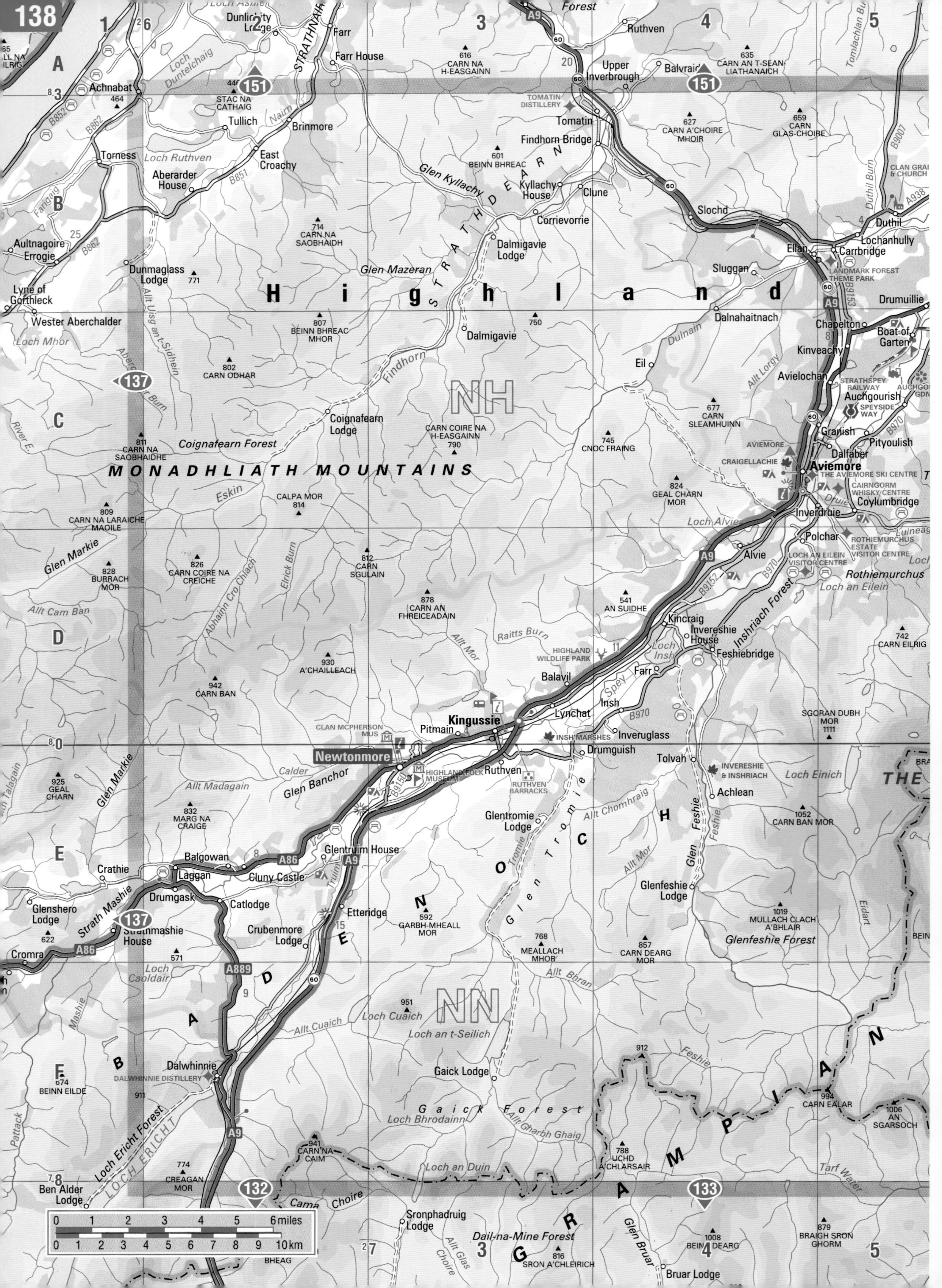
Highland
MONADHLIATH MOUNTAINS
NH
NN
GRAMPIAN
NOCHD
ADBA
Gaick Forest
Dunlichity Lodge
Farr
Farr House
STRATHNAIRN
Loch Duntelchaig
Achnabat
STAC NA CATHAIG
Tullich
Brinmore
Torness
Loch Ruthven
East Croachy
Aberarder House
Aultnagoire
Errogie
Lyne of Gorthleck
Wester Aberchalder
Dunmaglass Lodge
Loch Mhor
Allt Uisg an t-Sidhein
Ruthven
Upper Inverbrough
Balvraid
CARN NA H-EASGAINN
CARN AN T-SEAN-LIATHANAICH
TOMATIN DISTILLERY
Tomatin
Findhorn Bridge
CARN A'CHOIRE MHOIR
CARN GLAS-CHOIRE
BEINN BHREAC
Glen Kyllachy
STRATHDEARN
Kyllachy House
Clune
Corrievorrie
Slochd
CARN NA SAOBHAIDH
Dalmigavie Lodge
Glen Mazeran
Dalmigavie
BEINN BHREAC MHOR
CARN ODHAR
Findhorn
Coignafearn Lodge
Coignafearn Forest
CARN NA SAOBHAIDHE
CARN COIRE NA H-EASGAINN
Eskin
CALPA MOR
CARN NA LARAICHE MAOILE
Glen Markie
BURRACH MOR
CARN COIRE NA CREICHE
Abhainn Cro Chlach
Elrick Burn
CARN SGULAIN
CARN AN FHREICEADAIN
Allt Cam Ban
A'CHAILLEACH
CARN BAN
Allt Mor
Raitts Burn
CNOC FRAING
GEAL CHARN MOR
Eil
Dulnain
Dalnahaitnach
Sluggan
Duthil
Lochanhully
Carrbridge
Ellan
LANDMARK FOREST THEME PARK
Drumuillie
Chapelton
Boat of Garten
Kinveachy
Avielochan
STRATHSPEY RAILWAY
Auchgourish
SPEYSIDE WAY
Granish
Pityoulish
Dalfaber
AVIEMORE
CRAIGELLACHIE
Aviemore
THE AVIEMORE SKI CENTRE
CAIRNGORM WHISKY CENTRE
Coylumbridge
Inverdruie
Loch Alvie
Polchar
ROTHIEMURCHUS ESTATE VISITOR CENTRE
Alvie
LOCH AN EILEIN VISITOR CENTRE
Rothiemurchus
Loch an Eilein
Inshriach Forest
CARN SLEAMHUINN
AN SUIDHE
Kincraig
Invereshie House
Feshiebridge
Loch Insh
HIGHLAND WILDLIFE PARK
Balavil
Farr
Spey
Insh
Lynchat
Kingussie
Pitmain
CLAN MCPHERSON MUS
Newtonmore
INSH MARSHES
Inveruglass
Drumguish
Tolvah
SGORAN DUBH MOR
INVERESHIE & INSHRIACH
Loch Einich
Achlean
Ruthven
RUTHVEN BARRACKS
HIGHLAND FOLK MUSEUM
Calder
Glen Banchor
Allt Madagain
GEAL CHARN
MARG NA CRAIGE
Glentromie Lodge
Allt Chomhraig
Glen Tromie
CARN BAN MOR
Balgowan
Crathie
Laggan
Cluny Castle
Glentruim House
Truim
Allt Mor
Glen Feshie
Glenfeshie Lodge
Drumgask
Catlodge
Strath Mashie
Glenshero Lodge
Strathmashie House
Etteridge
GARBH-MHEALL MOR
MULLACH CLACH A'BHLAIR
Glenfeshie Forest
Eidart
Cromra
Crubenmore Lodge
Loch Caoldair
MEALLACH MHOR
CARN DEARG MOR
Allt Bhran
Mashie
Loch Cuaich
Allt Cuaich
Loch an t-Seilich
Feshie
Dalwhinnie
DALWHINNIE DISTILLERY
BEINN EILDE
Gaick Lodge
CARN EALAR
AN SGARSOCH
Loch Bhrodainn
Allt Gharbh Ghaig
Loch Ericht Forest
LOCH ERICHT
Pattack
CARN NA CAIM
UCHD A'CHLARSAIR
CREAGAN MOR
Loch an Duin
Tarf Water
Ben Alder Lodge
Cama Choire
Sronphadruig Lodge
Dail-na-Mine Forest
Glen Bruar
BEINN DEARG
BRAIGH SRON GHORM
SRON A'CHLEIRICH
Allt Glas Choire
Bruar Lodge
BHEAG
0 1 2 3 4 5 6 miles
0 1 2 3 4 5 6 7 8 9 10 km
A9
A86
A889
A938
B851
B852
B862
B9152
B9153
B970
B9150
B9007
137
151
132
133

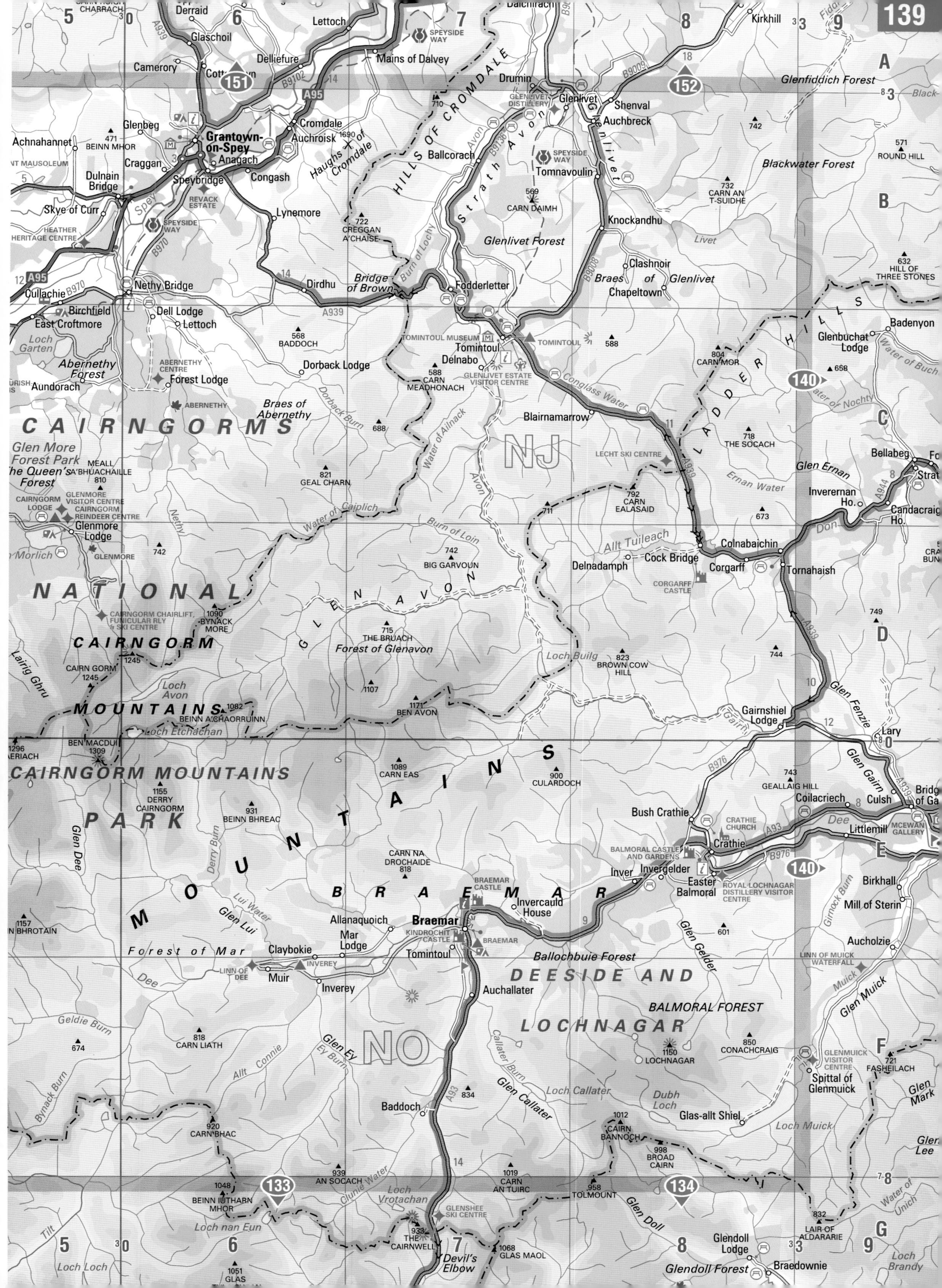

Derraid
Lettoch
SPEYSIDE WAY
Dalchirach
Kirkhill
Glaschoil
Dulliefure
Mains of Dalvey
Camerory
151
B9102
A95
HILLS OF CROMDALE
Drumin
GLENLIVET DISTILLERY
Glenlivet
Shenval
Auchbreck
152
B9009
Glenfiddich Forest
Glenbeg
Achnahannet
471
BEINN MHOR
Grantown-on-Spey
Cromdale
Auchroisk
Haughs of Cromdale
Anagach
Craggan
Ballcorach
Strath Avon
SPEYSIDE WAY
Tomnavoulin
742
571
ROUND HILL
Blackwater Forest
Dulnain Bridge
Speybridge
Congash
569
CARN DAIMH
732
CARN AN T-SUIDHE
Skye of Curr
Spey
REVACK ESTATE
Lynemore
722
CREGGAN A'CHAISE
Knockandhu
HEATHER HERITAGE CENTRE
Glenlivet Forest
Livet
632
HILL OF THREE STONES
A95
B970
Nethy Bridge
Cullachie
Birchfield
Dirdhu
Bridge of Brown
Burn of Lochy
Fodderletter
B9008
Clashnoir
Braes of Glenlivet
Chapeltown
East Croftmore
Dell Lodge
Lettoch
A939
LADDER HILLS
Badenyon
Glenbuchat Lodge
Loch Garten
568
BADDOCH
TOMINTOUL MUSEUM
Tomintoul
TOMINTOUL
588
804
CARN MOR
Water of Buchat
Abernethy Forest
ABERNETHY CENTRE
Forest Lodge
Aundorach
Dorback Lodge
Delnabo
588
CARN MEADHONACH
GLENLIVET ESTATE VISITOR CENTRE
Conglass Water
140
658
Water of Nochty
ABERNETHY
Braes of Abernethy
Dorback Burn
Water of Ailnack
Blairnamarrow
CAIRNGORMS
688
NJ
718
THE SOCACH
Glen More Forest Park
The Queen's Forest
MEALL A'BHUACHAILLE
810
821
GEAL CHARN
LECHT SKI CENTRE
A939
Bellabeg
Glen Ernan
Ernan Water
CAIRNGORM LODGE
GLENMORE VISITOR CENTRE
CAIRNGORM REINDEER CENTRE
Glenmore Lodge
792
CARN EALASAID
711
Inverernan Ho.
A944
Candacraig Ho.
673
Water of Caiplich
Nethy
Burn of Loin
Loch Morlich
GLENMORE
742
742
BIG GARVOUN
Allt Tuileach
Cock Bridge
Delnadamph
Colnabaichin
Corgarff
Tornahaish
Don
CORGARFF CASTLE
NATIONAL
GLEN AVON
1090
BYNACK MORE
CAIRNGORM CHAIRLIFT, FUNICULAR RLY & SKI CENTRE
749
715
THE BRUACH
Forest of Glenavon
CAIRNGORM
Lairig Ghru
CAIRN GORM
1245
1245
Loch Avon
1107
Loch Builg
823
BROWN COW HILL
744
Glen Fenzie
MOUNTAINS
1082
BEINN A'CHAORRUINN
1171
BEN AVON
Gairnshiel Lodge
Gairn
Lary
Loch Etchachan
1296
BRAERIACH
BEN MACDUI
1309
CAIRNGORM MOUNTAINS
1089
CARN EAS
900
CULARDOCH
B976
743
GEALLAIG HILL
Glen Gairn
A939
1155
DERRY CAIRNGORM
931
BEINN BHREAC
PARK
MOUNTAINS
Bush Crathie
CRATHIE CHURCH
Coilacriech
Culsh
Glen Dee
Derry Burn
CARN NA DROCHAIDE
818
BALMORAL CASTLE AND GARDENS
Crathie
A93
Dee
Littlemill
MCEWAN GALLERY
B976
BRAEMAR
BRAEMAR CASTLE
Inver
Invergelder
Easter Balmoral
ROYAL LOCHNAGAR DISTILLERY VISITOR CENTRE
140
Birkhall
Mill of Sterin
Lui Water
Glen Lui
Allanaquoich
Braemar
Invercauld House
Girnock Burn
1157
BEINN BHROTAIN
KINDROCHIT CASTLE
BRAEMAR
601
Glen Gelder
Aucholzie
Forest of Mar
Claybokie
Mar Lodge
Tomintoul
Ballochbuie Forest
LINN OF DEE
INVEREY
Muir
Inverey
DEESIDE AND
LINN OF MUICK WATERFALL
Dee
Auchallater
Muick
Glen Muick
BALMORAL FOREST
Geldie Burn
LOCHNAGAR
674
818
CARN LIATH
Glen Ey
Ey Burn
Allt Connie
NO
Callater Burn
1150
LOCHNAGAR
850
CONACHCRAIG
GLENMUICK VISITOR CENTRE
721
FASHEILACH
Spittal of Glenmuick
Glen Mark
Bynack Burn
834
Glen Callater
Loch Callater
Dubh Loch
Baddoch
A93
Glas-allt Shiel
Loch Muick
920
CARN BHAC
1012
CAIRN BANNOCH
998
BROAD CAIRN
Glen Lee
939
AN SOCACH
1019
CARN AN TUIRC
Glenshee
1048
BEINN IUTHARN MHOR
133
Clunie Water
Loch Vrotachan
958
TOLMOUNT
134
Glen Doll
Water of Unich
GLENSHEE SKI CENTRE
832
LAIR OF ALDARARIE
Tilt
Loch nan Eun
933
THE CAIRNWELL
1068
GLAS MAOL
Glendoll Lodge
Devil's Elbow
Loch Loch
1051
GLAS
Glendoll Forest
Braedownie
Loch Brandy
A
B
C
D
E
F
G
5
6
7
8
9

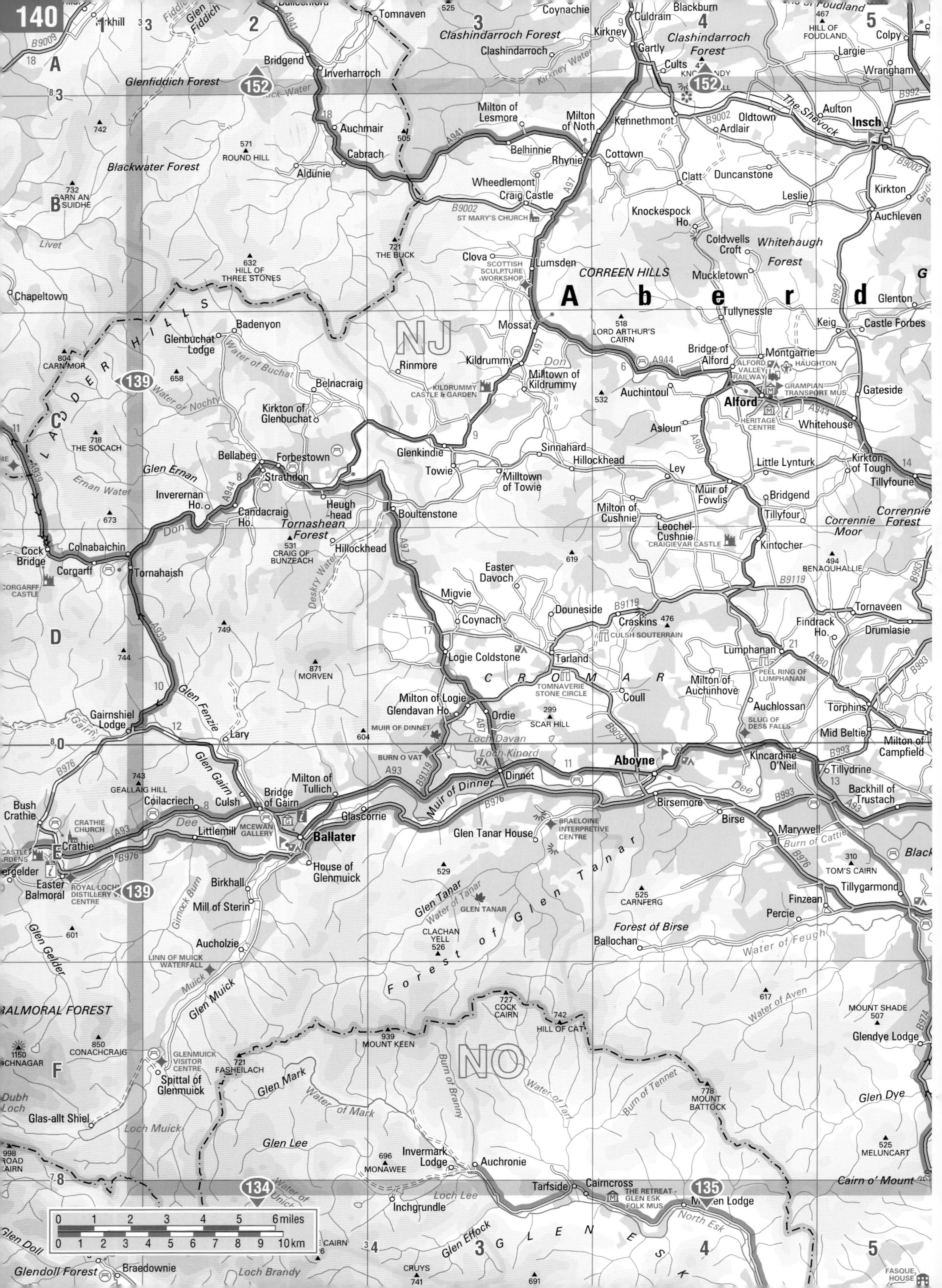
Tomnaven
Coynachie
Culdrain
Blackburn
HILL OF FOULAND
Colpy
Glen Fiddich
Clashindarroch Forest
Kirkney
Gartly
Clashindarroch Forest
Clashindarroch
Largie
Bridgend
Inverharroch
Glenfiddich Forest
Cults
Wrangham
Milton of Lesmore
Milton of Noth
Kennethmont
Oldtown
Aulton
Insch
The Shevock
Auchmair
ROUND HILL
Cabrach
Belhinnie
Rhynie
Ardlair
Cottown
Blackwater Forest
Aldunie
Clatt
Duncanstone
Wheedlemont
Craig Castle
Leslie
Kirkton
CARN AN SUIDHE
ST MARY'S CHURCH
Knockespock Ho.
Auchleven
Livet
THE BUCK
Coldwells Croft
Whitehaugh Forest
HILL OF THREE STONES
Clova
SCOTTISH SCULPTURE WORKSHOP
Lumsden
CORREEN HILLS
Muckletown
Chapeltown
A b e r d
Glenton
LADDER HILLS
Tullynessle
Badenyon
Glenbuchat Lodge
NJ
Mossat
LORD ARTHUR'S CAIRN
Keig
Castle Forbes
CARN MOR
Water of Buchat
Rinmore
Kildrummy
Don
Bridge of Alford
Montgarrie
ALFORD VALLEY RAILWAY
HAUGHTON
Belnacraig
KILDRUMMY CASTLE & GARDEN
Milltown of Kildrummy
Auchintoul
GRAMPIAN TRANSPORT MUS
Gateside
Water of Nochty
Alford
HERITAGE CENTRE
Whitehouse
Kirkton of Glenbuchat
Asloun
THE SOCACH
Glenkindie
Sinnahard
Hillockhead
Kirkton of Tough
Bellabeg
Forbestown
Little Lynturk
Glen Ernan
Strathdon
Towie
Milltown of Towie
Ley
Tillyfourie
Ernan Water
Muir of Fowlis
Bridgend
Inverernan Ho.
Heugh-head
Candacraig Ho.
Boultenstone
Milton of Cushnie
Tillyfour
Corrennie Forest
Tornashean Forest
Corrennie Moor
Leochel-Cushnie
Cock Bridge
Colnabaichin
CRAIG OF BUNZEACH
Hillockhead
CRAIGIEVAR CASTLE
Kintocher
Corgarff
Tornahaish
Deskry Water
BENAQUHALLIE
CORGARFF CASTLE
Easter Davoch
Migvie
Douneside
Tornaveen
Coynach
Craskins
Findrack Ho.
Drumlasie
CULSH SOUTERRAIN
Logie Coldstone
Tarland
Lumphanan
MORVEN
C R O M A R
PEEL RING OF LUMPHANAN
Milton of Auchinhove
Glen Fenzie
TOMNAVERIE STONE CIRCLE
Coull
Milton of Logie
Glendavan Ho.
Ordie
Auchlossan
Torphins
Gairnshiel Lodge
SCAR HILL
SLUG OF DESS FALLS
Lary
MUIR OF DINNET
Loch Davan
Mid Beltie
Milton of Campfield
Gairn
Glen Gairn
BURN O VAT
Loch Kinord
Aboyne
Kincardine O'Neil
Tillydrine
GEALLAIG HILL
Milton of Tullich
Dinnet
Bush Crathie
Coilacriech
Culsh
Bridge of Gairn
Muir of Dinnet
Backhill of Trustach
CRATHIE CHURCH
Dee
MCEWAN GALLERY
Glascorrie
Birsemore
Birse
Crathie
Littlemill
Ballater
Glen Tanar House
BRAELOINE INTERPRETIVE CENTRE
Marywell
Burn of Cattie
Easter Balmoral
House of Glenmuick
TOM'S CAIRN
ROYAL LOCHNAGAR DISTILLERY VISITOR CENTRE
Birkhall
Glen Tanar
Water of Tanar
GLEN TANAR
Tillygarmond
CARNFERG
Finzean
Percie
Mill of Sterin
Girnock Burn
Forest of Glen Tanar
Forest of Birse
Glen Gelder
CLACHAN YELL
Aucholzie
Ballochan
Water of Feugh
LINN OF MUICK WATERFALL
Muick
Glen Muick
Water of Aven
MOUNT SHADE
BALMORAL FOREST
COCK CAIRN
HILL OF CAT
Glendye Lodge
MOUNT KEEN
CONACHCRAIG
LOCHNAGAR
GLENMUICK VISITOR CENTRE
FASHEILACH
NO
Water of Tarf
Burn of Tennet
MOUNT BATTOCK
Spittal of Glenmuick
Glen Mark
Burn of Branny
Water of Mark
Glen Dye
Dubh Loch
Glas-allt Shiel
Loch Muick
Glen Lee
MELUNCART
Invermark Lodge
Auchronie
MONAWEE
Cairn o' Mount
Tarfside
Cairncross
THE RETREAT GLEN ESK FOLK MUS
Inchgrundle
Loch Lee
Millden Lodge
North Esk
Glen Doll
Glen Effock
G L E N E S K
Glendoll Forest
Braedownie
Loch Brandy
CRUYS
FASQUE HOUSE
0 1 2 3 4 5 6 miles
0 1 2 3 4 5 6 7 8 9 10 km
A93
A97
A939
A944
A941
A980
B9002
B976
B993
B9119
B9094
152
139
134
135

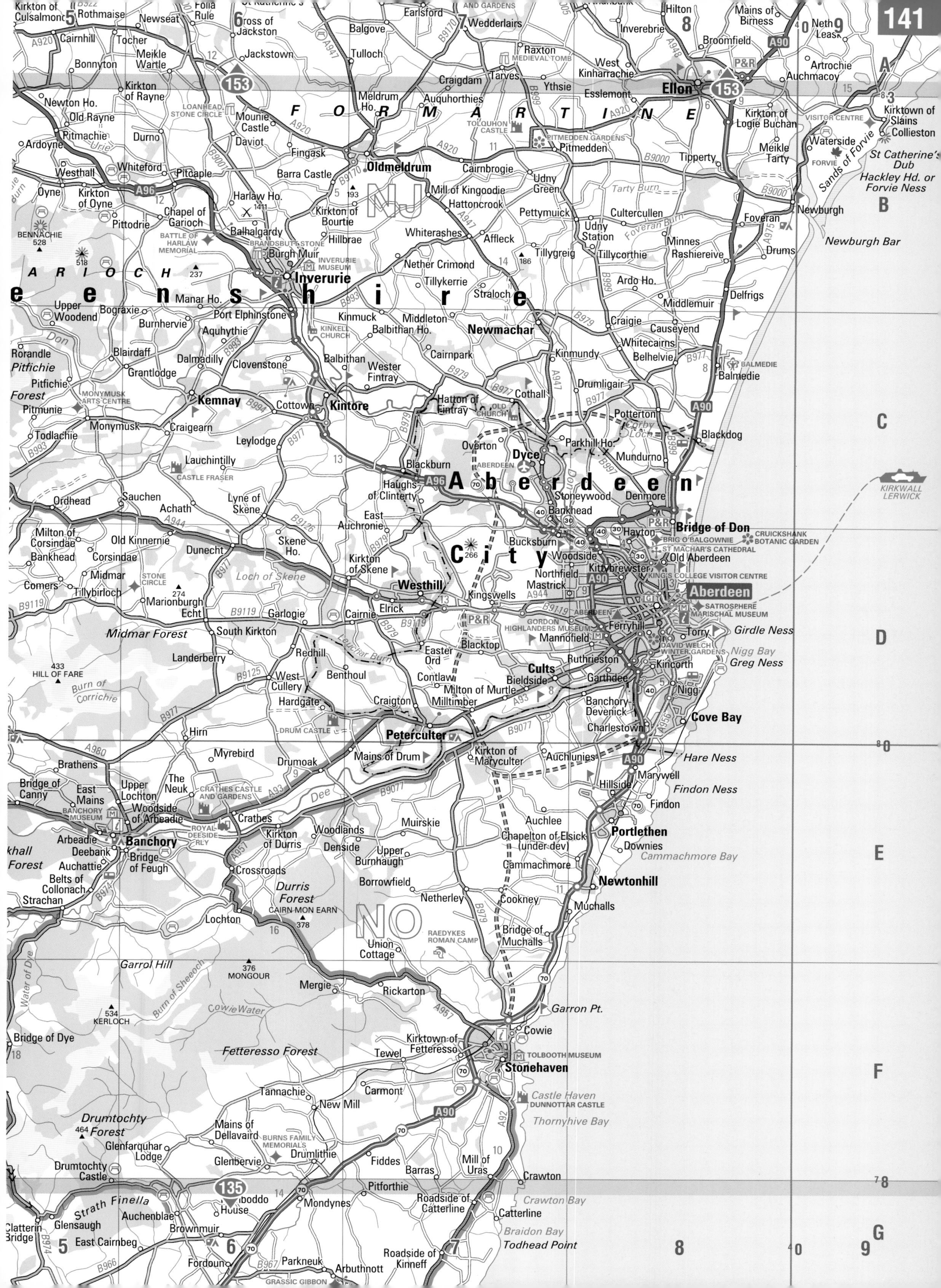
Kirkton of Culsalmond
Rothmaise
Newseat
Folla Rule
Cross of Jackston
Earlsford
Wedderlairs
Hilton
Mains of Birness
Neth Leask
Cairnhill
Tocher
Meikle Wartle
Jackstown
Balgove
Tulloch
Raxton
MEDIEVAL TOMB
Inverebrie
Broomfield
Bonnyton
West Kinharrachie
Artrochie
Auchmacoy
Kirkton of Rayne
Craigdam
Tarves
Ythsie
Esslemont
Ellon
Newton Ho.
LOANHEAD STONE CIRCLE
Meldrum Ho.
Auquhorthies
Old Rayne
F O R M A R T I N E
TOLQUHON CASTLE
Kirkton of Logie Buchan
VISITOR CENTRE
Kirktown of Slains
Collieston
Pitmachie
Durno
Mounie Castle
Daviot
PITMEDDEN GARDENS
Pitmedden
Ardoyne
Fingask
Oldmeldrum
Tipperty
Meikle Tarty
Waterside
FORVIE
Sands of Forvie
St Catherine's Dub
Hackley Hd. or Forvie Ness
Westhall
Whiteford
Pitcaple
Barra Castle
Cairnbrogie
Udny Green
Tarty Burn
Oyne
Kirkton of Oyne
Harlaw Ho.
Mill of Kingoodie
Hattoncrook
Pettymuick
Cultercullen
Foveran
Newburgh
Chapel of Garioch
Pittodrie
Kirkton of Bourtie
Udny Station
Foveran Burn
Minnes
Rashiereive
BENNACHIE
BATTLE OF HARLAW MEMORIAL
Balhalgardy
BRANDSBUTT STONE
Hillbrae
Whiterashes
Affleck
Tillygreig
Tillycorthie
Drums
Newburgh Bar
Burgh Muir
INVERURIE MUSEUM
Nether Crimond
G A R I O C H
Inverurie
Tillykerrie
Ardo Ho.
Delfrigs
Manar Ho.
Straloch
Middlemuir
A b e r d e e n s h i r e
Upper Woodend
Bograxie
Port Elphinstone
Kinmuck
Middleton
Craigie
Causeyend
Burnhervie
Aquhythie
KINKELL CHURCH
Balbithan Ho.
Newmachar
Whitecairns
Rorandle
Pitfichie
Blairdaff
Dalmadilly
Clovenstone
Balbithan
Cairnpark
Kinmundy
Belhelvie
BALMEDIE
Balmedie
Grantlodge
Wester Fintray
Drumligair
Pitfichie Forest
MONYMUSK ARTS CENTRE
Kemnay
Cottown
Kintore
Hatton of Fintray
Cothall
OLD CHURCH
Potterton
Pitmunie
Monymusk
Craigearn
Corby Loch
Blackdog
Todlachie
Leylodge
Overton
Dyce
Parkhill Ho.
Mundurno
Lauchintilly
CASTLE FRASER
Blackburn
ABERDEEN
Haughs of Clinterty
A b e r d e e n
Stoneywood
Denmore
KIRKWALL LERWICK
Sauchen
Ordhead
Achath
Lyne of Skene
Bankhead
Bridge of Don
East Auchronie
Hayton
CRUICKSHANK BOTANIC GARDEN
BRIG O' BALGOWNIE
ST MACHAR'S CATHEDRAL
Milton of Corsindae
Old Kinnernie
Skene Ho.
Bucksburn
C i t y
Woodside
Old Aberdeen
Bankhead
Corsindae
Dunecht
Kirkton of Skene
Kittybrewster
Northfield
KING'S COLLEGE VISITOR CENTRE
Midmar
STONE CIRCLE
Loch of Skene
Mastrick
Aberdeen
Comers
Tillybirloch
Westhill
SATROSPHERE
MARISCHAL MUSEUM
Marionburgh
Elrick
Kingswells
Echt
Garlogie
Cairnie
GORDON HIGHLANDERS MUSEUM
Ferryhill
Midmar Forest
South Kirkton
Mannofield
Torry
Girdle Ness
Redhill
Leuchar Burn
Easter Ord
Blacktop
DAVID WELCH WINTER GARDENS
Nigg Bay
Landerberry
Ruthrieston
Kincorth
Greg Ness
HILL OF FARE
Benthoul
Cults
Burn of Corrichie
West Cullery
Contlaw
Bieldside
Garthdee
Milton of Murtle
Nigg
Hardgate
Craigton
Milltimber
Banchory Devenick
Cove Bay
Charlestown
Hirn
DRUM CASTLE
Peterculter
Myrebird
Kirkton of Maryculter
Auchlunies
Hare Ness
Brathens
Drumoak
Mains of Drum
Maywell
Bridge of Canny
Upper Lochton
The Neuk
CRATHES CASTLE AND GARDENS
Hillside
East Mains
Findon Ness
Findon
BANCHORY MUSEUM
Woodside of Arbeadie
Dee
Crathes
Auchlee
Portlethen
Muirskie
Arbeadie
ROYAL DEESIDE RLY
Kirkton of Durris
Woodlands
Chapelton of Elsick (under dev)
Downies
Banchory
Deebank
Bridge of Feugh
Denside
Upper Burnhaugh
Cammachmore Bay
Auchattie
Crossroads
Cammachmore
Belts of Collonach
Durris Forest
Borrowfield
Newtonhill
Strachan
Netherley
Cookney
Muchalls
CAIRN-MON-EARN
Lochton
RAEDYKES ROMAN CAMP
Bridge of Muchalls
Union Cottage
Garrol Hill
MONGOUR
Water of Dye
Burn of Sheeoch
Mergie
Rickarton
Cowie Water
KERLOCH
Garron Pt.
Cowie
Bridge of Dye
Fetteresso Forest
Kirktown of Fetteresso
Tewel
TOLBOOTH MUSEUM
Stonehaven
Tannachie
Carmont
Castle Haven
DUNNOTTAR CASTLE
New Mill
Drumtochty Forest
Thornyhive Bay
Mains of Dellavaird
BURNS FAMILY MEMORIALS
Glenfarquhar Lodge
Drumlithie
Glenbervie
Fiddes
Mill of Uras
Drumtochty Castle
Barras
Crawton
Pitforthie
Strath Finella
Monboddo House
Mondynes
Roadside of Catterline
Crawton Bay
Auchenblae
Catterline
Glensaugh
Clatterin Bridge
Brownmuir
Braidon Bay
East Cairnbeg
Todhead Point
Parkneuk
Roadside of Kinneff
Fordoun
Arbuthnott
GRASSIC GIBBON
NJ
NO
A
B
C
D
E
F
G

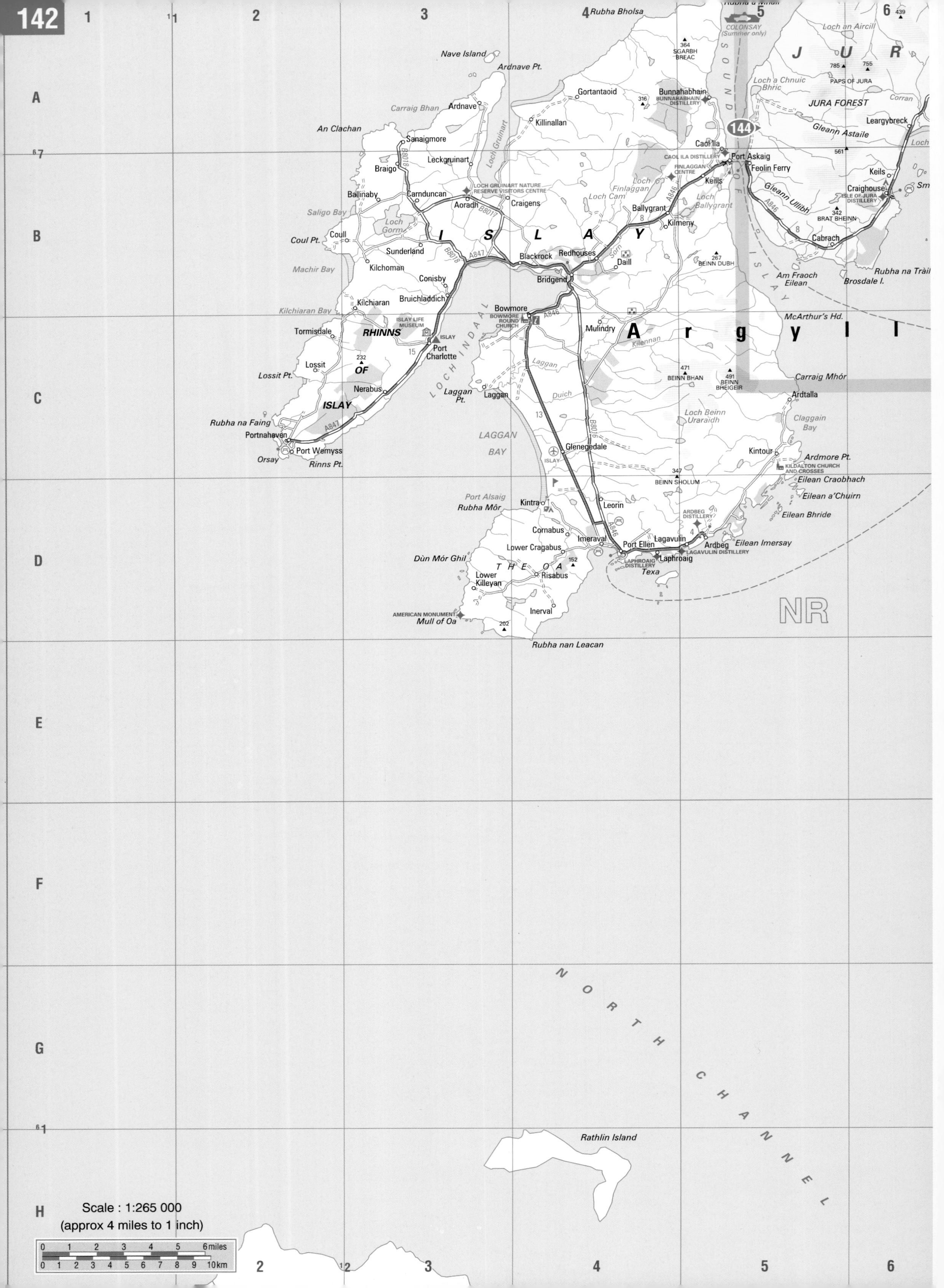

Rubha Bholsa
COLONSAY (Summer only)
SOUND OF ISLAY
J U R
Loch an Aircill
785
755
PAPS OF JURA
Loch a Chnuic Bhric
JURA FOREST
Corran
Leargybreck
Gleann Astaile
561
Keils
Craighouse
ISLE OF JURA DISTILLERY
342 BRAT BHEINN
Gleann Ullibh
A846
Cabrach
Rubha na Tràill
Brosdale I.
Am Fraoch Eilean
McArthur's Hd.
Nave Island
Ardnave Pt.
364 SGARBH BREAC
Bunnahabhain
BUNNAHABHAIN DISTILLERY
144
316
Gortantaoid
Killinallan
Carraig Bhan
Ardnave
An Clachan
Sanaigmore
Loch Gruinart
Caol Ila
CAOL ILA DISTILLERY
Port Askaig
Feolin Ferry
FINLAGGAN CENTRE
Keills
Loch Finlaggan
Loch Cam
Loch Ballygrant
Ballygrant
Kilmeny
Leckgruinart
Braigo
B8018
LOCH GRUINART NATURE RESERVE VISITORS CENTRE
Ballinaby
Carnduncan
Aoradh
B8017
Craigens
Saligo Bay
Loch Gorm
I S L A Y
Coull
Coul Pt.
Sunderland
Machir Bay
Kilchoman
Conisby
A847
Blackrock
Redhouses
Daill
267 BEINN DUBH
Bridgend
Bruichladdich
Kilchiaran
Kilchiaran Bay
ISLAY LIFE MUSEUM
Bowmore
BOWMORE ROUND CHURCH
A846
Mulindry
Tormisdale
RHINNS
ISLAY
Port Charlotte
15
232
OF
ISLAY
Lossit
Lossit Pt.
Nerabus
LOCH INDAAL
Laggan Pt.
Laggan
Laggan
Duich
A r g y l l
Kilennan
471 BEINN BHAN
491 BEINN BHEIGEIR
Carraig Mhór
Ardtalla
Rubha na Faing
Portnahaven
Orsay
Port Wemyss
Rinns Pt.
13
LAGGAN BAY
B8016
Glenegedale
Loch Beinn Uraraidh
Claggain Bay
Kintour
Ardmore Pt.
KILDALTON CHURCH AND CROSSES
Eilean Craobhach
Eilean a'Chuirn
347 BEINN SHOLUM
Port Alsaig
Rubha Mór
Kintra
Leorin
Eilean Bhride
ARDBEG DISTILLERY
Cornabus
Imeraval
Port Ellen
Lagavulin
Ardbeg
Eilean Imersay
LAGAVULIN DISTILLERY
Lower Cragabus
Dùn Mór Ghil
THE OA
152
LAPHROAIG DISTILLERY
Laphroaig
Texa
Lower Killeyan
Risabus
Inerval
AMERICAN MONUMENT
Mull of Oa
202
Rubha nan Leacan
NR
NORTH CHANNEL
Rathlin Island
A
B
C
D
E
F
G
H
1
2
3
4
5
6
Scale : 1:265 000
(approx 4 miles to 1 inch)
0 1 2 3 4 5 6 miles
0 1 2 3 4 5 6 7 8 9 10 km

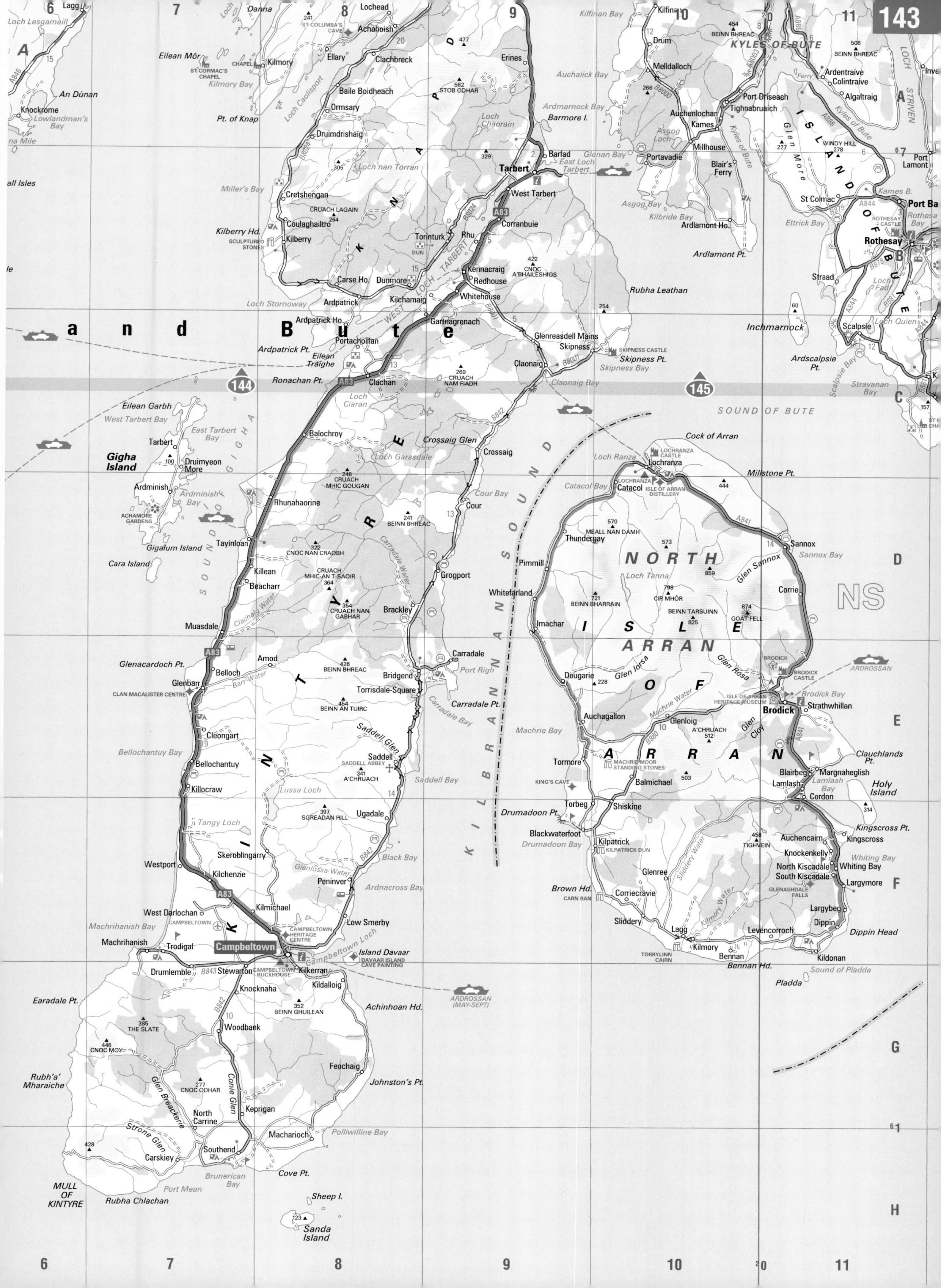
Argyll and Bute
KINTYRE
KNAPDALE
ISLE OF ARRAN
NORTH ARRAN
ISLAND OF BUTE
NS
144
145
Tarbert
West Tarbert
Campbeltown
Brodick
Rothesay
Port Bannatyne
Lamlash
Kilberry
Kennacraig
Redhouse
Whitehouse
Clachan
Tayinloan
Muasdale
Glenbarr
Bellochantuy
Westport
Kilchenzie
Machrihanish
Drumlemble
Stewarton
Kilkerran
Knocknaha
Woodbank
Southend
Carskiey
Machariocl
Keprigan
North Carrine
Feochaig
Saddell
Carradale
Grogport
Cour
Crossaig
Claonaig
Skipness
Lochranza
Catacol
Pirnmill
Imachar
Dougarie
Tormore
Blackwaterfoot
Shiskine
Kilpatrick
Corriecravie
Sliddery
Lagg
Kilmory
Bennan
Kildonan
Dippin
Whiting Bay
Kingscross
Cordon
Blairbeg
Corrie
Sannox
Tighnabruaich
Kames
Millhouse
Portavadie
Ardlamont Ho.
Gigha Island
Cara Island
Sanda Island
Holy Island
Pladda
Inchmarnock
Mull of Kintyre
Kilbrannan Sound
Sound of Bute
Sound of Gigha
Goat Fell 874
Campbeltown Loch
Island Davaar
Ardrossan
Ardrossan (May-Sept)
Kyles of Bute
A83
A841
B842
B843
B8001
B880
A844
6
7
8
9
10
11
A
B
C
D
E
F
G
H

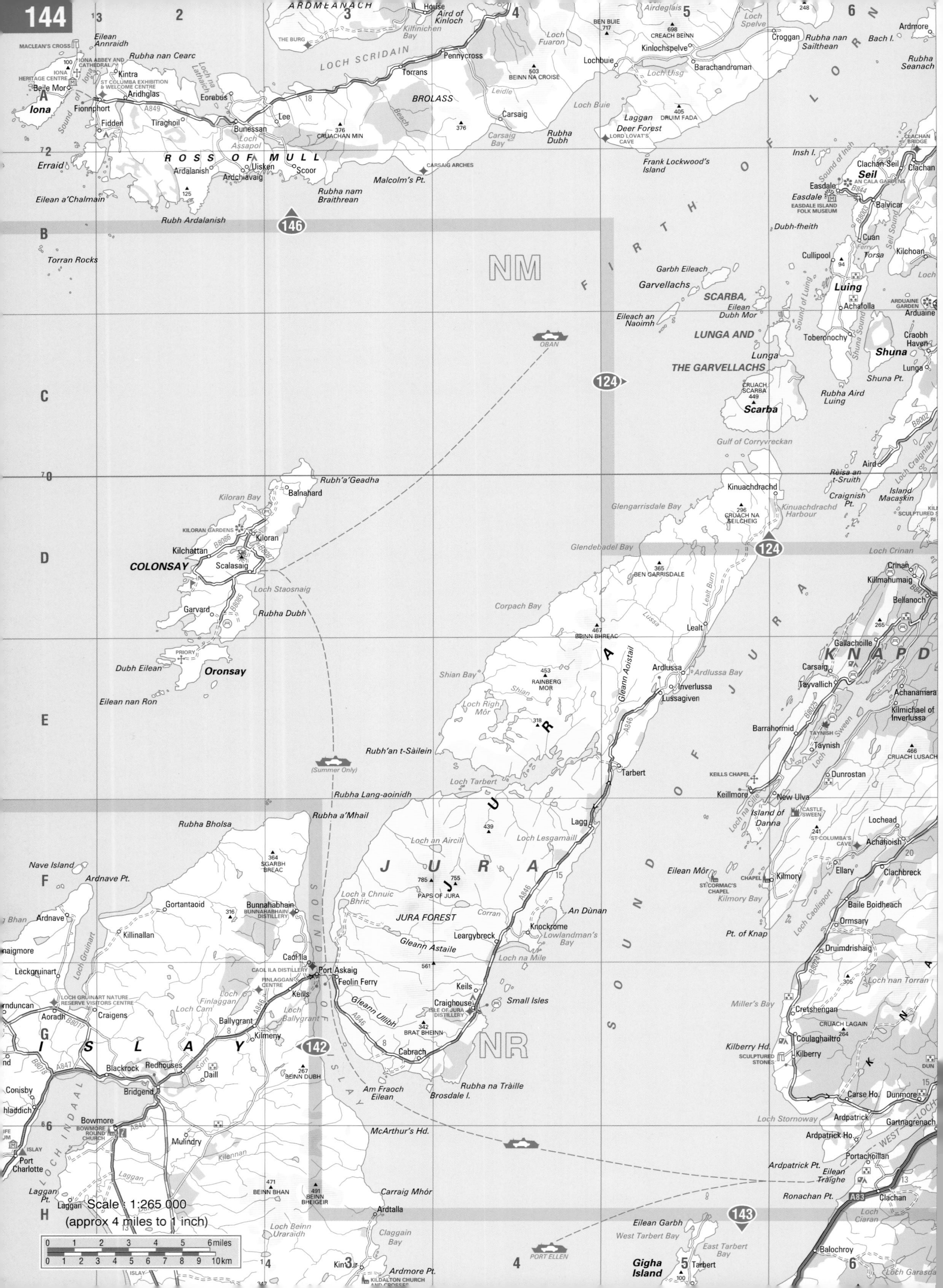
ARDMEANACH
House
Aird of Kinloch
Kilfinichen Bay
THE BURG
LOCH SCRIDAIN
Pennycross
Torrans
BEN BUIE 717
Loch Fuaron
503 BEINN NA CROISE
Airdeglais
698 CREACH BEINN
Loch Spelve
Kinlochspelve
Lochbuie
Loch Uisg
Barachandroman
Croggan
Rubha nan Sailthean
Bach I.
Ardmore
Rubha Seanach
Eilean Annraidh
MACLEAN'S CROSS
IONA ABBEY AND CATHEDRAL
Rubha nan Cearc
IONA HERITAGE CENTRE
Kintra
ST COLUMBA EXHIBITION & WELCOME CENTRE
Loch na Lathaich
Baile Mor
Iona
Sound of Iona
Aridhglas
Eorabus
Fionnphort
Fidden
Tiraghoil
Bunessan
Lee
Loch Assapol
376 CRUACHAN MIN
BROLASS
Leidle
Beach
376
Carsaig
Carsaig Bay
Loch Buie
Rubha Dubh
Laggan Deer Forest
405 DRUIM FADA
LORD LOVAT'S CAVE
Erraid
ROSS OF MULL
Ardalanish
Uisken
Scoor
Ardchiavaig
CARSAIG ARCHES
Eilean a'Chalmain
125
Rubha nam Braithrean
Malcolm's Pt.
Frank Lockwood's Island
Rubh Ardalanish
146
Insh I.
Sound of Insh
Seil
Clachan-Seil
Clachan
CLACHAN BRIDGE
Easdale
AN CALA GARDENS
EASDALE ISLAND FOLK MUSEUM
Balvicar
Dubh-fheith
Torran Rocks
FIRTH OF LORN
NM
Garbh Eileach
Garvellachs
Cuan
Cullipool
Torsa
Kilchoan
Luing
94
Achafolla
ARDUAINE GARDEN
Arduaine
SCARBA, LUNGA AND THE GARVELLACHS
Eilean Dubh Mor
Eileach an Naoimh
Lunga
Toberonochy
Shuna Sound
Craobh Haven
Shuna
OBAN
124
CRUACH SCARBA 449
Scarba
Shuna Pt.
Rubha Aird Luing
Gulf of Corryvreckan
B8002
Aird
Loch Craignish
Rèisa an t-Sruith
Craignish Pt.
Island Macaskin
SCULPTURED
Rubh'a'Geadha
Balnahard
Kiloran Bay
KILORAN GARDENS
Kiloran
Kilchattan
COLONSAY
Scalasaig
Loch Staosnaig
Garvard
Rubha Dubh
PRIORY
Dubh Eilean
Oronsay
Eilean nan Ron
Kinuachdrachd
296 CRUACH NA SEILCHEIG
Kinuachdrachd Harbour
Glengarrisdale Bay
Glendebadel Bay
365 BEN GARRISDALE
Loch Crinan
Crinan
Kilmahumaig
Bellanoch
Corpach Bay
Lussa
Lealt Burn
Lealt
467 BEINN BHREAC
Gallachoille
KNAPDALE
Carsaig
Tayvallich
Ardlussa
Ardlussa Bay
Inverlussa
Lussagiven
Shian Bay
453 RAINBERG MOR
Shian
Loch Righ Mòr
318
Gleann Aoistail
A846
Achanamara
Kilmichael of Inverlussa
Barrahormid
TAYNISH
Taynish
Loch Sween
466 CRUACH LUSACH
Rubh'an t-Sàilein
(Summer Only)
Tarbert
Loch Tarbert
Dunrostan
KEILLS CHAPEL
Keillmore
New Ulva
Island of Danna
CASTLE SWEEN
Loch na Cille
Rubha Lang-aoinidh
Rubha a'Mhail
Rubha Bholsa
Lagg
439
Loch an Aircill
Loch Lesgamaill
Lochead
241 ST COLUMBA'S CAVE
Achahoish
SOUND OF JURA
JURA
364 SGARBH BREAC
Nave Island
Ardnave Pt.
785
755
PAPS OF JURA
Eilean Mòr
ST CORMAC'S CHAPEL
CHAPEL
Kilmory
Kilmory Bay
Ellary
Clachbreck
Loch a Chnuic Bhric
Gortantaoid
Bunnahabhain
BUNNAHABHAIN DISTILLERY
316
JURA FOREST
Corran
An Dùnan
Ardnave
Killinallan
Loch Gruinart
Sound of Islay
Knockrome
Lowlandman's Bay
Leargybreck
Gleann Astaile
Baile Boidheach
Ormsary
Loch Caolisport
Pt. of Knap
Caol Ila
CAOL ILA DISTILLERY
Port Askaig
Feolin Ferry
FINLAGGAN CENTRE
561
Loch na Mile
Druimdrishaig
Leckgruinart
Keills
Loch Finlaggan
Craighouse
ISLE OF JURA DISTILLERY
Small Isles
Gleann Ullibh
305
Loch nan Torran
Miller's Bay
LOCH GRUINART NATURE RESERVE VISITORS CENTRE
Aoradh
Craigens
Loch Cam
Ballygrant
Loch Ballygrant
Kilmeny
342 BRAT BHEINN
Cretshengan
CRUACH LAGAIN 264
Coulaghailtro
ISLAY
142
Cabrach
NR
Kilberry Hd.
SCULPTURED STONES
Kilberry
B8017
A847
Blackrock
Redhouses
Daill
267 BEINN DUBH
Rubha na Tràille
Conisby
Bridgend
Am Fraoch Eilean
Brosdale I.
Carse Ho.
Dunmore
Bowmore
BOWMORE ROUND CHURCH
A846
Loch Stornoway
Ardpatrick
Gartnagrenach
Mulindry
McArthur's Hd.
Ardpatrick Ho.
WEST LOCH TARBERT
ISLAY
Port Charlotte
LOCH INDAAL
Kilennan
Laggan
Portachillan
Ardpatrick Pt.
Eilean Traighe
471 BEINN BHAN
491 BEINN BHEIGEIR
Carraig Mhór
Ronachan Pt.
A83
Clachan
Laggan Pt.
Laggan
Scale 1:265 000
(approx 4 miles to 1 inch)
Ardtalla
143
Eilean Garbh
West Tarbert Bay
Loch Ciaran
Loch Beinn Uraraidh
Claggain Bay
PORT ELLEN
East Tarbert Bay
Gigha Island
Tarbert
100
Balochroy
Loch Garasdal
Kintour
Ardmore Pt.
KILDALTON CHURCH AND CROSSES
0 1 2 3 4 5 6 miles
0 1 2 3 4 5 6 7 8 9 10 km

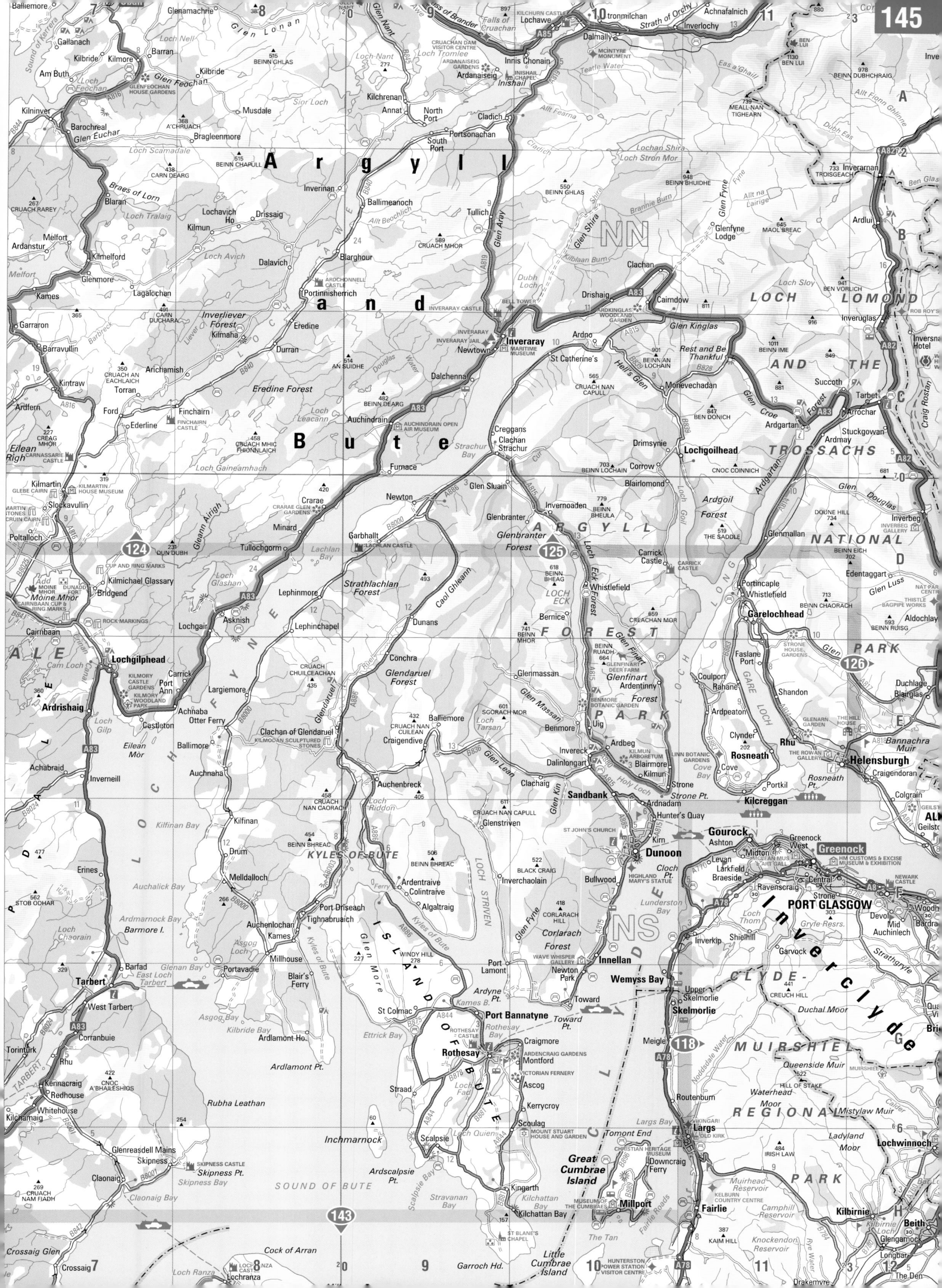

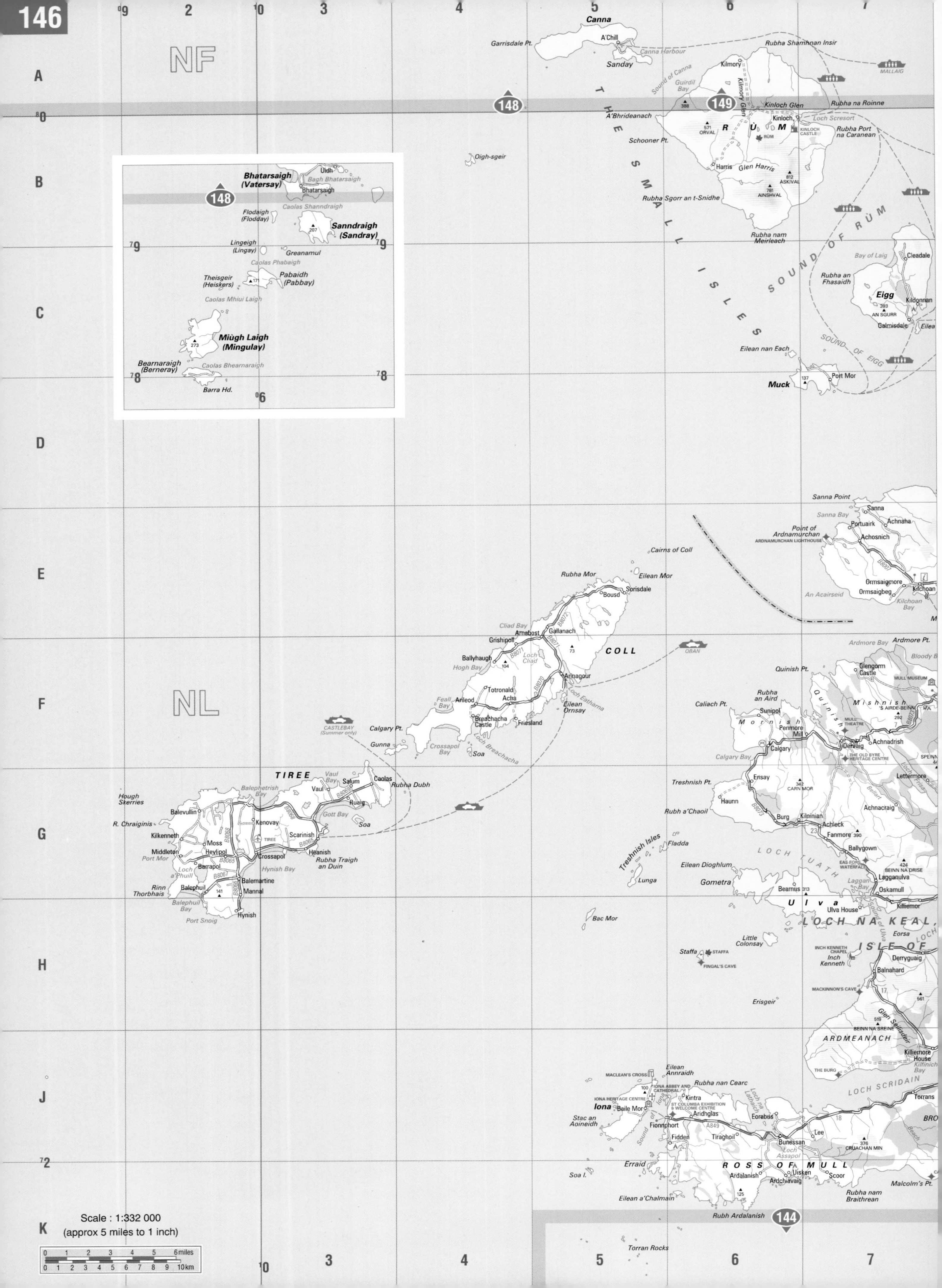

NF

148

Canna
Garrisdale Pt.
A'Chill
Sanday
Canna Harbour
Sound of Canna
Rubha Shamhnan Insir

MALLAIG

Kilmory
Guirdil Bay
Kilmory Glen
Kinloch Glen
Kinloch
Loch Scresort
Rubha na Roinne

149

571
ORVAL
R Ū M
KINLOCH
CASTLE
Rubha Port na Caranean

Schooner Pt.
Harris
Glen Harris
812
ASKIVAL
781
AINSHVAL

Rubha Sgorr an t-Snidhe

T H E
S M A L L
I S L E S

Rubha nam Meirleach

S O U N D
O F
R Ū M

Bay of Laig
Cleadale
Rubha an Fhasaidh
Eigg
393
AN SGURR
Kildonnan
Eilea
Galmisdale

Oigh-sgeir

SOUND OF EIGG

Eilean nan Each

Muck
137
Port Mor

Bhatarsaigh (Vatersay)
Ùidh
Bagh Bhatarsaigh
Bhatarsaigh

148

Caolas Shanndraigh
Flodaigh (Flodday)
207
Sanndraigh (Sandray)

Lingeigh (Lingay)
Greanamul
Caolas Phabaigh

Theisgeir (Heiskers)
171
Pabaidh (Pabbay)
Caolas Mhiui Laigh

273
Miùgh Laigh (Mingulay)

Bearnaraigh (Berneray)
Caolas Bhearnaraigh
Barra Hd.

Sanna Point
Sanna Bay
Sanna
Portuairk
Achnaha
Point of Ardnamurchan
ARDNAMURCHAN LIGHTHOUSE
Achosnich

An Acairseid
Ormsaigmore
Ormsaigbeg
Kilchoan
Kilchoan Bay

Cairns of Coll
Eilean Mor
Rubha Mor
Bousd
Sorisdale

Cliad Bay
Arnabost
Gallanach
Grishipoll
73
COLL

Ballyhaugh
104
Loch Cliad
Hogh Bay
Totronald
Acha
Arinagour
OBAN

Ardmore Bay
Ardmore Pt.
Bloody B

Quinish Pt.
Glengorm Castle
MULL MUSEUM

Rubha an Aird
M i s h n i s h
S'Airde-Beinn
292

Arileod
Eilean Ornsay
Breachacha
Castle
Friesland

Feall Bay

Caliach Pt.
M o r n i s h
Sunipol
Penmore
Mill
Calgary
MULL THEATRE
Dervaig
Achnadrish
THE OLD BYRE HERITAGE CENTRE
SPEINN

Calgary Pt.
Gunna
CASTLEBAY (Summer only)
Crossapol Bay
Soa

TIREE
Balephetrish Bay
Vaul
Salum
Caolas
Rubha Dubh
Calgary Bay

Treshnish Pt.
Ensay
342
CARN MOR
Lettermore

Hough Skerries
Balevullin
Vaul
Ruaig
Rubh a'Chaoil
Haunn
Burg
Kilninian
390
Achleck
Fanmore
Achnacraig

R. Chraiginis
Kenovay
Gott Bay
Soa
TIREE
Scarinish
Treshnish Isles
Fladda
EAS FORS WATERFALL
Ballygown
BEINN NA DRISE
424
Lagganulva

Kilkenneth
Moss
Heylipol
Crossapol
Heanish
Rubha Traigh an Duin
Lunga
Gometra
Bearnus
313
U l v a
Oskamull
L O C H T U A T H
Killiemor

Middleton
Port Mor
Barrapol
Loch a'Phuill
B8065
Balemartine
141
Mannal
Ulva House
L O C H N A K E A L
ISLE OF
Eorsa

Rinn Thorbhais
Balephuil
Balephuil Bay
Port Snoig
Hynish
Bac Mor
Little Colonsay
INCH KENNETH CHAPEL
Inch Kenneth
Derryguaig
Balnahard

Staffa
FINGAL'S CAVE
MACKINNON'S CAVE
561
17

Erisgeir
A R D M E A N A C H
515
BEINN NA SREINE
Killiemore House
Kilfinich Bay
Glen Seilisdeir

THE BURG
L O C H S C R I D A I N

MACLEAN'S CROSS
Eilean Annraidh
Rubha nan Cearc
Torrans
IONA HERITAGE CENTRE
FIONA ABBEY AND CATHEDRAL
100
Kintra
ST COLUMBA EXHIBITION & WELCOME CENTRE
Iona
Baile Mor
Stac an Aoineadh
Fionnphort
Ardnglas
Eorabus
Lee
BRO

Fidden
A849
Bunessan
376
CRUACHAN MIN

Erraid
Soa I.
Uisken
Scoor
Malcolm's Pt.
Ardalanish
Ardchiavaig
125
R O S S O F M U L L
Rubha nam Braithrean

Eilean a'Chalmain
Rubh Ardalanish

144

Torran Rocks

NL

Scale : 1:332 000
(approx 5 miles to 1 inch)

0 1 2 3 4 5 6 miles
0 1 2 3 4 5 6 7 8 9 10km

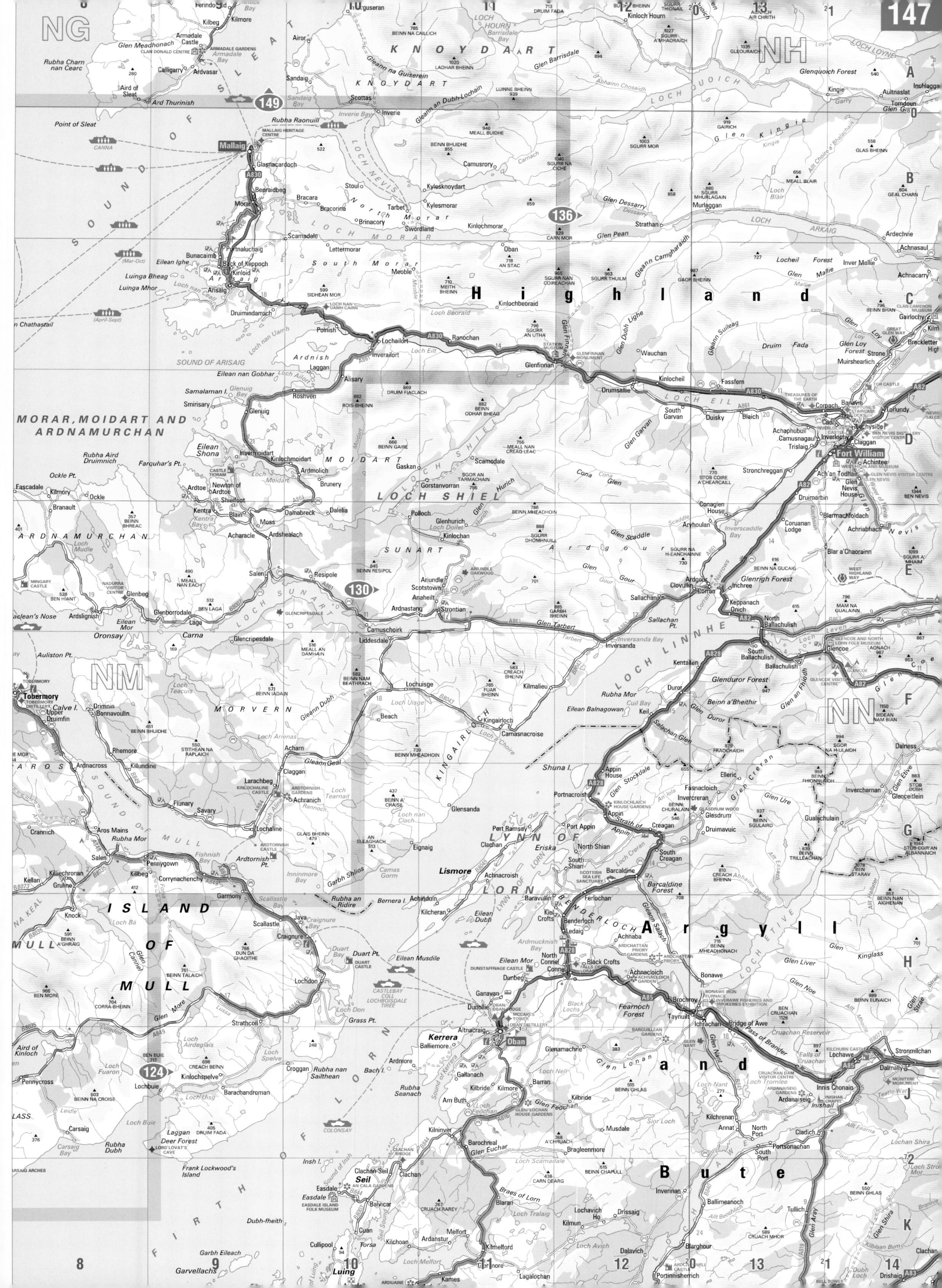

NG
NH
NM
NN
149
136
130
124
KNOYDART
Highland
Argyll and Bute
MORAR, MOIDART AND ARDNAMURCHAN
SOUND OF SLEAT
SOUND OF ARISAIG
LOCH SHIEL
LOCH SUNART
LOCH LINNHE
LOCH EIL
LOCH ARKAIG
LOCH QUOICH
LOCH NEVIS
LOCH MORAR
LOCH HOURN
LOCH LOYNE
LOCH ETIVE
LOCH AWE
SOUND OF MULL
LYNN OF LORN
FIRTH OF LORN
ISLAND OF MULL
MORVERN
SUNART
MOIDART
ARDNAMURCHAN
KINGAIRLOCH
BENDERLOCH
Mallaig
Fort William
Oban
Tobermory
Armadale
Ardvasar
Inverie
Glasnacardoch
Morar
Arisaig
Lochailort
Glenfinnan
Kinlocheil
Corpach
Banavie
Caol
Inverlochy
Glenuig
Kinlochmoidart
Acharacle
Salen
Strontian
Kilchoan
Ardgour
Corran
Onich
North Ballachulish
South Ballachulish
Ballachulish
Glencoe
Kentallen
Duror
Appin
Portnacroish
Port Appin
Creagan
Barcaldine
Benderloch
Ledaig
North Connel
Connel
Dunbeg
Taynuilt
Bridge of Awe
Lochawe
Dalmally
Kilmore
Kilninver
Kilmelford
Craignure
Lochaline
Lismore
Kerrera
Seil
Easdale
Luing
Inveraray
Glen Coe
Glen Nevis
Glen Etive
Glen More
Glen Tarbert
Glen Finnan
Loch Ba
Lochbuie
Carsaig
Pennyghael
Garvellachs
A82
A828
A830
A861
A884
A848
A849
A85
A816
A819
A83
8
9
10
11
12
13
14
A
B
C
D
E
F
G
H
J
K

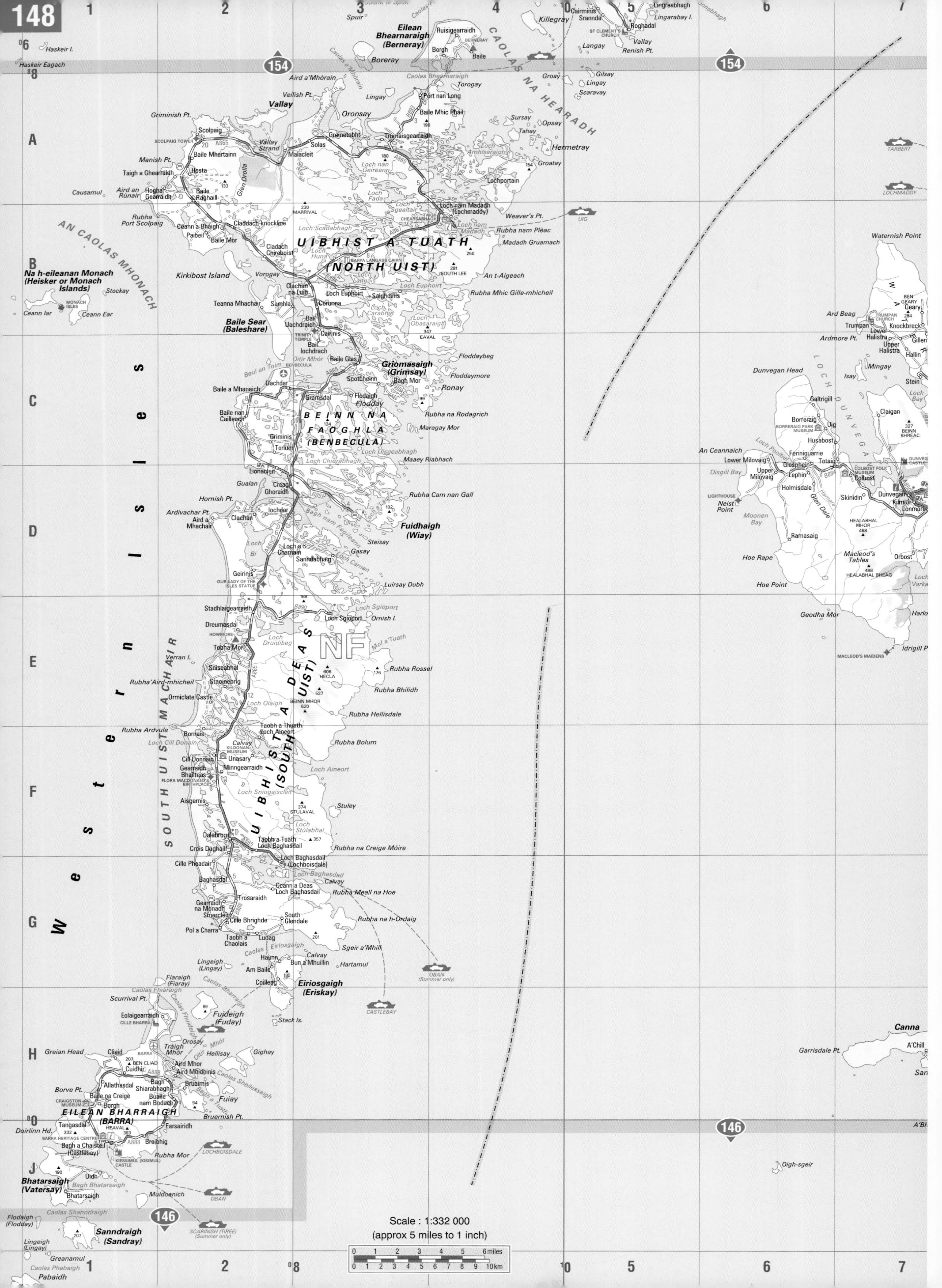

Eilean Bhearnaraigh (Berneray)
Ruisigearraidh
Borgh
Baile
Boreray
Caolas Bhearnaraigh
Caolas na Hearadh
Killegray
Cairminis
Srannda
Roghadal
Lingreabhagh
Lingarabay I.
St Clement's Church
Langay
Vallay
Renish Pt.
Haskeir I.
Haskeir Eagach
154
Aird a'Mhòrain
Groay
Gilsay
Lingay
Scaravay
Torogay
Port nan Long
Veilish Pt.
Vallay
Oronsay
Baile Mhic Phail
Griminish Pt.
Scolpaig
Scolpaig Tower
Baile Mhartainn
Vallay Strand
Solas
Malacleit
Greinetobht
Trumaisgearraidh
Sursay
Opsay
Tahay
Hermetray
Groatay
Manish Pt.
Taigh a Ghearraidh
Hosta
Causamul
Aird an Runair
Hogha Gearraidh
Baile Raghaill
Glen Drolla
Loch nan Geireann
Loch Fada
Lochportain
Loch nam Madadh (Lochmaddy)
Marrival
Rubha Port Scolpaig
Claddach-knockline
Ceann a Bhaigh
Paibeil
Baile Mor
Loch Scadabhagh
Weaver's Pt.
Rubha nam Pleac
Madadh Gruamach
An Caolas Mhonach
Uibhist a Tuath (North Uist)
Cladach Chireboist
Loch Hunn
Barpa Langass Cairn
South Lee
An t-Aigeach
Na h-eileanan Monach (Heisker or Monach Islands)
Stockay
Ceann Iar
Ceann Ear
Monach Isles
Kirkibost Island
Vorogay
Clachan na Luib
Loch Euphort
Saighdinis
Rubha Mhic Gille-mhicheil
Teanna Mhachair
Samhla
Corunna
Loch Carabhat
Loch Obasaraigh
Eaval
Baile Sear (Baleshare)
Uachdrach
Trinity Temple
Cairinis
Baile Iochdrach
Oitir Mhòr
Baile Glas
Benbecula
Griomasaigh (Grimsay)
Floddaybeg
Floddaymore
Beul an Toim
Uachdar
Scotbheinn
Bagh Mor
Ronay
Baile a Mhanaich
Gramsdal
Flodaigh
Flodday
Baile nan Cailleach
Beinn na Faoghla (Benbecula)
Rubha na Rodagrich
Maragay Mor
Griminis
Torlum
Loch Uisgeabhagh
Loch Chiurabhagh
Maaey Riabhach
Lionacleit
Gualan
Creag Ghoraidh
Rubha Cam nan Gall
Hornish Pt.
Iochdar
Ardivachar Pt.
Aird a Mhachair
Clachan
Bagh nam Faoileann
Fuidhaigh (Wiay)
Loch Bi
Loch a Charnain
Steisay
Gasay
Sanndabhaig
Loch Càrnan
Geirinis
Our Lady of the Isles Statue
Luirsay Dubh
Stadhlaigearraidh
Loch Sgioport
Ornish I.
Dreumasdal
Howmore
Loch Druidibeg
Tobha Mor
Mol a'Tuath
NF
Verran I.
Sniseabhal
Rubha Rossel
Hecla
Rubha'Aird-mhicheil
Staoinebrig
Rubha Bhilidh
Ormiclate Castle
Loch Olaigh
Beinn Mhor
Uibhist a Deas (South Uist)
Rubha Hellisdale
Rubha Ardvule
Taobh a Thuath Loch Aineort
Bornais
Loch Cill Donnain
Rubha Bolum
Calvay
Kildonan Museum
Cill Donnain
Unasary
Gearraidh Bhailteas
Minngearraidh
Loch Aineort
Flora Macdonald's Birthplace
Loch Sniogaiscleit
South Uist Machair
Stuley
Aisgernis
Stulaval
Loch Stùlabhal
Dalabrog
Taobh a Tuath Loch Baghasdail
Rubha na Creige Mòire
Crois Dughaill
Cille Pheadair
Loch Baghasdail (Lochboisdale)
Loch Baghasdail
Calvay
Baghasdal
Ceann a Deas Loch Baghasdail
Rubha Meall na Hoe
Trosaraidh
Gearraidh na Monadh
Smercleit
Cille Bhrighde
South Glendale
Rubha na h-Ordaig
Pol a Charra
Taobh a Chaolais
Ludag
Caolas Eiriosgaigh
Sgeir a'Mhill
Haunn
Calvay
Bun a'Mhuillin
Hartamul
Lingeigh (Lingay)
Am Baile
Coilleag
Eiriosgaigh (Eriskay)
Oban (Summer only)
Fiaraigh (Fiaray)
Caolas Fhiaraigh
Caolas Bharraigh
Castlebay
Scurrival Pt.
Fuideigh (Fuday)
Eolaigearraidh
Cille Bharra
Stack Is.
Orosay
Traigh Mhor
Hellisay
Gighay
Greian Head
Cliaid
Ben Cliad
Barra
Aird Mhor
Aird Mhidhinis
Cuidhir
Caolas Sheileasaigh
Borve Pt.
Allathasdal
Bagh Shiarabhagh
Baile na Creige
Buaile nam Bodach
Bruairnis
Fuiay
Craigston Museum
Borgh
Eilean Bharraigh (Barra)
Bruernish Pt.
Tangasdal
Heaval
Earsairidh
Dorlinn Hd.
Barra Heritage Centre
Bagh a Chaisteil (Castlebay)
Breibhig
Kiessimul (Kisimul) Castle
Rubha Mor
Lochboisdale
Bhatarsaigh (Vatersay)
Uidh
Bagh Bhatarsaigh
Bhatarsaigh
Muldoanich
Oban
Caolas Shanndraigh
Flodaigh (Flodday)
146
Sandraigh (Sandray)
Scarinish (Tiree) (Summer only)
Lingeigh (Lingay)
Greanamul
Caolas Phabaigh
Pabaidh
Western Isles
Tarbert
Lochmaddy
Uig
Waternish Point
Ben Geary
Geary
Ard Beag
Trumpan Church
Trumpan
Knockbreck
Lower Halistra
Upper Halistra
Gillen
Ardmore Pt.
Hallin
Dunvegan Head
Isay
Mingay
Loch Dunvegan
Stein
Galtrigill
Claigan
Borreraig
Borreraig Park Museum
Uig
Beinn Bhreac
Husabost
An Ceannaich
Loch Pooltiel
Feriniquarrie
Totaig
Lower Milovaig
Glasphein
Colbost Folk Museum
Colbost
Dunvegan Castle
Oisgill Bay
Upper Milovaig
Lephin
Holmisdale
Hamara
Glen Dale
Skinidin
Dunvegan
Kilmuir
Lonmore
Lighthouse
Neist Point
Moonen Bay
Healabhal Mhor
Ramasaig
Hoe Rape
Macleod's Tables
Healabhal Bheag
Orbost
Hoe Point
Geodha Mor
Macleod's Maidens
Idrigill P
Canna
A'Chill
Garrisdale Pt.
Oigh-sgeir
Scale : 1:332 000
(approx 5 miles to 1 inch)
0 1 2 3 4 5 6 miles
0 1 2 3 4 5 6 7 8 9 10 km

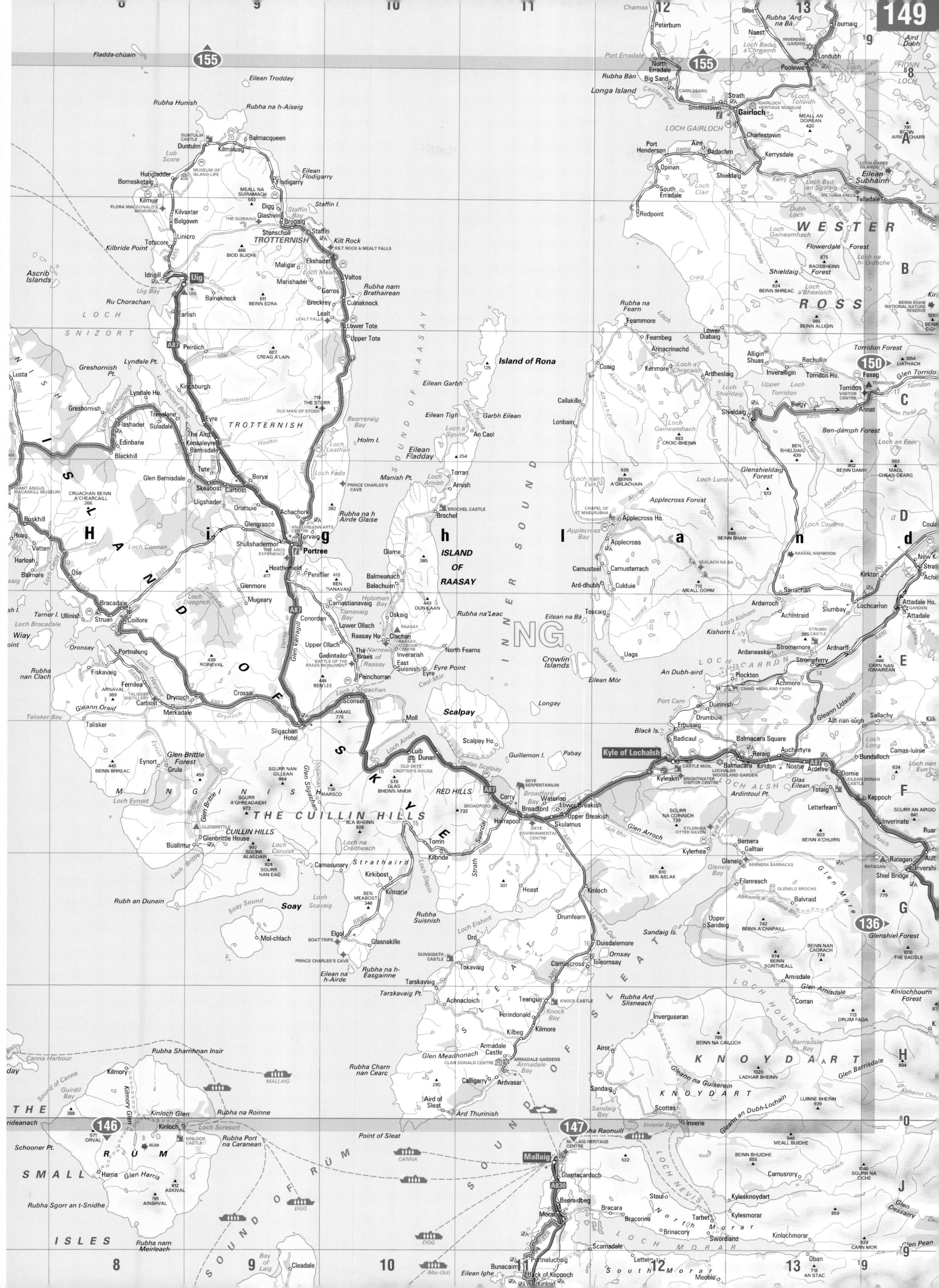

149
155
150
136
146
147
8
9
10
11
12
13
A
B
C
D
E
F
G
H
J
Fladda-chùain
Eilean Trodday
Rubha Hunish
Rubha na h-Aiseig
Duntulm Castle
Duntulm
Kilmaluag
Balmacqueen
Lub Score
Hungladder
Museum of Island Life
Bornesketaig
Eilean Flodigarry
Flodigarry
Kilmuir
Flora MacDonald's Memorial
Kilvaxter
Balgown
Meall na Suiramach
543
Digg
The Quiraing
Glashvin
Staffin Bay
Staffin I.
Brogaig
Linicro
Stenscholl
Staffin
Totscore
Trotternish
Kilt Rock
Kilt Rock & Mealt Falls
Kilbride Point
466
Biod Buidhe
Maligar
Elishader
Ascrib Islands
Idrigill
Uig
Uig Bay
Loch Mealt
Valtos
Marishader
Balnaknock
611
Beinn Edra
Garros
Rubha nam Brathairean
Ru Chorachan
Breckrey
Culnaknock
Loch
Earlish
Lealt
Lealt Falls
Snizort
Lower Tote
Upper Tote
A87
Peinlich
607
Creag A'Lain
Greshornish Pt.
Lyndale Pt.
Lusta
Kingsburgh
Lyndale Ho.
719
The Storr
Old Man of Storr
Greshornish
Treaslane
Suladale
Flashader
Eyre
The Aird
Trotternish
Bearreraig Bay
Edinbane
Kensaleyre
Bernisdale
Holm I.
Blackhill
Loch Leathan
Tote
Borve
Glen Bernisdale
Skeabost
Carbost
Loch Fada
Prince Charles's Cave
Cruachan Beinn A'Chearcaill
266
Giant Angus MacAskill Museum
Uigshader
Drumuie
Achachork
392
Rubha na h Airde Glaise
Roskhill
Glengrasco
An Tuireann Arts Centre
Torvaig
Roag
Shulishadermor
The Aros Experience
Portree
Vatten
Loch Cannan
Harlosh
Ose
Heatherfield
Penifiler
Balmore
417
413
Ben Tianavaig
Glenmore
Loch Duagrich
Mugeary
Tarner I.
Ullinish
Bracadale
Struan
Coillore
Camastianavaig
Tianavaig Bay
Conordan
Loch Bracadale
Wiay
Oronsay
Portnalong
Lower Ollach
Upper Ollach
The Braes
Gedintailor
Battle of the Braes Monument
Narrows of Raasay
Rubha nan Clach
Fiskavaig
Loch Harport
439
Roineval
Fernilea
Arnaval
369
Talisker Distillery
Carbost
Drynoch
Crossal
444
Ben Lee
Peinchorran
Gleann Oraid
Merkadale
Drynoch
Loch Sligachan
Sconser
Talisker Bay
Talisker
Sligachan Hotel
Glamaig
775
Eynort
Glen Brittle Forest
445
Beinn Bhreac
Grula
459
Sgurr nan Gillean
964
Glen Sligachan
736
Marsco
Loch Eynort
Sgurr A'Ghreadaidh
973
Glen Brittle
The Cuillin Hills
Glenbrittle
Cuillin Hills
Glenbrittle House
Bualintur
Loch Coruisk
992
Sgurr Alasdair
924
Sgurr nan Eag
Loch Brittle
Bla Bheinn
928
Loch na Creitheach
Camasunary
Strathaird
Rubh an Dunain
Soay Sound
Soay
Loch Scavaig
Kirkibost
Ben Meabost
346
Kilmarie
Mol-chlach
Elgol
Boat Trips
Glasnakille
Prince Charles's Cave
Eilean na h-Airde
Rubha na h-Easgainne
Island of Rona
125
Eilean Garbh
Eilean Tigh
Caol Rona
Garbh Eilean
Loch a' Sguirr
An Caol
Eilean Fladday
254
Manish Pt.
Torran
Loch Arnish
Arnish
Brochel Castle
Brochel
Sound of Raasay
Island of Raasay
Glame
385
Balmeanach
Balachuim
Holoman Bay
443
Dun Caan
Oskaig
Raasay
Raasay Ho.
Clachan
Raasay Outdoor Centre
Inverarish
East Suisnish
Rubha na'Leac
North Fearns
Eyre Point
Eyre
Caol Mòr
Scalpay
Moll
Loch Ainort
Luib
Dunan
Old Skye Crofter's House
570
Glas Bheinn Mhor
Scalpay Ho.
Caolas Scalpay
Red Hills
Broadford
732
Corry
Harrapool
Skye Serpentarium
Broadford Bay
Waterloo
Lower Breakish
Upper Breakish
Skulamus
Skye Environmental Centre
Torrin
Kilbride
Strath Suardal
B8083
301
Heast
Rubha Suisnish
Loch Eishort
Ord
Dunsgiath Castle
Tokavaig
Tarskavaig
Tarskavaig Pt.
Achnacloich
Sleat
Teangue
Knock Castle
Ferindonald
Knock Bay
Kilbeg
Kilmore
Armadale Castle
Clan Donald Centre
Armadale Gardens
Armadale Bay
Glen Meadhonach
Rubha Charn nan Cearc
280
Calligarry
Ardvasar
Aird of Sleat
Ard Thurinish
Point of Sleat
Skye
Inner Sound
Crowlin Islands
Eilean Mór
Eilean na Bà
Longay
Guillamon I.
Pabay
Kyle of Lochalsh
Kyleakin
Castle Moil
Bright Water Visitor Centre
Lochalsh Woodland Garden
Balmacara
Balmacara Square
Reraig
Kirkton
Nostie
Auchertyre
Ardelve
Dornie
Eilean Donan Castle
Glas Eilean
Totaig
Loch Alsh
Ardintoul Pt.
Sgurr na Coinnich
739
Kylerhea Otter Haven
Kyle Rhea
Glen Arroch
Allt Mór
Kylerhea
Bernera
Galltair
Bernera Barracks
Glenelg
Glenelg Bay
610
Ben Aslak
Eilanreach
Glenelg Brochs
Balvraid
Kinloch
Drumfearn
Loch na Dal
Duisdalemore
Ornsay
Isleornsay
Camuscross
Sandaig Is.
Upper Sandaig
742
Beinn A'Chapaill
974
Beinn Sgritheall
Beinn nan Caorach
774
Arnisdale
Glen Arnisdale
Corran
Loch Hourn
Rubha Ard Slisneach
Inverguseran
785
Beinn na Caillich
Airor
Knoydart
Gleann na Guiserein
1020
Ladhar Bheinn
Barrisdale Bay
Glen Barrisdale
Sandaig
Sandaig Bay
Scottas
Luinne Bheinn
939
Inverie Bay
Inverie
Gleann an Dubh-Lochain
946
Meall Buidhe
Rubha Raonuill
Mallaig Heritage Centre
Mallaig
522
Beinn Bhuidhe
855
Loch Nevis
Camusrory
Glasnacardoch
A830
Stoul
Kylesknoydart
Beoraidbeg
Bracara
Bracorina
North Morar
Tarbet
Kylesmorar
Morar
Brinacory
Swordland
Loch Morar
Kinlochmorar
Scamadale
Letterm...
Portnaluchaig
South Morar
Oban
718
An Stac
Meoble
Back of Keppoch
Kinloid
Bunacaimb
Eilean Ighe
(Mar-Oct)
Eigg
Cleadale
Bay of Laig
Sound of Rùm
Canna
Mallaig
Canna Harbour
Sound of Canna
Rubha Shamhnan Insir
Kilmory
Guirdil Bay
Kilmory Glen
388
Kinloch Glen
Rubha na Roinne
Kinloch
Loch Scresort
Kinloch Castle
Rubha Port na Caranean
571
Orval
Rùm
Schooner Pt.
Harris
Glen Harris
812
Askival
781
Ainshval
Rubha Sgorr an t-Snidhe
Small Isles
Rubha nam Meirleach
The
Chamas
Peterburn
Brae
Naast
Rubha 'Ard na Bà
Tournaig
Aird Dubh
Loch Bad a' Chreamh
Inverewe Garden
Londubh
Poolewe
Loch Kernsary
Fionn Loch
Port Erradale
North Erradale
Rubha Bàn
Big Sand
Longa Island
Caolas Beag
Carn Dearg
Strath
Gairloch Heritage Museum
Smithstown
Gairloch
Loch Tollaidh
Meall an Doirean
420
Loch Gairloch
Charlestown
791
Beinn Airigh Charr
Port Henderson
Aird
Badachro
B8056
Kerrysdale
Opinan
Shieldaig
Loch Bad an Sgalaig
Eilean Subhainn
Loch Maree Islands
Victoria Falls
Talladale
South Erradale
Loch Clàir
Redpoint
Dubh Loch
Loch Gaineamhach
Wester Ross
Flowerdale Forest
875
Baosbheinn Forest
Shieldaig Forest
624
Beinn Bhreac
Loch a'Bhealaich
Beinn Eighe National Nature Reserve
Ross
985
Beinn Alligin
Rubha na Fearn
Fearnmore
Loch Torridon
Fearnbeg
Lower Diabaig
Arinacrinachd
Torridon Forest
Alligin Shuas
Rechullin
1054
Liathach
Cuaig
Kenmore
Loch a' Chracaich
Inveralligin
Torridon Ho.
Fasag
Glen Torridon
Ardheslaig
Upper Loch Torridon
Torridon Visitor Centre
Loch Shieldaig
Callakille
Shieldaig
Balgy
Annat
Lonbain
Loch Gaineamhach
A896
Ben-damph Forest
693
Croic-Bheinn
Ben Shieldaig
439
Loch an Eoin
902
Beinn Damh
993
Maol Chean-Dearg
626
Beinn A'Chlachain
Loch nan Eun
Loch Lundie
Glenshieldaig Forest
513
Applecross Forest
Chapel of St Maelrubha
Applecross Ho.
Loch Coultrie
Applecross Bay
896
Beinn Bhan
Applecross
Rassal Ashwood
New Kelso
Camusteel
Camusterrach
Bealach na Ba
Ard-dhubh
Culduie
710
Meall Gorm
Kirkton
Sanachan
Ardarroch
Achintraid
Slumbay
Lochcarron
Attadale Ho.
Attadale
Toscaig
Loch Kishorn
Kishorn I.
395
Strome Castle
Ardaneaskan
Stromemore
Ardnarff
Stromeferry
Uags
Loch Carron
An Dubh-aird
Plockton
Craig Highland Farm
Achmore
Carn nan Iomairean
Duirinish
Drumbuie
Port Cam
Gleann Udalain
Sallachy
Alt-nan-sùgh
Black Is.
Erbusaig
Badicaul
Bundalloch
Camas-luinie
634
Keppoch
Letterfearn
Sgurr an Airgid
841
Inverinate
603
Beinn A'Chuirn
Loch Duich
Ratagan
Shiel Bridge
Glen More
779
Glenshiel Forest
1010
The Saddle
Kinlochhourn Forest
713
Druim Fada
894
Glen Dessarry
Glen Pean
829
Carn Mor
1040
Sgurr na Ciche
859
Islands
Highlands
NG

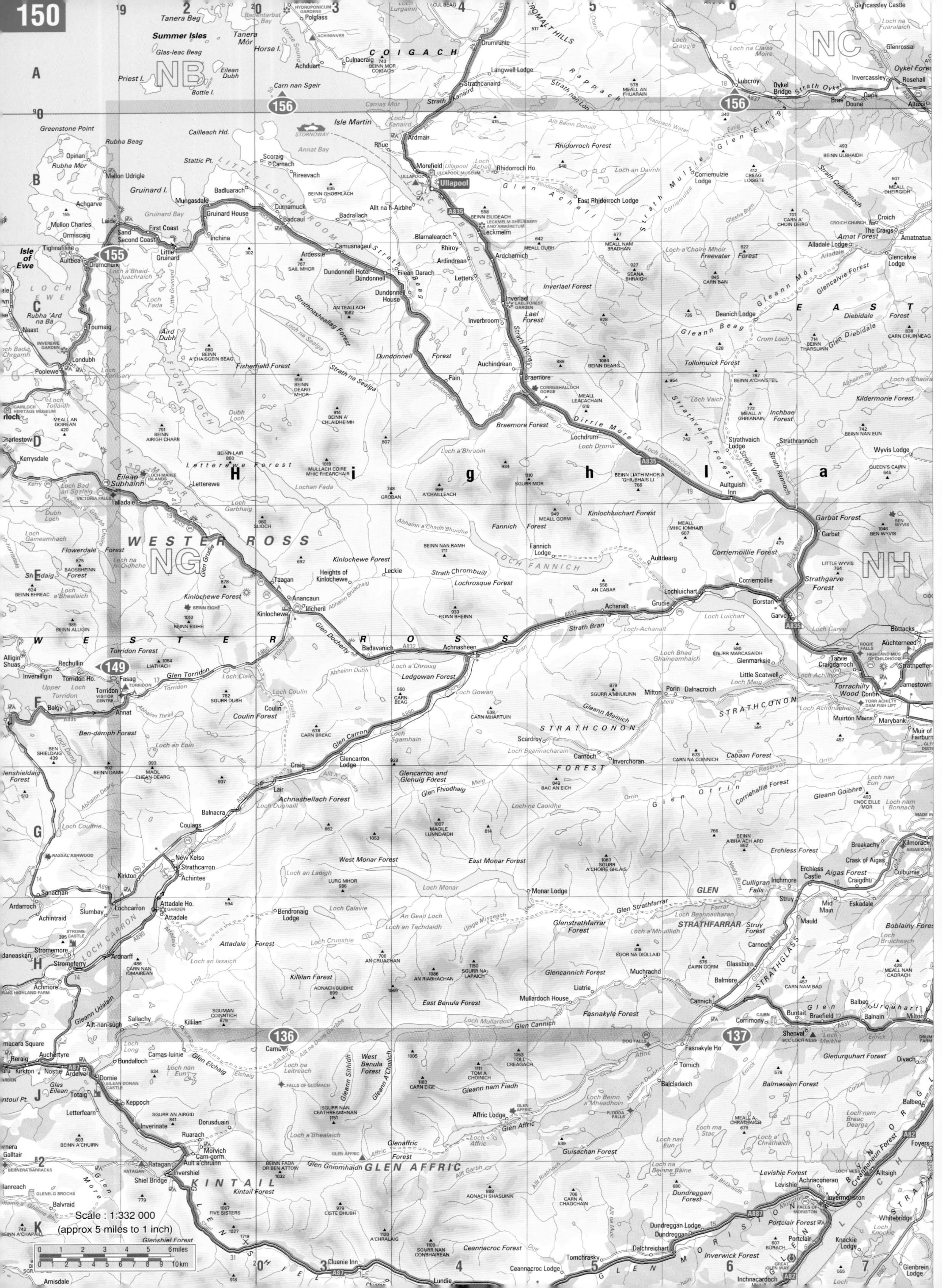
150
Summer Isles
Tanera Beg
Tanera Mór
Glas-leac Beag
Horse I.
Priest I.
Eilean Dubh
Bottle I.
NB
NC
NG
NH
COIGACH
Polglass
Achiltibuie
Culnacraig
Achduart
Carn nan Sgeir
Isle Martin
Drumrunie
Langwell Lodge
Strathcanaird
Strath Kanaird
Rappach
Strath nan Lon
Lubcroy
Oykel Bridge
Strath Oykel
Invercassley
Rosehall
Glencassley Castle
Glenrossal
Oykel Forest
Altass
Doune
Bree
Oape
Greenstone Point
Rubha Beag
Cailleach Hd.
Opinan
Rubha Mor
Mellon Udrigle
Static Pt.
Scoraig
Carnach
Rireavach
Annat Bay
Ardmair
Rhue
Morefield
Ullapool
Rhidorroch Forest
Rhidorroch Ho.
Glen Achall
East Rhidorroch Lodge
Strath Mulzie
Corriemulzie Lodge
Glen Einig
Strath Cuileannach
Croick
The Craigs
Amatnatua
Amat Forest
Gruinard I.
Badluarach
Mungasdale
Gruinard House
Dundonnell Hotel
Dundonnell
Dundonnell House
Achgarve
Mellon Charles
Ormiscaig
Laide
Sand
First Coast
Second Coast
Inchina
Little Gruinard
Isle of Ewe
Aultbea
Drumchork
Loch Ewe
Rubha 'Ard na Bà
Naast
Tournaig
Poolewe
Londubh
Loch Broom
Ardessie
Camusnagaul
Strath Beag
Badrallach
Allt na h-Airbhe
Blarnalearoch
Rhiroy
Ardindrean
Letters
Leckmelm
Ardcharnich
Inverlael
Lael Forest
Inverlael Forest
Inverbroom
Strath More
Auchindrean
Braemore
Freevater Forest
Alladale Lodge
Glencalvie Lodge
Glencalvie Forest
Gleann Mór
Deanich Lodge
Gleann Beag
EAST
Diebidale
Tollomuick Forest
Kildermorie Forest
Strathnasheallag Forest
Fisherfield Forest
Strath na Sealga
Fain
Braemore Forest
Dirrie More
Lochdrum
Loch Droma
Loch Glascarnoch
Loch Vaich
Strathvaich Lodge
Strathvaich Forest
Strathrannoch
Inchbae Forest
Wyvis Lodge
Kerrysdale
Charlestown
Eilean Subhainn
Loch Maree
Letterewe
Letterewe Forest
Talladale
Highland
Fannich Forest
Kinlochluichart Forest
Aultguish Inn
Garbat Forest
Garbat
WESTER ROSS
Flowerdale Forest
Kinlochewe Forest
Heights of Kinlochewe
Leckie
Strath Chrombuill
Lochrosque Forest
Loch Fannich
Fannich Lodge
Aultdearg
Corriemoillie Forest
Corriemoillie
Strathgarve Forest
Taagan
Anancaun
Kinlochewe
Incheril
Kinlochewe Forest
Glen Docherty
Achanalt
Strath Bran
Grudie
Lochluichart
Gorstan
Garve
Torridon Forest
Rechullin
Torridon Ho.
Inveralligin
Alligin Shuas
Fasag
Torridon
Annat
Balgy
Glen Torridon
Badavanich
Achnasheen
Ledgowan Forest
Glenmarksie
Little Scatwell
Milton
Porin
Dalnacroich
Strathpeffer
Tarvie
Craigdarroch
Torrachilty Wood
Contin
Jamestown
Ben-damph Forest
Coulin Forest
Coulin
Glen Carron
STRATHCONON
Scardroy
Carnoch
Inverchoran
Muirton Mains
Marybank
Craig
Glencarron Lodge
Glencarron and Glenuig Forest
Glen Fhiodhaig
Cabaan Forest
Glen Orrin
Corriehallie Forest
Lair
Achnashellach Forest
Balnacra
Coulags
West Monar Forest
East Monar Forest
New Kelso
Strathcarron
Achintee
Kirkton
Monar Lodge
Culligran Falls
Erchless Forest
Erchless Castle
Aigas Forest
Craigdhu
Breakachy
Crask of Aigas
Culburnie
Kilmorack
Sanachan
Ardarroch
Achintraid
Slumbay
Lochcarron
Attadale Ho.
Attadale
Bendronaig Lodge
Loch Calavie
Glen Strathfarrar
Glenstrathfarrar Forest
GLEN STRATHFARRAR
Struy Forest
Struy
Mid Main
Eskadale
Mauld
Strome Castle
Stromemore
Stromeferry
Ardnarff
Attadale Forest
Killilan Forest
Glencannich Forest
Muchrachd
Glassburn
Carnoch
Balmore
Achmore
East Benula Forest
Mullardoch House
Liatrie
Fasnakyle Forest
Cannich
Strathglass
Balbeg
Glen Urquhart
Buntait
Braefield
Balnain
Milton
Allt-nan-sùgh
Sallachy
Killilan
Glen Cannich
Corrimony
Shenval
Auchertyre
Nostie
Ardelve
Kirkton
Reraig
Dornie
Bundalloch
Camas-luinie
Glen Elchaig
Carnach
West Benula Forest
Fasnakyle Ho
Tomich
Glenurquhart Forest
Divach
Balmacaan Forest
Totaig
Keppoch
Letterfearn
Invernate
Dorusduain
Ruarach
Morvich
Gleann nam Fiadh
Affric Lodge
Glen Affric
Balcladaich
Bunloit
Foyers
Ratagan
Ault a' chruinn
Shiel Bridge
Invershiel
Glen Gniomhaidh
GLEN AFFRIC
Glenaffric Forest
Guisachan Forest
KINTAIL
Kintail Forest
Dundreggan Forest
Levishie Forest
Levishie
Achnaconeran
Alltsigh
Invermoriston
Glenshiel Forest
Portclair Forest
Portclair
Dundreggan Lodge
Dundreggan
Ceannacroc Forest
Ceannacroc Lodge
Dalchreichart
Tomchrasky
Inverwick Forest
Knockie Lodge
Whitebridge
Glenbrein Lodge
Cluanie Inn
Lundie
Arnisdale
GLEN MORISTON
GLEN SHIEL
Scale : 1:332 000
(approx 5 miles to 1 inch)
6 miles
10 km
A835
A832
A890
A896
A87
A831
A82
156
155
149
136
137

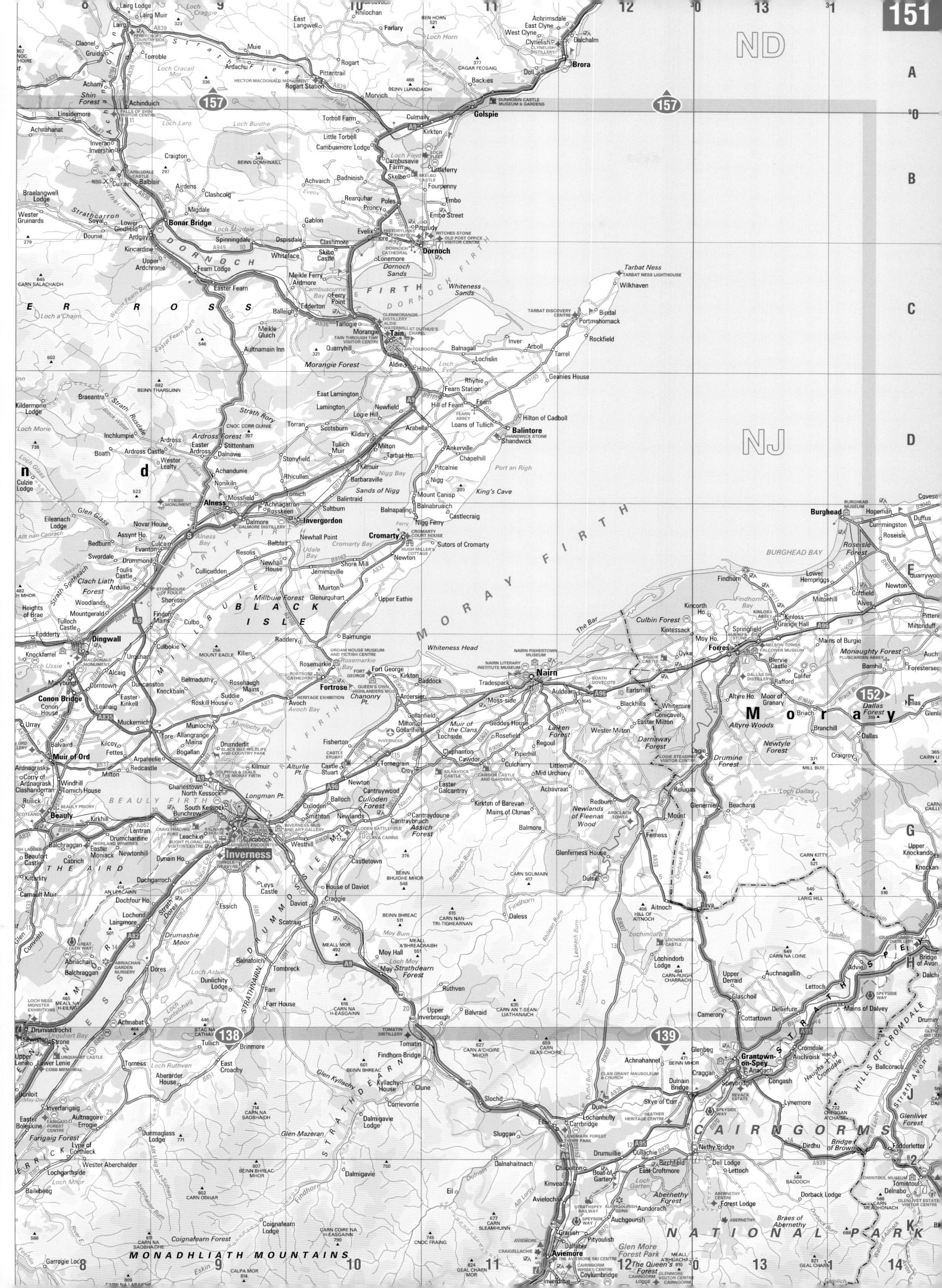

ND
NJ
A
B
C
D
E
F
G
H
J
K
8
9
10
11
12
13
14
157
157
152
138
139
Lairg Lodge
Lairg Muir
Lairg
Loch Craggie
Rhilochan
East Langwell
Farlary
BEN HORN 521
Loch Horn
Achrimsdale
East Clyne
West Clyne
Clynelish
Dalchalm
Brora
Claonel
Gruids
Torroble
Muie
Strath Fleet
Ardachu
Rogart
Pittentrail
Rogart Station
HECTOR MACDONALD MONUMENT
Loch Cracail Mor
CAGAR FEOSAIG
Doll
Backies
BEINN LUNNDAIDH
Achany
Shin Forest
Morvich
Achinduich
FALLS OF SHIN VISITOR CENTRE
DUNROBIN CASTLE MUSEUM & GARDENS
Golspie
Linsidemore
Loch Laro
Loch Buidhe
Torboll Farm
Culmaily
Kirkton
Achnahanat
Little Torboll
Inveran
Invershin
Cambusmore Lodge
Loch Fleet
Craigton
BEINN DOMHNAILL
Cambusavie Farm
Littleferry
CARBISDALE CASTLE
Culrain
Balblair
Skelbo
Fourpenny
Airdens
Clashcoig
Achvaich
Badninish
Braelangwell Lodge
Embo
Migdale
Rearquhar
Poles
Strathcarron
Soyal
Proncy
Embo Street
Wester Gruinards
Bonar Bridge
Lower Gledfield
Gablon
Pitgrudy
Dounie
Ardgay
Spinningdale
Loch Migdale
Ospisdale
Clashmore
Evelix
Camore
WITCHES STONE
OLD POST OFFICE VISITOR CENTRE
Kincardine
DORNOCH
A949
Skibo Castle
HISTORYLINKS EXHIBITION
DORNOCH CATHEDRAL
Dornoch
Whiteface
Lonemore
Upper Ardchronie
Dornoch Sands
Fearn Lodge
Meikle Ferry
Ardmore
CARN SALACHAIDH
Easter Fearn
Cambuscurrie Bay
Ferry Point
FIRTH
DORNOCH
Whiteness Sands
Tarbat Ness
TARBAT NESS LIGHTHOUSE
Wilkhaven
E R R O S S
Loch a' Chairn
Balleigh
Edderton
GLENMORANGIE DISTILLERY
ALDIE WATERMILL
ST DUTHUS'S CHAPEL
TARBAT DISCOVERY CENTRE
Bindal
Portmahomack
Tarlogie
Morangie
Meikle Gluich
Tain
TAIN THROUGH TIME VISITOR CENTRE
Rockfield
Aultnamain Inn
Quarryhill
Balnagall
Inver
Arboll
Tarrel
Morangie Forest
Lochslin
Aldie
Hilton
Loch Eye
BEINN THARSUINN
Rhynie
Geanies House
Fearn Station
Braeantra
Strath Rusdale
East Lamington
Fearn
Kildermorie Lodge
Lamington
Hill of Fearn
FEARN ABBEY
Newfield
Logie Hill
Loans of Tullich
Hilton of Cadboll
Loch Morie
Strath Rory
Torran
Scotsburn
Arabella
Balintore
Shandwick
SHANDWICK STONE
CNOC CORR GUINIE
Ardross Forest
Kildary
Inchlumpie
Ardross
Easter Ardross
Stittenham
Tullich Muir
Milton
Ankerville
Boath
Ardross Castle
Dalnavie
Wester Lealty
Stonyfield
Tarbat Ho.
Chapelhill
Port an Righ
Achandunie
Kilmuir
Pitcalnie
Rhicullen
Nigg Bay
Nigg
Culzie Lodge
Nonikiln
Barbaraville
Sands of Nigg
Mount Canisp
King's Cave
Tomich
FYRISH MONUMENT
Mossfield
Balintraid
Alness
Achnagarron
Rosskeen
Saltburn
Balnapaling
Balnabruaich
Glen Glass
Eileanach Lodge
Novar House
Dalmore
DALMORE DISTILLERY
Invergordon
Nigg Ferry
Castlecraig
Allt nan Caorach
Assynt Ho.
Alness Bay
Newhall Point
Cromarty
CROMARTY COURT HOUSE
Redburn
Evanton
Culcairn
Balblair
Cromarty Bay
HUGH MILLER'S COTTAGE
Sutors of Cromarty
Swordale
Resolis
Udale Bay
Drummond
Newhall House
Shore Mill
Newton
Foulis Castle
Clach Liath Forest
Cullicudden
Jemimaville
Ardullie
STOREHOUSE OF FOULIS
Muirton
Shoreton
Millbuie Forest
Glenurquhart
Upper Eathie
Heights of Brae
Woodlands
BLACK ISLE
MORAY FIRTH
Mountgerald
Findon Mains
Culbo
Tulloch Castle
Fodderty
Dingwall
Raddery
Balmungie
Knockfarrel
MACDONALD MONUMENT
Loch Ussie
Culbokie
MOUNT EAGLE
Killen
GROAM HOUSE MUSEUM AND PICTISH CENTRE
Whiteness Head
NAIRN FISHERTOWN MUSEUM
Alcaig
Urquhart
Rosemarkie
Rosemarkie Bay
NAIRN LITERARY INSTITUTE MUSEUM
Maryburgh
Corntown
Duncanston
Belmaduthy
Rosehaugh Mains
FORTROSE CATHEDRAL
Fortrose
Fort George
QUEEN'S OWN HIGHLANDERS MUSEUM
Kirkton
Baddock
Tradespark
Nairn
BOATH DOVECOTE
Conon Bridge
Conon House
Knockbain
Easter Kinkell
Suddie
Roskill House
HERITAGE EXHIBITION
Avoch
Avoch Bay
Chanonry Pt.
Ardersier
Moss-side
Auldearn
Urray
Muckernich
Munlochy
Munlochy Bay
Gollanfield
Milton of Gollanfield
Muir of the Clans
Lochside
Geddes House
Balvaird
Kilcoy
Tore
Allangrange Mains
Bogallan
Drumderfit
BLACK ISLE WILDLIFE AND COUNTRY PARK
Fisherton
Rosefield
Clephanton
Cawdor
Regoul
Muir of Ord
Fettes
Arpafeelie
Redcastle
Kilmuir
Castle Stuart
Alturlie Pt.
Tornagrain
Croy
KILRAVOCK CASTLE
CAWDOR CASTLE AND GARDENS
Piperhill
Culcharry
Mid Urchany
Ardnagrask
Corry of Ardnagrask
Clashandorran
Windhill
Tomich House
Milton
DOLPHINS & SEALS OF THE MORAY FIRTH
Charlestown
North Kessock
Longman Pt.
Newton
Cantraywood
Easter Galcantray
Achavraat
Ruilick
BEAULY PRIORY
Beauly
BEAULY FIRTH
South Kessock
Bunchrew
Balloch
Culloden
Culloden Forest
Smithton
Newlands
Cantraydoune
Cantraybruich
Kirkton of Barevan
Mains of Clunas
Kirkhill
Lentran
Drumchardine
Easter Moniack
Balchraggan
Beaufort Castle
Cabrich
Newtonhill
BALNAIN HOUSE
Leachkin
Culcabock
Inverness
INVERNESS MUS AND ART GALLERY
CULLODEN BATTLEFIELD
CLAVA CAIRNS
Westhill
Assich Forest
Balmore
THE AIRD
Dunain Ho.
Castletown
Kiltarlity
Dochgarroch
Leys Castle
House of Daviot
Daviot
Craggie
BEINN BHUIDHE MHOR
Camault Muir
Dochfour Ho.
Strath Dores
Essich
Scatraig
BEINN BHREAC
CARN NAN TRI-TIGHEARNAN
Lochend
Laimgmore
Drumashie Moor
Moy Burn
MEALL A' BHREACRAIBH
MEALL MOR
Moy Hall
Loch Moy
Strathdearn Forest
Moy
Convinth
GREAT GLEN WAY
Abriachan
ABRIACHAN GARDEN NURSERY
Dores
Loch Ashie
Balnafoich
Tombreck
Balchraggan
Dunlichity Lodge
Farr
Farr House
Ruthven
LOCH NESS MONSTER EXHIBITIONS
MEALL NA H-EILRIG
Loch Duntelchaig
STRATHNAIRN
DRUMMOSSIE
CARN NA H-EASGAINN
Upper Inverbrough
Balvraid
CARN AN T-SEAN LIATHANAICH
Achnabat
Drumnadrochit
Urquhart Bay
Lewiston
Strone
STAC NA CATHAIG
Tullich
Brinmore
TOMATIN DISTILLERY
Tomatin
CARN A'CHOIRE MHOIR
CARN GLAS-CHOIRE
Upper Lenie
Lower Lenie
URQUHART CASTLE
COBB MEMORIAL
Torness
Loch Ruthven
East Croachy
Aberarder House
BEINN BHREAC
Findhorn Bridge
Kyllachy House
Clune
Glen Kyllachy
Strathdearn
Slochd
Bunloit
Inverfarigaig
Aultnagoire
Errogie
FARIGAIG FOREST CENTRE
CARN NA SAOBHAIDH
Corrievorrie
Dalmigavie Lodge
Easter Boleskine
Farigaig Forest
Dunmaglass Lodge
Glen Mazeran
Sluggan
Lyne of Corthleck
Wester Aberchalder
BEINN BHREAC MHOR
Dalmigavie
Dalnahaitnach
Lochgarthside
Loch Mhor
Dulnain
CARN ODHAR
Eil
Bailebeag
Coignafearn Lodge
CARN COIRE NA H-EASGAINN
CARN SLEAMHUINN
Findhorn
Coignafearn Forest
CARN NA SAOBHAIDHE
CNOC FRAING
MONADHLIATH MOUNTAINS
Garrogie Lodge
CALPA MOR
GEAL CHARN MOR
CRAIGELLACHIE
Aviemore
Auldearn
Earlsmill
Blackhills
Whitemire
Conicavel
Easter Milton
Wester Milton
Laiken Forest
Darnaway Forest
LOGIE STEADING VISITOR CENTRE
Littlemill
Redburn
Newlands of Fleenas Wood
ARDCLACH TOWER
Relugas
Logie
Glenernie
Beachans
Mount
Ferness
Glenferness House
CARN SGUMAIN
Dulsie
HILL OF AITNOCH
Aitnoch
Dava
Daless
Lochindorb
LOCHINDORB CASTLE
Lochindorb Lodge
CARN-RUIGH CHARRACH
CARN NA LOINE
Upper Derraid
Auchnagallin
Lettoch
SPEYSIDE WAY
Glaschoil
Dellefure
Mains of Dalvey
Camerory
Cottartown
STRATHSPEY
Advie
Bridge of Avon
Dalchi
Drumin
HILLS OF CROMDALE
Glenbeg
Grantown-on-Spey
Anagach
Cromdale
Auchroisk
Haughs of Cromdale
Achnahannet
BEINN MHOR
CLAN GRANT MAUSOLEUM & CHURCH
Craggan
Speybridge
REVACK ESTATE
Congash
Ballcorach
Strath Avon
Dulnain Bridge
Skye of Curr
HEATHER HERITAGE CENTRE
SPEYSIDE HEATHER
Lynemore
CREGGAN A'CHAISE
Glenlivet Forest
Duthil
Lochanhully
Carrbridge
LANDMARK FOREST THEME PARK
Ellan
CAIRNGORMS
Nethy Bridge
Dirdhu
Bridge of Brown
Fodderletter
Drumuillie
Cullachie
Chapelton
Boat of Garten
East Croftmore
Birchfield
Dell Lodge
Lettoch
BADDOCH
TOMINTOUL MUSEUM
Tomintoul
Delnabo
GLENLIVET ESTATE VISITOR CENTRE
CARN MEADHONACH
Loch Garten
Abernethy Forest
ABERNETHY CENTRE
Forest Lodge
Dorback Lodge
Kinveachy
Avielochan
STRATHSPEY RAILWAY
AUCHGOURISH GDNS
Aundorach
Auchgourish
ABERNETHY
Braes of Abernethy
NATIONAL PARK
Granish
Dalfaber
Pityoulish
Glen More Forest Park
MEALL A'BHUACHAILLE
GEAL CHARN
Coylumbridge
Inverdruie
CAIRNGORM WHISKY CENTRE
The Queen's Forest
GLENMORE VISITOR CENTRE
CAIRNGORM LODGE
Burghead
BURGHEAD MUSEUM
Hopeman
Covesea
Duffus
Cummingston
Roseisle
Roseisle Forest
BURGHEAD BAY
Findhorn
Lower Hempriggs
Quarrywood
Newton
Coltfield
Alves
Milltonhill
Findhorn Bay
KINLOSS ABBEY
Kinloss
Culbin Forest
Kincorth Ho.
Kintessack
The Bar
Moy Ho.
Springfield
Grange Hall
Pittendreich
Miltonduff
Mains of Burgie
Dyke
Forres
NELSON TOWER
FALCONER MUSEUM
Monaughty Forest
PLUSCARDEN ABBEY
Auchtertyre
Forestersea
BRODIE CASTLE
Blervie Castle
Barnhill
DALLAS DHU DISTILLERY
Rafford
Califer
Altyre Ho.
Moor of Granary
Dallas Forest
Moray
Altyre Woods
Branchill
Dallas
Newtyle Forest
Drumine Forest
Craigroy
MILL BUIE
Loch Dallas
Lossie
Upper Knockando
Knockan
CARN KITTY
LARIG HILL
Findhorn
Divie
Dorback Burn
Allt a' Ghealaich
Burn of Tulchan
CRAGGANMORE DISTILLERY
Culloden
A9
A96
A82
A862
A835
A832
A939
A940
A95
B9006
B9091
B9090
B851
B862
B852
B861
B9154
B9007
B970
B9153
B9176
B9163
B9169
B9165
B9166
B9175
B817
B9092
B9089
B9010
B9040
B9012
B9102
B9101

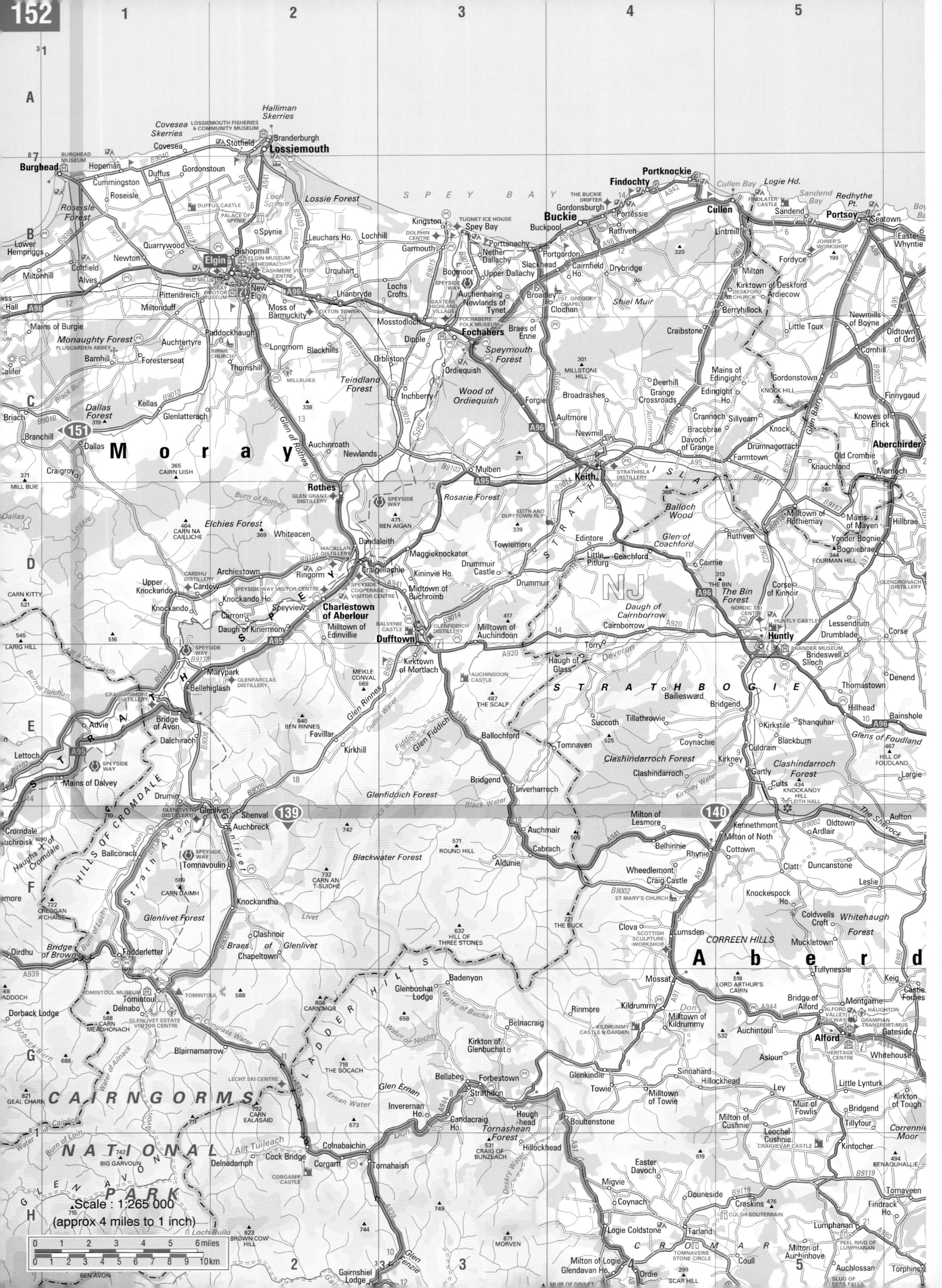
1
2
3
4
5
A
B
C
D
E
F
G
H
Halliman Skerries
Covesea Skerries
LOSSIEMOUTH FISHERIES & COMMUNITY MUSEUM
Branderburgh
Lossiemouth
Stotfield
Covesea
Burghead
BURGHEAD MUSEUM
Hopeman
Duffus
Gordonstoun
Cummingston
Roseisle
Roseisle Forest
DUFFUS CASTLE
PALACE OF SPYNIE
Loch Spynie
Lossie Forest
SPEY BAY
Spynie
Lower Hempriggs
Quarrywood
Bishopmill
Elgin
ELGIN MUSEUM
CATHEDRAL
CASHMERE VISITOR CENTRE
Newton
Coltfield
Alves
Miltonhill
OLD MILLS
MORAY MOTOR MUSEUM
New Elgin
Pittendreich
Miltonduff
Hall
Mains of Burgie
Monaughty Forest
PLUSCARDEN ABBEY
Barnhill
Foresterseat
Auchtertyre
Paddockhaugh
BIRNIE CHURCH
Thornhill
Moss of Barmuckity
COXTON TOWER
Longmorn
Blackhills
Leuchars Ho.
Lochhill
Urquhart
Lhanbryde
Lochs Crofts
Kingston
DOLPHIN CENTRE
TUGNET ICE HOUSE
Spey Bay
Garmouth
Porttanachy
Nether Dallachy
Upper Dallachy
Bogmoor
SPEYSIDE WAY
BAXTERS HIGHLAND VILLAGE
Auchenhalrig
Newlands of Tynet
Mosstodloch
FOCHABERS FOLK MUSEUM
Fochabers
Braes of Enzie
Speymouth Forest
Dipple
Orbliston
Teindland Forest
MILLBUIES
Ordiequish
Wood of Ordiequish
Inchberry
Forgie
Kellas
Glenlatterach
Dallas Forest
Black Burn
Briach
Branchill
151
Dallas
Moray
Glen of Rothes
338
Auchinroath
Newlands
Rothes
GLEN GRANT DISTILLERY
SPEYSIDE WAY
471 BEN AIGAN
Mulben
Rosarie Forest
365 CAIRN UISH
371 MILL BUIE
Craigroy
Burn of Rothes
Elchies Forest
404 CARN NA CAILLICHE
369
Whiteacen
MACALLAN DISTILLERY
Dandaleith
Maggieknockater
Craigellachie
Kininvie Ho.
Drummuir Castle
Drummuir
Towiemore
Archiestown
CARDHU DISTILLERY
Cardow
Upper Knockando
Ringorm
SPEYSIDE WAY VISITOR CENTRE
SPEYSIDE COOPERAGE VISITOR CENTRE
Midtown of Buchromb
Knockando Ho.
Knockando
Speyview
Charlestown of Aberlour
Carron
Daugh of Kinermony
Milltown of Edinvillie
BALVENIE CASTLE
Dufftown
GLENFIDDICH DISTILLERY
Milltown of Auchindoun
CARN KITTY 521
545 LARIG HILL
516
SPEYSIDE WAY
Marypark
Bellehiglash
GLENFARCLAS DISTILLERY
Kirktown of Mortlach
MEIKLE CONVAL 569
AUCHINDOUN CASTLE
487 THE SCALP
CRAGGANMORE DISTILLERY
Advie
Bridge of Avon
Dalchirach
840 BEN RINNES
Favillar
Kirkhill
Glen Rinnes
Glen Fiddich
Ballochford
Lettoch
SPEYSIDE WAY
Mains of Dalvey
Drumin
Glenfiddich Forest
Bridgend
Inverharroch
GLENLIVET DISTILLERY
Glenlivet
Shenval
Auchbreck
139
742
Cromdale
Auchroisk
Haughs of Cromdale
HILLS OF CROMDALE
Ballcorach
SPEYSIDE WAY
Tomnavoulin
571 ROUND HILL
Blackwater Forest
Auchmair
Cabrach
Aldunie
732 CARN AN T-SUIDHE
569 CARN DAIMH
Strath Avon
722 CREGGAN A'CHAISE
Glenlivet Forest
Knockandhu
Clashnoir
Braes of Glenlivet
Chapeltown
632 HILL OF THREE STONES
Dirdhu
Bridge of Brown
Fodderletter
Badenyon
Glenbuchat Lodge
TOMINTOUL MUSEUM
Tomintoul
Delnabo
GLENLIVET ESTATE VISITOR CENTRE
TOMINTOUL
588
Dorback Lodge
588 CARN MEADHONACH
804 CARN MOR
658
LADDER HILLS
Blairnamarrow
688
718 THE SOCACH
LECHT SKI CENTRE
821 GEAL CHARN
CAIRNGORMS
NATIONAL PARK
792 CARN EALASAID
Glen Ernan
Inverernan Ho.
673
Colnabaichin
Cock Bridge
Corgarff
CORGARFF CASTLE
Delnadamph
742 BIG GARVOUN
Tornahaish
715
Scale : 1:265 000
(approx 4 miles to 1 inch)
823 BROWN COW HILL
744
749
BEN AVON
Gairnshiel Lodge
Glen Fenzie
Findochty
Portknockie
Cullen Bay
Logie Hd.
Cullen
THE BUCKIE DRIFTER
Gordonsburgh
Portessie
Buckie
Buckpool
Rathven
FINDLATER CASTLE
Sandend
Sandend Bay
Redhythe Pt.
Portsoy
Seatown
Easter Whyntie
Lintmill
JOINER'S WORKSHOP
Portgordon
Cairnfield Ho.
Drybridge
320
Slackhead
Milton
Fordyce
199
Broadley
ST. GREGORY'S CHAPEL
Clochan
Shiel Muir
Kirktown of Deskford
DESKFORD CHURCH
Ardiecow
Berryhillock
Craibstone
Little Toux
Newmills of Boyne
Oldtown of Ord
Cornhill
301 MILLSTONE HILL
Mains of Edingight
Gordonstown
Deerhill
Grange Crossroads
Edingight Ho.
KNOCK HILL 430
Broadrashes
Crannoch
Sillyearn
Bracobrae
Knock
Finnygaud
Knowes of Elrick
Aultmore
Newmill
Davoch of Grange
Drumnagorrach
Aberchirder
Farmtown
Old Crombie
Knauchland
Marnoch
311
Keith
STRATHISLA DISTILLERY
STRATH ISLA
366
265
Balloch Wood
Milltown of Rothiemay
Mains of Mayen
Hillbrae
KEITH AND DUFFTOWN RLY
339
Edintore
Glen of Coachford
Ruthven
Yonder Bognie
Bogniebrae
344 FOURMAN HILL
Little Pitlurg
Coachford
Cairnie
313 THE BIN
The Bin Forest
NJ
Corse of Kinnoir
GLENDRONACH DISTILLERY
Daugh of Cairnborrow
Cairnborrow
NORDIC SKI CENTRE
HUNTLY CASTLE
Huntly
Lessendrum
Drumblade
Corse
417
Torry
BRANDER MUSEUM
Brideswell
Slioch
Haugh of Glass
Deveron
STRATHBOGIE
Bailiesward
Bridgend
Thomastown
Denend
Hillhead
Bainshole
Succoth
Tillathrowie
Kirkstile
Shanquhar
Glens of Foudland
Tomnaven
525
Coynachie
Blackburn
Culdrain
467 HILL OF FOUDLAND
Clashindarroch Forest
Clashindarroch
Kirkney
Gartly
Clashindarroch Forest
Largie
Cults
434 KNOCKANDY HILL
LEITH HALL
Kirkney Water
The Shevock
Milton of Lesmore
140
Kennethmont
Oldtown
Aulton
Ardlair
Milton of Noth
Belhinnie
Rhynie
Cottown
505
Wheedlemont
Craig Castle
Clatt
Duncanstone
Leslie
ST MARY'S CHURCH
Knockespock Ho.
721 THE BUCK
Clova
SCOTTISH SCULPTURE WORKSHOP
Lumsden
CORREEN HILLS
Coldwells Croft
Whitehaugh Forest
Muckletown
Aberd
Mossat
Tullynessle
518 LORD ARTHUR'S CAIRN
Keig
Castle Forbes
Kildrummy
Milltown of Kildrummy
Bridge of Alford
Montgarrie
ALFORD VALLEY RAILWAY
HAUGHTON
GRAMPIAN TRANSPORT MUS
Rinmore
KILDRUMMY CASTLE & GARDEN
532
Auchintoul
Alford
Gateside
HERITAGE CENTRE
Whitehouse
Belnacraig
Kirkton of Glenbuchat
Asloun
Glenkindie
Sinnahard
Hillockhead
Little Lynturk
Bellabeg
Forbestown
Strathdon
Towie
Milltown of Towie
Ley
Kirkton of Tough
Muir of Fowlis
Bridgend
Candacraig Ho.
Heugh-head
Boultenstone
Milton of Cushnie
Tillyfour
Tornashean Forest
Leochel-Cushnie
CRAIGIEVAR CASTLE
Correnie Moor
531 CRAIG OF BUNZEACH
Hillockhead
Kintocher
619
494 BENAQUHALLIE
Easter Davoch
Migvie
Coynach
Douneside
Craskins
476
CULSH SOUTERRAIN
Tornaveen
Findrack Ho.
Lumphanan
871 MORVEN
Logie Coldstone
Tarland
CROMAR
PEEL RING OF LUMPHANAN
TOMNAVERIE STONE CIRCLE
Coull
Milton of Auchinhove
Milton of Logie
Glendavan Ho.
Ordie
299 SCAR HILL
Auchlossan
Torphins
MUIR OF DINNET
SLUG OF DESS FALLS
A96
A95
A941
A920
A97
A939
A944
A980
A98
A942
A990
B9040
B9012
B9013
B9103
B9015
B9014
B9016
B9018
B9022
B9023
B9010
B9102
B9138
B9008
B9009
B9002
B9117
B9115
B9119
0 1 2 3 4 5 6 miles
0 1 2 3 4 5 6 7 8 9 10 km

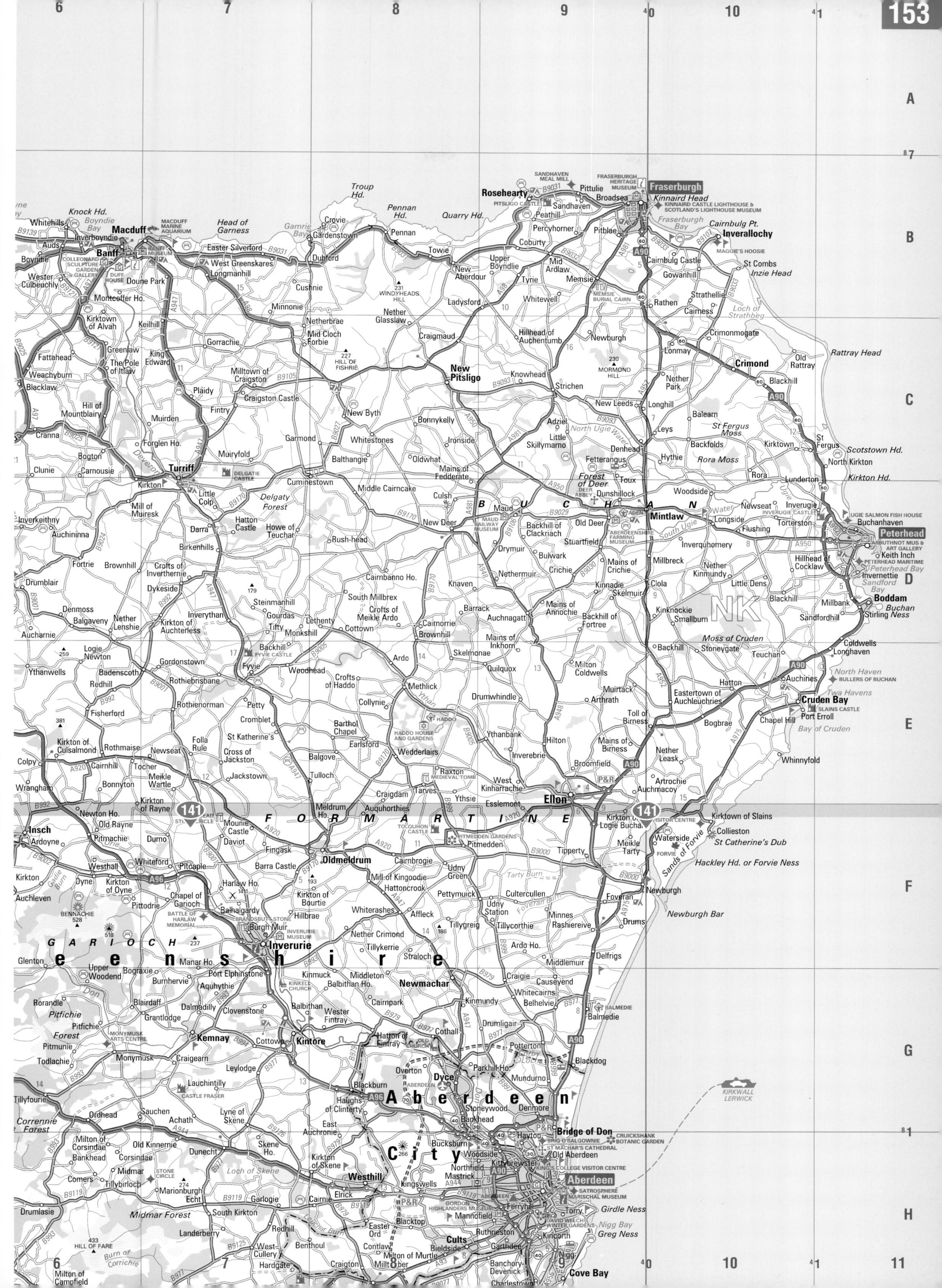

Fraserburgh
Rosehearty
Sandhaven
Pittulie
Broadsea
Kinnaird Head
Kinnaird Castle Lighthouse & Scotland's Lighthouse Museum
Fraserburgh Bay
Cairnbulg Pt.
Inverallochy
Maggie's Hoosie
Cairnbulg Castle
St Combs
Inzie Head
Gowanhill
Troup Hd.
Pennan Hd.
Quarry Hd.
Knock Hd.
Boyndie Bay
Head of Garness
Gamrie Bay
Crovie
Gardenstown
Pennan
Whitehills
Macduff
Macduff Marine Aquarium
Inverboyndie
Banff
Banff Museum
Duff House
Auds
Boyndie
Wester Culbeuchly
Doune Park
Easter Silverford
West Greenskares
Longmanhill
Dubford
Towie
New Aberdour
Upper Boyndie
Coburty
Percyhorner
Pitblae
Peathill
Pitsligo Castle
Sandhaven Meal Mill
Fraserburgh Heritage Museum
Mid Ardlaw
Memsie
Memsie Burial Cairn
Tyrie
Whitewell
Ladysford
Rathen
Strathellie
Cairness
Loch of Strathbeg
Crimonmogate
Rattray Head
Old Rattray
Crimond
Blackhill
Lonmay
Nether Park
Longhill
New Leeds
Newburgh
Mormond Hill
Strichen
Knowhead
Hillhead of Auchentumb
Craigmaud
Nether Glasslaw
Windyheads Hill
Cushnie
Minnonie
Montcoffer Ho.
Kirktown of Alvah
Keilhill
Netherbrae
Mid Cloch Forbie
Hill of Fishrie
Gorrachie
King Edward
Greenlaw
The Pole of Itlaw
Fattahead
Weachyburn
Blacklaw
Hill of Mountblairy
Milltown of Craigston
Craigston Castle
Plaidy
Fintry
Muirden
Forglen Ho.
Cranna
Bogton
Clunie
Carnousie
Turriff
Delgatie Castle
Muiryfold
Garmond
New Byth
Whitestones
Balthangie
Bonnykelly
Ironside
Oldwhat
Mains of Fedderate
New Pitsligo
Adziel
North Ugie Water
Little Skillymarno
Leys
Balearn
St Fergus Moss
Backfolds
Kirktown
St Fergus
Scotstown Hd.
North Kirkton
Kirkton Hd.
Hythie
Rora Moss
Rora
Lunderton
Denhead
Fetterangus
Forest of Deer
Deer Abbey
Toux
Dunshillock
Woodside
Newseat
Inverugie
Ugie Salmon Fish House
Buchanhaven
Peterhead
Arbuthnot Mus & Art Gallery
Keith Inch
Peterhead Maritime
Peterhead Bay
Invernettie
Sandford Bay
Boddam
Buchan Ness
Stirling Ness
Kirkton
Little Colp
Cuminestown
Middle Cairncake
Culsh
Delgaty Forest
Mill of Muiresk
Inverkeithny
Auchininna
Darra
Hatton Castle
Howe of Teuchar
Rush-head
New Deer
Maud
Maud Railway Museum
B U C H A N
Aden
Aberdeenshire Farming Museum
Mintlaw
Old Deer
Backhill of Clackriach
Stuartfield
South Ugie
Longside
Torterston
Flushing
Inverquhomery
Birkenhills
Fortrie
Brownhill
Crofts of Inverthernie
Drumblair
Dykeside
Cairnbanno Ho.
Drymuir
Bulwark
Crichie
Mains of Crichie
Millbreck
Nether Kinmundy
Hillhead of Cocklaw
Little Dens
Blackhill
Millbank
Sandfordhill
Knaven
Nethermuir
Kinnadie
Clola
Skelmuir
Steinmanhill
South Millbrex
Crofts of Meikle Ardo
Denmoss
Balgaveny
Nether Lenshie
Kirkton of Auchterless
Inverythan
Gourdas
Tifty
Lethenty
Monkshill
Cottown
Cairnorrie
Brownhill
Barrack
Auchnagatt
Mains of Annochie
Backhill of Fortree
Kinknockie
Smallburn
NK
Moss of Cruden
Aucharnie
Logie Newton
Backhill
Fyvie
Fyvie Castle
Ardo
Skelmonae
Mains of Inkhorn
Quilquox
Backhill
Stoneygate
Teuchan
Coldwells
Longhaven
North Haven
Bullers of Buchan
Ythanwells
Badenscoth
Gordonstown
Rothiebrisbane
Woodhead
Crofts of Haddo
Methlick
Milton Coldwells
Redhill
Rothienorman
Petty
Cromblet
Collynie
Drumwhindle
Muirtack
Arthrath
Hatton
Auchiries
Eastertown of Auchleuchries
Cruden Bay
Twa Havens
Slains Castle
Port Erroll
Bay of Cruden
Fisherford
Kirkton of Culsalmond
Rothmaise
Newseat
Folla Rule
St Katherine's
Barthol Chapel
Earlsford
Haddo
Haddo House and Gardens
Ythanbank
Hilton
Toll of Birness
Bogbrae
Chapel Hill
Mains of Birness
Nether Leask
Whinnyfold
Colpy
Cairnhill
Tocher
Meikle Wartle
Cross of Jackston
Jackston
Balgove
Wedderlairs
Tulloch
Raxton
Medieval Tomb
West Kinharrachie
Inverebrie
Broomfield
Artrochie
Auchmacoy
Wrangham
Bonnyton
Kirkton of Rayne
Newton Ho.
Old Rayne
Craigdam
Tarves
Ythsie
Esslemont
Ellon
Meldrum Ho.
Auquhorthies
F O R M A R T I N E
Kirkton of Logie Buchan
Kirktown of Slains
Visitor Centre
Collieston
St Catherine's Dub
Insch
Ardoyne
Pitmachie
Durno
Mounie Castle
Daviot
Tolquhon Castle
Pitmedden Gardens
Pitmedden
Tipperty
Waterside
Forvie
Sands of Forvie
Meikle Tarty
Hackley Hd. or Forvie Ness
Whiteford
Westhall
Pitcaple
Fingask
Oldmeldrum
Barra Castle
Cairnbrogie
Udny Green
Tarty Burn
Kirkton
Oyne
Kirkton of Oyne
Gadie Burn
Harlaw Ho.
Mill of Kingoodie
Hattoncrook
Kirkton of Bourtie
Pettymuick
Cultercullen
Foveran
Foveran Burn
Newburgh
Newburgh Bar
Auchleven
Pittodrie
Chapel of Garioch
Balhalgardy
Battle of Harlaw Memorial
Brandsbutt Stone
Whiterashes
Affleck
Udny Station
Tillycorthie
Minnes
Rashiereive
Drums
Bennachie
Burgh Muir
Inverurie Museum
Hillbrae
Tillygreig
G A R I O C H
Nether Crimond
Inverurie
Tillykerrie
Straloch
Ardo Ho.
Middlemuir
Delfrigs
Glenton
e e n s h i r e
Manar Ho.
Upper Woodend
Bograxie
Port Elphinstone
Kinmuck
Middleton
Burnhervie
Aquhythie
Kinkell Church
Balbithan Ho.
Newmachar
Craigie
Causeyend
Whitecairns
Belhelvie
Balmedie
Rorandle
Pitfichie
Forest
Blairdaff
Dalmadilly
Grantlodge
Clovenstone
Cairnpark
Kinmundy
Balbithan
Wester Fintray
Drumligair
Monymusk Arts Centre
Pitmunie
Kemnay
Cottown
Kintore
Hatton of Fintray
Old Church
Cothall
Potterton
Todlachie
Monymusk
Craigearn
Leylodge
Parkhill Ho.
Bishops Loch
Blackdog
Lauchintilly
Castle Fraser
Overton
Dyce
Mundurno
Kirkwall
Lerwick
Tillyfourie
Blackburn
Haughs of Clinterty
Aberdeen
A b e r d e e n
Denmore
Stoneywood
Ordhead
Sauchen
Lyne of Skene
Achath
Bankhead
Bridge of Don
Corrennie Forest
East Auchronie
Hayton
Cruickshank Botanic Garden
Brig o' Balgownie
St Machar's Cathedral
Old Aberdeen
Milton of Corsindae
Old Kinnernie
Skene Ho.
Bucksburn
Bankhead
Corsindae
Dunecht
Kirkton of Skene
C i t y
Woodside
Kittybrewster
King's College Visitor Centre
Loch of Skene
Westhill
Northfield
Mastrick
Comers
Midmar
Stone Circle
Tillybirloch
Marionburgh
Echt
Elrick
Kingswells
Satrosphere
Marischal Museum
Drumlasie
Garlogie
Cairnie
Gordon Highlanders Museum
Ferryhill
Torry
Girdle Ness
Midmar Forest
South Kirkton
Mannofield
David Welch Winter Gardens
Nigg Bay
Redhill
Blacktop
Landerberry
Easter Ord
Ruthrieston
Kincorth
Greg Ness
Hill of Fare
Burn of Corrichie
West Cullery
Benthoul
Contlaw
Cults
Bieldside
Garthdee
Nigg
Hardgate
Craigton
Milton of Murtle
Millt
Banchory-Devenick
Charlestown
Cove Bay
Milton of Campfield

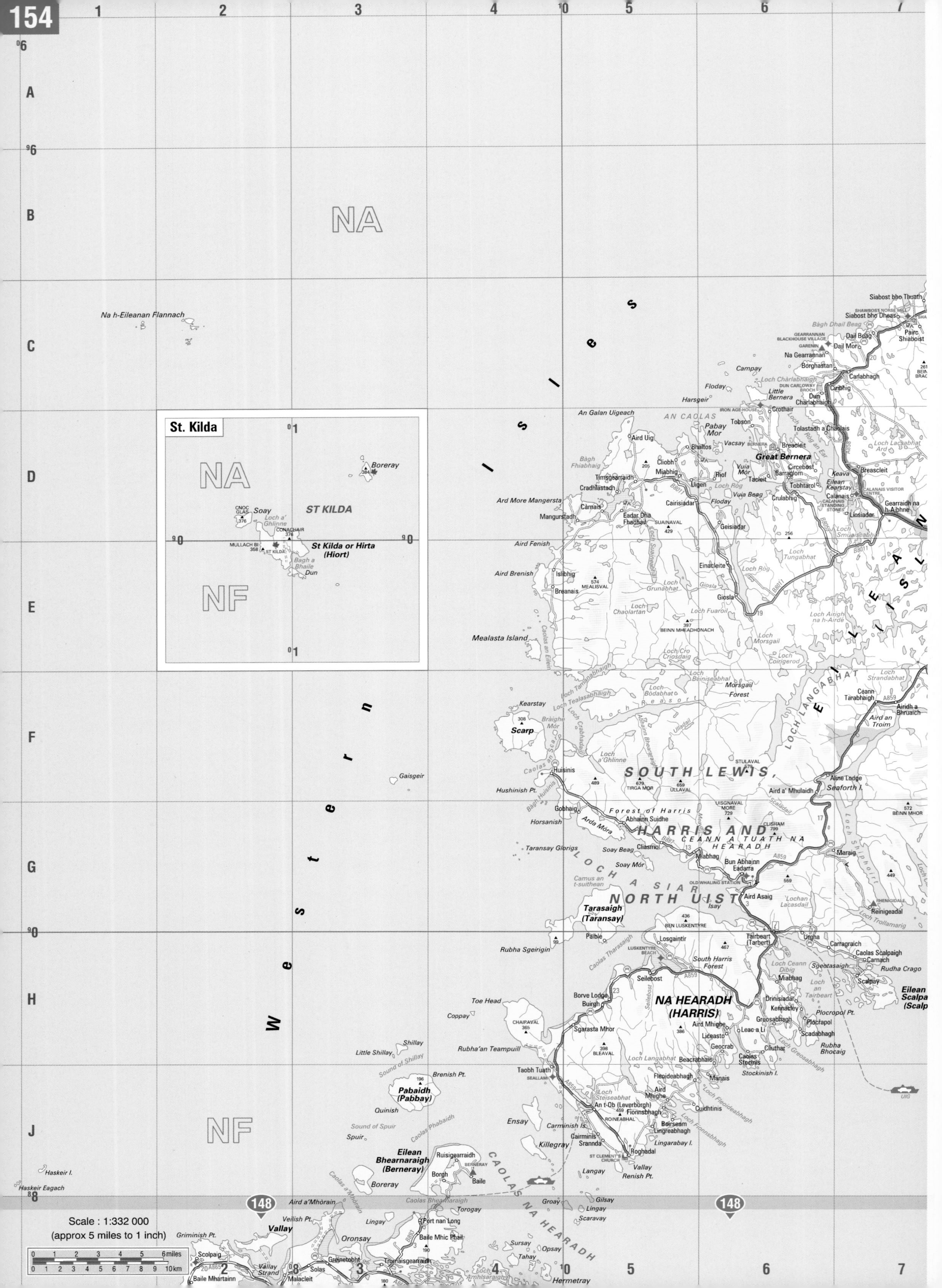

NA
NF
Na h-Eileanan Flannach
St. Kilda
Boreray
Soay
ST KILDA
St Kilda or Hirta (Hiort)
Bagh a Bhaile
Dun
Western Isles
Gaisgeir
Scarp
Kearstay
Huisinis
Hushinish Pt.
Mealasta Island
Aird Brenish
Aird Fenish
Ard More Mangersta
An Galan Uigeach
Aird Uig
Great Bernera
Little Bernera
Pabay Mor
Vacsay
Campay
Floday
Harsgeir
Siabost bho Thuath
Siabost bho Dheas
Dail Beag
Dail Mor
Na Gearrannan
Borghastan
Carlabhagh
Breascleit
Calanais
Linsiadar
Gearraidh na h-Aibhne
Tobson
Crothair
Circebost
Barraglom
Tobhtarol
Cliobh
Miabhig
Uigen
Timsgearraidh
Cradhlastadh
Carnais
Eadar Dha Fhadhail
Cairisiadar
Geisiadar
Mangurstadh
Islibhig
Breanais
Einacleite
Giosla
SOUTH LEWIS,
HARRIS AND
NORTH UIST
Forest of Harris
Abhainn Suidhe
Morsgail Forest
LOCH LANGABHAT
Loch Reasort
Ceann Tarabhaigh
Airidh a Bhruaich
Aird an Troim
Aline Lodge
Seaforth I.
Aird a' Mhulaidh
Maraig
Reinigeadal
Bun Abhainn Eadarra
Miabhag
Cliasmol
Soay Beag
Soay Mòr
Taransay Glorigs
Horsanish
Gobhaig
Arda Mòra
LOCH A SIAR
Tarasaigh (Taransay)
Paible
Rubha Sgeirigin
Aird Asaig
Tairbeart (Tarbert)
Urgha
Carragraich
Caolas Scalpaigh
Carnach
Rudha Crago
Scalpay
Eilean Scalpay (Scalpay)
Losgaintir
South Harris Forest
Seilebost
Borve Lodge
Buirgh
NA HEARADH (HARRIS)
Sgarasta Mhor
Toe Head
Coppay
Rubha'an Teampuill
Taobh Tuath
Shillay
Little Shillay
Sound of Shillay
Pabaidh (Pabbay)
Brenish Pt.
Quinish
Sound of Spuir
Spuir
Ensay
Killegray
Carminish Is.
An t-Ob (Leverburgh)
Fionnsbhagh
Roghadal
Renish Pt.
Lingarabay I.
Stockinish I.
Manais
Beacrabhaic
Geocrab
Leac a Li
Liceasto
Drinisiadar
Kennacley
Greosabhagh
Plocrapol Pt.
Scadabhagh
Rubha Bhocaig
Eilean Bhearnaraigh (Berneray)
Ruisigearraidh
Borgh
Baile
Boreray
CAOLAS NA HEARADH
Langay
Groay
Gilsay
Lingay
Scaravay
Haskeir I.
Haskeir Eagach
Aird a'Mhòrain
Vallay
Oronsay
Port nan Long
Baile Mhic Phail
Sursay
Opsay
Tahay
Hermetray
Scolpaig
Griminish Pt.
Baile Mhàrtainn
Malacleit
Solas
Greinetobht
148
Scale : 1:332 000
(approx 5 miles to 1 inch)

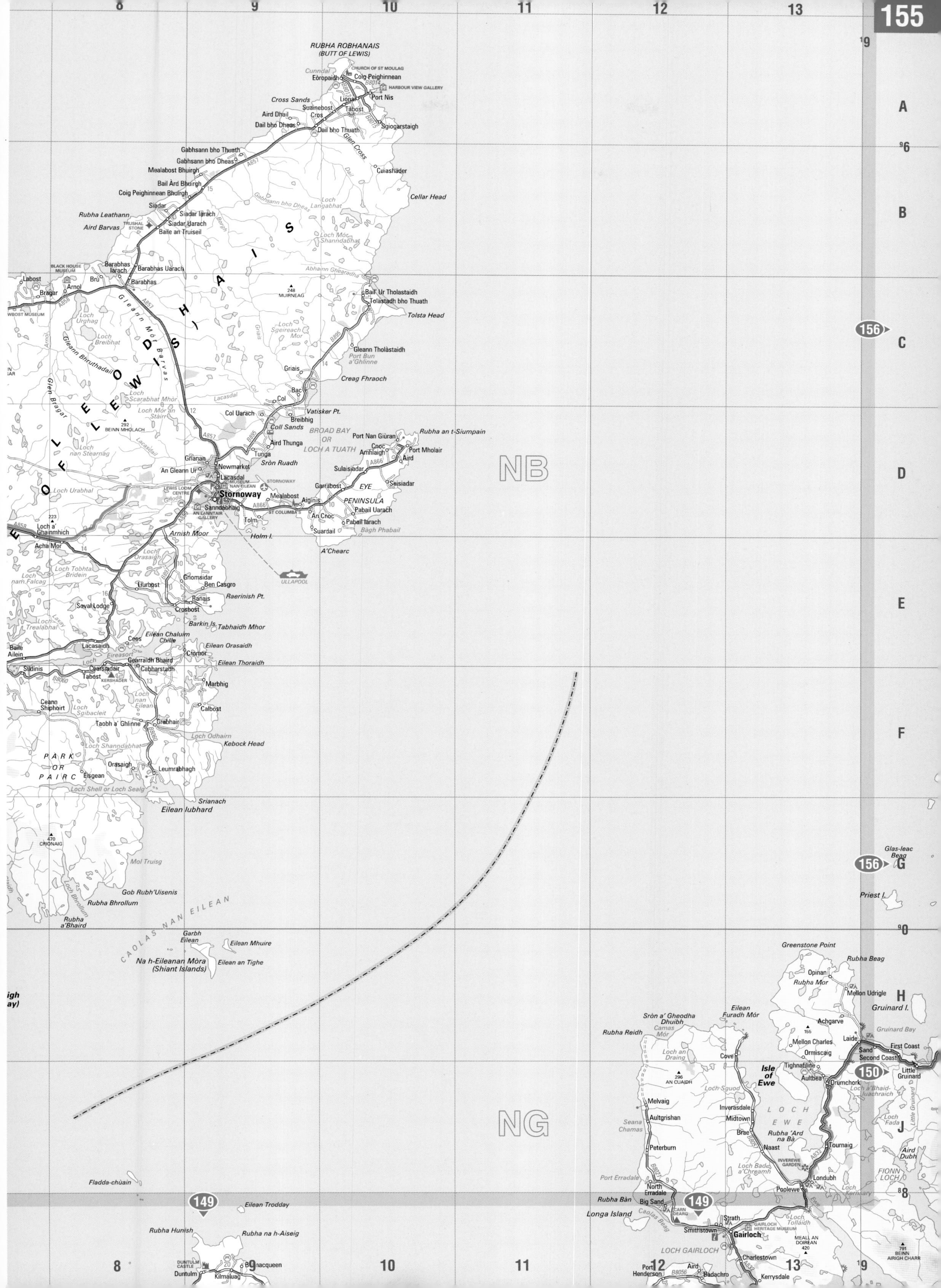
155
RUBHA ROBHANAIS
(BUTT OF LEWIS)
Cunndal
CHURCH OF ST MOLUAG
Eòropaidh
Coig Peighinnean
HARBOUR VIEW GALLERY
Lional
Port Nis
Cross Sands
Suainebost
Tàbost
Aird Dhail
Cros
Dail bho Dheas
Dail bho Thuath
Sgiogarstaigh
Glen Cross
Gabhsann bho Thuath
Gabhsann bho Dheas
Cuiashader
Mealabost Bhuirgh
Bail Àrd Bhuirgh
Coig Peighinnean Bhuirgh
Cellar Head
Siadar
Siadar Iarach
Siadar Uarach
Baile an Truiseil
Rubha Leathann
Aird Barvas
TRUSHAL STONE
Loch Langabhat
Loch Mòr Shanndabhat
BLACK HOUSE MUSEUM
Barabhas Iarach
Barabhas Uarach
Barabhas
Abhainn Ghearadha
Labost
Brù
Arnol
Bragar
248 MUIRNEAG
Bail' Ur Tholastaidh
Tolastadh bho Thuath
Tolsta Head
Loch Urghag
Loch Breibhat
Gleann Bhruthadail
Gleann Mòr Barvas
Loch Sgeireach Mor
Gleann Tholàstaidh
Port Bun a' Ghlinne
Griais
Creag Fhraoch
Bac
Glen Bragar
Loch Scarabhat Mhòr
Loch Mòr an Stàirr
Lacasdal
Col
Col Uarach
Vatisker Pt.
Breibhig
Coll Sands
292 BEINN MHOLACH
BROAD BAY OR LOCH A TUATH
Port Nan Giùran
Rubha an t-Siumpain
Aird Thunga
Cnoc Amhlaigh
Port Mholair
Aird
Loch nan Stearnag
Tunga
Giùran
Sròn Ruadh
An Gleann Ur
Newmarket
Lacasdal
Sulaisiadar
NB
STORNOWAY
MUSEUM NAN EILEAN
Seisiadar
Loch Urabhal
LEWIS LOOM CENTRE
Stornoway
Garrabost
EYE
Mealabost
Aiginis
PENINSULA
Sanndabhaig
Pabail Uarach
AN LANNTAIR GALLERY
ST COLUMBA'S
An Cnoc
Pabail Iarach
223
Loch a' Ghainmhich
Tolm
Suardail
Bàgh Phabail
Arnish Moor
Holm I.
A' Chearc
Acha Mor
Loch Orasaigh
Loch Tobhta Bridein
Loch nam Falcag
ULLAPOOL
Griomsidar
Liurbost
Ben Casgro
Ranais
Raerinish Pt.
Soval Lodge
Crosbost
Loch Trealabhal
Barkin Is.
Tabhaidh Mhor
Eilean Chaluim Chille
Ceos
Baile Ailein
Lacasaidh
Eilean Orasaidh
Cromor
Eireasort
Gearraidh Bhaird
Eilean Thoraidh
Sildinis
Ceann Shìphoirt
Tabost
KERSHADER
Cabharstadh
Marbhig
Loch nan Eilean
Loch Sgibacleit
Calbost
Taobh a' Ghlinne
Grabhair
Loch Odhairn
Kebock Head
Loch Shanndabhat
PARK OR PAIRC
Orasaigh
Eisgean
Leumrabhagh
Loch Sheil or Loch Sealg
Srianach
Eilean Iubhard
470 CRIONAIG
Mol Truisg
Gob Rubh' Uisenis
Loch Bhrollum
Rubha Bhrollum
Rubha a' Bhàird
CAOLAS NAN EILEAN
Garbh Eilean
Eilean Mhuire
Na h-Eileanan Mòra (Shiant Islands)
Eilean an Tighe
Fladda-chùain
149
Eilean Trodday
Rubha Hunish
Rubha na h-Aiseig
DUNTULM CASTLE
Duntulm
Bornacqueen
Kilmaluag
NG
156
Glas-leac Beag
Priest I.
Greenstone Point
Rubha Beag
Opinan
Rubha Mor
Mellon Udrigle
Gruinard I.
Achgarve
Gruinard Bay
Laide
Sròn a' Gheodha Dhuibh
Eilean Furadh Mór
Camas Mór
Rubha Reidh
Loch an Draing
155
Mellon Charles
Ormiscaig
Sand
First Coast
Second Coast
Cove
Tighnafiline
Isle of Ewe
Aultbea
Drumchork
150
Little Gruinard
296 AN CUAIDH
Loch Sguod
Loch a' Bhaid-luachraich
Melvaig
Inverasdale
LOCH EWE
Aultgrishan
Midtown
Seana Chamas
Rubha 'Ard na Bà
Brae
Naast
Tournaig
Loch Fada
Little Gruinard
Peterburn
Aird Dubh
INVEREWE GARDEN
Loch Bad a' Chreamh
FIONN LOCH
Port Erradale
Londubh
North Erradale
Poolewe
Loch Kernsary
Rubha Bàn
Big Sand
Longa Island
Caolas Beag
CARN DEARG
Loch Tollaidh
Strath
GAIRLOCH HERITAGE MUSEUM
Smithstown
Gairloch
MEALL AN DOIREAN 420
791 BEINN AIRIGH CHARR
LOCH GAIRLOCH
Charlestown
Port Henderson
Aird
Badachro
Kerrysdale
8
9
10
11
12
13
19
A
B
C
D
E
F
G
H
J

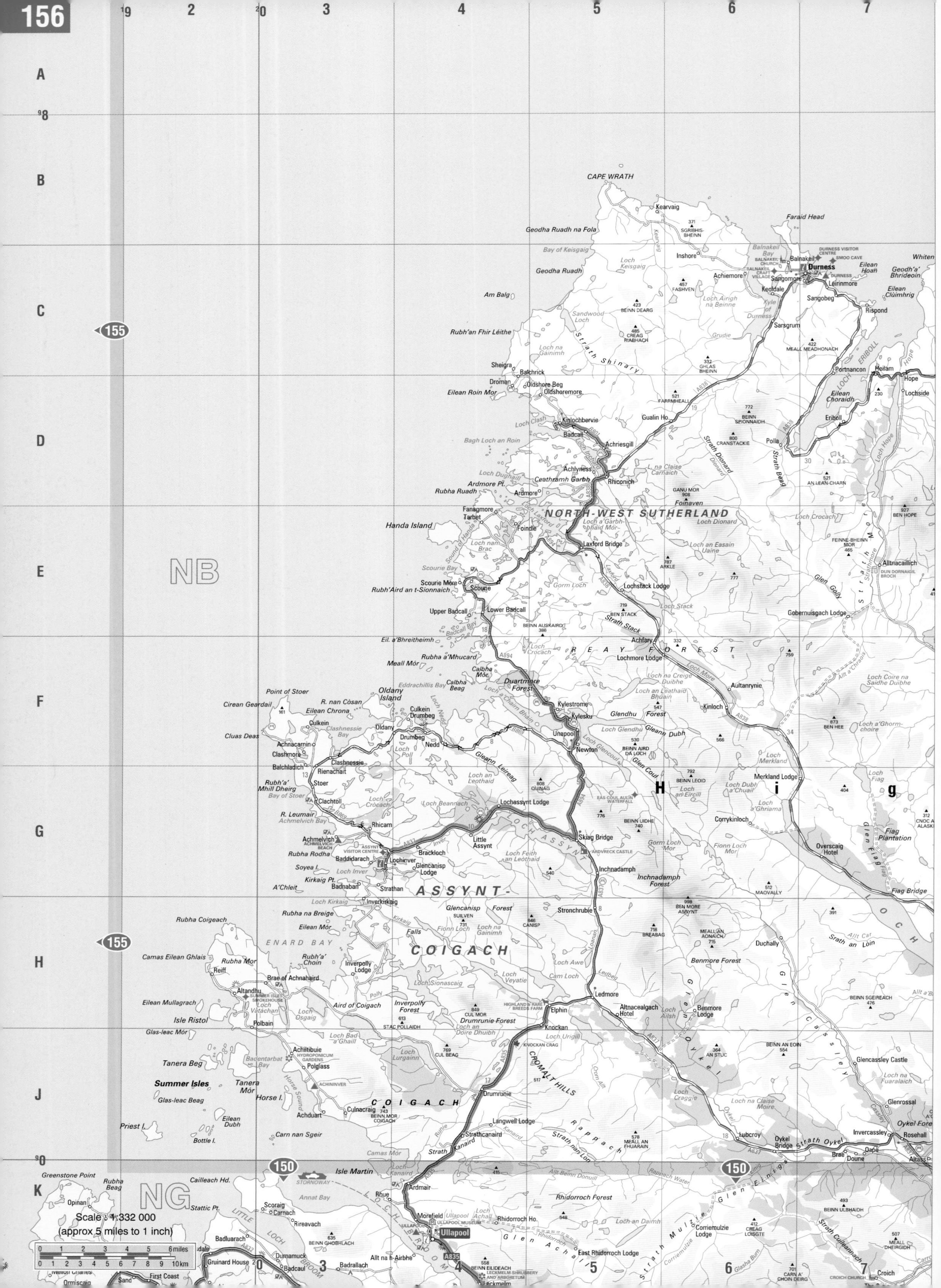

CAPE WRATH
Kearvaig
Faraid Head
Geodha Ruadh na Fola
Bay of Keisgaig
Loch Keisgaig
Inshore
Balnakeil
Durness
Geodha Ruadh
Achiemore
Sangomore
Keoldale
Leirinmore
Sangobeg
Am Balg
Rispond
Sandwood Loch
Rubh'an Fhir Léithe
Sarsgrum
Sheigra
Balchrick
Droman
Oldshore Beg
Oldshoremore
Eilean Roin Mor
Kinlochbervie
Badcall
Achriesgill
Gualin Ho.
Portnancon
Heilam
Hope
Lochside
Eriboll
Polla
Bagh Loch an Roin
Loch Clash
Achlyness
Rhiconich
Ardmore Pt.
Rubha Ruadh
Ardmore
Fanagmore
Tarbet
Handa Island
Foindle
NORTH-WEST SUTHERLAND
Foinaven
Loch Dionard
Laxford Bridge
Scourie Bay
Scourie More
Scourie
Rubh'Aird an t-Sionnaich
Lochstack Lodge
Upper Badcall
Lower Badcall
Gobernuisgach Lodge
Loch Stack
Strath Stack
REAY FOREST
Achfary
Lochmore Lodge
Eil. a'Bhreitheimh
Rubha a'Mhucard
Meall Mór
Calbha Mór
Calbha Beag
Duartmore Forest
Aultanrynie
Point of Stoer
Oldany Island
Cirean Geardail
R. nan Còsan
Eilean Chrona
Culkein Drumbeg
Culkein
Oldany
Kylestrome
Kylesku
Glendhu
Kinloch
Cluas Deas
Achnacarnin
Clashmore
Balchladich
Drumbeg
Nedd
Unapool
Newton
Clashnessie
Rienachait
Gleann Leireag
Glen Coul
Merkland Lodge
Stoer
Rubh'a' Mhill Dheirg
Bay of Stoer
Clachtoll
Loch Beannach
Lochassynt Lodge
R. Leumair
Achmelvich Bay
Rhicarn
Achmelvich
Little Assynt
LOCH ASSYNT
Skiag Bridge
Corrykinloch
Overscaig Hotel
Rubha Rodha
Baddidarach
Brackloch
Lochinver
Glencanisp Lodge
Inchnadamph
Inchnadamph Forest
Soyea I.
Loch Inver
Kirkaig Pt.
Badnaban
Strathan
A'Chleit
ASSYNT
Flag Bridge
Loch Kirkaig
Inverkirkaig
Glencanisp Forest
Stronchrubie
Rubha Coigeach
Rubha na Breige
Eilean Mór
Falls
ENARD BAY
COIGACH
Camas Eilean Ghlais
Rubha Mor
Rubh'a' Choin
Inverpolly Lodge
Duchally
Benmore Forest
Reiff
Brae of Achnahaird
Loch Sionascaig
Loch Veyatie
Cam Loch
Loch Awe
Altandhu
Eilean Mullagrach
Aird of Coigach
Ledmore
Isle Ristol
Inverpolly Forest
Drumrunie Forest
Elphin
Altnacealgach Hotel
Benmore Lodge
Glas-leac Mór
Polbain
Knockan
Loch Urigill
Achiltibuie
Polglass
CROMALT HILLS
Tanera Beg
Summer Isles
Tanera Mór
Glencassley Castle
Glas-leac Beag
Horse I.
Drumrunie
Culnacraig
Achduart
Glenrossal
Eilean Dubh
Priest I.
Carn nan Sgeir
Langwell Lodge
Strathcanaird
Invercassley
Rosehall
Bottle I.
Strath Kanaird
Lubcroy
Oykel Bridge
Strath Oykel
Brae
Doune
Altass
Camas Mòr
Isle Martin
Greenstone Point
Rubha Beag
Cailleach Hd.
Ardmair
Rhidorroch Forest
Opinan
Stattic Pt.
Scoraig
Carnach
Rhue
Morefield
Ullapool
Rhidorroch Ho.
Corriemulzie Lodge
Rireavach
Badluarach
Dundonnell
Gruinard House
Badcaul
Badrallach
Allt na h-Airbhe
East Rhidorroch Lodge
Croick
Sand
First Coast
NB
NG
Scale 1:332 000
(approx 5 miles to 1 inch)
155
150

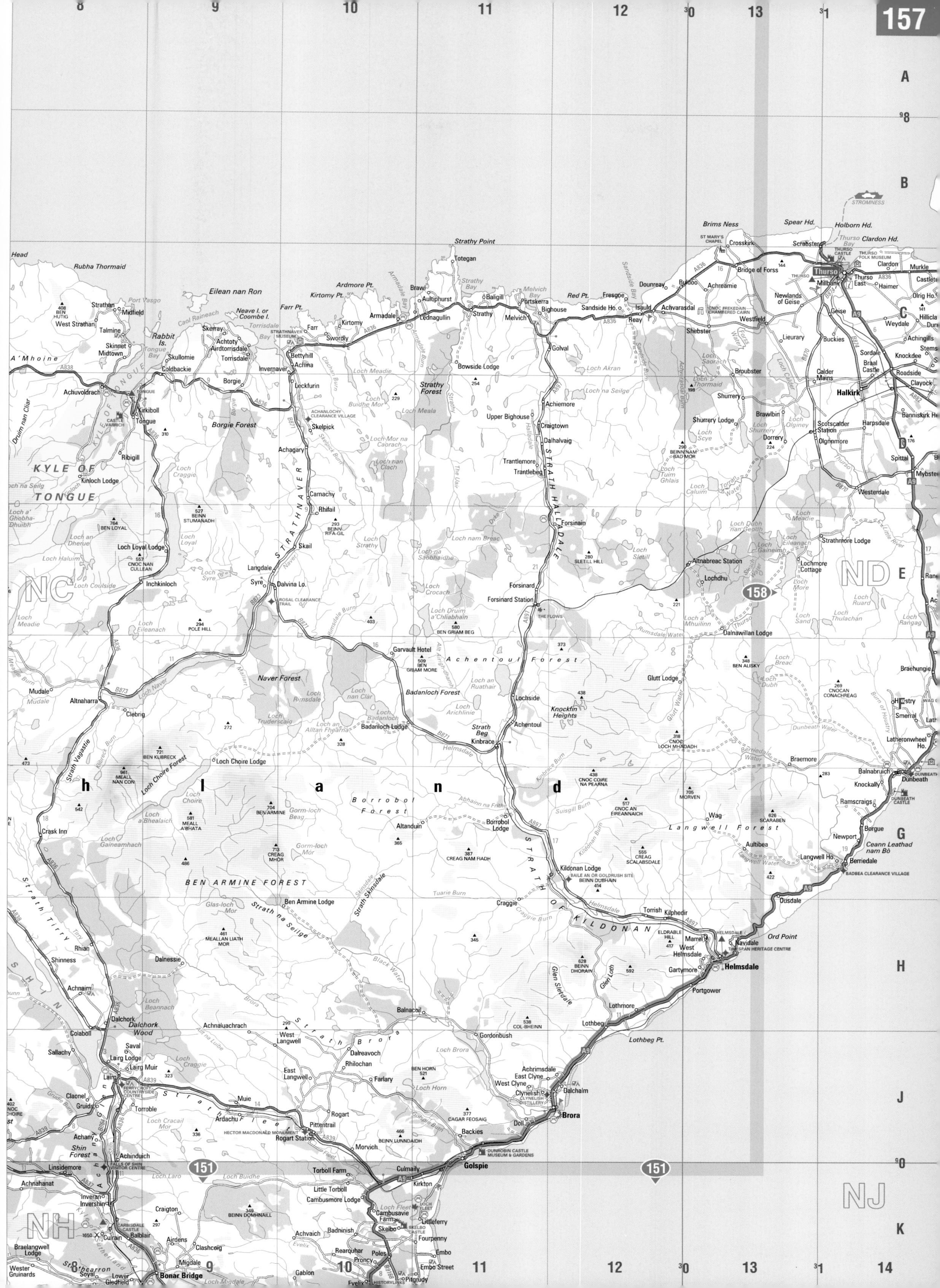
Strathy Point
Brims Ness
Spear Hd.
Holborn Hd.
Clardon Hd.
Rubha Thormaid
Eilean nan Ron
Ardmore Pt.
Kirtomy Pt.
Farr Pt.
Neave I. or Coombe I.
Rabbit Is.
A'Mhoine
Thurso
Scrabster
Crosskirk
Bridge of Forss
Dounreay
Buldoo
Achreamie
Newlands of Geise
Reay
Isauld
Achvarasdal
Sandside Ho.
Fresgoe
Red Pt.
Melvich
Portskerra
Bighouse
Baligill
Strathy
Aultiphurst
Brawl
Lednagullin
Armadale
Kirtomy
Farr
Swordly
Bettyhill
Achina
Invernaver
Skerray
Achtoty
Airdtorrisdale
Torrisdale
Skullomie
Coldbackie
Borgie
Tongue
Kirkiboll
Achuvoldrach
Strathan
Midfield
West Strathan
Talmine
Skinnet
Midtown
Ribigill
KYLE OF TONGUE
Kinloch Lodge
Ben Loyal
Loch Loyal Lodge
Inchkinloch
Borgie Forest
Strathy Forest
Bowside Lodge
Golval
Achiemore
Upper Bighouse
Craigtown
Dalhalvaig
Trantlemore
Trantlebeg
STRATH HALLADALE
Forsinain
Forsinard
Forsinard Station
Skelpick
Leckfurin
Achagary
Carnachy
Rhifail
STRATHNAVER
Skail
Langdale
Syre
Dalvina Lo.
Garvault Hotel
Achentoul Forest
Badanloch Forest
Badanloch Lodge
Naver Forest
Kinbrace
Achentoul
Lochside
Knockfin Heights
Mudale
Altnaharra
Clebrig
Loch Choire Lodge
Loch Choire Forest
Strath Vagastie
Crask Inn
Highland
Borrobol Forest
Altanduin
Borrobol Lodge
BEN ARMINE FOREST
Ben Armine Lodge
Strath na Seilge
Strath Skinsdale
Kildonan Lodge
STRATH OF KILDONAN
Craggie
Torrish
Kilphedir
Marrel
West Helmsdale
Navidale
Helmsdale
Gartymore
Portgower
Lothmore
Lothbeg
Lothbeg Pt.
Ord Point
Glen Loth
Glen Sletdale
Balnacoil
Gordonbush
Strath Brora
Loch Brora
Achrimsdale
East Clyne
West Clyne
Clynelish
Dalchalm
Brora
Doll
Backies
Golspie
Culmaily
Kirkton
Littleferry
Embo
Embo Street
Skelbo
Fourpenny
Cambusavie Farms
Loch Fleet
Cambusmore Lodge
Little Torboll
Torboll Farm
Morvich
Rogart Station
Pittentrail
Rogart
Muie
Ardachu
Strath Fleet
East Langwell
West Langwell
Dalreavoch
Rhilochan
Farlary
Achnaluachrach
Dalchork Wood
Dalchork
Colaboll
Sallachy
Saval
Lairg Lodge
Lairg Muir
Lairg
Torroble
Achinduich
Shin Forest
Inveran
Invershin
Culrain
Balblair
Airdens
Clashcraig
Migdale
Bonar Bridge
Craigton
Linsidemore
Achnahanat
Braelangwell Lodge
Achvaich
Badninish
Rearquhar
Proncy
Poles
Pitgrudy
Gablon
Dalnessie
Rhian
Shinness
Achnairn
Strath Tirry
Clardon
Millbank
Thurso East
Haimer
Murkle
Castletown
Olrig Ho.
Geise
Weydale
Hillicla
Westfield
Shebster
Lieurary
Buckies
Achingills
Sordale
Braal Castle
Knockdee
Stemster
Roadside
Broubster
Calder Mains
Halkirk
Clayock
Shurrery
Shurrery Lodge
Brawlbin
Scotscalder Station
Olgrinmore
Harpsdale
Banniskirk Ho.
Dorrery
Spittal
Mybster
Westerdale
Strathmore Lodge
Lochmore Cottage
Altnabreac Station
Lochdhu
Dalnawillan Lodge
Glutt Lodge
Braehungie
Latheronwheel Ho.
Braemore
Balnabruich
Dunbeath
Knockally
Ramscraigs
Berriedale
Borgue
Newport
Langwell Ho.
Langwell Forest
Aultibea
Wag
Ousdale
Ceann Leathad nam Bò
NC
ND
NH
NJ
158
151

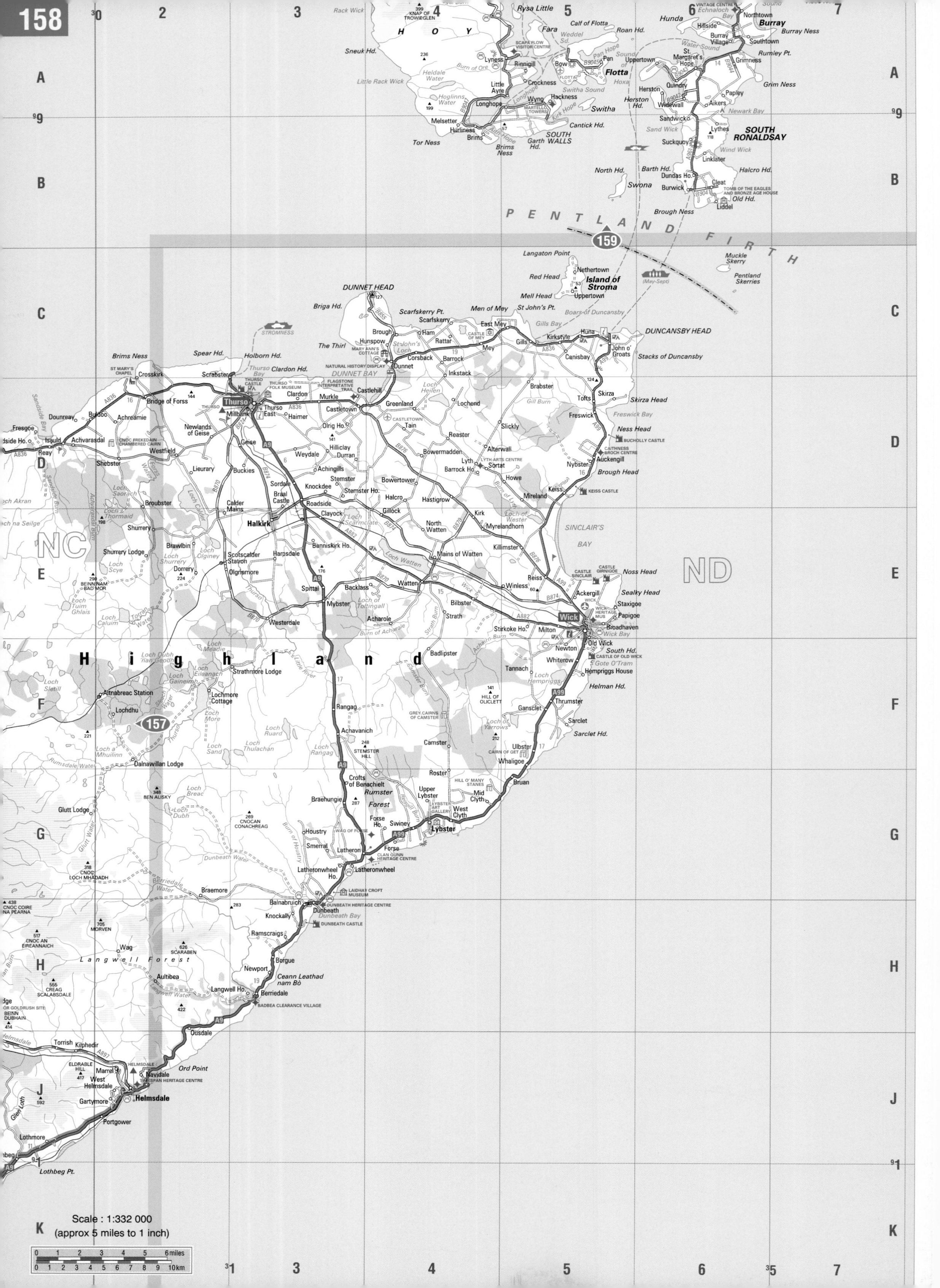
158
HOY
Rysa Little
Fara
Calf of Flotta
Roan Hd.
Hunda
Burray
Northtown
Burray Ness
Southtown
Burray Village
Hillside
Sneuk Hd.
Lyness
Rinnigill
Bow
Pan
Flotta
Uppertown
St. Margaret's Hope
Grimness
Rumley Pt.
Heldale Water
Little Rack Wick
Rack Wick
Little Ayre
Crockness
Swithа Sound
Hoxa
Herston
Quindry
Papley
Grim Ness
Hoglinns Water
Wyng
Hackness
Longhope
Herston Hd.
Widewall
Aikers
Newark Bay
Melsetter
Hurliness
Brims
Swithа
Cantick Hd.
Sandwick
Lythes
SOUTH RONALDSAY
Tor Ness
Garth Hd.
SOUTH WALLS
Brims Ness
Sand Wick
Suckquoy
Wind Wick
Linklater
North Hd.
Barth Hd.
Dundas Ho.
Halcro Hd.
Swona
Burwick
Cleat
TOMB OF THE EAGLES AND BRONZE AGE HOUSE
Old Hd.
Liddel
Brough Ness
PENTLAND FIRTH
159
Langaton Point
Nethertown
Red Head
Island of Stroma
Mell Head
Uppertown
Muckle Skerry
Pentland Skerries
(May-Sept)
DUNNET HEAD
Briga Hd.
Scarfskerry Pt.
Men of Mey
St John's Pt.
Boars of Duncansby
Scarfskerry
East Mey
Gills Bay
STROMNESS
Brough
Ham
CASTLE OF MEY
Huna
DUNCANSBY HEAD
The Thirl
Hunspow
Rattar
Mey
Gills
Kirkstyle
Canisbay
John o' Groats
Stacks of Duncansby
MARY ANN'S COTTAGE
Corsback
Barrock
Brims Ness
Spear Hd.
Holborn Hd.
NATURAL HISTORY DISPLAY
Dunnet
Inkstack
Thurso Bay
Clardon Hd.
DUNNET BAY
ST MARY'S CHAPEL
Crosskirk
Scrabster
THURSO CASTLE
THURSO FOLK MUSEUM
FLAGSTONE INTERPRETATIVE TRAIL
Brabster
Clardon
Murkle
Castlehill
Loch Heilen
Tofts
Skirza
Skirza Head
Bridge of Forss
Thurso
Greenland
Lochend
Gill Burn
Freswick Bay
Dounreay
Buldoo
Achreamie
Millbank
Thurso East
Haimer
Castletown
Freswick
Ness Head
Fresgoe
Newlands of Geise
Olrig Ho.
CASTLETOWN
Tain
Slickly
BUCHOLLY CASTLE
Sandside Ho.
Isauld
Achvarasdal
CNOC FREKEDAIN CHAMBERED CAIRN
Reay
Westfield
Geise
Hilliclay
Durran
Reaster
Alterwall
CAITHNESS BROCH CENTRE
Auckengill
Weydale
Bowermadden
LYTH ARTS CENTRE
Lyth
Sortat
Nybster
Brough Head
Shebster
Lieurary
Buckies
Achingills
Barrock Ho.
Howe
Stemster
Loch Saorach
Sordale
Knockdee
Stemster Ho.
Bowertower
Keiss
KEISS CASTLE
Loch Akran
Broubster
Calder Mains
Braal Castle
Roadside
Halcro
Hastigrow
Mireland
Loch Calder
Loch Thormaid
Halkirk
Clayock
Loch Scarmclate
Gillock
Kirk
Loch of Wester
SINCLAIR'S BAY
Loch na Seilge
Shurrery
NC
North Watten
Myrelandhorn
Killimster
Brawlbin
Banniskirk Ho.
Shurrery Lodge
Loch Shurrery
Loch Olginey
Scotscalder Station
Harpsdale
Loch Watten
Mains of Watten
Loch Scye
Dorrery
Olgrinmore
Spittal
Backlass
Watten
Winless
Reiss
CASTLE SINCLAIR
CASTLE GIRNIGOE
Noss Head
ND
BEINN NAM BAD MOR
Mybster
Loch of Toftingall
Bilbster
Ackergill
Sealky Head
Staxigoe
Loch Tuim Ghlais
Loch Caluim
Torran Water
Westerdale
Acharole
Strath
Wick
WICK HERITAGE MUS
Papigoe
Burn of Acharole
Stirkoke Ho.
Milton
Broadhaven
Wick Bay
Loch Meadie
Old Wick
South Hd.
Loch Dubh nan Geodh
Newton
Highland
Badlipster
Whiterow
CASTLE OF OLD WICK
Gote O'Tram
Loch Eileanach
Strathmore Lodge
Tannach
Loch Hempriggs
Hempriggs House
Loch Sletill
Loch Gaineimh
Little River
Altnabreac Station
Lochmore Cottage
Helman Hd.
HILL OF OLICLETT
Lochdhu
Rangag
GREY CAIRNS OF CAMSTER
Gansclet
Thrumster
157
Loch More
Achavanich
Loch Ruard
Loch of Yarrows
Sarclet
Sarclet Hd.
Loch Rangag
STEMSTER HILL
Camster
Loch a' Mhuilinn
Loch Sand
Loch Thulachan
CAIRN OF GET
Ulbster
Whaligoe
Rumsdale Water
Dalnawillan Lodge
Roster
HILL O' MANY STANES
Bruan
Loch Breac
Crofts of Benachielt
Rumster Forest
Upper Lybster
Mid Clyth
BEN ALISKY
Glutt Lodge
Loch Dubh
Braehungie
LYBSTER ART GALLERY
West Clyth
CNOCAN CONACHREAG
Forse Ho.
Swiney
Lybster
Houstry
WAG OF FORSE
Smerral
Latheron
Forse
CLAN GUNN HERITAGE CENTRE
Dunbeath Water
Latheronwheel Ho.
Latheronwheel
CNOC LOCH MHADADH
Berriedale Water
LAIDHAY CROFT MUSEUM
Braemore
Balnabruich
DUNBEATH HERITAGE CENTRE
CNOC COIRE NA PEARNA
Dunbeath
Knockally
Dunbeath Bay
MORVEN
DUNBEATH CASTLE
Ramscraigs
CNOC AN EIREANNAICH
Wag
SCARABEN
Langwell Forest
Borgue
Newport
Ceann Leathad nam Bò
CREAG SCALABSDALE
Aultibea
Langwell Ho.
Langwell Water
Berriedale
BADBEA CLEARANCE VILLAGE
BEINN DUBHAIN
Ousdale
Torrish
Kilphedir
Helmsdale
HELMSDALE
Ord Point
ELDRABLE HILL
Marrel
Navidale
TIMESPAN HERITAGE CENTRE
West Helmsdale
Helmsdale
Gartymore
Glen Loth
Portgower
Lothmore
Lothbeg Pt.
Scale : 1:332 000
(approx 5 miles to 1 inch)
0 1 2 3 4 5 6 miles
0 1 2 3 4 5 6 7 8 9 10 km

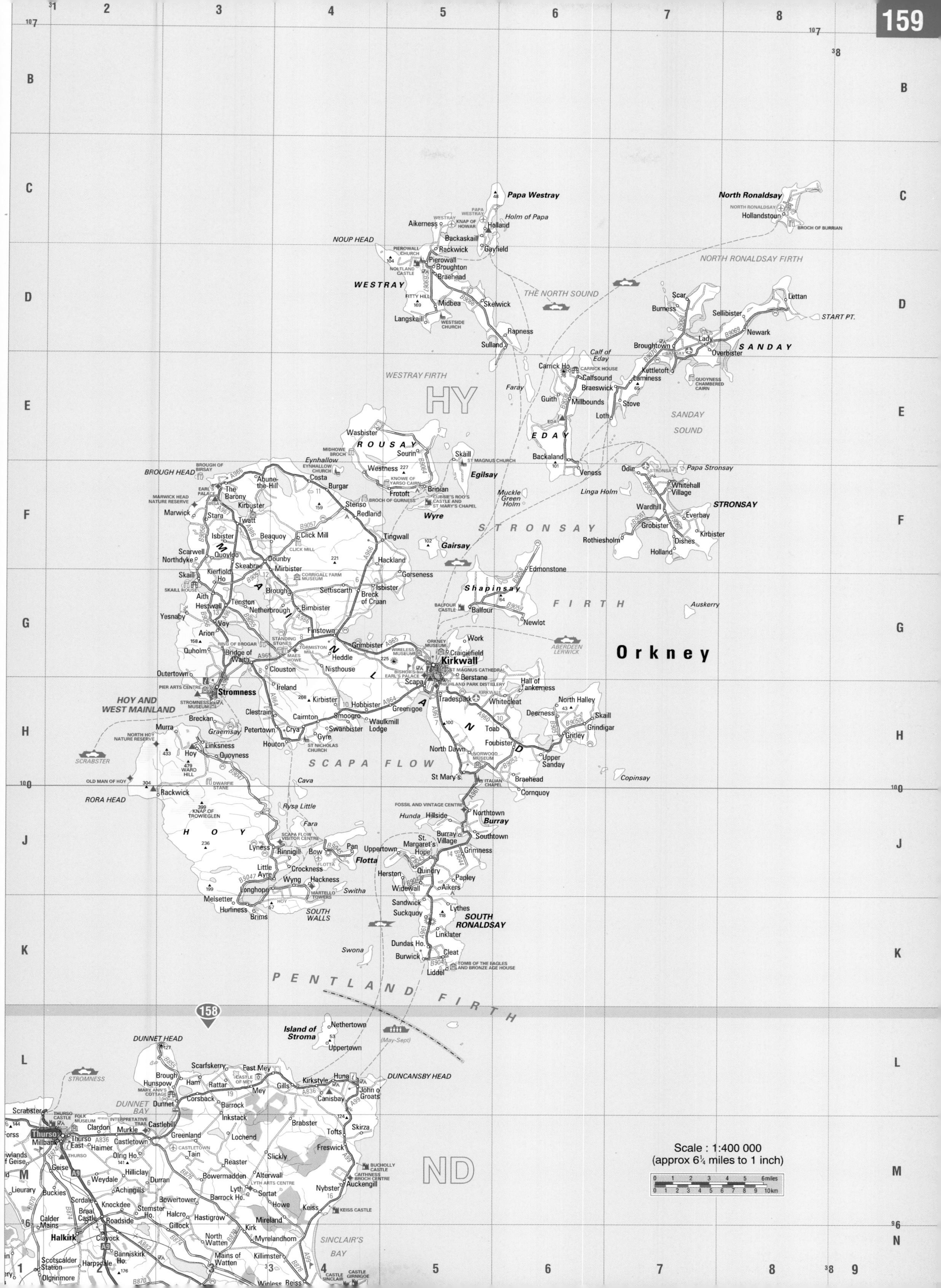

Scale : 1:400 000
(approx 6¼ miles to 1 inch)

0 1 2 3 4 5 6 miles
0 1 2 3 4 5 6 7 8 9 10km

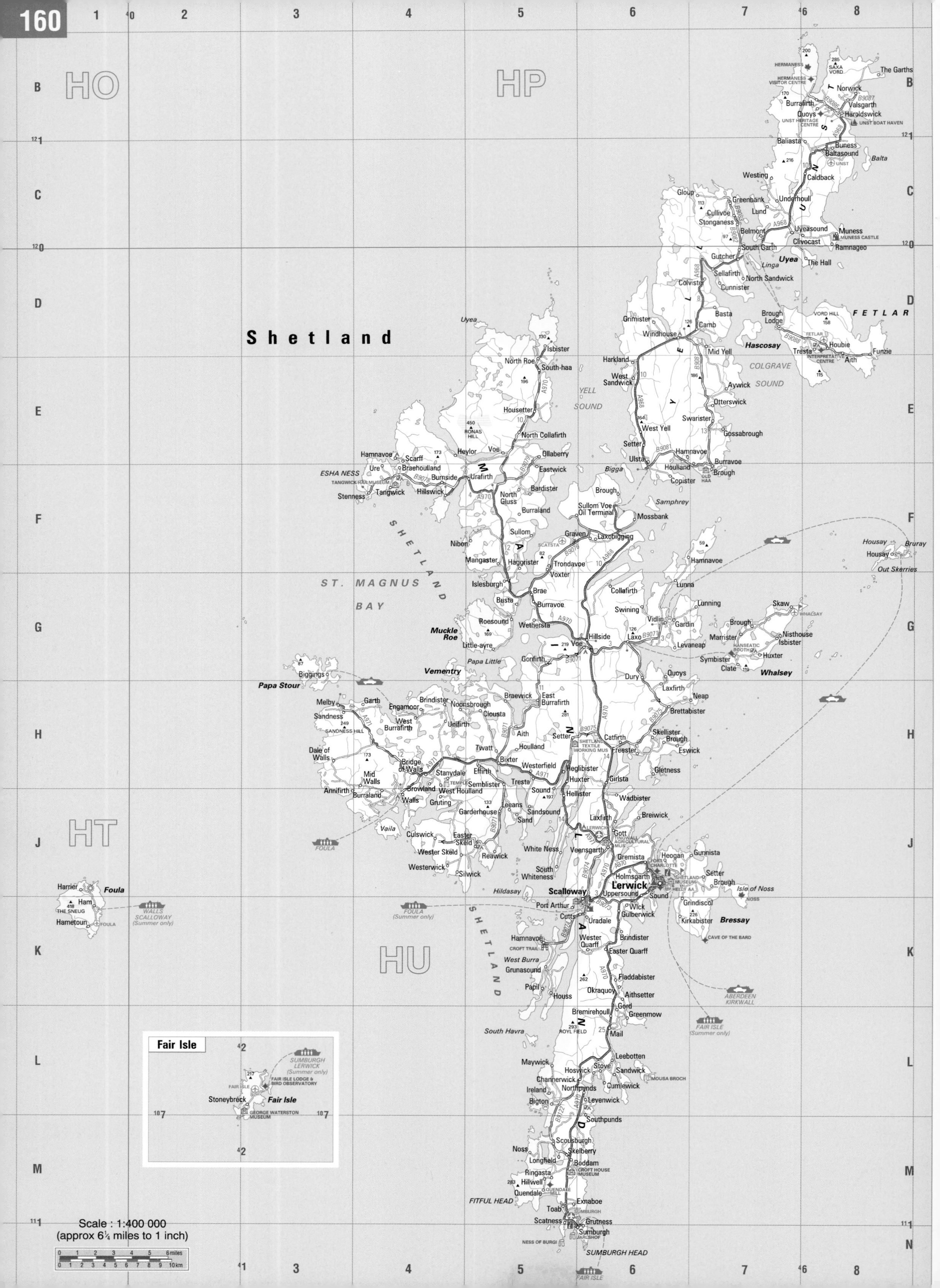
Shetland
HO
HP
HT
HU
Hermaness
Saxa Vord
The Garths
Hermaness Visitor Centre
Norwick
Burrafirth
Valsgarth
Quoys
Haroldswick
Unst Heritage Centre
Unst Boat Haven
Baliasta
Buness
Baltasound
Balta
Unst
Westing
Caldback
Gloup
Greenbank
Underhoull
Cullivoe
Lund
Stonganess
Belmont
Uyeasound
Muness
Muness Castle
South Garth
Clivocast
Ramnageo
Gutcher
Linga
Uyea
The Hall
Sellafirth
North Sandwick
Colvister
Cunnister
Basta
Brough Lodge
Vord Hill
Fetlar
Grimister
Camb
Windhouse
Houbie
Funzie
Mid Yell
Hascosay
Tresta
Interpretative Centre
Aith
Harkland
Colgrave Sound
West Sandwick
Yell Sound
Aywick
Otterswick
Yell
West Yell
Swarister
Gossabrough
Setter
Hamnavoe
Ulsta
Burravoe
Houlland
Brough
Copister
Old Haa
Bigga
Samphrey
Uyea
Isbister
North Roe
South-haa
Housetter
Ronas Hill
North Collafirth
Hamnavoe
Scarff
Heylor
Voe
Ollaberry
Esha Ness
Ure
Braehoulland
Eastwick
Tangwick Haa Museum
Burnside
Urafirth
Tangwick
Hillswick
Bardister
Stenness
North Gluss
Burraland
Sullom Voe Oil Terminal
Mossbank
Sullom
Graven
Laxobigging
Scatsta
Nibon
Mangaster
Haggrister
Trondavoe
Voxter
Shetland
St. Magnus Bay
Islesburgh
Hamnavoe
Lunna
Brae
Collafirth
Busta
Burravoe
Swining
Lunning
Skaw
Whalsay
Roesound
Wethersta
Vidlin
Gardin
Brough
Nisthouse
Muckle Roe
Hillside
Laxo
Marrister
Isbister
Little-ayre
Voe
Levaneap
Hanseatic Booth
Huxter
Papa Little
Gonfirth
Symbister
Clate
Whalsay
Vementry
Dury
Quoys
Biggings
Papa Stour
Braewick
East Burrafirth
Laxfirth
Neap
Melby
Garth
Brindister
Noonsbrough
Sandness
Engamoor
Clousta
Brettabister
Sandness Hill
West Burrafirth
Unifirth
Aith
Setter
Catfirth
Skellister
Brough
Dale of Walls
Twatt
Houlland
Shetland Textile Working Mus
Freester
Eswick
Bridge of Walls
Bixter
Westerfield
Mid Walls
Stanydale
Effirth
Heglibister
Girlsta
Gletness
Temple
Semblister
Tresta
Huxter
Annifirth
Burraland
Browland
West Houlland
Sound
Hellister
Wadbister
Walls
Gruting
Garderhouse
Leeans
Sand
Sandsound
Breiwick
Vaila
Laxfirth
Lerwick
Culswick
Easter Skeld
Gott
Tingwall Agricultural Mus
Foula
White Ness
Veensgarth
Gremista
Heogan
Gunnista
Wester Skeld
Reawick
Westerwick
Silwick
South Whiteness
Holmsgarth
Fort Charlotte
Shetland Museum
Setter
Harrier
Foula
Hildasay
Scalloway
Lerwick
Brough
Isle of Noss
Ham
The Sneug
Hametoun
Walls Scalloway (Summer only)
Foula (Summer only)
Port Arthur
Uppersound
Sound
Noss
Cutts
Wick
Gulberwick
Grindiscol
Kirkabister
Bressay
Uradale
Brindister
Cave of the Bard
Hamnavoe
Croft Trail
Wester Quarff
Easter Quarff
West Burra
Grunasound
Fladdabister
Papil
Houss
Okraquoy
Aithsetter
Aberdeen Kirkwall
Bremirehoull
Gord
Greenmow
Fair Isle (Summer only)
South Havra
Royl Field
Mail
Fair Isle
Sumburgh Lerwick (Summer only)
Fair Isle Lodge & Bird Observatory
Stoneybreck
Fair Isle
George Waterston Museum
Leebotten
Maywick
Stove
Sandwick
Hoswick
Mousa Broch
Channerwick
Cumlewick
Ireland
Northpunds
Bigton
Levenwick
Southpunds
Scousburgh
Noss
Skelberry
Longfield
Boddam
Croft House Museum
Ringasta
Hillwell
Quendale
Quendale Mill
Fitful Head
Exnaboe
Toab
Sumburgh
Scatness
Grutness
Sumburgh
Jarlshof
Ness of Burgi
Sumburgh Head
Fair Isle
Housay
Bruray
Out Skerries
Scale : 1:400 000
(approx 6¼ miles to 1 inch)
6 miles
10 km

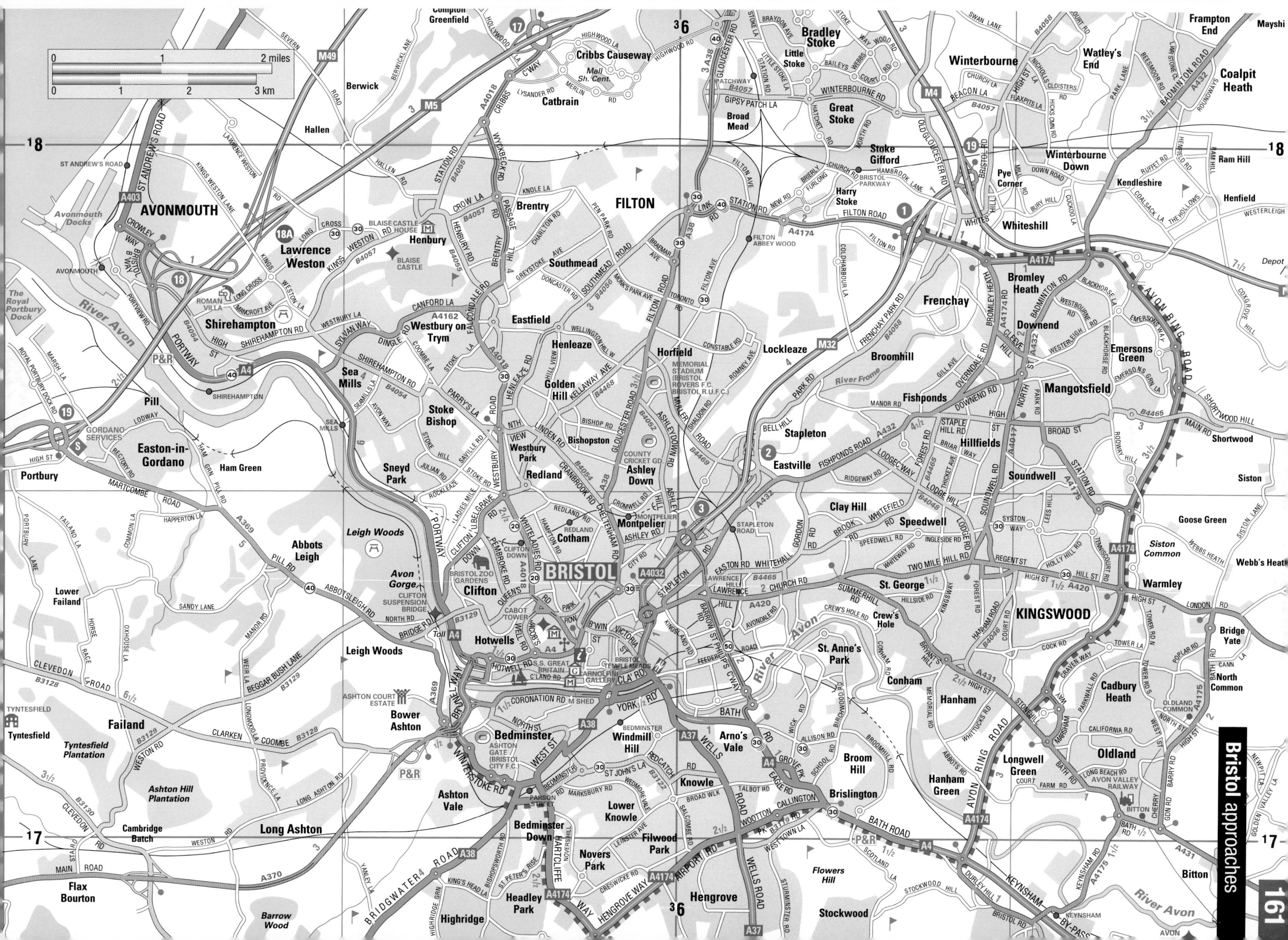
BRISTOL
AVONMOUTH
FILTON
KINGSWOOD
Avonmouth Docks
The Royal Portbury Dock
River Avon
River Frome
Avon Gorge
Clifton Suspension Bridge
Leigh Woods
Frampton End
Coalpit Heath
Watley's End
Winterbourne
Winterbourne Down
Kendleshire
Whiteshill
Pye Corner
Bromley Heath
Downend
Mangotsfield
Emersons Green
Siston Common
Warmley
Bridge Yate
North Common
Cadbury Heath
Oldland
Bitton
Longwell Green
Hanham
Hanham Green
Conham
Crew's Hole
St. George
Speedwell
Soundwell
Hillfields
Fishponds
Frenchay
Broomhill
Stapleton
Eastville
Clay Hill
St. Anne's Park
Broom Hill
Brislington
Stockwood
Flowers Hill
Arno's Vale
Knowle
Hengrove
Filwood Park
Lower Knowle
Novers Park
Windmill Hill
Bedminster
Bedminster Down
Headley Park
Highridge
Ashton Vale
Bower Ashton
Long Ashton
Barrow Wood
Ashton Hill Plantation
Cambridge Batch
Flax Bourton
Failand
Lower Failand
Tyntesfield
Tyntesfield Plantation
Abbots Leigh
Ham Green
Pill
Easton-in-Gordano
Portbury
Gordano Services
Shirehampton
Sea Mills
Sneyd Park
Stoke Bishop
Westbury on Trym
Henbury
Blaise Castle
Lawrence Weston
Hallen
Berwick
Catbrain
Cribbs Causeway
Brentry
Southmead
Henleaze
Eastfield
Golden Hill
Westbury Park
Redland
Cotham
Bishopston
Horfield
Ashley Down
Montpelier
Clifton
Hotwells
Lockleaze
Great Stoke
Stoke Gifford
Harry Stoke
Bradley Stoke
Little Stoke
Broad Mead
Patchway
Hartcliffe
Keynsham

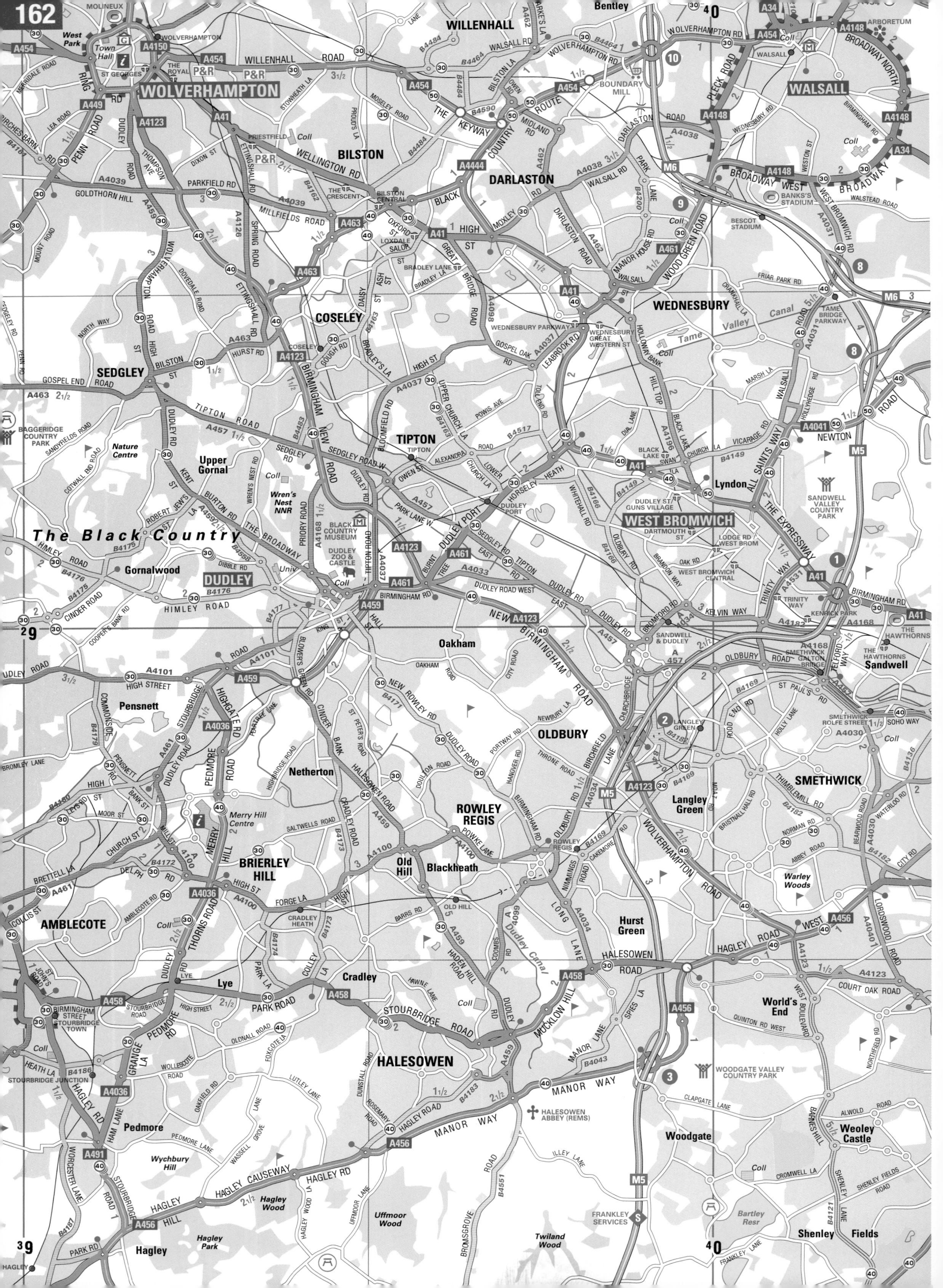
WOLVERHAMPTON
WILLENHALL
Bentley
WALSALL
BILSTON
DARLASTON
WEDNESBURY
COSELEY
SEDGLEY
TIPTON
Upper Gornal
Wren's Nest NNR
Nature Centre
Baggeridge Country Park
The Black Country
Gornalwood
DUDLEY
Black Country Museum
Dudley Zoo & Castle
WEST BROMWICH
Lyndon
Newton
Sandwell Valley Country Park
Oakham
OLDBURY
Sandwell
SMETHWICK
Langley Green
Pensnett
Netherton
ROWLEY REGIS
Merry Hill Centre
BRIERLEY HILL
Old Hill
Blackheath
Warley Woods
AMBLECOTE
Cradley Heath
Hurst Green
Lye
Cradley
World's End
HALESOWEN
Woodgate Valley Country Park
Halesowen Abbey (rems)
Pedmore
Wychbury Hill
Hagley Wood
Uffmoor Wood
Woodgate
Weoley Castle
Frankley Services
Bartley Resr
Twiland Wood
Hagley Park
Hagley
Shenley
Fields

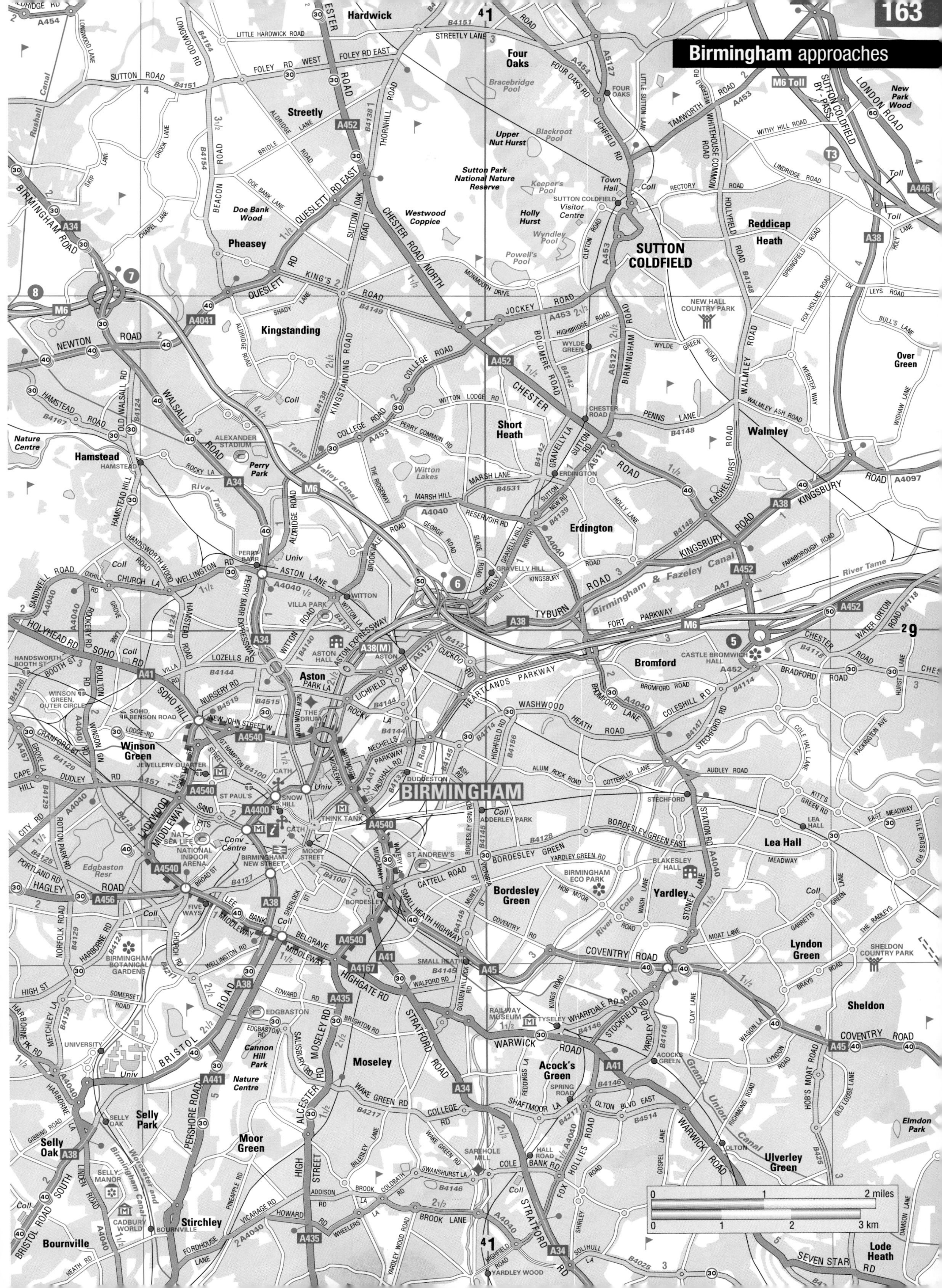
BIRMINGHAM
SUTTON COLDFIELD
Erdington
Aston
Bromford
Lea Hall
Yardley
Moseley
Selly Oak
Bournville
0 1 2 miles
0 1 2 3 km

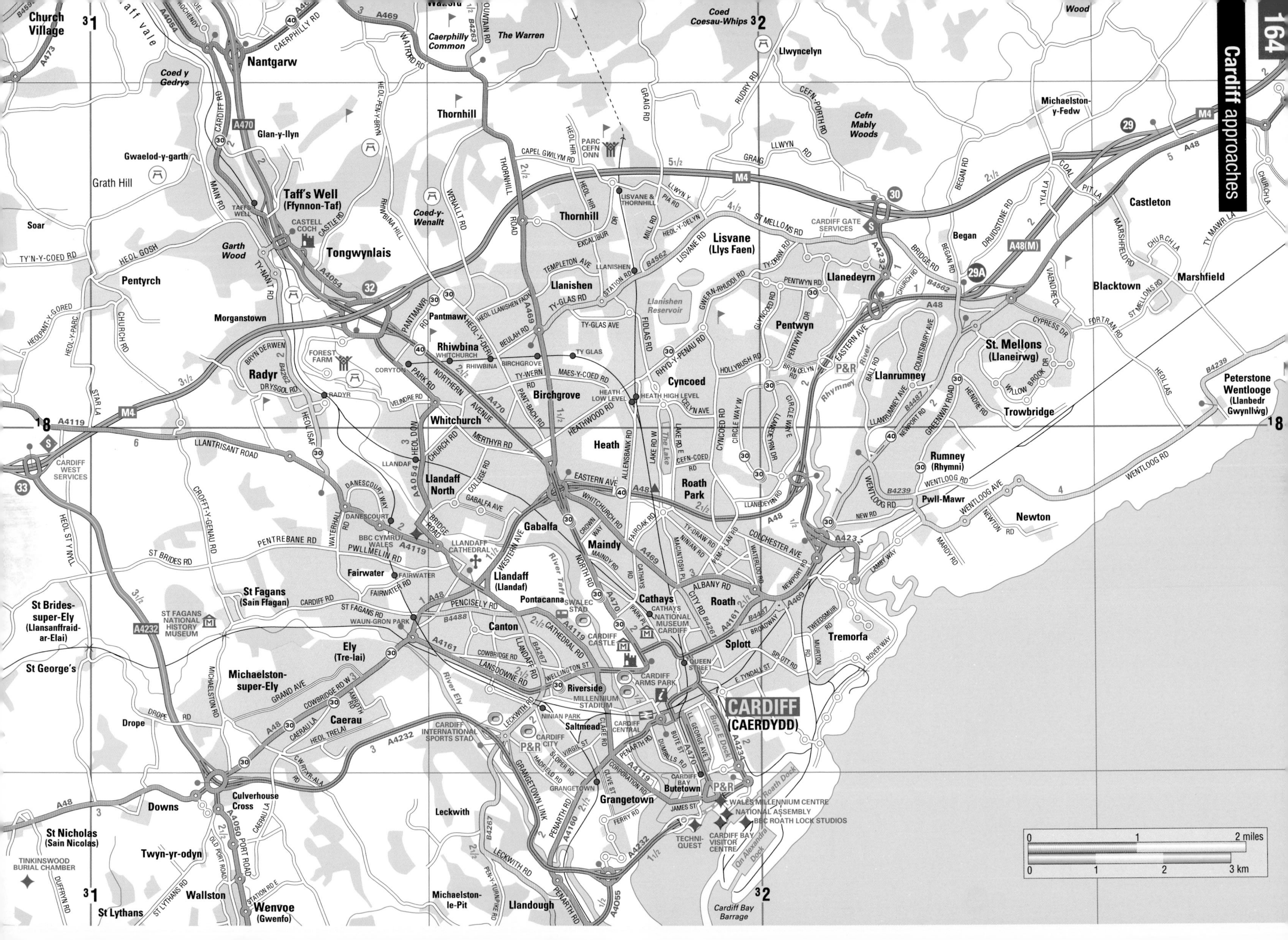
CARDIFF
(CAERDYDD)
Church Village
Nantgarw
Coed y Gedrys
Caerphilly Common
The Warren
Coed Coesau-Whips
Llwyncelyn
Wood
Michaelston-y-Fedw
Cefn Mably Woods
Thornhill
Glan-y-llyn
Gwaelod-y-garth
Grath Hill
Taff's Well (Ffynnon-Taf)
Castell Coch
Coed-y-Wenallt
Castleton
Marshfield
Blacktown
Began
Soar
Garth Wood
Tongwynlais
Lisvane (Llys Faen)
Cardiff Gate Services
Llanedeyrn
Pentyrch
Morganstown
Llanishen
Llanishen Reservoir
Pentwyn
St. Mellons (Llaneirwg)
Pantmawr
Rhiwbina
Forest Farm
Radyr
Cyncoed
Llanrumney
Peterstone Wentlooge (Llanbedr Gwynllŵg)
Trowbridge
Birchgrove
Whitchurch
Heath
The Lake
Rumney (Rhymni)
Cardiff West Services
Llandaff North
Roath Park
Pwll-Mawr
Newton
Gabalfa
Maindy
Llandaff Cathedral
Llandaff (Llandaf)
Pontacanna
Fairwater
St Fagans (Sain Ffagan)
St Fagans National History Museum
Cathays
Cathays National Museum Cardiff
Roath
Tremorfa
St Brides-super-Ely (Llansanffraid-ar-Elai)
Canton
Cardiff Castle
Splott
Ely (Tre-lai)
St George's
Cardiff Arms Park
Michaelston-super-Ely
Riverside
Millennium Stadium
Saltmead
Cardiff Central
Drope
Caerau
Cardiff International Sports Stad
Cardiff City
Butetown
Culverhouse Cross
Downs
Grangetown
Leckwith
Wales Millennium Centre
National Assembly
BBC Roath Lock Studios
Techniquest
Cardiff Bay Visitor Centre
St Nicholas (Sain Nicolas)
Tinkinswood Burial Chamber
Twyn-yr-odyn
Wallston
Wenvoe (Gwenfo)
St Lythans
Michaelston-le-Pit
Llandough
Cardiff Bay Barrage
Bute E Dock
Roath Dock
On Alexandra Dock
River Taff
River Ely
Rhymney River
M4
A48(M)
A48
A470
A469
A4232
A4161
A4119
A4054
A4055
A4160
A4050
A4234
B4562
B4239
B4267
B4262
B4488
B4263
0 1 2 miles
0 1 2 3 km

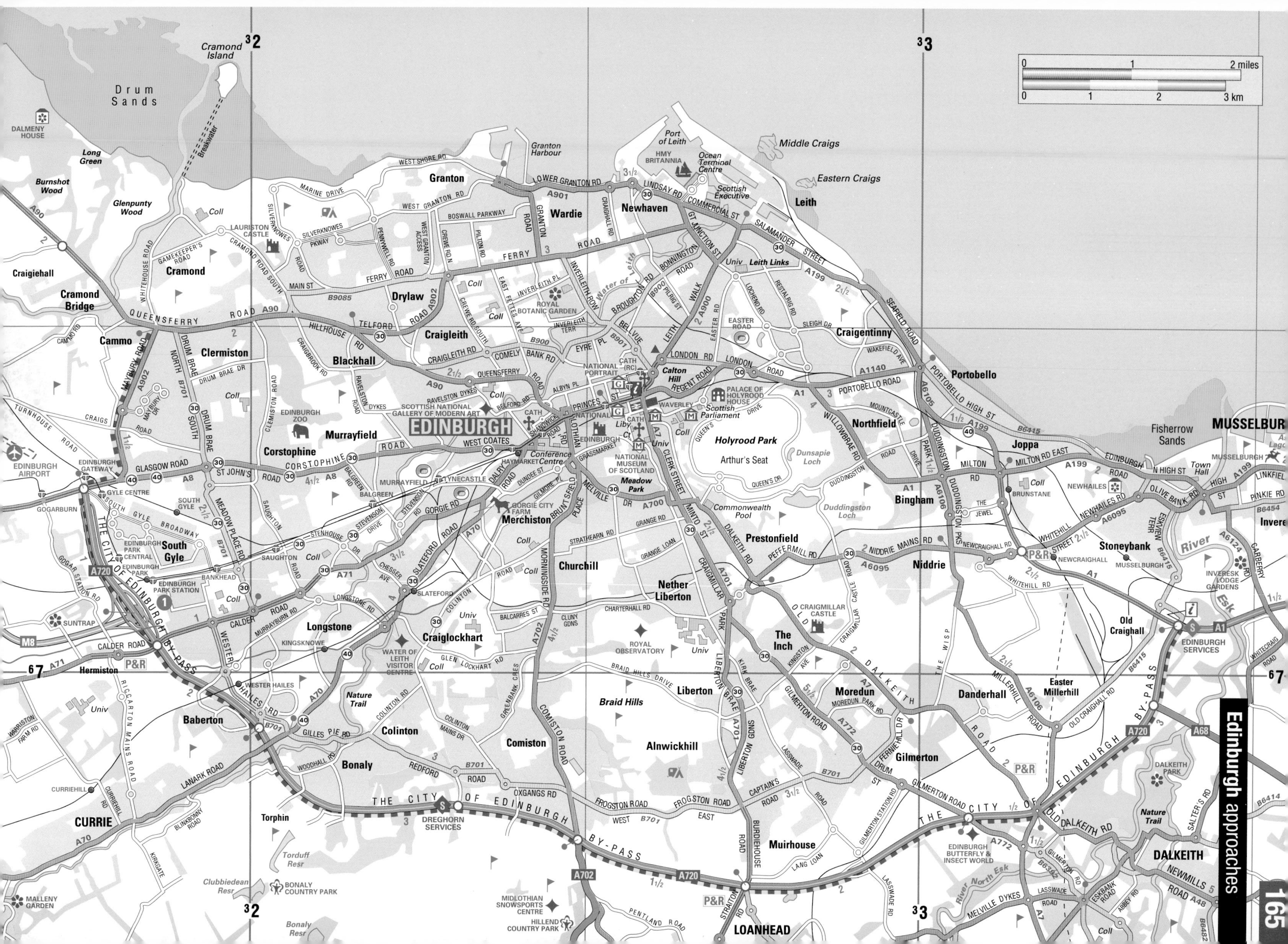
EDINBURGH
Leith
Newhaven
Wardie
Granton
Drylaw
Craigleith
Blackhall
Murrayfield
Corstophine
Clermiston
Cramond
Cramond Bridge
Cammo
Craigiehall
South Gyle
Baberton
Currie
Harmiston
Longstone
Colinton
Bonaly
Torphin
Craiglockhart
Merchiston
Comiston
Churchill
Nether Liberton
Liberton
Alnwickhill
Braid Hills
Muirhouse
LOANHEAD
The Inch
Moredun
Gilmerton
Prestonfield
Niddrie
Bingham
Danderhall
Northfield
Craigentinny
Portobello
Joppa
Stoneybank
Old Craighall
Easter Millerhill
DALKEITH
MUSSELBURGH
Fisherrow Sands
Holyrood Park
Arthur's Seat
Duddingston Loch
Calton Hill
Port of Leith
Granton Harbour
Middle Craigs
Eastern Craigs
Cramond Island
Drum Sands
Glenpunty Wood
Long Green
Burnshot Wood
DALMENY HOUSE
EDINBURGH AIRPORT
EDINBURGH ZOO
ROYAL OBSERVATORY
ROYAL BOTANIC GARDEN
Scottish Parliament
DREGHORN SERVICES
EDINBURGH SERVICES
MIDLOTHIAN SNOWSPORTS CENTRE
HILLEND COUNTRY PARK
BONALY COUNTRY PARK
MALLENY GARDEN
SUNTRAP
THE CITY OF EDINBURGH BY-PASS
A720
A1
A7
A70
A71
A8
A90
M8
33
32
67
0 1 2 miles
0 1 2 3 km

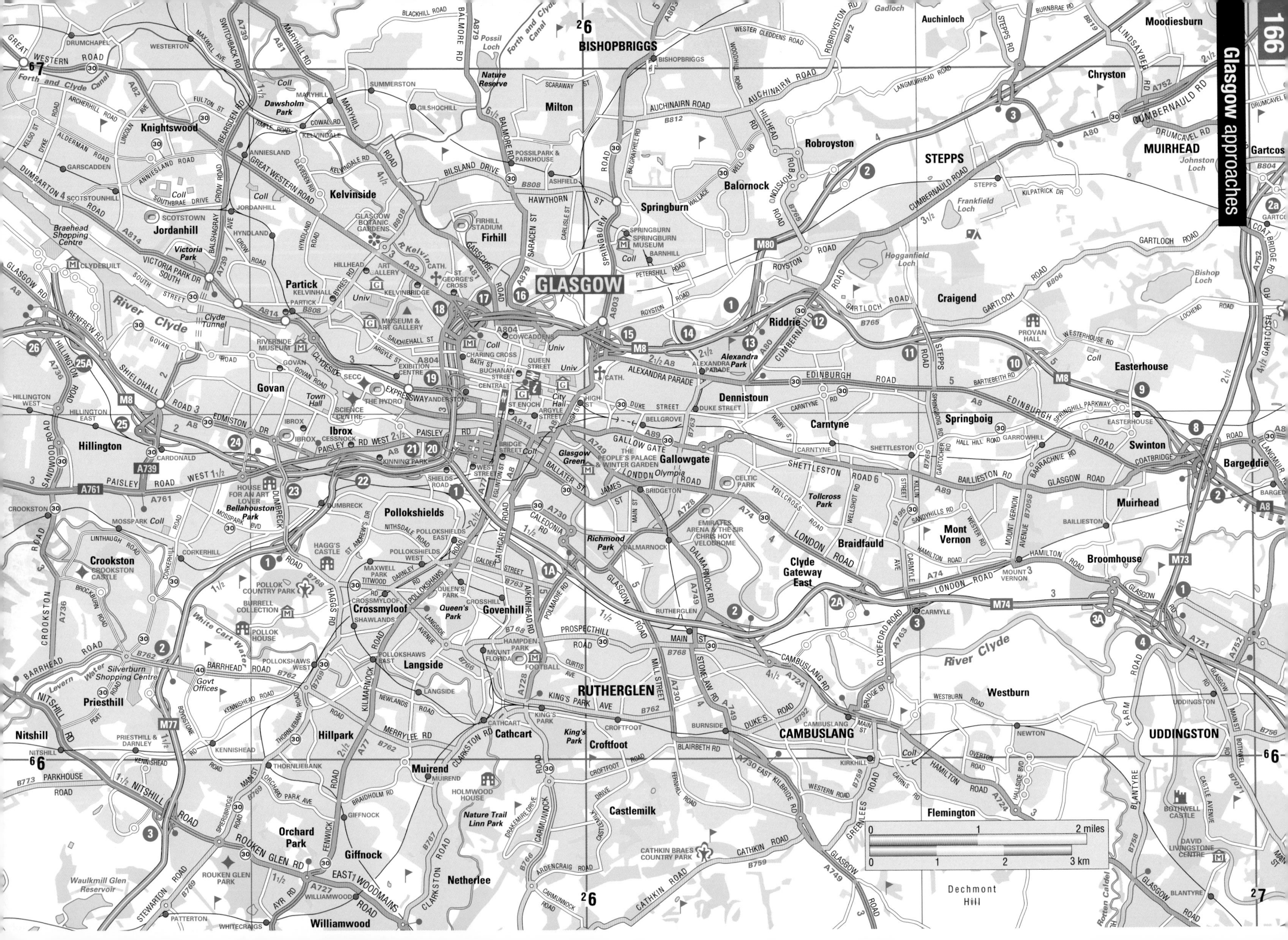
GLASGOW
Moodiesburn
Auchinloch
Chryston
MUIRHEAD
Gartcosh
STEPPS
Robroyston
Balornock
Springburn
BISHOPBRIGGS
Milton
Firhill
Kelvinside
Knightswood
Jordanhill
Partick
Govan
Ibrox
Hillington
Crookston
Priesthill
Nitshill
Pollokshields
Crossmyloof
Langside
Govanhill
Cathcart
Muirend
Netherlee
Giffnock
Hillpark
Orchard Park
Williamwood
RUTHERGLEN
Castlemilk
Croftfoot
CAMBUSLANG
Flemington
Westburn
UDDINGSTON
Broomhouse
Mont Vernon
Braidfauld
Clyde Gateway East
Carntyne
Dennistoun
Riddrie
Craigend
Springboig
Easterhouse
Swinton
Bargeddie
Muirhead
Gallowgate
Dechmont Hill
River Clyde
Forth and Clyde Canal
White Cart Water
Pollok Country Park
Rouken Glen Park
Cathkin Braes Country Park
Bellahouston Park
Queen's Park
Victoria Park
Dawsholm Park
Alexandra Park
Tollcross Park
Richmond Park
King's Park
Glasgow Green
Possil Loch
Hogganfield Loch
Frankfield Loch
Bishop Loch
Johnston Loch
Waulkmill Glen Reservoir
Braehead Shopping Centre
Silverburn Shopping Centre
0 1 2 miles
0 1 2 3 km
M8
M73
M74
M77
M80

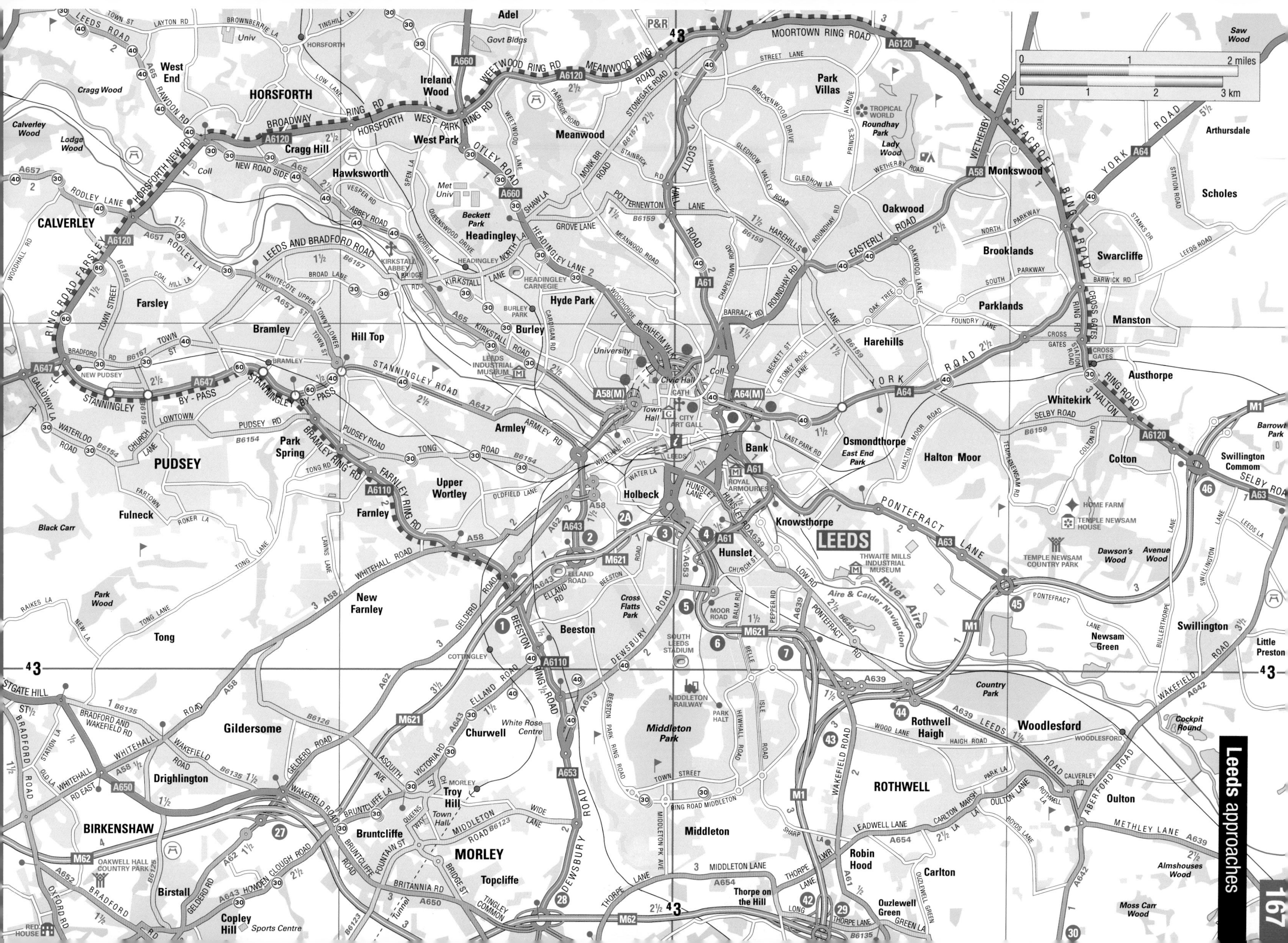
LEEDS
Scholes
Arthursdale
Swarcliffe
Manston
Austhorpe
Whitekirk
Colton
Swillington
Swillington Common
Little Preston
Newsam Green
Woodlesford
Oulton
Rothwell
Rothwell Haigh
Carlton
Robin Hood
Ouzlewell Green
Thorpe on the Hill
Middleton
Middleton Park
Morley
Topcliffe
Churwell
Troy Hill
Bruntcliffe
Gildersome
Drighlington
Birkenshaw
Birstall
Copley Hill
Tong
Fulneck
Black Carr
Pudsey
Farsley
Calverley
Horsforth
Cragg Hill
Hawksworth
West End
West Park
Ireland Wood
Adel
Meanwood
Headingley
Hyde Park
Burley
Armley
Bramley
Hill Top
Upper Wortley
Farnley
New Farnley
Beeston
Holbeck
Hunslet
Knowsthorpe
Bank
Osmondthorpe
Halton Moor
Harehills
Oakwood
Park Villas
Monkswood
Brooklands
Parklands
Park Spring
Roundhay Park
Temple Newsam House
Temple Newsam Country Park
Thwaite Mills Industrial Museum
Leeds Industrial Museum
River Aire
Aire & Calder Navigation
Middleton Railway
South Leeds Stadium
White Rose Centre
Oakwell Hall Country Park
Tropical World
University
Civic Hall
Town Hall
RING ROAD
OUTER RING ROAD
MOORTOWN RING ROAD
YORK ROAD
SELBY ROAD
PONTEFRACT LANE
WAKEFIELD ROAD
DEWSBURY ROAD
STANNINGLEY ROAD
BRADFORD ROAD
M1
M62
M621
A64
A58
A61
A65
A6120

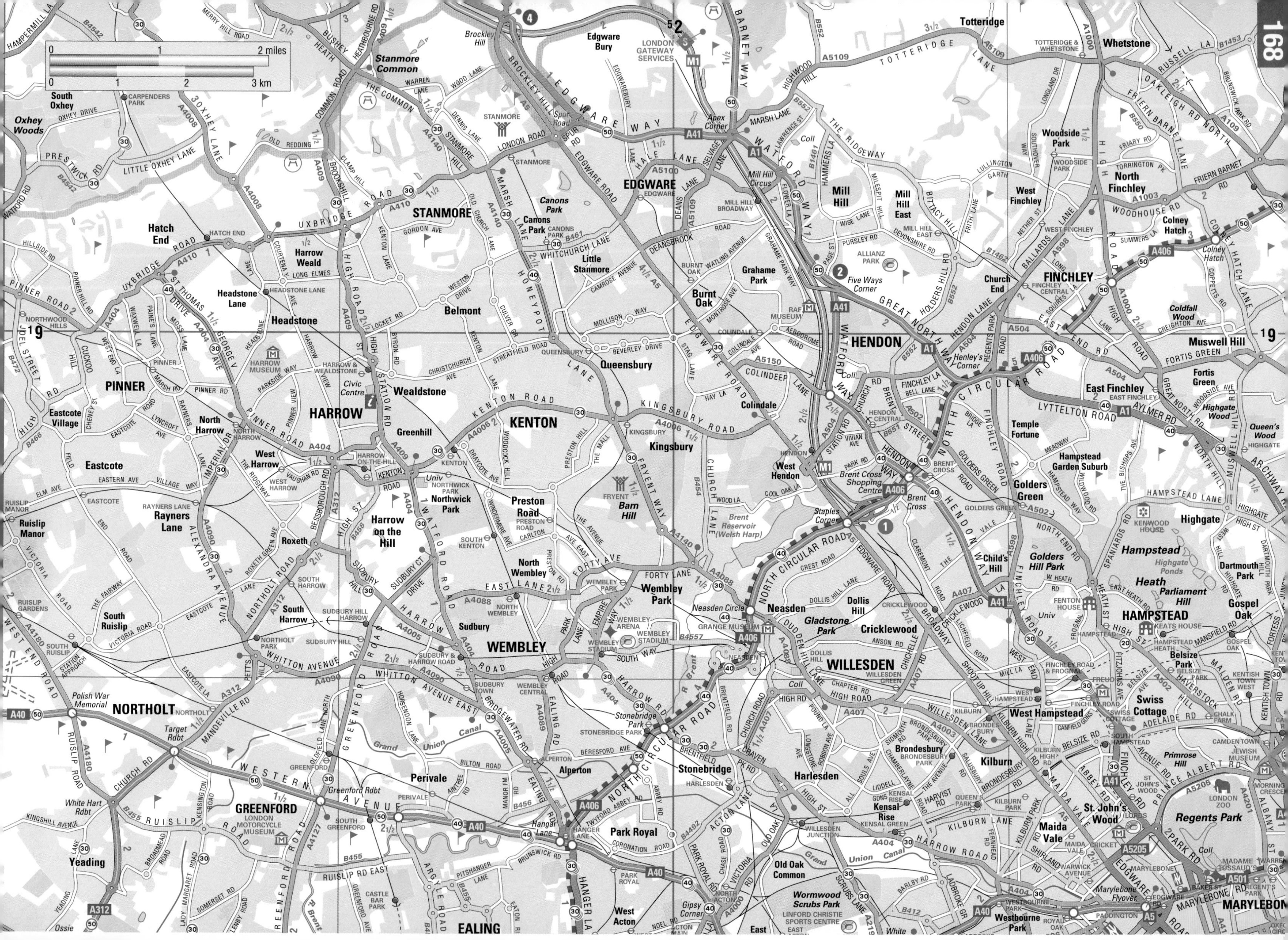
Whetstone
Totteridge
Woodside Park
North Finchley
Colney Hatch
FINCHLEY
West Finchley
Church End
Muswell Hill
Fortis Green
East Finchley
Hampstead Garden Suburb
Temple Fortune
Golders Green
Highgate
Hampstead Heath
HAMPSTEAD
Dartmouth Park
Gospel Oak
Belsize Park
Swiss Cottage
Primrose Hill
Regents Park
MARYLEBONE
St. John's Wood
Maida Vale
West Hampstead
Kilburn
Child's Hill
Golders Hill Park
Mill Hill
Mill Hill East
HENDON
Brent Cross
West Hendon
Colindale
Grahame Park
Burnt Oak
EDGWARE
Edgware Bury
Canons Park
Little Stanmore
Queensbury
Kingsbury
Cricklewood
Dollis Hill
WILLESDEN
Gladstone Park
Brondesbury
Kensal Rise
Harlesden
Neasden
Wembley Park
Stonebridge
Park Royal
West Acton
Alperton
Barn Hill
STANMORE
Stanmore Common
Belmont
KENTON
Preston Road
North Wembley
WEMBLEY
Sudbury
Wealdstone
Greenhill
HARROW
Harrow on the Hill
Northwick Park
Harrow Weald
Headstone
Headstone Lane
West Harrow
Roxeth
South Harrow
North Harrow
Rayners Lane
Hatch End
PINNER
Eastcote
Eastcote Village
Ruislip Manor
South Ruislip
NORTHOLT
GREENFORD
Perivale
EALING
Yeading
South Oxhey
Oxhey Woods
Wormwood Scrubs Park
Old Oak Common
Westbourne Park
Brockley Hill

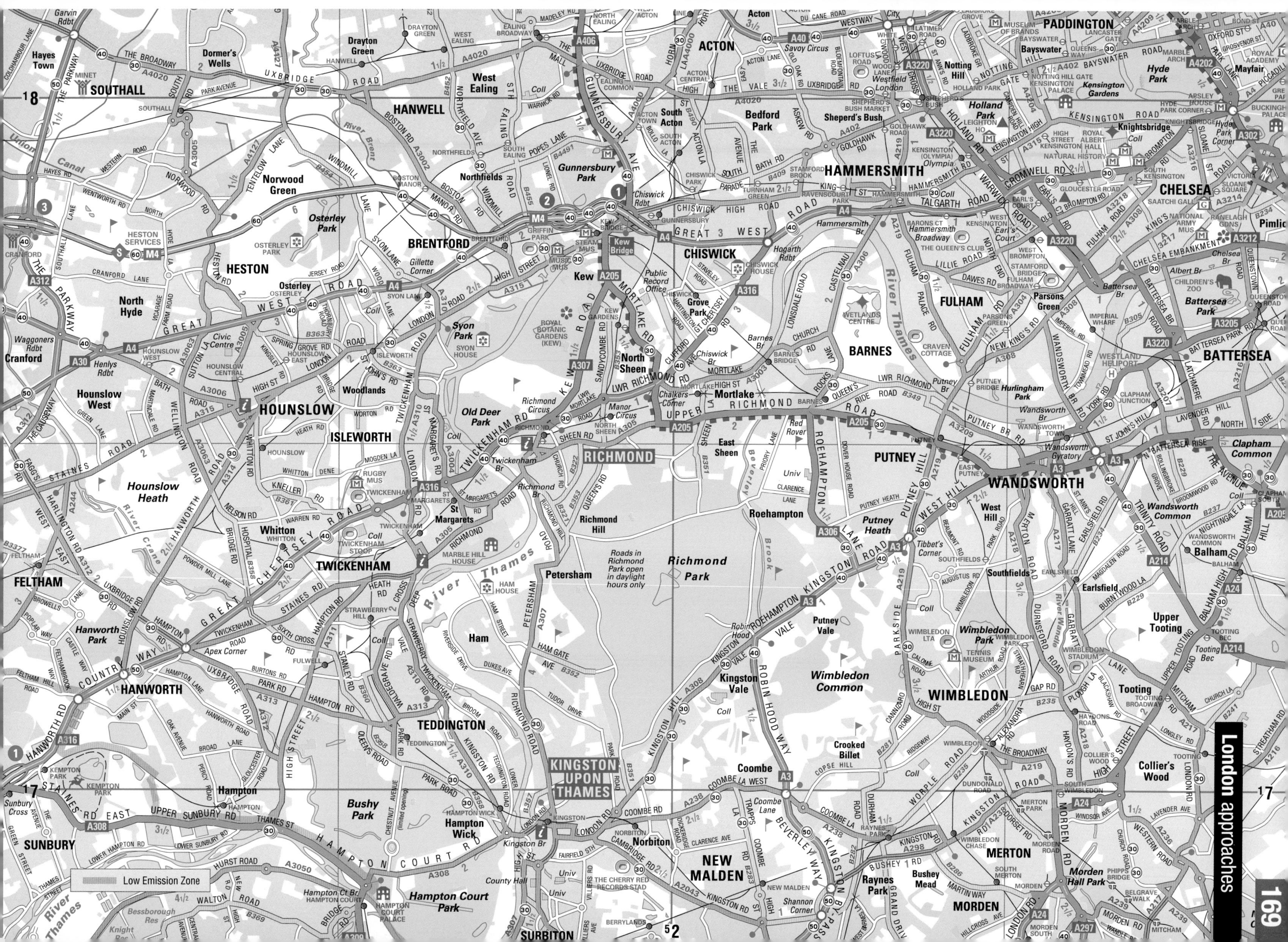
Hayes Town
Dormer's Wells
SOUTHALL
Drayton Green
West Ealing
HANWELL
ACTON
South Acton
Bedford Park
Shepherd's Bush
Notting Hill
Holland Park
PADDINGTON
Bayswater
Hyde Park
Kensington Gardens
Knightsbridge
Mayfair
Norwood Green
Osterley Park
HESTON
BRENTFORD
Northfields
Gunnersbury Park
HAMMERSMITH
CHELSEA
Pimlico
North Hyde
Osterley
Cranford
Hounslow West
HOUNSLOW
Woodlands
ISLEWORTH
Syon Park
Kew
CHISWICK
Grove Park
North Sheen
BARNES
FULHAM
Parsons Green
BATTERSEA
Battersea Park
Old Deer Park
RICHMOND
Mortlake
East Sheen
PUTNEY
WANDSWORTH
Clapham Common
Hounslow Heath
Whitton
TWICKENHAM
St Margarets
Richmond Hill
Petersham
Richmond Park
Roehampton
Putney Heath
West Hill
Southfields
Earlsfield
Wandsworth Common
Balham
Upper Tooting
FELTHAM
Hanworth Park
HANWORTH
Ham
Kingston Vale
Putney Vale
Wimbledon Common
Wimbledon Park
WIMBLEDON
Tooting
TEDDINGTON
Bushy Park
Hampton
Hampton Wick
KINGSTON UPON THAMES
Coombe
Crooked Billet
Collier's Wood
SUNBURY
Hampton Court Park
Norbiton
NEW MALDEN
Raynes Park
Bushey Mead
MERTON
MORDEN
Morden Hall Park
SURBITON
River Thames
Low Emission Zone

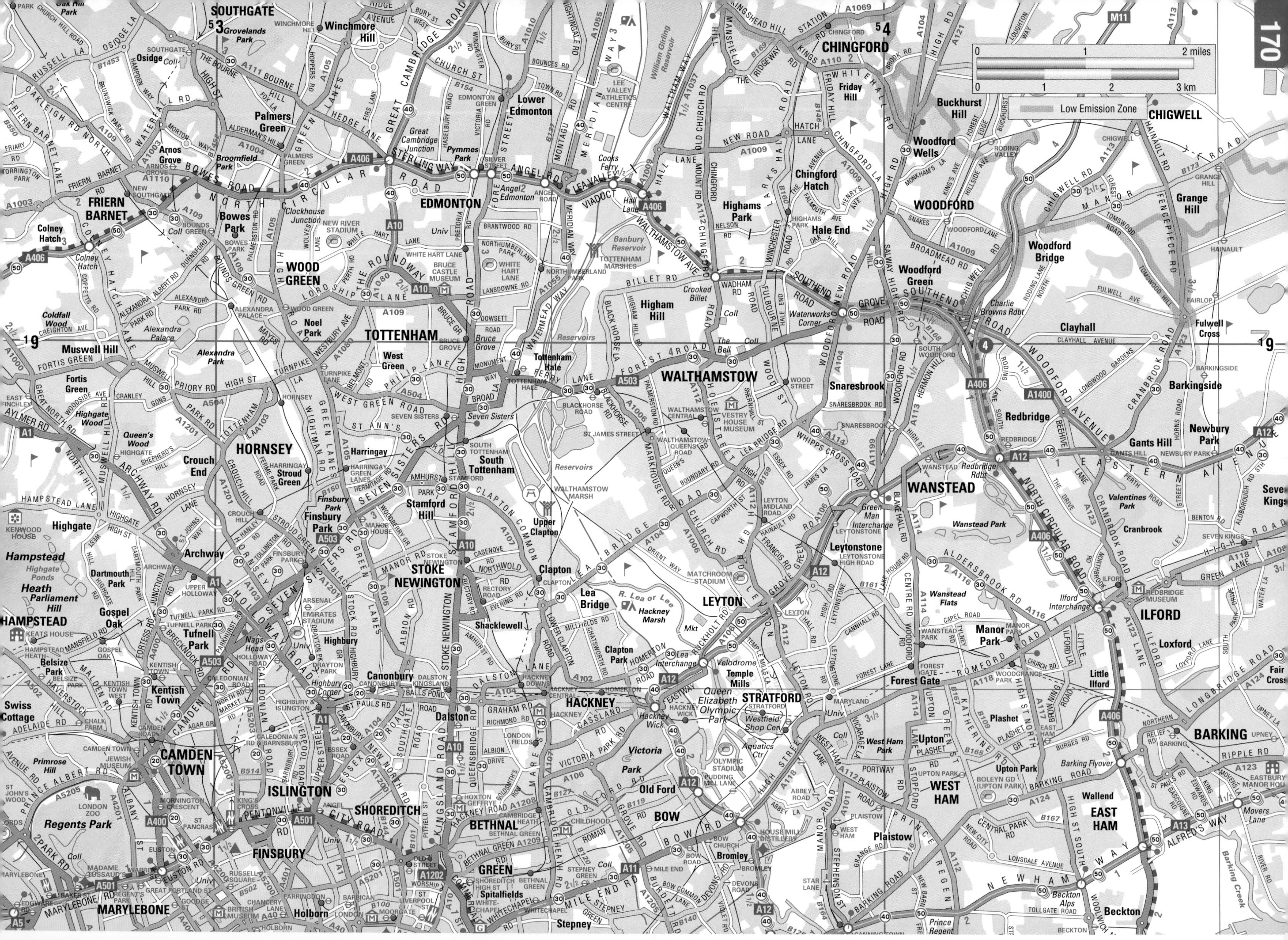
SOUTHGATE
Winchmore Hill
CHINGFORD
Friday Hill
Buckhurst Hill
CHIGWELL
Low Emission Zone
Osidge
Palmers Green
Lower Edmonton
Arnos Grove
Great Cambridge Junction
Pymmes Park
Woodford Wells
Chingford Hatch
Grange Hill
FRIERN BARNET
Bowes Park
EDMONTON
Highams Park
WOODFORD
Hale End
Colney Hatch
WOOD GREEN
Woodford Bridge
Woodford Green
Higham Hill
Noel Park
TOTTENHAM
Clayhall
Fulwell Cross
Muswell Hill
Alexandra Palace
Alexandra Park
West Green
Tottenham Hale
WALTHAMSTOW
Snaresbrook
Barkingside
Fortis Green
Redbridge
Newbury Park
Gants Hill
Highgate Wood
Queen's Wood
HORNSEY
Harringay
South Tottenham
Crouch End
Stroud Green
WANSTEAD
Seven Kings
Valentines Park
Cranbrook
Highgate
Stamford Hill
Finsbury Park
Upper Clapton
Wanstead Park
Hampstead Heath
Archway
Leytonstone
Dartmouth Park
Parliament Hill
STOKE NEWINGTON
Clapton
Lea Bridge
Hackney Marsh
LEYTON
Wanstead Flats
ILFORD
HAMPSTEAD
Gospel Oak
Shacklewell
Manor Park
Tufnell Park
Highbury
Clapton Park
Loxford
Belsize Park
Kentish Town
Canonbury
Temple Mills
Forest Gate
Little Ilford
Swiss Cottage
HACKNEY
STRATFORD
Queen Elizabeth Olympic Park
Dalston
Hackney Wick
Plashet
BARKING
CAMDEN TOWN
Primrose Hill
Victoria Park
Upton
West Ham Park
Upton Park
ISLINGTON
Old Ford
WEST HAM
Wallend
Regents Park
SHOREDITCH
BETHNAL GREEN
BOW
EAST HAM
Plaistow
FINSBURY
Bromley
MARYLEBONE
Holborn
Spitalfields
Stepney
Beckton
Beckton Alps

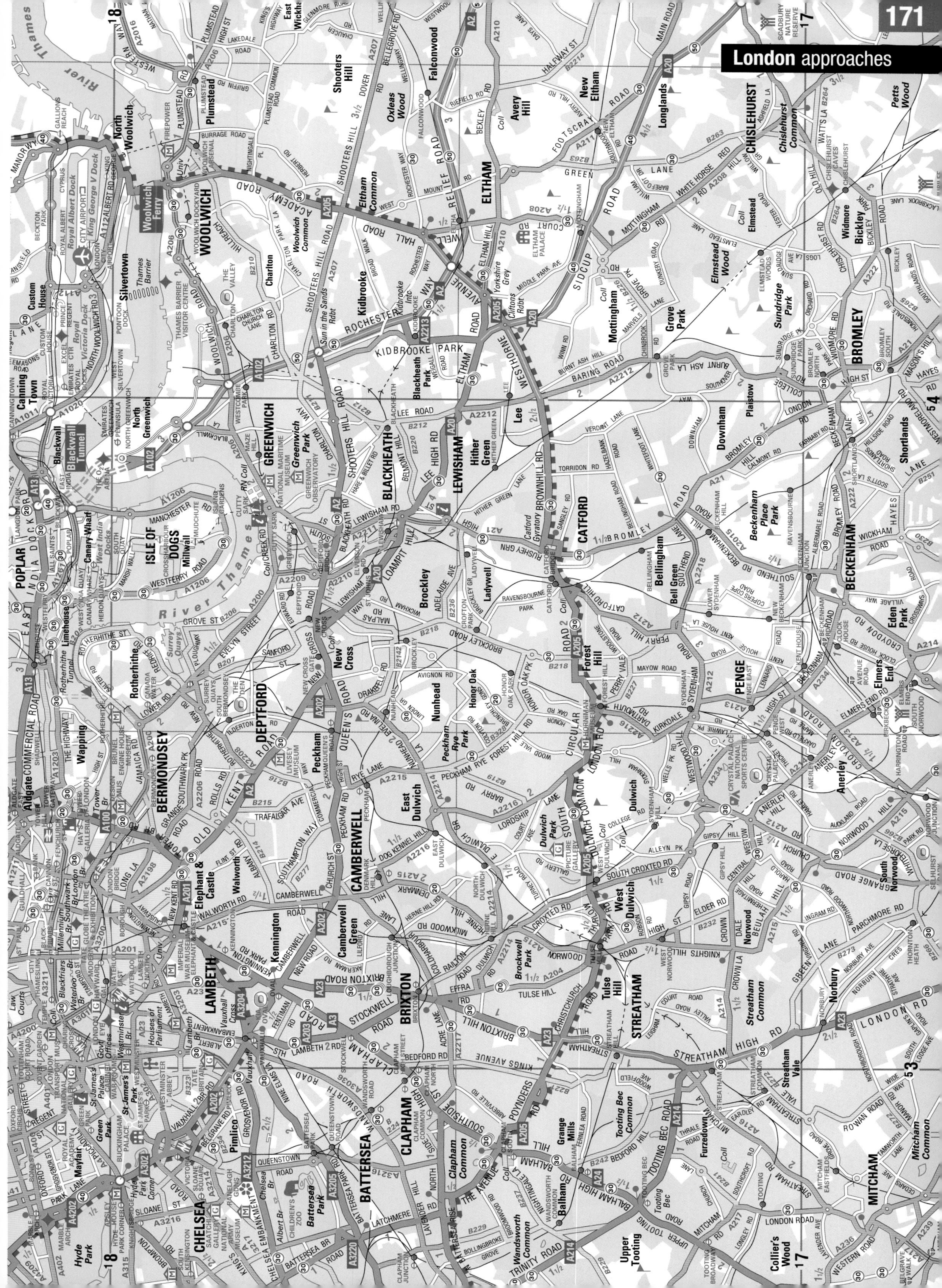
River Thames
North Woolwich
Plumstead
Shooters Hill
Falconwood
New Eltham
Longlands
Chislehurst
Avery Hill
Oxleas Wood
Woolwich
Woolwich Ferry
Eltham Common
Woolwich Common
Eltham
Charlton
Kidbrooke
Silvertown
Thames Barrier
Custom House
Canning Town
North Greenwich
Greenwich
Greenwich Park
Blackheath
Blackheath Park
Lewisham
Lee
Hither Green
Mottingham
Grove Park
Elmstead Wood
Sundridge Park
Bromley
Widmore
Bickley
Petts Wood
Plaistow
Downham
Shortlands
Catford
Bellingham
Beckenham Place Park
Beckenham
Isle of Dogs
Millwall
Canary Wharf
Poplar
Limehouse
Rotherhithe
Deptford
Brockley
Ladywell
New Cross
Nunhead
Honor Oak
Forest Hill
Penge
Eden Park
Elmers End
Bermondsey
Wapping
Aldgate
Peckham
Peckham Rye Park
East Dulwich
Dulwich
Sydenham
Anerley
Camberwell
Walworth
Elephant & Castle
Kennington
Camberwell Green
West Dulwich
South Norwood
Lambeth
Brixton
Brockwell Park
Tulse Hill
Streatham
Norbury
Streatham Common
Streatham Vale
Clapham
Clapham Common
Battersea
Battersea Park
Chelsea
Pimlico
Mayfair
Hyde Park
Green Park
Balham
Tooting Bec Common
Upper Tooting
Furzedown
Mitcham
Mitcham Common
Collier's Wood
Wandsworth Common
Grange Mills

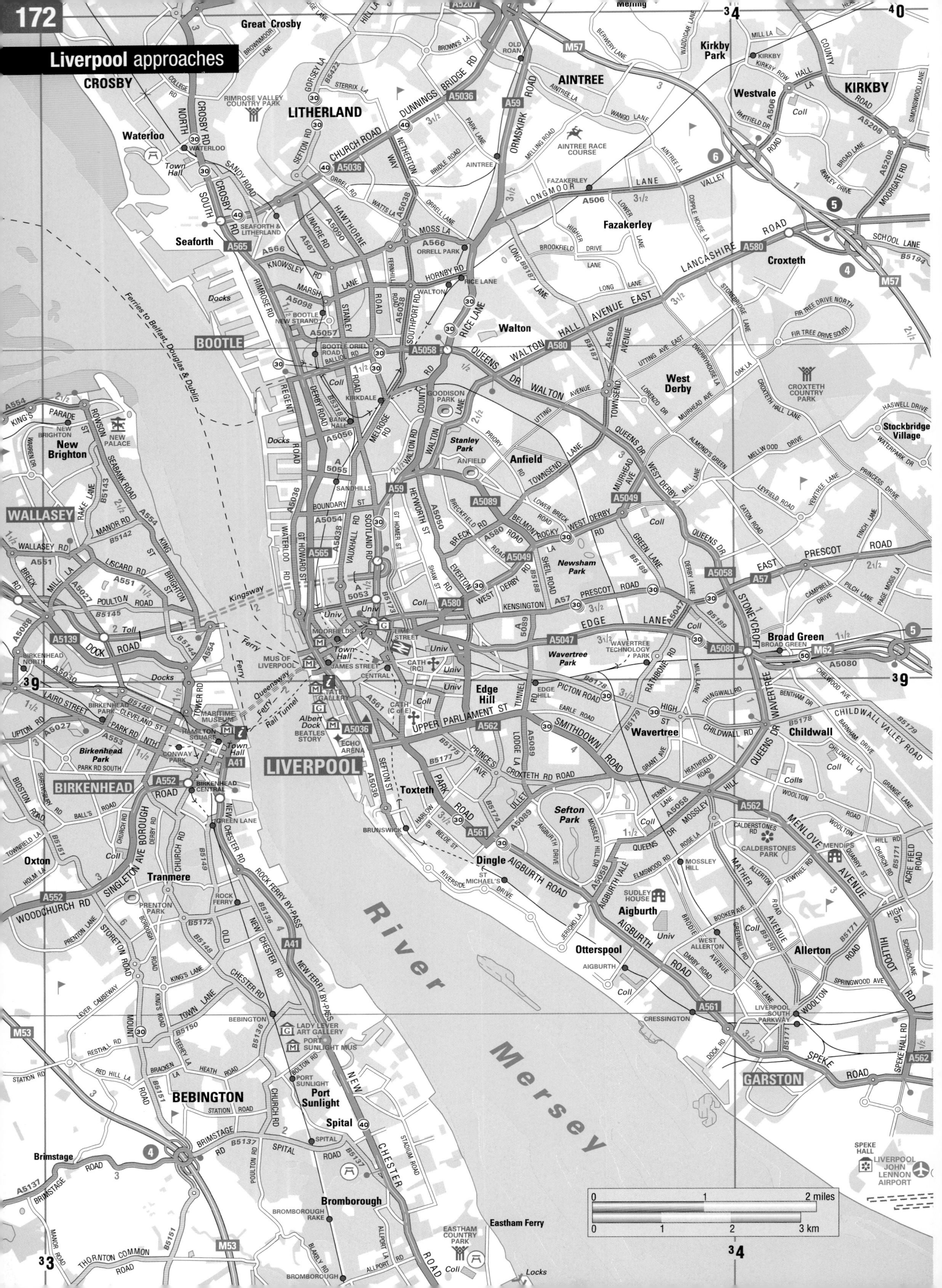
Great Crosby
CROSBY
Waterloo
Town Hall
Seaforth
LITHERLAND
RIMROSE VALLEY COUNTRY PARK
AINTREE
AINTREE RACE COURSE
Kirkby Park
KIRKBY
Westvale
Fazakerley
Croxteth
Docks
BOOTLE
Ferries to Belfast, Douglas & Dublin
Walton
West Derby
CROXTETH COUNTRY PARK
Stockbridge Village
New Brighton
NEW PALACE
Stanley Park
Anfield
WALLASEY
Newsham Park
Kingsway
Broad Green
Wavertree Park
WAVERTREE TECHNOLOGY PARK
Edge Hill
MUS OF LIVERPOOL
MARITIME MUSEUM
TATE GALLERY
Albert Dock
BEATLES STORY
ECHO ARENA
Queensway
Rail Tunnel
Birkenhead Park
BIRKENHEAD
LIVERPOOL
Wavertree
Childwall
Toxteth
Sefton Park
Oxton
Tranmere
Dingle
CALDERSTONES PARK
MENDIPS
SUDLEY HOUSE
Aigburth
River Mersey
Otterspool
Allerton
LIVERPOOL SOUTH PARKWAY
GARSTON
LADY LEVER ART GALLERY
PORT SUNLIGHT MUS
Port Sunlight
BEBINGTON
Spital
Brimstage
Bromborough
Eastham Ferry
EASTHAM COUNTRY PARK
Locks
SPEKE HALL
LIVERPOOL JOHN LENNON AIRPORT
0
1
2 miles
0
1
2
3 km

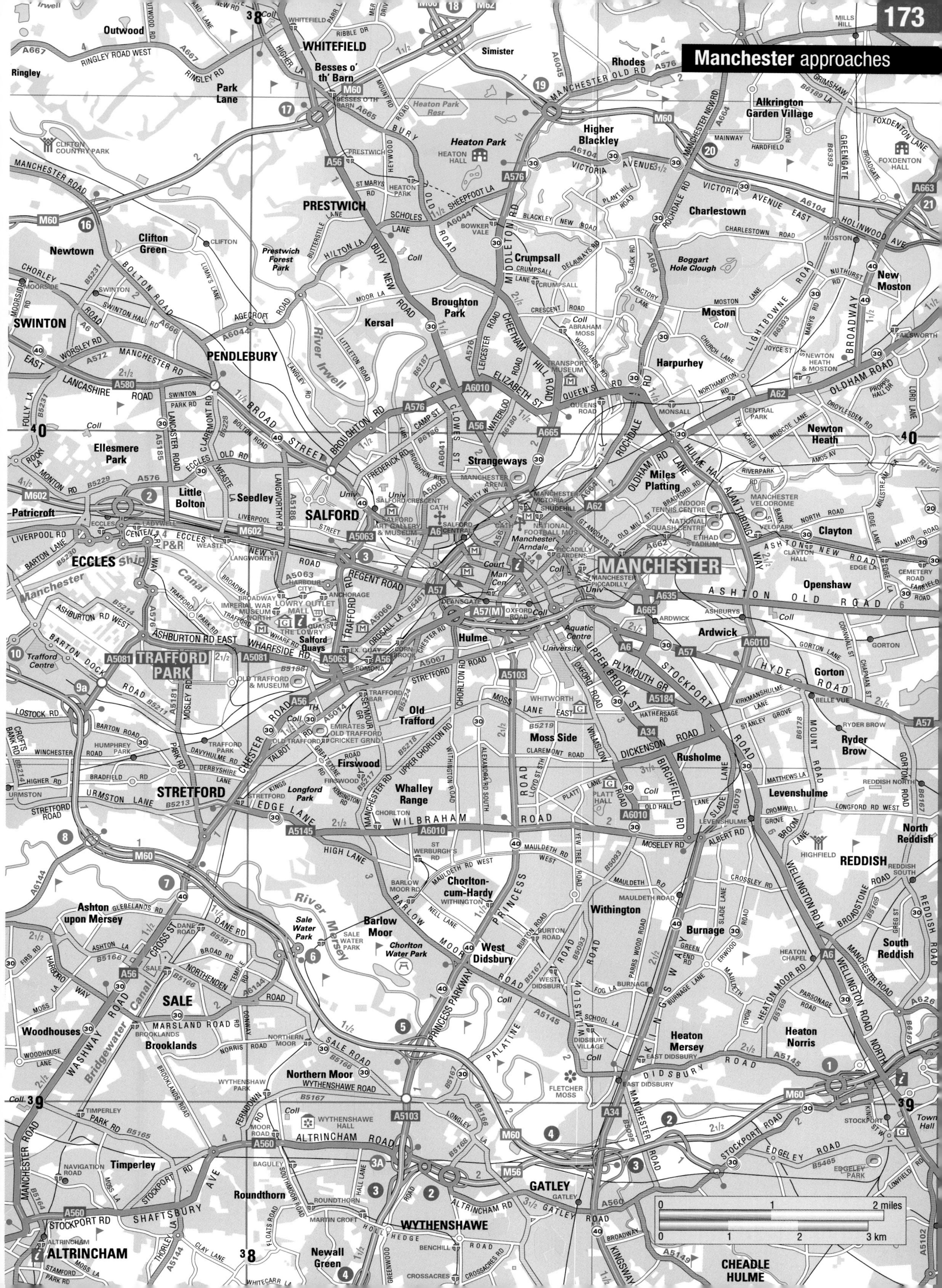
MANCHESTER
SALFORD
WHITEFIELD
Besses o' th' Barn
PRESTWICH
Outwood
Ringley
Park Lane
Simister
Rhodes
Alkrington Garden Village
Heaton Park
Higher Blackley
Charlestown
Crumpsall
Kersal
Broughton Park
Prestwich Forest Park
Clifton Green
Newtown
SWINTON
PENDLEBURY
Moston
New Moston
Harpurhey
Ellesmere Park
Little Bolton
Seedley
Patricroft
ECCLES
Strangeways
Miles Platting
Newton Heath
Clayton
Openshaw
Ardwick
Hulme
TRAFFORD PARK
Trafford Centre
Salford Quays
Old Trafford
Gorton
Ryder Brow
Moss Side
Rusholme
Firswood
Whalley Range
Longford Park
STRETFORD
Levenshulme
North Reddish
REDDISH
South Reddish
Chorlton-cum-Hardy
Withington
Burnage
Barlow Moor
West Didsbury
Ashton upon Mersey
SALE
Woodhouses
Brooklands
Heaton Mersey
Heaton Norris
Northern Moor
Fletcher Moss
Timperley
Roundthorn
WYTHENSHAWE
GATLEY
ALTRINCHAM
Newall Green
CHEADLE HULME
River Irwell
River Mersey
Manchester Ship Canal
Bridgewater Canal
M60
M602
M56
A57(M)
0 1 2 miles
0 1 2 3 km

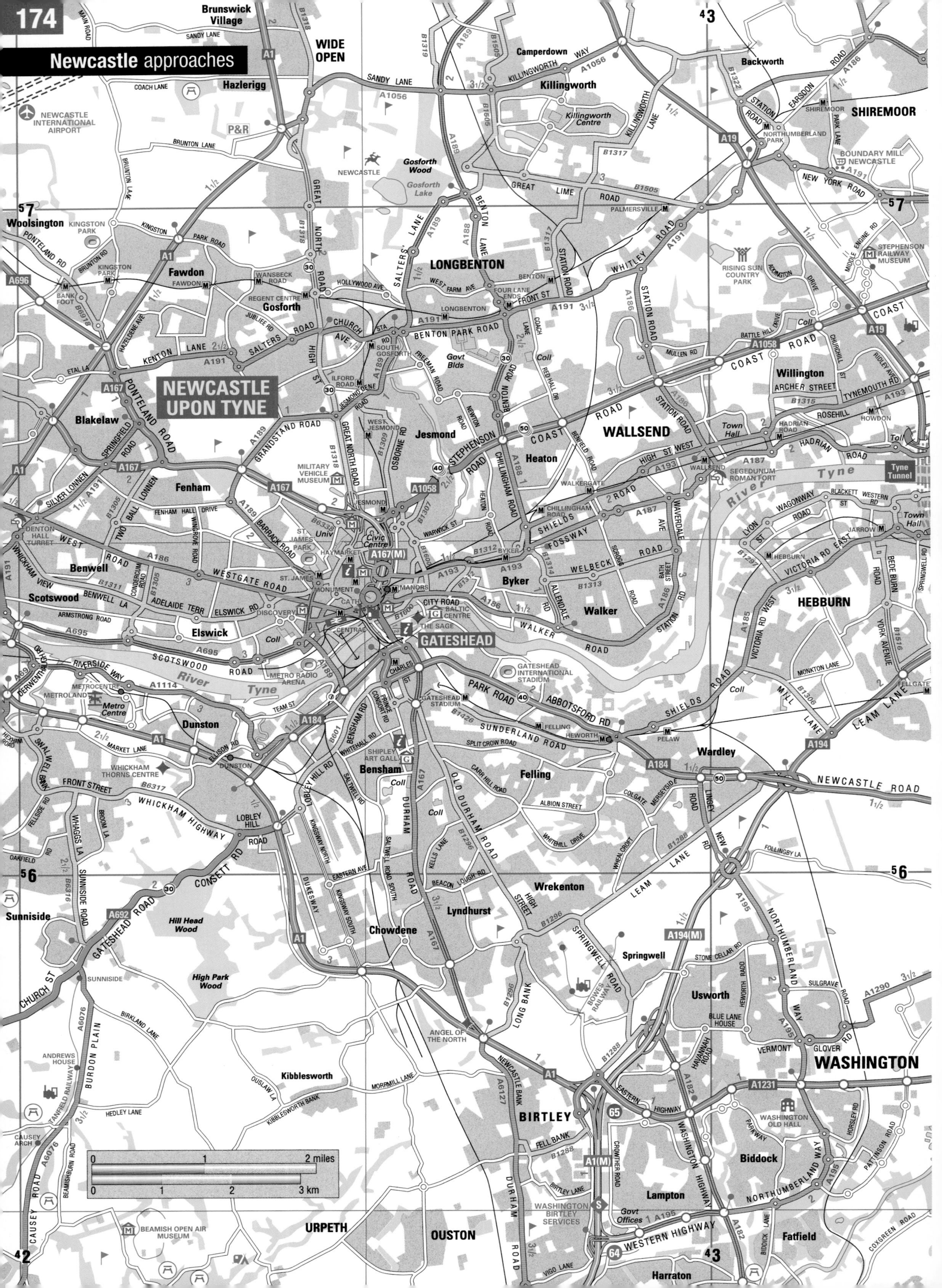
Brunswick Village
WIDE OPEN
Hazlerigg
Camperdown
Killingworth
Killingworth Centre
Backworth
SHIREMOOR
NEWCASTLE INTERNATIONAL AIRPORT
P&R
Gosforth Wood
Gosforth Lake
NEWCASTLE
BOUNDARY MILL NEWCASTLE
Woolsington
KINGSTON PARK
Fawdon
Gosforth
LONGBENTON
RISING SUN COUNTRY PARK
STEPHENSON RAILWAY MUSEUM
Govt Blds
NEWCASTLE UPON TYNE
Willington
Blakelaw
Jesmond
WALLSEND
Town Hall
Heaton
Fenham
MILITARY VEHICLE MUSEUM
SEGEDUNUM ROMAN FORT
River Tyne
Tyne Tunnel
Civic Centre
Benwell
Byker
Scotswood
HEBBURN
Walker
Elswick
GATESHEAD
GATESHEAD INTERNATIONAL STADIUM
METRO RADIO ARENA
METROLAND
Metro Centre
Dunston
Wardley
WHICKHAM THORNS CENTRE
Bensham
Felling
LOBLEY HILL
Wrekenton
Sunniside
Lyndhurst
Hill Head Wood
Chowdene
Springwell
High Park Wood
Usworth
BOWES RAILWAY
BLUE LANE HOUSE
ANGEL OF THE NORTH
VERMONT
GLOVER
WASHINGTON
ANDREWS HOUSE
Kibblesworth
BIRTLEY
WASHINGTON OLD HALL
CAUSEY ARCH
Biddock
Lampton
WASHINGTON BIRTLEY SERVICES
Govt Offices
BEAMISH OPEN AIR MUSEUM
URPETH
OUSTON
Fatfield
Harraton
0 1 2 miles
0 1 2 3 km

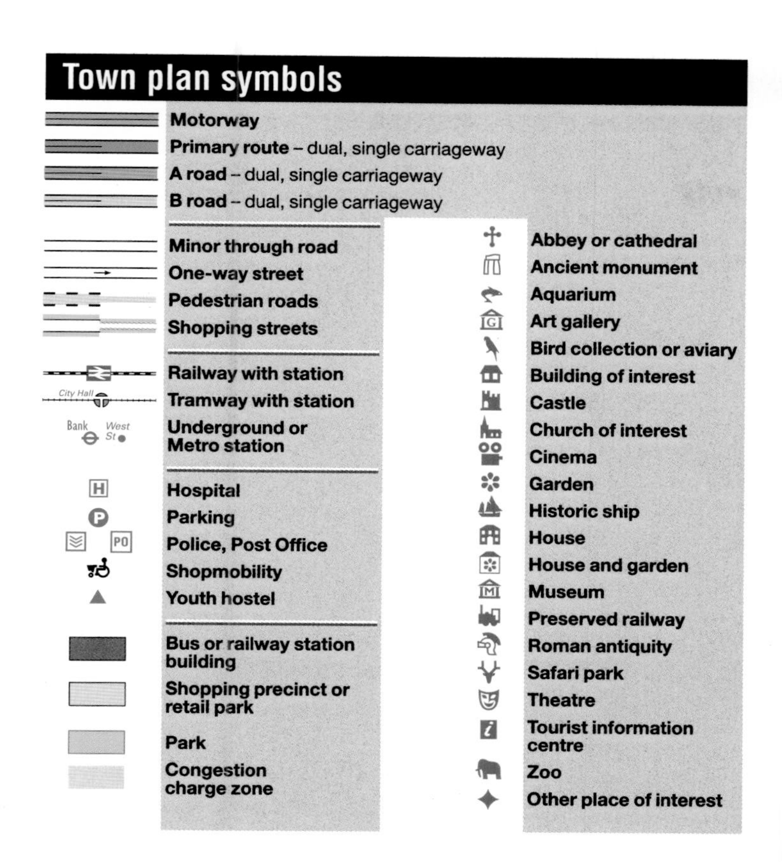

Town plan symbols

Motorway
Primary route – dual, single carriageway
A road -- dual, single carriageway
B road -- dual, single carriageway

Minor through road
One-way street
Pedestrian roads
Shopping streets

Railway with station
Tramway with station
Underground or Metro station

H　Hospital
P　Parking
Police, Post Office
Shopmobility
▲　Youth hostel

Bus or railway station building
Shopping precinct or retail park
Park
Congestion charge zone

✝ Abbey or cathedral
Ancient monument
Aquarium
Art gallery
Bird collection or aviary
Building of interest
Castle
Church of interest
Cinema
Garden
Historic ship
House
House and garden
Museum
Preserved railway
Roman antiquity
Safari park
Theatre
ℹ Tourist information centre
Zoo
✦ Other place of interest

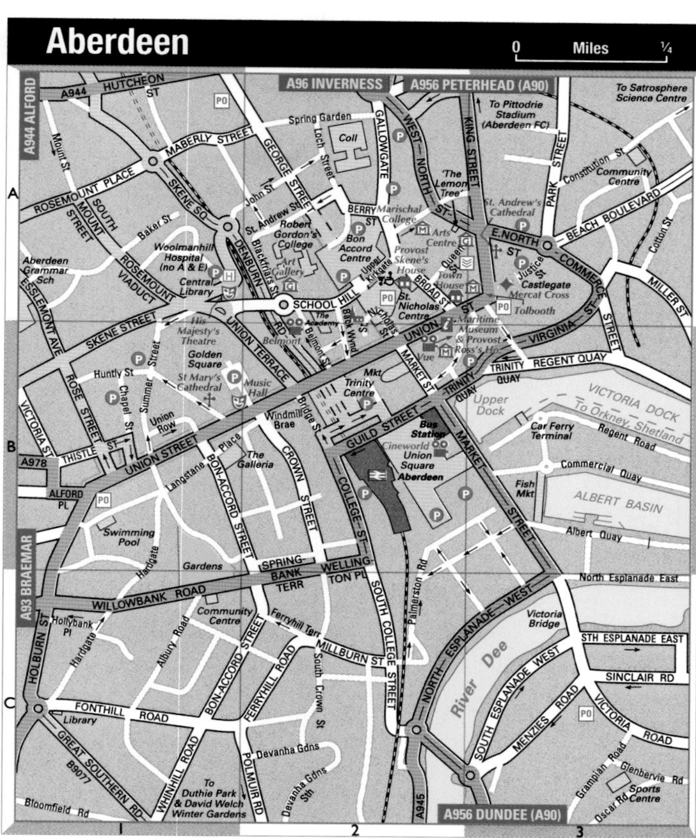

Aberdeen

Bath

Blackpool

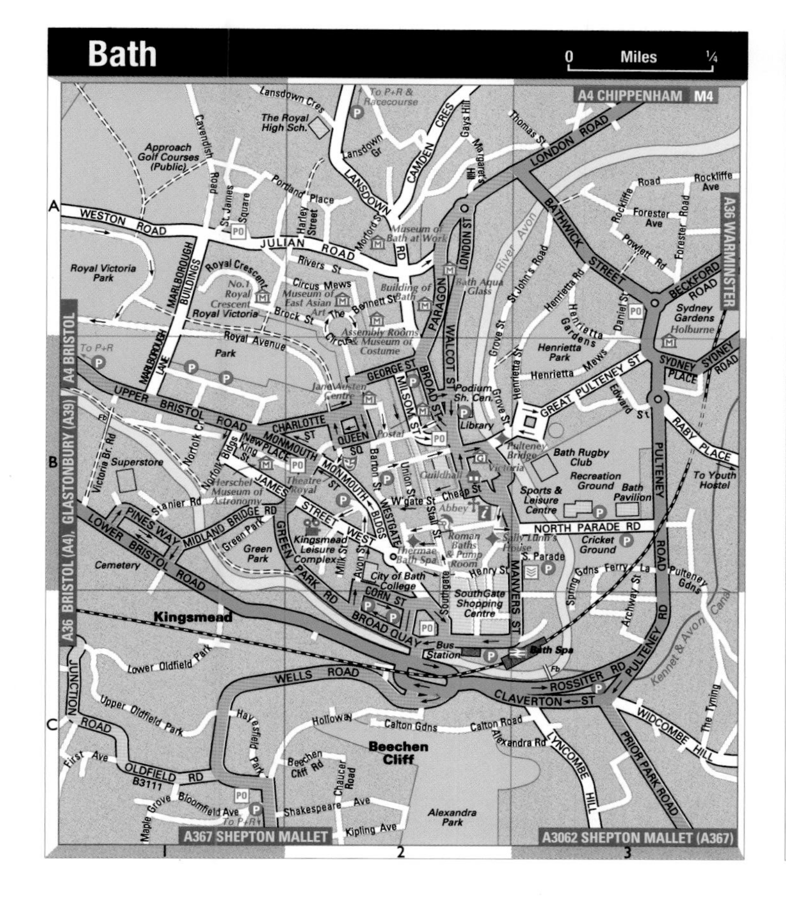

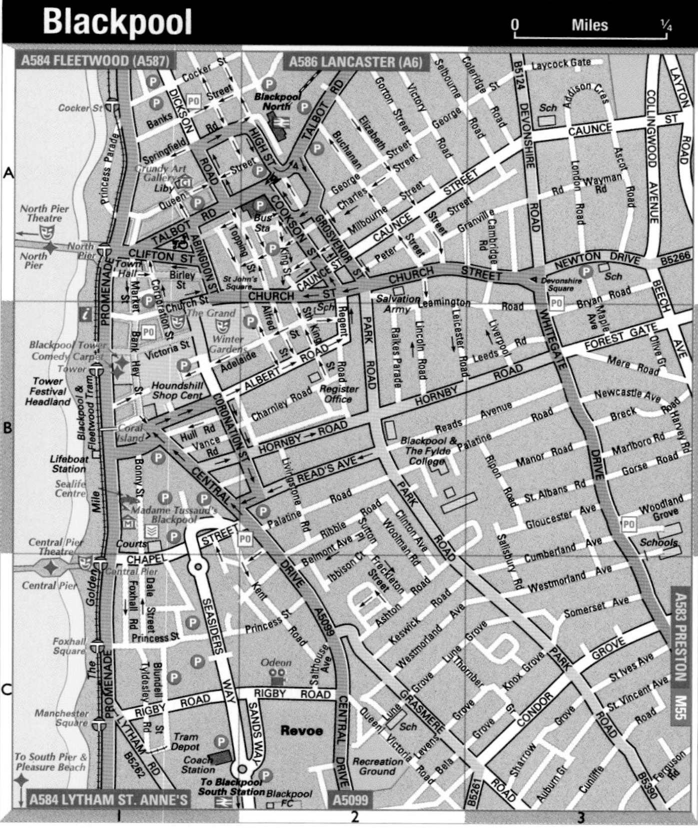

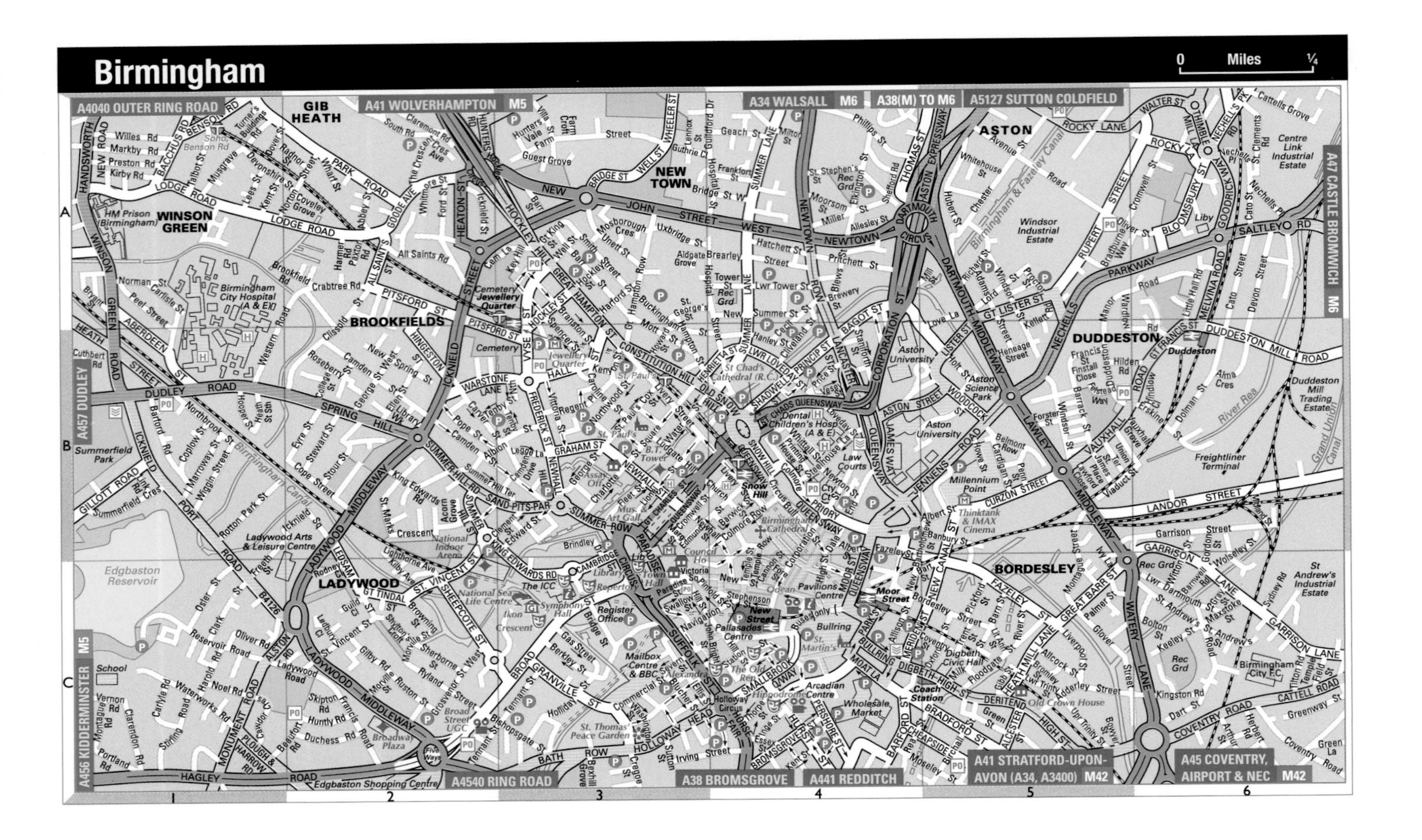
Birmingham
0 Miles ¼
A4040 OUTER RING ROAD
A41 WOLVERHAMPTON M5
A34 WALSALL M6
A38(M) TO M6
A5127 SUTTON COLDFIELD
A47 CASTLE BROMWICH M6
A457 DUDLEY
A456 KIDDERMINSTER M5
A4540 RING ROAD
A38 BROMSGROVE
A441 REDDITCH
A41 STRATFORD-UPON-AVON (A34, A3400) M42
A45 COVENTRY, AIRPORT & NEC M42
GIB HEATH
WINSON GREEN
NEW TOWN
ASTON
BROOKFIELDS
DUDDESTON
LADYWOOD
BORDESLEY
HM Prison (Birmingham)
Birmingham City Hospital (A & E)
Windsor Industrial Estate
Aston University
Aston Science Park
Millennium Point
Thinktank & IMAX Cinema
Snow Hill
New Street
Moor Street
Duddeston
Birmingham Cathedral
St. Chad's Cathedral (R.C.)
Children's Hosp (A & E)
Law Courts
The ICC
National Indoor Arena
Symphony Hall
Repertory
Town Hall
Council Ho
Mailbox Centre & BBC
Pallasades Centre
Bullring
St. Martin's
Coach Station
Wholesale Market
Digbeth Civic Hall
Old Crown House
Edgbaston Reservoir
Ladywood Arts & Leisure Centre
Summerfield Park
Edgbaston Shopping Centre
Broadway Plaza
St. Thomas' Peace Garden
Freightliner Terminal
Centre Link Industrial Estate
Duddeston Mill Trading Estate
St. Andrew's Industrial Estate
Birmingham City F.C.
Grand Union Canal
Birmingham & Fazeley Canal
River Rea
1 2 3 4 5 6
A B C

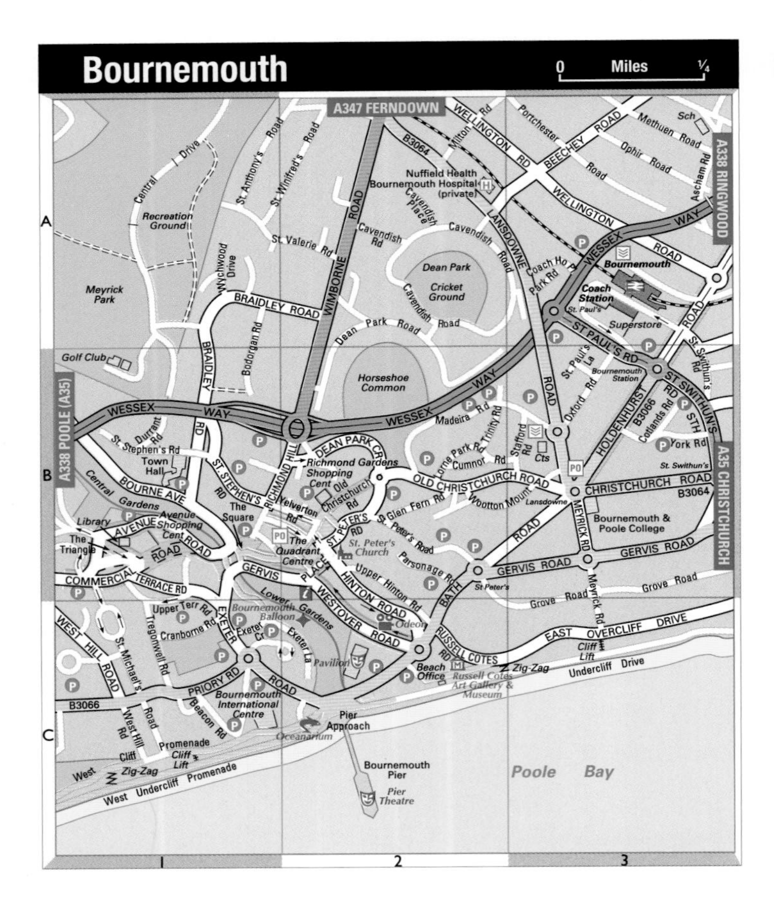
Bournemouth
0 Miles ¼
A347 FERNDOWN
A338 RINGWOOD
A338 POOLE (A35)
A35 CHRISTCHURCH
Nuffield Health Bournemouth Hospital (private)
Recreation Ground
Meyrick Park
Dean Park Cricket Ground
Horseshoe Common
Bournemouth
Coach Station
Superstore
Golf Club
Town Hall
Richmond Gardens Shopping Cent
The Square
The Triangle
Library
St. Peter's Church
Bournemouth & Poole College
Bournemouth Gardens
Bournemouth Balloon
Pavilion
Odeon
Bournemouth International Centre
Pier Approach
Oceanarium
Bournemouth Pier
Pier Theatre
Russell Cotes Art Gallery & Museum
Beach Office
Zig-Zag
Cliff Lift
Poole Bay
1 2 3
A B C

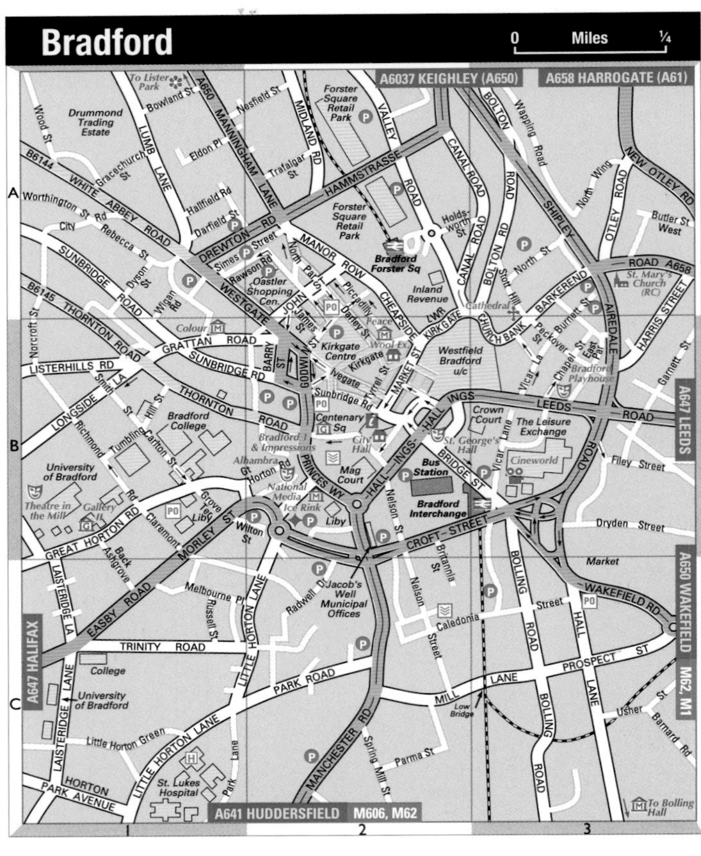
Bradford
0 Miles ¼
A6037 KEIGHLEY (A650)
A658 HARROGATE (A61)
A647 LEEDS
A650 WAKEFIELD M62, M1
A647 HALIFAX
A641 HUDDERSFIELD M606, M62
To Lister Park
Drummond Trading Estate
Forster Square Retail Park
Bradford Forster Sq
Inland Revenue
Cathedral
Oastler Shopping Cen
Kirkgate Centre
Westfield Bradford u/c
Crown Court
The Leisure Exchange
Cineworld
St. Mary's Church (RC)
Bradford Playhouse
Colour Museum
Bradford College
University of Bradford
Theatre in the Mill
Gallery II
Alhambra
National Media Museum
Ice Rink
Centenary Sq
City Hall
Mag Court
Bus Station
Bradford Interchange
Jacob's Well Municipal Offices
College
St. Lukes Hospital
To Bolling Hall
1 2 3
A B C

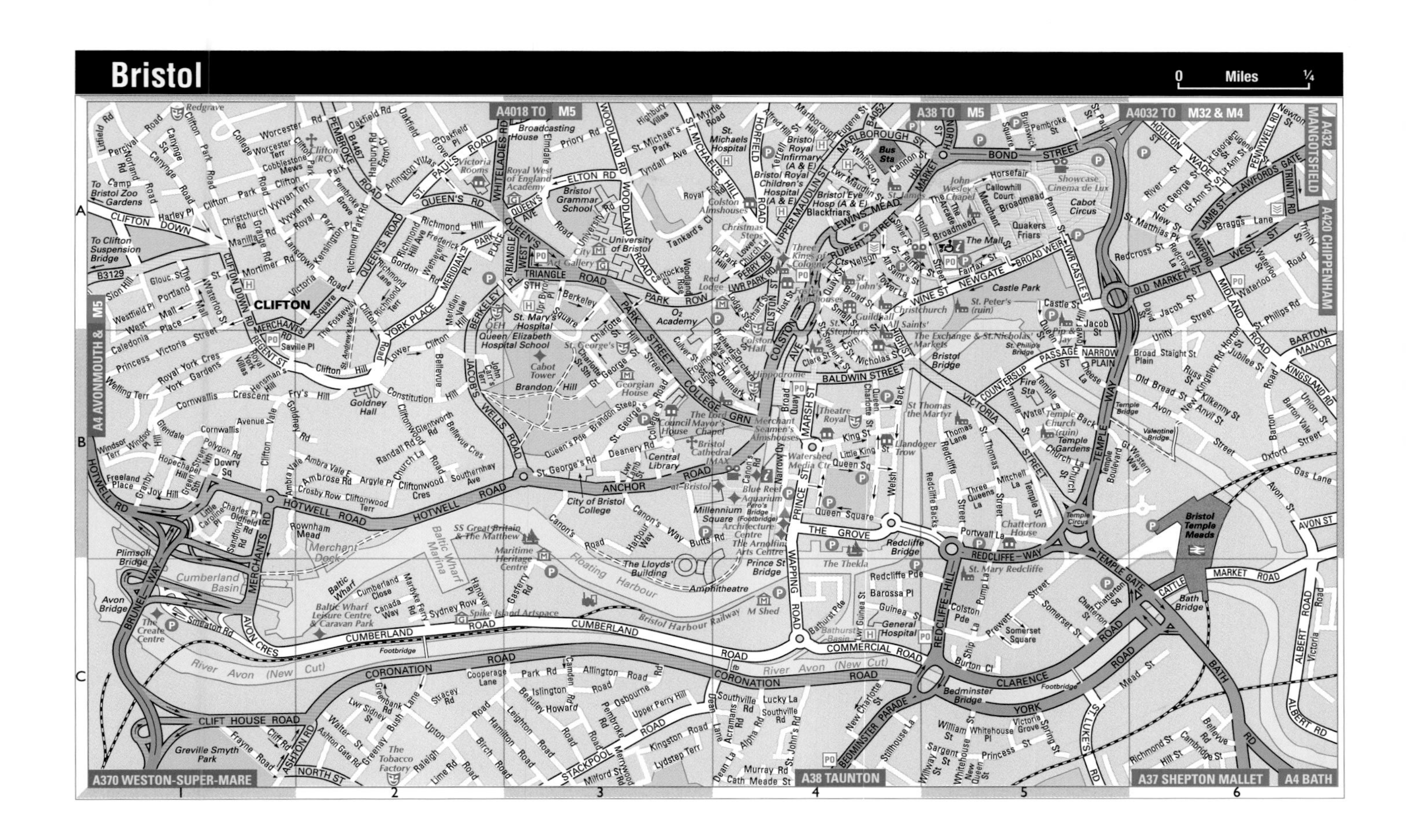
Bristol
0 Miles ¼
A4018 TO M5
A38 TO M5
A4032 TO M32 & M4
A432 MANGOTSFIELD
A420 CHIPPENHAM
A4 AVONMOUTH & M5
A370 WESTON-SUPER-MARE
A38 TAUNTON
A37 SHEPTON MALLET
A4 BATH
CLIFTON

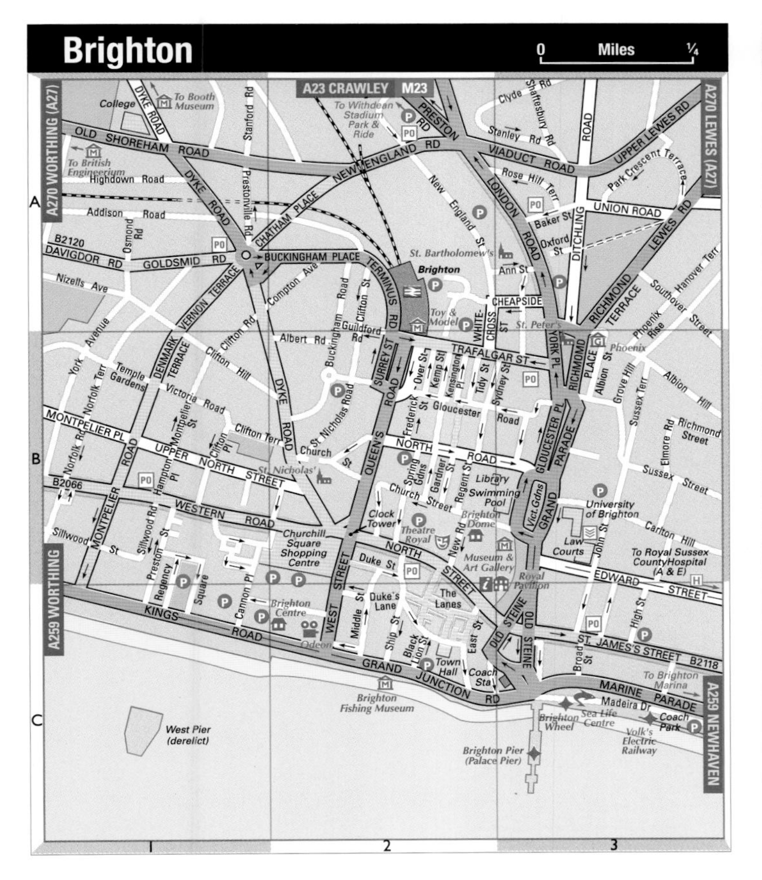
Brighton
0 Miles ¼
A23 CRAWLEY M23
A270 WORTHING (A27)
A270 LEWES (A27)
A259 WORTHING
A259 NEWHAVEN

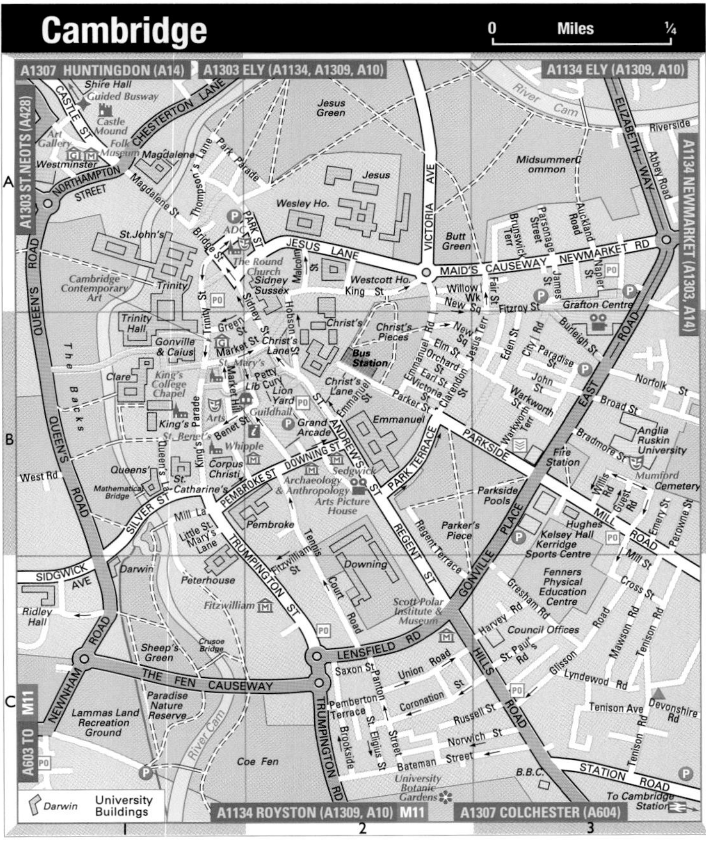
Cambridge
0 Miles ¼
A1307 HUNTINGDON (A14)
A1303 ELY (A1134, A1309, A10)
A1134 ELY (A1309, A10)
A1303 ST.NEOTS (A428)
A1134 NEWMARKET (A1303, A14)
A603 TO M11
A1134 ROYSTON (A1309, A10) M11
A1307 COLCHESTER (A604)
University Buildings

Canterbury

0   Miles   ¼

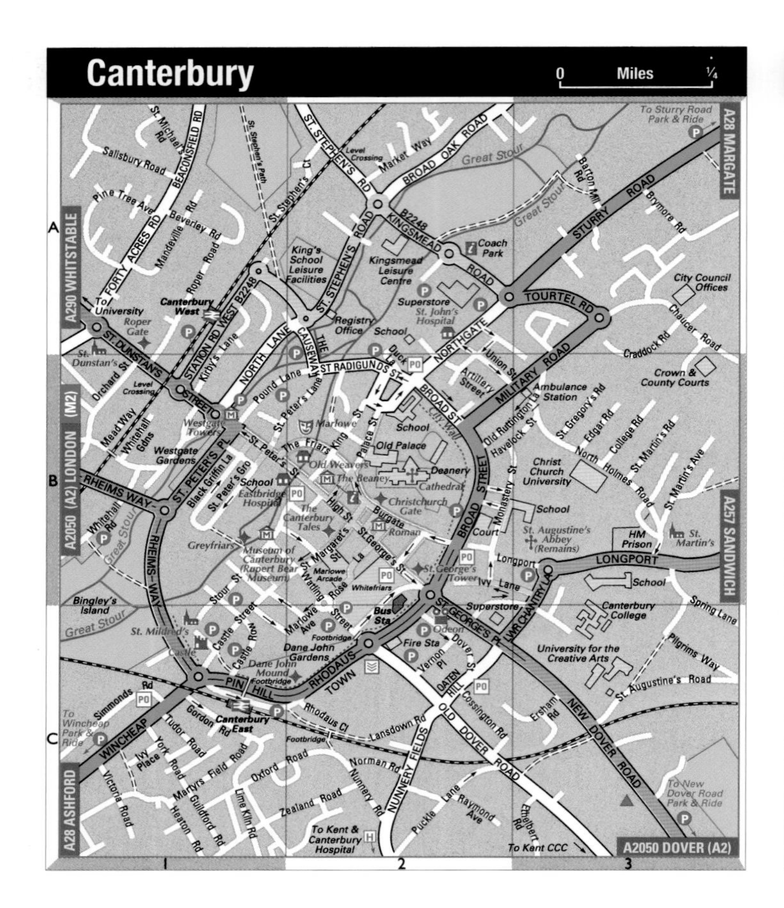

Cardiff / Caerdydd

0   Miles   ¼

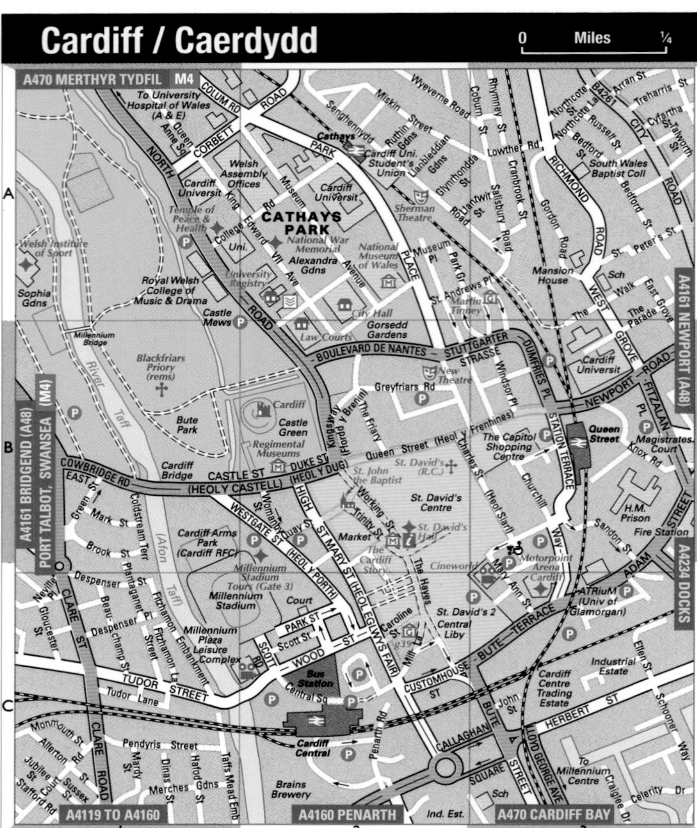

Cheltenham

0   Miles   ¼

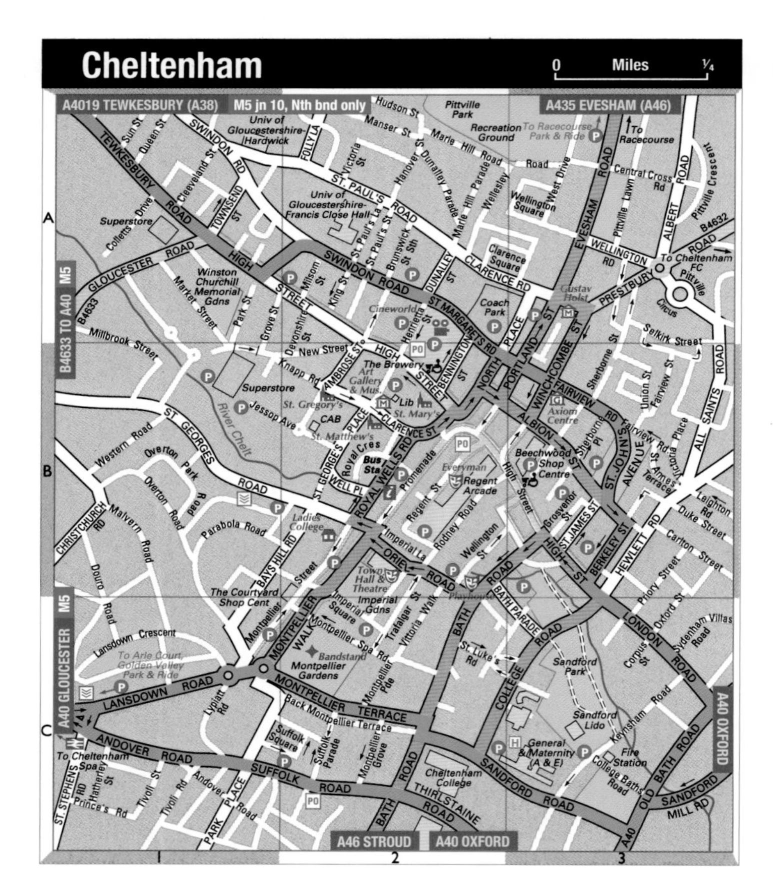

Chester

0   Miles   ¼

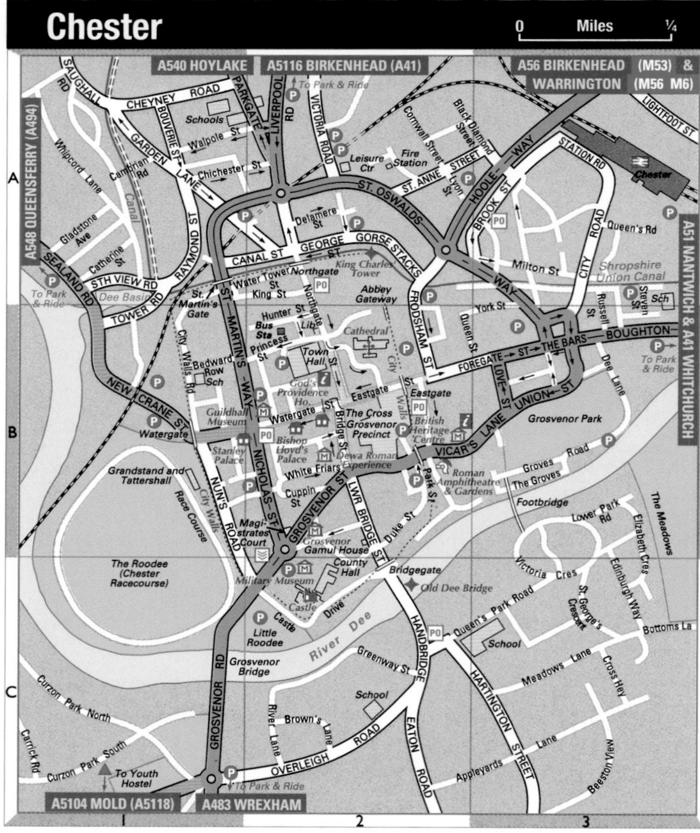

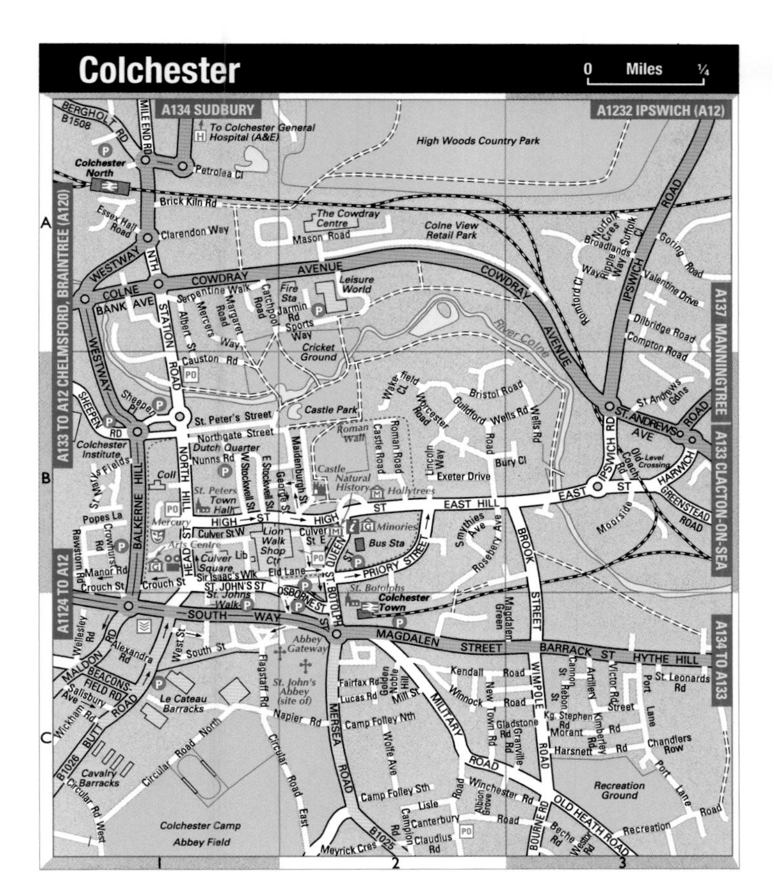
Colchester
0 Miles ¼
A134 SUDBURY
A1232 IPSWICH (A12)
To Colchester General Hospital (A&E)
High Woods Country Park
Colchester North
Petrolea Cl
Brick Kiln Rd
The Cowdray Centre
Mason Road
Colne View Retail Park
Clarendon Way
Essex Hall Road
COWDRAY AVENUE
WESTWAY
Leisure World
Serpentine Walk
Valentine Drive
Dilbridge Road
Compton Road
River Colne
Cricket Ground
Causton Rd
Bristol Road
St Andrews Gdns
Castle Park
St. Peter's Street
Northgate Street
Dutch Quarter
Nunns Rd
Colchester Institute
Castle
Roman Wall
Natural History
Hollytrees
Exeter Drive
Bury Cl
EAST HILL
EAST ST
HARWICH ROAD
GREENSTEAD ROAD
Moorside
Popes La
Minories
Bus Sta
PRIORY STREET
Mercury Arts Centre
Culver Sq
Lion Walk Shop Ctr
Crouch St
ST. JOHN'S ST
St. Botolphs
Colchester Town
SOUTH WAY
MAGDALEN STREET
BARRACK ST
HYTHE HILL
Abbey Gateway
St. John's Abbey (site of)
Le Cateau Barracks
Kendall Road
St. Leonards Rd
Napier Rd
Camp Folley Nth
Harsnett Rd
Chandlers Row
Cavalry Barracks
Circular Road North
Recreation Ground
Colchester Camp Abbey Field
Meyrick Cres
Recreation Rd
A133 TO A12 CHELMSFORD, BRAINTREE (A120)
A1124 TO A12
A137 MANNINGTREE
A133 CLACTON-ON-SEA
A134 TO A133
A
B
C
1
2
3

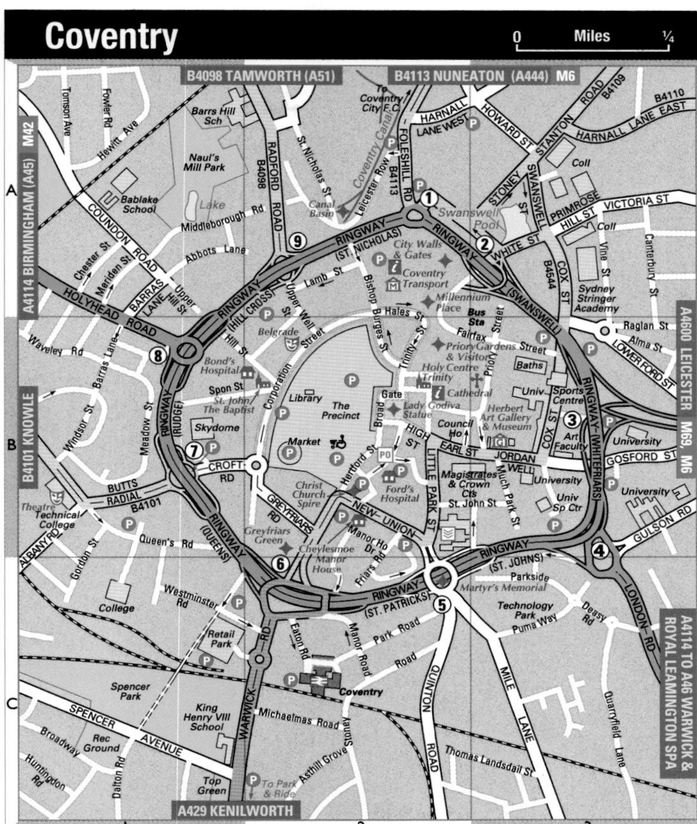
Coventry
0 Miles ¼
B4098 TAMWORTH (A51)
B4113 NUNEATON (A444) M6
To Coventry City F.C.
Barrs Hill Sch
Naul's Mill Park
Bablake School
Middleborough Rd
Abbots Lane
Swanswell Pool
VICTORIA ST
City Walls & Gates
Coventry Transport
Millennium Place
Bus Sta
Priory Gardens & Visitor Ctr
Holy Trinity
Cathedral
Herbert Art Gallery & Museum
Sydney Stringer Academy
Raglan St
Belgrade
Bond's Hospital
Library
The Precinct
Lady Godiva Statue
Council Ho
Skydome
Market
CROFT RD
Christ Church Spire
Ford's Hospital
Magistrates & Crown Cts
University
Sports Centre
Art Faculty
Univ Sp Ctr
GOSFORD ST
Technical College
Greyfriars Green
Cheylesmoe Manor House
Queen's Rd
RINGWAY (ST. JOHNS)
Parkside
Martyr's Memorial
Technology Park
Puma Way
College
Westminster Rd
Retail Park
Spencer Park
Coventry
King Henry VIII School
Michaelmas Road
Rec Ground
Top Green
To Park & Ride
Thomas Landsdail St
Quarryfield Lane
A429 KENILWORTH
A4114 BIRMINGHAM (A45)
M42
B4101 KNOWLE
A4600 LEICESTER
M69, M6
A4114 TO A46 WARWICK & ROYAL LEAMINGTON SPA
A
B
C
1
2
3

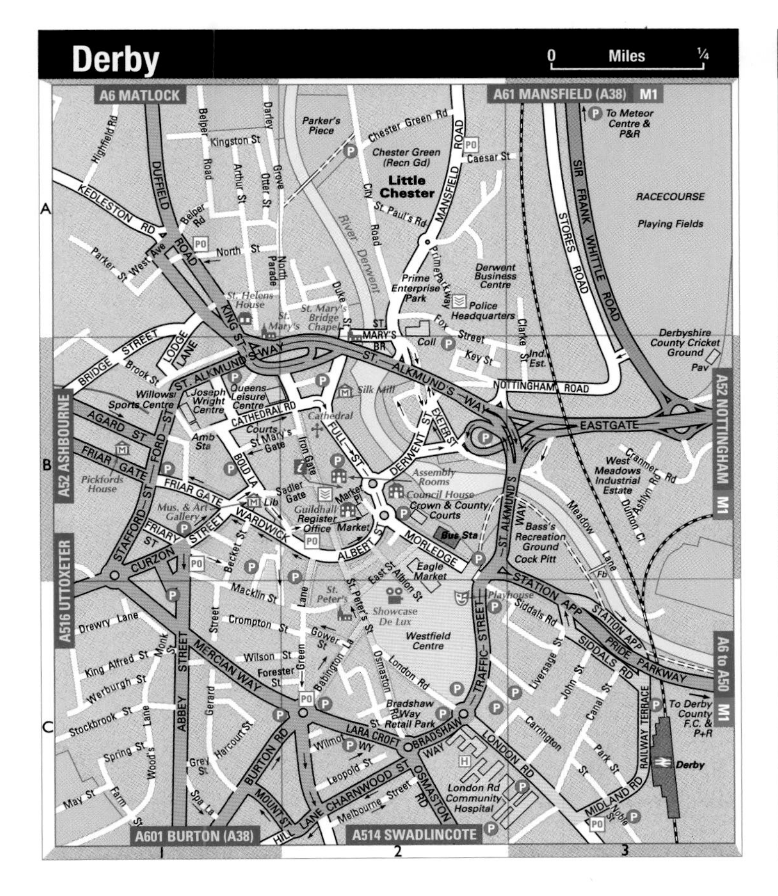
Derby
0 Miles ¼
A6 MATLOCK
A61 MANSFIELD (A38) M1
To Meteor Centre & P&R
Parker's Piece
Chester Green Rd
Chester Green (Recn Gd)
Little Chester
RACECOURSE
Playing Fields
KEDLESTON RD
SIR FRANK WHITTLE ROAD
St. Helens House
St. Mary's Bridge Chapel
River Derwent
Prime Enterprise Park
Derwent Business Centre
Police Headquarters
Derbyshire County Cricket Ground
BRIDGE STREET
Willows Sports Centre
Joseph Wright Centre
Queens Leisure Centre
Silk Mill
Cathedral
ST. ALKMUND'S WAY
NOTTINGHAM ROAD
EASTGATE
Pickfords House
FRIAR GATE
Assembly Rooms
Council House
Crown & County Courts
West Meadows Industrial Estate
Mus. & Art Gallery
Guildhall
Market
Bus Sta
Bass's Recreation Ground
Cock Pitt
CURZON
Eagle Market
MORLEDGE
STATION APP
Showcase De Lux
Westfield Centre
Drewry Lane
MERCIAN WAY
ABBEY STREET
King Alfred St
Stockbrook St
LARA CROFT WY
Bradshaw Way Retail Park
BRADSHAW WAY
LONDON RD
PRIDE PARKWAY
To Derby County F.C. & P+R
Derby
London Rd Community Hospital
MIDLAND RD
A601 BURTON (A38)
A514 SWADLINCOTE
A52 ASHBOURNE
A516 UTTOXETER
A52 NOTTINGHAM M1
A6 to A50 M1
A
B
C
1
2
3

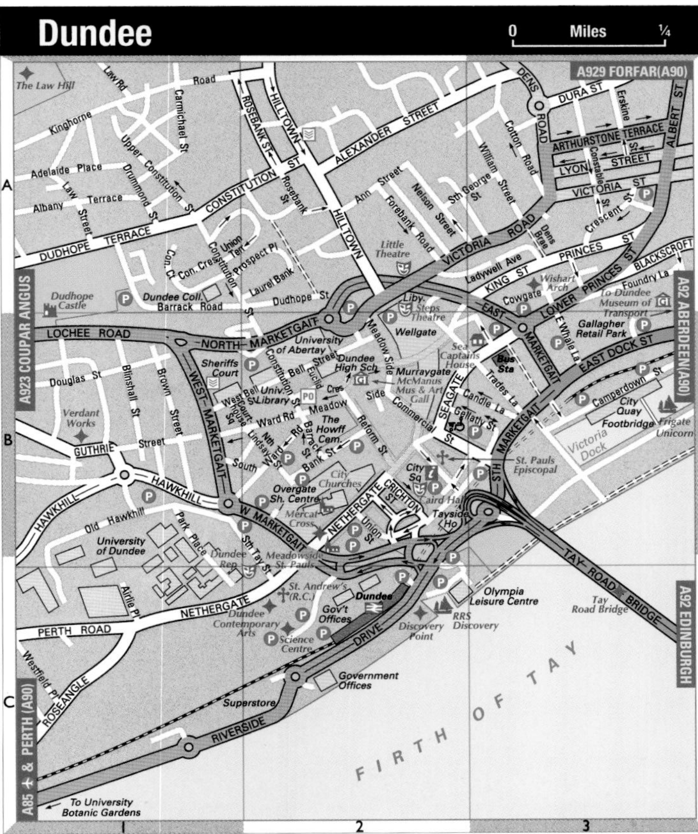
Dundee
0 Miles ¼
A929 FORFAR(A90)
The Law Hill
Law Rd
HILLTOWN
ALEXANDER STREET
DURA ST
ARTHURSTONE TERRACE
Adelaide Place
CONSTITUTION ST
LYON STREET
VICTORIA ST
Albany Terrace
DUDHOPE TERRACE
Little Theatre
VICTORIA ROAD
PRINCES ST
BLACKSCROFT
Dudhope Castle
Dundee Coll.
Barrack Road
Dudhope St
Lib.
Steps Theatre
Wellgate
Wishart Arch
To Dundee Museum of Transport
Gallagher Retail Park
LOCHEE ROAD
NORTH MARKETGAIT
University of Abertay
Sheriffs Court
Dundee High Sch
Murraygate
McManus Mus & Art Gall
Bus Sta
EAST DOCK ST
Douglas St
Camperdown
City Quay
Footbridge
Frigate Unicorn
Verdant Works
GUTHRIE Street
Ward Rd
The Howff Cem.
Victoria Dock
St. Pauls Episcopal
HAWKHILL
Overgate Sh. Centre
City Churches
City Sq
Caird Hall
Tayside Ho
University of Dundee
Dundee Rep
St. Andrew's (R.C.)
Dundee
Gov't Offices
Olympia Leisure Centre
Tay Road Bridge
RRS Discovery
Discovery Point
Dundee Contemporary Arts
Science Centre
PERTH ROAD
NETHERGATE
RIVERSIDE
Superstore
Government Offices
FIRTH OF TAY
To University Botanic Gardens
A923 COUPAR ANGUS
A92 ABERDEEN(A90)
A92 EDINBURGH
A85 & PERTH (A90)
A
B
C
1
2
3

Edinburgh

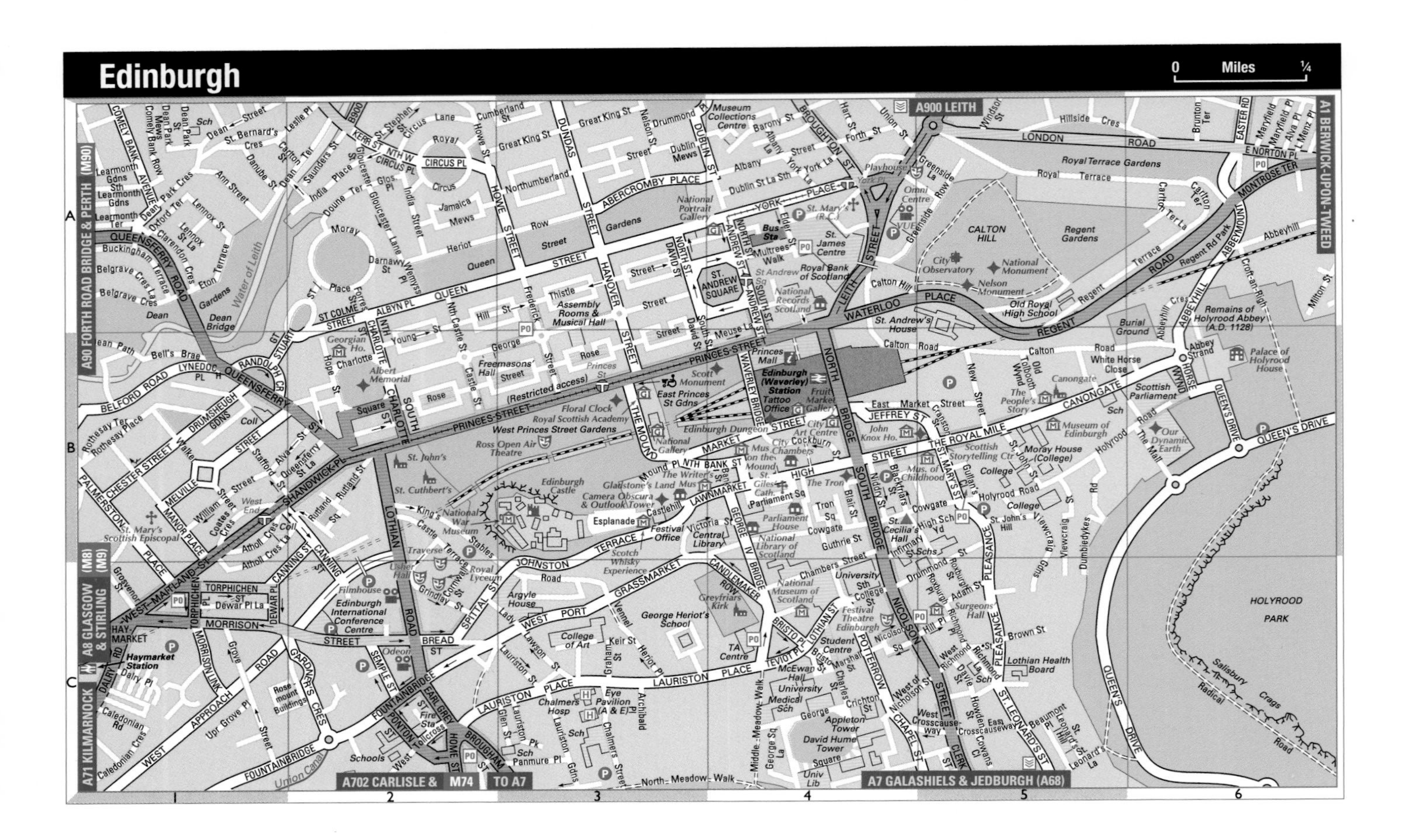

Durham

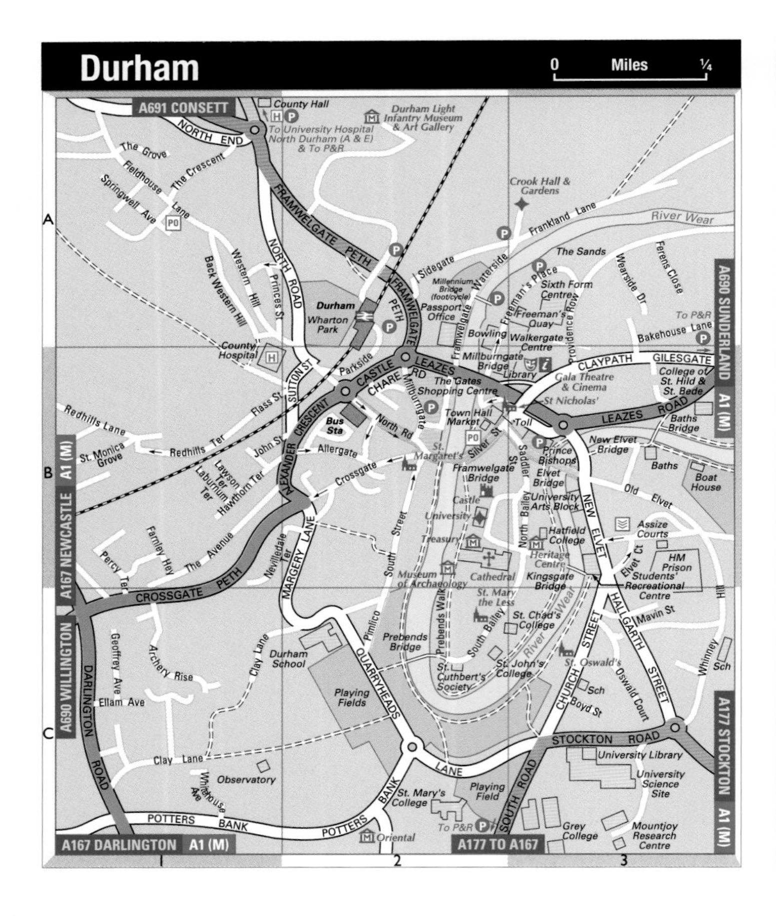

Exeter

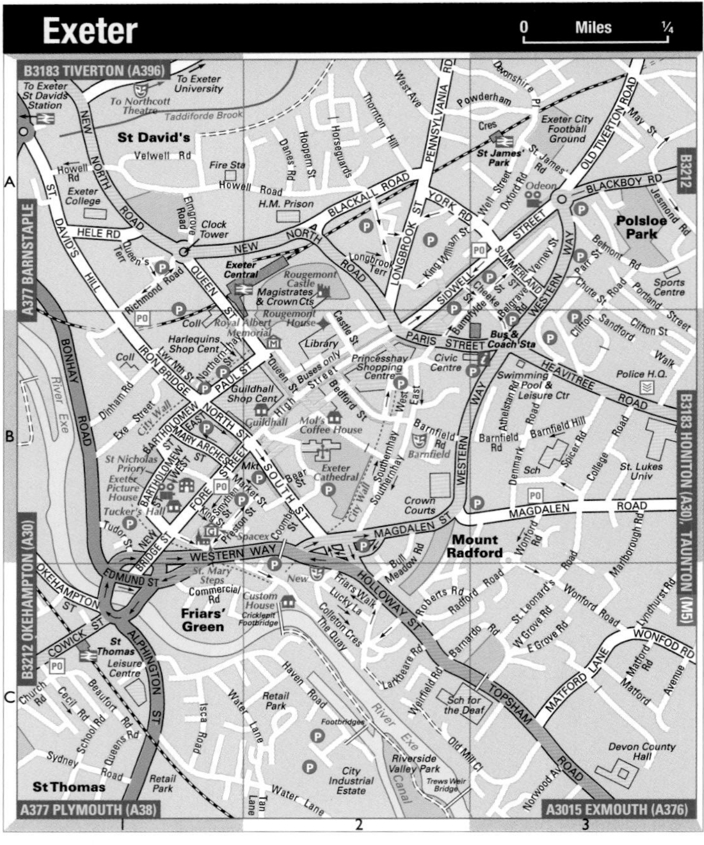

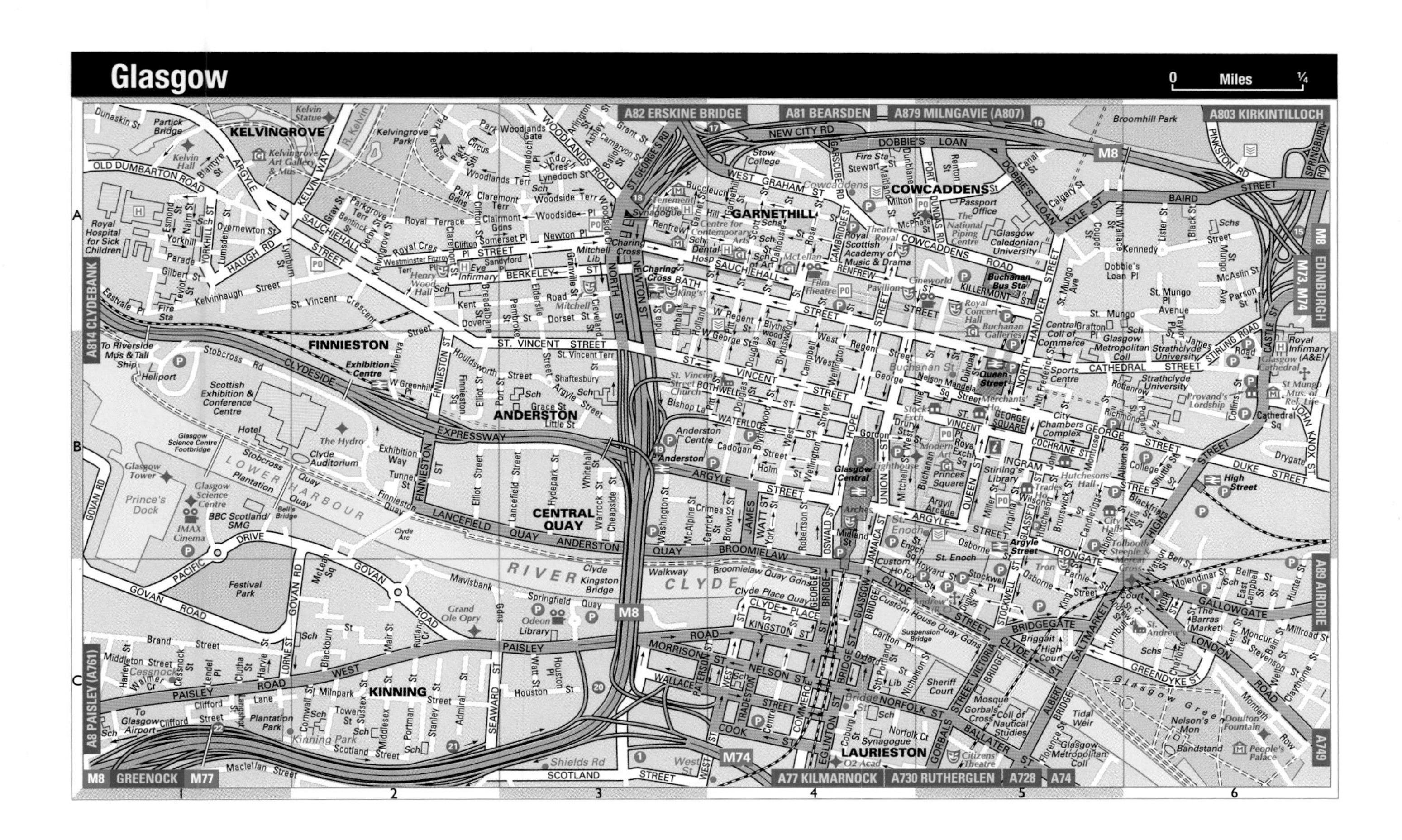

Glasgow

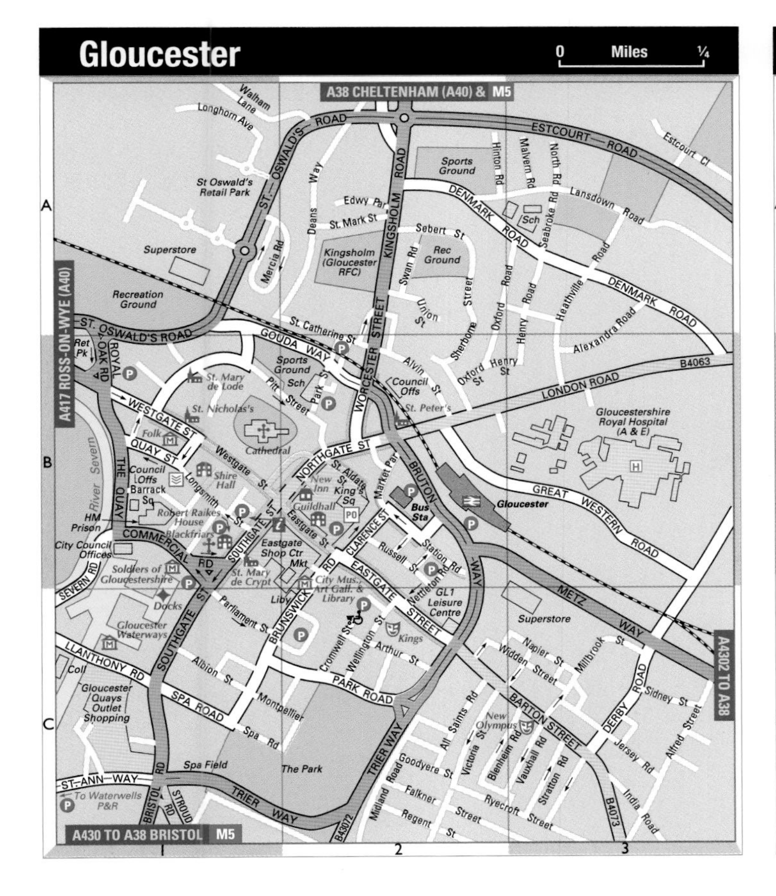

Gloucester

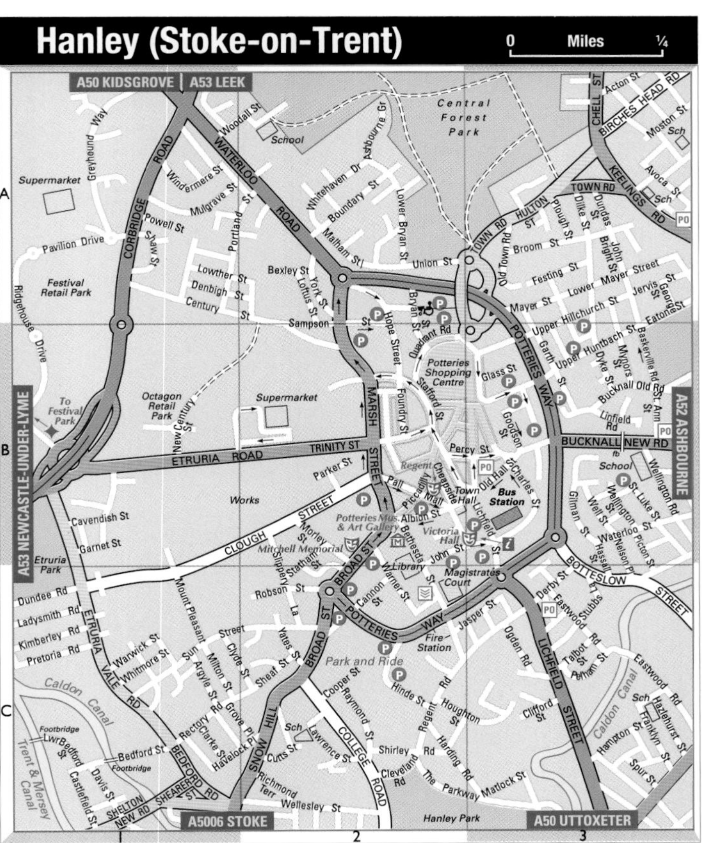

Hanley (Stoke-on-Trent)

Harrogate

0   Miles   ¼

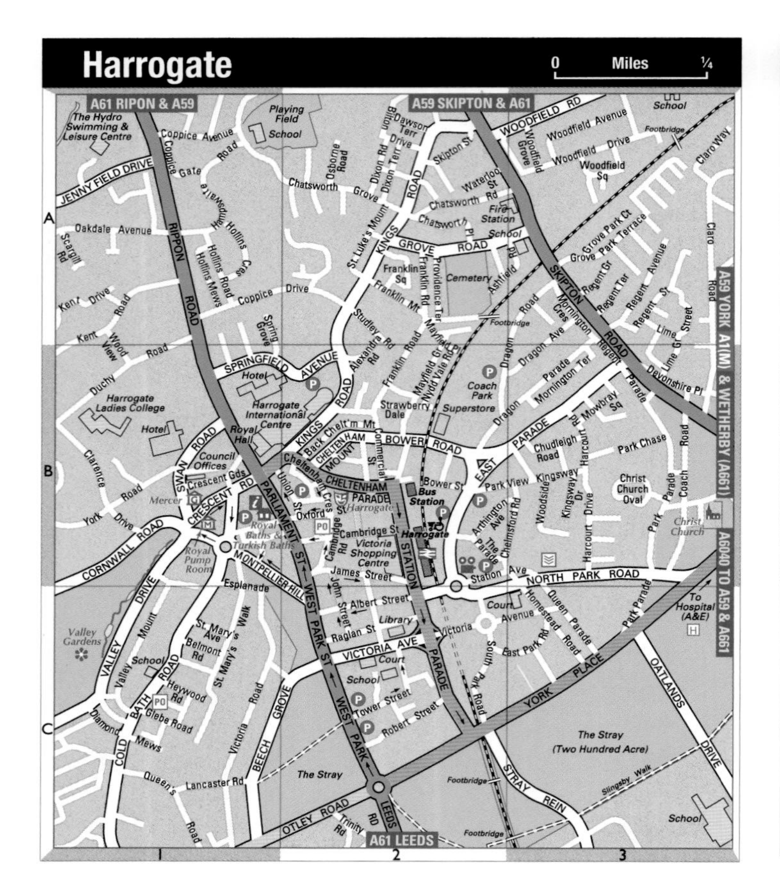

Hull

0   Miles   ¼

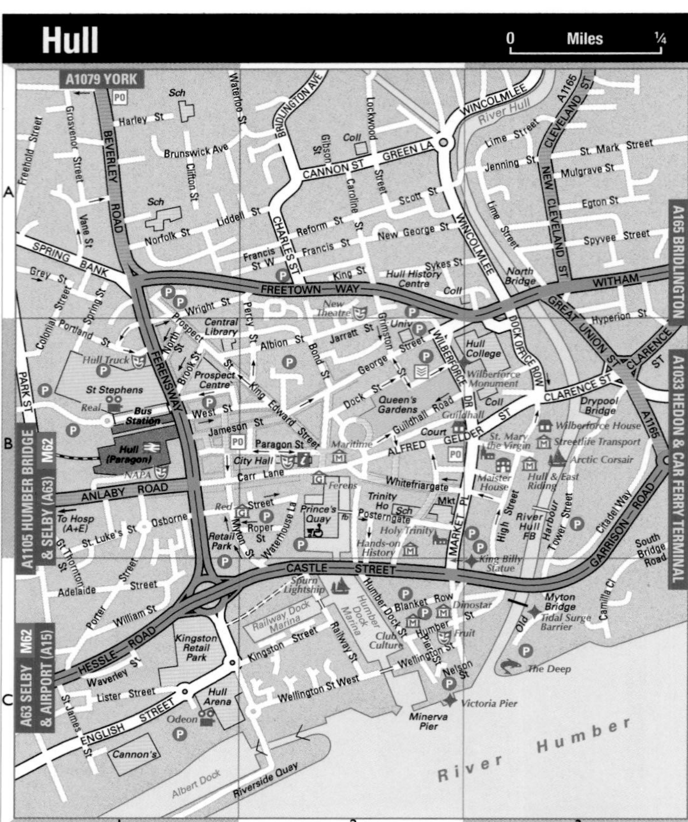

Ipswich

0   Miles   ¼

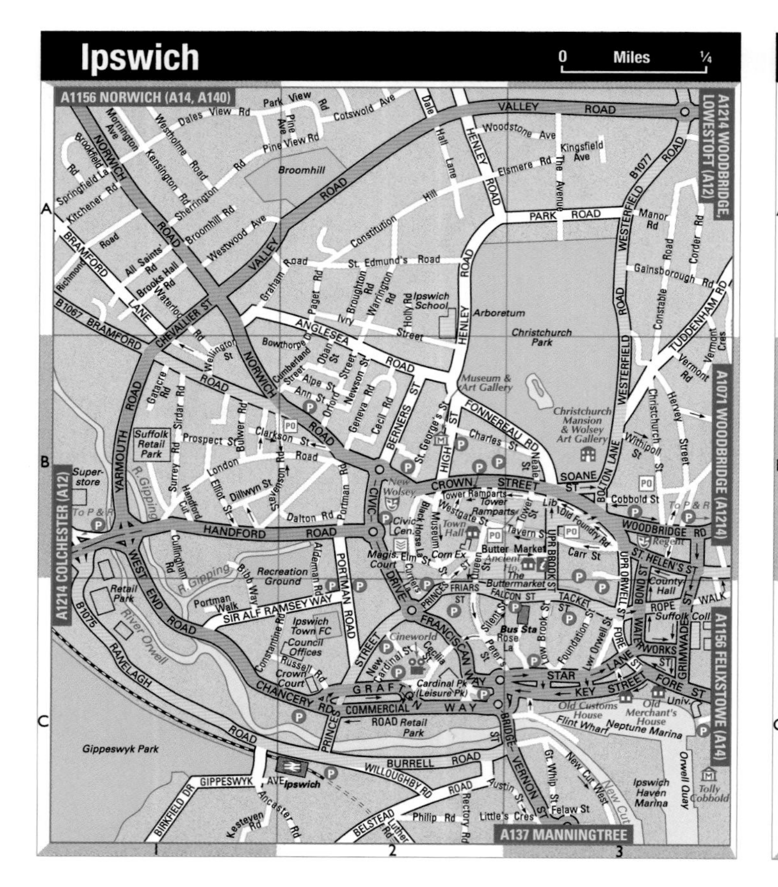

Leicester

0   Miles   ¼

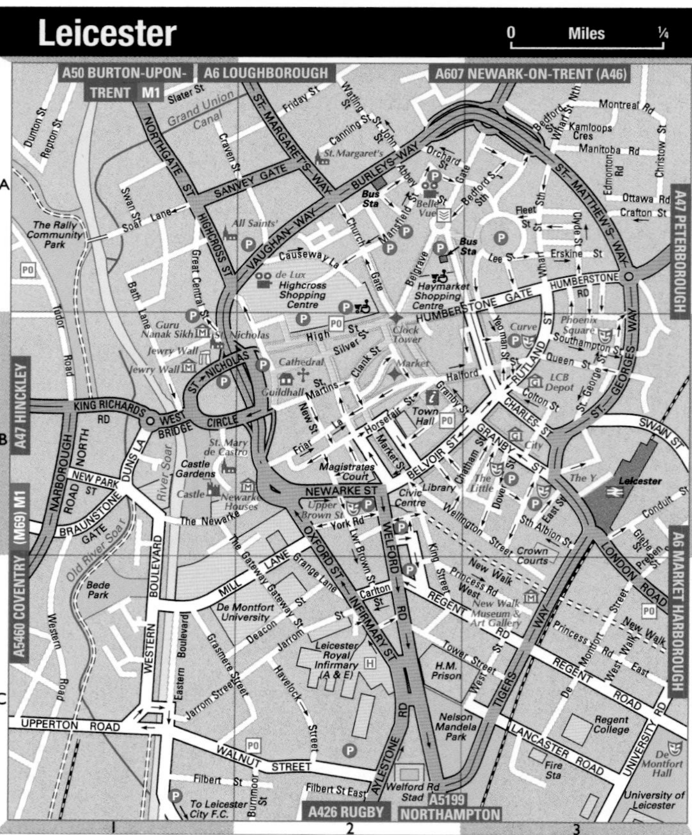

Leeds

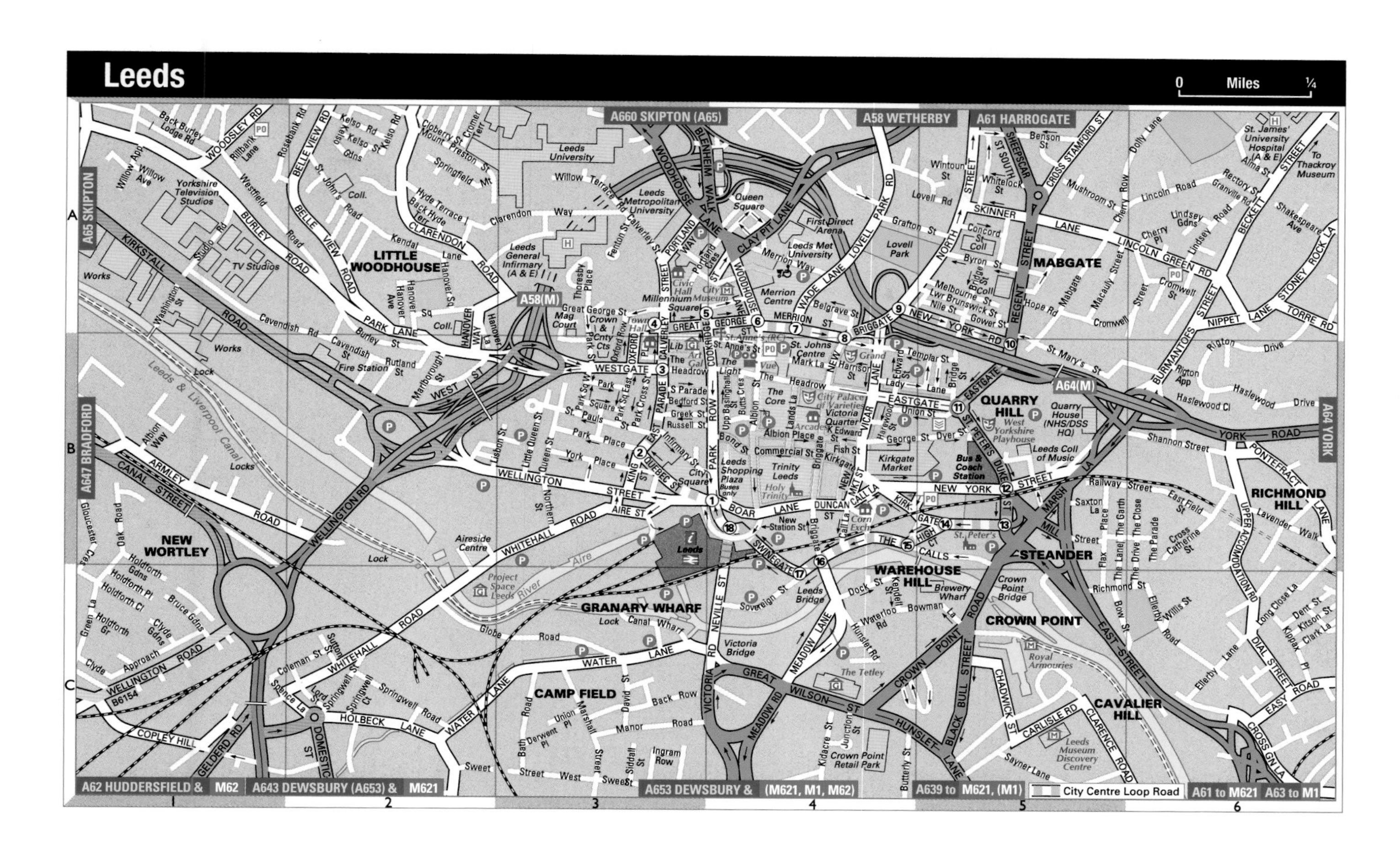

Liverpool

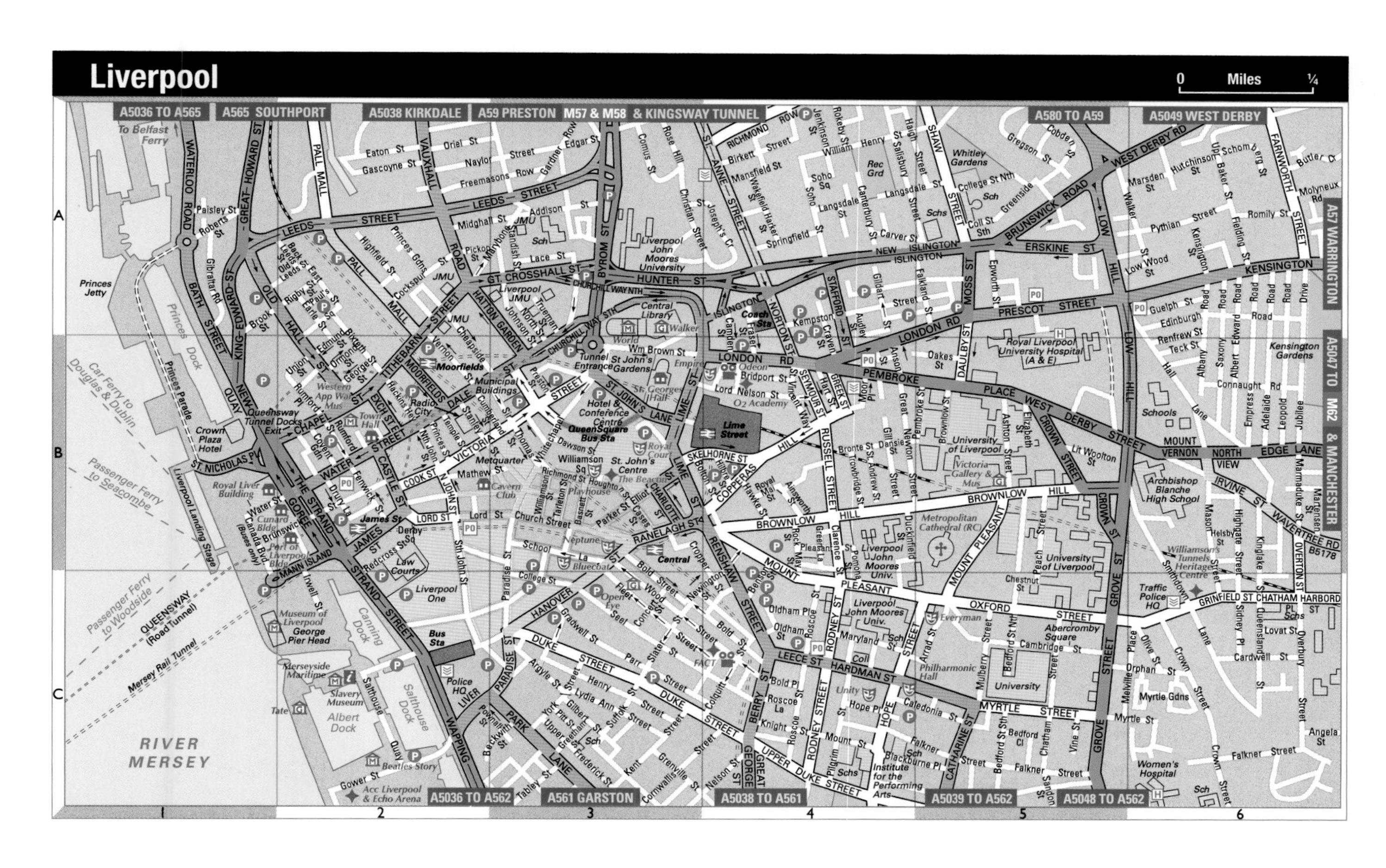

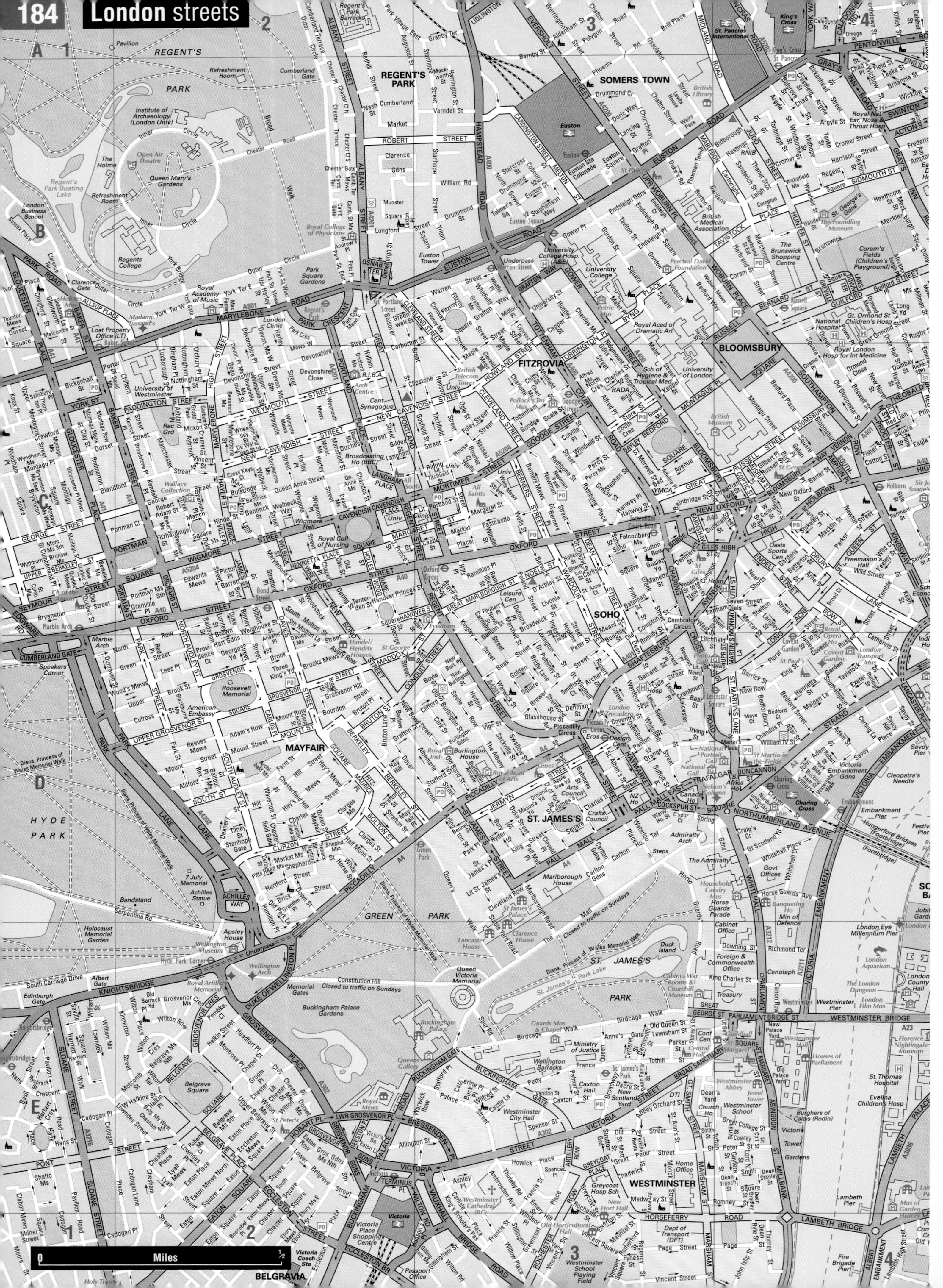

REGENT'S PARK
Institute of Archaeology (London Univ)
Open Air Theatre
Queen Mary's Gardens
Regent's Park Boating Lake
London Business School
Regents College
Madame Tussaud's
Lost Property Office (LT)
MARYLEBONE ROAD
EUSTON ROAD
SOMERS TOWN
St. Pancras International
King's Cross
British Library
Euston
University College Hosp. (A&E)
University College
FITZROVIA
BLOOMSBURY
British Museum
University of London
Royal Acad of Dramatic Art
Sch of Hygiene & Tropical Med
University of Westminster
Wallace Collection
Royal Coll of Nursing
Broadcasting Ho (BBC)
OXFORD STREET
MAYFAIR
Roosevelt Memorial
American Embassy
SOHO
Piccadilly Circus
Leisure Cen
Cambridge Circus
Royal Opera Ho
Covent Garden
London Transport Mus
St. James's
Burlington House
Royal Acad of Arts
National Portrait Gall
National Gall
TRAFALGAR SQUARE
Nelson's Column
Charing Cross
Embankment
Hungerford Bridges (Footbridge)
Cleopatra's Needle
Savoy Pier
Admiralty Arch
The Admiralty
Horse Guards' Parade
Banqueting Ho
Min of Defence
London Eye Millennium Pier
London Aquarium
County Hall
The London Dungeon
WESTMINSTER BRIDGE
Houses of Parliament
Westminster Abbey
Westminster Pier
St. Thomas' Hospital
Evelina Children's Hosp
Burghers of Calais (Rodin)
Victoria Tower Gardens
LAMBETH BRIDGE
Lambeth Pier
Fire Brigade Pier
WESTMINSTER
Westminster Cathedral (RC)
Victoria
Victoria Coach Sta
Victoria Place Shopping Centre
Dept of Transport (DFT)
Westminster School Playing Field
BELGRAVIA
Belgrave Square
Buckingham Palace
Buckingham Palace Gardens
Queen Victoria Memorial
Royal Mews
Queens Gallery
Wellington Barracks
Guards Mus & Chapel
Ministry of Justice
New Scotland Yard
GREEN PARK
ST. JAMES'S PARK
Duck Island
Clarence House
Lancaster House
Marlborough House
HYDE PARK
Speakers' Corner
Marble Arch
Apsley House
Wellington Museum
Wellington Arch
Hyde Park Corner
Holocaust Memorial Garden
7 July Memorial
Achilles Statue
Serpentine Rd
KNIGHTSBRIDGE
Diana, Princess of Wales Memorial Walk
Miles
0
½

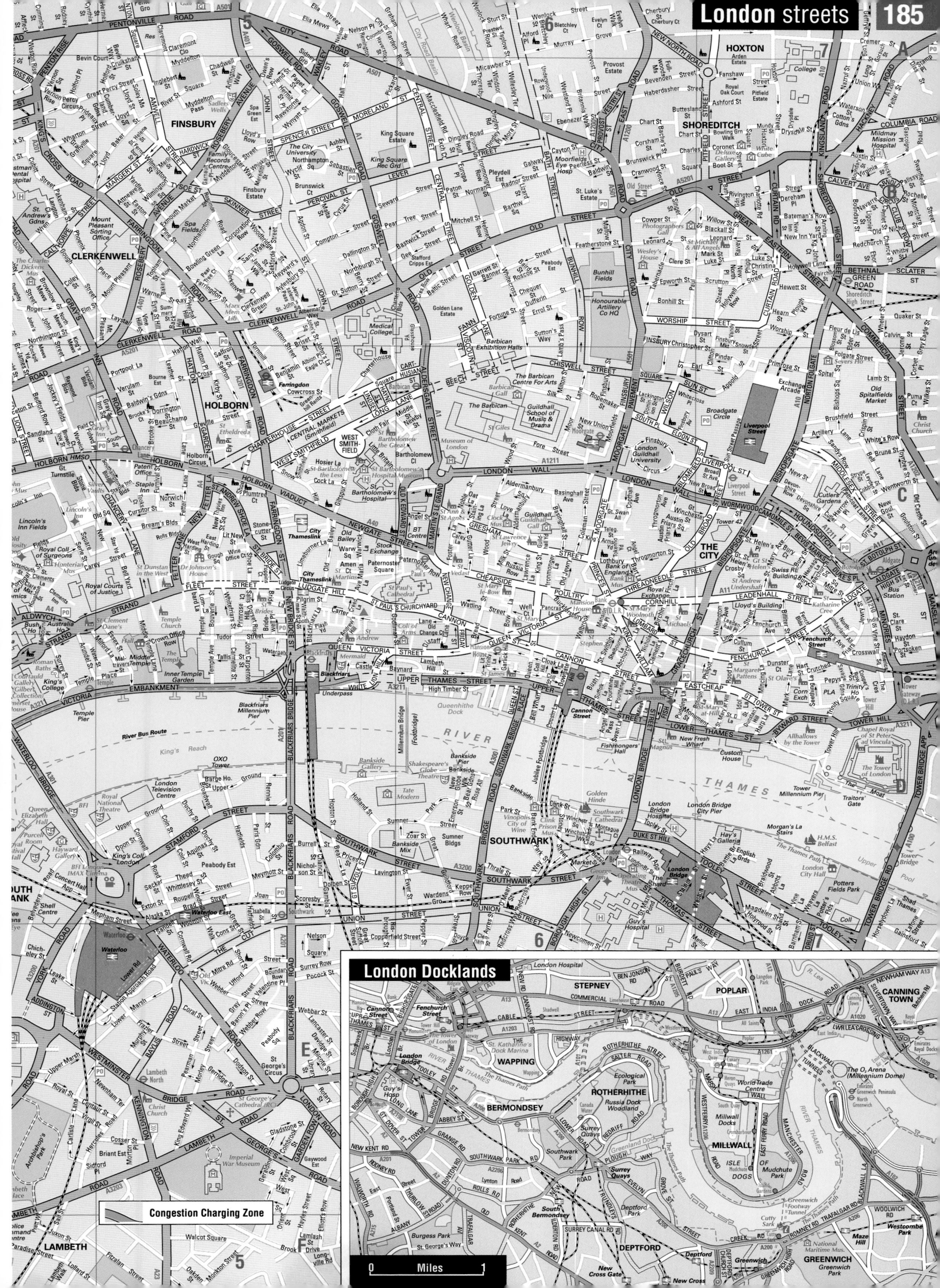

FINSBURY
CLERKENWELL
HOLBORN
HOXTON
SHOREDITCH
THE CITY
SOUTHWARK
LAMBETH
PENTONVILLE ROAD
CITY ROAD
GOSWELL ROAD
OLD STREET
CLERKENWELL ROAD
FARRINGDON ROAD
HOLBORN VIADUCT
NEWGATE STREET
LONDON WALL
FLEET STREET
STRAND
VICTORIA EMBANKMENT
UPPER THAMES STREET
QUEEN VICTORIA STREET
CANNON STREET
CHEAPSIDE
BISHOPSGATE
LEADENHALL STREET
FENCHURCH STREET
TOWER HILL
TOWER BRIDGE
LONDON BRIDGE
SOUTHWARK STREET
BLACKFRIARS BRIDGE
WATERLOO BRIDGE
WESTMINSTER BRIDGE ROAD
KENNINGTON ROAD
LAMBETH ROAD
St Paul's Cathedral
The Barbican
Museum of London
Bank of England
Liverpool Street
Fenchurch Street
Cannon Street
Blackfriars
Waterloo
Waterloo East
London Bridge
The Tower of London
Tate Modern
Shakespeare's Globe Theatre
Southwark Cathedral
Imperial War Museum
RIVER THAMES
Congestion Charging Zone
London Docklands
STEPNEY
POPLAR
CANNING TOWN
WAPPING
ROTHERHITHE
BERMONDSEY
MILLWALL
ISLE OF DOGS
DEPTFORD
GREENWICH
The O2 Arena (Millennium Dome)
World Trade Centre
Surrey Quays
Southwark Park
Burgess Park
Miles
0
1

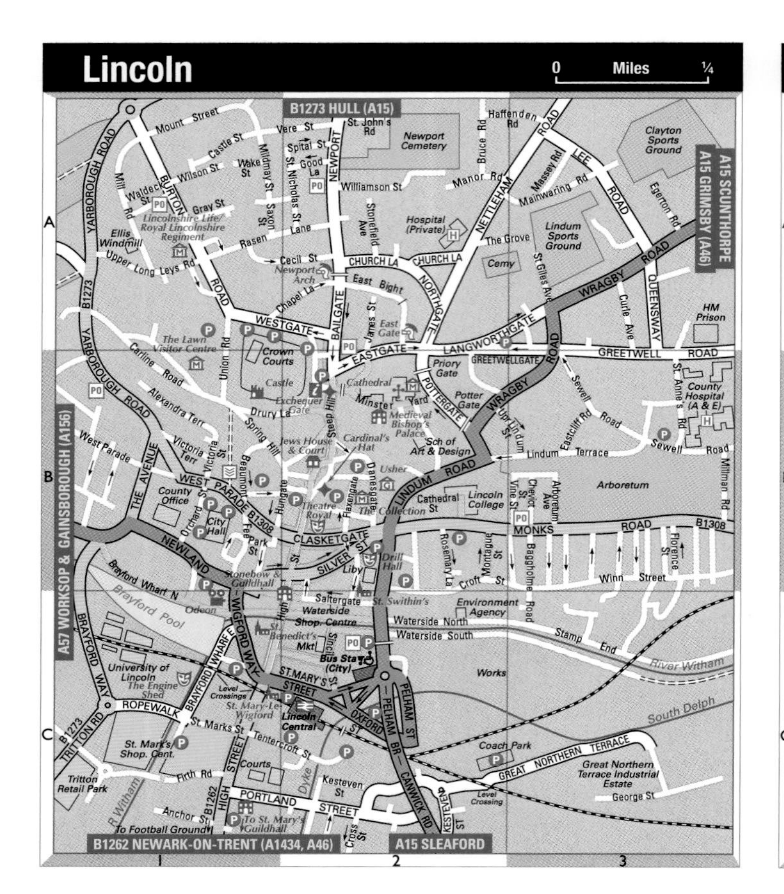
Lincoln
0 Miles ¼
B1273 HULL (A15)
A15 SCUNTHORPE
A15 GRIMSBY (A46)
A57 WORKSOP & GAINSBOROUGH (A156)
B1262 NEWARK-ON-TRENT (A1434, A46)
A15 SLEAFORD
Newport Cemetery
Clayton Sports Ground
Hospital (Private)
Lindum Sports Ground
Lincolnshire Life/ Royal Lincolnshire Regiment
Ellis Windmill
Newport Arch
HM Prison
The Lawn Visitor Centre
Crown Courts
Castle
Cathedral
Minster Yard
Medieval Bishop's Palace
County Hospital (A & E)
Sch of Art & Design
Arboretum
Cathedral
Lincoln College
County Office
City Hall
Theatre Royal
Usher
Drill Hall
Stonebow & Guildhall
Brayford Pool
Odeon
Saltergate
Waterside Shop. Centre
Environment Agency
Bus Station (City)
Works
River Witham
South Delph
University of Lincoln The Engine Shed
Lincoln Central
St. Mark's Shop. Cent.
Coach Park
Great Northern Terrace Industrial Estate
Tritton Retail Park
To Football Ground
WESTGATE
EASTGATE
NEWLAND
WEST PARADE
CLASKETGATE
WIGFORD WAY
ROPEWALK
PORTLAND STREET
GREAT NORTHERN TERRACE
LINDUM ROAD
WRAGBY ROAD
MONKS ROAD
GREETWELL ROAD
1
2
3
A
B
C

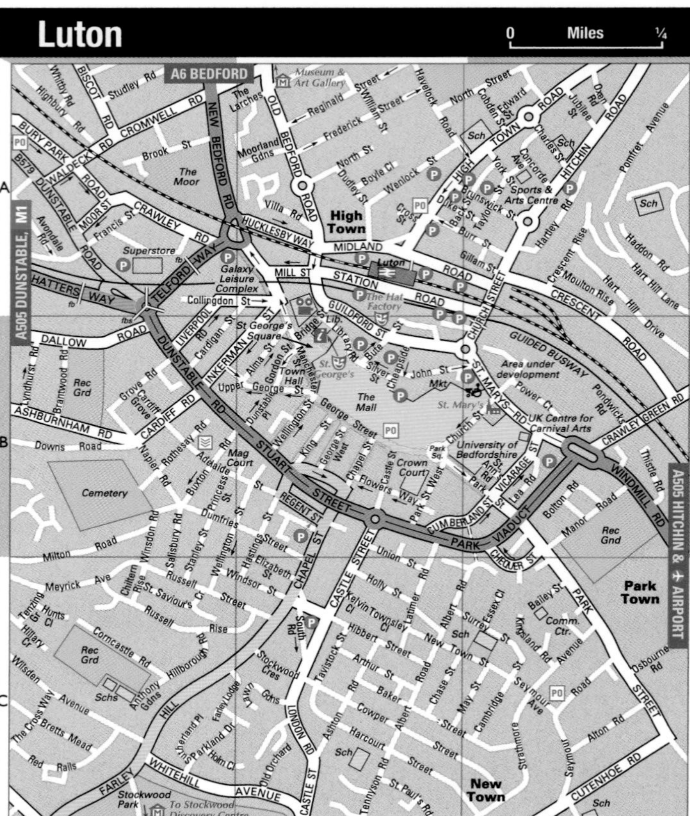
Luton
0 Miles ¼
A6 BEDFORD
A505 DUNSTABLE, M1
A505 HITCHIN & AIRPORT
Museum & Art Gallery
The Moor
High Town
Superstore
Galaxy Leisure Complex
Luton
The Hat Factory
Town Hall
The Mall
Area under development
UK Centre for Carnival Arts
University of Bedfordshire
Crown Court
Mag Court
Cemetery
Rec Grd
Park Town
New Town
To Stockwood Discovery Centre
Stockwood Park
GUIDED BUSWAY
CRAWLEY GREEN RD
DUNSTABLE RD
NEW BEDFORD RD
HATTERS WAY
STUART STREET
PARK VIADUCT
WINDMILL RD
CASTLE ST
LONDON RD
WHITEHILL AVENUE
CUTENHOE RD
1
2
3
A
B
C

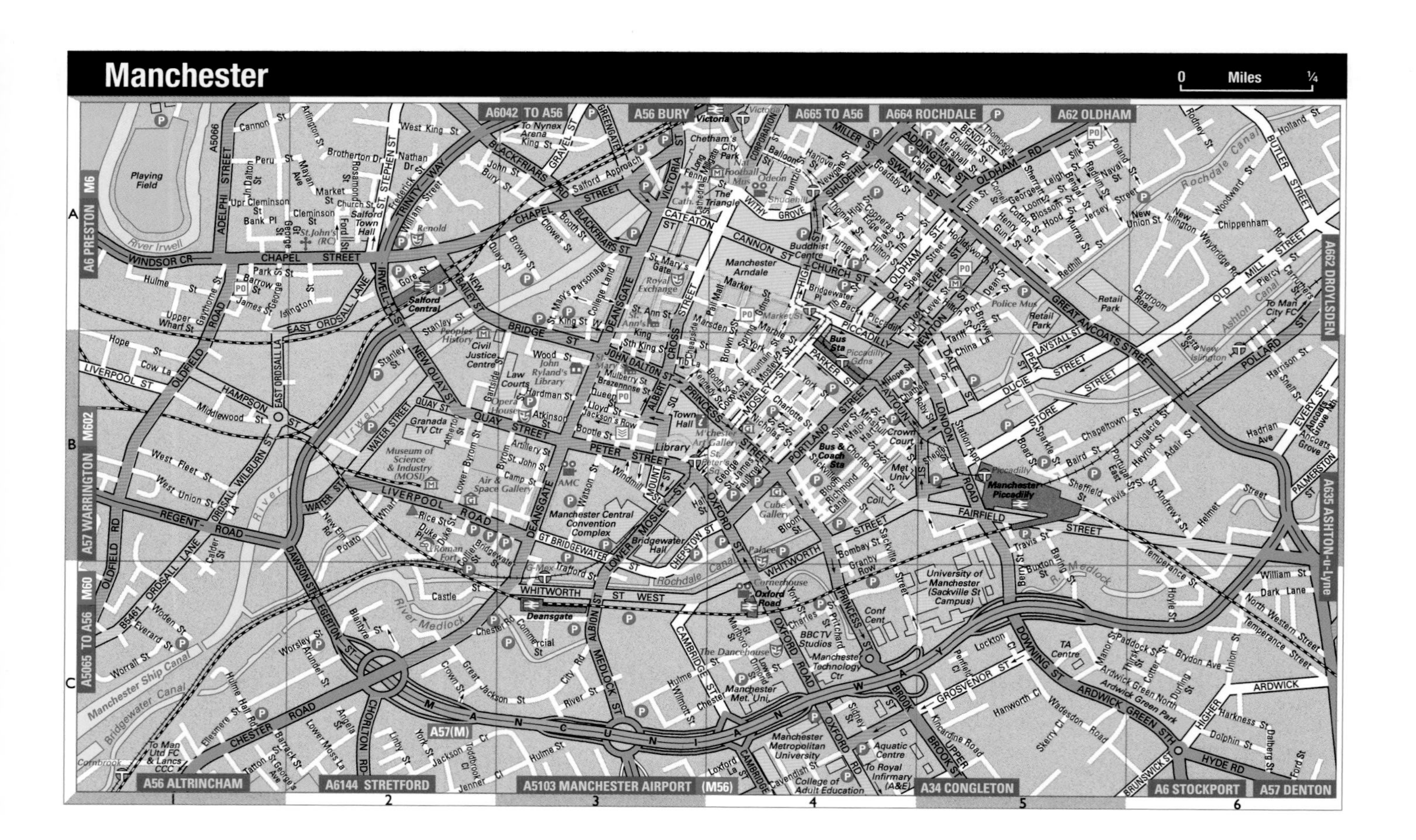
Manchester
0 Miles ¼
A6042 TO A56
A56 BURY
A665 TO A56
A664 ROCHDALE
A62 OLDHAM
A6 PRESTON M6
M602
A57 WARRINGTON
M60
A5065 TO A56
A662 DROYLSDEN
A635 ASHTON-u-Lyne
A56 ALTRINCHAM
A6144 STRETFORD
A5103 MANCHESTER AIRPORT (M56)
A34 CONGLETON
A6 STOCKPORT
A57 DENTON
Playing Field
Victoria
Chetham's
Manchester Arndale
Royal Exchange
Salford Central
Granada TV Ctr
Museum of Science & Industry (MOSI)
Air & Space Gallery
Civil Justice Centre
John Rylands Library
Opera House
Town Hall
Library
Manchester Central Convention Complex
Bridgewater Hall
Piccadilly Gdns
Bus & Coach Sta
Manchester Piccadilly
University of Manchester (Sackville St Campus)
Oxford Road
Deansgate
BBC TV Studios
Manchester Technology Ctr
Manchester Met. Uni.
Manchester Metropolitan University
Aquatic Centre
To Royal Infirmary (A&E)
College of Adult Education
Retail Park
Police Mus
To Man City FC
To Man Utd FC & Lancs CCC
River Irwell
River Medlock
Rochdale Canal
Ashton Canal
Manchester Ship Canal
Bridgewater Canal
CHAPEL STREET
LIVERPOOL ROAD
DEANSGATE
PICCADILLY
GREAT ANCOATS STREET
OLDHAM RD
REGENT ROAD
CHESTER ROAD
MANCUNIAN WAY
A57(M)
OXFORD ROAD
PRINCESS ST
FAIRFIELD STREET
ARDWICK GREEN STH
HYDE RD
1
2
3
4
5
6
A
B
C

Maidstone

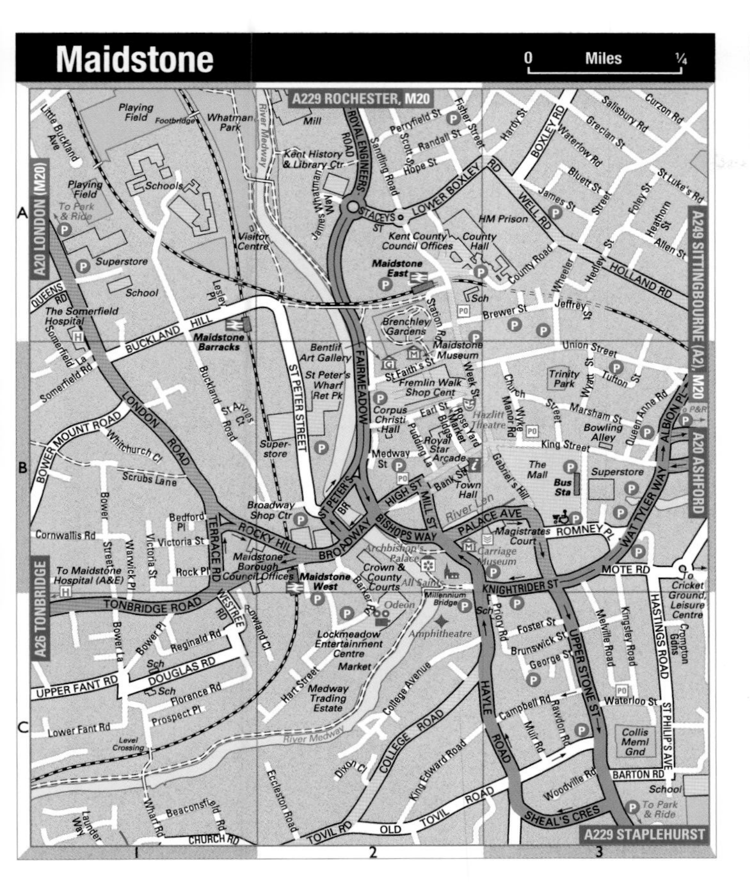

Middlesbrough

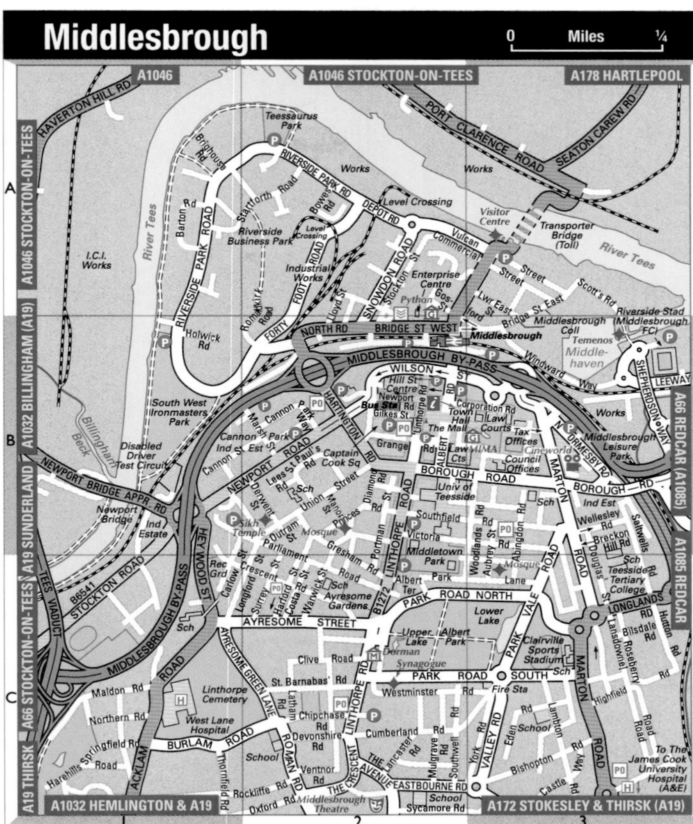

Milton Keynes

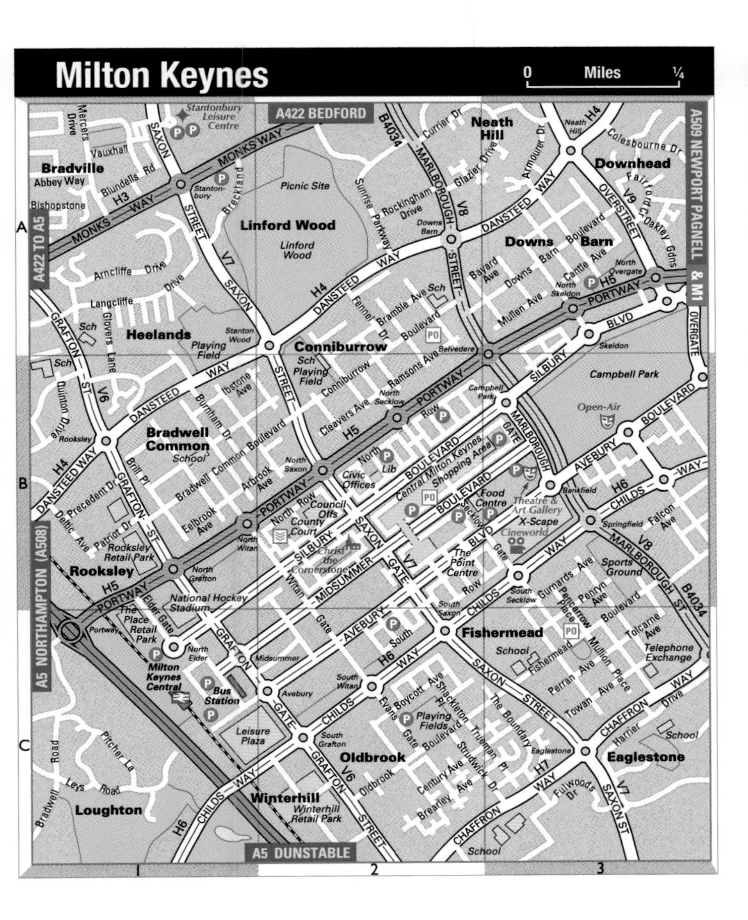

Newcastle upon Tyne

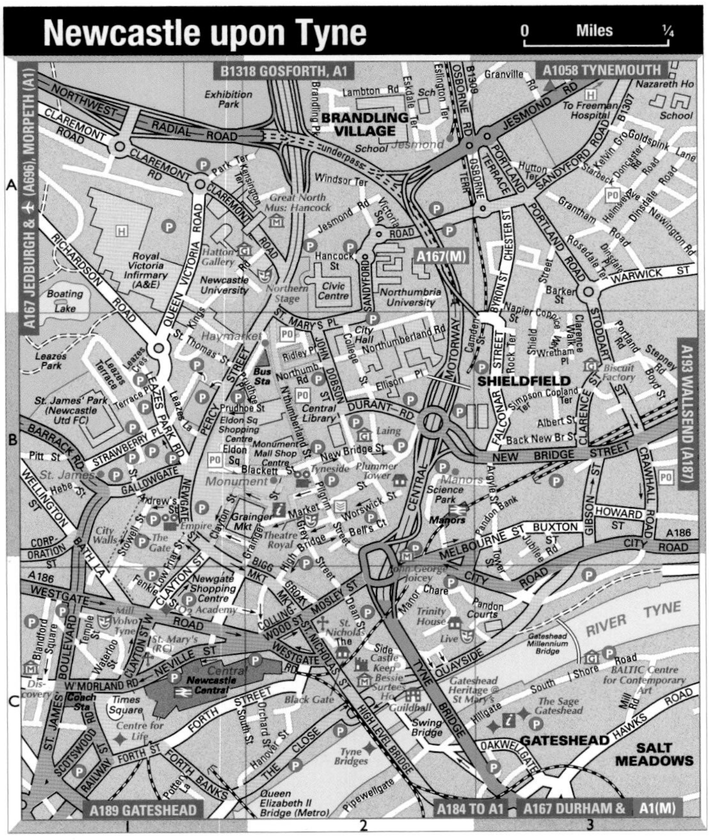

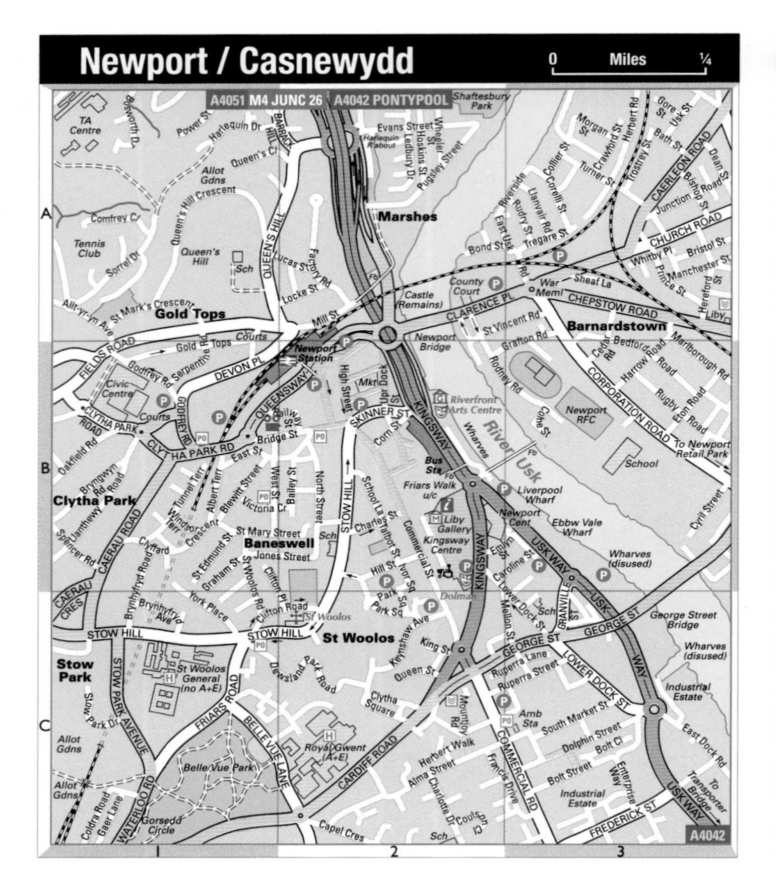

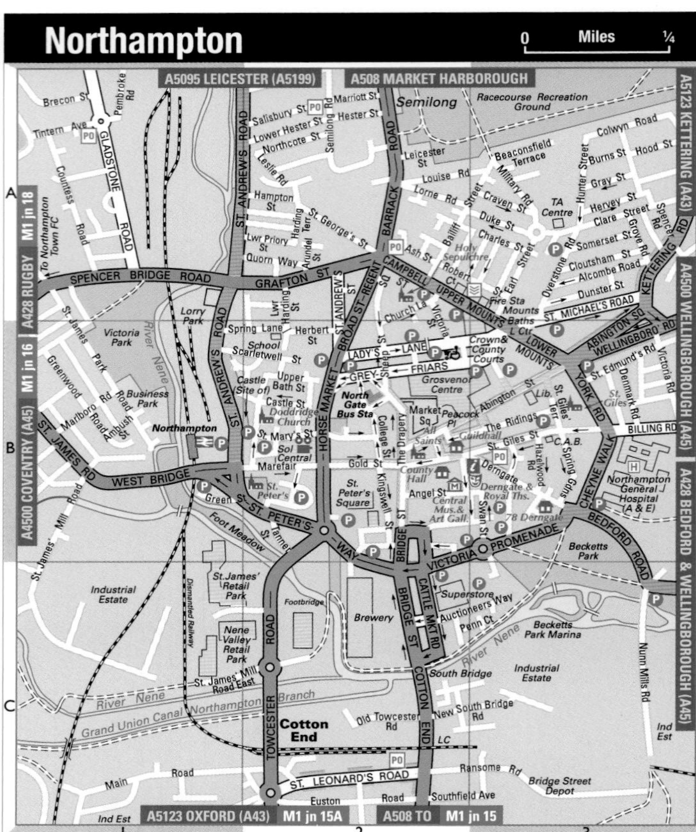

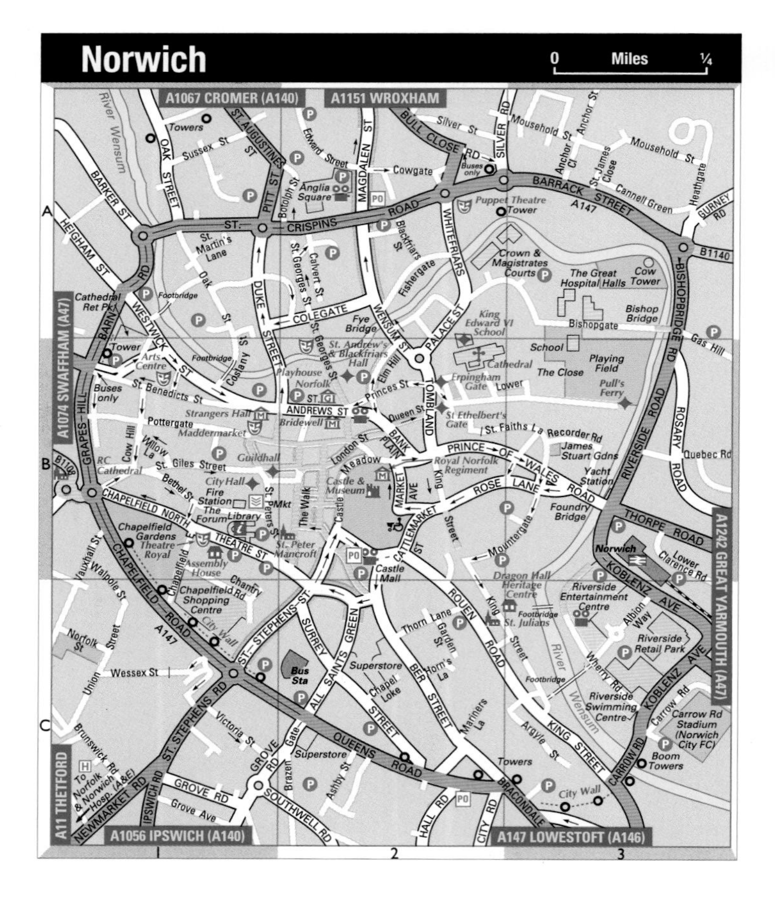

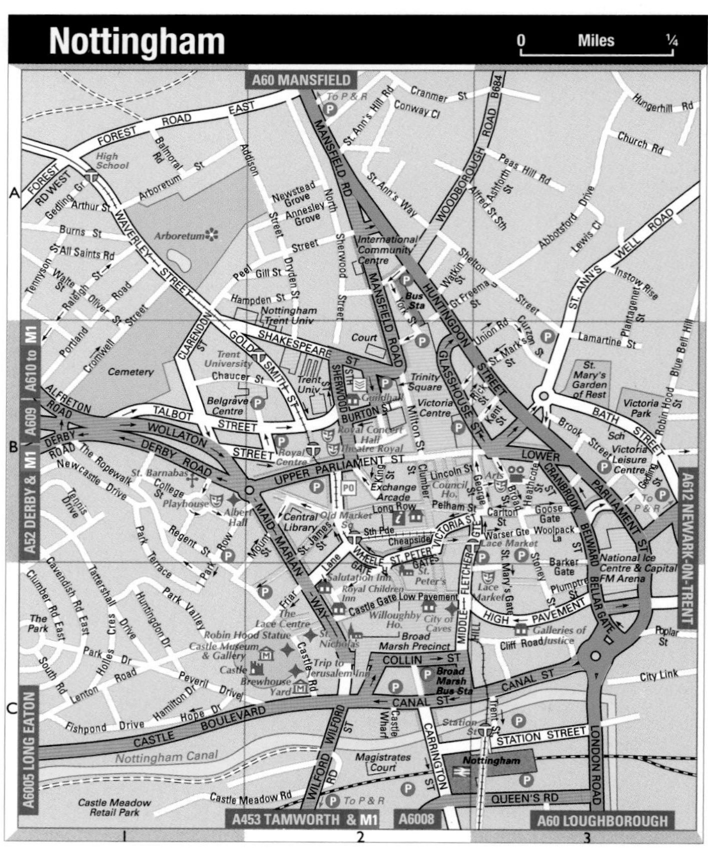

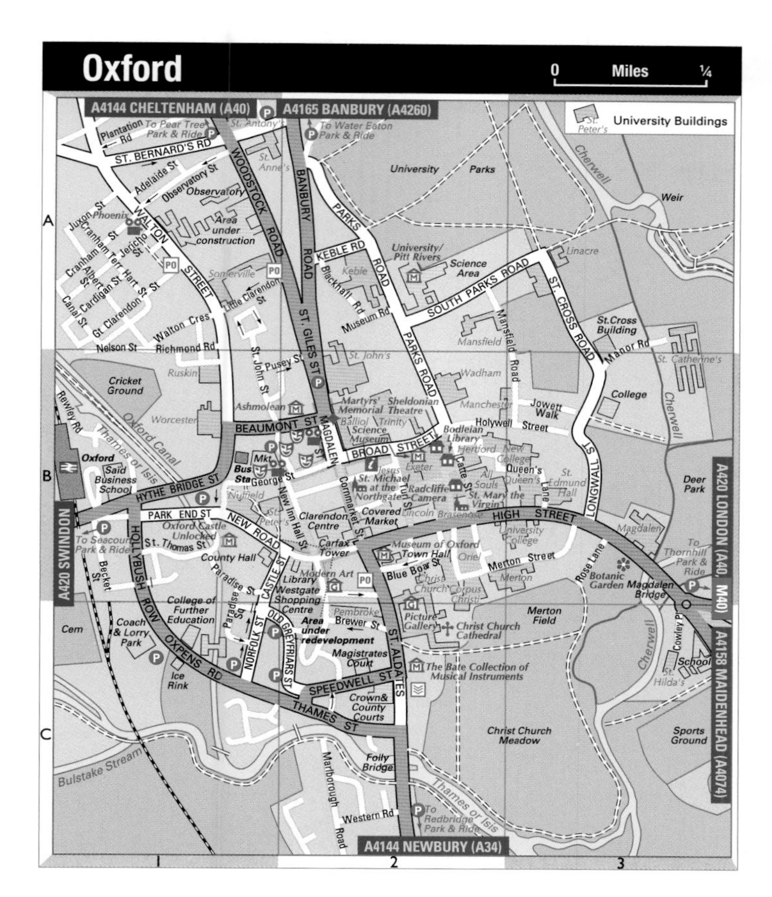
Oxford
0 Miles ¼
A4144 CHELTENHAM (A40)
A4165 BANBURY (A4260)
University Buildings
University Parks
WOODSTOCK ROAD
BANBURY ROAD
PARKS ROAD
KEBLE RD
SOUTH PARKS ROAD
ST. CROSS ROAD
St.Cross Building
Manor Rd
College
Deer Park
A420 LONDON (A40, M40)
A4158 MAIDENHEAD (A4074)
A420 SWINDON
WALTON STREET
Observatory St
Area under construction
Nelson St
Richmond Rd
Cricket Ground
Ashmolean
BEAUMONT ST
ST. GILES ST
MAGDALEN ST
BROAD STREET
HOLYWELL Street
Bodleian Library
Radcliffe Camera
Clarendon Centre
Carfax Tower
HIGH STREET
Covered Market
Museum of Oxford Town Hall
Merton Street
Botanic Garden
Magdalen Bridge
Merton Field
Christ Church Cathedral
Picture Gallery
Modern Art
Westgate Shopping Centre
Area under redevelopment
Magistrates Court
Crown & County Courts
The Bate Collection of Musical Instruments
SPEEDWELL ST
THAMES ST
ST ALDATES
Christ Church Meadow
Sports Ground
Folly Bridge
Western Rd
A4144 NEWBURY (A34)
Oxford Said Business School
HYTHE BRIDGE ST
PARK END ST
NEW ROAD
Oxford Castle Unlocked
County Hall
College of Further Education
Coach & Lorry Park
OXPENS RD
Ice Rink
Cem
Bulstake Stream
Thames or Isis
Oxford Canal
Cherwell
1 2 3
A B C

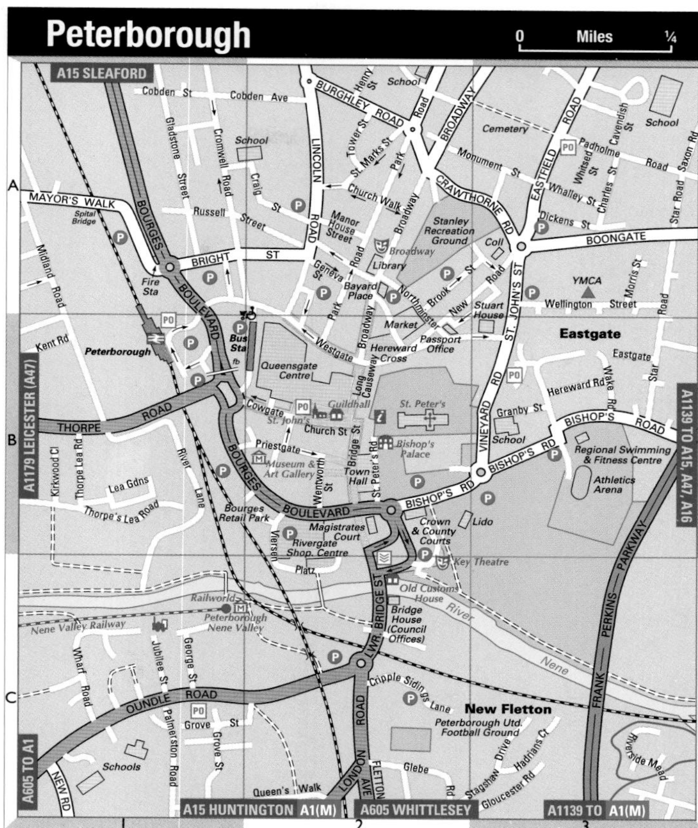
Peterborough
0 Miles ¼
A15 SLEAFORD
Cobden St
Cobden Ave
BURGHLEY ROAD
BROADWAY
Cemetery
School
MAYOR'S WALK
BOURGES BOULEVARD
LINCOLN ROAD
Stanley Recreation Ground
BRIGHT ST
BOONGATE
YMCA
Wellington Street
Eastgate
Peterborough
Queensgate Centre
Guildhall
St. Peter's
Westgate
Hereward Cross
Passport Office
THORPE ROAD
A1179 LEICESTER (A47)
A1139 TO A15, A47, A16
BISHOP'S ROAD
Regional Swimming & Fitness Centre
Athletics Arena
Museum & Art Gallery
Bishop's Palace
Town Hall
Bourges Retail Park
Magistrates Court
Rivergate Shop. Centre
Crown & County Courts
Lido
Key Theatre
Old Customs House
Bridge House (Council Offices)
Railworld
Peterborough Nene Valley
Nene Valley Railway
River Nene
OUNDLE ROAD
LONDON ROAD
New Fletton
Peterborough Utd. Football Ground
FRANK PERKINS PARKWAY
Schools
Queen's Walk
A605 TO A1
A15 HUNTINGTON A1(M)
A605 WHITTLESEY
A1139 TO A1(M)
1 2 3
A B C

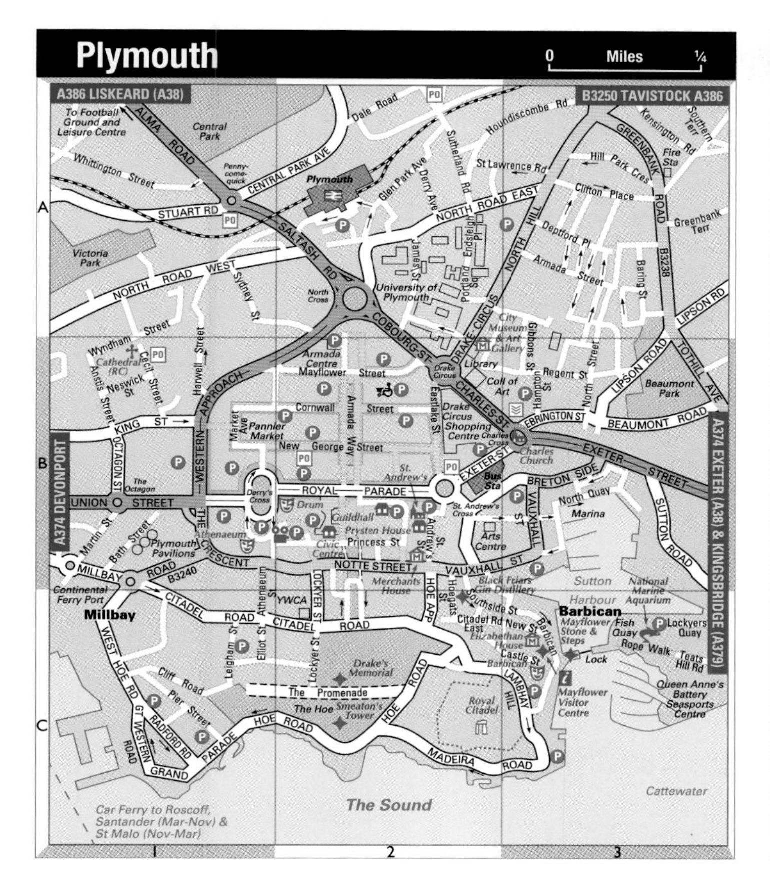
Plymouth
0 Miles ¼
A386 LISKEARD (A38)
B3250 TAVISTOCK A386
To Football Ground and Leisure Centre
Central Park
ALMA ROAD
Whittington Street
CENTRAL PARK AVE
Plymouth
STUART RD
SALTASH RD
NORTH ROAD EAST
NORTH ROAD WEST
Victoria Park
North Cross
University of Plymouth
COBOURG ST
DRAKE CIRCUS
City Museum & Art Gallery
Library
Coll of Art
LIPSON ROAD
Beaumont Park
BEAUMONT ROAD
EXETER STREET
A374 EXETER (A38) & KINGSBRIDGE (A379)
A374 DEVONPORT
KING ST
WESTERN APPROACH
Armada Centre
Mayflower Street
Cornwall Street
Pannier Market
New George Street
Drake Circus Shopping Centre
Charles Church
UNION STREET
ROYAL PARADE
The Octagon
Derry's Cross
Guildhall
Pryston House
Civic Centre
Athenaeum
NOTTE STREET
VAUXHALL ST
Merchants House
Arts Centre
Black Friars Gin Distillery
National Marine Aquarium
Sutton Harbour
Barbican
Mayflower Stone & Steps
Fish Quay
Lockyers Quay
Rope Walk
Continental Ferry Port
Millbay
MILLBAY ROAD
CITADEL ROAD
Drake's Memorial
The Promenade
The Hoe
Smeaton's Tower
HOE ROAD
Royal Citadel
MADEIRA ROAD
Mayflower Visitor Centre
Queen Anne's Battery Seaports Centre
The Sound
Cattewater
Car Ferry to Roscoff, Santander (Mar-Nov) & St Malo (Nov-Mar)
1 2 3
A B C

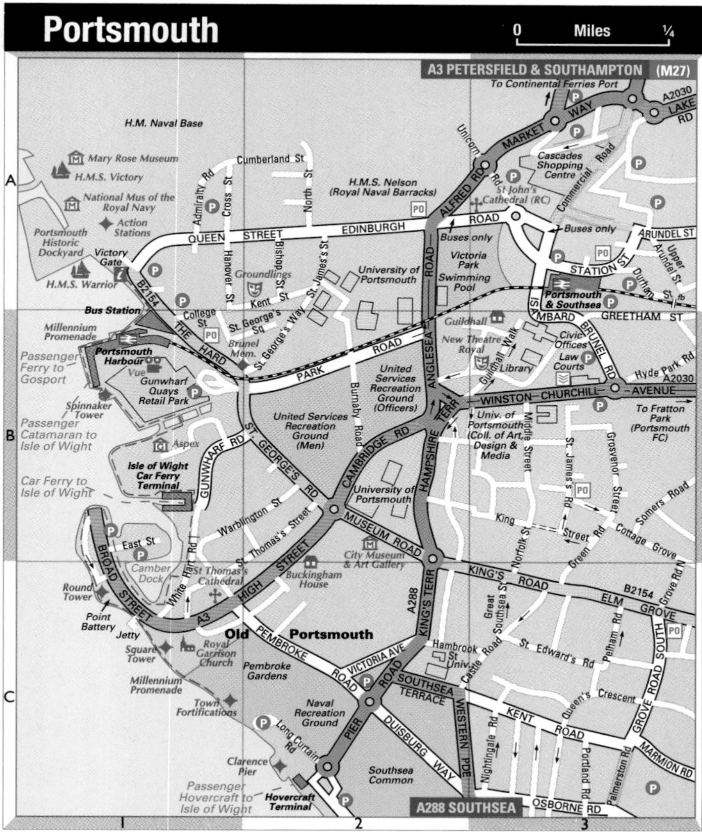
Portsmouth
0 Miles ¼
A3 PETERSFIELD & SOUTHAMPTON (M27)
To Continental Ferries Port
H.M. Naval Base
Mary Rose Museum
H.M.S. Victory
National Mus of the Royal Navy
Action Stations
Portsmouth Historic Dockyard
H.M.S. Warrior
Victory Gate
Cumberland St
H.M.S. Nelson (Royal Naval Barracks)
QUEEN STREET
EDINBURGH ROAD
MARKET WAY
Cascades Shopping Centre
St John's Cathedral (RC)
Buses only
Victoria Park
Swimming Pool
University of Portsmouth
ARUNDEL ST
STATION ST
Portsmouth & Southsea
GREETHAM ST
Bus Station
Millennium Promenade
Passenger Ferry to Gosport
Portsmouth Harbour
Gunwharf Quays Retail Park
Spinnaker Tower
Passenger Catamaran to Isle of Wight
Isle of Wight Car Ferry Terminal
Car Ferry to Isle of Wight
Guildhall
New Theatre Royal
Civic Offices
Library
Law Courts
WINSTON CHURCHILL AVENUE
Univ. of Portsmouth (Coll. of Art, Design & Media)
United Services Recreation Ground (Men)
United Services Recreation Ground (Officers)
CAMBRIDGE RD
ANGLESEA RD
HAMPSHIRE TERR
MUSEUM ROAD
City Museum & Art Gallery
Buckingham House
St Thomas's Cathedral
Old Portsmouth
Royal Garrison Church
Pembroke Gardens
BROAD STREET
Round Tower
Point Battery
Square Tower
Millennium Promenade
Town Fortifications
Naval Recreation Ground
Clarence Pier
Passenger Hovercraft to Isle of Wight
Hovercraft Terminal
Southsea Common
KING'S ROAD
ELM GROVE
KENT ROAD
A288 SOUTHSEA
OSBORNE RD
To Fratton Park (Portsmouth FC)
1 2 3
A B C

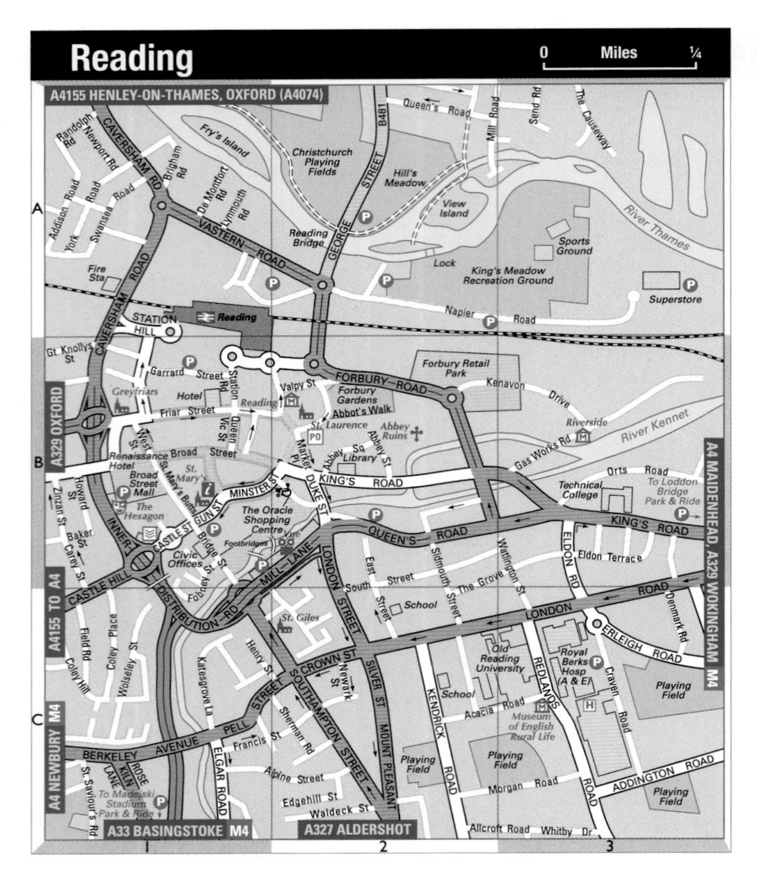
Reading
0 Miles ¼
A4155 HENLEY-ON-THAMES, OXFORD (A4074)
A329 OXFORD
A4 MAIDENHEAD, A329 WOKINGHAM
A4155 TO A4
A4 NEWBURY M4
M4
A33 BASINGSTOKE M4
A327 ALDERSHOT
Christchurch Playing Fields
Hill's Meadow
View Island
River Thames
Sports Ground
King's Meadow Recreation Ground
Reading Bridge
Superstore
Reading
Forbury Retail Park
Forbury Gardens
Abbot's Walk
Abbey Ruins
River Kennet
Riverside
Technical College
To Loddon Bridge Park & Ride
The Oracle Shopping Centre
Broad Street Mall
The Hexagon
Civic Offices
St. Giles
Old Reading University
Royal Berks Hosp (A & E)
Museum of English Rural Life
Playing Field
To Madejski Stadium Park & Ride
FORBURY ROAD
KING'S ROAD
QUEEN'S ROAD
LONDON ROAD
LONDON STREET
SOUTHAMPTON STREET
BERKELEY AVENUE
ELGAR ROAD
ADDINGTON ROAD
VASTERN ROAD
CAVERSHAM ROAD
1
2
3
A
B
C

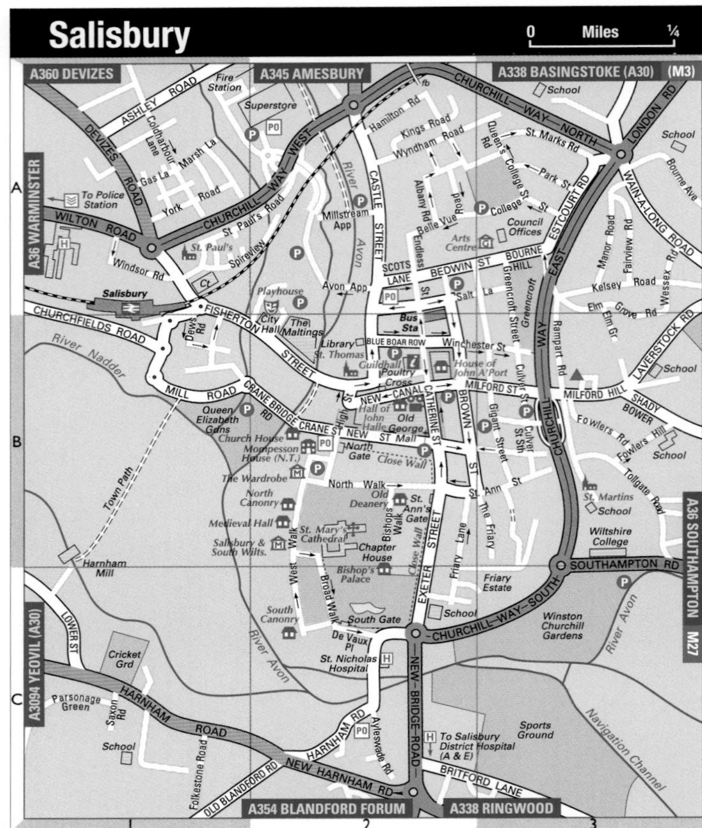
Salisbury
0 Miles ¼
A360 DEVIZES
A345 AMESBURY
A338 BASINGSTOKE (A30) (M3)
A36 WARMINSTER
A36 SOUTHAMPTON M27
A3094 YEOVIL (A30)
A354 BLANDFORD FORUM
A338 RINGWOOD
Salisbury
River Nadder
River Avon
To Police Station
Millstream App
Playhouse
City Hall
The Maltings
Library
Guildhall
Poultry Cross
House of John A'Port
Hall of John Halle
Church House
Mompesson House (N.T.)
The Wardrobe
North Canonry
Medieval Hall
Salisbury & South Wilts.
St. Mary's Cathedral
Chapter House
Bishop's Palace
South Canonry
South Gate
St. Nicholas Hospital
Harnham Mill
Town Path
Cricket Grd
Friary Estate
Winston Churchill Gardens
To Salisbury District Hospital (A & E)
Sports Ground
Navigation Channel
Wiltshire College
CHURCHILL WAY NORTH
CHURCHILL WAY SOUTH
CHURCHILL WAY WEST
CHURCHILL WAY EAST
WILTON ROAD
HARNHAM ROAD
NEW HARNHAM RD
BRITFORD LANE
SOUTHAMPTON RD
1
2
3
A
B
C

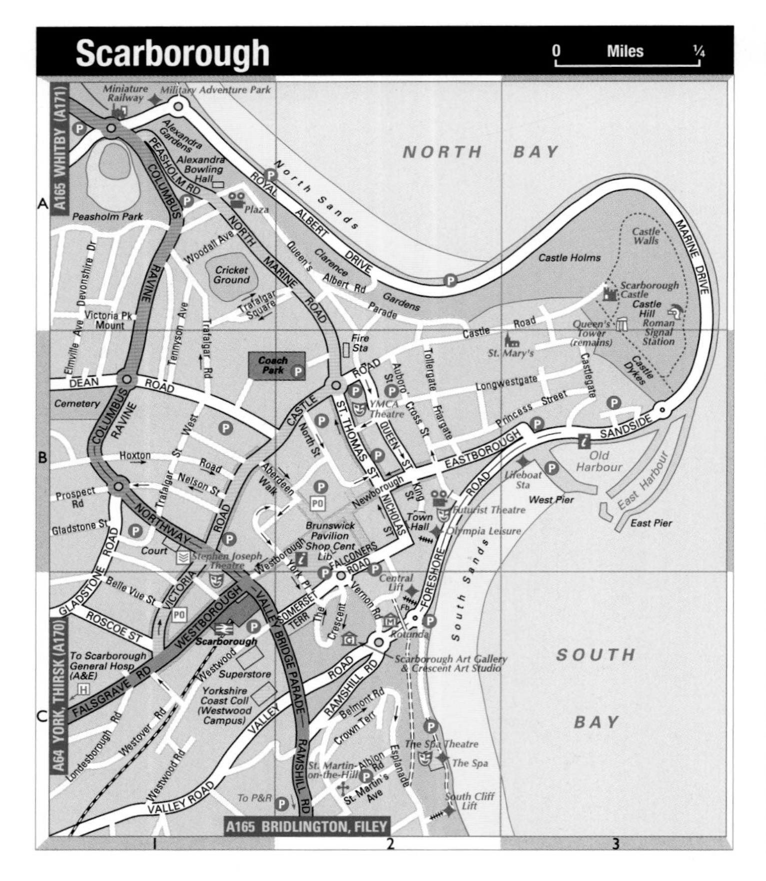
Scarborough
0 Miles ¼
NORTH BAY
SOUTH BAY
North Sands
South Sands
A165 WHITBY (A171)
A64 YORK, THIRSK (A170)
A165 BRIDLINGTON, FILEY
Miniature Railway
Military Adventure Park
Peasholm Park
Alexandra Gardens
Alexandra Bowling Hall
Cricket Ground
Castle Holms
Castle Walls
Scarborough Castle
Castle Hill Roman Signal Station
Castle Dykes
Queen's Tower (remains)
St. Mary's
Coach Park
YMCA Theatre
Old Harbour
East Harbour
West Pier
East Pier
Lifeboat Sta
Futurist Theatre
Olympia Leisure
Town Hall
Brunswick Pavilion Shop Cent
Stephen Joseph Theatre
Scarborough
Superstore
Yorkshire Coast Coll (Westwood Campus)
To Scarborough General Hosp (A&E)
Scarborough Art Gallery & Crescent Art Studio
Rotunda
Central Lift
The Spa Theatre
The Spa
South Cliff Lift
St. Martin-on-the-Hill
To P&R
ROYAL ALBERT DRIVE
MARINE DRIVE
NORTH MARINE ROAD
COLUMBUS RAVINE
NORTHWAY
WESTBOROUGH
VALLEY BRIDGE PARADE
VALLEY ROAD
FALSGRAVE RD
FORESHORE ROAD
SANDSIDE
1
2
3
A
B
C

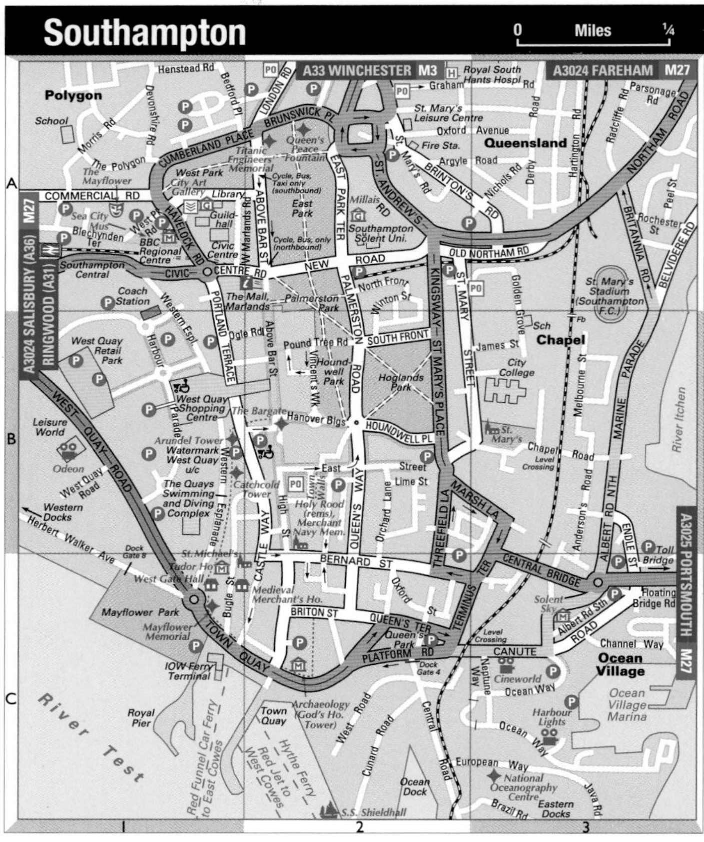
Southampton
0 Miles ¼
A33 WINCHESTER M3
A3024 FAREHAM M27
A3024 SALISBURY (A36) RINGWOOD (A31) M27
A3025 PORTSMOUTH M27
Polygon
Queensland
Chapel
Ocean Village
Royal South Hants Hospl
St. Mary's Leisure Centre
Queen's Peace Fountain
Titanic Engineers' Memorial
West Park
City Art Gallery
Library
Guildhall
Civic Centre
BBC Regional Centre
Sea City Mus
Southampton Central
East Park
Southampton Solent Uni.
Coach Station
The Mall, Marlands
Palmerston Park
West Quay Retail Park
West Quay Shopping Centre
The Bargate
Hoglands Park
Houndwell Park
Arundel Tower
Watermark West Quay u/c
Catchcold Tower
The Quays Swimming and Diving Complex
Holy Rood (rems), Merchant Navy Mem
St. Michael's
Tudor Ho
Medieval Merchant's Ho.
Mayflower Park
Mayflower Memorial
IOW Ferry Terminal
Royal Pier
Town Quay
Archaeology (God's Ho. Tower)
Red Funnel Car Ferry to East Cowes
Red Jet to West Cowes
Hythe Ferry
Ocean Dock
S.S. Shieldhall
National Oceanography Centre
Eastern Docks
Western Docks
River Test
River Itchen
St. Mary's Stadium (Southampton F.C.)
City College
Cineworld
Harbour Lights
Ocean Village Marina
Leisure World
Odeon
Toll Bridge
Floating Bridge Rd
Solent Sky
WEST QUAY ROAD
KINGSWAY
ST MARY'S PLACE
CENTRAL BRIDGE
TOWN QUAY
PLATFORM RD
CANUTE
NORTHAM ROAD
MARINE PARADE
COMMERCIAL RD
1
2
3
A
B
C

Sheffield

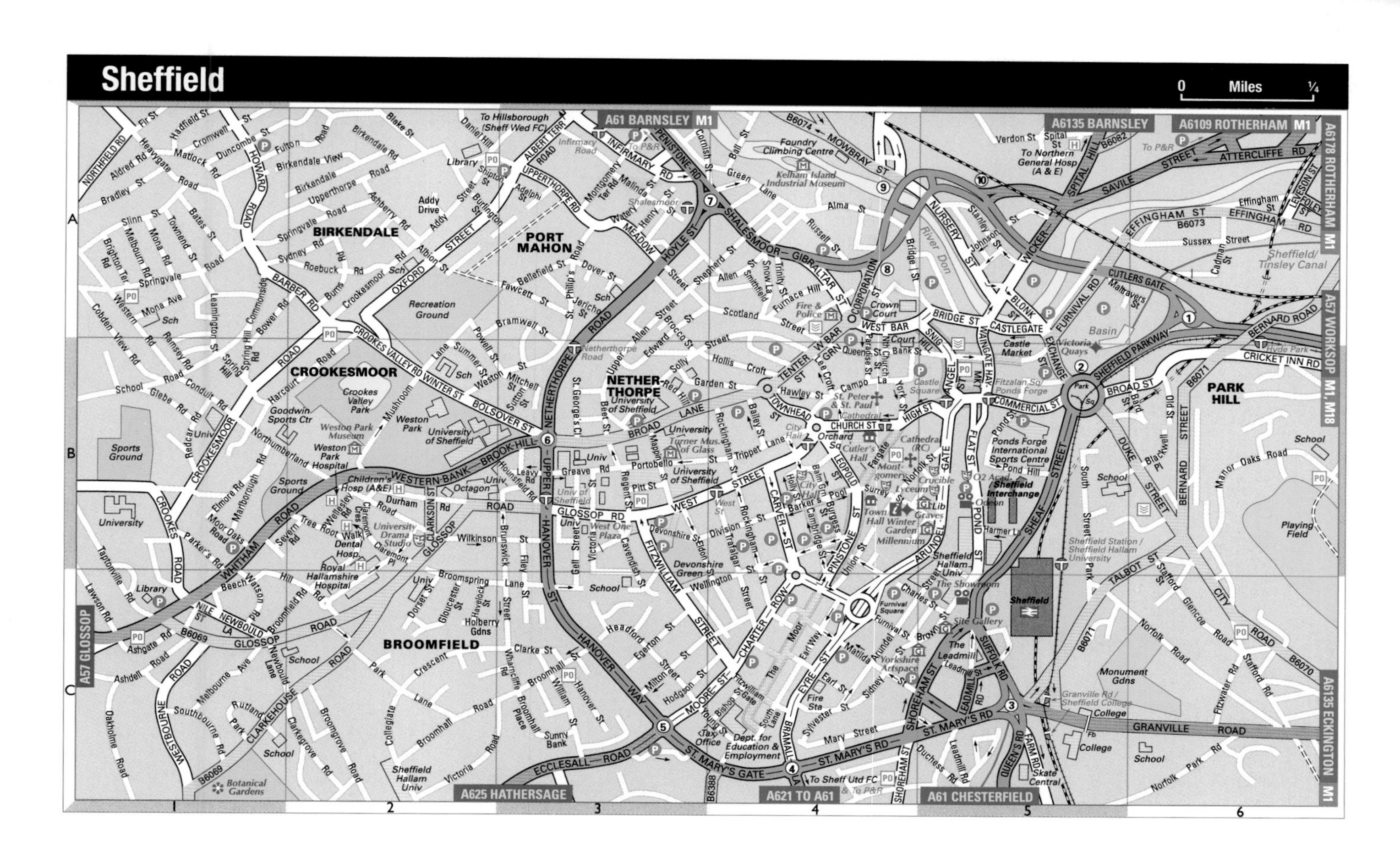

Southend-on-Sea

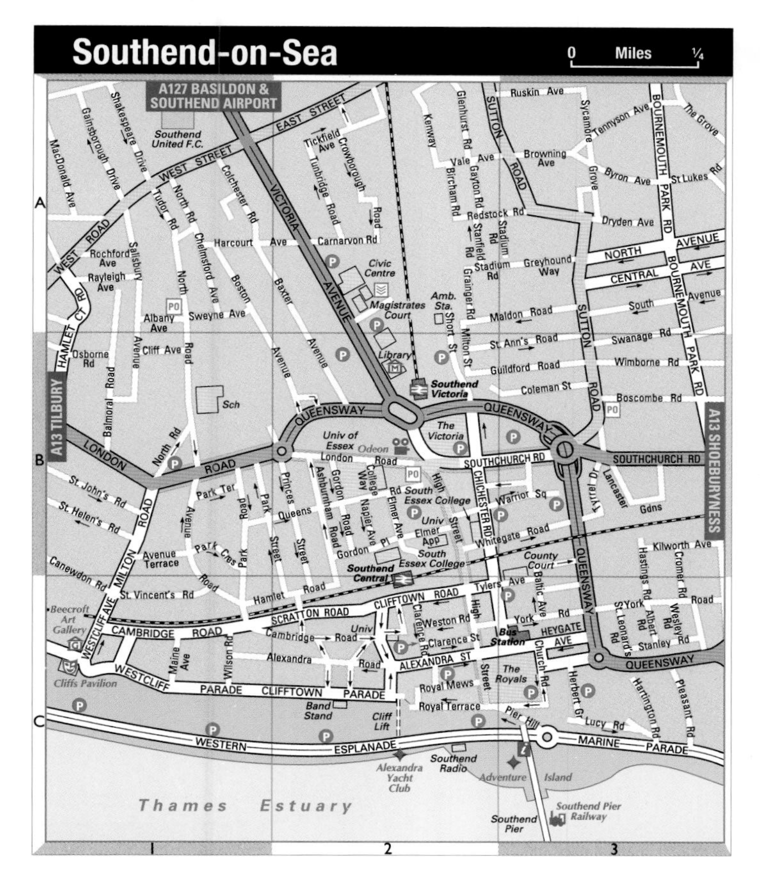

Stoke

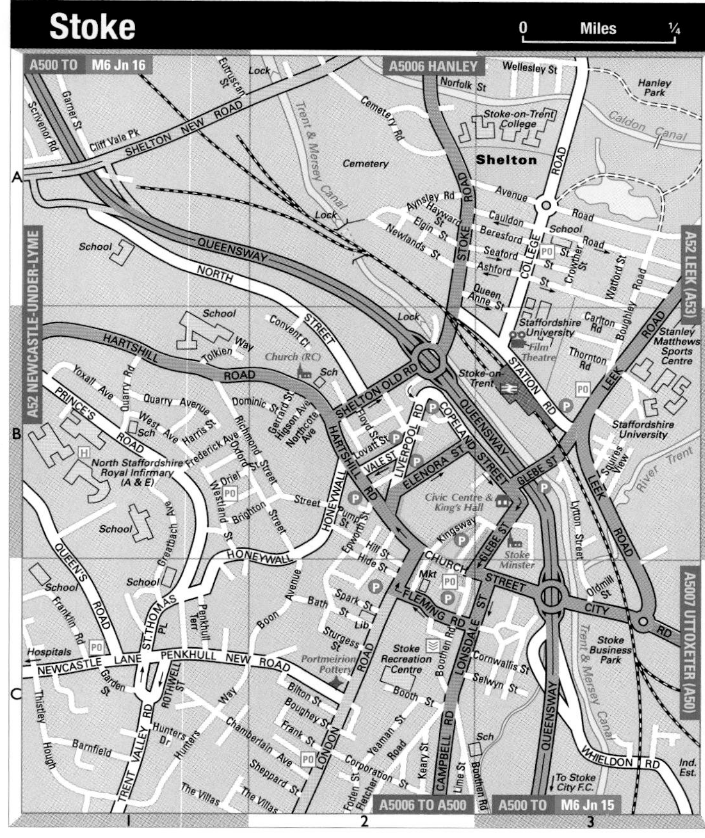

Stratford-upon-Avon

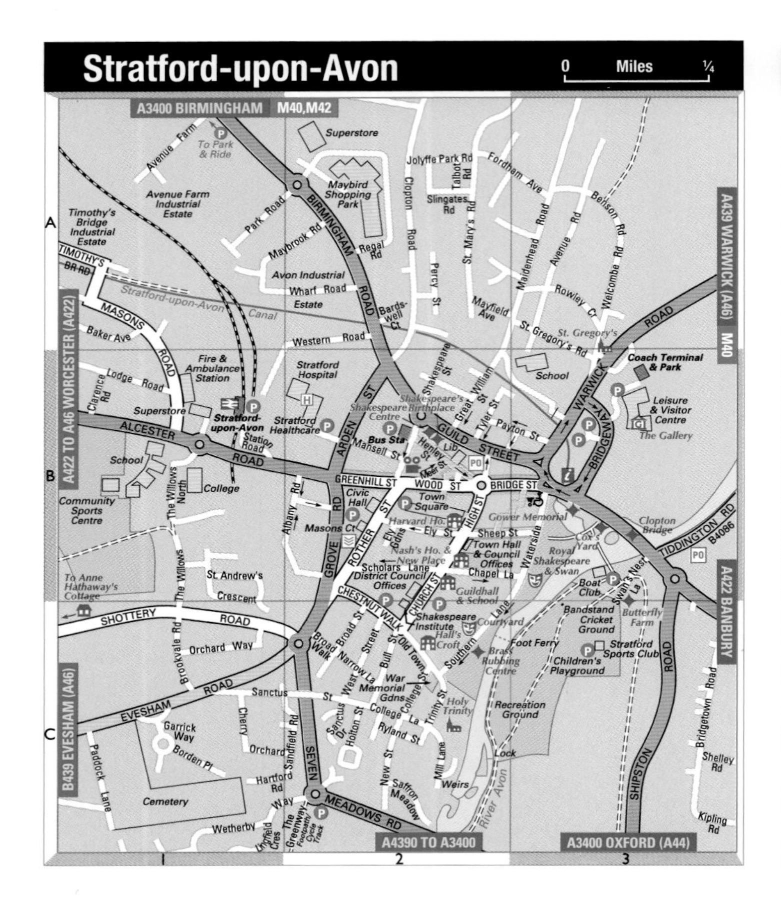

Sunderland

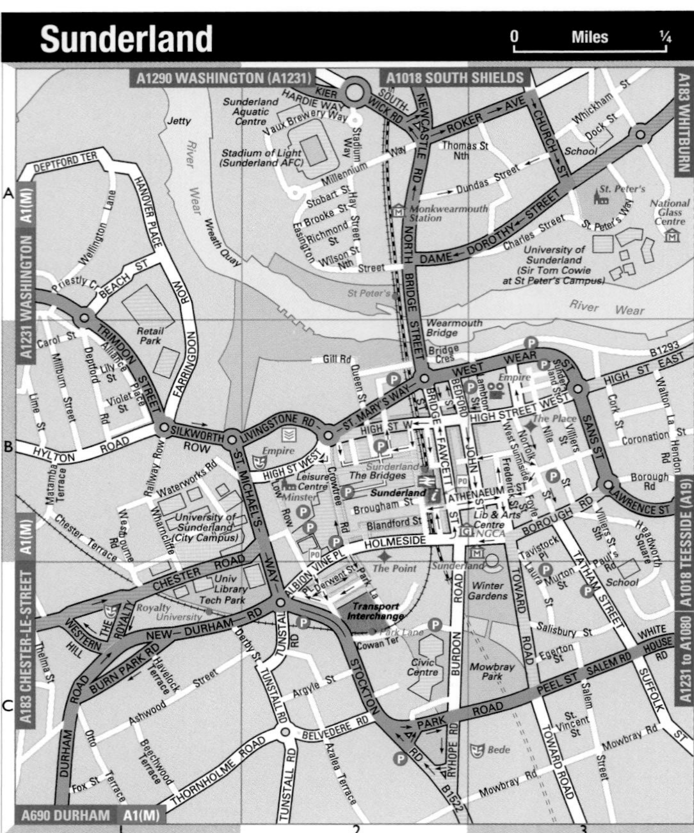

Swansea / Abertawe

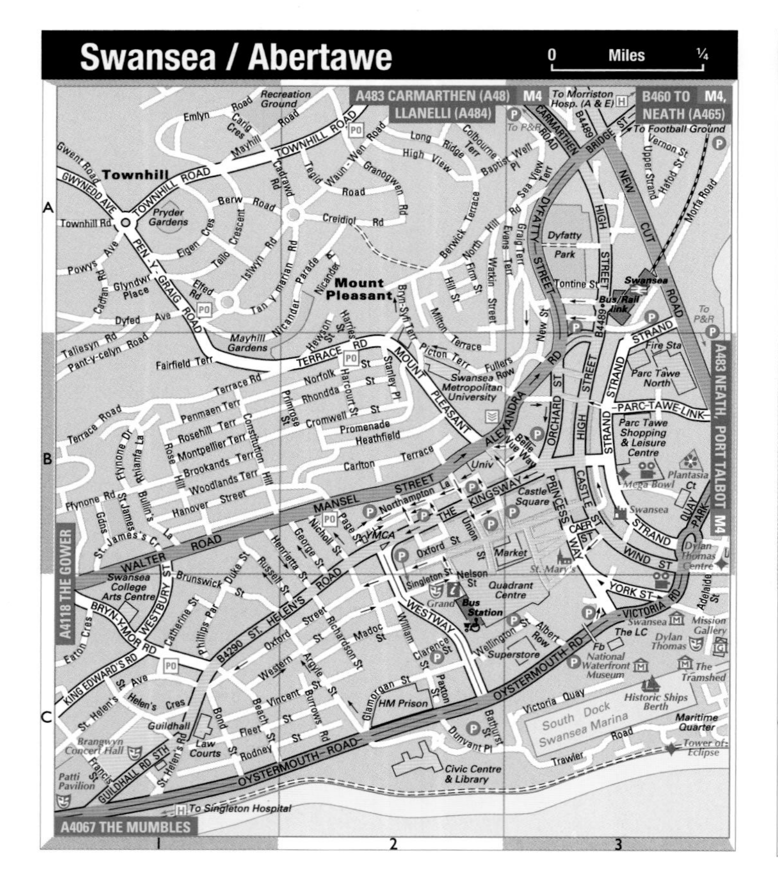

Swindon

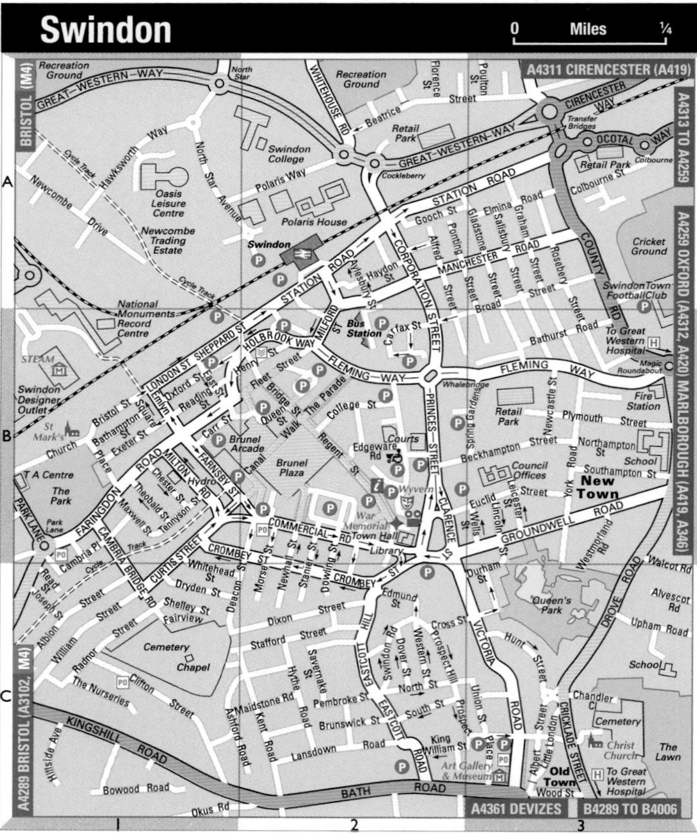

Taunton

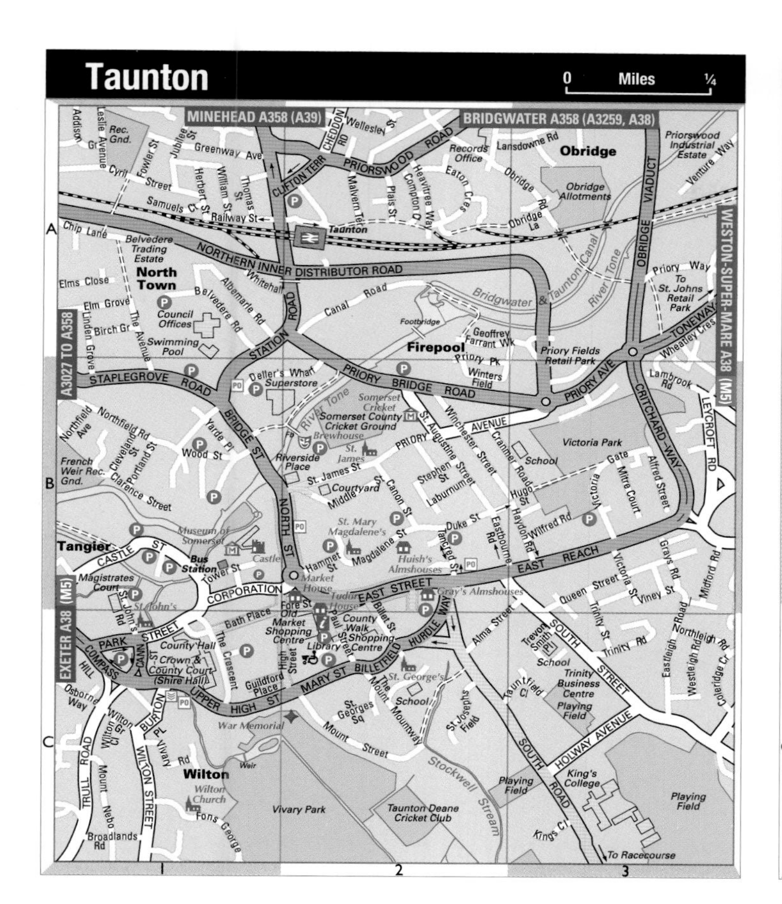

Telford

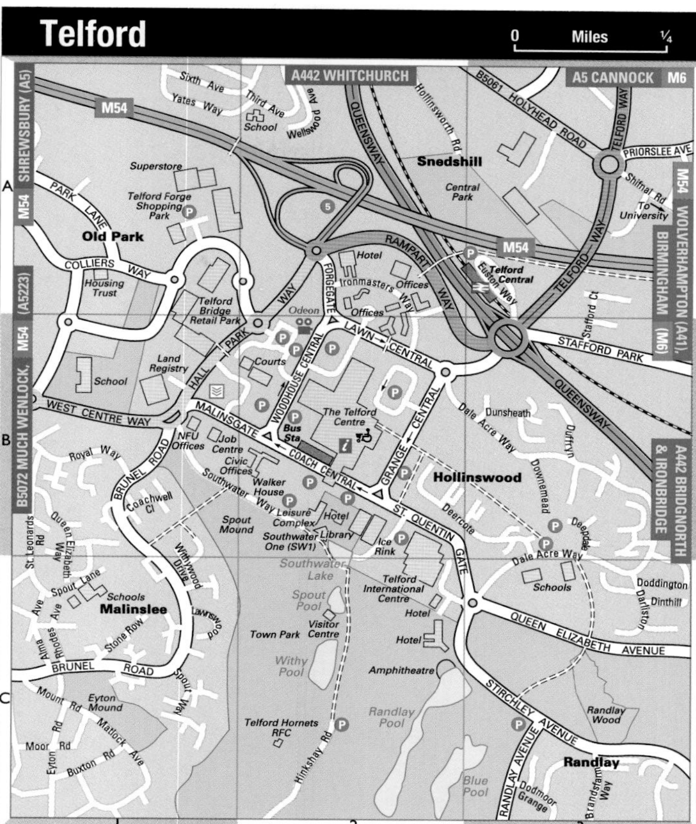

Winchester

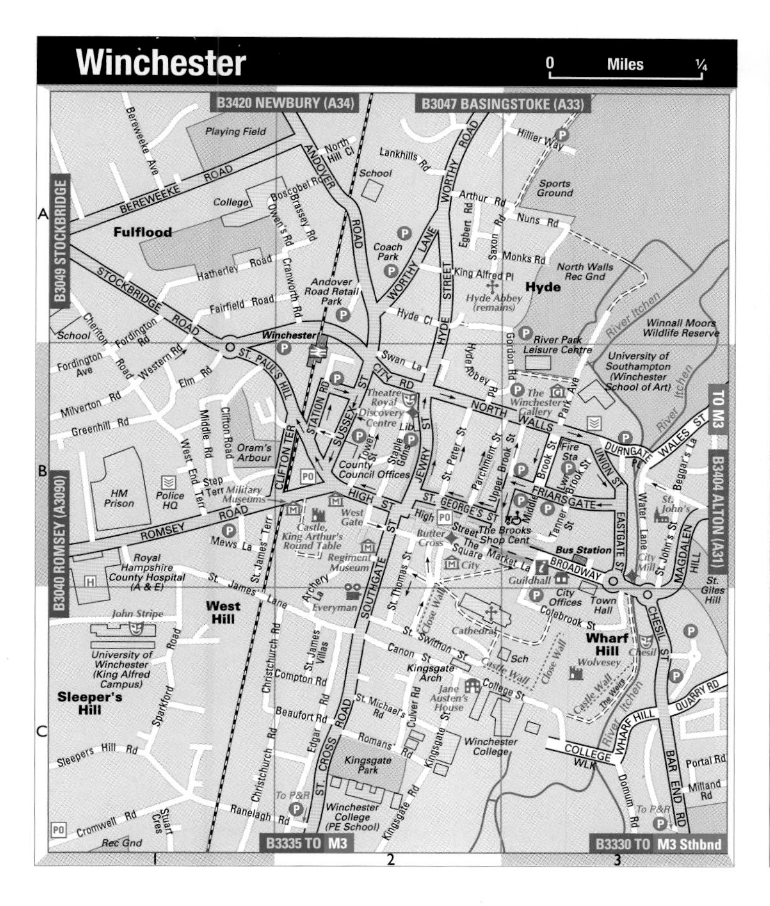

Windsor

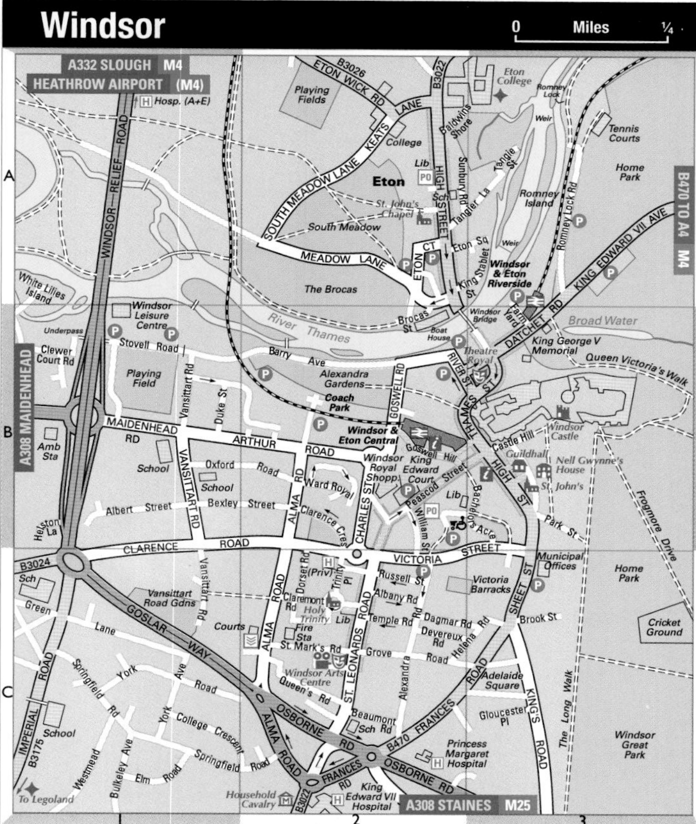

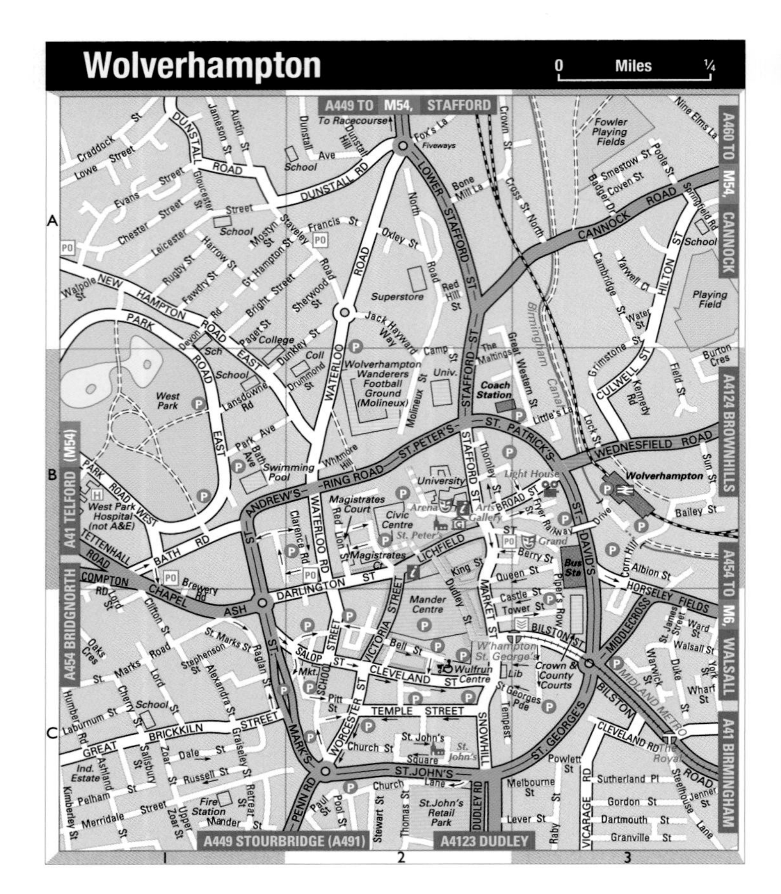
Wolverhampton
0 Miles ¼
A449 TO M54, STAFFORD
A460 TO M54, CANNOCK
A4124 BROWNHILLS
A454 TO M6, WALSALL
A41 BIRMINGHAM
A4123 DUDLEY
A449 STOURBRIDGE (A491)
A454 BRIDGNORTH
A41 TELFORD (M54)
West Park
Wolverhampton Wanderers Football Ground (Molineux)
Coach Station
Wolverhampton
Mander Centre
Wulfrun Centre
West Park Hospital (not A&E)
Ring Road
Playing Field
Fowler Playing Fields
Industrial Estate
Crown & County Courts
St. John's Retail Park
Swimming Pool
Magistrates Court
Civic Centre
Superstore
University
Birmingham Canal
1
2
3
A
B
C

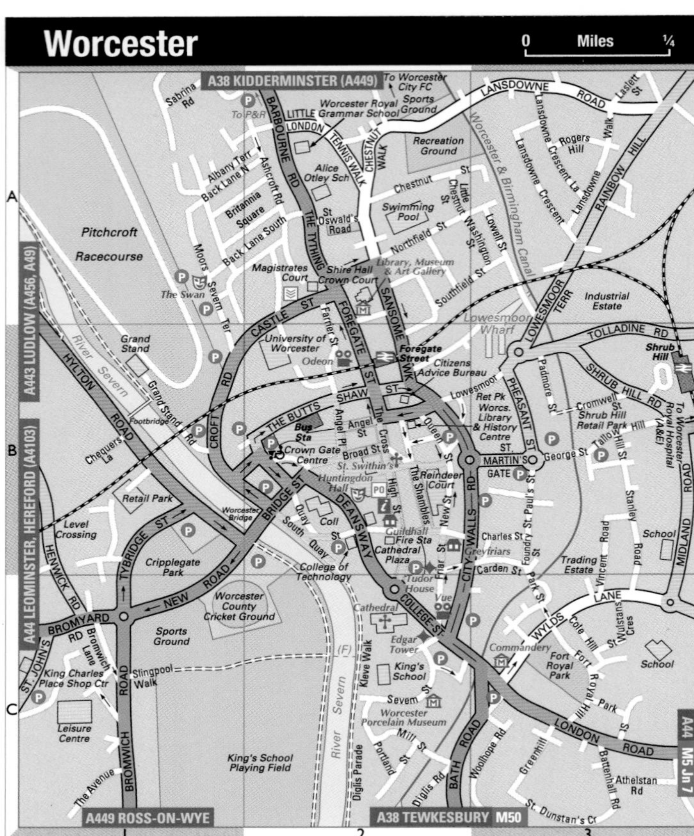
Worcester
0 Miles ¼
A38 KIDDERMINSTER (A449)
A443 LUDLOW (A456, A49)
A44 LEOMINSTER, HEREFORD (A4103)
A449 ROSS-ON-WYE
A38 TEWKESBURY M50
A44 M5 Jn 7
Pitchcroft Racecourse
Grand Stand
River Severn
Worcester County Cricket Ground
Cathedral
Worcester & Birmingham Canal
University of Worcester
Foregate Street
Crowngate Centre
Industrial Estate
Shrub Hill
Shrub Hill Retail Park
Worcester Royal Hospital (A&E)
King's School Playing Field
Worcester Porcelain Museum
Commandery
Fort Royal Park
Trading Estate
Leisure Centre
Sports Ground
Cripplegate Park
Retail Park
Level Crossing
Lowesmoor Wharf
1
2
3
A
B
C

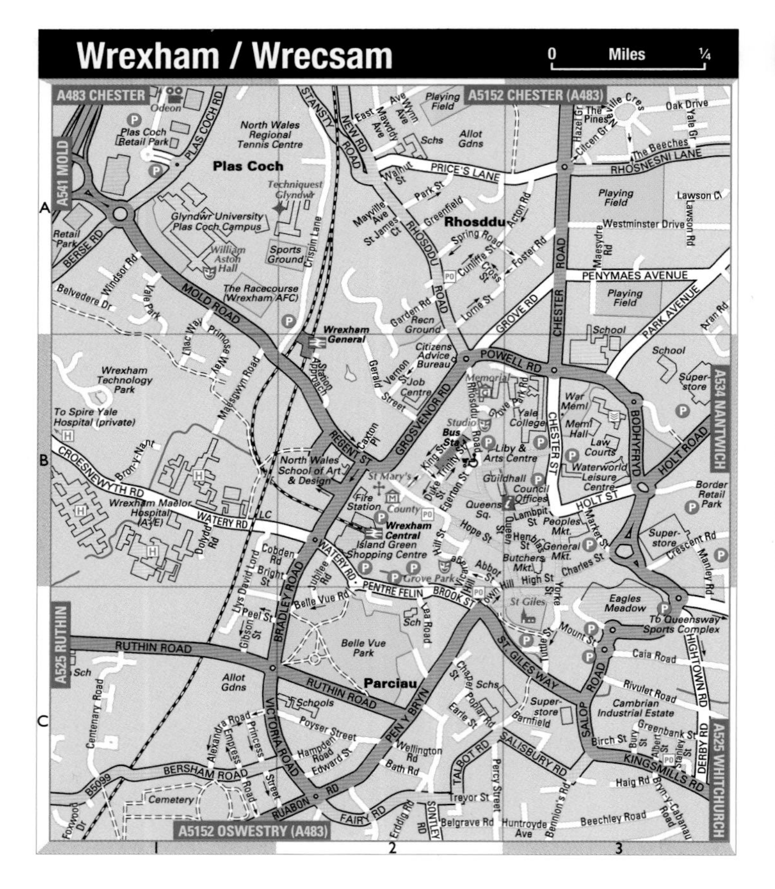
Wrexham / Wrecsam
0 Miles ¼
A483 CHESTER
A5152 CHESTER (A483)
A541 MOLD
A534 NANTWICH
A525 RUTHIN
A525 WHITCHURCH
A5152 OSWESTRY (A483)
Plas Coch
Rhosddu
Parciau
Glyndŵr University Plas Coch Campus
The Racecourse (Wrexham AFC)
Wrexham General
Wrexham Central
Wrexham Technology Park
Wrexham Maelor Hospital (A&E)
North Wales Regional Tennis Centre
North Wales School of Art & Design
Island Green Shopping Centre
Waterworld Leisure Centre
Eagles Meadow
To Queensway Sports Complex
Cambrian Industrial Estate
Belle Vue Park
To Spire Yale Hospital (private)
1
2
3
A
B
C

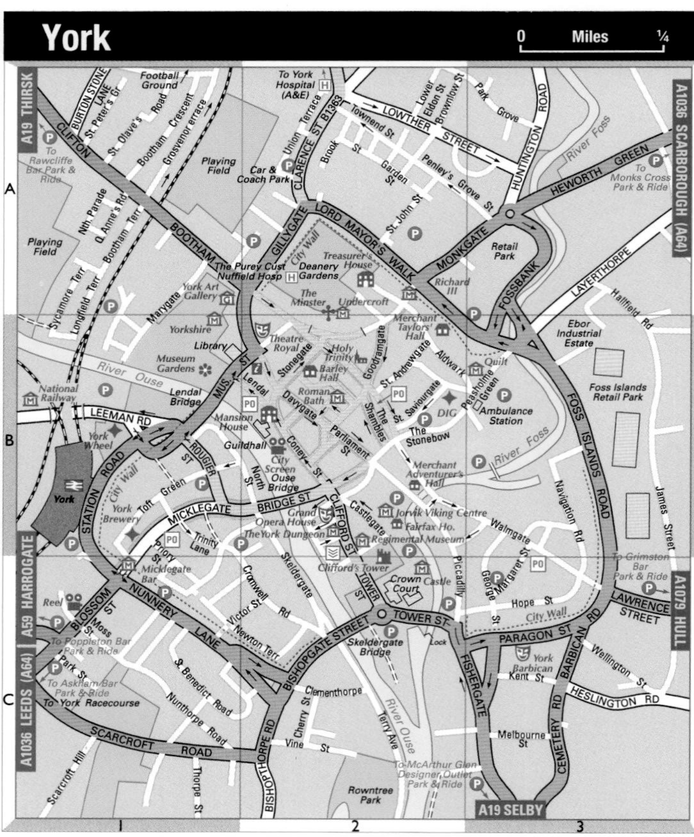
York
0 Miles ¼
A19 THIRSK
A1036 SCARBOROUGH (A64)
A1079 HULL
A19 SELBY
A1036 LEEDS (A64)
A59 HARROGATE
To York Hospital (A&E)
York
National Railway Museum
The Minster
City Wall
River Ouse
River Foss
Foss Islands Retail Park
Ebor Industrial Estate
Jorvik Viking Centre
Clifford's Tower
Museum Gardens
Yorkshire Museum
Merchant Adventurers' Hall
Treasurer's House
York Barbican
To Askham Bar Park & Ride
To York Racecourse
To Poppleton Bar Park & Ride
To Rawcliffe Bar Park & Ride
To Monks Cross Park & Ride
To Grimston Bar Park & Ride
To McArthur Glen Designer Outlet Park & Ride
Rowntree Park
1
2
3
A
B
C

Town plan indexes

Tivoli St C1
Town Hall & Theatre B2
Townsend St A1
Trafalgar St C2
Union St B3
Univ of Gloucestershire (Francis Close Hall) A2
Univ of Gloucestershire (Hardwick) A1
Victoria Pl B3
Victoria St A2
Vittoria Walk C2
Wel Pl B2
Wellesley Rd A2
Wellington Rd A3
Wellington Sq A3
Wellington St B2
West Drive A3
Western Rd B1
Winchcombe St B3
Winston Churchill Memorial Gdns A1

Chester 178

Abbey Gateway A2
Appleyards La C3
Bedward Row B1
Beeston View C3
Bishop Lloyd's Pal B2
Black Diamond St A2
Bottoms La C3
Boughton B3
Bouverie St A1
Bridge St B2
Bridgegate C2
British Heritage Centre B2
Brook St A3
Brown's La C2
Bus Station B2
Cambrian Rd A1
Canal St A2
Carrick Rd C1
Castle C2
Castle Dr C2
Cathedral B2
Catherine St A1
Chester A3
Cheyney Rd A1
Chichester St A1
City Rd A3
City Walls B1/B2
City Walls Rd B1
Cornwall St A2
County Hall C2
Cross Hey C3
Cuppin St B2
Curzon Park North C1
Curzon Park South C1
Dee Basin A1
Dee La B3
Delamere St A2
Dewa Roman Experience B2
Duke St B2
Eastgate B2
Eastgate St B2
Eaton Rd C2
Edinburgh Way C3
Elizabeth Cr B3
Fire Station A2
Foregate St B2
Frodsham St B2
Gamul House B2
Garden La A1
George St A2
Gladstone Ave A1
God's Providence House B2
Gorse Stacks A2
Greenway St C2
Grosvenor Bridge C1
Grosvenor Mus B2
Grosvenor Park B3
Grosvenor Precinct B2
Grosvenor Rd C1
Grosvenor St B2
Groves Rd B3
Guildhall Museum B1
Handbridge C2
Hartington St C3
Hoole Way A2
Hunter St B2
Information Ctr B2
King Charles' Tower A2
King St A2
Leisure Centre A2
Library B2
Lightfoot St A3
Little Roodee C2
Liverpool Rd A2
Love St B3
Lower Bridge St B2
Lower Park Rd B3
Lyon St A2
Magistrates Court B2
Meadows La C3
Military Museum C2
Milton St A3
New Crane St B1
Nicholas St B2
Northgate A2
Northgate St A2
Nun's Rd B1
Old Dee Bridge C2
Overleigh Rd C2
Park St B2
Police Station B2
Post Office A2/A3/B2/C2
Princess St B2
Queen St B2
Queen's Park Rd C3
Queen's Rd A3
Race Course B1
Raymond St A1
River La C2
Roman Amphitheatre & Gardens B2
Roodee, The (Chester Racecourse) B1
Russell St A3
St Anne St A2
St George's Cr C3
St Martin's Gate A1
St Martin's Way B1
St Oswalds Way A2
Saughall Rd A1
Sealand Rd A1
South View Rd A1
Stanley Palace B1
Station Rd A3
Steven St A3
The Bars B3
The Cross B2
The Groves B3
The Meadows B3
Tower Rd B1
Town Hall B2
Union St B3
Vicar's La B2
Victoria Cr C3
Victoria Rd A2
Walpole St A1
Water Tower St A1
Watergate B1
Watergate St B2
Whipcord La A1
White Friars B2
York St B3

Colchester 179

Abbey Gateway C2
Albert St A1
Albion Grove C2
Alexandra Rd C1
Artillery St C3
Arts Centre B1
Balkerne Hill B1
Barrack St C3
Beaconsfield Rd C1
Beche Rd C3
Bergholt Rd A1
Bourne Rd C3
Brick Kiln Rd A1
Bristol Rd B2
Broadlands Way A3
Brook St B3
Bury Cl B2
Bus Sta B2
Butt Rd C1
Camp Folley North C2
Camp Folley South C2
Campion Rd C2
Cannon St C3
Canterbury Rd C2
Castle B2
Castle Park B2
Castle Rd B2
Catchpool Rd A1
Causton Rd B1
Cavalry Barracks C1
Chandlers Row C3
Circular Rd East C2
Circular Rd North C1
Circular Rd West C1
Clarendon Way A1
Claudius Rd C2
Colchester Camp Abbey Field C1
Colchester Institute B1
Colchester A1
Colchester Town C2
Colne Bank Ave A1
Colne View Retail Pk A2
Compton Rd A3
Cowdray Ave A1/A2
Cowdray Centre, The A2
Crouch St B1
Crowhurst Rd B1
Culver Square Sh Ctr B1
Culver St East B2
Culver St West B1
Dilbridge Rd A3
East Hill B2
East St B3
East Stockwell St B1
Eld La B1
Essex Hall Rd A1
Exeter Dr B2
Fairfax Rd C2
Fire Station A2
Flagstaff Rd C1
George St B2
Gladstone Rd C2
Golden Noble Hill C2
Goring Rd A3
Granville Rd C3
Greenstead Rd B3
Guildford Rd B2
Harsnett Rd C3
Harwich Rd B3
Head St B1
High St B1/B2
High Woods Ctry Pk A2
Hollytrees B2
Hythe Hill C3
Information Ctr B2
Ipswich Rd A3
Jarmin Rd A2
Kendall Rd C2
Kimberley Rd C3
King Stephen Rd C3
Le Cateau Barracks C1
Leisure World A2
Library B1
Lincoln Way B2
Lion Walk Sh Ctr B1
Lisle Rd C2
Lucas Rd C2
Magdalen Green C3
Magdalen St C2
Maidenburgh St B2
Maldon Rd C1
Manor Rd B1
Margaret Rd A1
Mason Rd A2
Mercers Way A1
Mercury B1
Mersea Rd C2
Meyrick Cr C2
Mile End Rd A1
Military Rd C2
Mill St C2
Minories B2
Moorside B3
Morant Rd C3
Napier Rd C2
Natural History B2
New Town Rd C2
Norfolk Cr A3
North Hill B1
North Station Rd A1
Northgate St B1
Nunns Rd B1
Odeon B1
Old Coach Rd B3
Old Heath Rd C3
Osborne St B2
Petrolea Cl A1
Police Station C1
Popes La B1
Port La C3
Post Office B1/B2/C2
Priory St B2
Queen St B2
Rawstorn Rd B1
Rebon St C3
Recreation Rd C3
Ripple Way A3
Roman Rd B2
Roman Wall B2
Romford Cl A3
Rosebery Ave B2
St Andrews Ave B3
St Andrews Gdns B3
St Botolph St B2
St Botolphs B2
St John's Abbey (site of) C2
St John's St B1
St Johns Walk Sh Ctr B1
St Leonards Rd C3
St Marys Fields B1
St Peters B1
St Peter's St B1
Salisbury Ave C1
Serpentine Walk A1
Sheepen Pl B1
Sheepen Rd B1
Sir Isaac's Walk B1
Smythies Ave B2
South St C1
South Way C1
Sports Way A2
Suffolk Cl A3
Town Hall B1
Valentine Dr A3
Victor Rd C3
Wakefield Cl B2
Wellesley Rd C1
Wells Rd B2/B3
West St C1
West Stockwell St B1
Weston Rd C3
Westway A1
Wickham Rd C1
Wimpole Rd C3
Winchester Rd C2
Winnock Rd C2
Wolfe Ave C2
Worcester Rd B2

Coventry 179

Abbots La A1
Albany Rd B1
Alma St B3
Art Faculty B3
Asthill Grove C2
Bablake School A1
Barras La A1/B1
Barrs Hill School A1
Belgrade B2
Bishop Burges St A2
Bond's Hospital B1
Broad Gate B2
Broadway C1
Bus Station A3
Butts Radial B1
Canal Basin A2
Canterbury St A3
Cathedral B3
Chester St A1
Cheylesmore Manor House B2
Christ Church Spire B2
City Walls & Gates A2
Corporation St B2
Council House B2
Coundon Rd A1
Coventry Station C2
Coventry Transport Museum A2
Cox St A3
Croft Rd B1
Dalton Rd C1
Deasy Rd C3
Earl St B2
Eaton Rd C2
Fairfax St B2
Foleshill Rd A2
Ford's Hospital B2
Fowler Rd A1
Friars Rd C2
Gordon St C1
Gosford St B3
Greyfriars Green B2
Greyfriars Rd B2
Gulson Rd B3
Hales St A2
Harnall Lane East A3
Harnall Lane West A2
Herbert Art Gallery & Museum B3
Hertford St B2
Hewitt Ave A1
High St B2
Hill St B1
Holy Trinity B2
Holyhead Rd A1
Howard St A3
Huntingdon Rd C1
Information Ctr B2
Jordan Well B3
King Henry VIII School C1
Lady Godiva Statue B2
Lamb St A2
Leicester Row A2
Library B2
Little Park St B2
London Rd C3
Lower Ford St B3
Magistrates & Crown Courts B2
Manor House Drive B2
Manor Rd C2
Market B2
Martyr's Memorial C2
Meadow St B1
Meriden St A1
Michaelmas Rd C2
Middleborough Rd A1
Mile La C3
Millennium Place A2
Much Park St B3
Naul's Mill Park A1
New Union B2
Park Rd C2
Parkside C3
Post Office B2
Primrose Hill St A3
Priory Gardens & Visitor Centre B2
Priory St B3
Puma Way C3
Quarryfield La C3
Queen's Rd B1
Quinton Rd C2
Radford Rd A2
Raglan St B3
Retail Park C1
Ringway (Hill Cross) A1
Ringway (Queens) B1
Ringway (Rudge) B1
Ringway (St Johns) B3
Ringway (St Nicholas) A2
Ringway (St Patricks) C2
Ringway (Swanswell) A2
Ringway (Whitefriars) B3
St John St B2
St John The Baptist B2
St Nicholas St A2
Skydome B1
Spencer Ave C1
Spencer Park C1
Spon St B1
Sports Centre B3
Stoney Rd C2
Stoney Stanton Rd A3
Swanswell Pool A3
Sydney Stringer Academy A3
Technical College B1
Technology Park C3
The Precinct B2
Theatre B1
Thomas Landsdail St C2
Tomson Ave A1
Top Green C1
Trinity St B2
University B3
University Sports Ctr B3
Upper Hill St A1
Upper Well St A2
Victoria St A3
Vine St A3
Warwick Rd C2
Waveley Rd B1
Westminster Rd C1
White St A3
Windsor St B1

Derby 179

Abbey St C1
Agard St B1
Albert St B2
Albion St B2
Ambulance Station B1
Arthur St A1
Ashlyn Rd B3
Assembly Rooms B2
Babington La C2
Becket St B1
Belper Rd A1
Bold La B1
Bradshaw Way C2
Bradshaw Way Retail Park C2
Bridge St B1
Brook St B1
Burton Rd C1
Bus Station B2
Caesar St A2
Canal St C3
Carrington St C3
Cathedral B2
Cathedral Rd B1
Charnwood St C2
Chester Green Rd A2
City Rd A2
Clarke St A3
Cock Pitt B3
Council House B2
Courts B1
Cranmer Rd B3
Crompton St C1
Crown & County Courts B2
Curzon St B1
Darley Grove A1
Derby C3
Derbyshire County Cricket Ground B3
Derwent Business Centre A2
Derwent St B2
Drewry La C1
Duffield Rd A1
Duke St A2
Dunton Cl B3
Eagle Market C2
Eastgate B3
East St B2
Exeter St B2
Farm St C1
Ford St B1
Forester St C1
Fox St A2
Friar Gate B1
Friary St B1
Full St B2
Gerard St C1
Gower St C2
Green La C2
Grey St C1
Guildhall B2
Harcourt St C1
Highfield Rd A1
Hill La C2
Information Ctr B2
Iron Gate B2
John St C3
Joseph Wright Ctr B1
Kedleston Rd A1
Key St B2
King Alfred St C1
King St A1
Kingston St A1
Lara Croft Way C2
Leopold St C2
Library B1
Liversage St C3
Lodge La B1
London Rd C2
London Rd Community Hospital C2
Macklin St C1
Mansfield Rd A2
Market B2
Market Pl B2
May St C1
Meadow La B3
Melbourne St C2
Mercian Way C1
Midland Rd C3
Monk St C1
Morledge B2
Mount St C1
Museum and Art Gallery B1
Noble St C3
North Parade A1
North St A1
Nottingham Rd B3
Osmaston Rd C2
Otter St A1
Park St C3
Parker St A1
Pickfords House B1
Playhouse C2
Police HQ A2
Police Station B2
Post Office A1/A2/B1/B2/C2/C3
Prime Enterprise Pk A2
Pride Parkway C3
Prime Parkway A2
Queens Leisure Ctr B1
Racecourse A3
Railway Terr C3
Register Office B2
Sadler Gate B1
St Alkmund's Way B1/B2
St Helens House A1
St Mary's A1
St Mary's Bridge A2
St Mary's Bridge Chapel A2
St Mary's Gate B1
St Paul's Rd A2
St Peter's C2
St Peter's St C2
Showcase De Lux C2
Siddals Rd C3
Silk Mill B2
Sir Frank Whittle Rd A3
Spa La C1
Spring St C1
Stafford St B1
Station Approach C3
Stockbrook St C1
Stores Rd A3
Traffic St C2
Wardwick B1
Werburgh St C1
West Ave A1
Westfield Centre C2
West Meadows Industrial Estate B3
Wharf Rd A2
Wilmot St C2
Wilson St C1
Wood's La C1

Dundee 179

Adelaide Pl A1
Airlie Pl C1
Albany Terr A1
Albert St A3
Alexander St A2
Ann St A2
Arthurstone Terr A3
Bank St B2
Barrack Rd A1
Barrack St B2
Bell St B2
Blackscroft A3
Blinshall St B1
Brown St B1
Bus Station B3
Caird Hall B2
Camperdown St B3
Candle La B3
Carmichael St A1
City Churches B2
City Quay B3
City Sq B2
Commercial St B2
Constable St A3
Constitution Ct A1
Constitution Cres A1
Constitution St A1/B2
Cotton Rd A3
Courthouse Sq B1
Cowgate A3
Crescent St A3
Crichton St B2
Dens Brae A3
Dens Rd A3
Discovery Point C2
Douglas St B1
Drummond St A1
Dudhope Castle A1
Dudhope St A2
Dudhope Terr A1
Dundee C2
Dundee College A1
Dundee Contemporary Arts C2
Dundee High School B2
Dundee Repertory C2
Dura St A3
East Dock St B3
East Whale La B3
East Marketgait B3
Erskine St A3
Euclid Cr B2
Forebank Rd A2
Foundry La A3
Frigate Unicorn B3
Gallagher Retail Park B3
Gellatly St B3
Government Offices C2
Guthrie St B1
Hawkhill B1
Hilltown A2
Howff Cemetery, The B2
Information Ctr B2
King St A3
Kinghorne Rd A1
Ladywell Ave A3
Laurel Bank A2
Law Hill, The A1
Law Rd A1
Law St A1
Library A2
Little Theatre A2
Lochee Rd B1
Lower Princes St A3
Lyon St A3
McManus Museum & Art Gallery B2
Meadow Side B2
Meadowside St Pauls B2
Mercat Cross B2
Murraygate B2
Nelson St A2
Nethergate B2/C1
North Marketgait B2
North Lindsay St B2
Old Hawkhill B1
Olympia Leisure Ctr C3
Overgate Sh Ctr B2
Park Pl B1
Perth Rd C1
Police Station A2/B1
Post Office B2
Princes St A3
Prospect Pl A2
Reform St B2
Riverside Dr C2
Roseangle C1
Rosebank St A2
RRS Discovery C2
St Andrew's C2
St Pauls Episcopal B3
Science Centre C2
Seagate B2
Sheriffs Court B1
South George St A2
South Marketgait B3
South Tay St B2
South Ward Rd B2
Steps A2
Tay Road Bridge C3
Tayside House B2
Trades La B3
Union St B2
Union Terr A1
University Library B2
Univ of Abertay B2
Univ of Dundee B1
Upper Constitution St A1
Verdant Works B1
Victoria Dock B3
Victoria Rd A2
Victoria St A3
West Marketgait B1/B2
Ward Rd B1
Wellgate B2
West Bell St B1
Westfield Pl C1
William St A3
Wishart Arch A3

Durham 180

Alexander Cr B2
Allergate B2
Archery Rise C1
Assize Courts B3
Back Western Hill A1
Bakehouse La A3
Baths B3
Baths Bridge B3
Boat House B3
Bowling A2
Boyd St C3
Bus Station B2
Castle B2
Castle Chare B2
Cathedral B2
Church St C3
Clay La C1
Claypath B3
College of St Hild & St Bede B3
County Hall A1
County Hospital B1
Crook Hall & Gardens A3
Crossgate B2
Crossgate Peth C1
Darlington Rd C1
Durham A2
Durham Light Infantry Museum & Arts Gallery A2
Durham School C2
Ellam Ave C1
Elvet Bridge B3
Elvet Court B3
Farnley Hey B1
Ferens Cl A3
Fieldhouse La A1
Flass St B1
Framwelgate A2
Framewelgate Bridge B2
Framwelgate Peth A2
Framwelgate Waterside A2
Frankland La A3
Freeman's Pl A3
Freeman's Quay Leisure Centre A3
Gala Theatre & Cinema B3
Gates Sh Ctr, The B2
Geoffrey Ave C1
Gilesgate B3
Grey College C3
Hallgarth St C3
Hatfield College B3
Hawthorn Terr B1
Heritage Centre B3
HM Prison B3
Information Ctr B3
John St B1
Kingsgate Bridge B3
Laburnum Terr B1
Lawson Terr B1
Leazes Rd B2/B3
Library B2
Margery La B2
Market B2
Mavin St C3
Millburngate B2
Millburngate Bridge B2
Millennium Bridge (foot/cycle) A2
Mountjoy Research Centre C3
Museum of Archaeology B2
Nevilledale Terr B1
New Elvet B3
New Elvet Bridge B3
North Bailey B3
North End A1
North Rd A1/B2
Observatory C1
Old Elvet B3
Oriental Museum C2
Oswald Court C3
Parkside B2
Passport Office A2
Percy Terr B1
Pimlico C2
Police Station B3
Post Office A1/B2
Potters Bank C1/C2
Prebends Bridge C2
Prebends Walk C2
Prince Bishops Shopping Centre B3
Princes St A1
Providence Row A3
Quarryheads La C2
Redhills La B1
Redhills Terr B1
Saddler St B3
St Chad's College C3
St Cuthbert's Society C2
St John's College C2
St Margaret's B2
St Mary The Less C2
St Mary's College C2
St Monica Grove B1
St Nicholas' B3
St Oswald's C3
Sidegate A2
Silver St B2
Add Sixth Form Centre (Durham Gilesgate) A3
South Bailey C2
South Rd C3
South St B2
Springwell Ave A1
Stockton Rd C3
Students' Rec Centre B3
Sutton St B2
The Avenue B1
The Crescent A1
The Grove A1
The Sands A3
Town Hall B2
Treasury Museum B2
University B2
University Arts Block B3
University Library C3
Univ Science Site C3
Walkergate Centre A3
Wearside Dr A3
Western Hill A1
Wharton Park A2
Whinney Hill C3
Whitehouse Ave C1

Edinburgh 180

Abbey Strand B6
Abbeyhill A6
Abbeyhill Cr B6
Abbeymount A6
Abercromby Pl A3
Adam St C5
Albany La A4
Albany St A4
Albert Memorial B2
Albyn Pl A2
Alva Pl A6
Alva St B1
Ann St A1
Appleton Tower C4
Archibald Pl C3
Argyle House C3
Assembly Rooms & Musical Hall A3
Atholl Cr B1
Atholl Crescent La C1
Bank St B4
Barony St A4
Beaumont Pl C5
Belford Rd B1
Belgrave Cr A1
Belgrave Crescent La A1
Bell's Brae B1
Blackfriars St B4
Blair St B4
Bread St C2
Bristo Pl C4
Bristo St C4
Brougham St C2
Broughton St A4
Brown St C5
Brunton Terr A6
Buckingham Terr A1
Burial Ground A6
Bus Station A4
Caledonian Cr C1
Caledonian Rd C1
Calton Hill A4
Calton Hill A5
Calton Rd B4
Camera Obscura & Outlook Tower B3
Candlemaker Row C4
Canning St B2
Canongate B5
Canongate B5
Carlton St A1
Carlton Terr A6
Carlton Terrace La A6
Castle St B2
Castle Terr B2
Castlehill B3
Central Library B4
Chalmers Hospital C3
Chalmers St C3
Chambers St C4
Chapel St C4
Charles St C4
Charlotte Sq B2
Chester St B1
Circus La A2
Circus Pl A2
City Art Centre B4
City Chambers B4
City Observatory A5
Clarendon Cr A1
Clerk St C5
Coates Cr B1
Cockburn St B4
College of Art C3
Comely Bank Ave A1
Comely Bank Row A1
Cornwall St C2
Cowans Cl C5
Cowgate B4
Cranston St B5
Crichton St C4
Croft-An-Righ A6
Cumberland St A2
Dalry Pl C1
Dalry Rd C1
Danube St A1
Darnawy St A2
David Hume Tower C4
Davie St C5
Dean Bridge A1
Dean Gdns A1
Dean Park Cr A1
Dean Park Mews A1
Dean Park St A1
Dean Path B1
Dean St A1
Dean Terr A1
Dewar Pl C1
Dewar Place La C1
Doune Terr A2
Drummond Pl A3
Drummond St C5
Drumsheugh Gdns B1
Dublin Mews A3
Dublin St A4
Dublin St La South A4
Dumbiedykes Rd B5
Dundas St A3
Earl Grey St C2
East Crosscauseway C5
East Market St B4
East Norton Pl A6
East Princes St Gdns B3
Easter Rd A6
Edinburgh (Waverley) B4
Edinburgh Castle B3
Edinburgh Dungeon B4
Edinburgh Int Conference Ctr C2
Elder St A4
Esplanade B3
Eton Terr A1
Eye Pavilion C3
Festival Office B3
Festival Theatre Edinburgh C4
Filmhouse C2
Fire Station C2
Floral Clock B3
Forres St A2
Forth St A4
Fountainbridge C2
Frederick St A3
Freemasons' Hall B3
Fruit Market B4
Gardner's Crescent C2
George Heriot's School C3
George IV Bridge B4
George Sq C4
George Sq La C4
George St B3
Georgian House B2
Gladstone's Land B3
Glen St C3
Gloucester La A2
Gloucester Pl A2
Gloucester St A2
Graham St C3
Grassmarket C3
Great King St A3
Great Stuart B1
Greenside La A5
Greenside Row A5
Greyfriars Kirk C4
Grindlay St C2
Grosvenor St C1
Grove St C1
Gullan's Cl B5
Guthrie St B4
Hanover St A3
Hart St A4
Haymarket C1
Haymarket Sta C1
Heriot Pl C3
Heriot Row A2
High School Yard B5
High St B4
Hill Pl C5
Hill St A2
Hillside Cr A5
Holyrood Park C6
Holyrood Rd B5
Home St C2
Hope St B2
Horse Wynd B6
Howden St C5
Howe St A2
India Pl A2
India St A2
Infirmary St B4
Information Ctr B4
Jamaica Mews A2
Jeffrey St B4
John Knox House B4
Johnston Terr C3
Keir St C3
Kerr St A2
King's Stables Rd B2
Lady Lawson St C3
Lauriston Gdns C3
Lauriston Park C3
Lauriston Pl C3
Lauriston St C3
Lawnmarket B3
Learmonth Gdns A1
Learmonth Terr A1
Leith St A4
Lennox St A1
Lennox St La A1
Leslie Pl A2
London Rd A5
Lothian Health Board C5
Lothian Rd B2
Lothian St C4
Lower Menz Pl A6
Lynedoch Pl B1
Manor Pl B1
Market St B4
Marshall St C4
Maryfield A6
Maryfield Pl A6
McEwan Hall C4
Medical School C4
Melville St B1
Meuse La B4
Middle Meadow Wk C4
Milton St A6
Montrose Terr A6
Moray House (Coll) B5
Moray Place A2
Morrison Link C1
Morrison St C1
Mound Pl B3
Multrees Walk A4
Mus Collections Ctr A4
Museum of Childhood B5
Museum of Edinburgh B5
Museum on the Mound B4
National Gallery B3
National Library of Scotland B4
National Monument A5
National Museum of Scotland C4
National Portrait Gallery B4
National Records Scotland A4
Nelson Monument A5
Nelson St A3
New St B5
Nicolson Sq C4
Nicolson St C4
Niddry St B4
North Bridge B4
North Meadow Walk C3
North Bank St B3
North Castle St A2
North Charlotte St A2
North St Andrew St A4
North St David St A3
North West Circus Place A2
Northumberland St A3
Odeon C2
Old Royal High School A5
Old Tolbooth Wynd B5
Omni Centre A4
Our Dynamic Earth B6
Oxford Terr A1
Palace of Holyrood House B6
Palmerston Pl B1
Panmure Pl C3
Parliament House B4
Parliament Sq B4
People's Story, The B5
Playhouse Theatre A4
Pleasance C5
Police Station A4
Ponton St C2
Post Office A3/A4/B5/C1/C2/C4/C5
Potterrow C4
Princes Mall B4
Princes St B3
Princes St B3
Queen St A2
Queen Street Gdns A3
Queen's Dr B6/C6
Queensferry Rd A1
Queensferry St B1
Queensferry St La B2
Radical Rd C6
Randolph Cr B1
Regent Gdns A5
Regent Pl A5
Regent Rd B5
Regent Rd Park A6
Regent Terr A5
Remains of Holyrood Abbey (AD 1128) A6
Richmond La C5
Richmond Pl C5
Rose St B2
Rosemount Bldgs C1
Ross Open Air Theatre B3
Rothesay Pl B1
Rothesay Terr B1
Roxburgh Pl C5
Roxburgh St C5
Royal Bank of Scotland A4
Royal Circus A2
Royal Lyceum C2
Royal Scottish Academy B3
Royal Terrace A5
Royal Terrace Gdns A5
Rutland Sq B2
Rutland St B2
St Andrew Sq A4
St Andrew Sq A4
St Andrew's House A4
St Bernard's Cr A1
St Cecilia's Hall B4
St Colme St A2
St Cuthbert's B2
St Giles' B4
St James Centre A4
St John St B5
St John's B2
St John's Hill B5
St Leonard's Hill C5
St Leonard's La C5
St Leonard's St C5
St Mary's A4
St Mary's Scottish Episcopal B1
St Mary's St B5
St Stephen St A2
Salisbury Crags C6
Saunders St A2
Scotch Whisky Experience B3
Scott Monument B4
Scottish Parliament B6
Scottish Storytelling Centre B5
Semple St C2
Shandwick Pl B2
South Bridge B4
South Charlotte St B2
South College St C4
South Learmonth Gdns A1
South St Andrew St A4
South St David St A3
Spittal St C2
Stafford St B1
Student Centre C4
Surgeons' Hall C5
TA Centre C4
Tattoo Office B4
Teviot Pl C4
The Mall B6
The Mound B3
The Royal Mile B5
The Writer's Mus B4
Thistle St A3
Torphichen Pl C1
Torphichen St C1
Traverse Theatre B2
Tron Sq B4
Tron, The B4
Union St A4
University C4
University Library C4
Upper Grove Pl C1
Usher Hall C2
Vennel C3
Victoria St B3
Viewcraig Gdns B5
Viewcraig St B5
VUE A4
Walker St B1
Waterloo Pl A4
Waverley Bridge B4
Wemyss Pl A2
West Approach Rd C1
West Crosscauseway C5
West End C1
West Maitland St C1
West of Nicholson St C4
West Port C3
West Princes St Gdns B3
West Richmond St C5
West Tollcross C2
White Horse Cl B5
William St B1
Windsor St A5
York La A4
York Pl A4
York Pl A4
Young St B2

Exeter 180

Alphington St . . . C1
Athelstan Rd . . . B3
Bampfylde St . . . B2
Barnardo Rd . . . C3
Barnfield Hill . . . B3
Barnfield Rd . . . B2/B3
Barnfield Theatre . . . B2
Bartholomew St E . . . B1
Bartholomew St W . . . B1
Bear St . . . B2
Beaufort Rd . . . C1
Bedford St . . . B2
Belgrave Rd . . . A3
Belmont Rd . . . A3
Blackall Rd . . . A2
Blackboy Rd . . . A3
Bonhay Rd . . . B1
Bull Meadow Rd . . . C2
Bus & Coach Sta . . . B3
Castle St . . . B2
Cecil Rd . . . C1
Cheeke St . . . A3
Church Rd . . . C1
Chute St . . . A3
City Industrial Estate C2
City Wall . . . B1/B2
Civic Centre . . . B2
Clifton Rd . . . B3
Clifton St . . . B3
Clock Tower . . . A1
College Rd . . . B3
Colleton Cr . . . C2
Commercial Rd . . . C1
Coombe St . . . B2
Cowick St . . . C1
Crown Courts . . . B2
Custom House . . . C2
Danes' Rd . . . A2
Denmark Rd . . . B3
Devon County Hall . . . C3
Devonshire Pl . . . A3
Dinham Rd . . . B1
East Grove Rd . . . C3
Edmund St . . . C1
Elmgrove Rd . . . A1
Exe St . . . B1
Exeter Cathedral . . . B2
Exeter Central Sta . . . A1
Exeter City Football Ground . . . A3
Exeter College . . . A1
Exeter Picture Ho . . . B1
Fire Station . . . A1
Fore St . . . B1
Friars Walk . . . C2
Guildhall . . . B2
Guildhall Sh Ctr . . . B2
Harlequins Sh Ctr . . . B1
Haven Rd . . . C2
Heavitree Rd . . . B3
Hele Rd . . . A1
High St . . . B2
HM Prison . . . A2
Holloway St . . . C2
Hoopern St . . . A2
Horseguards . . . A2
Howell Rd . . . A1
Information Ctr . . . B3
Iron Bridge . . . B1
Isca Rd . . . C1
Jesmond Rd . . . A3
King William St . . . A2
King St . . . B1
Larkbeare Rd . . . C2
Leisure Centre . . . C1
Library . . . B2
Longbrook St . . . A2
Longbrook Terr . . . A2
Lower North St . . . B1
Lucky La . . . C2
Lyndhurst Rd . . . C3
Magdalen Rd . . . B3
Magdalen St . . . B2
Magistrates & Crown Courts . . . A2
Market . . . B2
Market St . . . B2
Marlborough Rd . . . C3
Mary Arches St . . . B1
Matford Ave . . . C3
Matford La . . . C3
Matford Rd . . . C3
May St . . . A3
Mol's Coffee Ho . . . B2
New Theatre . . . C2
New Bridge St . . . B1
New North Rd . . . A1/A2
North St . . . B1
Northernhay St . . . B1
Norwood Ave . . . C3
Odeon . . . A3
Okehampton St . . . C1
Old Mill Cl . . . C2
Old Tiverton Rd . . . A3
Oxford Rd . . . A3
Paris St . . . B2
Parr St . . . A3
Paul St . . . B1
Pennsylvania Rd . . . A2
Police HQ . . . B3
Portland Street . . . A3
Post Office . . . A3/B1/B3/C1
Powderham Cr . . . A3
Preston St . . . B1
Princesshay Sh Ctr . . . B2
Queen St . . . A1
Queens Rd . . . C1
Queen's Terr . . . A1
Radford Rd . . . C2
Richmond Rd . . . A1
Roberts Rd . . . C2
Rougemont Castle . . . A2
Rougemont House . . . B2
Royal Albert Memorial Mus . . . B2
St David's Hill . . . A1
St James' Pk Sta . . . A3
St James' Rd . . . A3
St Leonard's Rd . . . C3
St Lukes University . . . B3
St Mary Steps . . . C1
St Nicholas Priory . . . B1
St Thomas Sta . . . C1
Sandford Walk . . . B3
School for the Deaf . . . C2
School Rd . . . C1
Sidwell St . . . A2
Smythen St . . . B1
South St . . . B2
Southernhay East . . . B2
Southernhay West . . . B2
Spacex Gallery . . . B1
Spicer Rd . . . B3
Sports Centre . . . A3
Summerland St . . . A3
Swimming Pool & Leisure Centre . . . B3
Sydney Rd . . . C1
Tan La . . . C2
The Quay . . . C2
Thornton Hill . . . A2
Topsham Rd . . . C3
Tucker's Hall . . . B1
Tudor St . . . B1
Velwell Rd . . . A1
Verney St . . . A3
Water La . . . C1/C2
Weirfield Rd . . . C2
Well St . . . A3
West Ave . . . A2
West Grove Rd . . . C3
Western Way . . . A3/B1/B2
Wonford Rd . . . B3/C3
York Rd . . . A2

Glasgow 181

Admiral St . . . C2
Albert Bridge . . . C5
Albion St . . . B5
Anderston . . . B3
Anderston Centre . . . B3
Anderston Quay . . . B3
Arches . . . B4
Argyle St . . . A1/A2/B3/B4/B5
Argyle Street . . . B5
Argyll Arcade . . . B5
Arlington St . . . A3
Arts Centre . . . B3
Ashley St . . . A3
Bain St . . . C6
Baird St . . . A6
Baliol St . . . A3
Ballater St . . . C5
Barras, The (Market) C6
Bath St . . . A3
BBC Scotland/SMG . . . B1
Bell St . . . C6
Bell's Bridge . . . B1
Bentinck St . . . A2
Berkeley St . . . A3
Bishop La . . . B3
Black St . . . A6
Blackburn St . . . C2
Blackfriars St . . . B6
Blantyre St . . . A1
Blythswood Sq . . . A4
Blythswood St . . . B4
Bothwell St . . . B4
Brand St . . . C1
Breadalbane St . . . A2
Bridge St . . . C4
Bridge St . . . C4
Bridgegate . . . C5
Briggait . . . C5
Broomhill Park . . . A6
Broomielaw . . . B4
Broomielaw Quay Gdns . . . B3
Brown St . . . B4
Brunswick St . . . B5
Buccleuch St . . . A3
Buchanan Bus Sta . . . A5
Buchanan Galleries . . . A5
Buchanan St . . . B5
Buchanan St . . . B5
Cadogan St . . . B4
Caledonian Univ . . . A5
Calgary St . . . A5
Cambridge St . . . A4
Canal St . . . A5
Candleriggs . . . B5
Carlton Pl . . . C4
Carnarvon St . . . A3
Carrick St . . . B4
Castle St . . . B6
Cathedral Sq . . . B6
Cathedral St . . . B5
Central College of Commerce . . . B5
Ctr for Contemporary Arts . . . A4
Centre St . . . C4
Cessnock . . . C1
Cessnock St . . . C1
Charing Cross . . . A3
Charlotte St . . . C6
Cheapside St . . . B3
Cineworld . . . A5
Citizens' Theatre . . . C5
City Chambers Complex . . . B5
City Halls . . . B5
Clairmont Gdns . . . A2
Claremont St . . . A2
Claremont Terr . . . A2
Claythorne St . . . C6
Cleveland St . . . A3
Clifford La . . . C1
Clifford St . . . C1
Clifton Pl . . . A2
Clifton St . . . A2
Clutha St . . . C1
Clyde Arc . . . B2
Clyde Auditorium . . . B2
Clyde Pl . . . C4
Clyde Place Quay . . . C4
Clyde St . . . C5
Clyde Walkway . . . C3
Clydeside Expressway . . . B2
Coburg St . . . C4
Cochrane St . . . B5
College of Nautical Studies . . . C5
College St . . . B6
Collins St . . . B6
Commerce St . . . C4
Cook St . . . C4
Cornwall St . . . C2
Couper St . . . A5
Cowcaddens . . . A4
Cowcaddens Rd . . . A4
Crimea St . . . B3
Custom House . . . C4
Custom House Quay Gdns . . . C4
Dalhousie St . . . A4
Dental Hospital . . . A4
Derby St . . . A2
Dobbie's Loan . . . A4/A5
Dobbie's Loan Pl . . . A5
Dorset St . . . A3
Douglas St . . . B4
Doulton Fountain . . . C6
Dover St . . . A2
Drury St . . . B4
Drygate . . . B6
Duke St . . . B6
Dunaskin St . . . A1
Dunblane St . . . A4
Dundas St . . . B5
Dunlop St . . . C5
East Campbell St . . . C6
Eastvale Pl . . . A1
Eglinton St . . . C4
Elderslie St . . . A3
Elliot St . . . B2
Elmbank St . . . A3
Esmond St . . . A1
Exhibition Centre . . . B2
Exhibition Way . . . B2
Eye Infirmary . . . A2
Festival Park . . . C1
Film Theatre . . . A4
Finnieston Quay . . . B2
Finnieston Sq . . . B2
Finnieston St . . . B2
Fitzroy Pl . . . A2
Florence St . . . C5
Fox St . . . C5
Gallowgate . . . C6
Garnet St . . . A3
Garnethill St . . . A4
Garscube Rd . . . A4
George Sq . . . B5
George St . . . B5
George V Bridge . . . C4
Gilbert St . . . A1
Glasgow Bridge . . . C4
Glasgow Cathedral . . . B6
Glasgow Central . . . B4
Glasgow Green . . . C6
Glasgow Metropolitan College . . . B5/C5
Glasgow Tower . . . B1
Glasgow Science Centre . . . B1
Glasgow Science Centre Footbridge . . . B1
Glassford St . . . B5
Glebe St . . . A6
Gorbals Cross . . . C5
Gorbals St . . . C5
Gordon St . . . B4
Govan Rd . . . B1/C1/C2
Grace St . . . B3
Grand Ole Opry . . . C2
Grafton Pl . . . A5
Grant St . . . A3
Granville St . . . A3
Gray St . . . A2
Greendyke St . . . C6
Grey Eagle St . . . B7
Harley St . . . C1
Harvie St . . . C1
Haugh Rd . . . A1
Heliport . . . B1
Henry Wood Hall . . . A2
High Court . . . C5
High St . . . B6
High Street . . . B6
Hill St . . . A3
Holland St . . . A3
Holm St . . . B4
Hope St . . . A5
Houldsworth St . . . B2
Houston Pl . . . C3
Houston St . . . C3
Howard St . . . C5
Hunter St . . . C6
Hutcheson St . . . B5
Hutchesons Hall . . . B5
Hydepark St . . . B3
Hydro The . . . B2
Imax Cinema . . . B1
India St . . . A3
Information Ctr . . . B5
Ingram St . . . B5
Jamaica St . . . B4
James Watt St . . . B4
John Knox St . . . B6
John St . . . B5
Kelvin Hall . . . A1
Kelvin Statue . . . A2
Kelvin Way . . . A2
Kelvingrove Art Gallery & Museum . . . A1
Kelvingrove Park . . . A2
Kelvingrove St . . . A2
Kelvinhaugh St . . . A1
Kennedy St . . . A6
Kent Rd . . . A2
Killermont St . . . A5
King St . . . B5
King's . . . A3
Kingston Bridge . . . C3
Kingston St . . . C4
Kinning Park . . . C2
Kyle St . . . A5
Lancefield Quay . . . B2
Lancefield St . . . B3
Langshot St . . . C1
Lendel Pl . . . C1
Lighthouse . . . B4
Lister St . . . A6
Little St . . . B3
London Rd . . . C6
Lorne St . . . C1
Lower Harbour . . . B1
Lumsden St . . . A1
Lymburn St . . . A1
Lyndoch Cr . . . A3
Lynedoch Pl . . . A3
Lynedoch St . . . A3
Maclellan St . . . C1
Mair St . . . C2
Maitland St . . . A4
Mansell St . . . C7
Mavisbank Gdns . . . C2
Mcalpine St . . . B3
Mcaslin St . . . A6
McLean Sq . . . C2
McLellan Gallery . . . A4
McPhater St . . . A4
Merchants' House . . . B5
Middlesex St . . . C2
Middleton St . . . C1
Midland St . . . B4
Miller St . . . B5
Millroad St . . . C6
Milnpark St . . . C2
Milton St . . . A4
Minerva St . . . B2
Mitchell Library . . . A3
Mitchell St West . . . B4
Mitchell Theatre . . . A3
Modern Art Gallery . . . B5
Moir St . . . C6
Molendinar St . . . C6
Moncur St . . . C6
Montieth Row . . . C6
Montrose St . . . B5
Morrison St . . . C3
Mosque . . . C5
Nairn St . . . A1
Nelson Mandela Sq . . . B5
Nelson St . . . C4
Nelson's Monument C6
New City Rd . . . A4
Newton St . . . A3
Newton Pl . . . A3
Nicholson St . . . C4
Nile St . . . B5
Norfolk Court . . . C4
Norfolk St . . . C4
North Frederick St . . . B5
North Hanover St . . . B5
North Portland St . . . B6
North St . . . A3
North Wallace St . . . A5
O2 Academy . . . C4
Odeon . . . C3
Old Dumbarton Rd . . . A1
Osborne St . . . B5/C5
Oswald St . . . B4
Overnewton St . . . A1
Oxford St . . . C4
Pacific Dr . . . B1
Paisley Rd . . . C3
Paisley Rd West . . . C1
Park Circus . . . A2
Park Gdns . . . A2
Park St South . . . A2
Park Terr . . . A2
Parkgrove Terr . . . A2
Parnie St . . . C5
Parson St . . . A6
Partick Bridge . . . A1
Passport Office . . . A5
Pavilion Theatre . . . A4
Pembroke St . . . A3
People's Palace . . . C6
Pinkston Rd . . . A6
Piping Centre, The National . . . A5
Pitt St . . . A4/B4
Plantation Park . . . C1
Plantation Quay . . . B1
Police Sta . . . A4/A6/B5
Port Dundas Rd . . . A5
Port St . . . B2
Portman St . . . C2
Prince's Dock . . . B1
Princes Sq . . . B5
Provand's Lordship . . . B6
Queen St . . . B5
Queen Street . . . B5
Renfrew St . . . A3/A4
Renton St . . . A5
Richmond St . . . B5
Robertson St . . . B4
Rose St . . . A4
Rottenrow . . . B5
Royal Concert Hall . . . A5
Royal Crescent . . . A2
Royal Exchange Sq . . . B5
Royal Highland Fusiliers Mus . . . A3
Royal Hospital for Sick Children . . . A1
Royal Infirmary . . . B6
Royal Scottish Academy of Music & Drama . . . A4
Royal Terr . . . A2
Rutland Cr . . . C2
St Kent St . . . C6
St Andrew's (RC) . . . C5
St Andrew's . . . C6
St Andrew's St . . . C5
St Enoch . . . B5
St Enoch Sh Ctr . . . B5
St Enoch Sq . . . B4
St George's Rd . . . A3
St James Rd . . . B6
St Mungo Ave . . . A5/A6
St Mungo Museum of Religious Life . . . B6
St Mungo Pl . . . A6
St Vincent Cr . . . A2
St Vincent Pl . . . B5
St Vincent St . . . B3/B4
St Vincent Street Church . . . B4
St Vincent Terr . . . B3
Saltmarket . . . C5
Sandyford Pl . . . A3
Sauchiehall St . . . A2/A4
School of Art . . . A4
Sclater St . . . B7
Scotland St . . . C2
Scott St . . . A4
Scottish Exhibition & Conference Centre . . . B1
Seaward St . . . C2
Shaftesbury St . . . B3
Sheriff Court . . . C5
Shields Rd . . . C3
Shuttle St . . . B6
Somerset Pl . . . A2
South Portland St . . . C4
Springburn Rd . . . A6
Springfield Quay . . . C3
Stanley St . . . C2
Stevenson St . . . C6
Stewart St . . . A4
Stirling Rd . . . B6
Stirling's Library . . . B5
Stobcross Quay . . . B1
Stobcross Rd . . . B1
Stock Exchange . . . B5
Stockwell Pl . . . C5
Stockwell St . . . B5
Stow College . . . A4
Strathclyde Univ . . . B6
Sussex St . . . C2
Synagogues . . . A3/C4
Taylor Pl . . . A6
Tenement House . . . A3
Teviot St . . . A1
Theatre Royal . . . A4
Tolbooth Steeple & Mercat Cross . . . C6
Tower St . . . C2
Trades House . . . B5
Tradeston St . . . C4
Transport Mus . . . A1
Tron . . . C5
Trongate . . . B5
Tunnel St . . . B2
Turnbull St . . . C5
Union St . . . B4
Victoria Bridge . . . C5
Virginia St . . . B5
West Greenhill Pl . . . B2
West Regent St . . . A4
Wallace St . . . C3
Walls St . . . B6
Walmer Cr . . . C1
Warrock St . . . B3
Washington St . . . B3
Waterloo St . . . B4
Watson St . . . B6
Watt St . . . C3
Wellington St . . . B4
West Campbell St . . . B4
West George St . . . B4
West Graham St . . . A4
West Regent St . . . B4
West St . . . C4
West St . . . C4
Westminster Terr . . . A2
Whitehall St . . . B3
Wilkes St . . . C7
Wilson St . . . B5
Woodlands Gate . . . A3
Woodlands Rd . . . A3
Woodlands Terr . . . A2
Woodside Cr . . . A3
Woodside Pl . . . A3
Woodside Terr . . . A3
York St . . . B4
Yorkhill Pde . . . A1
Yorkhill St . . . A1

Gloucester 181

Albion St . . . C1
Alexandra Rd . . . B3
Alfred St . . . C3
All Saints Rd . . . C2
Alvin St . . . B2
Arthur St . . . C2
Barton St . . . C2
Barrack Square . . . B1
Blackfriars . . . B1
Blenheim Rd . . . C2
Bristol Rd . . . C1
Brunswick Rd . . . C2
Bruton Way . . . B2
Bus Station . . . B2
City Council Offices . . . B1
City Museum, Art Gallery & Library . . . B2
Clarence St . . . B2
Commercial Rd . . . B1
Cromwell St . . . C2
Deans Way . . . A2
Denmark Rd . . . A3
Derby Rd . . . C3
Docks . . . C1
Eastgate Sh Ctr . . . B1
Eastgate St . . . B2
Edwy Pde . . . A2
Estcourt Cl . . . A3
Estcourt Rd . . . A3
Falkner St . . . C2
Folk Museum . . . B1
GL1 Leisure Centre . . . C2
Gloucester Cath . . . B1
Gloucester Quays Outlet Shopping . . . C1
Gloucester Sta . . . B2
Gloucestershire Royal Hospital (A&E) . . . B3
Gloucester Waterways Mus . . . C1
Goodyere St . . . C2
Gouda Way . . . A1
Great Western Rd . . . B3
Guildhall . . . B2
Heathville Rd . . . A3
Henry Rd . . . B3
Henry St . . . B2
Hinton Rd . . . A2
HM Prison . . . B1
India Rd . . . C3
Information Ctr . . . B1
Jersey Rd . . . C3
King's . . . C2
King's Sq . . . B2
Kingsholm (Gloucester RFC) . . . A2
Kingsholm Rd . . . A2
Lansdown Rd . . . A3
Library . . . C2
Llanthony Rd . . . C1
London Rd . . . B3
Longhorn Ave . . . A1
Longsmith St . . . B1
Malvern Rd . . . A3
Market Pde . . . B2
Mercia Rd . . . A1
Metz Way . . . C3
Midland Rd . . . C2
Millbrook St . . . C3
Market . . . B2
Montpellier . . . C1
Napier St . . . C3
Nettleton Rd . . . C2
New Inn . . . B2
New Olympus . . . C3
North Rd . . . A3
Northgate St . . . B2
Oxford Rd . . . A2
Oxford St . . . B2
Park & Ride Gloucester . . . A1
Park Rd . . . C2
Park St . . . B2
Parliament St . . . C1
Pitt St . . . B1
Police Station . . . B1
Post Office . . . B2
Quay St . . . B1
Recreation Gd . . . A1/A2
Regent St . . . C2
Robert Raikes Ho . . . B1
Royal Oak Rd . . . B1
Russell St . . . B2
Ryecroft St . . . C2
St Aldate St . . . B2
St Ann Way . . . C1
St Catherine St . . . A2
St Mark St . . . A2
St Mary de Crypt . . . B1
St Mary de Lode . . . B1
St Nicholas's . . . B1
St Oswald's Rd . . . A1
St Oswald's Ret Pk . . . A1
St Peter's . . . B2
Seabroke Rd . . . A3
Sebert St . . . A2
Severn Rd . . . C1
Sherborne St . . . B2
Shire Hall . . . B1
Sidney St . . . C3
Soldiers of Gloucestershire . . . B1
Southgate St . . . B1/C1
Spa Field . . . C1
Spa Rd . . . C1
Sports Ground . . . A2/B2
Station Rd . . . B2
Stratton Rd . . . C3
Stroud Rd . . . C1
Superstore . . . A1
Swan Rd . . . A2
The Park . . . C2
The Quay . . . B1
Trier Way . . . C1/C2
Union St . . . A2
Vauxhall Rd . . . C3
Victoria St . . . C2
Walham Lane . . . A1
Wellington St . . . C2
Westgate Retail Park . . . B1
Westgate St . . . B1
Widden St . . . C2
Worcester St . . . B2

Hanley (Stoke-on-Trent) 181

Acton St . . . A3
Albion St . . . B2
Argyle St . . . C1
Ashbourne Gr . . . A2
Avoca St . . . A3
Baskerville Rd . . . B3
Bedford Rd . . . C1
Bedford St . . . C1
Bethesda St . . . B2
Bexley St . . . A2
Birches Head Rd . . . A3
Botteslow St . . . C3
Boundary St . . . A2
Broad St . . . C2
Broom St . . . A3
Bryan St . . . A2
Bucknall New Rd . . . B3
Bucknall Old Rd . . . B3
Bus Station . . . B3
Cannon St . . . C2
Castlefield St . . . C1
Hanley Park . . . C2
Cavendish St . . . B1
Central Forest Pk . . . A2
Charles St . . . B3
Cheapside . . . B2
Chell St . . . A3
Clarke St . . . C1
Cleveland Rd . . . C2
Clifford St . . . C3
Clough St . . . B2
Clyde St . . . C1
College Rd . . . C2
Cooper St . . . C2
Corbridge Rd . . . A1
Cutts St . . . C2
Davis St . . . C1
Denbigh St . . . A1
Derby St . . . C3
Dilke St . . . A3
Dundas St . . . A3
Dundee Rd . . . C1
Dyke St . . . B3
Eastwood Rd . . . C3
Eaton St . . . A3
Etruria Park . . . B1
Etruria Rd . . . B1
Etruria Vale Rd . . . C1
Festing St . . . A3
Festival Retail Park . . . A1
Fire Station . . . C2
Foundry St . . . B2
Franklyn St . . . C3
Garnet St . . . B1
Garth St . . . B3
George St . . . A3
Gilman St . . . B3
Glass St . . . B3
Goodson St . . . B3
Greyhound Way . . . A1
Grove Pl . . . C1
Hampton St . . . C3
Hanley Park . . . C2
Harding Rd . . . C2
Hassall St . . . B3
Havelock Pl . . . C1
Hazlehurst St . . . C3
Hinde St . . . C2
Hope St . . . B2
Houghton St . . . C2
Hulton St . . . A3
Information Ctr . . . B3
Jasper St . . . C2
Jervis St . . . A3
John Bright St . . . A3
John St . . . B2
Keelings Rd . . . A3
Kimberley Rd . . . C1
Ladysmith Rd . . . C1
Lawrence St . . . C2
Leek Rd . . . C3
Library . . . C2
Lichfield St . . . C3
Linfield Rd . . . B3
Loftus St . . . A2
Lower Bedford St . . . C1
Lower Bryan St . . . A2
Lower Mayer St . . . A3
Lowther St . . . A1
Magistrates Court . . . C2
Malham St . . . A2
Marsh St . . . B2
Matlock St . . . C3
Mayer St . . . B3
Milton St . . . C1
Mitchell Memorial Theatre . . . B2
Morley St . . . B2
Moston St . . . A3
Mount Pleasant . . . C1
Mulgrave St . . . A1
Mynors St . . . B3
Nelson Pl . . . B3
New Century St . . . B1
Octagon Retail Park . . . B1
Ogden Rd . . . C3
Old Hall St . . . B3
Old Town Rd . . . A3
Pall Mall . . . B2
Palmerston St . . . C3
Park and Ride . . . C2
Parker St . . . B2
Pavilion Dr . . . A1
Pelham St . . . C3
Percy St . . . B2
Piccadilly . . . B2
Picton St . . . B3
Plough St . . . A3
Police Station . . . C2
Portland St . . . A1
Post Office . . . A3/B3/C3
Potteries Museum & Art Gallery . . . B2
Potteries Sh Ctr . . . B2
Potteries Way . . . C2
Powell St . . . A1
Pretoria Rd . . . C1
Quadrant Rd . . . B2
Ranelagh St . . . C2
Raymond St . . . C2
Rectory Rd . . . C1
Regent Rd . . . C2
Regent Theatre . . . B2
Richmond Terr . . . C2
Ridgehouse Dr . . . A1
Robson St . . . C2
St Ann St . . . B3
St Luke St . . . B3
Sampson St . . . B2
Shaw St . . . A1
Sheaf St . . . C2
Shearer St . . . C1
Shelton New Rd . . . C1
Shirley Rd . . . C2
Slippery La . . . B2
Snow Hill . . . C2
Spur St . . . C3
Stafford St . . . B2
Statham St . . . B2
Stubbs La . . . C3
Sun St . . . C1
Supermarket . . . A1/B2
Talbot St . . . C3
The Parkway . . . C2
Town Hall . . . B2
Town Rd . . . A3
Trinity St . . . B2
Union St . . . A2
Upper Hillchurch St . . . A3
Upper Huntbach St . . . B3
Victoria Hall Theatre . . . B3
Warner St . . . C2
Warwick St . . . C1
Waterloo Rd . . . A1
Waterloo St . . . B3
Well St . . . B3
Wellesley St . . . C2
Wellington Rd . . . B3
Wellington St . . . B3
Whitehaven Dr . . . A2
Whitmore St . . . C1
Windermere St . . . A1
Woodall St . . . A1
Yates St . . . C2
York St . . . A2

Harrogate 182

Albert St . . . C2
Alexandra Rd . . . B2
Arthington Ave . . . B2
Ashfield Rd . . . A2
Back Cheltenham Mount . . . B2
Beech Grove . . . C1
Belmont Rd . . . C1
Bilton Dr . . . A2
Bower Rd . . . B2
Bower St . . . B2
Bus Station . . . B2
Cambridge Rd . . . B2
Cambridge St . . . B2
Cemetery . . . A2
Chatsworth Pl . . . A2
Chatsworth Grove . . . A2
Chatsworth Rd . . . A2
Chelmsford Rd . . . B3
Cheltenham Cr . . . B2
Cheltenham Mt . . . B2
Cheltenham Pde . . . B2
Christ Church . . . B3
Christ Church Oval . . . B3
Chudleigh Rd . . . B3
Clarence Dr . . . B1
Claro Rd . . . A3
Claro Way . . . A3
Coach Park . . . B2
Coach Rd . . . B3
Cold Bath Rd . . . C1
Commercial St . . . B2
Coppice Ave . . . A1
Coppice Dr . . . A1
Coppice Gate . . . A1
Cornwall Rd . . . B1
Council Offices . . . B1
Court . . . C3
Crescent Gdns . . . B1
Crescent Rd . . . B1
Dawson Terr . . . A2
Devonshire Pl . . . B3
Diamond Mews . . . C1
Dixon Rd . . . A2
Dixon Terr . . . A2
Dragon Ave . . . B3
Dragon Parade . . . B2
Dragon Rd . . . B2
Duchy Rd . . . B1
East Parade . . . B2
East Park Rd . . . C3
Esplanade . . . B1
Fire Station . . . A2
Franklin Mount . . . A2
Franklin Rd . . . B2
Franklin Square . . . A2
Glebe Rd . . . C1
Grove Park Court . . . A3
Grove Park Terrace . . . A3
Grove Rd . . . A2
Hampswaite Rd . . . A1
Harcourt Dr . . . B3
Harcourt Rd . . . B3
Harrogate . . . B2
Harrogate Int Ctr . . . B1
Harrogate Ladies College . . . B1
Harrogate Theatre . . . B2
Heywood Rd . . . C1
Hollins Cr . . . A1
Hollins Mews . . . A1
Hollins Rd . . . A1
Homestead Rd . . . C3
Hydro L Ctr, The . . . A1
Information Ctr . . . B1
James St . . . B2
Jenny Field Dr . . . A1
John St . . . B2
Kent Dr . . . A1
Kent Rd . . . A1
Kings Rd . . . A2
Kingsway . . . B3
Kingsway Dr . . . B3
Lancaster Rd . . . C1
Leeds Rd . . . C2
Lime Grove . . . B3
Lime St . . . A3
Mayfield Grove . . . B2
Mayfield Pl . . . A2
Mercer . . . B1
Montpellier Hill . . . B1
Mornington Cr . . . A3
Mornington Terr . . . B3
Mowbray Sq . . . B3
North Park Rd . . . B3
Nydd Vale Rd . . . B2
Oakdale Ave . . . A1
Oatlands Dr . . . C3
Odeon . . . B2
Osborne Rd . . . A2
Otley Rd . . . C2
Oxford St . . . B2
Park Chase . . . B3
Park Parade . . . B3
Park View . . . B2
Parliament St . . . B1
Police Station . . . B3
Post Office . . . B2/C1
Providence Terr . . . A2
Queen Parade . . . C3
Queen's Rd . . . C1
Raglan St . . . C2
Regent Ave . . . A3
Regent Grove . . . A3
Regent Parade . . . A3
Regent St . . . A3
Regent Terr . . . A3
Rippon Rd . . . A1
Robert St . . . C2
Royal Baths & Turkish Baths . . . B1
Royal Pump Room . . . B1
St Luke's Mount . . . A2
St Mary's Ave . . . C1
St Mary's Walk . . . C1
Scargill Rd . . . A1
Skipton Rd . . . A3
Skipton St . . . A2
Slingsby Walk . . . C3
South Park Rd . . . C2
Spring Grove . . . A1
Springfield Ave . . . B1
Station Ave . . . B2
Station Parade . . . B2
Strawberry Dale . . . B2
Stray Rein . . . C3
Studley Rd . . . A2
Superstore . . . B2
Swan Rd . . . B1
The Parade . . . B2
The Stray . . . C2/C3
Tower St . . . C2
Trinity Rd . . . C2
Union St . . . B2
Valley Dr . . . C1
Valley Gardens . . . C1
Valley Mount . . . C1
Victoria Ave . . . C2
Victoria Rd . . . C1
Victoria Shopping Centre . . . B2
Waterloo St . . . A2
West Park . . . C2
West Park St . . . C2
Wood View . . . A1
Woodfield Ave . . . A3
Woodfield Dr . . . A3
Woodfield Grove . . . A3
Woodfield Rd . . . A3
Woodfield Square . . . A3
Woodside . . . B3
York Pl . . . C3
York Rd . . . B1

Hull 182

Adelaide St . . . C1
Albert Dock . . . C1
Albion St . . . B2
Alfred Gelder St . . . B2
Anlaby Rd . . . B1
Arctic Corsair . . . B3
Beverley Rd . . . A1
Blanket Row . . . C2
Bond St . . . B2
Bridlington Ave . . . A2
Brook St . . . B1
Brunswick Ave . . . A1
Bus Station . . . B1
Camilla Cl . . . C3
Cannon St . . . A2
Cannon's . . . C1
Caroline St . . . A2
Carr La . . . B2
Castle St . . . C2
Central Library . . . B1
Charles St . . . A2
Citadel Way . . . B3
City Hall . . . B2
City Hall Theatre . . . B2
Clarence St . . . B3
Cleveland St . . . A3
Clifton St . . . A1
Club Culture . . . C2
Colonial St . . . B1
Court . . . B2
Deep, The . . . C3
Dock Office Row . . . B3
Dock St . . . B2
Dinostar . . . C2
Drypool Bridge . . . B3
Egton St . . . A3
English St . . . C1
Ferens Gallery . . . B2
Ferensway . . . B1
Francis St . . . A2
Francis St West . . . A2
Freehold St . . . A1
Freetown Way . . . A2
Fruit Theatre . . . C2
Garrison Rd . . . B3
George St . . . B2
Gibson St . . . A2
Great Thornton St . . . B1
Great Union St . . . A3
Green La . . . A2
Grey St . . . A1
Grimston St . . . B2
Grosvenor St . . . A1
Guildhall . . . B2
Guildhall Rd . . . B2
Hands-on History . . . B2
Harley St . . . A1
Hessle Rd . . . C1
High St . . . B3
Holy Trinity . . . B2
Hull & East Riding Museum . . . B3
Hull Arena . . . C1
Hull College . . . B3
Hull History Centre . . . A2
Hull (Paragon) Sta . . . B1
Hull Truck Theatre . . . B1
Humber Dock Marina C2
Humber Dock St . . . C2
Humber St . . . C2
Hyperion St . . . A3
Information Ctr . . . B2
Jameson St . . . B1
Jarratt St . . . B2
Jenning St . . . A3
King Billy Statue . . . C2
King Edward St . . . B2
King St . . . A2
Kingston Retail Park C1
Kingston St . . . C2
Liddell St . . . A1
Lime St . . . A3
Lister St . . . C1
Lockwood St . . . A2
Maister House . . . B3
Maritime Mus . . . B2
Market . . . B2
Market Place . . . B2
Minerva Pier . . . C2
Mulgrave St . . . A3
Myton Bridge . . . C3
Myton St . . . B1
NAPA (Northern Academy of Performing Arts) . . . B1
Nelson St . . . C2
New Cleveland St . . . A3
New George St . . . A2
New Theatre . . . A2
Norfolk St . . . A1
North Bridge . . . A3
North St . . . B1
Odeon . . . C1
Old Harbour . . . C3
Osborne St . . . B1
Paragon St . . . B2
Park St . . . B1
Percy St . . . A2
Pier St . . . C2
Police Station . . . B2
Post Office . . . A1/B1/B2
Porter St . . . C1
Portland St . . . B1
Posterngate . . . B2
Prince's Quay . . . B2
Prospect Centre . . . B1
Prospect St . . . B1
Queen's Gdns . . . B2
Railway Dock Marina C2
Railway St . . . C2
Real . . . B1
Red Gallery . . . B1
Reform St . . . A2
Retail Park . . . B1
River Hull Footbridge B3
Riverside Quay . . . C2
Roper St . . . B2
St James St . . . C1
St Luke's St . . . B1
St Mark St . . . A3
St Mary the Virgin . . . B3
St Stephens Sh Ctr . . . B1
Scott St . . . A2
South Bridge Rd . . . B3
Spring Bank . . . A1
Spring St . . . B1
Spurn Lightship . . . C2
Spyvee St . . . A3
Streetlife Transport Museum . . . B3
Sykes St . . . A2
Tidal Surge Barrier . . . C3
Tower St . . . B3
Trinity House . . . B2
University . . . B2
Vane St . . . A1
Victoria Pier . . . C2
Waterhouse La . . . B2
Waterloo St . . . A1
Waverley St . . . C1
Wellington St . . . C2
Wellington St West . . . C2
West St . . . B1
Whitefriargate . . . B2
Wilberforce Dr . . . B2
Wilberforce Ho . . . B3
Wilberforce Monument . . . B3
William St . . . C1
Wincolmlee . . . A3
Witham . . . A3
Wright St . . . A1

Ipswich 182

Alderman Rd . . . B2
All Saints' Rd . . . A1
Alpe St . . . B2
Ancaster Rd . . . C1
Ancient House . . . B3
Anglesea Rd . . . B2
Ann St . . . B2
Arboretum . . . A2
Austin St . . . C2
Belstead Rd . . . C2
Berners St . . . B2
Bibb Way . . . B1
Birkfield Dr . . . C1
Black Horse La . . . B2
Bolton La . . . B3
Bond St . . . C3
Bowthorpe Cl . . . B2
Bramford La . . . A1
Bramford Rd . . . A1
Bridge St . . . C2
Brookfield Rd . . . A1
Brooks Hall Rd . . . A1
Broomhill . . . A2
Broomhill Rd . . . A1
Broughton Rd . . . A2
Bulwer Rd . . . B1
Burrell Rd . . . C2
Butter Market . . . B2
Buttermarket Shopping Ctr, The . . . B3
Cardinal Park Leisure Park . . . C2
Carr St . . . B3
Cecil Rd . . . B2
Cecilia St . . . C2
Chancery Rd . . . C2
Charles St . . . B2
Chevallier St . . . A1
Christchurch Mansion & Wolsey Art Gallery . . . B3
Christchurch Park . . . A3
Christchurch St . . . B3
Cineworld . . . C2
Civic Centre . . . B2
Civic Dr . . . B2
Clarkson St . . . B1
Cobbold St . . . B3
Commercial Rd . . . C2
Constable Rd . . . A3
Constantine Rd . . . C1
Constitution Hill . . . A2
Corder Rd . . . A3
Corn Exchange . . . B2
Cotswold Ave . . . A2
Council Offices . . . C2
County Hall . . . B3
Crown Court . . . C2
Crown St . . . B2
Cullingham Rd . . . B1
Cumberland St . . . B2

Curriers La B2
Dale Hall La A2
Dales View Rd A1
Dalton Rd B2
Dillwyn St B1
Elliot St B1
Elm St B2
Elsmere Rd A3
Falcon St C2
Felaw St C3
Flint Wharf C3
Fonnereau Rd B2
Fore St C3
Foundation St C3
Franciscan Way C2
Friars St C2
Gainsborough Rd A3
Gatacre Rd B1
Geneva Rd B2
Gippeswyk Ave C1
Gippeswyk Park C1
Grafton Way C2
Graham Rd A1
Grimwade St C3
Great Whip St C3
Handford Cut B1
Handford Rd B1
Henley Rd A2
Hervey St B3
High St B2
Holly Rd A2
Information Ctr B3
Ipswich Haven Marina C3
Ipswich School A2
Ipswich Station C2
Ipswich Town FC (Portman Road) C2
Ivry St A2
Kensington Rd A1
Kesteven Rd C1
Key St C3
Kingsfield Ave A3
Kitchener Rd A1
Magistrates Court B2
Little's Cr C2
London Rd B1
Low Brook St C3
Lower Orwell St C3
Luther Rd C2
Manor Rd A3
Mornington Ave A1
Mus & Art Gallery B2
Museum St B2
Neale St B3
New Cardinal St C2
New Cut East C3
New Cut West C3
New Wolsey B2
Newson St B2
Norwich Rd A1/B1
Oban St B2
Old Customs Ho C3
Old Foundry Rd B3
Old Merchant's House C3
Orford St B2
Paget Rd A2
Park Rd A3
Park View Rd A2
Peter's St C2
Philip Rd C2
Pine Ave A2
Pine View Rd A2
Police Station B2
Portman Rd B2
Portman Walk C1
Post Office B2/B3
Princes St C2
Prospect St B1
Queen St B2
Ranelagh Rd C1
Recreation Ground B1
Rectory Rd C2
Regent Theatre B3
Retail Park C1
Retail Park C2
Richmond Rd A1
Rope Walk C3
Rose La C2
Russell Rd C2
St Edmund's Rd A2
St George's St B2
St Helen's St B3
Sherrington Rd A1
Silent St C2
Sir Alf Ramsey Way C1
Sirdar Rd B1
Soane St B3
Springfield La A1
Star La C3
Stevenson Rd B1
Suffolk College C3
Suffolk Retail Park B1
Superstore B1
Surrey Rd B1
Tacket St C3
Tavern St B3
The Avenue A3
Tolly Cobbold Mus C3
Tower Ramparts B2
Tower Ramparts Shopping Centre B2
Tower St B3
Town Hall B2
Tuddenham Rd A3
Upper Brook St B3
Upper Orwell St B3
University C3
Valley Rd A2
Vermont Cr B3
Vermont Rd B3
Vernon St C3
Warrington Rd A2
Waterloo Rd A1
Waterworks St C3
Wellington St B1
West End Rd B1
Westerfield Rd A3
Westgate St B2
Westholme Rd A1
Westwood Ave A1
Willoughby Rd C2
Withipoll St B3
Woodbridge Rd B3
Woodstone Ave A3
Yarmouth Rd B1

Leeds 183

Aire St B3
Aireside Centre B2
Albion Pl B4
Albion St B4
Albion Way B1
Alma St A6
Arcades B4
Armley Rd B1
Back Burley Lodge Rd A1
Back Hyde Terr A2
Back Row C3
Bath Rd C3
Beckett St A6
Bedford St B3
Belgrave St A4
Belle View Rd A2
Benson St A5
Black Bull St C5
Blenheim Walk A3
Boar La B4
Bond St B4
Bow St C5
Bowman La C4
Brewery C4
Bridge St A5/B5
Briggate B4
Bruce Gdns C1
Burley Rd A1
Burley St B1
Burmantofts St B6
Bus & Coach Station B5
Butterly St C4
Butts Cr B4
Brewery Wharf C5
Byron St A5
Call La B4
Calverley St A3/B3
Canal St B1
Canal Wharf C3
Carlisle Rd C5
Cavendish Rd A1
Cavendish St A2
Chadwick St C5
Cherry Pl A6
Cherry Row A5
City Museum A4
City Palace of Varieties B4
City Sq B3
Civic Hall A3
Clarence Road C5
Clarendon Rd A2
Clarendon Way A3
Clark La C6
Clay Pit La A4
Cloberry St A2
Clyde Approach C1
Clyde Gdns C1
Coleman St C2
Commercial St B4
Concord St A5
Cookridge St A4
Copley Hill C1
Corn Exchange B4
Cromer Terr A2
Cromwell St A5
Cross Catherine St B6
Cross Green La C6
Cross Stamford St A5
Crown & County Courts A3
Crown Point Bridge C5
Crown Point Ret Pk C4
Crown Point Rd C4
David St C3
Dent St C6
Derwent Pl C3
Dial St C6
Dock St C4
Dolly La A6
Domestic St C2
Duke St B5
Duncan St B4
Dyer St C5
East Field St B6
East Pde B3
East St C5
Eastgate B5
Easy Rd C6
Edward St B4
Ellerby La C6
Ellerby Rd C6
Fenton St A3
Fire Station B2
Fish St B4
Flax Pl B5
Gelderd Rd C1
George St B4
Globe Rd C2
Gloucester Cr B1
Gower St A5
Grafton St A4
Grand Theatre B4
Granville Rd A6
Great George St A3
Great Wilson St C4
Greek St B3
Green La C1
Hanover Ave A2
Hanover La A2
Hanover Sq A2
Hanover Way A2
Harewood St B4
Harrison St B4
Haslewood Cl B6
Haslewood Drive B6
High Court B5
Holbeck La C2
Holdforth Cl C1
Holdforth Gdns B1
Holdforth Gr C1
Holdforth Pl C1
Holy Trinity B4
Hope Rd A5
Hunslet La C4
Hunslet Rd C4
Hyde Terr A2
Infirmary St B3
Information Ctr B3
Ingram Row C3
Junction St C4
Kelso Gdns A2
Kelso Rd A2
Kelso St A2
Kendal La A2
Kendell St C4
Kidacre St C4
King Edward St B4
King St B3
Kippax Pl C6
Kirkgate B4
Kirkgate Market B4
Kirkstall Rd A1
Kitson St C6
Lady La B4
Lands La B4
Lavender Walk B6
Leeds Art Gallery B3
Leeds Bridge C4
Leeds College of Music B5
Leeds General Infirmary (A&E) A3
Leeds Metropolitan University A3/A4
Leeds Museum Discovery Centre C5
Leeds Sh Plaza B4
Leeds Station B3
Leeds University A3
Library B3
Lincoln Green Rd A6
Lincoln Rd A6
Lindsey Gdns A6
Lindsey Rd A6
Lisbon St B3
Little Queen St B3
Long Close La C6
Lord St C2
Lovell Park A4
Lovell Park Rd A4
Lovell Rd A5
Lower Brunswick St A5
Mabgate A5
Macauly St A5
Magistrates Court A3
Manor Rd C3
Mark La B4
Marlborough St B2
Marsh La B5
Marshall St C3
Meadow La C4
Meadow Rd C4
Melbourne St A5
Merrion Centre A4
Merrion St A4
Merrion Way A4
Mill St B5
Millennium Sq A3
Mount Preston St A2
Mushroom St A5
Neville St C4
New Briggate A4/B4
New Market St B4
New Station St B4
New York Rd A5
New York St B5
Nile St A5
Nippet La A6
North St A4
Northern St B3
Oak Rd B1
Oxford Pl B3
Oxford Row A3
Park Cross St B3
Park La A2
Park Pl B3
Park Row B4
Park Sq B3
Park Sq East B3
Park Sq West B3
Park St B3
Police Station B5
Pontefract La B6
Portland Cr A3
Portland Way A3
Post Office B4/B5
Project Space Leeds C2
Quarry House (NHS/DSS Headquarters) B5
Quebec St B3
Queen St B3
Railway St B5
Rectory St A6
Regent St A5
Richmond St C5
Rigton Approach B6
Rigton Dr B6
Rillbank La A1
Rosebank Rd A1
Royal Armouries C5
Russell St B3
Rutland St B2
St Anne's Cath (RC) A4
St Anne's St B4
St James' Hospital A6
St Johns Centre B4
St John's Rd A2
St Mary's St B5
St Pauls St B3
St Peter's B5
Saxton La B5
Sayner La C5
Shakespeare Ave A6
Shannon St B6
Sheepscar St South A5
Siddall St C3
Skinner La A5
South Pde B3
Sovereign St C4
Spence La C2
Springfield Mount A2
Springwell Ct C2
Springwell Rd C2
Springwell St C2
Stoney Rock La A6
Studio Rd A1
Sutton St C2
Sweet St C3
Sweet St West C3
Swinegate B4
Templar St B5
The Calls B5
The Close B6
The Core B4
The Drive B6
The Garth B5
The Headrow B3/B4
The Lane B5
The Light B4
The Parade B6
The Tetley C4
Thoresby Pl A3
Torre Rd A6
Town Hall A3
Union Pl C3
Union St B5
Upper Accomodation Rd B6
Upper Basinghall St B4
Vicar La B4
Victoria Bridge C4
Victoria Quarter B4
Victoria Rd C4
Vue B4
Wade La A4
Washington St A1
Water La C3
Waterloo Rd C4
Wellington Rd B2/C1
Wellington St B3
West St B2
West Yorkshire Playhouse B5
Westfield Rd A1
Westgate B3
Whitehall Rd B3/C2
Whitelock St A5
Willis St C6
Willow Approach A1
Willow Ave A1
Willow Terrace Rd A3
Wintoun St A5
Woodhouse La A3/A4
Woodsley Rd A1
York Pl B3
York Rd B6
Yorkshire Television Studios A1

Leicester 182

Abbey St A2
All Saints' A1
Aylestone Rd C2
Bath La A1
Bede Park C1
Bedford St A3
Bedford St South A3
Belgrave Gate A2
Belle Vue A2
Belvoir St B2
Braunstone Gate B1
Burleys Way A2
Burnmoor St C2
Bus Station A2
Canning St A2
Carlton St C2
Castle B1
Castle Gardens B1
Cathedral B2
Causeway La A2
Charles St B3
Chatham St B2
Christow St A3
Church Gate A2
City Gallery B3
Civic Centre B2
Clank St B2
Clock Tower B2
Clyde St A3
Colton St B3
Conduit St B3
Crafton St A3
Craven St A1
Crown Courts B3
Curve B3
De Lux A2
De Montfort Hall C3
De Montfort St C3
De Montfort Univ C1
Deacon St C2
Dover St B3
Duns La B1
Dunton St A1
East St B3
Eastern Boulevard C1
Edmonton Rd A3
Erskine St A3
Filbert St C1
Filbert St East C2
Fire Station C3
Fleet St A3
Friar La B2
Friday St A2
Gateway St C2
Glebe St B3
Granby St B3
Grange La C2
Grasmere St C1
Great Central St A1
Guildhall B2
Guru Nanak Sikh Museum B1
Halford St B2
Havelock St C2
Haymarket Sh Ctr A2
High St A2
Highcross St A1
Highcross Sh Ctr A2
HM Prison C2
Horsefair St B2
Humberstone Gate B2
Humberstone Rd A3
Infirmary St C2
Information Ctr B2
Jarrom St C2
Jewry Wall B1
Kamloops Cr A3
King Richards Rd B1
King St B2
Lancaster Rd C3
LCB Depot B3
Lee St A3
Leicester Royal Infirmary (A&E) C2
Leicester Station B3
Library B2
Little Theatre, The B3
London Rd C3
Lower Brown St B2
Magistrates Court B2
Manitoba Rd A3
Mansfield St A2
Market B2
Market St B2
Mill La C2
Montreal Rd A3
Narborough Rd N B1
Nelson Mandela Pk C2
New Park St B1
New St B2
New Walk C3
New Walk Museum & Art Gallery C3
Newarke Houses B2
Newarke St B2
Northgate St A1
Orchard St A2
Ottawa Rd A3
Oxford St C2
Upper Brown St B2
Phoenix Square B3
Police Station A3
Post Office A1/B2/C2/C3
Prebend St C3
Princess Rd East C3
Princess Rd West C3
Queen St B3
Regent College C3
Regent Rd C2/C3
Repton St A1
Rutland St B3
St George St B3
St Georges Way B3
St John St A2
St Margaret's A2
St Margaret's Way A2
St Martins B2
St Mary de Castro B1
St Matthew's Way A3
St Nicholas B1
St Nicholas Circle B1
Sanvey Gate A2
Silver St B2
Slater St A1
Soar La A1
South Albion St B3
Southampton St B3
Swain St B3
Swan St A1
The Gateway C2
The Newarke B1
The Rally Com Park A2
Tigers Way C3
Tower St C3
Town Hall B2
Tudor Rd B1
Univ of Leicester C3
University Rd C3
Upperton Rd C1
Vaughan Way A2
Walnut St C2
Watling St A2
Welford Rd B2
Welford Rd Stadium C2
Wellington St B2
West Bridge B1
West St C3
West Walk C3
Western Boulevard C1
Western Rd C1
Wharf St North A3
Wharf St South A3
Y' Theatre, The B3
Yeoman St B3
York Rd B2

Lincoln 186

Alexandra Terr B1
Anchor St C1
Arboretum B3
Arboretum Ave B3
Baggholme Rd B3
Bailgate A2
Beaumont Fee B1
Brayford Way C1
Brayford Wharf East C1
Brayford Wharf North B1
Bruce Rd A2
Burton Rd A1
Bus Station (City) C2
Canwick Rd C2
Cardinal's Hat B2
Carline Rd B1
Castle B1
Castle St A1
Cathedral B2
Cathedral St B2
Cecil St A2
Chapel La A2
Cheviot St B3
Church La A2
City Hall B1
Clasketgate B2
Clayton Sports Gd A3
Coach Park C2
Collection, The B2
County Hospital (A&E) B3
County Office B1
Courts C1
Croft St B2
Cross St C2
Crown Courts B1
Curle Ave A3
Danesgate B2
Drill Hall B2
Drury La B1
East Bight A2
East Gate A2
Eastcliff Rd B3
Eastgate B2
Egerton Rd A3
Ellis Windmill A1
Engine Shed, The C1
Environment Agency C2
Exchequer Gate B2
Firth Rd C1
Flaxengate B2
Florence St B3
George St C3
Good La A2
Gray St A1
Great Northern Terr C3
Great Northern Terr Industrial Estate C3
Greetwell Rd B3
Greetwellgate B3
Haffenden Rd A2
High St B2/C1
HM Prison A3
Hospital (Private) A2
Hungate B2
James St A2
Jews House & Ct B2
Kesteven St C2
Langworthgate A2
Lawn Visitor Centre, The B1
Lee Rd A3
Library B2
Lincoln College B2
Lincoln Central Station C2
Lincolnshire Life/Royal Lincolnshire Regiment Mus A1
Lindum Rd B2
Lindum Sports Gd A3
Lindum Terr B3
Mainwaring Rd A3
Manor Rd A2
Market C2
Massey Rd A3
Medieval Bishop's Palace B2
Mildmay St A1
Mill Rd A1
Millman Rd B3
Minster Yard B2
Monks Rd B3
Montague St B2
Mount St A1
Nettleham Rd A2
Newland B1
Newport A2
Newport Arch A2
Newport Cemetery A2
Northgate A2
Odeon C1
Orchard St B1
Oxford St C2
Park St B1
Pelham Bridge C2
Pelham St C2
Police Station B1
Portland St C2
Post Office A1/A2/B1/B3/C2
Potter Gate B2
Priory Gate B2
Queensway A3
Rasen La A1
Ropewalk C1
Rosemary La B2
St Anne's Rd B3
St Benedict's C1
St Giles Ave A3
St John's Rd A2
St Marks St C1
St Mark's Sh Ctr C1
St Mary-Le-Wigford C1
St Mary's St C2
St Nicholas St A2
St Swithin's B2
Saltergate C1
Saxon St A1
Sch of Art & Design B2
Sewell Rd B3
Silver St B2
Sincil St C2
Spital St A2
Spring Hill B1
Stamp End C3
Steep Hill B2
Stonebow & Guildhall C2
Stonefield Ave A2
Tentercroft St C1
The Avenue B1
The Grove A3
Theatre Royal B2
Tritton Retail Park C1
Tritton Rd C1
Union Rd B1
University of Lincoln C1
Upper Lindum St B3
Upper Long Leys Rd A1
Usher B2
Vere St A2
Victoria St B1
Victoria Terr B1
Vine St B3
Wake St A1
Waldeck St A1
Waterside Sh Ctr C2
Waterside North C2
Waterside South C2
West Pde B1
Westgate A2
Wigford Way C1
Williamson St A2
Wilson St A1
Winn St B3
Wragby Rd A3
Yarborough Rd A1

Liverpool 183

Abercromby Sq C5
Acc Liverpool C2
Addison St A3
Adelaide Rd B6
Ainsworth St B4
Albany Rd B6
Albert Dock C2
Albert Edward Rd B6
Angela St C6
Anson St B4
Archbishop Blanche High School B6
Argyle St C3
Arrad St C4
Ashton St B5
Audley St A4
Back Leeds St A2
Basnett St B3
Bath St A1
Beatles Story C2
Beckwith St C3
Bedford Close C5
Bedford St North C5
Bedford St South C5
Benson St C4
Berry St C4
Birkett St A4
Bixteth St B2
Blackburne Place C4
Bluecoat B3
Bold Place C4
Bold St C4
Bolton St B3
Bridport St B4
Bronte St B4
Brook St A1
Brownlow Hill B4/B5
Brownlow St B5
Brunswick Rd A5
Brunswick St B1
Bus Station C2
Butler Cr A6
Byrom St A3
Caledonia St C4
Cambridge St C5
Camden St A4
Canada Blvd B1
Canning Dock C2
Canterbury St A4
Cardwell St C6
Carver St A4
Cases St B3
Castle St B2
Catherine St C5
Cavern Club B3
Central Library A3
Central Station B3
Chapel St B2
Charlotte St B3
Chatham Place C6
Chatham St C5
Cheapside B2
Chestnut St C5
Christian St A3
Church St B3
Churchill Way North A3
Churchill Way South B3
Clarence St B4
Coach Station A4
Cobden St A5
Cockspur St A2
College St C3
College St North A5
College St South A5
Colquitt St C4
Comus St A3
Concert St C3
Connaught Rd B6
Cook St B2
Copperas Hill B4
Cornwallis St C3
Covent Garden B2
Craven St A4
Cropper St B3
Crown St B5/C6
Cumberland St B2
Cunard Building B1
Dale St B2
Dansie St B4
Daulby St B5
Dawson St B3
Derby Sq B2
Drury La B2
Duckinfield St B4
Duke St C3
Earle St A2
East St A2
Eaton St A2
Echo Arena C2
Edgar St A3
Edge La B6
Edinburgh Rd A6
Edmund St B2
Elizabeth St B5
Elliot St B3
Empire Theatre B4
Empress Rd B6
Epworth St A5
Erskine St A5
Everyman Theatre C5
Exchange St East B2
Fact Centre, The C4
Falkland St A5
Falkner St C5/C6
Farnworth St A6
Fenwick St B2
Fielding St A6
Fleet St C3
Fraser St A4
Freemasons Row A2
Gardner Row A3
Gascoyne St A2
George Pier Head C1
George St B2
Gibraltar Road A1
Gilbert St C3
Gildart St A4
Gill St B4
Goree B2
Gower St C2
Gradwell St C3
Great Crosshall St A3
Great George St C4
Great Howard St A1
Great Newton St B4
Greek St B4
Green La B4
Greenside A5
Greetham St C3
Gregson St A5
Grenville St C3
Grinfield St C6
Grove St C5
Guelph St A6
Hackins Hey B2
Haigh St A4
Hall La B6
Hanover St B3
Harbord St C6
Hardman St C4
Harker St A4
Hart St B4
Hatton Garden A2
Hawke St B4
Helsby St B6
Henry St C3
HM Customs & Excise National Mus C2
Highfield St A2
Highgate St B6
Hilbre St B4
Hope Place C4
Hope St C4
Houghton St B3
Hunter St A3
Hutchinson St A6
Information Ctr C2
Institute For The Performing Arts C4
Irvine St B6
Irwell St B2
Islington A4
James St B2
James St Station B2
Jenkinson St A4
Johnson St A3
Jubilee Drive B6
Kempston St A4
Kensington A6
Kensington Gdns B6
Kensington St A6
Kent St C3
King Edward St A1
Kinglake St B6
Knight St C4
Lace St A3
Langsdale St A4
Law Courts C2
Leece St C4
Leeds St A2
Leopold Rd B6
Lime St B3
Lime St Station B4
Little Woolton St B5
Liver St C2
Liverpool John Moores University A3/B4/C4
Liverpool Landing Stage B1
Liverpool One C2
London Rd A4/B4
Lord Nelson St B4
Lord St B2
Lovat St C6
Low Hill A5
Low Wood St A6
Lydia Ann St C3
Mansfield St A4
Marmaduke St B6
Marsden St A6
Martensen St B6
Marybone A3
Maryland St C4
Mason St B6
Mathew St B2
May St B4
Melville Place C6
Merseyside Maritime Museum C2
Metquarter B3
Metropolitan Cathedral (RC) B5
Midghall St A2
Molyneux Rd A6
Moor Place B4
Moorfields B2
Moorfields Sta B2
Moss St A5
Mount Pleasant B4/B5
Mount St C4
Mount Vernon B6
Mulberry St C5
Municipal Buildings B2
Mus of Liverpool C2
Myrtle Gdns C6
Myrtle St C5
Naylor St A2
Nelson St C4
Neptune Theatre B3
New Islington A4
New Quay B1
Newington St C3
North John St B2
North St A3
North View B6
Norton St A4
Oakes St B5
O2 Academy
Odeon B4
Old Hall St A1
Old Leeds St A2
Oldham Place C4
Oldham St C4
Olive St C6
Open Eye Gallery C3
Oriel St A2
Ormond St B2
Orphan St C6
Overbury St C6
Overton St B6
Oxford St C5
Paisley St A1
Pall Mall A2
Paradise St C3
Park La C3
Parker St B3
Parr St C3
Peach St B5
Pembroke Place B4
Pembroke St B5
Philharmonic Hall C5
Pickop St A2
Pilgrim St C4
Pitt St C3
Playhouse Theatre B3
Pleasant St B4
Police HQ C2
Police Station A4/B4
Pomona St B4
Port of Liverpool Building B2
Post Office A2/A4/A5/A6/B2/B3/B4/C4
Pownall St C2
Prescot St A5
Preston St B3
Princes Dock A1
Princes Gdns A2
Princes Jetty A1
Princes Pde B1
Princes St B2
Pythian St A6
Queen Square Bus Station B3
Queensland St C6
Queensway Tunnel (Docks exit) B1
Queensway Tunnel (Entrance) B3
Radio City B2
Ranelagh St B3
Redcross St B2
Renfrew St B6
Renshaw St B4
Richmond Row A4
Richmond St B3
Rigby St A2
Roberts St A1
Rock St B4
Rodney St C4
Rokeby St A4
Romily St A6
Roscoe La C4
Roscoe St C4
Rose Hill A3
Royal Ct Theatre B3
Royal Liver Building B1
Royal Liverpool Hospital (A&E) B5
Royal Mail St B4
Rumford Place B2
Rumford St B2
Russell St B4
St Andrew St B4
St Anne St A4
St Georges Hall B3
St John's Centre B3
St John's Gdns B3
St John's La B3
St Joseph's Cr A4
St Minishull St B5
St Nicholas Place B1
St Paul's Sq A2
St Vincent Way B4
Salisbury St A4
Salthouse Dock C2
Salthouse Quay C2
Sandon St C5
Saxony Rd B6
Schomberg St A6
School La B2
Seel St C3
Seymour St B4
Shaw St A5
Sidney Place C6
Sir Thomas St B3
Skelhorne St B4
Slater St C3
Slavery Museum C2
Smithdown La B6
Soho Sq A4
Soho St A4
South John St B2
Springfield A4
Stafford St A4
Standish St A3
Stanley St B2
Strand St C2
Suffolk St C3
Tabley St C3
Tarleton St B3
Tate Gallery C2
Teck St B6
Temple St B2
The Beacon B3
The Strand B2
Tithebarn St B2
Town Hall B2
Traffic Police HQ C6
Trowbridge St B4
Trueman St A3
Union St B2
Unity Theatre C4
University C5
Univ of Liverpool B5
Upper Duke St C4
Upper Frederick St C3
Upper Baker St A6
Vauxhall Rd A2
Vernon St B2
Victoria Gallery & Museum B5
Victoria St B2
Vine St C5
Wakefield St A4
Walker Art Gallery A3
Walker St A6
Wapping C2
Water St B1/B2
Waterloo Rd A1
Wavertree Rd B6
West Derby Rd A6
West Derby St B5
Whitechapel B3
Western Approaches War Museum B2
Whitley Gdns A5
William Brown St B3
William Henry St A4
Williamson Sq B3
Williamson St B3
Williamson's Tunnels Heritage Centre C6
Women's Hospital C6
Wood St B3
World Museum, Liverpool A3
York St C3

London 184

Abbey Orchard St E3
Abchurch La D6
Abingdon St E4
Achilles Way D2
Acton St B4
Addington St E4
Air St D3
Albany St B2
Albemarle St D3
Albert Embankment F4
Aldenham St A3
Aldersgate St C6
Alford St D2
Aldgate C7
Aldgate High St C7
Aldwych C4
Allsop Pl B1
Amwell St B5
Andrew Borde St C3
Angel A5
Appold St C7
Argyle Sq B4
Argyle St B4
Argyll St C3
Arnold Circus B7
Artillery La C7
Artillery Row E3
Association of Photographers Gallery B6
Baker St B1
Baker St B1
Baldwin's Gdns C5
Baltic St B6
Bank C6
Bank Museum C6
Bank of England C6
Bankside D6
Bankside Gallery D5
Banner St B6
Barbican C6
Barbican Gallery C6
Basil St E1
Bastwick St B6
Bateman's Row B7
Bath St B6
Bayley St C3
Baylis Rd E5
Beak St D3
Bedford Row C4
Bedford Sq C3
Bedford St D4
Bedford Way B3
Beech St C6
Belgrave Pl E2
Belgrave Sq E2
Bell La C7
Belvedere Rd E4
Berkeley Sq D2
Berkeley St D2
Bernard St B4
Berners Pl C3
Berners St C3
Berwick St C3
Bethnal Green Rd B7
Bevenden St B6
Bevis Marks C7
BFI (British Film Institute) D4
BFI London IMAX Cinema D5
Bidborough St B4
Binney St C2
Birdcage Walk E3
Bishopsgate C7
Blackfriars D5
Blackfriars Bridge D5
Blackfriars Rd E5
Blandford St C1
Blomfield St C6
Bloomsbury St C3
Bloomsbury Way C4
Bolton St D2
Bond St C2
Borough High St E6
Boswell St C4
Bow St C4
Bowling Green La B5
Brad St D5
Bressenden Pl E3
Brewer St D3
Brick St D2
Bridge St E4
Britannia Walk B6
British Film Institute (BFI) D4
British Library B3
British Museum C4
Britton St B5
Broad Sanctuary E3
Broadway E3
Brook Dr F5
Brook St D2
Brunswick Pl B6
Brunswick Sq B4
Brushfield St C7
Bruton St D2
Bryanston St C1
BT Centre C6
Buckingham Gate E3
Buckingham Palace E3
Buckingham Pal Rd F2
Bunhill Row B6
Byward St D7

Cabinet War Rooms & Churchill Mus E3
Cadogan La E2
Cadogan Pl E1
Cadogan Sq F1
Caledonian Rd A4
Calshot St A4
Calthorpe St B4
Calvert Ave B7
Cambridge Circus C3
Camomile St C7
Cannon St D6
Cannon St D6
Carey St C4
Carlisle La E4
Carlisle Pl E3
Carlton House Terr D3
Carmelite St D5
Carnaby St C3
Carter La C5
Carthusian St C6
Cartwright Gdns B4
Castle Baynard St D5
Cavendish Pl C2
Cavendish Sq C2
Caxton Hall E3
Caxton St E3
Central St B6
Chalton St B3
Chancery Lane C5
Chapel St E2
Charing Cross D4
Charing Cross Rd C3
Charles II St D3
Charles Sq B6
Charles St D2
Charlotte Rd B7
Charlotte St C3
Chart St B6
Charterhouse Sq C5
Charterhouse St C5
Cheapside C6
Chenies St C3
Chesham St E2
Chester Sq F2
Chesterfield Hill D2
Chiltern St C2
Chiswell St C6
City Garden Row A5
City Rd B6
City Thameslink C5
City University, The B5
Claremont Sq A5
Clarges St D2
Clerkenwell Cl B5
Clerkenwell Green B5
Clerkenwell Rd B5
Cleveland St C3
Clifford St D3
Clink Prison Mus D6
Clock Museum C6
Club Row B7
Cockspur St D3
Coleman St C6
Columbia Rd B7
Commercial St C7
Compton St B5
Conduit St D2
Constitution Hill E2
Copperfield St E5
Coptic St C4
Cornhill C6
Cornwall Rd D5
Coronet St B7
Courtauld Gallery D4
Covent Garden D4
Covent Garden D4
Cowcross St C5
Cowper St B6
Cranbourn St D3
Craven St D4
Crawford St C1
Creechurch La C7
Cremer St A7
Cromer St B4
Cumberland Gate D1
Cumberland Terr A2
Curtain Rd B7
Curzon St D2
D'arblay St C3
Davies St C2
Dean St C3
Deluxe Gallery B7
Denmark St C3
Dering St C2
Devonshire St C2
Diana, Princess of Wales Memorial Walk E3
Dingley Rd B6
Dorset St C1
Doughty St B4
Dover St D2
Downing St E4
Druid St E7
Drummond St B3
Drury La C4
Drysdale St B7
Duchess St C2
Dufferin St B6
Duke of Wellington Place E2
Duke St C2
Duke St D3
Duke St Hill D6
Duke's Place C7
Duncannon St D4
East Rd B6
Eastcastle St C3
Eastcheap D7
Eastman Dental Hospital B4
Eaton Place E2
Eaton Square E2
Eccleston St E2
Edgware Rd C1
Eldon St C6
Embankment D4
Endell St C4
Endsleigh Pl B3
Euston B3
Euston Rd B3
Euston Square B3
Evelina Children's Hospital E4
Eversholt St A3
Exmouth Market B5
Fann St B6
Farringdon C5
Farringdon Rd C5
Farringdon St C5
Featherstone St B6
Fenchurch St D7
Fenchurch St D7
Fetter La C5
Finsbury Circus C6
Finsbury Pavement C6
Finsbury Sq B6
Fitzalan St F5
Fitzmaurice Pl D2
Fleet St C5
Floral St D4
Florence Nightingale Museum E4
Folgate St C7
Foot Hospital B3
Fore St C6
Foster La C6
Francis St F3
Frazier St E5
Freemason's Hall C4
Friday St C6
Gainsford St E7
Garden Row E5
Gee St B6
George St C1
Gerrard St D3
Giltspur St C5
Glasshouse St D3
Gloucester Pl C1
Golden Hinde D6
Golden La B6
Golden Sq D3
Goodge St C3
Goodge St C3
Gordon Sq B3
Goswell Rd B5
Gough St B4
Goulston St C7
Gower St B3
Gracechurch St D6
Grafton Way B3
Gray's Inn Rd B4
Great College St E4
Great Cumberland Pl C1
Great Eastern St B7
Great Guildford St D6
Great Marlborough St C3
Great Ormond St B4
Great Ormond St Children's Hospl B4
Great Percy St B4
Great Peter St E3
Great Portland St B2
Great Portland St C2
Great Queen St C4
Great Russell St C3
Great Scotland Yd D4
Great Smith St E3
Great Suffolk St E5
Great Titchfield St C3
Great Tower St D7
Great Windmill St D3
Greek St C3
Green Park D3
Green St D2
Greencoat Pl F3
Gresham St C6
Greville St B4/C5
Greycoat Hosp Sch E3
Greycoat Pl E3
Grosvenor Cres E2
Grosvenor Gdns E2
Grosvenor Pl E2
Grosvenor Sq D2
Grosvenor St D2
Guards Museum and Chapel E3
Guildhall Art Gallery C6
Guilford St B4
Guy's Hospital D6
Haberdasher St B6
Hackney Rd B7
Half Moon St D2
Halkin St E2
Hall St B5
Hallam St C2
Hampstead Rd B3
Hanover Sq C2
Hans Cres E1
Hanway St C3
Hardwick St B5
Harley St C2
Harrison St B4
Hastings St B4
Hatfields D5
Hayles St F5
Haymarket D3
Hayne St C5
Hay's Galleria D7
Hay's Mews D2
Hayward Gallery D4
Helmet Row B6
Herbrand St B4
Hercules Rd E4
Hertford St D2
High Holborn C4
Hill St D2
HMS Belfast D7
Hobart Pl E2
Holborn C4
Holborn C5
Holborn Viaduct C5
Holland St D5
Holmes Mus B1
Holywell La B7
Horse Guards' Rd D3
Houndsditch C7
Houses of Parliament E4
Howland St C3
Hoxton Sq B7
Hoxton St B7
Hunter St B4
Hunterian Mus C4
Hyde Park D1
Hyde Park Cnr E2
Imperial War Mus E5
Inner Circle B2
Inst of Archaeology (London Univ) B2
Ironmonger Row B6
James St C2
James St D4
Jermyn St D3
Jockey's Fields C4
John Carpenter St D5
John St B4
Judd St B4
Kennington Rd E5
King Charles St E4
King's Coll London D5
King St D3
King St C6
King William St C6
Kingley St C3
King's Cross A4
King's Cross Rd B4
King's Cross St Pancras A4
King's Rd E2
Kingsland Rd B7
Kingsway C4
Kinnerton St E2
Knightsbridge E1
Lamb St C7
Lambeth Bridge F4
Lambeth High St F4
Lambeth North E5
Lambeth Palace E4
Lambeth Palace Rd E4
Lambeth Rd E5
Lambeth Walk F4
Lamb's Conduit St C4
Lancaster Pl D4
Langham Pl C2
Leadenhall St C7
Leake St E4
Leather La C5
Leicester Sq D3
Leicester St D3
Leonard St B6
Lever St B6
Lexington St D3
Lidlington Pl A3
Lime St D7
Lincoln's Inn Fields C4
Lindsey St C5
Lisle St D3
Liverpool St C7
Liverpool St C7
Lloyd Baker St B5
Lloyd Sq B5
Lombard St C6
London Aquarium E4
London Bridge D6
London Bridge Hospital D6
London City Hall D7
London Dungeon, The E4
London Film Mus E4
London Guildhall University C6
London Rd E5
London Transport Museum D4
London Wall C6
London-Eye E4
Long Acre D4
Long La C5
Longford St B2
Lower Belgrave St E2
Lower Grosvenor Pl E2
Lower Marsh E5
Lower Thames St D6
Lowndes St E2
Ludgate Circus C5
Ludgate Hill C5
Luxborough St C2
Lyall St E2
Macclesfield Rd B6
Madame Tussaud's B2
Maddox St D2
Malet St C3
Manchester Sq C2
Manchester St C2
Mandeville Pl C2
Mansell St D7
Mansion House D6
Mansion House D6
Maple St C3
Marble Arch C1
Marble Arch D1
Marchmont St B4
Margaret St C3
Margery St B5
Mark La D7
Marlborough Rd D3
Marshall St C3
Marsham St E3
Marylebone High St C2
Marylebone La C2
Marylebone Rd B2
Marylebone St C2
Mecklenburgh Sq B4
Middle Temple La C5
Middlesex St (Petticoat La) C7
Midland Rd A3
Minories C7
Monck St E3
Monmouth St C4
Montagu Pl C1
Montagu Sq C1
Montagu St C4
Montague Pl C3
Monument D6
Monument St D6
Monument, The D6
Moor La C6
Moorfields C6
Moorfields Eye Hospital B6
Moorgate C6
Moorgate C6
Moreland St B5
Morley St E5
Mortimer St C3
Mount Pleasant B5
Mount St D2
Murray Gr A6
Museum of Garden History E4
Mus of London C6
Museum St C4
Myddelton Sq B5
Myddelton St B5
National Gallery D3
National Hospital B4
National Portrait Gallery D3
Neal St C4
Nelson's Column D4
New Bond St C2/D2
New Bridge St C5
New Cavendish St C2
New Change C6
New Fetter La C5
New Inn Yard B7
New North Rd A6
New Oxford St C3
New Scotland Yard E3
New Sq C4
Newgate St C5
Newton St C4
Nile St B6
Noble St C6
Noel St C3
North Audley St D2
North Cres C3
North Row D2
Northampton Sq B5
Northington St B4
Northumberland Ave D4
Norton Folgate C7
Nottingham Pl C2
Obstetric Hosp B3
Old Bailey C5
Old Broad St C6
Old Compton St C3
Old County Hall E4
Old Gloucester St C4
Old King Edward St C6
Old Nichol St B7
Old Paradise St F4
Old Spitalfields Mkt C7
Old St B6
Old St B6
Old Vic E5
Open Air Theatre B2
Operating Theatre Museum D6
Orange St D3
Orchard St C2
Ossulston St A3
Outer Circle B1
Oxford Circus C3
Oxford St C2/C3
Paddington St C2
Palace St E3
Pall Mall D3
Pall Mall East D3
Pancras Rd A4
Panton St D3
Paris Gdn D5
Park Cres B2
Park La D2
Park Rd B1
Park St D2
Park St D6
Parker St C4
Parliament Sq E4
Parliament St E4
Paternoster Sq C5
Paul St B6
Pear Tree St B5
Penton Rise B4
Penton St A5
Pentonville Rd A4/A5
Percival St B5
Petticoat La (Middlesex St) C7
Petty France E3
Phoenix Pl B4
Phoenix Rd A3
Photo Gallery D3
Piccadilly D2
Piccadilly Circus D3
Pitfield St B7
Pollock's Toy Mus C3
Polygon Rd A3
Pont St E1
Portland Pl C2
Portman Mews C2
Portman Sq C2
Portman St C1
Portugal St C4
Poultry C6
Primrose St C7
Princes St C6
Procter St C4
Provost St B6
Quaker St B7
Queen Anne St C2
Queen Elizabeth Hall D4
Queen Sq B4
Queen St D6
Queen Street Pl D6
Queen Victoria St D5
Queens Gallery E3
Radnor St B6
Rathbone Pl C3
Rawstorne St B5
Red Lion Sq C4
Red Lion St C4
Redchurch St B7
Redcross Way D6
Regency St F3
Regent Sq B4
Regent St C3
Regent's Park B2
Richmond Terr E4
Ridgmount St C3
Rivington St B7
Robert St B2
Rochester Row F3
Ropemaker St C6
Rosebery Ave B5
Roupell St D5
Royal Acad of Arts D3
Royal Academy of Dramatic Art B3
Royal Acad of Music B2
Royal Artillery Memorial E2
Royal Coll of Nursing C2
Royal College of Surgeons C4
Royal Festival Hall D4
Royal London Hospital for Integrated Medicine C4
Royal National Theatre D5
Royal National Throat, Nose and Ear Hospital B4
Royal Opera House D4
Russell Sq B3
Russell Square B4
Sackville St D3
Sadlers Wells B5
Saffron Hill C5
Savile Row D3
Savoy Pl D4
Savoy St D4
School of Hygiene & Tropical Medicine C3
Scrutton St B7
Sekforde St B5
Serpentine Rd D1
Seven Dials C4
Seward St B5
Seymour St C1
Shad Thames D7
Shaftesbury Ave D3
Shakespeare's Globe Theatre D6
Shepherd Market D2
Sherwood St D3
Shoe La C5
Shoreditch High St B7
Shoreditch High St B7
Shorts Gdns C4
Sidmouth St B4
Silk St C6
Sir John Soane's Museum C4
Skinner St B5
Sloane St E1
Snow Hill C5
Soho Sq C3
Somerset House D4
South Audley St D2
South Carriage Dr E1
South Molton St C2
South Pl C6
South St D2
Southampton Row C4
Southampton St D4
Southwark D5
Southwark Bridge D6
Southwark Bridge Rd D6
Southwark Cath D6
Southwark St D6
Speakers' Corner D1
Spencer St B5
Spital Sq C7
St Alban's St D3
St Andrew St C5
St Bartholomew's Hospital C5
St Botolph St C7
St Bride St C5
St George's Circus E5
St George's Rd E5
St Giles High St C3
St James's Palace D3
St James's Park E3
St James's St D3
St John St B5
St Margaret St E4
St Mark's Hosp B5
St Martin's La D4
St Martin's Le Grand C6
St Mary Axe C7
St Pancras Int A4
St Paul's C6
St Paul's Cath C6
St Paul's Churchyard C5
St Peter's Hosp D4
St Thomas' Hosp E4
St Thomas St D6
Stamford St D5
Stanhope St B3
Stephenson Way B3
Stock Exchange C5
Stoney St D6
Strand C5
Stratton St D2
Sumner St D5
Sutton's Way B6
Swanfield St B7
Swinton St B4
Tabernacle St B6
Tate Modern D6
Tavistock Pl B4
Tavistock Sq B3
Tea & Coffee Mus D6
Temple D5
Temple Ave D5
Temple Pl D4
Terminus Pl E2
Thayer St C2
The Barbican Centre for Arts C5
The Brunswick Sh Ctr B4
The Cut E5
The Mall E3
Theobald's Rd C4
Thorney St F4
Threadneedle St C6
Throgmorton St C6
Tonbridge St B4
Tooley St D7
Torrington Pl B3
Tothill St E3
Tottenham Court Rd B3
Tottenham Ct Rd C3
Tottenham St C3
Tower Bridge D7
Tower Bridge App D7
Tower Bridge Rd E7
Tower Hill D7
Tower Hill D7
Tower of London, The D7
Toynbee St C7
Trafalgar Square D3
Trinity Sq D7
Trocadero Centre D3
Tudor St D5
Turnmill St C5
Ufford St E5
Union St D5
Univ Coll Hospl B3
University of London C3
Univ of Westminster C2
University St B3
Upper Belgrave St E2
Upper Berkeley St C1
Upper Brook St D2
Upper Grosvenor St D2
Upper Ground D5
Upper Montague St C1
Upper St Martin's La D4
Upper Thames St D6
Upper Wimpole St C2
Upper Woburn Pl B3
Vere St C2
Vernon Pl C4
Vestry St B6
Victoria E2
Victoria Emb D4
Victoria Pl Sh Ctr F2
Victoria St E3
Villiers St D4
Vincent Sq F3
Vinopolis City of Wine D6
Virginia Rd B7
Wakley St B5
Walbrook C6
Wallace Collection C2
Wardour St C3/D3
Warner St B5
Warren St B3
Warren St B3
Waterloo E5
Waterloo Bridge D4
Waterloo East D5
Waterloo Rd E5
Watling St C6
Webber St E5
Welbeck St C2
Wellington Arch E2
Wellington Mus E2
Wells St C3
Wenlock St A6
Wentworth St C7
West Smithfield C5
West Sq E5
Westminster E4
Westminster Abbey E4
Westminster Bridge E4
Westminster Bridge Rd E5
Westminster Cathedral (RC) E3
Westminster City Hall E3
Westminster Hall E4
Weymouth St C2
Wharf Rd A6
Wharton St B4
Whitcomb St D3
White Cube B7
White Lion Hill D5
White Lion St A5
Whitecross St B6
Whitefriars St C5
Whitehall D4
Whitehall Pl D4
Wigmore Hall C2
Wigmore St C2
William IV St D4
Wilmington Sq B5
Wilson St C6
Wilton Cres E2
Wimpole St C2
Windmill Walk D5
Woburn Pl B4
Woburn Sq B3
Women's Hosp C6
Wood St C6
Woodbridge St B5
Wootton St D5
Wormwood St C7
Worship St B6
Wren St B4
Wynyatt St B5
York Rd E4
York St C1
York Terrace East B2
York Terrace West B2
York Way A4

Luton 186

Adelaide St B1
Albert Rd C2
Alma St B2
Alton Rd C3
Anthony Gdns C1
Arthur St C2
Ashburnham Rd B1
Ashton Rd C2
Avondale Rd A1
Back St A2
Bailey St C3
Baker St C2
Biscot Rd A1
Bolton Rd B3
Boyle Cl A2
Brantwood Rd B1
Bretts Mead C1
Bridge St B2
Brook St A1
Brunswick St A3
Burr St A3
Bury Park Rd A1
Bute St B2
Buxton Rd B2
Cambridge St C3
Cardiff Grove B1
Cardiff Rd B1
Cardigan St A2
Castle St B2/C2
Chapel St C2
Charles St A3
Chase St C2
Cheapside B2
Chequer St C3
Chiltern Rise C1
Church St B2/B3
Cinema A2
Cobden St A3
Collingdon St A1
Community Centre C3
Concorde Ave A3
Corncastle Rd C1
Cowper St C2
Crawley Green Rd B3
Crawley Rd A1
Crescent Rise A3
Crescent Rd A3
Cromwell Rd A1
Cross St A2
Crown Court B2
Cumberland St B2
Cutenhoe Rd C3
Dallow Rd B1
Downs Rd B1
Dudley St A2
Duke St A2
Dumfries St B1
Dunstable Place B2
Dunstable Rd A1/B1
Edward St A3
Elizabeth St C2
Essex Cl C3
Farley Hill C1
Farley Lodge C1
Flowers Way B2
Francis St A1
Frederick St A2
Galaxy L Complex A2
George St B2
George St West B2
Gillam St A3
Gordon St B2
Grove Rd B1
Guildford St A2
Haddon Rd A3
Harcourt St C2
Hart Hill Drive A3
Hart Hill Lane A3
Hartley Rd A3
Hastings St B2
Hat Factory, The B2
Hatters Way A1
Havelock Rd A2
Hibbert St C2
High Town Rd A3
Highbury Rd A1
Hightown Com Sports & Arts Ctr A3
Hillary Cres C1
Hillborough Rd C1
Hitchin Rd A3
Holly St C2
Holm C1
Hucklesby Way A2
Hunts Cl C1
Information Ctr B2
Inkerman St A2
John St B2
Jubilee St A3
Kelvin Cl C2
King St B2
Kingsland Rd C3
Latimer Rd C2
Lawn Gdns C2
Lea Rd B3
Library B2
Library Rd B2
Liverpool Rd B1
London Rd C2
Luton Station A2
Lyndhurst Rd B1
Magistrates Court B2
Mall, The B2
Manchester St B2
Manor Rd B3
May St C3
Meyrick Ave C1
Midland Rd A2
Mill St A2
Milton Rd B1
Moor St A1
Moor, The A1
Moorland Gdns A2
Moulton Rise A3
Museum & Art Gallery A2
Napier Rd B1
New Bedford Rd A1
New Town St C2
North St A3
Old Bedford Rd A2
Old Orchard C2
Osbourne Rd C3
Oxen Rd A3
Park Sq B2
Park St B3/C3
Park St West B2
Park Viaduct B3
Parkland Drive C1
Police Station B1
Pomfret Ave A3
Pondwicks Rd B3
Post Office A1/A2/B2/C3
Power Court B3
Princess St B1
Red Rails C1
Regent St B2
Reginald St A2
Rothesay Rd B1
Russell Rise C1
Russell St C1
St Ann's Rd B3
St George's B2
St George's Square B2
St Mary's B3
St Marys Rd B3
St Paul's Rd C2
St Saviour's Cres C1
Salisbury Rd B1
Seymour Ave C3
Seymour Rd C3
Silver St B2
South Rd C2
Stanley St B1
Station Rd A2
Stockwood Cres C2
Stockwood Park C1
Strathmore Ave C2
Stuart St B2
Studley Rd A1
Surrey St C3
Sutherland Place C1
Tavistock St C2
Taylor St A3
Telford Way A1
Tennyson Rd C2
Tenzing Grove C1
The Cross Way C1
The Larches A2
Thistle Rd B3
Town Hall B2
Townsley Cl C2
UK Centre for Carnival Arts B3
Union St B2
Univ of Bedfordshire B3
Upper George St B2
Vicarage St B3
Villa Rd A2
Waldeck Rd A1
Wellington St B1/B2
Wenlock St A2
Whitby Rd A1
Whitehill Ave C1
William St A2
Wilsden Ave C1
Windmill Rd B3
Windsor St C2
Winsdon Rd B1
York St A3

Maidstone 187

Albion Pl B3
All Saints B2
Allen St A3
Amphitheatre C2
Archbishop's Palace B2
Bank St B2
Barker Rd C2
Barton Rd C3
Beaconsfield Rd C1
Bedford Pl B1
Bentlif Art Gallery B2
Bishops Way B2
Bluett St A3
Bower La C1
Bower Mount Rd B1
Bower Pl C1
Bower St B1
Bowling Alley B3
Boxley Rd A3
Brenchley Gardens A2
Brewer St A3
Broadway B2
Broadway Sh Ctr B2
Brunswick St C3
Buckland Hill A1
Buckland Rd B1
Bus Station B3
Campbell Rd C3
Carriage Museum B2
Church Rd C1
Church St B3
Cinema C2
College Ave C2
College Rd C2
Collis Memorial Gdn C3
Cornwallis Rd B1
Corpus Christi Hall B2
County Hall A2
County Rd A3
Crompton Gdns C3
Crown & County Courts B2
Curzon Rd A3
Dixon Cl C2
Douglas Rd C1
Earl St B2
Eccleston Rd C2
Fairmeadow B2
Fisher St A2
Florence Rd C1
Foley St A3
Foster St C3
Fremlin Walk Sh Ctr B2
Gabriel's Hill B3
George St C3
Grecian St A3
Hardy St A3
Hart St C2
Hastings Rd C3
Hayle Rd C3
Hazlitt Theatre B2
Heathorn St A3
Hedley St A3
High St B2
HM Prison A3
Holland Rd A3
Hope St A2
Information Ctr B2
James St A3
James Whatman Way A2
Jeffrey St A3
Kent County Council Offices A2
Kent History & Library Centre A2
King Edward Rd C2
King St B3
Kingsley Rd C3
Knightrider St B3
Launder Way C1
Lesley Pl A1
Little Buckland Ave A1
Lockmeadow Leisure Complex C2
London Rd B1
Lower Boxley Rd A2
Lower Fant Rd C1
Magistrates Court B3
Maidstone Barracks Station A1
Maidstone Borough Council Offices B1
Maidstone East Station A2
Maidstone Mus B2
Maidstone West Station B2
Market C2
Market Buildings B2
Marsham St B3
Medway St B2
Medway Trading Est C2
Melville Rd C3
Mill St B2
Millennium Bridge C2
Mote Rd B3
Muir Rd C3
Old Tovil Rd C2
Palace Ave B3
Perryfield St A2
Police Station B3
Post Office A2/B2/B3/C3
Priory Rd C3
Prospect Pl C1
Pudding La B2
Queen Anne Rd B3
Queens Rd A1
Randall St A2
Rawdon Rd C3
Reginald Rd C1
Rock Pl B1
Rocky Hill B1
Romney Pl B3
Rose Yard B2
Rowland Cl C1
Royal Engineers' Rd A2
Royal Star Arcade B2
St Annes Ct B1
St Faith's St B2
St Luke's Rd A3
St Peter's Br B2
St Peter's Wharf Retail Park B2
St Peter St B2
St Philip's Ave C3
Salisbury Rd A3
Sandling Rd A2
Scott St A2
Scrubs La B1
Sheal's Cres C3
Somerfield La B1
Somerfield Rd B1
Staceys St A2
Station Rd A2
Superstore A1/B2/B3
Terrace Rd B1
The Mall B3
The Somerfield Hospital A1
Tonbridge Rd C1
Tovil Rd C2
Town Hall B2
Trinity Park B3
Tufton St B3
Union St B3
Upper Fant Rd C1
Upper Stone St C3
Victoria St B1
Visitor Centre A1
Warwick Pl B1
Wat Tyler Way B3
Waterloo St C3
Waterlow Rd A3
Week St B2
Well Rd A3
Westree Rd C1
Wharf Rd C1
Whatman Park A1
Wheeler St A3
Whitchurch Cl B1
Woodville Rd C3
Wyatt St B3
Wyke Manor Rd B3

Manchester 186

Adair St B6
Addington St A5
Adelphi St A1
Air & Space Gallery B2
Albert Sq B3
Albion St C3
AMC Great Northern B3
Ancoats Gr B6
Ancoats Gr North B6
Angela St C2
Aquatic Centre C4
Ardwick Green Park C5
Ardwick Green North C5
Ardwick Green South C5
Arlington St A2
Artillery St B3
Arundel St C2
Atherton St B2
Atkinson St B3
Aytoun St B4
Back Piccadilly A4
Baird St B5
Balloon St A4
Bank Pl A1
Baring St B5
Barrack St C1
Barrow St A1
BBC TV Studios C4
Bendix St A5
Bengal St A5
Berry St C5
Blackfriars Rd A3
Blackfriars St A3
Blantyre St C2
Bloom St B4
Blossom St A5
Boad St B5
Bombay St B4
Booth St A3
Booth St B4
Bootle St B3
Brazennose St B3
Brewer St A5
Bridge St A3
Bridgewater Hall B3
Bridgewater Pl A4
Bridgewater St B2
Brook St C4
Brotherton Dr A2
Brown St A3
Brown St B4
Brunswick St C6
Brydon Ave C6
Buddhist Centre A4
Bury St A2
Bus & Coach Station B4
Bus Station B4
Butler St A6
Buxton St C5
Byrom St B3
Cable St A5
Calder St B1
Cambridge St C3/C4
Camp St B3
Canal St B4
Cannon St A1
Cannon St A4
Cardroom Rd A6
Carruthers St A6
Castle St C2
Cateaton St A3
Cathedral A3
Cathedral St A3
Cavendish St C4
Chapel St A1/A3
Chapeltown St B5
Charles St C4
Charlotte St B4
Chatham St B4
Cheapside A3
Chepstow St B3
Chester Rd C1/C2
Chester St C4
Chetham's (Dept Store) A3
China La B5
Chippenham Rd A6
Chorlton Rd C2
Chorlton St B4
Church St A2
Church St A4
City Park A4
City Rd C3
Civil Justice Centre B2
Cleminson St A2
Clowes St A3
College Land A3
Coll of Adult Ed C4
Collier St B2
Commercial St C3
Conference Centre C4
Cooper St B4
Copperas St A4
Cornbrook C1
Cornell St A5
Cornerhouse C4
Corporation St A4
Cotter St C6
Cotton St A5
Cow La B1
Cross St B3
Crown Court B4
Crown St C2
Cube Gallery B4
Dalberg St C6
Dale St A4/B5
Dancehouse, The C4
Dantzic St A4
Dark La C6
Dawson St C2
Dean St A5
Deansgate A3/B3
Deansgate Sta C3
Dolphin St C6
Downing St C5
Ducie St B5
Duke Pl B2
Duke St B2
Durling St C6
East Ordsall La A2/B1
Edge St A4
Egerton St C2
Ellesmere St C1
Everard St C1
Every St B6
Fairfield St B5
Faulkner St B4
Fennel St A3
Ford St A2
Ford St C6
Fountain St B4
Frederick St A2
Gartside St B2
Gaythorne St A1
George Leigh St A5
George St A1
George St B4
G-Mex C3
Goadsby St A4
Gore St A2
Goulden St A5
Granada TV Centre B2
Granby Row C4
Gravel St A3
Great Ancoats St A5
Great Bridgewater St B3
Great George St A1
Great Jackson St C2
Great Marlborough St C4
Greengate A3
Grosvenor St C5

Gun St A5
Hadrian Ave B6
Hall St B3
Hampson St B1
Hanover St A4
Hanworth Cl C5
Hardman St B3
Harkness St C6
Harrison St B6
Hart St B4
Helmet St B6
Henry St A5
Heyrod St B6
High St A4
Higher Ardwick C6
Hilton St A4/A5
Holland St A6
Hood St A5
Hope St B1
Hope St B4
Houldsworth St A5
Hoyle St C6
Hulme Hall Rd C1
Hulme St A1
Hulme St C3
Hyde Rd C6
Information Ctr B3
Irwell St A2
Islington St A2
Jackson Cr C2
Jackson's Row B3
James St A1
Jenner Cl C2
Jersey St A5
John Dalton St A1
John Dalton St B3
John Ryland's Liby B3
John St A2
Kennedy St B3
Kincardine Rd C5
King St A3
King St West A3
Law Courts B3
Laystall St B5
Lever St A5
Library B3
Linby St C2
Little Lever St A4
Liverpool Rd B2
Liverpool St B1
Lloyd St B3
Lockton Cl C5
London Rd B5
Long Millgate A3
Longacre St B6
Loom St A5
Lower Byrom St B2
Lower Mosley St B3
Lower Moss La C2
Lower Ormond St C4
Loxford La C4
Luna St A5
Major St B4
Manchester Arndale A4
Manchester Art Gallery B4
Manchester Central Convention Complex B3
Manchester Metropolitan University B4/C4
Manchester Piccadilly Sta B5
Manchester Technology Centre C4
Mancunian Way C3
Manor St C5
Marble St A4
Market St A2
Market St A4
Market St A4
Marsden St A3
Marshall St A5
Mayan Ave A2
Medlock St C3
Middlewood St B1
Miller St A4
Minshull St B4
Mosley St A4
Mount St B3
Mulberry St B3
Murray St A5
Museum of Science & Industry (MOSI) B2
Nathan Dr A2
National Football Museum A4
Naval St A5
New Bailey St A2
New Elm Rd B2
New Islington A6
New Islington Sta B6
New Quay St B2
New Union St A6
Newgate St A4
Newton St A5
Nicholas St B4
North Western St C6
Oak St A4
Odeon A4
Old Mill St A6
Oldfield Rd A1/C1
Oldham Rd A5
Oldham St A4
Opera House B3
Ordsall La C1
Oxford Rd C4
Oxford Rd C4
Oxford St B4
Paddock St C6
Palace Theatre B4
Pall Mall A3
Palmerston St B6
Park St A1
Parker St B4
Peak St B5
Penfield Cl C5
Peoples' History Museum B2
Peru St A1
Peter St B3
Piccadilly A4
Piccadilly B5
Piccadilly Gdns B4
Piercy St A6
Poland St A5
Police Museum A5
Police Station B3/B5
Pollard St B6
Port St A5
Portland St B4
Portugal St East B5
Post Office A1/A4/A5/B3
Potato Wharf B2
Princess St B3/C4
Pritchard St C4
Quay St A2
Quay St B2
Queen St B3
Radium St A5
Redhill St A5
Regent Rd B1
Renold Theatre A2
Retail Park A5
Rice St B2
Richmond St B4
River St C3
Roby St B5
Rodney St A6
Roman Fort B2
Rosamond St A2
Royal Exchange A3
Sackville St B4
St Andrew's St B6
St Ann St A3
St Ann's A3
St George's Ave C1
St James St B4
St John St B3
St John's Cath (RC) A2
St Mary's B3
St Mary's Gate A3
St Mary's Parsonage A3
St Peter's Sq B3
St Stephen St A2
Salford Approach A3
Salford Central A2
Sheffield St B5
Shepley St B5
Sherratt St A5
Shudehill A4
Shudehill A4
Sidney St C4
Silk St A5
Silver St B4
Skerry Cl C5
Snell St B6
South King St B3
Sparkle St B5
Spear St A4
Spring Gdns A4
Stanley St A2/B2
Station Approach B5
Store St B5
Swan St A4
Tariff St B5
Tatton St C1
Temperance St B6/C6
The Triangle A4
Thirsk St C6
Thomas St A4
Thompson St A5
Tib La B3
Tib St A4
Town Hall (Manchester) B3
Town Hall (Salford) A2
Trafford St C3
Travis St B5
Trinity Way A2
Turner St A4
Union St C6
Univ of Manchester (Sackville Street Campus) C5
Upper Brook St C5
Upper Cleminson St A1
Upper Wharf St A1
Vesta St B6
Victoria A4
Victoria Station A4
Victoria St A3
Wadesdon Rd C5
Water St B2
Watson St B3
West Fleet St B1
West King St A2
West Mosley St B4
West Union St B1
Weybridge Rd A6
Whitworth St B4
Whitworth St West C3
Wilburn St B1
William St A2
William St C6
Wilmott St C3
Windmill St B3
Windsor Cr A1
Withy Gr A4
Woden St C1
Wood St B3
Woodward St A6
Worrall St C1
Worsley St C2
York St B4
York St C2
York St C4

Middlesbrough 187

Abingdon Rd C3
Acklam Rd C1
Albert Park C2
Albert Rd B2
Albert Terr C2
Aubrey St C3
Ayresome Gdns C2
Ayresome Green La C1
Ayresome St C2
Barton Rd A1
Bilsdale Rd C3
Bishopton Rd C3
Borough Rd B2/B3
Bowes Rd A2
Breckon Hill Rd B3
Bridge St East B3
Bridge St West B2
Brighouse Rd A1
Burlam Rd C1
Bus Station B2
Cannon Park B1
Cannon Park Way B2
Cannon St B1
Captain Cook Sq B2
Carlow St C1
Castle Way C3
Chipchase Rd C2
Cineworld B3
Clairville Sports Stadium C3
Cleveland Centre B2
Clive Rd C2
Commercial St A2
Corporation Rd B2
Costa St C2
Council Offices B3
Crescent Rd C2
Cumberland Rd C2
Depot Rd A2
Derwent St B2
Devonshire Rd C2
Diamond Rd B2
Disabled Driver Test Circuit B1
Dorman Museum C2
Douglas St B3
Eastbourne Rd C2
Eden Rd C3
Enterprise Centre A2
Forty Foot Rd A2
Gilkes St B2
Gosford St A2
Grange Rd B2
Gresham Rd B2
Harehills Rd C1
Harford St C2
Hartington Rd B2
Haverton Hill Rd A1
Hey Wood St B1
Highfield Rd C3
Hill St Centre B2
Holwick Rd B1
Hutton Rd C3
ICI Works A1
Information Ctr B2
Lambton Rd C3
Lancaster Rd C2
Lansdowne Rd C3
Latham Rd C2
Law Courts B2/B3
Lees Rd B2
Leeway B3
Linthorpe Cemetery C1
Linthorpe Rd B2
Lloyd St B2
Longford St C2
Longlands Rd C3
Lower East St A3
Lower Lake C3
Maldon Rd C1
Manor St B2
Marsh St B2
Marton Rd B3
Middlehaven B3
Middlesbrough By-Pass B2/C1
Middlesbrough Coll B3
Middlesbrough L Pk B3
Middlesbrough Station B2
Middlesbrough Theatre C2
Middletown Park C2
MIMA B3
Mosque B2
Mosque C3
Mulgrave Rd C2
North Ormesby Rd B3
Newport Bridge B1
Newport Bridge Approach Rd B1
Newport Rd B2
North Rd B2
Northern Rd C1
Outram St B2
Oxford Rd C2
Park La C2
Park Rd North C2
Park Rd South C2
Park Vale Rd C3
Parliament Rd B1
Police Station A2
Port Clarence Rd A3
Portman St B2
Post Office B2/B3/C1/C2/C3
Princes Rd B2
Python A2
Riverside Bsns Park A2
Riverside Park Rd A1
Riverside Stadium (Middlesbrough FC) B3
Rockliffe Rd C2
Romaldkirk Rd B1
Roman Rd C2
Roseberry Rd C3
St Barnabas' Rd C2
St Paul's Rd B2
Saltwells Rd B3
Scott's Rd A3
Seaton Carew Rd A3
Shepherdson Way B3
Sikh Temple B2
Snowdon Rd A2
South West Ironmasters Park B1
Southfield Rd B2
Southwell Rd C2
Springfield Rd C1
Startforth Rd A2
Stockton Rd C1
Stockton St A2
Surrey St C2
Sycamore Rd C2
Synagogue C2
Tax Offices B3
Tees Viaduct C1
Teessaurus Park A2
Teesside Tertiary College C3
Temenos B3
The Avenue C2
The Crescent C2
Thornfield Rd C1
Town Hall B2
Transporter Bridge (Toll) A3
Union St B2
Univ of Teesside B2
Upper Lake C2
Valley Rd C3
Ventnor Rd C2
Victoria Rd B2
Visitor Centre A3
Vulcan St A2
Warwick St C2
Wellesley Rd B3
West Lane Hospl C1
Westminster Rd C2
Wilson St B2
Windward Way B3
Woodlands Rd B2
York Rd C3

Milton Keynes 187

Abbey Way A1
Arbrook Ave B1
Armourer Dr A3
Arncliffe Dr A1
Avebury C2
Avebury Blvd C2
Bankfield B3
Bayard Ave A2
Belvedere A2
Bishopstone A1
Blundells Rd A1
Boycott Ave C2
Bradwell Comm Blvd B1
Bradwell Rd C1
Bramble Ave A2
Brearley Ave C2
Breckland A1
Brill Place B1
Burnham Dr B1
Bus Station C1
Campbell Park B3
Cantle Ave A3
Central Milton Keynes Shopping Area B2
Century Ave C2
Chaffron Way C3
Childs Way C1
Christ the Cornerstone B2
Cineworld B2
Civic Offices B2
Cleavers Ave B2
Colesbourne Dr A3
Conniburrow Blvd B2
County Court B2
Currier Dr A2
Dansteed Way A2/A3/B1
Deltic Ave B1
Downs Barn A2
Downs Barn Blvd A3
Eaglestone C3
Eelbrook Ave B1
Elder Gate B1
Evans Gate C2
Fairford Cr A3
Falcon Ave B3
Fennel Dr A2
Fishermead Blvd C3
Food Centre B3
Fulwoods Dr C3
Glazier Dr A2
Glovers La A1
Grafton Gate C1
Grafton St A1/C2
Gurnards Ave B3
Harrier Dr C3
Ibstone Ave B1
Langcliffe Dr A1
Leisure Plaza C1
Leys Rd C1
Library B2
Linford Wood A2
Marlborough Gate B3
Marlborough St A2/B3
Mercers Dr A1
Midsummer C2
Midsummer Blvd B2
Milton Keynes Central C1
Monks Way A1
Mullen Ave A3
Mullion Pl C3
National Hockey Stadium B1
Neath Hill A3
North Elder C1
North Grafton B1
North Overgate A3
North Row B2
North Saxon B2
North Secklow B2
North Skeldon A3
North Witan B1
Oakley Gdns A3
Oldbrook Blvd C2
Open-Air Theatre B3
Overgate A3
Overstreet A3
Patriot Dr B1
Pencarrow Pl B3
Penryn Ave B3
Perran Ave C3
Pitcher La C1
Place Retail Pk, The C1
Point Centre, The B2
Police Station B2
Portway B2
Post Office A2/B2/C3
Precedent Dr B1
Quinton Dr B1
Ramsons Ave B2
Rockingham Dr A2
Rooksley B1
Rooksley Retail Park C1
Saxon Gate B2
Saxon St A1/C3
Secklow Gate B2
Shackleton Pl C2
Silbury Blvd B2
Skeldon A3
South Grafton C2
South Row C2
South Saxon C2
South Secklow B3
South Witan C2
Springfield B3
Stanton Wood A1
Stantonbury A1
Stantonbury L Ctr A1
Strudwick Dr C2
Sunrise Parkway A2
Telephone Exchange C3
The Boundary C3
Theatre & Art Gallery B3
Tolcarne Ave C3
Towan Ave C3
Trueman Pl C2
Vauxhall A1
Winterhill Retail Park C2
Witan Gate B2
X-Scape B3

Newcastle upon Tyne 187

Albert St B3
Argyle St B3
Back New Bridge St B3
BALTIC Centre for Contemporary Art C3
Barker St A3
Barrack Rd B1
Bath La B1
Bell's Court B2
Bessie Surtees Ho C2
Bigg Market C2
Biscuit Factory B3
Black Gate C2
Blackett St B2
Blandford Sq C1
Boating Lake A1
Boyd St B3
Brandling Park A2
Bus Station B2
Buxton St B3
Byron St A3
Camden St B2
Castle Keep C2
Central C1
Central Library B2
Central Motorway B2
Chester St A3
City Hall B2
City Rd B3/C3
City Walls C1
Civic Centre A2
Claremont Rd A1
Clarence St B3
Clarence Walk B3
Clayton St C1/B1
Clayton St West C1
Coach Station C1
College St B2
Collingwood St C2
Copland Terr B3
Coppice Way B3
Corporation St B1
Courts C3
Crawhall Rd B3
Dean St C2
Discovery C1
Dinsdale Pl A3
Dinsdale Rd A3
Doncaster Rd A3
Durant Rd B2
Eldon Sq B1
Eldon Sq Sh Ctr B2
Ellison Pl B2
Empire B1
Eskdale Terr A2
Eslington Terr A2
Exhibition Park A1
Falconar St B3
Fenkle St C1
Forth Banks C1
Forth St C1
Gallowgate B1
Gateshead Heritage @ St Mary's C3
Gateshead Millennium Bridge C3
Gibson St B3
Goldspink La A3
Grainger Market B2
Grainger St B2
Grantham Rd A3
Granville Rd A3
Great North Mus:Hancock A2
Grey St B2
Groat Market C2
Guildhall C2
Hancock St A2
Hanover St C2
Hatton Gallery A1
Hawks Rd C3
Haymarket B2
Heber St B1
Helmsley Rd A3
High Bridge B2
High Level Bridge C2
Hillgate C3
Howard St B3
Hutton Terr A3
Information Ctr C3
Jesmond A2
Jesmond Rd A2/A3
John Dobson St B2
John George Joicey Museum C2
Jubilee Rd B3
Kelvin Gr A3
Kensington Terr A2
Laing Gallery B2
Lambton Rd A2
Leazes Cr B1
Leazes La B1
Leazes Park B1
Leazes Park Rd B1
Leazes Terr B1
Live C2
Low Friar St C1
Manor Chare C2
Manors B2
Manors Station B2
Market St B2
Melbourne St B2
Mill Rd C3
Mill Volvo Tyne C1
Monument B2
Monument Mall Shopping Centre B2
Morpeth St A2
Mosley St C2
Napier St A3
Nazareth House A3
New Bridge St B2/B3
Newcastle Central Station C1
Newcastle University A1
Newgate Sh Ctr C1
Newgate St B1
Newington Rd A3
Northern Stage Theatre A2
Northumberland Rd B2
Northumberland St B2
Northumbria Univ A2
Northwest Radial Rd A1
O2 Academy C1
Oakwellgate C3
Orchard St C1
Osborne Rd A2
Osborne Terr A3
Pandon C3
Pandon Bank B3
Park Terr A1
Percy St B1
Pilgrim St B2
Pipewellgate C2
Pitt St B1
Plummer Tower A2
Police Station B2
Portland Rd A3/B3
Portland Terr A3
Post Office A3/B1/B2/B3
Pottery La C1
Prudhoe Pl B1
Prudhoe St B1
Quayside C2
Queen Elizabeth II Bridge C2
Queen Victoria Rd A1
Richardson Rd A1
Ridley Pl B2
Rock Terr B3
Rosedale Terr A3
Royal Victoria Infirmary A1
Sage Gateshead, The C3
St Andrew's St B1
St James B1
St James' Blvd C1
St James' Park (Newcastle Utd FC) B1
St Mary's (RC) C1
St Mary's Place B2
St Nicholas C2
St Nicholas St C2
St Thomas' St B1
Sandyford Rd A2/A3
Science Park B2
Shield St B3
Shieldfield B3
Simpson Terr B3
South Shore Rd C3
South St C1
Starbeck Ave A3
Stepney Rd B3
Stoddart St B3
Stowell St B1
Strawberry Pl B1
Swing Bridge C2
Temple St C1
Terrace Pl B1
The Close C2
The Gate B1
The Side C2
Theatre Royal B2
Times Sq C1
Tower St B3
Trinity House C2
Tyne Bridge C2
Tyne Bridges C2
Tyneside B2
Victoria Sq A2
Warwick St A3
Waterloo St C1
Wellington St B1
Westgate Rd C1/C2
Windsor Terr A2
Worswick St B2
Wretham Pl B3

Newport Casnewydd 188

Albert Terr B1
Allt-yr-Yn Ave A1
Alma St C2
Ambulance Station C3
Bailey St B2
Barrack Hill A2
Bath St A3
Bedford Rd B3
Belle Vue La C1
Belle Vue Park C1
Bishop St A3
Blewitt St B1
Bolt Cl C3
Bolt St C3
Bond St A2
Bosworth Dr A1
Bridge St B1
Bristol St A3
Bryngwyn Rd B1
Brynhyfryd Ave C1
Brynhyfryd Rd C1
Bus Station B2
Caerau Cres C1
Caerau Rd B1
Caerleon Rd A3
Capel Cres C2
Cardiff Rd C2
Caroline St B3
Castle (Remains) A2
Cedar Rd B3
Charles St B2
Charlotte Dr C2
Chepstow Rd A3
Church Rd A3
City Cinema B1
Civic Centre B1
Clarence Pl A2
Clifton Pl B1
Clifton Rd C1
Clyffard Cres B1
Clytha Park Rd B1
Clytha Sq C2
Coldra Rd C1
Collier St A3
Colne St B3
Comfrey Cl A1
Commercial Rd C3
Commercial St B2
Corelli St A3
Corn St B2
Corporation Rd B3
Coulson Cl C2
County Court A2
Courts A1
Courts B1
Crawford St A3
Cyril St B3
Dean St A3
Devon Pl B1
Dewsland Park Rd C2
Dolman B2
Dolphin St C3
East Dock Rd C3
East St B1
East Usk Rd A3
Ebbw Vale Wharf B3
Emlyn St B2
Enterprise Way C3
Eton Rd B3
Evans St A2
Factory Rd A2
Fields Rd B1
Francis Dr C2
Frederick St C3
Friars Rd C1
Gaer La C1
George St C3
George St Bridge C3
Godfrey Rd B1
Gold Tops B1
Gore St A3
Gorsedd Circle C1
Grafton Rd A3
Graham St B1
Granville St C3
Harlequin Dr A1
Harrow Rd B3
Herbert Rd A3
Herbert Walk C2
Hereford St A3
High St B2
Hill St B2
Hoskins St A2
Information Ctr B2
Ivor Sq B2
Jones St B1
Junction Rd A3
Keynshaw Ave C2
King St C2
Kingsway B2
Kingsway Centre B2
Ledbury Dr A2
Library A3
Library, Museum & Art Gallery B2
Liverpool Wharf B3
Llanthewy Rd B1
Llanvair Rd A3
Locke St A2
Lower Dock St C3
Lucas St A2
Manchester St A3
Market B2
Marlborough Rd B3
Mellon St C3
Mill St A2
Morgan St A3
Mountjoy Rd C2
Newport Bridge A2
Newport Ctr B2
Newport RFC B3
Newport Station B2
North St B2
Oakfield Rd B1
Park Sq C2
Police Station A3/C2
Post Office B1/B2/C1/C3
Power St A1
Prince St A3
Pugsley St A2
Queen St C2
Queen's Cl A1
Queen's Hill A1
Queen's Hill Cres A1
Queensway B2
Railway St B2
Riverfront Arts Centre B2
Riverside A3
Rodney Rd B2
Royal Gwent (A&E) C2
Rudry St A3
Rugby Rd B3
Ruperra La C3
Ruperra St C3
St Edmund St B1
St Mark's Cres A1
St Mary St B1
St Vincent Rd A3
St Woolos C2
St Woolos General (no A+E) C1
St Woolos Rd B1
School La B2
Serpentine Rd B1
Shaftesbury Park A2
Sheaf La A3
Skinner St B2
Sorrel Dr A1
South Market St C3
Spencer Rd B1
Stow Hill B2/C1/C2
Stow Park Ave C1
Stow Park Dr C1
TA Centre A1
Talbot St B2
Tennis Club A1
Tregare St A3
Trostrey St A3
Tunnel Terr B1
Turner St A3
Upper Dock St B2
Usk St A3
Usk Way B3/C3
Victoria Cr B1
War Memorial A3
Waterloo Rd C1
West St B1
Wharves B2
Wheeler St A2
Whitby Pl A3
Windsor Terr B1
York Pl C1

Northampton 188

78 Derngate B3
Abington Sq B3
Abington St B3
Alcombe St A3
All Saints' B2
Ambush St B1
Angel St B2
Arundel St A2
Ash St A2
Auctioneers Way C2
Bailiff St A2
Barrack Rd A2
Beaconsfield Terr A3
Becketts Park C3
Becketts Park Marina C3
Bedford Rd B3
Billing Rd B3
Brecon St A1
Brewery C2
Bridge St C2
Broad St B2
Burns St A3
Bus Station B2
Campbell St A2
Castle (Site of) B2
Castle St B2
Cattle Market Rd C2
Central Museum & Art Gallery B2
Charles St A3
Cheyne Walk B3
Church La A2
Clare St A3
Cloutsham St A3
College St B2
Colwyn Rd A3
Cotton End C2
Countess Rd A1
County Hall B2
Court A2
Craven St A3
Crown & County Courts B3
Denmark Rd B3
Derngate B3
Derngate & Royal Theatres B3
Doddridge Church B2
Duke St A3
Dunster St A3
Earl St A3
Euston Rd C2
Fire Station A3
Foot Meadow B2
Gladstone Rd A1
Gold St B2
Grafton St A2
Gray St A3
Green St B1
Greenwood Rd B1
Greyfriars B2
Grosvenor Centre B2
Grove Rd A3
Guildhall B2
Hampton St A2
Harding Terr A2
Hazelwood Rd B3
Herbert St B2
Hervey St A3
Hester St A2
Holy Sepulchre A2
Hood St A3
Horse Market B2
Hunter St A3
Information Ctr B1
Kettering Rd A3
Kingswell St B2
Lady's La B2
Leicester St A2
Leslie Rd A2
Library B3
Lorne Rd A2
Lorry Park A1
Louise Rd A2
Lower Harding St A2
Lower Hester St A2
Lower Mounts B3
Lower Priory St A2
Main Rd C1
Marefair B2
Market Sq B2
Marlboro Rd B1
Marriott St A2
Military Rd A3
Mounts Baths L Ctr A3
Nene Valley Retail Pk C1
New South Bridge Rd C2
Northampton General Hospital (A&E) B3
Northampton Sta B1
Northcote St A2
Nunn Mills Rd C3
Old Towcester Rd C2
Overstone Rd A3
Peacock Pl B2
Pembroke Rd A1
Penn Court C2
Police Station B3
Post Office A1/A2/B3/C2
Quorn Way A2
Ransome Rd C3
Regent Sq A2
Robert St A2
St Andrew's Rd B1
St Andrew's St A2
St Edmund's Rd B3
St George's St A2
St Giles B3
St Giles St B3
St Giles' Terr B3
St James' Mill Rd B1
St James' Mill Rd East C1
St James Park Rd B1
St James Retail Park C1
St James Rd B1
St Leonard's Rd C2
St Mary's St B2
St Michael's Rd A3
St Peter's B2
St Peter's Sq Sh Prec B2
St Peter's Way B2
Salisbury St A2
Scarletwell St B2
Semilong Rd A2
Sheep St B2
Sol Central (L Ctr) B2
Somerset St A3
South Bridge C2
Southfield Ave C2
Spencer Bridge Rd A1
Spencer Rd A3
Spring Gdns B3
Spring La B2
Swan St B3
TA Centre A3
Tanner St B2
The Drapery B2
The Ridings B3
Tintern Ave A1
Towcester Rd C2
Upper Bath St B2
Upper Mounts A2
Victoria Park A1
Victoria Promenade B2
Victoria Rd B3
Victoria St A2
Wellingborough Rd B3
West Bridge B1
York Rd B3

Norwich 188

Albion Way C3
All Saints Green C2
Anchor Cl A3
Anchor St A3
Anglia Sq A2
Argyle St C3
Arts Centre B1
Ashby St C2
Assembly House B1
Bank Plain B2
Barker St A1
Barn Rd A1
Barrack St A3
Ber St C2
Bethel St B1
Bishop Bridge A3
Bishopbridge Rd A3
Bishopgate A3
Blackfriars St A2
Botolph St A2
Bracondale C3
Brazen Gate C2
Bridewell B2
Brunswick Rd C1
Bull Close Rd A2
Bus Station C2
Calvert St A2
Cannell Green A3
Carrow Rd C3
Castle Mall B2
Castle Meadow B2
Castle & Mus B2
Cathedral B2
Cathedral Retail Pk A1
Cattlemarket St B2
Chantry Rd C1
Chapel Loke C2
Chapelfield East B1
Chapelfield Gdns B1
Chapelfield North B1
Chapelfield Rd B1
Chapelfield Sh Ctr C1
City Hall B1
City Rd C2
City Wall C1/C3
Colegate A2
Coslany St B1
Cow Hill B1
Cow Tower A3
Cowgate A2
Crown & Magistrates Courts A2
Dragon Hall Heritage Centre C3
Duke St A1
Edward St A2
Elm Hill B2
Erpingham Gate B2
Fire Station B1
Fishergate A2
Foundry Bridge B3
Fye Bridge A2
Garden St C2
Gas Hill B3
Grapes Hill B1
Great Hospital Halls, The A3
Grove Ave C1
Grove Rd C1
Guildhall A1
Gurney Rd A3
Hall Rd C2
Heathgate A3
Heigham St A1
Horn's La C2
Information Ctr B1
Ipswich Rd C1
James Stuart Gdns B3
King Edward VI School B2
King St B2
King St C3
Koblenz Ave C3
Library B1
London St B2
Lower Clarence Rd B3
Lower Cl B3
Maddermarket B1
Magdalen St A2
Mariners La C2
Market B2
Market Ave B2
Mountergate B3
Mousehold St A3
Newmarket Rd C1
Norfolk Gallery B2
Norfolk St C1
Norwich City FC C3
Norwich Station B3
Oak St A1
Palace St A2
Pitt St A1
Playhouse B2
Post Office A2/B2/C2
Pottergate B1
Prince of Wales Rd B2
Princes St B2
Pull's Ferry B3
Puppet Theatre A2
Quebec Rd B3
Queen St B2
Queens Rd C2
RC Cathedral B1
Recorder Rd B3
Riverside Entertainment Ctr C3
Riverside Swimming Centre C3
Riverside Retail Park C3
Riverside Rd B3
Rosary Rd B3
Rose La B2
Rouen Rd C2
Royal Norfolk Regiment Mus B2
St Andrew's & Blackfriars Hall B2
St Andrews St B2
St Augustines St A1
St Benedicts St B1
St Ethelbert's Gate B2
St Faiths La B3
St Georges St A2
St Giles St B1
St James Cl A3
St Julians C2
St Martin's La A1
St Peter Mancroft B2
St Peters St B1
St Stephens Rd C1
St Stephens St C1
Silver Rd A2
Silver St A2
Southwell Rd C2
Strangers Hall B1
Superstore C2
Surrey St C2
Sussex St A1
The Close B3
The Forum B1
The Walk B2
Theatre Royal B1
Theatre St B1
Thorn La C2
Thorpe Rd B3
Tombland B2
Union St C1
Vauxhall St B1
Victoria St C1
Walpole St B1
Wensum St A2
Wessex St C1
Westwick St A1
Wherry Rd C3
Whitefriars A2
Willow La B1
Yacht Station B3

Nottingham 188

Abbotsford Dr A3
Addison St A1
Albert Hall B1
Alfred St South A3
Alfreton Rd B1
All Saints Rd A1
Annesley Gr A2
Arboretum A1
Arboretum St A1
Arthur St A1
Arts Theatre B3
Ashforth St A3
Balmoral Rd A1
Barker Gate B3
Bath St B3
Belgrave Centre B1
Bellar Gate B3
Belward St B3
Blue Bell Hill Rd B3
Brewhouse Yard C2
Broad Marsh Bus Sta C2
Broad Marsh Prec C2

Broad St B3
Brook St B3
Burns St A1
Burton St B2
Bus Station A2
Canal St C2
Carlton St B3
Carrington St C2
Castle Blvd C1
Castle C2
Castle Gate C2
Castle Meadow Retail Park C1
Castle Meadow Rd C1
Castle Museum & Gallery C2
Castle Rd C2
Castle Wharf C2
Cavendish Rd East C1
Cemetery B1
Chaucer St B1
Cheapside B2
Church Rd A3
City Link B3
City of Caves C2
Clarendon St B1
Cliff Rd C3
Clumber Rd East C1
Clumber St B2
College St B1
Collin St C2
Conway Cl A2
Council House B2
Court B2
Cranbrook St B3
Cranmer St A2
Cromwell St B1
Curzon St B3
Derby Rd B1
Dryden St A2
Exchange Arcade B2
Fishpond Dr C1
Fletcher Gate B3
Forest Rd East A1
Forest Rd West A1
Friar La C2
Galleries of Justice C3
Gedling Gr A1
Gedling St B3
George St B3
Gill St A2
Glasshouse St B2
Goldsmith St B2
Goose Gate B3
Great Freeman St A2
Guildhall B2
Hamilton Dr C1
Hampden St A1
Heathcote St B3
High Pavement C3
High School A1
Holles Cr C1
Hope Dr C1
Hungerhill Rd A3
Huntingdon Dr C1
Huntingdon St A2
Information Ctr B2
Instow Rise A3
Int Com Ctr A2
Kent St B3
King St B2
Lace Centre, The C2
Lace Market B3
Lace Mkt Theatre C3
Lamartine St B3
Lenton Rd C1
Lewis Cl A3
Lincoln St B2
London Rd C3
Long Row B2
Low Pavement C2
Lower Parliament St B3
Magistrates Court C2
Maid Marian Way B2
Mansfield Rd A2/B2
Middle Hill C2
Milton St B2
Mount St B2
National Ice Centre C3
Newcastle Dr B1
Newstead Gr A2
North Sherwood St A2
Nottingham Arena C3
Nottingham Sta C3
Nottingham Trent University A2/B2
Old Market Sq B2
Oliver St A1
Park Dr C1
Park Row C1
Park Terr B1
Park Valley C1
Peas Hill Rd A3
Peel St A1
Pelham St B2
Peveril Dr C1
Plantagenet St A3
Playhouse Theatre B1
Plumptre St C3
Police Station B2
Poplar St C3
Portland Rd B1
Post Office B2
Queen's Rd C3
Raleigh St A1
Regent St B1
Rick St B3
Robin Hood Statue C2
Robin Hood St B3
Royal Centre B2
Royal Children Inn C2
Royal Concert Hall B2
St Ann's Hill Rd A2
St Ann's Way A2
St Ann's Well Rd A3
St Barnabas B1
St James' St B2
St Mark's St B3
St Mary's Gdn of Rest B3
St Mary's Gate B3
St Nicholas C2
St Peter's C2
St Peter's Gate B2
Salutation Inn C2
Shakespeare St B2
Shelton St A2
South Pde B2
South Rd C1
South Sherwood St B2
Station St C3
Station Street C3
Stoney St B3
Talbot St B1
Tattershall Dr C1
Tennis Dr B1
Tennyson St A1
The Park C1
The Ropewalk B1
Theatre Royal B2
Trent St C3
Trent University B2
Trinity Square Sh Ctr B2
Trip to Jerusalem Inn C2
Union Rd B3
Upper Parliament St B2
Victoria Centre B2
Victoria Leisure Ctr B3
Victoria Park B3
Victoria St B2
Walter St A1
Warser Gate B3
Watkin St A2
Waverley St A1
Wheeler Gate B2
Wilford Rd C2
Wilford St C2
Willoughby House C2
Wollaton St B1
Woodborough Rd A2
Woolpack La B3
York St A2

Oxford 189

Adelaide St A1
Albert St A1
All Souls (Coll) B2
Ashmolean Mus B2
Balliol (Coll) B2
Banbury Rd A2
Bate Collection of Musical Instruments C2
Beaumont St B1
Becket St B1
Blackhall Rd A2
Blue Boar St B2
Bodleian Library B2
Botanic Garden B3
Brasenose (Coll) B2
Brewer St C2
Broad St B2
Burton-Taylor Theatre B2
Bus Station B1
Canal St A1
Cardigan St A1
Carfax Tower B2
Castle B1
Castle St B1
Catte St B2
Cemetery C1
Christ Church (Coll) B2
Christ Church Cath C2
Christ Church Mdw C2
Clarendon Centre B2
Coach & Lorry Park C1
College B3
Coll of Further Ed C1
Cornmarket St B2
Corpus Christi (Coll) B2
County Hall B1
Covered Market B2
Cowley Pl C3
Cranham St A1
Cranham Terr A1
Cricket Ground B1
Crown & County Courts C2
Deer Park B3
Exeter (Coll) B3
Folly Bridge C2
George St B1
Great Clarendon St A1
Hart St A1
Hertford (Coll) B2
High St B3
Hollybush Row B1
Holywell St B2
Hythe Bridge St B1
Ice Rink C1
Information Ctr B2
Jericho St A1
Jesus (Coll) B2
Jowett Walk B3
Juxon St A1
Keble (Coll) A2
Keble Rd A2
Library B2
Linacre (Coll) A3
Lincoln (Coll) B2
Little Clarendon St A1
Longwall St B3
Magdalen (Coll) B3
Magdalen Bridge B2
Magdalen St B2
Magistrate's Court C2
Manchester (Coll) B2
Manor Rd B3
Mansfield (Coll) A2
Mansfield Rd A3
Market B1
Marlborough Rd C2
Martyrs' Memorial B2
Merton Field B3
Merton (Coll) B3
Merton St B2
Mus of Modern Art B2
Museum of Oxford B2
Museum Rd A2
New College (Coll) B3
New Inn Hall St B2
New Rd B1
New Theatre B2
Norfolk St C1
Nuffield (Coll) B1
Observatory A1
Observatory St A1
Odeon B1/B2
Old Fire Station B1
Old Greyfriars St C2
Oriel (Coll) B2
Oxford Station B1
Oxford Story, The B2
Oxford University Research Centres A1
Oxpens Rd C1
Paradise Sq C1
Paradise St B1
Park End St B1
Parks Rd A2/B2
Pembroke (Coll) C2
Phoenix A1
Picture Gallery C2
Plantation Rd A1
Playhouse B2
Police Station C2
Post Office A1/B2
Pusey St B1
Queen's La B3
Queen's (Coll) B3
Radcliffe Camera B2
Rewley Rd B1
Richmond Rd A1
Rose La B3
Ruskin (Coll) B1
Saïd Business School B1
St Aldates C2
St Anne's (Coll) A1
St Antony's (Coll) A1
St Bernard's Rd A1
St Catherine's (Coll) B3
St Cross Building A3
St Cross Rd A3
St Edmund Hall (Coll) B3
St Giles St A2
St Hilda's (Coll) C3
St John St B2
St John's (Coll) B2
St Mary the Virgin B2
St Michael at the Northgate B2
St Peter's (Coll) B1
St Thomas St B1
Science Area A2
Science Museum B2
Sheldonian Theatre B2
Somerville (Coll) A1
South Parks Rd A2
Speedwell St C2
Sports Ground C3
Thames St C2
Town Hall B2
Trinity (Coll) B2
Turl St B2
University Coll (Coll) B3
University Museum & Pitt Rivers Museum A2
University Parks A2
Wadham (Coll) B2
Walton Cr A1
Walton St A1
Western Rd C2
Westgate Sh Ctr B2
Woodstock Rd A1
Worcester (Coll) B1

Peterborough 189

Athletics Arena B3
Bishop's Palace B2
Bishop's Rd B2/B3
Boongate A3
Bourges Boulevard A1
Bourges Retail Pk B1/B2
Bridge House (Council Offices) C2
Bridge St B2
Bright St A1
Broadway A2
Broadway A2
Brook St A2
Burghley Rd A2
Bus Station B2
Cavendish St A3
Charles St A3
Church St B2
Church Walk A2
Cobden Ave A1
Cobden St A1
Cowgate B2
Craig St A2
Crawthorne Rd A2
Cripple Sidings La C2
Cromwell Rd A1
Dickens St A3
Eastfield Rd A3
Eastgate B3
Fire Station A1
Fletton Ave C2
Frank Perkins Parkway C3
Geneva St A2
George St C1
Gladstone St A1
Glebe Rd C2
Gloucester Rd C3
Granby St B3
Grove St C1
Guildhall B2
Hadrians Ct C3
Henry St A2
Hereward Cross (Sh) B2
Hereward Rd B3
Information Ctr B2
Jubilee St C1
Key Theatre C2
Kent Rd B1
Kirkwood Cl B1
Lea Gdns B1
Library A2
Lincoln Rd A2
London Rd C2
Long Causeway B2
Lower Bridge St C2
Magistrates Court B2
Manor House St A2
Mayor's Walk A1
Midland Rd A1
Monument St A2
Morris St A3
Mus & Art Gallery B2
Nene Valley Railway C1
New Rd A2
New Rd C1
Northminster A2
Old Customs Ho C2
Oundle Rd C1
Padholme Rd A3
Palmerston Rd C1
Park Rd A2
Passport Office B2
Peterborough Station B1
Peterborough Nene Valley C1
Peterborough United FC C2
Police Station B2
Post Office A3/B1/B2/B3/C1
Priestgate B2
Queen's Walk C2
Queensgate Centre B2
Railworld C1
Regional Swimming & Fitness Centre B3
River La B1
Rivergate Sh Ctr B2
Riverside Mead C3
Russell St A1
St John's B2
St John's St A3
St Marks St A2
St Peter's B2
St Peter's Rd B2
Saxon Rd A3
Spital Bridge A1
Stagshaw Dr C3
Star Rd B3
Thorpe Lea Rd B1
Thorpe Rd B1
Thorpe's Lea Rd B1
Tower St A2
Town Hall B2
Viersen Platz B2
Vineyard Rd B3
Wake Rd B3
Wellington St A3
Wentworth St B2
Westgate B2
Whalley St A3
Wharf Rd C1
Whitsed St A3
YMCA A3

Plymouth 189

Alma Rd A1
Anstis St B1
Armada Centre B2
Armada St A3
Armada Way B2
Arts Centre B2
Athenaeum B1
Athenaeum St C1
Barbican C3
Barbican C3
Baring St A3
Bath St B1
Beaumont Park B3
Beaumont Rd B3
Black Friars Gin Distillery C2
Breton Side B3
Bus Station B2
Castle St C3
Cathedral (RC) B1
Cecil St B1
Central Park A1
Central Park Ave A2
Charles Church B3
Charles Cross B3
Charles St B2
City Museum & Art Gallery B2
Citadel Rd C2
Citadel Rd East C2
Civic Centre B2
Cliff Rd C1
Clifton Pl A3
Cobourg St A2
College of Art B2
Continental Ferry Port B1
Cornwall St B2
Dale Rd A2
Deptford Pl A3
Derry Ave A2
Derry's Cross B1
Drake Circus B2
Drake Cir Sh Ctr B2
Drake's Memorial C2
Drum B2
Eastlake St B2
Ebrington St B3
Elizabethan Ho C3
Elliot St C1
Endsleigh Pl A2
Exeter St B3
Fire Station A3
Fish Quay C3
Gibbons St A3
Glen Park Ave A2
Grand Pde C1
Great Western Rd C1
Greenbank Rd A3
Greenbank Terr A3
Guildhall B2
Hampton St B3
Harwell St B1
Hill Park Cr A3
Hoe Approach B2
Hoe Rd C2
Hoegate St C2
Houndiscombe Rd A2
Information Ctr C3
James St A2
Kensington Rd A3
King St B1
Lambhay Hill C3
Leigham St C1
Library B2
Lipson Rd A3/B3
Lockyer St C2
Lockyers Quay C3
Madeira Rd C2
Marina B3
Market Ave B1
Martin St B1
Mayflower Stone & Steps C3
Mayflower St B2
Mayflower Visitor Centre C3
Merchants House B2
Millbay Rd B1
National Marine Aquarium C3
Neswick St B1
New George St B2
New St C3
North Cross A2
North Hill A3
North Quay B2
North Rd East A2
North Rd West A1
North St B3
Notte St B2
Octagon St B1
Pannier Market B1
Pennycomequick A1
Pier St C1
Plymouth Pavilions B1
Plymouth Station A2
Police Station B3
Portland Sq A2
Post Office A1/B1/B2
Princess St B2
Prysten House B2
Queen Anne's Battery Seasports Centre C3
Radford Rd C1
Regent St B3
Rope Walk C3
Royal Citadel C2
Royal Pde B2
St Andrew's B2
St Andrew's Cross B2
St Andrew's St B2
St Lawrence Rd A2
Saltash Rd A2
Smeaton's Tower C2
Southern Terr A3
Southside St C2
Stuart Rd A1
Sutherland Rd A2
Sutton Rd B3
Sydney St A1
Teats Hill Rd C3
The Crescent B1
The Hoe C2
The Octagon B1
The Promenade C2
Tothill Ave B3
Union St B1
Univ of Plymouth A2
Vauxhall St B2/3
Victoria Park A1
West Hoe Rd C1
Western Approach B1
Whittington St A1
Wyndham St B1
YMCA B2
YWCA C2

Portsmouth 189

Action Stations C1
Admiralty Rd A1
Alfred Rd A2
Anglesea Rd B2
Arundel St B3
Aspex B1
Bishop St A2
Broad St C1
Buckingham Ho C2
Burnaby Rd B2
Bus Station B1
Camber Dock C1
Cambridge Rd B2
Car Ferry to Isle of Wight B1
Cascades Sh Ctr A3
Castle Rd C3
City Museum & Art Gallery B2
Civic Offices B3
Clarence Pier C2
College St B1
Commercial Rd A3
Cottage Gr B3
Cross St A1
Cumberland St A2
Duisburg Way C2
Durham St A3
East St B1
Edinburgh Rd A2
Elm Gr C3
Great Southsea St C3
Green Rd B3
Greetham St B3
Grosvenor St B3
Groundlings A2
Grove Rd North C3
Grove Rd South C3
Guildhall B3
Guildhall Walk B3
Gunwharf Quays Retail Park B1
Gunwharf Rd B1
Hambrook St C2
Hampshire Terr B2
Hanover St A1
High St C2
HM Naval Base A1
HMS Nelson (Royal Naval Barracks) A2
HMS Victory A1
HMS Warrior A1
Hovercraft Terminal C2
Hyde Park Rd B3
Information Ctr A1/B3
Isambard Brunel Rd B3
Isle of Wight Car Ferry Terminal B1
Kent Rd C3
Kent St A2
King St B3
King's Rd C3
King's Terr C2
Lake Rd A3
Law Courts B3
Library B3
Long Curtain Rd C2
Market Way A3
Marmion Rd C3
Mary Rose Museum A1
Middle St B3
Millennium Prom B1/C1
Museum Rd B2
National Museum of the Royal Navy A1
Naval Recreation Gd C2
Nightingale Rd C3
Norfolk St B3
North St A2
Osborne Rd C3
Park Rd B2
Passenger Catamaran to Isle of Wight B1
Passenger Ferry to Gosport B1
Pelham Rd C3
Pembroke Gdns C2
Pier Rd C2
Point Battery C1
Police Station B3
Portsmouth & Southsea A3
Portsmouth Harbour B1
Portsmouth Historic Dockyard A1
Post Office A2/A3/B1/B3/C3
Queen St A1
Queen's Cr C3
Round Tower C1
Royal Garrison Church C1
St Edward's Rd C3
St George's Rd B2
St George's Sq B1
St George's Way B2
St James's Rd B3
St James's St A2
St John's Cathedral (RC) A3
St Thomas's Cath C1
St Thomas's St B2
Somers Rd B3
Southsea Common C2
Southsea Terr C2
Spinnaker Tower B1
Square Tower C1
Station St A3
Swimming Pool A2
The Hard B1
Town Fortifications C1
Unicorn Rd A2
United Services Recreation Ground B2
University of Portsmouth A2/B2
University of Portsmouth – College of Art, Design and Media B3
Upper Arundel St A3
Victoria Ave C2
Victoria Park A2
Victory Gate A1
Vue B1
Warblington St B1
Western Pde C2
White Hart Rd C1
Winston Churchill Ave B3

Reading 190

Abbey Ruins B2
Abbey Sq B2
Abbey St B2
Abbot's Walk B2
Acacia Rd C2
Addington Rd C3
Addison Rd A1
Allcroft Rd C3
Alpine St C2
Baker St B1
Berkeley Ave C1
Bridge St B1
Brigham Rd A1
Broad St B1
Broad Street Mall B1
Carey St B1
Castle Hill C1
Castle St B1
Caversham Rd A1
Christchurch Playing Fields A2
Magistrate's Court B1
Civic Offices B1
Coley Hill C1
Coley Pl C1
Craven Rd C3
Crown St C2
De Montfort Rd A1
Denmark Rd C3
East St B2
Edgehill St C2
Eldon Rd B3
Eldon Terrace B3
Elgar Rd C1
Erleigh Rd C3
Field Rd C1
Fire Station A1
Fobney St B1
Forbury Gdns B2
Forbury Retail Park B2
Forbury Rd B2
Francis St C1
Friar St B1
Garrard St B1
Gas Works Rd B3
George St A2
Great Knollys St B1
Greyfriars B1
Gun St B1
Henry St C1
Hexagon Theatre, The B1
Hill's Meadow A2
Howard St B1
Information Ctr B1
Inner Distribution Rd B1
Katesgrove La C1
Kenavon Dr B2
Kendrick Rd C2
King's Mdw Rec Gd A2
King's Rd B2
Library B2
London Rd C3
London St B2
Lynmouth Rd A1
Market Pl B2
Mill La B2
Mill Rd A2
Minster St B1
Morgan Rd C3
Mount Pleasant C2
Museum of English Rural Life C3
Napier Rd A2
Newark St C2
Newport Rd A1
Old Reading Univ C3
Oracle Sh Ctr, The B1
Orts Rd B3
Pell St C1
Queen Victoria St B1
Queen's Rd A2
Queen's Rd B2
Police Station B1
Post Office B2
Randolph Rd A1
Reading Bridge A2
Reading Station A1
Redlands Rd C3
Renaissance Hotel B1
Riverside Mus B3
Rose Kiln La C1
Royal Berks Hospital (A&E) C3
St Giles C2
St Laurence B2
St Mary's B1
St Mary's Butts B1
St Saviour's Rd C1
Send Rd A3
Sherman Rd C2
Sidmouth St B2
Silver St C2
South St B2
Southampton St C2
Station Hill A1
Station Rd B1
Superstore A3
Swansea Rd A1
Technical College B3
The Causeway A3
The Grove B2
Valpy St B2
Vastern Rd A1
Vue B2
Waldeck St C2
Watlington St B3
West St B1
Whitby Dr C3
Wolseley St C1
York Rd A1
Zinzan St B1

Salisbury 190

Albany Rd A2
Arts Centre A3
Ashley Rd A1
Avon Approach A2
Ayleswade Rd C2
Bedwin St A2
Belle Vue A2
Bishop's Palace C2
Bishops Walk B2
Blue Boar Row B2
Bourne Ave A3
Bourne Hill A3
Britford La C2
Broad Walk C2
Brown St B2
Bus Station B2
Castle St A2
Catherine St B2
Chapter House B2
Church House B2
Churchfields Rd B1
Churchill Way East B3
Churchill Way North A3
Churchill Way South C2
Churchill Way West A1
City Hall B2
Close Wall B2
Coldharbour La A1
College St A3
Council Offices A3
Court A1
Crane Bridge Rd B2
Crane St B2
Cricket Ground C1
Culver St South B3
De Vaux Pl C2
Devizes Rd A1
Dews Rd B1
Elm Grove B3
Elm Grove Rd A3
Endless St A2
Estcourt Rd A3
Exeter St C2
Fairview Rd A3
Fire Station A1
Fisherton St A1
Folkestone Rd C1
Fowlers Hill B3
Fowlers Rd B3
Friary Estate C3
Friary La B2
Gas La A1
Gigant St B3
Greencroft B3
Greencroft St A3
Guildhall B2
Hall of John Halle B2
Hamilton Rd A2
Harnham Mill B1
Harnham Rd C1/C2
High St B2
Hospital A1
House of John A'Port B2
Information Ctr B2
Kelsey Rd A3
King's Rd A2
Laverstock Rd B3
Library B2
London Rd A3
Lower St C1
Maltings, The B2
Manor Rd A3
Marsh La A1
Medieval Hall B2
Milford Hill B3
Milford St B3
Mill Rd B1
Millstream Approach A2
Mompesson House (NT) B2
New Bridge Rd C2
New Canal B2
New Harnham Rd C2
New St B2
North Canonry B2
North Gate B2
North Walk B2
Old George Hall B2
Old Blandford Rd C1
Old Deanery B2
Park St A3
Parsonage Green C1
Playhouse Theatre A2
Post Office A2/B2/C2
Poultry Cross B2
Queen Elizabeth Gdns B1
Queen's Rd A3
Rampart Rd B3
St Ann's Gate B2
St Ann St B2
St Marks Rd A3
St Martins B3
St Mary's Cath B2
St Nicholas Hospital C2
St Paul's A1
St Paul's Rd A1
St Thomas B2
Salisbury & South Wiltshire Museum B2
Salisbury General Hospital (A&E) C2
Salisbury Station A1
Salt La A3
Saxon Rd C1
Scots La A2
Shady Bower B3
South Canonry C2
South Gate C2
Southampton Rd B2
Spire View A1
Sports Ground C3
The Friary B3
Tollgate Rd B3
Town Path B1
Wain-a-Long Rd A3
Wardrobe, The B2
Wessex Rd A3
West Walk C2
Wilton Rd A1
Wiltshire College B3
Winchester St B3
Windsor Rd A1
Winston Churchill Gdns C3
Wyndham Rd A2
YHA B3
York Rd A1

Scarborough 190

Aberdeen Walk B2
Albert Rd A2
Albion Rd C2
Alexandra Bowling Hall A1
Alexandra Gardens A1
Auborough St B2
Belle Vue St C1
Belmont Rd C2
Brunswick Pavilion Shopping Centre B2
Castle Dykes B3
Castlegate B3
Castle Holms A3
Castle Hill A3
Castle Rd B2
Castle Walls A3
Cemetery B1
Central Lift C2
Clarence Gardens A2
Coach Park B1
Columbus Ravine A1
Court B1
Cricket Ground C1
Cross St B2
Crown Terr C2
Dean Rd B1
Devonshire Dr A1
East Harbour B3
East Pier B3
Eastborough B2
Elmville Ave B1
Esplanade C2
Falconers Rd B2
Falsgrave Rd C1
Fire Station B2
Foreshore Rd B2
Friargate B2
Futurist Theatre B2
Gladstone Rd B1
Gladstone St B1
Hoxton Rd B1
Information Ctr B2/B3
King St B2
Library B2
Lifeboat Station B3
Londesborough Rd C1
Longwestgate B3
Marine Dr A3
Military Adventure Park A1
Miniature Railway A1
Nelson St B1
Newborough B2
Nicolas St B2
North Marine Rd A1
North St B2
Northway B1
Old Harbour B3
Olympia Leisure B2
Peasholm Park A1
Peasholm Rd A1
Plaza A1
Police Station B1
Post Office B2/C1
Princess St B3
Prospect Rd B1
Queen St B2
Queen's Parade A2
Queen's Tower (Remains) A3
Ramshill Rd C2
Roman Signal Sta A3
Roscoe St C1
Rotunda Museum C2
Royal Albert Dr A2
St Martin-on-the-Hill C2
St Martin's Ave C2
St Mary's B3
St Thomas St B2
Sandside B3
Scarborough Art Gallery and Crescent Art Studio C2
Scarborough Castle A3
Scarborough C1
Somerset Terr C2
South Cliff Lift C2
Spa, The C2
Spa Theatre, The C2
Stephen Joseph Theatre B1
Tennyson Ave B1
The Crescent C2
Tollergate B2
Town Hall B2
Trafalgar Rd B1
Trafalgar Square A1
Trafalgar St West B1
Valley Bridge Parade C2
Valley Rd C1
Vernon Rd C2
Victoria Park Mount A1
Victoria Rd B1
West Pier B3
Westborough C1
Westover Rd C1
Westwood C1
Woodall Ave A1
YMCA Theatre B2
York Pl B2
Yorkshire Coast College (Westwood Campus) C1

Sheffield 191

Addy Dr A2
Addy St A2
Adelphi St A3
Albert Terrace Rd A3
Albion St A2
Aldred Rd A1
Allen St A4
Alma St A4
Angel St B5
Arundel Gate B5
Arundel St C4
Ashberry Rd A2
Ashdell Rd C1
Ashgate Rd C1
Athletics Centre B2
Attercliffe Rd A6
Bailey St B4
Ball St A4
Balm Green B4
Bank St B4
Barber Rd A2
Bard St B5
Barker's Pool B4
Bates St A1
Beech Hill Rd C1
Beet St B3
Bellefield St A3
Bernard Rd A6
Bernard St B6
Birkendale A2
Birkendale Rd A2
Birkendale View A1
Bishop St C4
Blackwell Pl B6
Blake St A2
Blonk St A5
Bolsover St B2
Botanical Gdns C1
Bower Rd A1
Bradley St A1
Bramall La C4
Bramwell St A3
Bridge St A4/A5
Brighton Terrace Rd A1
Broad La B3
Broad St B6
Brocco St A3
Brook Hill B3
Broomfield Rd C1
Broomgrove Rd C2
Broomhall Pl C3
Broomhall Rd C2
Broomhall St C3
Broomspring La C2
Brown St C5
Brunswick St B3
Burgess St B4
Burlington St A2
Burns Rd A2
Cadman St A6
Cambridge St B4
Campo La B4
Carver St B4
Castle Market B5
Castle Square B5
Castlegate A5
Cathedral (RC) B4
Cathedral B4
Cavendish St B3
Charles St C4
Charter Row C4
Children's Hospital (A&E) B2
Church St B4
City Hall B4
City Hall B4
City Rd C6
Claremont Cr B2
Claremont Pl B2
Clarke St C3
Clarkegrove Rd C2
Clarkehouse Rd C1
Clarkson St B2
Cobden View Rd A1
Collegiate Cr C2
Commercial St B5
Commonside A1
Conduit Rd B1
Cornish St A3
Corporation St A4
Court B4
Cricket Inn Rd B6
Cromwell St A1
Crookes Rd B1
Crookes Valley Park B2
Crookes Valley Rd B2
Crookesmoor Rd A2
Crown Court A4
Crucible Theatre B5
Cutlers Gate A6
Cutler's Hall B4
Daniel Hill A2
Dental Hospital B2
Dept for Education & Employment C4
Devonshire Green B3
Devonshire St B3
Division St B4
Dorset St C2
Dover St A3
Duchess Rd C5
Duke St B5
Duncombe St A1
Durham Rd B2
Earl St C4
Earl Way C4
Ecclesall Rd C3
Edward St B3
Effingham Rd A6
Effingham St A6
Egerton St C3
Eldon St B3
Elmore Rd B1
Exchange St B5
Eyre St C4
Fargate B4
Farm Rd C5
Fawcett St A3
Filey St B3
Fire & Police Mus A4
Fire Station C4
Fir St A1
Fitzalan Sq/Ponds Forge B5
Fitzwater Rd C6
Fitzwilliam Gate C4
Fitzwilliam St B3
Flat St B5
Foley St A6
Foundry Climbing Ctr A4
Fulton Rd A1
Furnace Hill A4
Furnival Rd A5
Furnival Sq C4
Furnival St C4
Garden St B3
Gell St B3
Gibraltar St A4
Glebe Rd B1
Glencoe Rd C6
Glossop Rd B2/B3/C1
Gloucester St C2
Granville Rd C6
Granville Rd/Sheffield College C5
Graves Gallery B5
Greave Rd B3
Green La A4
Hadfield St A1
Hanover St C3
Hanover Way C3
Harcourt Rd B1
Harmer La B5
Havelock St C2
Hawley St B4
Haymarket B5
Headford St C3
Heavygate Rd A1
Henry St A3
High St B4
Hodgson St C3
Holberry Gdns C2

Hollis Croft B4
Holly St B4
Hounsfield Rd B3
Howard Rd A1
Hoyle St A3
Hyde Park A6
Infirmary Rd A3
Infirmary Rd A3
Information Ctr B4
Jericho St A3
Johnson St A5
Kelham Island Ind Mus A4
Lawson Rd C1
Leadmill Rd C5
Leadmill St C5
Leadmill, The C5
Leamington St A1
Leavy Rd B3
Lee Croft B4
Leopold St B4
Leveson St A6
Library A2
Library B5
Library C1
Lyceum Theatre B5
Malinda St A3
Maltravers St A5
Manor Oaks Rd B6
Mappin St B3
Marlborough Rd B1
Mary St C4
Matilda St C4
Matlock Rd A1
Meadow St A3
Melbourn Rd A1
Melbourne Ave C1
Millennium Galleries B5
Milton St C3
Mitchell St B3
Mona Ave A1
Mona Rd A1
Montgomery Terr Rd A3
Montgomery Theatre B4
Monument Gdns C6
Moor Oaks Rd B1
Moore St C3
Mowbray St A4
Mushroom La B2
Netherthorpe Rd B3
Netherthorpe Rd B3
Newbould La C1
Nile St C1
Norfolk Park Rd C6
Norfolk Rd C6
Norfolk St B4
North Church St B4
Northfield Rd A1
Northumberland Rd B1
Nursery St A5
O2 Academy B5
Oakholme Rd C1
Octagon B2
Odeon B5
Old St B6
Orchard Square B5
Oxford St A2
Paradise St B4
Park La C2
Park Sq B5
Parker's Rd B1
Pearson Building (Univ) C2
Penistone Rd A3
Pinstone St B4
Pitt St B3
Police Station A4/B5
Pond Hill B5
Pond St B5
Ponds Forge International Sports Centre B5
Portobello St B3
Post Office A1/A2/B3/B4/B5/B6/C1/C3/C4/C6
Powell St A2
Queen St B4
Queen's Rd C5
Ramsey Rd B1
Red Hill B3
Redcar Rd B1
Regent St B3
Rockingham St B4
Roebuck Rd A2
Royal Hallamshire Hospital C2
Russell St A4
Rutland Park C1
St George's Cl B3
St Mary's Gate C3
St Mary's Rd C4/C5
St Peter & St Paul Cathedral B4
St Philip's Rd A3
Savile St A5
School Rd B1
Scotland St A4
Severn Rd B1
Shalesmoor A4
Shalesmoor A3
Sheaf St B5
Sheffield Hallam University B5
Sheffield Ice Sports Ctr – Skate Central C5
Sheffield Interchange B5
Sheffield Parkway A6
Sheffield Station C5
Sheffield Sta/Sheffield Hallam Univ B5
Sheffield University B2
Shepherd St A3
Shipton St A2
Shoreham St C4
Showroom, The C5
Shrewsbury Rd C5
Sidney St C4
Site Gallery C5
Slinn St A1
Smithfield A4
Snig Hill A5
Snow La A4
Solly St B3
Southbourne Rd C1
South La C4
South Street Park B5
Spital Hill A5
Spital St A5
Spring Hill B1
Spring Hill Rd B1
Springvale Rd A1
Stafford Rd C6
Stafford St B6
Stanley St A5
Suffolk Rd C5
Summer St B2
Sunny Bank C3
Surrey St B4
Sussex St A6
Sutton St B3
Sydney Rd A2
Sylvester St C4
Talbot St B5
Taptonville Rd B1
Tax Office C4
Tenter St B4
The Moor C4
Town Hall B4
Townend St A1
Townhead St B4
Trafalgar St B4
Tree Root Walk B2
Trinity St A4
Trippet La B4
Turner Museum of Glass B3
Union St B4
Univ Drama Studio B2
Univ of Sheffield B3
Upper Allen St A3
Upper Hanover St B3
Upperthorpe Rd A2/A3
Verdon St A5
Victoria Quays B5
Victoria Rd C2
Victoria St B3
Waingate B5
Watery St A3
Watson Rd C1
Wellesley Rd B2
Wellington St C3
West Bar A4
West Bar Green A4
West One Plaza B3
West St B3
West St B4
Westbourne Rd C1
Western Bank B2
Western Rd A1
Weston Park B2
Weston Park Hospl B2
Weston Park Mus B2
Weston St A2
Wharncliffe Rd C3
Whitham Rd B1
Wicker A5
Wilkinson St B2
William St C3
Winter Garden B4
Winter St B2
York St B4
Yorkshire Artspace C5
Young St C4

Southampton 190

Above Bar St A2
Albert Rd North B3
Albert Rd South C3
Anderson's Rd B3
Archaeology Mus (God's Ho Tower) C2
Argyle Rd A2
Arundel Tower B1
Bargate, The B2
BBC Regional Centre A1
Bedford Pl A1
Belvidere Rd A3
Bernard St C2
Blechynden Terr A1
Brazil Rd C3
Brinton's Rd A2
Britannia Rd A3
Briton St C2
Brunswick Pl A1
Bugle St C1
Canute Rd C3
Castle Way C2
Catchcold Tower B1
Central Bridge C3
Central Rd C2
Channel Way C3
Chapel Rd B3
Cineworld C3
City Art Gallery A1
City College B3
Civic Centre A1
Civic Centre Rd A1
Coach Station B1
Commercial Rd A1
Cumberland Pl A1
Cunard Rd C2
Derby Rd A3
Devonshire Rd A1
Dock Gate 4 C2
Dock Gate 8 B1
East Park A2
East Park Terrace A2
East St B2
Endle St B3
European Way C2
Fire Station A2
Floating Bridge Rd C3
Golden Gr A3
Graham Rd A2
Guildhall A1
Hanover Bldgs B2
Harbour Lights C3
Harbour Pde B1
Hartington Rd A3
Havelock Rd A1
Henstead Rd A1
Herbert Walker Ave B1
High St B2
Hoglands Park B2
Holy Rood (Rems), Merchant Navy Memorial B2
Houndwell Park B2
Houndwell Pl B2
Hythe Ferry C2
Information Ctr A1
Isle of Wight Ferry Terminal C1
James St B3
Java Rd C2
Kingsway A2
Leisure World B1
Library A1
Lime St B2
London Rd A2
Marine Pde B3
Marsh La B2
Mayflower Meml C1
Mayflower Park C1
Mayflower Theatre, The A1
Medieval Merchant's House C1
Melbourne St B3
Millais A2
Morris Rd A1
National Oceanography Centre C3
Neptune Way C3
New Rd A2
Nichols Rd A3
North Front A2
Northam Rd A3
Ocean Dock C2
Ocean Village Marina C3
Ocean Way C3
Odeon B1
Ogle Rd B1
Old Northam Rd A2
Orchard La B2
Oxford Ave A2
Oxford St C2
Palmerston Park A2
Palmerston Rd A2
Parsonage Rd A3
Peel St A3
Platform Rd C2
Police Station A1
Portland Terr B1
Post Office A2/A3/B2
Pound Tree Rd B2
Quays Swimming & Diving Complex, The B1
Queen's Park C2
Queen's Peace Fountain A2
Queen's Terr C2
Queen's Way B2
Radcliffe Rd A3
Rochester St A3
Royal Pier C1
Royal South Hants Hospital A2
Sea City Mus A1
St Andrew's Rd A2
St Mary St A2
St Mary's B3
St Mary's Leisure Ctr A2
St Mary's Pl B2
St Mary's Rd A2
St Mary's Stadium (Southampton FC) A3
St Michael's C1
Solent Sky C3
South Front B2
Southampton Central Station A1
Southampton Solent University A2
SS Shieldhall C2
Terminus Terr C2
The Mall, Marlands A1
The Polygon A1
Threefield La B2
Titanic Engineers' Memorial A2
Town Quay C1
Town Walls B2
Tudor House C1
Vincent's Walk B2
West Gate Hall C1
West Marlands Rd A1
West Park A1
West Park Rd A1
West Quay Rd B1
West Quay Retail Pk B1
West Quay Sh Ctr B1
West Rd C2
Western Esplanade B1
Winton St A2

Southend-on-Sea 191

Adventure Island C3
Albany Ave A1
Albert Rd C3
Alexandra Rd C2
Alexandra St C2
Alexandra Yacht Club C2
Ashburnham Rd B2
Ave Rd B1
Avenue Terr B1
Balmoral Rd B1
Baltic Ave B3
Baxter Ave A2/B2
Beecroft Art Gallery C1
Bircham Rd A2
Boscombe Rd B3
Boston Ave A1/B2
Bournemouth Pk Rd A3
Browning Ave A3
Bus Station C3
Byron Ave A3
Cambridge Rd C1/C2
Canewdon Rd B1
Carnarvon Rd A2
Central Ave A3
Chelmsford Ave A1
Chichester Rd B2
Church Rd C3
Civic Centre A2
Clarence Rd C2
Clarence St C2
Cliff Ave B1
Cliffs Pavilion C1
Clifftown Parade C2
Clifftown Rd C2
Colchester Rd A1
College Way B2
Coleman St B3
County Court B3
Cromer Rd B3
Crowborough Rd A2
Dryden Ave A3
East St A2
Elmer App B2
Elmer Ave B2
Gainsborough Dr A1
Gayton Rd A2
Glenhurst Rd A2
Gordon Pl B2
Gordon Rd B2
Grainger Rd A2
Greyhound Way A3
Guildford Rd B3
Hamlet Ct Rd B1
Hamlet Rd C1
Harcourt Ave A1
Hartington Rd C3
Hastings Rd B3
Herbert Gr C3
Heygate Ave C3
High St B2/C2
Information Ctr C3
Kenway A2
Kilworth Ave B3
Lancaster Gdns B3
Library B2
London Rd B1
Lucy Rd C3
MacDonald Ave A1
Magistrates Court A2
Maldon Rd A2
Maine Ave C1
Marine Rd C1
Marine Parade C3
Milton Rd B1
Milton St B2
Napier Ave B2
North Ave A3
North Rd A1/B1
Odeon B2
Osborne Rd B1
Park Cres B1
Park Rd B1
Park St B1
Park Terr B1
Pier Hill C3
Pleasant Rd C3
Police Station A2
Post Office B2/B3
Princes St B2
Queens Rd B2
Queensway B2/B3/C3
Rayleigh Ave A1
Redstock Rd A2
Rochford Ave A1
Royal Mews C2
Royal Terr C2
Royals Sh Ctr, The C3
Ruskin Ave A3
St Ann's Rd B3
St Helen's Rd B1
St John's Rd B1
St Leonard's Rd C3
St Lukes Rd A3
St Vincent's Rd C1
Salisbury Ave A1/B1
Scratton Rd C2
Shakespeare Dr A1
Short St A2
South Ave A3
Southchurch Rd B3
South Essex College B2
Southend Central B2
Southend Pier Railway C3
Southend Radio C2
Southend United FC A1
Southend Victoria B2
Stadium Rd A2
Stanfield Rd A2
Stanley Rd C3
Sutton Rd A3/B3
Swanage Rd B3
Sweyne Ave A1
Sycamore Gr A3
Tennyson Ave A3
The Grove A3
Tickfield Ave A2
Tudor Rd A1
Tunbridge Rd A2
Tylers Ave B3
Tyrrel Dr B3
Univ of Essex B2/C2
Vale Ave A2
Victoria Ave A2
Victoria Sh Ctr, The B2
Warrior Sq B3
Wesley Rd C3
West Rd A1
West St A1
Westcliff Ave C1
Westcliff Parade C1
Western Esplanade C1
Weston Rd C2
Whitegate Rd B3
Wilson Rd C1
Wimborne Rd B3
York Rd C3

Stoke 191

Ashford St A3
Avenue Rd A3
Aynsley Rd A2
Barnfield C1
Bath St C2
Beresford St A3
Bilton St C2
Boon Ave C2
Booth St C2
Boothen Rd C2/C3
Boughey St C2
Boughley Rd B3
Brighton St B1
Campbell Rd C2
Carlton Rd B2
Cauldon Rd A3
Cemetery A2
Cemetery Rd A2
Chamberlain Ave C1
Church (RC) B2
Church St C2
City Rd C3
Civic Centre & King's Hall B3
Cliff Vale Pk A1
College Rd A3
Convent Cl B2
Copeland St B2
Cornwallis St C3
Corporation St C2
Crowther St A3
Dominic St B1
Elenora St B2
Elgin St B2
Epworth St A3
Etruscan St A1
Film Theatre B3
Fleming Rd C2
Fletcher Rd C2
Floyd St B2
Foden St C2
Frank St C2
Franklin Rd C1
Frederick Ave B1
Garden St C2
Garner St A2
Gerrard St B2
Glebe St B3
Greatbach Ave B1
Hanley Park A3
Harris St B1
Hartshill Rd B1
Hayward St A2
Hide St B2
Higson Ave B2
Hill St B2
Honeywall B2
Hunters Dr C1
Hunters Way C1
Keary St C2
Kingsway B2
Leek Rd B3
Library C2
Lime St C2
Liverpool Rd B2
London Rd C2
Lonsdale St C2
Lovatt St B2
Lytton St B3
Market A2
Newcastle La C1
Newlands St A2
Norfolk St A2
North St A1/B2
North Staffordshire Royal Infirmary (A&E) B1
Northcote Ave B2
Oldmill St C3
Oriel St B1
Oxford St B1
Penkhull New Rd C1
Penkhull St C1
Police Station C2
Portmeirion Pottery C2
Post Office A3/B1/B3/C1/C2
Prince's Rd B1
Pump St B2
Quarry Ave B2
Quarry Rd B1
Queen Anne St A3
Queen's Rd C1
Queensway A1/B2/C3
Richmond St B1
Rothwell St C1
St Peter's B3
St Thomas Pl C1
Scrivenor Rd A1
Seaford St A3
Selwyn St C3
Shelton New Rd A1
Shelton Old Rd B2
Sheppard St C2
Spark St C2
Spencer Rd B3
Spode St C2
Squires View B3
Staffordshire Univ B3
Stanley Matthews Sports Centre B3
Station Rd B3
Stoke Business Park C3
Stoke Recreation Ctr C2
Stoke Rd A2
Stoke-on-Trent Coll A3
Stoke-on-Trent Station B3
Sturgess St C2
The Villas C1
Thistley Hough C1
Thornton Rd B3
Tolkien Way B1
Trent Valley Rd C1
Vale St B2
Watford St A3
Wellesley St A3
West Ave B1
Westland St B1
Yeaman St C2
Yoxall Ave B1

Stratford-upon-Avon 192

Albany Rd B1
Alcester Rd B1
Ambulance Station B1
Arden St B1
Avenue Farm A1
Ave Farm Ind Est A1
Avenue Rd A3
Avon Industrial Est A2
Baker Ave A1
Bandstand C3
Benson Rd A3
Birmingham Rd A2
Boat Club B3
Borden Pl C1
Brass Rubbing Ctr C2
Bridge St B2
Bridgetown Rd C3
Bridgeway B3
Broad St C2
Broad Walk C2
Brookvale Rd C1
Bull St C2
Bus Station B2
Butterfly Farm C3
Cemetery C1
Chapel La B2
Cherry Orchard C1
Chestnut Walk B2
Children's Playground C3
Church St C2
Civic Hall B2
Clarence Rd B1
Clopton Bridge B3
Clopton Rd A2
Coach Terminal & Pk B3
College B1
College La C2
College St C2
Com Sports Centre B1
Council Offices (District) B2
Courtyard C2
Cox's Yard B3
Cricket Ground C3
Ely Gdns B2
Ely St B2
Evesham Rd C1
Fire Station B1
Foot Ferry C3
Fordham Ave A2
Garrick Way C1
Gower Memorial B3
Great William St B2
Greenhill St B2
Grove Rd B2
Guild St B2
Guildhall & School B2
Hall's Croft C2
Hartford Rd C1
Harvard House B2
Henley St B2
High St B2
Holton St C2
Holy Trinity C2
Information Ctr B3
Jolyffe Park Rd A2
Kipling Rd C3
Leisure & Visitor Ctr B3
Library B2
Lodge Rd B1
Maidenhead Rd A3
Mansell St B2
Masons Court B2
Masons Rd A1
Maybird Shopping Pk A2
Maybrook Rd A1
Mayfield Ave A2
Meer St B2
Mill La C2
Moat House Hotel B3
Narrow La C2
Nash's House & New Place B2
New St C2
Old Town C2
Orchard Way C1
Paddock La C1
Park Rd A1
Payton St B2
Percy St A2
Police Station B2
Post Office B2/B3
Recreation Ground C2
Regal Road A2
Rother St B2
Rowley Cr A3
Royal Shakespeare Theatre B3
Ryland St C2
Saffron Meadow C2
St Andrew's Cr B1
St Gregory's A3
St Gregory's Rd A3
St Mary's Rd A2
Sanctus Dr C2
Sanctus St C1
Sandfield Rd C2
Scholars La B2
Seven Meadows Rd C2
Shakespeare Ctr B2
Shakespeare Inst C2
Shakespeare St B2
Shakespeare's Birthplace B2
Sheep St B2
Shelley Rd C3
Shipston Rd C3
Shottery Rd C1
Slingates Rd A2
Southern La C2
Station Rd B1
Stratford Healthcare B2
Stratford Hospital B2
Stratford Sports Club B1
Stratford-upon-Avon Station B1
Swan's Nest La B3
Swan Theatre B3
Talbot Rd A2
The Greenway C2
The Willows B1
The Willows North B1
Tiddington Rd B3
Timothy's Bridge Industrial Estate A1
Timothy's Bridge Rd A1
Town Hall & Council Offices B2
Town Sq B2
Trinity St C2
Tyler St B2
War Memorial Gdns B3
Warwick Rd B3
Waterside B3
Welcombe Rd A3
West St C2
Western Rd A2
Wharf Rd A2
Wood St B2

Sunderland 192

Albion Pl C2
Alliance Pl B1
Argyle St C2
Ashwood St C1
Athenaeum St B2
Azalea Terr C2
Beach St A1
Bede Theatre C3
Bedford St B2
Beechwood Terr C1
Belvedere Rd C2
Blandford St B2
Borough Rd B3
Bridge Cr B2
Bridge St B2
Brooke St A2
Brougham St B2
Burdon Rd C2
Burn Park C1
Burn Park Rd C1
Burn Park Tech Park C1
Carol St B1
Charles St A3
Chester Rd C1
Chester Terr B1
Church St A3
Civic Centre C2
Cork St B3
Coronation St B3
Cowan Terr C2
Crowtree Rd B2
Dame Dorothy St A2
Deptford Rd B1
Deptford Terr A1
Derby St C2
Derwent St C2
Dock St A3
Dundas St A2
Durham Rd C1
Easington St A2
Egerton St C3
Empire B2
Empire Theatre B2
Farringdon Row B1
Fawcett St B2
Fox St C1
Foyle St B3
Frederick St B3
Gill Rd B2
Hanover Pl A1
Havelock Terrace C1
Hay St A2
Headworth Sq B3
Hendon Rd B3
High St East B3
High St West B2/B3
Holmeside B2
Hylton Rd B1
Information Ctr B2
John St B3
Kier Hardie Way A2
Lambton St B3
Laura St C3
Lawrence St B3
Leisure Centre B2
Library & Arts Ctr B3
Lily St B1
Lime St B1
Livingstone Rd B2
Low Row B2
Matamba Terr B1
Millburn St B1
Millennium Way A2
Minster B2
Monkwearmouth Station Museum A2
Mowbray Park C3
Mowbray Rd C3
Murton St C3
National Glass Ctr A3
New Durham Rd C1
Newcastle Rd A2
Nile St B3
Norfolk St B3
North Bridge St A2
Northern Gallery for Contemporary Art B3
Otto Terr C1
Park La C2
Park Lane C2
Park Rd C2
Paul's Rd B3
Peel St C3
Police Station B2
Post Office B2
Priestly Cr A1
Queen St B2
Railway Row B1
Retail Park B1
Richmond St A2
Roker Ave A2
Royalty Theatre C1
Ryhope Rd C2
St Mary's Way B2
St Michael's Way B2
St Peter's A3
St Peter's A2
St Peter's Way A3
St Vincent St C3
Salem Rd C3
Salem St C3
Salisbury St C3
Sans St B3
Silkworth Row B1
Southwick Rd A2
Stadium of Light (Sunderland AFC) A2
Stadium Way A2
Stobart St A2
Stockton Rd C2
Suffolk St C3
Sunderland Aquatic Centre A2
Sunderland B2
Sunderland Mus B3
Sunderland Sta B2
Sunderland St B3
Tatham St C3
Tavistock Pl B3
The Bridges B2
The Place B3
The Royalty C1
Thelma St C1
Thomas St North A2
Thornholme Rd C1
Toward Rd C3
Transport Interchange C2
Trimdon St Way B1
Tunstall Rd C2
University C1
University Library C1
Univ of Sunderland (City Campus) B1
Univ of Sunderland (Sir Tom Cowie at St Peter's Campus) A3
Vaux Brewery Way A2
Villiers St B3
Villiers St South B3
Vine Pl C2
Violet St B1
Walton La B3
Waterworks Rd B1
Wearmouth Bridge B2
Wellington La A1
West Sunniside B3
West Wear St B3
Westbourne Rd B1
Western Hill C1
Wharncliffe B1
Whickham St A3
White House Rd C3
Wilson St North A2
Winter Gdns C3
Wreath Quay A1

Swansea 192
Abertawe

Adelaide St C3
Albert Row C3
Alexandra Rd B3
Argyle St C1
Baptist Well Pl A2
Beach St C1
Belle Vue Way B3
Berw Rd A1
Berwick Terr A2
Bond St C1
Brangwyn Concert Hall C1
Bridge St A3
Brookands Terr B1
Brunswick St C1
Bryn-Syfi Terr A2
Bryn-y-Mor Rd C1
Bullins La B1
Burrows Rd C1
Bus/Rail link A3
Bus Station C2
Cadfan Rd A1
Cadrawd Rd A1
Caer St B3
Carig Cr A1
Carlton Terr B2
Carmarthen Rd A3
Castle Square B3
Castle St B3
Catherine St C1
Cinema C3
Civic Ctr & Library C2
Clarence St C2
Colbourne Terr A2
Constitution Hill B1
Court B3
Creidiol Rd A2
Cromwell St B2
Duke St B1
Dunvant Pl C2
Dyfatty Park A3
Dyfatty St A3
Dyfed Ave A1
Dylan Thomas Ctr B3
Dylan Thomas Theatre C3
Eaton Cr C1
Eigen Cr A1
Elfed Rd A1
Emlyn Rd A1
Evans Terr A3
Fairfield Terr B1
Ffynone Dr B1
Ffynone Rd B1
Fire Station B3
Firm St A2
Fleet St C1
Francis St C1
Fullers Row B2
George St B2
Glamorgan St C2
Glyndŵr Pl A1
Graig Terr A3
Grand Theatre C2
Granogwen Rd A2
Guildhall C1
Guildhall Rd South C1
Gwent Rd A1
Gwynedd Ave A1
Hafod St A3
Hanover St B1
Harcourt St B2
Harries St A2
Heathfield B2
Henrietta St B1
Hewson St B2
High St A3/B3
High View A2
Hill St A2
Historic Ships Berth C3
HM Prison C2
Information Ctr C2
Islwyn Rd A1
King Edward's Rd C1
Law Courts C1
Long Ridge A2
Madoc St C2
Mansel St B2
Maritime Quarter C3
Market B3
Mayhill Gdns B1
Mayhill Rd A1
Mega Bowl B3
Milton Terr A2
Mission Gallery C3
Montpellier Terr B1
Morfa Rd A3
Mount Pleasant B2
National Waterfront Museum C3
Nelson St C2
New Cut Rd A3
New St A3
Nicander Pde A2
Nicander Pl A2
Nicholl St B2
Norfolk St B2
North Hill Rd A2
Northampton La B2
Orchard St B3
Oxford St B2
Oystermouth Rd C1
Page St B2
Pant-y-Celyn Rd B1
Parc Tawe Link B3
Parc Tawe North B3
Parc Tawe Sh & L Ctr B3
Patti Pavilion C1
Paxton St C2
Penmaen Terr B1
Pen-y-Graig Rd A1
Phillips Pde C1
Picton Terr B2
Plantasia B3
Police Station B2
Post Office A1/A2/B2/C1
Powys Ave A1
Primrose St B2
Princess Way B3
Promenade B2
Pryder Gdns A1
Quadrant Centre C2
Quay Park B3
Rhianfa La B1
Rhondda St B2
Richardson St C2
Rodney St C1
Rose Hill B1
Rosehill Terr B1
Russell St B1
St Helen's Ave C1
St Helen's Cr C1
St Helen's Rd C1
St James Gdns B1
St James's Cr B1
St Mary's B3
Sea View Terr A3
Singleton St C2
South Dock C3
Stanley Pl B2
Strand B3
Swansea Castle B3
Swansea College Arts Centre C1
Swansea Metropolitan University B2
Swansea Museum C3
Swansea Station A3
Taliesyn Rd B1
Tan y Marian Rd A1
Tegid Rd A2
Teilo Cres A1
Terrace Rd B1/B2
The Kingsway B2
The LC C3
Tontine St A3
Tower of Eclipse C3
Townhill Rd A1
Tramshed The C3
Trawler Rd C3
Union St B2
Upper Strand A3
Vernon St A3
Victoria Quay C3
Victoria Rd B3
Vincent St C1
Walter Rd B1
Watkin St A2
Waun-Wen Rd A2
Wellington St C2
Westbury St C1
Western St C1
Westway C2
William St C2
Wind St B3
Woodlands Terr B1
YMCA B2
York St C3

Swindon 192

Albert St C3
Albion St C1
Alfred St A2
Alvescot Rd C3
Art Gallery & Mus C3
Ashford Rd C1
Aylesbury St A2
Bath Rd C2
Bathampton St B1
Bathurst Rd B3
Beatrice St A2
Beckhampton St B3
Bowood Rd C1
Bristol St B1
Broad St A3
Brunel Arcade B2
Brunel Plaza B2
Brunswick St C2
Bus Station B2
Cambria Bridge Rd B1
Cambria Place B1
Canal Walk B2
Carfax St B2
Carr St B1
Cemetery C1/C3
Chandler Cl C3
Chapel C1
Chester St B1
Christ Church C3
Church Place B1
Cirencester Way A3
Clarence St B2
Clifton St C1
Cockleberry A2
Colbourne A3
Colbourne St A3
College St B2
Commercial Rd B2
Corporation St A2
Council Offices B3
County Rd A3
Courts B2
Cricket Ground A3
Cricklade Street C3
Crombey St B1/C2
Cross St C2
Curtis St B1
Deacon St C1
Designer Outlet (Great Western) B1
Dixon St C2
Dover St C2
Dowling St C2
Drove Rd C3
Dryden St C1
Durham St C3
East St B1
Eastcott Hill C2
Eastcott Rd C2
Edgeware Rd B2
Edmund St C2
Elmina Rd A3
Emlyn Square B1
Euclid St B3
Exeter St B1
Fairview C1
Faringdon Rd B1
Farnsby St B1
Fire Station B3
Fleet St B2
Fleming Way B2/B3
Florence St A2
Gladstone St A3
Gooch St A2
Graham St A3
Great Western Way A1/A2
Groundwell Rd B3
Hawksworth Way A1
Haydon St A2
Henry St B2
Hillside Ave C1
Holbrook Way B2
Hunt St C3
Hydro B1
Hythe Rd C2
Information Ctr B2
Joseph St C1
Kent Rd C2
King William St C2
Kingshill Rd C1
Lansdown Rd C2
Leicester St B3
Library B2
Lincoln St B3
Little London C3
London St B1
Magic B3
Maidstone Rd C2
Manchester Rd A3
Maxwell St B1
Milford St B2
Milton Rd B1
Morse St C2
National Monuments Record Centre B1
Newcastle St B3
Newcombe Drive A1
Newcombe Trading Estate A1
Newhall St C2
North St C2
North Star Ave A1
North Star A1
Northampton St B3
Oasis Leisure Centre A1
Ocotal Way A3
Okus Rd C1
Old Town C3
Oxford St B1
Park Lane B1
Park Lane B1
Pembroke St C2
Plymouth St B3
Polaris House A2
Polaris Way A2
Police Station B2
Ponting St A2
Post Office B1/B2/C1/C3
Poulton St A3
Princes St B2
Prospect Hill C2
Prospect Place C2
Queen St B2
Queen's Park C3
Radnor St C1
Read St C1
Reading St B1
Regent St B2
Retail Park A2/A3/B3

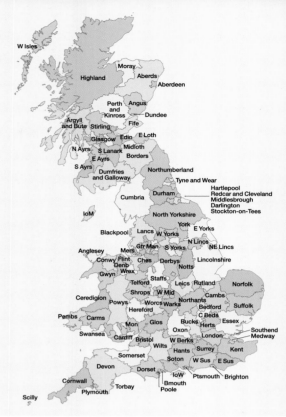

Abbreviations used in the index

Abbreviation	Name
Aberdeen	Aberdeen City
Aberds	Aberdeenshire
Ald	Alderney
Anglesey	Isle of Anglesey
Angus	Angus
Argyll	Argyll and Bute
Bath	Bath and North East Somerset
Bedford	Bedford
Bl Gwent	Blaenau Gwent
Blackburn	Blackburn with Darwen
Blackpool	Blackpool
Bmouth	Bournemouth
Borders	Scottish Borders
Brack	Bracknell
Bridgend	Bridgend
Brighton	City of Brighton and Hove
Bristol	City and County of Bristol
Bucks	Buckinghamshire
C Beds	Central Bedfordshire
Caerph	Caerphilly
Cambs	Cambridgeshire
Cardiff	Cardiff
Carms	Carmarthenshire
Ceredig	Ceredigion
Ches E	Cheshire East
Ches W	Cheshire West and Chester
Clack	Clackmannanshire
Conwy	Conwy
Corn	Cornwall
Cumb	Cumbria
Darl	Darlington
Denb	Denbighshire
Derby	City of Derby
Derbys	Derbyshire
Devon	Devon
Dorset	Dorset
Dumfries	Dumfries and Galloway
Dundee	Dundee City
Durham	Durham
E Ayrs	East Ayrshire
E Dunb	East Dunbartonshire
E Loth	East Lothian
E Renf	East Renfrewshire
E Sus	East Sussex
E Yorks	East Riding of Yorkshire
Edin	City of Edinburgh
Essex	Essex
Falk	Falkirk
Fife	Fife
Flint	Flintshire
Glasgow	City of Glasgow
Glos	Gloucestershire
Gtr Man	Greater Manchester
Guern	Guernsey
Gwyn	Gwynedd
Halton	Halton
Hants	Hampshire
Hereford	Herefordshire
Herts	Hertfordshire
Highld	Highland
Hrtlpl	Hartlepool
Hull	Hull
IoM	Isle of Man
IoW	Isle of Wight
Invclyd	Inverclyde
Jersey	Jersey
Kent	Kent
Lancs	Lancashire
Leicester	City of Leicester
Leics	Leicestershire
Lincs	Lincolnshire
London	Greater London
Luton	Luton
M Keynes	Milton Keynes
M Tydf	Merthyr Tydfil
Mbro	Middlesbrough
Medway	Medway
Mers	Merseyside
Midloth	Midlothian
Mon	Monmouthshire
Moray	Moray
N Ayrs	North Ayrshire
N Lincs	North Lincolnshire
N Lanark	North Lanarkshire
N Som	North Somerset
N Yorks	North Yorkshire
NE Lincs	North East Lincolnshire
Neath	Neath Port Talbot
Newport	City and County of Newport
Norf	Norfolk
Northants	Northamptonshire
Northumb	Northumberland
Nottingham	City of Nottingham
Notts	Nottinghamshire
Orkney	Orkney
Oxon	Oxfordshire
Pboro	Peterborough
Pembs	Pembrokeshire
Perth	Perth and Kinross
Plym	Plymouth
Poole	Poole
Powys	Powys
Ptsmth	Portsmouth
Reading	Reading
Redcar	Redcar and Cleveland
Renfs	Renfrewshire
Rhondda	Rhondda Cynon Taff
Rutland	Rutland
S Ayrs	South Ayrshire
S Glos	South Gloucestershire
S Lanark	South Lanarkshire
S Yorks	South Yorkshire
Scilly	Scilly
Shetland	Shetland
Shrops	Shropshire
Slough	Slough
Som	Somerset
Soton	Southampton
Staffs	Staffordshire
Southend	Southend-on-Sea
Stirling	Stirling
Stockton	Stockton-on-Tees
Stoke	Stoke-on-Trent
Suff	Suffolk
Sur	Surrey
Swansea	Swansea
Swindon	Swindon
T&W	Tyne and Wear
Telford	Telford and Wrekin
Thurrock	Thurrock
Torbay	Torbay
Torf	Torfaen
V Glam	The Vale of Glamorgan
W Berks	West Berkshire
W Dunb	West Dunbartonshire
W Isles	Western Isles
W Loth	West Lothian
W Mid	West Midlands
W Sus	West Sussex
W Yorks	West Yorkshire
Warks	Warwickshire
Warr	Warrington
Wilts	Wiltshire
Windsor	Windsor and Maidenhead
Wokingham	Wokingham
Worcs	Worcestershire
Wrex	Wrexham
York	City of York

How to use the index

Example

Trudoxhill Som **24** E2

- grid square
- page number
- county or unitary authority

Index to road maps of Britain

A

Ab Kettleby Leics 64 B4
Ab Lench Worcs 50 D5
Abbas Combe Som 12 B5
Abberley Worcs 50 C2
Abberton Essex 43 C6
Abberton Worcs 50 D4
Abberwick Northumb 117 C7
Abbess Roding Essex 42 C1
Abbey Devon 11 C6
Abbey-cwm-hir Powys 48 B2
Abbey Dore Hereford 49 F5
Abbey Field Essex 43 B5
Abbey Hulton Stoke 75 E6
Abbey St Bathans Borders 122 C3
Abbey Town Cumb 107 D8
Abbey Village Lancs 86 B4
Abbey Wood London 29 B5
Abbeydale S Yorks 88 F4
Abbeystead Lancs 93 D5
Abbots Bickington Devon 9 C5
Abbots Bromley Staffs 62 B4
Abbots Langley Herts 40 D3
Abbots Leigh N Som 23 B7
Abbots Morton Worcs 50 D5
Abbots Ripton Cambs 54 B3
Abbots Salford Warks 51 D5
Abbotsbury Dorset 12 F3
Abbotsham Devon 9 B6
Abbotskerswell Devon 7 C6
Abbotsley Cambs 54 D3
Abbotswood Hants 14 B4
Abbotts Ann Hants 25 E8
Abcott Shrops 49 B5
Abdon Shrops 61 F5
Aber Ceredig 46 E3
Aber-Arad Carms 46 F2
Aber-banc Ceredig 46 E2
Aber Cowarch Gwyn 59 C5
Aber-Giâr Carms 46 E4
Aber-gwynfi Neath 34 E2
Aber-Hirnant Gwyn 72 F3
Aber-nant Rhondda 34 D4
Aber-Rhiwlech Gwyn 59 B6
Aber-Village Powys 35 B5
Aberaeron Ceredig 46 C3
Aberaman Rhondda 34 D4
Aberangell Gwyn 58 C5
Aberarder Highld 137 F7
Aberarder House Highld 138 B2
Aberarder Lodge Highld 137 F8
Aberargie Perth 128 C3
Aberarth Ceredig 46 C3
Aberavon Neath 33 E8
Aberbeeg Bl Gwent 35 D6
Abercanaid M Tydf 34 D4
Abercarn Caerph 35 E6
Abercastle Pembs 44 B3
Abercegir Powys 58 D5
Aberchirder Aberds 152 C6
Abercraf Powys 34 C2
Abercrombie Fife 129 D7
Abercych Pembs 45 E4
Abercynafon Powys 34 C4
Abercynon Rhondda 34 E4
Aberdalgie Perth 128 B2
Aberdâr = Aberdare Rhondda 34 D3
Aberdare = Aberdâr Rhondda 34 D3
Aberdaron Gwyn 70 E2
Aberdaugleddau = Milford Haven Pembs 44 E4
Aberdeen Aberdeen 141 D8
Aberdesach Gwyn 82 F4
Aberdour Fife 128 F3
Aberdovey Gwyn 58 E3
Aberdulais Neath 34 D1
Aberedw Powys 48 E2
Abereiddy Pembs 44 B2
Abererch Gwyn 70 D4
Aberfan M Tydf 34 D4
Aberfeldy Perth 133 E5
Aberffraw Anglesey 82 E3
Aberffrwd Ceredig 47 B5
Aberford W Yorks 95 F7
Aberfoyle Stirling 126 D4
Abergavenny = Y Fenni Mon 35 C6
Abergele Conwy 72 B3
Abergorlech Carms 46 F4
Abergwaun = Fishguard Pembs 44 B4
Abergwesyn Powys 47 D7
Abergwili Carms 33 B5
Abergwynant Gwyn 58 C3
Abergwyngregyn Gwyn 83 D6
Abergynolwyn Gwyn 58 D3
Aberhonddu = Brecon Powys 34 B4
Aberhosan Powys 58 E5
Aberkenfig Bridgend 34 F2
Aberlady E Loth 129 F6
Aberlemno Angus 135 D5
Aberllefenni Gwyn 58 D4
Abermagwr Ceredig 47 B5
Abermaw = Barmouth Gwyn 58 C3
Abermeurig Ceredig 46 D4
Abermule Powys 59 E8
Abernaint Powys 59 B8
Abernant Carms 32 B4
Abernethy Perth 128 C3
Abernyte Perth 134 F2
Aberpennar = Mountain Ash Rhondda 34 E4
Aberporth Ceredig 45 D4
Abersoch Gwyn 70 E4
Abersychan Torf 35 D6
Abertawe = Swansea Swansea 33 E7
Aberteifi = Cardigan Ceredig 45 E3
Aberthin V Glam 22 B2
Abertillery = Abertyleri Bl Gwent 35 D6
Abertridwr Caerph 35 F5
Abertridwr Powys 59 C7
Abertyleri = Abertillery Bl Gwent 35 D6
Abertysswg Caerph 35 D5
Aberuthven Perth 127 C8
Aberyscir Powys 34 B3
Aberystwyth Ceredig 58 F2
Abhainn Suidhe W Isles 154 G5
Abingdon-on-Thames Oxon 38 E4
Abinger Common Sur 28 E2
Abinger Hammer Sur 27 E8
Abington S Lanark 114 B2
Abington Pigotts Cambs 54 E4
Ablington Glos 37 D8
Ablington Wilts 25 E6
Abney Derbys 75 B8
Aboyne Aberds 140 E4
Abram Gtr Man 86 D4
Abriachan Highld 151 H8
Abridge Essex 41 E7
Abronhill N Lanark 119 B7
Abson S Glos 24 B2
Abthorpe Northants 52 E4
Abune-the-Hill Orkney 159 F3
Aby Lincs 79 B7
Acaster Malbis York 95 E8
Acaster Selby N Yorks 95 E8
Accrington Lancs 87 B5
Acha Argyll 146 F4
Acha Mor W Isles 155 E8
Achabraid Argyll 145 E7
Achachork Highld 149 D9
Achafolla Argyll 124 D3
Achagary Highld 157 D10
Achahoish Argyll 144 F6
Achalader Perth 133 E8
Achallader Argyll 131 E7
Ach'an Todhair Highld 130 B4
Achanalt Highld 150 E5
Achanamara Argyll 144 E6
Achandunie Highld 151 D9
Achany Highld 157 J8
Achaphubuil Highld 130 B4
Acharacle Highld 147 E9
Acharn Highld 147 F10
Acharn Perth 132 E4
Acharole Highld 158 E4
Achath Aberds 141 C6
Achavanich Highld 158 F3
Achavraat Highld 151 G12
Achddu Carms 33 D5
Achduart Highld 156 J3
Achentoul Highld 157 F11
Achfary Highld 156 F5
Achgarve Highld 155 H13
Achiemore Highld 156 C6
Achiemore Highld 157 D11
A'Chill Highld 148 H7
Achiltibuie Highld 156 J3
Achina Highld 157 C10
Achinduich Highld 157 J8
Achinduin Argyll 124 B4
Achingills Highld 158 D3
Achintee Highld 131 B5
Achintee Highld 150 G2
Achintraid Highld 149 E13
Achlean Highld 138 E4
Achleck Argyll 146 G7
Achluachrach Highld 137 F5
Achlyness Highld 156 D5
Achmelvich Highld 156 G3
Achmore Highld 149 E13
Achmore Stirling 132 F2
Achnaba Argyll 124 B5
Achnaba Argyll 145 E8
Achnabat Highld 151 H8
Achnacarnin Highld 156 F3
Achnacarry Highld 136 F4
Achnacloich Argyll 125 B5
Achnacloich Highld 149 H10
Achnaconeran Highld 137 C7
Achnacraig Argyll 146 G7
Achnacroish Argyll 130 E2
Achnadrish Argyll 146 F7
Achnafalnich Argyll 125 C8
Achnagarron Highld 151 E9
Achnaha Highld 146 E7
Achnahanat Highld 151 B8
Achnahannet Highld 139 B5
Achnairn Highld 157 H8
Achnaluachrach Highld 157 J9
Achnasaul Highld 136 F4
Achnasheen Highld 150 F4
Achosnich Highld 146 E7
Achranich Highld 147 G10
Achreamie Highld 157 C13
Achriabhach Highld 131 C5
Achriesgill Highld 156 D5
Achrimsdale Highld 157 J12
Achtoty Highld 157 C9
Achurch Northants 65 F7
Achuvoldrach Highld 157 D8
Achvaich Highld 151 B10
Achvarasdal Highld 157 C12
Ackergill Highld 158 E5
Acklam Mbro 102 C2
Acklam N Yorks 96 C3
Ackleton Shrops 61 E7
Acklington Northumb 117 D8
Ackton W Yorks 88 B5
Ackworth Moor Top W Yorks 88 C5
Acle Norf 69 C7
Acock's Green W Mid 62 F5
Acol Kent 31 C7
Acomb Northumb 110 C2
Acomb York 95 D8
Aconbury Hereford 49 F7
Acre Lancs 87 B5
Acre Street W Sus 15 E8
Acrefair Wrex 73 E6
Acton Ches E 74 D3
Acton Dorset 13 G7
Acton London 41 F5
Acton Shrops 60 F3
Acton Suff 56 E2
Acton Wrex 73 D7
Acton Beauchamp Hereford 49 D8
Acton Bridge Ches W 74 B2
Acton Burnell Shrops 60 D5
Acton Green Hereford 49 D8
Acton Pigott Shrops 60 D5
Acton Round Shrops 61 E6
Acton Scott Shrops 60 F4
Acton Trussell Staffs 62 C3
Acton Turville S Glos 37 F5
Adbaston Staffs 61 B7
Adber Dorset 12 B3
Adderley Shrops 74 E3
Adderstone Northumb 123 F7
Addiewell W Loth 120 C2
Addingham W Yorks 94 E3
Addington Bucks 39 B7
Addington Kent 29 D7
Addington London 28 C4
Addinston Borders 121 D8
Addiscombe London 28 C4
Addlestone Sur 27 C8
Addlethorpe Lincs 79 C8
Adel W Yorks 95 F5
Adeney Telford 61 C7
Adfa Powys 59 D7
Adforton Hereford 49 B6
Adisham Kent 31 D6
Adlestrop Glos 38 B2
Adlingfleet E Yorks 90 B2
Adlington Lancs 86 C4
Admaston Staffs 62 B4
Admaston Telford 61 C6
Admington Warks 51 E7
Adstock Bucks 52 F5
Adstone Northants 52 D3
Adversane W Sus 16 B4
Advie Highld 152 E1
Adwalton W Yorks 88 B3
Adwell Oxon 39 E6
Adwick le Street S Yorks 89 D6
Adwick upon Dearne S Yorks 89 D5
Adziel Aberds 153 C9
Ae Village Dumfries 114 F2
Affleck Aberds 141 B7
Affpuddle Dorset 13 E6
Affric Lodge Highld 136 B4
Afon-wen Flint 72 B5
Afton IoW 14 F4
Agglethorpe N Yorks 101 F5
Agneash IoM 84 D4
Aigburth Mers 85 F4
Aiginis W Isles 155 D9
Aike E Yorks 97 E6
Aikerness Orkney 159 C5
Aikers Orkney 159 J5
Aiketgate Cumb 108 E4
Aikton Cumb 108 D2
Ailey Hereford 48 E5
Ailstone Warks 51 D7
Ailsworth Pboro 65 E8
Ainderby Quernhow N Yorks 102 F1
Ainderby Steeple N Yorks 101 E8
Aingers Green Essex 43 B7
Ainsdale Mers 85 C4
Ainsdale-on-Sea Mers 85 C4
Ainstable Cumb 108 E5
Ainsworth Gtr Man 87 C5
Ainthorpe N Yorks 103 D5
Aintree Mers 85 E4
Aird Argyll 124 E3
Aird Dumfries 104 C4
Aird Highld 149 A12
Aird W Isles 155 D10
Aird a Mhachair W Isles 148 D2
Aird a' Mhulaidh W Isles 154 F6
Aird Asaig W Isles 154 G6
Aird Dhail W Isles 155 A9
Aird Mhidhinis W Isles 148 H2
Aird Mhighe W Isles 154 H6
Aird Mhighe W Isles 154 J5
Aird Mhor W Isles 148 H2
Aird of Sleat Highld 149 H10
Aird Thunga W Isles 155 D9
Aird Uig W Isles 154 D5
Airdens Highld 151 B9
Airdrie N Lanark 119 C7
Airdtorrisdale Highld 157 C9
Airidh a Bhruaich W Isles 154 F7
Airieland Dumfries 106 D4
Airmyn E Yorks 89 B8
Airntully Perth 133 F7
Airor Highld 149 H12
Airth Falk 127 F7
Airton N Yorks 94 D2
Airyhassen Dumfries 105 E7
Aisby Lincs 78 F3
Aisby Lincs 90 E2
Aisgernis W Isles 148 F2
Aiskew N Yorks 101 F7
Aislaby N Yorks 103 D6
Aislaby N Yorks 103 F5
Aislaby Stockton 102 C2
Aisthorpe Lincs 78 A2
Aith Orkney 159 G3
Aith Shetland 160 D8
Aith Shetland 160 H5
Aithsetter Shetland 160 K6
Aitkenhead S Ayrs 112 D3
Aitnoch Highld 151 H12
Akeld Northumb 117 B5
Akeley Bucks 52 F5
Akenham Suff 56 E5
Albaston Corn 6 B2
Alberbury Shrops 60 C3
Albourne W Sus 17 C6
Albrighton Shrops 60 C4
Albrighton Shrops 62 D2
Alburgh Norf 69 F5
Albury Herts 41 B7
Albury Sur 27 E8
Albury End Herts 41 B7
Alby Hill Norf 81 D7
Alcaig Highld 151 F8
Alcaston Shrops 60 F4
Alcester Warks 51 D5
Alciston E Sus 18 E2
Alcombe Som 21 E8
Alcombe Wilts 24 C3
Alconbury Cambs 54 B2
Alconbury Weston Cambs 54 B2
Aldbar Castle Angus 135 D5
Aldborough N Yorks 95 C7
Aldborough Norf 81 D7
Aldbourne Wilts 25 B7
Aldbrough E Yorks 97 F8
Aldbrough St John N Yorks 101 C7
Aldbury Herts 40 C2
Aldcliffe Lancs 92 C4
Aldclune Perth 133 C6
Aldeburgh Suff 57 D8
Aldeby Norf 69 E7
Aldenham Herts 40 E4
Alderbury Wilts 14 B2
Aldercar Derbys 76 E4
Alderford Norf 68 C4
Alderholt Dorset 14 C2
Alderley Glos 36 E4
Alderley Edge Ches E 74 B5
Aldermaston W Berks 26 C3
Aldermaston Wharf W Berks 26 C4
Alderminster Warks 51 E7
Alder's End Hereford 49 E8
Aldersey Green Ches W 73 D8
Aldershot Hants 27 D6
Alderton Glos 50 F5
Alderton Northants 52 E5
Alderton Shrops 60 B4
Alderton Suff 57 E7
Alderton Wilts 37 F5
Alderwasley Derbys 76 D3
Aldfield N Yorks 95 C5
Aldford Ches W 73 D8
Aldham Essex 43 B5
Aldham Suff 56 E4
Aldie Highld 151 C10
Aldingbourne W Sus 16 D3
Aldingham Cumb 92 B2
Aldington Kent 19 B7
Aldington Worcs 51 E5
Aldington Frith Kent 19 B7
Aldochlay Argyll 126 E2
Aldreth Cambs 54 B5
Aldridge W Mid 62 D4
Aldringham Suff 57 C8
Aldsworth Glos 38 C1
Aldunie Moray 140 B2
Aldwark Derbys 76 D2
Aldwark N Yorks 95 C7
Aldwick W Sus 16 E3
Aldwincle Northants 65 F7
Aldworth W Berks 26 B3
Alexandria W Dunb 118 B3
Alfardisworthy Devon 8 C4
Alfington Devon 11 E6
Alfold Sur 27 F8
Alfold Bars W Sus 27 F8
Alfold Crossways Sur 27 F8
Alford Aberds 140 C4
Alford Lincs 79 B7
Alford Som 23 F8
Alfreton Derbys 76 D4
Alfrick Worcs 50 D2
Alfrick Pound Worcs 50 D2
Alfriston E Sus 18 E2
Algaltraig Argyll 145 F9
Algarkirk Lincs 79 F5
Alhampton Som 23 F8
Aline Lodge W Isles 154 F6
Alisary Highld 147 D10
Alkborough N Lincs 90 B2
Alkerton Oxon 51 E8
Alkham Kent 31 E6
Alkington Shrops 74 F2
Alkmonton Derbys 75 F8
All Cannings Wilts 25 C5
All Saints South Elmham Suff 69 F6
All Stretton Shrops 60 E4
Alladale Lodge Highld 150 C7
Allaleigh Devon 7 D6
Allanaquoich Aberds 139 E7
Allangrange Mains Highld 151 F9
Allanton Borders 122 D4
Allanton N Lanark 119 D8
Allathasdal W Isles 148 H1
Allendale Town Northumb 109 D8
Allenheads Northumb 109 E8
Allens Green Herts 41 C7
Allensford Durham 110 D3
Allensmore Hereford 49 F6
Allenton Derby 76 F3
Aller Som 12 B2
Allerby Cumb 107 F7
Allerford Som 21 E8
Allerston N Yorks 103 F6
Allerthorpe E Yorks 96 E3
Allerton Mers 86 F2
Allerton W Yorks 94 F4
Allerton Bywater W Yorks 88 B5
Allerton Mauleverer N Yorks 95 D7
Allesley W Mid 63 F7
Allestree Derby 76 F3
Allet Corn 3 B6
Allexton Leics 64 D5
Allgreave Ches E 75 C6
Allhallows Medway 30 B2
Allhallows-on-Sea Medway 30 B2
Alligin Shuas Highld 149 C13
Allimore Green Staffs 62 C2
Allington Lincs 77 E8
Allington Wilts 25 C5
Allington Wilts 25 F7
Allithwaite Cumb 92 B3
Alloa Clack 127 E7
Allonby Cumb 107 E7
Alloway S Ayrs 112 C3
Allt Carms 33 D6
Allt na h-Airbhe Highld 150 B4
Allt-nan-sùgh Highld 136 B2
Alltchaorunn Highld 131 D5
Alltforgan Powys 59 B6
Alltmawr Powys 48 E2
Alltnacaillich Highld 156 E7
Alltsigh Highld 137 C7
Alltwalis Carms 46 F3
Alltwen Neath 33 D8
Alltyblaca Ceredig 46 E4
Allwood Green Suff 56 B4
Almeley Hereford 48 D5
Almer Dorset 13 E7
Almholme S Yorks 89 D6
Almington Staffs 74 F4
Alminstone Cross Devon 8 B5
Almondbank Perth 128 B2
Almondbury W Yorks 88 C2
Almondsbury S Glos 36 F3
Alne N Yorks 95 C7
Alness Highld 151 E9
Alnham Northumb 117 C5
Alnmouth Northumb 117 C8
Alnwick Northumb 117 C7
Alperton London 40 F4
Alphamstone Essex 56 F2
Alpheton Suff 56 D2
Alphington Devon 10 E4
Alport Derbys 76 C2
Alpraham Ches E 74 D2
Alresford Essex 43 B6
Alrewas Staffs 63 C5
Alsager Ches E 74 D4
Alsagers Bank Staffs 74 E5
Alsop en le Dale Derbys 75 D8
Alston Cumb 109 E7
Alston Devon 11 D8
Alstone Glos 50 F4
Alstonefield Staffs 75 D8
Alswear Devon 10 B2
Altandhu Highld 156 H2
Altanduin Highld 157 G11
Altarnun Corn 8 F4
Altass Highld 156 J7
Alterwall Highld 158 D4
Altham Lancs 93 F7
Althorne Essex 43 E5
Althorpe N Lincs 90 D2
Alticry Dumfries 105 D6
Altnabreac Station Highld 157 E13
Altnacealgach Hotel Highld 156 H5
Altnacraig Argyll 124 C4
Altnafeadh Highld 131 D6
Altnaharra Highld 157 F8
Altofts W Yorks 88 B4
Alton Derbys 76 C3
Alton Hants 26 F5
Alton Staffs 75 E7
Alton Pancras Dorset 12 D5
Alton Priors Wilts 25 C6
Altrincham Gtr Man 87 F5
Altrua Highld 136 F5
Altskeith Stirling 126 D3
Altyre Ho. Moray 151 F13
Alva Clack 127 E7
Alvanley Ches W 73 B8
Alvaston Derby 76 F3
Alvechurch Worcs 50 B5
Alvecote Warks 63 D6
Alvediston Wilts 13 B7
Alveley Shrops 61 F7
Alverdiscott Devon 9 B7
Alverstoke Hants 15 E7
Alverstone IoW 15 F6
Alverton Notts 77 E7
Alves Moray 152 B1
Alvescot Oxon 38 D2
Alveston S Glos 36 F3
Alveston Warks 51 D7
Alvie Highld 138 D4
Alvingham Lincs 91 E7
Alvington Glos 36 D3
Alwalton Cambs 65 E8
Alweston Dorset 12 C4
Alwinton Northumb 116 D5
Alwoodley W Yorks 95 E5
Alyth Perth 134 E2
Am Baile W Isles 148 G2
Am Buth Argyll 124 C4
Amatnatua Highld 150 B7
Amber Hill Lincs 78 E5
Ambergate Derbys 76 D3
Amberley Glos 37 D5
Amberley W Sus 16 C4
Amble Northumb 117 D8
Amblecote W Mid 62 F2
Ambler Thorn W Yorks 87 B8
Ambleside Cumb 99 D5
Ambleston Pembs 44 C5
Ambrosden Oxon 39 C6
Amcotts N Lincs 90 C2
Amersham Bucks 40 E2
Amesbury Wilts 25 E6
Amington Staffs 63 D6
Amisfield Dumfries 114 F2
Amlwch Anglesey 82 B4
Amlwch Port Anglesey 82 B4
Ammanford = Rhydaman Carms 33 C7
Amod Argyll 143 E8
Amotherby N Yorks 96 B3
Ampfield Hants 14 B5
Ampleforth N Yorks 95 B8
Ampney Crucis Glos 37 D7
Ampney St Mary Glos 37 D7
Ampney St Peter Glos 37 D7
Amport Hants 25 E7
Ampthill C Beds 53 F8
Ampton Suff 56 B2
Amroth Pembs 32 D2
Amulree Perth 133 F5
An Caol Highld 149 C11
An Cnoc W Isles 155 D9
An Gleann Ur W Isles 155 D9
An t-Ob = Leverburgh W Isles 154 J5
Anagach Highld 139 B6
Anaheilt Highld 130 C2
Anancaun Highld 150 E3
Ancaster Lincs 78 E2
Anchor Shrops 59 F8
Anchorsholme Blackpool 92 E3
Ancroft Northumb 123 E5
Ancrum Borders 116 B2
Anderby Lincs 79 B8
Anderson Dorset 13 E6
Anderton Ches W 74 B3
Andover Hants 25 E8
Andover Down Hants 25 E8
Andoversford Glos 37 C7
Andreas IoM 84 C4
Anfield Mers 85 E4
Angersleigh Som 11 C6
Angle Pembs 44 E3
Angmering W Sus 16 D4
Angram N Yorks 95 E8
Angram N Yorks 100 E3
Anie Stirling 126 C4
Ankerville Highld 151 D11
Anlaby E Yorks 90 B4
Anmer Norf 80 E3
Anna Valley Hants 25 E8
Annan Dumfries 107 C8
Annat Argyll 125 C6
Annat Highld 149 C13
Annbank S Ayrs 112 B4
Annesley Notts 76 D5
Annesley Woodhouse Notts 76 D4
Annfield Plain Durham 110 D4
Anniffirth Shetland 160 J3
Annitsford T&W 111 B5
Annscroft Shrops 60 D4
Ansdell Lancs 85 B4
Ansford Som 23 F8
Ansley Warks 63 E6
Anslow Staffs 63 B6
Anslow Gate Staffs 63 B5
Anstey Herts 54 F5
Anstey Leics 64 D2
Anstruther Easter Fife 129 D7
Anstruther Wester Fife 129 D7
Ansty Hants 26 E5
Ansty W Sus 17 B6
Ansty Warks 63 F7

Ansty Wilts 13 B7
Anthill Common Hants 15 C7
Anthorn Cumb 107 D8
Antingham Norf 81 D8
Anton's Gowt Lincs 79 E5
Antonshill Falk 127 F7
Antony Corn 5 D8
Anwick Lincs 78 D4
Anwoth Dumfries 106 D2
Aoradh Argyll 142 B3
Apes Hall Cambs 67 E5
Apethorpe Northants 65 E7
Apeton Staffs 62 C2
Apley Lincs 78 B4
Apperknowle Derbys 76 B3
Apperley Glos 37 B5
Apperley Bridge W Yorks 94 F4
Appersett N Yorks 100 E3
Appin Argyll 130 E3
Appin House Argyll 130 E3
Appleby N Lincs 90 C3
Appleby-in-Westmorland Cumb 100 B1
Appleby Magna Leics 63 D7
Appleby Parva Leics 63 D7
Applecross Highld 149 D12
Applecross Ho. Highld 149 D12
Appledore Devon 11 C5
Appledore Devon 20 F3
Appledore Kent 19 C6
Appledore Heath Kent 19 B6
Appleford Oxon 39 E5
Applegarthtown Dumfries 114 F4
Appleshaw Hants 25 E8
Applethwaite Cumb 98 B4
Appleton Halton 86 F3
Appleton Oxon 38 D4
Appleton-le-Moors N Yorks 103 F5
Appleton-le-Street N Yorks 96 B3
Appleton Roebuck N Yorks 95 E8
Appleton Thorn Warr 86 F4
Appleton Wiske N Yorks 102 D1
Appletreehall Borders 115 C8
Appletreewick N Yorks 94 C3
Appley Som 11 B5
Appley Bridge Lancs 86 D3
Apse Heath IoW 15 F6
Apsley End C Beds 54 F2
Apuldram W Sus 16 D2
Aquhythie Aberds 141 C6
Arabella Highld 151 D11
Arbeadie Aberds 141 E5
Arberth = Narberth Pembs 32 C2
Arbirlot Angus 135 E6
Arboll Highld 151 C11
Arborfield Wokingham 27 C5
Arborfield Cross Wokingham 27 C5
Arborfield Garrison Wokingham 27 C5
Arbour-thorne S Yorks 88 F4
Arbroath Angus 135 E6
Arbuthnott Aberds 135 B7
Archiestown Moray 152 D2
Arclid Ches E 74 C4
Ard-dhubh Highld 149 D12
Ardachu Highld 157 J9
Ardalanish Argyll 146 K6
Ardanaiseig Argyll 125 C6
Ardaneaskan Highld 149 E13
Ardanstur Argyll 124 D4
Ardargie House Hotel Perth 128 C2
Ardarroch Highld 149 E13
Ardbeg Argyll 142 D5
Ardbeg Argyll 145 E10
Ardcharnich Highld 150 C4
Ardchiavaig Argyll 146 K6
Ardchullarie More Stirling 126 C4
Ardchyle Stirling 126 B4
Arddleen Powys 60 C2
Ardechvie Highld 136 E4
Ardeley Herts 41 B6
Ardelve Highld 149 F13
Arden Argyll 126 F2
Ardens Grafton Warks 51 D6
Ardentinny Argyll 145 E10
Ardentraive Argyll 145 F9
Ardeonaig Stirling 132 F3
Ardersier Highld 151 F10
Ardessie Highld 150 C3
Ardfern Argyll 124 E4
Ardgartan Argyll 125 E8
Ardgay Highld 151 B8
Ardgour Highld 130 C4
Ardheslaig Highld 149 C12
Ardiecow Moray 152 B5
Ardindrean Highld 150 C4
Ardingly W Sus 17 B7
Ardington Oxon 38 F4
Ardlair Aberds 140 B4
Ardlamont Ho. Argyll 145 G8
Ardleigh Essex 43 B6
Ardler Perth 134 E2
Ardley Oxon 39 B5
Ardlui Argyll 126 C2
Ardlussa Argyll 144 E5
Ardmair Highld 150 B4
Ardmay Argyll 125 E8
Ardminish Argyll 143 D7
Ardmolich Highld 147 D10
Ardmore Argyll 124 C3
Ardmore Highld 151 C10
Ardmore Highld 156 D5
Ardnacross Argyll 147 G8
Ardnadam Argyll 145 F10
Ardnagrask Highld 151 G8
Ardnarff Highld 149 E13
Ardnastang Highld 130 C2
Ardnave Argyll 142 A3
Ardno Argyll 125 E7
Ardo Aberds 153 E8
Ardo Ho. Aberds 141 B8
Ardoch Perth 133 F7
Ardochy House Highld 136 D5
Ardoyne Aberds 141 B5
Ardpatrick Argyll 144 G6
Ardpatrick Ho. Argyll 144 H6
Ardpeaton Argyll 145 E11
Ardrishaig Argyll 145 E7
Ardross Fife 129 D7
Ardross Highld 151 D9
Ardross Castle Highld 151 D9
Ardrossan N Ayrs 118 E2
Ardshealach Highld 147 E9
Ardsley S Yorks 88 D4
Ardslignish Highld 147 E8
Ardtalla Argyll 142 C5
Ardtalnaig Perth 132 F4
Ardtoe Highld 147 D9
Ardtrostan Perth 127 B5
Arduaine Argyll 124 D3
Ardullie Highld 151 E8
Ardvasar Highld 149 H11
Ardvorlich Perth 126 B5
Ardwell Dumfries 104 E5
Ardwell Mains Dumfries 104 E5
Ardwick Gtr Man 87 E6
Areley Kings Worcs 50 B3
Arford Hants 27 F6
Argoed Caerph 35 E5
Argoed Mill Powys 47 C8
Arichamish Argyll 124 E5
Arichastlich Argyll 125 B8
Aridhglas Argyll 146 J6
Arileod Argyll 146 F4
Arinacrinachd Highld 149 C12
Arinagour Argyll 146 F5
Arion Orkney 159 G3
Arisaig Highld 147 C9
Ariundle Highld 130 C2
Arkendale N Yorks 95 C6
Arkesden Essex 55 F5
Arkholme Lancs 93 B5
Arkle Town N Yorks 101 D5
Arkleton Dumfries 115 E6
Arkley London 41 E5
Arksey S Yorks 89 D6
Arkwright Town Derbys 76 B4
Arle Glos 37 B6
Arlecdon Cumb 98 C2
Arlesey C Beds 54 F2
Arleston Telford 61 C6
Arley Ches E 86 F4
Arlingham Glos 36 C4
Arlington Devon 20 E5
Arlington E Sus 18 E2
Arlington Glos 37 D8
Armadale Highld 157 C10
Armadale W Loth 120 C2
Armadale Castle Highld 149 H11
Armathwaite Cumb 108 E5
Arminghall Norf 69 D5
Armitage Staffs 62 C4
Armley W Yorks 95 F5
Armscote Warks 51 E7
Armthorpe S Yorks 89 D7
Arnabost Argyll 146 F5
Arncliffe N Yorks 94 B2
Arncroach Fife 129 D7
Arne Dorset 13 F7
Arnesby Leics 64 E3
Arngask Perth 128 C3
Arnisdale Highld 149 G13
Arnish Highld 149 D10
Arniston Engine Midloth 121 C6
Arnol W Isles 155 C8
Arnold E Yorks 97 E7
Arnold Notts 77 E5
Arnprior Stirling 126 E5
Arnside Cumb 92 B4
Aros Mains Argyll 147 G8
Arowry Wrex 73 F8
Arpafeelie Highld 151 F9
Arrad Foot Cumb 99 F5
Arram E Yorks 97 E6
Arrathorne N Yorks 101 E7
Arreton IoW 15 F6
Arrington Cambs 54 D4
Arrivain Argyll 125 B8
Arrochar Argyll 125 E8
Arrow Warks 51 D5
Arthington W Yorks 95 E5
Arthingworth Northants 64 F4
Arthog Gwyn 58 C3
Arthrath Aberds 153 E9
Arthurstone Perth 134 E2
Artrochie Aberds 153 E10
Arundel W Sus 16 D4
Aryhoulan Highld 130 C4
Asby Cumb 98 B2
Ascog Argyll 145 G10
Ascot Windsor 27 C7
Ascott Warks 51 F8
Ascott-under-Wychwood Oxon 38 C3
Asenby N Yorks 95 B6
Asfordby Leics 64 C4
Asfordby Hill Leics 64 C4
Asgarby Lincs 78 E4
Asgarby Lincs 79 C6
Ash Kent 29 C6
Ash Kent 31 D6
Ash Som 12 B2
Ash Sur 27 D6
Ash Bullayne Devon 10 D2
Ash Green Warks 63 F7
Ash Magna Shrops 74 F2
Ash Mill Devon 10 B2
Ash Priors Som 11 B6
Ash Street Suff 56 E4
Ash Thomas Devon 10 C5
Ash Vale Sur 27 D6
Ashampstead W Berks 26 B3
Ashbocking Suff 57 D5
Ashbourne Derbys 75 E8
Ashbrittle Som 11 B5
Ashburton Devon 7 C5
Ashbury Devon 9 E7
Ashbury Oxon 38 F2
Ashby N Lincs 90 D3
Ashby by Partney Lincs 79 C7
Ashby cum Fenby NE Lincs 91 D6
Ashby de la Launde Lincs 78 D3
Ashby-de-la-Zouch Leics 63 C7
Ashby Folville Leics 64 C4
Ashby Magna Leics 64 E2
Ashby Parva Leics 64 F2
Ashby Puerorum Lincs 79 B6
Ashby St Ledgers Northants 52 C3
Ashby St Mary Norf 69 D6
Ashchurch Glos 50 F4
Ashcombe Devon 7 B7
Ashcott Som 23 F6
Ashdon Essex 55 E6
Ashe Hants 26 E3
Asheldham Essex 43 D5
Ashen Essex 55 E8
Ashendon Bucks 39 C7
Ashfield Carms 33 B7
Ashfield Stirling 127 D6
Ashfield Suff 57 C6
Ashfield Green Suff 57 B6
Ashfold Crossways W Sus 17 B6
Ashford Devon 20 F4
Ashford Hants 14 C2
Ashford Kent 30 E4
Ashford Sur 27 B8
Ashford Bowdler Shrops 49 B7
Ashford Carbonell Shrops 49 B7
Ashford Hill Hants 26 C3
Ashford in the Water Derbys 75 C8
Ashgill S Lanark 119 E7
Ashill Devon 11 C5
Ashill Norf 67 D8
Ashill Som 11 C8
Ashingdon Essex 42 E4
Ashington Northumb 117 F8
Ashington Som 12 B3
Ashington W Sus 16 C5
Ashintully Castle Perth 133 C8
Ashkirk Borders 115 B7
Ashlett Hants 15 D5
Ashleworth Glos 37 B5
Ashley Cambs 55 C7
Ashley Ches E 87 F5
Ashley Devon 9 C8
Ashley Dorset 14 D2
Ashley Glos 37 E6
Ashley Hants 14 E3
Ashley Hants 25 F8
Ashley Northants 64 E4
Ashley Staffs 74 F4
Ashley Green Bucks 40 D2
Ashley Heath Dorset 14 D2
Ashley Heath Staffs 74 F4
Ashmanhaugh Norf 69 B6
Ashmansworth Hants 26 D2
Ashmansworthy Devon 8 C5
Ashmore Dorset 13 C7
Ashorne Warks 51 D8
Ashover Derbys 76 C3
Ashow Warks 51 B8
Ashprington Devon 7 D6
Ashreigney Devon 9 C8
Ashstead Sur 28 D2
Ashton Ches W 74 C2
Ashton Corn 2 D5
Ashton Hants 15 C6
Ashton Hereford 49 C7
Ashton Involyd 118 B2
Ashton Northants 53 E5
Ashton Northants 65 F7
Ashton Common Wilts 24 D3
Ashton-In-Makerfield Gtr Man 86 E3
Ashton Keynes Wilts 37 E7
Ashton under Hill Worcs 50 F4
Ashton-under-Lyne Gtr Man 87 E7
Ashton upon Mersey Gtr Man 87 E5
Ashurst Hants 14 C4
Ashurst Kent 18 B2
Ashurst W Sus 17 C5
Ashurstwood W Sus 28 F5
Ashwater Devon 9 E5
Ashwell Herts 54 F3
Ashwell Rutland 65 C5
Ashwell Som 11 C8
Ashwellthorpe Norf 68 E4
Ashwick Som 23 E8
Ashwicken Norf 67 C7
Ashybank Borders 115 C8
Askam in Furness Cumb 92 B2
Askern S Yorks 89 C6
Askerswell Dorset 12 E3
Askett Bucks 39 D8
Askham Cumb 99 B7
Askham Notts 77 B7
Askham Bryan York 95 E8
Askham Richard York 95 E8
Asknish Argyll 145 D8
Askrigg N Yorks 100 E4
Askwith N Yorks 94 E4
Aslackby Lincs 78 F3
Aslacton Norf 68 E4
Aslockton Notts 77 F7
Asloun Aberds 140 C4
Aspatria Cumb 107 E8
Aspenden Herts 41 B6
Asperton Lincs 79 F5
Aspley Guise C Beds 53 F7
Aspley Heath C Beds 53 F7
Aspull Gtr Man 86 D4
Asselby E Yorks 89 B8
Asserby Lincs 79 B7
Assington Suff 56 F3
Assynt Ho. Highld 151 E8
Astbury Ches E 74 C5
Astcote Northants 52 D4
Asterley Shrops 60 D3
Asterton Shrops 60 E3
Asthall Oxon 38 C2
Asthall Leigh Oxon 38 C3
Astley Shrops 60 C5
Astley Warks 63 F7
Astley Worcs 50 C2
Astley Abbotts Shrops 61 E7
Astley Bridge Gtr Man 86 C5
Astley Cross Worcs 50 C3
Astley Green Gtr Man 86 E5
Aston Ches E 74 E3
Aston Ches W 74 B2
Aston Derbys 88 F2
Aston Hereford 49 B6
Aston Herts 41 B5
Aston Oxon 38 D3
Aston S Yorks 89 F5
Aston Shrops 60 B5
Aston Staffs 74 E4
Aston Telford 61 D6
Aston W Mid 62 F4
Aston Wokingham 39 F7
Aston Abbotts Bucks 39 B8
Aston Botterell Shrops 61 F6
Aston-By-Stone Staffs 75 F6
Aston Cantlow Warks 51 D6
Aston Clinton Bucks 40 C1
Aston Crews Hereford 36 B3
Aston Cross Glos 50 F4
Aston End Herts 41 B5
Aston Eyre Shrops 61 E6
Aston Fields Worcs 50 C4
Aston Flamville Leics 63 E8
Aston Ingham Hereford 36 B3
Aston juxta Mondrum Ches E 74 D3
Aston le Walls Northants 52 D2
Aston Magna Glos 51 F6
Aston Munslow Shrops 60 F5
Aston on Clun Shrops 60 F3
Aston-on-Trent Derbys 63 B8
Aston Rogers Shrops 60 D3
Aston Rowant Oxon 39 E7
Aston Sandford Bucks 39 D7
Aston Somerville Worcs 50 F5
Aston Subedge Glos 51 E6
Aston Tirrold Oxon 39 F5
Aston Upthorpe Oxon 39 F5
Astrop Northants 52 F3
Astwick C Beds 54 F3
Astwood M Keynes 53 E7
Astwood Worcs 50 D3
Astwood Bank Worcs 50 C5
Aswarby Lincs 78 F3
Aswardby Lincs 79 B6
Atch Lench Worcs 50 D5
Atcham Shrops 60 D5
Athelhampton Dorset 13 E5
Athelington Suff 57 B6
Athelney Som 11 B8
Athelstaneford E Loth 121 B8
Atherington Devon 9 B7
Atherstone Warks 63 E7
Atherstone on Stour Warks 51 D7
Atherton Gtr Man 86 D4
Atley Hill N Yorks 101 D7
Atlow Derbys 76 E2
Attadale Highld 150 H2
Attadale Ho. Highld 150 H2
Attenborough Notts 76 F5
Atterby Lincs 90 E3
Attercliffe S Yorks 88 F4
Attleborough Norf 68 E3
Attleborough Warks 63 E7
Attlebridge Norf 68 C4
Atwick E Yorks 97 D7
Atworth Wilts 24 C3
Aubourn Lincs 78 C2
Auchagallon N Ayrs 143 E9
Auchallater Aberds 139 F7
Aucharnie Aberds 153 D6
Auchattie Aberds 141 E5
Auchavan Angus 134 C1
Auchbreck Moray 139 B8
Auchenback E Renf 118 D5
Auchenbainzie Dumfries 113 E8
Auchenblae Aberds 135 B7
Auchenbrack Dumfries 113 E7
Auchenbreck Argyll 145 E9
Auchencairn Dumfries 106 D4
Auchencairn Dumfries 114 F2
Auchencairn N Ayrs 143 F11
Auchencrosh S Ayrs 104 B5
Auchencrow Borders 122 C4
Auchendinny Midloth 121 C5
Auchengray S Lanark 120 D2
Auchenhalrig Moray 152 B3
Auchenheath S Lanark 119 E8
Auchenlochan Argyll 145 F8
Auchenmalg Dumfries 105 D6
Auchensoul S Ayrs 112 E2
Auchentiber N Ayrs 118 E3
Auchertyre Highld 149 F13
Auchgourish Highld 138 C5
Auchincarroch W Dunb 126 F3
Auchindrain Argyll 125 E6
Auchindrean Highld 150 C4
Auchininna Aberds 153 D6
Auchinleck E Ayrs 113 B5
Auchinloch N Lanark 119 B6
Auchinroath Moray 152 C2
Auchintoul Aberds 140 C4
Auchiries Aberds 153 E10
Auchlee Aberds 141 E7
Auchleven Aberds 140 B5
Auchlochan S Lanark 119 F8
Auchlossan Aberds 140 D4
Auchlunies Aberds 141 E7
Auchlyne Stirling 126 B4
Auchmacoy Aberds 153 E9
Auchmair Moray 140 B2
Auchmantle Dumfries 105 C5
Auchmillan E Ayrs 112 B5
Auchmithie Angus 135 E6
Auchmuirbridge Fife 128 D4
Auchmull Angus 135 B5
Auchnacree Angus 134 C4
Auchnagallin Highld 151 H13
Auchnagatt Aberds 153 D9
Auchnaha Argyll 145 E8
Auchnashelloch Perth 127 C6
Aucholzie Aberds 140 E2
Auchrannie Angus 134 D2
Auchroisk Highld 139 B6
Auchronie Angus 140 F3
Auchterarder Perth 127 C8
Auchteraw Highld 137 D6
Auchterderran Fife 128 E4
Auchterhouse Angus 134 F3
Auchtermuchty Fife 128 C4
Auchterneed Highld 150 F7
Auchtertool Fife 128 E4
Auchtertyre Moray 152 C1
Auchtubh Stirling 126 B4
Auckengill Highld 158 D5
Auckley S Yorks 89 D7
Audenshaw Gtr Man 87 E7
Audlem Ches E 74 E3
Audley Staffs 74 D4
Audley End Essex 56 F2
Auds Aberds 153 B6
Aughton E Yorks 96 F3
Aughton Lancs 85 D4
Aughton Lancs 93 C5
Aughton S Yorks 89 F5
Aughton Wilts 25 D7
Aughton Park Lancs 86 D2
Auldearn Highld 151 F12
Aulden Hereford 49 D6
Auldgirth Dumfries 114 F2
Auldhame E Loth 129 F7
Auldhouse S Lanark 119 D6
Ault a'chruinn Highld 136 B2
Aultanrynie Highld 156 F6
Aultbea Highld 155 J13
Aultdearg Highld 150 E5
Aultgrishan Highld 155 J12
Aultguish Inn Highld 150 D6
Aultibea Highld 157 G13
Aultiphurst Highld 157 C11
Aultmore Moray 152 C4
Aultnagoire Highld 137 B8
Aultnamain Inn Highld 151 C9
Aultnaslat Highld 136 D4
Aulton Aberds 140 B5
Aundorach Highld 139 C5
Aunsby Lincs 78 F3
Auquhorthies Aberds 141 B7
Aust S Glos 36 F2
Austendike Lincs 66 B2
Austerfield S Yorks 89 E7
Austrey Warks 63 D6
Austwick N Yorks 93 C7
Authorpe Lincs 91 F8
Authorpe Row Lincs 79 B8
Avebury Wilts 25 C6
Aveley Thurrock 42 F1
Avening Glos 37 E5
Averham Notts 77 D7
Aveton Gifford Devon 6 E4
Avielochan Highld 138 C5
Aviemore Highld 138 C4
Avington Hants 26 F3
Avington W Berks 25 C8
Avoch Highld 151 F10
Avon Hants 14 E2
Avon Dassett Warks 52 E2
Avonbridge Falk 120 B2
Avonmouth Bristol 23 B7
Avonwick Devon 6 D5
Awbridge Hants 14 B4
Awhirk Dumfries 104 D4
Awkley S Glos 36 F2
Awliscombe Devon 11 D6
Awre Glos 36 D4
Awsworth Notts 76 E4
Axbridge Som 23 D6
Axford Hants 26 E4
Axford Wilts 25 B7
Axminster Devon 11 E7
Axmouth Devon 11 E7
Axton Flint 85 F2
Aycliff Kent 31 E7
Aycliffe Durham 101 B7
Aydon Northumb 110 C3
Aylburton Glos 36 D3
Ayle Northumb 109 E7
Aylesbeare Devon 10 E5
Aylesbury Bucks 39 C8
Aylesby NE Lincs 91 D6
Aylesford Kent 29 D8
Aylesham Kent 31 D6
Aylestone Leicester 64 D2
Aylmerton Norf 81 D7
Aylsham Norf 81 E7
Aylton Hereford 49 F8
Aymestrey Hereford 49 C6
Aynho Northants 52 F3
Ayot St Lawrence Herts 40 C4
Ayot St Peter Herts 41 C5
Ayr S Ayrs 112 B3
Aysgarth N Yorks 101 F5
Ayside Cumb 99 F5
Ayston Rutland 65 D5
Aythorpe Roding Essex 42 C1
Ayton Borders 122 C5
Aywick Shetland 160 E7
Azerley N Yorks 95 B5

B

Babbacombe Torbay 7 C7
Babbinswood Shrops 73 F7
Babcary Som 12 B3
Babel Carms 47 F7
Babell Flint 73 B5
Babraham Cambs 55 D6
Babworth Notts 89 F7
Bac W Isles 155 C9
Bachau Anglesey 82 C4
Back of Keppoch Highld 147 C9
Back Rogerton E Ayrs 113 B5
Backaland Orkney 159 E6
Backaskaill Orkney 159 C5
Backbarrow Cumb 99 F5
Backe Carms 32 C3
Backfolds Aberds 153 C10
Backford Ches W 73 B8
Backford Cross Ches W 73 B7
Backhill Aberds 153 E7
Backhill Aberds 153 E10
Backhill of Clackriach Aberds 153 D9
Backhill of Fortree Aberds 153 D9
Backhill of Trustach Aberds 140 E5
Backies Highld 157 J11
Backlass Highld 158 E4
Backwell N Som 23 C6
Backworth T&W 111 B6
Bacon End Essex 42 C2
Baconsthorpe Norf 81 D7
Bacton Hereford 49 F5
Bacton Norf 81 D9
Bacton Suff 56 C4
Bacton Green Suff 56 C4
Bacup Lancs 87 B6
Badachro Highld 149 A12
Badanloch Lodge Highld 157 F10
Badavanich Highld 150 F4
Badbury Swindon 38 F1
Badby Northants 52 D3
Badcall Highld 156 D5
Badcaul Highld 150 B3
Baddeley Green Stoke 75 D6
Baddesley Clinton Warks 51 B7
Baddesley Ensor Warks 63 E6
Baddidarach Highld 156 G3
Baddoch Aberds 139 F7
Baddock Highld 151 F10
Badenscoth Aberds 153 E7
Badenyon Aberds 140 C2
Badger Shrops 61 E7
Badger's Mount Kent 29 C5
Badgeworth Glos 37 C6
Badgworth Som 23 D5
Badicaul Highld 149 F12
Badingham Suff 57 C7
Badlesmere Kent 30 D4
Badlipster Highld 158 F4
Badluarach Highld 150 B2
Badminton S Glos 37 F5
Badnaban Highld 156 G3
Badninish Highld 151 B10
Badrallach Highld 150 B3
Badsey Worcs 51 E5
Badshot Lea Sur 27 E6
Badsworth W Yorks 89 C5
Badwell Ash Suff 56 C3
Bae Colwyn = Colwyn Bay Conwy 83 D8
Bag Enderby Lincs 79 B6
Bagby N Yorks 102 F2
Bagendon Glos 37 D7
Bagh a Chaisteil = Castlebay W Isles 148 J1
Bagh Mor W Isles 148 C3
Bagh Shiarabhagh W Isles 148 H2
Baghasdal W Isles 148 G2
Bagillt Flint 73 B6
Baginton Warks 51 B8
Baglan Neath 33 E8
Bagley Shrops 60 B4
Bagnall Staffs 75 D6
Bagnor W Berks 26 C2
Bagshot Sur 27 C7
Bagshot Wilts 25 C8
Bagthorpe Norf 80 D3
Bagthorpe Notts 76 D4
Bagworth Leics 63 D8
Bagwy Llydiart Hereford 35 B8
Bail Àrd Bhuirgh W Isles 155 B9
Bail Uachdraich W Isles 148 B3
Baildon W Yorks 94 F4
Baile W Isles 154 J4
Baile a Mhanaich W Isles 148 C2
Baile Ailein W Isles 155 E7
Baile an Truiseil W Isles 155 B8
Baile Boidheach Argyll 144 F6
Baile Glas W Isles 148 C3
Baile Mhartainn W Isles 148 A2
Baile Mhic Phail W Isles 148 A3
Baile Mor Argyll 146 J5
Baile Mor W Isles 148 B2
Baile na Creige W Isles 148 H1
Baile nan Cailleach W Isles 148 C2
Baile Raghaill W Isles 148 A2
Bailebeag Highld 137 C8
Baileyhead Cumb 108 B5
Bailiesward Aberds 152 E4
Baillieston Glasgow 119 C6
Bail'lochdrach W Isles 148 C3
Bail'Ur Tholastaidh W Isles 155 C10
Bainbridge N Yorks 100 E4
Bainsford Falk 127 F7
Bainshole Aberds 152 E6
Bainton E Yorks 97 D5
Bainton Pboro 65 D7
Bairnkine Borders 116 C2
Baker Street Thurrock 42 F2
Baker's End Herts 41 C6
Bakewell Derbys 76 C2
Bala = Y Bala Gwyn 72 F3
Balachuirn Highld 149 D10
Balavil Highld 138 D3
Balbeg Highld 137 B7
Balbeg Highld 150 H7
Balbeggie Perth 128 B3
Balbithan Aberds 141 C6
Balbithan Ho. Aberds 141 C7
Balblair Highld 151 B8
Balblair Highld 151 E10
Balby S Yorks 89 D6
Balchladich Highld 156 F3
Balchraggan Highld 151 G8
Balchraggan Highld 151 H8
Balchrick Highld 156 D4
Balchrystie Fife 129 D6
Balcladaich Highld 137 B5
Balcombe W Sus 28 F4
Balcombe Lane W Sus 28 F4
Balcomie Fife 129 C8
Balcurvie Fife 128 D5
Baldersby N Yorks 95 B6
Baldersby St James N Yorks 95 B6
Balderstone Lancs 93 F6
Balderton Ches W 73 C7
Balderton Notts 77 D8
Baldhu Corn 3 B6
Baldinnie Fife 129 C6
Baldock Herts 54 F3
Baldovie Dundee 134 F4
Baldrine IoM 84 D4
Baldslow E Sus 18 D4
Baldwin IoM 84 D3
Baldwinholme Cumb 108 D3
Baldwin's Gate Staffs 74 E4
Bale Norf 81 D6
Balearn Aberds 153 C10
Balemartine Argyll 146 G2
Balephuil Argyll 146 G2
Balerno Edin 120 C4
Balevullin Argyll 146 G2
Balfield Angus 135 C5
Balfour Orkney 159 G5
Balfron Stirling 126 F4
Balfron Station Stirling 126 F4
Balgaveny Aberds 153 D6
Balgavies Angus 135 D5
Balgonar Fife 128 E2
Balgove Aberds 153 E8
Balgowan Highld 138 E2
Balgown Highld 149 B8
Balgrochan E Dunb 119 B6
Balgy Highld 149 C13
Balhaldie Stirling 127 D7
Balhalgardy Aberds 141 B6
Balham London 28 B3
Balhary Perth 134 E2
Baliasta Shetland 160 C8
Baligill Highld 157 C11
Balintore Angus 134 D2
Balintore Highld 151 D11
Balintraid Highld 151 D10
Balk N Yorks 102 F2
Balkeerie Angus 134 E3
Balkemback Angus 134 F3
Balkholme E Yorks 89 B8
Balkissock S Ayrs 104 A5
Ball Shrops 60 B3
Ball Haye Green Staffs 75 D6
Ball Hill Hants 26 C2
Ballabeg IoM 84 E2
Ballacannel IoM 84 D4
Ballachulish Highld 130 D4
Ballajora IoM 84 C4
Ballaleigh IoM 84 D3
Ballamodha IoM 84 E2
Ballantrae S Ayrs 104 A4
Ballaquine IoM 84 D4
Ballards Gore Essex 43 E5
Ballasalla IoM 84 C3
Ballasalla IoM 84 E2
Ballater Aberds 140 E2
Ballaugh IoM 84 C3
Ballaveare IoM 84 E3
Ballcorach Moray 139 B7
Ballechin Perth 133 D6
Balleigh Highld 151 C10
Ballencrieff E Loth 121 B7
Ballentoul Perth 133 C5
Ballidon Derbys 76 D2
Balliemore Argyll 124 C4
Balliemore Argyll 145 E9
Ballikinrain Stirling 126 F4
Ballimeanoch Argyll 125 D6
Ballimore Argyll 145 E8
Ballimore Stirling 126 C4
Ballinaby Argyll 142 B3
Ballindean Perth 128 B4
Ballingdon Suff 56 E2
Ballinger Common Bucks 40 D2
Ballingham Hereford 49 F7
Ballingry Fife 128 E3
Ballinlick Perth 133 E6
Ballinluig Perth 133 D6
Ballintuim Perth 133 D8
Balloch Angus 134 D3
Balloch Highld 151 G10
Balloch N Lanark 119 B7
Balloch W Dunb 126 F2
Ballochan Aberds 140 E4
Ballochford Moray 152 E3
Ballochmorrie S Ayrs 112 F2
Balls Cross W Sus 16 B3
Balls Green Essex 43 B6
Ballygown Argyll 146 G7
Ballygrant Argyll 142 B4
Ballyhaugh Argyll 146 F4
Balmacara Highld 149 F13
Balmacara Square Highld 149 F13
Balmaclellan Dumfries 106 B3
Balmacneil Perth 133 D6
Balmacqueen Highld 149 A9
Balmae Dumfries 106 E3
Balmaha Stirling 126 E3
Balmalcolm Fife 128 D5
Balmeanach Highld 149 D10
Balmedie Aberds 141 C8
Balmer Heath Shrops 73 F8
Balmerino Fife 129 B5
Balmerlawn Hants 14 D4
Balmichael N Ayrs 143 E10
Balmirmer Angus 135 F5
Balmore Highld 149 D7
Balmore Highld 150 H6
Balmore Highld 151 G11
Balmore Perth 133 D6
Balmule Fife 128 F4
Balmullo Fife 129 B6
Balmungie Highld 151 F10
Balnaboth Angus 134 C3
Balnabruaich Highld 151 E10
Balnabruich Highld 158 H3
Balnacoil Highld 157 H11
Balnacra Highld 150 G2
Balnafoich Highld 151 H9
Balnagall Highld 151 C11
Balnaguard Perth 133 D6
Balnahard Argyll 144 D3
Balnahard Argyll 146 H7
Balnain Highld 150 H7
Balnakeil Highld 156 C6
Balnaknock Highld 149 B9
Balnapaling Highld 151 E10
Balne N Yorks 89 C6
Balochroy Argyll 143 C8
Balone Fife 129 C6
Balornock Glasgow 119 C6
Balquharn Perth 133 F7
Balquhidder Stirling 126 B4
Balsall W Mid 51 B7
Balsall Common W Mid 51 B7
Balsall Heath W Mid 62 F4
Balscott Oxon 51 E8
Balsham Cambs 55 D6
Baltasound Shetland 160 C8
Balterley Staffs 74 D4
Baltersan Dumfries 105 C8
Balthangie Aberds 153 C8
Baltonsborough Som 23 F7
Balvaird Highld 151 F8
Balvicar Argyll 124 D3
Balvraid Highld 149 G13
Balvraid Highld 151 H11
Bamber Bridge Lancs 86 B3
Bambers Green Essex 42 B1
Bamburgh Northumb 123 F7
Bamff Perth 134 D2
Bamford Derbys 88 F3
Bamford Gtr Man 87 C6
Bampton Cumb 99 C7
Bampton Devon 10 B4
Bampton Oxon 38 D3
Bampton Grange Cumb 99 C7
Banavie Highld 131 B5
Banbury Oxon 52 E2
Bancffosfelen Carms 33 C5
Banchory Aberds 141 E5
Banchory-Devenick Aberds 141 D8
Bancycapel Carms 33 C5
Bancyfelin Carms 32 C4
Bancyffordd Carms 46 F3
Bandirran Perth 134 F2
Banff Aberds 153 B6
Bangor Gwyn 83 D5
Bangor-is-y-coed Wrex 73 E7
Banham Norf 68 F3
Bank Hants 14 D3
Bank Newton N Yorks 94 D2
Bank Street Worcs 49 C8
Bankend Dumfries 107 C7
Bankfoot Perth 133 F7
Bankglen E Ayrs 113 C6
Bankhead Aberdeen 141 C7
Bankhead Aberds 141 D5
Banknock Falk 119 B7
Banks Cumb 109 C5
Banks Lancs 85 B4
Bankshill Dumfries 114 F4
Banningham Norf 81 E8
Banniskirk Ho. Highld 158 E3
Bannister Green Essex 42 B2
Bannockburn Stirling 127 E7
Banstead Sur 28 D3
Bantham Devon 6 E4
Banton N Lanark 119 B7
Banwell N Som 23 D5
Banyard's Green Suff 57 B6
Bapchild Kent 30 C3
Bar Hill Cambs 54 C4
Barabhas W Isles 155 C8
Barabhas Iarach W Isles 155 C8
Barabhas Uarach W Isles 155 B8
Barachandroman Argyll 124 C2
Barassie S Ayrs 118 F3
Baravullin Argyll 124 E4
Barbaraville Highld 151 D10
Barber Booth Derbys 88 F2
Barbieston S Ayrs 112 C4
Barbon Cumb 99 F8
Barbridge Ches E 74 D3
Barbrook Devon 21 E6
Barby Northants 52 B3
Barcaldine Argyll 130 E3
Barcheston Warks 51 F7
Barcombe E Sus 17 C8
Barcombe Cross E Sus 17 C8
Barden N Yorks 101 E6
Barden Scale N Yorks 94 D3
Bardennoch Dumfries 113 E5
Bardfield Saling Essex 42 B2
Bardister Shetland 160 F5
Bardney Lincs 78 C4
Bardon Leics 63 C8
Bardon Mill Northumb 109 C7
Bardowie E Dunb 119 B5
Bardrainney Invclyd 118 B3
Bardsea Cumb 92 B3
Bardsey W Yorks 95 E6
Bardwell Suff 56 B3
Bare Lancs 92 C4
Barfad Argyll 145 G7
Barford Norf 68 D4
Barford Warks 51 C7
Barford St John Oxon 52 F2
Barford St Martin Wilts 25 F5
Barford St Michael Oxon 52 F2
Barfrestone Kent 31 D6
Bargod = Bargoed Caerph 35 E5
Bargoed = Bargod Caerph 35 E5
Bargrennan Dumfries 105 B7
Barham Cambs 54 B2
Barham Kent 31 D6
Barham Suff 56 D5
Barharrow Dumfries 106 D3
Barhill Dumfries 106 C5
Barholm Lincs 65 C7
Barkby Leics 64 D3
Barkestone-le-Vale Leics 77 F7
Barkham Wokingham 27 C5
Barking London 41 F7
Barking Suff 56 D4
Barking Tye Suff 56 D4
Barkingside London 41 F7
Barkisland W Yorks 87 C8
Barkston Lincs 78 E2
Barkston N Yorks 95 F7
Barkway Herts 54 F4
Barlaston Staffs 75 F5
Barlavington W Sus 16 C3
Barlborough Derbys 76 B4
Barlby N Yorks 96 F2
Barlestone Leics 63 D8
Barley Herts 54 F4
Barley Lancs 93 E8
Barley Mow T&W 111 D5
Barleythorpe Rutland 64 D5
Barling Essex 43 F5
Barlow Derbys 76 B3
Barlow N Yorks 89 B7
Barlow T&W 110 C4
Barmby Moor E Yorks 96 E3
Barmby on the Marsh E Yorks 89 B7
Barmer Norf 80 D4
Barmoor Castle Northumb 123 F5
Barmoor Lane End Northumb 123 F6
Barmouth = Abermaw Gwyn 58 C3
Barmpton Darl 101 C8
Barmston E Yorks 97 D7
Barnack Pboro 65 D7
Barnacle Warks 63 F7
Barnard Castle Durham 101 C5
Barnard Gate Oxon 38 C4
Barnardiston Suff 55 E8
Barnbarroch Dumfries 106 D5
Barnburgh S Yorks 89 D5
Barnby Suff 69 F7
Barnby Dun S Yorks 89 D7
Barnby in the Willows Notts 77 D8
Barnby Moor Notts 89 F7
Barnes Street Kent 29 E7
Barnet London 41 E5
Barnetby le Wold N Lincs 90 D4
Barney Norf 81 D5
Barnham Suff 56 B2
Barnham W Sus 16 D3
Barnham Broom Norf 68 D3
Barnhead Angus 135 D6
Barnhill Ches W 73 D8
Barnhill Dundee 134 F4
Barnhill Moray 152 C1
Barnhills Dumfries 104 B3
Barningham Durham 101 C5
Barningham Suff 56 B3
Barnoldby le Beck NE Lincs 91 D6
Barnoldswick Lancs 93 E8
Barns Green W Sus 16 B5
Barnsley Glos 37 D7
Barnsley S Yorks 88 D4
Barnstaple Devon 20 F4
Barnston Essex 42 C2
Barnston Mers 85 F3
Barnstone Notts 77 F7
Barnt Green Worcs 50 B5
Barnton Ches W 74 B3
Barnton Edin 120 B4
Barnwell All Saints Northants 65 F7
Barnwell St Andrew Northants 65 F7
Barnwood Glos 37 C5
Barochreal Argyll 124 C4
Barons Cross Hereford 49 D6
Barr S Ayrs 112 E2
Barra Castle Aberds 141 B6
Barrachan Dumfries 105 E7
Barrack Aberds 153 D8
Barraglom W Isles 154 D6
Barrahormid Argyll 144 E6
Barran Argyll 124 C4
Barrapol Argyll 146 G2
Barras Aberds 141 F7
Barras Cumb 100 C3
Barrasford Northumb 110 B2
Barravullin Argyll 124 E4
Barregarrow IoM 84 D3
Barrhead E Renf 118 D4
Barrhill S Ayrs 112 F2
Barrington Cambs 54 E4
Barrington Som 11 C8
Barripper Corn 2 C5
Barrmill N Ayrs 118 D3
Barrock Highld 158 C4
Barrock Ho. Highld 158 D4
Barrow Lancs 93 F7
Barrow Rutland 65 C5
Barrow Suff 55 C8
Barrow Green Kent 30 C3
Barrow Gurney N Som 23 C7
Barrow Haven N Lincs 90 B4
Barrow-in-Furness Cumb 92 C2
Barrow Island Cumb 92 C1
Barrow Nook Lancs 86 D2
Barrow Street Wilts 24 F3
Barrow upon Humber N Lincs 90 B4
Barrow upon Soar Leics 64 C2
Barrow upon Trent Derbys 63 B7
Barroway Drove Norf 67 D5
Barrowburn Northumb 116 C4
Barrowby Lincs 77 F8
Barrowcliff N Yorks 103 F8
Barrowden Rutland 65 D6
Barrowford Lancs 93 F8
Barrows Green Ches E 74 D3
Barrows Green Cumb 99 F7
Barrow's Green Mers 86 F3
Barry Angus 135 F5
Barry = Y Barri V Glam 22 C3
Barry Island V Glam 22 C3
Barsby Leics 64 C3
Barsham Suff 69 F6
Barston W Mid 51 B7
Bartestree Hereford 49 E7
Barthol Chapel Aberds 153 E8
Barthomley Ches E 74 D4
Bartley Hants 14 C4
Bartley Green W Mid 62 F4
Bartlow Cambs 55 E6
Barton Cambs 54 D5
Barton Ches W 73 D8
Barton Glos 37 B8
Barton Lancs 85 D4
Barton Lancs 92 F5
Barton N Yorks 101 D7
Barton Oxon 39 D5
Barton Torbay 7 C7
Barton Warks 51 D6
Barton Bendish Norf 67 D7
Barton Hartshorn Bucks 52 F4
Barton in Fabis Notts 76 F5
Barton in the Beans Leics 63 D7
Barton-le-Clay C Beds 53 F8
Barton-le-Street N Yorks 96 B3
Barton-le-Willows N Yorks 96 C3
Barton Mills Suff 55 B8
Barton on Sea Hants 14 E3
Barton on the Heath Warks 51 F7
Barton St David Som 23 F7
Barton Seagrave Northants 53 B6
Barton Stacey Hants 26 E2
Barton Turf Norf 69 B6
Barton-under-Needwood Staffs 63 C5
Barton-upon-Humber N Lincs 90 B4
Barton Waterside N Lincs 90 B4
Barugh S Yorks 88 D4
Barway Cambs 55 B6
Barwell Leics 63 E8
Barwick Herts 41 C6
Barwick Som 12 C3
Barwick in Elmet W Yorks 95 F6
Baschurch Shrops 60 B4
Bascote Warks 52 C2
Basford Green Staffs 75 D6
Bashall Eaves Lancs 93 E6
Bashley Hants 14 E3
Basildon Essex 42 F3
Basingstoke Hants 26 D4
Baslow Derbys 76 B2
Bason Bridge Som 22 E5
Bassaleg Newport 35 F6
Bassenthwaite Cumb 108 F2
Bassett Soton 14 C5
Bassingbourn Cambs 54 E4
Bassingfield Notts 77 F6
Bassingham Lincs 78 C2
Bassingthorpe Lincs 65 B6
Basta Shetland 160 D7
Baston Lincs 65 C8
Bastwick Norf 69 C7
Baswick Steer E Yorks 97 E6
Batchworth Heath Herts 40 E3
Batcombe Dorset 12 D4
Batcombe Som 23 F8
Bate Heath Ches E 74 B3
Batford Herts 40 C4
Bath Bath 24 C2
Bathampton Bath 24 C2
Bathealton Som 11 B5
Batheaston Bath 24 C2
Bathford Bath 24 C2
Bathgate W Loth 120 C2
Bathley Notts 77 D7
Bathpool Corn 5 B7
Bathpool Som 11 B7
Bathville W Loth 120 C2
Batley W Yorks 88 B3
Batsford Glos 51 F6
Battersby N Yorks 102 D3
Battersea London 28 B3
Battisborough Cross Devon 6 E3
Battisford Suff 56 D4
Battisford Tye Suff 56 D4
Battle E Sus 18 D4
Battle Powys 48 F2
Battledown Glos 37 B6
Battlefield Shrops 60 C5
Battlesbridge Essex 42 E3
Battlesden C Beds 40 B2
Battlesea Green Suff 57 B6
Battleton Som 10 B4
Battram Leics 63 D8
Battramsley Hants 14 E4
Baughton Worcs 50 E3
Baughurst Hants 26 D3

Baulking Oxon 38 E3
Baumber Lincs 78 B5
Baunton Glos 37 D7
Baverstock Wilts 24 F5
Bawburgh Norf 68 D4
Bawdeswell Norf 81 E6
Bawdrip Som 22 F5
Bawdsey Suff 57 E7
Bawtry S Yorks 89 E7
Baxenden Lancs 87 B5
Baxterley Warks 63 E6
Baybridge Hants 15 B6
Baycliff Cumb 92 B2
Baydon Wilts 25 B7
Bayford Herts 41 D6
Bayford Som 12 B5
Bayles Cumb 109 E7
Baylham Suff 56 D5
Baynard's Green Oxon 39 B5
Bayston Hill Shrops 60 D4
Baythorn End Essex 55 E8
Bayton Worcs 49 B8
Beach Highld 130 D1
Beachampton Bucks 53 F5
Beachamwell Norf 67 D7
Beachans Moray 151 G13
Beacharr Argyll 143 D7
Beachborough Kent 19 B8
Beachley Glos 36 E2
Beacon Devon 11 D6
Beacon End Essex 43 B5
Beacon Hill Sur 27 F6
Beacon's Bottom Bucks 39 E7
Beaconsfield Bucks 40 F2
Beacrabhaic W Isles 154 H6
Beadlam N Yorks 102 F4
Beadlow C Beds 54 F2
Beadnell Northumb 117 B8
Beaford Devon 9 C7
Beal N Yorks 89 B6
Beal Northumb 123 E6
Beamhurst Staffs 75 F7
Beaminster Dorset 12 D2
Beamish Durham 110 D5
Beamsley N Yorks 94 D3
Bean Kent 29 B6
Beanacre Wilts 24 C4
Beanley Northumb 117 C6
Beaquoy Orkney 159 F4
Bear Cross Bmouth 13 E8
Beardwood Blackburn 86 B4
Beare Green Sur 28 E2
Bearley Warks 51 C6
Bearnus Argyll 146 G6
Bearpark Durham 110 E5
Bearsbridge Northumb 109 D7
Bearsden E Dunb 118 B5
Bearsted Kent 29 D8
Bearstone Shrops 74 F4
Bearwood Hereford 49 D5
Bearwood Poole 13 E8
Bearwood W Mid 62 F4
Beattock Dumfries 114 D3
Beauchamp Roding Essex 42 C1
Beauchief S Yorks 88 F4
Beaufort Bl Gwent 35 C5
Beaufort Castle Highld 151 G8
Beaulieu Hants 14 D4
Beauly Highld 151 G8
Beaumaris Anglesey 83 D6
Beaumont Cumb 108 D3
Beaumont Essex 43 B7
Beaumont Hill Darl 101 C7
Beausale Warks 51 B7
Beauworth Hants 15 B6
Beaworthy Devon 9 E6
Beazley End Essex 42 B3
Bebington Mers 85 F4
Bebside Northumb 117 F8
Beccles Suff 69 E7
Becconsall Lancs 86 B2
Beck Foot Cumb 99 E8
Beck Hole N Yorks 103 D6
Beck Row Suff 55 B7
Beck Side Cumb 98 F4
Beckbury Shrops 61 D7
Beckenham London 28 C4
Beckermet Cumb 98 D2
Beckfoot Cumb 98 D3
Beckfoot Cumb 107 E7
Beckford Worcs 50 F4
Beckhampton Wilts 25 C5
Beckingham Lincs 77 D8
Beckingham Notts 89 F8
Beckington Som 24 D3
Beckley E Sus 19 C5
Beckley Hants 14 E3
Beckley Oxon 39 C5
Beckton London 41 F7
Beckwithshaw N Yorks 95 D5
Becontree London 41 F7
Bed-y-coedwr Gwyn 71 E8
Bedale N Yorks 101 F7
Bedburn Durham 110 F4
Bedchester Dorset 13 C6
Beddau Rhondda 34 F4
Beddgelert Gwyn 71 C6
Beddingham E Sus 17 D8
Beddington London 28 C4
Bedfield Suff 57 C6
Bedford Bedford 53 D8
Bedham W Sus 16 B4
Bedhampton Hants 15 D8
Bedingfield Suff 57 C5
Bedlam N Yorks 95 C5
Bedlington Northumb 117 F8
Bedlington Station Northumb 117 F8
Bedlinog M Tydf 34 D4
Bedminster Bristol 23 B7
Bedmond Herts 40 D3
Bednall Staffs 62 C3
Bedrule Borders 116 C2
Bedstone Shrops 49 B5
Bedwas Caerph 35 F5
Bedworth Warks 63 F7
Bedworth Heath Warks 63 F7
Beeby Leics 64 D3
Beech Hants 26 F4
Beech Staffs 75 F5
Beech Hill Gtr Man 86 D3
Beech Hill W Berks 26 C4
Beechingstoke Wilts 25 D5
Beedon W Berks 26 B2
Beeford E Yorks 97 D7
Beeley Derbys 76 C2
Beelsby NE Lincs 91 D6
Beenham W Berks 26 C3
Beeny Corn 8 E3
Beer Devon 11 F7
Beer Hackett Dorset 12 C3
Beercrocombe Som 11 B8
Beesands Devon 7 E6
Beesby Lincs 91 F8
Beeson Devon 7 E6
Beeston C Beds 54 E2
Beeston Ches W 74 D2
Beeston Norf 68 C2
Beeston Notts 76 F5
Beeston W Yorks 95 F5
Beeston Regis Norf 81 C7
Beeswing Dumfries 107 C5
Beetham Cumb 92 B4
Beetley Norf 68 C2
Begbroke Oxon 38 C4
Begelly Pembs 32 D2
Beggar's Bush Powys 48 C4
Beguildy Powys 48 B3
Beighton Norf 69 D6
Beighton S Yorks 88 F5
Beighton Hill Derbys 76 D2
Beith N Ayrs 118 D3
Bekesbourne Kent 31 D5
Belaugh Norf 69 C5
Belbroughton Worcs 50 B4
Belchamp Otten Essex 56 E2
Belchamp St Paul Essex 55 E8
Belchamp Walter Essex 56 E2
Belchford Lincs 79 B5
Belford Northumb 123 F7
Belhaven E Loth 122 B2
Belhelvie Aberds 141 C8
Belhinnie Aberds 140 B3
Bell Bar Herts 41 D5
Bell Busk N Yorks 94 D2
Bell End Worcs 50 B4
Bell o'th'Hill Ches W 74 E2
Bellabeg Aberds 140 C2
Bellamore S Ayrs 112 F2
Bellanoch Argyll 144 D6
Bellaty Angus 134 D2
Belleau Lincs 79 B7
Bellehiglash Moray 152 E1
Bellerby N Yorks 101 E6
Bellever Devon 6 B4
Belliehill Angus 135 C5
Bellingdon Bucks 40 D2
Bellingham Northumb 116 F4
Belloch Argyll 143 E7
Bellochantuy Argyll 143 E7
Bells Yew Green E Sus 18 B3
Bellsbank E Ayrs 112 D4
Bellshill N Lanark 119 C7
Bellshill Northumb 123 F7
Bellspool Borders 120 F4
Bellsquarry W Loth 120 C3
Belmaduthy Highld 151 F9
Belmesthorpe Rutland 65 C7
Belmont Blackburn 86 C4
Belmont London 28 C3
Belmont S Ayrs 112 B3
Belmont Shetland 160 C7
Belnacraig Aberds 140 C2
Belowda Corn 4 C4
Belper Derbys 76 E3
Belper Lane End Derbys 76 E3
Belsay Northumb 110 B4
Belses Borders 115 B8
Belsford Devon 7 D5
Belstead Suff 56 E5
Belston S Ayrs 112 B3
Belstone Devon 9 E8
Belthorn Blackburn 86 B5
Beltinge Kent 31 C5
Beltoft N Lincs 90 D2
Belton Leics 63 B8
Belton Lincs 78 F2
Belton N Lincs 89 D8
Belton Norf 69 D7
Belton in Rutland Rutland 64 D5
Beltring Kent 29 E7
Belts of Collonach Aberds 141 E5
Belvedere London 29 B5
Belvoir Leics 77 F8
Bembridge IoW 15 F7
Bemersyde Borders 121 F8
Bemerton Wilts 25 F6
Bempton E Yorks 97 B7
Ben Alder Lodge Highld 132 B2
Ben Armine Lodge Highld 157 H10
Ben Casgro W Isles 155 E9
Benacre Suff 69 F8
Benbuie Dumfries 113 E7
Benderloch Argyll 124 B5
Bendronaig Lodge Highld 150 H3
Benenden Kent 18 B5
Benfield Dumfries 105 C7
Bengate Norf 69 B6
Bengeworth Worcs 50 E5
Benhall Green Suff 57 C7
Benhall Street Suff 57 C7
Benholm Aberds 135 C8
Beningbrough N Yorks 95 D8
Benington Herts 41 B5
Benington Lincs 79 E6
Benllech Anglesey 82 C5
Benmore Argyll 145 E10
Benmore Stirling 126 B3
Benmore Lodge Highld 156 H6
Bennacott Corn 8 E4
Bennan N Ayrs 143 F10
Benniworth Lincs 91 F6
Benover Kent 29 E8
Bensham T&W 110 C5
Benslie N Ayrs 118 E3
Benson Oxon 39 E6
Bent Aberds 135 B6
Bent Gate Lancs 87 B5
Benthall Northumb 117 B8
Benthall Shrops 61 D6
Bentham Glos 37 C6
Benthoul Aberdeen 141 D7
Bentlawnt Shrops 60 D3
Bentley E Yorks 97 F6
Bentley Hants 27 E5
Bentley S Yorks 89 D6
Bentley Suff 56 F5
Bentley Warks 63 E6
Bentley Worcs 50 C4
Bentley Heath W Mid 51 B6
Benton Devon 21 F5
Bentpath Dumfries 115 E6
Bents W Loth 120 C2
Bentworth Hants 26 E4
Benvie Dundee 134 F3
Benwick Cambs 66 E3
Beoley Worcs 51 C5
Beoraidbeg Highld 147 B9
Bepton W Sus 16 C2
Berden Essex 41 B7
Bere Alston Devon 6 C2
Bere Ferrers Devon 6 C2
Bere Regis Dorset 13 E6
Berepper Corn 3 D5
Bergh Apton Norf 69 D6
Berinsfield Oxon 39 E5
Berkeley Glos 36 E3
Berkhamsted Herts 40 D2
Berkley Som 24 E3
Berkswell W Mid 51 B7
Bermondsey London 28 B4
Bernera Highld 149 F13
Bernice Argyll 145 D10
Bernisdale Highld 149 C9
Berrick Salome Oxon 39 E6
Berriedale Highld 158 H3
Berrier Cumb 99 B5
Berriew Powys 59 D8
Berrington Northumb 123 E6
Berrington Shrops 60 D5
Berrow Som 22 D5
Berrow Green Worcs 50 D2
Berry Down Cross Devon 20 E4
Berry Hill Glos 36 C2
Berry Hill Pembs 45 E2
Berry Pomeroy Devon 7 C6
Berryhillock Moray 152 B5
Berrynarbor Devon 20 E4
Bersham Wrex 73 E7
Berstane Orkney 159 G5
Berwick E Sus 18 E2
Berwick Bassett Wilts 25 B5
Berwick Hill Northumb 110 B4
Berwick St James Wilts 25 F5
Berwick St John Wilts 13 B7
Berwick St Leonard Wilts 24 F4
Berwick-upon-Tweed Northumb 123 D5
Bescar Lancs 85 C4
Besford Worcs 50 E4
Bessacarr S Yorks 89 D7
Bessels Leigh Oxon 38 D4
Bessingby E Yorks 97 C7
Bessingham Norf 81 D7
Bestbeech Hill E Sus 18 B3
Besthorpe Norf 68 E3
Besthorpe Notts 77 C8
Bestwood Nottingham 77 E5
Bestwood Village Notts 77 E5
Beswick E Yorks 97 E6
Betchworth Sur 28 E3
Bethania Ceredig 46 C4
Bethania Gwyn 71 C8
Bethania Gwyn 83 F6
Bethel Anglesey 82 D3
Bethel Gwyn 72 F3
Bethel Gwyn 82 E5
Bethersden Kent 30 E3
Bethesda Gwyn 83 E6
Bethesda Pembs 32 C1
Bethlehem Carms 33 B7
Bethnal Green London 41 F6
Betley Staffs 74 E4
Betsham Kent 29 B7
Betteshanger Kent 31 D7
Bettiscombe Dorset 11 E8
Bettisfield Wrex 73 F8
Betton Shrops 60 D3
Betton Shrops 74 F3
Bettws Bridgend 34 F3
Bettws Mon 35 C6
Bettws Newport 35 E6
Bettws Cedewain Powys 59 E8
Bettws Gwerfil Goch Denb 72 E4
Bettws Ifan Ceredig 46 E2
Bettws Newydd Mon 35 D7
Bettws-y-crwyn Shrops 60 F2
Bettyhill Highld 157 C10
Betws Carms 33 C7
Betws Bledrws Ceredig 46 D4
Betws-Garmon Gwyn 82 F5
Betws-y-Coed Conwy 83 F7
Betws-yn-Rhos Conwy 72 B3
Beulah Ceredig 45 E4
Beulah Powys 47 D8
Bevendean Brighton 17 D7
Bevercotes Notts 77 B6
Beverley E Yorks 97 F6
Beverston Glos 37 E5
Bevington Glos 36 E3
Bewaldeth Cumb 108 F2
Bewcastle Cumb 109 B5
Bewdley Worcs 50 B2
Bewerley N Yorks 94 C4
Bewholme E Yorks 97 D7
Bexhill E Sus 18 E4
Bexley London 29 B5
Bexleyheath London 29 B5
Bexwell Norf 67 D6
Beyton Suff 56 C3
Bhaltos W Isles 154 D5
Bhatarsaigh W Isles 148 J1
Bibury Glos 37 D8
Bicester Oxon 39 B5
Bickenhall Som 11 C7
Bickenhill W Mid 63 F5
Bicker Lincs 78 F5
Bickershaw Gtr Man 86 D4
Bickerstaffe Lancs 86 D2
Bickerton Ches E 74 D2
Bickerton N Yorks 95 D7
Bickington Devon 7 B5
Bickington Devon 20 F4
Bickleigh Devon 6 C3
Bickleigh Devon 10 D4
Bickleton Devon 20 F4
Bickley London 28 C5
Bickley Moss Ches W 74 E2
Bicknacre Essex 42 D3
Bicknoller Som 22 F3
Bicknor Kent 30 D2
Bickton Hants 14 C2
Bicton Shrops 60 C4
Bicton Shrops 60 F2
Bidborough Kent 29 E6
Biddenden Kent 19 B5
Biddenham Bedford 53 E8
Biddestone Wilts 24 B3
Biddisham Som 23 D5
Biddlesden Bucks 52 E4
Biddlestone Northumb 117 D5
Biddulph Staffs 75 D5
Biddulph Moor Staffs 75 D6
Bideford Devon 9 B6
Bidford-on-Avon Warks 51 D6
Bidston Mers 85 E3
Bielby E Yorks 96 E3
Bieldside Aberdeen 141 D7
Bierley IoW 15 G6
Bierley W Yorks 94 F4
Bierton Bucks 39 C8
Big Sand Highld 149 A12
Bigbury Devon 6 E4
Bigbury on Sea Devon 6 E4
Bigby Lincs 90 D4
Biggar Cumb 92 C1
Biggar S Lanark 120 F3
Biggin Derbys 75 D8
Biggin Derbys 76 E2
Biggin N Yorks 95 F8
Biggin Hill London 28 D5
Biggings Shetland 160 G3
Biggleswade C Beds 54 E2
Bighouse Highld 157 C11
Bighton Hants 26 F4
Bignor W Sus 16 C3
Bigton Shetland 160 L5
Bilberry Corn 4 C5
Bilborough Nottingham 76 E5
Bilbrook Som 22 E2
Bilbrough N Yorks 95 E8
Bilbster Highld 158 E4
Bildershaw Durham 101 B7
Bildeston Suff 56 E3
Billericay Essex 42 E2
Billesdon Leics 64 D4
Billesley Warks 51 D6
Billingborough Lincs 78 F4
Billinge Mers 86 D3
Billingford Norf 81 E6
Billingham Stockton 102 B2
Billinghay Lincs 78 D4
Billingley S Yorks 88 D5
Billingshurst W Sus 16 B4
Billingsley Shrops 61 F7
Billington C Beds 40 B2
Billington Lancs 93 F7
Billockby Norf 69 C7
Billy Row Durham 110 F4
Bilsborrow Lancs 92 F5
Bilsby Lincs 79 B7
Bilsham W Sus 16 D3
Bilsington Kent 19 B7
Bilson Green Glos 36 C3
Bilsthorpe Notts 77 C6
Bilsthorpe Moor Notts 77 D6
Bilston Midloth 121 C5
Bilston W Mid 62 E3
Bilstone Leics 63 D7
Bilting Kent 30 E4
Bilton E Yorks 97 F7
Bilton Northumb 117 C8
Bilton Warks 52 B2
Bilton in Ainsty N Yorks 95 E7
Bimbister Orkney 159 G4
Binbrook Lincs 91 E6
Binchester Blocks Durham 110 F5
Bincombe Dorset 12 F4
Bindal Highld 151 C12
Binegar Som 23 E8
Binfield Brack 27 B6
Binfield Heath Oxon 26 B5
Bingfield Northumb 110 B2
Bingham Notts 77 F7
Bingley W Yorks 94 F4
Bings Heath Shrops 60 C5
Binham Norf 81 D5
Binley Hants 26 D2
Binley W Mid 51 B8
Binley Woods Warks 51 B8
Binniehill Falk 119 B8
Binsoe N Yorks 94 B5
Binstead IoW 15 E6
Binsted Hants 27 E5
Binton Warks 51 D6
Bintree Norf 81 E6
Binweston Shrops 60 D3
Birch Essex 43 C5
Birch Gtr Man 87 D6
Birch Green Essex 43 C5
Birch Heath Ches W 74 C2
Birch Hill Ches W 74 B2
Birch Vale Derbys 87 F8
Bircham Newton Norf 80 D3
Bircham Tofts Norf 80 D3
Birchanger Essex 41 B8
Birchencliffe W Yorks 88 C2
Bircher Hereford 49 C6
Birchgrove Cardiff 22 B3
Birchgrove Swansea 33 E8
Birchington Kent 31 C6
Birchmoor Warks 63 D6
Birchover Derbys 76 C2
Birchwood Lincs 78 C2
Birchwood Warr 86 E4
Bircotes Notts 89 E7
Birdbrook Essex 55 E8
Birdforth N Yorks 95 B7
Birdham W Sus 16 E2
Birdholme Derbys 76 C3
Birdingbury Warks 52 C2
Birdlip Glos 37 C6
Birds Edge W Yorks 88 D3
Birdsall N Yorks 96 C4
Birdsgreen Shrops 61 F7
Birdsmoor Gate Dorset 11 D8
Birdston E Dunb 119 B6
Birdwell S Yorks 88 D4
Birdwood Glos 36 C4
Birgham Borders 122 F3
Birkby N Yorks 101 D8
Birkdale Mers 85 C4
Birkenhead Mers 85 F4
Birkenhills Aberds 153 D7
Birkenshaw N Lanark 119 C6
Birkenshaw W Yorks 88 B3
Birkhall Aberds 140 E2
Birkhill Angus 134 F3
Birkhill Borders 114 C5
Birkholme Lincs 65 B6
Birkin N Yorks 89 B6
Birley Hereford 49 D6
Birling Kent 29 C7
Birling Northumb 117 D8
Birling Gap E Sus 18 F2
Birlingham Worcs 50 E4
Birmingham W Mid 62 F4
Birnam Perth 133 E7
Birse Aberds 140 E4
Birsemore Aberds 140 E4
Birstall Leics 64 D2
Birstall W Yorks 88 B3
Birstwith N Yorks 94 D5
Birthorpe Lincs 78 F4
Birtley Hereford 49 C5
Birtley Northumb 109 B8
Birtley T&W 111 D5
Birts Street Worcs 50 F2
Bisbrooke Rutland 65 E5
Biscathorpe Lincs 91 F6
Biscot Luton 40 B3
Bish Mill Devon 10 B2
Bisham Windsor 39 F8
Bishampton Worcs 50 D4
Bishop Auckland Durham 101 B7
Bishop Burton E Yorks 97 F5
Bishop Middleham Durham 111 F6
Bishop Monkton N Yorks 95 C6
Bishop Norton Lincs 90 E3
Bishop Sutton Bath 23 D7
Bishop Thornton N Yorks 95 C5
Bishop Wilton E Yorks 96 D3
Bishopbridge Lincs 90 E4
Bishopbriggs E Dunb 119 C6
Bishopmill Moray 152 B2
Bishops Cannings Wilts 24 C5
Bishop's Castle Shrops 60 F3
Bishop's Caundle Dorset 12 C4
Bishop's Cleeve Glos 37 B6
Bishops Frome Hereford 49 E8
Bishop's Green Essex 42 C2
Bishop's Hull Som 11 B7
Bishop's Itchington Warks 51 D8
Bishops Lydeard Som 11 B6
Bishops Nympton Devon 10 B2
Bishop's Offley Staffs 61 B7
Bishop's Stortford Herts 41 B7
Bishop's Sutton Hants 26 F4
Bishop's Tachbrook Warks 51 C8
Bishops Tawton Devon 20 F4
Bishop's Waltham Hants 15 C6
Bishop's Wood Staffs 62 D2
Bishopsbourne Kent 31 D5
Bishopsteignton Devon 7 B7
Bishopstoke Hants 15 C5
Bishopston Swansea 33 F6
Bishopstone Bucks 39 C8
Bishopstone E Sus 17 D8
Bishopstone Hereford 49 E6
Bishopstone Swindon 38 F2
Bishopstone Wilts 13 B8
Bishopstrow Wilts 24 E3
Bishopswood Som 11 C7
Bishopsworth Bristol 23 C7
Bishopthorpe York 95 E8
Bishopton Darl 102 B1
Bishopton Dumfries 105 E8
Bishopton N Yorks 95 B6
Bishopton Renfs 118 B4
Bishopton Warks 51 D6
Bishton Newport 35 F7
Bisley Glos 37 D6
Bisley Sur 27 D7
Bispham Blackpool 92 E3
Bispham Green Lancs 86 C2
Bissoe Corn 3 B6
Bisterne Close Hants 14 D3
Bitchfield Lincs 65 B6
Bittadon Devon 20 E4
Bittaford Devon 6 D4
Bittering Norf 68 C2
Bitterley Shrops 49 B7
Bitterne Soton 15 C5
Bitteswell Leics 64 F2
Bitton S Glos 23 C8
Bix Oxon 39 F7
Bixter Shetland 160 H5
Blaby Leics 64 E2
Black Bourton Oxon 38 D2
Black Callerton T&W 110 C4
Black Clauchrie S Ayrs 112 F2
Black Corries Lodge Highld 131 D6
Black Crofts Argyll 124 B5
Black Dog Devon 10 D3
Black Heddon Northumb 110 B3
Black Lane Gtr Man 87 D5
Black Marsh Shrops 60 E3
Black Mount Argyll 131 E6
Black Notley Essex 42 B3
Black Pill Swansea 33 E7
Black Tar Pembs 44 E4
Black Torrington Devon 9 D6
Blackacre Dumfries 114 E3
Blackadder West Borders 122 D4
Blackawton Devon 7 D6
Blackborough Devon 11 D5
Blackborough End Norf 67 C6
Blackboys E Sus 18 C2
Blackbrook Derbys 76 E3
Blackbrook Mers 86 E3
Blackbrook Staffs 74 F4
Blackburn Aberds 141 C7
Blackburn Aberds 152 E5
Blackburn Blackburn 86 B4
Blackburn W Loth 120 C2
Blackcraig Dumfries 113 F7
Blackden Heath Ches E 74 B4
Blackdog Aberds 141 C8
Blackfell T&W 111 D5
Blackfield Hants 14 D5
Blackford Cumb 108 C3
Blackford Perth 127 D7
Blackford Som 12 B4
Blackford Som 23 E6
Blackfordby Leics 63 C7
Blackgang IoW 15 G5
Blackhall Colliery Durham 111 F7
Blackhall Mill T&W 110 D4
Blackhall Rocks Durham 111 F7
Blackham E Sus 29 F5
Blackhaugh Borders 121 F7
Blackheath Essex 43 B6
Blackheath Suff 57 B8
Blackheath Sur 27 E8
Blackheath W Mid 62 F3
Blackhill Aberds 153 C10
Blackhill Aberds 153 D10
Blackhill Highld 149 C8
Blackhills Highld 151 F12
Blackhills Moray 152 C2
Blackhorse S Glos 23 B8
Blackland Wilts 24 C5
Blacklaw Aberds 153 C6
Blackley Gtr Man 87 D6
Blacklunans Perth 134 C1
Blackmill Bridgend 34 F3
Blackmoor Hants 27 F5
Blackmoor Gate Devon 21 E5
Blackmore Essex 42 D2
Blackmore End Essex 55 F8
Blackmore End Herts 40 C4
Blackness Falk 120 B3
Blacknest Hants 27 E5
Blacko Lancs 93 E8
Blackpool Blackpool 92 F3
Blackpool Devon 7 E6
Blackpool Pembs 32 C1
Blackpool Gate Cumb 108 B5
Blackridge W Loth 119 C8
Blackrock Argyll 142 B4
Blackrock Mon 35 C6
Blackrod Gtr Man 86 C4
Blackshaw Dumfries 107 C7
Blackshaw Head W Yorks 87 B7
Blacksmith's Green Suff 56 C5
Blackstone W Sus 17 C6
Blackthorn Oxon 39 C6
Blackthorpe Suff 56 C3
Blacktoft E Yorks 90 B2
Blacktop Aberdeen 141 D7
Blacktown Newport 35 F6
Blackwall Tunnel London 41 F6
Blackwater Corn 3 B6
Blackwater Hants 27 D6
Blackwater IoW 15 F6
Blackwaterfoot N Ayrs 143 F9
Blackwell Darl 101 C7
Blackwell Derbys 75 B8
Blackwell Derbys 76 D4
Blackwell W Sus 28 F4
Blackwell Warks 51 E7
Blackwell Worcs 50 B4
Blackwood = Coed Duon Caerph 35 E5
Blackwood S Lanark 119 E7
Blackwood Hill Staffs 75 D6
Blacon Ches W 73 C7
Bladnoch Dumfries 105 D8
Bladon Oxon 38 C4
Blaen-gwynfi Neath 34 E2
Blaen-waun Carms 32 B3
Blaen-y-coed Carms 32 B4
Blaen-y-Cwm Denb 72 F4
Blaen-y-cwm Gwyn 71 E8
Blaen-y-cwm Powys 59 B7
Blaenannerch Ceredig 45 E4
Blaenau Ffestiniog Gwyn 71 C8
Blaenavon Torf 35 D6
Blaencelyn Ceredig 46 D2
Blaendyryn Powys 47 F8
Blaenffos Pembs 45 F3
Blaengarw Bridgend 34 E3
Blaengwrach Neath 34 D2
Blaenpennal Ceredig 46 C5
Blaenplwyf Ceredig 46 B4
Blaenporth Ceredig 45 E4
Blaenrhondda Rhondda 34 D3
Blaenycwm Ceredig 47 B7
Blagdon N Som 23 D7
Blagdon Torbay 7 C6
Blagdon Hill Som 11 C7
Blagill Cumb 109 E7
Blaguegate Lancs 86 D2
Blaich Highld 130 B4
Blain Highld 147 E9
Blaina Bl Gwent 35 D6
Blair Atholl Perth 133 C5
Blair Drummond Stirling 127 E6
Blairbeg N Ayrs 143 E11
Blairdaff Aberds 141 C5
Blairglas Argyll 126 F2
Blairgowrie Perth 134 E1
Blairhall Fife 128 F2
Blairingone Perth 127 E8
Blairland N Ayrs 118 E3
Blairlogie Stirling 127 E7
Blairlomond Argyll 125 F7
Blairmore Argyll 145 E10
Blairnamarrow Moray 139 C8
Blairquhosh Stirling 126 F4
Blair's Ferry Argyll 145 G8
Blairskaith E Dunb 119 B5
Blaisdon Glos 36 C4
Blakebrook Worcs 50 B3
Blakedown Worcs 50 B3
Blakelaw Borders 122 F3
Blakeley Staffs 62 E2
Blakeley Lane Staffs 75 E6
Blakemere Hereford 49 E5
Blakeney Glos 36 D3
Blakeney Norf 81 C6
Blakenhall Ches E 74 E4
Blakenhall W Mid 62 E3
Blakeshall Worcs 62 F2
Blakesley Northants 52 D4
Blanchland Northumb 110 D2
Bland Hill N Yorks 94 D5
Blandford Forum Dorset 13 D6
Blandford St Mary Dorset 13 D6
Blanefield Stirling 119 B5
Blankney Lincs 78 C3
Blantyre S Lanark 119 D6
Blar a'Chaorainn Highld 131 C5
Blaran Argyll 124 D4
Blarghour Argyll 125 D6
Blarmachfoldach Highld 130 C4
Blarnalearoch Highld 150 B4
Blashford Hants 14 D2
Blaston Leics 64 E5
Blatherwycke Northants 65 E6
Blawith Cumb 98 F4
Blaxhall Suff 57 D7
Blaxton S Yorks 89 D7
Blaydon T&W 110 C4
Bleadon N Som 22 D5
Bleak Hey Nook Gtr Man 87 D8
Blean Kent 30 C5
Bleasby Lincs 90 F5
Bleasby Notts 77 E7
Bleasdale Lancs 93 E5
Bleatarn Cumb 100 C2
Blebocraigs Fife 129 C6
Bleddfa Powys 48 C4
Bledington Glos 38 B2
Bledlow Bucks 39 D7
Bledlow Ridge Bucks 39 E7
Blegbie E Loth 121 C7
Blencarn Cumb 109 F6
Blencogo Cumb 107 E8
Blendworth Hants 15 C8
Blenheim Park Norf 80 D4
Blennerhasset Cumb 107 E8
Blervie Castle Moray 151 F13
Bletchingdon Oxon 39 C5
Bletchingley Sur 28 D4
Bletchley M Keynes 53 F6
Bletchley Shrops 74 F3
Bletherston Pembs 32 B1
Bletsoe Bedford 53 D8
Blewbury Oxon 39 F5
Blickling Norf 81 E7
Blidworth Notts 77 D5
Blindburn Northumb 116 C4
Blindcrake Cumb 107 F8
Blindley Heath Sur 28 E4
Blisland Corn 5 B6
Bliss Gate Worcs 50 B2
Blissford Hants 14 C2
Blisworth Northants 52 D5
Blithbury Staffs 62 B4
Blitterlees Cumb 107 D8
Blockley Glos 51 F6
Blofield Norf 69 D6
Blofield Heath Norf 69 C6
Blo' Norton Norf 56 B4
Bloomfield Borders 115 B8
Blore Staffs 75 E8
Blount's Green Staffs 75 F7
Blowick Mers 85 C4
Bloxham Oxon 52 F2
Bloxholm Lincs 78 D3
Bloxwich W Mid 62 D3
Bloxworth Dorset 13 E6
Blubberhouses N Yorks 94 D4
Blue Anchor Som 22 E2
Blue Anchor Swansea 33 E6
Blue Row Essex 43 C6
Blundeston Suff 69 E8
Blunham C Beds 54 D2
Blunsdon St Andrew Swindon 37 F8
Bluntington Worcs 50 B3
Bluntisham Cambs 54 B4
Blunts Corn 5 C8
Blyborough Lincs 90 E3
Blyford Suff 57 B8
Blymhill Staffs 62 C2
Blyth Northumb 117 F9
Blyth Notts 89 F7
Blyth Bridge Borders 120 E4
Blythburgh Suff 57 B8
Blythe Borders 121 E8
Blythe Bridge Staffs 75 E6
Blyton Lincs 90 E2
Boarhills Fife 129 C7
Boarhunt Hants 15 D7
Boar's Head Gtr Man 86 D3
Boars Hill Oxon 38 D4
Boarshead E Sus 18 B2
Boarstall Bucks 39 C6
Boasley Cross Devon 9 E6
Boat of Garten Highld 138 C5
Boath Highld 151 D8
Bobbing Kent 30 C2
Bobbington Staffs 62 E2
Bobbingworth Essex 41 D8
Bocaddon Corn 5 D6
Bochastle Stirling 126 D5
Bocking Essex 42 B3
Bocking Churchstreet Essex 42 B3
Boddam Aberds 153 D11
Boddam Shetland 160 M5
Boddington Glos 37 B5
Bodedern Anglesey 82 C3
Bodelwyddan Denb 72 B4
Bodenham Hereford 49 D7
Bodenham Wilts 14 B2
Bodenham Moor Hereford 49 D7
Bodermid Gwyn 70 E2
Bodewryd Anglesey 82 B3
Bodfari Denb 72 B4
Bodffordd Anglesey 82 D4
Bodham Norf 81 C7
Bodiam E Sus 18 C4
Bodicote Oxon 52 F2
Bodieve Corn 4 B4
Bodinnick Corn 5 D6
Bodle Street Green E Sus 18 D3
Bodmin Corn 5 C5
Bodney Norf 67 E8
Bodorgan Anglesey 82 E3
Bodsham Kent 30 E5
Boduan Gwyn 70 D4
Bodymoor Heath Warks 63 E5
Bogallan Highld 151 F9
Bogbrae Aberds 153 E10
Bogend Borders 122 E3
Bogend S Ayrs 118 F3
Boghall W Loth 120 C2
Boghead S Lanark 119 E7
Bogmoor Moray 152 B3
Bogniebrae Aberds 152 D5
Bognor Regis W Sus 16 E3
Bograxie Aberds 141 C6
Bogside N Lanark 119 D8
Bogton Aberds 153 C6
Bogue Dumfries 113 F6
Bohenie Highld 137 F5
Bohortha Corn 3 C7
Bohuntine Highld 137 F5
Boirseam W Isles 154 J5
Bojewyan Corn 2 C2
Bolam Durham 101 B6
Bolam Northumb 117 F6
Bolberry Devon 6 F4
Bold Heath Mers 86 F3
Boldon T&W 111 C6
Boldon Colliery T&W 111 C6
Boldre Hants 14 E4
Boldron Durham 101 C5
Bole Notts 89 F8
Bolehill Derbys 76 D2
Boleside Borders 121 F7
Bolham Devon 10 C4
Bolham Water Devon 11 C6
Bolingey Corn 4 D2
Bollington Ches E 75 B6
Bollington Cross Ches E 75 B6
Bolney W Sus 17 B6
Bolnhurst Bedford 53 D8
Bolshan Angus 135 D6
Bolsover Derbys 76 B4
Bolsterstone S Yorks 88 E3
Bolstone Hereford 49 F7
Boltby N Yorks 102 F2
Bolter End Bucks 39 E7
Bolton Cumb 99 B8
Bolton E Loth 121 B8
Bolton E Yorks 96 D3
Bolton Gtr Man 86 D5
Bolton Northumb 117 C7
Bolton Abbey N Yorks 94 D3
Bolton Bridge N Yorks 94 D3
Bolton-by-Bowland Lancs 93 E7
Bolton-le-Sands Lancs 92 C4
Bolton Low Houses Cumb 108 E2
Bolton-on-Swale N Yorks 101 E7
Bolton Percy N Yorks 95 E8
Bolton Town End Lancs 92 C4
Bolton upon Dearne S Yorks 89 D5
Boltonfellend Cumb 108 C4
Boltongate Cumb 108 E2
Bolventor Corn 5 B6
Bomere Heath Shrops 60 C4
Bon-y-maen Swansea 33 E7
Bonar Bridge Highld 151 B9
Bonawe Argyll 125 B6
Bonby N Lincs 90 C4
Boncath Pembs 45 F4
Bonchester Bridge Borders 115 C8
Bonchurch IoW 15 G6
Bondleigh Devon 9 D8
Bonehill Devon 6 B5
Bonehill Staffs 63 D5
Bo'ness Falk 127 F8
Bonhill W Dunb 118 B3
Boningale Shrops 62 D2
Bonjedward Borders 116 B2
Bonkle N Lanark 119 D8
Bonnavoulin Highld 147 F8
Bonnington Edin 120 C4
Bonnington Kent 19 B7
Bonnybank Fife 129 D5
Bonnybridge Falk 127 F7
Bonnykelly Aberds 153 C8
Bonnyrigg and Lasswade Midloth 121 C6
Bonnyton Aberds 153 E6
Bonnyton Angus 134 F3
Bonnyton Angus 135 D6
Bonsall Derbys 76 D2
Bonskeid House Perth 133 C5
Bont Mon 35 C7
Bont-Dolgadfan Powys 59 D5
Bont-goch Ceredig 58 F3
Bont-newydd Conwy 72 B4
Bont Newydd Gwyn 71 C8
Bont Newydd Gwyn 71 E8
Bontddu Gwyn 58 C3
Bonthorpe Lincs 79 B7
Bontnewydd Ceredig 46 C5
Bontnewydd Gwyn 82 F4
Bontuchel Denb 72 D4
Bonvilston V Glam 22 B2
Booker Bucks 39 E8
Boon Borders 121 E8
Boosbeck Redcar 102 C4
Boot Cumb 98 D3
Boot Street Suff 57 E6
Booth W Yorks 87 B8
Booth Wood W Yorks 87 C8
Boothby Graffoe Lincs 78 D2
Boothby Pagnell Lincs 78 F2
Boothen Stoke 75 E5
Boothferry E Yorks 89 B8
Boothville Northants 53 C5
Bootle Cumb 98 F3
Bootle Mers 85 E4
Booton Norf 81 E7
Boquhan Stirling 126 F4
Boraston Shrops 49 B8
Borden Kent 30 C2
Borden W Sus 16 B2
Bordley N Yorks 94 C2
Bordon Hants 27 F6
Bordon Camp Hants 27 F5
Boreham Essex 42 D3
Boreham Wilts 24 E3
Boreham Street E Sus 18 D3
Borehamwood Herts 40 E4
Boreland Dumfries 114 E4
Boreland Stirling 132 F2
Borgh W Isles 148 H1
Borgh W Isles 154 J4
Borghastan W Isles 154 C7
Borgie Highld 157 D9
Borgue Dumfries 106 E3
Borgue Highld 158 H3
Borley Essex 56 E2
Bornais W Isles 148 F2
Bornesketaig Highld 149 A8
Borness Dumfries 106 E3
Borough Green Kent 29 D7
Boroughbridge N Yorks 95 C6
Borras Head Wrex 73 D7
Borreraig Highld 148 C6
Borrobol Lodge Highld 157 G11
Borrowash Derbys 76 F4
Borrowby N Yorks 102 F2
Borrowdale Cumb 98 C4
Borrowfield Aberds 141 E7
Borth Ceredig 58 E3
Borth-y-Gest Gwyn 71 D6
Borthwickbrae Borders 115 C7
Borthwickshiels Borders 115 C7
Borve Highld 149 D9
Borve Lodge W Isles 154 H5
Borwick Lancs 92 B5
Bosavern Corn 2 C2
Bosbury Hereford 49 E8
Boscastle Corn 8 E3
Boscombe Bmouth 14 E2
Boscombe Wilts 25 F7
Boscoppa Corn 4 D5
Bosham W Sus 16 D2
Bosherston Pembs 44 F4
Boskenna Corn 2 D3
Bosley Ches E 75 C6
Bossall N Yorks 96 C3
Bossiney Corn 8 F2
Bossingham Kent 31 E5
Bossington Som 21 E7
Bostock Green Ches W 74 C3
Boston Lincs 79 E6
Boston Long Hedges Lincs 79 E6
Boston Spa W Yorks 95 E7
Boston West Lincs 79 E5
Boswinger Corn 3 B8
Botallack Corn 2 C2
Botany Bay London 41 E5
Botcherby Cumb 108 D4
Botcheston Leics 63 D8
Botesdale Suff 56 B4
Bothal Northumb 117 F8
Bothamsall Notts 77 B6
Bothel Cumb 107 F8
Bothenhampton Dorset 12 E2
Bothwell S Lanark 119 D7
Botley Bucks 40 D2
Botley Hants 15 C6
Botley Oxon 38 D4
Botolph Claydon Bucks 39 B7
Botolphs W Sus 17 D5
Bottacks Highld 150 E7
Bottesford Leics 77 F8
Bottesford N Lincs 90 D2
Bottisham Cambs 55 C6
Bottlesford Wilts 25 D6
Bottom Boat W Yorks 88 B4
Bottom House Staffs 75 D7
Bottom o'th'Moor Gtr Man 86 C4
Bottom of Hutton Lancs 86 B2
Bottomcraig Fife 129 B5
Botusfleming Corn 6 C2
Botwnnog Gwyn 70 D3
Bough Beech Kent 29 E5
Boughrood Powys 48 F3
Boughspring Glos 36 E2
Boughton Norf 67 D6
Boughton Northants 53 C5
Boughton Notts 77 C6
Boughton Aluph Kent 30 E4
Boughton Lees Kent 30 E4
Boughton Malherbe Kent 30 E2
Boughton Monchelsea Kent 29 D8
Boughton Street Kent 30 D4
Boulby Redcar 103 C5
Boulden Shrops 60 F5
Boulmer Northumb 117 C8
Boulston Pembs 44 D4
Boultenstone Aberds 140 C3
Boultham Lincs 78 C2
Bourn Cambs 54 D4
Bourne Lincs 65 B7
Bourne End Bucks 40 F1
Bourne End C Beds 53 E7
Bourne End Herts 40 D3
Bournemouth Bmouth 13 E8
Bournes Green Glos 37 D6
Bournes Green Southend 43 F5
Bournheath Worcs 50 B4
Bournmoor Durham 111 D6
Bournville W Mid 62 F4
Bourton Dorset 24 F2
Bourton N Som 23 C5
Bourton Oxon 38 F2
Bourton Shrops 61 E5
Bourton on Dunsmore Warks 52 B2
Bourton on the Hill Glos 51 F6
Bourton-on-the-Water Glos 38 B1
Bousd Argyll 146 E5
Boustead Hill Cumb 108 D2
Bouth Cumb 99 F5
Bouthwaite N Yorks 94 B4
Boveney Bucks 27 B7
Boverton V Glam 21 C8
Bovey Tracey Devon 7 B6
Bovingdon Herts 40 D3
Bovingdon Green Bucks 39 F8
Bovingdon Green Herts 40 D3
Bovinger Essex 41 D8
Bovington Camp Dorset 13 F6
Bow Borders 121 E7
Bow Devon 10 D2
Bow Orkney 159 J4
Bow Brickhill M Keynes 53 F7
Bow of Fife Fife 128 C5
Bow Street Ceredig 58 F3
Bowbank Durham 100 B4
Bowburn Durham 111 F6
Bowcombe IoW 15 F5
Bowd Devon 11 E6
Bowden Borders 121 F8
Bowden Devon 7 E6
Bowden Hill Wilts 24 C4
Bowderdale Cumb 100 D1
Bowdon Gtr Man 87 F5
Bower Northumb 116 F3
Bower Hinton Som 12 C2
Bowerchalke Wilts 13 B8
Bowerhill Wilts 24 C4
Bowermadden Highld 158 D4
Bowers Gifford Essex 42 F3
Bowershall Fife 128 E2
Bowertower Highld 158 D4
Bowes Durham 100 C4
Bowgreave Lancs 92 E4
Bowgreen Gtr Man 87 F5
Bowhill Borders 115 B7
Bowhouse Dumfries 107 C7
Bowland Bridge Cumb 99 F6
Bowley Hereford 49 D7
Bowlhead Green Sur 27 F7
Bowling W Dunb 118 B4
Bowling W Yorks 94 F4
Bowling Bank Wrex 73 E7
Bowling Green Worcs 50 D3
Bowmanstead Cumb 99 E5
Bowmore Argyll 142 C4
Bowness-on-Solway Cumb 108 C2
Bowness-on-Windermere Cumb 99 E6
Bowsden Northumb 123 E5
Bowside Lodge Highld 157 C11
Bowston Cumb 99 E6
Bowthorpe Norf 68 D4
Box Glos 37 D5
Box Wilts 24 C3
Box End Bedford 53 E8
Boxbush Glos 36 C4
Boxford Suff 56 E3
Boxford W Berks 26 B2
Boxgrove W Sus 16 D3
Boxley Kent 29 D8
Boxmoor Herts 40 D3
Boxted Essex 56 F4
Boxted Suff 56 D2
Boxted Cross Essex 56 F4
Boxted Heath Essex 56 F4
Boxworth Cambs 54 C4
Boxworth End Cambs 54 C4
Boyden Gate Kent 31 C6
Boylestone Derbys 75 F8
Boyndie Aberds 153 B6
Boynton E Yorks 97 C7
Boysack Angus 135 E6
Boyton Corn 8 E5
Boyton Suff 57 E7
Boyton Wilts 24 F4
Boyton Cross Essex 42 D2
Boyton End Suff 55 E8
Bozeat Northants 53 D7

Braid IoM 84 E3
Braal Castle Highld 158 D3
Brabling Green Suff 57 C6
Brabourne Kent 30 E4
Brabourne Lees Kent 30 E4
Brabster Highld 158 D5
Bracadale Highld 149 E8
Bracara Highld 147 B10
Braceborough Lincs 65 C7
Bracebridge Lincs 78 C2
Bracebridge Heath Lincs 78 C2
Bracebridge Low Fields Lincs 78 C2
Braceby Lincs 78 F3
Bracewell Lancs 93 E8
Brackenfield Derbys 76 D3
Brackenthwaite Cumb 108 E2
Brackenthwaite N Yorks 95 D5
Bracklesham W Sus 16 E2
Brackletter Highld 136 F4
Brackley Argyll 143 D8
Brackley Northants 52 F3
Brackloch Highld 156 G4
Bracknell Brack 27 C6
Braco Perth 127 D7
Bracobrae Moray 152 C5
Bracon Ash Norf 68 E4
Bracorina Highld 147 B10
Bradbourne Derbys 76 D2
Bradbury Durham 101 B8
Bradda IoM 84 F1
Bradden Northants 52 E4
Braddock Corn 5 C6
Bradeley Stoke 75 D5
Bradenham Bucks 39 E8
Bradenham Norf 68 D2
Bradenstoke Wilts 24 B5
Bradfield Essex 56 F5
Bradfield Norf 81 D8
Bradfield W Berks 26 B4
Bradfield Combust Suff 56 D2
Bradfield Green Ches E 74 D3
Bradfield Heath Essex 43 B7
Bradfield St Clare Suff 56 D3
Bradfield St George Suff 56 C3
Bradford Corn 5 B6
Bradford Derbys 76 C2
Bradford Devon 9 D6
Bradford Northumb 123 F7
Bradford W Yorks 94 F4
Bradford Abbas Dorset 12 C3
Bradford Leigh Wilts 24 C3
Bradford-on-Avon Wilts 24 C3
Bradford-on-Tone Som 11 B6
Bradford Peverell Dorset 12 E4
Brading IoW 15 F7
Bradley Derbys 76 E2
Bradley Hants 26 E4
Bradley NE Lincs 91 D6
Bradley Staffs 62 C2
Bradley W Mid 62 E3
Bradley W Yorks 88 B2
Bradley Green Worcs 50 C4
Bradley in the Moors Staffs 75 E7
Bradley Stoke S Glos 36 F3
Bradlow Hereford 50 F2
Bradmore Notts 77 F5
Bradmore W Mid 62 E2
Bradninch Devon 10 D5
Bradnop Staffs 75 D7
Bradpole Dorset 12 E2
Bradshaw Gtr Man 86 C5
Bradshaw W Yorks 87 C8
Bradstone Devon 9 F5
Bradwall Green Ches E 74 C4
Bradway S Yorks 88 F4
Bradwell Derbys 88 F2
Bradwell Essex 42 B4
Bradwell M Keynes 53 F6
Bradwell Norf 69 D8
Bradwell Staffs 74 E5
Bradwell Grove Oxon 38 D2
Bradwell on Sea Essex 43 D6
Bradwell Waterside Essex 43 D5
Bradworthy Devon 8 C5
Bradworthy Cross Devon 8 C5
Brae Dumfries 107 B5
Brae Highld 155 J13
Brae Highld 156 J7
Brae Shetland 160 G5
Brae of Achnahaird Highld 156 H3
Brae Roy Lodge Highld 137 E6
Braeantra Highld 151 D8
Braedownie Angus 134 B2
Braefield Highld 150 H7
Braegrum Perth 128 B2
Braehead Dumfries 105 D8
Braehead Orkney 159 D5
Braehead Orkney 159 H6
Braehead S Lanark 119 F8
Braehead S Lanark 120 D2
Braehead of Lunan Angus 135 D6
Braehoulland Shetland 160 F4
Braehungie Highld 158 G3
Braelangwell Lodge Highld 151 B8
Braemar Aberds 139 E7
Braemore Highld 150 D4
Braemore Highld 158 G2
Braes of Enzie Moray 152 C3
Braeside Involyd 118 B2
Braeswick Orkney 159 E7
Braewick Shetland 160 H5
Brafferton Darl 101 B7
Brafferton N Yorks 95 B7
Brafield-on-the-Green Northants 53 D6
Bragar W Isles 155 C7
Bragbury End Herts 41 B5
Bragleenmore Argyll 124 C5
Braichmelyn Gwyn 83 E6
Braid Edin 120 C5
Braides Lancs 92 D4
Braidley N Yorks 101 F5
Braidwood S Lanark 119 E8
Braigo Argyll 142 B3
Brailsford Derbys 76 E2
Brainshaugh Northumb 117 D8
Braintree Essex 42 B3
Braiseworth Suff 56 B5
Braishfield Hants 14 B4
Braithwaite Cumb 98 B4
Braithwaite S Yorks 89 C7
Braithwaite W Yorks 94 E3
Braithwell S Yorks 89 E6
Bramber W Sus 17 C5
Bramcote Notts 76 F5
Bramcote Warks 63 F8
Bramdean Hants 15 B7
Bramerton Norf 69 D5
Bramfield Herts 41 C5
Bramfield Suff 57 B7
Bramford Suff 56 E5
Bramhall Gtr Man 87 F6
Bramham W Yorks 95 E7
Bramhope W Yorks 95 E5
Bramley Hants 26 D4
Bramley S Yorks 89 E5
Bramley Sur 27 E8
Bramley W Yorks 94 F5
Bramling Kent 31 D6
Brampford Speke Devon 10 E4
Brampton Cambs 54 B3
Brampton Cumb 100 B1
Brampton Cumb 108 C5
Brampton Derbys 76 B3
Brampton Hereford 49 F6
Brampton Lincs 77 B8
Brampton Norf 81 E8
Brampton S Yorks 88 D5
Brampton Suff 69 F7
Brampton Abbotts Hereford 36 B3
Brampton Ash Northants 64 F4
Brampton Bryan Hereford 49 B5
Brampton en le Morthen S Yorks 89 F5
Bramshall Staffs 75 F7
Bramshaw Hants 14 C3
Bramshill Hants 26 C5
Bramshott Hants 27 F6
Bran End Essex 42 B2
Branault Highld 147 E8
Brancaster Norf 80 C3
Brancaster Staithe Norf 80 C3
Brancepeth Durham 110 F5
Branch End Northumb 110 C3
Branchill Moray 151 F13
Brand Green Glos 36 B4
Branderburgh Moray 152 A2
Brandesburton E Yorks 97 E7
Brandeston Suff 57 C6
Brandhill Shrops 49 B6
Brandis Corner Devon 9 D6
Brandiston Norf 81 E7
Brandon Durham 110 F5
Brandon Lincs 78 E2
Brandon Northumb 117 C6
Brandon Suff 67 F7
Brandon Warks 52 B2
Brandon Bank Cambs 67 F6
Brandon Creek Norf 67 E6
Brandon Parva Norf 68 D3
Brandsby N Yorks 95 B8
Brandy Wharf Lincs 90 E4
Brane Corn 2 D3
Branksome Poole 13 E8
Branksome Park Poole 13 E8
Bransby Lincs 77 B8
Branscombe Devon 11 F6
Bransford Worcs 50 D2
Bransgore Hants 14 E2
Branshill Clack 127 E7
Bransholme Hull 97 F7
Branson's Cross Worcs 51 B5
Branston Leics 64 B5
Branston Lincs 78 C3
Branston Staffs 63 B6
Branston Booths Lincs 78 C3
Branstone IoW 15 F6
Bransty Cumb 98 C1
Brant Broughton Lincs 78 D2
Brantham Suff 56 F5
Branthwaite Cumb 98 B2
Branthwaite Cumb 108 F2
Brantingham E Yorks 90 B3
Branton Northumb 117 C6
Branton S Yorks 89 D7
Branxholm Park Borders 115 C7
Branxholme Borders 115 C7
Branxton Northumb 122 F4
Brassey Green Ches W 74 C2
Brassington Derbys 76 D2
Brasted Kent 29 D5
Brasted Chart Kent 29 D5
Brathens Aberds 141 E5
Bratoft Lincs 79 C7
Brattleby Lincs 90 F3
Bratton Telford 61 C6
Bratton Wilts 24 D4
Bratton Clovelly Devon 9 E6
Bratton Fleming Devon 20 F5
Bratton Seymour Som 12 B4
Braughing Herts 41 B6
Braunston Northants 52 C3
Braunston-in-Rutland Rutland 64 D5
Braunstone Town Leicester 64 D2
Braunton Devon 20 F3
Brawby N Yorks 96 B3
Brawl Highld 157 C11
Brawlbin Highld 158 E2
Bray Windsor 27 B7
Bray Shop Corn 5 B8
Bray Wick Windsor 27 B6
Braybrooke Northants 64 F4
Braye Ald 16
Brayford Devon 21 F5
Braystones Cumb 98 D2
Braythorn N Yorks 94 E5
Brayton N Yorks 95 F9
Brazacott Corn 8 E4
Breach Kent 30 C2
Breachacha Castle Argyll 146 F4
Breachwood Green Herts 40 B4
Breacleit W Isles 154 D6
Breaden Heath Shrops 73 F8
Breadsall Derbys 76 F3
Breadstone Glos 36 D4
Breage Corn 2 D5
Breakachy Highld 150 G7
Bream Glos 36 D3
Breamore Hants 14 C2
Brean Som 22 D4
Breanais W Isles 154 E4
Brearton N Yorks 95 C6
Breascleit W Isles 154 D7
Breaston Derbys 76 F4
Brechfa Carms 46 F4
Brechin Angus 135 C5
Breck of Cruan Orkney 159 G4
Breckan Orkney 159 H3
Breckrey Highld 149 B10
Brecon = Aberhonddu Powys 34 B4
Bredbury Gtr Man 87 E7
Brede E Sus 18 D5
Bredenbury Hereford 49 D8
Bredfield Suff 57 D6
Bredgar Kent 30 C2
Bredhurst Kent 29 C8
Bredicot Worcs 50 D4
Bredon Worcs 50 F4
Bredon's Norton Worcs 50 F4
Bredwardine Hereford 48 E5
Breedon on the Hill Leics 63 B8
Breibhig W Isles 148 J1
Breibhig W Isles 155 D9
Breich W Loth 120 C2
Breightmet Gtr Man 86 D5
Breighton E Yorks 96 F3
Breinton Hereford 49 F6
Breinton Common Hereford 49 E6
Breiwick Shetland 160 J6
Bremhill Wilts 24 B4
Bremirehoull Shetland 160 L6
Brenchley Kent 29 E7
Brendon Devon 21 E6
Brenkley T&W 110 B5
Brent Eleigh Suff 56 E3
Brent Knoll Som 22 D5
Brent Pelham Herts 54 F5
Brentford London 28 B2
Brentingby Leics 64 C4
Brentwood Essex 42 E1
Brenzett Kent 19 C7
Brereton Staffs 62 C4
Brereton Green Ches E 74 C4
Brereton Heath Ches E 74 C5
Bressingham Norf 68 F3
Bretby Derbys 63 B6
Bretford Warks 52 B2
Bretforton Worcs 51 E5
Bretherdale Head Cumb 99 D7
Bretherton Lancs 86 B2
Brettabister Shetland 160 H6
Brettenham Norf 68 F2
Brettenham Suff 56 D3
Bretton Derbys 76 B2
Bretton Flint 73 C7
Brewer Street Sur 28 D4
Brewlands Bridge Angus 134 C1
Brewood Staffs 62 D2
Briach Moray 151 F13
Briants Puddle Dorset 13 E6
Brick End Essex 42 B1
Brickendon Herts 41 D6
Bricket Wood Herts 40 D4
Bricklehampton Worcs 50 E4
Bride IoM 84 B4
Bridekirk Cumb 107 F8
Bridell Pembs 45 E3
Bridestowe Devon 9 F7
Brideswell Aberds 152 E5
Bridford Devon 10 F3
Bridfordmills Devon 10 F3
Bridge Kent 31 D5
Bridge End Lincs 78 F4
Bridge Green Essex 55 F5
Bridge Hewick N Yorks 95 B6
Bridge of Alford Aberds 140 C4
Bridge of Allan Stirling 127 E6
Bridge of Avon Moray 152 E1
Bridge of Awe Argyll 125 C6
Bridge of Balgie Perth 132 E2
Bridge of Cally Perth 133 D8
Bridge of Canny Aberds 141 E5
Bridge of Craigisla Angus 134 D2
Bridge of Dee Dumfries 106 D4
Bridge of Don Aberdeen 141 C8
Bridge of Dun Angus 135 D6
Bridge of Dye Aberds 141 F5
Bridge of Earn Perth 128 C3
Bridge of Ericht Perth 132 D2
Bridge of Feugh Aberds 141 E6
Bridge of Forss Highld 157 C13
Bridge of Gairn Aberds 140 E2
Bridge of Gaur Perth 132 D2
Bridge of Muchalls Aberds 141 E7
Bridge of Oich Highld 137 D6
Bridge of Orchy Argyll 125 B8
Bridge of Waith Orkney 159 G3
Bridge of Walls Shetland 160 H4
Bridge of Weir Renfs 118 C3
Bridge Sollers Hereford 49 E6
Bridge Street Suff 56 E2
Bridge Trafford Ches W 73 B8
Bridge Yate S Glos 23 B8
Bridgefoot Angus 134 F3
Bridgefoot Cumb 98 B2
Bridgehampton Som 12 B3
Bridgehill Durham 110 D3
Bridgemary Hants 15 D6
Bridgemont Derbys 87 F8
Bridgend Aberds 140 C4
Bridgend Aberds 152 E5
Bridgend Angus 135 C5
Bridgend Argyll 142 B4
Bridgend Argyll 143 E8
Bridgend Argyll 145 D7
Bridgend = Pen-Y-Bont Ar Ogwr Bridgend 21 B8
Bridgend Cumb 99 C5
Bridgend Fife 129 C5
Bridgend Moray 152 E3
Bridgend N Lanark 119 B6
Bridgend Pembs 45 E3
Bridgend W Loth 120 B3
Bridgend of Lintrathen Angus 134 D2
Bridgerule Devon 8 D4
Bridges Shrops 60 E3
Bridgeton Glasgow 119 C6
Bridgetown Corn 8 F5
Bridgetown Som 21 F8
Bridgham Norf 68 F2
Bridgnorth Shrops 61 E7
Bridgtown Staffs 62 D3
Bridgwater Som 22 F5
Bridlington E Yorks 97 C7
Bridport Dorset 12 E2
Bridstow Hereford 36 B2
Brierfield Lancs 93 F8
Brierley Glos 36 C3
Brierley Hereford 49 D6
Brierley S Yorks 88 C5
Brierley Hill W Mid 62 F3
Briery Hill Bl Gwent 35 D5
Brig o'Turk Stirling 126 D4
Brigg N Lincs 90 D4
Briggswath N Yorks 103 D6
Brigham Cumb 107 F7
Brigham E Yorks 97 D6
Brighouse W Yorks 88 B2
Brighstone IoW 14 F5
Brightgate Derbys 76 D2
Brighthampton Oxon 38 D3
Brightling E Sus 18 C3
Brightlingsea Essex 43 C6
Brighton Brighton 17 D7
Brighton Corn 4 D4
Brighton Hill Hants 26 E4
Brightons Falk 120 B2
Brightwalton W Berks 26 B2
Brightwell Suff 57 E6
Brightwell Baldwin Oxon 39 E6
Brightwell cum Sotwell Oxon 39 E5
Brignall Durham 101 C5
Brigsley NE Lincs 91 D6
Brigsteer Cumb 99 F6
Brigstock Northants 65 F6
Brill Bucks 39 C6
Brilley Hereford 48 E4
Brimaston Pembs 44 C4
Brimfield Hereford 49 C7
Brimington Derbys 76 B4
Brimley Devon 7 B5
Brimpsfield Glos 37 C6
Brimpton W Berks 26 C3
Brims Orkney 159 K3
Brimscombe Glos 37 D5
Brimstage Mers 85 F4
Brinacory Highld 147 B10
Brind E Yorks 96 F3
Brindister Shetland 160 H4
Brindister Shetland 160 K6
Brindle Lancs 86 B4
Brindley Ford Stoke 75 D5
Brineton Staffs 62 C2
Bringhurst Leics 64 E5
Brington Cambs 53 B8
Brinian Orkney 159 F5
Briningham Norf 81 D6
Brinkhill Lincs 79 B6
Brinkley Cambs 55 D7
Brinklow Warks 52 B2
Brinkworth Wilts 37 F7
Brinmore Highld 138 B2
Brinscall Lancs 86 B4
Brinsea N Som 23 C6
Brinsley Notts 76 E4
Brinsop Hereford 49 E6
Brinsworth S Yorks 88 F5
Brinton Norf 81 D6
Brisco Cumb 108 D4
Brisley Norf 81 E5
Brislington Bristol 23 B8
Bristol Bristol 23 B7
Briston Norf 81 D6
Britannia Lancs 87 B6
Britford Wilts 14 B2
Brithdir Gwyn 58 C4
British Legion Village Kent 29 D8
Briton Ferry Neath 33 E8
Britwell Salome Oxon 39 E6
Brixham Torbay 7 D7
Brixton Devon 6 D3
Brixton London 28 B4
Brixton Deverill Wilts 24 F3
Brixworth Northants 52 B5
Brize Norton Oxon 38 D3
Broad Blunsdon Swindon 38 E1
Broad Campden Glos 51 F6
Broad Chalke Wilts 13 B8
Broad Green C Beds 53 E7
Broad Green Essex 42 B4
Broad Green Worcs 50 D2
Broad Haven Pembs 44 D3
Broad Heath Worcs 49 C8
Broad Hill Cambs 55 B6
Broad Hinton Wilts 25 B6
Broad Laying Hants 26 C2
Broad Marston Worcs 51 E6
Broad Oak Carms 33 B6
Broad Oak Cumb 98 E3
Broad Oak Dorset 12 E2
Broad Oak Dorset 13 C5
Broad Oak E Sus 18 C5
Broad Oak E Sus 18 D5
Broad Oak Hereford 36 B1
Broad Oak Mers 86 E3
Broad Street Kent 30 D2
Broad Street Green Essex 42 D4
Broad Town Wilts 25 B5
Broadbottom Gtr Man 87 E7
Broadbridge W Sus 16 D2
Broadbridge Heath W Sus 28 F2
Broadclyst Devon 10 E4
Broadfield Gtr Man 87 C6
Broadfield Lancs 86 B3
Broadfield Pembs 32 D2
Broadfield W Sus 28 F3
Broadford Highld 149 F11
Broadford Bridge W Sus 16 B4
Broadhaugh Borders 115 D7
Broadhaven Highld 158 E5
Broadheath Gtr Man 87 F5
Broadhembury Devon 11 D6
Broadhempston Devon 7 C6
Broadholme Derbys 76 E3
Broadholme Lincs 77 B8
Broadland Row E Sus 18 D5
Broadlay Carms 32 D4
Broadley Lancs 87 C6
Broadley Moray 152 B3
Broadley Common Essex 41 D7
Broadmayne Dorset 12 F5
Broadmeadows Borders 121 F7
Broadmere Hants 26 E4
Broadmoor Pembs 32 D1
Broadoak Kent 31 C5
Broadrashes Moray 152 C4
Broadsea Aberds 153 B9
Broadstairs Kent 31 C7
Broadstone Poole 13 E8
Broadstone Shrops 60 F5
Broadtown Lane Wilts 25 B5
Broadwas Worcs 50 D2
Broadwater Herts 41 B5
Broadwater W Sus 17 D5
Broadway Carms 32 D3
Broadway Pembs 44 D3
Broadway Som 11 C8
Broadway Suff 57 B7
Broadway Worcs 51 F5
Broadwell Glos 36 C2
Broadwell Glos 38 B2
Broadwell Oxon 38 D2
Broadwell Warks 52 C2
Broadwell House Northumb 110 D2
Broadwey Dorset 12 F4
Broadwindsor Dorset 12 D2
Broadwood Kelly Devon 9 D8
Broadwoodwidger Devon 9 F6
Brobury Hereford 48 E5
Brochel Highld 149 D10
Brochloch Dumfries 113 E5
Brochroy Argyll 125 B6
Brockamin Worcs 50 D2
Brockbridge Hants 15 C7
Brockdam Northumb 117 B7
Brockdish Norf 57 B6
Brockenhurst Hants 14 D4
Brocketsbrae S Lanark 119 F8
Brockford Street Suff 56 C5
Brockhall Northants 52 C4
Brockham Sur 28 E2
Brockhampton Glos 37 B7
Brockhampton Hereford 49 F7
Brockholes W Yorks 88 C2
Brockhurst Derbys 76 C3
Brockhurst Hants 15 D7
Brocklebank Cumb 108 E3
Brocklesby Lincs 90 C5
Brockley N Som 23 C6
Brockley Green Suff 56 D2
Brockleymoor Cumb 108 F4
Brockton Shrops 60 D3
Brockton Shrops 60 F3
Brockton Shrops 61 D7
Brockton Shrops 61 E5
Brockton Telford 61 C7
Brockweir Glos 36 D2
Brockwood Hants 15 B7
Brockworth Glos 37 C5
Brocton Staffs 62 C3
Brodick N Ayrs 143 E11
Brodsworth S Yorks 89 D6
Brogaig Highld 149 B9
Brogborough C Beds 53 F7
Broken Cross Ches E 75 B5
Broken Cross Ches W 74 B3
Brokenborough Wilts 37 F6
Bromborough Mers 85 F4
Brome Suff 56 B5
Brome Street Suff 57 B5
Bromeswell Suff 57 D7
Bromfield Cumb 107 E8
Bromfield Shrops 49 B6
Bromham Bedford 53 D8
Bromham Wilts 24 C4
Bromley London 28 C5
Bromley W Mid 62 F3
Bromley Common London 28 C5
Bromley Green Kent 19 B6
Brompton Medway 29 C8
Brompton N Yorks 102 E1
Brompton N Yorks 103 F7
Brompton-on-Swale N Yorks 101 E7
Brompton Ralph Som 22 F2
Brompton Regis Som 21 F8
Bromsash Hereford 36 B3
Bromsberrow Heath Glos 50 F2
Bromsgrove Worcs 50 B4
Bromyard Hereford 49 D8
Bromyard Downs Hereford 49 D8
Bronaber Gwyn 71 D8
Brongest Ceredig 46 E2
Bronington Wrex 73 F8
Bronllys Powys 48 F3
Bronnant Ceredig 46 C5
Bronwydd Arms Carms 33 B5
Bronydd Powys 48 E4
Bronygarth Shrops 73 F6
Brook Carms 32 D3
Brook Hants 14 B4
Brook Hants 14 C3
Brook IoW 14 F4
Brook Kent 30 E4
Brook Sur 27 E8
Brook Sur 27 F7
Brook End Bedford 53 C8
Brook Hill Hants 14 C3
Brook Street Kent 19 B6
Brook Street Kent 29 E6
Brook Street W Sus 17 B7
Brooke Norf 69 E5
Brooke Rutland 64 D5
Brookenby Lincs 91 E6
Brookend Glos 36 E2
Brookfield Renfs 118 C4
Brookhouse Lancs 92 C5
Brookhouse Green Ches E 74 C5
Brookland Kent 19 C6
Brooklands Dumfries 106 B5
Brooklands Gtr Man 87 E5
Brooklands Shrops 74 E2
Brookmans Park Herts 41 D5
Brooks Powys 59 E8
Brooks Green W Sus 16 B5
Brookthorpe Glos 37 C5
Brookville Norf 67 E7
Brookwood Sur 27 D7
Broom C Beds 54 E2
Broom S Yorks 88 E5
Broom Warks 51 D5
Broom Worcs 50 B4
Broom Green Norf 81 E5
Broom Hill Dorset 13 D8
Broome Norf 69 E6
Broome Shrops 60 F4
Broome Park Northumb 117 C7
Broomedge Warr 86 F5
Broomer's Corner W Sus 16 B5
Broomfield Aberds 153 E9
Broomfield Essex 42 C3
Broomfield Kent 30 D2
Broomfield Kent 31 C5
Broomfield Som 22 F4
Broomfleet E Yorks 90 B2
Broomhall Ches E 74 E3
Broomhall Windsor 27 C7
Broomhaugh Northumb 110 C3
Broomhill Norf 67 D6
Broomhill Northumb 117 D8
Broomhill S Yorks 88 D5
Broomholm Norf 81 D9
Broomley Northumb 110 C3
Broompark Durham 110 E5
Broom's Green Glos 50 F2
Broomy Lodge Hants 14 C3
Brora Highld 157 J12
Broseley Shrops 61 D6
Brotherhouse Bar Lincs 66 C2
Brotherstone Borders 122 F2
Brothertoft Lincs 79 E5
Brotherton N Yorks 89 B5
Brotton Redcar 102 C4
Broubster Highld 157 C13
Brough Cumb 100 C2
Brough Derbys 88 F2
Brough E Yorks 90 B3
Brough Highld 158 C4
Brough Notts 77 D8
Brough Orkney 159 G4
Brough Shetland 160 F6
Brough Shetland 160 F7
Brough Shetland 160 G7
Brough Shetland 160 H6
Brough Shetland 160 J7
Brough Lodge Shetland 160 D7
Brough Sowerby Cumb 100 C2
Broughall Shrops 74 E2
Broughton Borders 120 F4
Broughton Cambs 54 B3
Broughton Flint 73 C7
Broughton Hants 25 F8
Broughton Lancs 92 F5
Broughton M Keynes 53 E6
Broughton N Lincs 90 D3
Broughton N Yorks 94 D2
Broughton N Yorks 96 B3
Broughton Northants 53 B6
Broughton Orkney 159 D5
Broughton Oxon 52 F2
Broughton V Glam 21 B8
Broughton Astley Leics 64 E2
Broughton Beck Cumb 98 F4
Broughton Common Wilts 24 C3
Broughton Gifford Wilts 24 C3
Broughton Hackett Worcs 50 D4
Broughton in Furness Cumb 98 F4
Broughton Mills Cumb 98 E4
Broughton Moor Cumb 107 F7
Broughton Park Gtr Man 87 D6
Broughton Poggs Oxon 38 D2
Broughtown Orkney 159 D7
Broughty Ferry Dundee 134 F4
Browhouses Dumfries 108 C2
Browland Shetland 160 H4
Brown Candover Hants 26 F3
Brown Edge Lancs 85 C4
Brown Edge Staffs 75 D6
Brown Heath Ches W 73 C8
Brownhill Aberds 153 D6
Brownhill Aberds 153 D8
Brownhill Blackburn 93 F6
Brownhill Shrops 60 B4
Brownhills Fife 129 C7
Brownhills W Mid 62 D4
Brownlow Ches E 74 C5
Brownlow Heath Ches E 74 C5
Brownmuir Aberds 135 B7
Brown's End Glos 50 F2
Brownshill Glos 37 D5
Brownston Devon 6 D4
Brownyside Northumb 117 B7
Broxa N Yorks 103 E7
Broxbourne Herts 41 D6
Broxburn E Loth 122 B2
Broxburn W Loth 120 B3
Broxholme Lincs 78 B2
Broxted Essex 42 B1
Broxton Ches W 73 D8
Broxwood Hereford 49 D5
Broyle Side E Sus 17 C8
Brù W Isles 155 C8
Bruairnis W Isles 148 H2
Bruan Highld 158 G5
Bruar Lodge Perth 133 B5
Brucehill W Dunb 118 B3
Bruera Ches W 73 C8
Bruern Abbey Oxon 38 B2
Bruichladdich Argyll 142 B3
Bruisyard Suff 57 C7
Brumby N Lincs 90 D2
Brund Staffs 75 C8
Brundall Norf 69 D6
Brundish Suff 57 C6
Brundish Street Suff 57 B6
Brunery Highld 147 D10
Brunshaw Lancs 93 F8
Brunswick Village T&W 110 B5
Bruntcliffe W Yorks 88 B3
Bruntingthorpe Leics 64 E3
Brunton Fife 128 B5
Brunton Northumb 117 B8
Brunton Wilts 25 D7
Brushford Devon 9 D8
Brushford Som 10 B4
Bruton Som 23 F8
Bryanston Dorset 13 D6
Brydekirk Dumfries 107 B8
Bryher Scilly 2 E3
Brymbo Wrex 73 D6
Brympton Som 12 C3
Bryn Carms 33 D6
Bryn Gtr Man 86 D3
Bryn Neath 34 E2
Bryn Shrops 60 F2
Bryn-coch Neath 33 E8
Bryn Du Anglesey 82 D3
Bryn Gates Gtr Man 86 D3
Bryn-glas Conwy 83 E8
Bryn Golau Rhondda 34 F3
Bryn-Iwan Carms 46 F2
Bryn-mawr Gwyn 70 D3
Bryn-nantllech Conwy 72 C3
Bryn-penarth Powys 59 D8
Bryn Rhyd-yr-Arian Conwy 72 C3
Bryn Saith Marchog Denb 72 D4
Bryn Sion Gwyn 59 C5
Bryn-y-gwenin Mon 35 C7
Bryn-y-maen Conwy 83 D8
Bryn-yr-eryr Gwyn 70 C4
Brynamman Carms 33 C8
Brynberian Pembs 45 F3
Brynbryddan Neath 34 E1
Brynbuga = Usk Mon 35 D7
Bryncae Rhondda 34 F3
Bryncethin Bridgend 34 F3
Bryncir Gwyn 71 C5
Bryncroes Gwyn 70 D3
Bryncrug Gwyn 58 D3
Bryneglwys Denb 72 E5
Brynford Flint 73 B5
Bryngwran Anglesey 82 D3
Bryngwyn Ceredig 45 E4
Bryngwyn Mon 35 D7
Bryngwyn Powys 48 E3
Brynhenllan Pembs 45 F2
Brynhoffnant Ceredig 46 D2
Brynithel Bl Gwent 35 D6
Brynmawr Bl Gwent 35 C5
Brynmenyn Bridgend 34 F3
Brynmill Swansea 33 E7
Brynna Rhondda 34 F3
Brynrefail Anglesey 82 C4
Brynrefail Gwyn 83 E5
Brynsadler Rhondda 34 F4
Brynsiencyn Anglesey 82 E4
Brynteg Anglesey 82 C4
Brynteg Ceredig 46 E3
Buaile nam Bodach W Isles 148 H2
Bualintur Highld 149 F9
Buarthmeini Gwyn 72 F2
Bubbenhall Warks 51 B8
Bubwith E Yorks 96 F3
Buccleuch Borders 115 C6
Buchanhaven Aberds 153 D11
Buchanty Perth 127 B8
Buchlyvie Stirling 126 E4
Buckabank Cumb 108 E3
Buckden Cambs 54 C2
Buckden N Yorks 94 B2
Buckenham Norf 69 D6
Buckerell Devon 11 D6
Buckfast Devon 6 C5
Buckfastleigh Devon 6 C5
Buckhaven Fife 129 E5
Buckholm Borders 121 F7
Buckholt Mon 36 C2
Buckhorn Weston Dorset 13 B5
Buckhurst Hill Essex 41 E7
Buckie Moray 152 B4
Buckies Highld 158 D3
Buckingham Bucks 52 F4
Buckland Bucks 40 C1
Buckland Devon 6 E4
Buckland Glos 51 F5
Buckland Hants 14 E4
Buckland Herts 54 F4
Buckland Kent 31 E7
Buckland Oxon 38 E3
Buckland Sur 28 D3
Buckland Brewer Devon 9 B6
Buckland Common Bucks 40 D2
Buckland Dinham Som 24 D2
Buckland Filleigh Devon 9 D6
Buckland in the Moor Devon 6 B5
Buckland Monachorum Devon 6 C2
Buckland Newton Dorset 12 D4
Buckland St Mary Som 11 C7
Bucklebury W Berks 26 B3
Bucklegate Lincs 79 F6
Bucklerheads Angus 134 F4
Bucklers Hard Hants 14 E5
Bucklesham Suff 57 E6
Buckley = Bwcle Flint 73 C6
Bucklow Hill Ches E 86 F5
Buckminster Leics 65 B5
Bucknall Lincs 78 C4
Bucknall Stoke 75 E6
Bucknell Oxon 39 B5
Bucknell Shrops 49 B5
Buckpool Moray 152 B4
Buck's Cross Devon 8 B5
Bucks Green W Sus 27 F8
Bucks Horn Oak Hants 27 E6
Buck's Mills Devon 9 B5
Bucksburn Aberdeen 141 D7
Buckshaw Village Lancs 86 B3
Buckskin Hants 26 D4
Buckton E Yorks 97 B7
Buckton Hereford 49 B5
Buckton Northumb 123 F6
Buckworth Cambs 54 B2
Budbrooke Warks 51 C7
Budby Notts 77 C6
Budd's Titson Corn 8 D4
Bude Corn 8 D4
Budlake Devon 10 E4
Budle Northumb 123 F7
Budleigh Salterton Devon 11 F5
Budock Water Corn 3 C6
Buerton Ches E 74 E3
Buffler's Holt Bucks 52 F4
Bugbrooke Northants 52 D4
Buglawton Ches E 75 C5
Bugle Corn 4 D5
Bugley Wilts 24 E3
Bugthorpe E Yorks 96 D3
Buildwas Shrops 61 D6
Builth Road Powys 48 D2
Builth Wells = Llanfair-Ym-Muallt Powys 48 D2
Buirgh W Isles 154 H5
Bulby Lincs 65 B7
Bulcote Notts 77 E6
Buldoo Highld 157 C12
Bulford Wilts 25 E6
Bulford Camp Wilts 25 E6
Bulkeley Ches E 74 D2
Bulkington Warks 63 F7
Bulkington Wilts 24 D4
Bulkworthy Devon 9 C5
Bull Hill Hants 14 E4
Bullamoor N Yorks 102 E1
Bullbridge Derbys 76 D3
Bullbrook Brack 27 C6
Bulley Glos 36 C4
Bullgill Cumb 107 F7
Bullington Hants 26 E2
Bullington Lincs 78 B3
Bull's Green Herts 41 C5
Bullwood Argyll 145 F10
Bulmer Essex 56 E2
Bulmer N Yorks 96 C2
Bulmer Tye Essex 56 F2
Bulphan Thurrock 42 F2
Bulverhythe E Sus 18 E4
Bulwark Aberds 153 D9
Bulwell Nottingham 76 E5
Bulwick Northants 65 E6
Bumble's Green Essex 41 D7
Bun a'Mhuillin W Isles 148 G2
Bun Abhainn Eadarra W Isles 154 G6
Bun Loyne Highld 136 D5
Bunacaimb Highld 147 C9
Bunarkaig Highld 136 F4
Bunbury Ches E 74 D2
Bunbury Heath Ches E 74 D2
Bunchrew Highld 151 G9
Bundalloch Highld 149 F13
Buness Shetland 160 C8
Bunessan Argyll 146 J6
Bungay Suff 69 F6
Bunker's Hill Lincs 78 B2
Bunker's Hill Lincs 79 D5
Bunkers Hill Oxon 38 C4
Bunloit Highld 137 B8
Bunnahabhain Argyll 142 A5
Bunny Notts 64 B2
Buntait Highld 150 H6
Buntingford Herts 41 B6
Bunwell Norf 68 E4
Burbage Derbys 75 B7
Burbage Leics 63 E8
Burbage Wilts 25 C7
Burchett's Green Windsor 39 F8
Burcombe Wilts 25 F5
Burcot Oxon 39 E5
Burcott Bucks 40 B1
Burdon T&W 111 D6
Bures Suff 56 F3
Bures Green Suff 56 F3
Burford Ches E 74 D3
Burford Oxon 38 C2
Burford Shrops 49 C7
Burg Argyll 146 G6
Burgar Orkney 159 F4
Burgate Hants 14 C2
Burgate Suff 56 B4
Burgess Hill W Sus 17 C7
Burgh Suff 57 D6
Burgh by Sands Cumb 108 D3
Burgh Castle Norf 69 D7
Burgh Heath Sur 28 D3
Burgh le Marsh Lincs 79 C8
Burgh Muir Aberds 141 B6
Burgh next Aylsham Norf 81 E8
Burgh on Bain Lincs 91 F6
Burgh St Margaret Norf 69 C7
Burgh St Peter Norf 69 E7
Burghclere Hants 26 C2
Burghead Moray 151 E14
Burghfield W Berks 26 C4
Burghfield Common W Berks 26 C4
Burghfield Hill W Berks 26 C4
Burghill Hereford 49 E6
Burghwallis S Yorks 89 C6
Burham Kent 29 C8
Buriton Hants 15 B8
Burland Ches E 74 D3
Burlawn Corn 4 B4
Burleigh Brack 27 C6
Burlescombe Devon 11 C5
Burleston Dorset 13 E5
Burley Hants 14 D3
Burley Rutland 65 C5
Burley W Yorks 95 F5
Burley Gate Hereford 49 E7
Burley in Wharfedale W Yorks 94 E4
Burley Lodge Hants 14 D3
Burley Street Hants 14 D3
Burleydam Ches E 74 E3
Burlingjobb Powys 48 D4
Burlow E Sus 18 D2
Burlton Shrops 60 B4
Burmarsh Kent 19 B7
Burmington Warks 51 F7
Burn N Yorks 89 B6
Burn of Cambus Stirling 127 D6
Burnaston Derbys 76 F2
Burnbank S Lanark 119 D7
Burnby E Yorks 96 E4
Burncross S Yorks 88 E4
Burneside Cumb 99 E7
Burness Orkney 159 D7
Burneston N Yorks 101 F8
Burnett Bath 23 C8
Burnfoot Borders 115 C7
Burnfoot Borders 115 C8
Burnfoot E Ayrs 112 D4
Burnfoot Perth 127 D8
Burnham Bucks 40 F2
Burnham N Lincs 90 C4
Burnham Deepdale Norf 80 C4
Burnham Green Herts 41 C5
Burnham Market Norf 80 C4
Burnham Norton Norf 80 C4
Burnham-on-Crouch Essex 43 E5
Burnham-on-Sea Som 22 E5
Burnham Overy Staithe Norf 80 C4
Burnham Overy Town Norf 80 C4
Burnham Thorpe Norf 80 C4
Burnhead Dumfries 113 E8
Burnhead S Ayrs 112 D2
Burnhervie Aberds 141 C6
Burnhill Green Staffs 61 D7
Burnhope Durham 110 E4
Burnhouse N Ayrs 118 D3
Burniston N Yorks 103 E8
Burnlee W Yorks 88 D2
Burnley Lancs 93 F8
Burnley Lane Lancs 93 F8
Burnmouth Borders 123 C5
Burnopfield Durham 110 D4
Burnsall N Yorks 94 C3
Burnside Angus 135 D5
Burnside E Ayrs 113 C5
Burnside Fife 128 D3
Burnside S Lanark 119 C6
Burnside Shetland 160 F4
Burnside W Loth 120 B3
Burnside of Duntrune Angus 134 F4
Burnswark Dumfries 107 B8
Burnt Heath Derbys 76 B2
Burnt Houses Durham 101 B6
Burnt Yates N Yorks 95 C5
Burntcommon Sur 27 D8
Burnthouse Corn 3 C6
Burntisland Fife 128 F4
Burnton E Ayrs 112 D4
Burntwood Staffs 62 D4
Burnwynd Edin 120 C4
Burpham Sur 27 D8
Burpham W Sus 16 D4
Burradon Northumb 117 D5
Burradon T&W 111 B5
Burrafirth Shetland 160 B8
Burraland Shetland 160 F5
Burraland Shetland 160 J4
Burras Corn 3 C5
Burravoe Shetland 160 F7
Burravoe Shetland 160 G5
Burray Village Orkney 159 J5
Burrells Cumb 100 C1
Burrelton Perth 134 F2
Burridge Devon 20 F4
Burridge Hants 15 C6
Burrill N Yorks 101 F7
Burringham N Lincs 90 D2
Burrington Devon 9 C8
Burrington Hereford 49 B6
Burrington N Som 23 D6
Burrough Green Cambs 55 D7
Burrough on the Hill Leics 64 C4
Burrow-bridge Som 11 B8
Burrowhill Sur 27 C7
Burry Swansea 33 E5
Burry Green Swansea 33 E5
Burry Port = Porth Tywyn Carms 33 D5
Burscough Lancs 86 C2
Burscough Bridge Lancs 86 C2
Bursea E Yorks 96 F4
Burshill E Yorks 97 E6
Bursledon Hants 15 D5
Burslem Stoke 75 E5
Burstall Suff 56 E4
Burstock Dorset 12 D2
Burston Norf 68 F4
Burston Staffs 75 F6
Burstow Sur 28 E4
Burstwick E Yorks 91 B6
Burtersett N Yorks 100 F3
Burtle Som 23 E5
Burton Ches W 73 B7
Burton Ches W 74 C2
Burton Dorset 14 E2
Burton Lincs 78 B2
Burton Northumb 123 F7
Burton Pembs 44 E4
Burton Som 22 E3
Burton Wilts 24 B3
Burton Agnes E Yorks 97 C7
Burton Bradstock Dorset 12 F2
Burton Dassett Warks 51 D8
Burton Fleming E Yorks 97 B6
Burton Green W Mid 51 B7
Burton Green Wrex 73 D7
Burton Hastings Warks 63 E8
Burton-in-Kendal Cumb 92 B5
Burton in Lonsdale N Yorks 93 B6
Burton Joyce Notts 77 E6
Burton Latimer Northants 53 B7
Burton Lazars Leics 64 C4
Burton-le-Coggles Lincs 65 B6
Burton Leonard N Yorks 95 C6
Burton on the Wolds Leics 64 B2
Burton Overy Leics 64 E3
Burton Pedwardine Lincs 78 E4
Burton Pidsea E Yorks 97 F8
Burton Salmon N Yorks 89 B5
Burton Stather N Lincs 90 C2
Burton upon Stather N Lincs 90 C2
Burton upon Trent Staffs 63 B6
Burtonwood Warr 86 E3
Burwardsley Ches W 74 D2
Burwarton Shrops 61 F6
Burwash E Sus 18 C3
Burwash Common E Sus 18 C3
Burwash Weald E Sus 18 C3
Burwell Cambs 55 C6
Burwell Lincs 79 B6
Burwen Anglesey 82 B4
Burwick Orkney 159 K5
Bury Cambs 66 F2
Bury Gtr Man 87 C6
Bury Som 10 B4
Bury W Sus 16 C4
Bury Green Herts 41 B7
Bury St Edmunds Suff 56 C2
Burythorpe N Yorks 96 C3
Busby E Renf 119 D5
Buscot Oxon 38 E2
Bush Bank Hereford 49 D6
Bush Crathie Aberds 139 E8
Bush Green Norf 68 F5
Bushbury W Mid 62 D3
Bushby Leics 64 D3
Bushey Herts 40 E4
Bushey Heath Herts 40 E4
Bushley Worcs 50 F3
Bushton Wilts 25 B5
Buslingthorpe Lincs 90 F4
Busta Shetland 160 G5
Butcher's Cross E Sus 18 C2
Butcombe N Som 23 C7
Butetown Cardiff 22 B3
Butleigh Som 23 F7
Butleigh Wootton Som 23 F7
Butler's Cross Bucks 39 D8
Butler's End Warks 63 F6
Butlers Marston Warks 51 E8
Butley Suff 57 D7
Butley High Corner Suff 57 E7
Butt Green Ches E 74 D3
Butterburn Cumb 109 B6
Buttercrambe N Yorks 96 D3
Butterknowle Durham 101 B6
Butterleigh Devon 10 D4
Buttermere Cumb 98 C3
Buttermere Wilts 25 C8
Buttershaw W Yorks 88 B2
Butterstone Perth 133 E7
Butterton Staffs 75 D7
Butterwick Durham 102 B1
Butterwick Lincs 79 E6
Butterwick N Yorks 96 B3
Butterwick N Yorks 97 B5
Buttington Powys 60 D2
Buttonoak Worcs 50 B2
Butt's Green Hants 14 B4
Buttsash Hants 14 D5
Buxhall Suff 56 D4
Buxhall Fen Street Suff 56 D4
Buxley Borders 122 D4
Buxted E Sus 17 B8
Buxton Derbys 75 B7

Buxton Norf 81 E8
Buxworth Derbys 87 F8
Bwcle = Buckley Flint 73 C6
Bwlch Powys 35 B5
Bwlch-Llan Ceredig 46 D4
Bwlch-y-cibau Powys 59 C8
Bwlch-y-fadfa Ceredig 46 E3
Bwlch-y-ffridd Powys 59 E7
Bwlch-y-sarnau Powys 48 B2
Bwlchgwyn Wrex 73 D6
Bwlchnewydd Carms 32 B4
Bwlchtocyn Gwyn 70 E4
Bwlchyddar Powys 59 B8
Bwlchygroes Pembs 45 F4
Byermoor T&W 110 D4
Byers Green Durham 110 F5
Byfield Northants 52 D3
Byfleet Sur 27 C8
Byford Hereford 49 E5
Bygrave Herts 54 F3
Byker T&W 111 C5
Bylchau Conwy 72 C3
Byley Ches W 74 C4
Bynea Carms 33 E6
Byrness Northumb 116 D3
Bythorn Cambs 53 B8
Byton Hereford 49 C5
Byworth W Sus 16 B3

C

Cabharstadh W Isles 155 E8
Cablea Perth 133 F6
Cabourne Lincs 90 D5
Cabrach Argyll 144 G3
Cabrach Moray 140 B2
Cabrich Highld 151 G8
Cabus Lancs 92 E4
Cackle Street E Sus 17 B8
Cadbury Devon 10 D4
Cadbury Barton Devon 9 C8
Cadder E Dunb 119 B6
Caddington C Beds 40 C3
Caddonfoot Borders 121 F7
Cade Street E Sus 18 C3
Cadeby Leics 63 D8
Cadeby S Yorks 89 D6
Cadeleigh Devon 10 D4
Cadgwith Corn 3 E6
Cadham Fife 128 D4
Cadishead Gtr Man 86 E5
Cadle Swansea 33 E7
Cadley Lancs 92 F5
Cadley Wilts 25 C7
Cadley Wilts 25 D7
Cadmore End Bucks 39 E7
Cadnam Hants 14 C3
Cadney N Lincs 90 D4
Cadole Flint 73 C6
Cadoxton V Glam 22 C3
Cadoxton-Juxta-Neath Neath 34 E1
Cadshaw Blackburn 86 C5
Cadzow S Lanark 119 D7
Caeathro Gwyn 82 E4
Caehopkin Powys 34 C2
Caenby Lincs 90 F4
Caenby Corner Lincs 90 F3
Caér-bryn Carms 33 C6
Caer Llan Mon 36 D1
Caerau Bridgend 34 E2
Caerau Cardiff 22 B3
Caerdeon Gwyn 58 C3
Caerdydd = Cardiff Cardiff 22 B3
Caerfarchell Pembs 44 C2
Caerffili = Caerphilly Caerph 35 F5
Caerfyrddin = Carmarthen Carms 33 B5
Caergeiliog Anglesey 82 D3
Caergwrle Flint 73 D7
Caergybi = Holyhead Anglesey 82 C2
Caerleon = Caerllion Newport 35 E7
Caerllion = Caerleon Newport 35 E7
Caernarfon Gwyn 82 E4
Caerphilly = Caerffili Caerph 35 F5
Caersws Powys 59 E7
Caerwedros Ceredig 46 D2
Caerwent Mon 36 E1
Caerwych Gwyn 71 D7
Caerwys Flint 72 B5
Caethle Gwyn 58 E3
Caim Anglesey 83 C6
Caio Carms 47 F5
Cairinis W Isles 148 B3
Cairisiadar W Isles 154 D5
Cairminis W Isles 154 J5
Cairnbaan Argyll 145 D7
Cairnbanno Ho. Aberds 153 D8
Cairnborrow Aberds 152 D4
Cairnbrogie Aberds 141 B7
Cairnbulg Castle Aberds 153 B10
Cairncross Angus 134 B4
Cairncross Borders 122 C4
Cairndow Argyll 125 D7
Cairness Aberds 153 B10
Cairneyhill Fife 128 F2
Cairnfield Ho. Moray 152 B4
Cairngaan Dumfries 104 F5
Cairngarroch Dumfries 104 E4
Cairnhill Aberds 153 E6
Cairnie Aberds 141 D7
Cairnie Aberds 152 D4
Cairnorrie Aberds 153 D8
Cairnpark Aberds 141 C7
Cairnryan Dumfries 104 C4
Cairnton Orkney 159 H4
Caister-on-Sea Norf 69 C8
Caistor Lincs 90 D5
Caistor St Edmund Norf 68 D5
Caistron Northumb 117 D5
Caitha Bowland Borders 121 E7
Calais Street Suff 56 F3
Calanais W Isles 154 D7
Calbost W Isles 155 F9
Calbourne IoW 14 F5
Calceby Lincs 79 B6
Calcot Row W Berks 26 B4
Calcott Kent 31 C5
Caldback Shetland 160 C8
Caldbeck Cumb 108 F3
Caldbergh N Yorks 101 F5
Caldecote Cambs 54 D4
Caldecote Cambs 65 F8
Caldecote Herts 54 F3
Caldecote Northants 52 D4
Caldecott Northants 53 C7
Caldecott Oxon 38 E4
Caldecott Rutland 65 E5
Calder Bridge Cumb 98 D2
Calder Hall Cumb 98 D2
Calder Mains Highld 158 E2
Calder Vale Lancs 92 E5
Calderbank N Lanark 119 C7
Calderbrook Gtr Man 87 C7
Caldercruix N Lanark 119 C8
Caldermill S Lanark 119 E6
Calderwood S Lanark 119 D6
Caldhame Angus 134 E4
Caldicot Mon 36 F1
Caldwell Derbys 63 C6
Caldwell N Yorks 101 C6
Caldy Mers 85 F3
Caledrhydiau Ceredig 46 D3
Calfsound Orkney 159 E6
Calgary Argyll 146 F6
Califer Moray 151 F13
California Falk 120 B2
California Norf 69 C8
Calke Derbys 63 B7
Callakille Highld 149 C11
Callaly Northumb 117 D6
Callander Stirling 126 D5
Callaughton Shrops 61 E6
Callestick Corn 4 D2
Calligarry Highld 149 H11
Callington Corn 5 C8
Callow Hereford 49 F6
Callow End Worcs 50 E3
Callow Hill Wilts 37 F7
Callow Hill Worcs 50 B2
Callows Grave Worcs 49 C7
Calmore Hants 14 C4
Calmsden Glos 37 D7
Calne Wilts 24 B5
Calow Derbys 76 B4
Calshot Hants 15 D5
Calstock Corn 6 C2
Calstone Wellington Wilts 24 C5
Calthorpe Norf 81 D7
Calthwaite Cumb 108 E4
Calton N Yorks 94 D2
Calton Staffs 75 D8
Calveley Ches E 74 D2
Calver Derbys 76 B2
Calver Hill Hereford 49 E5
Calverhall Shrops 74 F3
Calverleigh Devon 10 C4
Calverley W Yorks 94 F5
Calvert Bucks 39 B6
Calverton M Keynes 53 F5
Calverton Notts 77 E6
Calvine Perth 133 C5
Calvo Cumb 107 D8
Cam Glos 36 E4
Camas-luinie Highld 136 B2
Camasnacroise Highld 130 D2
Camastianavaig Highld 149 E10
Camasunary Highld 149 G10
Camault Muir Highld 151 G8
Camb Shetland 160 D7
Camber E Sus 19 D6
Camberley Sur 27 C6
Camberwell London 28 B4
Camblesforth N Yorks 89 B7
Cambo Northumb 117 F6
Cambois Northumb 117 F9
Camborne Corn 3 B5
Cambourne Cambs 54 D4
Cambridge Cambs 55 D5
Cambridge Glos 36 D4
Cambridge Town Southend 43 F5
Cambus Clack 127 E7
Cambusavie Farm Highld 151 B10
Cambusbarron Stirling 127 E6
Cambuskenneth Stirling 127 E7
Cambuslang S Lanark 119 C6
Cambusmore Lodge Highld 151 B10
Camden London 41 F5
Camelford Corn 8 F3
Camelsdale Sur 27 F6
Camerory Highld 151 H13
Camer's Green Worcs 50 F2
Camerton Bath 23 D8
Camerton Cumb 107 F7
Camerton E Yorks 91 B6
Camghouran Perth 132 D2
Cammachmore Aberds 141 E8
Cammeringham Lincs 90 F3
Camore Highld 151 B10
Camp Hill Warks 63 E7
Campbeltown Argyll 143 F8
Camperdown T&W 111 B5
Campmuir Perth 134 F2
Campsall S Yorks 89 C6
Campsey Ash Suff 57 D7
Campton C Beds 54 F2
Camptown Borders 116 C2
Camrose Pembs 44 C4
Camserney Perth 133 E5
Camster Highld 158 F4
Camuschoirk Highld 130 C1
Camuscross Highld 149 G11
Camusnagaul Highld 130 B4
Camusnagaul Highld 150 C3
Camusrory Highld 147 B11
Camusteel Highld 149 D12
Camusterrach Highld 149 D12
Camusvrachan Perth 132 E3
Canada Hants 14 C3
Canadia E Sus 18 D4
Canal Side S Yorks 89 C7
Candacraig Ho. Aberds 140 C2
Candlesby Lincs 79 C7
Candy Mill S Lanark 120 E3
Cane End Oxon 26 B4
Canewdon Essex 42 E4
Canford Bottom Dorset 13 D8
Canford Cliffs Poole 13 F8
Canford Magna Poole 13 E8
Canham's Green Suff 56 C4
Canholes Derbys 75 B7
Canisbay Highld 158 C5
Cann Dorset 13 B6
Cann Common Dorset 13 B6
Cannard's Grave Som 23 E8
Cannich Highld 150 H6
Cannington Som 22 F4
Cannock Staffs 62 D3
Cannock Wood Staffs 62 C4
Canon Bridge Hereford 49 E6
Canon Frome Hereford 49 E8
Canon Pyon Hereford 49 E6
Canonbie Dumfries 108 B3
Canons Ashby Northants 52 D3
Canonstown Corn 2 C4
Canterbury Kent 30 D5
Cantley Norf 69 D6
Cantley S Yorks 89 D7
Cantlop Shrops 60 D5
Canton Cardiff 22 B3
Cantraybruich Highld 151 G10
Cantraydoune Highld 151 G10
Cantraywood Highld 151 G10
Cantsfield Lancs 93 B6
Canvey Island Essex 42 F3
Canwick Lincs 78 C2
Canworthy Water Corn 8 E4
Caol Highld 131 B5
Caol Ila Argyll 142 A5
Caolas Argyll 146 G3
Caolas Scalpaigh W Isles 154 H7
Caolas Stocinis W Isles 154 H6
Capel Sur 28 E2
Capel Bangor Ceredig 58 F3
Capel Betws Lleucu Ceredig 46 D5
Capel Carmel Gwyn 70 E2
Capel Coch Anglesey 82 C4
Capel Curig Conwy 83 F7
Capel Cynon Ceredig 46 E2
Capel Dewi Carms 33 B5
Capel Dewi Ceredig 46 E3
Capel Dewi Ceredig 58 F3
Capel Garmon Conwy 83 F8
Capel-gwyn Anglesey 82 D3
Capel Gwyn Carms 33 B5
Capel Gwynfe Carms 33 B8
Capel Hendre Carms 33 C6
Capel Hermon Gwyn 71 E8
Capel Isaac Carms 33 B6
Capel Iwan Carms 45 F4
Capel le Ferne Kent 31 F6
Capel Llanilltern Cardiff 34 F4
Capel Mawr Anglesey 82 D4
Capel St Andrew Suff 57 E7
Capel St Mary Suff 56 F4
Capel Seion Ceredig 46 B5
Capel Tygwydd Ceredig 45 E4
Capel Uchaf Gwyn 70 C5
Capel-y-graig Gwyn 82 E5
Capelulo Conwy 83 D7
Capenhurst Ches W 73 B7
Capernwray Lancs 92 B5
Capheaton Northumb 117 F6
Cappercleuch Borders 115 B5
Capplegill Dumfries 114 D4
Capton Devon 7 D6
Caputh Perth 133 F7
Car Colston Notts 77 E7
Carbis Bay Corn 2 C4
Carbost Highld 149 D9
Carbost Highld 149 E8
Carbrook S Yorks 88 F4
Carbrooke Norf 68 D2
Carburton Notts 77 B6
Carcant Borders 121 D6
Carcary Angus 135 D6
Carclaze Corn 4 D5
Carcroft S Yorks 89 C6
Cardenden Fife 128 E4
Cardeston Shrops 60 C3
Cardiff = Caerdydd Cardiff 22 B3
Cardigan = Aberteifi Ceredig 45 E3
Cardington Bedford 53 E8
Cardington Shrops 60 E5
Cardinham Corn 5 C6
Cardonald Glasgow 118 C5
Cardow Moray 152 D1
Cardrona Borders 121 F6
Cardross Argyll 118 B3
Cardurnock Cumb 107 D8
Careby Lincs 65 C7
Careston Castle Angus 135 D5
Carew Pembs 32 D1
Carew Cheriton Pembs 32 D1
Carew Newton Pembs 32 D1
Carey Hereford 49 F7
Carfrae E Loth 121 C8
Cargenbridge Dumfries 107 B6
Cargill Perth 134 F1
Cargo Cumb 108 D3
Cargreen Corn 6 C2
Carham Northumb 122 F4
Carhampton Som 22 E2
Carharrack Corn 3 B6
Carie Perth 132 D3
Carie Perth 132 F3
Carines Corn 4 D2
Carisbrooke IoW 15 F5
Cark Cumb 92 B3
Carlabhagh W Isles 154 C7
Carland Cross Corn 4 D3
Carlby Lincs 65 C7
Carlecotes S Yorks 88 D2
Carlesmoor N Yorks 94 B4
Carleton Cumb 99 B7
Carleton Cumb 108 D4
Carleton Lancs 92 F3
Carleton N Yorks 94 E2
Carleton Forehoe Norf 68 D3
Carleton Rode Norf 68 E4
Carlin How Redcar 103 C5
Carlingcott Bath 23 D8
Carlisle Cumb 108 D4
Carlops Borders 120 D4
Carlton Bedford 53 D7
Carlton Cambs 55 D7
Carlton Leics 63 D7
Carlton N Yorks 89 B7
Carlton N Yorks 101 C6
Carlton N Yorks 101 F5
Carlton N Yorks 102 F4
Carlton Notts 77 E6
Carlton S Yorks 88 C4
Carlton Stockton 102 B1
Carlton Suff 57 C7
Carlton W Yorks 88 B4
Carlton Colville Suff 69 F8
Carlton Curlieu Leics 64 E3
Carlton Husthwaite N Yorks 95 B7
Carlton in Cleveland N Yorks 102 D3
Carlton in Lindrick Notts 89 F6
Carlton le Moorland Lincs 78 D2
Carlton Miniott N Yorks 102 F1
Carlton on Trent Notts 77 C7
Carlton Scroop Lincs 78 E2
Carluke S Lanark 119 D8
Carmarthen = Caerfyrddin Carms 33 B5
Carmel Anglesey 82 C3
Carmel Carms 33 C6
Carmel Flint 73 B5
Carmel Guern 16
Carmel Gwyn 82 F4
Carmont Aberds 141 F7
Carmunnock Glasgow 119 D6
Carmyle Glasgow 119 C6
Carmyllie Angus 135 E5
Carn-gorm Highld 136 B2
Carnaby E Yorks 97 C7
Carnach Highld 136 B3
Carnach Highld 150 B3
Carnach W Isles 154 H7
Carnachy Highld 157 D10
Càrnais W Isles 154 D5
Carnbee Fife 129 D7
Carnbo Perth 128 D2
Carnbrea Corn 3 B5
Carnduff S Lanark 119 E6
Carnduncan Argyll 142 B3
Carne Corn 3 C8
Carnforth Lancs 92 B4
Carnhedryn Pembs 44 C3
Carnhell Green Corn 2 C5
Carnkie Corn 3 C5
Carnkie Corn 3 C6
Carno Powys 59 E6
Carnoch Highld 150 F5
Carnoch Highld 150 H6
Carnock Fife 128 F2
Carnon Downs Corn 3 B6
Carnousie Aberds 153 C6
Carnoustie Angus 135 F5
Carnwath S Lanark 120 E2
Carnyorth Corn 2 C2
Carperby N Yorks 101 F5
Carpley Green N Yorks 100 F4
Carr S Yorks 89 E6
Carr Hill T&W 111 C5
Carradale Argyll 143 E9
Carragraich W Isles 154 H6
Carrbridge Highld 138 B5
Carrefour Selous Jersey 17
Carreg-wen Pembs 45 E4
Carreglefn Anglesey 82 C3
Carrick Argyll 145 E8
Carrick Fife 129 B6
Carrick Castle Argyll 145 D10
Carrick Ho. Orkney 159 E6
Carriden Falk 128 F2
Carrington Gtr Man 86 E5
Carrington Lincs 79 D6
Carrington Midloth 121 C6
Carrog Conwy 71 C8
Carrog Denb 72 E5
Carron Falk 127 F7
Carron Moray 152 D2
Carron Bridge Stirling 127 F6
Carronbridge Dumfries 113 E8
Carronshore Falk 127 F7
Carrshield Northumb 109 E8
Carrutherstown Dumfries 107 B8
Carrville Durham 111 E6
Carsaig Argyll 144 E6
Carsaig Argyll 147 J8
Carscreugh Dumfries 105 D6
Carse Gray Angus 134 D4
Carse Ho. Argyll 144 G6
Carsegowan Dumfries 105 D8
Carseriggan Dumfries 105 C7
Carsethorn Dumfries 107 D6
Carshalton London 28 C3
Carsington Derbys 76 D2
Carskiey Argyll 143 H7
Carsluith Dumfries 105 D8
Carsphairn Dumfries 113 E5
Carstairs S Lanark 120 E2
Carstairs Junction S Lanark 120 E2
Carswell Marsh Oxon 38 E3
Carter's Clay Hants 14 B4
Carterton Oxon 38 D2
Carterway Heads Northumb 110 D3
Carthew Corn 4 D5
Carthorpe N Yorks 101 F8
Cartington Northumb 117 D6
Cartland S Lanark 119 E8
Cartmel Cumb 92 B3
Cartmel Fell Cumb 99 F6
Carway Carms 33 D5
Cary Fitzpaine Som 12 B3
Cas-gwent = Chepstow Mon 36 E2
Cascob Powys 48 C4
Cashlie Perth 132 E1
Cashmoor Dorset 13 C7
Casnewydd = Newport Newport 35 F7
Cassey Compton Glos 37 C7
Cassington Oxon 38 C4
Cassop Durham 111 F6
Castell Denb 72 C5
Castell-Howell Ceredig 46 E3
Castell-Nedd = Neath Neath 33 E8
Castell Newydd Emlyn = Newcastle Emlyn Carms 46 E2
Castell-y-bwch Torf 35 E6
Castellau Rhondda 34 F4
Casterton Cumb 93 B6
Castle Acre Norf 67 C8
Castle Ashby Northants 53 D6
Castle Bolton N Yorks 101 E5
Castle Bromwich W Mid 62 F5
Castle Bytham Lincs 65 C6
Castle Caereinion Powys 59 D8
Castle Camps Cambs 55 E7
Castle Carrock Cumb 108 D5
Castle Cary Som 23 F8
Castle Combe Wilts 24 B3
Castle Donington Leics 63 B8
Castle Douglas Dumfries 106 C4
Castle Eaton Swindon 37 E8
Castle Eden Durham 111 F7
Castle Forbes Aberds 140 C5
Castle Frome Hereford 49 E8
Castle Green Sur 27 C7
Castle Gresley Derbys 63 C6
Castle Heaton Northumb 122 E5
Castle Hedingham Essex 55 F8
Castle Hill Kent 29 E7
Castle Huntly Perth 128 B5
Castle Kennedy Dumfries 104 D5
Castle O'er Dumfries 115 E5
Castle Pulverbatch Shrops 60 D4
Castle Rising Norf 67 B6
Castle Stuart Highld 151 G10
Castlebay = Bagh a Chaisteil W Isles 148 J1
Castlebythe Pembs 32 B1
Castlecary N Lanark 119 B7
Castlecraig Highld 151 E11
Castlefairn Dumfries 113 F7
Castleford W Yorks 88 B5
Castlehill Borders 120 F5
Castlehill Highld 158 D3
Castlehill W Dunb 118 B3
Castlemaddy Dumfries 113 F5
Castlemartin Pembs 44 F4
Castlemilk Dumfries 107 B8
Castlemilk Glasgow 119 D6
Castlemorris Pembs 44 B4
Castlemorton Worcs 50 F2
Castleside Durham 110 E3
Castlethorpe M Keynes 53 E6
Castleton Angus 134 E3
Castleton Argyll 145 E7
Castleton Derbys 88 F2
Castleton Gtr Man 87 C6
Castleton N Yorks 102 D4
Castleton Newport 35 F6
Castletown Ches W 73 D8
Castletown Highld 151 G10
Castletown Highld 158 D3
Castletown IoM 84 F2
Castletown T&W 111 D6
Castleweary Borders 115 D7
Castley N Yorks 95 E5
Caston Norf 68 E2
Castor Pboro 65 E8
Catacol N Ayrs 143 D10
Catbrain S Glos 36 F2
Catbrook Mon 36 D2
Catchall Corn 2 D3
Catchems Corner W Mid 51 B7
Catchgate Durham 110 D4
Catcleugh Northumb 116 D3
Catcliffe S Yorks 88 F5
Catcott Som 23 F5
Caterham Sur 28 D4
Catfield Norf 69 B6
Catfirth Shetland 160 H6
Catford London 28 B4
Catforth Lancs 92 F4
Cathays Cardiff 22 B3
Cathcart Glasgow 119 C5
Cathedine Powys 35 B5
Catherington Hants 15 C7
Catherton Shrops 49 B8
Catlodge Highld 138 E2
Catlowdy Cumb 108 B4
Catmore W Berks 38 F4
Caton Lancs 92 C5
Caton Green Lancs 92 C5
Catrine E Ayrs 113 B5
Cat's Ash Newport 35 E7
Catsfield E Sus 18 D4
Catshill Worcs 50 B4
Cattal N Yorks 95 D7
Cattawade Suff 56 F5
Catterall Lancs 92 E4
Catterick N Yorks 101 E7
Catterick Bridge N Yorks 101 E7
Catterick Garrison N Yorks 101 E6
Catterlen Cumb 108 F4
Catterline Aberds 135 B8
Catterton N Yorks 95 E8
Catthorpe Leics 52 B3
Cattistock Dorset 12 E3
Catton N Yorks 95 B6
Catton Northumb 109 D8
Catwick E Yorks 97 E7
Catworth Cambs 53 B8
Caudlesprings Norf 68 D2
Caulcott Oxon 39 B5
Cauldcots Angus 135 E6
Cauldhame Stirling 126 E5
Cauldmill Borders 115 C8
Cauldon Staffs 75 E7
Caulkerbush Dumfries 107 D6
Caulside Dumfries 115 F7
Caunsall Worcs 62 F2
Caunton Notts 77 D7
Causeway End Dumfries 105 C8
Causeway Foot W Yorks 94 F3
Causeway-head Stirling 127 E6
Causewayend S Lanark 120 F3
Causewayhead Cumb 107 D8
Causey Park Bridge Northumb 117 E7
Causeyend Aberds 141 C8
Cautley Cumb 100 E1
Cavendish Suff 56 E2
Cavendish Bridge Leics 63 B8
Cavenham Suff 55 C8
Caversfield Oxon 39 B5
Caversham Reading 26 B5
Caverswall Staffs 75 E6
Cavil E Yorks 96 F3
Cawdor Highld 151 F11
Cawkwell Lincs 79 B5
Cawood N Yorks 95 F8
Cawsand Corn 6 D2
Cawston Norf 81 E7
Cawthorne S Yorks 88 D3
Cawthorpe Lincs 65 B7
Cawton N Yorks 96 B2
Caxton Cambs 54 D4
Caynham Shrops 49 B7
Caythorpe Lincs 78 E2
Caythorpe Notts 77 E6
Cayton N Yorks 103 F8
Ceann a Bhaigh W Isles 148 B2
Ceann a Deas Loch Baghasdail W Isles 148 G2
Ceann Shiphoirt W Isles 155 F7
Ceann Tarabhaigh W Isles 154 F7
Ceannacroc Lodge Highld 136 C5
Cearsiadair W Isles 155 E8
Cefn Berain Conwy 72 C3
Cefn-brith Conwy 72 D3
Cefn Canol Powys 73 F6
Cefn-coch Conwy 83 E8
Cefn Coch Powys 59 B8
Cefn-coed-y-cymmer M Tydf 34 D4
Cefn Cribbwr Bridgend 34 F2
Cefn Cross Bridgend 34 F2
Cefn-ddwysarn Gwyn 72 F3
Cefn Einion Shrops 60 F2
Cefn-gorwydd Powys 47 E8
Cefn-mawr Wrex 73 E6
Cefn-y-bedd Flint 73 D7
Cefn-y-pant Carms 32 B2
Cefneithin Carms 33 C6
Cei-bach Ceredig 46 D3
Ceinewydd = New Quay Ceredig 46 D2
Ceint Anglesey 82 D4
Cellan Ceredig 46 E5
Cellarhead Staffs 75 E6
Cemaes Anglesey 82 B3
Cemmaes Powys 58 D5
Cemmaes Road Powys 58 D5
Cenarth Carms 45 E4
Cenin Gwyn 71 C5
Central Invclyd 118 B2
Ceos W Isles 155 E8
Ceres Fife 129 C6
Cerne Abbas Dorset 12 D4
Cerney Wick Glos 37 E7
Cerrigceinwen Anglesey 82 D4
Cerrigydrudion Conwy 72 E3
Cessford Borders 116 B3
Ceunant Gwyn 82 E5
Chaceley Glos 50 F3
Chacewater Corn 3 B6
Chackmore Bucks 52 F4
Chacombe Northants 52 E2
Chad Valley W Mid 62 F4
Chadderton Gtr Man 87 D7
Chadderton Fold Gtr Man 87 D6
Chaddesden Derby 76 F3
Chaddesley Corbett Worcs 50 B3
Chaddleworth W Berks 26 B2
Chadlington Oxon 38 B3
Chadshunt Warks 51 D8
Chadwell Leics 64 B4
Chadwell St Mary Thurrock 29 B7
Chadwick End W Mid 51 B7
Chadwick Green Mers 86 E3
Chaffcombe Som 11 C8
Chagford Devon 10 F2
Chailey E Sus 17 C7
Chain Bridge Lincs 79 E6
Chainbridge Cambs 66 D4
Chainhurst Kent 29 E8
Chalbury Dorset 13 D8
Chalbury Common Dorset 13 D8
Chaldon Sur 28 D4
Chaldon Herring Dorset 13 F5
Chale IoW 15 G5
Chale Green IoW 15 G5
Chalfont Common Bucks 40 E3
Chalfont St Giles Bucks 40 E2
Chalfont St Peter Bucks 40 E3
Chalford Glos 37 D5
Chalgrove Oxon 39 E6
Chalk Kent 29 B7
Challacombe Devon 21 E5
Challoch Dumfries 105 C7
Challock Kent 30 D4
Chalton C Beds 40 B3
Chalton Hants 15 C8
Chalvington E Sus 18 E2
Chancery Ceredig 46 B4
Chandler's Ford Hants 14 B5
Channel Tunnel Kent 19 B8
Channerwick Shetland 160 L6
Chantry Som 24 E2
Chantry Suff 56 E5
Chapel Fife 128 E4
Chapel Allerton Som 23 D6
Chapel Allerton W Yorks 95 F6
Chapel Amble Corn 4 B4
Chapel Brampton Northants 52 C5
Chapel Chorlton Staffs 74 F5
Chapel-en-le-Frith Derbys 87 F8
Chapel End Warks 63 E7
Chapel Green Warks 52 C2
Chapel Green Warks 63 F6
Chapel Haddlesey N Yorks 89 B6
Chapel Head Cambs 66 F3
Chapel Hill Aberds 153 E10
Chapel Hill Lincs 78 D5
Chapel Hill Mon 36 E2
Chapel Hill N Yorks 95 E6
Chapel Lawn Shrops 48 B5
Chapel-le-Dale N Yorks 93 B7
Chapel Milton Derbys 87 F8
Chapel of Garioch Aberds 141 B6
Chapel Row W Berks 26 C3
Chapel St Leonards Lincs 79 B8
Chapel Stile Cumb 99 D5
Chapelgate Lincs 66 B4
Chapelhall N Lanark 119 C7
Chapelhill Dumfries 114 E3
Chapelhill Highld 151 D11
Chapelhill N Ayrs 118 E2
Chapelhill Perth 128 B4
Chapelhill Perth 133 F7
Chapelknowe Dumfries 108 B3
Chapelton Angus 135 E6
Chapelton Devon 9 B7
Chapelton Highld 138 C5
Chapelton S Lanark 119 E6
Chapeltown Blackburn 86 C5
Chapeltown Moray 139 B8
Chapeltown S Yorks 88 E4
Chapmans Well Devon 9 E5
Chapmanslade Wilts 24 E3
Chapmore End Herts 41 C6
Chappel Essex 42 B4
Chard Som 11 D8
Chardstock Devon 11 D8
Charfield S Glos 36 E4
Charford Worcs 50 C4
Charing Kent 30 E3
Charing Cross Dorset 14 C2
Charing Heath Kent 30 E3
Charingworth Glos 51 F7
Charlbury Oxon 38 C3
Charlcombe Bath 24 C2
Charlecote Warks 51 D7
Charles Devon 21 F5
Charles Tye Suff 56 D4
Charlesfield Dumfries 107 C8
Charleston Angus 134 E3
Charleston Renfs 118 C4
Charlestown Aberdeen 141 D8
Charlestown Corn 4 D5
Charlestown Derbys 87 E8
Charlestown Dorset 12 G4
Charlestown Fife 128 F2
Charlestown Gtr Man 87 D6
Charlestown Highld 149 A13
Charlestown Highld 151 G9
Charlestown W Yorks 87 B7
Charlestown of Aberlour Moray 152 D2
Charlesworth Derbys 87 E8
Charleton Devon 7 E5
Charlton Hants 25 E8
Charlton Herts 40 B4
Charlton London 28 B5
Charlton Northants 52 F3
Charlton Northumb 116 F4
Charlton Som 23 D8
Charlton Telford 61 C5
Charlton W Sus 16 C2
Charlton Wilts 13 B7
Charlton Wilts 25 D6
Charlton Wilts 37 F6
Charlton Worcs 50 E5
Charlton Abbots Glos 37 B7
Charlton Adam Som 12 B3
Charlton-All-Saints Wilts 14 B2
Charlton Down Dorset 12 E4
Charlton Horethorne Som 12 B4
Charlton Kings Glos 37 B6
Charlton Mackerell Som 12 B3
Charlton Marshall Dorset 13 D6
Charlton Musgrove Som 12 B5
Charlton on Otmoor Oxon 39 C5
Charltons Redcar 102 C4
Charlwood Sur 28 E3
Charlynch Som 22 F4
Charminster Dorset 12 E4
Charmouth Dorset 11 E8
Charndon Bucks 39 B6
Charney Bassett Oxon 38 E3
Charnock Richard Lancs 86 C3
Charsfield Suff 57 D6
Chart Corner Kent 29 D8
Chart Sutton Kent 30 E2
Charter Alley Hants 26 D3
Charterhouse Som 23 D6
Charterville Allotments Oxon 38 C3
Chartham Kent 30 D5
Chartham Hatch Kent 30 D5
Chartridge Bucks 40 D2
Charvil Wokingham 27 B5
Charwelton Northants 52 D3
Chasetown Staffs 62 D4
Chastleton Oxon 38 B2
Chasty Devon 8 D5
Chatburn Lancs 93 E7
Chatcull Staffs 74 F4
Chatham Medway 29 C8
Chathill Northumb 117 B7
Chattenden Medway 29 B8
Chatteris Cambs 66 F3
Chattisham Suff 56 E4
Chatto Borders 116 C3
Chatton Northumb 117 B6
Chawleigh Devon 10 C2
Chawley Oxon 38 D4
Chawston Bedford 54 D2
Chawton Hants 26 F5
Cheadle Gtr Man 87 F6
Cheadle Staffs 75 E7
Cheadle Heath Gtr Man 87 F6
Cheadle Hulme Gtr Man 87 F6
Cheam London 28 C3
Cheapside Sur 27 D8
Chearsley Bucks 39 C7
Chebsey Staffs 62 B2
Checkendon Oxon 39 F6
Checkley Ches E 74 E4
Checkley Hereford 49 F7
Checkley Staffs 75 F7
Chedburgh Suff 55 D8
Cheddar Som 23 D6
Cheddington Bucks 40 C2
Cheddleton Staffs 75 D6
Cheddon Fitzpaine Som 11 B7
Chedglow Wilts 37 E6
Chedgrave Norf 69 E6
Chedington Dorset 12 D2
Chediston Suff 57 B7
Chedworth Glos 37 C7
Chedzoy Som 22 F5
Cheeklaw Borders 122 D3
Cheeseman's Green Kent 19 B7
Cheglinch Devon 20 E4
Cheldon Devon 10 C2
Chelford Ches E 74 B5
Chell Heath Stoke 75 D5
Chellaston Derby 76 F3
Chellington Bedford 53 D7
Chelmarsh Shrops 61 F7
Chelmer Village Essex 42 D3
Chelmondiston Suff 57 F6
Chelmorton Derbys 75 C8
Chelmsford Essex 42 D3
Chelsea London 28 B3
Chelsfield London 29 C5
Chelsworth Suff 56 E3
Cheltenham Glos 37 B6
Chelveston Northants 53 C7
Chelvey N Som 23 C6
Chelwood Bath 23 C8
Chelwood Common E Sus 17 B8
Chelwood Gate E Sus 17 B8
Chelworth Wilts 37 E6
Chelworth Green Wilts 37 E7
Chemistry Shrops 74 E2
Chenies Bucks 40 E3
Cheny Longville Shrops 60 F4
Chepstow = Cas-gwent Mon 36 E2
Chequerfield W Yorks 89 B5
Cherhill Wilts 24 B5
Cherington Glos 37 E6
Cherington Warks 51 F7
Cheriton Devon 21 E6
Cheriton Hants 15 B6
Cheriton Kent 19 B8
Cheriton Swansea 33 E5
Cheriton Bishop Devon 10 E2
Cheriton Fitzpaine Devon 10 D3
Cheriton or Stackpole Elidor Pembs 44 F4
Cherrington Telford 61 B6
Cherry Burton E Yorks 97 E5
Cherry Hinton Cambs 55 D5
Cherry Orchard Worcs 50 D3
Cherry Willingham Lincs 78 B3
Cherrybank Perth 128 B3
Chertsey Sur 27 C8
Cheselbourne Dorset 13 E5
Chesham Bucks 40 D2
Chesham Bois Bucks 40 E2
Cheshunt Herts 41 D6
Cheslyn Hay Staffs 62 D3
Chessington London 28 C2
Chester Ches W 73 C8
Chester-Le-Street Durham 111 D5
Chester Moor Durham 111 E5
Chesterblade Som 23 E8
Chesterfield Derbys 76 B3
Chesters Borders 116 B2
Chesters Borders 116 C2
Chesterton Cambs 55 C5
Chesterton Cambs 65 E8
Chesterton Glos 37 D7
Chesterton Oxon 39 B5
Chesterton Shrops 61 E7
Chesterton Staffs 74 E5
Chesterton Warks 51 D8
Chesterwood Northumb 109 C8
Chestfield Kent 30 C5
Cheston Devon 6 D4
Cheswardine Shrops 61 B7
Cheswick Northumb 123 E6
Chetnole Dorset 12 D4
Chettiscombe Devon 10 C4
Chettisham Cambs 66 F5
Chettle Dorset 13 C7
Chetton Shrops 61 E6
Chetwode Bucks 39 B6
Chetwynd Aston Telford 61 C7
Cheveley Cambs 55 C7
Chevening Kent 29 D5
Chevington Suff 55 D8
Chevithorne Devon 10 C4
Chew Magna Bath 23 C7
Chew Stoke Bath 23 C7
Chewton Keynsham Bath 23 C8
Chewton Mendip Som 23 D7
Chicheley M Keynes 53 E7
Chichester W Sus 16 D2
Chickerell Dorset 12 F4
Chicklade Wilts 24 F4
Chicksgrove Wilts 24 F4
Chidden Hants 15 C7
Chiddingfold Sur 27 F7
Chiddingly E Sus 18 D2
Chiddingstone Kent 29 E5
Chiddingstone Causeway Kent 29 E6
Chiddingstone Hoath Kent 29 E5
Chideock Dorset 12 E2
Chidham W Sus 15 D8
Chidswell W Yorks 88 B3
Chieveley W Berks 26 B2
Chignall St James Essex 42 D2
Chignall Smealy Essex 42 C2
Chigwell Essex 41 E7
Chigwell Row Essex 41 E7
Chilbolton Hants 25 F8
Chilcomb Hants 15 B6
Chilcombe Dorset 12 E3
Chilcompton Som 23 D8
Chilcote Leics 63 C6
Child Okeford Dorset 13 C6
Childer Thornton Ches W 73 B7
Childrey Oxon 38 F3
Child's Ercall Shrops 61 B6
Childswickham Worcs 51 F5
Childwall Mers 86 F2
Childwick Green Herts 40 C4
Chilfrome Dorset 12 E3
Chilgrove W Sus 16 C2
Chilham Kent 30 D4
Chilhampton Wilts 25 F5
Chilla Devon 9 D6
Chillaton Devon 9 F6
Chillenden Kent 31 D6
Chillerton IoW 15 F5
Chillesford Suff 57 D7
Chillingham Northumb 117 B6
Chillington Devon 7 E5
Chillington Som 11 C8
Chilmark Wilts 24 F4
Chilson Oxon 38 C3
Chilsworthy Corn 6 B2
Chilsworthy Devon 8 D5
Chilthorne Domer Som 12 C3
Chiltington E Sus 17 C7
Chilton Bucks 39 C6
Chilton Durham 101 B7
Chilton Oxon 38 F4
Chilton Cantelo Som 12 B3
Chilton Foliat Wilts 25 B8
Chilton Lane Durham 111 F6
Chilton Polden Som 23 F5
Chilton Street Suff 55 E8
Chilton Trinity Som 22 F4
Chilvers Coton Warks 63 E7
Chilwell Notts 76 F5
Chilworth Hants 14 C5
Chilworth Sur 27 E8
Chimney Oxon 38 D3
Chineham Hants 26 D4
Chingford London 41 E6
Chinley Derbys 87 F8
Chinley Head Derbys 87 F8
Chinnor Oxon 39 D7
Chipnall Shrops 74 F4
Chippenhall Green Suff 57 B6
Chippenham Cambs 55 C7
Chippenham Wilts 24 B4
Chipperfield Herts 40 D3
Chipping Herts 54 F4
Chipping Lancs 93 E6
Chipping Campden Glos 51 F6
Chipping Hill Essex 42 C4
Chipping Norton Oxon 38 B3
Chipping Ongar Essex 42 D1
Chipping Sodbury S Glos 36 F4
Chipping Warden Northants 52 E2
Chipstable Som 10 B5
Chipstead Kent 29 D5
Chipstead Sur 28 D3
Chirbury Shrops 60 E2
Chirk = Y Waun Wrex 73 F6
Chirk Bank Shrops 73 F6
Chirmorrie S Ayrs 105 B6
Chirnside Borders 122 D4
Chirnsidebridge Borders 122 D4
Chirton Wilts 25 D5
Chisbury Wilts 25 C7
Chiselborough Som 12 C2
Chiseldon Swindon 25 B6
Chiserley W Yorks 87 B8
Chislehampton Oxon 39 E5
Chislehurst London 28 B5
Chislet Kent 31 C6
Chiswell Green Herts 40 D4
Chiswick London 28 B3
Chiswick End Cambs 54 E4
Chisworth Derbys 87 E7
Chithurst W Sus 16 B2
Chittering Cambs 55 B5
Chitterne Wilts 24 E4
Chittlehamholt Devon 9 B8
Chittlehampton Devon 9 B8
Chittoe Wilts 24 C4
Chivenor Devon 20 F4
Chobham Sur 27 C7
Choicelee Borders 122 D3
Cholderton Wilts 25 E7
Cholesbury Bucks 40 D2
Chollerford Northumb 110 B2
Chollerton Northumb 110 B2
Cholmondeston Ches E 74 C3
Cholsey Oxon 39 F5
Cholstrey Hereford 49 D6
Chop Gate N Yorks 102 E3
Choppington Northumb 117 F8
Chopwell T&W 110 D4
Chorley Ches E 74 D2
Chorley Lancs 86 C3
Chorley Shrops 61 F6
Chorley Staffs 62 C4
Chorleywood Herts 40 E3
Chorlton cum Hardy Gtr Man 87 E6
Chorlton Lane Ches W 73 E8
Choulton Shrops 60 F3
Chowdene T&W 111 D5
Chowley Ches W 73 D8
Chrishall Essex 54 F5
Christchurch Cambs 66 E4
Christchurch Dorset 14 E2
Christchurch Glos 36 C2
Christchurch Newport 35 F7
Christian Malford Wilts 24 B4
Christleton Ches W 73 C8
Christmas Common Oxon 39 E7
Christon N Som 23 D5
Christon Bank Northumb 117 B8
Christow Devon 10 F3
Chryston N Lanark 119 B6
Chudleigh Devon 7 B6
Chudleigh Knighton Devon 7 B6
Chulmleigh Devon 9 C8
Chunal Derbys 87 E8
Church Lancs 86 B5
Church Aston Telford 61 C7
Church Brampton Northants 52 C5
Church Broughton Derbys 76 F2
Church Crookham Hants 27 D6
Church Eaton Staffs 62 C2
Church End C Beds 40 B2
Church End C Beds 53 F7
Church End C Beds 54 F2
Church End Cambs 66 D3
Church End Cambs 66 F2
Church End E Yorks 97 D6
Church End Essex 42 B3
Church End Essex 55 D6
Church End Hants 26 D4
Church End Lincs 78 F5
Church End Warks 63 E6
Church End Warks 63 E6
Church End Wilts 24 B5
Church Enstone Oxon 38 B3
Church Fenton N Yorks 95 F8
Church Green Devon 11 E6
Church Green Norf 68 E3
Church Gresley Derbys 63 C6
Church Hanborough Oxon 38 C4
Church Hill Ches W 74 C3
Church Houses N Yorks 102 E4
Church Knowle Dorset 13 F7
Church Laneham Notts 77 B8
Church Langton Leics 64 E4
Church Lawford Warks 52 B2
Church Lawton Ches E 74 D5
Church Leigh Staffs 75 F7
Church Lench Worcs 50 D5
Church Mayfield Staffs 75 E8
Church Minshull Ches E 74 C3
Church Norton W Sus 16 E2
Church Preen Shrops 60 E5
Church Pulverbatch Shrops 60 D4
Church Stoke Powys 60 E2
Church Stowe Northants 52 D4
Church Street Kent 29 B8
Church Stretton Shrops 60 E4
Church Town N Lincs 89 D8
Church Town Sur 28 D4
Church Village Rhondda 34 F4
Church Warsop Notts 77 C5
Churcham Glos 36 C4
Churchbank Shrops 48 B4
Churchbridge Staffs 62 D3
Churchdown Glos 37 C5
Churchend Essex 42 B2
Churchend Essex 43 E6
Churchend S Glos 36 E4
Churchfield W Mid 62 E4
Churchgate Street Essex 41 C7
Churchill Devon 11 D8
Churchill Devon 20 E4
Churchill N Som 23 D6
Churchill Oxon 38 B2
Churchill Worcs 50 B3
Churchill Worcs 50 D4
Churchinford Som 11 C7
Churchover Warks 64 F2
Churchstanton Som 11 C6
Churchstow Devon 6 E5
Churchtown Derbys 76 C2
Churchtown IoM 84 C4
Churchtown Lancs 92 E4

Churchtown Mers 85 C4
Churnsike Lodge Northumb 109 B6
Churston Ferrers Torbay 7 D7
Churt Sur 27 F6
Churton Ches W 73 D8
Churwell W Yorks 88 B3
Chute Standen Wilts 25 D8
Chwilog Gwyn 70 D5
Chyandour Corn 2 C3
Cilan Uchaf Gwyn 70 E3
Cilcain Flint 73 C5
Cilcennin Ceredig 46 C4
Cilfor Gwyn 71 D7
Cilfrew Neath 34 D1
Cilfynydd Rhondda 34 E4
Cilgerran Pembs 45 E3
Cilgwyn Carms 33 B8
Cilgwyn Gwyn 82 F4
Cilgwyn Pembs 45 F2
Ciliau Aeron Ceredig 46 D3
Cill Donnain W Isles 148 F2
Cille Bhrighde W Isles 148 G2
Cille Pheadair W Isles 148 G2
Cilmery Powys 48 D2
Cilsan Carms 33 B6
Ciltalgarth Gwyn 72 E2
Cilwendeg Pembs 45 F4
Cilybebyll Neath 33 D8
Cilycwm Carms 47 F6
Cimla Neath 34 E1
Cinderford Glos 36 C3
Cippyn Pembs 45 E3
Circebost W Isles 154 D6
Cirencester Glos 37 D7
Ciribhig W Isles 154 C6
City London 41 F6
City Powys 60 F2
City Dulas Anglesey 82 C4
Clachaig Argyll 145 E10
Clachan Argyll 124 D3
Clachan Argyll 125 D7
Clachan Argyll 130 E2
Clachan Argyll 144 H6
Clachan Highld 149 E10
Clachan W Isles 148 D2
Clachan na Luib W Isles 148 B3
Clachan of Campsie E Dunb 119 B6
Clachan of Glendaruel Argyll 145 E8
Clachan-Seil Argyll 124 D3
Clachan Strachur Argyll 125 E6
Clachaneasy Dumfries 105 B7
Clachanmore Dumfries 104 E4
Clachbreck Argyll 144 F6
Clachnabrain Angus 134 C3
Clachtoll Highld 156 G3
Clackmannan Clack 127 E8
Clacton-on-Sea Essex 43 C7
Cladach Chireboist W Isles 148 B2
Claddach-knockline W Isles 148 B2
Cladich Argyll 125 C6
Claggan Highld 131 B5
Claggan Highld 147 G9
Claigan Highld 148 C7
Claines Worcs 50 D3
Clandown Bath 23 D8
Clanfield Hants 15 C7
Clanfield Oxon 38 D2
Clanville Hants 25 E8
Claonaig Argyll 145 H7
Claonel Highld 157 J8
Clap Hill Kent 19 B7
Clapgate Dorset 13 D8
Clapgate Herts 41 B7
Clapham Bedford 53 D8
Clapham London 28 B3
Clapham N Yorks 93 C7
Clapham W Sus 16 D4
Clappers Borders 122 D5
Clappersgate Cumb 99 D5
Clapton Som 12 D2
Clapton-in-Gordano N Som 23 B6
Clapton-on-the-Hill Glos 38 C1
Clapworthy Devon 9 B8
Clara Vale T&W 110 C4
Clarach Ceredig 58 F3
Clarbeston Pembs 32 B1
Clarbeston Road Pembs 32 B1
Clarborough Notts 89 F8
Clardon Highld 158 D3
Clare Suff 55 E8
Clarebrand Dumfries 106 C4
Clarencefield Dumfries 107 C7
Clarilaw Borders 115 C8
Clark's Green Sur 28 F2
Clarkston E Renf 119 D5
Clashandorran Highld 151 G8
Clashcoig Highld 151 B9
Clashindarroch Aberds 152 E4
Clashmore Highld 151 C10
Clashmore Highld 156 F3
Clashnessie Highld 156 F3
Clashnoir Moray 139 B8
Clate Shetland 160 G7
Clathy Perth 127 C8
Clatt Aberds 140 B4
Clatter Powys 59 E6
Clatterford IoW 15 F5
Clatterin Bridge Aberds 135 B6
Clatworthy Som 22 F2
Claughton Lancs 92 E5
Claughton Lancs 93 C5
Claughton Mers 85 F4
Claverdon Warks 51 C6
Claverham N Som 23 C6
Clavering Essex 55 F5
Claverley Shrops 61 E7
Claverton Bath 24 C2
Clawdd-newydd Denb 72 D4
Clawthorpe Cumb 92 B5
Clawton Devon 9 E5
Claxby Lincs 79 B7
Claxby Lincs 90 E5
Claxton N Yorks 96 C2
Claxton Norf 69 D6
Clay Common Suff 69 F7
Clay Coton Northants 52 B3
Clay Cross Derbys 76 C3
Clay Hill W Berks 26 B3
Clay Lake Lincs 66 B2
Claybokie Aberds 139 E6
Claybrooke Magna Leics 63 F8
Claybrooke Parva Leics 63 F8
Claydon Oxon 52 D2
Claydon Suff 56 D5
Claygate Dumfries 108 B3
Claygate Kent 29 E8
Claygate Sur 28 C2
Claygate Cross Kent 29 D7
Clayhanger Devon 10 B5
Clayhanger W Mid 62 D4
Clayhidon Devon 11 C6
Clayhill E Sus 18 C5
Clayhill Hants 14 D4
Clayock Highld 158 E3
Claypole Lincs 77 E8
Clayton S Yorks 89 D5
Clayton Staffs 75 E5
Clayton W Sus 17 C6
Clayton W Yorks 94 F4
Clayton Green Lancs 86 B3
Clayton-le-Moors Lancs 93 F7
Clayton-le-Woods Lancs 86 B3
Clayton West W Yorks 88 C3
Clayworth Notts 89 F8
Cleadale Highld 146 C7
Cleadon T&W 111 C6
Clearbrook Devon 6 C3
Clearwell Glos 36 D2
Cleasby N Yorks 101 C7
Cleat Orkney 159 K5
Cleatlam Durham 101 C6
Cleator Cumb 98 C2
Cleator Moor Cumb 98 C2
Clebrig Highld 157 F8
Cleckheaton W Yorks 88 B2
Clee St Margaret Shrops 61 F5
Cleedownton Shrops 61 F5
Cleehill Shrops 49 B7
Cleethorpes NE Lincs 91 D7
Cleeton St Mary Shrops 49 B8
Cleeve N Som 23 C6
Cleeve Hill Glos 37 B6
Cleeve Prior Worcs 51 E5
Clegyrnant Powys 59 D6
Clehonger Hereford 49 F6
Cleish Perth 128 E2
Cleland N Lanark 119 D8
Clench Common Wilts 25 C6
Clenchwarton Norf 67 B5
Clent Worcs 50 B4
Cleobury Mortimer Shrops 49 B8
Cleobury North Shrops 61 F6
Cleongart Argyll 143 E7
Clephanton Highld 151 F11
Clerklands Borders 115 B8
Clestrain Orkney 159 H4
Cleuch Head Borders 115 C8
Cleughbrae Dumfries 107 B7
Clevancy Wilts 25 B5
Clevedon N Som 23 B6
Cleveley Oxon 38 B3
Cleveleys Lancs 92 E3
Cleverton Wilts 37 F6
Clevis Bridgend 21 B7
Clewer Som 23 D6
Cley next the Sea Norf 81 C6
Cliaid W Isles 148 H1
Cliasmol W Isles 154 G5
Cliburn Cumb 99 B7
Click Mill Orkney 159 F4
Cliddesden Hants 26 E4
Cliff End E Sus 19 D5
Cliffburn Angus 135 E6
Cliffe Medway 29 B8
Cliffe N Yorks 96 F2
Cliffe Woods Medway 29 B8
Clifford Hereford 48 E4
Clifford W Yorks 95 E7
Clifford Chambers Warks 51 D6
Clifford's Mesne Glos 36 B4
Cliffsend Kent 31 C7
Clifton Bristol 23 B7
Clifton C Beds 54 F2
Clifton Cumb 99 B7
Clifton Derbys 75 E8
Clifton Lancs 92 F4
Clifton N Yorks 94 E4
Clifton Northumb 117 F8
Clifton Nottingham 77 F5
Clifton Oxon 52 F2
Clifton S Yorks 89 E6
Clifton Stirling 131 F7
Clifton Worcs 50 E3
Clifton York 95 D8
Clifton Campville Staffs 63 C6
Clifton Green Gtr Man 87 D5
Clifton Hampden Oxon 39 E5
Clifton Reynes M Keynes 53 D7
Clifton upon Dunsmore Warks 52 B3
Clifton upon Teme Worcs 50 C2
Cliftoncote Borders 116 B4
Cliftonville Kent 31 B7
Climaen gwyn Neath 33 D8
Climping W Sus 16 D4
Climpy S Lanark 120 D2
Clink Som 24 E2
Clint N Yorks 95 D5
Clint Green Norf 68 C3
Clintmains Borders 122 F2
Cliobh W Isles 154 D5
Clippesby Norf 69 C7
Clipsham Rutland 65 C6
Clipston Northants 64 F4
Clipstone Notts 77 C5
Clitheroe Lancs 93 E7
Cliuthar W Isles 154 H6
Clive Shrops 60 B5
Clivocast Shetland 160 C8
Clixby Lincs 90 D5
Clocaenog Denb 72 D4
Clochan Moray 152 B4
Clock Face Mers 86 E3
Clockmill Borders 122 D3
Cloddiau Powys 60 D2
Clodock Hereford 35 B7
Clola Aberds 153 D10
Clophill C Beds 53 F8
Clopton Northants 65 F7
Clopton Suff 57 D6
Clopton Corner Suff 57 D6
Clopton Green Suff 55 D8
Close Clark IoM 84 E2
Closeburn Dumfries 113 E8
Closworth Som 12 C3
Clothall Herts 54 F3
Clotton Ches W 74 C2
Clough Foot W Yorks 87 B7
Cloughton N Yorks 103 E8
Cloughton Newlands N Yorks 103 E8
Clousta Shetland 160 H5
Clouston Orkney 159 G3
Clova Aberds 140 B3
Clova Angus 134 B3
Clove Lodge Durham 100 C4
Clovelly Devon 8 B5
Clovenfords Borders 121 F7
Clovenstone Aberds 141 C6
Clovullin Highld 130 C4
Clow Bridge Lancs 87 B6
Clowne Derbys 76 B4
Clows Top Worcs 50 B2
Cloy Wrex 73 E7
Cluanie Inn Highld 136 C3
Cluanie Lodge Highld 136 C3
Clun Shrops 60 F3
Clunbury Shrops 60 F3
Clunderwen Carms 32 C2
Clune Highld 138 B3
Clunes Highld 136 F5
Clungunford Shrops 49 B5
Clunie Aberds 153 C6
Clunie Perth 133 E8
Clunton Shrops 60 F3
Cluny Fife 128 E4
Cluny Castle Highld 138 E2
Clutton Bath 23 D8
Clutton Ches W 73 D8
Clwt-grugoer Conwy 72 C3
Clwt-y-bont Gwyn 83 E5
Clydach Mon 35 C6
Clydach Swansea 33 D7
Clydach Vale Rhondda 34 E3
Clydebank W Dunb 118 B4
Clydey Pembs 45 F4
Clyffe Pypard Wilts 25 B5
Clynder Argyll 145 E11
Clyne Neath 34 D2
Clynelish Highld 157 J11
Clynnog-fawr Gwyn 82 F4
Clyro Powys 48 E4
Clyst Honiton Devon 10 E4
Clyst Hydon Devon 10 D5
Clyst St George Devon 10 F4
Clyst St Lawrence Devon 10 D5
Clyst St Mary Devon 10 E4
Cnoc Amhlaigh W Isles 155 D10
Cnwch-coch Ceredig 47 B5
Coachford Aberds 152 D4
Coad's Green Corn 5 B7
Coal Aston Derbys 76 B3
Coalbrookdale Telford 61 D6
Coalbrookvale Bl Gwent 35 D5
Coalburn S Lanark 119 F8
Coalburns T&W 110 C4
Coalcleugh Northumb 109 E8
Coaley Glos 36 D4
Coalhall E Ayrs 112 C4
Coalhill Essex 42 E3
Coalpit Heath S Glos 36 F3
Coalport Telford 61 D6
Coalsnaughton Clack 127 E8
Coaltown of Balgonie Fife 128 E4
Coaltown of Wemyss Fife 128 E5
Coalville Leics 63 C8
Coalway Glos 36 C2
Coat Som 12 B2
Coatbridge N Lanark 119 C7
Coatdyke N Lanark 119 C7
Coate Swindon 38 F1
Coate Wilts 24 C5
Coates Cambs 66 E3
Coates Glos 37 D6
Coates Lancs 93 E8
Coates Notts 90 F2
Coates W Sus 16 C3
Coatham Redcar 102 B3
Coatham Mundeville Darl 101 B7
Coatsgate Dumfries 114 D3
Cobbaton Devon 9 B8
Cobbler's Green Norf 69 E5
Coberley Glos 37 C6
Cobham Kent 29 C7
Cobham Sur 28 C2
Cobholm Island Norf 69 D8
Cobleland Stirling 126 E4
Cobnash Hereford 49 C6
Coburty Aberds 153 B9
Cock Bank Wrex 73 E7
Cock Bridge Aberds 139 D8
Cock Clarks Essex 42 D4
Cockayne N Yorks 102 E4
Cockayne Hatley Cambs 54 E3
Cockburnspath Borders 122 B3
Cockenzie and Port Seton E Loth 121 B7
Cockerham Lancs 92 D4
Cockermouth Cumb 107 F8
Cockernhoe Green Herts 40 B4
Cockfield Durham 101 B6
Cockfield Suff 56 D3
Cockfosters London 41 E5
Cocking W Sus 16 C2
Cockington Torbay 7 C6
Cocklake Som 23 E6
Cockley Beck Cumb 98 D4
Cockley Cley Norf 67 D7
Cockshutt Shrops 60 B4
Cockthorpe Norf 81 C5
Cockwood Devon 10 F4
Cockyard Hereford 49 F6
Codda Corn 5 B6
Coddenham Suff 56 D5
Coddington Ches W 73 D8
Coddington Hereford 50 E2
Coddington Notts 77 D8
Codford St Mary Wilts 24 F4
Codford St Peter Wilts 24 F4
Codicote Herts 41 C5
Codmore Hill W Sus 16 B4
Codnor Derbys 76 E4
Codrington S Glos 24 B2
Codsall Staffs 62 D2
Codsall Wood Staffs 62 D2
Coed Duon = Blackwood Caerph 35 E5
Coed Mawr Gwyn 83 D5
Coed Morgan Mon 35 C7
Coed-Talon Flint 73 D6
Coed-y-bryn Ceredig 46 E2
Coed-y-paen Mon 35 E7
Coed-yr-ynys Powys 35 B5
Coed Ystumgwern Gwyn 71 E6
Coedely Rhondda 34 F4
Coedkernew Newport 35 F6
Coedpoeth Wrex 73 D6
Coedway Powys 60 C3
Coelbren Powys 34 C2
Coffinswell Devon 7 C6
Cofton Hackett Worcs 50 B5
Cogan V Glam 22 B3
Cogenhoe Northants 53 C6
Cogges Oxon 38 D3
Coggeshall Essex 42 B4
Coggeshall Hamlet Essex 42 B4
Coggins Mill E Sus 18 C2
Coig Peighinnean W Isles 155 A10
Coig Peighinnean Bhuirgh W Isles 155 B9
Coignafearn Lodge Highld 138 C2
Coilacriech Aberds 140 E2
Coilantogle Stirling 126 D4
Coilleag W Isles 148 G2
Coillore Highld 149 E8
Coity Bridgend 34 F3
Col W Isles 155 C9
Col Uarach W Isles 155 D9
Colaboll Highld 157 H8
Colan Corn 4 C3
Colaton Raleigh Devon 11 F5
Colbost Highld 148 D7
Colburn N Yorks 101 E6
Colby Cumb 100 B1
Colby IoM 84 E2
Colby Norf 81 D8
Colchester Essex 43 B6
Colcot V Glam 22 C3
Cold Ash W Berks 26 C3
Cold Ashby Northants 52 B4
Cold Ashton S Glos 24 B2
Cold Aston Glos 37 C8
Cold Blow Pembs 32 C2
Cold Brayfield M Keynes 53 D7
Cold Hanworth Lincs 90 F4
Cold Harbour Lincs 78 F2
Cold Hatton Telford 61 B6
Cold Hesledon Durham 111 E7
Cold Higham Northants 52 D4
Cold Kirby N Yorks 102 F3
Cold Newton Leics 64 D4
Cold Northcott Corn 8 F4
Cold Norton Essex 42 D4
Cold Overton Leics 64 C5
Coldbackie Highld 157 D9
Coldbeck Cumb 100 D2
Coldblow London 29 B6
Coldean Brighton 17 D7
Coldeast Devon 7 B6
Colden W Yorks 87 B7
Colden Common Hants 15 B5
Coldfair Green Suff 57 C8
Coldham Cambs 66 D4
Coldharbour Glos 36 D2
Coldharbour Kent 29 D6
Coldharbour Sur 28 E2
Coldingham Borders 122 C5
Coldrain Perth 128 D2
Coldred Kent 31 E6
Coldridge Devon 9 D8
Coldstream Angus 134 F3
Coldstream Borders 122 F4
Coldwaltham W Sus 16 C4
Coldwells Aberds 153 D11
Coldwells Croft Aberds 140 B4
Coldyeld Shrops 60 E3
Cole Som 23 F8
Cole Green Herts 41 C5
Cole Henley Hants 26 D2
Colebatch Shrops 60 F3
Colebrook Devon 10 D5
Colebrooke Devon 10 E2
Coleby Lincs 78 C2
Coleby N Lincs 90 C2
Coleford Devon 10 D2
Coleford Glos 36 C2
Coleford Som 23 E8
Colehill Dorset 13 D8
Coleman's Hatch E Sus 29 F5
Colemere Shrops 73 F8
Colemore Hants 26 F5
Coleorton Leics 63 C8
Colerne Wilts 24 B3
Cole's Green Suff 57 C6
Coles Green Suff 56 E4
Colesbourne Glos 37 C6
Colesden Bedford 54 D2
Coleshill Bucks 40 E2
Coleshill Oxon 38 E2
Coleshill Warks 63 F6
Colestocks Devon 11 D5
Colgate W Sus 28 F3
Colgrain Argyll 126 F2
Colinsburgh Fife 129 D6
Colinton Edin 120 C5
Colintraive Argyll 145 F9
Colkirk Norf 80 E5
Collace Perth 134 F2
Collafirth Shetland 160 G6
Collaton St Mary Torbay 7 D6
College Milton S Lanark 119 D6
Collessie Fife 128 C4
Collier Row London 41 E8
Collier Street Kent 29 E8
Collier's End Herts 41 B6
Collier's Green Kent 18 B4
Colliery Row T&W 111 E6
Collieston Aberds 141 B9
Collin Dumfries 107 B7
Collingbourne Ducis Wilts 25 D7
Collingbourne Kingston Wilts 25 D7
Collingham Notts 77 C8
Collingham W Yorks 95 E6
Collington Hereford 49 C8
Collingtree Northants 53 D5
Collins Green Warr 86 E3
Colliston Angus 135 E6
Collycroft Warks 63 F7
Collynie Aberds 153 E8
Collyweston Northants 65 D6
Colmonell S Ayrs 104 A5
Colmworth Bedford 54 D2
Coln Rogers Glos 37 D7
Coln St Aldwyn's Glos 37 D8
Coln St Dennis Glos 37 C7
Colnabaichin Aberds 139 D8
Colnbrook Slough 27 B8
Colne Cambs 54 B4
Colne Lancs 93 E8
Colne Edge Lancs 93 E8
Colne Engaine Essex 56 F2
Colney Norf 68 D4
Colney Heath Herts 41 D5
Colney Street Herts 40 D4
Colpy Aberds 153 E6
Colquhar Borders 121 E6
Colsterdale N Yorks 101 F6
Colsterworth Lincs 65 B6
Colston Bassett Notts 77 F6
Coltfield Moray 151 E14
Colthouse Cumb 99 E5
Coltishall Norf 69 C5
Coltness N Lanark 119 D8
Colton Cumb 99 F5
Colton N Yorks 95 E8
Colton Norf 68 D4
Colton Staffs 62 B4
Colton W Yorks 95 F6
Colva Powys 48 D4
Colvend Dumfries 107 D5
Colvister Shetland 160 D7
Colwall Green Hereford 50 E2
Colwall Stone Hereford 50 E2
Colwell Northumb 110 B2
Colwich Staffs 62 B4
Colwick Notts 77 E6
Colwinston V Glam 21 B8
Colworth W Sus 16 D3
Colwyn Bay = Bae Colwyn Conwy 83 D8
Colyford Devon 11 E7
Colyton Devon 11 E7
Combe Hereford 48 C5
Combe Oxon 38 C4
Combe W Berks 25 C8
Combe Common Sur 27 F7
Combe Down Bath 24 C2
Combe Florey Som 22 F3
Combe Hay Bath 24 D2
Combe Martin Devon 20 E4
Combe Moor Hereford 49 C5
Combe Raleigh Devon 11 D6
Combe St Nicholas Som 11 C8
Combeinteignhead Devon 7 B7
Comberbach Ches W 74 B3
Comberton Cambs 54 D4
Comberton Hereford 49 C6
Combpyne Devon 11 E7
Combridge Staffs 75 F7
Combrook Warks 51 D8
Combs Derbys 75 B7
Combs Suff 56 D4
Combs Ford Suff 56 D4
Combwich Som 22 E4
Comers Aberds 141 D5
Comins Coch Ceredig 58 F3
Commercial End Cambs 55 C6
Commins Capel Betws Ceredig 46 D5
Commins Coch Powys 58 D5
Common Edge Blackpool 92 F3
Common Side Derbys 76 B3
Commondale N Yorks 102 C4
Commonmoor Corn 5 C7
Commonside Ches W 74 B2
Compstall Gtr Man 87 E7
Compton Devon 7 C6
Compton Hants 15 B5
Compton Sur 27 E6
Compton Sur 27 E7
Compton W Berks 26 B3
Compton W Sus 15 C8
Compton Wilts 25 D6
Compton Abbas Dorset 13 C6
Compton Abdale Glos 37 C7
Compton Bassett Wilts 24 B5
Compton Beauchamp Oxon 38 F2
Compton Bishop Som 23 D5
Compton Chamberlayne Wilts 13 B8
Compton Dando Bath 23 C8
Compton Dundon Som 23 F6
Compton Martin Bath 23 D7
Compton Pauncefoot Som 12 B4
Compton Valence Dorset 12 E3
Comrie Fife 128 F2
Comrie Perth 127 B6
Conaglen House Highld 130 C4
Conchra Argyll 145 E9
Concraigie Perth 133 E8
Conder Green Lancs 92 D4
Conderton Worcs 50 F4
Condicote Glos 38 B1
Condorrat N Lanark 119 B7
Condover Shrops 60 D4
Coney Weston Suff 56 B3
Coneyhurst W Sus 16 B5
Coneysthorpe N Yorks 96 B3
Coneythorpe N Yorks 95 D6
Conford Hants 27 F6
Congash Highld 139 B6
Congdon's Shop Corn 5 B7
Congerstone Leics 63 D7
Congham Norf 80 E3
Congl-y-wal Gwyn 71 C8
Congleton Ches E 75 C5
Congresbury N Som 23 C6
Congreve Staffs 62 C3
Conicavel Moray 151 F12
Coningsby Lincs 78 D5
Conington Cambs 54 C4
Conington Cambs 65 F8
Conisbrough S Yorks 89 E6
Conisby Argyll 142 B3
Conisholme Lincs 91 E8
Coniston Cumb 99 E5
Coniston E Yorks 97 F7
Coniston Cold N Yorks 94 D2
Conistone N Yorks 94 C2
Connah's Quay Flint 73 C6
Connel Argyll 124 B5
Connel Park E Ayrs 113 C6
Connor Downs Corn 2 C4
Conon Bridge Highld 151 F8
Conon House Highld 151 F8
Cononley N Yorks 94 E2
Conordan Highld 149 E10
Consall Staffs 75 E6
Consett Durham 110 D4
Constable Burton N Yorks 101 E6
Constantine Corn 3 D6
Constantine Bay Corn 4 B3
Contin Highld 150 F7
Contlaw Aberdeen 141 D7
Conwy Conwy 83 D7
Conyer Kent 30 C3
Conyers Green Suff 56 C2
Cooden E Sus 18 E4
Cooil IoM 84 E3
Cookbury Devon 9 D6
Cookham Windsor 40 F1
Cookham Dean Windsor 40 F1
Cookham Rise Windsor 40 F1
Cookhill Worcs 51 D5
Cookley Suff 57 B7
Cookley Worcs 62 F2
Cookley Green Oxon 39 E6
Cookney Aberds 141 E7
Cookridge W Yorks 95 E5
Cooksbridge E Sus 17 C8
Cooksmill Green Essex 42 D2
Coolham W Sus 16 B5
Cooling Medway 29 B8
Coombe Corn 4 D4
Coombe Corn 8 C4
Coombe Hants 15 B7
Coombe Wilts 25 D6
Coombe Bissett Wilts 14 B2
Coombe Hill Glos 37 B5
Coombe Keynes Dorset 13 F6
Coombes W Sus 17 D5
Coopersale Common Essex 41 D7
Cootham W Sus 16 C4
Copdock Suff 56 E5
Copford Green Essex 43 B5
Copgrove N Yorks 95 C6
Copister Shetland 160 F6
Cople Bedford 54 E2
Copley Durham 101 B5
Coplow Dale Derbys 75 B8
Copmanthorpe York 95 E8
Coppathorne Corn 8 D4
Coppenhall Staffs 62 C3
Coppenhall Moss Ches E 74 D4
Copperhouse Corn 2 C4
Coppingford Cambs 65 F8
Copplestone Devon 10 D2
Coppull Lancs 86 C3
Coppull Moor Lancs 86 C3
Copsale W Sus 17 B5
Copster Green Lancs 93 F6
Copston Magna Warks 63 F8
Copt Heath W Mid 51 B6
Copt Hewick N Yorks 95 B6
Copt Oak Leics 63 C8
Copthorne Shrops 60 C4
Copthorne Sur 28 F4
Copy's Green Norf 80 D5
Copythorne Hants 14 C4
Corbets Tey London 42 F1
Corbridge Northumb 110 C2
Corby Northants 65 F5
Corby Glen Lincs 65 B6
Cordon N Ayrs 143 E11
Coreley Shrops 49 B8
Cores End Bucks 40 F2
Corfe Som 11 C7
Corfe Castle Dorset 13 F7
Corfe Mullen Dorset 13 E7
Corfton Shrops 60 F4
Corgarff Aberds 139 D8
Corhampton Hants 15 B7
Corlae Dumfries 113 E6
Corley Warks 63 F7
Corley Ash Warks 63 F6
Corley Moor Warks 63 F6
Cornaa IoM 84 D4
Cornabus Argyll 142 D4
Cornel Conwy 83 E7
Corner Row Lancs 92 F4
Corney Cumb 98 E3
Cornforth Durham 111 F6
Cornhill Aberds 152 C5
Cornhill-on-Tweed Northumb 122 F4
Cornholme W Yorks 87 B7
Cornish Hall End Essex 55 F7
Cornquoy Orkney 159 J6
Cornsay Durham 110 E4
Cornsay Colliery Durham 110 E4
Corntown Highld 151 F8
Corntown V Glam 21 B8
Cornwell Oxon 38 B2
Cornwood Devon 6 D4
Cornworthy Devon 7 D6
Corpach Highld 130 B4
Corpusty Norf 81 D7
Corran Highld 130 C4
Corran Highld 149 H13
Corranbuie Argyll 145 G7
Corrany IoM 84 D4
Corrie N Ayrs 143 D11
Corrie Common Dumfries 114 F5
Corriecravie N Ayrs 143 F10
Corriemoillie Highld 150 E6
Corriemulzie Lodge Highld 150 B6
Corrievarkie Lodge Perth 132 B2
Corrievorrie Highld 138 B3
Corrimony Highld 150 H6
Corringham Lincs 90 E2
Corringham Thurrock 42 F3
Corris Gwyn 58 D4
Corris Uchaf Gwyn 58 D4
Corrour Shooting Lodge Highld 131 C8
Corrow Argyll 125 E7
Corry Highld 149 F11
Corry of Ardnagrask Highld 151 G8
Corrykinloch Highld 156 G6
Corrymuckloch Perth 133 F5
Corrynachenchy Argyll 147 G9
Cors-y-Gedol Gwyn 71 E6
Corsback Highld 158 C4
Corscombe Dorset 12 D3
Corse Aberds 152 D6
Corse Glos 36 B4
Corse Lawn Worcs 50 F3
Corse of Kinnoir Aberds 152 D5
Corsewall Dumfries 104 C4
Corsham Wilts 24 B3
Corsindae Aberds 141 D5
Corsley Wilts 24 E3
Corsley Heath Wilts 24 E3
Corsock Dumfries 106 B4
Corston Bath 23 C8
Corston Wilts 37 F6
Corstorphine Edin 120 B4
Cortachy Angus 134 D3
Corton Suff 69 E8
Corton Wilts 24 E4
Corton Denham Som 12 B4
Coruanan Lodge Highld 130 C4
Corunna W Isles 148 B3
Corwen Denb 72 E4
Coryton Devon 9 F6
Coryton Thurrock 42 F3
Cosby Leics 64 E2
Coseley W Mid 62 E3
Cosgrove Northants 53 E5
Cosham Ptsmth 15 D7
Cosheston Pembs 32 D1
Cossall Notts 76 E4
Cossington Leics 64 C3
Cossington Som 23 E5
Costa Orkney 159 F4
Costessey Norf 68 C4
Costock Notts 64 B2
Coston Leics 64 B5
Cote Oxon 38 D3
Cotebrook Ches W 74 C2
Cotehill Cumb 108 D4
Cotes Cumb 99 F6
Cotes Leics 64 B2
Cotes Staffs 74 F5
Cotesbach Leics 64 F2
Cotgrave Notts 77 F6
Cothall Aberds 141 C7
Cotham Notts 77 E7
Cothelstone Som 22 F3
Cotherstone Durham 101 C5
Cothill Oxon 38 E4
Cotleigh Devon 11 D7
Cotmanhay Derbys 76 E4
Cotmaton Devon 11 F6
Coton Cambs 54 D5
Coton Northants 52 B4
Coton Staffs 62 B2
Coton Staffs 75 F6
Coton Clanford Staffs 62 B2
Coton Hill Shrops 60 C4
Coton Hill Staffs 75 F6
Coton in the Elms Derbys 63 C6
Cott Devon 7 C5
Cottam E Yorks 97 C5
Cottam Lancs 92 F5
Cottam Notts 77 B8
Cottartown Highld 151 H13
Cottenham Cambs 54 C5
Cotterdale N Yorks 100 E3
Cottered Herts 41 B6
Cotteridge W Mid 50 B5
Cotterstock Northants 65 E7
Cottesbrooke Northants 52 B5
Cottesmore Rutland 65 C6
Cotteylands Devon 10 C4
Cottingham E Yorks 97 F6
Cottingham Northants 64 E5
Cottingley W Yorks 94 F4
Cottisford Oxon 52 F3
Cotton Staffs 75 E7
Cotton Suff 56 C4
Cotton End Bedford 53 E8
Cottown Aberds 140 B4
Cottown Aberds 141 C6
Cottown Aberds 153 D8
Cotwalton Staffs 75 F6
Couch's Mill Corn 5 D6
Coughton Hereford 36 B2
Coughton Warks 51 C5
Coulaghailtro Argyll 144 G6
Coulags Highld 150 G2
Coulby Newham Mbro 102 C3
Coulderton Cumb 98 D1
Coulin Highld 150 F3
Coull Aberds 140 D4
Coull Argyll 142 B3
Coulport Argyll 145 E11
Coulsdon London 28 D3
Coulston Wilts 24 D4
Coulter S Lanark 120 F3
Coulton N Yorks 96 B2
Cound Shrops 61 D5
Coundon Durham 101 B7
Coundon W Mid 63 F7
Coundon Grange Durham 101 B7
Countersett N Yorks 100 F4
Countess Wilts 25 E6
Countess Wear Devon 10 F4
Countesthorpe Leics 64 E2
Countisbury Devon 21 E6
County Oak W Sus 28 F3
Coup Green Lancs 86 B3
Coupar Angus Perth 134 E2
Coupland Northumb 122 F5
Cour Argyll 143 D9
Courance Dumfries 114 E3
Court-at-Street Kent 19 B7
Court Henry Carms 33 B6
Courteenhall Northants 53 D5
Courtsend Essex 43 E6
Courtway Som 22 F4
Cousland Midloth 121 C6
Cousley Wood E Sus 18 B3
Cove Argyll 145 E11
Cove Borders 122 B3
Cove Devon 10 C4
Cove Hants 27 D6
Cove Highld 155 H13
Cove Bay Aberdeen 141 D8
Cove Bottom Suff 57 B8
Covehithe Suff 69 F8
Coven Staffs 62 D3
Coveney Cambs 66 F4
Covenham St Bartholomew Lincs 91 E7
Covenham St Mary Lincs 91 E7
Coventry W Mid 51 B8
Coverack Corn 3 E6
Coverham N Yorks 101 F6
Covesea Moray 152 A1
Covington Cambs 53 B8
Covington S Lanark 120 F2
Cow Ark Lancs 93 E6
Cowan Bridge Lancs 93 B6
Cowbeech E Sus 18 D3
Cowbit Lincs 66 C2
Cowbridge Lincs 79 E6
Cowbridge Som 21 E8
Cowbridge = Y Bont-Faen V Glam 21 B8
Cowdale Derbys 75 B7
Cowden Kent 29 E5
Cowdenbeath Fife 128 E3
Cowdenburn Borders 120 D5
Cowers Lane Derbys 76 E3
Cowes IoW 15 E5
Cowesby N Yorks 102 F2
Cowfold W Sus 17 B6
Cowgill Cumb 100 F2
Cowie Aberds 141 F7
Cowie Stirling 127 F7
Cowley Devon 10 E4
Cowley Glos 37 C6
Cowley London 40 F3
Cowley Oxon 39 D5
Cowleymoor Devon 10 C4
Cowling Lancs 86 C3
Cowling N Yorks 94 E2
Cowling N Yorks 101 F7
Cowlinge Suff 55 D8
Cowpe Lancs 87 B6
Cowpen Northumb 117 F8
Cowpen Bewley Stockton 102 B2
Cowplain Hants 15 C7
Cowshill Durham 109 E8
Cowslip Green N Som 23 C6
Cowstrandburn Fife 128 E2
Cowthorpe N Yorks 95 D7
Cox Common Suff 69 F6
Cox Green Windsor 27 B6
Cox Moor Notts 76 D5
Coxbank Ches E 74 E3
Coxbench Derbys 76 E3
Coxford Norf 80 E4
Coxford Soton 14 C4
Coxheath Kent 29 D8
Coxhill Kent 31 E6
Coxhoe Durham 111 F6
Coxley Som 23 E7
Coxwold N Yorks 95 B8
Coychurch Bridgend 21 B8
Coylton S Ayrs 112 B4
Coylumbridge Highld 138 C5
Coynach Aberds 140 D3
Coynachie Aberds 152 E4
Coytrahen Bridgend 34 F2
Crabadon Devon 7 D5
Crabbs Cross Worcs 50 C5
Crabtree W Sus 17 B6
Crackenthorpe Cumb 100 B1
Crackington Haven Corn 8 E3
Crackley Warks 51 B7
Crackleybank Shrops 61 C7
Crackpot N Yorks 100 E4
Cracoe N Yorks 94 C2
Craddock Devon 11 C5
Cradhlastadh W Isles 154 D5
Cradley Hereford 50 E2
Cradley Heath W Mid 62 F3
Crafthole Corn 5 D8
Cragg Vale W Yorks 87 B8
Craggan Highld 139 B6
Craggie Highld 151 H10
Craggie Highld 157 H11
Craghead Durham 110 D5
Crai Powys 34 B2
Craibstone Moray 152 C4
Craichie Angus 135 E5
Craig Dumfries 106 B3
Craig Dumfries 106 C3
Craig Highld 150 G3
Craig Castle Aberds 140 B3
Craig-cefn-parc Swansea 33 D7
Craig Penllyn V Glam 21 B8
Craig-y-don Conwy 83 C7
Craig-y-nos Powys 34 C2
Craiganor Lodge Perth 132 D3
Craigdam Aberds 153 E8
Craigdarroch Dumfries 113 E7
Craigdarroch Highld 150 F7
Craigdhu Highld 150 G7
Craigearn Aberds 141 C6
Craigellachie Moray 152 D2
Craigencross Dumfries 104 C4
Craigend Perth 128 B3
Craigend Stirling 127 F6
Craigendive Argyll 145 E9
Craigendoran Argyll 126 F2
Craigens Argyll 142 B3
Craigens E Ayrs 113 C5
Craighat Stirling 126 F3
Craighead Fife 129 D8
Craighlaw Mains Dumfries 105 C7
Craighouse Argyll 144 G4
Craigie Aberds 141 C8
Craigie Dundee 134 F4
Craigie Perth 128 B3
Craigie Perth 133 E8
Craigie S Ayrs 118 F4
Craigiefield Orkney 159 G5
Craigielaw E Loth 121 B7
Craiglockhart Edin 120 B5
Craigmalloch E Ayrs 112 E4
Craigmaud Aberds 153 C8
Craigmillar Edin 121 B5
Craigmore Argyll 145 G10
Craignant Shrops 73 F6
Craigneuk N Lanark 119 C7
Craigneuk N Lanark 119 D7
Craignure Argyll 124 B3
Craigo Angus 135 C6
Craigow Perth 128 D2
Craigrothie Fife 129 C5
Craigroy Moray 151 F14
Craigruie Stirling 126 B3
Craigston Castle Aberds 153 C7
Craigton Aberdeen 141 D7
Craigton Angus 134 D3
Craigton Angus 135 F5
Craigton Highld 151 B9
Craigtown Highld 157 D11
Craik Borders 115 D6
Crail Fife 129 D8
Crailing Borders 116 B2
Crailinghall Borders 116 B2
Craiselound N Lincs 89 E8
Crakehill N Yorks 95 B7
Crakemarsh Staffs 75 F7
Crambe N Yorks 96 C3
Cramlington Northumb 111 B5
Cramond Edin 120 B4
Cramond Bridge Edin 120 B4
Cranage Ches E 74 C4
Cranberry Staffs 74 F5
Cranborne Dorset 13 C8
Cranbourne Brack 27 B7
Cranbrook, Devon 10 E5
Cranbrook Kent 18 B4
Cranbrook Common Kent 18 B4
Crane Moor S Yorks 88 D4
Crane's Corner Norf 68 C2
Cranfield C Beds 53 E7
Cranford London 28 B2
Cranford St Andrew Northants 53 B7
Cranford St John Northants 53 B7
Cranham Glos 37 C5
Cranham London 42 F1
Crank Mers 86 E3
Crank Wood Gtr Man 86 D4
Cranleigh Sur 27 F8
Cranley Suff 57 B5
Cranmer Green Suff 56 B4
Cranmore IoW 14 E4
Cranna Aberds 153 C6
Crannich Argyll 147 G8
Crannoch Moray 152 C4
Cranoe Leics 64 E4
Cransford Suff 57 C7
Cranshaws Borders 122 C2
Cranstal IoM 84 B4
Crantock Corn 4 C2
Cranwell Lincs 78 E3
Cranwich Norf 67 E7
Cranworth Norf 68 D2
Craobh Haven Argyll 124 E3
Crapstone Devon 6 C3
Crarae Argyll 125 F5
Crask Inn Highld 157 G8
Crask of Aigas Highld 150 G7
Craskins Aberds 140 D4
Craster Northumb 117 C8
Craswall Hereford 48 F4
Cratfield Suff 57 B7
Crathes Aberds 141 E6
Crathie Aberds 139 E8
Crathie Highld 137 E8
Crathorne N Yorks 102 D2
Craven Arms Shrops 60 F4
Crawcrook T&W 110 C4
Crawford Lancs 86 D2
Crawford S Lanark 114 B2
Crawfordjohn S Lanark 113 B8
Crawick Dumfries 113 C7
Crawley Hants 26 F2
Crawley Oxon 38 C3
Crawley W Sus 28 F3
Crawley Down W Sus 28 F4
Crawleyside Durham 110 E2
Crawshawbooth Lancs 87 B6
Crawton Aberds 135 B8
Cray N Yorks 94 B2
Cray Perth 133 C8
Crayford London 29 B6
Crayke N Yorks 95 B8
Crays Hill Essex 42 E3
Cray's Pond Oxon 39 F6
Creacombe Devon 10 C3
Creag Ghoraidh W Isles 148 D2
Creagan Argyll 130 E3
Creaguaineach Lodge Highld 131 C7
Creaksea Essex 43 E5
Creaton Northants 52 B5
Creca Dumfries 108 B2
Credenhill Hereford 49 E6
Crediton Devon 10 D3
Creebridge Dumfries 105 C8
Creech Heathfield Som 11 B7
Creech St Michael Som 11 B7
Creed Corn 3 B8
Creekmouth London 41 F7
Creeting Bottoms Suff 56 D5
Creeting St Mary Suff 56 D4
Creeton Lincs 65 B7
Creetown Dumfries 105 D8
Creg-ny-Baa IoM 84 D3
Creggans Argyll 125 E6
Cregneash IoM 84 F1
Cregrina Powys 48 D3
Creich Fife 128 B5
Creigiau Cardiff 34 F4
Cremyll Corn 6 D2
Creslow Bucks 39 B8
Cressage Shrops 61 D5
Cressbrook Derbys 75 B8
Cresselly Pembs 32 D1
Cressing Essex 42 B3
Cresswell Northumb 117 E8
Cresswell Staffs 75 F6
Cresswell Quay Pembs 32 D1
Creswell Derbys 76 B5
Cretingham Suff 57 C6
Cretshengan Argyll 144 G6
Crewe Ches E 74 D4
Crewe Ches W 73 D8
Crewgreen Powys 60 C3
Crewkerne Som 12 D2
Crianlarich Stirling 126 B2
Cribyn Ceredig 46 D4
Criccieth Gwyn 71 D5
Crich Derbys 76 D3
Crichie Aberds 153 D9
Crichton Midloth 121 C6
Crick Mon 36 E1
Crick Northants 52 B3
Crickadarn Powys 48 E2
Cricket Malherbie Som 11 C8
Cricket St Thomas Som 11 D8
Crickheath Shrops 60 B2
Crickhowell Powys 35 C6
Cricklade Wilts 37 E8
Cricklewood London 41 F5
Cridling Stubbs N Yorks 89 B6
Crieff Perth 127 B7
Criggion Powys 60 C2
Crigglestone W Yorks 88 C4
Crimond Aberds 153 C10
Crimonmogate Aberds 153 C10
Crimplesham Norf 67 D6
Crinan Argyll 144 D6
Cringleford Norf 68 D4
Cringles W Yorks 94 E3
Crinow Pembs 32 C2
Cripplesease Corn 2 C4
Cripplestyle Dorset 13 C8
Cripp's Corner E Sus 18 C4
Croasdale Cumb 98 C2
Crock Street Som 11 C8
Crockenhill Kent 29 C6
Crockernwell Devon 10 E2
Crockerton Wilts 24 E3
Crocketford or Ninemile Bar Dumfries 106 B5
Crockey Hill York 96 E2
Crockham Hill Kent 28 D5
Crockleford Heath Essex 43 B6
Crockness Orkney 159 J4
Croes-goch Pembs 44 B3
Croes-lan Ceredig 46 E2
Croes-y-mwyalch Torf 35 E7
Croeserw Neath 34 E2
Croesor Gwyn 71 C7
Croesyceiliog Carms 33 C5
Croesyceiliog Torf 35 E7
Croesywaun Gwyn 82 F5
Croft Leics 64 E2
Croft Lincs 79 C8
Croft Pembs 45 E3
Croft Warr 86 E4
Croft-on-Tees N Yorks 101 D7
Croftamie Stirling 126 F3
Croftmalloch W Loth 120 C2
Crofton W Yorks 88 C4

Crofton Wilts 25 C7
Crofts of Benachielt Highld 158 G3
Crofts of Haddo Aberds 153 E8
Crofts of Inverthernie Aberds 153 D7
Crofts of Meikle Ardo Aberds 153 D8
Crofty Swansea 33 E6
Croggan Argyll 124 C3
Croglin Cumb 109 E5
Croich Highld 150 B7
Crois Dughaill W Isles 148 F2
Cromarty Highld 151 E10
Cromblet Aberds 153 E7
Cromdale Highld 139 B6
Cromer Herts 41 B5
Cromer Norf 81 C8
Cromford Derbys 76 D2
Cromhall S Glos 36 E3
Cromhall Common S Glos 36 F3
Cromor W Isles 155 E9
Cromra Highld 137 E8
Cromwell Notts 77 C7
Cronberry E Ayrs 113 B6
Crondall Hants 27 E5
Cronk-y-Voddy IoM 84 D3
Cronton Mers 86 F2
Crook Cumb 99 E6
Crook Durham 110 F4
Crook of Devon Perth 128 D2
Crookedholm E Ayrs 118 F4
Crookes S Yorks 88 F4
Crookham Northumb 122 F5
Crookham W Berks 26 C3
Crookham Village Hants 27 D5
Crookhaugh Borders 114 B4
Crookhouse Borders 116 B3
Crooklands Cumb 99 F7
Cropredy Oxon 52 E2
Cropston Leics 64 C2
Cropthorne Worcs 50 E4
Cropton N Yorks 103 F5
Cropwell Bishop Notts 77 F6
Cropwell Butler Notts 77 F6
Cros W Isles 155 A10
Crosbost W Isles 155 E8
Crosby Cumb 107 F7
Crosby IoM 84 E3
Crosby N Lincs 90 C2
Crosby Garrett Cumb 100 D2
Crosby Ravensworth Cumb 99 C8
Crosby Villa Cumb 107 F7
Croscombe Som 23 E7
Cross Som 23 D6
Cross Ash Mon 35 C8
Cross-at-Hand Kent 29 E8
Cross Green Devon 9 F5
Cross Green Suff 56 D2
Cross Green Suff 56 D3
Cross Green Warks 51 D8
Cross-hands Carms 32 B2
Cross Hands Carms 33 C6
Cross Hands Pembs 32 C1
Cross Hill Derbys 76 E4
Cross Houses Shrops 60 D5
Cross in Hand E Sus 18 C2
Cross in Hand Leics 64 F2
Cross Inn Ceredig 46 C4
Cross Inn Ceredig 46 D2
Cross Inn Rhondda 34 F4
Cross Keys Kent 29 D6
Cross Lane Head Shrops 61 E7
Cross Lanes Corn 3 D5
Cross Lanes N Yorks 95 C8
Cross Lanes Wrex 73 E7
Cross Oak Powys 35 B5
Cross of Jackston Aberds 153 E7
Cross o'th'hands Derbys 76 E2
Cross Street Suff 57 B5
Crossaig Argyll 143 C9
Crossal Highld 149 E9
Crossapol Argyll 146 G2
Crossburn Falk 119 B8
Crossbush W Sus 16 D4
Crosscanonby Cumb 107 F7
Crossdale Street Norf 81 D8
Crossens Mers 85 C4
Crossflatts W Yorks 94 E4
Crossford Fife 128 F2
Crossford S Lanark 119 E8
Crossgate Lincs 66 B2
Crossgatehall E Loth 121 C6
Crossgates Fife 128 F3
Crossgates Powys 48 C2
Crossgill Lancs 93 C5
Crosshill E Ayrs 112 B4
Crosshill Fife 128 E3
Crosshill S Ayrs 112 D3
Crosshouse E Ayrs 118 F3
Crossings Cumb 108 B5
Crosskeys Caerph 35 E6
Crosskirk Highld 157 B13
Crosslanes Shrops 60 C3
Crosslee Borders 115 C6
Crosslee Renfs 118 C4
Crossmichael Dumfries 106 C4
Crossmoor Lancs 92 F4
Crossroads Aberds 141 E6
Crossroads E Ayrs 118 F4
Crossway Hereford 49 F8
Crossway Mon 35 C8
Crossway Powys 48 D2
Crossway Green Worcs 50 C3
Crossways Dorset 13 F5
Crosswell Pembs 45 F3
Crosswood Ceredig 47 B5
Crosthwaite Cumb 99 E6
Croston Lancs 86 C2
Crostwick Norf 69 C5
Crostwight Norf 69 B6
Crothair W Isles 154 D6
Crouch Kent 29 D7
Crouch Hill Dorset 12 C5
Crouch House Green Kent 28 E5
Croucheston Wilts 13 B8
Croughton Northants 52 F3
Crovie Aberds 153 B8
Crow Edge S Yorks 88 D2
Crow Hill Hereford 36 B3
Crowan Corn 2 C5
Crowborough E Sus 18 B2
Crowcombe Som 22 F3
Crowdecote Derbys 75 C8
Crowden Derbys 87 E8
Crowell Oxon 39 E7
Crowfield Northants 52 E4
Crowfield Suff 56 D5
Crowhurst E Sus 18 D4
Crowhurst Sur 28 E4
Crowhurst Lane End Sur 28 E4
Crowland Lincs 66 C2
Crowlas Corn 2 C4
Crowle N Lincs 89 C8
Crowle Worcs 50 D4
Crowmarsh Gifford Oxon 39 F6
Crown Corner Suff 57 B6
Crownhill Plym 6 D2
Crownland Suff 56 C4
Crownthorpe Norf 68 D3
Crowntown Corn 2 C5
Crows-an-wra Corn 2 D2
Crowshill Norf 68 D2
Crowsnest Shrops 60 D3
Crowthorne Brack 27 C6
Crowton Ches W 74 B2
Croxall Staffs 63 C5
Croxby Lincs 91 E5
Croxdale Durham 111 F5
Croxden Staffs 75 F7
Croxley Green Herts 40 E3
Croxton Cambs 54 C3
Croxton N Lincs 90 C4
Croxton Norf 67 F8
Croxton Staffs 74 F4
Croxton Kerrial Leics 64 B5
Croxtonbank Staffs 74 F4
Croy Highld 151 G10
Croy N Lanark 119 B7
Croyde Devon 20 F3
Croydon Cambs 54 E4
Croydon London 28 C4
Crubenmore Lodge Highld 138 E2
Cruckmeole Shrops 60 D4
Cruckton Shrops 60 C4
Cruden Bay Aberds 153 E10
Crudgington Telford 61 C6
Crudwell Wilts 37 E6
Crug Powys 48 B3
Crugmeer Corn 4 B4
Crugybar Carms 47 F5
Crulabhig W Isles 154 D6
Crumlin = Crymlyn Caerph 35 E6
Crumpsall Gtr Man 87 D6
Crundale Kent 30 E4
Crundale Pembs 44 D4
Cruwys Morchard Devon 10 C3
Crux Easton Hants 26 D2
Crwbin Carms 33 C5
Crya Orkney 159 H4
Cryers Hill Bucks 40 E1
Crymlyn = Crumlin Caerph 35 E6
Crymlyn Gwyn 83 D6
Crymych Pembs 45 F3
Crynant Neath 34 D1
Crynfryn Ceredig 46 C4
Cuaig Highld 149 C12
Cuan Argyll 124 D3
Cubbington Warks 51 C8
Cubeck N Yorks 100 F4
Cubert Corn 4 D2
Cubley S Yorks 88 D3
Cubley Common Derbys 75 F8
Cublington Bucks 39 B8
Cublington Hereford 49 F6
Cuckfield W Sus 17 B7
Cucklington Som 13 B5
Cuckney Notts 77 B5
Cuckoo Hill Notts 89 E8
Cuddesdon Oxon 39 D6
Cuddington Bucks 39 C7
Cuddington Ches W 74 B3
Cuddington Heath Ches W 73 E8
Cuddy Hill Lancs 92 F4
Cudham London 28 D5
Cudliptown Devon 6 B3
Cudworth S Yorks 88 D4
Cudworth Som 11 C8
Cuffley Herts 41 D6
Cuiashader W Isles 155 B10
Cuidhir W Isles 148 H1
Cuidhtinis W Isles 154 J5
Culbo Highld 151 E9
Culbokie Highld 151 F9
Culburnie Highld 150 G7
Culcabock Highld 151 G9
Culcairn Highld 151 E9
Culcharry Highld 151 F11
Culcheth Warr 86 E4
Culdrain Aberds 152 E5
Culduie Highld 149 D12
Culford Suff 56 B2
Culgaith Cumb 99 B8
Culham Oxon 39 E5
Culkein Highld 156 F3
Culkein Drumbeg Highld 156 F4
Culkerton Glos 37 E6
Cullachie Highld 139 B5
Cullen Moray 152 B5
Cullercoats T&W 111 B6
Cullicudden Highld 151 E9
Cullingworth W Yorks 94 F3
Cullipool Argyll 124 D3
Cullivoe Shetland 160 C7
Culloch Perth 127 C6
Culloden Highld 151 G10
Cullompton Devon 10 D5
Culmaily Highld 151 B11
Culmazie Dumfries 105 D7
Culmington Shrops 60 F4
Culmstock Devon 11 C6
Culnacraig Highld 156 J3
Culnaknock Highld 149 B10
Culpho Suff 57 E6
Culrain Highld 151 B8
Culross Fife 127 F8
Culroy S Ayrs 112 C3
Culsh Aberds 140 E2
Culsh Aberds 153 D8
Culshabbin Dumfries 105 D7
Culswick Shetland 160 J4
Cultercullen Aberds 141 B8
Cults Aberdeen 141 D7
Cults Aberds 152 E5
Cults Dumfries 105 E8
Culverstone Green Kent 29 C7
Culverthorpe Lincs 78 E3
Culworth Northants 52 E3
Culzie Lodge Highld 151 D8
Cumbernauld N Lanark 119 B7
Cumbernauld Village N Lanark 119 B7
Cumberworth Lincs 79 B8
Cuminestown Aberds 153 C8
Cumlewick Shetland 160 L6
Cummersdale Cumb 108 D3
Cummertrees Dumfries 107 C8
Cummingston Moray 152 B1
Cumnock E Ayrs 113 B5
Cumnor Oxon 38 D4
Cumrew Cumb 108 D5
Cumwhinton Cumb 108 D4
Cumwhitton Cumb 108 D5
Cundall N Yorks 95 B7
Cunninghamhead N Ayrs 118 E3
Cunnister Shetland 160 D7
Cupar Fife 129 C5
Cupar Muir Fife 129 C5
Cupernham Hants 14 B4
Curbar Derbys 76 B2
Curbridge Hants 15 C6
Curbridge Oxon 38 D3
Curdridge Hants 15 C6
Curdworth Warks 63 E5
Curland Som 11 C7
Curlew Green Suff 57 C7
Currarie S Ayrs 112 E1
Curridge W Berks 26 B2
Currie Edin 120 C4
Curry Mallet Som 11 B8
Curry Rivel Som 11 B8
Curtisden Green Kent 29 E8
Curtisknowle Devon 6 D5
Cury Corn 3 D5
Cushnie Aberds 153 B7
Cushuish Som 22 F3
Cusop Hereford 48 E4
Cutcloy Dumfries 105 F8
Cutcombe Som 21 F8
Cutgate Gtr Man 87 C6
Cutiau Gwyn 58 C3
Cutlers Green Essex 55 F6
Cutnall Green Worcs 50 C3
Cutsdean Glos 51 F5
Cutthorpe Derbys 76 B3
Cutts Shetland 160 K6
Cuxham Oxon 39 E6
Cuxton Medway 29 C8
Cuxwold Lincs 91 D5
Cwm Bl Gwent 35 D5
Cwm Denb 72 B4
Cwm Swansea 33 E7
Cwm-byr Carms 46 F5
Cwm-Cewydd Gwyn 59 C5
Cwm-cou Ceredig 45 E4
Cwm-Dulais Swansea 33 D7
Cwm-felin-fach Caerph 35 E5
Cwm Ffrwd-oer Torf 35 D6
Cwm-hesgen Gwyn 71 E8
Cwm-hwnt Rhondda 34 D3
Cwm Irfon Powys 47 E7
Cwm-Llinau Powys 58 D5
Cwm-mawr Carms 33 C6
Cwm-parc Rhondda 34 E3
Cwm Penmachno Conwy 71 C8
Cwm-y-glo Carms 33 C6
Cwm-y-glo Gwyn 82 E5
Cwmafan Neath 34 E1
Cwmaman Rhondda 34 E4
Cwmann Carms 46 E4
Cwmavon Torf 35 D6
Cwmbâch Rhondda 34 D4
Cwmbach Carms 32 B3
Cwmbach Carms 33 D5
Cwmbach Powys 48 D2
Cwmbach Powys 48 F3
Cwmbelan Powys 59 F6
Cwmbrân = Cwmbran Torf 35 E6
Cwmbran = Cwmbrân Torf 35 E6
Cwmbrwyno Ceredig 58 F4
Cwmcarn Caerph 35 E6
Cwmcarvan Mon 36 D1
Cwmcych Carms 45 F4
Cwmdare Rhondda 34 D3
Cwmderwen Powys 59 D6
Cwmdu Carms 46 F5
Cwmdu Powys 35 B5
Cwmdu Swansea 33 E7
Cwmduad Carms 46 F2
Cwmdwr Carms 47 F6
Cwmfelin Bridgend 34 F2
Cwmfelin M Tydf 34 D4
Cwmfelin Boeth Carms 32 C2
Cwmfelin Mynach Carms 32 B3
Cwmffrwd Carms 33 C5
Cwmgiedd Powys 34 C1
Cwmgors Neath 33 C8
Cwmgwili Carms 33 C6
Cwmgwrach Neath 34 D2
Cwmhiraeth Carms 46 F2
Cwmifor Carms 33 B7
Cwmisfael Carms 33 C5
Cwmllynfell Neath 33 C8
Cwmorgan Pembs 45 F4
Cwmpengraig Carms 46 F2
Cwmrhos Powys 35 B5
Cwmsychpant Ceredig 46 E3
Cwmtillery Bl Gwent 35 D6
Cwmwysg Powys 34 B2
Cwmyoy Mon 35 B6
Cwmystwyth Ceredig 47 B6
Cwrt Gwyn 58 D3
Cwrt-newydd Ceredig 46 E3
Cwrt-y-cadno Carms 47 E5
Cwrt-y-gollen Powys 35 C6
Cydweli = Kidwelly Carms 33 D5
Cyffordd Llandudno = Llandudno Junction Conwy 83 D7
Cyffylliog Denb 72 D4
Cyfronydd Powys 59 D8
Cymer Neath 34 E2
Cyncoed Cardiff 35 F5
Cynghordy Carms 47 E7
Cynheidre Carms 33 D5
Cynwyd Denb 72 E4
Cynwyl Elfed Carms 32 B4
Cywarch Gwyn 59 C5

D

Dacre Cumb 99 B6
Dacre N Yorks 94 C4
Dacre Banks N Yorks 94 C4
Daddry Shield Durham 109 F8
Dadford Bucks 52 F4
Dadlington Leics 63 E8
Dafarn Faig Gwyn 71 C5
Dafen Carms 33 D6
Daffy Green Norf 68 D2
Dagenham London 41 F7
Daglingworth Glos 37 D6
Dagnall Bucks 40 C2
Dail Beag W Isles 154 C7
Dail bho Dheas W Isles 155 A9
Dail bho Thuath W Isles 155 A9
Dail Mor W Isles 154 C7
Daill Argyll 142 B4
Dailly S Ayrs 112 D2
Dairsie or Osnaburgh Fife 129 C6
Daisy Hill Gtr Man 86 D4
Dalabrog W Isles 148 F2
Dalavich Argyll 125 D5
Dalbeattie Dumfries 106 C5
Dalblair E Ayrs 113 C6
Dalbog Angus 135 B5
Dalbury Derbys 76 F2
Dalby IoM 84 E2
Dalby N Yorks 96 B2
Dalchalloch Perth 132 C4
Dalchalm Highld 157 J12
Dalchenna Argyll 125 E6
Dalchirach Moray 152 E1
Dalchork Highld 157 H8
Dalchreichart Highld 137 C5
Dalchruin Perth 127 C6
Dalderby Lincs 78 C5
Dale Pembs 44 E3
Dale Abbey Derbys 76 F4
Dale Head Cumb 99 C6
Dale of Walls Shetland 160 H3
Dalelia Highld 147 E10
Daless Highld 151 H11
Dalfaber Highld 138 C5
Dalgarven N Ayrs 118 E2
Dalgety Bay Fife 128 F3
Dalginross Perth 127 B6
Dalguise Perth 133 E6
Dalhalvaig Highld 157 D11
Dalham Suff 55 C8
Dalinlongart Argyll 145 E10
Dalkeith Midloth 121 C6
Dallam Warr 86 E3
Dallas Moray 151 F14
Dalleagles E Ayrs 113 C5
Dallinghoo Suff 57 D6
Dallington E Sus 18 D3
Dallington Northants 52 C5
Dallow N Yorks 94 B4
Dalmadilly Aberds 141 C6
Dalmally Argyll 125 C7
Dalmarnock Glasgow 119 C6
Dalmary Stirling 126 E4
Dalmellington E Ayrs 112 D4
Dalmeny Edin 120 B4
Dalmigavie Highld 138 C3
Dalmigavie Lodge Highld 138 B3
Dalmore Highld 151 E9
Dalmuir W Dunb 118 B4
Dalnabreck Highld 147 E9
Dalnacardoch Lodge Perth 132 B4
Dalnacroich Highld 150 F6
Dalnaglar Castle Perth 133 C8
Dalnahaitnach Highld 138 B4
Dalnaspidal Lodge Perth 132 B3
Dalnavaid Perth 133 C7
Dalnavie Highld 151 D9
Dalnawillan Lodge Highld 157 E13
Dalness Highld 131 D5
Dalnessie Highld 157 H9
Dalqueich Perth 128 D2
Dalreavoch Highld 157 J10
Dalry N Ayrs 118 E2
Dalrymple E Ayrs 112 C3
Dalserf S Lanark 119 D8
Dalston Cumb 108 D3
Dalswinton Dumfries 114 F2
Dalton Dumfries 107 B8
Dalton Lancs 86 D2
Dalton N Yorks 95 B7
Dalton N Yorks 101 D6
Dalton Northumb 110 B4
Dalton Northumb 110 D2
Dalton S Yorks 89 E5
Dalton-in-Furness Cumb 92 B2
Dalton-le-Dale Durham 111 E7
Dalton-on-Tees N Yorks 101 D7
Dalton Piercy Hrtlpl 111 F7
Dalveich Stirling 126 B5
Dalvina Lodge Highld 157 E9
Dalwhinnie Highld 138 F2
Dalwood Devon 11 D7
Dalwyne S Ayrs 112 E3
Dam Green Norf 68 F3
Dam Side Lancs 92 E4
Damerham Hants 14 C2
Damgate Norf 69 D7
Damnaglaur Dumfries 104 F5
Damside Borders 120 E4
Danbury Essex 42 D3
Danby N Yorks 103 D5
Danby Wiske N Yorks 101 E8
Dandaleith Moray 152 D2
Danderhall Midloth 121 C6
Dane End Herts 41 B6
Danebridge Ches E 75 C6
Danehill E Sus 17 B8
Danemoor Green Norf 68 D3
Danesford Shrops 61 E7
Daneshill Hants 26 D4
Dangerous Corner Lancs 86 C3
Danskine E Loth 121 C8
Darcy Lever Gtr Man 86 D5
Darenth Kent 29 B6
Daresbury Halton 86 F3
Darfield S Yorks 88 D5
Darfoulds Notts 77 B5
Dargate Kent 30 C4
Darite Corn 5 C7
Darlaston W Mid 62 E3
Darley N Yorks 94 D5
Darley Bridge Derbys 76 C2
Darley Head N Yorks 94 D4
Darlingscott Warks 51 E7
Darlington Darl 101 C7
Darliston Shrops 74 F2
Darlton Notts 77 B7
Darnall S Yorks 88 F4
Darnick Borders 121 F8
Darowen Powys 58 D5
Darra Aberds 153 D7
Darracott Devon 20 F3
Darras Hall Northumb 110 B4
Darrington W Yorks 89 B5
Darsham Suff 57 C8
Dartford Kent 29 B6
Dartford Crossing Kent 29 B6
Dartington Devon 7 C5
Dartmeet Devon 6 B4
Dartmouth Devon 7 D6
Darton S Yorks 88 D4
Darvel E Ayrs 119 F5
Darwell Hole E Sus 18 D3
Darwen Blackburn 86 B4
Datchet Windsor 27 B7
Datchworth Herts 41 C5
Datchworth Green Herts 41 C5
Daubhill Gtr Man 86 D5
Daugh of Kinermony Moray 152 D2
Dauntsey Wilts 37 F6
Dava Moray 151 H13
Davenham Ches W 74 B3
Davenport Green Ches E 74 B5
Daventry Northants 52 C3
David's Well Powys 48 B2
Davidson's Mains Edin 120 B5
Davidstow Corn 8 F3
Davington Dumfries 115 D5
Daviot Aberds 141 B6
Daviot Highld 151 H10
Davoch of Grange Moray 152 C4
Davyhulme Gtr Man 87 E5
Daw's House Corn 8 F5
Dawley Telford 61 D6
Dawlish Devon 7 B7
Dawlish Warren Devon 7 B7
Dawn Conwy 83 D8
Daws Heath Essex 42 F4
Daw's House Corn 8 F5
Dawsmere Lincs 79 F7
Dayhills Staffs 75 F6
Daylesford Glos 38 B2
Ddôl-Cownwy Powys 59 C7
Ddrydwy Anglesey 82 D3
Deadwater Northumb 116 E2
Deaf Hill Durham 111 F6
Deal Kent 31 D7
Deal Hall Essex 43 E6
Dean Cumb 98 B2
Dean Devon 6 C5
Dean Devon 20 E4
Dean Dorset 13 C7
Dean Hants 15 C6
Dean Som 23 E8
Dean Prior Devon 6 C5
Dean Row Ches E 87 F6
Deanburnhaugh Borders 115 C6
Deane Gtr Man 86 D4
Deane Hants 26 D3
Deanich Lodge Highld 150 C6
Deanland Dorset 13 C7
Deans W Loth 120 C3
Deanscales Cumb 98 B2
Deanshanger Northants 53 F5
Deanston Stirling 127 D6
Dearham Cumb 107 F7
Debach Suff 57 D6
Debden Essex 41 E7
Debden Essex 55 F6
Debden Cross Essex 55 F6
Debenham Suff 57 C5
Dechmont W Loth 120 B3
Deddington Oxon 52 F2
Dedham Essex 56 F4
Dedham Heath Essex 56 F4
Deebank Aberds 141 E5
Deene Northants 65 E6
Deenethorpe Northants 65 E6
Deepcar S Yorks 88 E3
Deepcut Sur 27 D7
Deepdale Cumb 100 F2
Deeping Gate Lincs 65 D8
Deeping St James Lincs 65 D8
Deeping St Nicholas Lincs 66 C2
Deerhill Moray 152 C4
Deerhurst Glos 37 B5
Deerness Orkney 159 H6
Defford Worcs 50 E4
Defynnog Powys 34 B3
Deganwy Conwy 83 D7
Deighton N Yorks 102 D1
Deighton W Yorks 88 C2
Deighton York 96 E2
Deiniolen Gwyn 83 E5
Delabole Corn 8 F2
Delamere Ches W 74 C2
Delfrigs Aberds 141 B8
Dell Lodge Highld 139 C6
Delliefure Highld 151 H13
Delnabo Moray 139 C7
Delnadamph Aberds 139 D8
Delph Gtr Man 87 D7
Delves Durham 110 E4
Delvine Perth 133 E8
Dembleby Lincs 78 F3
Denaby Main S Yorks 89 E5
Denbigh = Dinbych Denb 72 C4
Denbury Devon 7 C6
Denby Derbys 76 E3
Denby Dale W Yorks 88 D3
Denchworth Oxon 38 E3
Dendron Cumb 92 B2
Denel End C Beds 53 F8
Denend Aberds 152 E6
Denford Northants 53 B7
Dengie Essex 43 D5
Denham Bucks 40 F3
Denham Suff 55 C8
Denham Suff 57 B5
Denham Street Suff 57 B5
Denhead Aberds 153 C9
Denhead Fife 129 C6
Denhead of Arbilot Angus 135 E5
Denhead of Gray Dundee 134 F3
Denholm Borders 115 C8
Denholme W Yorks 94 F3
Denholme Clough W Yorks 94 F3
Denio Gwyn 70 D4
Denmead Hants 15 C7
Denmore Aberdeen 141 C8
Denmoss Aberds 153 D6
Dennington Suff 57 C6
Denny Falk 127 F7
Denny Lodge Hants 14 D4
Dennyloanhead Falk 127 F7
Denshaw Gtr Man 87 C7
Denside Aberds 141 E7
Densole Kent 31 E6
Denston Suff 55 D8
Denstone Staffs 75 E8
Dent Cumb 100 F2
Denton Cambs 65 F8
Denton Darl 101 C7
Denton E Sus 17 D8
Denton Gtr Man 87 E7
Denton Kent 31 E6
Denton Lincs 77 F8
Denton N Yorks 94 E4
Denton Norf 69 F5
Denton Northants 53 D6
Denton Oxon 39 D5
Denton's Green Mers 86 E2
Denver Norf 67 D6
Denwick Northumb 117 C8
Deopham Norf 68 D3
Deopham Green Norf 68 E3
Depden Suff 55 D8
Depden Green Suff 55 D8
Deptford London 28 B4
Deptford Wilts 24 F5
Derby Derby 76 F3
Derbyhaven IoM 84 F2
Dereham Norf 68 C2
Deri Caerph 35 D5
Derril Devon 8 D5
Derringstone Kent 31 E6
Derrington Staffs 62 B2
Derriton Devon 8 D5
Derry Hill Wilts 24 B4
Derryguaig Argyll 146 H7
Derrythorpe N Lincs 90 D2
Dersingham Norf 80 D2
Dervaig Argyll 146 F7
Derwen Denb 72 D4
Derwenlas Powys 58 E4
Desborough Northants 64 F5
Desford Leics 63 D8
Detchant Northumb 123 F6
Detling Kent 29 D8
Deuddwr Powys 60 C2
Devauden Mon 36 E1
Devil's Bridge Ceredig 47 B6
Devizes Wilts 24 C5
Devol Invclyd 118 B3
Devonport Plym 6 D2
Devonside Clack 127 E8
Devoran Corn 3 C6
Dewar Borders 121 E6
Dewlish Dorset 13 E5
Dewsbury W Yorks 88 B3
Dewsbury Moor W Yorks 88 B3
Dewshall Court Hereford 49 F6
Dhoon IoM 84 D4
Dhoor IoM 84 C4
Dhowin IoM 84 B4
Dial Post W Sus 17 C5
Dibden Hants 14 D5
Dibden Purlieu Hants 14 D5
Dickleburgh Norf 68 F4
Didbrook Glos 51 F5
Didcot Oxon 39 F5
Diddington Cambs 54 C2
Diddlebury Shrops 60 F5
Didley Hereford 49 F6
Didling W Sus 16 C2
Didmarton Glos 37 F5
Didsbury Gtr Man 87 E6
Didworthy Devon 6 C4
Digby Lincs 78 D3
Digg Highld 149 B9
Diggle Gtr Man 87 D8
Digmoor Lancs 86 D2
Digswell Park Herts 41 C5
Dihewyd Ceredig 46 D3
Dilham Norf 69 B6
Dilhorne Staffs 75 E6
Dillarburn S Lanark 119 E8
Dillington Cambs 54 C2
Dilston Northumb 110 C2
Dilton Marsh Wilts 24 E3
Dilwyn Hereford 49 D6
Dinas Carms 45 F4
Dinas Gwyn 70 D3
Dinas Cross Pembs 45 F2
Dinas Dinlle Gwyn 82 F4
Dinas-Mawddwy Gwyn 59 C5
Dinas Powys V Glam 22 B3
Dinbych = Denbigh Denb 72 C4
Dinbych-Y-Pysgod = Tenby Pembs 32 D2
Dinder Som 23 E7
Dinedor Hereford 49 F7
Dingestow Mon 36 C1
Dingle Mers 85 F4
Dingleden Kent 18 B5
Dingley Northants 64 F4
Dingwall Highld 151 F8
Dinlabyre Borders 115 E8
Dinmael Conwy 72 E4
Dinnet Aberds 140 E3
Dinnington S Yorks 89 F6
Dinnington Som 12 C2
Dinnington T&W 110 B5
Dinorwic Gwyn 83 E5
Dinton Bucks 39 C7
Dinton Wilts 24 F5
Dinwoodie Mains Dumfries 114 E4
Dinworthy Devon 8 C5
Dippen N Ayrs 143 F11
Dippenhall Sur 27 E6
Dipple Moray 152 C3
Dipple S Ayrs 112 D2
Diptford Devon 6 D5
Dipton Durham 110 D4
Dirdhu Highld 139 B6
Dirleton E Loth 129 F7
Dirt Pot Northumb 109 E8
Discoed Powys 48 C4
Diseworth Leics 63 B8
Dishes Orkney 159 F7
Dishforth N Yorks 95 B6
Disley Ches E 87 F7
Diss Norf 56 B5
Disserth Powys 48 D2
Distington Cumb 98 B2
Ditchampton Wilts 25 F5
Ditcheat Som 23 F8
Ditchingham Norf 69 E6
Ditchling E Sus 17 C7
Ditherington Shrops 60 C5
Dittisham Devon 7 D6
Ditton Halton 86 F2
Ditton Kent 29 D8
Ditton Green Cambs 55 D7
Ditton Priors Shrops 61 F6
Divach Highld 137 B7
Divlyn Carms 47 F6
Dixton Glos 50 F4
Dixton Mon 36 C2
Dobcross Gtr Man 87 D7
Dobwalls Corn 5 C7
Doc Penfro = Pembroke Dock Pembs 44 E4
Doccombe Devon 10 F2
Dochfour Ho. Highld 151 H9
Dochgarroch Highld 151 G9
Docking Norf 80 D3
Docklow Hereford 49 D7
Dockray Cumb 99 B5
Dockroyd W Yorks 94 F3
Dodburn Borders 115 D7
Doddinghurst Essex 42 E1
Doddington Cambs 66 E3
Doddington Kent 30 D3
Doddington Lincs 78 B2
Doddington Northumb 123 F5
Doddington Shrops 49 B8
Doddiscombsleigh Devon 10 F3
Dodford Northants 52 C4
Dodford Worcs 50 B4
Dodington S Glos 24 A2
Dodleston Ches W 73 C7
Dods Leigh Staffs 75 F7
Dodworth S Yorks 88 D4
Doe Green Warr 86 F3
Doe Lea Derbys 76 C4
Dog Village Devon 10 E4
Dogdyke Lincs 78 D5
Dogmersfield Hants 27 D5
Dogridge Wilts 37 F7
Dogsthorpe Pboro 65 D8
Dol-fôr Powys 58 D5
Dôl-y-Bont Ceredig 58 F3
Dol-y-cannau Powys 48 E4
Dolanog Powys 59 C7
Dolau Powys 48 C3
Dolau Rhondda 34 F3
Dolbenmaen Gwyn 71 C6
Dolfach Powys 59 D6
Dolfor Powys 59 F8
Dolgarrog Conwy 83 E7
Dolgellau Gwyn 58 C4
Dolgran Carms 46 F3
Dolhendre Gwyn 72 F2
Doll Highld 157 J11
Dollar Clack 127 E8
Dolley Green Powys 48 C4
Dollwen Ceredig 58 F3
Dolphin Flint 73 B5
Dolphinholme Lancs 92 D5
Dolphinton S Lanark 120 E4
Dolton Devon 9 C7
Dolwen Conwy 83 D8
Dolwen Powys 59 D6
Dolwyd Conwy 83 D8
Dolwyddelan Conwy 83 F7
Dolyhir Powys 48 D4
Doncaster S Yorks 89 D6
Dones Green Ches W 74 B3
Donhead St Andrew Wilts 13 B7
Donhead St Mary Wilts 13 B7
Donibristle Fife 128 F3
Donington Lincs 78 F5
Donington on Bain Lincs 91 F6
Donington South Ing Lincs 78 F5
Donisthorpe Leics 63 C7
Donkey Town Sur 27 C7
Donnington Glos 38 B1
Donnington Hereford 50 F2
Donnington Shrops 61 D5
Donnington Telford 61 C7
Donnington W Berks 26 C2
Donnington W Sus 16 D2
Donnington Wood Telford 61 C7
Donyatt Som 11 C8
Doonfoot S Ayrs 112 C3
Dorback Lodge Highld 139 C6
Dorchester Dorset 12 E4
Dorchester Oxon 39 E5
Dordon Warks 63 D6
Dore S Yorks 88 F4
Dores Highld 151 H8
Dorking Sur 28 E2
Dormansland Sur 28 E5
Dormanstown Redcar 102 B3
Dormington Hereford 49 E7
Dormston Worcs 50 D4
Dornal S Ayrs 105 B6
Dorney Bucks 27 B7
Dornie Highld 149 F13
Dornoch Highld 151 C10
Dornock Dumfries 108 C2
Dorrery Highld 158 E2
Dorridge W Mid 51 B6
Dorrington Lincs 78 D3
Dorrington Shrops 60 D4
Dorsington Warks 51 E6
Dorstone Hereford 48 E5
Dorton Bucks 39 C6
Dorusduain Highld 136 B2
Dosthill Staffs 63 E6
Dottery Dorset 12 E2
Doublebois Corn 5 C6
Dougarie N Ayrs 143 E9
Doughton Glos 37 E5
Douglas IoM 84 E3
Douglas S Lanark 119 F8
Douglas & Angus Dundee 134 F4
Douglas Water S Lanark 119 F8
Douglas West S Lanark 119 F8
Douglastown Angus 134 E4
Doulting Som 23 E8
Dounby Orkney 159 F3
Doune Highld 156 J7
Doune Stirling 127 D6
Doune Park Aberds 153 B7
Douneside Aberds 140 D3
Dounie Highld 151 B8
Dounreay Highld 157 C12
Dousland Devon 6 C3
Dovaston Shrops 60 B3
Dove Holes Derbys 75 B7
Dovenby Cumb 107 F7
Dover Kent 31 E7
Dovercourt Essex 57 F6
Doverdale Worcs 50 C3
Doveridge Derbys 75 F8
Doversgreen Sur 28 E3
Dowally Perth 133 E7
Dowbridge Lancs 92 F4
Dowdeswell Glos 37 C6
Dowlais M Tydf 34 D4
Dowland Devon 9 C7
Dowlish Wake Som 11 C8
Down Ampney Glos 37 E8
Down Hatherley Glos 37 B5
Down St Mary Devon 10 D2
Down Thomas Devon 6 D3
Downcraig Ferry N Ayrs 145 H10
Downderry Corn 5 D8
Downe London 28 C5
Downend IoW 15 F6
Downend S Glos 23 B8
Downend W Berks 26 B2
Downfield Dundee 134 F3
Downgate Corn 5 B8
Downham Essex 42 E3
Downham Lancs 93 E7
Downham Northumb 122 F4
Downham Market Norf 67 D6
Downhead Som 23 E8
Downhill Perth 133 F7
Downhill T&W 111 D6
Downholland Cross Lancs 85 D4
Downholme N Yorks 101 E6
Downies Aberds 141 E8
Downley Bucks 39 E8
Downside Som 23 E8
Downside Sur 28 D2
Downton Hants 14 E3
Downton Wilts 14 B2
Downton on the Rock Hereford 49 B6
Dowsby Lincs 65 B8
Dowsdale Lincs 66 C2
Dowthwaitehead Cumb 99 B5
Doxey Staffs 62 B3
Doxford Northumb 117 B7
Doxford Park T&W 111 D6
Doynton S Glos 24 B2
Draffan S Lanark 119 E7
Dragonby N Lincs 90 C3
Drakeland Corner Devon 6 D3
Drakemyre N Ayrs 118 D2
Drake's Broughton Worcs 50 E4
Drakes Cross Worcs 51 B5
Drakewalls Corn 6 B2
Draughton N Yorks 94 D3
Draughton Northants 53 B5
Drax N Yorks 89 B7
Draycote Warks 52 B2
Draycott Derbys 76 F4
Draycott Glos 51 F6
Draycott Som 23 D6
Draycott in the Clay Staffs 63 B5
Draycott in the Moors Staffs 75 E6
Drayford Devon 10 C2
Drayton Leics 64 E5
Drayton Lincs 78 F5
Drayton Norf 68 C4
Drayton Oxon 38 E4
Drayton Oxon 52 E2
Drayton Ptsmth 15 D7
Drayton Som 12 B2
Drayton Worcs 50 B4
Drayton Bassett Staffs 63 D5
Drayton Beauchamp Bucks 40 C2
Drayton Parslow Bucks 39 B8
Drayton St Leonard Oxon 39 E5
Dre-fach Carms 33 C7
Dre-fach Ceredig 46 E4
Drebley N Yorks 94 D3
Dreemskerry IoM 84 C4
Dreenhill Pembs 44 D4
Drefach Carms 33 C6
Drefach Carms 46 F2
Drefelin Carms 46 F2
Dreghorn N Ayrs 118 F3
Drellingore Kent 31 E6
Drem E Loth 121 B8
Dresden Stoke 75 E6
Dreumasdal W Isles 148 E2
Drewsteignton Devon 10 E2
Driby Lincs 79 B6
Driffield E Yorks 97 D6
Driffield Glos 37 E7
Drigg Cumb 98 E2
Drighlington W Yorks 88 B3
Drimnin Highld 147 F8
Drimpton Dorset 12 D2
Drimsynie Argyll 125 E7
Drinisiadar W Isles 154 H6
Drinkstone Suff 56 C3
Drinkstone Green Suff 56 C3
Drishaig Argyll 125 D7
Drissaig Argyll 124 D5
Drochil Borders 120 E4
Drointon Staffs 62 B4
Droitwich Spa Worcs 50 C3
Droman Highld 156 D4
Dron Perth 128 C3
Dronfield Derbys 76 B3
Dronfield Woodhouse Derbys 76 B3
Drongan E Ayrs 112 C4
Dronley Angus 134 F3
Droxford Hants 15 C7
Droylsden Gtr Man 87 E7
Druid Denb 72 E4
Druidston Pembs 44 D3
Druimarbin Highld 130 B4
Druimavuic Argyll 130 E4
Druimdrishaig Argyll 144 F6
Druimindarroch Highld 147 C9
Druimyeon More Argyll 143 C7
Drum Argyll 145 F8
Drum Perth 128 D2
Drumbeg Highld 156 F4
Drumblade Aberds 152 D5
Drumblair Aberds 153 D6
Drumbuie Dumfries 113 F5
Drumbuie Highld 149 E12
Drumburgh Cumb 108 D2
Drumburn Dumfries 107 C6
Drumchapel Glasgow 118 B5
Drumchardine Highld 151 G8
Drumchork Highld 155 J13
Drumclog S Lanark 119 F6
Drumderfit Highld 151 F9
Drumeldrie Fife 129 D6
Drumelzier Borders 120 F4
Drumfearn Highld 149 G11
Drumgask Highld 138 E2
Drumgley Angus 134 D4
Drumguish Highld 138 E3
Drumin Moray 152 E1
Drumlasie Aberds 140 D5
Drumlemble Argyll 143 G7
Drumligair Aberds 141 C8
Drumlithie Aberds 141 F6
Drummoddie Dumfries 105 E7
Drummond Highld 151 E9
Drummore Dumfries 104 F5
Drummuir Moray 152 D3
Drummuir Castle Moray 152 D3
Drumnadrochit Highld 137 B8
Drumnagorrach Moray 152 C5
Drumoak Aberds 141 E6
Drumpark Dumfries 107 A5
Drumphail Dumfries 105 C6
Drumrash Dumfries 106 B3
Drumrunie Highld 156 J4
Drums Aberds 141 B8
Drumsallie Highld 130 B3
Drumstinchall Dumfries 107 D5
Drumsturdy Angus 134 F4
Drumtochty Castle Aberds 135 B6
Drumtroddan Dumfries 105 E7
Drumuie Highld 149 D9
Drumuillie Highld 138 B5
Drumvaich Stirling 127 D5
Drumwhindle Aberds 153 E9
Drunkendub Angus 135 E6
Drury Flint 73 C6
Drury Square Norf 68 C2
Dry Doddington Lincs 77 E8
Dry Drayton Cambs 54 C4
Drybeck Cumb 100 C1
Drybridge Moray 152 B4
Drybridge N Ayrs 118 F3
Drybrook Glos 36 C3
Dryburgh Borders 121 F8
Dryhope Borders 115 B5
Drylaw Edin 120 B5
Drym Corn 2 C5
Drymen Stirling 126 F3
Drymuir Aberds 153 D9
Drynoch Highld 149 E9
Dryslwyn Carms 33 B6
Dryton Shrops 61 D5
Dubford Aberds 153 B8
Dubton Angus 135 D5
Duchally Highld 156 H6
Duchlage Argyll 126 F2
Duck Corner Suff 57 E7
Duckington Ches W 73 D8
Ducklington Oxon 38 D3
Duckmanton Derbys 76 B4
Duck's Cross Bedford 54 D2
Duddenhoe End Essex 55 F5
Duddingston Edin 121 B5
Duddington Northants 65 D6
Duddleswell E Sus 17 B8
Duddo Northumb 122 E5
Duddon Ches W 74 C2
Duddon Bridge Cumb 98 F4
Dudleston Shrops 73 F7
Dudleston Heath Shrops 73 F7
Dudley T&W 111 B5
Dudley W Mid 62 E3
Dudley Port W Mid 62 E3
Duffield Derbys 76 E3
Duffryn Neath 34 E2
Duffryn Newport 35 F6
Dufftown Moray 152 E3
Duffus Moray 152 B1
Dufton Cumb 100 B1
Duggleby N Yorks 96 C4
Duirinish Highld 149 E12
Duisdalemore Highld 149 G12
Duisky Highld 130 B4
Dukestown Bl Gwent 35 C5
Dukinfield Gtr Man 87 E7
Dulas Anglesey 82 C4
Dulcote Som 23 E7
Dulford Devon 11 D5
Dull Perth 133 E5
Dullatur N Lanark 119 B7
Dullingham Cambs 55 D7
Dulnain Bridge Highld 139 B5
Duloe Bedford 54 C2
Duloe Corn 5 D7
Dulsie Highld 151 G12
Dulverton Som 10 B4
Dulwich London 28 B4
Dumbarton W Dunb 118 B3
Dumbleton Glos 50 F5
Dumcrieff Dumfries 114 D4
Dumfries Dumfries 107 B6
Dumgoyne Stirling 126 F4
Dummer Hants 26 E3
Dumpford W Sus 16 B2
Dumpton Kent 31 C7
Dun Angus 135 D6
Dun Charlabhaigh W Isles 154 C6
Dunain Ho. Highld 151 G9
Dunalastair Perth 132 D4
Dunan Highld 149 F10
Dunans Argyll 145 D9
Dunball Som 22 E5
Dunbar E Loth 122 B2
Dunbeath Highld 158 H3
Dunbeg Argyll 124 B4
Dunblane Stirling 127 D6
Dunbog Fife 128 C4
Duncanston Highld 151 F8
Duncanstone Aberds 140 B4
Dunchurch Warks 52 B2
Duncote Northants 52 D4
Duncow Dumfries 114 F2
Duncraggan Stirling 126 D4
Duncrievie Perth 128 D3
Duncton W Sus 16 C3
Dundas Ho. Orkney 159 K5
Dundee Dundee 134 F4
Dundeugh Dumfries 113 F5
Dundon Som 23 F6
Dundonald S Ayrs 118 F3
Dundonnell Highld 150 C3
Dundonnell Hotel Highld 150 C3
Dundonnell House Highld 150 C4
Dundraw Cumb 108 E2
Dundreggan Highld 137 C6
Dundreggan Lodge Highld 137 C6
Dundrennan Dumfries 106 E4
Dundry N Som 23 C7
Dunecht Aberds 141 D6
Dunfermline Fife 128 F2
Dunfield Glos 37 E8
Dunford Bridge S Yorks 88 D2
Dungworth S Yorks 88 F3
Dunham Notts 77 B8
Dunham-on-the-Hill Ches W 73 B8

E

F

Felingwm uchaf Carms 33 B6
Felinwynt Ceredig 45 D4
Felixkirk N Yorks 102 F2
Felixstowe Suff 57 F6
Felixstowe Ferry Suff 57 F7
Felkington Northumb 122 E5
Felkirk W Yorks 88 C4
Fell Side Cumb 108 F3
Felling T&W 111 C5
Felmersham Bedford 53 D7
Felmingham Norf 81 E8
Felpham W Sus 16 E3
Felsham Suff 56 D3
Felsted Essex 42 B2
Feltham London 28 B2
Felthorpe Norf 68 C4
Felton Hereford 49 E7
Felton N Som 23 C7
Felton Northumb 117 D7
Felton Butler Shrops 60 C3
Feltwell Norf 67 E7
Fen Ditton Cambs 55 C5
Fen Drayton Cambs 54 C4
Fen End W Mid 51 B7
Fen Side Lincs 79 D6
Fenay Bridge W Yorks 88 C2
Fence Lancs 93 F8
Fence Houses T&W 111 D6
Fengate Norf 81 E7
Fengate Pboro 66 E2
Fenham Northumb 123 E6
Fenhouses Lincs 79 E5
Feniscliffe Blackburn 86 B4
Feniscowles Blackburn 86 B4
Feniton Devon 11 E6
Fenlake Bedford 53 E8
Fenny Bentley Derbys 75 D8
Fenny Bridges Devon 11 E6
Fenny Compton Warks 52 D2
Fenny Drayton Leics 63 E7
Fenny Stratford M Keynes 53 F6
Fenrother Northumb 117 E7
Fenstanton Cambs 54 C4
Fenton Cambs 54 B4
Fenton Lincs 77 B8
Fenton Lincs 77 D8
Fenton Stoke 75 E5
Fenton Barns E Loth 129 F7
Fenton Town Northumb 123 F5
Fenwick E Ayrs 118 E4
Fenwick Northumb 110 B3
Fenwick Northumb 123 E6
Fenwick S Yorks 89 C6
Feochaig Argyll 143 G8
Feock Corn 3 C7
Feolin Ferry Argyll 144 G3
Ferindonald Highld 149 H11
Feriniquarrie Highld 148 C6
Ferlochan Argyll 138 E3
Fern Angus 134 C4
Ferndale Rhondda 34 E4
Ferndown Dorset 13 D8
Ferness Highld 151 G12
Ferney Green Cumb 99 E6
Fernham Oxon 38 E2
Fernhill Heath Worcs 50 D3
Fernhurst W Sus 16 B2
Fernie Fife 128 C5
Ferniegair S Lanark 119 D7
Fernilea Highld 149 E8
Fernilee Derbys 75 B7
Ferrensby N Yorks 95 C6
Ferring W Sus 16 D4
Ferry Hill Cambs 66 F3
Ferry Point Highld 151 C10
Ferrybridge W Yorks 89 B5
Ferryden Angus 135 D7
Ferryhill Aberdeen 141 D8
Ferryhill Durham 111 F5
Ferryhill Station Durham 111 F6
Ferryside Carms 32 C4
Fersfield Norf 68 F3
Fersit Highld 131 B7
Ferwig Ceredig 45 E3
Feshiebridge Highld 138 D4
Fetcham Sur 28 D2
Fetterangus Aberds 153 C9
Fettercairn Aberds 135 B6
Fettes Highld 151 F8
Fewcott Oxon 39 B5
Fewston N Yorks 94 D4
Ffair-Rhos Ceredig 47 C6
Ffairfach Carms 33 B7
Ffaldybrenin Carms 46 E5
Ffarmers Carms 47 E5
Ffawyddog Powys 35 C6
Fforest Carms 33 D6
Fforest-fâch Swansea 33 E7
Ffos-y-ffin Ceredig 46 C3
Ffostrasol Ceredig 46 E2
Ffridd-Uchaf Gwyn 83 F5
Ffrith Wrex 73 D6
Ffrwd Gwyn 82 F4
Ffynnon ddrain Carms 33 B5
Ffynnon-oer Ceredig 46 D4
Ffynnongroyw Flint 85 F2
Fidden Argyll 146 J6
Fiddes Aberds 141 F7
Fiddington Glos 50 F4
Fiddington Som 22 E4
Fiddleford Dorset 13 C6
Fiddlers Hamlet Essex 41 D7
Field Staffs 75 F7
Field Broughton Cumb 99 F5
Field Dalling Norf 81 D6
Field Head Leics 63 D8
Fifehead Magdalen Dorset 13 B5
Fifehead Neville Dorset 13 C5
Fifield Oxon 38 C2
Fifield Wilts 25 D6
Fifield Windsor 27 B7
Fifield Bavant Wilts 13 B8
Figheldean Wilts 25 E6
Filands Wilts 37 F6
Filby Norf 69 C7
Filey N Yorks 97 A7
Filgrave M Keynes 53 E6
Filkins Oxon 38 D2
Filleigh Devon 9 B8
Filleigh Devon 10 C2
Fillingham Lincs 90 F3
Fillongley Warks 63 F6
Filton S Glos 23 B8
Fimber E Yorks 96 C4
Finavon Angus 134 D4
Finchairn Argyll 124 E5
Fincham Norf 67 D6
Finchampstead Wokingham 27 C5
Finchdean Hants 15 C8
Finchingfield Essex 55 F7
Finchley London 41 E5
Findern Derbys 76 F3
Findhorn Moray 151 E13
Findhorn Bridge Highld 138 B4
Findo Gask Perth 128 B2
Findochty Moray 152 B4
Findon Aberds 141 E8
Findon W Sus 16 D5
Findon Mains Highld 151 E9
Findrack Ho. Aberds 140 D5
Finedon Northants 53 B7
Fingal Street Suff 57 C6
Fingask Aberds 141 B6
Fingerpost Worcs 50 B2
Fingest Bucks 39 E7
Finghall N Yorks 101 F6
Fingland Cumb 108 D2
Fingland Dumfries 113 C7
Finglesham Kent 31 D7
Fingringhoe Essex 43 B6
Finlarig Stirling 132 F2
Finmere Oxon 52 F4
Finnart Perth 132 D2
Finningham Suff 56 C4
Finningley S Yorks 89 E7
Finnygaud Aberds 152 C5
Finsbury London 41 F6
Finstall Worcs 50 C4
Finsthwaite Cumb 99 F5
Finstock Oxon 38 C3
Finstown Orkney 159 G4
Fintry Aberds 153 C7
Fintry Dundee 134 F4
Fintry Stirling 126 F5
Finzean Aberds 140 E5
Fionnphort Argyll 146 J6
Fionnsbhagh W Isles 154 J5
Fir Tree Durham 110 F4
Firbeck S Yorks 89 F6
Firby N Yorks 96 C3
Firby N Yorks 101 F7
Firgrove Gtr Man 87 C7
Firsby Lincs 79 C7
Firsdown Wilts 25 F7
First Coast Highld 150 B2
Fishbourne IoW 15 E6
Fishbourne W Sus 16 D2
Fishburn Durham 111 F6
Fishcross Clack 127 E7
Fisher Place Cumb 99 C5
Fisherford Aberds 153 E6
Fisher's Pond Hants 15 B5
Fisherstreet W Sus 27 F7
Fisherton Highld 151 F10
Fisherton S Ayrs 112 C2
Fishguard = Abergwaun Pembs 44 B4
Fishlake S Yorks 89 C7
Fishleigh Barton Devon 9 B7
Fishponds Bristol 23 B8
Fishpool Glos 36 B3
Fishtoft Lincs 79 E6
Fishtoft Drove Lincs 79 E6
Fishtown of Usan Angus 135 D7
Fishwick Borders 122 D5
Fiskavaig Highld 149 E8
Fiskerton Lincs 78 B3
Fiskerton Notts 77 D7
Fitling E Yorks 97 F8
Fittleton Wilts 25 E6
Fittleworth W Sus 16 C4
Fitton End Cambs 66 C4
Fitz Shrops 60 C4
Fitzhead Som 11 B6
Fitzwilliam W Yorks 88 C5
Fiunary Highld 147 G9
Five Acres Glos 36 C2
Five Ashes E Sus 18 C2
Five Oak Green Kent 29 E7
Five Oaks Jersey 17
Five Oaks W Sus 16 B4
Five Roads Carms 33 D5
Fivecrosses Ches W 74 B2
Fivehead Som 11 B8
Flack's Green Essex 42 C3
Flackwell Heath Bucks 40 F1
Fladbury Worcs 50 E4
Fladdabister Shetland 160 K6
Flagg Derbys 75 C8
Flamborough E Yorks 97 B8
Flamstead Herts 40 C3
Flamstead End Herts 41 D6
Flansham W Sus 16 D3
Flanshaw W Yorks 88 B4
Flasby N Yorks 94 D2
Flash Staffs 75 C7
Flashader Highld 149 C8
Flask Inn N Yorks 103 D7
Flaunden Herts 40 D3
Flawborough Notts 77 E7
Flawith N Yorks 95 C7
Flax Bourton N Som 23 C7
Flaxby N Yorks 95 D6
Flaxholme Derbys 76 E3
Flaxley Glos 36 C3
Flaxpool Som 22 F3
Flaxton N Yorks 96 C2
Fleckney Leics 64 E3
Flecknoe Warks 52 C3
Fledborough Notts 77 B8
Fleet Hants 15 D8
Fleet Hants 27 D6
Fleet Lincs 66 B3
Fleet Hargate Lincs 66 B3
Fleetham Northumb 117 B7
Fleetlands Hants 15 D6
Fleetville Herts 40 D4
Fleetwood Lancs 92 E3
Flemingston V Glam 22 B2
Flemington S Lanark 119 D6
Flempton Suff 56 C2
Fleoideabhagh W Isles 154 J5
Fletchertown Cumb 108 E2
Fletching E Sus 17 B8
Flexbury Corn 8 D4
Flexford Sur 27 E7
Flimby Cumb 107 F7
Flimwell E Sus 18 B4
Flint = Y Fflint Flint 73 B6
Flint Mountain Flint 73 B6
Flintham Notts 77 E7
Flinton E Yorks 97 F8
Flintsham Hereford 48 D5
Flitcham Norf 80 E3
Flitton C Beds 53 F8
Flitwick C Beds 53 F8
Flixborough N Lincs 90 C2
Flixborough Stather N Lincs 90 C2
Flixton Gtr Man 86 E5
Flixton N Yorks 97 B6
Flixton Suff 69 F6
Flockton W Yorks 88 C3
Flodaigh W Isles 148 C3
Flodden Northumb 122 F5
Flodigarry Highld 149 A9
Flood's Ferry Cambs 66 E3
Flookburgh Cumb 92 B3
Florden Norf 68 E4
Flore Northants 52 C4
Flotterton Northumb 117 D5
Flowton Suff 56 E4
Flush House W Yorks 88 D2
Flushing Aberds 153 D10
Flushing Corn 3 C7
Flyford Flavell Worcs 50 D4
Foals Green Suff 57 B6
Fobbing Thurrock 42 F3
Fochabers Moray 152 C3
Fochriw Caerph 35 D5
Fockerby N Lincs 90 C2
Fodderletter Moray 139 B7
Fodderty Highld 151 F8
Foel Powys 59 C6
Foel-gastell Carms 33 C6
Foffarty Angus 134 E4
Foggathorpe E Yorks 96 F3
Fogo Borders 122 E3
Fogorig Borders 122 E3
Foindle Highld 156 E4
Folda Angus 134 C1
Fole Staffs 75 F7
Foleshill W Mid 63 F7
Folke Dorset 12 C4
Folkestone Kent 31 F6
Folkingham Lincs 78 F3
Folkington E Sus 18 E2
Folksworth Cambs 65 F8
Folkton N Yorks 97 B6
Folla Rule Aberds 153 E7
Follifoot N Yorks 95 D6
Folly Gate Devon 9 E7
Fonthill Bishop Wilts 24 F4
Fonthill Gifford Wilts 24 F4
Fontmell Magna Dorset 13 C6
Fontwell W Sus 16 D3
Foolow Derbys 75 B8
Foots Cray London 29 B5
Forbestown Aberds 140 C2
Force Mills Cumb 99 E5
Forcett N Yorks 101 C6
Ford Argyll 124 E4
Ford Bucks 39 D7
Ford Devon 9 B6
Ford Glos 37 B7
Ford Northumb 122 F5
Ford Shrops 60 C4
Ford Staffs 75 D7
Ford W Sus 16 D3
Ford Wilts 24 B3
Ford End Essex 42 C2
Ford Street Som 11 C6
Fordcombe Kent 29 E6
Fordell Fife 128 F3
Forden Powys 60 D2
Forder Green Devon 7 C5
Fordham Cambs 55 B7
Fordham Essex 43 B5
Fordham Norf 67 E6
Fordhouses W Mid 62 D3
Fordingbridge Hants 14 C2
Fordon E Yorks 97 B6
Fordoun Aberds 135 B7
Ford's Green Suff 56 C4
Fordstreet Essex 43 B5
Fordwells Oxon 38 C3
Fordwich Kent 31 D5
Fordyce Aberds 152 B5
Forebridge Staffs 62 B3
Forest Durham 109 F8
Forest Becks Lancs 93 D7
Forest Gate London 41 F7
Forest Green Sur 28 E2
Forest Hall Cumb 99 D7
Forest Head Cumb 109 D5
Forest Hill Oxon 39 D5
Forest Lane Head N Yorks 95 D6
Forest Lodge Argyll 131 E6
Forest Lodge Highld 139 C6
Forest Lodge Perth 133 B6
Forest Mill Clack 127 E8
Forest Row E Sus 28 F5
Forest Town Notts 77 C5
Forestburn Gate Northumb 117 E6
Foresterseat Moray 152 C1
Forestside W Sus 15 C8
Forfar Angus 134 D4
Forgandenny Perth 128 C2
Forge Powys 58 E4
Forge Side Torf 35 D6
Forgewood N Lanark 119 D7
Forgie Moray 152 C3
Forglen Ho. Aberds 153 C6
Formby Mers 85 D4
Forncett End Norf 68 E4
Forncett St Mary Norf 68 E4
Forncett St Peter Norf 68 E4
Forneth Perth 133 E7
Fornham All Saints Suff 56 C2
Fornham St Martin Suff 56 C2
Forres Moray 151 F13
Forrest Lodge Dumfries 113 F5
Forrestfield N Lanark 119 C8
Forsbrook Staffs 75 E6
Forse Highld 158 G4
Forse Ho. Highld 158 G4
Forsinain Highld 157 E12
Forsinard Highld 157 E11
Forsinard Station Highld 157 E11
Forston Dorset 12 E4
Fort Augustus Highld 137 D6
Fort George Guern 16
Fort George Highld 151 F10
Fort William Highld 131 B5
Forteviot Perth 128 C2
Forth S Lanark 120 D2
Forth Road Bridge Edin 120 B4
Forthampton Glos 50 F3
Fortingall Perth 132 E4
Forton Hants 26 E2
Forton Lancs 92 D4
Forton Shrops 60 C4
Forton Som 11 D8
Forton Staffs 61 B7
Forton Heath Shrops 60 C4
Fortrie Aberds 153 D6
Fortrose Highld 151 F10
Fortuneswell Dorset 12 G4
Forty Green Bucks 40 E2
Forty Hill London 41 E6
Forward Green Suff 56 D4
Fosbury Wilts 25 D8
Fosdyke Lincs 79 F6
Foss Perth 132 D4
Foss Cross Glos 37 D7
Fossebridge Glos 37 C7
Foster Street Essex 41 D7
Fosterhouses S Yorks 89 C7
Foston Derbys 75 F8
Foston Lincs 77 E8
Foston N Yorks 96 C2
Foston on the Wolds E Yorks 97 D7
Fotherby Lincs 91 E7
Fotheringhay Northants 65 E7
Foubister Orkney 159 H6
Foul Mile E Sus 18 D3
Foulby W Yorks 88 C4
Foulden Borders 122 D5
Foulden Norf 67 E7
Foulis Castle Highld 151 E8
Foulridge Lancs 93 E8
Foulsham Norf 81 E6
Fountainhall Borders 121 E7
Four Ashes Staffs 62 F2
Four Ashes Suff 56 B4
Four Crosses Powys 59 D7
Four Crosses Powys 60 C2
Four Crosses Wrex 73 D6
Four Elms Kent 29 E5
Four Forks Som 22 F4
Four Gotes Cambs 66 C4
Four Lane Ends Ches W 74 C2
Four Lanes Corn 3 C5
Four Marks Hants 26 F4
Four Mile Bridge Anglesey 82 D2
Four Oaks E Sus 19 C5
Four Oaks W Mid 62 E5
Four Oaks W Mid 63 F6
Four Roads Carms 33 D5
Four Roads IoM 84 F2
Four Throws Kent 18 C4
Fourlane Ends Derbys 76 D3
Fourlanes End Ches E 74 D5
Fourpenny Highld 151 B11
Fourstones Northumb 109 C8
Fovant Wilts 13 B8
Foveran Aberds 141 B8
Fowey Corn 5 D6
Fowley Common Warr 86 E4
Fowlis Angus 134 F3
Fowlis Wester Perth 127 B8
Fowlmere Cambs 54 E5
Fownhope Hereford 49 F7
Fox Corner Sur 27 D7
Fox Lane Hants 27 D6
Fox Street Essex 43 B6
Foxbar Renfs 118 C4
Foxcombe Hill Oxon 38 D4
Foxdale IoM 84 E2
Foxearth Essex 56 E2
Foxfield Cumb 98 F4
Foxham Wilts 24 B4
Foxhole Corn 4 D4
Foxhole Swansea 33 E7
Foxholes N Yorks 97 B6
Foxhunt Green E Sus 18 D2
Foxley Norf 81 E6
Foxley Wilts 37 F5
Foxt Staffs 75 E7
Foxton Cambs 54 E5
Foxton Durham 102 B1
Foxton Leics 64 E4
Foxup N Yorks 93 B8
Foxwist Green Ches W 74 C3
Foxwood Shrops 49 B8
Foy Hereford 36 B2
Foyers Highld 137 B7
Fraddam Corn 2 C4
Fraddon Corn 4 D4
Fradley Staffs 63 C5
Fradswell Staffs 75 F6
Fraisthorpe E Yorks 97 C7
Framfield E Sus 17 B8
Framingham Earl Norf 69 D5
Framingham Pigot Norf 69 D5
Framlingham Suff 57 C6
Frampton Dorset 12 E4
Frampton Lincs 79 F6
Frampton Cotterell S Glos 36 F3
Frampton Mansell Glos 37 D6
Frampton on Severn Glos 36 D4
Frampton West End Lincs 79 E5
Framsden Suff 57 D5
Framwellgate Moor Durham 111 E5
Franche Worcs 50 B3
Frankby Mers 85 F3
Frankley Worcs 62 F3
Frank's Bridge Powys 48 D3
Frankton Warks 52 B2
Frant E Sus 18 B2
Fraserburgh Aberds 153 B9
Frating Green Essex 43 B6
Fratton Ptsmth 15 E7
Freathy Corn 5 D8
Freckenham Suff 55 B7
Freckleton Lancs 86 B2
Freeby Leics 64 B5
Freehay Staffs 75 E7
Freeland Oxon 38 C4
Freester Shetland 160 H6
Freethorpe Norf 69 D7
Freiston Lincs 79 E6
Fremington Devon 20 F4
Fremington N Yorks 101 E5
Frenchay S Glos 23 B8
Frenchbeer Devon 9 F8
Frenich Stirling 126 D3
Frensham Sur 27 E6
Fresgoe Highld 157 C12
Freshfield Mers 85 D3
Freshford Bath 24 C2
Freshwater IoW 14 F4
Freshwater Bay IoW 14 F4
Freshwater East Pembs 32 E1
Fressingfield Suff 57 B6
Freston Suff 57 F5
Freswick Highld 158 D5
Fretherne Glos 36 D4
Frettenham Norf 68 C5
Freuchie Fife 128 D4
Freuchies Angus 134 C2
Freystrop Pembs 44 D4
Friar's Gate E Sus 29 F5
Friarton Perth 128 B3
Friday Bridge Cambs 66 D4
Friday Street E Sus 18 E3
Fridaythorpe E Yorks 96 D4
Friern Barnet London 41 E5
Friesland Argyll 146 F4
Friesthorpe Lincs 90 F4
Frieston Lincs 78 E2
Frieth Bucks 39 E7
Frilford Oxon 38 E4
Frilsham W Berks 26 B3
Frimley Sur 27 D6
Frimley Green Sur 27 D6
Frindsbury Medway 29 B8
Fring Norf 80 D3
Fringford Oxon 39 B6
Frinsted Kent 30 D2
Frinton-on-Sea Essex 43 B8
Friockheim Angus 135 E5
Friog Gwyn 58 C3
Frisby on the Wreake Leics 64 C3
Friskney Lincs 79 D7
Friskney Eaudike Lincs 79 D7
Friskney Tofts Lincs 79 D7
Friston E Sus 18 F2
Friston Suff 57 C8
Fritchley Derbys 76 D3
Frith Bank Lincs 79 E6
Frith Common Worcs 49 C8
Fritham Hants 14 C3
Frithelstock Devon 9 C6
Frithelstock Stone Devon 9 C6
Frithville Lincs 79 D6
Frittenden Kent 30 E2
Frittiscombe Devon 7 E6
Fritton Norf 68 E5
Fritton Norf 69 D7
Fritwell Oxon 39 B5
Frizinghall W Yorks 94 F4
Frizington Cumb 98 C2
Frocester Glos 36 D4
Frodesley Shrops 60 D5
Frodingham N Lincs 90 C2
Frodsham Ches W 74 B2
Frogden Borders 116 B3
Froggatt Derbys 76 B2
Froghall Staffs 75 E7
Frogmore Devon 7 E5
Frogmore Hants 27 D6
Frognall Lincs 65 C8
Frogshail Norf 81 D8
Frolesworth Leics 64 E2
Frome Som 24 E2
Frome St Quintin Dorset 12 D3
Fromes Hill Hereford 49 E8
Fron Denb 72 C4
Fron Gwyn 70 D4
Fron Gwyn 82 F5
Fron Powys 48 C2
Fron Powys 59 E8
Fron Powys 60 D2
Froncysyllte Wrex 73 E6
Frongoch Gwyn 72 F3
Frostenden Suff 69 F7
Frosterley Durham 110 F3
Frotoft Orkney 159 F5
Froxfield Wilts 25 C7
Froxfield Green Hants 15 B8
Froyle Hants 27 E5
Fryerning Essex 42 D2
Fryton N Yorks 96 B2
Fulbeck Lincs 78 D2
Fulbourn Cambs 55 D6
Fulbrook Oxon 38 C2
Fulford Som 11 B7
Fulford Staffs 75 F6
Fulford York 96 E2
Fulham London 28 B3
Fulking W Sus 17 C6
Full Sutton E Yorks 96 D3
Fullarton Glasgow 119 C6
Fullarton N Ayrs 118 F3
Fuller Street Essex 42 C3
Fuller's Moor Ches W 73 D8
Fullerton Hants 25 F8
Fulletby Lincs 79 B5
Fullwood E Ayrs 118 D4
Fulmer Bucks 40 F2
Fulmodestone Norf 81 D5
Fulnetby Lincs 78 B3
Fulstow Lincs 91 E7
Fulwell T&W 111 D6
Fulwood Lancs 92 F5
Fulwood S Yorks 88 F4
Fundenhall Norf 68 E4
Fundenhall Street Norf 68 E4
Funtington W Sus 15 D8
Funtley Hants 15 D6
Funtullich Perth 127 B6
Funzie Shetland 160 D8
Furley Devon 11 D7
Furnace Argyll 125 E6
Furnace Carms 33 D6
Furnace End Warks 63 E6
Furneaux Pelham Herts 41 B7
Furness Vale Derbys 87 F8
Furze Platt Windsor 40 F1
Furzehill Devon 21 E6
Fyfett Som 11 C7
Fyfield Essex 42 D1
Fyfield Glos 38 D2
Fyfield Hants 25 E7
Fyfield Oxon 38 E4
Fyfield Wilts 25 C6
Fylingthorpe N Yorks 103 D7
Fyvie Aberds 153 E7

G

Gabhsann bho Dheas W Isles 155 B9
Gabhsann bho Thuath W Isles 155 B9
Gablon Highld 151 B10
Gabroc Hill E Ayrs 118 D4
Gaddesby Leics 64 C3
Gadebridge Herts 40 D3
Gaer Powys 35 B5
Gaerllwyd Mon 35 E8
Gaerwen Anglesey 82 D4
Gagingwell Oxon 38 B4
Gaick Lodge Highld 138 F3
Gailey Staffs 62 C3
Gainford Durham 101 C6
Gainsborough Lincs 90 E2
Gainsborough Suff 57 E5
Gainsford End Essex 55 F8
Gairloch Highld 149 A13
Gairlochy Highld 136 F4
Gairney Bank Perth 128 E3
Gairnshiel Lodge Aberds 139 D8
Gaisgill Cumb 99 D8
Gaitsgill Cumb 108 E3
Galashiels Borders 121 F7
Galgate Lancs 92 D4
Galhampton Som 12 B4
Gallaberry Dumfries 114 F2
Gallachoille Argyll 144 E6
Gallanach Argyll 124 C4
Gallanach Argyll 146 E5
Gallantry Bank Ches E 74 D2
Gallatown Fife 128 E4
Galley Common Warks 63 E7
Galley Hill Cambs 54 C4
Galleyend Essex 42 D3
Galleywood Essex 42 D3
Gallin Perth 132 E2
Gallowfauld Angus 134 E4
Gallows Green Staffs 75 E7
Galltair Highld 149 F13
Galmisdale Highld 146 C7
Galmpton Devon 6 E4
Galmpton Torbay 7 D6
Galphay N Yorks 95 B5
Galston E Ayrs 118 F5
Galtrigill Highld 148 C6
Gamblesby Cumb 109 F6
Gamesley Derbys 87 E8
Gamlingay Cambs 54 D3
Gammersgill N Yorks 101 F5
Gamston Notts 77 B7
Ganarew Hereford 36 C2
Ganavan Argyll 124 B4
Gang Corn 5 C8
Ganllwyd Gwyn 71 E8
Gannochy Angus 135 B5
Gannochy Perth 128 B3
Gansclet Highld 158 F5
Ganstead E Yorks 97 F7
Ganthorpe N Yorks 96 B2
Ganton N Yorks 97 B5
Garbat Highld 150 E7
Garbhallt Argyll 125 F6
Garboldisham Norf 68 F3
Garden City Flint 73 C7
Garden Village W Yorks 95 F7
Garden Village Wrex 73 D7
Gardenstown Aberds 153 B7
Garderhouse Shetland 160 J5
Gardham E Yorks 97 E5
Gardin Shetland 160 G6
Gare Hill Som 24 E2
Garelochhead Argyll 145 D11
Garford Oxon 38 E4
Garforth W Yorks 95 F7
Gargrave N Yorks 94 D2
Gargunnock Stirling 127 E6
Garlic Street Norf 68 F5
Garlieston Dumfries 105 E8
Garlinge Green Kent 30 D5
Garlogie Aberds 141 D6
Garmond Aberds 153 C8
Garmony Argyll 147 G9
Garmouth Moray 152 B3
Garn-yr-erw Torf 35 C6
Garnant Carms 33 C7
Garndiffaith Torf 35 D6
Garndolbenmaen Gwyn 71 C5
Garnedd Conwy 83 F7
Garnett Bridge Cumb 99 E7
Garnfadryn Gwyn 70 D3
Garnkirk N Lanark 119 C6
Garnlydan Bl Gwent 35 C5
Garnswllt Swansea 33 D7
Garrabost W Isles 155 D10
Garraron Argyll 124 E4
Garras Corn 3 D6
Garreg Gwyn 71 C7
Garrick Perth 127 C7
Garrigill Cumb 109 E7
Garriston N Yorks 101 E6
Garroch Dumfries 113 F5
Garrogie Lodge Highld 137 C8
Garros Highld 149 B9
Garrow Perth 133 E5
Garryhorn Dumfries 113 E5
Garsdale Cumb 100 F2
Garsdale Head Cumb 100 E2
Garsdon Wilts 37 F6
Garshall Green Staffs 75 F6
Garsington Oxon 39 D5
Garstang Lancs 92 E4
Garston Mers 86 F2
Garswood Mers 86 E3
Gartcosh N Lanark 119 C6
Garth Bridgend 34 E2
Garth Gwyn 83 D5
Garth Powys 47 E8
Garth Shetland 160 H4
Garth Wrex 73 E6
Garth Row Cumb 99 E7
Garthamlock Glasgow 119 C6
Garthbrengy Powys 48 F2
Garthdee Aberdeen 141 D8
Gartheli Ceredig 46 D4
Garthmyl Powys 59 E8
Garthorpe Leics 64 B5
Garthorpe N Lincs 90 C2
Gartly Aberds 152 E5
Gartmore Stirling 126 E4
Gartnagrenach Argyll 144 H6
Gartness N Lanark 119 C7
Gartness Stirling 126 F4
Gartocharn W Dunb 126 F3
Garton E Yorks 97 F8
Garton-on-the-Wolds E Yorks 97 D5
Gartsherrie N Lanark 119 C7
Gartymore Highld 157 H13
Garvald E Loth 121 B8
Garvamore Highld 137 E8
Garvard Argyll 144 D2
Garvault Hotel Highld 157 F10
Garve Highld 150 E6
Garvestone Norf 68 D3
Garvock Aberds 135 B7
Garvock Invclyd 118 B2
Garway Hereford 36 B1
Garway Hill Hereford 35 B8
Gaskan Highld 130 B1
Gastard Wilts 24 C3
Gasthorpe Norf 68 F2
Gatcombe IoW 15 F5
Gate Burton Lincs 90 F2
Gate Helmsley N Yorks 96 D2
Gateacre Mers 86 F2
Gatebeck Cumb 99 F7
Gateford Notts 89 F6
Gateforth N Yorks 89 B6
Gatehead E Ayrs 118 F3
Gatehouse Northumb 116 F3
Gatehouse of Fleet Dumfries 106 D3
Gatelawbridge Dumfries 114 E2
Gateley Norf 81 E5
Gatenby N Yorks 101 F8
Gateshead T&W 111 C5
Gatesheath Ches W 73 C8
Gateside Aberds 140 C5
Gateside Angus 134 E4
Gateside E Renf 118 D4
Gateside Fife 128 D3
Gateside N Ayrs 118 D3
Gathurst Gtr Man 86 D3
Gatley Gtr Man 87 F6
Gattonside Borders 121 F8
Gatwick Airport W Sus 28 E3
Gaufron Powys 47 C8
Gaulby Leics 64 D3
Gauldry Fife 129 B5
Gaunt's Common Dorset 13 D8
Gautby Lincs 78 B4
Gavinton Borders 122 D3
Gawber S Yorks 88 D4
Gawcott Bucks 52 F4
Gawsworth Ches E 75 C5
Gawthorpe W Yorks 88 B3
Gawthrop Cumb 100 F1
Gawthwaite Cumb 98 F4
Gay Street W Sus 16 B4
Gaydon Warks 51 D8
Gayfield Orkney 159 C5
Gayhurst M Keynes 53 E6
Gayle N Yorks 100 F3
Gayles N Yorks 101 D6
Gayton Mers 85 F3
Gayton Norf 67 C7
Gayton Northants 52 D5
Gayton Staffs 62 B3
Gayton le Marsh Lincs 91 F8
Gayton le Wold Lincs 91 F6
Gayton Thorpe Norf 67 C7
Gaywood Norf 67 B6
Gazeley Suff 55 C8
Geanies House Highld 151 D11
Gearraidh Bhailteas W Isles 148 F2
Gearraidh Bhaird W Isles 155 E8
Gearraidh na h-Aibhne W Isles 154 D7
Gearraidh na Monadh W Isles 148 G2
Geary Highld 148 B7
Geddes House Highld 151 F11
Gedding Suff 56 D3
Geddington Northants 65 F5
Gedintailor Highld 149 E10
Gedling Notts 77 E6
Gedney Lincs 66 B4
Gedney Broadgate Lincs 66 B4
Gedney Drove End Lincs 66 B4
Gedney Dyke Lincs 66 B4
Gedney Hill Lincs 66 C3
Gee Cross Gtr Man 87 E7
Geilston Argyll 118 B3
Geirinis W Isles 148 D2
Geise Highld 158 D3
Geisiadar W Isles 154 D6
Geldeston Norf 69 E6
Gell Conwy 83 E8
Gelli Pembs 32 C1
Gelli Rhondda 34 E3
Gellideg M Tydf 34 D4
Gellifor Denb 72 C5
Gelligaer Caerph 35 E5
Gellilydan Gwyn 71 D7
Gellinudd Neath 33 D8
Gellyburn Perth 133 F7
Gellywen Carms 32 B3
Gelston Dumfries 106 D4
Gelston Lincs 78 E2
Gembling E Yorks 97 D7
Gentleshaw Staffs 62 C4
Geocrab W Isles 154 H6
George Green Bucks 40 F3
George Nympton Devon 10 B2
Georgefield Dumfries 115 E5
Georgeham Devon 20 F3
Georgetown Bl Gwent 35 D5
Gerlan Gwyn 83 E6
Germansweek Devon 9 E6
Germoe Corn 2 D4
Gerrans Corn 3 C7
Gerrards Cross Bucks 40 F3
Gestingthorpe Essex 56 F2
Geuffordd Powys 60 C2
Gib Hill Ches W 74 B3
Gibbet Hill Warks 64 F2
Gibbshill Dumfries 106 B4
Gidea Park London 41 F8
Gidleigh Devon 9 F8
Giffnock E Renf 119 D5
Gifford E Loth 121 C8
Giffordland N Ayrs 118 E2
Giffordtown Fife 128 C4
Giggleswick N Yorks 93 C8
Gilberdyke E Yorks 90 B2
Gilchriston E Loth 121 C7
Gilcrux Cumb 107 F8
Gildersome W Yorks 88 B3
Gildingwells S Yorks 89 F6
Gileston V Glam 22 C2
Gilfach Caerph 35 E5
Gilfach Goch Rhondda 34 F3
Gilfachrheda Ceredig 46 D3
Gillamoor N Yorks 102 F4
Gillar's Green Mers 86 E2
Gillen Highld 148 C7
Gilling East N Yorks 96 B2
Gilling West N Yorks 101 D6
Gillingham Dorset 13 B6
Gillingham Medway 29 C8
Gillingham Norf 69 E7
Gillock Highld 158 E4
Gillow Heath Staffs 75 D5
Gills Highld 158 C5
Gill's Green Kent 18 B4
Gilmanscleuch Borders 115 B6
Gilmerton Edin 121 C5
Gilmerton Perth 127 B7
Gilmonby Durham 100 C4
Gilmorton Leics 64 F2
Gilmourton S Lanark 119 E6
Gilsland Northumb 109 C6
Gilsland Spa Cumb 109 C6
Gilston Borders 121 D7
Gilston Herts 41 C7
Gilwern Mon 35 C6
Gimingham Norf 81 D8
Giosla W Isles 154 E6
Gipping Suff 56 C4
Gipsey Bridge Lincs 79 E5
Girdle Toll N Ayrs 118 E3
Girlsta Shetland 160 H6
Girsby N Yorks 102 D1
Girtford C Beds 54 D2
Girthon Dumfries 106 D3
Girton Cambs 54 C5
Girton Notts 77 C8
Girvan S Ayrs 112 E1
Gisburn Lancs 93 E8
Gisleham Suff 69 F8
Gislingham Suff 56 B4
Gissing Norf 68 F4
Gittisham Devon 11 E6
Gladestry Powys 48 D4
Gladsmuir E Loth 121 B7
Glais Swansea 33 D8
Glaisdale N Yorks 103 D5
Glame Highld 149 D10
Glamis Angus 134 E3
Glan Adda Gwyn 83 D5
Glan Conwy Conwy 83 D8
Glan-Conwy Conwy 83 F8
Glan-Duar Carms 46 E4
Glan-Dwyfach Gwyn 71 C5
Glan Gors Anglesey 82 D4
Glan-rhyd Gwyn 82 F4
Glan-traeth Anglesey 82 D2
Glan-y-don Flint 73 B5
Glan-y-nant Powys 59 F6
Glan-y-wern Gwyn 71 D7
Glan-yr-afon Anglesey 83 C6
Glan-yr-afon Gwyn 72 E3
Glan-yr-afon Gwyn 72 E4
Glanaman Carms 33 C7
Glandford Norf 81 C6
Glandwr Pembs 32 B2
Glandy Cross Carms 32 B2
Glandyfi Ceredig 58 E3
Glangrwyney Powys 35 C6
Glanmule Powys 59 E8
Glanrafon Ceredig 58 F3
Glanrhyd Gwyn 70 D3
Glanrhyd Pembs 45 E3
Glanton Northumb 117 C6
Glanton Pike Northumb 117 C6
Glanvilles Wootton Dorset 12 D4
Glapthorn Northants 65 E7
Glapwell Derbys 76 C4
Glas-allt Shiel Aberds 139 F8
Glasbury Powys 48 F3
Glaschoil Highld 151 H13
Glascoed Denb 72 B3
Glascoed Mon 35 D7
Glascoed Powys 59 C8
Glascorrie Aberds 140 E2
Glascote Staffs 63 D6
Glascwm Powys 48 D3
Glasdrum Argyll 130 E4
Glasfryn Conwy 72 D3
Glasgow Glasgow 119 C5
Glashvin Highld 149 B9
Glasinfryn Gwyn 83 E5
Glasnacardoch Highld 147 B9
Glasnakille Highld 149 G10
Glasphein Highld 148 D6
Glaspwll Powys 58 E4
Glassburn Highld 150 H6
Glasserton Dumfries 105 F8
Glassford S Lanark 119 E7
Glasshouse Hill Glos 36 B4
Glasshouses N Yorks 94 C4
Glasslie Fife 128 D4
Glasson Cumb 108 C2
Glasson Lancs 92 D4
Glassonby Cumb 109 F5
Glasterlaw Angus 135 D5
Glaston Rutland 65 D5
Glastonbury Som 23 F7
Glatton Cambs 65 F8
Glazebrook Warr 86 E4
Glazebury Warr 86 E4
Glazeley Shrops 61 F7
Gleadless S Yorks 88 F4
Gleadsmoss Ches E 74 C5
Gleann Tholàstaidh W Isles 155 C10
Gleaston Cumb 92 B2
Gleiniant Powys 59 E6
Glemsford Suff 56 E2
Glen Dumfries 106 B5
Glen Dumfries 106 D2
Glen Auldyn IoM 84 C4
Glen Bernisdale Highld 149 D9
Glen Ho Borders 121 F5
Glen Mona IoM 84 D4
Glen Nevis House Highld 131 B5
Glen Parva Leics 64 E2
Glen Sluain Argyll 125 F6
Glen Tanar House Aberds 140 E3
Glen Trool Lodge Dumfries 112 F4
Glen Village Falk 119 B8
Glen Vine IoM 84 E3
Glenamachrie Argyll 124 C5
Glenbarr Argyll 143 E7
Glenbeg Highld 139 B6
Glenbeg Highld 147 E8
Glenbervie Aberds 141 F6
Glenboig N Lanark 119 C7
Glenborrodale Highld 147 E9
Glenbranter Argyll 125 F7
Glenbreck Borders 114 B3
Glenbrein Lodge Highld 137 C7
Glenbrittle House Highld 149 F9
Glenbuchat Lodge Aberds 140 C2
Glenbuck E Ayrs 113 B7
Glenburn Renfs 118 C4
Glencalvie Lodge Highld 150 C7
Glencanisp Lodge Highld 156 G4
Glencaple Dumfries 107 C6
Glencarron Lodge Highld 150 F3
Glencarse Perth 128 B3
Glencassley Castle Highld 156 J7
Glenceitlein Highld 131 E5
Glencoe Highld 130 D4
Glencraig Fife 128 E3
Glencripesdale Highld 147 F9
Glencrosh Dumfries 113 F7
Glendavan Ho. Aberds 140 D3
Glendevon Perth 127 D8
Glendoe Lodge Highld 137 D7
Glendoebeg Highld 137 D7
Glendoick Perth 128 B4
Glendoll Lodge Angus 134 B2
Glendoune S Ayrs 112 E1
Glenduckie Fife 128 C4
Glendye Lodge Aberds 140 F5
Gleneagles Hotel Perth 127 C8
Gleneagles House Perth 127 D8
Glenegedale Argyll 142 C4
Glenelg Highld 149 G13
Glenernie Moray 151 G13
Glenfarg Perth 128 C3
Glenfarquhar Lodge Aberds 141 F6
Glenferness House Highld 151 G12
Glenfeshie Lodge Highld 138 E4
Glenfield Leics 64 D2
Glenfinnan Highld 147 C11
Glenfoot Perth 128 C3
Glenfyne Lodge Argyll 125 D8
Glengap Dumfries 106 D3
Glengarnock N Ayrs 118 D3
Glengorm Castle Argyll 146 F7
Glengrasco Highld 149 D9
Glenhead Farm Angus 134 C2
Glenhoul Dumfries 113 F6
Glenhurich Highld 130 C2
Glenkerry Borders 115 C5
Glenkiln Dumfries 106 B5
Glenkindie Aberds 140 C3
Glenlatterach Moray 152 C1
Glenlee Dumfries 113 F6
Glenlichorn Perth 127 C6
Glenlivet Moray 139 B7
Glenlochsie Perth 133 B7
Glenloig N Ayrs 143 E10
Glenluce Dumfries 105 D6
Glenmallan Argyll 125 F8
Glenmarksie Highld 150 F6
Glenmassan Argyll 145 E10
Glenmavis N Lanark 119 C7
Glenmaye IoM 84 E2
Glenmidge Dumfries 113 F8
Glenmore Argyll 124 D4
Glenmore Highld 149 D9
Glenmore Lodge Highld 139 D5
Glenmoy Angus 134 C4
Glenogil Angus 134 C4
Glenprosen Lodge Angus 134 C2
Glenprosen Village Angus 134 C3
Glenquiech Angus 134 C4
Glenreasdell Mains Argyll 145 H7
Glenree N Ayrs 143 F10
Glenridding Cumb 99 C5
Glenrossal Highld 156 J7
Glenrothes Fife 128 D4
Glensanda Highld 130 E2
Glensaugh Aberds 135 B6
Glenshero Lodge Highld 137 E8
Glenstockadale Dumfries 104 C4
Glenstriven Argyll 145 F9
Glentaggart S Lanark 113 B8
Glentham Lincs 90 E4
Glentirranmuir Stirling 127 E5
Glenton Aberds 140 B5
Glentress Borders 121 F5
Glentromie Lodge Highld 138 E3
Glentrool Village Dumfries 105 B7
Glentruan IoM 84 B4
Glentruim House Highld 138 E2
Glentworth Lincs 90 F3
Glenuig Highld 147 D9
Glenurquhart Highld 151 E10
Glespin S Lanark 113 B8
Gletness Shetland 160 H6
Glewstone Hereford 36 B2
Glinton Pboro 65 D8
Glooston Leics 64 E4
Glororum Northumb 123 F7
Glossop Derbys 87 E8
Gloster Hill Northumb 117 D8
Gloucester Glos 37 C5
Gloup Shetland 160 C7
Glusburn N Yorks 94 E3
Glutt Lodge Highld 157 F12
Glutton Bridge Staffs 75 C7
Glympton Oxon 38 B4
Glyn-Ceiriog Wrex 73 F6
Glyn-cywarch Gwyn 71 D7
Glyn Ebwy = Ebbw Vale Bl Gwent 35 D5
Glyn-neath = Glynedd Neath 34 D2
Glynarthen Ceredig 46 E2
Glynbrochan Powys 59 F6
Glyncoch Rhondda 34 E4
Glyncorrwg Neath 34 E2
Glynde E Sus 17 D8
Glyndebourne E Sus 17 C8
Glyndyfrdwy Denb 72 E5
Glynedd = Glyn-neath Neath 34 D2
Glynogwr Bridgend 34 F3
Glyntaff Rhondda 34 F4
Glyntawe Powys 34 C2
Gnosall Staffs 62 B2
Gnosall Heath Staffs 62 B2
Goadby Leics 64 E4
Goadby Marwood Leics 64 B4
Goat Lees Kent 30 E4
Goatacre Wilts 24 B5
Goathill Dorset 12 C4
Goathland N Yorks 103 D6
Goathurst Som 22 F4
Gobernuisgach Lodge Highld 156 E7
Gobhaig W Isles 154 G5
Gobowen Shrops 73 F7
Godalming Sur 27 E7
Godley Gtr Man 87 E7
Godmanchester Cambs 54 B3
Godmanstone Dorset 12 E4
Godmersham Kent 30 D4
Godney Som 23 E6
Godolphin Cross Corn 2 C5
Godre'r-graig Neath 34 D1
Godshill Hants 14 C2
Godshill IoW 15 F6
Godstone Sur 28 D4
Godwinscroft Hants 14 E2
Goetre Mon 35 D7
Goferydd Anglesey 82 C2
Goff's Oak Herts 41 D6
Gogar Edin 120 B4
Goginan Ceredig 58 F3
Golan Gwyn 71 C6
Golant Corn 5 D6
Golberdon Corn 5 B8
Golborne Gtr Man 86 E4
Golcar W Yorks 88 C2
Gold Hill Norf 66 E5
Goldcliff Newport 35 F7
Golden Cross E Sus 18 D2
Golden Green Kent 29 E7
Golden Grove Carms 33 C6

Golden Hill Hants 14 E3
Golden Pot Hants 26 E5
Golden Valley Glos 37 B6
Goldenhill Stoke 75 D5
Golders Green London 41 F5
Goldhanger Essex 43 D5
Golding Shrops 60 D5
Goldington Bedford 53 D8
Goldsborough N Yorks 95 D6
Goldsborough N Yorks 103 C6
Goldsithney Corn 2 C4
Goldsworthy Devon 9 B5
Goldthorpe S Yorks 89 D5
Gollanfield Highld 151 F11
Golspie Highld 157 J11
Golval Highld 157 C11
Gomeldon Wilts 25 F6
Gomersal W Yorks 88 B3
Gomshall Sur 27 E8
Gonalston Notts 77 E6
Gonfirth Shetland 160 G5
Good Easter Essex 42 C2
Gooderstone Norf 67 D7
Goodleigh Devon 20 F5
Goodmanham E Yorks 96 E4
Goodnestone Kent 30 C4
Goodnestone Kent 31 D6
Goodrich Hereford 36 C2
Goodrington Torbay 7 D6
Goodshaw Lancs 87 B6
Goodwick = Wdig Pembs 44 B4
Goodworth Clatford Hants 25 E8
Goole E Yorks 89 B8
Goonbell Corn 3 B6
Goonhavern Corn 4 D2
Goose Eye W Yorks 94 E3
Goose Green Gtr Man 86 D3
Goose Green Norf 68 F4
Goose Green W Sus 16 C5
Gooseham Corn 8 C4
Goosey Oxon 38 E3
Goosnargh Lancs 93 F5
Goostrey Ches E 74 B4
Gorcott Hill Warks 51 C5
Gord Shetland 160 L6
Gordon Borders 122 E2
Gordonbush Highld 157 J11
Gordonsburgh Moray 152 B4
Gordonstoun Moray 152 B1
Gordonstown Aberds 152 C5
Gordonstown Aberds 153 E7
Gore Kent 31 D7
Gore Cross Wilts 24 D5
Gore Pit Essex 42 C4
Gorebridge Midloth 121 C6
Gorefield Cambs 66 C4
Gorey Jersey 17
Gorgie Edin 120 B5
Goring Oxon 39 F6
Goring-by-Sea W Sus 16 D5
Goring Heath Oxon 26 B4
Gorleston-on-Sea Norf 69 D8
Gornalwood W Mid 62 E3
Gorrachie Aberds 153 C7
Gorran Churchtown Corn 3 B8
Gorran Haven Corn 3 B9
Gorrenberry Borders 115 E7
Gors Ceredig 46 B5
Gorse Hill Swindon 38 F1
Gorsedd Flint 73 B5
Gorseinon Swansea 33 E6
Gorseness Orkney 159 G5
Gorsgoch Ceredig 46 D3
Gorslas Carms 33 C6
Gorsley Glos 36 B3
Gorstan Highld 150 E6
Gorstanvorran Highld 130 B2
Gorsteyhill Staffs 74 D4
Gorsty Hill Staffs 62 B5
Gortantaoid Argyll 142 A4
Gorton Gtr Man 87 E6
Gosbeck Suff 57 D5
Gosberton Lincs 78 F5
Gosberton Clough Lincs 65 B8
Gosfield Essex 42 B3
Gosford Hereford 49 C7
Gosforth Cumb 98 D2
Gosforth T&W 110 C5
Gosmore Herts 40 B4
Gosport Hants 15 E7
Gossabrough Shetland 160 E7
Gossington Glos 36 D4
Goswick Northumb 123 E6
Gotham Notts 76 F5
Gotherington Glos 37 B6
Gott Shetland 160 J6
Goudhurst Kent 18 B4
Goulceby Lincs 79 B5
Gourdas Aberds 153 D7
Gourdon Aberds 135 B8
Gourock Invclyd 118 B2
Govan Glasgow 119 C5
Govanhill Glasgow 119 C5
Goveton Devon 7 E5
Govilon Mon 35 C6
Gowanhill Aberds 153 B10
Gowdall E Yorks 89 B7
Gowerton Swansea 33 E6
Gowkhall Fife 128 F2
Gowthorpe E Yorks 96 D3
Goxhill E Yorks 97 E7
Goxhill N Lincs 90 B5
Goxhill Haven N Lincs 90 B5
Goytre Neath 34 F1
Grabhair W Isles 155 F8
Graby Lincs 65 B7
Grade Corn 3 E6
Graffham W Sus 16 C3
Grafham Cambs 54 C2
Grafham Sur 27 E8
Grafton Hereford 49 F6
Grafton N Yorks 95 C7
Grafton Oxon 38 D2
Grafton Shrops 60 C4
Grafton Worcs 49 C7
Grafton Flyford Worcs 50 D4
Grafton Regis Northants 53 E5
Grafton Underwood Northants 65 F6
Grafty Green Kent 30 E2
Graianrhyd Denb 73 D6
Graig Conwy 83 D8
Graig Denb 72 B4
Graig-fechan Denb 72 D5
Grain Medway 30 B2
Grainsby Lincs 91 E6
Grainthorpe Lincs 91 E7
Grampound Corn 3 B8
Grampound Road Corn 4 D4
Gramsdal W Isles 148 C3
Granborough Bucks 39 B7
Granby Notts 77 F7
Grandborough Warks 52 C2
Grandtully Perth 133 D6
Grange Cumb 98 C4
Grange E Ayrs 118 F4
Grange Medway 29 C8
Grange Mers 85 F3
Grange Perth 128 B4
Grange Crossroads Moray 152 C4
Grange Hall Moray 151 E13
Grange Hill Essex 41 E7
Grange Moor W Yorks 88 C3
Grange of Lindores Fife 128 C4
Grange-over-Sands Cumb 92 B4
Grange Villa Durham 110 D5
Grangemill Derbys 76 D2
Grangemouth Falk 127 F8
Grangepans Falk 128 F2
Grangetown Cardiff 22 B3
Grangetown Redcar 102 B3
Granish Highld 138 C5
Gransmoor E Yorks 97 D7
Granston Pembs 44 B3
Grantchester Cambs 54 D5
Grantham Lincs 78 F2
Grantley N Yorks 94 C5
Grantlodge Aberds 141 C6
Granton Dumfries 114 D3
Granton Edin 120 B5
Granton-on-Spey Highld 139 B6
Grantshouse Borders 122 C4
Grappenhall Warr 86 F4
Grasby Lincs 90 D4
Grasmere Cumb 99 D5
Grasscroft Gtr Man 87 D7
Grassendale Mers 85 F4
Grassholme Durham 100 B4
Grassington N Yorks 94 C3
Grassmoor Derbys 76 C4
Grassthorpe Notts 77 C7
Grateley Hants 25 E7
Gratwich Staffs 75 F7
Graveley Cambs 54 C3
Graveley Herts 41 B5
Gravelly Hill W Mid 62 E5
Gravels Shrops 60 D3
Graven Shetland 160 F6
Graveney Kent 30 C4
Gravesend Herts 41 B7
Gravesend Kent 29 B7
Grayingham Lincs 90 E3
Grayrigg Cumb 99 E7
Grays Thurrock 29 B7
Grayshott Hants 27 F6
Grayswood Sur 27 F7
Graythorp Hrtlpl 102 B3
Grazeley Wokingham 26 C4
Greasbrough S Yorks 88 E5
Greasby Mers 85 F3
Great Abington Cambs 55 E6
Great Addington Northants 53 B7
Great Alne Warks 51 D6
Great Altcar Lancs 85 D4
Great Amwell Herts 41 C6
Great Asby Cumb 100 C1
Great Ashfield Suff 56 C3
Great Ayton N Yorks 102 C3
Great Baddow Essex 42 D3
Great Bardfield Essex 55 F7
Great Barford Bedford 54 D2
Great Barr W Mid 62 E4
Great Barrington Glos 38 C2
Great Barrow Ches W 73 C8
Great Barton Suff 56 C2
Great Barugh N Yorks 96 B3
Great Bavington Northumb 117 F5
Great Bealings Suff 57 E6
Great Bedwyn Wilts 25 C7
Great Bentley Essex 43 B7
Great Billing Northants 53 C6
Great Bircham Norf 80 D3
Great Blakenham Suff 56 D5
Great Blencow Cumb 108 F4
Great Bolas Telford 61 B6
Great Bookham Sur 28 D2
Great Bourton Oxon 52 E2
Great Bowden Leics 64 F4
Great Bradley Suff 55 D7
Great Braxted Essex 42 C4
Great Bricett Suff 56 D4
Great Brickhill Bucks 53 F7
Great Bridge W Mid 62 E3
Great Bridgeford Staffs 62 B2
Great Brington Northants 52 C4
Great Bromley Essex 43 B6
Great Broughton Cumb 107 F7
Great Broughton N Yorks 102 D3
Great Budworth Ches W 74 B3
Great Burdon Darl 101 C8
Great Burgh Sur 28 D3
Great Burstead Essex 42 E2
Great Busby N Yorks 102 D3
Great Canfield Essex 42 C1
Great Carlton Lincs 91 F8
Great Casterton Rutland 65 D7
Great Chart Kent 30 E3
Great Chatwell Staffs 61 C7
Great Chesterford Essex 55 E6
Great Cheverell Wilts 24 D4
Great Chishill Cambs 54 F5
Great Clacton Essex 43 C7
Great Cliff W Yorks 88 C4
Great Clifton Cumb 98 B2
Great Coates NE Lincs 91 D6
Great Comberton Worcs 50 E4
Great Corby Cumb 108 D4
Great Cornard Suff 56 E2
Great Cowden E Yorks 97 E8
Great Coxwell Oxon 38 E2
Great Crakehall N Yorks 101 E7
Great Cransley Northants 53 B6
Great Cressingham Norf 67 D8
Great Crosby Mers 85 E4
Great Cubley Derbys 75 F8
Great Dalby Leics 64 C4
Great Denham Bedford 53 E8
Great Doddington Northants 53 C6
Great Dunham Norf 67 C8
Great Dunmow Essex 42 B2
Great Durnford Wilts 25 F6
Great Easton Essex 42 B2
Great Easton Leics 64 E5
Great Eccleston Lancs 92 E4
Great Edstone N Yorks 103 F5
Great Ellingham Norf 68 E3
Great Elm Som 24 E2
Great Eversden Cambs 54 D4
Great Fencote N Yorks 101 E7
Great Finborough Suff 56 D4
Great Fransham Norf 67 C8
Great Gaddesden Herts 40 C3
Great Gidding Cambs 65 F8
Great Givendale E Yorks 96 D4
Great Glemham Suff 57 C7
Great Glen Leics 64 E3
Great Gonerby Lincs 77 F8
Great Gransden Cambs 54 D3
Great Green Norf 69 F5
Great Green Suff 56 D3
Great Habton N Yorks 96 B3
Great Hale Lincs 78 E4
Great Hallingbury Essex 41 C8
Great Hampden Bucks 39 D8
Great Harrowden Northants 53 B6
Great Harwood Lancs 93 F7
Great Haseley Oxon 39 D6
Great Hatfield E Yorks 97 E7
Great Haywood Staffs 62 B4
Great Heath W Mid 63 F7
Great Heck N Yorks 89 B6
Great Henny Essex 56 F2
Great Hinton Wilts 24 D4
Great Hockham Norf 68 E2
Great Holland Essex 43 C8
Great Horkesley Essex 56 F3
Great Hormead Herts 41 B6
Great Horton W Yorks 94 F4
Great Horwood Bucks 53 F5
Great Houghton Northants 53 D5
Great Houghton S Yorks 88 D5
Great Hucklow Derbys 75 B8
Great Kelk E Yorks 97 D7
Great Kimble Bucks 39 D8
Great Kingshill Bucks 40 E1
Great Langton N Yorks 101 E7
Great Leighs Essex 42 C3
Great Lever Gtr Man 86 D5
Great Limber Lincs 90 D5
Great Linford M Keynes 53 E6
Great Livermere Suff 56 B2
Great Longstone Derbys 76 B2
Great Lumley Durham 111 E5
Great Lyth Shrops 60 D4
Great Malvern Worcs 50 E2
Great Maplestead Essex 56 F2
Great Marton Blackpool 92 F3
Great Massingham Norf 80 E3
Great Melton Norf 68 D4
Great Milton Oxon 39 D6
Great Missenden Bucks 40 D1
Great Mitton Lancs 93 F7
Great Mongeham Kent 31 D7
Great Moulton Norf 68 E4
Great Munden Herts 41 B6
Great Musgrave Cumb 100 C2
Great Ness Shrops 60 C3
Great Notley Essex 42 B3
Great Oakley Essex 43 B7
Great Oakley Northants 65 F5
Great Offley Herts 40 B4
Great Ormside Cumb 100 C2
Great Orton Cumb 108 D3
Great Ouseburn N Yorks 95 C7
Great Oxendon Northants 64 F4
Great Oxney Green Essex 42 D2
Great Palgrave Norf 67 C8
Great Parndon Essex 41 D7
Great Paxton Cambs 54 C3
Great Plumpton Lancs 92 F3
Great Plumstead Norf 69 C6
Great Ponton Lincs 78 F2
Great Preston W Yorks 88 B5
Great Raveley Cambs 66 F2
Great Rissington Glos 38 C1
Great Rollright Oxon 51 F8
Great Ryburgh Norf 81 E5
Great Ryle Northumb 117 C6
Great Ryton Shrops 60 D4
Great Saling Essex 42 B3
Great Salkeld Cumb 109 F5
Great Sampford Essex 55 F7
Great Sankey Warr 86 F3
Great Saxham Suff 55 C8
Great Shefford W Berks 25 B8
Great Shelford Cambs 55 D5
Great Smeaton N Yorks 101 D8
Great Snoring Norf 80 D5
Great Somerford Wilts 37 F6
Great Stainton Darl 101 B8
Great Stambridge Essex 42 E4
Great Staughton Cambs 54 C2
Great Steeping Lincs 79 C7
Great Stonar Kent 31 D7
Great Strickland Cumb 99 B7
Great Stukeley Cambs 54 B3
Great Sturton Lincs 78 B5
Great Sutton Ches W 73 B7
Great Sutton Shrops 60 F5
Great Swinburne Northumb 110 B2
Great Tew Oxon 38 B3
Great Tey Essex 42 B4
Great Thurkleby N Yorks 95 B7
Great Thurlow Suff 55 D7
Great Torrington Devon 9 C6
Great Tosson Northumb 117 D6
Great Totham Essex 42 C4
Great Totham Essex 42 C4
Great Tows Lincs 91 E6
Great Urswick Cumb 92 B2
Great Wakering Essex 43 F5
Great Waldingfield Suff 56 E3
Great Walsingham Norf 80 D5
Great Waltham Essex 42 C2
Great Warley Essex 42 E1
Great Washbourne Glos 50 F4
Great Weldon Northants 65 F6
Great Welnetham Suff 56 D2
Great Wenham Suff 56 F4
Great Whittington Northumb 110 B3
Great Wigborough Essex 43 C5
Great Wilbraham Cambs 55 D6
Great Wishford Wilts 25 F5
Great Witcombe Glos 37 C6
Great Witley Worcs 50 C2
Great Wolford Warks 51 F7
Great Wratting Suff 55 E7
Great Wymondley Herts 41 B5
Great Wyrley Staffs 62 D3
Great Wytheford Shrops 61 C5
Great Yarmouth Norf 69 D8
Great Yeldham Essex 55 F8
Greater Doward Hereford 36 C2
Greatford Lincs 65 C7
Greatgate Staffs 75 E7
Greatham Hants 27 F5
Greatham Hrtlpl 102 B2
Greatham W Sus 16 C4
Greatstone on Sea Kent 19 C7
Greatworth Northants 52 E3
Greave Lancs 87 B6
Greeba IoM 84 D3
Green Denb 72 C4
Green End Bedford 54 D2
Green Hammerton N Yorks 95 D7
Green Lane Powys 59 E8
Green Ore Som 23 D7
Green St Green London 29 C5
Green Street Herts 40 E4
Greenbank Shetland 160 C7
Greenburn W Loth 120 C2
Greendikes Northumb 117 B6
Greenfield C Beds 53 F8
Greenfield Flint 73 B5
Greenfield Gtr Man 87 D7
Greenfield Highld 136 D5
Greenfield Oxon 39 E7
Greenford London 40 F4
Greengairs N Lanark 119 B7
Greenham W Berks 26 C2
Greenhaugh Northumb 116 F3
Greenhead Northumb 109 C6
Greenhill Falk 119 B8
Greenhill Kent 31 C5
Greenhill Leics 63 C8
Greenhill London 40 F4
Greenhills N Ayrs 118 D3
Greenhithe Kent 29 B6
Greenholm E Ayrs 118 F5
Greenholme Cumb 99 D7
Greenhouse Borders 115 B8
Greenhow Hill N Yorks 94 C4
Greenigoe Orkney 159 H5
Greenland Highld 158 D4
Greenlands Bucks 39 F7
Greenlaw Aberds 153 C6
Greenlaw Borders 122 E3
Greenlea Dumfries 107 B7
Greenloaning Perth 127 D7
Greenmount Gtr Man 87 C5
Greenmow Shetland 160 L6
Greenock Invclyd 118 B2
Greenock West Invclyd 118 B2
Greenodd Cumb 99 F5
Greenrow Cumb 107 D8
Greens Norton Northants 52 E4
Greenside T&W 110 C4
Greensidehill Northumb 117 C5
Greenstead Green Essex 42 B4
Greensted Essex 41 D8
Greenwich London 28 B4
Greet Glos 50 F5
Greete Shrops 49 B7
Greetham Lincs 79 B6
Greetham Rutland 65 C6
Greetland W Yorks 87 B8
Gregg Hall Cumb 99 E6
Gregson Lane Lancs 86 B3
Greinetobht W Isles 148 A3
Greinton Som 23 F6
Gremista Shetland 160 J6
Grenaby IoM 84 E2
Grendon Northants 53 C6
Grendon Warks 63 D6
Grendon Common Warks 63 E6
Grendon Green Hereford 49 D7
Grendon Underwood Bucks 39 B6
Grenofen Devon 6 B2
Grenoside S Yorks 88 E4
Greosabhagh W Isles 154 H6
Gresford Wrex 73 D7
Gresham Norf 81 D7
Greshornish Highld 149 C8
Gressenhall Norf 68 C2
Gressingham Lancs 93 C5
Gresty Green Ches E 74 D4
Greta Bridge Durham 101 C5
Gretna Dumfries 108 C3
Gretna Green Dumfries 108 C3
Gretton Glos 50 F5
Gretton Northants 65 E5
Gretton Shrops 60 E5
Grewelthorpe N Yorks 94 B5
Grey Green N Lincs 89 D8
Greygarth N Yorks 94 B4
Greynor Carms 33 D6
Greysouthen Cumb 98 B2
Greystoke Cumb 108 F4
Greystone Angus 135 E5
Greystone Dumfries 107 B6
Greywell Hants 26 D5
Griais W Isles 155 C9
Grianan W Isles 155 D9
Gribthorpe E Yorks 96 F3
Gridley Corner Devon 9 E5
Griff Warks 63 F7
Griffithstown Torf 35 E6
Grimbister Orkney 159 G4
Grimblethorpe Lincs 91 F6
Grimeford Village Lancs 86 C4
Grimethorpe S Yorks 88 D5
Griminis W Isles 148 C2
Grimister Shetland 160 D6
Grimley Worcs 50 C3
Grimness Orkney 159 J5
Grimoldby Lincs 91 F7
Grimpo Shrops 60 B3
Grimsargh Lancs 93 F5
Grimsbury Oxon 52 E2
Grimsby NE Lincs 91 C6
Grimscote Northants 52 D4
Grimscott Corn 8 D4
Grimsthorpe Lincs 65 B7
Grimston E Yorks 97 F8
Grimston Leics 64 B3
Grimston Norf 80 E3
Grimston York 96 D2
Grimstone Dorset 12 E4
Grinacombe Moor Devon 9 E6
Grindale E Yorks 97 B7
Grindigar Orkney 159 H6
Grindiscol Shetland 160 K6
Grindle Shrops 61 D7
Grindleford Derbys 76 B2
Grindleton Lancs 93 E7
Grindley Staffs 62 B4
Grindley Brook Shrops 74 E2
Grindlow Derbys 75 B8
Grindon Northumb 122 E5
Grindon Staffs 75 D7
Grindonmoor Gate Staffs 75 D7
Gringley on the Hill Notts 89 E8
Grinsdale Cumb 108 D3
Grinshill Shrops 60 B5
Grinton N Yorks 101 E5
Griomsidar W Isles 155 E8
Grishipoll Argyll 146 F4
Grisling Common E Sus 17 B8
Gristhorpe N Yorks 103 F8
Griston Norf 68 E2
Gritley Orkney 159 H6
Grittenham Wilts 37 F7
Grittleton Wilts 37 F5
Grizebeck Cumb 98 F4
Grizedale Cumb 99 E5
Grobister Orkney 159 F7
Groby Leics 64 D2
Groes Conwy 72 C4
Groes Neath 34 F1
Groes-faen Rhondda 34 F4
Groes-lwyd Powys 60 C2
Groesffordd Marli Denb 72 B4
Groeslon Gwyn 82 E5
Groeslon Gwyn 82 F4
Grogport Argyll 143 D9
Gromford Suff 57 D7
Gronant Flint 72 A4
Groombridge E Sus 18 B2
Grosmont Mon 35 B8
Grosmont N Yorks 103 D6
Groton Suff 56 E3
Groudle Glen IoM 84 E4
Grougfoot Falk 120 B3
Grouville Jersey 17
Grove Dorset 12 G5
Grove Kent 31 C6
Grove Notts 77 B7
Grove Oxon 38 E4
Grove Park London 28 B5
Grove Vale W Mid 62 E4
Grovesend Swansea 33 D6
Grudie Highld 150 E6
Gruids Highld 157 J8
Gruinard House Highld 150 B2
Grula Highld 149 F8
Gruline Argyll 147 G8
Grunasound Shetland 160 K5
Grundisburgh Suff 57 D6
Grunsagill Lancs 93 D7
Gruting Shetland 160 J4
Grutness Shetland 160 N6
Gualachulain Highld 131 E5
Gualin Ho. Highld 156 D6
Guardbridge Fife 129 C6
Guarlford Worcs 50 E3
Guay Perth 133 E7
Guestling Green E Sus 19 D5
Guestling Thorn E Sus 18 D5
Guestwick Norf 81 E6
Guestwick Green Norf 81 E6
Guide Blackburn 86 B5
Guide Post Northumb 117 F8
Guilden Morden Cambs 54 E3
Guilden Sutton Ches W 73 C8
Guildford Sur 27 E7
Guildtown Perth 133 F8
Guilsborough Northants 52 B4
Guilsfield Powys 60 C2
Guilton Kent 31 D6
Guineaford Devon 20 F4
Guisborough Redcar 102 C4
Guiseley W Yorks 94 E4
Guist Norf 81 E5
Guith Orkney 159 E6
Guiting Power Glos 37 B7
Gulberwick Shetland 160 K6
Gullane E Loth 129 F6
Gulval Corn 2 C3
Gulworthy Devon 6 B2
Gumfreston Pembs 32 D2
Gumley Leics 64 E3
Gummow's Shop Corn 4 D3
Gun Hill E Sus 18 D2
Gunby E Yorks 96 F3
Gunby Lincs 65 B6
Gundleton Hants 26 F4
Gunn Devon 20 F5
Gunnerside N Yorks 100 E4
Gunnerton Northumb 110 B2
Gunness N Lincs 90 C2
Gunnislake Corn 6 B2
Gunnista Shetland 160 J7
Gunthorpe Norf 81 D6
Gunthorpe Notts 77 E6
Gunthorpe Pboro 65 D8
Gunville IoW 15 F5
Gunwalloe Corn 3 D5
Gurnard IoW 15 E5
Gurnett Ches E 75 B6
Gurney Slade Som 23 E8
Gurnos Powys 34 D1
Gussage All Saints Dorset 13 C8
Gussage St Michael Dorset 13 C7
Guston Kent 31 E7
Gutcher Shetland 160 D7
Guthrie Angus 135 D5
Guyhirn Cambs 66 D3
Guyhirn Gull Cambs 66 D3
Guy's Head Lincs 66 B4
Guy's Marsh Dorset 13 B6
Guyzance Northumb 117 D8
Gwaenysgor Flint 72 A4
Gwalchmai Anglesey 82 D3
Gwaun-Cae-Gurwen Neath 33 C8
Gwaun-Leision Neath 33 C8
Gwbert Ceredig 45 E3
Gweek Corn 3 D6
Gwehelog Mon 35 D7
Gwenddwr Powys 48 E2
Gwennap Corn 3 C6
Gwenter Corn 3 E6
Gwernaffield Flint 73 C6
Gwernesney Mon 35 D8
Gwernogle Carms 46 F4
Gwernymynydd Flint 73 C6
Gwersyllt Wrex 73 D7
Gwespyr Flint 85 F2
Gwithian Corn 2 B4
Gwredog Anglesey 82 C4
Gwyddelwern Denb 72 E4
Gwyddgrug Carms 46 F3
Gwydyr Uchaf Conwy 83 E7
Gwynfryn Wrex 73 D6
Gwystre Powys 48 C2
Gwytherin Conwy 83 E8
Gyfelia Wrex 73 E7
Gyffin Conwy 83 D7
Gyre Orkney 159 H4
Gyrn-goch Gwyn 70 C5

H

Habberley Shrops 60 D3
Habergham Lancs 93 F8
Habrough NE Lincs 90 C5
Haceby Lincs 78 F3
Hacheston Suff 57 D7
Hackbridge London 28 C3
Hackenthorpe S Yorks 88 F5
Hackford Norf 68 D3
Hackforth N Yorks 101 E7
Hackland Orkney 159 F4
Hackleton Northants 53 D6
Hackness N Yorks 103 E7
Hackness Orkney 159 J4
Hackney London 41 F6
Hackthorn Lincs 90 F3
Hackthorpe Cumb 99 B7
Haconby Lincs 65 B8
Hacton London 41 F8
Hadden Borders 122 F3
Haddenham Bucks 39 D7
Haddenham Cambs 55 B5
Haddington E Loth 121 B8
Haddington Lincs 78 C2
Haddiscoe Norf 69 E7
Haddon Cambs 65 E8
Haddon Ches E 75 C6
Hade Edge W Yorks 88 D2
Hademore Staffs 63 D5
Hadfield Derbys 87 E8
Hadham Cross Herts 41 C7
Hadham Ford Herts 41 B7
Hadleigh Essex 42 F4
Hadleigh Suff 56 E4
Hadley Telford 61 C6
Hadley End Staffs 62 B5
Hadlow Kent 29 E7
Hadlow Down E Sus 18 C2
Hadnall Shrops 60 C5
Hadstock Essex 55 E6
Hady Derbys 76 B3
Hadzor Worcs 50 C4
Haffenden Quarter Kent 30 E2
Hafod-Dinbych Conwy 83 F8
Hafod-Iom Conwy 83 D8
Haggate Lancs 93 F8
Haggbeck Cumb 108 B4
Haggerston Northumb 123 E6
Haggrister Shetland 160 F5
Hagley Hereford 49 E7
Hagley Worcs 62 F3
Hagworthingham Lincs 79 C6
Haigh Gtr Man 86 D4
Haigh S Yorks 88 C3
Haigh Moor W Yorks 88 B3
Haighton Green Lancs 93 F5
Hail Weston Cambs 54 C2
Haile Cumb 98 D2
Hailes Glos 50 F5
Hailey Herts 41 C6
Hailey Oxon 38 C3
Hailsham E Sus 18 E2
Haimer Highld 158 D3
Hainault London 41 E7
Hainford Norf 68 C5
Hainton Lincs 91 F5
Hairmyres S Lanark 119 D6
Haisthorpe E Yorks 97 C7
Hakin Pembs 44 E3
Halam Notts 77 D6
Halbeath Fife 128 F3
Halberton Devon 10 C5
Halcro Highld 158 D4
Hale Gtr Man 87 F5
Hale Halton 86 F2
Hale Hants 14 C2
Hale Bank Halton 86 F2
Hale Street Kent 29 E7
Halebarns Gtr Man 87 F5
Hales Norf 69 E6
Hales Staffs 74 F4
Hales Place Kent 30 D5
Halesfield Telford 61 D7
Halesgate Lincs 66 B3
Halesowen W Mid 62 F3
Halesworth Suff 57 B7
Halewood Mers 86 F2
Halford Shrops 60 F4
Halford Warks 51 E7
Halfpenny Furze Carms 32 C3
Halfpenny Green Staffs 62 E2
Halfway Carms 46 F5
Halfway Carms 47 F7
Halfway W Berks 26 C2
Halfway Bridge W Sus 16 B3
Halfway House Shrops 60 C3
Halfway Houses Kent 30 B3
Halifax W Yorks 87 B8
Halket E Ayrs 118 D4
Halkirk Highld 158 E3
Halkyn Flint 73 B6
Hall Dunnerdale Cumb 98 E4
Hall Green W Mid 62 F5
Hall Green W Yorks 88 C4
Hall Grove Herts 41 C5
Hall of Tankerness Orkney 159 H6
Hall of the Forest Shrops 60 F2
Halland E Sus 18 D2
Hallaton Leics 64 E4
Hallatrow Bath 23 D8
Hallbankgate Cumb 109 D5
Hallen S Glos 36 F2
Halliburton Borders 122 E2
Hallin Highld 148 C7
Halling Medway 29 C8
Hallington Lincs 91 F7
Hallington Northumb 110 B2
Halliwell Gtr Man 86 C5
Halloughton Notts 77 D6
Hallow Worcs 50 D3
Hallrule Borders 115 C8
Halls E Loth 122 B2
Hall's Green Herts 41 B5
Hallsands Devon 7 F6
Hallthwaites Cumb 98 F3
Hallworthy Corn 8 F3
Hallyburton House Perth 134 F2
Hallyne Borders 120 E4
Halmer End Staffs 74 E4
Halmore Glos 36 D3
Halmyre Mains Borders 120 E4
Halnaker W Sus 16 D3
Halsall Lancs 85 C4
Halse Northants 52 E3
Halse Som 11 B6
Halsetown Corn 2 C4
Halsham E Yorks 91 B6
Halsinger Devon 20 F4
Halstead Essex 56 F2
Halstead Kent 29 C5
Halstead Leics 64 D4
Halstock Dorset 12 D3
Haltham Lincs 78 C5
Haltoft End Lincs 79 E6
Halton Bucks 40 C1
Halton Halton 86 F3
Halton Lancs 92 C5
Halton Northumb 110 C2
Halton W Yorks 95 F6
Halton Wrex 73 F7
Halton East N Yorks 94 D3
Halton Gill N Yorks 93 B8
Halton Holegate Lincs 79 C7
Halton Lea Gate Northumb 109 D6
Halton West N Yorks 93 D8
Haltwhistle Northumb 109 C7
Halvergate Norf 69 D7
Halwell Devon 7 D5
Halwill Devon 9 E6
Halwill Junction Devon 9 D6
Ham Devon 11 D7
Ham Glos 36 E3
Ham Highld 158 C4
Ham Kent 31 D7
Ham London 28 B2
Ham Shetland 160 K1
Ham Wilts 25 C8
Ham Common Dorset 13 B6
Ham Green Hereford 50 E2
Ham Green Kent 19 C5
Ham Green Kent 30 C2
Ham Green N Som 23 B7
Ham Green Worcs 50 C5
Ham Street Som 23 F7
Hamble-le-Rice Hants 15 D5
Hambleden Bucks 39 F7
Hambledon Hants 15 C7
Hambledon Sur 27 F7
Hambleton Lancs 92 E3
Hambleton N Yorks 95 F8
Hambridge Som 11 B8
Hambrook S Glos 23 B8
Hambrook W Sus 15 D8
Hameringham Lincs 79 C6
Hamerton Cambs 54 B2
Hametoun Shetland 160 K1
Hamilton S Lanark 119 D7
Hammer W Sus 27 F6
Hammerpot W Sus 16 D4
Hammersmith London 28 B3
Hammerwich Staffs 62 D4
Hammerwood E Sus 28 F5
Hammond Street Herts 41 D6
Hammoon Dorset 13 C6
Hamnavoe Shetland 160 E4
Hamnavoe Shetland 160 E6
Hamnavoe Shetland 160 F6
Hamnavoe Shetland 160 K5
Hampden Park E Sus 18 E3
Hamperden End Essex 55 F6
Hampnett Glos 37 C7
Hampole S Yorks 89 C6
Hampreston Dorset 13 E8
Hampstead London 41 F5
Hampstead Norreys W Berks 26 B3
Hampsthwaite N Yorks 95 D5
Hampton London 28 C2
Hampton Shrops 61 F7
Hampton Worcs 50 E5
Hampton Bishop Hereford 49 F7
Hampton Heath Ches W 73 E8
Hampton in Arden W Mid 63 F6
Hampton Loade Shrops 61 F7
Hampton Lovett Worcs 50 C3
Hampton Lucy Warks 51 D7
Hampton on the Hill Warks 51 C7
Hampton Poyle Oxon 39 C5
Hamrow Norf 80 E5
Hamsey E Sus 17 C8
Hamsey Green London 28 D4
Hamstall Ridware Staffs 62 C5
Hamstead IoW 14 E5
Hamstead W Mid 62 E4
Hamstead Marshall W Berks 26 C2
Hamsterley Durham 110 D4
Hamsterley Durham 110 F4
Hamstreet Kent 19 B7
Hamworthy Poole 13 E7
Hanbury Staffs 63 B5
Hanbury Worcs 50 C4
Hanbury Woodend Staffs 63 B5
Hanby Lincs 78 F3
Hanchurch Staffs 74 E5
Handbridge Ches W 73 C8
Handcross W Sus 17 B6
Handforth Ches E 87 F6
Handley Ches W 73 D8
Handsacre Staffs 62 C4
Handsworth S Yorks 88 F5
Handsworth W Mid 62 E4
Handy Cross Devon 9 B6
Hanford Stoke 75 E5
Hanging Langford Wilts 24 F5
Hangleton W Sus 16 D4
Hanham S Glos 23 B8
Hankelow Ches E 74 E3
Hankerton Wilts 37 E6
Hankham E Sus 18 E3
Hanley Stoke 75 E5
Hanley Castle Worcs 50 E3
Hanley Child Worcs 49 C8
Hanley Swan Worcs 50 E3
Hanley William Worcs 49 C8
Hanlith N Yorks 94 C2
Hanmer Wrex 73 F8
Hannah Lincs 79 B8
Hannington Hants 26 D3
Hannington Northants 53 B6
Hannington Swindon 38 E1
Hannington Wick Swindon 38 E1
Hansel Village S Ayrs 118 F3
Hanslope M Keynes 53 E6
Hanthorpe Lincs 65 B7
Hanwell London 40 F4
Hanwell Oxon 52 E2
Hanwood Shrops 60 D4
Hanworth London 28 B2
Hanworth Norf 81 D7
Happendon S Lanark 119 F8
Happisburgh Norf 69 A6
Happisburgh Common Norf 69 B6
Hapsford Ches W 73 B8
Hapton Lancs 93 F7
Hapton Norf 68 E4
Harberton Devon 7 D5
Harbertonford Devon 7 D5
Harbledown Kent 30 D5
Harborne W Mid 62 F4
Harborough Magna Warks 52 B2
Harbottle Northumb 117 D5
Harbury Warks 51 D8
Harby Leics 77 F7
Harby Notts 77 B8
Harcombe Devon 11 E6
Harden W Mid 62 D4
Harden W Yorks 94 F3
Hardenhuish Wilts 24 B4
Hardgate Aberds 141 D6
Hardham W Sus 16 C4
Hardingham Norf 68 D3
Hardingstone Northants 53 D5
Hardington Som 24 D2
Hardington Mandeville Som 12 C3
Hardington Marsh Som 12 D3
Hardley Hants 14 D5
Hardley Street Norf 69 D6
Hardmead M Keynes 53 E7
Hardrow N Yorks 100 E3
Hardstoft Derbys 76 C4
Hardway Hants 15 D7
Hardway Som 24 F2
Hardwick Bucks 39 C8
Hardwick Cambs 54 D4
Hardwick Norf 67 C6
Hardwick Norf 68 F5
Hardwick Northants 53 C6
Hardwick Notts 77 B6
Hardwick Oxon 38 D3
Hardwick Oxon 39 B5
Hardwick W Mid 62 E4
Hardwicke Glos 36 C4
Hardwicke Glos 37 B6
Hardwicke Hereford 48 E4
Hardy's Green Essex 43 B5
Hare Green Essex 43 B6
Hare Hatch Wokingham 27 B6
Hare Street Herts 41 B6
Hareby Lincs 79 C6
Hareden Lancs 93 D6
Harefield London 40 E3
Harehills W Yorks 95 F6
Harehope Northumb 117 B6
Haresceugh Cumb 109 E6
Harescombe Glos 37 C5
Haresfield Glos 37 C5
Hareshaw N Lanark 119 C8
Hareshaw Head Northumb 116 F4
Harewood W Yorks 95 E6
Harewood End Hereford 36 B2
Harford Carms 46 E5
Harford Devon 6 D4
Hargate Norf 68 E4
Hargatewall Derbys 75 B8
Hargrave Ches W 73 C8
Hargrave Northants 53 B8
Hargrave Suff 55 D8
Harker Cumb 108 C3
Harkland Shetland 160 E6
Harkstead Suff 57 F5
Harlaston Staffs 63 C6
Harlaw Ho. Aberds 141 B6
Harlaxton Lincs 77 F8
Harle Syke Lancs 93 F8
Harlech Gwyn 71 D6
Harlequin Notts 77 F6
Harlescott Shrops 60 C5
Harlesden London 41 F5
Harleston Devon 7 E5
Harleston Norf 68 F5
Harleston Suff 56 D4
Harlestone Northants 52 C5
Harley S Yorks 88 E4
Harley Shrops 61 D5
Harleyholm S Lanark 120 F2
Harlington C Beds 53 F8
Harlington London 27 B8
Harlington S Yorks 89 D5
Harlosh Highld 149 D7
Harlow Essex 41 C7
Harlow Hill N Yorks 95 D5
Harlow Hill Northumb 110 C3
Harlthorpe E Yorks 96 F3
Harlton Cambs 54 D4
Harman's Cross Dorset 13 F7
Harmby N Yorks 101 F6
Harmer Green Herts 41 C5
Harmer Hill Shrops 60 B4
Harmondsworth London 27 B8
Harmston Lincs 78 C2
Harnham Northumb 110 B3
Harnhill Glos 37 D7
Harold Hill London 41 E8
Harold Wood London 41 E8
Haroldston West Pembs 44 D3
Haroldswick Shetland 160 B8
Harome N Yorks 102 F4
Harpenden Herts 40 C4
Harpford Devon 11 E5
Harpham E Yorks 97 C6
Harpley Norf 80 E3
Harpley Worcs 49 C8
Harpole Northants 52 C4
Harpsdale Highld 158 E3
Harpsden Oxon 39 F7
Harpswell Lincs 90 F3
Harpur Hill Derbys 75 B7
Harpurhey Gtr Man 87 D6
Harraby Cumb 108 D4
Harrapool Highld 149 F11
Harrier Shetland 160 J1
Harrietfield Perth 127 B8
Harrietsham Kent 30 D2
Harrington Cumb 98 B1
Harrington Lincs 79 B6
Harrington Northants 64 F4
Harringworth Northants 65 E6
Harris Highld 146 B6
Harrogate N Yorks 95 D6
Harrold Bedford 53 D7
Harrow London 40 F4
Harrow on the Hill London 40 F4
Harrow Street Suff 56 F3
Harrow Weald London 40 E4
Harrowbarrow Corn 5 C8
Harrowden Bedford 53 E8
Harrowgate Hill Darl 101 C7
Harston Cambs 54 D5
Harston Leics 77 F8
Harswell E Yorks 96 E4
Hart Hrtlpl 111 F7
Hart Common Gtr Man 86 D4
Hart Hill Luton 40 B4
Hart Station Hrtlpl 111 F7
Hartburn Northumb 117 F6
Hartburn Stockton 102 C2
Hartest Suff 56 D2
Hartfield E Sus 29 F5
Hartford Cambs 54 B3
Hartford Ches W 74 B3
Hartford End Essex 42 C2
Hartfordbridge Hants 27 D5
Hartforth N Yorks 101 D6
Harthill Ches W 74 D2
Harthill N Lanark 120 C2
Harthill S Yorks 89 F5
Hartington Derbys 75 C8
Hartland Devon 8 B4
Hartlebury Worcs 50 B3
Hartlepool Hrtlpl 111 F8
Hartley Cumb 100 D2
Hartley Kent 18 B4
Hartley Kent 29 C7
Hartley Northumb 111 B6
Hartley Westpall Hants 26 D4
Hartley Wintney Hants 27 D5
Hartlip Kent 30 C2
Hartoft End N Yorks 103 E5
Harton N Yorks 96 C3
Harton Shrops 60 F4
Harton T&W 111 C6
Hartpury Glos 36 B4
Hartshead W Yorks 88 B2
Hartshill Warks 63 E7
Hartshorne Derbys 63 B7
Hartsop Cumb 99 C6
Hartwell Northants 53 D5
Hartwood N Lanark 119 D8
Harvieston Stirling 126 F4
Harvington Worcs 51 E5
Harvington Cross Worcs 51 E5
Harwell Oxon 38 F4
Harwich Essex 57 F6
Harwood Durham 109 F8
Harwood Gtr Man 86 C5
Harwood Dale N Yorks 103 E7
Harworth Notts 89 E7
Hasbury W Mid 62 F3
Hascombe Sur 27 E7
Haselbech Northants 52 B5
Haselbury Plucknett Som 12 C2
Haseley Warks 51 C7
Haselor Warks 51 D6
Hasfield Glos 37 B5
Hasguard Pembs 44 E3
Haskayne Lancs 85 D4
Hasketon Suff 57 D6
Hasland Derbys 76 C3
Haslemere Sur 27 F7
Haslingden Lancs 87 B5
Haslingfield Cambs 54 D5
Haslington Ches E 74 D4
Hassall Ches E 74 D4
Hassall Green Ches E 74 D4
Hassell Street Kent 30 E4
Hassendean Borders 115 B8
Hassingham Norf 69 D6
Hassocks W Sus 17 C6
Hassop Derbys 76 B2
Hastigrow Highld 158 D4
Hastingleigh Kent 30 E4
Hastings E Sus 18 E5
Hastingwood Essex 41 D7
Hastoe Herts 40 D2
Haswell Durham 111 E6
Haswell Plough Durham 111 E6
Hatch C Beds 54 E2
Hatch Hants 26 D4
Hatch Wilts 13 B7
Hatch Beauchamp Som 11 B8
Hatch End London 40 E4
Hatch Green Som 11 C8
Hatchet Gate Hants 14 D4
Hatching Green Herts 40 C4
Hatchmere Ches W 74 B2
Hatcliffe NE Lincs 91 D6
Hatfield Hereford 49 D7
Hatfield Herts 41 D5
Hatfield S Yorks 89 D7
Hatfield Worcs 50 D3
Hatfield Broad Oak Essex 41 C8
Hatfield Garden Village Herts 41 D5
Hatfield Heath Essex 41 C8
Hatfield Hyde Herts 41 C5
Hatfield Peverel Essex 42 C3
Hatfield Woodhouse S Yorks 89 D7
Hatford Oxon 38 E3
Hatherden Hants 25 D8
Hatherleigh Devon 9 D7
Hathern Leics 63 B8
Hatherop Glos 38 D1
Hathersage Derbys 88 F3
Hathershaw Gtr Man 87 D7

Hatherton Ches E 74 E3
Hatherton Staffs 62 C3
Hatley St George Cambs 54 D3
Hatt Corn 5 C8
Hattingley Hants 26 F4
Hatton Aberds 153 E10
Hatton Derbys 63 B6
Hatton Lincs 78 B4
Hatton Shrops 60 E4
Hatton Warks 51 C7
Hatton Warr 86 F3
Hatton Castle Aberds 153 D7
Hatton Heath Ches W 73 C8
Hatton of Fintray Aberds 141 C7
Hattoncrook Aberds 141 B7
Haugh E Ayrs 112 B4
Haugh Gtr Man 87 C7
Haugh Lincs 79 B7
Haugh Head Northumb 117 B6
Haugh of Glass Moray 152 E4
Haugh of Urr Dumfries 106 C5
Haugham Lincs 91 F7
Haughley Suff 56 C4
Haughley Green Suff 56 C4
Haughs of Clinterty Aberdeen 141 C7
Haughton Notts 77 B6
Haughton Shrops 60 B3
Haughton Shrops 61 C5
Haughton Shrops 61 D7
Haughton Shrops 61 E6
Haughton Staffs 62 B2
Haughton Castle Northumb 110 B2
Haughton Green Gtr Man 87 E7
Haughton Moss Ches E 74 D2
Haultwick Herts 41 B6
Haunn Argyll 146 G6
Haunn W Isles 148 G2
Haunton Staffs 63 C6
Hauxley Northumb 117 D8
Hauxton Cambs 54 D5
Havant Hants 15 D8
Haven Hereford 49 D6
Haven Bank Lincs 78 D5
Haven Side E Yorks 91 B5
Havenstreet IoW 15 E6
Havercroft W Yorks 88 C4
Haverfordwest = Hwlffordd Pembs 44 D4
Haverhill Suff 55 E7
Haverigg Cumb 92 B1
Havering-atte-Bower London 41 E8
Haveringland Norf 81 E7
Haversham M Keynes 53 E6
Haverthwaite Cumb 99 F5
Haverton Hill Stockton 102 B2
Hawarden = Penarlâg Flint 73 C7
Hawcoat Cumb 92 B2
Hawen Ceredig 46 E2
Hawes N Yorks 100 F3
Hawes' Green Norf 68 E5
Hawes Side Blackpool 92 F3
Hawford Worcs 50 C3
Hawick Borders 115 C8
Hawk Green Gtr Man 87 F7
Hawkchurch Devon 11 D8
Hawkedon Suff 55 D8
Hawkenbury Kent 18 B2
Hawkenbury Kent 30 E2
Hawkeridge Wilts 24 D3
Hawkerland Devon 11 F5
Hawkes End W Mid 63 F7
Hawkesbury S Glos 36 F4
Hawkesbury Warks 63 F7
Hawkesbury Upton S Glos 36 F4
Hawkhill Northumb 117 C8
Hawkhurst Kent 18 B4
Hawkinge Kent 31 F6
Hawkley Hants 15 B8
Hawkridge Som 21 F7
Hawkshead Cumb 99 E5
Hawkshead Hill Cumb 99 E5
Hawksland S Lanark 119 F8
Hawkswick N Yorks 94 B2
Hawksworth Notts 77 E7
Hawksworth W Yorks 94 E4
Hawksworth W Yorks 95 F5
Hawkwell Essex 42 E4
Hawley Hants 27 D6
Hawley Kent 29 B6
Hawling Glos 37 B7
Hawnby N Yorks 102 F3
Haworth W Yorks 94 F3
Hawstead Suff 56 D2
Hawthorn Durham 111 E7
Hawthorn Rhondda 35 F5
Hawthorn Wilts 24 C3
Hawthorn Hill Brack 27 B6
Hawthorn Hill Lincs 78 D5
Hawthorpe Lincs 65 B7
Hawton Notts 77 D7
Haxby York 96 D2
Haxey N Lincs 89 D8
Hay Green Norf 66 C5
Hay-on-Wye = Y Gelli Gandryll Powys 48 E4
Hay Street Herts 41 B6
Haydock Mers 86 E3
Haydon Dorset 12 C4
Haydon Bridge Northumb 109 C8
Haydon Wick Swindon 37 F8
Haye Corn 5 C8
Hayes London 28 C5
Hayes London 40 F4
Hayfield Derbys 87 F8
Hayfield Fife 128 E4
Hayhill E Ayrs 112 C4
Hayhillock Angus 135 E5
Hayle Corn 2 C4
Haynes C Beds 53 E8
Haynes Church End C Beds 53 E8
Hayscastle Pembs 44 C3
Hayscastle Cross Pembs 44 C4
Hayshead Angus 135 E6
Hayton Aberdeen 141 D8
Hayton Cumb 107 E8
Hayton Cumb 108 D5
Hayton E Yorks 96 E4
Hayton Notts 89 F8
Hayton's Bent Shrops 60 F5
Haytor Vale Devon 7 B5
Haywards Heath W Sus 17 B7
Haywood S Yorks 89 C6
Haywood Oaks Notts 77 D6
Hazel Grove Gtr Man 87 F7
Hazel Street Kent 18 B3
Hazelbank S Lanark 119 E8
Hazelbury Bryan Dorset 12 D5
Hazeley Hants 26 D5
Hazelhurst Gtr Man 87 D7
Hazelslade Staffs 62 C4
Hazelton Glos 37 C7
Hazelton Walls Fife 128 B5
Hazelwood Derbys 76 E3
Hazlemere Bucks 40 E1
Hazlerigg T&W 110 B5
Hazlewood N Yorks 94 D3
Hazon Northumb 117 D7
Heacham Norf 80 D2
Head of Muir Falk 127 F7
Headbourne Worthy Hants 26 F2
Headbrook Hereford 48 D5
Headcorn Kent 30 E2
Headingley W Yorks 95 F5
Headington Oxon 39 D5
Headlam Durham 101 C6
Headless Cross Worcs 50 C5
Headley Hants 26 C3
Headley Hants 27 F6
Headley Sur 28 D3
Headon Notts 77 B7
Heads S Lanark 119 E7
Heads Nook Cumb 108 D4
Heage Derbys 76 D3
Healaugh N Yorks 95 E7
Healaugh N Yorks 101 E5
Heald Green Gtr Man 87 F6
Heale Devon 20 E5
Heale Som 23 E8
Healey Gtr Man 87 C6
Healey N Yorks 101 F6
Healey Northumb 110 D3
Healing NE Lincs 91 C6
Heamoor Corn 2 C3
Heanish Argyll 146 G3
Heanor Derbys 76 E4
Heanton Punchardon Devon 20 F4
Heapham Lincs 90 F2
Hearthstane Borders 114 B4
Heasley Mill Devon 21 F6
Heast Highld 149 G11
Heath Cardiff 22 B3
Heath Derbys 76 C4
Heath and Reach C Beds 40 B2
Heath End Hants 26 C3
Heath End Sur 27 E6
Heath End Warks 51 C7
Heath Hayes Staffs 62 C4
Heath Hill Shrops 61 C7
Heath House Som 23 E6
Heath Town W Mid 62 E3
Heathcote Derbys 75 C8
Heather Leics 63 C7
Heatherfield Highld 149 D9
Heathfield Devon 7 B6
Heathfield E Sus 18 C2
Heathfield Som 11 B6
Heathhall Dumfries 107 B6
Heathrow Airport London 27 B8
Heathstock Devon 11 D7
Heathton Shrops 62 E2
Heatley Warr 86 F5
Heaton Lancs 92 C4
Heaton Staffs 75 C6
Heaton T&W 111 C5
Heaton W Yorks 94 F4
Heaton Moor Gtr Man 87 E6
Heaverham Kent 29 D6
Heaviley Gtr Man 87 F7
Heavitree Devon 10 E4
Hebburn T&W 111 C6
Hebden N Yorks 94 C3
Hebden Bridge W Yorks 87 B7
Hebron Anglesey 82 C4
Hebron Carms 32 B2
Hebron Northumb 117 F7
Heck Dumfries 114 F3
Heckfield Hants 26 C5
Heckfield Green Suff 57 B5
Heckfordbridge Essex 43 B5
Heckington Lincs 78 E4
Heckmondwike W Yorks 88 B3
Heddington Wilts 24 C4
Heddle Orkney 159 G4
Heddon-on-the-Wall Northumb 110 C4
Hedenham Norf 69 E6
Hedge End Hants 15 C5
Hedgerley Bucks 40 F2
Hedging Som 11 B8
Hedley on the Hill Northumb 110 D3
Hednesford Staffs 62 C4
Hedon E Yorks 91 B5
Hedsor Bucks 40 F2
Hedworth T&W 111 C6
Hegdon Hill Hereford 49 D7
Heggerscales Cumb 100 C3
Heglibister Shetland 160 H5
Heighington Darl 101 B7
Heighington Lincs 78 C3
Heights of Brae Highld 151 E8
Heights of Kinlochewe Highld 150 E3
Heilam Highld 156 C7
Heiton Borders 122 F3
Hele Devon 10 D4
Hele Devon 20 E4
Helensburgh Argyll 145 E11
Helford Corn 3 D6
Helford Passage Corn 3 D6
Helhoughton Norf 80 E4
Helions Bumpstead Essex 55 E7
Hellaby S Yorks 89 E6
Helland Corn 5 B5
Hellesdon Norf 68 C5
Hellidon Northants 52 D3
Hellifield N Yorks 93 D8
Hellingly E Sus 18 D2
Hellington Norf 69 D6
Hellister Shetland 160 J5
Helm Northumb 117 E7
Helmdon Northants 52 E3
Helmingham Suff 57 D5
Helmington Row Durham 110 F4
Helmsdale Highld 157 H13
Helmshore Lancs 87 B5
Helmsley N Yorks 102 F4
Helperby N Yorks 95 C7
Helperthorpe N Yorks 97 B5
Helpringham Lincs 78 E4
Helpston Pboro 65 D8
Helsby Ches W 73 B8
Helsey Lincs 79 B8
Helston Corn 3 D5
Helstone Corn 8 F2
Helton Cumb 99 B7
Helwith Bridge N Yorks 93 C8
Hemblington Norf 69 C6
Hemel Hempstead Herts 40 D3
Hemingbrough N Yorks 96 F2
Hemingby Lincs 78 B5
Hemingford Abbots Cambs 54 B3
Hemingford Grey Cambs 54 B3
Hemingstone Suff 57 D5
Hemington Leics 63 B8
Hemington Northants 65 F7
Hemington Som 24 D2
Hemley Suff 57 E6
Hemlington Mbro 102 C3
Hemp Green Suff 57 C7
Hempholme E Yorks 97 D6
Hempnall Norf 68 E5
Hempnall Green Norf 68 E5
Hempriggs House Highld 158 F5
Hempstead Essex 55 F7
Hempstead Medway 29 C8
Hempstead Norf 69 B7
Hempstead Norf 81 D7
Hempsted Glos 37 C5
Hempton Norf 80 E5
Hempton Oxon 52 F2
Hemsby Norf 69 C7
Hemswell Lincs 90 E3
Hemswell Cliff Lincs 90 F3
Hemsworth W Yorks 88 C5
Hemyock Devon 11 C6
Hen-feddau fawr Pembs 45 F4
Henbury Bristol 23 B7
Henbury Ches E 75 B5
Hendon London 41 F5
Hendon T&W 111 D7
Hendre Flint 73 C5
Hendre-ddu Conwy 83 E8
Hendreforgan Rhondda 34 F3
Hendy Carms 33 D6
Heneglwys Anglesey 82 D4
Henfield W Sus 17 C6
Henford Devon 9 E5
Henghurst Kent 19 B6
Hengoed Caerph 35 E5
Hengoed Powys 48 D4
Hengoed Shrops 73 F6
Hengrave Suff 56 C2
Henham Essex 41 B8
Heniarth Powys 59 D8
Henlade Som 11 B7
Henley Shrops 49 B7
Henley Som 23 F6
Henley Suff 57 D5
Henley W Sus 16 B2
Henley-in-Arden Warks 51 C6
Henley-on-Thames Oxon 39 F7
Henley's Down E Sus 18 D4
Henllan Ceredig 46 E2
Henllan Denb 72 C4
Henllan Amgoed Carms 32 B2
Henllys Torf 35 E6
Henlow C Beds 54 F2
Hennock Devon 10 F3
Henny Street Essex 56 F2
Henryd Conwy 83 D7
Henry's Moat Pembs 32 B1
Hensall N Yorks 89 B6
Henshaw Northumb 109 C7
Hensingham Cumb 98 C1
Henstead Suff 69 F7
Henstridge Som 12 C5
Henstridge Ash Som 12 B5
Henstridge Marsh Som 12 B5
Henton Oxon 39 D7
Henton Som 23 E6
Henwood Corn 5 B7
Heogan Shetland 160 J6
Heol-las Swansea 33 E7
Heol Senni Powys 34 B3
Heol-y-Cyw Bridgend 34 F3
Hepburn Northumb 117 B6
Hepple Northumb 117 D5
Hepscott Northumb 117 F8
Heptonstall W Yorks 87 B7
Hepworth Suff 56 B3
Hepworth W Yorks 88 D2
Herbrandston Pembs 44 E3
Hereford Hereford 49 E7
Heriot Borders 121 D6
Hermiston Edin 120 B4
Hermitage Borders 115 E8
Hermitage Dorset 12 D4
Hermitage W Berks 26 B3
Hermitage W Sus 15 D8
Hermon Anglesey 82 E3
Hermon Carms 33 B7
Hermon Carms 46 F2
Hermon Pembs 45 F4
Herne Kent 31 C5
Herne Bay Kent 31 C5
Herner Devon 9 B7
Hernhill Kent 30 C4
Herodsfoot Corn 5 C7
Herongate Essex 42 E2
Heronsford S Ayrs 104 A5
Herriard Hants 26 E4
Herringfleet Suff 69 E7
Herringswell Suff 55 B8
Hersden Kent 31 C6
Hersham Corn 8 D4
Hersham Sur 28 C2
Herstmonceux E Sus 18 D3
Herston Orkney 159 J5
Hertford Herts 41 C6
Hertford Heath Herts 41 C6
Hertingfordbury Herts 41 C6
Hesket Newmarket Cumb 108 F3
Hesketh Bank Lancs 86 B2
Hesketh Lane Lancs 93 E6
Heskin Green Lancs 86 C3
Hesleden Durham 111 F7
Hesleyside Northumb 116 F4
Heslington York 96 D2
Hessay York 95 D8
Hessenford Corn 5 D8
Hessett Suff 56 C3
Hessle E Yorks 90 B4
Hest Bank Lancs 92 C4
Heston London 28 B2
Hestwall Orkney 159 G3
Heswall Mers 85 F3
Hethe Oxon 39 B5
Hethersett Norf 68 D4
Hethersgill Cumb 108 C4
Hethpool Northumb 116 B4
Hett Durham 111 F5
Hetton N Yorks 94 D2
Hetton-le-Hole T&W 111 E6
Hetton Steads Northumb 123 F6
Heugh Northumb 110 B3
Heugh-head Aberds 140 C2
Heveningham Suff 57 B7
Hever Kent 29 E5
Heversham Cumb 99 F6
Hevingham Norf 81 E7
Hewas Water Corn 3 B8
Hewelsfield Glos 36 D2
Hewish N Som 23 C6
Hewish Som 12 D2
Heworth York 96 D2
Hexham Northumb 110 C2
Hextable Kent 29 B6
Hexton Herts 54 F2
Hexworthy Devon 6 B4
Hey Lancs 93 E8
Heybridge Essex 42 D4
Heybridge Essex 42 E2
Heybridge Basin Essex 42 D4
Heybrook Bay Devon 6 E3
Heydon Cambs 54 E5
Heydon Norf 81 E7
Heydour Lincs 78 F3
Heylipol Argyll 146 G2
Heylor Shetland 160 E4
Heysham Lancs 92 C4
Heyshott W Sus 16 C2
Heyside Gtr Man 87 D7
Heytesbury Wilts 24 E4
Heythrop Oxon 38 B3
Heywood Gtr Man 87 C6
Heywood Wilts 24 D3
Hibaldstow N Lincs 90 D3
Hickleton S Yorks 89 D5
Hickling Norf 69 B7
Hickling Notts 64 B3
Hickling Green Norf 69 B7
Hickling Heath Norf 69 B7
Hickstead W Sus 17 B6
Hidcote Boyce Glos 51 E6
High Ackworth W Yorks 88 C5
High Angerton Northumb 117 F6
High Bankhill Cumb 109 E5
High Barnes T&W 111 D6
High Beach Essex 41 E7
High Bentham N Yorks 93 C6
High Bickington Devon 9 B8
High Birkwith N Yorks 93 B7
High Blantyre S Lanark 119 D6
High Bonnybridge Falk 119 B8
High Bradfield S Yorks 88 E3
High Bray Devon 21 F5
High Brooms Kent 29 E6
High Bullen Devon 9 B7
High Buston Northumb 117 D8
High Callerton Northumb 110 B4
High Catton E Yorks 96 D3
High Cogges Oxon 38 D3
High Coniscliffe Darl 101 C7
High Cross Hants 15 B8
High Cross Herts 41 C6
High Easter Essex 42 C2
High Eggborough N Yorks 89 B6
High Ellington N Yorks 101 F6
High Ercall Telford 61 C5
High Etherley Durham 101 B6
High Garrett Essex 42 B3
High Grange Durham 110 F4
High Green Norf 68 D4
High Green S Yorks 88 E4
High Green Worcs 50 E3
High Halden Kent 19 B5
High Halstow Medway 29 B8
High Ham Som 23 F6
High Harrington Cumb 98 B2
High Hatton Shrops 61 B6
High Hawsker N Yorks 103 D7
High Hesket Cumb 108 E4
High Hesleden Durham 111 F7
High Hoyland S Yorks 88 C3
High Hunsley E Yorks 97 F5
High Hurstwood E Sus 17 B8
High Hutton N Yorks 96 C3
High Ireby Cumb 108 F2
High Kelling Norf 81 C7
High Kilburn N Yorks 95 B8
High Lands Durham 101 B6
High Lane Gtr Man 87 F7
High Lane Worcs 49 C8
High Laver Essex 41 D8
High Legh Ches E 86 F5
High Leven Stockton 102 C2
High Littleton Bath 23 D8
High Lorton Cumb 98 B3
High Marishes N Yorks 96 B4
High Marnham Notts 77 B8
High Melton S Yorks 89 D6
High Mickley Northumb 110 C3
High Mindork Dumfries 105 D7
High Newton Cumb 99 F6
High Newton-by-the-Sea Northumb 117 B8
High Nibthwaite Cumb 98 F4
High Offley Staffs 61 B7
High Ongar Essex 42 D1
High Onn Staffs 62 C2
High Roding Essex 42 C2
High Row Cumb 108 F3
High Salvington W Sus 16 D5
High Sellafield Cumb 98 D2
High Shaw N Yorks 100 E3
High Spen T&W 110 D4
High Stoop Durham 110 E4
High Street Corn 4 D4
High Street Kent 18 B4
High Street Suff 56 E2
High Street Suff 57 B8
High Street Suff 57 D8
High Street Green Suff 56 D4
High Throston Hrtlpl 111 F7
High Toynton Lincs 79 C5
High Trewhitt Northumb 117 D6
High Valleyfield Fife 128 F2
High Westwood Durham 110 D4
High Wray Cumb 99 E5
High Wych Herts 41 C7
High Wycombe Bucks 40 E1
Higham Derbys 76 D3
Higham Kent 29 B8
Higham Lancs 93 F8
Higham Suff 55 C8
Higham Suff 56 F4
Higham Dykes Northumb 110 B4
Higham Ferrers Northants 53 C7
Higham Gobion C Beds 54 F2
Higham on the Hill Leics 63 E7
Higham Wood Kent 29 E6
Highampton Devon 9 D6
Highbridge Highld 136 F4
Highbridge Som 22 E5
Highbrook W Sus 28 F4
Highburton W Yorks 88 C2
Highbury Som 23 E8
Highclere Hants 26 C2
Highcliffe Dorset 14 E3
Higher Ansty Dorset 13 D5
Higher Ashton Devon 10 F3
Higher Ballam Lancs 92 F3
Higher Bartle Lancs 92 F5
Higher Boscaswell Corn 2 C2
Higher Burwardsley Ches W 74 D2
Higher Clovelly Devon 8 B5
Higher End Gtr Man 86 D3
Higher Kinnerton Flint 73 C7
Higher Penwortham Lancs 86 B3
Higher Town Scilly 2 E4
Higher Walreddon Devon 6 B2
Higher Walton Lancs 86 B3
Higher Walton Warr 86 F3
Higher Wheelton Lancs 86 B4
Higher Whitley Ches W 86 F4
Higher Wincham Ches W 74 B3
Higher Wych Ches W 73 E8
Highfield E Yorks 96 F3
Highfield Gtr Man 86 D5
Highfield N Ayrs 118 D3
Highfield Oxon 39 B5
Highfield S Yorks 88 F4
Highfield T&W 110 D4
Highfields Cambs 54 D4
Highfields Northumb 123 D5
Highgate London 41 F5
Highlane Ches E 75 C5
Highlane Derbys 88 F5
Highlaws Cumb 107 E8
Highleadon Glos 36 B4
Highleigh W Sus 16 E2
Highley Shrops 61 F7
Highmoor Cross Oxon 39 F7
Highmoor Hill Mon 36 F1
Highnam Glos 36 C4
Highnam Green Glos 36 B4
Highsted Kent 30 C3
Highstreet Green Essex 55 F8
Hightae Dumfries 107 B7
Hightown Ches E 75 C5
Hightown Mers 85 D4
Hightown Green Suff 56 D3
Highway Wilts 24 B5
Highweek Devon 7 B6
Highworth Swindon 38 E2
Hilborough Norf 67 D8
Hilcote Derbys 76 D4
Hilcott Wilts 25 D6
Hilden Park Kent 29 E6
Hildenborough Kent 29 E6
Hildersham Cambs 55 E6
Hilderstone Staffs 75 F6
Hilderthorpe E Yorks 97 C7
Hilfield Dorset 12 D4
Hilgay Norf 67 E6
Hill Pembs 32 D2
Hill S Glos 36 E3
Hill W Mid 62 E5
Hill Brow W Sus 15 B8
Hill Dale Lancs 86 C2
Hill Dyke Lincs 79 E6
Hill End Durham 110 F3
Hill End Fife 128 E2
Hill End N Yorks 94 D3
Hill Head Hants 15 D6
Hill Head Northumb 110 C2
Hill Mountain Pembs 44 E4
Hill of Beath Fife 128 E3
Hill of Fearn Highld 151 D11
Hill of Mountblairy Aberds 153 C6
Hill Ridware Staffs 62 C4
Hill Top Durham 100 B4
Hill Top Hants 14 D5
Hill Top W Mid 62 E3
Hill Top W Yorks 88 C4
Hill View Dorset 13 E7
Hillam N Yorks 89 B6
Hillbeck Cumb 100 C2
Hillborough Kent 31 C6
Hillbrae Aberds 141 B6
Hillbrae Aberds 152 D6
Hillbutts Dorset 13 D7
Hillclifflane Derbys 76 E2
Hillcommon Som 11 B6
Hillend Fife 128 F3
Hillerton Devon 10 E2
Hillesden Bucks 39 B6
Hillesley Glos 36 F4
Hillfarance Som 11 B6
Hillhead Aberds 152 E5
Hillhead Devon 7 D7
Hillhead S Ayrs 112 C4
Hillhead of Auchentumb Aberds 153 C9
Hillhead of Cocklaw Aberds 153 D10
Hillhouse Borders 121 D8
Hilliclay Highld 158 D3
Hillingdon London 40 F3
Hillington Glasgow 118 C5
Hillington Norf 80 E3
Hillmorton Warks 52 B3
Hillockhead Aberds 140 C3
Hillockhead Aberds 140 D2
Hillside Aberds 141 E8
Hillside Angus 135 C7
Hillside Mers 85 C4
Hillside Orkney 159 J5
Hillside Shetland 160 G6
Hillswick Shetland 160 F4
Hillway IoW 15 F7
Hillwell Shetland 160 M5
Hilmarton Wilts 24 B5
Hilperton Wilts 24 D3
Hilsea Ptsmth 15 D7
Hilston E Yorks 97 F8
Hilton Aberds 153 E9
Hilton Cambs 54 C3
Hilton Cumb 100 B2
Hilton Derbys 76 F2
Hilton Dorset 13 D5
Hilton Durham 101 B6
Hilton Highld 151 C10
Hilton Shrops 61 E7
Hilton Stockton 102 C2
Hilton of Cadboll Highld 151 D11
Himbleton Worcs 50 D4
Himley Staffs 62 E2
Hincaster Cumb 99 F7
Hinckley Leics 63 E8
Hinderclay Suff 56 B4
Hinderton Ches W 73 B7
Hinderwell N Yorks 103 C5
Hindford Shrops 73 F7
Hindhead Sur 27 F6
Hindley Gtr Man 86 D4
Hindley Green Gtr Man 86 D4
Hindlip Worcs 50 D3
Hindolveston Norf 81 E6
Hindon Wilts 24 F4
Hindringham Norf 81 D5
Hingham Norf 68 D3
Hinstock Shrops 61 B6
Hintlesham Suff 56 E4
Hinton Hants 14 E3
Hinton Hereford 48 F5
Hinton Northants 52 D3
Hinton S Glos 24 B2
Hinton Shrops 60 D4
Hinton Ampner Hants 15 B6
Hinton Blewett Bath 23 D7
Hinton Charterhouse Bath 24 D2
Hinton-in-the-Hedges Northants 52 F3
Hinton Martell Dorset 13 D8
Hinton on the Green Worcs 50 E5
Hinton Parva Swindon 38 F2
Hinton St George Som 12 C2
Hinton St Mary Dorset 13 C5
Hinton Waldrist Oxon 38 E3
Hints Shrops 49 B8
Hints Staffs 63 D5
Hinwick Bedford 53 C7
Hinxhill Kent 30 E4
Hinxton Cambs 55 E5
Hinxworth Herts 54 E3
Hipperholme W Yorks 88 B2
Hipswell N Yorks 101 E6
Hirael Gwyn 83 D5
Hiraeth Carms 32 B2
Hirn Aberds 141 D6
Hirnant Powys 59 B7
Hirst N Lanark 119 C8
Hirst Northumb 117 F8
Hirst Courtney N Yorks 89 B7
Hirwaen Denb 72 C5
Hirwaun Rhondda 34 D3
Hiscott Devon 9 B7
Histon Cambs 54 C5
Hitcham Suff 56 D3
Hitchin Herts 40 B4
Hither Green London 28 B4
Hittisleigh Devon 10 E2
Hive E Yorks 96 F4
Hixon Staffs 62 B4
Hoaden Kent 31 D6
Hoaldalbert Mon 35 B7
Hoar Cross Staffs 62 B5
Hoarwithy Hereford 36 B2
Hoath Kent 31 C6
Hobarris Shrops 48 B5
Hobbister Orkney 159 H4
Hobkirk Borders 115 C8
Hobson Durham 110 D4
Hoby Leics 64 C3
Hockering Norf 68 C3
Hockerton Notts 77 D7
Hockley Essex 42 E4
Hockley Heath W Mid 51 B6
Hockliffe C Beds 40 B2
Hockwold cum Wilton Norf 67 F7
Hockworthy Devon 10 C5
Hoddesdon Herts 41 D6
Hoddlesden Blackburn 86 B5
Hoddom Mains Dumfries 107 B8
Hoddomcross Dumfries 107 B8
Hodgeston Pembs 32 E1
Hodley Powys 59 E8
Hodnet Shrops 61 B6
Hodthorpe Derbys 76 B5
Hoe Hants 15 C6
Hoe Norf 68 C2
Hoe Gate Hants 15 C7
Hoff Cumb 100 C1
Hog Patch Sur 27 E6
Hoggard's Green Suff 56 D2
Hoggeston Bucks 39 B8
Hogha Gearraidh W Isles 148 A2
Hoghton Lancs 86 B4
Hognaston Derbys 76 D2
Hogsthorpe Lincs 79 B8
Holbeach Lincs 66 B3
Holbeach Bank Lincs 66 B3
Holbeach Clough Lincs 66 B3
Holbeach Drove Lincs 66 C3
Holbeach Hurn Lincs 66 B3
Holbeach St Johns Lincs 66 C3
Holbeach St Marks Lincs 79 F6
Holbeach St Matthew Lincs 79 F7
Holbeck Notts 76 B5
Holbeck W Yorks 95 F5
Holbeck Woodhouse Notts 76 B5
Holberrow Green Worcs 50 D5
Holbeton Devon 6 D4
Holborn London 41 F6
Holbrook Derbys 76 E3
Holbrook S Yorks 88 F5
Holbrook Suff 57 F5
Holburn Northumb 123 F6
Holbury Hants 14 D5
Holcombe Devon 7 B7
Holcombe Som 23 E8
Holcombe Rogus Devon 11 C5
Holcot Northants 53 C5
Holden Lancs 93 E7
Holdenby Northants 52 C4
Holdenhurst Bmouth 14 E2
Holdgate Shrops 61 F5
Holdingham Lincs 78 E3
Holditch Dorset 11 D8
Hole-in-the-Wall Hereford 36 B3
Holefield Borders 122 F4
Holehouses Ches E 74 B4
Holemoor Devon 9 D6
Holestane Dumfries 113 E8
Holford Som 22 E3
Holgate York 95 D8
Holker Cumb 92 B3
Holkham Norf 80 C4
Hollacombe Devon 9 D5
Holland Orkney 159 C5
Holland Orkney 159 F7
Holland Fen Lincs 78 E5
Holland-on-Sea Essex 43 C8
Hollandstoun Orkney 159 C8
Hollee Dumfries 108 C2
Hollesley Suff 57 E7
Hollicombe Torbay 7 C6
Hollingbourne Kent 30 D2
Hollington Derbys 76 F2
Hollington E Sus 18 D4
Hollington Staffs 75 F7
Hollington Grove Derbys 76 F2
Hollingworth Gtr Man 87 E8
Hollins Gtr Man 87 D6
Hollins Green Warr 86 E4
Hollins Lane Lancs 92 D4
Hollinsclough Staffs 75 C7
Hollinwood Gtr Man 87 D7
Hollinwood Shrops 74 F2
Hollocombe Devon 9 C8
Hollow Meadows S Yorks 88 F3
Holloway Derbys 76 D3
Hollowell Northants 52 B4
Holly End Norf 66 D4
Holly Green Worcs 50 E3
Hollybush Caerph 35 D5
Hollybush E Ayrs 112 C3
Hollybush Worcs 50 F2
Hollym E Yorks 91 B7
Hollywood Worcs 51 B5
Holmbridge W Yorks 88 D2
Holmbury St Mary Sur 28 E2
Holmbush Corn 4 D5
Holmcroft Staffs 62 B3
Holme Cambs 65 F8
Holme Cumb 92 B5
Holme N Yorks 102 F1
Holme Notts 77 D8
Holme W Yorks 88 D2
Holme Chapel Lancs 87 B6
Holme Green N Yorks 95 E8
Holme Hale Norf 67 D8
Holme Lacy Hereford 49 F7
Holme Marsh Hereford 48 D5
Holme next the Sea Norf 80 C3
Holme-on-Spalding-Moor E Yorks 96 F4
Holme on the Wolds E Yorks 97 E5
Holme Pierrepont Notts 77 F6
Holme St Cuthbert Cumb 107 E8
Holme Wood W Yorks 94 F4
Holmer Hereford 49 E7
Holmer Green Bucks 40 E2
Holmes Chapel Ches E 74 C4
Holmesfield Derbys 76 B3
Holmeswood Lancs 86 C2
Holmewood Derbys 76 C4
Holmfirth W Yorks 88 D2
Holmhead Dumfries 113 F7
Holmhead E Ayrs 113 B5
Holmisdale Highld 148 D6
Holmpton E Yorks 91 B7
Holmrook Cumb 98 E2
Holmsgarth Shetland 160 J6
Holmwrangle Cumb 108 E5
Holne Devon 6 C5
Holnest Dorset 12 D4
Holsworthy Devon 8 D5
Holsworthy Beacon Devon 9 D5
Holt Dorset 13 D8
Holt Norf 81 D6
Holt Wilts 24 C3
Holt Worcs 50 C3
Holt Wrex 73 D8
Holt End Hants 26 F4
Holt End Worcs 51 C5
Holt Fleet Worcs 50 C3
Holt Heath Worcs 50 C3
Holt Park W Yorks 95 E5
Holtby York 96 D2
Holton Oxon 39 D6
Holton Som 12 B4
Holton Suff 57 B7
Holton cum Beckering Lincs 90 F5
Holton Heath Dorset 13 E7
Holton le Clay Lincs 91 D6
Holton le Moor Lincs 90 E4
Holton St Mary Suff 56 F4
Holwell Dorset 12 C5
Holwell Herts 54 F2
Holwell Leics 64 B4
Holwell Oxon 38 D2
Holwick Durham 100 B4
Holworth Dorset 13 F5
Holy Cross Worcs 50 B4
Holy Island Northumb 123 E7
Holybourne Hants 26 E5
Holyhead = Caergybi Anglesey 82 C2
Holymoorside Derbys 76 C3
Holyport Windsor 27 B6
Holystone Northumb 117 D5
Holytown N Lanark 119 C7
Holywell Cambs 54 B4
Holywell Corn 4 D2
Holywell Dorset 12 D3
Holywell E Sus 18 F2
Holywell = Treffynnon Flint 73 B5
Holywell Northumb 111 B6
Holywell Green W Yorks 87 C8
Holywell Lake Som 11 B6
Holywell Row Suff 55 B8
Holywood Dumfries 114 F2
Hom Green Hereford 36 B2
Homer Shrops 61 D6
Homersfield Suff 69 F5
Homington Wilts 14 B2
Honey Hill Kent 30 C5
Honey Street Wilts 25 C6
Honey Tye Suff 56 F3
Honeyborough Pembs 44 E4
Honeybourne Worcs 51 E6
Honeychurch Devon 9 D8
Honiley Warks 51 B7
Honing Norf 69 B6
Honingham Norf 68 C4
Honington Lincs 78 E2
Honington Suff 56 B3
Honington Warks 51 E7
Honiton Devon 11 D6
Honley W Yorks 88 C2
Hoo Green Ches E 86 F5
Hoo St Werburgh Medway 29 B8
Hood Green S Yorks 88 D4
Hooe E Sus 18 E3
Hooe Plym 6 D3
Hooe Common E Sus 18 D3
Hook E Yorks 89 B8
Hook Hants 26 D5
Hook London 28 C2
Hook Pembs 44 D4
Hook Wilts 37 F7
Hook Green Kent 18 B3
Hook Green Kent 29 C7
Hook Norton Oxon 51 F8
Hooke Dorset 12 E3
Hookgate Staffs 74 F4
Hookway Devon 10 E3
Hookwood Sur 28 E3
Hoole Ches W 73 C8
Hooley Sur 28 D3
Hoop Mon 36 D2
Hooton Ches W 73 B7
Hooton Levitt S Yorks 89 E6
Hooton Pagnell S Yorks 89 D5
Hooton Roberts S Yorks 89 E5
Hop Pole Lincs 65 C8
Hope Derbys 88 F2
Hope Devon 6 F4
Hope Highld 156 B7
Hope Powys 60 D2
Hope Shrops 60 D3
Hope Staffs 75 D8
Hope = Yr Hôb Flint 73 D7
Hope Bagot Shrops 49 B7
Hope Bowdler Shrops 60 E4
Hope End Green Essex 42 B1
Hope Green Ches E 87 F7
Hope Mansell Hereford 36 C3
Hope under Dinmore Hereford 49 D7
Hopeman Moray 152 B1
Hope's Green Essex 42 F3
Hopesay Shrops 60 F3
Hopley's Green Hereford 48 D5
Hopperton N Yorks 95 D7
Hopstone Shrops 61 E7
Hopton Shrops 60 B3
Hopton Shrops 61 B5
Hopton Staffs 62 B3
Hopton Suff 56 B3
Hopton Cangeford Shrops 60 F5
Hopton Castle Shrops 49 B5
Hopton on Sea Norf 69 D8
Hopton Wafers Shrops 49 B8
Hoptonheath Shrops 49 B5
Hopwas Staffs 63 D5
Hopwood Gtr Man 87 D6
Hopwood Worcs 50 B5
Horam E Sus 18 D2
Horbling Lincs 78 F4
Horbury W Yorks 88 C3
Horcott Glos 38 D1
Horden Durham 111 E7
Horderley Shrops 60 F4
Hordle Hants 14 E3
Hordley Shrops 73 F7
Horeb Carms 33 B6
Horeb Carms 33 D5
Horeb Ceredig 46 E2
Horfield Bristol 23 B8
Horham Suff 57 B6
Horkesley Heath Essex 43 B5
Horkstow N Lincs 90 C3
Horley Oxon 52 E2
Horley Sur 28 E3
Hornblotton Green Som 23 F7
Hornby Lancs 93 C5
Hornby N Yorks 101 E7
Hornby N Yorks 102 D1
Horncastle Lincs 79 C5
Hornchurch London 41 F8
Horncliffe Northumb 122 E5
Horndean Borders 122 E4
Horndean Hants 15 C8
Horndon Devon 6 B3
Horndon on the Hill Thurrock 42 F2
Horne Sur 28 E4
Horniehaugh Angus 134 C4
Horning Norf 69 C6
Horninghold Leics 64 E5
Horninglow Staffs 63 B6
Horningsea Cambs 55 C5
Horningsham Wilts 24 E3
Horningtoft Norf 80 E5
Horns Corner Kent 18 C4
Horns Cross Devon 9 B5
Horns Cross E Sus 18 C5
Hornsby Cumb 108 D5
Hornsea E Yorks 97 E8
Hornsea Bridge E Yorks 97 E8
Hornsey London 41 F6
Hornton Oxon 51 E8
Horrabridge Devon 6 C3
Horringer Suff 56 C2
Horringford IoW 15 F6
Horse Bridge Staffs 75 D6
Horsebridge Devon 6 B2
Horsebridge Hants 25 F8
Horsebrook Staffs 62 C2
Horsehay Telford 61 D6
Horseheath Cambs 55 E7
Horsehouse N Yorks 101 F5
Horsell Sur 27 D7
Horseman's Green Wrex 73 E8
Horseway Cambs 66 F4
Horsey Norf 69 B7
Horsford Norf 68 C4
Horsforth W Yorks 94 F5
Horsham W Sus 28 F2
Horsham Worcs 50 D2
Horsham St Faith Norf 68 C5
Horsington Lincs 78 C4
Horsington Som 12 B5
Horsley Derbys 76 E3
Horsley Glos 37 E5
Horsley Northumb 110 C3
Horsley Northumb 116 E4
Horsley Cross Essex 43 B7
Horsley Woodhouse Derbys 76 E3
Horsleycross Street Essex 43 B7
Horsleyhill Borders 115 C8
Horsleyhope Durham 110 E3
Horsmonden Kent 29 E7
Horspath Oxon 39 D5
Horstead Norf 69 C5
Horsted Keynes W Sus 17 B7
Horton Bucks 40 C2
Horton Dorset 13 D8
Horton Lancs 93 D8
Horton Northants 53 D6
Horton S Glos 36 F4
Horton Shrops 60 B4
Horton Som 11 C8
Horton Staffs 75 D6
Horton Swansea 33 F5
Horton Wilts 25 C5
Horton Windsor 27 B8
Horton-cum-Studley Oxon 39 C5
Horton Green Ches W 73 E8
Horton Heath Hants 15 C5
Horton in Ribblesdale N Yorks 93 B8
Horton Kirby Kent 29 C6
Hortonlane Shrops 60 C4
Horwich Gtr Man 86 C4
Horwich End Derbys 87 F8
Horwood Devon 9 B7
Hose Leics 64 B4
Hoselaw Borders 122 F4
Hoses Cumb 98 E4
Hosh Perth 127 B7
Hosta W Isles 148 A2
Hoswick Shetland 160 L6
Hotham E Yorks 96 F4
Hothfield Kent 30 E3
Hoton Leics 64 B2
Houbie Shetland 160 D8
Houdston S Ayrs 112 E1
Hough Ches E 74 D4
Hough Ches E 75 B5
Hough Green Halton 86 F2
Hough-on-the-Hill Lincs 78 E2
Hougham Lincs 77 E8
Houghton Cambs 54 B3
Houghton Cumb 108 D4
Houghton Hants 25 F8
Houghton Pembs 44 E4
Houghton W Sus 16 C4
Houghton Conquest C Beds 53 E8
Houghton Green E Sus 19 C6
Houghton Green Warr 86 E4
Houghton-le-Side Darl 101 B7
Houghton-Le-Spring T&W 111 E6
Houghton on the Hill Leics 64 D3
Houghton Regis C Beds 40 B3
Houghton St Giles Norf 80 D5
Houlland Shetland 160 F7
Houlland Shetland 160 H5
Houlsyke N Yorks 103 D5
Hound Hants 15 D5
Hound Green Hants 26 D5
Houndslow Borders 122 E2
Houndwood Borders 122 C4
Hounslow London 28 B2
Hounslow Green Essex 42 C2
Housay Shetland 160 F8
House of Daviot Highld 151 G10
House of Glenmuick Aberds 140 E2
Housetter Shetland 160 E5
Houss Shetland 160 K5
Houston Renfs 118 C4
Houstry Highld 158 G3
Houton Orkney 159 H4
Hove Brighton 17 D6
Hoveringham Notts 77 E6
Hoveton Norf 69 C6
Hovingham N Yorks 96 B2
How Cumb 108 D5
How Caple Hereford 49 F8
How End C Beds 53 E8
How Green Kent 29 E5
Howbrook S Yorks 88 E4
Howden Borders 116 B2
Howden E Yorks 89 B8
Howden-le-Wear Durham 110 F4
Howe Highld 158 D5
Howe N Yorks 101 F8
Howe Norf 69 D5
Howe Bridge Gtr Man 86 D4
Howe Green Essex 42 D3
Howe of Teuchar Aberds 153 D7
Howe Street Essex 42 C2
Howe Street Essex 55 F7
Howell Lincs 78 E4
Howey Powys 48 D2
Howgate Midloth 120 D5
Howick Northumb 117 C8
Howle Durham 101 B5
Howle Telford 61 B6
Howlett End Essex 55 F6
Howley Som 11 D7
Hownam Borders 116 C3
Hownam Mains Borders 116 B3
Howpasley Borders 115 D6
Howsham N Lincs 90 D4
Howsham N Yorks 96 C3
Howslack Dumfries 114 D3
Howtel Northumb 122 F4
Howton Hereford 35 B8
Howtown Cumb 99 C6
Howwood Renfs 118 C3
Hoxne Suff 57 B5
Hoy Orkney 159 H3
Hoylake Mers 85 F3
Hoyland S Yorks 88 D4
Hoylandswaine S Yorks 88 D3
Hubberholme N Yorks 94 B2
Hubbert's Bridge Lincs 79 E5
Huby N Yorks 95 C8
Huby N Yorks 95 E5
Hucclecote Glos 37 C5
Hucking Kent 30 D2
Hucknall Notts 76 E5
Huddersfield W Yorks 88 C2
Huddington Worcs 50 D4
Hudswell N Yorks 101 D6
Huggate E Yorks 96 D4
Hugglescote Leics 63 C8
Hugh Town Scilly 2 E4
Hughenden Valley Bucks 40 E1
Hughley Shrops 61 E5
Huish Devon 9 C7
Huish Wilts 25 C6
Huish Champflower Som 11 B5
Huish Episcopi Som 12 B2
Huisinis W Isles 154 F4
Hulcott Bucks 40 C1
Hulland Derbys 76 E2
Hulland Ward Derbys 76 E2
Hullavington Wilts 37 F5
Hullbridge Essex 42 E4
Hulme Gtr Man 87 E6

Kirkton of Auchterhouse Angus 134 F3
Kirkton of Auchterless Aberds 153 D7
Kirkton of Barevan Highld 151 G11
Kirkton of Bourtie Aberds 141 B7
Kirkton of Collace Perth 134 F1
Kirkton of Craig Angus 135 D7
Kirkton of Culsalmond Aberds 153 E6
Kirkton of Durris Aberds 141 E6
Kirkton of Glenbuchat Aberds 140 C2
Kirkton of Glenisla Angus 134 C2
Kirkton of Kingoldrum Angus 134 D3
Kirkton of Largo Fife 129 D6
Kirkton of Lethendy Perth 133 E8
Kirkton of Logie Buchan Aberds 141 B8
Kirkton of Maryculter Aberds 141 E7
Kirkton of Menmuir Angus 135 C5
Kirkton of Monikie Angus 135 F5
Kirkton of Oyne Aberds 141 B5
Kirkton of Rayne Aberds 153 F6
Kirkton of Skene Aberds 141 D7
Kirkton of Tough Aberds 140 C5
Kirktonhill Borders 121 D7
Kirktown Aberds 153 C10
Kirktown of Alvah Aberds 153 B6
Kirktown of Deskford Moray 152 B5
Kirktown of Fetteresso Aberds 141 F7
Kirktown of Mortlach Moray 152 E3
Kirktown of Slains Aberds 141 B9
Kirkurd Borders 120 E4
Kirkwall Orkney 159 G5
Kirkwhelpington Northumb 117 F5
Kirmington N Lincs 90 C5
Kirmond le Mire Lincs 91 E5
Kirn Argyll 145 F10
Kirriemuir Angus 134 D3
Kirstead Green Norf 69 E5
Kirtlebridge Dumfries 108 B2
Kirtleton Dumfries 115 F5
Kirtling Cambs 55 D7
Kirtling Green Cambs 55 D7
Kirtlington Oxon 38 C4
Kirtomy Highld 157 C10
Kirton Lincs 79 F6
Kirton Notts 77 C6
Kirton Suff 57 F6
Kirton End Lincs 79 E5
Kirton Holme Lincs 79 E5
Kirton in Lindsey N Lincs 90 E3
Kislingbury Northants 52 D4
Kites Hardwick Warks 52 C2
Kittisford Som 11 B5
Kittle Swansea 33 F6
Kitt's Green W Mid 63 F5
Kitt's Moss Gtr Man 87 F6
Kittybrewster Aberdeen 141 D8
Kitwood Hants 26 F4
Kivernoll Hereford 49 F6
Kiveton Park S Yorks 89 F5
Knaith Lincs 90 F2
Knaith Park Lincs 90 F2
Knap Corner Dorset 13 B6
Knaphill Sur 27 D7
Knapp Perth 134 F2
Knapp Som 11 B8
Knapthorpe Notts 77 D7
Knapton Norf 81 D9
Knapton York 95 D8
Knapton Green Hereford 49 D6
Knapwell Cambs 54 C4
Knaresborough N Yorks 95 D6
Knarsdale Northumb 109 D6
Knauchland Moray 152 C5
Knaven Aberds 153 D8
Knayton N Yorks 102 F2
Knebworth Herts 41 B5
Knedlington E Yorks 89 B8
Kneesall Notts 77 C7
Kneesworth Cambs 54 E4
Kneeton Notts 77 E7
Knelston Swansea 33 F5
Knenhall Staffs 75 F6
Knettishall Suff 68 F2
Knightacott Devon 21 F5
Knightcote Warks 51 D8
Knightley Dale Staffs 62 B2
Knighton Devon 6 E3
Knighton Leicester 64 D2
Knighton = Tref-Y-Clawdd Powys 48 B4
Knighton Staffs 61 B7
Knighton Staffs 74 E4
Knightswood Glasgow 118 C5
Knightwick Worcs 50 D2
Knill Hereford 48 C4
Knipton Leics 77 F8
Knitsley Durham 110 E4
Kniveton Derbys 76 D2
Knock Argyll 147 H8
Knock Cumb 100 B1
Knock Moray 152 C5
Knockally Highld 158 H3
Knockan Highld 156 H5
Knockandhu Moray 139 B8
Knockando Moray 152 D1
Knockando Ho. Moray 152 D2
Knockbain Highld 151 F9
Knockbreck Highld 148 B7
Knockbrex Dumfries 106 E2
Knockdee Highld 158 D3
Knockdolian S Ayrs 104 A5
Knockenkelly N Ayrs 143 F11
Knockentiber E Ayrs 118 F3
Knockespock Ho. Aberds 140 B4
Knockfarrel Highld 151 F8
Knockglass Dumfries 104 D4
Knockholt Kent 29 D5
Knockholt Pound Kent 29 D5
Knockie Lodge Highld 137 C7
Knockin Shrops 60 B3
Knockinlaw E Ayrs 118 F4
Knocklearn Dumfries 106 B4
Knocknaha Argyll 143 G7
Knocknain Dumfries 104 C3
Knockrome Argyll 144 F4
Knocksharry IoM 84 D2
Knodishall Suff 57 C8
Knolls Green Ches E 74 B5
Knolton Wrex 73 F7
Knolton Bryn Wrex 73 F7
Knook Wilts 24 E4
Knossington Leics 64 D5
Knott End-on-Sea Lancs 92 E3
Knotting Bedford 53 C8
Knotting Green Bedford 53 C8
Knottingley W Yorks 89 B6
Knotts Cumb 99 B6
Knotts Lancs 93 D7
Knotty Ash Mers 86 E2
Knotty Green Bucks 40 E2
Knowbury Shrops 49 B7
Knowe Dumfries 105 B7
Knowehead Dumfries 113 E6
Knowes of Elrick Aberds 152 C6
Knowesgate Northumb 117 F5
Knoweton N Lanark 119 D7
Knowhead Aberds 153 C9
Knowl Hill Windsor 27 B6
Knowle Bristol 23 B8
Knowle Devon 10 D2
Knowle Devon 11 F5
Knowle Devon 20 F3
Knowle Shrops 49 B7
Knowle W Mid 51 B6
Knowle Green Lancs 93 F6
Knowle Park W Yorks 94 E3
Knowlton Dorset 13 C8
Knowlton Kent 31 D6
Knowsley Mers 86 E2
Knowstone Devon 10 B3
Knox Bridge Kent 29 E8
Knucklas Powys 48 B4
Knuston Northants 53 C7
Knutsford Ches E 74 B4
Knutton Staffs 74 E5
Knypersley Staffs 75 D5
Kuggar Corn 3 E6
Kyle of Lochalsh Highld 149 F12
Kyleakin Highld 149 F12
Kylerhea Highld 149 F12
Kylesknoydart Highld 147 B11
Kylesku Highld 156 F5
Kylesmorar Highld 147 B11
Kylestrome Highld 156 F5
Kyllachy House Highld 138 B3
Kynaston Shrops 60 B3
Kynnersley Telford 61 C6
Kyre Magna Worcs 49 C8

L

La Fontenelle Guern 16
La Planque Guern 16
Labost W Isles 155 C7
Lacasaidh W Isles 155 E8
Lacasdal W Isles 155 D9
Laceby NE Lincs 91 D6
Lacey Green Bucks 39 E8
Lach Dennis Ches W 74 B4
Lackford Suff 55 B8
Lacock Wilts 24 C4
Ladbroke Warks 52 D2
Laddingford Kent 29 E7
Lade Bank Lincs 79 D6
Ladock Corn 4 D3
Lady Orkney 159 D7
Ladybank Fife 128 C5
Ladykirk Borders 122 E4
Ladysford Aberds 153 B9
Laga Highld 147 E9
Lagalochan Argyll 124 D4
Lagavulin Argyll 142 D5
Lagg Argyll 144 F4
Lagg N Ayrs 143 F10
Laggan Argyll 142 C3
Laggan Highld 137 E5
Laggan Highld 138 E2
Laggan Highld 147 D10
Laggan S Ayrs 112 F2
Lagganulva Argyll 146 G7
Laide Highld 155 H13
Laigh Fenwick E Ayrs 118 E4
Laigh Glengall S Ayrs 112 C3
Laighmuir E Ayrs 118 E4
Laindon Essex 42 F2
Lair Highld 150 G3
Lairg Highld 157 J8
Lairg Lodge Highld 157 J8
Lairg Muir Highld 157 J8
Lairgmore Highld 151 H8
Laisterdyke W Yorks 94 F4
Laithes Cumb 108 F4
Lake IoW 15 F6
Lake Wilts 25 F6
Lakenham Norf 68 D5
Lakenheath Suff 67 F7
Lakesend Norf 66 E5
Lakeside Cumb 99 F5
Laleham Sur 27 C8
Laleston Bridgend 21 B7
Lamarsh Essex 56 F2
Lamas Norf 81 E8
Lambden Borders 122 E3
Lamberhurst Kent 18 B3
Lamberhurst Quarter Kent 18 B3
Lamberton Borders 123 D5
Lambeth London 28 B4
Lambhill Glasgow 119 C5
Lambley Northumb 109 D6
Lambley Notts 77 E6
Lamborough Hill Oxon 38 D4
Lambourn W Berks 25 B8
Lambourne End Essex 41 E7
Lambs Green W Sus 28 F3
Lambston Pembs 44 D4
Lambton T&W 111 D5
Lamerton Devon 6 B2
Lamesley T&W 111 D5
Laminess Orkney 159 E7
Lamington Highld 151 D10
Lamington S Lanark 120 F2
Lamlash N Ayrs 143 E11
Lamloch Dumfries 112 E5
Lamonby Cumb 108 F4
Lamorna Corn 2 D3
Lamorran Corn 3 B7
Lampardbrook Suff 57 C6
Lampeter = Llanbedr Pont Steffan Ceredig 46 E4
Lampeter Velfrey Pembs 32 C2
Lamphey Pembs 32 D1
Lamplugh Cumb 98 B2
Lamport Northants 53 B5
Lamyatt Som 23 F8
Lana Devon 8 E5
Lanark S Lanark 119 E8
Lancaster Lancs 92 C4
Lanchester Durham 110 E4
Lancing W Sus 17 D5
Landbeach Cambs 55 C5
Landcross Devon 9 B6
Landerberry Aberds 141 D6
Landford Wilts 14 C3
Landford Manor Wilts 14 B3
Landimore Swansea 33 E5
Landkey Devon 20 F4
Landore Swansea 33 E7
Landrake Corn 5 C8
Landscove Devon 7 C5
Landshipping Pembs 32 C1
Landshipping Quay Pembs 32 C1
Landulph Corn 6 C2
Landwade Suff 55 C7
Lane Corn 4 C3
Lane End Bucks 39 E8
Lane End Cumb 98 E3
Lane End Dorset 13 E6
Lane End Hants 15 B6
Lane End IoW 15 F7
Lane End Lancs 93 E8
Lane Ends Lancs 93 D7
Lane Ends Lancs 93 F7
Lane Ends N Yorks 94 E2
Lane Head Derbys 75 B8
Lane Head Durham 101 C6
Lane Head Gtr Man 86 E4
Lane Head W Yorks 88 D2
Lane Side Lancs 87 B5
Laneast Corn 8 F4
Laneham Notts 77 B8
Lanehead Durham 109 E8
Lanehead Northumb 116 F3
Lanercost Cumb 109 C5
Laneshaw Bridge Lancs 94 E2
Lanfach Caerph 35 E6
Langar Notts 77 F7
Langbank Renfs 118 B3
Langbar N Yorks 94 D3
Langburnshiels Borders 115 D8
Langcliffe N Yorks 93 C8
Langdale Highld 157 E9
Langdale End N Yorks 103 E7
Langdon Corn 8 F5
Langdon Beck Durham 109 F8
Langdon Hills Essex 42 F2
Langdyke Fife 128 D5
Langenhoe Essex 43 C6
Langford C Beds 54 E2
Langford Devon 10 D5
Langford Essex 42 D4
Langford Notts 77 D8
Langford Oxon 38 D2
Langford Budville Som 11 B6
Langham Essex 56 F4
Langham Norf 81 C6
Langham Rutland 64 C5
Langham Suff 56 C3
Langhaugh Borders 120 F5
Langho Lancs 93 F7
Langholm Dumfries 115 F6
Langleeford Northumb 117 B5
Langley Ches E 75 B6
Langley Hants 14 D5
Langley Herts 41 B5
Langley Kent 30 D2
Langley Northumb 109 C8
Langley Slough 27 B8
Langley W Sus 16 B2
Langley Warks 51 C6
Langley Burrell Wilts 24 B4
Langley Common Derbys 76 F2
Langley Heath Kent 30 D2
Langley Lower Green Essex 54 F5
Langley Marsh Som 11 B5
Langley Park Durham 110 E5
Langley Street Norf 69 D6
Langley Upper Green Essex 54 F5
Langney E Sus 18 E3
Langold Notts 89 F6
Langore Corn 8 F5
Langport Som 12 B2
Langrick Lincs 79 E5
Langridge Bath 24 C2
Langridge Ford Devon 9 B7
Langrigg Cumb 107 E8
Langrish Hants 15 B8
Langsett S Yorks 88 D3
Langshaw Borders 121 F8
Langside Perth 127 C6
Langskaill Orkney 159 D5
Langstone Hants 15 D8
Langstone Newport 35 E7
Langthorne N Yorks 101 E7
Langthorpe N Yorks 95 C6
Langthwaite N Yorks 101 D5
Langtoft E Yorks 97 C6
Langtoft Lincs 65 C8
Langton Durham 101 C6
Langton Lincs 78 C5
Langton Lincs 79 B6
Langton N Yorks 96 C3
Langton by Wragby Lincs 78 B4
Langton Green Kent 18 B2
Langton Green Suff 56 B5
Langton Herring Dorset 12 F4
Langton Matravers Dorset 13 G8
Langtree Devon 9 C6
Langwathby Cumb 109 F5
Langwell Ho. Highld 158 H3
Langwell Lodge Highld 156 J4
Langwith Derbys 76 C5
Langwith Junction Derbys 76 C5
Langworth Lincs 78 B3
Lanivet Corn 4 C5
Lanlivery Corn 5 D5
Lanner Corn 3 C6
Lanreath Corn 5 D6
Lansallos Corn 5 D6
Lansdown Glos 37 B6
Lanteglos Highway Corn 5 D6
Lanton Borders 116 B2
Lanton Northumb 122 F5
Lapford Devon 10 D2
Laphroaig Argyll 142 D4
Lapley Staffs 62 C2
Lapworth Warks 51 B6
Larachbeg Highld 147 G9
Larbert Falk 127 F7
Larden Green Ches E 74 D2
Largie Aberds 152 E6
Largiemore Argyll 145 E8
Largoward Fife 129 D6
Largs N Ayrs 118 D2
Largybeg N Ayrs 143 F11
Largymore N Ayrs 143 F11
Larkfield Invclyd 118 B2
Larkhall S Lanark 119 D7
Larkhill Wilts 25 E6
Larling Norf 68 F2
Larriston Borders 115 E8
Lartington Durham 101 C5
Lary Aberds 140 D2
Lasham Hants 26 E4
Lashenden Kent 30 E2
Lassington Glos 36 B4
Lassodie Fife 128 E3
Lastingham N Yorks 103 E5
Latcham Som 23 E6
Latchford Herts 41 B6
Latchford Warr 86 F4
Latchingdon Essex 42 D4
Latchley Corn 6 B2
Lately Common Warr 86 E4
Lathbury M Keynes 53 E6
Latheron Highld 158 G3
Latheronwheel Highld 158 G3
Latheronwheel Ho. Highld 158 G3
Lathones Fife 129 D6
Latimer Bucks 40 E3
Latteridge S Glos 36 F3
Lattiford Som 12 B4
Latton Wilts 37 E7
Latton Bush Essex 41 D7
Lauchintilly Aberds 141 C6
Lauder Borders 121 E8
Laugharne Carms 32 C4
Laughterton Lincs 77 B8
Laughton E Sus 18 D2
Laughton Leics 64 F3
Laughton Lincs 78 F3
Laughton Lincs 90 E2
Laughton Common S Yorks 89 F6
Laughton en le Morthen S Yorks 89 F6
Launcells Corn 8 D4
Launceston Corn 8 F5
Launton Oxon 39 B6
Laurencekirk Aberds 135 B7
Laurieston Dumfries 106 C3
Laurieston Falk 120 B2
Lavendon M Keynes 53 D7
Lavenham Suff 56 E3
Laverhay Dumfries 114 E4
Laversdale Cumb 108 C4
Laverstock Wilts 25 F6
Laverstoke Hants 26 E2
Laverton Glos 51 F5
Laverton N Yorks 94 B5
Laverton Som 24 D2
Lavister Wrex 73 D7
Law S Lanark 119 D8
Lawers Perth 127 B6
Lawers Perth 132 F3
Lawford Essex 56 F4
Lawhitton Corn 9 F5
Lawkland N Yorks 93 C7
Lawley Telford 61 D6
Lawnhead Staffs 62 B2
Lawrenny Pembs 32 D1
Lawshall Suff 56 D2
Lawton Hereford 49 D6
Laxey IoM 84 D4
Laxfield Suff 57 B6
Laxfirth Shetland 160 H6
Laxfirth Shetland 160 J6
Laxford Bridge Highld 156 E5
Laxo Shetland 160 G6
Laxobigging Shetland 160 F6
Laxton E Yorks 89 B8
Laxton Northants 65 E6
Laxton Notts 77 C7
Laycock W Yorks 94 E3
Layer Breton Essex 43 C5
Layer de la Haye Essex 43 C5
Layer Marney Essex 43 C5
Layham Suff 56 E4
Laylands Green W Berks 25 C8
Laytham E Yorks 96 F3
Layton Blackpool 92 F3
Lazenby Redcar 102 B3
Lazonby Cumb 108 F5
Le Planel Guern 16
Le Skerne Haughton Darl 101 C8
Le Villocq Guern 16
Lea Derbys 76 D3
Lea Hereford 36 B3
Lea Lincs 90 F2
Lea Shrops 60 D4
Lea Shrops 60 F3
Lea Wilts 37 F6
Lea Marston Warks 63 E6
Lea Town Lancs 92 F4
Leabrooks Derbys 76 D4
Leac a Li W Isles 154 H6
Leachkin Highld 151 G9
Leadburn Midloth 120 D5
Leaden Roding Essex 42 C1
Leadenham Lincs 78 D2
Leadgate Cumb 109 E7
Leadgate Durham 110 D4
Leadgate T&W 110 D4
Leadhills S Lanark 113 C8
Leafield Oxon 38 C3
Leagrave Luton 40 B3
Leake N Yorks 102 E2
Leake Commonside Lincs 79 D6
Lealholm N Yorks 103 D5
Lealt Argyll 144 D5
Lealt Highld 149 B10
Leamington Hastings Warks 52 C2
Leamonsley Staffs 62 D5
Leamside Durham 111 E6
Leanaig Highld 151 F8
Leargybreck Argyll 144 F4
Leasgill Cumb 99 F6
Leasingham Lincs 78 E3
Leasingthorne Durham 101 B7
Leasowe Mers 85 E3
Leatherhead Sur 28 D2
Leatherhead Common Sur 28 D2
Leathley N Yorks 94 E5
Leaton Shrops 60 C4
Leaveland Kent 30 D4
Leavening N Yorks 96 C3
Leaves Green London 28 C5
Leazes Durham 110 D4
Lebberston N Yorks 103 F8
Lechlade-on-Thames Glos 38 E2
Leck Lancs 93 B6
Leckford Hants 25 F8
Leckfurin Highld 157 D10
Leckgruinart Argyll 142 B3
Leckhampstead Bucks 52 F5
Leckhampstead W Berks 26 B2
Leckhampstead Thicket W Berks 26 B2
Leckhampton Glos 37 C6
Leckie Highld 150 E3
Leckmelm Highld 150 B4
Leckwith V Glam 22 B3
Leconfield E Yorks 97 E6
Ledaig Argyll 124 B5
Ledburn Bucks 40 B2
Ledbury Hereford 50 F2
Ledcharrie Stirling 126 B4
Ledgemoor Hereford 49 D6
Ledicot Hereford 49 C6
Ledmore Highld 156 H5
Lednagullin Highld 157 C10
Ledsham Ches W 73 B7
Ledsham W Yorks 89 B5
Ledston W Yorks 88 B5
Ledston Luck W Yorks 95 F7
Ledwell Oxon 38 B4
Lee Argyll 146 J7
Lee Devon 20 E3
Lee Hants 14 C4
Lee Lancs 93 D5
Lee Shrops 73 F8
Lee Brockhurst Shrops 60 B5
Lee Clump Bucks 40 D2
Lee Mill Devon 6 D4
Lee Moor Devon 6 C3
Lee-on-the-Solent Hants 15 D6
Leeans Shetland 160 J5
Leebotten Shetland 160 L6
Leebotwood Shrops 60 E4
Leece Cumb 92 C2
Leechpool Pembs 44 D4
Leeds Kent 30 D2
Leeds W Yorks 95 F5
Leedstown Corn 2 C5
Leek Staffs 75 D6
Leek Wootton Warks 51 C7
Leekbrook Staffs 75 D6
Leeming N Yorks 101 F7
Leeming Bar N Yorks 101 E7
Lees Derbys 76 F2
Lees Gtr Man 87 D7
Lees W Yorks 94 F3
Leeswood Flint 73 C6
Legbourne Lincs 91 F7
Legerwood Borders 121 E8
Legsby Lincs 90 F5
Leicester Leicester 64 D2
Leicester Forest East Leics 64 D2
Leigh Dorset 12 D4
Leigh Glos 37 B5
Leigh Gtr Man 86 D4
Leigh Kent 29 E6
Leigh Shrops 60 D3
Leigh Sur 28 E3
Leigh Wilts 37 E7
Leigh Worcs 50 D2
Leigh Beck Essex 42 F4
Leigh Common Som 12 B5
Leigh Delamere Wilts 24 B3
Leigh Green Kent 19 B6
Leigh on Sea Southend 42 F4
Leigh Park Hants 15 D8
Leigh Sinton Worcs 50 D2
Leigh upon Mendip Som 23 E8
Leigh Woods N Som 23 B7
Leighswood W Mid 62 D4
Leighterton Glos 37 E5
Leighton N Yorks 94 B4
Leighton Powys 60 D2
Leighton Shrops 61 D6
Leighton Som 24 E2
Leighton Bromswold Cambs 54 B2
Leighton Buzzard C Beds 40 B2
Leinthall Earls Hereford 49 C6
Leinthall Starkes Hereford 49 C6
Leintwardine Hereford 49 B6
Leire Leics 64 E2
Leirinmore Highld 156 C7
Leiston Suff 57 C8
Leitfie Perth 134 E2
Leith Edin 121 B5
Leitholm Borders 122 E3
Lelant Corn 2 C4
Lelley E Yorks 97 F8
Lem Hill Worcs 50 B2
Lemmington Hall Northumb 117 C7
Lempitlaw Borders 122 F3
Lenchwick Worcs 50 E5
Lendalfoot S Ayrs 112 F1
Lendrick Lodge Stirling 126 D4
Lenham Kent 30 D2
Lenham Heath Kent 30 E3
Lennel Borders 122 E4
Lennoxtown E Dunb 119 B6
Lenton Lincs 78 F3
Lenton Nottingham 77 F5
Lentran Highld 151 G8
Lenwade Norf 68 C3
Leny Ho. Stirling 126 D5
Lenzie E Dunb 119 B6
Leoch Angus 134 F3
Leochel-Cushnie Aberds 140 C4
Leominster Hereford 49 D6
Leonard Stanley Glos 37 D5
Leorin Argyll 142 D4
Lepe Hants 15 E5
Lephin Highld 148 D6
Lephinchapel Argyll 145 D8
Lephinmore Argyll 145 D8
Leppington N Yorks 96 C3
Lepton W Yorks 88 C3
Lerryn Corn 5 D6
Lerwick Shetland 160 J6
Lesbury Northumb 117 C8
Leslie Aberds 140 B4
Leslie Fife 128 D4
Lesmahagow S Lanark 119 F8
Lesnewth Corn 8 E3
Lessendrum Aberds 152 D5
Lessingham Norf 69 B6
Lessonhall Cumb 108 D2
Leswalt Dumfries 104 C4
Letchmore Heath Herts 40 E4
Letchworth Herts 54 F3
Letcombe Bassett Oxon 38 F3
Letcombe Regis Oxon 38 F3
Letham Angus 135 E5
Letham Falk 127 F7
Letham Fife 128 C5
Letham Perth 128 B2
Letham Grange Angus 135 E6
Lethenty Aberds 153 D8
Letheringham Suff 57 D6
Letheringsett Norf 81 D6
Lettaford Devon 10 F2
Lettan Orkney 159 D8
Letterewe Highld 150 D2
Letterfearn Highld 149 F13
Letterfinlay Highld 137 E5
Lettermorar Highld 147 C10
Lettermore Argyll 146 G7
Letters Highld 150 C4
Letterston Pembs 44 C4
Lettoch Highld 139 C6
Lettoch Highld 151 H13
Letton Hereford 48 E5
Letton Hereford 49 B5
Letton Green Norf 68 D2
Letty Green Herts 41 C5
Letwell S Yorks 89 F6
Leuchars Fife 129 B6
Leuchars Ho. Moray 152 B2
Leumrabhagh W Isles 155 F8
Levan Invclyd 118 B2
Levaneap Shetland 160 G6
Levedale Staffs 62 C2
Leven E Yorks 97 E7
Leven Fife 129 D5
Levencorroch N Ayrs 143 F11
Levens Cumb 99 F6
Levens Green Herts 41 B6
Levenshulme Gtr Man 87 E6
Levenwick Shetland 160 L6
Leverburgh = An t-Ob W Isles 154 J5
Leverington Cambs 66 C4
Leverton Lincs 79 E7
Leverton Highgate Lincs 79 E7
Leverton Lucasgate Lincs 79 E7
Leverton Outgate Lincs 79 E7
Levington Suff 57 F6
Levisham N Yorks 103 E6
Levishie Highld 137 C7
Lew Oxon 38 D3
Lewannick Corn 8 F4
Lewdown Devon 9 F6
Lewes E Sus 17 C8
Leweston Pembs 44 C4
Lewisham London 28 B4
Lewiston Highld 137 B8
Lewistown Bridgend 34 F3
Lewknor Oxon 39 E7
Leworthy Devon 8 D5
Leworthy Devon 21 F5
Lewtrenchard Devon 9 F6
Lexden Essex 43 B5
Ley Aberds 140 C4
Ley Corn 5 C6
Leybourne Kent 29 D7
Leyburn N Yorks 101 E6
Leyfields Staffs 63 D6
Leyhill Bucks 40 D2
Leyland Lancs 86 B3
Leylodge Aberds 141 C6
Leymoor W Yorks 88 C2
Leys Aberds 153 C10
Leys Perth 134 F2
Leys Castle Highld 151 G9
Leys of Cossans Angus 134 E3
Leysdown-on-Sea Kent 30 B4
Leysmill Angus 135 E6
Leysters Pole Hereford 49 C7
Leyton London 41 F6
Leytonstone London 41 F6
Lezant Corn 5 B8
Leziate Norf 67 C6
Lhanbryde Moray 152 B2
Liatrie Highld 150 H5
Libanus Powys 34 B3
Libberton S Lanark 120 E2
Liberton Edin 121 C5
Liceasto W Isles 154 H6
Lichfield Staffs 62 D5
Lickey Worcs 50 B4
Lickey End Worcs 50 B4
Lickfold W Sus 16 B3
Liddel Orkney 159 K5
Liddesdale Highld 130 D1
Liddington Swindon 38 F2
Lidgate Suff 55 D8
Lidget S Yorks 89 D7
Lidget Green W Yorks 94 F4
Lidgett Notts 77 C6
Lidlington C Beds 53 F7
Lidstone Oxon 38 B3
Lieurary Highld 158 D2
Liff Angus 134 F3
Lifton Devon 9 F5
Liftondown Devon 9 F5
Lighthorne Warks 51 D8
Lightwater Sur 27 C7
Lightwood Stoke 75 E6
Lightwood Green Ches E 74 E3
Lightwood Green Wrex 73 E7
Lilbourne Northants 52 B3
Lilburn Tower Northumb 117 B6
Lilleshall Telford 61 C7
Lilley Herts 40 B4
Lilley W Berks 26 B2
Lilliesleaf Borders 115 B8
Lillingstone Dayrell Bucks 52 F5
Lillingstone Lovell Bucks 52 E5
Lillington Dorset 12 C4
Lillington Warks 51 C8
Lilliput Poole 13 E8
Lilstock Som 22 E3
Lilyhurst Shrops 61 C7
Limbury Luton 40 B3
Limebrook Hereford 49 C5
Limefield Gtr Man 87 C6
Limekilnburn S Lanark 119 D7
Limekilns Fife 128 F2
Limerigg Falk 119 B8
Limerstone IoW 14 F5
Limington Som 12 B3
Limpenhoe Norf 69 D6
Limpley Stoke Wilts 24 C2
Limpsfield Sur 28 D5
Limpsfield Chart Sur 28 D5
Linby Notts 76 D5
Linchmere W Sus 27 F6
Lincluden Dumfries 107 B6
Lincoln Lincs 78 B2
Lincomb Worcs 50 C3
Lincombe Devon 6 D5
Lindal in Furness Cumb 92 B2
Lindale Cumb 99 F6
Lindean Borders 121 F7
Lindfield W Sus 17 B7
Lindford Hants 27 F6
Lindifferon Fife 128 C5
Lindley W Yorks 88 C2
Lindley Green N Yorks 94 E5
Lindores Fife 128 C4
Lindridge Worcs 49 C8
Lindsell Essex 42 B2
Lindsey Suff 56 E3
Linford Hants 14 D2
Linford Thurrock 29 B7
Lingague IoM 84 E2
Lingards Wood W Yorks 87 C8
Lingbob W Yorks 94 F3
Lingdale Redcar 102 C4
Lingen Hereford 49 C5
Lingfield Sur 28 E4
Lingreabhagh W Isles 154 J5
Lingwood Norf 69 D6
Linicro Highld 149 B8
Linkenholt Hants 25 D8
Linkhill Kent 18 C5
Linkinhorne Corn 5 B8
Linklater Orkney 159 K5
Linksness Orkney 159 H3
Linktown Fife 128 E4
Linley Shrops 60 E3
Linley Green Hereford 49 D8
Linlithgow W Loth 120 B3
Linlithgow Bridge W Loth 120 B2
Linshiels Northumb 116 D4
Linsiadar W Isles 154 D7
Linsidemore Highld 151 B8
Linslade C Beds 40 B2
Linstead Parva Suff 57 B7
Linstock Cumb 108 D4
Linthwaite W Yorks 88 C2
Lintlaw Borders 122 D4
Lintmill Moray 152 B5
Linton Borders 116 B3
Linton Cambs 55 E6
Linton Derbys 63 C6
Linton Hereford 36 B3
Linton Kent 29 E8
Linton N Yorks 94 C2
Linton Northumb 117 E8
Linton W Yorks 95 E6
Linton-on-Ouse N Yorks 95 C7
Linwood Hants 14 D2
Linwood Lincs 90 F5
Linwood Renfs 118 C4
Lionacleit W Isles 148 D2
Lional W Isles 155 A10
Liphook Hants 27 F6
Liscard Mers 85 E4
Liscombe Som 21 F7
Liskeard Corn 5 C7
L'Islet Guern 16
Liss Hants 15 B8
Liss Forest Hants 15 B8
Lissett E Yorks 97 D7
Lissington Lincs 90 F5
Lisvane Cardiff 35 F5
Liswerry Newport 35 F7
Litcham Norf 67 C8
Litchborough Northants 52 D4
Litchfield Hants 26 D2
Litherland Mers 85 E4
Litlington Cambs 54 E4
Litlington E Sus 18 E2
Little Abington Cambs 55 E6
Little Addington Northants 53 B7
Little Alne Warks 51 C6
Little Altcar Mers 85 D4
Little Asby Cumb 100 D1
Little Assynt Highld 156 G4
Little Aston Staffs 62 D4
Little Atherfield IoW 15 F5
Little Ayre Orkney 159 J4
Little-ayre Shetland 160 G5
Little Ayton N Yorks 102 C3
Little Baddow Essex 42 D3
Little Badminton S Glos 37 F5
Little Ballinluig Perth 133 D6
Little Bampton Cumb 108 D2
Little Bardfield Essex 55 F7
Little Barford Bedford 54 D2
Little Barningham Norf 81 D7
Little Barrington Glos 38 C2
Little Barrow Ches W 73 B8
Little Barugh N Yorks 96 B3
Little Bavington Northumb 110 B2
Little Bealings Suff 57 E6
Little Bedwyn Wilts 25 C7
Little Bentley Essex 43 B7
Little Berkhamsted Herts 41 D5
Little Billing Northants 53 C6
Little Birch Hereford 49 F7
Little Blakenham Suff 56 E5
Little Blencow Cumb 108 F4
Little Bollington Ches E 86 F5
Little Bookham Sur 28 D2
Little Bowden Leics 64 F4
Little Bradley Suff 55 D7
Little Brampton Shrops 60 F3
Little Brechin Angus 135 C5
Little Brickhill M Keynes 53 F7
Little Brington Northants 52 C4
Little Bromley Essex 43 B6
Little Broughton Cumb 107 F7
Little Budworth Ches W 74 C2
Little Burstead Essex 42 E2
Little Bytham Lincs 65 C7
Little Carlton Lincs 91 F7
Little Carlton Notts 77 D7
Little Casterton Rutland 65 D7
Little Cawthorpe Lincs 91 F7
Little Chalfont Bucks 40 E2
Little Chart Kent 30 E3
Little Chesterford Essex 55 E6
Little Cheverell Wilts 24 D4
Little Chishill Cambs 54 F5
Little Clacton Essex 43 C7
Little Clifton Cumb 98 B2
Little Colp Aberds 153 D7
Little Comberton Worcs 50 E4
Little Common E Sus 18 E4
Little Compton Warks 51 F7
Little Cornard Suff 56 F2
Little Cowarne Hereford 49 D8
Little Coxwell Oxon 38 E2
Little Crakehall N Yorks 101 E7
Little Cressingham Norf 67 D8
Little Crosby Mers 85 D4
Little Dalby Leics 64 C4
Little Dawley Telford 61 D6
Little Dens Aberds 153 D10
Little Dewchurch Hereford 49 F7
Little Downham Cambs 66 F5
Little Driffield E Yorks 97 D6
Little Dunham Norf 67 C8
Little Dunkeld Perth 133 E7
Little Dunmow Essex 42 B2
Little Easton Essex 42 B2
Little Eaton Derbys 76 E3
Little Eccleston Lancs 92 E4
Little Ellingham Norf 68 E3
Little End Essex 41 D8
Little Eversden Cambs 54 D4
Little Faringdon Oxon 38 D2
Little Fencote N Yorks 101 E7
Little Fenton N Yorks 95 F8
Little Finborough Suff 56 D4
Little Fransham Norf 68 C2
Little Gaddesden Herts 40 C2
Little Gidding Cambs 65 F8
Little Glemham Suff 57 D7
Little Glenshee Perth 133 F6
Little Gransden Cambs 54 D3
Little Green Som 24 E2
Little Grimsby Lincs 91 E7
Little Gruinard Highld 150 C2
Little Habton N Yorks 96 B3
Little Hadham Herts 41 B7
Little Hale Lincs 78 E4
Little Hallingbury Essex 41 C7
Little Hampden Bucks 40 D1
Little Harrowden Northants 53 B6
Little Haseley Oxon 39 D6
Little Hatfield E Yorks 97 E7
Little Hautbois Norf 81 E8
Little Haven Pembs 44 D3
Little Hay Staffs 62 D5
Little Hayfield Derbys 87 F8
Little Haywood Staffs 62 B4
Little Heath W Mid 63 F7
Little Hereford Hereford 49 C7
Little Horkesley Essex 56 F3
Little Horsted E Sus 17 C8
Little Horton W Yorks 94 F4
Little Horwood Bucks 53 F5
Little Houghton Northants 53 D6
Little Houghton S Yorks 88 D5
Little Hucklow Derbys 75 B8
Little Hulton Gtr Man 86 D5
Little Humber E Yorks 91 B5
Little Hungerford W Berks 26 B3
Little Irchester Northants 53 C7
Little Kimble Bucks 39 D8
Little Kineton Warks 51 D8
Little Kingshill Bucks 40 E1
Little Langdale Cumb 99 D5
Little Langford Wilts 25 F5
Little Laver Essex 41 D8
Little Leigh Ches W 74 B3
Little Leighs Essex 42 C3
Little Lever Gtr Man 87 D5
Little London Bucks 39 C6
Little London E Sus 18 D2
Little London Hants 25 E8
Little London Hants 26 D4
Little London Lincs 66 B2
Little London Lincs 66 B4
Little London Norf 81 E7
Little London Powys 59 F7
Little Longstone Derbys 75 B8
Little Lynturk Aberds 140 C4
Little Malvern Worcs 50 E2
Little Maplestead Essex 56 F2
Little Marcle Hereford 49 F8
Little Marlow Bucks 40 F1
Little Marsden Lancs 93 F8
Little Massingham Norf 80 E3
Little Melton Norf 68 D4
Little Mill Mon 35 D7
Little Milton Oxon 39 D6
Little Missenden Bucks 40 E2
Little Musgrave Cumb 100 C2
Little Ness Shrops 60 C4
Little Neston Ches W 73 B6
Little Newcastle Pembs 44 C4
Little Newsham Durham 101 C6
Little Oakley Essex 43 B8
Little Oakley Northants 65 F5
Little Orton Cumb 108 D3
Little Ouseburn N Yorks 95 C7
Little Paxton Cambs 54 C2
Little Petherick Corn 4 B4
Little Pitlurg Moray 152 D4
Little Plumpton Lancs 92 F3
Little Plumstead Norf 69 C6
Little Ponton Lincs 78 F2
Little Raveley Cambs 54 B3
Little Reedness E Yorks 90 B2
Little Ribston N Yorks 95 D6
Little Rissington Glos 38 C1
Little Ryburgh Norf 81 E5
Little Ryle Northumb 117 C6
Little Salkeld Cumb 109 F5
Little Sampford Essex 55 F7
Little Sandhurst Brack 27 C6
Little Saxham Suff 55 C8
Little Scatwell Highld 150 F6
Little Sessay N Yorks 95 B7
Little Shelford Cambs 54 D5
Little Singleton Lancs 92 F3
Little Skillymarno Aberds 153 C9
Little Smeaton N Yorks 89 C6
Little Snoring Norf 81 D5
Little Sodbury S Glos 36 F4
Little Somborne Hants 25 F8
Little Somerford Wilts 37 F6
Little Stainforth N Yorks 93 C8
Little Stainton Darl 101 B8
Little Stanney Ches W 73 B8
Little Staughton Bedford 54 C2
Little Steeping Lincs 79 C7
Little Stoke Staffs 75 F6
Little Stonham Suff 56 C5
Little Stretton Leics 64 D3
Little Stretton Shrops 60 E4
Little Strickland Cumb 99 C7
Little Stukeley Cambs 54 B3
Little Sutton Ches W 73 B7
Little Tew Oxon 38 B3
Little Thetford Cambs 55 B6
Little Thirkleby N Yorks 95 B7
Little Thurlow Suff 55 D7
Little Thurrock Thurrock 29 B7
Little Torboll Highld 151 B10
Little Torrington Devon 9 C6
Little Totham Essex 42 C4
Little Toux Aberds 152 C5
Little Town Cumb 98 C4
Little Town Lancs 93 F6
Little Urswick Cumb 92 B2
Little Wakering Essex 43 F5
Little Walden Essex 55 E6
Little Waldingfield Suff 56 E3
Little Walsingham Norf 80 D5
Little Waltham Essex 42 C3
Little Warley Essex 42 E2
Little Weighton E Yorks 97 F5
Little Weldon Northants 65 F6
Little Welnetham Suff 56 C2
Little Wenlock Telford 61 D6
Little Whittingham Green Suff 57 B6
Little Wilbraham Cambs 55 D6
Little Wishford Wilts 25 F5
Little Witley Worcs 50 C2
Little Wittenham Oxon 39 E5
Little Wolford Warks 51 F7
Little Wratting Suff 55 E7
Little Wymington Bedford 53 C7
Little Wymondley Herts 41 B5
Little Wyrley Staffs 62 D4
Little Yeldham Essex 55 F8
Littlebeck N Yorks 103 D6
Littleborough Gtr Man 87 C7
Littleborough Notts 90 F2
Littlebourne Kent 31 D6
Littlebredy Dorset 12 F3
Littlebury Essex 55 F6
Littlebury Green Essex 55 F5
Littledean Glos 36 C3
Littleferry Highld 151 B11
Littleham Devon 9 B6
Littleham Devon 10 F5
Littlehampton W Sus 16 D4
Littlehempston Devon 7 C6
Littlehoughton Northumb 117 C8
Littlemill Aberds 140 E2
Littlemill E Ayrs 112 C4
Littlemill Highld 151 F12
Littlemill Northumb 117 C8
Littlemoor Dorset 12 F4
Littlemore Oxon 39 D5
Littleover Derby 76 F3
Littleport Cambs 67 F5
Littlestone on Sea Kent 19 C7
Littlethorpe Leics 64 E2
Littlethorpe N Yorks 95 C6
Littleton Ches W 73 C8
Littleton Hants 26 F2
Littleton Perth 134 F2
Littleton Som 23 F6
Littleton Sur 27 C8
Littleton Sur 27 E7
Littleton Drew Wilts 37 F5
Littleton-on-Severn S Glos 36 F2
Littleton Pannell Wilts 24 D5
Littletown Durham 111 E6
Littlewick Green Windsor 27 B6
Littleworth Bedford 53 E8
Littleworth Glos 37 D5
Littleworth Oxon 38 E3
Littleworth Staffs 62 C4
Littleworth Worcs 50 D3
Litton Derbys 75 B8
Litton N Yorks 94 B2
Litton Som 23 D7
Litton Cheney Dorset 12 E3
Liurbost W Isles 155 E8
Liverpool Mers 85 E4
Liverpool Airport Mers 86 F2
Liversedge W Yorks 88 B3
Liverton Devon 7 B6
Liverton Redcar 103 C5
Livingston W Loth 120 C3
Livingston Village W Loth 120 C3
Lixwm Flint 73 B5
Lizard Corn 3 E6
Llaingoch Anglesey 82 C2
Llaithddu Powys 59 F7
Llan Powys 59 D5
Llan Ffestiniog Gwyn 71 C8
Llan-y-pwll Wrex 73 D7
Llanaber Gwyn 58 C3
Llanaelhaearn Gwyn 70 C4
Llanafan Ceredig 47 B5
Llanafan-fawr Powys 47 D8
Llanallgo Anglesey 82 C4
Llanandras = Presteigne Powys 48 C5
Llanarmon Gwyn 70 D5
Llanarmon Dyffryn Ceiriog Wrex 73 F5
Llanarmon-yn-Ial Denb 73 D5
Llanarth Ceredig 46 D3
Llanarth Mon 35 C7
Llanarthne Carms 33 B6
Llanasa Flint 85 F2
Llanbabo Anglesey 82 C3
Llanbadarn Fawr Ceredig 58 F3

Manar Ho. Aberds 141 B6
Manaton Devon 10 F2
Manby Lincs 91 F7
Mancetter Warks 63 E7
Manchester Gtr Man 87 E6
Manchester Airport Gtr Man 87 F6
Mancot Flint 73 C7
Mandally Highld 137 D5
Manea Cambs 66 F4
Manfield N Yorks 101 C7
Mangaster Shetland 160 F5
Mangotsfield S Glos 23 B8
Mangurstadh W Isles 154 D5
Mankinholes W Yorks 87 B7
Manley Ches W 74 B2
Mannal Argyll 146 G2
Mannerston W Loth 120 B3
Manningford Bohune Wilts 25 D6
Manningford Bruce Wilts 25 D6
Manningham W Yorks 94 F4
Mannings Heath W Sus 17 B6
Mannington Dorset 13 D8
Manningtree Essex 56 F4
Mannofield Aberdeen 141 D8
Manor London 41 F7
Manor Estate S Yorks 88 F4
Manorbier Pembs 32 E1
Manordeilo Carms 33 B7
Manorhill Borders 122 F2
Manorowen Pembs 44 B4
Mansel Lacy Hereford 49 E6
Manselfield Swansea 33 F6
Mansell Gamage Hereford 49 E5
Mansergh Cumb 99 F8
Mansfield E Ayrs 113 C6
Mansfield Notts 76 C5
Mansfield Woodhouse Notts 76 C5
Mansriggs Cumb 98 F4
Manston Dorset 13 C6
Manston Kent 31 C7
Manston W Yorks 95 F6
Manswood Dorset 13 D7
Manthorpe Lincs 65 C7
Manthorpe Lincs 78 F2
Manton N Lincs 90 D3
Manton Notts 77 B5
Manton Rutland 65 D5
Manton Wilts 25 C6
Manuden Essex 41 B7
Maperton Som 12 B4
Maple Cross Herts 40 E3
Maplebeck Notts 77 C7
Mapledurham Oxon 26 B4
Mapledurwell Hants 26 D4
Maplehurst W Sus 17 B5
Maplescombe Kent 29 C6
Mapleton Derbys 75 E8
Mapperley Derbys 76 E4
Mapperley Park Nottingham 77 E5
Mapperton Dorset 12 E3
Mappleborough Green Warks 51 C5
Mappleton E Yorks 97 E8
Mappowder Dorset 12 D5
Mar Lodge Aberds 139 E6
Maraig W Isles 154 G6
Marazanvose Corn 4 D3
Marazion Corn 2 C4
Marbhig W Isles 155 F9
Marbury Ches E 74 E2
March Cambs 66 E4
March S Lanark 114 C2
Marcham Oxon 38 E4
Marchamley Shrops 61 B5
Marchington Staffs 75 F8
Marchington Woodlands Staffs 62 B5
Marchroes Gwyn 70 E4
Marchwiel Wrex 73 E7
Marchwood Hants 14 C4
Marcross V Glam 21 C8
Marden Hereford 49 E7
Marden Kent 29 E8
Marden T&W 111 B6
Marden Wilts 25 D5
Marden Beech Kent 29 E8
Marden Thorn Kent 29 E8
Mardy Mon 35 C7
Marefield Leics 64 D4
Mareham le Fen Lincs 79 C5
Mareham on the Hill Lincs 79 C5
Marehay Derbys 76 E3
Marehill W Sus 16 C4
Maresfield E Sus 17 B8
Marfleet Hull 90 B5
Marford Wrex 73 D7
Margam Neath 34 F1
Margaret Marsh Dorset 13 C6
Margaret Roding Essex 42 C1
Margaretting Essex 42 D2
Margate Kent 31 B7
Margnaheglish N Ayrs 143 E11
Margrove Park Redcar 102 C4
Marham Norf 67 C7
Marhamchurch Corn 8 D4
Marholm Pboro 65 D8
Mariandyrys Anglesey 83 C6
Marianglas Anglesey 82 C5
Mariansleigh Devon 10 B2
Marionburgh Aberds 141 D6
Marishader Highld 149 B9
Marjoriebanks Dumfries 114 F3
Mark Dumfries 104 D5
Mark S Ayrs 104 B4
Mark Som 23 E5
Mark Causeway Som 23 E5
Mark Cross E Sus 17 C8
Mark Cross E Sus 18 B2
Markbeech Kent 29 E5
Markby Lincs 79 B7
Market Bosworth Leics 63 D8
Market Deeping Lincs 65 D8
Market Drayton Shrops 74 F3
Market Harborough Leics 64 F4
Market Lavington Wilts 24 D5
Market Overton Rutland 65 C5
Market Rasen Lincs 90 F5
Market Stainton Lincs 78 B5
Market Warsop Notts 77 C5
Market Weighton E Yorks 96 E4
Market Weston Suff 56 B3
Markethill Perth 134 F2
Markfield Leics 63 C8
Markham Caerph 35 D5
Markham Moor Notts 77 B7
Markinch Fife 128 D4
Markington N Yorks 95 C5
Marks Tey Essex 43 B5
Marksbury Bath 23 C8
Markyate Herts 40 C3
Marland Gtr Man 87 C6
Marlborough Wilts 25 C6
Marlbrook Hereford 49 D7
Marlbrook Worcs 50 B4
Marlcliff Warks 51 D5
Marldon Devon 7 C6
Marlesford Suff 57 D7
Marley Green Ches E 74 E2
Marley Hill T&W 110 D5
Marley Mount Hants 14 E3
Marlingford Norf 68 D4
Marloes Pembs 44 E2
Marlow Bucks 39 F8
Marlow Hereford 49 B6
Marlow Bottom Bucks 40 F1
Marlpit Hill Kent 28 E5
Marlpool Derbys 76 E4
Marnhull Dorset 13 C5
Marnoch Aberds 152 C5
Marnock N Lanark 119 C7
Marple Gtr Man 87 F7
Marple Bridge Gtr Man 87 F7
Marr S Yorks 89 D6
Marrel Highld 157 H13
Marrick N Yorks 101 E5
Marrister Shetland 160 G7
Marros Carms 32 D3
Marsden T&W 111 C6
Marsden W Yorks 87 C8
Marsett N Yorks 100 F4
Marsh Devon 11 C7
Marsh W Yorks 94 F3
Marsh Baldon Oxon 39 E5
Marsh Gibbon Bucks 39 B6
Marsh Green Devon 10 E5
Marsh Green Kent 28 E5
Marsh Green Staffs 75 D5
Marsh Lane Derbys 76 B4
Marsh Street Som 21 E8
Marshall's Heath Herts 40 C4
Marshalsea Dorset 11 D8
Marshalswick Herts 40 D4
Marsham Norf 81 E7
Marshaw Lancs 93 D5
Marshborough Kent 31 D7
Marshbrook Shrops 60 F4
Marshchapel Lincs 91 E7
Marshfield Newport 35 F6
Marshfield S Glos 24 B2
Marshgate Corn 8 E3
Marshland St James Norf 66 D5
Marshside Mers 85 C4
Marshwood Dorset 11 E8
Marske N Yorks 101 D6
Marske-by-the-Sea Redcar 102 B4
Marston Ches W 74 B3
Marston Hereford 49 D5
Marston Lincs 77 E8
Marston Oxon 39 D5
Marston Staffs 62 B3
Marston Staffs 62 C2
Marston Warks 63 E6
Marston Wilts 24 D4
Marston Doles Warks 52 D2
Marston Green W Mid 63 F5
Marston Magna Som 12 B3
Marston Meysey Wilts 37 E8
Marston Montgomery Derbys 75 F8
Marston Moretaine C Beds 53 E7
Marston on Dove Derbys 63 B6
Marston St Lawrence Northants 52 E3
Marston Stannett Hereford 49 D7
Marston Trussell Northants 64 F3
Marstow Hereford 36 C2
Marsworth Bucks 40 C2
Marten Wilts 25 D7
Marthall Ches E 74 B5
Martham Norf 69 C7
Martin Hants 13 C8
Martin Kent 31 E7
Martin Lincs 78 C5
Martin Lincs 78 D4
Martin Dales Lincs 78 C4
Martin Drove End Hants 13 B8
Martin Hussingtree Worcs 50 C3
Martin Mill Kent 31 E7
Martinhoe Devon 21 E5
Martinhoe Cross Devon 21 E5
Martinscroft Warr 86 F4
Martinstown Dorset 12 F4
Martlesham Suff 57 E6
Martlesham Heath Suff 57 E6
Martletwy Pembs 32 C1
Martley Worcs 50 D2
Martock Som 12 C2
Marton Ches E 75 C5
Marton E Yorks 97 F7
Marton Lincs 90 F2
Marton Mbro 102 C3
Marton N Yorks 95 C7
Marton N Yorks 103 F5
Marton Shrops 60 B4
Marton Shrops 60 D2
Marton Warks 52 C2
Marton-le-Moor N Yorks 95 B6
Martyr Worthy Hants 26 F3
Martyr's Green Sur 27 D8
Marwick Orkney 159 F3
Marwood Devon 20 F4
Mary Tavy Devon 6 B3
Marybank Highld 150 F7
Maryburgh Highld 151 F8
Maryhill Glasgow 119 C5
Marykirk Aberds 135 C6
Marylebone Gtr Man 86 D3
Marypark Moray 152 E1
Maryport Cumb 107 F7
Maryport Dumfries 104 F5
Maryton Angus 135 D6
Marywell Aberds 140 E4
Marywell Aberds 141 E8
Marywell Angus 135 E6
Masham N Yorks 101 F7
Mashbury Essex 42 C2
Masongill N Yorks 93 B6
Masonhill S Ayrs 112 B3
Mastin Moor Derbys 76 B4
Mastrick Aberdeen 141 D7
Matching Essex 41 C8
Matching Green Essex 41 C8
Matching Tye Essex 41 C8
Matfen Northumb 110 B3
Matfield Kent 29 E7
Mathern Mon 36 E2
Mathon Hereford 50 E2
Mathry Pembs 44 B3
Matlaske Norf 81 D7
Matlock Derbys 76 C2
Matlock Bath Derbys 76 D2
Matson Glos 37 C5
Matterdale End Cumb 99 B5
Mattersey Notts 89 F7
Mattersey Thorpe Notts 89 F7
Mattingley Hants 26 D5
Mattishall Norf 68 C3
Mattishall Burgh Norf 68 C3
Mauchline E Ayrs 112 B4
Maud Aberds 153 D9
Maugersbury Glos 38 B2
Maughold IoM 84 C4
Mauld Highld 150 H7
Maulden C Beds 53 F8
Maulds Meaburn Cumb 99 C8
Maunby N Yorks 102 F1
Maund Bryan Hereford 49 D7
Maundown Som 11 B5
Mautby Norf 69 C7
Mavis Enderby Lincs 79 C6
Maw Green Ches E 74 D4
Mawbray Cumb 107 E7
Mawdesley Lancs 86 C2
Mawdlam Bridgend 34 F2
Mawgan Corn 3 D6
Mawla Corn 3 B6
Mawnan Corn 3 D6
Mawnan Smith Corn 3 D6
Mawsley Northants 53 B6
Maxey Pboro 65 D8
Maxstoke Warks 63 F6
Maxton Borders 122 F2
Maxton Kent 31 E7
Maxwellheugh Borders 122 F3
Maxwelltown Dumfries 107 B6
Maxworthy Corn 8 E4
May Bank Staffs 75 E5
Mayals Swansea 33 E7
Maybole S Ayrs 112 D3
Mayfield E Sus 18 C2
Mayfield Midloth 121 C6
Mayfield Staffs 75 E8
Mayfield W Loth 120 C2
Mayford Sur 27 D7
Mayland Essex 43 D5
Maynard's Green E Sus 18 D2
Maypole Mon 36 C1
Maypole Scilly 2 E4
Maypole Green Essex 43 B5
Maypole Green Norf 69 E7
Maypole Green Suff 57 C6
Maywick Shetland 160 L5
Meadle Bucks 39 D8
Meadowtown Shrops 60 D3
Meaford Staffs 75 F5
Meal Bank Cumb 99 E7
Mealabost W Isles 155 D9
Mealabost Bhuirgh W Isles 155 B9
Mealsgate Cumb 108 E2
Meanwood W Yorks 95 F5
Mearbeck N Yorks 93 C8
Meare Som 23 E6
Meare Green Som 11 B8
Mears Ashby Northants 53 C6
Measham Leics 63 C7
Meath Green Sur 28 E3
Meathop Cumb 99 F6
Meaux E Yorks 97 F6
Meavy Devon 6 C3
Medbourne Leics 64 E4
Medburn Northumb 110 B4
Meddon Devon 8 C4
Meden Vale Notts 77 C5
Medlam Lincs 79 D6
Medmenham Bucks 39 F8
Medomsley Durham 110 D4
Medstead Hants 26 F4
Meer End W Mid 51 B7
Meerbrook Staffs 75 C6
Meers Bridge Lincs 91 F8
Meesden Herts 54 F5
Meeth Devon 9 D7
Meggethead Borders 114 B4
Meidrim Carms 32 B3
Meifod Denb 72 D4
Meifod Powys 59 C8
Meigle N Ayrs 118 C1
Meigle Perth 134 E2
Meikle Earnock S Lanark 119 D7
Meikle Ferry Highld 151 C10
Meikle Forter Angus 134 C1
Meikle Gluich Highld 151 C9
Meikle Pinkerton E Loth 122 B3
Meikle Strath Aberds 135 B6
Meikle Tarty Aberds 141 B8
Meikle Wartle Aberds 153 E7
Meikleour Perth 134 F1
Meinciau Carms 33 C5
Meir Stoke 75 E6
Meir Heath Staffs 75 E6
Melbourn Cambs 54 E4
Melbourne Derbys 63 B7
Melbourne E Yorks 96 E3
Melbourne S Lanark 120 E3
Melbury Abbas Dorset 13 B6
Melbury Bubb Dorset 12 D3
Melbury Osmond Dorset 12 D3
Melbury Sampford Dorset 12 D3
Melby Shetland 160 H3
Melchbourne Bedford 53 C8
Melcombe Bingham Dorset 13 D5
Melcombe Regis Dorset 12 F4
Meldon Devon 9 E7
Meldon Northumb 117 F7
Meldreth Cambs 54 E4
Meldrum Ho. Aberds 141 B7
Melfort Argyll 124 D4
Melgarve Highld 137 E7
Meliden Denb 72 A4
Melin-y-coed Conwy 83 E8
Melin-y-ddôl Powys 59 D7
Melin-y-grug Powys 59 D7
Melin-y-Wig Denb 72 E4
Melinbyrhedyn Powys 58 E5
Melincourt Neath 34 D2
Melkinthorpe Cumb 99 B7
Melkridge Northumb 109 C7
Melksham Wilts 24 C4
Melldalloch Argyll 145 F8
Melling Lancs 93 B5
Melling Mers 85 D4
Melling Mount Mers 86 D2
Mellis Suff 56 B5
Mellon Charles Highld 155 H13
Mellon Udrigle Highld 155 H13
Mellor Gtr Man 87 F7
Mellor Lancs 93 F6
Mellor Brook Lancs 93 F6
Mells Som 24 E2
Melmerby Cumb 109 F6
Melmerby N Yorks 95 B6
Melmerby N Yorks 101 F5
Melplash Dorset 12 E2
Melrose Borders 121 F8
Melsetter Orkney 159 K3
Melsonby N Yorks 101 D6
Meltham W Yorks 88 C2
Melton Suff 57 D6
Melton Constable Norf 81 D6
Melton Mowbray Leics 64 C4
Melton Ross N Lincs 90 C4
Meltonby E Yorks 96 D3
Melvaig Highld 155 J12
Melverley Shrops 60 C3
Melverley Green Shrops 60 C3
Melvich Highld 157 C11
Membury Devon 11 D7
Memsie Aberds 153 B9
Memus Angus 134 D4
Menabilly Corn 5 D5
Menai Bridge = Porthaethwy Anglesey 83 D5
Mendham Suff 69 F5
Mendlesham Suff 56 C5
Mendlesham Green Suff 56 C4
Menheniot Corn 5 C7
Mennock Dumfries 113 D8
Menston W Yorks 94 E4
Menstrie Clack 127 E7
Menthorpe N Yorks 96 F2
Mentmore Bucks 40 C2
Meoble Highld 147 C10
Meole Brace Shrops 60 C4
Meols Mers 85 E3
Meonstoke Hants 15 C7
Meopham Kent 29 C7
Meopham Station Kent 29 C7
Mepal Cambs 66 F4
Meppershall C Beds 54 F2
Merbach Hereford 48 E5
Mere Ches E 86 F5
Mere Wilts 24 F3
Mere Brow Lancs 86 C2
Mere Green W Mid 62 E5
Mereclough Lancs 93 F8
Mereside Blackpool 92 F3
Mereworth Kent 29 D7
Mergie Aberds 141 F6
Meriden W Mid 63 F6
Merkadale Highld 149 E8
Merkland Dumfries 106 B4
Merkland S Ayrs 112 E2
Merkland Lodge Highld 156 G7
Merley Poole 13 E8
Merlin's Bridge Pembs 44 D4
Merrington Shrops 60 B4
Merrion Pembs 44 F4
Merriott Som 12 C2
Merrivale Devon 6 B3
Merrow Sur 27 D8
Merrymeet Corn 5 C7
Mersham Kent 19 B7
Merstham Sur 28 D3
Merston W Sus 16 D2
Merstone IoW 15 F6
Merther Corn 3 B7
Merthyr Carms 32 B4
Merthyr Cynog Powys 47 F8
Merthyr-Dyfan V Glam 22 C3
Merthyr Mawr Bridgend 21 B7
Merthyr Tudful = Merthyr Tydfil M Tydf 34 D4
Merthyr Tydfil = Merthyr Tudful M Tydf 34 D4
Merthyr Vale M Tydf 34 E4
Merton Devon 9 C7
Merton London 28 B3
Merton Norf 68 E2
Merton Oxon 39 C5
Mervinslaw Borders 116 C2
Meshaw Devon 10 C2
Messing Essex 42 C4
Messingham N Lincs 90 D2
Metfield Suff 69 F5
Metheringham Lincs 78 C3
Methil Fife 129 E5
Methlem Gwyn 70 D2
Methley W Yorks 88 B4
Methlick Aberds 153 E8
Methven Perth 128 B2
Methwold Norf 67 E7
Methwold Hythe Norf 67 E7
Mettingham Suff 69 F6
Mevagissey Corn 3 B9
Mewith Head N Yorks 93 C7
Mexborough S Yorks 89 D5
Mey Highld 158 C4
Meysey Hampton Glos 37 E8
Miabhag W Isles 154 G5
Miabhag W Isles 154 H6
Miabhig W Isles 154 D5
Michaelchurch Hereford 36 B2
Michaelchurch Escley Hereford 48 F5
Michaelchurch on Arrow Powys 48 D4
Michaelston-le-Pit V Glam 22 B3
Michaelston-y-Fedw Newport 35 F6
Michaelstow Corn 5 B5
Michealston-super-Ely Cardiff 22 B3
Micheldever Hants 26 F3
Michelmersh Hants 14 B4
Mickfield Suff 56 C5
Mickle Trafford Ches W 73 C8
Micklebring S Yorks 89 E6
Mickleby N Yorks 103 C6
Mickleham Sur 28 D2
Mickleover Derby 76 F3
Micklethwaite W Yorks 94 E4
Mickleton Durham 100 B4
Mickleton Glos 51 E6
Mickletown W Yorks 88 B4
Mickley N Yorks 95 B5
Mickley Square Northumb 110 C3
Mid Ardlaw Aberds 153 B9
Mid Auchinlech Invclyd 118 B3
Mid Beltie Aberds 140 D5
Mid Calder W Loth 120 C3
Mid Cloch Forbie Aberds 153 C7
Mid Clyth Highld 158 G4
Mid Lavant W Sus 16 D2
Mid Main Highld 150 H7
Mid Urchany Highld 151 G11
Mid Walls Shetland 160 H4
Mid Yell Shetland 160 D7
Midbea Orkney 159 D5
Middle Assendon Oxon 39 F7
Middle Aston Oxon 38 B4
Middle Barton Oxon 38 B4
Middle Cairncake Aberds 153 D8
Middle Claydon Bucks 39 B7
Middle Drums Angus 135 D5
Middle Handley Derbys 76 B4
Middle Littleton Worcs 51 E5
Middle Maes-coed Hereford 48 F5
Middle Mill Pembs 44 C3
Middle Rasen Lincs 90 F4
Middle Rigg Perth 128 D2
Middle Tysoe Warks 51 E8
Middle Wallop Hants 25 F7
Middle Winterslow Wilts 25 F7
Middle Woodford Wilts 25 F6
Middlebie Dumfries 108 B2
Middleforth Green Lancs 86 B3
Middleham N Yorks 101 F6
Middlehope Shrops 60 F4
Middlemarsh Dorset 12 D4
Middlemuir Aberds 141 B8
Middlesbrough Mbro 102 B2
Middleshaw Cumb 99 F7
Middleshaw Dumfries 107 B8
Middlesmoor N Yorks 94 B3
Middlestone Durham 111 F5
Middlestone Moor Durham 110 F5
Middlestown W Yorks 88 C3
Middlethird Borders 122 E2
Middleton Aberds 141 C7
Middleton Argyll 146 G2
Middleton Cumb 99 F8
Middleton Derbys 75 C8
Middleton Derbys 76 D2
Middleton Essex 56 F2
Middleton Gtr Man 87 D6
Middleton Hants 26 E2
Middleton Hereford 49 C7
Middleton Lancs 92 D4
Middleton Midloth 121 D6
Middleton N Yorks 94 E4
Middleton N Yorks 103 F5
Middleton Norf 67 C6
Middleton Northants 64 F5
Middleton Northumb 117 F6
Middleton Northumb 123 F7
Middleton Perth 128 D3
Middleton Perth 133 E8
Middleton Shrops 49 B7
Middleton Shrops 60 B3
Middleton Shrops 60 E2
Middleton Suff 57 C8
Middleton Swansea 33 F5
Middleton W Yorks 88 B3
Middleton Warks 63 E5
Middleton Cheney Northants 52 E2
Middleton Green Staffs 75 F6
Middleton Hall Northumb 117 B5
Middleton-in-Teesdale Durham 100 B4
Middleton Moor Suff 57 C8
Middleton-on-Leven N Yorks 102 D2
Middleton-on-Sea W Sus 16 D3
Middleton on the Hill Hereford 49 C7
Middleton-on-the-Wolds E Yorks 96 E5
Middleton One Row Darl 102 C1
Middleton Priors Shrops 61 E6
Middleton Quernham N Yorks 95 B6
Middleton Scriven Shrops 61 F6
Middleton St George Darl 101 C8
Middleton Stoney Oxon 39 B5
Middleton Tyas N Yorks 101 D7
Middletown Cumb 98 D1
Middletown Powys 60 C3
Middlewich Ches E 74 C3
Middlewood Green Suff 56 C4
Middlezoy Som 23 F5
Middridge Durham 101 B7
Midfield Highld 157 C8
Midge Hall Lancs 86 B3
Midgeholme Cumb 109 D6
Midgham W Berks 26 C3
Midgley W Yorks 87 B8
Midgley W Yorks 88 C3
Midhopestones S Yorks 88 E3
Midhurst W Sus 16 B2
Midlem Borders 115 B8
Midmar Aberds 141 D5
Midsomer Norton Bath 23 D8
Midton Invclyd 118 B2
Midtown Highld 155 J13
Midtown Highld 157 C8
Midtown of Buchromb Moray 152 D3
Midville Lincs 79 D6
Midway Ches E 87 F7
Migdale Highld 151 B9
Migvie Aberds 140 D3
Milarrochy Stirling 126 E3
Milborne Port Som 12 C4
Milborne St Andrew Dorset 13 E6
Milborne Wick Som 12 B4
Milbourne Northumb 110 B4
Milburn Cumb 100 B1
Milbury Heath S Glos 36 E3
Milcombe Oxon 52 F2
Milden Suff 56 E3
Mildenhall Suff 55 B8
Mildenhall Wilts 25 C7
Mile Cross Norf 68 C5
Mile Elm Wilts 24 C4
Mile End Essex 43 B5
Mile End Glos 36 C2
Mile Oak Brighton 17 D6
Milebrook Powys 48 B5
Milebush Kent 29 E8
Mileham Norf 68 C2
Milesmark Fife 128 F2
Milfield Northumb 122 F5
Milford Derbys 76 E3
Milford Devon 8 B4
Milford Powys 59 E7
Milford Staffs 62 B3
Milford Sur 27 E7
Milford Wilts 14 B2
Milford Haven = Aberdaugleddau Pembs 44 E4
Milford on Sea Hants 14 E3
Milkwall Glos 36 D2
Milkwell Wilts 13 B7
Mill Bank W Yorks 87 B8
Mill Common Suff 69 F7
Mill End Bucks 39 F7
Mill End Herts 54 F4
Mill Green Essex 42 D2
Mill Green Norf 68 F4
Mill Green Suff 56 E3
Mill Hill London 41 E5
Mill Lane Hants 27 D5
Mill of Kingoodie Aberds 141 B7
Mill of Muiresk Aberds 153 D6
Mill of Sterin Aberds 140 E2
Mill of Uras Aberds 141 F7
Mill Place N Lincs 90 D3
Mill Side Cumb 99 F6
Mill Street Norf 68 C3
Milland W Sus 16 B2
Millarston Renfs 118 C4
Millbank Aberds 153 D11
Millbank Highld 158 D3
Millbeck Cumb 98 B4
Millbounds Orkney 159 E6
Millbreck Aberds 153 D10
Millbridge Sur 27 E6
Millbrook C Beds 53 F8
Millbrook Corn 6 D2
Millbrook Soton 14 C4
Millburn S Ayrs 112 B4
Millcombe Devon 7 E6
Millcorner E Sus 18 C5
Milldale Staffs 75 D8
Millden Lodge Angus 135 B5
Milldens Angus 135 D5
Millerhill Midloth 121 C6
Miller's Dale Derbys 75 B8
Miller's Green Derbys 76 D2
Millgreen Shrops 61 B6
Millhalf Hereford 48 E4
Millhayes Devon 11 D7
Millhead Lancs 92 B4
Millheugh S Lanark 119 D7
Millholme Cumb 99 E7
Millhouse Argyll 145 F8
Millhouse Cumb 108 F3
Millhouse Green S Yorks 88 D3
Millhousebridge Dumfries 114 F4
Millhouses S Yorks 88 F4
Millikenpark Renfs 118 C4
Millin Cross Pembs 44 D4
Millington E Yorks 96 D4
Millmeece Staffs 74 F5
Millom Cumb 98 F3
Millook Corn 8 E3
Millpool Corn 5 B6
Millport N Ayrs 145 H10
Millquarter Dumfries 113 F6
Millthorpe Lincs 78 F4
Millthrop Cumb 100 E1
Milltimber Aberdeen 141 D7
Milltown Corn 5 D6
Milltown Derbys 76 C3
Milltown Devon 20 F4
Milltown Dumfries 108 B3
Milltown of Aberdalgie Perth 128 B2
Milltown of Auchindoun Moray 152 D3
Milltown of Craigston Aberds 153 C7
Milltown of Edinvillie Moray 152 D2
Milltown of Kildrummy Aberds 140 C3
Milltown of Rothiemay Moray 152 D5
Milltown of Towie Aberds 140 C3
Milnathort Perth 128 D3
Milner's Heath Ches W 73 C8
Milngavie E Dunb 119 B5
Milnrow Gtr Man 87 C7
Milnshaw Lancs 87 B5
Milnthorpe Cumb 99 F6
Milo Carms 33 C6
Milson Shrops 49 B8
Milstead Kent 30 D3
Milston Wilts 25 E6
Milton Angus 134 E3
Milton Cambs 55 C5
Milton Cumb 109 C5
Milton Derbys 63 B7
Milton Dumfries 105 D6
Milton Dumfries 106 B5
Milton Dumfries 113 F8
Milton Highld 150 F6
Milton Highld 150 H7
Milton Highld 151 D10
Milton Highld 151 G8
Milton Highld 158 E5
Milton Moray 152 B5
Milton N Som 22 C5
Milton Notts 77 B7
Milton Oxon 38 E4
Milton Oxon 52 F2
Milton Pembs 32 D1
Milton Perth 127 C8
Milton Ptsmth 15 E7
Milton Stirling 126 D4
Milton Stoke 75 D6
Milton W Dunb 118 B4
Milton Abbas Dorset 13 D6
Milton Abbot Devon 6 B2
Milton Bridge Midloth 120 C5
Milton Bryan C Beds 53 F7
Milton Clevedon Som 23 F8
Milton Coldwells Aberds 153 E9
Milton Combe Devon 6 C2
Milton Damerel Devon 9 C5
Milton End Glos 37 D8
Milton Ernest Bedford 53 D8
Milton Green Ches W 73 D8
Milton Hill Oxon 38 E4
Milton Keynes M Keynes 53 F6
Milton Keynes Village M Keynes 53 F6
Milton Lilbourne Wilts 25 C6
Milton Malsor Northants 52 D5
Milton Morenish Perth 132 F3
Milton of Auchinhove Aberds 140 D4
Milton of Balgonie Fife 128 D5
Milton of Buchanan Stirling 126 E3
Milton of Campfield Aberds 140 D5
Milton of Campsie E Dunb 119 B6
Milton of Corsindae Aberds 141 D5
Milton of Cushnie Aberds 140 C4
Milton of Dalcapon Perth 133 D6
Milton of Edradour Perth 133 D6
Milton of Gollanfield Highld 151 F10
Milton of Lesmore Aberds 140 B3
Milton of Logie Aberds 140 D3
Milton of Murtle Aberdeen 141 D7
Milton of Noth Aberds 140 B4
Milton of Tullich Aberds 140 E2
Milton on Stour Dorset 13 B5
Milton Regis Kent 30 C3
Milton under Wychwood Oxon 38 C2
Miltonduff Moray 152 B1
Miltonhill Moray 151 E13
Miltonise Dumfries 105 B5
Milverton Som 11 B6
Milverton Warks 51 C8
Milwich Staffs 75 F6
Minard Argyll 125 F5
Minchinhampton Glos 37 D5
Mindrum Northumb 122 F4
Minehead Som 21 E8
Minera Wrex 73 D6
Minety Wilts 37 E7
Minffordd Gwyn 58 C4
Minffordd Gwyn 71 D6
Minffordd Gwyn 83 D5
Miningsby Lincs 79 C6
Minions Corn 5 B7
Minishant S Ayrs 112 C3
Minllyn Gwyn 59 C5
Minnes Aberds 141 B8
Minngearraidh W Isles 148 F2
Minnigaff Dumfries 105 C8
Minnonie Aberds 153 B7
Minskip N Yorks 95 C6
Minstead Hants 14 C3
Minsted W Sus 16 B2
Minster Kent 30 B3
Minster Kent 31 C7
Minster Lovell Oxon 38 C3
Minsterley Shrops 60 D3
Minsterworth Glos 36 C4
Minterne Magna Dorset 12 D4
Minting Lincs 78 B4
Mintlaw Aberds 153 D9
Minto Borders 115 B8
Minton Shrops 60 E4
Minwear Pembs 32 C1
Minworth W Mid 63 E5
Mirbister Orkney 159 F4
Mirehouse Cumb 98 C1
Mireland Highld 158 D5
Mirfield W Yorks 88 C3
Miserden Glos 37 D6
Miskin Rhondda 34 F4
Misson Notts 89 E7
Misterton Leics 64 F2
Misterton Notts 89 E8
Misterton Som 12 D2
Mistley Essex 56 F5
Mitcham London 28 C3
Mitchel Troy Mon 36 C1
Mitcheldean Glos 36 C3
Mitchell Corn 4 D3
Mitcheltroy Common Mon 36 D1
Mitford Northumb 117 F7
Mithian Corn 4 D2
Mitton Staffs 62 C2
Mixbury Oxon 52 F4
Moat Cumb 108 B4
Moats Tye Suff 56 D4
Mobberley Ches E 74 B4
Mobberley Staffs 75 E7
Moccas Hereford 49 E5
Mochdre Conwy 83 D8
Mochdre Powys 59 F7
Mochrum Dumfries 105 E7
Mockbeggar Hants 14 D2
Mockerkin Cumb 98 B2
Modbury Devon 6 D4
Moddershall Staffs 75 F6
Moelfre Anglesey 82 C5
Moelfre Powys 59 B8
Moffat Dumfries 114 D3
Moggerhanger C Beds 54 E2
Moira Leics 63 C7
Mol-chlach Highld 149 G9
Molash Kent 30 D4
Mold = Yr Wyddgrug Flint 73 C6
Moldgreen W Yorks 88 C2
Molehill Green Essex 42 B1
Molescroft E Yorks 97 E6
Molesden Northumb 117 F7
Molesworth Cambs 53 B8
Moll Highld 149 E10
Molland Devon 10 B3
Mollington Ches W 73 B7
Mollington Oxon 52 E2
Mollinsburn N Lanark 119 B7
Monachty Ceredig 46 C4
Monachylemore Stirling 126 C3
Monar Lodge Highld 150 G5
Monaughty Powys 48 C4
Monboddo House Aberds 135 B7
Mondynes Aberds 135 B7
Monevechadan Argyll 125 E7
Monewden Suff 57 D6
Moneydie Perth 128 B2
Moniaive Dumfries 113 E7
Monifieth Angus 134 F4
Monikie Angus 135 F4
Monimail Fife 128 C4
Monington Pembs 45 E3
Monk Bretton S Yorks 88 D4
Monk Fryston N Yorks 89 B6
Monk Sherborne Hants 26 D4
Monk Soham Suff 57 C6
Monk Street Essex 42 B2
Monken Hadley London 41 E5
Monkhopton Shrops 61 E6
Monkland Hereford 49 D6
Monkleigh Devon 9 B6
Monknash V Glam 21 B8
Monkokehampton Devon 9 D7
Monks Eleigh Suff 56 E3
Monk's Gate W Sus 17 B6
Monks Heath Ches E 74 B5
Monks Kirby Warks 63 F8
Monks Risborough Bucks 39 D8
Monkseaton T&W 111 B6
Monkshill Aberds 153 D7
Monksilver Som 22 F2
Monkspath W Mid 51 B6
Monkswood Mon 35 D7
Monkton Devon 11 D6
Monkton Kent 31 C6
Monkton Pembs 44 E4
Monkton S Ayrs 112 B3
Monkton Combe Bath 24 C2
Monkton Deverill Wilts 24 F3
Monkton Farleigh Wilts 24 C3
Monkton Heathfield Som 11 B7
Monkton Up Wimborne Dorset 13 C8
Monkwearmouth T&W 111 D6
Monkwood Hants 26 F4
Monmouth = Trefynwy Mon 36 C2
Monmouth Cap Mon 35 B7
Monnington on Wye Hereford 49 E5
Monreith Dumfries 105 E7
Monreith Mains Dumfries 105 E7
Mont Saint Guern 16
Montacute Som 12 C2
Montcoffer Ho. Aberds 153 B6
Montford Argyll 145 G10
Montford Shrops 60 C4
Montford Bridge Shrops 60 C4
Montgarrie Aberds 140 C4
Montgomery = Trefaldwyn Powys 60 E2
Montrave Fife 129 D5
Montrose Angus 135 D7
Montsale Essex 43 E6
Monxton Hants 25 E8
Monyash Derbys 75 C8
Monymusk Aberds 141 C5
Monzie Perth 127 B7
Monzie Castle Perth 127 B7
Moodiesburn N Lanark 119 B6
Moonzie Fife 128 C5
Moor Allerton W Yorks 95 F5
Moor Crichel Dorset 13 D7
Moor End E Yorks 96 F4
Moor End York 96 D2
Moor Monkton N Yorks 95 D8
Moor of Granary Moray 151 F13
Moor of Ravenstone Dumfries 105 E7
Moor Row Cumb 98 C2
Moor Street Kent 30 C2
Moorby Lincs 79 C5
Moordown Bmouth 13 E8
Moore Halton 86 F3
Moorend Glos 36 D4
Moorends S Yorks 89 C7
Moorgreen Notts 76 E4
Moorhall Derbys 76 B3
Moorhampton Hereford 49 E5
Moorhead W Yorks 94 F4
Moorhouse Cumb 108 D3
Moorhouse Notts 77 C7
Moorlinch Som 23 F5
Moorsholm Redcar 102 C4
Moorside Gtr Man 87 D7
Moorthorpe W Yorks 89 C5
Moortown Hants 14 D2
Moortown IoW 14 F5
Moortown Lincs 90 E4
Morangie Highld 151 C10
Morar Highld 147 B9
Morborne Cambs 65 E8
Morchard Bishop Devon 10 D2
Morcombelake Dorset 12 E2
Morcott Rutland 65 D6
Morda Shrops 60 B2
Morden Dorset 13 E7
Morden London 28 C3
Mordiford Hereford 49 F7
Mordon Durham 101 B8
More Shrops 60 E3
Morebath Devon 10 B4
Morebattle Borders 116 B3
Morecambe Lancs 92 C4
Morefield Highld 150 B4
Moreleigh Devon 7 D5
Morenish Perth 132 F2
Moresby Cumb 98 B1
Moresby Parks Cumb 98 C1
Morestead Hants 15 B6
Moreton Dorset 13 F6
Moreton Essex 41 D8
Moreton Mers 85 E3
Moreton Oxon 39 D6
Moreton Staffs 61 C7
Moreton Corbet Shrops 61 B5
Moreton-in-Marsh Glos 51 F7
Moreton Jeffries Hereford 49 E8
Moreton Morrell Warks 51 D8
Moreton on Lugg Hereford 49 E7
Moreton Pinkney Northants 52 E3
Moreton Say Shrops 74 F3
Moreton Valence Glos 36 D4
Moretonhampstead Devon 10 F2
Morfa Carms 33 C6
Morfa Carms 33 E6
Morfa Bach Carms 32 C4
Morfa Bychan Gwyn 71 D6
Morfa Dinlle Gwyn 82 F4
Morfa Glas Neath 34 D2
Morfa Nefyn Gwyn 70 C3
Morfydd Denb 72 E5
Morgan's Vale Wilts 14 B2
Moriah Ceredig 46 B5
Morland Cumb 99 B7
Morley Derbys 76 E3
Morley Durham 101 B6
Morley W Yorks 88 B3
Morley Green Ches E 87 F6
Morley St Botolph Norf 68 E3
Morningside Edin 120 B5
Morningside N Lanark 119 D8
Morningthorpe Norf 68 E5
Morpeth Northumb 117 F8
Morphie Aberds 135 C7
Morrey Staffs 62 C5
Morris Green Essex 55 F8
Morriston Swansea 33 E7
Morston Norf 81 C6
Mortehoe Devon 20 E3
Mortimer W Berks 26 C4
Mortimer West End Hants 26 C4
Mortimer's Cross Hereford 49 C6
Mortlake London 28 B3
Morton Cumb 108 D3
Morton Derbys 76 C4
Morton Lincs 65 B7
Morton Lincs 77 C8
Morton Lincs 90 E2
Morton Norf 68 C4
Morton Notts 77 D7
Morton S Glos 36 E3
Morton Shrops 60 B2
Morton Bagot Warks 51 C6
Morton-on-Swale N Yorks 101 E8
Morvah Corn 2 C3
Morval Corn 5 D7
Morvich Highld 136 B2
Morvich Highld 157 J10
Morville Shrops 61 E6
Morville Heath Shrops 61 E6
Morwenstow Corn 8 C4
Mosborough S Yorks 88 F5
Moscow E Ayrs 118 E4
Mosedale Cumb 108 F3
Moseley W Mid 62 E3
Moseley W Mid 62 F4
Moseley Worcs 50 D3
Moss Argyll 146 G2
Moss Highld 147 E9
Moss S Yorks 89 C6
Moss Wrex 73 D7
Moss Bank Mers 86 E3
Moss Edge Lancs 92 E4
Moss End Brack 27 B6
Moss of Barmuckity Moray 152 B2
Moss Pit Staffs 62 B3
Moss-side Highld 151 F11
Moss Side Lancs 92 F3
Mossat Aberds 140 C3
Mossbank Shetland 160 F6
Mossbay Cumb 98 B1
Mossblown S Ayrs 112 B4
Mossbrow Gtr Man 86 F5
Mossburnford Borders 116 C2
Mossdale Dumfries 106 B3
Mossend N Lanark 119 C7
Mosser Cumb 98 B3
Mossfield Highld 151 D9
Mossgiel E Ayrs 112 B4
Mosside Angus 134 D4
Mossley Ches E 75 C5
Mossley Gtr Man 87 D7
Mossley Hill Mers 85 F4
Mosstodloch Moray 152 B3
Mosston Angus 135 E5
Mossy Lea Lancs 86 C3
Mosterton Dorset 12 D2
Moston Gtr Man 87 D6
Moston Shrops 61 B5
Moston Green Ches E 74 C4
Mostyn Flint 85 F2
Mostyn Quay Flint 85 F2
Motcombe Dorset 13 B6
Mothecombe Devon 6 E4
Motherby Cumb 99 B6
Motherwell N Lanark 119 D7
Mottingham London 28 B5
Mottisfont Hants 14 B4
Mottistone IoW 14 F5
Mottram in Longdendale Gtr Man 87 E7
Mottram St Andrew Ches E 75 B5
Mouilpied Guern 16
Mouldsworth Ches W 74 B2
Moulin Perth 133 D6
Moulsecoomb Brighton 17 D7
Moulsford Oxon 39 F5
Moulsoe M Keynes 53 E7
Moulton Ches W 74 C3
Moulton Lincs 66 B3
Moulton N Yorks 101 D7
Moulton Northants 53 C5
Moulton Suff 55 C7
Moulton V Glam 22 B2
Moulton Chapel Lincs 66 C2
Moulton Eaugate Lincs 66 C3
Moulton Seas End Lincs 66 B3
Moulton St Mary Norf 69 D6
Mounie Castle Aberds 141 B6
Mount Corn 4 D2
Mount Corn 5 C6
Mount Highld 151 G12
Mount Bures Essex 56 F3
Mount Canisp Highld 151 D10
Mount Hawke Corn 3 B6
Mount Pleasant Ches E 74 D5
Mount Pleasant Derbys 63 C6
Mount Pleasant Derbys 76 E3
Mount Pleasant Flint 73 B6
Mount Pleasant Hants 14 E3
Mount Pleasant W Yorks 88 B3
Mount Sorrel Wilts 13 B8
Mount Tabor W Yorks 87 B8
Mountain W Yorks 94 F3
Mountain Ash = Aberpennar Rhondda 34 E4
Mountain Cross Borders 120 E4

Mountain Water Pembs 44 C4
Mountbenger Borders 115 B6
Mountfield E Sus 18 C4
Mountgerald Highld 151 E8
Mountjoy Corn 4 C3
Mountnessing Essex 42 E2
Mounton Mon 36 E2
Mountsorrel Leics 64 C2
Mousehole Corn 2 D3
Mousen Northumb 123 F7
Mouswald Dumfries 107 B7
Mow Cop Ches E 75 D5
Mowhaugh Borders 116 B4
Mowsley Leics 64 F3
Moxley W Mid 62 E3
Moy Highld 137 F7
Moy Highld 151 H10
Moy Hall Highld 151 H10
Moy Ho. Moray 151 E13
Moy Lodge Highld 137 F7
Moyles Court Hants 14 D2
Moylgrove Pembs 45 E3
Muasdale Argyll 143 D7
Much Birch Hereford 49 F7
Much Cowarne Hereford 49 E8
Much Dewchurch Hereford 49 F6
Much Hadham Herts 41 C7
Much Hoole Lancs 86 B2
Much Marcle Hereford 49 F8
Much Wenlock Shrops 61 D6
Muchalls Aberds 141 E8
Muchelney Som 12 B2
Muchlarnick Corn 5 D7
Muchrachd Highld 150 H5
Muckernich Highld 151 F8
Mucking Thurrock 42 F2
Muckleford Dorset 12 E4
Mucklestone Staffs 74 F4
Muckleton Shrops 61 B5
Muckletown Aberds 140 B4
Muckley Corner Staffs 62 D4
Muckton Lincs 91 F7
Mudale Highld 157 F8
Muddiford Devon 20 F4
Mudeford Dorset 14 E2
Mudford Som 12 C3
Mudgley Som 23 E6
Mugdock Stirling 119 B5
Mugeary Highld 149 E9
Mugginton Derbys 76 E2
Muggleswick Durham 110 E3
Muie Highld 157 J9
Muir Aberds 139 F6
Muir of Fairburn Highld 150 F7
Muir of Fowlis Aberds 140 C4
Muir of Ord Highld 151 F8
Muir of Pert Angus 134 F4
Muirden Aberds 153 C7
Muirdrum Angus 135 F5
Muirhead Angus 134 F3
Muirhead Fife 128 D4
Muirhead N Lanark 119 C6
Muirhead S Ayrs 118 F3
Muirhouselaw Borders 116 B2
Muirhouses Falk 128 F2
Muirkirk E Ayrs 113 B6
Muirmill Stirling 127 F6
Muirshearlich Highld 136 F4
Muirskie Aberds 141 E7
Muirtack Aberds 153 E9
Muirton Highld 151 E10
Muirton Perth 127 C8
Muirton Perth 128 B3
Muirton Mains Highld 150 F7
Muirton of Ardblair Perth 134 E1
Muirton of Ballochy Angus 135 C6
Muiryfold Aberds 153 C7
Muker N Yorks 100 E4
Mulbarton Norf 68 D4
Mulben Moray 152 C3
Mulindry Argyll 142 C4
Mullardoch House Highld 150 H5
Mullion Corn 3 E5
Mullion Cove Corn 3 E5
Mumby Lincs 79 B8
Munderfield Row Hereford 49 D8
Munderfield Stocks Hereford 49 D8
Mundesley Norf 81 D9
Mundford Norf 67 E8
Mundham Norf 69 E6
Mundon Essex 42 D4
Mundurno Aberdeen 141 C8
Munerigie Highld 137 D5
Muness Shetland 160 C8
Mungasdale Highld 150 B2
Mungrisdale Cumb 108 F3
Munlochy Highld 151 F9
Munsley Hereford 49 E8
Munslow Shrops 60 F5
Murchington Devon 9 F8
Murcott Oxon 39 C5
Murkle Highld 158 D3
Murlaggan Highld 136 E3
Murlaggan Highld 137 F6
Murra Orkney 159 H3
Murrayfield Edin 120 B5
Murrow Cambs 66 D3
Mursley Bucks 39 B8
Murthill Angus 134 D4
Murthly Perth 133 F7
Murton Cumb 100 B2
Murton Durham 111 E6
Murton Northumb 123 E5
Murton York 96 D2
Musbury Devon 11 E7
Muscoates N Yorks 102 F4
Musdale Argyll 124 C5
Musselburgh E Loth 121 B6
Muston Leics 77 F8
Muston N Yorks 97 B6
Mustow Green Worcs 50 B3
Mutehill Dumfries 106 E3
Mutford Suff 69 F7
Muthill Perth 127 C7
Mutterton Devon 10 D5
Muxton Telford 61 C7
Mybster Highld 158 E3
Myddfai Carms 34 B1
Myddle Shrops 60 B4
Mydroilyn Ceredig 46 D3
Myerscough Lancs 92 F4
Mylor Bridge Corn 3 C7
Mynachlog-ddu Pembs 45 F3
Myndtown Shrops 60 F3
Mynydd Bach Ceredig 47 B6
Mynydd-bach Mon 36 E1
Mynydd Bodafon Anglesey 82 C4
Mynydd-isa Flint 73 C6
Mynyddygarreg Carms 33 D5
Mynytho Gwyn 70 D4
Myrebird Aberds 141 E6
Myrelandhorn Highld 158 E4
Myreside Perth 128 B4
Myrtle Hill Carms 47 F6
Mytchett Sur 27 D6
Mytholm W Yorks 87 B7
Mytholmroyd W Yorks 87 B8
Myton-on-Swale N Yorks 95 C7
Mytton Shrops 60 C4

N

Na Gearrannan W Isles 154 C6
Naast Highld 155 J13
Naburn York 95 E8
Nackington Kent 31 D5
Nacton Suff 57 E6
Nafferton E Yorks 97 D6
Nailbridge Glos 36 C3
Nailsbourne Som 11 B7
Nailsea N Som 23 B6
Nailstone Leics 63 D8
Nailsworth Glos 37 E5
Nairn Highld 151 F11
Nalderswood Sur 28 E3
Nancegollan Corn 2 C5
Nancledra Corn 2 C3
Nanhoron Gwyn 70 D3
Nannau Gwyn 71 E8
Nannerch Flint 73 C5
Nanpantan Leics 64 C2
Nanpean Corn 4 D4
Nanstallon Corn 4 C5
Nant-ddu Powys 34 C4
Nant-glas Powys 47 C8
Nant Peris Gwyn 83 F6
Nant Uchaf Denb 72 D4
Nant-y-Bai Carms 47 E6
Nant-y-cafn Neath 34 D2
Nant-y-derry Mon 35 D7
Nant-y-ffin Carms 46 F4
Nant-y-moel Bridgend 34 E3
Nant-y-pandy Conwy 83 D6
Nanternis Ceredig 46 D2
Nantgaredig Carms 33 B5
Nantgarw Rhondda 35 F5
Nantglyn Denb 72 C4
Nantgwyn Powys 47 B8
Nantlle Gwyn 82 F5
Nantmawr Shrops 60 B2
Nantmel Powys 48 C2
Nantmor Gwyn 71 C7
Nantwich Ches E 74 D3
Nantycaws Carms 33 C5
Nantyffyllon Bridgend 34 E2
Nantyglo Bl Gwent 35 C5
Naphill Bucks 39 E8
Nappa N Yorks 93 D8
Napton on the Hill Warks 52 C2
Narberth = Arberth Pembs 32 C2
Narborough Leics 64 E2
Narborough Norf 67 C7
Nasareth Gwyn 82 F4
Naseby Northants 52 B4
Nash Bucks 53 F5
Nash Hereford 48 C5
Nash Newport 35 F7
Nash Shrops 49 B8
Nash Lee Bucks 39 D8
Nassington Northants 65 E7
Nasty Herts 41 B6
Nateby Cumb 100 D2
Nateby Lancs 92 E4
Natland Cumb 99 F7
Naughton Suff 56 E4
Naunton Glos 37 B8
Naunton Worcs 50 F3
Naunton Beauchamp Worcs 50 D4
Navenby Lincs 78 D2
Navestock Heath Essex 41 E8
Navestock Side Essex 42 E1
Navidale Highld 157 H13
Nawton N Yorks 102 F4
Nayland Suff 56 F3
Nazeing Essex 41 D7
Neacroft Hants 14 E2
Neal's Green Warks 63 F7
Neap Shetland 160 H7
Near Sawrey Cumb 99 E5
Neasham Darl 101 C8
Neath = Castell-Nedd Neath 33 E8
Neath Abbey Neath 33 E8
Neatishead Norf 69 B6
Nebo Anglesey 82 B4
Nebo Ceredig 46 C4
Nebo Conwy 83 F8
Nebo Gwyn 82 F4
Necton Norf 67 D8
Nedd Highld 156 F4
Nedderton Northumb 117 F8
Nedging Tye Suff 56 E4
Needham Norf 68 F5
Needham Market Suff 56 D4
Needingworth Cambs 54 B4
Needwood Staffs 63 B5
Neen Savage Shrops 49 B8
Neen Sollars Shrops 49 B8
Neenton Shrops 61 F6
Nefyn Gwyn 70 C4
Neilston E Renf 118 D4
Neinthirion Powys 59 D6
Neithrop Oxon 52 E2
Nelly Andrews Green Powys 60 D2
Nelson Caerph 35 E5
Nelson Lancs 93 F8
Nelson Village Northumb 111 B5
Nemphlar S Lanark 119 E8
Nempnett Thrubwell N Som 23 C7
Nene Terrace Lincs 66 D2
Nenthall Cumb 109 E7
Nenthead Cumb 109 E7
Nenthorn Borders 122 F2
Nerabus Argyll 142 C3
Nercwys Flint 73 C6
Nerston S Lanark 119 D6
Nesbit Northumb 123 F5
Ness Ches W 73 B7
Nesscliffe Shrops 60 C3
Neston Ches W 73 B6
Neston Wilts 24 C3
Nether Alderley Ches E 74 B5
Nether Blainslie Borders 121 E8
Nether Booth Derbys 88 F2
Nether Broughton Leics 64 B3
Nether Burrow Lancs 93 B6
Nether Cerne Dorset 12 E4
Nether Compton Dorset 12 C3
Nether Crimond Aberds 141 B7
Nether Dalgliesh Borders 115 D5
Nether Dallachy Moray 152 B3
Nether Exe Devon 10 D4
Nether Glasslaw Aberds 153 C8
Nether Handwick Angus 134 E3
Nether Haugh S Yorks 88 E5
Nether Heage Derbys 76 D3
Nether Heyford Northants 52 D4
Nether Hindhope Borders 116 C3
Nether Howecleuch S Lanark 114 C3
Nether Kellet Lancs 92 C5
Nether Kinmundy Aberds 153 D10
Nether Langwith Notts 76 B5
Nether Leask Aberds 153 E10
Nether Lenshie Aberds 153 D6
Nether Monynut Borders 122 C3
Nether Padley Derbys 76 B2
Nether Park Aberds 153 C10
Nether Poppleton York 95 D8
Nether Silton N Yorks 102 E2
Nether Stowey Som 22 F3
Nether Urquhart Fife 128 D3
Nether Wallop Hants 25 F8
Nether Wasdale Cumb 98 D3
Nether Whitacre Warks 63 E6
Nether Worton Oxon 52 F2
Netheravon Wilts 25 E6
Netherbrae Aberds 153 C7
Netherbrough Orkney 159 G4
Netherburn S Lanark 119 E8
Netherbury Dorset 12 E2
Netherby Cumb 108 B3
Netherby N Yorks 95 E6
Nethercote Warks 52 C3
Nethercott Devon 20 F3
Netherend Glos 36 D2
Netherfield E Sus 18 D4
Netherhampton Wilts 14 B2
Netherlaw Dumfries 106 E4
Netherley Aberds 141 E7
Netherley Mers 86 F2
Nethermill Dumfries 114 F3
Nethermuir Aberds 153 D9
Netherplace E Renf 118 D5
Netherseal Derbys 63 C6
Netherthird E Ayrs 113 C5
Netherthong W Yorks 88 D2
Netherthorpe S Yorks 89 F6
Netherton Angus 135 D5
Netherton Devon 7 B6
Netherton Hants 25 D8
Netherton Mers 85 D4
Netherton Northumb 117 D5
Netherton Oxon 38 E4
Netherton Perth 133 D8
Netherton Stirling 119 B5
Netherton W Mid 62 F3
Netherton W Yorks 88 C2
Netherton W Yorks 88 C3
Netherton Worcs 50 E4
Nethertown Cumb 98 D1
Nethertown Highld 158 C5
Netherwitton Northumb 117 E7
Netherwood E Ayrs 113 B6
Nethy Bridge Highld 139 B6
Netley Hants 15 D5
Netley Marsh Hants 14 C4
Netteswell Essex 41 C7
Nettlebed Oxon 39 F7
Nettlebridge Som 23 E8
Nettlecombe Dorset 12 E3
Nettleden Herts 40 C3
Nettleham Lincs 78 B3
Nettlestead Kent 29 D7
Nettlestead Green Kent 29 D7
Nettlestone IoW 15 E7
Nettlesworth Durham 111 E5
Nettleton Lincs 90 D5
Nettleton Wilts 24 B3
Neuadd Carms 33 B7
Nevendon Essex 42 E3
Nevern Pembs 45 E2
New Abbey Dumfries 107 C6
New Aberdour Aberds 153 B8
New Addington London 28 C4
New Alresford Hants 26 F3
New Alyth Perth 134 E2
New Arley Warks 63 F6
New Ash Green Kent 29 C7
New Barn Kent 29 C7
New Barnetby N Lincs 90 C4
New Barton Northants 53 C6
New Bewick Northumb 117 B6
New-bigging Angus 134 E2
New Bilton Warks 52 B2
New Bolingbroke Lincs 79 D6
New Boultham Lincs 78 B2
New Bradwell M Keynes 53 E6
New Brancepeth Durham 110 E5
New Bridge Wrex 73 E6
New Brighton Flint 73 C6
New Brighton Mers 85 E4
New Brinsley Notts 76 D4
New Broughton Wrex 73 D7
New Buckenham Norf 68 E3
New Byth Aberds 153 C8
New Catton Norf 68 C5
New Cheriton Hants 15 B6
New Costessey Norf 68 C4
New Cowper Cumb 107 E8
New Cross Ceredig 46 B5
New Cross London 28 B4
New Cumnock E Ayrs 113 C6
New Deer Aberds 153 D8
New Delaval Northumb 111 B5
New Duston Northants 52 C5
New Earswick York 96 D2
New Edlington S Yorks 89 E6
New Elgin Moray 152 B2
New Ellerby E Yorks 97 F7
New Eltham London 28 B5
New End Worcs 51 D5
New Farnley W Yorks 94 F5
New Ferry Mers 85 F4
New Fryston W Yorks 89 B5
New Galloway Dumfries 106 B3
New Gilston Fife 129 D6
New Grimsby Scilly 2 E3
New Hainford Norf 68 C5
New Hartley Northumb 111 B6
New Haw Sur 27 C8
New Hedges Pembs 32 D2
New Herrington T&W 111 D6
New Hinksey Oxon 39 D5
New Holkham Norf 80 D4
New Holland N Lincs 90 B4
New Houghton Derbys 76 C4
New Houghton Norf 80 E3
New Houses N Yorks 93 B8
New Humberstone Leicester 64 D3
New Hutton Cumb 99 E7
New Hythe Kent 29 D8
New Inn Carms 46 F3
New Inn Mon 36 D1
New Inn Pembs 45 F2
New Inn Torf 35 E7
New Invention Shrops 48 B4
New Invention W Mid 62 D3
New Kelso Highld 150 G2
New Kingston Notts 64 B2
New Lanark S Lanark 119 E8
New Lane Lancs 86 C2
New Lane End Warr 86 E4
New Leake Lincs 79 D7
New Leeds Aberds 153 C9
New Longton Lancs 86 B3
New Luce Dumfries 105 C5
New Malden London 28 C3
New Marske Redcar 102 B4
New Marton Shrops 73 F7
New Micklefield W Yorks 95 F7
New Mill Aberds 141 F6
New Mill Herts 40 C2
New Mill W Yorks 88 D2
New Mill Wilts 25 C6
New Mills Ches E 87 F5
New Mills Corn 4 D3
New Mills Derbys 87 F7
New Mills Powys 59 D7
New Milton Hants 14 E3
New Moat Pembs 32 B1
New Ollerton Notts 77 C6
New Oscott W Mid 62 E4
New Park N Yorks 95 D5
New Pitsligo Aberds 153 C8
New Polzeath Corn 4 B4
New Quay = Ceinewydd Ceredig 46 D2
New Rackheath Norf 69 C5
New Radnor Powys 48 C4
New Rent Cumb 108 F4
New Ridley Northumb 110 D3
New Road Side N Yorks 94 E2
New Romney Kent 19 C7
New Rossington S Yorks 89 E7
New Row Ceredig 47 B6
New Row Lancs 93 F6
New Row N Yorks 102 C4
New Sarum Wilts 25 F6
New Silksworth T&W 111 D6
New Stevenston N Lanark 119 D7
New Street Staffs 75 D7
New Street Lane Shrops 74 F3
New Swanage Dorset 13 F8
New Totley S Yorks 76 B3
New Town E Loth 121 B7
New Tredegar = Tredegar Newydd Caerph 35 D5
New Trows S Lanark 119 F8
New Ulva Argyll 144 E6
New Walsoken Cambs 66 D4
New Waltham NE Lincs 91 D6
New Whittington Derbys 76 B3
New Wimpole Cambs 54 E4
New Winton E Loth 121 B7
New Yatt Oxon 38 C3
New York Lincs 78 D5
New York N Yorks 94 C4
Newall W Yorks 94 E4
Newark Orkney 159 D8
Newark Pboro 66 D2
Newark-on-Trent Notts 77 D7
Newarthill N Lanark 119 D7
Newbarns Cumb 92 B2
Newbattle Midloth 121 C6
Newbiggin Cumb 92 C2
Newbiggin Cumb 98 E2
Newbiggin Cumb 99 B6
Newbiggin Cumb 99 B8
Newbiggin Cumb 109 E5
Newbiggin Durham 100 B4
Newbiggin N Yorks 100 E4
Newbiggin N Yorks 100 F4
Newbiggin-by-the-Sea Northumb 117 F9
Newbiggin-on-Lune Cumb 100 D2
Newbigging Angus 134 F4
Newbigging Angus 134 F4
Newbigging S Lanark 120 E3
Newbold Derbys 76 B3
Newbold Leics 63 C8
Newbold on Avon Warks 52 B2
Newbold on Stour Warks 51 E7
Newbold Pacey Warks 51 D7
Newbold Verdon Leics 63 D8
Newborough Anglesey 82 E4
Newborough Pboro 66 D2
Newborough Staffs 62 B5
Newbottle Northants 52 F3
Newbottle T&W 111 D6
Newbourne Suff 57 E6
Newbridge Caerph 35 E6
Newbridge Ceredig 46 D4
Newbridge Corn 2 C3
Newbridge Corn 5 C8
Newbridge Dumfries 107 B6
Newbridge Edin 120 B4
Newbridge Hants 14 C3
Newbridge IoW 14 F5
Newbridge Pembs 44 B4
Newbridge Green Worcs 50 F3
Newbridge-on-Usk Mon 35 E7
Newbridge on Wye Powys 48 D2
Newbrough Northumb 109 C8
Newbuildings Devon 10 D2
Newburgh Aberds 141 B8
Newburgh Aberds 153 C9
Newburgh Borders 115 C6
Newburgh Fife 128 C4
Newburgh Lancs 86 C2
Newburn T&W 110 C4
Newbury W Berks 26 C2
Newbury Park London 41 F7
Newby Cumb 99 B7
Newby Lancs 93 E8
Newby N Yorks 93 B7
Newby N Yorks 102 C3
Newby N Yorks 103 E8
Newby Bridge Cumb 99 F5
Newby East Cumb 108 D4
Newby West Cumb 108 D3
Newby Wiske N Yorks 102 F1
Newcastle Mon 35 C8
Newcastle Shrops 60 F2
Newcastle Emlyn = Castell Newydd Emlyn Carms 46 E2
Newcastle-under-Lyme Staffs 74 E5
Newcastle Upon Tyne T&W 110 C5
Newcastleton or Copshaw Holm Borders 115 F7
Newchapel Pembs 45 F4
Newchapel Powys 59 F6
Newchapel Staffs 75 D5
Newchapel Sur 28 E4
Newchurch Carms 32 B4
Newchurch IoW 15 F6
Newchurch Kent 19 B7
Newchurch Lancs 93 F8
Newchurch Mon 36 E1
Newchurch Powys 48 D4
Newchurch Staffs 62 B5
Newcott Devon 11 D7
Newcraighall Edin 121 B6
Newdigate Sur 28 E2
Newell Green Brack 27 B6
Newenden Kent 18 C5
Newent Glos 36 B4
Newerne Glos 36 D3
Newfield Durham 110 F5
Newfield Highld 151 D10
Newford Scilly 2 E4
Newfound Hants 26 D3
Newgale Pembs 44 C3
Newgate Norf 81 C6
Newgate Street Herts 41 D6
Newhall Ches E 74 E3
Newhall Derbys 63 B6
Newhall House Highld 151 E9
Newhall Point Highld 151 E10
Newham Northumb 117 B7
Newham Hall Northumb 117 B7
Newhaven Derbys 75 D8
Newhaven E Sus 17 D8
Newhaven Edin 121 B5
Newhey Gtr Man 87 C7
Newholm N Yorks 103 C6
Newhouse N Lanark 119 C7
Newick E Sus 17 B8
Newingreen Kent 19 B8
Newington Kent 19 B8
Newington Kent 30 C2
Newington Kent 31 C7
Newington Notts 89 E7
Newington Oxon 39 E6
Newington Shrops 60 F4
Newland Glos 36 D2
Newland Hull 97 F6
Newland N Yorks 89 B7
Newland Worcs 50 E2
Newlandrig Midloth 121 C6
Newlands Borders 115 E8
Newlands Highld 151 G10
Newlands Moray 152 C3
Newlands Northumb 110 D3
Newland's Corner Sur 27 E8
Newlands of Geise Highld 158 D2
Newlands of Tynet Moray 152 B3
Newlands Park Anglesey 82 C2
Newlandsmuir S Lanark 119 D6
Newlot Orkney 159 G6
Newlyn Corn 2 D3
Newmachar Aberds 141 C7
Newmains N Lanark 119 D8
Newmarket Suff 55 C7
Newmarket W Isles 155 D9
Newmill Borders 115 C7
Newmill Corn 2 C3
Newmill Moray 152 C4
Newmill of Inshewan Angus 134 C4
Newmills of Boyne Aberds 152 C5
Newmiln Perth 133 F8
Newmilns E Ayrs 118 F5
Newnham Cambs 54 D5
Newnham Glos 36 C3
Newnham Hants 26 D5
Newnham Herts 54 F3
Newnham Kent 30 D3
Newnham Northants 52 D3
Newnham Bridge Worcs 49 C8
Newpark Fife 129 C6
Newport Devon 20 F4
Newport E Yorks 96 F4
Newport Essex 55 F6
Newport Highld 158 H3
Newport IoW 15 F6
Newport = Casnewydd Newport 35 F7
Newport Norf 69 C8
Newport = Trefdraeth Pembs 45 F2
Newport Telford 61 C7
Newport-on-Tay Fife 129 B6
Newport Pagnell M Keynes 53 E6
Newpound Common W Sus 16 B4
Newquay Corn 4 C3
Newsbank Ches E 74 C5
Newseat Aberds 153 D10
Newseat Aberds 153 E7
Newsham N Yorks 101 C6
Newsham N Yorks 102 F1
Newsham Northumb 111 B6
Newsholme E Yorks 89 B8
Newsholme Lancs 93 D8
Newsome W Yorks 88 C2
Newstead Borders 121 F8
Newstead Northumb 117 B7
Newstead Notts 76 D5
Newthorpe N Yorks 95 F7
Newton Argyll 125 F6
Newton Borders 116 B2
Newton Bridgend 21 B7
Newton Cambs 54 E5
Newton Cambs 66 C4
Newton Cardiff 22 B4
Newton Ches W 73 C8
Newton Ches W 74 B2
Newton Ches W 74 D2
Newton Cumb 92 B2
Newton Derbys 76 D4
Newton Dorset 13 C5
Newton Dumfries 108 B2
Newton Dumfries 114 E4
Newton Gtr Man 87 E7
Newton Hereford 48 F5
Newton Hereford 49 D7
Newton Highld 151 E10
Newton Highld 151 G10
Newton Highld 156 F5
Newton Highld 158 F5
Newton Lancs 92 F4
Newton Lancs 93 B5
Newton Lancs 93 D6
Newton Lincs 78 F3
Newton Moray 152 B1
Newton Norf 67 C8
Newton Northants 65 F5
Newton Northumb 110 C3
Newton Notts 77 E6
Newton Perth 133 F5
Newton S Lanark 119 C6
Newton S Lanark 120 F2
Newton S Yorks 89 D6
Newton Staffs 62 B4
Newton Suff 56 E3
Newton Swansea 33 F7
Newton W Loth 120 B3
Newton Warks 52 B3
Newton Wilts 14 B3
Newton Abbot Devon 7 B6
Newton Arlosh Cumb 107 D8
Newton Aycliffe Durham 101 B7
Newton Bewley Hrtlpl 102 B2
Newton Blossomville M Keynes 53 D7
Newton Bromswold Northants 53 C7
Newton Burgoland Leics 63 D7
Newton by Toft Lincs 90 F4
Newton Ferrers Devon 6 E3
Newton Flotman Norf 68 E5
Newton Hall Northumb 110 C3
Newton Harcourt Leics 64 E3
Newton Heath Gtr Man 87 D6
Newton Ho. Aberds 141 B5
Newton Kyme N Yorks 95 E7
Newton-le-Willows Mers 86 E3
Newton-le-Willows N Yorks 101 F7
Newton Longville Bucks 53 F6
Newton Mearns E Renf 118 D5
Newton Morrell N Yorks 101 D7
Newton Mulgrave N Yorks 103 C5
Newton of Ardtoe Highld 147 D9
Newton of Balcanquhal Perth 128 C3
Newton of Falkland Fife 128 D4
Newton on Ayr S Ayrs 112 B3
Newton on Ouse N Yorks 95 D8
Newton-on-Rawcliffe N Yorks 103 E6
Newton-on-the-Moor Northumb 117 D7
Newton on Trent Lincs 77 B8
Newton Park Argyll 145 G10
Newton Poppleford Devon 11 F5
Newton Purcell Oxon 52 F4
Newton Regis Warks 63 D6
Newton Reigny Cumb 108 F4
Newton Solney Derbys 63 B6
Newton St Cyres Devon 10 E3
Newton St Faith Norf 68 C5
Newton St Loe Bath 24 C2
Newton St Petrock Devon 9 C6
Newton Stacey Hants 26 E2
Newton Stewart Dumfries 105 C8
Newton Tony Wilts 25 E7
Newton Tracey Devon 9 B7
Newton under Roseberry Redcar 102 C3
Newton upon Derwent E Yorks 96 E3
Newton Valence Hants 26 F5
Newtonairds Dumfries 113 F8
Newtongrange Midloth 121 C6
Newtonhill Aberds 141 E8
Newtonhill Highld 151 G8
Newtonmill Angus 135 C6
Newtonmore Highld 138 E3
Newtown Argyll 125 E6
Newtown Ches W 74 B2
Newtown Corn 3 D6
Newtown Cumb 107 E7
Newtown Cumb 108 C5
Newtown Derbys 87 F7
Newtown Devon 10 B2
Newtown Glos 36 D3
Newtown Glos 50 F4
Newtown Hants 14 B4
Newtown Hants 14 C3
Newtown Hants 15 C6
Newtown Hants 15 C7
Newtown Hants 15 D5
Newtown Hants 26 C2
Newtown Hereford 49 E8
Newtown Highld 137 D6
Newtown IoM 84 E3
Newtown IoW 14 E5
Newtown Northumb 117 B6
Newtown Northumb 117 D6
Newtown Northumb 123 F5
Newtown Poole 13 E8
Newtown = Y Drenewydd Powys 59 E8
Newtown Shrops 73 F8
Newtown Staffs 75 C6
Newtown Staffs 75 C7
Newtown Wilts 13 B7
Newtown Linford Leics 64 D2
Newtown St Boswells Borders 121 F8
Newtown Unthank Leics 63 D8
Newtyle Angus 134 E2
Neyland Pembs 44 E4
Niarbyl IoM 84 E2
Nibley S Glos 36 F3
Nibley Green Glos 36 E4
Nibon Shetland 160 F5
Nicholashayne Devon 11 C6
Nicholaston Swansea 33 F6
Nidd N Yorks 95 C6
Nigg Aberdeen 141 D8
Nigg Highld 151 D11
Nigg Ferry Highld 151 E10
Nightcott Som 10 B3
Nilig Denb 72 D4
Nine Ashes Essex 42 D1
Nine Mile Burn Midloth 120 D4
Nine Wells Pembs 44 C2
Ninebanks Northumb 109 D7
Ninfield E Sus 18 D4
Ningwood IoW 14 F4
Nisbet Borders 116 B2
Nisthouse Orkney 159 G4
Nisthouse Shetland 160 G7
Niton IoW 15 G6
Nitshill Glasgow 118 C5
No Man's Heath Ches W 74 E2
No Man's Heath Warks 63 D6
Noak Hill London 41 E8
Noblethorpe S Yorks 88 D3
Nobottle Northants 52 C4
Nocton Lincs 78 C3
Noke Oxon 39 C5
Nolton Pembs 44 D3
Nolton Haven Pembs 44 D3
Nomansland Devon 10 C3
Nomansland Wilts 14 C3
Noneley Shrops 60 B4
Nonikiln Highld 151 D9
Nonington Kent 31 D6
Noonsbrough Shetland 160 H4
Norbreck Blackpool 92 E3
Norbridge Hereford 50 E2
Norbury Ches E 74 E2
Norbury Derbys 75 E8
Norbury Shrops 60 E3
Norbury Staffs 61 B7
Nordelph Norf 67 D5
Norden Gtr Man 87 C6
Norden Heath Dorset 13 F7
Nordley Shrops 61 E6
Norham Northumb 122 E5
Norley Ches W 74 B2
Norleywood Hants 14 E4
Norman Cross Cambs 65 E8
Normanby N Lincs 90 C2
Normanby N Yorks 103 F5
Normanby Redcar 102 C3
Normanby-by-Spital Lincs 90 F4
Normanby by Stow Lincs 90 F2
Normanby le Wold Lincs 90 E5
Normandy Sur 27 D7
Norman's Bay E Sus 18 E3
Norman's Green Devon 11 D5
Normanstone Suff 69 E8
Normanton Derby 76 F3
Normanton Leics 77 E8
Normanton Lincs 78 E2
Normanton Notts 77 D7
Normanton Rutland 65 D6
Normanton W Yorks 88 B4
Normanton le Heath Leics 63 C7
Normanton on Soar Notts 64 B2
Normanton-on-the-Wolds Notts 77 F6
Normanton on Trent Notts 77 C7
Normoss Lancs 92 F3
Norney Sur 27 E7
Norrington Common Wilts 24 C3
Norris Green Mers 85 E4
Norris Hill Leics 63 C7
North Anston S Yorks 89 F6
North Aston Oxon 38 B4
North Baddesley Hants 14 C4
North Ballachulish Highld 130 C4
North Barrow Som 12 B4
North Barsham Norf 80 D5
North Benfleet Essex 42 F3
North Bersted W Sus 16 D3
North Berwick E Loth 129 F7
North Boarhunt Hants 15 C7
North Bovey Devon 10 F2
North Bradley Wilts 24 D3
North Brentor Devon 9 F6
North Brewham Som 24 F2
North Buckland Devon 20 E3
North Burlingham Norf 69 C6
North Cadbury Som 12 B4
North Cairn Dumfries 104 B3
North Carlton Lincs 78 B2
North Carrine Argyll 143 H7
North Cave E Yorks 96 F4
North Cerney Glos 37 D7
North Charford Wilts 14 C2
North Charlton Northumb 117 B7
North Cheriton Som 12 B4
North Cliff E Yorks 97 E8
North Cliffe E Yorks 96 F4
North Clifton Notts 77 B8
North Cockerington Lincs 91 E7
North Coker Som 12 C3
North Collafirth Shetland 160 E5
North Common E Sus 17 B7
North Connel Argyll 124 B5
North Cornelly Bridgend 34 F2
North Cotes Lincs 91 D7
North Cove Suff 69 F7
North Cowton N Yorks 101 D7
North Crawley M Keynes 53 E7
North Cray London 29 B5
North Creake Norf 80 D4
North Curry Som 11 B8
North Dalton E Yorks 96 D5
North Dawn Orkney 159 H5
North Deighton N Yorks 95 D6
North Duffield N Yorks 96 F2
North Elkington Lincs 91 E6
North Elmham Norf 81 E5
North Elmshall W Yorks 89 C5
North End Bucks 39 B8
North End E Yorks 97 F8
North End Essex 42 C2
North End Hants 26 C2
North End Lincs 78 E5
North End N Som 23 C6
North End Ptsmth 15 D7
North End Som 11 B7
North End W Sus 16 D5
North Erradale Highld 155 J12
North Fambridge Essex 42 E4
North Fearns Highld 149 E10
North Featherstone W Yorks 88 B5
North Ferriby E Yorks 90 B3
North Frodingham E Yorks 97 D7
North Gluss Shetland 160 F5
North Gorley Hants 14 C2
North Green Norf 68 F5
North Green Suff 57 C7
North Greetwell Lincs 78 B3
North Grimston N Yorks 96 C4
North Halley Orkney 159 H6
North Halling Medway 29 C8
North Hayling Hants 15 D8
North Hazelrigg Northumb 123 F6
North Heasley Devon 21 F6
North Heath W Sus 16 B4
North Hill Cambs 55 B5
North Hill Corn 5 B7
North Hinksey Oxon 38 D4
North Holmwood Sur 28 E2
North Howden E Yorks 96 F3
North Huish Devon 6 D5
North Hykeham Lincs 78 C2
North Johnston Pembs 44 D4
North Kelsey Lincs 90 D4
North Kelsey Moor Lincs 90 D4
North Kessock Highld 151 G9
North Killingholme N Lincs 90 C5
North Kilvington N Yorks 102 F2
North Kilworth Leics 64 F3
North Kirkton Aberds 153 C11
North Kiscadale N Ayrs 143 F11
North Kyme Lincs 78 D4
North Lancing W Sus 17 D5
North Lee Bucks 39 D8
North Leigh Oxon 38 C3
North Leverton with Habblesthorpe Notts 89 F8
North Littleton Worcs 51 E5
North Lopham Norf 68 F3
North Luffenham Rutland 65 D6
North Marden W Sus 16 C2
North Marston Bucks 39 B7
North Middleton Midloth 121 D6
North Middleton Northumb 117 B6
North Molton Devon 10 B2
North Moreton Oxon 39 F5
North Mundham W Sus 16 D2
North Muskham Notts 77 D7
North Newbald E Yorks 96 F5
North Newington Oxon 52 F2
North Newnton Wilts 25 D6
North Newton Som 22 F4
North Nibley Glos 36 E4
North Oakley Hants 26 D3
North Ockendon London 42 F1
North Ormesby Mbro 102 B3
North Ormsby Lincs 91 E6
North Otterington N Yorks 102 F1
North Owersby Lincs 90 E4
North Perrott Som 12 D2
North Petherton Som 22 F4
North Petherwin Corn 8 F4
North Pickenham Norf 67 D8
North Piddle Worcs 50 D4
North Poorton Dorset 12 E3
North Port Argyll 125 C6
North Queensferry Fife 128 F3
North Radworthy Devon 21 F6
North Rauceby Lincs 78 E3
North Reston Lincs 91 F7
North Rigton N Yorks 95 E5
North Rode Ches E 75 C5
North Roe Shetland 160 E5
North Runcton Norf 67 C6
North Sandwick Shetland 160 D7
North Scale Cumb 92 C1
North Scarle Lincs 77 C8
North Seaton Northumb 117 F8
North Shian Argyll 130 E3
North Shields T&W 111 C6
North Shoebury Southend 43 F5
North Shore Blackpool 92 F3
North Side Cumb 98 B2
North Side Pboro 66 E2
North Skelton Redcar 102 C4
North Somercotes Lincs 91 E8
North Stainley N Yorks 95 B5
North Stainmore Cumb 100 C3
North Stifford Thurrock 42 F2
North Stoke Bath 24 C2
North Stoke Oxon 39 F6
North Stoke W Sus 16 C4
North Street Hants 26 F4
North Street Kent 30 D4
North Street Medway 30 B2
North Street W Berks 26 B4
North Sunderland Northumb 123 F8
North Tamerton Corn 8 E5
North Tawton Devon 9 D8
North Thoresby Lincs 91 E6
North Tidworth Wilts 25 E7
North Togston Northumb 117 D8
North Tuddenham Norf 68 C3
North Walbottle T&W 110 C4
North Walsham Norf 81 D8
North Waltham Hants 26 E3
North Warnborough Hants 26 D5
North Water Bridge Angus 135 C6
North Watten Highld 158 E4
North Weald Bassett Essex 41 D7
North Wheatley Notts 89 F8
North Whilborough Devon 7 C6
North Wick Bath 23 C7
North Willingham Lincs 91 F5
North Wingfield Derbys 76 C4
North Witham Lincs 65 B6
North Woolwich London 28 B5
North Wootton Dorset 12 C4
North Wootton Norf 67 B6
North Wootton Som 23 E7
North Wraxall Wilts 24 B3
North Wroughton Swindon 38 F1
Northacre Norf 68 E2
Northallerton N Yorks 102 E1
Northam Devon 9 B6
Northam Soton 14 C5
Northampton Northants 53 C5
Northaw Herts 41 D5
Northbeck Lincs 78 E3
Northborough Pboro 65 D8
Northbourne Kent 31 D7
Northbridge Street E Sus 18 C4
Northchapel W Sus 16 B3
Northchurch Herts 40 D2
Northcott Devon 8 E5
Northdown Kent 31 B7
Northdyke Orkney 159 F3
Northend Bath 24 C2
Northend Bucks 39 E7
Northend Warks 51 D8
Northenden Gtr Man 87 E6
Northfield Aberdeen 141 D8
Northfield Borders 122 C5
Northfield E Yorks 90 B4
Northfield W Mid 50 B5
Northfields Lincs 65 D7
Northfleet Kent 29 B7
Northgate Lincs 65 B8
Northhouse Borders 115 D7
Northiam E Sus 18 C5
Northill C Beds 54 E2
Northington Hants 26 F3
Northlands Lincs 79 D6
Northlea Durham 111 D7
Northleach Glos 37 C8
Northleigh Devon 11 E6
Northlew Devon 9 E7
Northmoor Oxon 38 D4
Northmoor Green or Moorland Som 22 F5
Northmuir Angus 134 D3
Northney Hants 15 D8
Northolt London 40 F4
Northop Flint 73 C6
Northop Hall Flint 73 C6
Northorpe Lincs 65 C7
Northorpe Lincs 78 F5
Northorpe Lincs 90 E2
Northover Som 12 B3
Northover Som 23 F6
Northowram W Yorks 88 B2
Northport Dorset 13 F7
Northpunds Shetland 160 L6
Northrepps Norf 81 D8
Northtown Orkney 159 J5
Northway Glos 50 F4
Northwich Ches W 74 B3
Northwick S Glos 36 F2
Northwold Norf 67 E7
Northwood Derbys 76 C2
Northwood IoW 15 E5
Northwood Kent 31 C7
Northwood London 40 E3
Northwood Shrops 73 F8
Northwood Green Glos 36 C4
Norton E Sus 17 D8
Norton Glos 37 B5
Norton Halton 86 F3
Norton Herts 54 F3
Norton IoW 14 F4
Norton Mon 35 C8
Norton Northants 52 C4
Norton Notts 77 B5
Norton Powys 48 C5
Norton S Yorks 89 C6
Norton Shrops 60 F4
Norton Shrops 61 D5
Norton Shrops 61 D7
Norton Stockton 102 B2
Norton Suff 56 C3
Norton W Sus 16 D3
Norton W Sus 16 E2
Norton Wilts 37 F5
Norton Worcs 50 D3
Norton Worcs 50 E5
Norton Bavant Wilts 24 E4
Norton Bridge Staffs 75 F5
Norton Canes Staffs 62 D4
Norton Canon Hereford 49 E5
Norton Corner Norf 81 E6
Norton Disney Lincs 77 D8
Norton East Staffs 62 D4
Norton Ferris Wilts 24 F2
Norton Fitzwarren Som 11 B6
Norton Green IoW 14 F4
Norton Hawkfield Bath 23 C7
Norton Heath Essex 42 D2
Norton in Hales Shrops 74 F4
Norton-in-the-Moors Stoke 75 D5
Norton-Juxta-Twycross Leics 63 D7
Norton-le-Clay N Yorks 95 B7
Norton Lindsey Warks 51 C7
Norton Malreward Bath 23 C8
Norton Mandeville Essex 42 D1
Norton-on-Derwent N Yorks 96 B3
Norton St Philip Som 24 D2
Norton sub Hamdon Som 12 C2
Norton Woodseats S Yorks 88 F4

Norwell Notts 77 C7
Norwell Woodhouse Notts 77 C7
Norwich Norf 68 D5
Norwick Shetland 160 B8
Norwood Derbys 89 F5
Norwood Hill Sur 28 E3
Norwoodside Cambs 66 E4
Noseley Leics 64 E4
Noss Shetland 160 M5
Noss Mayo Devon 6 E3
Nosterfield N Yorks 101 F7
Nostie Highld 149 F13
Notgrove Glos 37 B8
Nottage Bridgend 21 B7
Nottingham Nottingham 77 F5
Nottington Dorset 12 F4
Notton W Yorks 88 C4
Notton Wilts 24 C4
Nounsley Essex 42 C3
Noutard's Green Worcs 50 C2
Novar House Highld 151 E9
Nox Shrops 60 C4
Nuffield Oxon 39 F6
Nun Hills Lancs 87 B6
Nun Monkton N Yorks 95 D8
Nunburnholme E Yorks 96 E4
Nuncargate Notts 76 D5
Nuneaton Warks 63 E7
Nuneham Courtenay Oxon 39 E5
Nunney Som 24 E2
Nunnington N Yorks 96 B2
Nunnykirk Northumb 117 E6
Nunsthorpe NE Lincs 91 D6
Nunthorpe Mbro 102 C3
Nunthorpe York 96 D2
Nunton Wilts 14 B2
Nunwick N Yorks 95 B6
Nupend Glos 36 D4
Nursling Hants 14 C4
Nursted Hants 15 B8
Nutbourne W Sus 15 D8
Nutbourne W Sus 16 C4
Nutfield Sur 28 D4
Nuthall Notts 76 E5
Nuthampstead Herts 54 F5
Nuthurst W Sus 17 B5
Nutley E Sus 17 B8
Nutley Hants 26 E4
Nutwell S Yorks 89 D7
Nybster Highld 158 D5
Nyetimber W Sus 16 E2
Nyewood W Sus 16 B2
Nymet Rowland Devon 10 D2
Nymet Tracey Devon 10 D2
Nympsfield Glos 37 D5
Nynehead Som 11 B6
Nyton W Sus 16 D3

O

Oad Street Kent 30 C2
Oadby Leics 64 D3
Oak Cross Devon 9 E7
Oakamoor Staffs 75 E7
Oakbank W Loth 120 C3
Oakdale Caerph 35 E5
Oake Som 11 B6
Oaken Staffs 62 D2
Oakenclough Lancs 92 E5
Oakengates Telford 61 C7
Oakenholt Flint 73 B6
Oakenshaw Durham 110 F5
Oakenshaw W Yorks 88 B2
Oakerthorpe Derbys 76 D3
Oakes W Yorks 88 C2
Oakfield Torf 35 E7
Oakford Ceredig 46 D3
Oakford Devon 10 B4
Oakfordbridge Devon 10 B4
Oakgrove Ches E 75 C6
Oakham Rutland 65 D5
Oakhanger Hants 27 F5
Oakhill Som 23 E8
Oakhurst Kent 29 D6
Oakington Cambs 54 C5
Oaklands Herts 41 C5
Oaklands Powys 48 D2
Oakle Street Glos 36 C4
Oakley Bedford 53 D8
Oakley Bucks 39 C6
Oakley Fife 128 F2
Oakley Hants 26 D3
Oakley Oxon 39 D7
Oakley Poole 13 E8
Oakley Suff 57 B5
Oakley Green Windsor 27 B7
Oakley Park Powys 59 F6
Oakmere Ches W 74 C2
Oakridge Glos 37 D6
Oakridge Hants 26 D4
Oaks Shrops 60 D4
Oaks Green Derbys 75 F8
Oaksey Wilts 37 E6
Oakthorpe Leics 63 C7
Oakwoodhill Sur 28 F2
Oakworth W Yorks 94 F3
Oape Highld 156 J7
Oare Kent 30 C4
Oare Som 21 E7
Oare W Berks 26 B3
Oare Wilts 25 C6
Oasby Lincs 78 F3
Oathlaw Angus 134 D4
Oatlands N Yorks 95 D6
Oban Argyll 124 C4
Oban Highld 147 C11
Oborne Dorset 12 C4
Obthorpe Lincs 65 C7
Occlestone Green Ches W 74 C3
Occold Suff 57 B5
Ochiltree E Ayrs 112 B4
Ochtermuthill Perth 127 C7
Ochtertyre Perth 127 B7
Ockbrook Derbys 76 F4
Ockham Sur 27 D8
Ockle Highld 147 D8
Ockley Sur 28 F2
Ocle Pychard Hereford 49 E7
Octon E Yorks 97 C6
Octon Cross Roads E Yorks 97 C6
Odcombe Som 12 C3
Odd Down Bath 24 C2
Oddendale Cumb 99 C7
Odder Lincs 78 B2
Oddingley Worcs 50 D4
Oddington Glos 38 B2
Oddington Oxon 39 C5
Odell Bedford 53 D7
Odie Orkney 159 F7
Odiham Hants 26 D5
Odstock Wilts 14 B2
Odstone Leics 63 D7
Offchurch Warks 51 C8
Offenham Worcs 51 E5
Offham E Sus 17 C7
Offham Kent 29 D7
Offham W Sus 16 D4
Offord Cluny Cambs 54 C3
Offord Darcy Cambs 54 C3
Offton Suff 56 E4
Offwell Devon 11 E6
Ogbourne Maizey Wilts 25 B6
Ogbourne St Andrew Wilts 25 B6
Ogbourne St George Wilts 25 B7
Ogil Angus 134 C4
Ogle Northumb 110 B4
Ogmore V Glam 21 B7
Ogmore-by-Sea V Glam 21 B7
Ogmore Vale Bridgend 34 E3
Okeford Fitzpaine Dorset 13 C6
Okehampton Devon 9 E7
Okehampton Camp Devon 9 E7
Okraquoy Shetland 160 K6
Old Northants 53 B5
Old Aberdeen Aberdeen 141 D8
Old Alresford Hants 26 F3
Old Arley Warks 63 E6
Old Basford Nottingham 76 E5
Old Basing Hants 26 D4
Old Bewick Northumb 117 B6
Old Bolingbroke Lincs 79 C6
Old Bramhope W Yorks 94 E5
Old Brampton Derbys 76 B3
Old Bridge of Tilt Perth 133 C5
Old Bridge of Urr Dumfries 106 C4
Old Buckenham Norf 68 E3
Old Burghclere Hants 26 D2
Old Byland N Yorks 102 F3
Old Cassop Durham 111 F6
Old Castleton Borders 115 E8
Old Catton Norf 68 C5
Old Clee NE Lincs 91 D6
Old Cleeve Som 22 E2
Old Clipstone Notts 77 C6
Old Colwyn Conwy 83 D8
Old Coulsdon London 28 D4
Old Crombie Aberds 152 C5
Old Dailly S Ayrs 112 E2
Old Dalby Leics 64 B3
Old Deer Aberds 153 D9
Old Denaby S Yorks 89 E5
Old Edlington S Yorks 89 E6
Old Eldon Durham 101 B7
Old Ellerby E Yorks 97 F7
Old Felixstowe Suff 57 F7
Old Fletton Pboro 65 E8
Old Glossop Derbys 87 E8
Old Goole E Yorks 89 B8
Old Hall Powys 59 F6
Old Heath Essex 43 B6
Old Heathfield E Sus 18 C2
Old Hill W Mid 62 F3
Old Hunstanton Norf 80 C2
Old Hurst Cambs 54 B3
Old Hutton Cumb 99 F7
Old Kea Corn 3 B7
Old Kilpatrick W Dunb 118 B4
Old Kinnernie Aberds 141 D6
Old Knebworth Herts 41 B5
Old Langho Lancs 93 F7
Old Laxey IoM 84 D4
Old Leake Lincs 79 D7
Old Malton N Yorks 96 B3
Old Micklefield W Yorks 95 F7
Old Milton Hants 14 E3
Old Milverton Warks 51 C7
Old Monkland N Lanark 119 C7
Old Netley Hants 15 D5
Old Philpstoun W Loth 120 B3
Old Quarrington Durham 111 F6
Old Radnor Powys 48 D4
Old Rattray Aberds 153 C10
Old Rayne Aberds 141 B5
Old Romney Kent 19 C7
Old Sodbury S Glos 36 F4
Old Somerby Lincs 78 F2
Old Stratford Northants 53 E5
Old Thirsk N Yorks 102 F2
Old Town Cumb 99 F7
Old Town Cumb 108 E4
Old Town Northumb 116 E4
Old Town Scilly 2 E4
Old Trafford Gtr Man 87 E6
Old Tupton Derbys 76 C3
Old Warden C Beds 54 E2
Old Weston Cambs 53 B8
Old Whittington Derbys 76 B3
Old Wick Highld 158 E5
Old Windsor Windsor 27 B7
Old Wives Lees Kent 30 D4
Old Woking Sur 27 D8
Old Woodhall Lincs 78 C5
Oldany Highld 156 F4
Oldberrow Warks 51 C6
Oldborough Devon 10 D2
Oldbury Shrops 61 E7
Oldbury W Mid 62 F3
Oldbury Warks 63 E7
Oldbury-on-Severn S Glos 36 E3
Oldbury on the Hill Glos 37 F5
Oldcastle Bridgend 21 B8
Oldcastle Mon 35 B7
Oldcotes Notts 89 F6
Oldfallow Staffs 62 C3
Oldfield Worcs 50 C3
Oldford Som 24 D2
Oldham Gtr Man 87 D7
Oldhamstocks E Loth 122 B3
Oldland S Glos 23 B8
Oldmeldrum Aberds 141 B7
Oldshore Beg Highld 156 D4
Oldshoremore Highld 156 D5
Oldstead N Yorks 102 F3
Oldtown Aberds 140 B4
Oldtown of Ord Aberds 152 C6
Oldway Swansea 33 F6
Oldways End Devon 10 B3
Oldwhat Aberds 153 C8
Olgrinmore Highld 158 E2
Oliver's Battery Hants 15 B5
Ollaberry Shetland 160 E5
Ollerton Ches E 74 B4
Ollerton Notts 77 C6
Ollerton Shrops 61 B6
Olmarch Ceredig 46 D5
Olney M Keynes 53 D6
Olrig Ho. Highld 158 D3
Olton W Mid 62 F5
Olveston S Glos 36 F3
Olwen Ceredig 46 E4
Ombersley Worcs 50 C3
Ompton Notts 77 C6
Onchan IoM 84 E3
Onecote Staffs 75 D7
Onen Mon 35 C8
Ongar Hill Norf 67 B5
Ongar Street Hereford 49 C5
Onibury Shrops 49 B6
Onich Highld 130 C4
Onllwyn Neath 34 C2
Onneley Staffs 74 E4
Onslow Village Sur 27 E7
Onthank E Ayrs 118 E4
Openwoodgate Derbys 76 E3
Opinan Highld 149 A12
Opinan Highld 155 H13
Orange Lane Borders 122 E3
Orange Row Norf 66 B5
Orasaigh W Isles 155 F8
Orbliston Moray 152 C3
Orbost Highld 148 D7
Orby Lincs 79 C7
Orchard Hill Devon 9 B6
Orchard Portman Som 11 B7
Orcheston Wilts 25 E5
Orcop Hereford 36 B1
Orcop Hill Hereford 36 B1
Ord Highld 149 G11
Ordhead Aberds 141 C5
Ordie Aberds 140 D3
Ordiequish Moray 152 C3
Ordsall Notts 89 F7
Ore E Sus 18 D5
Oreton Shrops 61 F6
Orford Suff 57 E8
Orford Warr 86 E4
Orgreave Staffs 63 C5
Orlestone Kent 19 B6
Orleton Hereford 49 C6
Orleton Worcs 49 C8
Orlingbury Northants 53 B6
Ormesby Redcar 102 C3
Ormesby St Margaret Norf 69 C7
Ormesby St Michael Norf 69 C7
Ormiclate Castle W Isles 148 E2
Ormiscaig Highld 155 H13
Ormiston E Loth 121 C7
Ormsaigbeg Highld 146 E7
Ormsaigmore Highld 146 E7
Ormsary Argyll 144 F6
Ormsgill Cumb 92 B1
Ormskirk Lancs 86 D2
Orpington London 29 C5
Orrell Gtr Man 86 D3
Orrell Mers 85 E4
Orrisdale IoM 84 C3
Orroland Dumfries 106 E4
Orsett Thurrock 42 F2
Orslow Staffs 62 C2
Orston Notts 77 E7
Orthwaite Cumb 108 F2
Ortner Lancs 92 D5
Orton Cumb 99 D8
Orton Northants 53 B6
Orton Longueville Pboro 65 E8
Orton-on-the-Hill Leics 63 D7
Orton Waterville Pboro 65 E8
Orwell Cambs 54 D4
Osbaldeston Lancs 93 F6
Osbaldwick York 96 D2
Osbaston Shrops 60 B3
Osbournby Lincs 78 F3
Oscroft Ches W 74 C2
Ose Highld 149 D8
Osgathorpe Leics 63 C8
Osgodby Lincs 90 E4
Osgodby N Yorks 96 F2
Osgodby N Yorks 103 F8
Oskaig Highld 149 E10
Oskamull Argyll 146 G7
Osmaston Derby 76 F3
Osmaston Derbys 76 E2
Osmington Dorset 12 F5
Osmington Mills Dorset 12 F5
Osmotherley N Yorks 102 E2
Ospisdale Highld 151 C10
Ospringe Kent 30 C4
Ossett W Yorks 88 B3
Ossington Notts 77 C7
Ostend Essex 43 E5
Oswaldkirk N Yorks 96 B2
Oswaldtwistle Lancs 86 B5
Oswestry Shrops 60 B2
Otford Kent 29 D6
Otham Kent 29 D8
Othery Som 23 F5
Otley Suff 57 D6
Otley W Yorks 94 E5
Otter Ferry Argyll 145 E8
Otterbourne Hants 15 B5
Otterburn N Yorks 93 D8
Otterburn Northumb 116 E4
Otterburn Camp Northumb 116 E4
Otterham Corn 8 E3
Otterhampton Som 22 E4
Ottershaw Sur 27 C8
Otterswick Shetland 160 E7
Otterton Devon 11 F5
Ottery St Mary Devon 11 E6
Ottinge Kent 31 E5
Ottringham E Yorks 91 B6
Oughterby Cumb 108 D2
Oughtershaw N Yorks 100 F3
Oughterside Cumb 107 E8
Oughtibridge S Yorks 88 E4
Oughtrington Warr 86 F4
Oulston N Yorks 95 B8
Oulton Cumb 108 D2
Oulton Norf 81 E7
Oulton Staffs 75 F6
Oulton Suff 69 E8
Oulton W Yorks 88 B4
Oulton Broad Suff 69 E8
Oulton Street Norf 81 E7
Oundle Northants 65 F7
Ousby Cumb 109 F6
Ousdale Highld 158 H2
Ousden Suff 55 D8
Ousefleet E Yorks 90 B2
Ouston Durham 111 D5
Ouston Northumb 110 B3
Out Newton E Yorks 91 B7
Out Rawcliffe Lancs 92 E4
Outertown Orkney 159 G3
Outgate Cumb 99 E5
Outhgill Cumb 100 D2
Outlane W Yorks 87 C8
Outwell Norf 66 D5
Outwick Hants 14 C2
Outwood Sur 28 E4
Outwood W Yorks 88 B4
Outwoods Staffs 61 C7
Ovenden W Yorks 87 B8
Ovenscloss Borders 121 F7
Over Cambs 54 B4
Over Ches W 74 C3
Over S Glos 36 F2
Over Compton Dorset 12 C3
Over Green W Mid 63 E5
Over Haddon Derbys 76 C2
Over Hulton Gtr Man 86 D4
Over Kellet Lancs 92 B5
Over Kiddington Oxon 38 B4
Over Knutsford Ches E 74 B4
Over Monnow Mon 36 C2
Over Norton Oxon 38 B3
Over Peover Ches E 74 B4
Over Silton N Yorks 102 E2
Over Stowey Som 22 F3
Over Stratton Som 12 C2
Over Tabley Ches E 86 F5
Over Wallop Hants 25 F7
Over Whitacre Warks 63 E6
Over Worton Oxon 38 B4
Overbister Orkney 159 D7
Overbury Worcs 50 F4
Overcombe Dorset 12 F4
Overgreen Derbys 76 B3
Overleigh Som 23 F6
Overley Green Warks 51 D5
Overpool Ches W 73 B7
Overscaig Hotel Highld 156 G7
Overseal Derbys 63 C6
Oversland Kent 30 D4
Overstone Northants 53 C6
Overstrand Norf 81 C8
Overthorpe Northants 52 E2
Overton Aberdeen 141 C7
Overton Ches W 74 B2
Overton Dumfries 107 C6
Overton Hants 26 E3
Overton Lancs 92 D4
Overton N Yorks 95 D8
Overton Shrops 49 B7
Overton Swansea 33 F5
Overton W Yorks 88 C3
Overton = Owrtyn Wrex 73 E7
Overton Bridge Wrex 73 E7
Overtown N Lanark 119 D8
Oving Bucks 39 B7
Oving W Sus 16 D3
Ovingdean Brighton 17 D7
Ovingham Northumb 110 C3
Ovington Durham 101 C6
Ovington Essex 55 E8
Ovington Hants 26 F3
Ovington Norf 68 D2
Ovington Northumb 110 C3
Ower Hants 14 C4
Owermoigne Dorset 13 F5
Owlbury Shrops 60 E3
Owler Bar Derbys 76 B2
Owlerton S Yorks 88 F4
Owl's Green Suff 57 C6
Owlswick Bucks 39 D7
Owmby Lincs 90 D4
Owmby-by-Spital Lincs 90 F4
Owrtyn = Overton Wrex 73 E7
Owslebury Hants 15 B6
Owston Leics 64 D4
Owston S Yorks 89 C6
Owston Ferry N Lincs 90 D2
Owstwick E Yorks 97 F8
Owthorne E Yorks 91 B7
Owthorpe Notts 77 F6
Oxborough Norf 67 D7
Oxcombe Lincs 79 B6
Oxen Park Cumb 99 F5
Oxenholme Cumb 99 F7
Oxenhope W Yorks 94 F3
Oxenton Glos 50 F4
Oxenwood Wilts 25 D8
Oxford Oxon 39 D5
Oxhey Herts 40 E4
Oxhill Warks 51 E8
Oxley W Mid 62 D3
Oxley Green Essex 43 C5
Oxley's Green E Sus 18 C3
Oxnam Borders 116 C2
Oxshott Sur 28 C2
Oxspring S Yorks 88 D3
Oxted Sur 28 D4
Oxton Borders 121 D7
Oxton Notts 77 D6
Oxwich Swansea 33 F5
Oxwick Norf 80 E5
Oykel Bridge Highld 156 J6
Oyne Aberds 141 B5

P

Pabail Iarach W Isles 155 D10
Pabail Uarach W Isles 155 D10
Pace Gate N Yorks 94 D4
Packington Leics 63 C7
Padanaram Angus 134 D4
Padbury Bucks 52 F5
Paddington London 41 F5
Paddlesworth Kent 19 B8
Paddock Wood Kent 29 E7
Paddockhaugh Moray 152 C2
Paddockhole Dumfries 115 F5
Padfield Derbys 87 E8
Padiham Lancs 93 F7
Padog Conwy 83 F8
Padside N Yorks 94 D4
Padstow Corn 4 B4
Padworth W Berks 26 C4
Page Bank Durham 110 F5
Pagham W Sus 16 E2
Paglesham Churchend Essex 43 E5
Paglesham Eastend Essex 43 E5
Paibeil W Isles 148 B2
Paible W Isles 154 H5
Paignton Torbay 7 C6
Pailton Warks 63 F8
Painscastle Powys 48 E3
Painshawfield Northumb 110 C3
Painsthorpe E Yorks 96 D4
Painswick Glos 37 D5
Pairc Shiaboist W Isles 154 C7
Paisley Renfs 118 C4
Pakefield Suff 69 E8
Pakenham Suff 56 C3
Pale Gwyn 72 F3
Palestine Hants 25 E7
Paley Street Windsor 27 B6
Palfrey W Mid 62 E4
Palgowan Dumfries 112 F3
Palgrave Suff 56 B5
Pallion T&W 111 D6
Palmarsh Kent 19 B8
Palnackie Dumfries 106 D5
Palnure Dumfries 105 C8
Palterton Derbys 76 C4
Pamber End Hants 26 D4
Pamber Green Hants 26 D4
Pamber Heath Hants 26 C4
Pamphill Dorset 13 D7
Pampisford Cambs 55 E5
Pan Orkney 159 J4
Panbride Angus 135 F5
Pancrasweek Devon 8 D4
Pandy Gwyn 58 D3
Pandy Mon 35 B7
Pandy Powys 59 D6
Pandy Wrex 73 F5
Pandy Tudur Conwy 83 E8
Panfield Essex 42 B3
Pangbourne W Berks 26 B4
Pannal N Yorks 95 D6
Panshanger Herts 41 C5
Pant Shrops 60 B2
Pant-glâs Powys 58 E4
Pant-glas Carms 33 B6
Pant-glas Gwyn 71 C5
Pant-glas Shrops 73 F6
Pant-lasau Swansea 33 E7
Pant Mawr Powys 59 F5
Pant-teg Carms 33 B5
Pant-y-Caws Carms 32 B2
Pant-y-dwr Powys 47 B8
Pant-y-ffridd Powys 59 D8
Pant-y-Wacco Flint 72 B5
Pant-yr-awel Bridgend 34 F3
Pantgwyn Carms 33 B6
Pantgwyn Ceredig 45 E4
Panton Lincs 78 B4
Pantperthog Gwyn 58 D4
Pantyffynnon Carms 33 C7
Pantymwyn Flint 73 C5
Panxworth Norf 69 C6
Papcastle Cumb 107 F8
Papigoe Highld 158 E5
Papil Shetland 160 K5
Papley Orkney 159 J5
Papple E Loth 121 B8
Papplewick Notts 76 D5
Papworth Everard Cambs 54 C3
Papworth St Agnes Cambs 54 C3
Par Corn 5 D5
Parbold Lancs 86 C2
Parbrook Som 23 F7
Parbrook W Sus 16 B4
Parc Gwyn 72 F2
Parc-Seymour Newport 35 E8
Parc-y-rhôs Carms 46 E4
Parcllyn Ceredig 45 D4
Pardshaw Cumb 98 B2
Parham Suff 57 C7
Park Dumfries 114 E2
Park Corner Oxon 39 F6
Park Corner Windsor 40 F1
Park End Mbro 102 C3
Park End Northumb 109 B8
Park Gate Hants 15 D6
Park Hill N Yorks 95 C6
Park Hill Notts 77 D6
Park Street W Sus 28 F2
Parkend Glos 36 D3
Parkeston Essex 57 F6
Parkgate Ches W 73 B6
Parkgate Dumfries 114 F3
Parkgate Kent 19 B5
Parkgate Sur 28 E3
Parkham Devon 9 B5
Parkham Ash Devon 9 B5
Parkhill Ho. Aberds 141 C7
Parkhouse Mon 36 D1
Parkhouse Green Derbys 76 C4
Parkhurst IoW 15 E5
Parkmill Swansea 33 F6
Parkneuk Aberds 135 B7
Parkstone Poole 13 E8
Parley Cross Dorset 13 E8
Parracombe Devon 21 E5
Parrog Pembs 45 F2
Parsley Hay Derbys 75 C8
Parson Cross S Yorks 88 E4
Parson Drove Cambs 66 D3
Parsonage Green Essex 42 D3
Parsonby Cumb 107 F8
Parson's Heath Essex 43 B6
Partick Glasgow 119 C5
Partington Gtr Man 86 E5
Partney Lincs 79 C7
Parton Cumb 98 B1
Parton Dumfries 106 B3
Parton Glos 37 B5
Partridge Green W Sus 17 C5
Parwich Derbys 75 D8
Passenham Northants 53 F5
Paston Norf 81 D9
Patchacott Devon 9 E6
Patcham Brighton 17 D7
Patching W Sus 16 D4
Patchole Devon 20 E5
Pateley Bridge N Yorks 94 C4
Paternoster Heath Essex 43 C5
Path of Condie Perth 128 C2
Pathe Som 23 F5
Pathhead Aberds 135 C7
Pathhead E Ayrs 113 C6
Pathhead Fife 128 E4
Pathhead Midloth 121 C6
Pathstruie Perth 128 C2
Patna E Ayrs 112 C4
Patney Wilts 25 D5
Patrick IoM 84 D2
Patrick Brompton N Yorks 101 E7
Patrington E Yorks 91 B7
Patrixbourne Kent 31 D5
Patterdale Cumb 99 C5
Pattingham Staffs 62 E2
Pattishall Northants 52 D4
Pattiswick Green Essex 42 B4
Patton Bridge Cumb 99 E7
Paul Corn 2 D3
Paulerspury Northants 52 E5
Paull E Yorks 91 B5
Paulton Bath 23 D8
Pavenham Bedford 53 D7
Pawlett Som 22 E5
Pawston Northumb 122 F4
Paxford Glos 51 F6
Paxton Borders 122 D5
Payhembury Devon 11 D5
Paythorne Lancs 93 D8
Peacehaven E Sus 17 D8
Peak Dale Derbys 75 B7
Peak Forest Derbys 75 B8
Peakirk Pboro 65 D8
Pearsie Angus 134 D3
Pease Pottage W Sus 28 F3
Peasedown St John Bath 24 D2
Peasemore W Berks 26 B2
Peasenhall Suff 57 C7
Peaslake Sur 27 E8
Peasley Cross Mers 86 E3
Peasmarsh E Sus 19 C5
Peaston E Loth 121 C7
Peastonbank E Loth 121 C7
Peat Inn Fife 129 D6
Peathill Aberds 153 B9
Peatling Magna Leics 64 E2
Peatling Parva Leics 64 F2
Peaton Shrops 60 F5
Peats Corner Suff 57 C5
Pebmarsh Essex 56 F2
Pebworth Worcs 51 E6
Pecket Well W Yorks 87 B7
Peckforton Ches E 74 D2
Peckham London 28 B4
Peckleton Leics 63 D8
Pedlinge Kent 19 B8
Pedmore W Mid 62 F3
Pedwell Som 23 F6
Peebles Borders 121 E5
Peel IoM 84 D2
Peel Common Hants 15 D6
Peel Park S Lanark 119 D6
Peening Quarter Kent 19 C5
Pegsdon C Beds 54 F2
Pegswood Northumb 117 F8
Pegwell Kent 31 C7
Peinchorran Highld 149 E10
Peinlich Highld 149 C9
Pelaw T&W 111 C5
Pelcomb Bridge Pembs 44 D4
Pelcomb Cross Pembs 44 D4
Peldon Essex 43 C5
Pellon W Yorks 87 B8
Pelsall W Mid 62 D4
Pelton Durham 111 D5
Pelutho Cumb 107 E8
Pelynt Corn 5 D7
Pemberton Gtr Man 86 D3
Pembrey Carms 33 D5
Pembridge Hereford 49 D5
Pembroke = Penfro Pembs 44 E4
Pembroke Dock = Doc Penfro Pembs 44 E4
Pembury Kent 29 E7
Pen-bont Rhydybeddau Ceredig 58 F3
Pen-clawdd Swansea 33 E6
Pen-ffordd Pembs 32 B1
Pen-groes-oped Mon 35 D7
Pen-llyn Anglesey 82 C3
Pen-lon Anglesey 82 E4
Pen-sarn Gwyn 70 C5
Pen-sarn Gwyn 71 E6
Pen-twyn Mon 36 D2
Pen-y-banc Carms 33 B7
Pen-y-bont Carms 32 B4
Pen-y-bont Gwyn 58 D4
Pen-y-bont Gwyn 71 E7
Pen-y-bont Powys 60 B2
Pen-Y-Bont Ar Ogwr = Bridgend Bridgend 21 B8
Pen-y-bryn Gwyn 58 C3
Pen-y-bryn Pembs 45 E3
Pen-y-cae Powys 34 C2
Pen-y-cae-mawr Mon 35 E8
Pen-y-cefn Flint 72 B5
Pen-y-clawdd Mon 36 D1
Pen-y-coedcae Rhondda 34 F4
Pen-y-fai Bridgend 34 F2
Pen-y-garn Carms 46 F4
Pen-y-garn Ceredig 58 F3
Pen-y-garnedd Anglesey 82 D5
Pen-y-gop Conwy 72 E3
Pen-y-graig Gwyn 70 D2
Pen-y-groes Carms 33 C6
Pen-y-groeslon Gwyn 70 D3
Pen-y-Gwryd Hotel Gwyn 83 F6
Pen-y-stryt Denb 73 D5
Pen-yr-heol Mon 35 C8
Pen-yr-Heolgerrig M Tydf 34 D4
Penallt Mon 36 C2
Penally Pembs 32 E2
Penalt Hereford 36 B2
Penare Corn 3 B8
Penarlâg = Hawarden Flint 73 C7
Penarth V Glam 22 B3
Penbryn Ceredig 45 D4
Pencader Carms 46 F3
Pencaenewydd Gwyn 70 C5
Pencaitland E Loth 121 C7
Pencarnisiog Anglesey 82 D3
Pencarreg Carms 46 E4
Pencelli Powys 34 B4
Pencoed Bridgend 34 F3
Pencombe Hereford 49 D7
Pencoyd Hereford 36 B2
Pencraig Hereford 36 B2
Pencraig Powys 59 B7
Pendeen Corn 2 C2
Penderyn Rhondda 34 D3
Pendine Carms 32 D3
Pendlebury Gtr Man 87 D5
Pendleton Lancs 93 F7
Pendock Worcs 50 F2
Pendoggett Corn 4 B5
Pendomer Som 12 C3
Pendoylan V Glam 22 B2
Pendre Bridgend 34 F3
Penegoes Powys 58 D4
Penfro = Pembroke Pembs 44 E4
Pengam Caerph 35 E5
Penge London 28 B4
Pengenffordd Powys 48 F3
Pengorffwysfa Anglesey 82 B4
Pengover Green Corn 5 C7
Penhale Corn 3 E5
Penhale Corn 4 D4
Penhalvaen Corn 3 C6
Penhill Swindon 38 F1
Penhow Newport 35 E8
Penhurst E Sus 18 D3
Peniarth Gwyn 58 D3
Penicuik Midloth 120 C5
Peniel Carms 33 B5
Peniel Denb 72 C4
Penifiler Highld 149 D9
Peninver Argyll 143 F8
Penisarwaun Gwyn 83 E5
Penistone S Yorks 88 D3
Penjerrick Corn 3 C6
Penketh Warr 86 F3
Penkill S Ayrs 112 E2
Penkridge Staffs 62 C3
Penley Wrex 73 F8
Penllergaer Swansea 33 E7
Penllyn V Glam 21 B8
Penmachno Conwy 83 F7
Penmaen Swansea 33 F6
Penmaenan Conwy 83 D7
Penmaenmawr Conwy 83 D7
Penmaenpool Gwyn 58 C3
Penmark V Glam 22 C2
Penmarth Corn 3 C6
Penmon Anglesey 83 C6
Penmore Mill Argyll 146 F7
Penmorfa Ceredig 46 D2
Penmorfa Gwyn 71 C6
Penmynydd Anglesey 82 D5
Penn Bucks 40 E2
Penn W Mid 62 E2
Penn Street Bucks 40 E2
Pennal Gwyn 58 D4
Pennan Aberds 153 B8
Pennant Ceredig 46 C4
Pennant Denb 72 D4
Pennant Denb 72 F4
Pennant Powys 59 E5
Pennant Melangell Powys 59 B7
Pennar Pembs 44 E4
Pennard Swansea 33 F6
Pennerley Shrops 60 E3
Pennington Cumb 92 B2
Pennington Gtr Man 86 E4
Pennington Hants 14 E4
Penny Bridge Cumb 99 F5
Pennycross Argyll 147 J8
Pennygate Norf 69 B6
Pennygown Argyll 147 G8
Pennymoor Devon 10 C3
Pennywell T&W 111 D6
Penparc Ceredig 45 E4
Penparc Pembs 44 B3
Penparcau Ceredig 58 F2
Penperlleni Mon 35 D7
Penpillick Corn 5 D5
Penpol Corn 3 C7
Penpoll Corn 5 D6
Penpont Dumfries 113 E8
Penpont Powys 34 B3
Penrhôs Mon 35 C8
Penrherber Carms 45 F4
Penrhiw goch Carms 33 C6
Penrhiw-llan Ceredig 46 E2
Penrhiw-pâl Ceredig 46 E2
Penrhiwceiber Rhondda 34 E4
Penrhos Gwyn 70 D4
Penrhos Powys 34 C1
Penrhosfeilw Anglesey 82 C2
Penrhyn Bay Conwy 83 C8
Penrhyn-coch Ceredig 58 F3
Penrhyndeudraeth Gwyn 71 D7
Penrhynside Conwy 83 C8
Penrice Swansea 33 F5
Penrith Cumb 108 F5
Penrose Corn 4 B3
Penruddock Cumb 99 B6
Penryn Corn 3 C6
Pensarn Carms 33 C5
Pensarn Conwy 72 B3
Pensax Worcs 50 C2
Pensby Mers 85 F3
Penselwood Som 24 F2
Pensford Bath 23 C8
Penshaw T&W 111 D6
Penshurst Kent 29 E6
Pensilva Corn 5 C7
Penston E Loth 121 B7
Pentewan Corn 3 B9
Pentir Gwyn 83 E5
Pentire Corn 4 C2
Pentlow Essex 56 E2
Pentney Norf 67 C7
Penton Mewsey Hants 25 E8
Pentraeth Anglesey 82 D5
Pentre Carms 33 C6
Pentre Powys 59 F7
Pentre Powys 60 E2
Pentre Rhondda 34 E3
Pentre Shrops 60 C3
Pentre Wrex 72 F5
Pentre Wrex 73 E6
Pentre-bâch Ceredig 46 E4
Pentre-bach Powys 47 F8
Pentre Berw Anglesey 82 D4
Pentre-bont Conwy 83 F7
Pentre-celyn Denb 72 D5
Pentre-Celyn Powys 59 D5
Pentre-chwyth Swansea 33 E7
Pentre-cwrt Carms 46 F2
Pentre Dolau-Honddu Powys 47 E8
Pentre-dwr Swansea 33 E7
Pentre-galar Pembs 45 F3
Pentre-Gwenlais Carms 33 C7
Pentre Gwynfryn Gwyn 71 E6
Pentre Halkyn Flint 73 B6
Pentre-Isaf Conwy 83 E8
Pentre Llanrhaeadr Denb 72 C4
Pentre-llwyn-llŵyd Powys 47 D8
Pentre-llyn Ceredig 46 B5
Pentre-llyn cymmer Conwy 72 D3
Pentre Meyrick V Glam 21 B8
Pentre-poeth Newport 35 F6
Pentre-rhew Ceredig 47 D5
Pentre-tafarn-y-fedw Conwy 83 E8
Pentre-ty-gwyn Carms 47 F7
Pentrebach M Tydf 34 D4
Pentrebach Swansea 33 D7
Pentrebeirdd Powys 59 C8
Pentrecagal Carms 46 E2
Pentredwr Denb 73 E5
Pentrefelin Carms 33 B6
Pentrefelin Ceredig 46 E5
Pentrefelin Conwy 83 D8
Pentrefelin Gwyn 71 D6
Pentrefoelas Conwy 83 F8
Pentregat Ceredig 46 D2
Pentreheyling Shrops 60 E2
Pentre'r Felin Conwy 83 E8
Pentre'r-felin Powys 47 F8
Pentrich Derbys 76 D3
Pentridge Dorset 13 C8
Pentyrch Cardiff 35 F5
Penuchadre V Glam 21 B7
Penuwch Ceredig 46 C4
Penwithick Corn 4 D5
Penwyllt Powys 34 C2
Penybanc Carms 33 C7
Penybont Powys 48 C3
Penybontfawr Powys 59 B7
Penycae Wrex 73 E6
Penycwm Pembs 44 C3
Penyffordd Flint 73 C7
Penyffridd Gwyn 82 F5
Penygarnedd Powys 59 B8
Penygraig Rhondda 34 E3
Penygroes Gwyn 82 F4
Penygroes Pembs 45 F3
Penyrheol Caerph 35 F5
Penysarn Anglesey 82 B4
Penywaun Rhondda 34 D3
Penzance Corn 2 C3
Peopleton Worcs 50 D4
Peover Heath Ches E 74 B4
Peper Harow Sur 27 E7
Perceton N Ayrs 118 E3
Percie Aberds 140 E4
Percyhorner Aberds 153 B9
Periton Som 21 E8
Perivale London 40 F4
Perkinsville Durham 111 D5
Perlethorpe Notts 77 B6
Perranarworthal Corn 3 C6
Perranporth Corn 4 D2
Perranuthnoe Corn 2 D4
Perranzabuloe Corn 4 D2
Perry Barr W Mid 62 E4
Perry Green Herts 41 C7
Perry Green Wilts 37 F6
Perry Street Kent 29 B7
Perryfoot Derbys 88 F2
Pershall Staffs 74 F5
Pershore Worcs 50 E4
Pert Angus 135 C6
Pertenhall Bedford 53 C8
Perth Perth 128 B3
Perthy Shrops 73 F7
Perton Staffs 62 E2
Pertwood Wilts 24 F3
Peter Tavy Devon 6 B3
Peterborough Pboro 65 E8
Peterburn Highld 155 J12
Peterchurch Hereford 48 F5
Peterculter Aberdeen 141 D7
Peterhead Aberds 153 D11
Peterlee Durham 111 E7
Peter's Green Herts 40 C4
Peters Marland Devon 9 C6
Petersfield Hants 15 B8
Peterston super-Ely V Glam 22 B2
Peterstone Wentlooge Newport 35 F6
Peterstow Hereford 36 B2
Petertown Orkney 159 H4
Petham Kent 30 D5
Petrockstow Devon 9 D7
Pett E Sus 19 D5
Pettaugh Suff 57 D5
Petteridge Kent 29 E7
Pettinain S Lanark 120 E2
Pettistree Suff 57 D6
Petton Devon 10 B5
Petton Shrops 60 B4
Petts Wood London 28 C5
Petty Aberds 153 E7
Pettycur Fife 128 F4
Pettymuick Aberds 141 B8
Petworth W Sus 16 B3
Pevensey E Sus 18 E3
Pevensey Bay E Sus 18 E3
Pewsey Wilts 25 C6
Philham Devon 8 B4
Philiphaugh Borders 115 B7
Phillack Corn 2 C4
Philleigh Corn 3 C7
Philpstoun W Loth 120 B3
Phocle Green Hereford 36 B3
Phoenix Green Hants 27 D5
Pica Cumb 98 B2
Piccotts End Herts 40 D3
Pickering N Yorks 103 F5
Picket Piece Hants 25 E8
Picket Post Hants 14 D2
Pickhill N Yorks 101 F8
Picklescott Shrops 60 E4
Pickletillem Fife 129 B6
Pickmere Ches E 74 B3
Pickney Som 11 B6
Pickstock Telford 61 B7
Pickwell Devon 20 E3
Pickwell Leics 64 C4
Pickworth Lincs 78 F3
Pickworth Rutland 65 C6
Picton Ches W 73 B8
Picton Flint 85 F2
Picton N Yorks 102 D2
Piddinghoe E Sus 17 D8
Piddington Northants 53 D6
Piddington Oxon 39 C6
Piddlehinton Dorset 12 E5
Piddletrenthide Dorset 12 E5
Pidley Cambs 54 B4
Piercebridge Darl 101 C7
Pierowall Orkney 159 D5
Pigdon Northumb 117 F7
Pikehall Derbys 75 D8
Pilgrims Hatch Essex 42 E1
Pilham Lincs 90 E2
Pill N Som 23 B7
Pillaton Corn 5 C8
Pillerton Hersey Warks 51 E8
Pillerton Priors Warks 51 E7
Pilleth Powys 48 C4
Pilley Hants 14 E4
Pilley S Yorks 88 D4
Pilling Lancs 92 E4
Pilling Lane Lancs 92 E3
Pillowell Glos 36 D3
Pillwell Dorset 13 C5
Pilning S Glos 36 F2
Pilsbury Derbys 75 C8
Pilsdon Dorset 12 E2
Pilsgate Pboro 65 D7
Pilsley Derbys 76 B2
Pilsley Derbys 76 C4
Pilton Devon 20 F4
Pilton Northants 65 F7
Pilton Rutland 65 D6
Pilton Som 23 E7
Pilton Green Swansea 33 F5
Pimperne Dorset 13 D7
Pin Mill Suff 57 F6
Pinchbeck Lincs 66 B2
Pinchbeck Bars Lincs 65 B8
Pinchbeck West Lincs 66 B2
Pincheon Green S Yorks 89 C7
Pinehurst Swindon 38 F1
Pinfold Lancs 85 C4
Pinged Carms 33 D5
Pinhoe Devon 10 E4
Pinkneys Green Windsor 40 F1
Pinley W Mid 51 B8
Pinminnoch S Ayrs 112 E1
Pinmore S Ayrs 112 E2
Pinmore Mains S Ayrs 112 E2
Pinner London 40 F4
Pinvin Worcs 50 E4
Pinwherry S Ayrs 112 F1
Pinxton Derbys 76 D4
Pipe and Lyde Hereford 49 E7
Pipe Gate Shrops 74 E4
Piperhill Highld 151 F11
Piper's Pool Corn 8 F4
Pipewell Northants 64 F5
Pippacott Devon 20 F4
Pipton Powys 48 F3
Pirbright Sur 27 D7
Pirnmill N Ayrs 143 D9
Pirton Herts 54 F2
Pirton Worcs 50 E3
Pisgah Ceredig 47 B5
Pisgah Stirling 127 D6
Pishill Oxon 39 F7
Pistyll Gwyn 70 C4
Pitagowan Perth 133 C5
Pitblae Aberds 153 B9
Pitcairngreen Perth 128 B2
Pitcalnie Highld 151 D11
Pitcaple Aberds 141 B6
Pitch Green Bucks 39 D7
Pitch Place Sur 27 D7
Pitchcombe Glos 37 D5
Pitchcott Bucks 39 B7
Pitchford Shrops 60 D5
Pitcombe Som 23 F8
Pitcorthie Fife 129 D7
Pitcox E Loth 122 B2
Pitcur Perth 134 F2
Pitfichie Aberds 141 C5
Pitforthie Aberds 135 B8
Pitgrudy Highld 151 B10
Pitkennedy Angus 135 D5
Pitkevy Fife 128 D4
Pitkierie Fife 129 D7
Pitlessie Fife 128 D5
Pitlochry Perth 133 D6
Pitmachie Aberds 141 B5
Pitmain Highld 138 D3
Pitmedden Aberds 141 B7
Pitminster Som 11 C7
Pitmuies Angus 135 E5
Pitmunie Aberds 141 C5
Pitney Som 12 B2
Pitscottie Fife 129 C6
Pitsea Essex 42 F3
Pitsford Northants 53 C5
Pitsmoor S Yorks 88 F4
Pitstone Bucks 40 C2
Pitstone Green Bucks 40 C2
Pittendreich Moray 152 B1
Pittentrail Highld 157 J10
Pittenweem Fife 129 D7
Pittington Durham 111 E6
Pittodrie Aberds 141 B5
Pitton Wilts 25 F7
Pittswood Kent 29 E7
Pittulie Aberds 153 B9
Pity Me Durham 111 E5
Pityme Corn 4 B4
Pityoulish Highld 138 C5
Pixey Green Suff 57 B6
Pixham Sur 28 D2
Pixley Hereford 49 F8
Place Newton N Yorks 96 B4
Plaidy Aberds 153 C7
Plains N Lanark 119 C7
Plaish Shrops 60 E5
Plaistow W Sus 27 F8
Plaitford Wilts 14 C3
Plank Lane Gtr Man 86 E4
Plas-canol Gwyn 58 C2
Plas Gogerddan Ceredig 58 F3
Plas Llwyngwern Powys 58 D4
Plas Nantyr Wrex 73 F5
Plas-yn-Cefn Denb 72 B4
Plastow Green Hants 26 C3
Platt Kent 29 D7
Platt Bridge Gtr Man 86 D4
Platts Common S Yorks 88 D4
Plawsworth Durham 111 E5
Plaxtol Kent 29 D7
Play Hatch Oxon 26 B5
Playden E Sus 19 C6
Playford Suff 57 E6
Playing Place Corn 3 B7
Playley Green Glos 50 F2
Plealey Shrops 60 D4
Plean Stirling 127 F7
Pleasington Blackburn 86 B4
Pleasley Derbys 76 C5
Pleckgate Blackburn 93 F6
Plenmeller Northumb 109 C7
Pleshey Essex 42 C2
Plockton Highld 149 E13
Plocrapol W Isles 154 H6
Ploughfield Hereford 49 E5
Plowden Shrops 60 F3
Ploxgreen Shrops 60 D3
Pluckley Kent 30 E3
Pluckley Thorne Kent 30 E3
Plumbland Cumb 107 F8
Plumley Ches E 74 B4
Plumpton Cumb 108 F4
Plumpton E Sus 17 C7
Plumpton Green E Sus 17 C7
Plumpton Head Cumb 108 F5
Plumstead London 29 B5
Plumstead Norf 81 D7
Plumtree Notts 77 F6
Plungar Leics 77 F7
Plush Dorset 12 D5
Plwmp Ceredig 46 D2
Plymouth Plym 6 D2
Plympton Plym 6 D3

Plymstock Plym 6 D3
Plymtree Devon 11 D5
Pockley N Yorks 102 F4
Pocklington E Yorks 96 E4
Pode Hole Lincs 66 B2
Podimore Som 12 B3
Podington Bedford 53 C7
Podmore Staffs 74 F4
Point Clear Essex 43 C6
Pointon Lincs 78 F4
Pokesdown Bmouth 14 E2
Pol a Charra W Isles 148 G2
Polbae Dumfries 105 B6
Polbain Highld 156 H2
Polbathic Corn 5 D8
Polbeth W Loth 120 C3
Polchar Highld 138 D4
Pole Elm Worcs 50 E3
Polebrook Northants 65 F7
Polegate E Sus 18 E2
Poles Highld 151 B10
Polesworth Warks 63 D6
Polgigga Corn 2 D2
Polglass Highld 156 J3
Polgooth Corn 4 D4
Poling W Sus 16 D4
Polkerris Corn 5 D5
Polla Highld 156 D6
Pollington E Yorks 89 C7
Polloch Highld 130 C1
Pollok Glasgow 118 C5
Pollokshields Glasgow 119 C5
Polmassick Corn 3 B8
Polmont Falk 120 B2
Polnessan E Ayrs 112 C4
Polnish Highld 147 C10
Polperro Corn 5 D7
Polruan Corn 5 D6
Polsham Som 23 E7
Polstead Suff 56 F3
Poltalloch Argyll 124 F4
Poltimore Devon 10 E4
Polton Midloth 121 C5
Polwarth Borders 122 D3
Polyphant Corn 8 F4
Polzeath Corn 4 B4
Ponders End London 41 E6
Pondersbridge Cambs 66 E2
Pondtail Hants 27 D6
Ponsanooth Corn 3 C6
Ponsworthy Devon 6 B5
Pont Aber Carms 33 B8
Pont Aber-Geirw Gwyn 71 E8
Pont-ar-gothi Carms 33 B6
Pont ar Hydfer Powys 34 B2
Pont-ar-llechau Carms 33 B8
Pont Cwm Pydew Denb 72 F4
Pont Cyfyng Conwy 83 F7
Pont Cysyllte Wrex 73 E6
Pont Dolydd Prysor Gwyn 71 D8
Pont-faen Powys 47 F8
Pont Fronwydd Gwyn 58 B5
Pont-gareg Pembs 45 E3
Pont-Henri Carms 33 D5
Pont-Llogel Powys 59 C7
Pont Pen-y-benglog Gwyn 83 E6
Pont Rhyd-goch Conwy 83 E6
Pont-Rhyd-sarn Gwyn 59 B5
Pont Rhyd-y-cyff Bridgend 34 F2
Pont-rhyd-y-groes Ceredig 47 B6
Pont-rug Gwyn 82 E5
Pont Senni = Sennybridge Powys 34 B3
Pont-siân Ceredig 46 E3
Pont-y-gwaith Rhondda 34 E4
Pont-Y-Pŵl = Pontypool Torf 35 D6
Pont-y-pant Conwy 83 F7
Pont y Pennant Gwyn 59 B6
Pont yr Afon-Gam Gwyn 71 C8
Pont-yr-hafod Pembs 44 C4
Pontamman Carms 33 C7
Pontantwn Carms 33 C5
Pontardawe Neath 33 D8
Pontarddulais Swansea 33 D6
Pontarsais Carms 33 B5
Pontblyddyn Flint 73 C6
Pontbren Araeth Carms 33 B7
Pontbren Llwyd Rhondda 34 D3
Pontefract W Yorks 89 B5
Ponteland Northumb 110 B4
Ponterwyd Ceredig 58 F4
Pontesbury Shrops 60 D3
Pontfadog Wrex 73 F6
Pontfaen Pembs 45 F2
Pontgarreg Ceredig 46 D2
Ponthir Torf 35 E7
Ponthirwaun Ceredig 45 E4
Pontllanfraith Caerph 35 E5
Pontlliw Swansea 33 D7
Pontllyfni Gwyn 82 F4
Pontlottyn Caerph 35 D5
Pontneddfechan Powys 34 D3
Pontnewydd Torf 35 E6
Pontrhydfendigaid Ceredig 47 C6
Pontrhydyfen Neath 34 E1
Pontrilas Hereford 35 B7
Pontrobert Powys 59 C8
Ponts Green E Sus 18 D3
Pontshill Hereford 36 B3
Pontsticill M Tydf 34 C4
Pontwgan Conwy 83 D7
Pontyates Carms 33 D5
Pontyberem Carms 33 C6
Pontyclun Rhondda 34 F4
Pontycymer Bridgend 34 E3
Pontyglasier Pembs 45 F3
Pontypool = Pont-Y-Pŵl Torf 35 D6
Pontypridd Rhondda 34 F4
Pontywaun Caerph 35 E6
Pooksgreen Hants 14 C4
Pool Corn 3 B5
Pool W Yorks 94 E5
Pool o'Muckhart Clack 128 D2
Pool Quay Powys 60 C2
Poole Poole 13 E8
Poole Keynes Glos 37 E6
Poolend Staffs 75 D6
Poolewe Highld 155 J13
Pooley Bridge Cumb 99 B6
Poolfold Staffs 75 D5
Poolhill Glos 36 B4
Poolsbrook Derbys 76 B4
Pootings Kent 29 E5
Pope Hill Pembs 44 D4
Popeswood Brack 27 C6
Popham Hants 26 E3
Poplar London 41 F6
Popley Hants 26 D4
Porchester Nottingham 77 E5
Porchfield IoW 14 E5
Porin Highld 150 F6
Poringland Norf 69 D5
Porkellis Corn 3 C5
Porlock Som 21 E7
Porlock Weir Som 21 E7
Port Ann Argyll 145 E8
Port Appin Argyll 130 E3
Port Arthur Shetland 160 K5
Port Askaig Argyll 142 B5
Port Bannatyne Argyll 145 G9
Port Carlisle Cumb 108 C2
Port Charlotte Argyll 142 C3
Port Clarence Stockton 102 B2
Port Driseach Argyll 145 F8
Port e Vullen IoM 84 C4
Port Ellen Argyll 142 D4
Port Elphinstone Aberds 141 C6
Port Erin IoM 84 F1
Port Erroll Aberds 153 E10
Port-Eynon Swansea 33 F5
Port Gaverne Corn 8 F2
Port Glasgow Invclyd 118 B3
Port Henderson Highld 149 A12
Port Isaac Corn 4 A4
Port Lamont Argyll 145 F9
Port Lion Pembs 44 E4
Port Logan Dumfries 104 E4
Port Mholair W Isles 155 D10
Port Mor Highld 146 D7
Port Mulgrave N Yorks 103 C5
Port Nan Giùran W Isles 155 D10
Port nan Long W Isles 148 A3
Port Nis W Isles 155 A10
Port of Menteith Stirling 126 D4
Port Quin Corn 4 A4
Port Ramsay Argyll 130 E2
Port St Mary IoM 84 F2
Port Sunlight Mers 85 F4
Port Talbot Neath 34 E1
Port Tennant Swansea 33 E7
Port Wemyss Argyll 142 C2
Port William Dumfries 105 E7
Portachoillan Argyll 144 H6
Portavadie Argyll 145 G8
Portbury N Som 23 B7
Portchester Hants 15 D7
Portclair Highld 137 C7
Portencalzie Dumfries 104 B4
Portencross N Ayrs 118 E1
Portesham Dorset 12 F4
Portessie Moray 152 B4
Portfield Gate Pembs 44 D4
Portgate Devon 9 F6
Portgordon Moray 152 B3
Portgower Highld 157 H13
Porth Corn 4 C3
Porth Rhondda 34 E4
Porth Navas Corn 3 D6
Porth Tywyn = Burry Port Carms 33 D5
Porth-y-waen Shrops 60 B2
Porthaethwy = Menai Bridge Anglesey 83 D5
Porthallow Corn 3 D6
Porthallow Corn 5 D7
Porthcawl Bridgend 21 B7
Porthcothan Corn 4 B3
Porthcurno Corn 2 D2
Porthgain Pembs 44 B3
Porthill Shrops 60 C4
Porthkerry V Glam 22 C2
Porthleven Corn 2 D5
Porthllechog Anglesey 82 B4
Porthmadog Gwyn 71 D6
Porthmeor Corn 2 C3
Portholland Corn 3 B8
Porthoustock Corn 3 D7
Porthpean Corn 4 D5
Porthtowan Corn 3 B5
Porthyrhyd Carms 33 C6
Porthyrhyd Carms 47 F6
Portincaple Argyll 145 D11
Portington E Yorks 96 F3
Portinnisherrich Argyll 125 D5
Portinscale Cumb 98 B4
Portishead N Som 23 B6
Portkil Argyll 145 E11
Portknockie Moray 152 B4
Portlethen Aberds 141 E8
Portling Dumfries 107 D5
Portloe Corn 3 C8
Portmahomack Highld 151 C12
Portmeirion Gwyn 71 D6
Portmellon Corn 3 B9
Portmore Hants 14 E4
Portnacroish Argyll 130 E3
Portnahaven Argyll 142 C2
Portnalong Highld 149 E8
Portnaluchaig Highld 147 C9
Portnancon Highld 156 C7
Portnellan Stirling 126 B3
Portobello Edin 121 B6
Porton Wilts 25 F6
Portpatrick Dumfries 104 D4
Portreath Corn 3 B5
Portree Highld 149 D9
Portscatho Corn 3 C7
Portsea Ptsmth 15 D7
Portskerra Highld 157 C11
Portskewett Mon 36 F2
Portslade Brighton 17 D6
Portslade-by-Sea Brighton 17 D6
Portsmouth Ptsmth 15 D7
Portsmouth W Yorks 87 B7
Portsonachan Argyll 125 C6
Portsoy Aberds 152 B5
Portswood Soton 14 C5
Portuairk Highld 146 E7
Portway Hereford 49 F6
Portway Worcs 51 B5
Portwrinkle Corn 5 D8
Poslingford Suff 55 E8
Postbridge Devon 6 B4
Postcombe Oxon 39 E7
Postling Kent 19 B8
Postwick Norf 69 D5
Potholm Dumfries 115 F6
Potsgrove C Beds 40 B2
Pott Row Norf 80 E3
Pott Shrigley Ches E 75 B6
Potten End Herts 40 D3
Potter Brompton N Yorks 97 B5
Potter Heigham Norf 69 C7
Potter Street Essex 41 D7
Potterhanworth Lincs 78 C3
Potterhanworth Booths Lincs 78 C3
Potterne Wilts 24 D4
Potterne Wick Wilts 24 D5
Potternewton W Yorks 95 F6
Potters Bar Herts 41 D5
Potter's Cross Staffs 62 F2
Potterspury Northants 53 E5
Potterton Aberds 141 C8
Potterton W Yorks 95 F7
Potto N Yorks 102 D2
Potton C Beds 54 E3
Poughill Corn 8 D4
Poughill Devon 10 D3
Poulshot Wilts 24 D4
Poulton Glos 37 D8
Poulton Mers 85 E4
Poulton-le-Fylde Lancs 92 F3
Pound Bank Worcs 50 B2
Pound Green E Sus 18 C2
Pound Green IoW 14 F4
Pound Green Worcs 50 B2
Pound Hill W Sus 28 F3
Poundfield E Sus 18 B2
Poundland S Ayrs 112 F1
Poundon Bucks 39 B6
Poundsgate Devon 6 B5
Poundstock Corn 8 E4
Powburn Northumb 117 C6
Powderham Devon 10 F4
Powerstock Dorset 12 E3
Powfoot Dumfries 107 C8
Powick Worcs 50 D3
Powmill Perth 128 E2
Poxwell Dorset 12 F5
Poyle Slough 27 B8
Poynings W Sus 17 C6
Poyntington Dorset 12 C4
Poynton Ches E 87 F7
Poynton Green Telford 61 C5
Poystreet Green Suff 56 D3
Praa Sands Corn 2 D4
Pratt's Bottom London 29 C5
Praze Corn 2 C4
Praze-an-Beeble Corn 2 C5
Predannack Wollas Corn 3 E5
Prees Shrops 74 F2
Prees Green Shrops 74 F2
Prees Heath Shrops 74 F2
Prees Higher Heath Shrops 74 F2
Prees Lower Heath Shrops 74 F2
Preesall Lancs 92 E3
Preesgweene Shrops 73 F6
Prenderguest Borders 122 D5
Prendwick Northumb 117 C6
Prengwyn Ceredig 46 E3
Prenteg Gwyn 71 C6
Prenton Mers 85 F4
Prescot Mers 86 E2
Prescott Shrops 60 B4
Pressen Northumb 122 F4
Prestatyn Denb 72 A4
Prestbury Ches E 75 B6
Prestbury Glos 37 B6
Presteigne = Llanandras Powys 48 C5
Presthope Shrops 61 E5
Prestleigh Som 23 E8
Preston Borders 122 D3
Preston Brighton 17 D7
Preston Devon 7 B6
Preston Dorset 12 F5
Preston E Loth 121 B8
Preston E Yorks 97 F7
Preston Glos 37 D7
Preston Glos 49 F8
Preston Herts 40 B4
Preston Kent 30 C4
Preston Kent 31 C6
Preston Lancs 86 B3
Preston Northumb 117 B7
Preston Rutland 65 D5
Preston Shrops 60 C5
Preston Wilts 24 B5
Preston Wilts 25 B7
Preston Bagot Warks 51 C6
Preston Bissett Bucks 39 B6
Preston Bowyer Som 11 B6
Preston Brockhurst Shrops 60 B5
Preston Brook Halton 86 F3
Preston Candover Hants 26 E4
Preston Capes Northants 52 D3
Preston Crowmarsh Oxon 39 E6
Preston Gubbals Shrops 60 C4
Preston on Stour Warks 51 E7
Preston on the Hill Halton 86 F3
Preston on Wye Hereford 49 E5
Preston Plucknett Som 12 C3
Preston St Mary Suff 56 D3
Preston-under-Scar N Yorks 101 E5
Preston upon the Weald Moors Telford 61 C6
Preston Wynne Hereford 49 E7
Prestonmill Dumfries 107 D6
Prestonpans E Loth 121 B6
Prestwich Gtr Man 87 D6
Prestwick Northumb 110 B4
Prestwick S Ayrs 112 B3
Prestwood Bucks 40 D1
Price Town Bridgend 34 E3
Prickwillow Cambs 67 F5
Priddy Som 23 D7
Priest Hutton Lancs 92 B5
Priest Weston Shrops 60 E2
Priesthaugh Borders 115 D7
Primethorpe Leics 64 E2
Primrose Green Norf 68 C3
Primrose Valley N Yorks 97 B7
Primrosehill Herts 40 D3
Princes Gate Pembs 32 C2
Princes Risborough Bucks 39 D8
Princethorpe Warks 52 B2
Princetown Caerph 35 C5
Princetown Devon 6 B3
Prion Denb 72 C4
Prior Muir Fife 129 C7
Prior Park Northumb 123 D5
Priors Frome Hereford 49 F7
Priors Hardwick Warks 52 D2
Priors Marston Warks 52 D2
Priorslee Telford 61 C7
Priory Wood Hereford 48 E4
Priston Bath 23 C8
Pristow Green Norf 68 F4
Prittlewell Southend 42 F4
Privett Hants 15 B7
Prixford Devon 20 F4
Probus Corn 3 B7
Proncy Highld 151 B10
Prospect Cumb 107 E8
Prudhoe Northumb 110 C3
Ptarmigan Lodge Stirling 126 D2
Pubil Perth 132 E1
Puckeridge Herts 41 B6
Puckington Som 11 C8
Pucklechurch S Glos 23 B8
Pucknall Hants 14 B4
Puckrup Glos 50 F3
Puddinglake Ches W 74 C4
Puddington Ches W 73 B7
Puddington Devon 10 C3
Puddledock Norf 68 E3
Puddletown Dorset 13 E5
Pudleston Hereford 49 D7
Pudsey W Yorks 94 F5
Pulborough W Sus 16 C4
Puleston Telford 61 B7
Pulford Ches W 73 D7
Pulham Dorset 12 D5
Pulham Market Norf 68 F4
Pulham St Mary Norf 68 F5
Pulloxhill C Beds 53 F8
Pumpherston W Loth 120 C3
Pumsaint Carms 47 E5
Puncheston Pembs 32 B1
Puncknowle Dorset 12 F3
Punnett's Town E Sus 18 C3
Purbrook Hants 15 D7
Purewell Dorset 14 E2
Purfleet Thurrock 29 B6
Puriton Som 22 E5
Purleigh Essex 42 D4
Purley London 28 C4
Purley W Berks 26 B4
Purlogue Shrops 48 B4
Purls Bridge Cambs 66 F4
Purse Caundle Dorset 12 C4
Purslow Shrops 60 F3
Purston Jaglin W Yorks 88 C5
Purton Glos 36 D3
Purton Glos 36 D3
Purton Wilts 37 F7
Purton Stoke Wilts 37 E7
Pury End Northants 52 E5
Pusey Oxon 38 E3
Putley Hereford 49 F8
Putney London 28 B3
Putsborough Devon 20 E3
Puttenham Herts 40 C1
Puttenham Sur 27 E7
Puxton N Som 23 C6
Pwll Carms 33 D5
Pwll-glas Denb 72 D5
Pwll-trap Carms 32 C3
Pwll-y-glaw Neath 34 E1
Pwllcrochan Pembs 44 E4
Pwllgloyw Powys 48 F2
Pwllheli Gwyn 70 D4
Pwllmeyric Mon 36 E2
Pye Corner Newport 35 F7
Pye Green Staffs 62 C3
Pyecombe W Sus 17 C6
Pyewipe NE Lincs 91 C6
Pyle = Y Pîl Bridgend 34 F2
Pyle IoW 15 G5
Pylle Som 23 F8
Pymoor Cambs 66 F4
Pyrford Sur 27 D8
Pyrton Oxon 39 E6
Pytchley Northants 53 B6
Pyworthy Devon 8 D5

Q

Quabbs Shrops 60 F2
Quadring Lincs 78 F5
Quainton Bucks 39 C7
Quarley Hants 25 E7
Quarndon Derbys 76 E3
Quarrier's Homes Invclyd 118 C3
Quarrington Lincs 78 E3
Quarrington Hill Durham 111 F6
Quarry Bank W Mid 62 F3
Quarryford E Loth 121 C8
Quarryhill Highld 151 C10
Quarrywood Moray 152 B1
Quarter S Lanark 119 D7
Quatford Shrops 61 E7
Quatt Shrops 61 F7
Quebec Durham 110 E4
Quedgeley Glos 37 C5
Queen Adelaide Cambs 67 F5
Queen Camel Som 12 B3
Queen Charlton Bath 23 C8
Queen Dart Devon 10 C3
Queen Oak Dorset 24 F2
Queen Street Kent 29 E7
Queen Street Wilts 37 F7
Queenborough Kent 30 B3
Queenhill Worcs 50 F3
Queen's Head Shrops 60 B3
Queen's Park Bedford 53 E8
Queen's Park Northants 53 C5
Queensbury W Yorks 94 F4
Queensferry Edin 120 B4
Queensferry Flint 73 C7
Queenstown Blackpool 92 F3
Queenzieburn N Lanark 119 B6
Quemerford Wilts 24 C5
Quendale Shetland 160 M5
Quendon Essex 55 F6
Queniborough Leics 64 C3
Quenington Glos 37 D8
Quernmore Lancs 92 D5
Quethiock Corn 5 C8
Quholm Orkney 159 G3
Quicks Green W Berks 26 B3
Quidenham Norf 68 F3
Quidhampton Hants 26 D3
Quidhampton Wilts 25 F6
Quilquox Aberds 153 E9
Quina Brook Shrops 74 F2
Quindry Orkney 159 J5
Quinton Northants 53 D5
Quinton W Mid 62 F3
Quintrell Downs Corn 4 C3
Quixhill Staffs 75 E8
Quoditch Devon 9 E6
Quoig Perth 127 B7
Quorndon Leics 64 C2
Quothquan S Lanark 120 F2
Quoyloo Orkney 159 F3
Quoyness Orkney 159 H3
Quoys Shetland 160 B8
Quoys Shetland 160 G6

R

Raasay Ho. Highld 149 E10
Rabbit's Cross Kent 29 E8
Raby Mers 73 B7
Rachan Mill Borders 120 F4
Rachub Gwyn 83 E6
Rackenford Devon 10 C3
Rackham W Sus 16 C4
Rackheath Norf 69 C5
Racks Dumfries 107 B7
Rackwick Orkney 159 D5
Rackwick Orkney 159 J3
Radbourne Derbys 76 F2
Radcliffe Gtr Man 87 D5
Radcliffe Northumb 117 D8
Radcliffe on Trent Notts 77 F6
Radclive Bucks 52 F4
Radcot Oxon 38 E2
Raddery Highld 151 F10
Radernie Fife 129 D6
Radford Semele Warks 51 C8
Radipole Dorset 12 F4
Radlett Herts 40 E4
Radley Oxon 39 E5
Radmanthwaite Notts 76 C5
Radmoor Shrops 61 B6
Radmore Green Ches E 74 D2
Radnage Bucks 39 E7
Radstock Bath 23 D8
Radstone Northants 52 E3
Radway Warks 51 E8
Radway Green Ches E 74 D4
Radwell Bedford 53 D8
Radwell Herts 54 F3
Radwinter Essex 55 F7
Radyr Cardiff 35 F5
Rafford Moray 151 F13
Ragdale Leics 64 C3
Raglan Mon 35 D8
Ragnall Notts 77 B8
Rahane Argyll 145 E11
Rainford Mers 86 D2
Rainford Junction Mers 86 D2
Rainham London 41 F8
Rainham Medway 30 C2
Rainhill Mers 86 E2
Rainhill Stoops Mers 86 E3
Rainow Ches E 75 B6
Rainton N Yorks 95 B6
Rainworth Notts 77 D5
Raisbeck Cumb 99 D8
Raise Cumb 109 E7
Rait Perth 128 B4
Raithby Lincs 79 C6
Raithby Lincs 91 F7
Rake W Sus 16 B2
Rakewood Gtr Man 87 C7
Ram Carms 46 E4
Ram Lane Kent 30 E3
Ramasaig Highld 148 D6
Rame Corn 3 C6
Rame Corn 6 E2
Rameldry Mill Bank Fife 128 D5
Ramnageo Shetland 160 C8
Rampisham Dorset 12 D3
Rampside Cumb 92 C2
Rampton Cambs 54 C5
Rampton Notts 77 B7
Ramsbottom Gtr Man 87 C5
Ramsbury Wilts 25 B7
Ramscraigs Highld 158 H3
Ramsdean Hants 15 B8
Ramsdell Hants 26 D3
Ramsden Oxon 38 C3
Ramsden Bellhouse Essex 42 E3
Ramsden Heath Essex 42 E3
Ramsey Cambs 66 F2
Ramsey Essex 57 F6
Ramsey IoM 84 C4
Ramsey Forty Foot Cambs 66 F3
Ramsey Heights Cambs 66 F2
Ramsey Island Essex 43 D5
Ramsey Mereside Cambs 66 F2
Ramsey St Mary's Cambs 66 F2
Ramseycleuch Borders 115 C5
Ramsgate Kent 31 C7
Ramsgill N Yorks 94 B4
Ramshorn Staffs 75 E7
Ramsnest Common Sur 27 F7
Ranais W Isles 155 E9
Ranby Lincs 78 B5
Ranby Notts 89 F7
Rand Lincs 78 B4
Randwick Glos 37 D5
Ranfurly Renfs 118 C3
Rangag Highld 158 F3
Rangemore Staffs 63 B5
Rangeworthy S Glos 36 F3
Rankinston E Ayrs 112 C4
Ranmoor S Yorks 88 F4
Ranmore Common Sur 28 D2
Rannerdale Cumb 98 C3
Rannoch Station Perth 131 D8
Ranochan Highld 147 C11
Ranskill Notts 89 F7
Ranton Staffs 62 B2
Ranworth Norf 69 C6
Raploch Stirling 127 E6
Rapness Orkney 159 D6
Rascal Moor E Yorks 96 F4
Rascarrel Dumfries 106 E4
Rashiereive Aberds 141 B8
Raskelf N Yorks 95 B7
Rassau Bl Gwent 35 C5
Rastrick W Yorks 88 B2
Ratagan Highld 136 C2
Ratby Leics 64 D2
Ratcliffe Culey Leics 63 E7
Ratcliffe on Soar Leics 63 B8
Ratcliffe on the Wreake Leics 64 C3
Rathen Aberds 153 B10
Rathillet Fife 129 B5
Rathmell N Yorks 93 D8
Ratho Edin 120 B4
Ratho Station Edin 120 B4
Rathven Moray 152 B4
Ratley Warks 51 E8
Ratlinghope Shrops 60 E4
Rattar Highld 158 C4
Ratten Row Lancs 92 E4
Rattery Devon 6 C5
Rattlesden Suff 56 D3
Rattray Perth 134 E1
Raughton Head Cumb 108 E3
Raunds Northants 53 B7
Ravenfield S Yorks 89 E5
Ravenglass Cumb 98 E2
Raveningham Norf 69 E6
Ravenscar N Yorks 103 D7
Ravenscraig Invclyd 118 B2
Ravensdale IoM 84 C3
Ravensden Bedford 53 D8
Ravenseat N Yorks 100 D3
Ravenshead Notts 77 D5
Ravensmoor Ches E 74 D3
Ravensthorpe Northants 52 B4
Ravensthorpe W Yorks 88 B3
Ravenstone Leics 63 C8
Ravenstone M Keynes 53 D6
Ravenstonedale Cumb 100 D2
Ravenstown Cumb 92 B3
Ravenstruther S Lanark 120 E2
Ravensworth N Yorks 101 D6
Raw N Yorks 103 D7
Rawcliffe E Yorks 89 B7
Rawcliffe York 95 D8
Rawcliffe Bridge E Yorks 89 B7
Rawdon W Yorks 94 F5
Rawmarsh S Yorks 88 E5
Rawreth Essex 42 E3
Rawridge Devon 11 D7
Rawtenstall Lancs 87 B6
Raxton Aberds 153 E8
Raydon Suff 56 F4
Raylees Northumb 117 E5
Rayleigh Essex 42 E4
Rayne Essex 42 B3
Rayners Lane London 40 F4
Raynes Park London 28 C3
Reach Cambs 55 C6
Read Lancs 93 F7
Reading Reading 26 B5
Reading Street Kent 19 B6
Reagill Cumb 99 C8
Rearquhar Highld 151 B10
Rearsby Leics 64 C3
Reaster Highld 158 D4
Reawick Shetland 160 J5
Reay Highld 157 C12
Rechullin Highld 149 C13
Reculver Kent 31 C6
Red Dial Cumb 108 E2
Red Hill Worcs 50 D3
Red Houses Jersey 17
Red Lodge Suff 55 B7
Red Rail Hereford 36 B2
Red Rock Gtr Man 86 D3
Red Roses Carms 32 C3
Red Row Northumb 117 E8
Red Street Staffs 74 D5
Red Wharf Bay Anglesey 82 C5
Redberth Pembs 32 D1
Redbourn Herts 40 C4
Redbourne N Lincs 90 E3
Redbrook Mon 36 C2
Redbrook Wrex 74 E2
Redburn Highld 151 E8
Redburn Highld 151 G12
Redburn Northumb 109 C7
Redcar Redcar 102 B4
Redcastle Angus 135 D6
Redcastle Highld 151 G8
Redcliff Bay N Som 23 B6
Redding Falk 120 B2
Reddingmuirhead Falk 120 B2
Reddish Gtr Man 87 E6
Redditch Worcs 50 C5
Rede Suff 56 D2
Redenhall Norf 69 F5
Redesdale Camp Northumb 116 E4
Redesmouth Northumb 116 F4
Redford Aberds 135 B7
Redford Angus 135 E5
Redford Durham 110 F3
Redfordgreen Borders 115 C6
Redgorton Perth 128 B2
Redgrave Suff 56 B4
Redhill Aberds 141 D6
Redhill Aberds 153 E6
Redhill N Som 23 C7
Redhill Sur 28 D3
Redhouse Argyll 145 G7
Redhouses Argyll 142 B4
Redisham Suff 69 F7
Redland Bristol 23 B7
Redland Orkney 159 F4
Redlingfield Suff 57 B5
Redlynch Som 23 F9
Redlynch Wilts 14 B3
Redmarley D'Abitot Glos 50 F2
Redmarshall Stockton 102 B1
Redmile Leics 77 F7
Redmire N Yorks 101 E5
Redmoor Corn 5 C5
Rednal Shrops 60 B3
Redpath Borders 121 F8
Redpoint Highld 149 B12
Redruth Corn 3 B5
Redvales Gtr Man 87 D6
Redwick Newport 35 F8
Redwick S Glos 36 F2
Redworth Darl 101 B7
Reed Herts 54 F4
Reedham Norf 69 D7
Reedness E Yorks 89 B8
Reeds Beck Lincs 78 C5
Reepham Lincs 78 B3
Reepham Norf 81 E6
Reeth N Yorks 101 E5
Regaby IoM 84 C4
Regoul Highld 151 F11
Reiff Highld 156 H2
Reigate Sur 28 D3
Reighton N Yorks 97 B7
Reighton Gap N Yorks 97 B7
Reinigeadal W Isles 154 G7
Reiss Highld 158 E5
Rejerrah Corn 4 D2
Releath Corn 3 C5
Relubbus Corn 2 C4
Relugas Moray 151 G12
Remenham Wokingham 39 F7
Remenham Hill Wokingham 39 F7
Remony Perth 132 E4
Rempstone Notts 64 B2
Rendcomb Glos 37 D7
Rendham Suff 57 C7
Rendlesham Suff 57 D7
Renfrew Renfs 118 C5
Renhold Bedford 53 D8
Renishaw Derbys 76 B4
Rennington Northumb 117 C8
Renton W Dunb 118 B3
Renwick Cumb 109 E5
Repps Norf 69 C7
Repton Derbys 63 B7
Reraig Highld 149 F13
Rescobie Angus 135 D5
Resipole Highld 147 E10
Resolis Highld 151 E9
Resolven Neath 34 D2
Reston Borders 122 C4
Reswallie Angus 135 D5
Retew Corn 4 D4
Retford Notts 89 F8
Rettendon Essex 42 E3
Rettendon Place Essex 42 E3
Revesby Lincs 79 C5
Revesby Bridge Lincs 79 C6
Rew Street IoW 15 E5
Rewe Devon 10 E4
Reydon Suff 57 B8
Reydon Smear Suff 57 B8
Reymerston Norf 68 D3
Reynalton Pembs 32 D1
Reynoldston Swansea 33 E5
Rezare Corn 5 B8
Rhaeadr Gwy = Rhayader Powys 47 C8
Rhandirmwyn Carms 47 E6
Rhayader = Rhaeadr Gwy Powys 47 C8
Rhedyn Gwyn 70 D3
Rhemore Highld 147 F8
Rhencullen IoM 84 C3
Rhes-y-cae Flint 73 B5
Rhewl Denb 72 C5
Rhewl Denb 73 E5
Rhian Highld 157 H8
Rhicarn Highld 156 G3
Rhiconich Highld 156 D5
Rhicullen Highld 151 D9
Rhidorroch Ho. Highld 150 B4
Rhifail Highld 157 E10
Rhigos Rhondda 34 D3
Rhilochan Highld 157 J10
Rhiroy Highld 150 C4
Rhisga = Risca Caerph 35 E6
Rhiw Gwyn 70 E3
Rhiwabon = Ruabon Wrex 73 E7
Rhiwbina Cardiff 35 F5
Rhiwbryfdir Gwyn 71 C7
Rhiwderin Newport 35 F6
Rhiwlas Gwyn 72 F3
Rhiwlas Gwyn 83 E5
Rhiwlas Powys 73 F5
Rhodes Gtr Man 87 D6
Rhodes Minnis Kent 31 E5
Rhodesia Notts 77 B5
Rhodiad Pembs 44 C2
Rhondda Rhondda 34 E3
Rhonehouse or Kelton Hill Dumfries 106 D4
Rhoose = Y Rhws V Glam 22 C2
Rhôs Carms 46 F2
Rhôs Neath 33 D8
Rhos-fawr Gwyn 70 D4
Rhos-goch Powys 48 E3
Rhos-hill Pembs 45 E3
Rhos-on-Sea Conwy 83 C8
Rhos-y-brithdir Powys 59 B8
Rhos-y-garth Ceredig 46 B5
Rhos-y-gwaliau Gwyn 72 F3
Rhos-y-llan Gwyn 70 D3
Rhos-y-Madoc Wrex 73 E7
Rhos-y-meirch Powys 48 C4
Rhosaman Carms 33 C8
Rhosbeirio Anglesey 82 B3
Rhoscefnhir Anglesey 82 D5
Rhoscolyn Anglesey 82 D2
Rhoscrowther Pembs 44 E4
Rhosesmor Flint 73 C6
Rhosgadfan Gwyn 82 F5
Rhosgoch Anglesey 82 C4
Rhoshirwaun Gwyn 70 E2
Rhoslan Gwyn 71 C5
Rhoslefain Gwyn 58 D2
Rhosllanerchrugog Wrex 73 E6
Rhosmaen Carms 33 B7
Rhosmeirch Anglesey 82 D4
Rhosneigr Anglesey 82 D3
Rhosnesni Wrex 73 D7
Rhosrobin Wrex 73 D7
Rhossili Swansea 33 F5
Rhosson Pembs 44 C2
Rhostryfan Gwyn 82 F4
Rhostyllen Wrex 73 E7
Rhosybol Anglesey 82 C4
Rhu Argyll 145 E11
Rhu Argyll 145 G7
Rhuallt Denb 72 B4
Rhuddall Heath Ches W 74 C2
Rhuddlan Ceredig 46 E3
Rhuddlan Denb 72 B4
Rhue Highld 150 B3
Rhulen Powys 48 E3
Rhunahaorine Argyll 143 D8
Rhuthun = Ruthin Denb 72 D5
Rhyd Gwyn 71 C7
Rhyd Powys 59 D6
Rhyd-Ddu Gwyn 83 F5
Rhyd-moel-ddu Powys 48 B2
Rhyd-Rosser Ceredig 46 C4
Rhyd-uchaf Gwyn 72 F3
Rhyd-wen Gwyn 58 C4
Rhyd-y-clafdy Gwyn 70 D4
Rhyd-y-foel Conwy 72 B3
Rhyd-y-fro Neath 33 D8
Rhyd-y-gwin Swansea 33 D7
Rhyd-y-meirch Mon 35 D7
Rhyd-y-meudwy Denb 72 D5
Rhyd-y-pandy Swansea 33 D7
Rhyd-y-sarn Gwyn 71 C7
Rhyd-yr-onen Gwyn 58 D3
Rhydaman = Ammanford Carms 33 C7
Rhydargaeau Carms 33 B5
Rhydcymerau Carms 46 F4
Rhydd Worcs 50 E3
Rhydding Neath 33 E8
Rhydfudr Ceredig 46 C4
Rhydlewis Ceredig 46 E2
Rhydlios Gwyn 70 D2
Rhydlydan Conwy 83 F8
Rhydness Powys 48 E3
Rhydowen Ceredig 46 E3
Rhydspence Hereford 48 E4
Rhydtalog Flint 73 D6
Rhydwyn Anglesey 82 C3
Rhydycroesau Powys 73 F6
Rhydyfelin Ceredig 46 B4
Rhydyfelin Rhondda 34 F4
Rhydymain Gwyn 58 B5
Rhydymwyn Flint 73 C6
Rhyl = Y Rhyl Denb 72 A4
Rhymney = Rhymni Caerph 35 D5
Rhymni = Rhymney Caerph 35 D5
Rhynd Fife 129 B6
Rhynd Perth 128 B3
Rhynie Aberds 140 B3
Rhynie Highld 151 D11
Ribbesford Worcs 50 B2
Ribblehead N Yorks 93 B7
Ribbleton Lancs 93 F5
Ribchester Lancs 93 F6
Ribigill Highld 157 D8
Riby Lincs 91 D5
Riby Cross Roads Lincs 91 D5
Riccall N Yorks 96 F2
Riccarton E Ayrs 118 F4
Richards Castle Hereford 49 C6
Richings Park Bucks 27 B8
Richmond London 28 B2
Richmond N Yorks 101 D6
Rickarton Aberds 141 F7
Rickinghall Suff 56 B4
Rickleton T&W 111 D5
Rickling Essex 55 F5
Rickmansworth Herts 40 E3
Riddings Cumb 108 B4
Riddings Derbys 76 D4
Riddlecombe Devon 9 C8
Riddlesden W Yorks 94 E3
Riddrie Glasgow 119 C6
Ridge Dorset 13 F7
Ridge Hants 14 C4
Ridge Wilts 24 F4
Ridge Green Sur 28 E4
Ridge Lane Warks 63 E6
Ridgebourne Powys 48 C2
Ridgehill N Som 23 C7
Ridgeway Cross Hereford 50 E2
Ridgewell Essex 55 E8
Ridgewood E Sus 17 C8
Ridgmont C Beds 53 F7
Riding Mill Northumb 110 C3
Ridleywood Wrex 73 D8
Ridlington Norf 69 A6
Ridlington Rutland 64 D5
Ridsdale Northumb 116 F5
Riechip Perth 133 E7
Riemore Perth 133 E7
Rienachait Highld 156 F3
Rievaulx N Yorks 102 F3
Rift House Hrtlpl 111 F7
Rigg Dumfries 108 C2
Riggend N Lanark 119 B7
Rigsby Lincs 79 B7
Rigside S Lanark 119 F8
Riley Green Lancs 86 B4
Rileyhill Staffs 62 C5
Rilla Mill Corn 5 B7
Rillington N Yorks 96 B4
Rimington Lancs 93 E8
Rimpton Som 12 B4
Rimswell E Yorks 91 B7
Rinaston Pembs 44 C4
Ringasta Shetland 160 M5
Ringford Dumfries 106 D3
Ringinglow S Yorks 88 F3
Ringland Norf 68 C4
Ringles Cross E Sus 17 B8
Ringmer E Sus 17 C8
Ringmore Devon 6 E4
Ringorm Moray 152 D2
Ring's End Cambs 66 D3
Ringsfield Suff 69 F7
Ringsfield Corner Suff 69 F7
Ringshall Herts 40 C2
Ringshall Suff 56 D4
Ringshall Stocks Suff 56 D4
Ringstead Norf 80 C3
Ringstead Northants 53 B7
Ringwood Hants 14 D2
Ringwould Kent 31 E7
Rinmore Aberds 140 C3
Rinnigill Orkney 159 J4
Rinsey Corn 2 D4
Riof W Isles 154 D6
Ripe E Sus 18 D2
Ripley Derbys 76 D3
Ripley Hants 14 E2
Ripley N Yorks 95 C5
Ripley Sur 27 D8
Riplingham E Yorks 97 F5
Ripon N Yorks 95 B6
Rippingale Lincs 65 B7
Ripple Kent 31 E7
Ripple Worcs 50 F3
Ripponden W Yorks 87 C8
Rireavach Highld 150 B3
Risabus Argyll 142 D4
Risbury Hereford 49 D7
Risby Suff 55 C8
Risca = Rhisga Caerph 35 E6
Rise E Yorks 97 E7
Riseden E Sus 18 B3
Risegate Lincs 66 B2
Riseholme Lincs 78 B2
Riseley Bedford 53 C8
Riseley Wokingham 26 C5
Rishangles Suff 57 C5
Rishton Lancs 93 F7
Rishworth W Yorks 87 C8
Rising Bridge Lancs 87 B5
Risley Derbys 76 F4
Risley Warr 86 E4
Risplith N Yorks 94 C5
Rispond Highld 156 C7
Rivar Wilts 25 C8
Rivenhall End Essex 42 C4
River Bank Cambs 55 C6
Riverhead Kent 29 D6
Rivington Lancs 86 C4
Roa Island Cumb 92 C2
Roachill Devon 10 B3
Road Green Norf 69 E5
Roade Northants 53 D5
Roadhead Cumb 108 B5
Roadmeetings S Lanark 119 E8
Roadside Highld 158 D3
Roadside of Catterline Aberds 135 B8
Roadside of Kinneff Aberds 135 B8
Roadwater Som 22 F2
Roag Highld 149 D7
Roath Cardiff 22 B3
Roberton Borders 115 C7
Roberton S Lanark 114 B2
Robertsbridge E Sus 18 C4
Roberttown W Yorks 88 B2
Robeston Cross Pembs 44 E3
Robeston Wathen Pembs 32 C1
Robin Hood W Yorks 88 B4
Robin Hood's Bay N Yorks 103 D7
Roborough Devon 6 C3
Roborough Devon 9 C7
Roby Mers 86 E2
Roby Mill Lancs 86 D3
Rocester Staffs 75 F8
Roch Pembs 44 C3
Roch Gate Pembs 44 C3
Rochdale Gtr Man 87 C6
Roche Corn 4 C4
Rochester Medway 29 C8
Rochester Northumb 116 E4
Rochford Essex 42 E4
Rock Corn 4 B4
Rock Northumb 117 B8
Rock W Sus 16 C5
Rock Worcs 50 B2
Rock Ferry Mers 85 F4
Rockbeare Devon 10 E5
Rockbourne Hants 14 C2
Rockcliffe Cumb 108 C3
Rockcliffe Dumfries 107 D5
Rockfield Highld 151 C12
Rockfield Mon 36 C1
Rockford Hants 14 D2
Rockhampton S Glos 36 E3
Rockingham Northants 65 E5
Rockland All Saints Norf 68 E2
Rockland St Mary Norf 69 D6
Rockland St Peter Norf 68 E2
Rockley Wilts 25 B6
Rockwell End Bucks 39 F7
Rockwell Green Som 11 B6
Rodborough Glos 37 D5
Rodbourne Swindon 37 F8
Rodbourne Wilts 37 F6
Rodbourne Cheney Swindon 37 F8
Rodd Hereford 48 C5
Roddam Northumb 117 B6
Rodden Dorset 12 F4
Rode Som 24 D3
Rode Heath Ches E 74 D5
Rodeheath Ches E 75 C5
Roden Telford 61 C5
Rodhuish Som 22 F2
Rodington Telford 61 C5
Rodley Glos 36 C4
Rodley W Yorks 94 F5
Rodmarton Glos 37 E6
Rodmell E Sus 17 D8
Rodmersham Kent 30 C3
Rodney Stoke Som 23 D6
Rodsley Derbys 76 E2
Rodway Som 22 F4
Rodwell Dorset 12 G4
Roe Green Herts 54 F4
Roecliffe N Yorks 95 C6
Roehampton London 28 B3
Roesound Shetland 160 G5
Roffey W Sus 28 F2
Rogart Highld 157 J10
Rogart Station Highld 157 J10
Rogate W Sus 16 B2
Rogerstone Newport 35 F6
Roghadal W Isles 154 J5
Rogiet Mon 36 F1
Rogue's Alley Cambs 66 D3
Roke Oxon 39 E6
Roker T&W 111 D7
Rollesby Norf 69 C7
Rolleston Leics 64 D4
Rolleston Notts 77 D7
Rolleston-on-Dove Staffs 63 B6
Rolston E Yorks 97 E8
Rolvenden Kent 18 B5
Rolvenden Layne Kent 19 B5
Romaldkirk Durham 100 B4
Romanby N Yorks 102 E1
Romannobridge Borders 120 E4
Romansleigh Devon 10 B2
Romford London 41 F8
Romiley Gtr Man 87 E7
Romsey Hants 14 B4
Romsey Town Cambs 55 D5
Romsley Shrops 61 F7
Romsley Worcs 50 B4
Ronague IoM 84 E2
Rookhope Durham 110 E2
Rookley IoW 15 F6
Rooks Bridge Som 23 D5
Roos E Yorks 97 F8
Roosebeck Cumb 92 C2
Rootham's Green Bedford 54 D2
Rootpark S Lanark 120 D2
Ropley Hants 26 F4
Ropley Dean Hants 26 F4
Ropsley Lincs 78 F2
Rora Aberds 153 C10
Rorandle Aberds 141 C5
Rorrington Shrops 60 D3
Roscroggan Corn 3 B5
Rose Corn 4 D2
Rose Ash Devon 10 B2
Rose Green W Sus 16 E3
Rose Grove Lancs 93 F8
Rose Hill E Sus 17 C8
Rose Hill Lancs 93 F8
Rose Hill Suff 57 E5
Roseacre Kent 29 D8
Roseacre Lancs 92 F4
Rosebank S Lanark 119 E8
Rosebrough Northumb 117 B7
Rosebush Pembs 32 B1
Rosecare Corn 8 E3
Rosedale Abbey N Yorks 103 E5
Roseden Northumb 117 B6
Rosefield Highld 151 F11

224 Shi–Sto

Shiregreen S Yorks 88 E4
Shirehampton Bristol 23 B7
Shiremoor T&W 111 B6
Shirenewton Mon 36 E1
Shireoaks Notts 89 F6
Shirkoak Kent 19 B6
Shirl Heath Hereford 49 D6
Shirland Derbys 76 D3
Shirley Derbys 76 E2
Shirley London 28 C4
Shirley Soton 14 C5
Shirley W Mid 51 B6
Shirrell Heath Hants 15 C6
Shirwell Devon 20 F4
Shirwell Cross Devon 20 F4
Shiskine N Ayrs 143 F10
Shobdon Hereford 49 C6
Shobnall Staffs 63 B6
Shobrooke Devon 10 D3
Shoby Leics 64 C3
Shocklach Ches W 73 E8
Shoeburyness Southend 43 F5
Sholden Kent 31 D7
Sholing Soton 14 C5
Shoot Hill Shrops 60 C4
Shop Corn 4 B3
Shop Corn 8 C4
Shop Corner Suff 57 F6
Shore Mill Highld 151 E10
Shoreditch London 41 F6
Shoreham Kent 29 C6
Shoreham-By-Sea W Sus 17 D6
Shoresdean Northumb 123 E5
Shoreswood Northumb 122 E5
Shoreton Highld 151 E9
Shorncote Glos 37 E7
Shorne Kent 29 B7
Short Heath W Mid 62 D3
Shortacombe Devon 9 F7
Shortgate E Sus 17 C8
Shortlanesend Corn 3 B7
Shortlees E Ayrs 118 F4
Shortstown Bedford 53 E8
Shorwell IoW 15 F5
Shoscombe Bath 24 D2
Shotatton Shrops 60 B3
Shotesham Norf 69 E5
Shotgate Essex 42 E3
Shotley Suff 57 F6
Shotley Bridge Durham 110 D3
Shotley Gate Suff 57 F6
Shotleyfield Northumb 110 D3
Shottenden Kent 30 D4
Shottermill Sur 27 F6
Shottery Warks 51 D6
Shotteswell Warks 52 E2
Shottisham Suff 57 E7
Shottle Derbys 76 E3
Shottlegate Derbys 76 E3
Shotton Durham 111 F7
Shotton Flint 73 C7
Shotton Northumb 122 F4
Shotton Colliery Durham 111 E6
Shotts N Lanark 119 C8
Shotwick Ches W 73 B7
Shouldham Norf 67 D6
Shouldham Thorpe Norf 67 D6
Shoulton Worcs 50 D3
Shover's Green E Sus 18 B3
Shrawardine Shrops 60 C4
Shrawley Worcs 50 C3
Shrewley Common Warks 51 C7
Shrewsbury Shrops 60 C4
Shrewton Wilts 25 E5
Shripney W Sus 16 D3
Shrivenham Oxon 38 F2
Shropham Norf 68 E2
Shrub End Essex 43 B5
Shucknall Hereford 49 E7
Shudy Camps Cambs 55 E7
Shulishadermor Highld 149 D9
Shurdington Glos 37 C6
Shurlock Row Windsor 27 B6
Shurrery Highld 157 D13
Shurrery Lodge Highld 157 D13
Shurton Som 22 E4
Shustoke Warks 63 E6
Shute Devon 10 D3
Shute Devon 11 E7
Shutford Oxon 51 E8
Shuthonger Glos 50 F3
Shutlanger Northants 52 D5
Shuttington Warks 63 D6
Shuttlewood Derbys 76 B4
Siabost bho Dheas W Isles 154 C7
Siabost bho Thuath W Isles 154 C7
Siadar W Isles 155 B8
Siadar Iarach W Isles 155 B8
Siadar Uarach W Isles 155 B8
Sibbaldbie Dumfries 114 F4
Sibbertoft Northants 64 F3
Sibdon Carwood Shrops 60 F4
Sibford Ferris Oxon 51 F8
Sibford Gower Oxon 51 F8
Sible Hedingham Essex 55 F8
Sibsey Lincs 79 D6
Sibson Cambs 65 E7
Sibson Leics 63 D7
Sibthorpe Notts 77 E7
Sibton Suff 57 C7
Sibton Green Suff 57 B7
Sicklesmere Suff 56 C2
Sicklinghall N Yorks 95 E6
Sid Devon 11 F6
Sidbury Devon 11 E6
Sidbury Shrops 61 F6
Sidcot N Som 23 D6
Sidcup London 29 B5
Siddick Cumb 107 F7
Siddington Ches E 74 B5
Siddington Glos 37 E7
Sidemoor Worcs 50 B4
Sidestrand Norf 81 D8
Sidford Devon 11 E6
Sidlesham W Sus 16 E2
Sidley E Sus 18 E4
Sidlow Sur 28 E3
Sidmouth Devon 11 F6
Sigford Devon 7 B5
Sigglesthorne E Yorks 97 E7
Sighthill Edin 120 B4
Sigingstone V Glam 21 B8
Signet Oxon 38 C2
Silchester Hants 26 C4
Sildinis W Isles 155 F7
Sileby Leics 64 C2
Silecroft Cumb 98 F3
Silfield Norf 68 E4
Silian Ceredig 46 D4
Silk Willoughby Lincs 78 E3
Silkstone S Yorks 88 D3
Silkstone Common S Yorks 88 D3
Silloth Cumb 107 D8
Sills Northumb 116 D4
Sillyearn Moray 152 C5
Siloh Carms 47 F6
Silpho N Yorks 103 E7
Silsden W Yorks 94 E3
Silsoe C Beds 53 F8
Silver End Essex 42 C4
Silverburn Midloth 120 C5
Silverdale Lancs 92 B4
Silverdale Staffs 74 E5
Silvergate Norf 81 E7
Silverhill E Sus 18 D4
Silverley's Green Suff 57 B6
Silverstone Northants 52 E4
Silverton Devon 10 D4
Silvington Shrops 49 B8
Silwick Shetland 160 J4
Simmondley Derbys 87 E8
Simonburn Northumb 109 B8
Simonsbath Som 21 F6
Simonstone Lancs 93 F7
Simprim Borders 122 E4
Simpson M Keynes 53 F6
Simpson Cross Pembs 44 D3
Sinclair's Hill Borders 122 D4
Sinclairston E Ayrs 112 C4
Sinderby N Yorks 101 F8
Sinderhope Northumb 109 D8
Sindlesham Wokingham 27 C5
Singdean Borders 115 D8
Singleborough Bucks 53 F5
Singleton Lancs 92 F3
Singleton W Sus 16 C2
Singlewell Kent 29 B7
Sinkhurst Green Kent 30 E2
Sinnahard Aberds 140 C3
Sinnington N Yorks 103 F5
Sinton Green Worcs 50 C3
Sipson London 27 B8
Sirhowy Bl Gwent 35 C5
Sisland Norf 69 E6
Sissinghurst Kent 18 B4
Sisterpath Borders 122 E3
Siston S Glos 23 B8
Sithney Corn 2 D5
Sittingbourne Kent 30 C2
Six Ashes Staffs 61 F7
Six Hills Leics 64 B3
Six Mile Bottom Cambs 55 D6
Sixhills Lincs 91 F5
Sixpenny Handley Dorset 13 C7
Sizewell Suff 57 C8
Skail Highld 157 E10
Skaill Orkney 159 E5
Skaill Orkney 159 G3
Skaill Orkney 159 H6
Skares E Ayrs 113 C5
Skateraw E Loth 122 B3
Skaw Shetland 160 G7
Skeabost Highld 149 D9
Skeabrae Orkney 159 F3
Skeeby N Yorks 101 D7
Skeffington Leics 64 D4
Skeffling E Yorks 91 C7
Skegby Notts 76 C4
Skegness Lincs 79 C8
Skelberry Shetland 160 M5
Skelbo Highld 151 B10
Skelbrooke S Yorks 89 C6
Skeldyke Lincs 79 F6
Skellingthorpe Lincs 78 B2
Skellister Shetland 160 H6
Skellow S Yorks 89 C6
Skelmanthorpe W Yorks 88 C3
Skelmersdale Lancs 86 D2
Skelmonae Aberds 153 E8
Skelmorlie N Ayrs 118 C1
Skelmuir Aberds 153 D9
Skelpick Highld 157 D10
Skelton Cumb 108 F4
Skelton E Yorks 89 B8
Skelton N Yorks 101 D5
Skelton Redcar 102 C4
Skelton York 95 D8
Skelton-on-Ure N Yorks 95 C6
Skelwick Orkney 159 D5
Skelwith Bridge Cumb 99 D5
Skendleby Lincs 79 C7
Skene Ho. Aberds 141 D6
Skenfrith Mon 36 B1
Skerne E Yorks 97 D6
Skeroblingarry Argyll 143 F8
Skerray Highld 157 C9
Skerton Lancs 92 C4
Sketchley Leics 63 E8
Sketty Swansea 33 E7
Skewen Neath 33 E8
Skewsby N Yorks 96 B2
Skeyton Norf 81 E8
Skiag Bridge Highld 156 G5
Skibo Castle Highld 151 C10
Skidbrooke Lincs 91 E8
Skidbrooke North End Lincs 91 E8
Skidby E Yorks 97 F6
Skilgate Som 10 B4
Skillington Lincs 65 B5
Skinburness Cumb 107 D8
Skinflats Falk 127 F8
Skinidin Highld 148 D7
Skinnet Highld 157 C8
Skinningrove Redcar 103 B5
Skipness Argyll 145 H7
Skippool Lancs 92 E3
Skipsea E Yorks 97 D7
Skipsea Brough E Yorks 97 D7
Skipton N Yorks 94 D2
Skipton-on-Swale N Yorks 95 B6
Skipwith N Yorks 96 F2
Skirbeck Lincs 79 E6
Skirbeck Quarter Lincs 79 E6
Skirlaugh E Yorks 97 F7
Skirling Borders 120 F3
Skirmett Bucks 39 F7
Skirpenbeck E Yorks 96 D3
Skirwith Cumb 109 F6
Skirza Highld 158 D5
Skulamus Highld 149 F11
Skullomie Highld 157 C9
Skyborry Green Shrops 48 B4
Skye of Curr Highld 139 B5
Skyreholme N Yorks 94 C3
Slackhall Derbys 87 F8
Slackhead Moray 152 B4
Slad Glos 37 D5
Slade Devon 20 E4
Slade Pembs 44 D4
Slade Green London 29 B6
Slaggyford Northumb 109 D6
Slaidburn Lancs 93 D7
Slaithwaite W Yorks 87 C8
Slaley Northumb 110 D2
Slamannan Falk 119 B8
Slapton Bucks 40 B2
Slapton Devon 7 E6
Slapton Northants 52 E4
Slatepit Dale Derbys 76 C3
Slattocks Gtr Man 87 D6
Slaugham W Sus 17 B6
Slaughterford Wilts 24 B3
Slawston Leics 64 E4
Sleaford Hants 27 F6
Sleaford Lincs 78 E3
Sleagill Cumb 99 C7
Sleapford Telford 61 C6
Sledge Green Worcs 50 F3
Sledmere E Yorks 96 C5
Sleightholme Durham 100 C4
Sleights N Yorks 103 D6
Slepe Dorset 13 E7
Slickly Highld 158 D4
Sliddery N Ayrs 143 F10
Sligachan Hotel Highld 149 F9
Slimbridge Glos 36 D4
Slindon Staffs 74 F5
Slindon W Sus 16 D3
Slinfold W Sus 28 F2
Sling Gwyn 83 E6
Slingsby N Yorks 96 B2
Slioch Aberds 152 E5
Slip End C Beds 40 C3
Slip End Herts 54 F3
Slipton Northants 53 B7
Slitting Mill Staffs 62 C4
Slochd Highld 138 B4
Slockavullin Argyll 124 F4
Sloley Norf 81 E8
Sloothby Lincs 79 B7
Slough Slough 27 B7
Slough Green W Sus 17 B6
Sluggan Highld 138 B4
Slumbay Highld 149 E13
Slyfield Sur 27 D7
Slyne Lancs 92 C4
Smailholm Borders 122 F2
Small Dole W Sus 17 C6
Small Hythe Kent 19 B5
Smallbridge Gtr Man 87 C7
Smallburgh Norf 69 B6
Smallburn Aberds 153 D10
Smallburn E Ayrs 113 B6
Smalley Derbys 76 E4
Smallfield Sur 28 E4
Smallridge Devon 11 D8
Smannell Hants 25 E8
Smardale Cumb 100 D2
Smarden Kent 30 E2
Smarden Bell Kent 30 E2
Smeatharpe Devon 11 C6
Smeeth Kent 19 B7
Smeeton Westerby Leics 64 E3
Smercleit W Isles 148 G2
Smerral Highld 158 G3
Smethwick W Mid 62 F4
Smirisary Highld 147 D9
Smisby Derbys 63 C7
Smith Green Lancs 92 D4
Smithfield Cumb 108 C4
Smithincott Devon 11 C5
Smith's Green Essex 42 B1
Smithstown Highld 149 A12
Smithton Highld 151 G10
Smithy Green Ches E 74 B4
Smockington Leics 63 F8
Smoogro Orkney 159 H4
Smythe's Green Essex 43 C5
Snaigow House Perth 133 E7
Snailbeach Shrops 60 D3
Snailwell Cambs 55 C7
Snainton N Yorks 103 F7
Snaith E Yorks 89 B7
Snape N Yorks 101 F7
Snape Suff 57 D7
Snape Green Lancs 85 C4
Snarestone Leics 63 D7
Snarford Lincs 90 F4
Snargate Kent 19 C6
Snave Kent 19 C7
Snead Powys 60 E3
Sneath Common Norf 68 F4
Sneaton N Yorks 103 D6
Sneatonthorpe N Yorks 103 D7
Snelland Lincs 90 F4
Snelston Derbys 75 E8
Snettisham Norf 80 D2
Sniseabhal W Isles 148 E2
Snitter Northumb 117 D6
Snitterby Lincs 90 E3
Snitterfield Warks 51 D7
Snitton Shrops 49 B7
Snodhill Hereford 48 E5
Snodland Kent 29 C7
Snowden Hill S Yorks 88 D3
Snowdown Kent 31 D6
Snowshill Glos 51 F5
Snydale W Yorks 88 C5
Soar Anglesey 82 D3
Soar Carms 33 B7
Soar Devon 6 F5
Soar-y-Mynydd Ceredig 47 D6
Soberton Hants 15 C7
Soberton Heath Hants 15 C7
Sockbridge Cumb 99 B7
Sockburn Darl 101 D8
Soham Cambs 55 B6
Soham Cotes Cambs 55 B6
Solas W Isles 148 A3
Soldon Cross Devon 8 C5
Soldridge Hants 26 F4
Sole Street Kent 29 C7
Sole Street Kent 30 E4
Solihull W Mid 51 B6
Sollers Dilwyn Hereford 49 D6
Sollers Hope Hereford 49 F8
Sollom Lancs 86 C2
Solva Pembs 44 C2
Somerby Leics 64 C4
Somerby Lincs 90 D4
Somercotes Derbys 76 D4
Somerford Dorset 14 E2
Somerford Keynes Glos 37 E7
Somerley W Sus 16 E2
Somerleyton Suff 69 E7
Somersal Herbert Derbys 75 F8
Somersby Lincs 79 B6
Somersham Cambs 54 B4
Somersham Suff 56 E4
Somerton Oxon 38 B4
Somerton Som 12 B2
Sompting W Sus 17 D5
Sonning Wokingham 27 B5
Sonning Common Oxon 39 F7
Sonning Eye Oxon 27 B5
Sontley Wrex 73 E7
Sopley Hants 14 E2
Sopwell Herts 40 D4
Sopworth Wilts 37 F5
Sorbie Dumfries 105 E8
Sordale Highld 158 D3
Sorisdale Argyll 146 E5
Sorn E Ayrs 113 B5
Sornhill E Ayrs 118 F5
Sortat Highld 158 D4
Sotby Lincs 78 B5
Sots Hole Lincs 78 C4
Sotterley Suff 69 F7
Soudley Shrops 61 B7
Soughton Flint 73 C6
Soulbury Bucks 40 B1
Soulby Cumb 100 C2
Souldern Oxon 52 F3
Souldrop Bedford 53 C7
Sound Ches E 74 E3
Sound Shetland 160 H5
Sound Shetland 160 J6
Sound Heath Ches E 74 E3
Soundwell S Glos 23 B8
Sourhope Borders 116 B4
Sourin Orkney 159 E5
Sourton Devon 9 E7
Soutergate Cumb 98 F4
South Acre Norf 67 C8
South Allington Devon 7 F5
South Alloa Falk 127 E7
South Ambersham W Sus 16 B3
South Anston S Yorks 89 F6
South Ascot Windsor 27 C7
South Ballachulish Highld 130 D4
South Balloch S Ayrs 112 E3
South Bank Redcar 102 B3
South Barrow Som 12 B4
South Beach Gwyn 70 D4
South Benfleet Essex 42 F3
South Bersted W Sus 16 D3
South Brent Devon 6 C4
South Brewham Som 24 F2
South Broomhill Northumb 117 E8
South Burlingham Norf 69 D6
South Cadbury Som 12 B4
South Cairn Dumfries 104 C3
South Carlton Lincs 78 B2
South Cave E Yorks 96 F5
South Cerney Glos 37 E7
South Chard Som 11 D8
South Charlton Northumb 117 B7
South Cheriton Som 12 B4
South Cliffe E Yorks 96 F4
South Clifton Notts 77 B8
South Cockerington Lincs 91 F7
South Cornelly Bridgend 34 F2
South Cove Suff 69 F7
South Creagan Argyll 130 E3
South Creake Norf 80 D4
South Croxton Leics 64 C3
South Croydon London 28 C4
South Dalton E Yorks 97 E5
South Darenth Kent 29 C6
South Duffield N Yorks 96 F2
South Elkington Lincs 91 F6
South Elmsall W Yorks 89 C5
South End Bucks 40 B1
South End Cumb 92 C2
South End N Lincs 90 B5
South Erradale Highld 149 A12
South Fambridge Essex 42 E4
South Fawley W Berks 38 F3
South Ferriby N Lincs 90 B3
South Garth Shetland 160 D7
South Garvan Highld 130 B3
South Glendale W Isles 148 G2
South Godstone Sur 28 E4
South Gorley Hants 14 C2
South Green Essex 42 E2
South Green Kent 30 C2
South-haa Shetland 160 E5
South Ham Hants 26 D4
South Hanningfield Essex 42 E3
South Harting W Sus 15 C8
South Hatfield Herts 41 D5
South Hayling Hants 15 E8
South Hazelrigg Northumb 123 F6
South Heath Bucks 40 D2
South Heighton E Sus 17 D8
South Hetton Durham 111 E6
South Hiendley W Yorks 88 C4
South Hill Corn 5 B8
South Hinksey Oxon 39 D5
South Hole Devon 8 B4
South Holme N Yorks 96 B2
South Holmwood Sur 28 E2
South Hornchurch London 41 F8
South Hykeham Lincs 78 C2
South Hylton T&W 111 D6
South Kelsey Lincs 90 E4
South Kessock Highld 151 G9
South Killingholme N Lincs 91 C5
South Kilvington N Yorks 102 F2
South Kilworth Leics 64 F3
South Kirkby W Yorks 88 C5
South Kirkton Aberds 141 D6
South Kiscadale N Ayrs 143 F11
South Kyme Lincs 78 E4
South Lancing W Sus 17 D5
South Leigh Oxon 38 D3
South Leverton Notts 89 F8
South Littleton Worcs 51 E5
South Lopham Norf 68 F3
South Luffenham Rutland 65 D6
South Malling E Sus 17 C8
South Marston Swindon 38 F1
South Middleton Northumb 117 B5
South Milford N Yorks 95 F7
South Millbrex Aberds 153 D8
South Milton Devon 6 E5
South Mimms Herts 41 D5
South Molton Devon 10 B2
South Moreton Oxon 39 F5
South Mundham W Sus 16 D2
South Muskham Notts 77 D7
South Newbald E Yorks 96 F5
South Newington Oxon 52 F2
South Newton Wilts 25 F5
South Normanton Derbys 76 D4
South Norwood London 28 C4
South Nutfield Sur 28 E4
South Ockendon Thurrock 42 F1
South Ormsby Lincs 79 B6
South Otterington N Yorks 102 F1
South Owersby Lincs 90 E4
South Oxhey Herts 40 E4
South Perrott Dorset 12 D2
South Petherton Som 12 C2
South Petherwin Corn 8 F5
South Pickenham Norf 67 D8
South Pool Devon 7 E5
South Port Argyll 125 C6
South Radworthy Devon 21 F6
South Rauceby Lincs 78 E3
South Raynham Norf 80 E4
South Reston Lincs 91 F8
South Runcton Norf 67 D6
South Scarle Notts 77 C8
South Shian Argyll 130 E3
South Shields T&W 111 C6
South Shore Blackpool 92 F3
South Somercotes Lincs 91 E8
South Stainley N Yorks 95 C6
South Stainmore Cumb 100 C3
South Stifford Thurrock 29 B7
South Stoke Oxon 39 F5
South Stoke W Sus 16 D4
South Street E Sus 17 C7
South Street Kent 30 C5
South Street Kent 30 D4
South Street London 28 D5
South Tawton Devon 9 E8
South Thoresby Lincs 79 B7
South Tidworth Wilts 25 E7
South Town Hants 26 F4
South View Hants 26 D4
South Walsham Norf 69 C6
South Warnborough Hants 26 E5
South Weald Essex 42 E1
South Weston Oxon 39 E7
South Wheatley Corn 8 E4
South Wheatley Notts 89 F8
South Whiteness Shetland 160 J5
South Widcombe Bath 23 D7
South Wigston Leics 64 E2
South Willingham Lincs 91 F5
South Wingfield Derbys 76 D3
South Witham Lincs 65 C6
South Wonston Hants 26 F2
South Woodham Ferrers Essex 42 E4
South Wootton Norf 67 B6
South Wraxall Wilts 24 C3
South Zeal Devon 9 E8
Southall London 40 F4
Southam Glos 37 B6
Southam Warks 52 C2
Southampton Soton 14 C5
Southborough Kent 29 E6
Southbourne Bmouth 14 E2
Southbourne W Sus 15 D8
Southburgh Norf 68 D2
Southburn E Yorks 97 D5
Southchurch Southend 43 F5
Southcott Wilts 25 D6
Southcourt Bucks 39 C8
Southdean Borders 116 D2
Southdene Mers 86 E2
Southease E Sus 17 D8
Southend Argyll 143 H7
Southend W Berks 26 B3
Southend Wilts 25 B6
Southend-on-Sea Southend 42 F4
Southernden Kent 30 E2
Southerndown V Glam 21 B7
Southerness Dumfries 107 D6
Southery Norf 67 E6
Southfield Northumb 111 B5
Southfleet Kent 29 B7
Southgate Ceredig 46 B4
Southgate London 41 E5
Southgate Norf 81 E7
Southgate Swansea 33 F6
Southill C Beds 54 E2
Southleigh Devon 11 E7
Southminster Essex 43 E5
Southmoor Oxon 38 E3
Southoe Cambs 54 C2
Southolt Suff 57 C5
Southorpe Pboro 65 D7
Southowram W Yorks 88 B2
Southport Mers 85 C4
Southpunds Shetland 160 L6
Southrepps Norf 81 D8
Southrey Lincs 78 C4
Southrop Glos 38 D1
Southrope Hants 26 E4
Southsea Ptsmth 15 E7
Southstoke Bath 24 C2
Southtown Norf 69 D8
Southtown Orkney 159 J5
Southwaite Cumb 108 E4
Southwark London 28 B4
Southwater W Sus 17 B5
Southwater Street W Sus 17 B5
Southway Som 23 E7
Southwell Dorset 12 G4
Southwell Notts 77 D6
Southwick Hants 15 D7
Southwick Northants 65 E7
Southwick T&W 111 D6
Southwick W Sus 17 D6
Southwick Wilts 24 D3
Southwold Suff 57 B9
Southwood Norf 69 D6
Southwood Som 23 F7
Soval Lodge W Isles 155 E8
Sowber Gate N Yorks 102 F1
Sowerby N Yorks 102 F2
Sowerby W Yorks 87 B8
Sowerby Bridge W Yorks 87 B8
Sowerby Row Cumb 108 F3
Sowood W Yorks 87 C8
Sowton Devon 10 E4
Soyal Highld 151 B8
Spa Common Norf 81 D8
Spacey Houses N Yorks 95 D6
Spadeadam Farm Cumb 109 B5
Spalding Lincs 66 B2
Spaldington E Yorks 96 F3
Spaldwick Cambs 54 B2
Spalford Notts 77 C8
Spanby Lincs 78 F3
Sparham Norf 68 C3
Spark Bridge Cumb 99 F5
Sparkford Som 12 B4
Sparkhill W Mid 62 F4
Sparkwell Devon 6 D3
Sparrow Green Norf 68 C2
Sparrowpit Derbys 87 F8
Sparsholt Hants 26 F2
Sparsholt Oxon 38 F3
Spartylea Northumb 109 E8
Spaunton N Yorks 103 F5
Spaxton Som 22 F4
Spean Bridge Highld 136 F5
Spear Hill W Sus 16 C5
Speen Bucks 39 E8
Speen W Berks 26 C2
Speeton N Yorks 97 B7
Speke Mers 86 F2
Speldhurst Kent 29 E6
Spellbrook Herts 41 C7
Spelsbury Oxon 38 B3
Spelter Bridgend 34 E2
Spencers Wood Wokingham 26 C5
Spennithorne N Yorks 101 F6
Spennymoor Durham 111 F5
Spetchley Worcs 50 D3
Spetisbury Dorset 13 D7
Spexhall Suff 69 F6
Spey Bay Moray 152 B3
Speybridge Highld 139 B6
Speyview Moray 152 D2
Spilsby Lincs 79 C7
Spindlestone Northumb 123 F7
Spinkhill Derbys 76 B4
Spinningdale Highld 151 C9
Spirthill Wilts 24 B4
Spital Hill S Yorks 89 E7
Spital in the Street Lincs 90 F3
Spithurst E Sus 17 C8
Spittal Dumfries 105 D7
Spittal E Loth 121 B7
Spittal Highld 158 E3
Spittal Northumb 123 D6
Spittal Pembs 44 C4
Spittal Stirling 126 F4
Spittal of Glenmuick Aberds 140 F2
Spittal of Glenshee Perth 133 B8
Spittalfield Perth 133 E8
Spixworth Norf 68 C5
Splayne's Green E Sus 17 B8
Spofforth N Yorks 95 D6
Spon End W Mid 51 B8
Spon Green Flint 73 C6
Spondon Derby 76 F4
Spooner Row Norf 68 E3
Sporle Norf 67 C8
Spott E Loth 122 B2
Spratton Northants 52 B5
Spreakley Sur 27 E6
Spreyton Devon 9 E8
Spridlington Lincs 90 F4
Spring Vale S Yorks 88 D3
Spring Valley IoM 84 E3
Springburn Glasgow 119 C6
Springfield Dumfries 108 C3
Springfield Essex 42 D3
Springfield Fife 128 C5
Springfield Moray 151 F13
Springfield W Mid 62 F4
Springhill Staffs 62 D3
Springholm Dumfries 106 C5
Springkell Dumfries 108 B2
Springside N Ayrs 118 F3
Springthorpe Lincs 90 F2
Springwell T&W 111 D5
Sproatley E Yorks 97 F7
Sproston Green Ches W 74 C4
Sprotbrough S Yorks 89 D6
Sproughton Suff 56 E5
Sprouston Borders 122 F3
Sprowston Norf 68 C5
Sproxton Leics 65 B5
Sproxton N Yorks 102 F4
Spurstow Ches E 74 D2
Spynie Moray 152 B2
Squires Gate Blackpool 92 F3
Srannda W Isles 154 J5
Sronphadruig Lodge Perth 132 B4
Stableford Shrops 61 E7
Stableford Staffs 74 F5
Stacey Bank S Yorks 88 E3
Stackhouse N Yorks 93 C8
Stackpole Pembs 44 F4
Staddiscombe Plym 6 D3
Staddlethorpe E Yorks 90 B2
Stadhampton Oxon 39 E6
Stadhlaigearraidh W Isles 148 E2
Staffield Cumb 108 E5
Staffin Highld 149 B9
Stafford Staffs 62 B3
Stagsden Bedford 53 E7
Stainburn Cumb 98 B2
Stainburn N Yorks 94 E5
Stainby Lincs 65 B6
Staincross S Yorks 88 C4
Staindrop Durham 101 B6
Staines-upon-Thames Sur 27 B8
Stainfield Lincs 65 B7
Stainfield Lincs 78 B4
Stainforth N Yorks 93 C8
Stainforth S Yorks 89 C7
Staining Lancs 92 F3
Stainland W Yorks 87 C8
Stainsacre N Yorks 103 D7
Stainsby Derbys 76 C4
Stainton Cumb 99 B6
Stainton Cumb 99 F7
Stainton Durham 101 C5
Stainton Mbro 102 C2
Stainton N Yorks 101 E6
Stainton S Yorks 89 E6
Stainton by Langworth Lincs 78 B3
Stainton le Vale Lincs 91 E5
Stainton with Adgarley Cumb 92 B2
Staintondale N Yorks 103 E7
Stair Cumb 98 B4
Stair E Ayrs 112 B4
Stairhaven Dumfries 105 D6
Staithes N Yorks 103 C5
Stake Pool Lancs 92 E4
Stakeford Northumb 117 F8
Stalbridge Dorset 12 C5
Stalbridge Weston Dorset 12 C5
Stalham Norf 69 B6
Stalham Green Norf 69 B6
Stalisfield Green Kent 30 D3
Stalling Busk N Yorks 100 F4
Stallingborough NE Lincs 91 C5
Stalmine Lancs 92 E3
Stalybridge Gtr Man 87 E7
Stambourne Essex 55 F8
Stambourne Green Essex 55 E8
Stamford Lincs 65 D7
Stamford Bridge Ches W 73 C8
Stamford Bridge E Yorks 96 D3
Stamfordham Northumb 110 B3
Stanah Cumb 99 C5
Stanborough Herts 41 C5
Stanbridge C Beds 40 B2
Stanbridge Dorset 13 D8
Stanbrook Worcs 50 E3
Stanbury W Yorks 94 F3
Stand Gtr Man 87 D5
Stand N Lanark 119 C7
Standburn Falk 120 B2
Standeford Staffs 62 D3
Standen Kent 30 E2
Standford Hants 27 F6
Standingstone Cumb 107 F7
Standish Gtr Man 86 C3
Standlake Oxon 38 D3
Standon Hants 14 B5
Standon Herts 41 B6
Standon Staffs 74 F5
Stane N Lanark 119 D8
Stanfield Norf 80 E5
Stanford C Beds 54 E2
Stanford Kent 19 B8
Stanford Bishop Hereford 49 D8
Stanford Bridge Worcs 50 C2
Stanford Dingley W Berks 26 B3
Stanford in the Vale Oxon 38 E3
Stanford-le-Hope Thurrock 42 F2
Stanford on Avon Northants 52 B3
Stanford on Soar Notts 64 B2
Stanford on Teme Worcs 50 C2
Stanford Rivers Essex 41 D8
Stanfree Derbys 76 B4
Stanghow Redcar 102 C4
Stanground Pboro 66 E2
Stanhoe Norf 80 D4
Stanhope Borders 114 B4
Stanhope Durham 110 F2
Stanion Northants 65 F6
Stanley Derbys 76 E4
Stanley Durham 110 D4
Stanley Lancs 86 D2
Stanley Perth 133 F8
Stanley Staffs 75 D6
Stanley W Yorks 88 B4
Stanley Common Derbys 76 E4
Stanley Gate Lancs 86 D2
Stanley Hill Hereford 49 E8
Stanlow Ches W 73 B8
Stanmer Brighton 17 D7
Stanmore Hants 15 B5
Stanmore London 40 E4
Stanmore W Berks 26 B2
Stannergate Dundee 134 F4
Stanningley W Yorks 94 F5
Stannington Northumb 110 B5
Stannington S Yorks 88 F4
Stansbatch Hereford 48 C5
Stansfield Suff 55 D8
Stanstead Suff 56 E2
Stanstead Abbotts Herts 41 C6
Stansted Kent 29 C7
Stansted Airport Essex 42 B1
Stansted Mountfitchet Essex 41 B8
Stanton Glos 51 F5
Stanton Mon 35 B7
Stanton Northumb 117 F7
Stanton Staffs 75 E8
Stanton Suff 56 B3
Stanton by Bridge Derbys 63 B7
Stanton-by-Dale Derbys 76 F4
Stanton Drew Bath 23 C7
Stanton Fitzwarren Swindon 38 E1
Stanton Harcourt Oxon 38 D4
Stanton Hill Notts 76 C4
Stanton in Peak Derbys 76 C2
Stanton Lacy Shrops 49 B6
Stanton Long Shrops 61 E5
Stanton-on-the-Wolds Notts 77 F6
Stanton Prior Bath 23 C8
Stanton St Bernard Wilts 25 C5
Stanton St John Oxon 39 D5
Stanton St Quintin Wilts 24 B4
Stanton Street Suff 56 C3
Stanton under Bardon Leics 63 C8
Stanton upon Hine Heath Shrops 61 B5
Stanton Wick Bath 23 C8
Stanwardine in the Fields Shrops 60 B4
Stanwardine in the Wood Shrops 60 B4
Stanway Essex 43 B5
Stanway Glos 51 F5
Stanway Green Suff 57 B6
Stanwell Sur 27 B8
Stanwell Moor Sur 27 B8
Stanwick Northants 53 B7
Stanwick-St-John N Yorks 101 C6
Stanwix Cumb 108 D4
Stanydale Shetland 160 H4
Staoinebrig W Isles 148 E2
Stape N Yorks 103 E5
Stapehill Dorset 13 D8
Stapeley Ches E 74 E3
Stapenhill Staffs 63 B6
Staple Kent 31 D6
Staple Som 22 E3
Staple Cross E Sus 18 C4
Staple Fitzpaine Som 11 C7
Staplefield W Sus 17 B6
Stapleford Cambs 55 D5
Stapleford Herts 41 C6
Stapleford Leics 64 C5
Stapleford Lincs 77 D8
Stapleford Notts 76 F4
Stapleford Wilts 25 F5
Stapleford Abbotts Essex 41 E8
Stapleford Tawney Essex 41 E8
Staplegrove Som 11 B7
Staplehay Som 11 B7
Staplehurst Kent 29 E8
Staplers IoW 15 F6
Stapleton Bristol 23 B8
Stapleton Cumb 108 B5
Stapleton Hereford 48 C5
Stapleton Leics 63 E8
Stapleton N Yorks 101 C7
Stapleton Shrops 60 D4
Stapleton Som 12 B2
Stapley Som 11 C6
Staploe Bedford 54 C2
Staplow Hereford 49 E8
Star Fife 128 D5
Star Pembs 45 F4
Star Som 23 D6
Stara Orkney 159 F3
Starbeck N Yorks 95 D6
Starbotton N Yorks 94 B2
Starcross Devon 10 F4
Stareton Warks 51 B8
Starkholmes Derbys 76 D3
Starlings Green Essex 55 F5
Starston Norf 68 F5
Startforth Durham 101 C5
Startley Wilts 37 F6
Stathe Som 11 B8
Stathern Leics 77 F7
Station Town Durham 111 F7
Staughton Green Cambs 54 C2
Staughton Highway Cambs 54 C2
Staunton Glos 36 B4
Staunton Glos 36 C2
Staunton in the Vale Notts 77 E8
Staunton on Arrow Hereford 49 C5
Staunton on Wye Hereford 49 E5
Staveley Cumb 99 E6
Staveley Cumb 99 F5
Staveley Derbys 76 B4
Staveley N Yorks 95 C6
Staverton Devon 7 C5
Staverton Glos 37 B5
Staverton Northants 52 C3
Staverton Wilts 24 C3
Staverton Bridge Glos 37 B5
Stawell Som 23 F5
Staxigoe Highld 158 E5
Staxton N Yorks 97 B6
Staylittle Powys 59 E5
Staynall Lancs 92 E3
Staythorpe Notts 77 D7
Stean N Yorks 94 B3
Stearsby N Yorks 96 B2
Steart Som 22 E4
Stebbing Essex 42 B2
Stebbing Green Essex 42 B2
Stedham W Sus 16 B2
Steele Road Borders 115 E8
Steen's Bridge Hereford 49 D7
Steep Hants 15 B8
Steep Marsh Hants 15 B8
Steeple Dorset 13 F7
Steeple Essex 43 D5
Steeple Ashton Wilts 24 D4
Steeple Aston Oxon 38 B4
Steeple Barton Oxon 38 B4
Steeple Bumpstead Essex 55 E7
Steeple Claydon Bucks 39 B6
Steeple Gidding Cambs 65 F8
Steeple Langford Wilts 24 F5
Steeple Morden Cambs 54 E3
Steeton W Yorks 94 E3
Stein Highld 148 C7
Steinmanhill Aberds 153 D7
Stelling Minnis Kent 30 E5
Stemster Highld 158 D3
Stemster Ho. Highld 158 D3
Stenalees Corn 4 D5
Stenhousemuir Falk 127 F7
Stenigot Lincs 91 F6
Stenness Shetland 160 F4
Stenscholl Highld 149 B9
Stenso Orkney 159 F4
Stenson Derbys 63 B7
Stenton E Loth 122 B2
Stenton Fife 128 E4
Stenwith Lincs 77 F8
Stepaside Pembs 32 D2
Stepping Hill Gtr Man 87 F7
Steppingley C Beds 53 F8
Stepps N Lanark 119 C6
Sterndale Moor Derbys 75 C8
Sternfield Suff 57 C7
Sterridge Devon 20 E4
Stert Wilts 24 D5
Stetchworth Cambs 55 D7
Stevenage Herts 41 B5
Stevenston N Ayrs 118 E2
Steventon Hants 26 E3
Steventon Oxon 38 E4
Stevington Bedford 53 D7
Stewartby Bedford 53 E8
Stewarton Argyll 143 G7
Stewarton E Ayrs 118 E4
Stewkley Bucks 40 B1
Stewton Lincs 91 F7
Steyne Cross IoW 15 F7
Steyning W Sus 17 C5
Steynton Pembs 44 E4
Stibb Corn 8 C4
Stibb Cross Devon 9 C6
Stibb Green Wilts 25 C7
Stibbard Norf 81 E5
Stibbington Cambs 65 E7
Stichill Borders 122 F3
Sticker Corn 4 D4
Stickford Lincs 79 D6
Sticklepath Devon 9 E8
Stickney Lincs 79 D6
Stiffkey Norf 81 C5
Stifford's Bridge Hereford 50 E2
Stillingfleet N Yorks 95 E8
Stillington N Yorks 95 C8
Stillington Stockton 102 B1
Stilton Cambs 65 F8
Stinchcombe Glos 36 E4
Stinsford Dorset 12 E5
Stirchley Telford 61 D7
Stirkoke Ho. Highld 158 E5
Stirling Aberds 153 D11
Stirling Stirling 127 E6
Stisted Essex 42 B3
Stithians Corn 3 C6
Stittenham Highld 151 D9
Stivichall W Mid 51 B8
Stixwould Lincs 78 C4
Stoak Ches W 73 B8
Stobieside S Lanark 119 F6
Stobo Borders 120 F4
Stoborough Dorset 13 F7
Stoborough Green Dorset 13 F7
Stobshiel E Loth 121 C7
Stobswood Northumb 117 E8
Stock Essex 42 E2
Stock Green Worcs 50 D4
Stock Wood Worcs 50 D5
Stockbridge Hants 25 F8
Stockbury Kent 30 C2
Stockcross W Berks 26 C2
Stockdalewath Cumb 108 E3
Stockerston Leics 64 E5
Stockheath Hants 15 D8
Stockiemuir Stirling 126 F4
Stocking Pelham Herts 41 B7
Stockingford Warks 63 E7
Stockland Devon 11 D7
Stockland Bristol Som 22 E4
Stockleigh English Devon 10 D3
Stockleigh Pomeroy Devon 10 D3
Stockley Wilts 24 C5
Stocklinch Som 11 C8
Stockport Gtr Man 87 E6
Stocksbridge S Yorks 88 E3
Stocksfield Northumb 110 C3
Stockton Hereford 49 C7
Stockton Norf 69 E6
Stockton Shrops 60 D2
Stockton Shrops 61 E7
Stockton Warks 52 C2
Stockton Wilts 24 F4
Stockton Heath Warr 86 F4
Stockton-on-Tees Stockton 102 C2
Stockton on Teme Worcs 50 C2
Stockton on the Forest York 96 D2
Stodmarsh Kent 31 C6
Stody Norf 81 D6
Stoer Highld 156 G3
Stoford Som 12 C3
Stoford Wilts 25 F5
Stogumber Som 22 F2
Stogursey Som 22 E4
Stoke Devon 8 B4
Stoke Hants 15 D8
Stoke Hants 26 D2
Stoke Medway 30 B2
Stoke Suff 57 E5
Stoke Abbott Dorset 12 D2
Stoke Albany Northants 64 F5
Stoke Ash Suff 56 B5
Stoke Bardolph Notts 77 E6
Stoke Bliss Worcs 49 C8
Stoke Bruerne Northants 52 E5
Stoke by Clare Suff 55 E8
Stoke-by-Nayland Suff 56 F3
Stoke Canon Devon 10 E4
Stoke Charity Hants 26 F2
Stoke Climsland Corn 5 B8
Stoke D'Abernon Sur 28 D2
Stoke Doyle Northants 65 F7
Stoke Dry Rutland 65 E5
Stoke Farthing Wilts 13 B8
Stoke Ferry Norf 67 E7
Stoke Fleming Devon 7 D6
Stoke Gabriel Devon 7 D6
Stoke Gifford S Glos 23 B8
Stoke Golding Leics 63 E7
Stoke Goldington M Keynes 53 E6
Stoke Green Bucks 40 F2
Stoke Hammond Bucks 40 B1
Stoke Heath Shrops 61 B6
Stoke Holy Cross Norf 68 D5
Stoke Lacy Hereford 49 E8
Stoke Lyne Oxon 39 B5
Stoke Mandeville Bucks 39 C8
Stoke Newington London 41 F6
Stoke on Tern Shrops 61 B6
Stoke-on-Trent Stoke 75 E5
Stoke Orchard Glos 37 B6
Stoke Poges Bucks 40 F2
Stoke Prior Hereford 49 D7
Stoke Prior Worcs 50 C4
Stoke Rivers Devon 20 F5
Stoke Rochford Lincs 65 B6
Stoke Row Oxon 39 F6
Stoke St Gregory Som 11 B8
Stoke St Mary Som 11 B7
Stoke St Michael Som 23 E8
Stoke St Milborough Shrops 61 F5

Stoke sub Hamdon Som 12 C2
Stoke Talmage Oxon 39 E6
Stoke Trister Som 12 B5
Stoke Wake Dorset 13 D5
Stokeford Dorset 13 F6
Stokeham Notts 77 B7
Stokeinteignhead Devon 7 B7
Stokenchurch Bucks 39 E7
Stokenham Devon 7 E6
Stokesay Shrops 60 F4
Stokesby Norf 69 C7
Stokesley N Yorks 102 D3
Stolford Som 22 E4
Ston Easton Som 23 D8
Stondon Massey Essex 42 D1
Stone Bucks 39 C7
Stone Glos 36 E3
Stone Kent 19 C6
Stone Kent 29 B6
Stone S Yorks 89 F6
Stone Staffs 75 F6
Stone Worcs 50 B3
Stone Allerton Som 23 D6
Stone Bridge Corner Pboro 66 D2
Stone Chair W Yorks 88 B2
Stone Cross E Sus 18 E3
Stone Cross Kent 31 D7
Stone-edge Batch N Som 23 B6
Stone House Cumb 100 F2
Stone Street Kent 29 D6
Stone Street Suff 56 F3
Stone Street Suff 69 F6
Stonebroom Derbys 76 D4
Stoneferry Hull 97 F7
Stonefield S Lanark 119 D6
Stonegate E Sus 18 C3
Stonegate N Yorks 103 D5
Stonegrave N Yorks 96 B2
Stonehaugh Northumb 109 B7
Stonehaven Aberds 141 F7
Stonehouse Glos 37 D5
Stonehouse Northumb 109 D6
Stonehouse S Lanark 119 E7
Stoneleigh Warks 51 B8
Stonely Cambs 54 C2
Stoner Hill Hants 15 B8
Stone's Green Essex 43 B7
Stonesby Leics 64 B5
Stonesfield Oxon 38 C3
Stonethwaite Cumb 98 C4
Stoney Cross Hants 14 C3
Stoney Middleton Derbys 76 B2
Stoney Stanton Leics 63 E8
Stoney Stoke Som 24 F2
Stoney Stratton Som 23 F8
Stoney Stretton Shrops 60 D3
Stoneybreck Shetland 160 N8
Stoneyburn W Loth 120 C2
Stoneygate Aberds 153 E10
Stoneygate Leicester 64 D3
Stoneyhills Essex 43 E5
Stoneykirk Dumfries 104 D4
Stoneywood Aberdeen 141 C7
Stoneywood Falk 127 F6
Stonganess Shetland 160 C7
Stonham Aspal Suff 56 D5
Stonnall Staffs 62 D4
Stonor Oxon 39 F7
Stonton Wyville Leics 64 E4
Stony Cross Hereford 50 E2
Stony Stratford M Keynes 53 E5
Stonyfield Highld 151 D9
Stoodleigh Devon 10 C4
Stopes S Yorks 88 F3
Stopham W Sus 16 C4
Stopsley Luton 40 B4
Stores Corner Suff 57 E7
Storeton Mers 85 F4
Stornoway W Isles 155 D9
Storridge Hereford 50 E2
Storrington W Sus 16 C4
Storrs Cumb 99 E5
Storth Cumb 99 F6
Storwood E Yorks 96 E3
Stotfield Moray 152 A2
Stotfold C Beds 54 F3
Stottesdon Shrops 61 F6
Stoughton Leics 64 D3
Stoughton Sur 27 D7
Stoughton W Sus 16 C2
Stoul Highld 147 B10
Stoulton Worcs 50 E4
Stour Provost Dorset 13 B5
Stour Row Dorset 13 B6
Stourbridge W Mid 62 F3
Stourpaine Dorset 13 D6
Stourport on Severn Worcs 50 B3
Stourton Staffs 62 F2
Stourton Warks 51 F7
Stourton Wilts 24 F2
Stourton Caundle Dorset 12 C5
Stove Orkney 159 E7
Stove Shetland 160 L6
Stoven Suff 69 F7
Stow Borders 121 E7
Stow Lincs 78 F3
Stow Lincs 90 F2
Stow Bardolph Norf 67 D6
Stow Bedon Norf 68 E2
Stow cum Quy Cambs 55 C6
Stow Longa Cambs 54 B2
Stow Maries Essex 42 E4
Stow-on-the-Wold Glos 38 B1
Stowbridge Norf 67 D6
Stowe Shrops 48 B5
Stowe-by-Chartley Staffs 62 B4
Stowe Green Glos 36 D2
Stowell Som 12 B4
Stowford Devon 9 F6
Stowlangtoft Suff 56 C3
Stowmarket Suff 56 D4
Stowting Kent 30 E5
Stowupland Suff 56 D4
Straad Argyll 145 G9
Strachan Aberds 141 E5
Stradbroke Suff 57 B6
Stradishall Suff 55 D8
Stradsett Norf 67 D6
Stragglethorpe Lincs 78 D2
Straid S Ayrs 112 E1
Straith Dumfries 113 F8
Straiton Edin 121 C5
Straiton S Ayrs 112 D3
Straloch Aberds 141 B7
Straloch Perth 133 C7
Stramshall Staffs 75 F7
Strang IoM 84 E3
Stranraer Dumfries 104 C4
Stratfield Mortimer W Berks 26 C4
Stratfield Saye Hants 26 C4
Stratfield Turgis Hants 26 D4
Stratford London 41 F6
Stratford St Andrew Suff 57 C7
Stratford St Mary Suff 56 F4
Stratford Sub Castle Wilts 25 F6
Stratford Tony Wilts 13 B8
Stratford-upon-Avon Warks 51 D6
Strath Highld 149 A12
Strath Highld 158 E4
Strathan Highld 136 E2
Strathan Highld 156 G3
Strathan Highld 157 C8
Strathaven S Lanark 119 E7
Strathblane Stirling 119 B5
Strathcanaird Highld 156 J4
Strathcarron Highld 150 G2
Strathcoil Argyll 124 B2
Strathdon Aberds 140 C2
Strathellie Aberds 153 B10
Strathkinness Fife 129 C6
Strathmashie House Highld 137 E8
Strathmiglo Fife 128 C4
Strathmore Lodge Highld 158 F3
Strathpeffer Highld 150 F7
Strathrannoch Highld 150 D6
Strathtay Perth 133 D6
Strathvaich Lodge Highld 150 D6
Strathwhillan N Ayrs 143 E11
Strathy Highld 157 C11
Strathyre Stirling 126 C4
Stratton Corn 8 D4
Stratton Dorset 12 E4
Stratton Glos 37 D7
Stratton Audley Oxon 39 B6
Stratton on the Fosse Som 23 D8
Stratton St Margaret Swindon 38 F1
Stratton St Michael Norf 68 E5
Stratton Strawless Norf 81 E8
Stravithie Fife 129 C7
Streat E Sus 17 C7
Streatham London 28 B4
Streatley C Beds 40 B3
Streatley W Berks 39 F5
Street Lancs 92 D5
Street N Yorks 103 D5
Street Som 23 F6
Street Dinas Shrops 73 F7
Street End Kent 30 D5
Street End W Sus 16 E2
Street Gate T&W 110 D5
Street Lydan Wrex 73 F8
Streethay Staffs 62 C5
Streetlam N Yorks 101 E8
Streetly W Mid 62 E4
Streetly End Cambs 55 E7
Strefford Shrops 60 F4
Strelley Notts 76 E5
Strensall York 96 C2
Stretcholt Som 22 E4
Strete Devon 7 E6
Stretford Gtr Man 87 E6
Strethall Essex 55 F5
Stretham Cambs 55 B6
Strettington W Sus 16 D2
Stretton Ches W 73 D8
Stretton Derbys 76 C3
Stretton Rutland 65 C6
Stretton Staffs 62 C2
Stretton Staffs 63 B6
Stretton Warr 86 F4
Stretton Grandison Hereford 49 E8
Stretton-on-Dunsmore Warks 52 B2
Stretton-on-Fosse Warks 51 F7
Stretton Sugwas Hereford 49 E6
Stretton under Fosse Warks 63 F8
Stretton Westwood Shrops 61 E5
Strichen Aberds 153 C9
Strines Gtr Man 87 F7
Stringston Som 22 E3
Strixton Northants 53 C7
Stroat Glos 36 E2
Stromeferry Highld 149 E13
Stromemore Highld 149 E13
Stromness Orkney 159 H3
Stronaba Highld 136 F5
Stronachlachar Stirling 126 C3
Stronchreggan Highld 130 B4
Stronchrubie Highld 156 H5
Strone Argyll 145 E10
Strone Highld 136 F4
Strone Highld 137 B8
Strone Invclyd 118 B2
Stronmilchan Argyll 125 C7
Strontian Highld 130 C2
Strood Medway 29 C8
Strood Green Sur 28 E3
Strood Green W Sus 16 B4
Strood Green W Sus 28 F2
Stroud Glos 37 D5
Stroud Hants 15 B8
Stroud Green Essex 42 E4
Stroxton Lincs 78 F2
Struan Highld 149 E8
Struan Perth 133 C5
Strubby Lincs 91 F8
Strumpshaw Norf 69 D6
Strutherhill S Lanark 119 E7
Struy Highld 150 H6
Stryt-issa Wrex 73 E6
Stuartfield Aberds 153 D9
Stub Place Cumb 98 E2
Stubbington Hants 15 D6
Stubbins Lancs 87 C5
Stubbs Cross Kent 19 B6
Stubb's Green Norf 69 E5
Stubbs Green Norf 69 E6
Stubhampton Dorset 13 C7
Stubton Lincs 77 E8
Stuckgowan Argyll 126 D2
Stuckton Hants 14 C2
Stud Green Windsor 27 B6
Studham C Beds 40 C3
Studland Dorset 13 F8
Studley Warks 51 C5
Studley Wilts 24 B4
Studley Roger N Yorks 95 B5
Stump Cross Essex 55 E6
Stuntney Cambs 55 B6
Sturbridge Staffs 74 F5
Sturmer Essex 55 E7
Sturminster Marshall Dorset 13 D7
Sturminster Newton Dorset 13 C5
Sturry Kent 31 C5
Sturton N Lincs 90 D3
Sturton by Stow Lincs 90 F2
Sturton le Steeple Notts 89 F8
Stuston Suff 56 B5
Stutton N Yorks 95 E7
Stutton Suff 57 F5
Styal Ches E 87 F6
Styrrup Notts 89 E7
Suainebost W Isles 155 A10
Suardail W Isles 155 D9
Succoth Aberds 152 E4
Succoth Argyll 125 E8
Suckley Worcs 50 D2
Suckquoy Orkney 159 K5
Sudborough Northants 65 F6
Sudbourne Suff 57 D8
Sudbrook Lincs 78 E2
Sudbrook Mon 36 F2
Sudbrooke Lincs 78 B3
Sudbury Derbys 75 F8
Sudbury London 40 F4
Sudbury Suff 56 E2
Suddie Highld 151 F9
Sudgrove Glos 37 D6
Suffield N Yorks 103 E7
Suffield Norf 81 D8
Sugnall Staffs 74 F4
Suladale Highld 149 C8
Sulaisiadar W Isles 155 D10
Sulby IoM 84 C3
Sulgrave Northants 52 E3
Sulham W Berks 26 B4
Sulhamstead W Berks 26 C4
Sulland Orkney 159 D6
Sullington W Sus 16 C4
Sullom Shetland 160 F5
Sullom Voe Oil Terminal Shetland 160 F5
Sully V Glam 22 C3
Sumburgh Shetland 160 N6
Summer Bridge N Yorks 94 C5
Summer-house Darl 101 C7
Summercourt Corn 4 D3
Summerfield Norf 80 D3
Summergangs Hull 97 F7
Summerleaze Mon 35 F8
Summersdale W Sus 16 D2
Summerseat Gtr Man 87 C5
Summertown Oxon 39 D5
Summit Gtr Man 87 D7
Sunbury-on-Thames Sur 28 C2
Sundaywell Dumfries 113 F8
Sunderland Argyll 142 B3
Sunderland Cumb 107 F8
Sunderland T&W 111 D6
Sunderland Bridge Durham 111 F5
Sundhope Borders 115 B6
Sundon Park Luton 40 B3
Sundridge Kent 29 D5
Sunipol Argyll 146 F6
Sunk Island E Yorks 91 C6
Sunningdale Windsor 27 C7
Sunninghill Windsor 27 C7
Sunningwell Oxon 38 D4
Sunniside Durham 110 F4
Sunniside T&W 110 D5
Sunnyhurst Blackburn 86 B4
Sunnylaw Stirling 127 E6
Sunnyside W Sus 28 F4
Sunton Wilts 25 D7
Surbiton London 28 C2
Surby IoM 84 E2
Surfleet Lincs 66 B2
Surfleet Seas End Lincs 66 B2
Surlingham Norf 69 D6
Sustead Norf 81 D7
Susworth Lincs 90 D2
Sutcombe Devon 8 C5
Suton Norf 68 E3
Sutors of Cromarty Highld 151 E11
Sutterby Lincs 79 B6
Sutterton Lincs 79 F5
Sutton C Beds 54 E3
Sutton Cambs 54 B5
Sutton Kent 31 E7
Sutton London 28 C3
Sutton Mers 86 E3
Sutton N Yorks 89 B5
Sutton Norf 69 B6
Sutton Notts 77 F7
Sutton Notts 89 F7
Sutton Oxon 38 D4
Sutton Pboro 65 E7
Sutton S Yorks 89 C6
Sutton Shrops 61 F7
Sutton Shrops 74 F3
Sutton Som 23 F8
Sutton Staffs 61 B7
Sutton Suff 57 E7
Sutton Sur 27 E8
Sutton W Sus 16 C3
Sutton at Hone Kent 29 B6
Sutton Bassett Northants 64 E4
Sutton Benger Wilts 24 B4
Sutton Bonington Notts 64 B2
Sutton Bridge Lincs 66 B4
Sutton Cheney Leics 63 D8
Sutton Coldfield W Mid 62 E5
Sutton Courtenay Oxon 39 E5
Sutton Crosses Lincs 66 B4
Sutton Grange N Yorks 95 B5
Sutton Green Sur 27 D8
Sutton Howgrave N Yorks 95 B6
Sutton In Ashfield Notts 76 D4
Sutton-in-Craven N Yorks 94 E3
Sutton in the Elms Leics 64 E2
Sutton Ings Hull 97 F7
Sutton Lane Ends Ches E 75 B6
Sutton Leach Mers 86 E3
Sutton Maddock Shrops 61 D7
Sutton Mallet Som 23 F5
Sutton Mandeville Wilts 13 B7
Sutton Manor Mers 86 E3
Sutton Montis Som 12 B4
Sutton on Hull Hull 97 F7
Sutton on Sea Lincs 91 F9
Sutton-on-the-Forest N Yorks 95 C8
Sutton on the Hill Derbys 76 F2
Sutton on Trent Notts 77 C7
Sutton Scarsdale Derbys 76 C4
Sutton Scotney Hants 26 F2
Sutton St Edmund Lincs 66 C3
Sutton St James Lincs 66 C3
Sutton St Nicholas Hereford 49 E7
Sutton under Brailes Warks 51 F8
Sutton-under-Whitestonecliffe N Yorks 102 F2
Sutton upon Derwent E Yorks 96 E3
Sutton Valence Kent 30 E2
Sutton Veny Wilts 24 E3
Sutton Waldron Dorset 13 C6
Sutton Weaver Ches W 74 B2
Sutton Wick Bath 23 D7
Swaby Lincs 79 B6
Swadlincote Derbys 63 C7
Swaffham Norf 67 D8
Swaffham Bulbeck Cambs 55 C6
Swaffham Prior Cambs 55 C6
Swafield Norf 81 D8
Swainby N Yorks 102 D2
Swainshill Hereford 49 E6
Swainsthorpe Norf 68 D5
Swainswick Bath 24 C2
Swalcliffe Oxon 51 F8
Swalecliffe Kent 30 C5
Swallow Lincs 91 D5
Swallowcliffe Wilts 13 B7
Swallowfield Wokingham 26 C5
Swallownest S Yorks 89 F5
Swallows Cross Essex 42 E2
Swan Green Ches W 74 B4
Swan Green Suff 57 B6
Swanage Dorset 13 G8
Swanbister Orkney 159 H4
Swanbourne Bucks 39 B8
Swanland E Yorks 90 B3
Swanley Kent 29 C6
Swanley Village Kent 29 C6
Swanmore Hants 15 C6
Swannington Leics 63 C8
Swannington Norf 68 C4
Swanscombe Kent 29 B7
Swansea = Abertawe Swansea 33 E7
Swanton Abbott Norf 81 E8
Swanton Morley Norf 68 C3
Swanton Novers Norf 81 D6
Swanton Street Kent 30 D2
Swanwick Derbys 76 D4
Swanwick Hants 15 D6
Swarby Lincs 78 E3
Swardeston Norf 68 D5
Swarister Shetland 160 E7
Swarkestone Derbys 63 B7
Swarland Northumb 117 D7
Swarland Estate Northumb 117 D7
Swarthmoor Cumb 92 B2
Swathwick Derbys 76 C3
Swaton Lincs 78 F4
Swavesey Cambs 54 C4
Sway Hants 14 E3
Swayfield Lincs 65 B6
Swaythling Soton 14 C5
Sweet Green Worcs 49 C8
Sweetham Devon 10 E3
Sweethouse Corn 5 C5
Sweffling Suff 57 C7
Swepstone Leics 63 C7
Swerford Oxon 51 F8
Swettenham Ches E 74 C5
Swetton N Yorks 94 B4
Swffryd Caerph 35 E6
Swiftsden E Sus 18 C4
Swilland Suff 57 D5
Swillington W Yorks 95 F6
Swimbridge Devon 9 B8
Swimbridge Newland Devon 20 F5
Swinbrook Oxon 38 C2
Swinderby Lincs 77 C8
Swindon Glos 37 B6
Swindon Staffs 62 E2
Swindon Swindon 38 F1
Swine E Yorks 97 F7
Swinefleet E Yorks 89 B8
Swineshead Bedford 53 C8
Swineshead Lincs 78 E5
Swineshead Bridge Lincs 78 E5
Swiney Highld 158 G4
Swinford Leics 52 B3
Swinford Oxon 38 D4
Swingate Notts 76 E5
Swingfield Minnis Kent 31 E6
Swingfield Street Kent 31 E6
Swinhoe Northumb 117 B8
Swinhope Lincs 91 E6
Swining Shetland 160 G6
Swinithwaite N Yorks 101 F5
Swinnow Moor W Yorks 94 F5
Swinscoe Staffs 75 E8
Swinside Hall Borders 116 C3
Swinstead Lincs 65 B7
Swinton Borders 122 E4
Swinton Gtr Man 87 D5
Swinton N Yorks 94 B5
Swinton N Yorks 96 B3
Swinton S Yorks 88 E5
Swintonmill Borders 122 E4
Swithland Leics 64 C2
Swordale Highld 151 E8
Swordland Highld 147 B10
Swordly Highld 157 C10
Sworton Heath Ches E 86 F4
Swydd-ffynnon Ceredig 47 C5
Swynnerton Staffs 75 F5
Swyre Dorset 12 F3
Sychtyn Powys 59 D6
Syde Glos 37 C6
Sydenham London 28 B4
Sydenham Oxon 39 D7
Sydenham Damerel Devon 6 B2
Syderstone Norf 80 D4
Sydling St Nicholas Dorset 12 E4
Sydmonton Hants 26 D2
Syerston Notts 77 E7
Syke Gtr Man 87 C6
Sykehouse S Yorks 89 C7
Sykes Lancs 93 D6
Syleham Suff 57 B6
Sylen Carms 33 D6
Symbister Shetland 160 G7
Symington S Ayrs 118 F3
Symington S Lanark 120 F2
Symonds Yat Hereford 36 C2
Symondsbury Dorset 12 E2
Synod Inn Ceredig 46 D3
Syre Highld 157 E9
Syreford Glos 37 B7
Syresham Northants 52 E4
Syston Leics 64 C3
Syston Lincs 78 E2
Sytchampton Worcs 50 C3
Sywell Northants 53 C6

T

Taagan Highld 150 E3
Tàbost W Isles 155 A10
Tabost W Isles 155 F8
Tackley Oxon 38 B4
Tacleit W Isles 154 D6
Tacolneston Norf 68 E4
Tadcaster N Yorks 95 E7
Taddington Derbys 75 B8
Taddiport Devon 9 C6
Tadley Hants 26 C4
Tadlow C Beds 54 E3
Tadmarton Oxon 51 F8
Tadworth Sur 28 D3
Tafarn-y-gelyn Denb 73 C5
Tafarnau-bach Bl Gwent 35 C5
Taff's Well Rhondda 35 F5
Tafolwern Powys 59 D5
Tai Conwy 83 E7
Tai-bach Powys 59 B8
Tai-mawr Conwy 72 E3
Tai-Ucha Denb 72 D4
Taibach Neath 34 F1
Taigh a Ghearraidh W Isles 148 A2
Tain Highld 151 C10
Tain Highld 158 D4
Tainant Wrex 73 E6
Tainlon Gwyn 82 F4
Tairbeart = Tarbert W Isles 154 G6
Tai'r-Bull Powys 34 B3
Tairgwaith Neath 33 C8
Takeley Essex 42 B1
Takeley Street Essex 41 B8
Tal-sarn Ceredig 46 D4
Tal-y-bont Ceredig 58 F3
Tal-y-bont Conwy 83 E7
Tal-y-bont Gwyn 71 E6
Tal-y-bont Gwyn 83 D6
Tal-y-cafn Conwy 83 D7
Tal-y-llyn Gwyn 58 D4
Tal-y-wern Powys 58 D5
Talachddu Powys 48 F2
Talacre Flint 85 F2
Talardd Gwyn 59 B5
Talaton Devon 11 E5
Talbenny Pembs 44 D3
Talbot Green Rhondda 34 F4
Talbot Village Poole 13 E8
Tale Devon 11 D5
Talerddig Powys 59 D6
Talgarreg Ceredig 46 D3
Talgarth Powys 48 F3
Talisker Highld 149 E8
Talke Staffs 74 D5
Talkin Cumb 109 D5
Talla Linnfoots Borders 114 B4
Talladale Highld 150 D2
Tallarn Green Wrex 73 E8
Tallentire Cumb 107 F8
Talley Carms 46 F5
Tallington Lincs 65 D7
Talmine Highld 157 C8
Talog Carms 32 B4
Talsarn Carms 34 B1
Talsarnau Gwyn 71 D7
Talskiddy Corn 4 C4
Talwrn Anglesey 82 D4
Talwrn Wrex 73 E6
Talybont-on-Usk Powys 35 B5
Talygarn Rhondda 34 F4
Talyllyn Powys 35 B5
Talysarn Gwyn 82 F4
Talywain Torf 35 D6
Tame Bridge N Yorks 102 D3
Tamerton Foliot Plym 6 C2
Tamworth Staffs 63 D6
Tan Hinon Powys 59 F5
Tan-lan Conwy 83 E7
Tan-lan Gwyn 71 C7
Tan-y-bwlch Gwyn 71 C7
Tan-y-fron Conwy 72 C3
Tan-y-graig Anglesey 82 D5
Tan-y-graig Gwyn 70 D4
Tan-y-groes Ceredig 45 E4
Tan-y-pistyll Powys 59 B7
Tan-yr-allt Gwyn 82 F4
Tandem W Yorks 88 C2
Tanden Kent 19 B6
Tandridge Sur 28 D4
Tanerdy Carms 33 B5
Tanfield Durham 110 D4
Tanfield Lea Durham 110 D4
Tangasdal W Isles 148 J1
Tangiers Pembs 44 D4
Tangley Hants 25 D8
Tanglwst Carms 46 F2
Tangmere W Sus 16 D3
Tangwick Shetland 160 F4
Tankersley S Yorks 88 D4
Tankerton Kent 30 C5
Tannach Highld 158 F5
Tannachie Aberds 141 F6
Tannadice Angus 134 D4
Tannington Suff 57 C6
Tansley Derbys 76 D3
Tansley Knoll Derbys 76 C3
Tansor Northants 65 E7
Tantobie Durham 110 D4
Tanton N Yorks 102 C3
Tanworth-in-Arden Warks 51 B6
Tanygrisiau Gwyn 71 C7
Tanyrhydiau Ceredig 47 C6
Taobh a Chaolais W Isles 148 G2
Taobh a Thuath Loch Aineort W Isles 148 F2
Taobh a Tuath Loch Baghasdail W Isles 148 F2
Taobh a'Ghlinne W Isles 155 F8
Taobh Tuath W Isles 154 J4
Taplow Bucks 40 F2
Tapton Derbys 76 B3
Tarbat Ho. Highld 151 D10
Tarbert Argyll 143 C7
Tarbert Argyll 144 E5
Tarbert Argyll 145 G7
Tarbert = Tairbeart W Isles 154 G6
Tarbet Argyll 126 D2
Tarbet Highld 147 B10
Tarbet Highld 156 E4
Tarbock Green Mers 86 F2
Tarbolton S Ayrs 112 B4
Tarbrax S Lanark 120 D3
Tardebigge Worcs 50 C5
Tarfside Angus 134 B4
Tarland Aberds 140 D3
Tarleton Lancs 86 B2
Tarlogie Highld 151 C10
Tarlscough Lancs 86 C2
Tarlton Glos 37 E6
Tarnbrook Lancs 93 D5
Tarporley Ches W 74 C2
Tarr Som 22 F3
Tarrant Crawford Dorset 13 D7
Tarrant Gunville Dorset 13 C7
Tarrant Hinton Dorset 13 C7
Tarrant Keyneston Dorset 13 D7
Tarrant Launceston Dorset 13 D7
Tarrant Monkton Dorset 13 D7
Tarrant Rawston Dorset 13 D7
Tarrant Rushton Dorset 13 D7
Tarrel Highld 151 C11
Tarring Neville E Sus 17 D8
Tarrington Hereford 49 E8
Tarsappie Perth 128 B3
Tarskavaig Highld 149 H10
Tarves Aberds 153 E8
Tarvie Highld 150 F7
Tarvie Perth 133 C7
Tarvin Ches W 73 C8
Tasburgh Norf 68 E5
Tasley Shrops 61 E6
Taston Oxon 38 B3
Tatenhill Staffs 63 B6
Tathall End M Keynes 53 E6
Tatham Lancs 93 C6
Tathwell Lincs 91 F7
Tatling End Bucks 40 F3
Tatsfield Sur 28 D5
Tattenhall Ches W 73 D8
Tattenhoe M Keynes 53 F6
Tatterford Norf 80 E4
Tattersett Norf 80 D4
Tattershall Lincs 78 D5
Tattershall Bridge Lincs 78 D4
Tattershall Thorpe Lincs 78 D5
Tattingstone Suff 56 F5
Tatworth Som 11 D8
Taunton Som 11 B7
Taverham Norf 68 C4
Tavernspite Pembs 32 C2
Tavistock Devon 6 B2
Taw Green Devon 9 E8
Tawstock Devon 9 B7
Taxal Derbys 75 B7
Tay Bridge Dundee 129 B6
Tayinloan Argyll 143 D7
Taymouth Castle Perth 132 E4
Taynish Argyll 144 E6
Taynton Glos 36 B4
Taynton Oxon 38 C2
Taynuilt Argyll 125 B6
Tayport Fife 129 B6
Tayvallich Argyll 144 E6
Tealby Lincs 91 E5
Tealing Angus 134 F4
Teangue Highld 149 H11
Teanna Mhachair W Isles 148 B2
Tebay Cumb 99 D8
Tebworth C Beds 40 B2
Tedburn St Mary Devon 10 E3
Teddington Glos 50 F4
Teddington London 28 B2
Tedstone Delamere Hereford 49 D8
Tedstone Wafre Hereford 49 D8
Teeton Northants 52 B4
Teffont Evias Wilts 24 F4
Teffont Magna Wilts 24 F4
Tegryn Pembs 45 F4
Teigh Rutland 65 C5
Teigncombe Devon 9 F8
Teigngrace Devon 7 B6
Teignmouth Devon 7 B7
Telford Telford 61 D6
Telham E Sus 18 D4
Tellisford Som 24 D3
Telscombe E Sus 17 D8
Telscombe Cliffs E Sus 17 D7
Templand Dumfries 114 F3
Temple Corn 5 B6
Temple Glasgow 118 C5
Temple Midloth 121 D6
Temple Balsall W Mid 51 B7
Temple Bar Carms 33 C6
Temple Bar Ceredig 46 D4
Temple Cloud Bath 23 D8
Temple Combe Som 12 B5
Temple Ewell Kent 31 E6
Temple Grafton Warks 51 D6
Temple Guiting Glos 37 B7
Temple Herdewyke Warks 51 D8
Temple Hirst N Yorks 89 B7
Temple Normanton Derbys 76 C4
Temple Sowerby Cumb 99 B8
Templehall Fife 128 E4
Templeton Devon 10 C3
Templeton Pembs 32 C2
Templeton Bridge Devon 10 C3
Templetown Durham 110 D4
Tempsford C Beds 54 D2
Ten Mile Bank Norf 67 E6
Tenbury Wells Worcs 49 C7
Tenby = Dinbych-Y-Pysgod Pembs 32 D2
Tendring Essex 43 B7
Tendring Green Essex 43 B7
Tenston Orkney 159 G3
Tenterden Kent 19 B5
Terling Essex 42 C3
Ternhill Shrops 74 F3
Terregles Banks Dumfries 107 B6
Terrick Bucks 39 D8
Terrington N Yorks 96 B2
Terrington St Clement Norf 66 C5
Terrington St John Norf 66 C5
Teston Kent 29 D8
Testwood Hants 14 C4
Tetbury Glos 37 E5
Tetbury Upton Glos 37 E5
Tetchill Shrops 73 F7
Tetcott Devon 8 E5
Tetford Lincs 79 B6
Tetney Lincs 91 D7
Tetney Lock Lincs 91 D7
Tetsworth Oxon 39 D6
Tettenhall W Mid 62 E2
Teuchan Aberds 153 E10
Teversal Notts 76 C4
Teversham Cambs 55 D5
Teviothead Borders 115 D7
Tewel Aberds 141 F7
Tewin Herts 41 C5
Tewkesbury Glos 50 F3
Teynham Kent 30 C3
Thackthwaite Cumb 98 B3
Thainston Aberds 135 B6
Thakeham W Sus 16 C5
Thame Oxon 39 D7
Thames Ditton Sur 28 C2
Thames Haven Thurrock 42 F3
Thamesmead London 41 F7
Thanington Kent 30 D5
Thankerton S Lanark 120 F2
Tharston Norf 68 E4
Thatcham W Berks 26 C3
Thatto Heath Mers 86 E3
Thaxted Essex 55 F7
The Aird Highld 149 C9
The Arms Norf 67 E8
The Bage Hereford 48 E4
The Balloch Perth 127 C7
The Barony Orkney 159 F3
The Bog Shrops 60 E3
The Bourne Sur 27 E6
The Braes Highld 149 E10
The Broad Hereford 49 C6
The Butts Som 24 E2
The Camp Glos 37 D6
The Camp Herts 40 D4
The Chequer Wrex 73 E8
The City Bucks 39 E7
The Common Wilts 25 F7
The Craigs Highld 150 B7
The Cronk IoM 84 C3
The Dell Suff 69 E7
The Den N Ayrs 118 D3
The Eals Northumb 116 F3
The Eaves Glos 36 D3
The Flatt Cumb 109 B5
The Four Alls Shrops 74 F3
The Garths Shetland 160 B8
The Green Cumb 98 F3
The Green Wilts 24 F3
The Grove Dumfries 107 B6
The Hall Shetland 160 D8
The Haven W Sus 27 F8
The Heath Norf 81 E7
The Heath Suff 56 F5
The Hill Cumb 98 F3
The Howe Cumb 99 F6
The Howe IoM 84 F1
The Hundred Hereford 49 C7
The Lee Bucks 40 D2
The Lhen IoM 84 B3
The Marsh Powys 60 E3
The Marsh Wilts 37 F7
The Middles Durham 110 D5
The Moor Kent 18 C4
The Mumbles = Y Mwmbwls Swansea 33 F7
The Murray S Lanark 119 D6
The Neuk Aberds 141 E6
The Oval Bath 24 C2
The Pole of Itlaw Aberds 153 C6
The Quarry Glos 36 E4
The Rhos Pembs 32 C1
The Rock Telford 61 D6
The Ryde Herts 41 D5
The Sands Sur 27 E6
The Stocks Kent 19 C6
The Throat Wokingham 27 C6
The Vauld Hereford 49 E7
The Wyke Shrops 61 D7
Theakston N Yorks 101 F8
Thealby N Lincs 90 C2
Theale Som 23 E6
Theale W Berks 26 B4
Thearne E Yorks 97 F6
Theberton Suff 57 C8
Theddingworth Leics 64 F3
Theddlethorpe All Saints Lincs 91 F8
Theddlethorpe St Helen Lincs 91 F8
Thelbridge Barton Devon 10 C2
Thelnetham Suff 56 B4
Thelveton Norf 68 F4
Thelwall Warr 86 F4
Themelthorpe Norf 81 E6
Thenford Northants 52 E3
Therfield Herts 54 F4
Thetford Lincs 65 C8
Thetford Norf 67 F8
Theydon Bois Essex 41 E7
Thickwood Wilts 24 B3
Thimbleby Lincs 78 C5
Thimbleby N Yorks 102 E2
Thingwall Mers 85 F3
Thirdpart N Ayrs 118 E1
Thirlby N Yorks 102 F2
Thirlestane Borders 121 E8
Thirn N Yorks 101 F7
Thirsk N Yorks 102 F2
Thirtleby E Yorks 97 F7
Thistleton Lancs 92 F4
Thistleton Rutland 65 C6
Thistley Green Suff 55 B7
Thixendale N Yorks 96 C4
Thockrington Northumb 110 B2
Tholomas Drove Cambs 66 D3
Tholthorpe N Yorks 95 C7
Thomas Chapel Pembs 32 D2
Thomas Close Cumb 108 E4
Thomastown Aberds 152 E5
Thompson Norf 68 E2
Thomshill Moray 152 C2
Thong Kent 29 B7
Thongsbridge W Yorks 88 D2
Thoralby N Yorks 101 F5
Thoresway Lincs 91 E5
Thorganby Lincs 91 E6
Thorganby N Yorks 96 E2
Thorgill N Yorks 103 E5
Thorington Suff 57 B8
Thorington Street Suff 56 F4
Thorlby N Yorks 94 D2
Thorley Herts 41 C7
Thorley Street Herts 41 C7
Thorley Street IoW 14 F4
Thormanby N Yorks 95 B7
Thornaby-on-Tees Stockton 102 C2
Thornage Norf 81 D6
Thornborough Bucks 52 F5
Thornborough N Yorks 95 B5
Thornbury Devon 9 D5
Thornbury Hereford 49 D8
Thornbury S Glos 36 E3
Thornbury W Yorks 94 F4
Thornby Northants 52 B4
Thorncliffe Staffs 75 D7
Thorncombe Dorset 11 D8
Thorncombe Dorset 13 D6
Thorncombe Street Sur 27 E8
Thorncote Green C Beds 54 E2
Thorncross IoW 14 F5
Thorndon Suff 56 C5
Thorndon Cross Devon 9 E7
Thorne S Yorks 89 C7
Thorne St Margaret Som 11 B5
Thorner W Yorks 95 E6
Thorney Notts 77 B8
Thorney Pboro 66 D2
Thorney Crofts E Yorks 91 B6
Thorney Green Suff 56 C4
Thorney Hill Hants 14 E2
Thorney Toll Pboro 66 D3
Thornfalcon Som 11 B7
Thornford Dorset 12 C4
Thorngumbald E Yorks 91 B6
Thornham Norf 80 C3
Thornham Magna Suff 56 B5
Thornham Parva Suff 56 B5
Thornhaugh Pboro 65 D7
Thornhill Cardiff 35 F5
Thornhill Cumb 98 D2
Thornhill Derbys 88 F2
Thornhill Dumfries 113 E8
Thornhill Soton 15 C5
Thornhill Stirling 127 E5
Thornhill W Yorks 88 C3
Thornhill Edge W Yorks 88 C3
Thornhill Lees W Yorks 88 C3
Thornholme E Yorks 97 C7
Thornley Durham 110 F4
Thornley Durham 111 F6
Thornliebank E Renf 118 D5
Thorns Suff 55 D8
Thorns Green Ches E 87 F5
Thornsett Derbys 87 F8
Thornthwaite Cumb 98 B4
Thornthwaite N Yorks 94 D4
Thornton Angus 134 E3
Thornton Bucks 53 F5
Thornton E Yorks 96 E3
Thornton Fife 128 E4
Thornton Lancs 92 E3
Thornton Leics 63 D8
Thornton Lincs 78 C5
Thornton Mbro 102 C2
Thornton Mers 85 D4
Thornton Northumb 123 E5
Thornton Pembs 44 E4
Thornton W Yorks 94 F4
Thornton Curtis N Lincs 90 C4
Thornton Heath London 28 C4
Thornton Hough Mers 85 F4
Thornton in Craven N Yorks 94 E2
Thornton-le-Beans N Yorks 102 E1
Thornton-le-Clay N Yorks 96 C2
Thornton-le-Dale N Yorks 103 F6
Thornton le Moor Lincs 90 E4
Thornton-le-Moor N Yorks 102 F1
Thornton-le-Moors Ches W 73 B8
Thornton-le-Street N Yorks 102 F2
Thornton Rust N Yorks 100 F4
Thornton Steward N Yorks 101 F6
Thornton Watlass N Yorks 101 F7
Thorntonhall S Lanark 119 D5
Thorntonloch E Loth 122 B3
Thorntonpark Northumb 122 E5
Thornwood Common Essex 41 D7
Thornydykes Borders 122 E2
Thoroton Notts 77 E7
Thorp Arch W Yorks 95 E7
Thorpe Derbys 75 D8
Thorpe E Yorks 97 E5
Thorpe Lincs 91 F8
Thorpe N Yorks 94 C3
Thorpe Norf 69 E7
Thorpe Notts 77 E7
Thorpe Sur 27 C8
Thorpe Abbotts Norf 57 B5
Thorpe Acre Leics 64 B2
Thorpe Arnold Leics 64 B4
Thorpe Audlin W Yorks 89 C5
Thorpe Bassett N Yorks 96 B4
Thorpe Bay Southend 43 F5
Thorpe by Water Rutland 65 E5
Thorpe Common Suff 57 F6
Thorpe Constantine Staffs 63 D6
Thorpe Culvert Lincs 79 C7
Thorpe End Norf 69 C5
Thorpe Fendykes Lincs 79 C7
Thorpe Green Essex 43 B7
Thorpe Green Suff 56 D3
Thorpe Hesley S Yorks 88 E4
Thorpe in Balne S Yorks 89 C6
Thorpe in the Fallows Lincs 90 F3
Thorpe Langton Leics 64 E4
Thorpe Larches Durham 102 B1
Thorpe-le-Soken Essex 43 B7
Thorpe le Street E Yorks 96 E4
Thorpe Malsor Northants 53 B6
Thorpe Mandeville Northants 52 E3
Thorpe Market Norf 81 D8
Thorpe Marriot Norf 68 C4
Thorpe Morieux Suff 56 D3
Thorpe on the Hill Lincs 78 C2
Thorpe Salvin S Yorks 89 F6
Thorpe Satchville Leics 64 C4
Thorpe St Andrew Norf 69 D5
Thorpe St Peter Lincs 79 C7
Thorpe Thewles Stockton 102 B2
Thorpe Tilney Lincs 78 D4
Thorpe Underwood N Yorks 95 D7
Thorpe Waterville Northants 65 F7
Thorpe Willoughby N Yorks 95 F8
Thorpeness Suff 57 D8
Thorrington Essex 43 C6
Thorverton Devon 10 D4
Thrandeston Suff 56 B5
Thrapston Northants 53 B7
Thrashbush N Lanark 119 C7
Threapland Cumb 107 F8
Threapland N Yorks 94 C2
Threapwood Ches W 73 E8
Threapwood Staffs 75 E7
Three Ashes Hereford 36 B2
Three Bridges W Sus 28 F3
Three Burrows Corn 3 B6
Three Chimneys Kent 18 B5
Three Cocks Powys 48 F3
Three Crosses Swansea 33 E6
Three Cups Corner E Sus 18 C3
Three Holes Norf 66 D5
Three Leg Cross E Sus 18 B3
Three Legged Cross Dorset 13 D8
Three Oaks E Sus 18 D5
Threehammer Common Norf 69 C6
Threekingham Lincs 78 F3
Threemile Cross Wokingham 26 C5
Threemilestone Corn 3 B6
Threemiletown W Loth 120 B3
Threlkeld Cumb 99 B5
Threshfield N Yorks 94 C2
Thrigby Norf 69 C7
Thringarth Durham 100 B4
Thringstone Leics 63 C8
Thrintoft N Yorks 101 E8
Thriplow Cambs 54 E5
Throckenholt Lincs 66 D3
Throcking Herts 54 F4
Throckley T&W 110 C4
Throckmorton Worcs 50 E4
Throphill Northumb 117 F7
Thropton Northumb 117 D6
Throsk Stirling 127 E7
Throwleigh Devon 9 E8
Throwley Kent 30 D3
Thrumpton Notts 76 F5
Thrumster Highld 158 F5
Thrunton Northumb 117 C6
Thrupp Glos 37 D5
Thrupp Oxon 38 C4
Thrushelton Devon 9 F6
Thrussington Leics 64 C3
Thruxton Hants 25 E7
Thruxton Hereford 49 F6
Thrybergh S Yorks 89 E5
Thulston Derbys 76 F4
Thundergay N Ayrs 143 D9
Thundersley Essex 42 F3
Thundridge Herts 41 C6
Thurcaston Leics 64 C2
Thurcroft S Yorks 89 F5
Thurgarton Norf 81 D7
Thurgarton Notts 77 E6
Thurgoland S Yorks 88 D3
Thurlaston Leics 64 E2
Thurlaston Warks 52 B2
Thurlbear Som 11 B7
Thurlby Lincs 65 C8
Thurlby Lincs 78 C2
Thurleigh Bedford 53 D8
Thurlestone Devon 6 E4
Thurloxton Som 22 F4
Thurlstone S Yorks 88 D3
Thurlton Norf 69 E7
Thurlwood Ches E 74 D5
Thurmaston Leics 64 D3
Thurnby Leics 64 D3
Thurne Norf 69 C7
Thurnham Kent 30 D2
Thurnham Lancs 92 D4
Thurning Norf 81 E6
Thurning Northants 65 F7
Thurnscoe S Yorks 89 D5
Thurnscoe East S Yorks 89 D5
Thursby Cumb 108 D3
Thursford Norf 81 D5
Thursley Sur 27 F7
Thurso Highld 158 D3
Thurso East Highld 158 D3
Thurstaston Mers 85 F3
Thurston Suff 56 C3
Thurstonfield Cumb 108 D3
Thurstonland W Yorks 88 C2
Thurton Norf 69 D6
Thurvaston Derbys 76 F2
Thuxton Norf 68 D3
Thwaite N Yorks 100 E3

Thwaite Suff 56 C5
Thwaite St Mary Norf 69 E6
Thwaites W Yorks 94 E3
Thwaites Brow W Yorks 94 E3
Thwing E Yorks 97 B6
Tibbermore Perth 128 B2
Tibberton Glos 36 B4
Tibberton Telford 61 B6
Tibberton Worcs 50 D4
Tibenham Norf 68 F4
Tibshelf Derbys 76 C4
Tibthorpe E Yorks 97 D5
Ticehurst E Sus 18 B3
Tichborne Hants 26 F3
Tickencote Rutland 65 D6
Tickenham N Som 23 B6
Tickhill S Yorks 89 E6
Ticklerton Shrops 60 E4
Ticknall Derbys 63 B7
Tickton E Yorks 97 E6
Tidcombe Wilts 25 D7
Tiddington Oxon 39 D6
Tiddington Warks 51 D7
Tidebrook E Sus 18 C3
Tideford Corn 5 D8
Tideford Cross Corn 5 C8
Tidenham Glos 36 E2
Tideswell Derbys 75 B8
Tidmarsh W Berks 26 B4
Tidmington Warks 51 F7
Tidpit Hants 13 C8
Tidworth Wilts 25 E7
Tiers Cross Pembs 44 D4
Tiffield Northants 52 D4
Tifty Aberds 153 D7
Tigerton Angus 135 C5
Tigh-na-Blair Perth 127 C6
Tighnabruaich Argyll 145 F8
Tighnafiline Highld 155 J13
Tigley Devon 7 C5
Tilbrook Cambs 53 C8
Tilbury Thurrock 29 B7
Tilbury Juxta Clare Essex 55 E8
Tile Cross W Mid 63 F5
Tile Hill W Mid 51 B7
Tilehurst Reading 26 B4
Tilford Sur 27 E6
Tilgate W Sus 28 F3
Tilgate Forest Row W Sus 28 F3
Tillathrowie Aberds 152 E4
Tilley Shrops 60 B5
Tillicoultry Clack 127 E8
Tillingham Essex 43 D5
Tillington Hereford 49 E6
Tillington W Sus 16 B3
Tillington Common Hereford 49 E6
Tillyarblet Angus 135 C5
Tillybirloch Aberds 141 D5
Tillycorthie Aberds 141 B8
Tillydrine Aberds 140 E5
Tillyfour Aberds 140 C4
Tillyfourie Aberds 140 C5
Tillygarmond Aberds 140 E5
Tillygreig Aberds 141 B7
Tillykerrie Aberds 141 B7
Tilmanstone Kent 31 D7
Tilney All Saints Norf 67 C5
Tilney High End Norf 67 C5
Tilney St Lawrence Norf 66 C5
Tilshead Wilts 24 E5
Tilstock Shrops 74 F2
Tilston Ches W 73 D8
Tilstone Fearnall Ches W 74 C2
Tilsworth C Beds 40 B2
Tilton on the Hill Leics 64 D4
Timberland Lincs 78 D4
Timbersbrook Ches E 75 C5
Timberscombe Som 21 E8
Timble N Yorks 94 D4
Timperley Gtr Man 87 F5
Timsbury Bath 23 D8
Timsbury Hants 14 B4
Timsgearraidh W Isles 154 D5
Timworth Green Suff 56 C2
Tincleton Dorset 13 E5
Tindale Cumb 109 D6
Tingewick Bucks 52 F4
Tingley W Yorks 88 B3
Tingrith C Beds 53 F8
Tingwall Orkney 159 F4
Tinhay Devon 9 F5
Tinshill W Yorks 95 F5
Tinsley S Yorks 88 E5
Tintagel Corn 8 F2
Tintern Parva Mon 36 D2
Tintinhull Som 12 C3
Tintwistle Derbys 87 E8
Tinwald Dumfries 114 F3
Tinwell Rutland 65 D7
Tipperty Aberds 141 B8
Tipsend Norf 66 E5
Tipton W Mid 62 E3
Tipton St John Devon 11 E5
Tiptree Essex 42 C4
Tir-y-dail Carms 33 C7
Tirabad Powys 47 E7
Tiraghoil Argyll 146 J6
Tirley Glos 37 B5
Tirphil Caerph 35 D5
Tirril Cumb 99 B7
Tisbury Wilts 13 B7
Tisman's Common W Sus 27 F8
Tissington Derbys 75 D8
Titchberry Devon 8 B4
Titchfield Hants 15 D6
Titchmarsh Northants 53 B8
Titchwell Norf 80 C3
Tithby Notts 77 F6
Titley Hereford 48 C5
Titlington Northumb 117 C7
Titsey Sur 28 D5
Tittensor Staffs 75 F5
Tittleshall Norf 80 E4
Tiverton Ches W 74 C2
Tiverton Devon 10 C4
Tivetshall St Margaret Norf 68 F4
Tivetshall St Mary Norf 68 F4
Tividale W Mid 62 E3
Tivy Dale S Yorks 88 D3
Tixall Staffs 62 B3
Tixover Rutland 65 D6
Toab Orkney 159 H6
Toab Shetland 160 M5
Toadmoor Derbys 76 D3
Tobermory Argyll 147 F8
Toberonochy Argyll 124 E3
Tobha Mor W Isles 148 E2
Tobhtarol W Isles 154 D6
Tobson W Isles 154 D6
Tocher Aberds 153 E6
Tockenham Wilts 24 B5
Tockenham Wick Wilts 37 F7
Tockholes Blackburn 86 B4
Tockington S Glos 36 F3
Tockwith N Yorks 95 D7
Todber Dorset 13 B6
Todding Hereford 49 B6
Toddington C Beds 40 B3
Toddington Glos 50 F5
Todenham Glos 51 F7
Todhills Cumb 108 C3
Todlachie Aberds 141 C5
Todmorden W Yorks 87 B7
Todrig Borders 115 C7
Todwick S Yorks 89 F5
Toft Cambs 54 D4
Toft Lincs 65 C7
Toft Hill Durham 101 B6
Toft Hill Lincs 78 C5
Toft Monks Norf 69 E7
Toft next Newton Lincs 90 F4
Toftrees Norf 80 E4
Tofts Highld 158 D5
Toftwood Norf 68 C2
Togston Northumb 117 D8
Tokavaig Highld 149 G11
Tokers Green Oxon 26 B5
Tolastadh a Chaolais W Isles 154 D6
Tolastadh bho Thuath W Isles 155 C10
Toll Bar S Yorks 89 D6
Toll End W Mid 62 E3
Toll of Birness Aberds 153 E10
Tolland Som 22 F3
Tollard Royal Wilts 13 C7
Tollbar End W Mid 51 B8
Toller Fratrum Dorset 12 E3
Toller Porcorum Dorset 12 E3
Tollerton N Yorks 95 C8
Tollerton Notts 77 F6
Tollesbury Essex 43 C5
Tolleshunt D'Arcy Essex 43 C5
Tolleshunt Major Essex 43 C5
Tolm W Isles 155 D9
Tolpuddle Dorset 13 E5
Tolvah Highld 138 E4
Tolworth London 28 C2
Tomatin Highld 138 B4
Tombreck Highld 151 H9
Tomchrasky Highld 137 C5
Tomdoun Highld 136 D4
Tomich Highld 137 B6
Tomich Highld 151 D9
Tomich House Highld 151 G8
Tomintoul Aberds 139 E7
Tomintoul Moray 139 C7
Tomnaven Moray 152 E4
Tomnavoulin Moray 139 B8
Ton-Pentre Rhondda 34 E3
Tonbridge Kent 29 E6
Tondu Bridgend 34 F2
Tonfanau Gwyn 58 D2
Tong Shrops 61 D7
Tong W Yorks 94 F5
Tong Norton Shrops 61 D7
Tonge Leics 63 B8
Tongham Sur 27 E6
Tongland Dumfries 106 D3
Tongue Highld 157 D8
Tongue End Lincs 65 C8
Tongwynlais Cardiff 35 F5
Tonna Neath 34 E1
Tonwell Herts 41 C6
Tonypandy Rhondda 34 E3
Tonyrefail Rhondda 34 F4
Toot Baldon Oxon 39 D5
Toot Hill Essex 41 D8
Toothill Hants 14 C4
Top of Hebers Gtr Man 87 D6
Topcliffe N Yorks 95 B7
Topcroft Norf 69 E5
Topcroft Street Norf 69 E5
Toppesfield Essex 55 F8
Toppings Gtr Man 86 C5
Topsham Devon 10 F4
Torbay Torbay 7 D7
Torbeg N Ayrs 143 F10
Torboll Farm Highld 151 B10
Torbrex Stirling 127 E6
Torbryan Devon 7 C6
Torcross Devon 7 E6
Tore Highld 151 F9
Torinturk Argyll 145 G7
Torksey Lincs 77 B8
Torlum W Isles 148 C2
Torlundy Highld 131 B5
Tormarton S Glos 24 B2
Tormisdale Argyll 142 C2
Tormitchell S Ayrs 112 E2
Tormore N Ayrs 143 E9
Tornagrain Highld 151 G10
Tornahaish Aberds 139 D8
Tornaveen Aberds 140 D5
Torness Highld 137 B8
Toronto Durham 110 F4
Torpenhow Cumb 108 F2
Torphichen W Loth 120 B2
Torphins Aberds 140 D5
Torpoint Corn 6 D2
Torquay Torbay 7 C7
Torquhan Borders 121 E7
Torran Argyll 124 E4
Torran Highld 149 D10
Torran Highld 151 D10
Torrance E Dunb 119 B6
Torrans Argyll 146 J7
Torranyard N Ayrs 118 E3
Torre Torbay 7 C7
Torridon Highld 150 F2
Torridon Ho. Highld 149 C13
Torrin Highld 149 F10
Torrisdale Highld 157 C9
Torrisdale-Square Argyll 143 E8
Torrish Highld 157 H12
Torrisholme Lancs 92 C4
Torroble Highld 157 J8
Torry Aberdeen 141 D8
Torry Aberds 152 E4
Torryburn Fife 128 F2
Torterston Aberds 153 D10
Torthorwald Dumfries 107 B7
Tortington W Sus 16 D4
Tortworth S Glos 36 E4
Torvaig Highld 149 D9
Torver Cumb 98 E4
Torwood Falk 127 F7
Torworth Notts 89 F7
Tosberry Devon 8 B4
Toscaig Highld 149 E12
Toseland Cambs 54 C3
Tosside N Yorks 93 D7
Tostock Suff 56 C3
Totaig Highld 148 C7
Totaig Highld 149 F13
Tote Highld 149 D9
Totegan Highld 157 C11
Tothill Lincs 91 F8
Totland IoW 14 F4
Totnes Devon 7 C6
Toton Notts 76 F5
Totronald Argyll 146 F4
Totscore Highld 149 B8
Tottenham London 41 E6
Tottenhill Norf 67 C6
Tottenhill Row Norf 67 C6
Totteridge London 41 E5
Totternhoe C Beds 40 B2
Tottington Gtr Man 87 C5
Totton Hants 14 C4
Touchen End Windsor 27 B6
Tournaig Highld 155 J13
Toux Aberds 153 C9
Tovil Kent 29 D8
Tow Law Durham 110 F4
Toward Argyll 145 G10
Towcester Northants 52 E4
Towednack Corn 2 C3
Tower End Norf 67 C6
Towersey Oxon 39 D7
Towie Aberds 140 C3
Towie Aberds 153 B8
Towiemore Moray 152 D3
Town End Cambs 66 E4
Town End Cumb 99 F6
Town Row E Sus 18 B2
Town Yetholm Borders 116 B4
Townend W Dunb 118 B4
Towngate Lincs 65 C8
Townhead Cumb 108 F5
Townhead Dumfries 106 E3
Townhead S Ayrs 112 D2
Townhead S Yorks 88 D2
Townhead of Greenlaw Dumfries 106 C4
Townhill Fife 128 F3
Townsend Bucks 39 D7
Townsend Herts 40 D4
Townshend Corn 2 C4
Towthorpe York 96 D2
Towton N Yorks 95 F7
Towyn Conwy 72 B3
Toxteth Mers 85 F4
Toynton All Saints Lincs 79 C6
Toynton Fen Side Lincs 79 C6
Toynton St Peter Lincs 79 C7
Toy's Hill Kent 29 D5
Trabboch E Ayrs 112 B4
Traboe Corn 3 D6
Tradespark Highld 151 F11
Tradespark Orkney 159 H5
Trafford Park Gtr Man 87 E5
Trallong Powys 34 B3
Tranent E Loth 121 B7
Tranmere Mers 85 F4
Trantlebeg Highld 157 D11
Trantlemore Highld 157 D11
Tranwell Northumb 117 F7
Trapp Carms 33 C7
Traprain E Loth 121 B8
Traquair Borders 121 F6
Trawden Lancs 94 F2
Trawsfynydd Gwyn 71 D8
Tre-Gibbon Rhondda 34 D3
Tre-Taliesin Ceredig 58 E3
Tre-vaughan Carms 32 B4
Tre-wyn Mon 35 B7
Trealaw Rhondda 34 E4
Treales Lancs 92 F4
Trearddur Anglesey 82 D2
Treaslane Highld 149 C8
Trebanog Rhondda 34 E4
Trebanos Neath 33 D8
Trebartha Corn 5 B7
Trebarwith Corn 8 F2
Trebetherick Corn 4 B4
Treborough Som 22 F2
Trebudannon Corn 4 C4
Trebullett Corn 5 B8
Treburley Corn 5 B8
Trebyan Corn 5 C5
Trecastle Powys 34 B2
Trecenydd Caerph 35 F5
Trecwn Pembs 44 B4
Trecynon Rhondda 34 D3
Tredavoe Corn 2 D3
Trederwen Powys 60 C2
Tredegar Bl Gwent 35 D5
Tredegar = Newydd New Tredegar Caerph 35 D5
Tredington Glos 37 B6
Tredington Warks 51 E7
Tredinnick Corn 4 B4
Tredomen Powys 48 F3
Tredunnock Mon 35 E7
Tredustan Powys 48 F3
Treen Corn 2 D2
Treeton S Yorks 88 F5
Tref-Y-Clawdd = Knighton Powys 48 B4
Trefaldwyn = Montgomery Powys 60 E2
Trefasser Pembs 44 B3
Trefdraeth Anglesey 82 D4
Trefdraeth = Newport Pembs 45 F2
Trefecca Powys 48 F3
Trefechan Ceredig 58 F2
Trefeglwys Powys 59 E6
Trefenter Ceredig 46 C5
Treffgarne Pembs 44 C4
Treffynnon = Holywell Flint 73 B5
Treffynnon Pembs 44 C3
Trefgarn Owen Pembs 44 C3
Trefil Bl Gwent 35 C5
Trefilan Ceredig 46 D4
Trefin Pembs 44 B3
Treflach Shrops 60 B2
Trefnanney Powys 60 C2
Trefnant Denb 72 B4
Trefonen Shrops 60 B2
Trefor Anglesey 82 C3
Trefor Gwyn 70 C4
Treforest Rhondda 34 F4
Trefriw Conwy 83 E7
Trefynwy = Monmouth Mon 36 C2
Tregadillett Corn 8 F4
Tregaian Anglesey 82 D4
Tregare Mon 35 C8
Tregaron Ceredig 47 D5
Tregarth Gwyn 83 E6
Tregeare Corn 8 F4
Tregeiriog Wrex 73 F5
Tregele Anglesey 82 B3
Tregidden Corn 3 D6
Treglemais Pembs 44 C3
Tregole Corn 8 E3
Tregonetha Corn 4 C4
Tregony Corn 3 B8
Tregoss Corn 4 C4
Tregoyd Powys 48 F4
Tregroes Ceredig 46 E3
Tregurrian Corn 4 C3
Tregynon Powys 59 E7
Trehafod Rhondda 34 E4
Treharris M Tydf 34 E4
Treherbert Rhondda 34 E3
Trekenner Corn 5 B8
Treknow Corn 8 F2
Trelan Corn 3 E6
Trelash Corn 8 E3
Trelassick Corn 4 D3
Trelawnyd Flint 72 B4
Trelech Carms 45 F4
Treleddyd-fawr Pembs 44 C2
Trelewis M Tydf 35 E5
Treligga Corn 8 F2
Trelights Corn 4 B4
Trelill Corn 4 B5
Trelissick Corn 3 C7
Trellech Mon 36 D2
Trelleck Grange Mon 36 D1
Trelogan Flint 85 F2
Trelystan Powys 60 D2
Tremadog Gwyn 71 C6
Tremail Corn 8 F3
Tremain Ceredig 45 E4
Tremaine Corn 8 F4
Tremar Corn 5 C7
Trematon Corn 5 D8
Tremeirchion Denb 72 B4
Trenance Corn 4 C3
Trenarren Corn 3 B9
Trench Telford 61 C6
Treneglos Corn 8 F4
Trenewan Corn 5 D6
Trent Dorset 12 C3
Trent Vale Stoke 75 E5
Trentham Stoke 75 E5
Trentishoe Devon 20 E5
Treoes V Glam 21 B8
Treorchy = Treorci Rhondda 34 E3
Treorci = Treorchy Rhondda 34 E3
Tre'r-ddôl Ceredig 58 E3
Trerulefoot Corn 5 D8
Tresaith Ceredig 45 D4
Tresawle Corn 3 B7
Trescott Staffs 62 E2
Trescowe Corn 2 C4
Tresham Glos 36 E4
Tresillian Corn 3 B7
Tresinwen Pembs 44 A4
Treskinnick Cross Corn 8 E4
Tresmeer Corn 8 F4
Tresparrett Corn 8 E3
Tresparrett Posts Corn 8 E3
Tressait Perth 133 C5
Tresta Shetland 160 D8
Tresta Shetland 160 H5
Treswell Notts 77 B7
Trethosa Corn 4 D4
Trethurgy Corn 4 D5
Tretio Pembs 44 C2
Tretire Hereford 36 B2
Tretower Powys 35 B5
Treuddyn Flint 73 D6
Trevalga Corn 8 F2
Trevalyn Wrex 73 D7
Trevanson Corn 4 B4
Trevarren Corn 4 C4
Trevarrian Corn 4 C3
Trevarrick Corn 3 B8
Trevaughan Carms 32 C2
Treveighan Corn 5 B5
Trevellas Corn 4 D2
Treverva Corn 3 C6
Trevethin Torf 35 D6
Trevigro Corn 5 C8
Treviscoe Corn 4 D4
Trevone Corn 4 B3
Trewarmett Corn 8 F2
Trewassa Corn 8 F3
Trewellard Corn 2 C2
Trewen Corn 8 F4
Trewennack Corn 3 D5
Trewern Powys 60 C2
Trewethern Corn 4 B5
Trewidland Corn 5 D7
Trewint Corn 8 E3
Trewint Corn 8 F4
Trewithian Corn 3 C7
Trewoofe Corn 2 D3
Trewoon Corn 4 D4
Treworga Corn 3 B7
Treworlas Corn 3 C7
Treyarnon Corn 4 B3
Treyford W Sus 16 C2
Trezaise Corn 4 D4
Triangle W Yorks 87 B8
Trickett's Cross Dorset 13 D8
Triffleton Pembs 44 C4
Trimdon Durham 111 F6
Trimdon Colliery Durham 111 F6
Trimdon Grange Durham 111 F6
Trimingham Norf 81 D8
Trimley Lower Street Suff 57 F6
Trimley St Martin Suff 57 F6
Trimley St Mary Suff 57 F6
Trimpley Worcs 50 B2
Trimsaran Carms 33 D5
Trimstone Devon 20 E3
Trinafour Perth 132 C4
Trinant Caerph 35 D6
Tring Herts 40 C2
Tring Wharf Herts 40 C2
Trinity Angus 135 C6
Trinity Jersey 17
Trisant Ceredig 47 B6
Trislaig Highld 130 B4
Trispen Corn 4 D3
Tritlington Northumb 117 E8
Trochry Perth 133 E6
Trodigal Argyll 143 F7
Troed-rhiwdalar Powys 47 D8
Troedyraur Ceredig 46 E2
Troedyrhiw M Tydf 34 D4
Tromode IoM 84 E3
Trondavoe Shetland 160 F5
Troon Corn 3 C5
Troon S Ayrs 118 F3
Trosaraidh W Isles 148 G2
Trossachs Hotel Stirling 126 D4
Troston Suff 56 B2
Trottiscliffe Kent 29 C7
Trotton W Sus 16 B2
Troutbeck Cumb 99 B5
Troutbeck Cumb 99 D6
Troutbeck Bridge Cumb 99 D6
Trow Green Glos 36 D2
Trowbridge Wilts 24 D3
Trowell Notts 76 F4
Trowle Common Wilts 24 D3
Trowley Bottom Herts 40 C3
Trows Borders 122 F2
Trowse Newton Norf 68 D5
Trudoxhill Som 24 E2
Trull Som 11 B7
Trumaisgearraidh W Isles 148 A3
Trumpan Highld 148 B7
Trumpet Hereford 49 F8
Trumpington Cambs 54 D5
Trunch Norf 81 D8
Trunnah Lancs 92 E3
Truro Corn 3 B7
Trusham Devon 10 F3
Trusley Derbys 76 F2
Trusthorpe Lincs 91 F9
Trysull Staffs 62 E2
Tubney Oxon 38 E4
Tuckenhay Devon 7 D6
Tuckhill Shrops 61 F7
Tuckingmill Corn 3 B5
Tuddenham Suff 55 B8
Tuddenham St Martin Suff 57 E5
Tudeley Kent 29 E7
Tudhoe Durham 111 F5
Tudorville Hereford 36 B2
Tudweiliog Gwyn 70 D3
Tuesley Sur 27 E7
Tuffley Glos 37 C5
Tufton Hants 26 E2
Tufton Pembs 32 B1
Tugby Leics 64 D4
Tugford Shrops 61 F5
Tullibardine Perth 127 C8
Tullibody Clack 127 E7
Tullich Argyll 125 D6
Tullich Highld 138 B2
Tullich Muir Highld 151 D10
Tulliemet Perth 133 D6
Tulloch Aberds 135 B7
Tulloch Aberds 153 E8
Tulloch Perth 128 B2
Tulloch Castle Highld 151 E8
Tullochgorm Argyll 125 F5
Tulloes Angus 135 E5
Tullybannocher Perth 127 B6
Tullybelton Perth 133 F7
Tullyfergus Perth 134 E2
Tullymurdoch Perth 134 D1
Tullynessle Aberds 140 C4
Tumble Carms 33 C6
Tumby Woodside Lincs 79 D5
Tummel Bridge Perth 132 D4
Tunga W Isles 155 D9
Tunstall E Yorks 97 F9
Tunstall Kent 30 C2
Tunstall Lancs 93 B6
Tunstall N Yorks 101 E7
Tunstall Norf 69 D7
Tunstall Stoke 75 D5
Tunstall Suff 57 D7
Tunstall T&W 111 D6
Tunstead Derbys 75 B8
Tunstead Gtr Man 87 D8
Tunstead Norf 81 E8
Tunworth Hants 26 E4
Tupsley Hereford 49 E7
Tupton Derbys 76 C3
Tur Langton Leics 64 E4
Turgis Green Hants 26 D4
Turin Angus 135 D5
Turkdean Glos 37 C8
Turleigh Wilts 24 C3
Turn Lancs 87 C6
Turnastone Hereford 49 F5
Turnberry S Ayrs 112 D2
Turnditch Derbys 76 E2
Turners Hill W Sus 28 F4
Turners Puddle Dorset 13 E6
Turnford Herts 41 D6
Turnhouse Edin 120 B4
Turnworth Dorset 13 D6
Turriff Aberds 153 C7
Turton Bottoms Blackburn 86 C5
Turves Cambs 66 E3
Turvey Bedford 53 D7
Turville Bucks 39 E7
Turville Heath Bucks 39 E7
Turweston Bucks 52 F4
Tushielaw Borders 115 C6
Tutbury Staffs 63 B6
Tutnall Worcs 50 B4
Tutshill Glos 36 E2
Tuttington Norf 81 E8
Tutts Clump W Berks 26 B3
Tuxford Notts 77 B7
Twatt Orkney 159 F3
Twatt Shetland 160 H5
Twechar E Dunb 119 B7
Tweedmouth Northumb 123 D5
Tweedsmuir Borders 114 B3
Twelve Heads Corn 3 B6
Twemlow Green Ches E 74 C4
Twenty Lincs 65 B8
Twerton Bath 24 C2
Twickenham London 28 B2
Twigworth Glos 37 B5
Twineham W Sus 17 C6
Twinhoe Bath 24 D2
Twinstead Essex 56 F2
Twinstead Green Essex 56 F2
Twiss Green Warr 86 E4
Twiston Lancs 93 E8
Twitchen Devon 21 F6
Twitchen Shrops 49 B5
Two Bridges Devon 6 B4
Two Dales Derbys 76 C2
Two Mills Ches W 73 B7
Twycross Leics 63 D7
Twyford Bucks 39 B6
Twyford Derbys 63 B7
Twyford Hants 15 B5
Twyford Leics 64 C4
Twyford Lincs 65 B6
Twyford Norf 81 E6
Twyford Wokingham 27 B5
Twyford Common Hereford 49 F7
Twyn-y-Sheriff Mon 35 D8
Twynholm Dumfries 106 D3
Twyning Glos 50 F3
Twyning Green Glos 50 F4
Twynllanan Carms 34 B1
Twynmynydd Carms 33 C7
Twywell Northants 53 B7
Ty-draw Conwy 83 F8
Ty-hen Carms 32 B4
Ty-hen Gwyn 70 D2
Ty-mawr Anglesey 82 C4
Ty Mawr Carms 46 E4
Ty Mawr Cwm Conwy 72 E3
Ty-nant Conwy 72 E3
Ty-nant Gwyn 59 B6
Ty-uchaf Powys 59 B7
Tyberton Hereford 49 F5
Tyburn W Mid 62 E5
Tycroes Carms 33 C7
Tycrwyn Powys 59 C8
Tydd Gote Lincs 66 C4
Tydd St Giles Cambs 66 C4
Tydd St Mary Lincs 66 C4
Tyddewi = St David's Pembs 44 C2
Tyddyn-mawr Gwyn 71 C6
Tye Green Essex 41 D7
Tye Green Essex 42 B3
Tye Green Essex 55 F6
Tyldesley Gtr Man 86 D4
Tyler Hill Kent 30 C5
Tylers Green Bucks 40 E2
Tylorstown Rhondda 34 E4
Tylwch Powys 59 F6
Tyn-y-celyn Wrex 73 F5
Tyn-y-coed Shrops 60 B2
Tyn-y-fedwen Powys 72 F5
Tyn-y-ffridd Powys 72 F5
Tyn-y-graig Powys 48 D2
Ty'n-y-groes Conwy 83 D7
Ty'n-y-maes Gwyn 83 E6
Tyn-y-pwll Anglesey 82 C4
Ty'n-yr-eithin Ceredig 47 C5
Tyncelyn Ceredig 46 C5
Tyndrum Stirling 131 F7
Tyne Tunnel T&W 111 C6
Tyneham Dorset 13 F6
Tynehead Midloth 121 D6
Tynemouth T&W 111 C6
Tynewydd Rhondda 34 E3
Tyninghame E Loth 122 B2
Tynron Dumfries 113 E8
Tynygongl Anglesey 82 C5
Tynygraig Ceredig 47 C5
Tŷ'r-felin-isaf Conwy 83 E8
Tyrie Aberds 153 B9
Tyringham M Keynes 53 E6
Tythecott Devon 9 C6
Tythegston Bridgend 21 B7
Tytherington Ches E 75 B6
Tytherington S Glos 36 F3
Tytherington Som 24 E2
Tytherington Wilts 24 E4
Tytherleigh Devon 11 D8
Tywardreath Corn 5 D5
Tywyn Conwy 83 D7
Tywyn Gwyn 58 D2

U

Uachdar W Isles 148 C2
Uags Highld 149 E12
Ubbeston Green Suff 57 B7
Ubley Bath 23 D7
Uckerby N Yorks 101 D7
Uckfield E Sus 17 B8
Uckington Glos 37 B6
Uddingston S Lanark 119 C6
Uddington S Lanark 119 F8
Udimore E Sus 19 D5
Udny Green Aberds 141 B7
Udny Station Aberds 141 B8
Udston S Lanark 119 D6
Udstonhead S Lanark 119 E7
Uffcott Wilts 25 B6
Uffculme Devon 11 C5
Uffington Lincs 65 D7
Uffington Oxon 38 F3
Uffington Shrops 60 C5
Ufford Pboro 65 D7
Ufford Suff 57 D6
Ufton Warks 51 C8
Ufton Nervet W Berks 26 C4
Ugadale Argyll 143 F8
Ugborough Devon 6 D4
Uggeshall Suff 69 F7
Ugglebarnby N Yorks 103 D6
Ughill S Yorks 88 E3
Ugley Essex 41 B8
Ugley Green Essex 41 B8
Ugthorpe N Yorks 103 C5
Uidh W Isles 148 J1
Uig Argyll 145 E10
Uig Highld 148 C6
Uig Highld 149 B8
Uigen W Isles 154 D5
Uigshader Highld 149 D9
Uisken Argyll 146 K6
Ulbster Highld 158 F5
Ulceby Lincs 79 B7
Ulceby N Lincs 90 C5
Ulceby Skitter N Lincs 90 C5
Ulcombe Kent 30 E2
Uldale Cumb 108 F2
Uley Glos 36 E4
Ulgham Northumb 117 E8
Ullapool Highld 150 B4
Ullenhall Warks 51 C6
Ullenwood Glos 37 C6
Ulleskelf N Yorks 95 E8
Ullesthorpe Leics 64 F2
Ulley S Yorks 89 F5
Ullingswick Hereford 49 E7
Ullinish Highld 149 E8
Ullock Cumb 98 B2
Ulnes Walton Lancs 86 C3
Ulpha Cumb 98 E3
Ulrome E Yorks 97 D7
Ulsta Shetland 160 E6
Ulva House Argyll 146 H7
Ulverston Cumb 92 B2
Ulwell Dorset 13 F8
Umberleigh Devon 9 B8
Unapool Highld 156 F5
Unasary W Isles 148 F2
Underbarrow Cumb 99 E6
Undercliffe W Yorks 94 F4
Underhoull Shetland 160 C7
Underriver Kent 29 D6
Underwood Notts 76 D4
Undy Mon 35 F8
Unifirth Shetland 160 H4
Union Cottage Aberds 141 E7
Union Mills IoM 84 E3
Union Street E Sus 18 B4
Unstone Derbys 76 B3
Unstone Green Derbys 76 B3
Unthank Cumb 108 F4
Unthank Cumb 109 E6
Unthank End Cumb 108 F4
Up Cerne Dorset 12 D4
Up Exe Devon 10 D4
Up Hatherley Glos 37 B6
Up Holland Lancs 86 D3
Up Marden W Sus 15 C8
Up Nately Hants 26 D4
Up Somborne Hants 25 F8
Up Sydling Dorset 12 D4
Upavon Wilts 25 D6
Upchurch Kent 30 C2
Upcott Hereford 48 D5
Upend Cambs 55 D7
Upgate Norf 68 C4
Uphall W Loth 120 B3
Uphall Station W Loth 120 B3
Upham Devon 10 D3
Upham Hants 15 B6
Uphampton Worcs 50 C3
Uphill N Som 22 D5
Uplawmoor E Renf 118 D4
Upleadon Glos 36 B4
Upleatham Redcar 102 C4
Uplees Kent 30 C3
Uploders Dorset 12 E3
Uplowman Devon 10 C5
Uplyme Devon 11 E8
Upminster London 42 F1
Upnor Medway 29 B8
Upottery Devon 11 D7
Upper Affcot Shrops 60 F4
Upper Ardchronie Highld 151 C9
Upper Arley Worcs 61 F7
Upper Arncott Oxon 39 C6
Upper Astrop Northants 52 F3
Upper Badcall Highld 156 E4
Upper Basildon W Berks 26 B3
Upper Beeding W Sus 17 C5
Upper Benefield Northants 65 F6
Upper Bighouse Highld 157 D11
Upper Boddington Northants 52 D2
Upper Borth Ceredig 58 F3
Upper Boyndlie Aberds 153 B9
Upper Brailes Warks 51 F8
Upper Breakish Highld 149 F11
Upper Breinton Hereford 49 E6
Upper Broadheath Worcs 50 D3
Upper Broughton Notts 64 B3
Upper Bucklebury W Berks 26 C3
Upper Burnhaugh Aberds 141 E7
Upper Caldecote C Beds 54 E2
Upper Catesby Northants 52 D3
Upper Chapel Powys 48 E2
Upper Church Village Rhondda 34 F4
Upper Chute Wilts 25 D7
Upper Clatford Hants 25 E8
Upper Clynnog Gwyn 71 C5
Upper Cumberworth W Yorks 88 D3
Upper Cwm-twrch Powys 34 C1
Upper Cwmbran Torf 35 E6
Upper Dallachy Moray 152 B3
Upper Dean Bedford 53 C8
Upper Denby W Yorks 88 D3
Upper Denton Cumb 109 C6
Upper Derraid Highld 151 H13
Upper Dicker E Sus 18 E2
Upper Dovercourt Essex 57 F6
Upper Druimfin Argyll 147 F8
Upper Dunsforth N Yorks 95 C7
Upper Eathie Highld 151 E10
Upper Elkstone Staffs 75 D7
Upper End Derbys 75 B7
Upper Farringdon Hants 26 F5
Upper Framilode Glos 36 C4
Upper Glenfintaig Highld 137 F5
Upper Gornal W Mid 62 E3
Upper Gravenhurst C Beds 54 F2
Upper Green Mon 35 C7
Upper Green W Berks 25 C8
Upper Grove Common Hereford 36 B2
Upper Hackney Derbys 76 C2
Upper Hale Sur 27 E6
Upper Halistra Highld 148 C7
Upper Halling Medway 29 C7
Upper Hambleton Rutland 65 D6
Upper Hardres Court Kent 31 D5
Upper Hartfield E Sus 29 F5
Upper Haugh S Yorks 88 E5
Upper Heath Shrops 61 F5
Upper Hellesdon Norf 68 C5
Upper Helmsley N Yorks 96 D2
Upper Hergest Hereford 48 D4
Upper Heyford Northants 52 D4
Upper Heyford Oxon 38 B4
Upper Hill Hereford 49 D6
Upper Hopton W Yorks 88 C2
Upper Horsebridge E Sus 18 D2
Upper Hulme Staffs 75 C7
Upper Inglesham Swindon 38 E2
Upper Inverbrough Highld 151 H11
Upper Killay Swansea 33 E6
Upper Knockando Moray 152 D1
Upper Lambourn W Berks 38 F3
Upper Leigh Staffs 75 F7
Upper Lenie Highld 137 B8
Upper Lochton Aberds 141 E5
Upper Longdon Staffs 62 C4
Upper Lybster Highld 158 G4
Upper Lydbrook Glos 36 C3
Upper Maes-coed Hereford 48 F5
Upper Midway Derbys 63 B6
Upper Milovaig Highld 148 D6
Upper Minety Wilts 37 E7
Upper Mitton Worcs 50 B3
Upper North Dean Bucks 39 E8
Upper Obney Perth 133 F7
Upper Ollach Highld 149 E10
Upper Padley Derbys 76 B2
Upper Pollicott Bucks 39 C7
Upper Poppleton York 95 D8
Upper Quinton Warks 51 E6
Upper Ratley Hants 14 B4
Upper Rissington Glos 38 C2
Upper Rochford Worcs 49 C8
Upper Sandaig Highld 149 G12
Upper Sanday Orkney 159 H6
Upper Sapey Hereford 49 C8
Upper Saxondale Notts 77 F6
Upper Seagry Wilts 37 F6
Upper Shelton C Beds 53 E7
Upper Sheringham Norf 81 C7
Upper Skelmorlie N Ayrs 118 C2
Upper Slaughter Glos 38 B1
Upper Soudley Glos 36 C3
Upper Stondon C Beds 54 F2
Upper Stowe Northants 52 D4
Upper Stratton Swindon 38 F1
Upper Street Hants 14 C2
Upper Street Norf 69 C6
Upper Street Norf 69 C6
Upper Street Suff 56 F5
Upper Strensham Worcs 50 F4
Upper Sundon C Beds 40 B3
Upper Swell Glos 38 B1
Upper Tean Staffs 75 F7
Upper Tillyrie Perth 128 D3
Upper Tooting London 28 B3
Upper Tote Highld 149 C10
Upper Town N Som 23 C7
Upper Treverward Shrops 48 B4
Upper Tysoe Warks 51 E8
Upper Upham Wilts 25 B7
Upper Wardington Oxon 52 E2
Upper Weald M Keynes 53 F5
Upper Weedon Northants 52 D4
Upper Wield Hants 26 F4
Upper Winchendon Bucks 39 C7
Upper Witton W Mid 62 E4
Upper Woodend Aberds 141 C5
Upper Woodford Wilts 25 F6
Upper Wootton Hants 26 D3
Upper Wyche Hereford 50 E2
Upperby Cumb 108 D4
Uppermill Gtr Man 87 D7
Uppersound Shetland 160 J6
Upperthong W Yorks 88 D2
Upperthorpe N Lincs 89 D8
Upperton W Sus 16 B3
Uppertown Derbys 76 C3
Uppertown Highld 158 C5
Uppertown Orkney 159 J5
Uppingham Rutland 65 E5
Uppington Shrops 61 D6
Upsall N Yorks 102 F2
Upshire Essex 41 D7
Upstreet Kent 31 C6
Upthorpe Suff 56 B3
Upton Cambs 54 B2
Upton Ches W 73 C8
Upton Corn 8 D4
Upton Dorset 12 F5
Upton Dorset 13 E7
Upton Hants 14 C4
Upton Hants 25 D8
Upton Leics 63 E7
Upton Lincs 90 F2
Upton Mers 85 F3
Upton Norf 69 C6
Upton Northants 52 C5
Upton Notts 77 B7
Upton Notts 77 D7
Upton Oxon 39 F5
Upton Pboro 65 D8
Upton Slough 27 B7
Upton Som 10 B4
Upton W Yorks 89 C5
Upton Bishop Hereford 36 B3
Upton Cheyney S Glos 23 C8
Upton Cressett Shrops 61 E6
Upton Cross Corn 5 B7
Upton Grey Hants 26 E4
Upton Hellions Devon 10 D3
Upton Lovell Wilts 24 E4
Upton Magna Shrops 61 C5
Upton Noble Som 24 F2
Upton Pyne Devon 10 E4
Upton Scudamore Wilts 24 E3
Upton St Leonard's Glos 37 C5
Upton Snodsbury Worcs 50 D4
Upton upon Severn Worcs 50 E3
Upton Warren Worcs 50 C4
Upwaltham W Sus 16 C3
Upware Cambs 55 B6
Upwell Norf 66 D4
Upwey Dorset 12 F4
Upwood Cambs 66 F2
Uradale Shetland 160 K6
Urafirth Shetland 160 F5
Urchfont Wilts 24 D5
Urdimarsh Hereford 49 E7
Ure Shetland 160 F4
Ure Bank N Yorks 95 B6
Urgha W Isles 154 H6
Urishay Common Hereford 48 F5
Urlay Nook Stockton 102 C1
Urmston Gtr Man 87 E5
Urpeth Durham 110 D5
Urquhart Highld 151 F8
Urquhart Moray 152 B2
Urra N Yorks 102 D3
Urray Highld 151 F8
Ushaw Moor Durham 110 E5
Usk = Brynbuga Mon 35 D7
Usselby Lincs 90 E4
Usworth T&W 111 D6
Utkinton Ches W 74 C2
Utley W Yorks 94 E3
Uton Devon 10 E3
Utterby Lincs 91 E7
Uttoxeter Staffs 75 F7
Uwchmynydd Gwyn 70 E2
Uxbridge London 40 F3
Uyeasound Shetland 160 C7
Uzmaston Pembs 44 D4

V

Valley Anglesey 82 D2
Valley Truckle Corn 8 F2
Valleyfield Dumfries 106 D3
Valsgarth Shetland 160 B8
Valtos Highld 149 B10
Van Powys 59 F6
Vange Essex 42 F3
Varteg Torf 35 D6
Vatten Highld 149 D7
Vaul Argyll 146 G3
Vaynor M Tydf 34 C4
Veensgarth Shetland 160 J6
Velindre Powys 48 F3
Vellow Som 22 F2
Veness Orkney 159 F6
Venn Green Devon 9 C5
Venn Ottery Devon 11 E5
Vennington Shrops 60 D3
Venny Tedburn Devon 10 E3
Ventnor IoW 15 G6
Vernham Dean Hants 25 D8
Vernham Street Hants 25 D8
Vernolds Common Shrops 60 F4
Verwood Dorset 13 D8
Veryan Corn 3 C8
Vicarage Devon 11 F7
Vickerstown Cumb 92 C1
Victoria Corn 4 C4
Victoria S Yorks 88 D2
Vidlin Shetland 160 G6
Viewpark N Lanark 119 C7
Vigo Village Kent 29 C7
Vinehall Street E Sus 18 C4
Vine's Cross E Sus 18 D2
Viney Hill Glos 36 D3
Virginia Water Sur 27 C8
Virginstow Devon 9 E5
Vobster Som 24 E2
Voe Shetland 160 E5
Voe Shetland 160 G6
Vowchurch Hereford 49 F5
Voxter Shetland 160 F5
Voy Orkney 159 G3

W

Wackerfield Durham 101 B6
Wacton Norf 68 E4
Wadbister Shetland 160 J6
Wadborough Worcs 50 E4
Waddesdon Bucks 39 C7
Waddingham Lincs 90 E3
Waddington Lancs 93 E7
Waddington Lincs 78 C2
Wadebridge Corn 4 B4
Wadeford Som 11 C8
Wadenhoe Northants 65 F7
Wadesmill Herts 41 C6
Wadhurst E Sus 18 B3
Wadshelf Derbys 76 B3
Wadsley S Yorks 88 E4
Wadsley Bridge S Yorks 88 E4
Wadworth S Yorks 89 E6
Waen Denb 72 C3
Waen Denb 72 C5
Waen Fach Powys 60 C2
Waen Goleugoed Denb 72 B4
Wag Highld 157 G13
Wainfleet All Saints Lincs 79 D7
Wainfleet Bank Lincs 79 D7
Wainfleet St Mary Lincs 79 D8
Wainfleet Tofts Lincs 79 D7
Wainhouse Corner Corn 8 E3
Wainscott Medway 29 B8
Wainstalls W Yorks 87 B8
Waitby Cumb 100 D2
Waithe Lincs 91 D6
Wake Lady Green N Yorks 102 E4
Wakefield W Yorks 88 B4
Wakerley Northants 65 E6
Wakes Colne Essex 42 B4
Walberswick Suff 57 B8
Walberton W Sus 16 D3
Walbottle T&W 110 C4
Walcot Lincs 78 F3
Walcot N Lincs 90 B2
Walcot Shrops 60 F3
Walcot Swindon 38 F1
Walcot Telford 61 C5
Walcot Green Norf 68 F4
Walcote Leics 64 F2
Walcote Warks 51 D6
Walcott Lincs 78 D4
Walcott Norf 69 A6
Walden N Yorks 101 F5
Walden Head N Yorks 100 F4
Walden Stubbs N Yorks 89 C6
Waldersey Cambs 66 D4
Walderslade Medway 29 C8
Walderton W Sus 15 C8
Walditch Dorset 12 E2
Waldley Derbys 75 F8
Waldridge Durham 111 D5
Waldringfield Suff 57 E6
Waldringfield Heath Suff 57 E6
Waldron E Sus 18 D2
Wales S Yorks 89 F5
Walesby Lincs 90 E5
Walesby Notts 77 B6
Walford Hereford 36 B2
Walford Hereford 49 B5
Walford Shrops 60 B4

Walford Heath Shrops 60 C4
Walgherton Ches E 74 E3
Walgrave Northants 53 B6
Walhampton Hants 14 E4
Walk Mill Lancs 93 F8
Walkden Gtr Man 86 D5
Walker T&W 111 C5
Walker Barn Ches E 75 B6
Walker Fold Lancs 93 E6
Walkerburn Borders 121 F6
Walkeringham Notts 89 E8
Walkerith Lincs 89 E8
Walkern Herts 41 B5
Walker's Green Hereford 49 E7
Walkerville N Yorks 101 E7
Walkford Dorset 14 E3
Walkhampton Devon 6 C3
Walkington E Yorks 97 F5
Walkley S Yorks 88 F4
Wall Northumb 110 C2
Wall Staffs 62 D5
Wall Bank Shrops 60 E5
Wall Heath W Mid 62 F2
Wall under Heywood Shrops 60 E5
Wallaceton Dumfries 113 F8
Wallacetown S Ayrs 112 B3
Wallacetown S Ayrs 112 D2
Wallands Park E Sus 17 C8
Wallasey Mers 85 E4
Wallcrouch E Sus 18 B3
Wallingford Oxon 39 F6
Wallington Hants 15 D6
Wallington Herts 54 F3
Wallington London 28 C3
Wallis Pembs 32 B1
Walliswood Sur 28 F2
Walls Shetland 160 J4
Wallsend T&W 111 C5
Wallston V Glam 22 B3
Wallyford E Loth 121 B6
Walmer Kent 31 D7
Walmer Bridge Lancs 86 B2
Walmersley Gtr Man 87 C6
Walmley W Mid 62 E5
Walpole Suff 57 B7
Walpole Cross Keys Norf 66 C5
Walpole Highway Norf 66 C5
Walpole Marsh Norf 66 C4
Walpole St Andrew Norf 66 C5
Walpole St Peter Norf 66 C5
Walsall W Mid 62 E4
Walsall Wood W Mid 62 D4
Walsden W Yorks 87 B7
Walsgrave on Sowe W Mid 63 F7
Walsham le Willows Suff 56 B3
Walshaw Gtr Man 87 C5
Walshford N Yorks 95 D7
Walsoken Cambs 66 C4
Walston S Lanark 120 E3
Walsworth Herts 54 F3
Walters Ash Bucks 39 E8
Walterston V Glam 22 B2
Walterstone Hereford 35 B7
Waltham Kent 30 E5
Waltham NE Lincs 91 D6
Waltham Abbey Essex 41 D6
Waltham Chase Hants 15 C6
Waltham Cross Herts 41 D6
Waltham on the Wolds Leics 64 B5
Waltham St Lawrence Windsor 27 B6
Walthamstow London 41 F6
Walton Cumb 108 C5
Walton Derbys 76 C3
Walton Leics 64 F2
Walton M Keynes 53 F6
Walton Mers 85 E4
Walton Pboro 65 D8
Walton Powys 48 D4
Walton Som 23 F6
Walton Staffs 75 F5
Walton Suff 57 F6
Walton Telford 61 C5
Walton W Yorks 88 C4
Walton W Yorks 95 E7
Walton Warks 51 D7
Walton Cardiff Glos 50 F4
Walton East Pembs 32 B1
Walton-in-Gordano N Som 23 B6
Walton-le-Dale Lancs 86 B3
Walton-on-Thames Sur 28 C2
Walton on the Hill Staffs 62 B3
Walton on the Hill Sur 28 D3
Walton-on-the-Naze Essex 43 B8
Walton on the Wolds Leics 64 C2
Walton-on-Trent Derbys 63 C6
Walton West Pembs 44 D3
Walwen Flint 73 B6
Walwick Northumb 110 B2
Walworth Darl 101 C7
Walworth Gate Darl 101 B7
Walwyn's Castle Pembs 44 D3
Wambrook Som 11 D7
Wanborough Sur 27 E7
Wanborough Swindon 38 F2
Wandsworth London 28 B3
Wangford Suff 57 B8
Wanlockhead Dumfries 113 C8
Wansford E Yorks 97 D6
Wansford Pboro 65 E7
Wanstead London 41 F7
Wanstrow Som 24 E2
Wanswell Glos 36 D3
Wantage Oxon 38 F3
Wapley S Glos 24 B2
Wappenbury Warks 51 C8
Wappenham Northants 52 E4
Warbleton E Sus 18 D3
Warblington Hants 15 D8
Warborough Oxon 39 E5
Warboys Cambs 66 F3
Warbreck Blackpool 92 F3
Warbstow Corn 8 E4
Warburton Gtr Man 86 F5
Warcop Cumb 100 C2
Ward End W Mid 62 F5
Ward Green Suff 56 C4
Warden Kent 30 B4
Warden Northumb 110 C2
Wardhill Orkney 159 F7
Wardington Oxon 52 E2
Wardlaw Borders 115 C5
Wardle Ches E 74 D3
Wardle Gtr Man 87 C7
Wardley Rutland 64 D5
Wardlow Derbys 75 B8
Wardy Hill Cambs 66 F4
Ware Herts 41 C6
Ware Kent 31 C6
Wareham Dorset 13 F7
Warehorne Kent 19 B6
Waren Mill Northumb 123 F7
Warenford Northumb 117 B7
Warenton Northumb 123 F7
Wareside Herts 41 C6
Waresley Cambs 54 D3
Waresley Worcs 50 B3
Warfield Brack 27 B6
Warfleet Devon 7 D6
Wargrave Wokingham 27 B5
Warham Norf 80 C5
Warhill Gtr Man 87 E7
Wark Northumb 109 B8
Wark Northumb 122 F4
Warkleigh Devon 9 B8
Warkton Northants 53 B6
Warkworth Northants 52 E2
Warkworth Northumb 117 D8
Warlaby N Yorks 101 E8
Warland W Yorks 87 B7
Warleggan Corn 5 C6
Warlingham Sur 28 D4
Warmfield W Yorks 88 B4
Warmingham Ches E 74 C4
Warmington Northants 65 E7
Warmington Warks 52 E2
Warminster Wilts 24 E3
Warmlake Kent 30 D2
Warmley S Glos 23 B8
Warmley Tower S Glos 23 B8
Warmonds Hill Northants 53 C7
Warmsworth S Yorks 89 D6
Warmwell Dorset 13 F5
Warndon Worcs 50 D3
Warnford Hants 15 B7
Warnham W Sus 28 F2
Warninglid W Sus 17 B6
Warren Ches E 75 B5
Warren Pembs 44 F4
Warren Heath Suff 57 E6
Warren Row Windsor 39 F8
Warren Street Kent 30 D3
Warrington M Keynes 53 D6
Warrington Warr 86 F4
Warsash Hants 15 D5
Warslow Staffs 75 D7
Warter E Yorks 96 D4
Warthermarske N Yorks 94 B5
Warthill N Yorks 96 D2
Wartling E Sus 18 E3
Wartnaby Leics 64 B4
Warton Lancs 86 B2
Warton Lancs 92 B4
Warton Northumb 117 D6
Warton Warks 63 D6
Warwick Warks 51 C7
Warwick Bridge Cumb 108 D4
Warwick on Eden Cumb 108 D4
Wasbister Orkney 159 E4
Wasdale Head Cumb 98 D3
Wash Common W Berks 26 C2
Washaway Corn 4 C5
Washbourne Devon 7 D5
Washfield Devon 10 C4
Washfold N Yorks 101 D5
Washford Som 22 E2
Washford Pyne Devon 10 C3
Washingborough Lincs 78 B3
Washington T&W 111 D6
Washington W Sus 16 C5
Wasing W Berks 26 C3
Waskerley Durham 110 E3
Wasperton Warks 51 D7
Wasps Nest Lincs 78 C3
Wass N Yorks 95 B8
Watchet Som 22 E2
Watchfield Oxon 38 E2
Watchfield Som 22 E5
Watchgate Cumb 99 E7
Watchhill Cumb 107 E8
Watcombe Torbay 7 C7
Watendlath Cumb 98 C4
Water Devon 10 F2
Water Lancs 87 B6
Water End E Yorks 96 F3
Water End Herts 40 C3
Water End Herts 41 D5
Water Newton Cambs 65 E8
Water Orton Warks 63 E5
Water Stratford Bucks 52 F4
Water Yeat Cumb 98 F4
Waterbeach Cambs 55 C5
Waterbeck Dumfries 108 B2
Waterden Norf 80 D4
Waterfall Staffs 75 D7
Waterfoot E Renf 119 D5
Waterfoot Lancs 87 B6
Waterford Hants 14 E4
Waterford Herts 41 C6
Waterhead Cumb 99 D5
Waterhead Dumfries 114 E4
Waterheads Borders 120 D5
Waterhouses Durham 110 E4
Waterhouses Staffs 75 D7
Wateringbury Kent 29 D7
Waterloo Gtr Man 87 D7
Waterloo Highld 149 F11
Waterloo Mers 85 E4
Waterloo N Lanark 119 D8
Waterloo Norf 68 C5
Waterloo Perth 133 F7
Waterloo Poole 13 E8
Waterloo Shrops 74 F2
Waterloo Port Gwyn 82 E4
Waterlooville Hants 15 D7
Watermeetings S Lanark 114 C2
Watermillock Cumb 99 B6
Waterperry Oxon 39 D6
Waterrow Som 11 B5
Water's Nook Gtr Man 86 D4
Waters Upton Telford 61 C6
Watersfield W Sus 16 C4
Waterside Aberds 141 B9
Waterside Blackburn 86 B5
Waterside Cumb 108 E2
Waterside E Ayrs 112 D4
Waterside E Ayrs 118 E4
Waterside E Dunb 119 B6
Waterside E Renf 118 D5
Waterstock Oxon 39 D6
Waterston Pembs 44 E4
Watford Herts 40 E4
Watford Northants 52 C4
Watford Gap Staffs 62 D5
Wath N Yorks 94 C4
Wath N Yorks 95 B6
Wath N Yorks 96 B2
Wath Brow Cumb 98 C2
Wath upon Dearne S Yorks 88 D5
Watlington Norf 67 C6
Watlington Oxon 39 E6
Watnall Notts 76 E5
Watten Highld 158 E4
Wattisfield Suff 56 B4
Wattisham Suff 56 D4
Wattlesborough Heath Shrops 60 C3
Watton E Yorks 97 D6
Watton Norf 68 D2
Watton at Stone Herts 41 C6
Wattston N Lanark 119 B7
Wattstown Rhondda 34 E4
Wauchan Highld 136 F2
Waulkmill Lodge Orkney 159 H4
Waun Powys 59 D5
Waun-y-clyn Carms 33 D5
Waunarlwydd Swansea 33 E7
Waunclunda Carms 47 F5
Waunfawr Gwyn 82 F5
Waungron Swansea 33 D6
Waunlwyd Bl Gwent 35 D5
Wavendon M Keynes 53 F7
Waverbridge Cumb 108 E2
Waverton Ches W 73 C8
Waverton Cumb 108 E2
Wavertree Mers 85 F4
Wawne E Yorks 97 F6
Waxham Norf 69 B7
Waxholme E Yorks 91 B7
Way Kent 31 C7
Way Village Devon 10 C3
Wayfield Medway 29 C8
Wayford Som 12 D2
Waymills Shrops 74 E2
Wayne Green Mon 35 C8
Wdig = Goodwick Pembs 44 B4
Weachyburn Aberds 153 C6
Weald Oxon 38 D3
Wealdstone London 40 F4
Weardley W Yorks 95 E5
Weare Som 23 D6
Weare Giffard Devon 9 B6
Wearhead Durham 109 F8
Weasdale Cumb 100 D1
Weasenham All Saints Norf 80 E4
Weasenham St Peter Norf 80 E4
Weatherhill Sur 28 E4
Weaverham Ches W 74 B3
Weaverthorpe N Yorks 97 B5
Webheath Worcs 50 C5
Wedderlairs Aberds 153 E8
Wedderlie Borders 122 D2
Weddington Warks 63 E7
Wedhampton Wilts 25 D5
Wedmore Som 23 E6
Wednesbury W Mid 62 E3
Wednesfield W Mid 62 D3
Weedon Bucks 39 C8
Weedon Bec Northants 52 D4
Weedon Lois Northants 52 E4
Weeford Staffs 62 D5
Week Devon 10 C2
Week St Mary Corn 8 E4
Weeke Hants 26 F2
Weekley Northants 65 F5
Weel E Yorks 97 F6
Weeley Essex 43 B7
Weeley Heath Essex 43 B7
Weem Perth 133 E5
Weeping Cross Staffs 62 B3
Weethley Gate Warks 51 D5
Weeting Norf 67 F7
Weeton E Yorks 91 B7
Weeton Lancs 92 F3
Weeton N Yorks 95 E5
Weetwood Hall Northumb 117 B6
Weir Lancs 87 B6
Weir Quay Devon 6 C2
Welborne Norf 68 D3
Welbourn Lincs 78 D2
Welburn N Yorks 96 C3
Welburn N Yorks 102 F4
Welbury N Yorks 102 D1
Welby Lincs 78 F2
Welches Dam Cambs 66 F4
Welcombe Devon 8 C4
Weld Bank Lancs 86 C3
Weldon Northumb 117 E7
Welford Northants 64 F3
Welford W Berks 26 B2
Welford-on-Avon Warks 51 D6
Welham Leics 64 E4
Welham Notts 89 F8
Welham Green Herts 41 D5
Well Hants 27 E5
Well Lincs 79 B7
Well N Yorks 101 F7
Well End Bucks 40 F1
Well Heads W Yorks 94 F3
Well Hill Kent 29 C5
Well Town Devon 10 D4
Welland Worcs 50 E2
Wellbank Angus 134 F4
Welldale Dumfries 107 C8
Wellesbourne Warks 51 D7
Welling London 29 B5
Wellingborough Northants 53 C6
Wellingham Norf 80 E4
Wellingore Lincs 78 D2
Wellington Cumb 98 D2
Wellington Hereford 49 E6
Wellington Som 11 B6
Wellington Telford 61 C6
Wellington Heath Hereford 50 E2
Wellington Hill W Yorks 95 F6
Wellow Bath 24 D2
Wellow IoW 14 F4
Wellow Notts 77 C6
Wellpond Green Herts 41 B7
Wells Som 23 E7
Wells Green Ches E 74 D3
Wells-Next-The-Sea Norf 80 C5
Wellsborough Leics 63 D7
Wellswood Torbay 7 C7
Wellwood Fife 128 F2
Welney Norf 66 E5
Welsh Bicknor Hereford 36 C2
Welsh End Shrops 74 F2
Welsh Frankton Shrops 73 F7
Welsh Hook Pembs 44 C4
Welsh Newton Hereford 36 C1
Welsh St Donats V Glam 22 B2
Welshampton Shrops 73 F8
Welshpool = Y Trallwng Powys 60 D2
Welton Cumb 108 E3
Welton E Yorks 90 B3
Welton Lincs 78 B3
Welton Northants 52 C3
Welton Hill Lincs 90 F4
Welton le Marsh Lincs 79 C7
Welton le Wold Lincs 91 F6
Welwick E Yorks 91 B7
Welwyn Herts 41 C5
Welwyn Garden City Herts 41 C5
Wem Shrops 60 B5
Wembdon Som 22 F4
Wembley London 40 F4
Wembury Devon 6 E3
Wembworthy Devon 9 D8
Wemyss Bay Involyd 118 C1
Wenallt Ceredig 47 B5
Wenallt Gwyn 72 E3
Wendens Ambo Essex 55 F6
Wendlebury Oxon 39 C5
Wendling Norf 68 C2
Wendover Bucks 40 D1
Wendron Corn 3 C5
Wendy Cambs 54 E4
Wenfordbridge Corn 5 B5
Wenhaston Suff 57 B8
Wennington Cambs 54 B3
Wennington Lancs 93 B6
Wennington London 41 F8
Wensley Derbys 76 C2
Wensley N Yorks 101 F5
Wentbridge W Yorks 89 C5
Wentnor Shrops 60 E3
Wentworth Cambs 55 B5
Wentworth S Yorks 88 E4
Wenvoe V Glam 22 B3
Weobley Hereford 49 D6
Weobley Marsh Hereford 49 D6
Wereham Norf 67 D6
Wergs W Mid 62 D2
Wern Powys 59 C6
Wern Powys 60 C2
Wernffrwd Swansea 33 E6
Wernyrheolydd Mon 35 C7
Werrington Corn 8 F5
Werrington Pboro 65 D8
Werrington Staffs 75 E6
Wervin Ches W 73 B8
Wesham Lancs 92 F4
Wessington Derbys 76 D3
West Acre Norf 67 C7
West Adderbury Oxon 52 F2
West Allerdean Northumb 123 E5
West Alvington Devon 6 E5
West Amesbury Wilts 25 E6
West Anstey Devon 10 B3
West Ashby Lincs 79 B5
West Ashling W Sus 16 D2
West Ashton Wilts 24 D3
West Auckland Durham 101 B6
West Ayton N Yorks 103 F7
West Bagborough Som 22 F3
West Barkwith Lincs 91 F5
West Barnby N Yorks 103 C6
West Barns E Loth 122 B2
West Barsham Norf 80 D5
West Bay Dorset 12 E2
West Beckham Norf 81 D7
West Bedfont Sur 27 B8
West Benhar N Lanark 119 C8
West Bergholt Essex 43 B5
West Bexington Dorset 12 F3
West Bilney Norf 67 C7
West Blatchington Brighton 17 D6
West Bowling W Yorks 94 F4
West Bradford Lancs 93 E7
West Bradley Som 23 F7
West Bretton W Yorks 88 C3
West Bridgford Notts 77 F5
West Bromwich W Mid 62 E4
West Buckland Devon 21 F5
West Buckland Som 11 B6
West Burrafirth Shetland 160 H4
West Burton N Yorks 101 F5
West Burton W Sus 16 C3
West Butterwick N Lincs 90 D2
West Byfleet Sur 27 C8
West Caister Norf 69 C8
West Calder W Loth 120 C3
West Camel Som 12 B3
West Challow Oxon 38 F3
West Chelborough Dorset 12 D3
West Chevington Northumb 117 E8
West Chiltington W Sus 16 C4
West Chiltington Common W Sus 16 C4
West Chinnock Som 12 C2
West Chisenbury Wilts 25 D6
West Clandon Sur 27 D8
West Cliffe Kent 31 E7
West Clyne Highld 157 J11
West Clyth Highld 158 G4
West Coker Som 12 C3
West Compton Dorset 12 E3
West Compton Som 23 E7
West Cowick E Yorks 89 B7
West Cranmore Som 23 E8
West Cross Swansea 33 F7
West Cullery Aberds 141 D6
West Curry Corn 8 E4
West Curthwaite Cumb 108 E3
West Darlochan Argyll 143 F7
West Dean W Sus 16 C2
West Dean Wilts 14 B3
West Deeping Lincs 65 D8
West Derby Mers 85 E4
West Dereham Norf 67 D6
West Didsbury Gtr Man 87 E6
West Ditchburn Northumb 117 B7
West Down Devon 20 E4
West Drayton London 27 B8
West Drayton Notts 77 B7
West Ella E Yorks 90 B4
West End Bedford 53 D7
West End E Yorks 96 F5
West End E Yorks 97 F7
West End Hants 15 C5
West End Lancs 86 B5
West End N Som 23 C6
West End N Yorks 94 D4
West End Norf 68 D2
West End Norf 69 C8
West End Oxon 38 D4
West End S Lanark 120 E2
West End S Yorks 89 D7
West End Suff 69 F7
West End Sur 27 C7
West End W Sus 17 C6
West End Wilts 13 B7
West End Wilts 24 B4
West End Green Hants 26 C4
West Farleigh Kent 29 D8
West Felton Shrops 60 B3
West Fenton E Loth 129 F6
West Ferry Dundee 134 F4
West Firle E Sus 17 D8
West Ginge Oxon 38 F4
West Grafton Wilts 25 C7
West Green Hants 26 D5
West Greenskares Aberds 153 B7
West Grimstead Wilts 14 B3
West Grinstead W Sus 17 B5
West Haddlesey N Yorks 89 B6
West Haddon Northants 52 B4
West Hagbourne Oxon 39 F5
West Hagley Worcs 62 F3
West Hall Cumb 109 C5
West Hallam Derbys 76 E4
West Halton N Lincs 90 B3
West Ham London 41 F7
West Handley Derbys 76 B3
West Hanney Oxon 38 E4
West Hanningfield Essex 42 E3
West Hardwick W Yorks 88 C5
West Harnham Wilts 14 B2
West Harptree Bath 23 D7
West Hatch Som 11 B7
West Head Norf 67 D5
West Heath Ches E 74 C5
West Heath Hants 26 D3
West Heath Hants 27 D6
West Helmsdale Highld 157 H13
West Hendred Oxon 38 F4
West Heslerton N Yorks 96 B5
West Hill Devon 11 E5
West Hill E Yorks 97 C7
West Hill N Som 23 B6
West Hoathly W Sus 28 F4
West Holme Dorset 13 F6
West Horndon Essex 42 F2
West Horrington Som 23 E7
West Horsley Sur 27 D8
West Horton Northumb 123 F6
West Hougham Kent 31 E6
West Houlland Shetland 160 H4
West-houses Derbys 76 D4
West Huntington York 96 D2
West Hythe Kent 19 B8
West Ilsley W Berks 38 F4
West Itchenor W Sus 15 D8
West Keal Lincs 79 C6
West Kennett Wilts 25 C6
West Kilbride N Ayrs 118 E2
West Kingsdown Kent 29 C6
West Kington Wilts 24 B3
West Kinharrachie Aberds 153 E9
West Kirby Mers 85 F3
West Knapton N Yorks 96 B4
West Knighton Dorset 12 F5
West Knoyle Wilts 24 F3
West Kyloe Northumb 123 E6
West Lambrook Som 12 C2
West Langdon Kent 31 E7
West Langwell Highld 157 J9
West Lavington W Sus 16 B2
West Lavington Wilts 24 D5
West Layton N Yorks 101 D6
West Lea Durham 111 E7
West Leake Notts 64 B2
West Learmouth Northumb 122 F4
West Leigh Devon 9 D8
West Lexham Norf 67 C8
West Lilling N Yorks 96 C2
West Linton Borders 120 D4
West Liss Hants 15 B8
West Littleton S Glos 24 B2
West Looe Corn 5 D7
West Luccombe Som 21 E7
West Lulworth Dorset 13 F6
West Lutton N Yorks 96 C5
West Lydford Som 23 F7
West Lyng Som 11 B8
West Lynn Norf 67 B6
West Malling Kent 29 D7
West Malvern Worcs 50 E2
West Marden W Sus 15 C8
West Marina E Sus 18 E4
West Markham Notts 77 B7
West Marsh NE Lincs 91 C6
West Marton N Yorks 93 D8
West Meon Hants 15 B7
West Mersea Essex 43 C6
West Milton Dorset 12 E3
West Minster Kent 30 B3
West Molesey Sur 28 C2
West Monkton Som 11 B7
West Moors Dorset 13 D8
West Morriston Borders 122 E2
West Muir Angus 135 C5
West Ness N Yorks 96 B2
West Newham Northumb 110 B3
West Newton E Yorks 97 F7
West Newton Norf 67 B6
West Norwood London 28 B4
West Ogwell Devon 7 B6
West Orchard Dorset 13 C6
West Overton Wilts 25 C6
West Park Hrtlpl 111 F7
West Parley Dorset 13 E8
West Peckham Kent 29 D7
West Pelton Durham 110 D5
West Pennard Som 23 F7
West Pentire Corn 4 C2
West Perry Cambs 54 C2
West Putford Devon 9 C5
West Quantoxhead Som 22 E3
West Rainton Durham 111 E6
West Rasen Lincs 90 F4
West Raynham Norf 80 E4
West Retford Notts 89 F7
West Rounton N Yorks 102 D2
West Row Suff 55 B7
West Rudham Norf 80 E4
West Runton Norf 81 C7
West Saltoun E Loth 121 C7
West Sandwick Shetland 160 E6
West Scrafton N Yorks 101 F5
West Sleekburn Northumb 117 F8
West Somerton Norf 69 C7
West Stafford Dorset 12 F5
West Stockwith Notts 89 E8
West Stoke W Sus 16 D2
West Stonesdale N Yorks 100 D3
West Stoughton Som 23 E6
West Stour Dorset 13 B5
West Stourmouth Kent 31 C6
West Stow Suff 56 B2
West Stowell Wilts 25 C6
West Strathan Highld 157 C8
West Stratton Hants 26 E3
West Street Kent 30 D3
West Tanfield N Yorks 95 B5
West Taphouse Corn 5 C6
West Tarbert Argyll 145 G7
West Thirston Northumb 117 E7
West Thorney W Sus 15 D8
West Thurrock Thurrock 29 B6
West Tilbury Thurrock 29 B7
West Tisted Hants 15 B7
West Tofts Norf 67 E8
West Tofts Perth 133 F8
West Torrington Lincs 90 F5
West Town Hants 15 E8
West Town N Som 23 C6
West Tytherley Hants 14 B3
West Tytherton Wilts 24 B4
West Walton Norf 66 C4
West Walton Highway Norf 66 C4
West Wellow Hants 14 C3
West Wemyss Fife 128 E5
West Wick N Som 23 C5
West Wickham Cambs 55 E7
West Wickham London 28 C4
West Williamston Pembs 32 D1
West Willoughby Lincs 78 E2
West Winch Norf 67 C6
West Winterslow Wilts 25 F7
West Wittering W Sus 15 E8
West Witton N Yorks 101 F5
West Woodburn Northumb 116 F4
West Woodhay W Berks 25 C8
West Woodlands Som 24 E2
West Worldham Hants 26 F5
West Worlington Devon 10 C2
West Worthing W Sus 16 D5
West Wratting Cambs 55 D7
West Wycombe Bucks 39 E8
West Wylam Northumb 110 C4
West Yell Shetland 160 E6
Westacott Devon 20 F4
Westbere Kent 31 C5
Westborough Lincs 77 E8
Westbourne Bmouth 13 E8
Westbourne Suff 56 E5
Westbourne W Sus 15 D8
Westbrook W Berks 26 B2
Westbury Bucks 52 F4
Westbury Shrops 60 D3
Westbury Wilts 24 D3
Westbury Leigh Wilts 24 D3
Westbury-on-Severn Glos 36 C4
Westbury on Trym Bristol 23 B7
Westbury-sub-Mendip Som 23 E7
Westby Lancs 92 F3
Westcliff-on-Sea Southend 42 F4
Westcombe Som 23 F8
Westcote Glos 38 B2
Westcott Bucks 39 C7
Westcott Devon 10 D5
Westcott Sur 28 E2
Westcott Barton Oxon 38 B4
Westdean E Sus 18 F2
Westdene Brighton 17 D6
Wester Aberchalder Highld 137 B8
Wester Balgedie Perth 128 D3
Wester Culbeuchly Aberds 153 B6
Wester Dechmont W Loth 120 C3
Wester Denoon Angus 134 E3
Wester Fintray Aberds 141 C7
Wester Gruinards Highld 151 B8
Wester Lealty Highld 151 D9
Wester Milton Highld 151 F12
Wester Newburn Fife 129 D6
Wester Quarff Shetland 160 K6
Wester Skeld Shetland 160 J4
Westerdale Highld 158 E3
Westerdale N Yorks 102 D4
Westerfield Shetland 160 H5
Westerfield Suff 57 E5
Westergate W Sus 16 D3
Westerham Kent 28 D5
Westerhope T&W 110 C4
Westerleigh S Glos 23 B9
Westerton Angus 135 D6
Westerton Durham 110 F5
Westerton W Sus 16 D2
Westerwick Shetland 160 J4
Westfield Cumb 98 B1
Westfield E Sus 18 D5
Westfield Hereford 50 E2
Westfield Highld 158 D2
Westfield N Lanark 119 B7
Westfield Norf 68 D2
Westfield W Loth 120 B2
Westfields Dorset 12 D5
Westfields of Rattray Perth 134 E1
Westgate Durham 110 F2
Westgate N Lincs 89 D8
Westgate Norf 80 C4
Westgate Norf 81 C5
Westgate on Sea Kent 31 B7
Westhall Aberds 141 B5
Westhall Suff 69 F7
Westham Dorset 12 G4
Westham E Sus 18 E3
Westham Som 23 E6
Westhampnett W Sus 16 D2
Westhay Som 23 E6
Westhead Lancs 86 D2
Westhide Hereford 49 E7
Westhill Aberds 141 D7
Westhill Highld 151 G10
Westhope Hereford 49 D6
Westhope Shrops 60 F4
Westhorpe Lincs 78 F5
Westhorpe Suff 56 C4
Westhoughton Gtr Man 86 D4
Westhouse N Yorks 93 B6
Westhumble Sur 28 D2
Westing Shetland 160 C7
Westlake Devon 6 D4
Westleigh Devon 9 B6
Westleigh Devon 11 C5
Westleigh Gtr Man 86 D4
Westleton Suff 57 C8
Westley Shrops 60 D3
Westley Suff 56 C2
Westley Waterless Cambs 55 D7
Westlington Bucks 39 C7
Westlinton Cumb 108 C3
Westmarsh Kent 31 C6
Westmeston E Sus 17 C7
Westmill Herts 41 B6
Westminster London 28 B4
Westmuir Angus 134 D3
Westness Orkney 159 F4
Westnewton Cumb 107 E8
Westnewton Northumb 122 F5
Westoe T&W 111 C6
Weston Bath 24 C2
Weston Ches E 74 D4
Weston Devon 11 F6
Weston Dorset 12 G4
Weston Halton 86 F3
Weston Hants 15 B8
Weston Herts 54 F3
Weston Lincs 66 B2
Weston N Yorks 94 E4
Weston Northants 52 E3
Weston Notts 77 C7
Weston Shrops 61 B5
Weston Shrops 61 E5
Weston Staffs 62 B3
Weston W Berks 25 B8
Weston Beggard Hereford 49 E7
Weston by Welland Northants 64 E4
Weston Colville Cambs 55 D7
Weston Coyney Stoke 75 E6
Weston Favell Northants 53 C5
Weston Green Cambs 55 D7
Weston Green Norf 68 C4
Weston Heath Shrops 61 C7
Weston Hills Lincs 66 B2
Weston-in-Gordano N Som 23 B6
Weston Jones Staffs 61 B7
Weston Longville Norf 68 C4
Weston Lullingfields Shrops 60 B4
Weston-on-the-Green Oxon 39 C5
Weston-on-Trent Derbys 63 B8
Weston Patrick Hants 26 E4
Weston Rhyn Shrops 73 F6
Weston-Sub-Edge Glos 51 E6
Weston-super-Mare N Som 22 C5
Weston Turville Bucks 40 C1
Weston under Lizard Staffs 62 C2
Weston under Penyard Hereford 36 B3
Weston under Wetherley Warks 51 C8
Weston Underwood Derbys 76 E2
Weston Underwood M Keynes 53 D6
Westonbirt Glos 37 F5
Westoncommon Shrops 60 B4
Westoning C Beds 53 F8
Westonzoyland Som 23 F5
Westow N Yorks 96 C3
Westport Argyll 143 F7
Westport Som 11 C8
Westrigg W Loth 120 C2
Westruther Borders 122 E2
Westry Cambs 66 E3
Westville Notts 76 E5
Westward Cumb 108 E2
Westward Ho! Devon 9 B6
Westwell Kent 30 E3
Westwell Oxon 38 D2
Westwell Leacon Kent 30 E3
Westwick Cambs 54 C5
Westwick Durham 101 C5
Westwick Norf 81 E8
Westwood Devon 10 E5
Westwood Wilts 24 D3
Westwoodside N Lincs 89 E8
Wetheral Cumb 108 D4
Wetherby W Yorks 95 E7
Wetherden Suff 56 C4
Wetheringsett Suff 56 C5
Wethersfield Essex 55 F8
Wethersta Shetland 160 G5
Wetherup Street Suff 56 C5
Wetley Rocks Staffs 75 E6
Wettenhall Ches E 74 C3
Wetton Staffs 75 D8
Wetwang E Yorks 96 D5
Wetwood Staffs 74 F4
Wexcombe Wilts 25 D7
Wexham Street Bucks 40 F2
Weybourne Norf 81 C7
Weybread Suff 68 F5
Weybridge Sur 27 C8
Weycroft Devon 11 E8
Weydale Highld 158 D3
Weyhill Hants 25 E8
Weymouth Dorset 12 G4
Whaddon Bucks 53 F6
Whaddon Cambs 54 E4
Whaddon Glos 37 C5
Whaddon Wilts 14 B2
Whale Cumb 99 B7
Whaley Derbys 76 B5
Whaley Bridge Derbys 87 F8
Whaley Thorns Derbys 76 B5
Whaligoe Highld 158 F5
Whalley Lancs 93 F7
Whalton Northumb 117 F7
Wham N Yorks 93 C7
Whaplode Lincs 66 B3
Whaplode Drove Lincs 66 C3
Whaplode St Catherine Lincs 66 B3
Wharfe N Yorks 93 C7
Wharles Lancs 92 F4
Wharncliffe Side S Yorks 88 E3
Wharram le Street N Yorks 96 C4
Wharton Ches W 74 C3
Wharton Green Ches W 74 C3
Whashton N Yorks 101 D6
Whatcombe Dorset 13 D6
Whatcote Warks 51 E8
Whatfield Suff 56 E4
Whatley Som 11 D8
Whatley Som 24 E2
Whatlington E Sus 18 D4
Whatstandwell Derbys 76 D3
Whatton Notts 77 F7
Whauphill Dumfries 105 E8
Whaw N Yorks 100 D4
Wheatacre Norf 69 E7
Wheatcroft Derbys 76 D3
Wheathampstead Herts 40 C4
Wheathill Shrops 61 F6
Wheatley Devon 10 E4
Wheatley Hants 27 E5
Wheatley Oxon 39 D5
Wheatley S Yorks 89 D6
Wheatley W Yorks 87 B8
Wheatley Hill Durham 111 F6
Wheaton Aston Staffs 62 C2
Wheddon Cross Som 21 F8
Wheedlemont Aberds 140 B3
Wheelerstreet Sur 27 E7
Wheelock Ches E 74 D4
Wheelock Heath Ches E 74 D4
Wheelton Lancs 86 B4
Wheen Angus 134 B3
Wheldrake York 96 E2
Whelford Glos 38 E1
Whelpley Hill Herts 40 D2
Whempstead Herts 41 B6
Whenby N Yorks 96 C2
Whepstead Suff 56 D2
Wherstead Suff 57 E5
Wherwell Hants 25 E8
Wheston Derbys 75 B8
Whetsted Kent 29 E7
Whetstone Leics 64 E2
Whicham Cumb 98 F3
Whichford Warks 51 F8
Whickham T&W 110 C5
Whiddon Down Devon 9 E8
Whigstreet Angus 134 E4
Whilton Northants 52 C4
Whim Farm Borders 120 D5
Whimble Devon 9 D5
Whimple Devon 10 E5
Whimpwell Green Norf 69 B6
Whinburgh Norf 68 D3
Whinnieliggate Dumfries 106 D4
Whinnyfold Aberds 153 E10
Whippingham IoW 15 E6
Whipsnade C Beds 40 C3
Whipton Devon 10 E4
Whirlow S Yorks 88 F4
Whisby Lincs 78 C2
Whissendine Rutland 64 C5
Whissonsett Norf 80 E5
Whistlefield Argyll 145 D10
Whistlefield Argyll 145 D11
Whistley Green Wokingham 27 B5
Whiston Mers 86 E2
Whiston Northants 53 C6
Whiston S Yorks 88 F5
Whiston Staffs 62 C2
Whiston Staffs 75 E7
Whitbeck Cumb 98 F3
Whitbourne Hereford 50 D2
Whitburn T&W 111 C7
Whitburn W Loth 120 C2
Whitburn Colliery T&W 111 C7
Whitby Ches W 73 B7
Whitby N Yorks 103 C6
Whitbyheath Ches W 73 B7
Whitchurch Bath 23 C8
Whitchurch Bucks 39 B7
Whitchurch Cardiff 35 F5
Whitchurch Devon 6 B2
Whitchurch Hants 26 E2
Whitchurch Hereford 36 C2
Whitchurch Oxon 26 B4
Whitchurch Pembs 44 C2
Whitchurch Shrops 74 E2
Whitchurch Canonicorum Dorset 11 E8
Whitchurch Hill Oxon 26 B4
Whitcombe Dorset 12 F5
Whitcott Keysett Shrops 60 F2
White Coppice Lancs 86 C4
White Lackington Dorset 12 E5
White Ladies Aston Worcs 50 D4
White Lund Lancs 92 C4
White Mill Carms 33 B5
White Ness Shetland 160 J5
White Notley Essex 42 C3
White Pit Lincs 79 B6
White Post Notts 77 D6
White Rocks Hereford 35 B8
White Roding Essex 42 C1
White Waltham Windsor 27 B6
Whiteacen Moray 152 D2
Whiteacre Heath Warks 63 E6
Whitebridge Highld 137 C7
Whitebrook Mon 36 D2
Whiteburn Borders 121 E8
Whitecairn Dumfries 105 D6
Whitecairns Aberds 141 C8
Whitecastle S Lanark 120 E3
Whitechapel Lancs 93 E5
Whitecleat Orkney 159 H6
Whitecraig E Loth 121 B6
Whitecroft Glos 36 D3
Whitecross Corn 4 B4
Whitecross Falk 120 B2
Whitecross Staffs 62 B2
Whiteface Highld 151 C10
Whitefarland N Ayrs 143 D9
Whitefaulds S Ayrs 112 D2
Whitefield Gtr Man 87 D6
Whitefield Perth 134 F1
Whiteford Aberds 141 B6
Whitegate Ches W 74 C3
Whitehall Blackburn 86 B4
Whitehall W Sus 16 B5
Whitehall Village Orkney 159 F7
Whitehaven Cumb 98 C1
Whitehill Hants 27 F5
Whitehills Aberds 153 B6
Whitehills S Lanark 119 D6
Whitehough Derbys 87 F8
Whitehouse Aberds 140 C5
Whitehouse Argyll 145 G7
Whiteinch Glasgow 118 C5
Whitekirk E Loth 129 F7
Whitelaw S Lanark 119 E6
Whiteleas T&W 111 C6
Whiteley Bank IoW 15 F6
Whiteley Green Ches E 75 B6
Whiteley Village Sur 27 C8
Whitemans Green W Sus 17 B7
Whitemire Moray 151 F12
Whitemoor Corn 4 D4
Whitemore Staffs 75 C5
Whitenap Hants 14 B4
Whiteoak Green Oxon 38 C3
Whiteparish Wilts 14 B3
Whiterashes Aberds 141 B7
Whiterow Highld 158 F5
Whiteshill Glos 37 D5
Whiteside Northumb 109 C7
Whiteside W Loth 120 C2
Whitesmith E Sus 18 D2
Whitestaunton Som 11 C7
Whitestone Devon 10 E3
Whitestone Devon 20 E3
Whitestone Warks 63 F7
Whitestones Aberds 153 C8
Whitestreet Green Suff 56 F3
Whitewall Corner N Yorks 96 B3
Whiteway Glos 37 C6
Whiteway Glos 37 E5
Whitewell Aberds 153 B9
Whitewell Lancs 93 E6
Whitewell Bottom Lancs 87 B6
Whiteworks Devon 6 B4
Whitfield Kent 31 E7
Whitfield Northants 52 F4
Whitfield Northumb 109 D7
Whitfield S Glos 36 E3
Whitford Devon 11 E7
Whitford Flint 72 B5
Whitgift E Yorks 90 B2
Whitgreave Staffs 62 B2
Whithorn Dumfries 105 E8
Whiting Bay N Ayrs 143 F11
Whitkirk W Yorks 95 F6
Whitland Carms 32 C2
Whitletts S Ayrs 112 B3
Whitley N Yorks 89 B6
Whitley Reading 26 B5
Whitley Wilts 24 C3
Whitley Bay T&W 111 B6
Whitley Chapel Northumb 110 D2
Whitley Lower W Yorks 88 C3
Whitley Row Kent 29 D5
Whitlock's End W Mid 51 B6
Whitminster Glos 36 D4
Whitmore Staffs 74 E5
Whitnage Devon 10 C5
Whitnash Warks 51 C8
Whitney-on-Wye Hereford 48 E4
Whitrigg Cumb 108 D2
Whitrigg Cumb 108 F2
Whitsbury Hants 14 C2
Whitsome Borders 122 D4
Whitson Newport 35 F7
Whitstable Kent 30 C5
Whitstone Corn 8 E4
Whittingham Northumb 117 C6
Whittingslow Shrops 60 F4
Whittington Glos 37 B7
Whittington Lancs 93 B6
Whittington Norf 67 E7
Whittington Shrops 73 F7
Whittington Staffs 62 F2
Whittington Staffs 63 D5
Whittington Worcs 50 D3
Whittle-le-Woods Lancs 86 B3
Whittlebury Northants 52 E4
Whittlesey Cambs 66 E2
Whittlesford Cambs 55 E5
Whittlestone Head Blackburn 86 C5
Whitton Borders 116 B3
Whitton N Lincs 90 B3
Whitton Northumb 117 D6
Whitton Powys 48 C4
Whitton Shrops 49 B7
Whitton Stockton 102 B1
Whitton Suff 56 E5
Whittonditch Wilts 25 B7
Whittonstall Northumb 110 D3
Whitway Hants 26 D2
Whitwell Derbys 76 B5
Whitwell Herts 40 B4
Whitwell IoW 15 G6
Whitwell N Yorks 101 E7

Whitwell Rutland 65 D6
Whitwell-on-the-Hill N Yorks 96 C3
Whitwell Street Norf 81 E7
Whitwick Leics 63 C8
Whitwood W Yorks 88 B5
Whitworth Lancs 87 C6
Whixall Shrops 74 F2
Whixley N Yorks 95 D7
Whoberley W Mid 51 B8
Whorlton Durham 101 C6
Whorlton N Yorks 102 D2
Whygate Northumb 109 B7
Whyle Hereford 49 C7
Whyteleafe Sur 28 D4
Wibdon Glos 36 E2
Wibsey W Yorks 88 A2
Wibtoft Leics 63 F8
Wichenford Worcs 50 C2
Wichling Kent 30 D3
Wick Bmouth 14 E2
Wick Devon 11 D6
Wick Highld 158 E5
Wick S Glos 24 B2
Wick Shetland 160 K6
Wick V Glam 21 B8
Wick W Sus 16 D4
Wick Wilts 14 B2
Wick Worcs 50 E4
Wick Hill Wokingham 27 C5
Wick St Lawrence N Som 23 C5
Wicken Cambs 55 B6
Wicken Northants 52 F5
Wicken Bonhunt Essex 55 F5
Wicken Green Village Norf 80 D4
Wickenby Lincs 90 F4
Wickersley S Yorks 89 E5
Wickford Essex 42 E3
Wickham Hants 15 C6
Wickham W Berks 25 B8
Wickham Bishops Essex 42 C4
Wickham Market Suff 57 D7
Wickham Skeith Suff 56 C4
Wickham St Paul Essex 56 F2
Wickham Street Suff 55 D8
Wickham Street Suff 56 C4
Wickhambreux Kent 31 D6
Wickhambrook Suff 55 D8
Wickhamford Worcs 51 E5
Wickhampton Norf 69 D7
Wicklewood Norf 68 D3
Wickmere Norf 81 D7
Wickwar S Glos 36 F4
Widdington Essex 55 F6
Widdrington Northumb 117 E8
Widdrington Station Northumb 117 E8
Wide Open T&W 110 B5
Widecombe in the Moor Devon 6 B5
Widegates Corn 5 D7
Widemouth Bay Corn 8 D4
Widewall Orkney 159 J5
Widford Essex 42 D2
Widford Herts 41 C7
Widham Wilts 37 F7
Widmer End Bucks 40 E1
Widmerpool Notts 64 B3
Widnes Halton 86 F3
Wigan Gtr Man 86 D3
Wiggaton Devon 11 E6
Wiggenhall St Germans Norf 67 C5
Wiggenhall St Mary Magdalen Norf 67 C5
Wiggenhall St Mary the Virgin Norf 67 C5
Wigginton Herts 40 C2
Wigginton Oxon 51 F8
Wigginton Staffs 63 D6
Wigginton York 95 D8
Wigglesworth N Yorks 93 D8
Wiggonby Cumb 108 D2
Wiggonholt W Sus 16 C4
Wighill N Yorks 95 E7
Wighton Norf 80 D5
Wigley Hants 14 C4
Wigmore Hereford 49 C6
Wigmore Medway 30 C2
Wigsley Notts 77 B8
Wigsthorpe Northants 65 F7
Wigston Leics 64 E3
Wigthorpe Notts 89 F6
Wigtoft Lincs 79 F5
Wigton Cumb 108 E2
Wigtown Dumfries 105 D8
Wigtwizzle S Yorks 88 E3
Wike W Yorks 95 E6
Wike Well End S Yorks 89 C7
Wilbarston Northants 64 F5
Wilberfoss E Yorks 96 D3
Wilberlee W Yorks 87 C8
Wilburton Cambs 55 B5
Wilby Norf 68 F3
Wilby Northants 53 C6
Wilby Suff 57 B6
Wilcot Wilts 25 C6
Wilcott Shrops 60 C3
Wilcrick Newport 35 F8
Wilday Green Derbys 76 B3
Wildboarclough Ches E 75 C6
Wilden Bedford 53 D8
Wilden Worcs 50 B3
Wildhern Hants 25 D8
Wildhill Herts 41 D5
Wildmoor Worcs 50 B4
Wildsworth Lincs 90 E2
Wilford Nottingham 77 F5
Wilkesley Ches E 74 E3
Wilkhaven Highld 151 C12
Wilkieston W Loth 120 C4
Willand Devon 10 C5
Willaston Ches E 74 D3
Willaston Ches W 73 B7
Willen M Keynes 53 E6
Willenhall W Mid 51 B8
Willenhall W Mid 62 E3
Willerby E Yorks 97 F6
Willerby N Yorks 97 B6
Willersey Glos 51 F6
Willersley Hereford 48 E5
Willesborough Kent 30 E4
Willesborough Lees Kent 30 E4
Willesden London 41 F5
Willett Som 22 F3
Willey Shrops 61 E6
Willey Warks 63 F8
Willey Green Sur 27 D7
Williamscott Oxon 52 E2
Willian Herts 54 F3
Willingale Essex 42 D1
Willingdon E Sus 18 E2
Willingham Cambs 54 B5
Willingham by Stow Lincs 90 F2
Willington Bedford 54 E2
Willington Derbys 63 B6
Willington Durham 110 F4
Willington T&W 111 C6
Willington Warks 51 F7
Willington Corner Ches W 74 C2
Willisham Tye Suff 56 D4
Willitoft E Yorks 96 F3
Williton Som 22 E2
Willoughbridge Staffs 74 E4
Willoughby Lincs 79 B7
Willoughby Warks 52 C3
Willoughby-on-the-Wolds Notts 64 B3
Willoughby Waterleys Leics 64 E2
Willoughton Lincs 90 E3
Willows Green Essex 42 C3
Willsbridge S Glos 23 B8
Willsworthy Devon 9 F7
Wilmcote Warks 51 D6
Wilmington Devon 11 E7
Wilmington E Sus 18 E2
Wilmington Kent 29 B6
Wilminstone Devon 6 B2
Wilmslow Ches E 87 F6
Wilnecote Staffs 63 D6
Wilpshire Lancs 93 F6
Wilsden W Yorks 94 F3
Wilsford Lincs 78 E3
Wilsford Wilts 25 D6
Wilsford Wilts 25 F6
Wilsill N Yorks 94 C4
Wilsley Pound Kent 18 B4
Wilsom Hants 26 F5
Wilson Leics 63 B8
Wilsontown S Lanark 120 D2
Wilstead Bedford 53 E8
Wilsthorpe Lincs 65 C7
Wilstone Herts 40 C2
Wilton Borders 115 C7
Wilton Cumb 98 C2
Wilton N Yorks 103 F6
Wilton Redcar 102 C3
Wilton Wilts 25 C7
Wilton Wilts 25 F5
Wimbish Essex 55 F6
Wimbish Green Essex 55 F7
Wimblebury Staffs 62 C4
Wimbledon London 28 B3
Wimblington Cambs 66 E4
Wimborne Minster Dorset 13 E8
Wimborne St Giles Dorset 13 C8
Wimbotsham Norf 67 D6
Wimpson Soton 14 C4
Wimpstone Warks 51 E7
Wincanton Som 12 B5
Wincham Ches W 74 B3
Winchburgh W Loth 120 B3
Winchcombe Glos 37 B7
Winchelsea E Sus 19 D6
Winchelsea Beach E Sus 19 D6
Winchester Hants 15 B5
Winchet Hill Kent 29 E8
Winchfield Hants 27 D5
Winchmore Hill Bucks 40 E2
Winchmore Hill London 41 E6
Wincle Ches E 75 C6
Wincobank S Yorks 88 E4
Windermere Cumb 99 E6
Winderton Warks 51 E8
Windhill Highld 151 G8
Windhouse Shetland 160 D6
Windlehurst Gtr Man 87 F7
Windlesham Sur 27 C7
Windley Derbys 76 E3
Windmill Hill E Sus 18 D3
Windmill Hill Som 11 C8
Windrush Glos 38 C1
Windsor N Lincs 89 C8
Windsor Windsor 27 B7
Windsoredge Glos 37 D5
Windygates Fife 128 D5
Windyknowe W Loth 120 C2
Windywalls Borders 122 F3
Wineham W Sus 17 B6
Winestead E Yorks 91 B6
Winewall Lancs 94 E2
Winfarthing Norf 68 F4
Winford IoW 15 F6
Winford N Som 23 C7
Winforton Hereford 48 E4
Winfrith Newburgh Dorset 13 F6
Wing Bucks 40 B1
Wing Rutland 65 D5
Wingate Durham 111 F7
Wingates Gtr Man 86 D4
Wingates Northumb 117 E7
Wingerworth Derbys 76 C3
Wingfield C Beds 40 B2
Wingfield Suff 57 B6
Wingfield Wilts 24 D3
Wingham Kent 31 D6
Wingmore Kent 31 E5
Wingrave Bucks 40 C1
Winkburn Notts 77 D7
Winkfield Brack 27 B7
Winkfield Row Brack 27 B6
Winkhill Staffs 75 D7
Winklebury Hants 26 D4
Winkleigh Devon 9 D8
Winksley N Yorks 95 B5
Winkton Dorset 14 E2
Winlaton T&W 110 C4
Winless Highld 158 E5
Winmarleigh Lancs 92 E4
Winnal Hereford 49 F6
Winnall Hants 15 B5
Winnersh Wokingham 27 B5
Winscales Cumb 98 B2
Winscombe N Som 23 D6
Winsford Ches W 74 C3
Winsford Som 21 F8
Winsham Som 11 D8
Winshill Staffs 63 B6
Winskill Cumb 109 F5
Winslade Hants 26 E4
Winsley Wilts 24 C3
Winslow Bucks 39 B7
Winson Glos 37 D7
Winson Green W Mid 62 F4
Winsor Hants 14 C4
Winster Cumb 99 E6
Winster Derbys 76 C2
Winston Durham 101 C6
Winston Suff 57 C5
Winston Green Suff 57 C5
Winstone Glos 37 D6
Winswell Devon 9 C6
Winter Gardens Essex 42 F3
Winterborne Clenston Dorset 13 D6
Winterborne Herringston Dorset 12 F4
Winterborne Houghton Dorset 13 D6
Winterborne Kingston Dorset 13 E6
Winterborne Monkton Dorset 12 F4
Winterborne Stickland Dorset 13 D6
Winterborne Whitechurch Dorset 13 D6
Winterborne Zelston Dorset 13 E6
Winterbourne S Glos 36 F3
Winterbourne W Berks 26 B2
Winterbourne Abbas Dorset 12 E4
Winterbourne Bassett Wilts 25 B6
Winterbourne Dauntsey Wilts 25 F6
Winterbourne Down S Glos 23 B8
Winterbourne Earls Wilts 25 F6
Winterbourne Gunner Wilts 25 F6
Winterbourne Monkton Wilts 25 B6
Winterbourne Steepleton Dorset 12 F4
Winterbourne Stoke Wilts 25 E5
Winterburn N Yorks 94 D2
Winteringham N Lincs 90 B3
Winterley Ches E 74 D4
Wintersett W Yorks 88 C4
Wintershill Hants 15 C6
Winterton N Lincs 90 C3
Winterton-on-Sea Norf 69 C7
Winthorpe Lincs 79 C8
Winthorpe Notts 77 D8
Winton Bmouth 13 E8
Winton Cumb 100 C2
Winton N Yorks 102 E2
Wintringham N Yorks 96 B4
Winwick Cambs 65 F8
Winwick Northants 52 B4
Winwick Warr 86 E4
Wirksworth Derbys 76 D2
Wirksworth Moor Derbys 76 D3
Wirswall Ches E 74 E2
Wisbech Cambs 66 D4
Wisbech St Mary Cambs 66 D4
Wisborough Green W Sus 16 B4
Wiseton Notts 89 F8
Wishaw N Lanark 119 D7
Wishaw Warks 63 E5
Wisley Sur 27 D8
Wispington Lincs 78 B5
Wissenden Kent 30 E3
Wissett Suff 57 B7
Wistanstow Shrops 60 F4
Wistanswick Shrops 61 B6
Wistaston Ches E 74 D3
Wistaston Green Ches E 74 D3
Wiston Pembs 32 C1
Wiston S Lanark 120 F2
Wiston W Sus 16 C5
Wistow Cambs 66 F2
Wistow N Yorks 95 F8
Wiswell Lancs 93 F7
Witcham Cambs 66 F4
Witchampton Dorset 13 D7
Witchford Cambs 55 B6
Witham Essex 42 C4
Witham Friary Som 24 E2
Witham on the Hill Lincs 65 C7
Withcall Lincs 91 F6
Withdean Brighton 17 D7
Witherenden Hill E Sus 18 C3
Witheridge Devon 10 C3
Witherley Leics 63 E7
Withern Lincs 91 F8
Withernsea E Yorks 91 B7
Withernwick E Yorks 97 E7
Withersdale Street Suff 69 F5
Withersfield Suff 55 E7
Witherslack Cumb 99 F6
Withiel Corn 4 C4
Withiel Florey Som 21 F8
Withington Glos 37 C7
Withington Gtr Man 87 E6
Withington Hereford 49 E7
Withington Shrops 61 C5
Withington Staffs 75 F7
Withington Green Ches E 74 B5
Withleigh Devon 10 C4
Withnell Lancs 86 B4
Withybrook Warks 63 F8
Withycombe Som 22 E2
Withycombe Raleigh Devon 10 F5
Withyham E Sus 29 F5
Withypool Som 21 F7
Witley Sur 27 F7
Witnesham Suff 57 D5
Witney Oxon 38 C3
Wittering Pboro 65 D7
Wittersham Kent 19 C5
Witton Angus 135 B5
Witton Worcs 50 C3
Witton Bridge Norf 69 A6
Witton Gilbert Durham 110 E5
Witton-le-Wear Durham 110 F4
Witton Park Durham 110 F4
Wiveliscombe Som 11 B5
Wivelrod Hants 26 F4
Wivelsfield E Sus 17 B7
Wivelsfield Green E Sus 17 B7
Wivenhoe Essex 43 B6
Wivenhoe Cross Essex 43 B6
Wiveton Norf 81 C6
Wix Essex 43 B7
Wixford Warks 51 D5
Wixhill Shrops 61 B5
Wixoe Suff 55 E8
Woburn C Beds 53 F7
Woburn Sands M Keynes 53 F7
Wokefield Park W Berks 26 C4
Woking Sur 27 D8
Wokingham Wokingham 27 C6
Wolborough Devon 7 B6
Wold Newton E Yorks 97 B6
Wold Newton NE Lincs 91 E6
Woldingham Sur 28 D4
Wolfclyde S Lanark 120 F3
Wolferton Norf 67 B6
Wolfhill Perth 134 F1
Wolf's Castle Pembs 44 C4
Wolfsdale Pembs 44 C4
Woll Borders 115 B7
Wollaston Northants 53 C7
Wollaston Shrops 60 C3
Wollaton Nottingham 76 F5
Wollerton Shrops 74 F3
Wollescote W Mid 62 F3
Wolsingham Durham 110 F3
Wolstanton Staffs 75 E5
Wolston Warks 52 B2
Wolvercote Oxon 38 D4
Wolverhampton W Mid 62 E3
Wolverley Shrops 73 F8
Wolverley Worcs 50 B3
Wolverton Hants 26 D3
Wolverton M Keynes 53 E6
Wolverton Warks 51 C7
Wolverton Common Hants 26 D3
Wolvesnewton Mon 36 E1
Wolvey Warks 63 F8
Wolviston Stockton 102 B2
Wombleton N Yorks 102 F4
Wombourne Staffs 62 E2
Wombwell S Yorks 88 D4
Womenswold Kent 31 D6
Womersley N Yorks 89 C6
Wonastow Mon 36 C1
Wonersh Sur 27 E8
Wonson Devon 9 F8
Wonston Hants 26 F2
Wooburn Bucks 40 F2
Wooburn Green Bucks 40 F2
Wood Dalling Norf 81 E6
Wood End Herts 41 B6
Wood End Warks 51 B6
Wood End Warks 63 E6
Wood Enderby Lincs 79 C5
Wood Field Sur 28 D2
Wood Green London 41 E6
Wood Hayes W Mid 62 D3
Wood Lanes Ches E 87 F7
Wood Norton Norf 81 E6
Wood Street Norf 69 B6
Wood Street Sur 27 D7
Wood Walton Cambs 66 F2
Woodacott Devon 9 D5
Woodale N Yorks 94 B3
Woodbank Argyll 143 G7
Woodbastwick Norf 69 C6
Woodbeck Notts 77 B7
Woodborough Notts 77 E6
Woodborough Wilts 25 D6
Woodbridge Dorset 12 C5
Woodbridge Suff 57 E6
Woodbury Devon 10 F5
Woodbury Salterton Devon 10 F5
Woodchester Glos 37 D5
Woodchurch Kent 19 B6
Woodchurch Mers 85 F3
Woodcombe Som 21 E8
Woodcote Oxon 39 F6
Woodcott Hants 26 D2
Woodcroft Glos 36 E2
Woodcutts Dorset 13 C7
Woodditton Cambs 55 D7
Woodeaton Oxon 39 C5
Woodend Cumb 98 E3
Woodend Northants 52 E4
Woodend W Sus 16 D2
Woodend Green Northants 52 E4
Woodfalls Wilts 14 B2
Woodfield Oxon 39 B5
Woodfield S Ayrs 112 B3
Woodford Corn 8 C4
Woodford Devon 7 D5
Woodford Glos 36 E3
Woodford Gtr Man 87 F6
Woodford London 41 E7
Woodford Northants 53 B7
Woodford Bridge London 41 E7
Woodford Halse Northants 52 D3
Woodgate Norf 68 C3
Woodgate W Mid 62 F3
Woodgate W Sus 16 D3
Woodgate Worcs 50 C4
Woodgreen Hants 14 C2
Woodhall Herts 41 C5
Woodhall Invclyd 118 B3
Woodhall N Yorks 100 E4
Woodhall Spa Lincs 78 C4
Woodham Sur 27 C8
Woodham Ferrers Essex 42 E3
Woodham Mortimer Essex 42 D4
Woodham Walter Essex 42 D4
Woodhaven Fife 129 B6
Woodhead Aberds 153 E7
Woodhey Gtr Man 87 C5
Woodhill Shrops 61 F7
Woodhorn Northumb 117 F8
Woodhouse Leics 64 C2
Woodhouse N Lincs 89 D8
Woodhouse S Yorks 88 F5
Woodhouse W Yorks 88 B4
Woodhouse W Yorks 95 F5
Woodhouse Eaves Leics 64 C2
Woodhouse Park Gtr Man 87 F6
Woodhouselee Midloth 120 C5
Woodhouselees Dumfries 108 B3
Woodhouses Staffs 63 C5
Woodhurst Cambs 54 B4
Woodingdean Brighton 17 D7
Woodkirk W Yorks 88 B3
Woodland Devon 7 C5
Woodland Durham 101 B5
Woodlands Aberds 141 E6
Woodlands Dorset 13 D8
Woodlands Hants 14 C4
Woodlands Highld 151 E8
Woodlands N Yorks 95 D6
Woodlands S Yorks 89 D6
Woodlands Park Windsor 27 B6
Woodlands St Mary W Berks 25 B8
Woodlane Staffs 62 B5
Woodleigh Devon 6 E5
Woodlesford W Yorks 88 B4
Woodley Gtr Man 87 E7
Woodley Wokingham 27 B5
Woodmancote Glos 36 E4
Woodmancote Glos 37 B6
Woodmancote Glos 37 D7
Woodmancote W Sus 15 D8
Woodmancote W Sus 17 C6
Woodmancott Hants 26 E3
Woodmansey E Yorks 97 F6
Woodmansterne Sur 28 D3
Woodminton Wilts 13 B8
Woodnesborough Kent 31 D7
Woodnewton Northants 65 E7
Woodplumpton Lancs 92 F5
Woodrising Norf 68 D2
Wood's Green E Sus 18 B3
Woodseaves Shrops 74 F3
Woodseaves Staffs 61 B7
Woodsend Wilts 25 B7
Woodsetts S Yorks 89 F6
Woodsford Dorset 13 E5
Woodside Aberdeen 141 D8
Woodside Aberds 153 D10
Woodside Brack 27 B7
Woodside Fife 129 D6
Woodside Hants 14 E4
Woodside Herts 41 D5
Woodside Perth 134 F2
Woodside of Arbeadie Aberds 141 E6
Woodstock Oxon 38 C4
Woodstock Pembs 32 B1
Woodthorpe Derbys 76 B4
Woodthorpe Leics 64 C2
Woodthorpe Lincs 91 F8
Woodthorpe York 95 E8
Woodton Norf 69 E5
Woodtown Devon 9 B6
Woodtown Devon 9 B6
Woodvale Mers 85 C4
Woodville Derbys 63 C7
Woodyates Dorset 13 C8
Woofferton Shrops 49 C7
Wookey Som 23 E7
Wookey Hole Som 23 E7
Wool Dorset 13 F6
Woolacombe Devon 20 E3
Woolage Green Kent 31 E6
Woolaston Glos 36 E2
Woolavington Som 22 E5
Woolbeding W Sus 16 B2
Wooldale W Yorks 88 D2
Wooler Northumb 117 B5
Woolfardisworthy Devon 8 B5
Woolfardisworthy Devon 10 D3
Woolfords Cottages S Lanark 120 D3
Woolhampton W Berks 26 C3
Woolhope Hereford 49 F8
Woolhope Cockshoot Hereford 49 F8
Woolland Dorset 13 D5
Woollaton Devon 9 C6
Woolley Bath 24 C2
Woolley Cambs 54 B2
Woolley Corn 8 C4
Woolley Derbys 76 C3
Woolley W Yorks 88 C4
Woolmer Green Herts 41 C5
Woolmere Green Worcs 50 C4
Woolpit Suff 56 C3
Woolscott Warks 52 C2
Woolsington T&W 110 C4
Woolstanwood Ches E 74 D3
Woolstaston Shrops 60 E4
Woolsthorpe Lincs 65 B6
Woolsthorpe Lincs 77 F8
Woolston Devon 6 E5
Woolston Shrops 60 B3
Woolston Shrops 60 F4
Woolston Soton 14 C5
Woolston Warr 86 F4
Woolstone M Keynes 53 F6
Woolstone Oxon 38 F2
Woolton Mers 86 F2
Woolton Hill Hants 26 C2
Woolverstone Suff 57 F5
Woolverton Som 24 D2
Woolwich London 28 B5
Woolwich Ferry London 28 B5
Woonton Hereford 49 D5
Wooperton Northumb 117 B6
Woore Shrops 74 E4
Wootten Green Suff 57 B6
Wootton Bedford 53 E8
Wootton Hants 14 E3
Wootton Hereford 48 D5
Wootton Kent 31 E6
Wootton N Lincs 90 C4
Wootton Northants 53 D5
Wootton Oxon 38 C4
Wootton Oxon 38 D4
Wootton Shrops 49 B6
Wootton Shrops 60 B3
Wootton Staffs 62 B2
Wootton Staffs 75 E8
Wootton Bridge IoW 15 E6
Wootton Common IoW 15 E6
Wootton Courtenay Som 21 E8
Wootton Fitzpaine Dorset 11 E8
Wootton Rivers Wilts 25 C6
Wootton St Lawrence Hants 26 D3
Wootton Wawen Warks 51 C6
Worcester Worcs 50 D3
Worcester Park London 28 C3
Wordsley W Mid 62 F2
Worfield Shrops 61 E7
Work Orkney 159 G5
Workington Cumb 98 B1
Worksop Notts 77 B5
Worlaby N Lincs 90 C4
World's End W Berks 26 B2
Worle N Som 23 C5
Worleston Ches E 74 D3
Worlingham Suff 69 F7
Worlington Suff 55 B7
Worlingworth Suff 57 C6
Wormald Green N Yorks 95 C6
Wormbridge Hereford 49 F6
Wormegay Norf 67 C6
Wormelow Tump Hereford 49 F6
Wormhill Derbys 75 B8
Wormingford Essex 56 F3
Worminghall Bucks 39 D6
Wormington Glos 50 F5
Worminster Som 23 E7
Wormit Fife 129 B5
Wormleighton Warks 52 D2
Wormley Herts 41 D6
Wormley Sur 27 F7
Wormley West End Herts 41 D6
Wormshill Kent 30 D2
Wormsley Hereford 49 E6
Worplesdon Sur 27 D7
Worrall S Yorks 88 E4
Worsbrough S Yorks 88 D4
Worsbrough Common S Yorks 88 D4
Worsley Gtr Man 86 D5
Worstead Norf 69 B6
Worsthorne Lancs 93 F8
Worston Lancs 93 E7
Worswell Devon 6 E3
Worth Kent 31 D7
Worth W Sus 28 F4
Worth Matravers Dorset 13 G7
Wortham Suff 56 B4
Worthen Shrops 60 D3
Worthenbury Wrex 73 E8
Worthing Norf 68 C2
Worthing W Sus 16 D5
Worthington Leics 63 B8
Worting Hants 26 D4
Wortley S Yorks 88 E4
Wortley W Yorks 95 F5
Worton N Yorks 100 E4
Worton Wilts 24 D4
Wortwell Norf 69 F5
Wotherton Shrops 60 D2
Wotter Devon 6 C3
Wotton Sur 28 E2
Wotton-under-Edge Glos 36 E4
Wotton Underwood Bucks 39 C6
Woughton on the Green M Keynes 53 F6
Wouldham Kent 29 C8
Wrabness Essex 57 F5
Wrafton Devon 20 F3
Wragby Lincs 78 B4
Wragby W Yorks 88 C5
Wragholme Lincs 91 E7
Wramplingham Norf 68 D4
Wrangbrook W Yorks 89 C5
Wrangham Aberds 153 E6
Wrangle Lincs 79 D7
Wrangle Bank Lincs 79 D7
Wrangle Lowgate Lincs 79 D7
Wrangway Som 11 C6
Wrantage Som 11 B8
Wrawby N Lincs 90 D4
Wraxall Dorset 12 D3
Wraxall N Som 23 B6
Wraxall Som 23 F8
Wray Lancs 93 C6
Wraysbury Windsor 27 B8
Wrayton Lancs 93 B6
Wrea Green Lancs 92 F3
Wreay Cumb 99 B6
Wreay Cumb 108 E4
Wrecclesham Sur 27 E6
Wrecsam = Wrexham Wrex 73 D7
Wrekenton T&W 111 D5
Wrelton N Yorks 103 F5
Wrenbury Ches E 74 E2
Wrench Green N Yorks 103 F7
Wreningham Norf 68 E4
Wrentham Suff 69 F7
Wrenthorpe W Yorks 88 B4
Wrentnall Shrops 60 D4
Wressle E Yorks 96 F3
Wressle N Lincs 90 D3
Wrestlingworth C Beds 54 E3
Wretham Norf 68 F2
Wretton Norf 67 E6
Wrexham = Wrecsam Wrex 73 D7
Wrexham Industrial Estate Wrex 73 E7
Wribbenhall Worcs 50 B2
Wrightington Bar Lancs 86 C3
Wrinehill Staffs 74 E4
Wrington N Som 23 C6
Writhlington Bath 24 D2
Writtle Essex 42 D2
Wrockwardine Telford 61 C6
Wroot N Lincs 89 D8
Wrotham Kent 29 D7
Wrotham Heath Kent 29 D7
Wroughton Swindon 37 F8
Wroxall IoW 15 G6
Wroxall Warks 51 B7
Wroxeter Shrops 61 D5
Wroxham Norf 69 C6
Wroxton Oxon 52 E2
Wyaston Derbys 75 E8
Wyberton Lincs 79 E6
Wyboston Bedford 54 D2
Wybunbury Ches E 74 E4
Wych Cross E Sus 28 F5
Wychbold Worcs 50 C4
Wyck Hants 27 F5
Wyck Rissington Glos 38 B1
Wycoller Lancs 94 F2
Wycomb Leics 64 B4
Wycombe Marsh Bucks 40 E1
Wyddial Herts 54 F4
Wye Kent 30 E4
Wyesham Mon 36 C2
Wyfordby Leics 64 C4
Wyke Dorset 13 B5
Wyke Shrops 61 D6
Wyke Sur 27 D7
Wyke W Yorks 88 B2
Wyke Regis Dorset 12 G4
Wykeham N Yorks 96 B4
Wykeham N Yorks 103 F7
Wyken W Mid 63 F7
Wykey Shrops 60 B3
Wylam Northumb 110 C4
Wylde Green W Mid 62 E5
Wyllie Caerph 35 E5
Wylye Wilts 24 F5
Wymering Ptsmth 15 D7
Wymeswold Leics 64 B3
Wymington Bedford 53 C7
Wymondham Leics 65 C5
Wymondham Norf 68 D4
Wyndham Bridgend 34 E3
Wynford Eagle Dorset 12 E3
Wyng Orkney 159 J4
Wynyard Village Stockton 102 B2
Wyre Piddle Worcs 50 E4
Wysall Notts 64 B3
Wythall Worcs 51 B5
Wytham Oxon 38 D4
Wythburn Cumb 99 C5
Wythenshawe Gtr Man 87 F6
Wythop Mill Cumb 98 B3
Wyton Cambs 54 B3
Wyverstone Suff 56 C4
Wyverstone Street Suff 56 C4
Wyville Lincs 65 B5
Wyvis Lodge Highld 150 D7

Y

Y Bala = Bala Gwyn 72 F3
Y Barri = Barry V Glam 22 C3
Y Bont-Faen = Cowbridge V Glam 21 B8
Y Drenewydd = Newtown Powys 59 E8
Y Felinheli Gwyn 82 E5
Y Fenni = Abergavenny Mon 35 C6
Y Fför Gwyn 70 D4
Y Fflint = Flint Flint 73 B6
Y-Ffrith Denb 72 A4
Y Gelli Gandryll = Hay-on-Wye Powys 48 E4
Y Mwmbwls = The Mumbles Swansea 33 F7
Y Pîl = Pyle Bridgend 34 F2
Y Rhws = Rhoose V Glam 22 C2
Y Rhyl = Rhyl Denb 72 A4
Y Trallwng = Welshpool Powys 60 D2
Y Waun = Chirk Wrex 73 F6
Yaddlethorpe N Lincs 90 D2
Yafford IoW 14 F5
Yafforth N Yorks 101 E8
Yalding Kent 29 D7
Yanworth Glos 37 C7
Yapham E Yorks 96 D3
Yapton W Sus 16 D3
Yarburgh Lincs 91 E7
Yarcombe Devon 11 D7
Yard Som 22 F2
Yardley W Mid 62 F5
Yardley Gobion Northants 53 E5
Yardley Hastings Northants 53 D6
Yardro Powys 48 D4
Yarkhill Hereford 49 E8
Yarlet Staffs 62 B3
Yarlington Som 12 B4
Yarlside Cumb 92 C2
Yarm Stockton 102 C2
Yarmouth IoW 14 F4
Yarnbrook Wilts 24 D3
Yarnfield Staffs 75 F5
Yarnscombe Devon 9 B7
Yarnton Oxon 38 C4
Yarpole Hereford 49 C6
Yarrow Borders 115 B6
Yarrow Feus Borders 115 B6
Yarsop Hereford 49 E6
Yarwell Northants 65 E7
Yate S Glos 36 F4
Yateley Hants 27 C6
Yatesbury Wilts 25 B5
Yattendon W Berks 26 B3
Yatton Hereford 49 C6
Yatton N Som 23 C6
Yatton Keynell Wilts 24 B3
Yaverland IoW 15 F7
Yaxham Norf 68 C3
Yaxley Cambs 65 E8
Yaxley Suff 56 B5
Yazor Hereford 49 E6
Yeading London 40 F4
Yeadon W Yorks 94 E5
Yealand Conyers Lancs 92 B5
Yealand Redmayne Lancs 92 B5
Yealmpton Devon 6 D3
Yearby Redcar 102 B4
Yearsley N Yorks 95 B8
Yeaton Shrops 60 C4
Yeaveley Derbys 75 E8
Yedingham N Yorks 96 B4
Yeldon Bedford 53 C8
Yelford Oxon 38 D3
Yelland Devon 20 F3
Yelling Cambs 54 C3
Yelvertoft Northants 52 B3
Yelverton Devon 6 C3
Yelverton Norf 69 D5
Yenston Som 12 B5
Yeo Mill Devon 10 B3
Yeoford Devon 10 E2
Yeolmbridge Corn 8 F5
Yeovil Som 12 C3
Yeovil Marsh Som 12 C3
Yeovilton Som 12 B3
Yerbeston Pembs 32 D1
Yesnaby Orkney 159 G3
Yetlington Northumb 117 D6
Yetminster Dorset 12 C3
Yettington Devon 11 F5
Yetts o'Muckhart Clack 128 D2
Yieldshields S Lanark 119 D8
Yiewsley London 40 F3
Ynys-meudwy Neath 33 D8
Ynysboeth Rhondda 34 E4
Ynysddu Caerph 35 E5
Ynysgyfflog Gwyn 58 C3
Ynyshir Rhondda 34 E4
Ynyslas Ceredig 58 E3
Ynystawe Swansea 33 D7
Ynysybwl Rhondda 34 E4
Yockenthwaite N Yorks 94 B2
Yockleton Shrops 60 C3
Yokefleet E Yorks 90 B2
Yoker W Dunb 118 C5
Yonder Bognie Aberds 152 D5
York York 95 D8
York Town Sur 27 C6
Yorkletts Kent 30 C4
Yorkley Glos 36 D3
Yorton Shrops 60 B5
Youlgreave Derbys 76 C2
Youlstone Devon 8 C4
Youlthorpe E Yorks 96 D3
Youlton N Yorks 95 C7
Young Wood Lincs 78 B4
Young's End Essex 42 C3
Yoxall Staffs 62 C5
Yoxford Suff 57 C7
Yr Hôb = Hope Flint 73 D7
Yr Wyddgrug = Mold Flint 73 C6
Ysbyty-Cynfyn Ceredig 47 B6
Ysbyty Ifan Conwy 72 E2
Ysbyty Ystwyth Ceredig 47 B6
Ysceifiog Flint 73 B5
Yspitty Carms 33 E6
Ystalyfera Neath 34 D1
Ystrad Rhondda 34 E3
Ystrad Aeron Ceredig 46 D4
Ystrad-mynach Caerph 35 E5
Ystradfellte Powys 34 C3
Ystradffin Carms 47 E6
Ystradgynlais Powys 34 C1
Ystradmeurig Ceredig 47 C6
Ystradowen Carms 33 C8
Ystradowen V Glam 22 B2
Ystumtuen Ceredig 47 B6
Ythanbank Aberds 153 E9
Ythanwells Aberds 153 E6
Ythsie Aberds 153 E8

Z

Zeal Monachorum Devon 10 D2
Zeals Wilts 24 F2
Zelah Corn 4 D3
Zennor Corn 2 C3

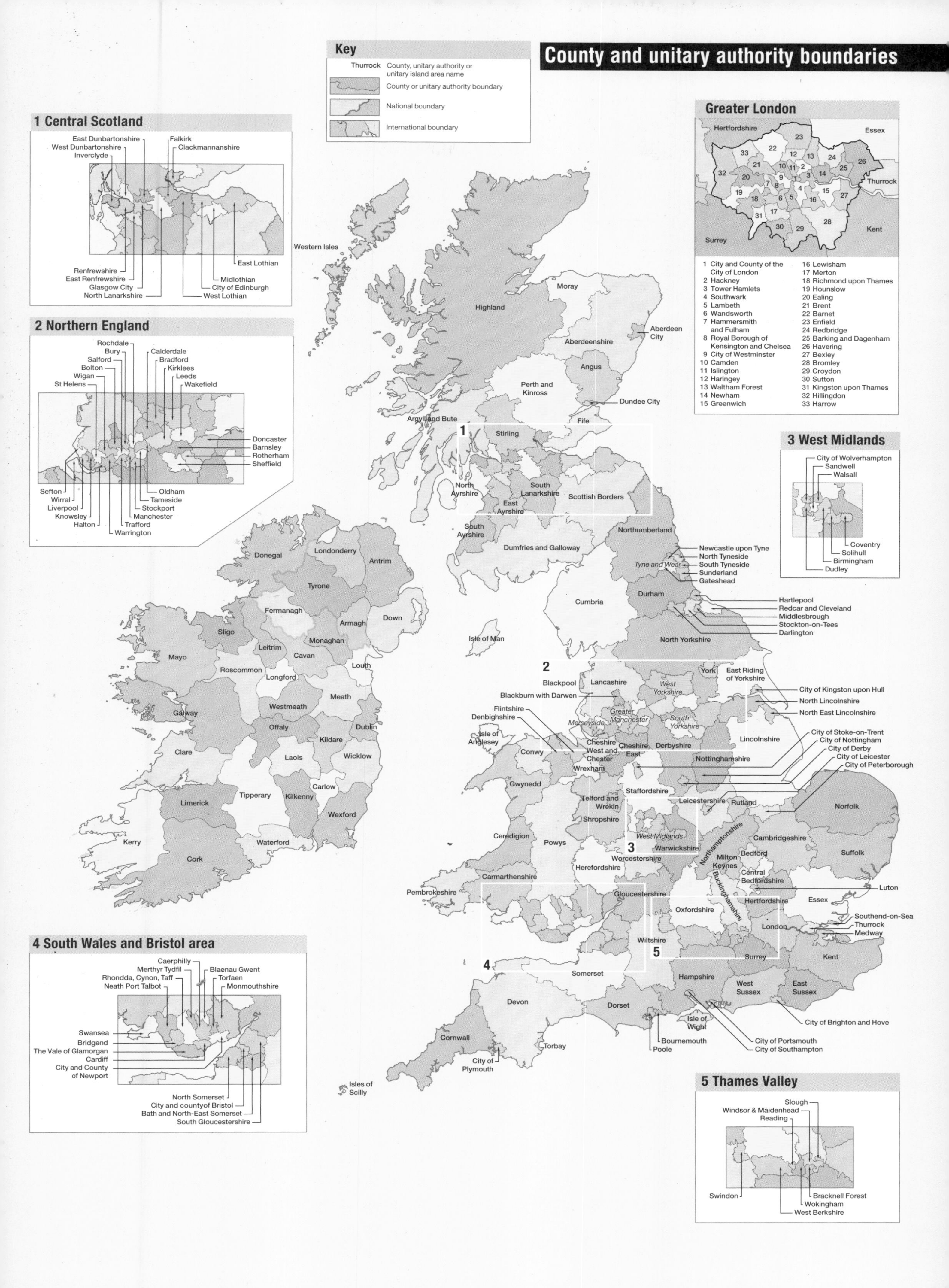

County and unitary authority boundaries
Key
Thurrock County, unitary authority or unitary island area name
County or unitary authority boundary
National boundary
International boundary
1 Central Scotland
East Dunbartonshire
West Dunbartonshire
Inverclyde
Falkirk
Clackmannanshire
Renfrewshire
East Renfrewshire
Glasgow City
North Lanarkshire
East Lothian
Midlothian
City of Edinburgh
West Lothian
2 Northern England
Rochdale
Bury
Salford
Bolton
Wigan
St Helens
Calderdale
Bradford
Kirklees
Leeds
Wakefield
Doncaster
Barnsley
Rotherham
Sheffield
Sefton
Wirral
Liverpool
Knowsley
Halton
Oldham
Tameside
Stockport
Manchester
Trafford
Warrington
Greater London
Hertfordshire
Essex
Thurrock
Kent
Surrey
1 City and County of the City of London
2 Hackney
3 Tower Hamlets
4 Southwark
5 Lambeth
6 Wandsworth
7 Hammersmith and Fulham
8 Royal Borough of Kensington and Chelsea
9 City of Westminster
10 Camden
11 Islington
12 Haringey
13 Waltham Forest
14 Newham
15 Greenwich
16 Lewisham
17 Merton
18 Richmond upon Thames
19 Hounslow
20 Ealing
21 Brent
22 Barnet
23 Enfield
24 Redbridge
25 Barking and Dagenham
26 Havering
27 Bexley
28 Bromley
29 Croydon
30 Sutton
31 Kingston upon Thames
32 Hillingdon
33 Harrow
3 West Midlands
City of Wolverhampton
Sandwell
Walsall
Coventry
Solihull
Birmingham
Dudley
Western Isles
Highland
Moray
Aberdeen City
Aberdeenshire
Angus
Perth and Kinross
Dundee City
Argyll and Bute
Fife
Stirling
North Ayrshire
South Lanarkshire
East Ayrshire
Scottish Borders
South Ayrshire
Dumfries and Galloway
Northumberland
Newcastle upon Tyne
North Tyneside
South Tyneside
Sunderland
Gateshead
Tyne and Wear
Cumbria
Durham
Hartlepool
Redcar and Cleveland
Middlesbrough
Stockton-on-Tees
Darlington
Isle of Man
North Yorkshire
Donegal
Londonderry
Antrim
Tyrone
Fermanagh
Armagh
Down
Monaghan
Sligo
Leitrim
Cavan
Mayo
Roscommon
Longford
Louth
Galway
Westmeath
Meath
Offaly
Dublin
Kildare
Clare
Laois
Wicklow
Carlow
Limerick
Tipperary
Kilkenny
Wexford
Kerry
Waterford
Cork
Blackpool
Lancashire
York
East Riding of Yorkshire
West Yorkshire
City of Kingston upon Hull
Blackburn with Darwen
North Lincolnshire
Flintshire
Denbighshire
Greater Manchester
Merseyside
South Yorkshire
North East Lincolnshire
Isle of Anglesey
Cheshire West and Chester
Cheshire East
Derbyshire
Lincolnshire
Conwy
Wrexham
Nottinghamshire
City of Stoke-on-Trent
City of Nottingham
City of Derby
City of Leicester
City of Peterborough
Gwynedd
Staffordshire
Telford and Wrekin
Leicestershire
Rutland
Norfolk
Shropshire
Northamptonshire
Ceredigion
Powys
West Midlands
Warwickshire
Cambridgeshire
Worcestershire
Bedford
Suffolk
Milton Keynes
Herefordshire
Central Bedfordshire
Carmarthenshire
Buckinghamshire
Luton
Pembrokeshire
Gloucestershire
Hertfordshire
Essex
Oxfordshire
Southend-on-Sea
Thurrock
Medway
London
Wiltshire
Surrey
Kent
Somerset
Hampshire
West Sussex
East Sussex
Devon
Dorset
Isle of Wight
City of Brighton and Hove
Cornwall
Bournemouth
Poole
City of Portsmouth
City of Southampton
Torbay
City of Plymouth
Isles of Scilly
4 South Wales and Bristol area
Caerphilly
Merthyr Tydfil
Rhondda, Cynon, Taff
Neath Port Talbot
Blaenau Gwent
Torfaen
Monmouthshire
Swansea
Bridgend
The Vale of Glamorgan
Cardiff
City and County of Newport
North Somerset
City and countyof Bristol
Bath and North-East Somerset
South Gloucestershire
5 Thames Valley
Slough
Windsor & Maidenhead
Reading
Swindon
Bracknell Forest
Wokingham
West Berkshire